INTERNATIONAL TRADE AND
INVESTMENT

INTERNATIONAL TRADE AND INVESTMENT

Regulating International Business

JOHN H. BARTON
Professor of Law
Stanford Law School

BART S. FISHER
Professorial Lecturer in International Relations
Johns Hopkins School of Advanced International Studies
Member, Bar of the District of Columbia

LITTLE, BROWN AND COMPANY
Boston   Toronto

Library of Congress Catalog Card No. 84-81756

ISBN 0-316-08280-5

Third Printing

MV NY

Published simultaneously in Canada
by Little, Brown & Company (Canada) Limited

Printed in the United States of America

To my family

John H. Barton

With greatest pleasure
I dedicate my work in this book
to
Margaret, Ross, and Ivan Fisher,
my parents and sister

Bart S. Fisher

SUMMARY OF CONTENTS

CONTENTS

Chapter III

REGULATION OF INTERNATIONAL TRADE: THE INSTITUTIONS   89

Chapter IV

RELIEF FROM FAIRLY PRICED FOREIGN COMPETITION

Chapter V

ANTIDUMPING DUTIES 273

Chapter VII

CUSTOMS: CLASSIFICATION AND VALUATION   393

Chapter VIII

NONTARIFF BARRIERS TO TRADE: STANDARDS AND GOVERNMENT PROCUREMENT

Chapter IX

DISPUTE SETTLEMENT AND ENFORCEMENT OF GATT RIGHTS

Chapter X

TRADE AND DEVELOPING NATIONS   503

Chapter XI

ANTITRUST ISSUES IN INTERNATIONAL TRADE   **551**

Chapter XII

THE USE OF TRADE CONTROLS FOR POLITICAL PURPOSES   631

PART 2

TECHNOLOGY IN INTERNATIONAL COMMERCE

669

Chapter XIII

THE TERRITORIAL STRUCTURE OF INTELLECTUAL PROPERTY RIGHTS

671

Chapter XVI

INVESTOR NATIONAL REGULATION OF PORTFOLIO INVESTMENT   813

Chapter XVIII

INVESTMENT DISPUTES   897

PREFACE

International business law is rapidly becoming a bread-and-butter area for the lawyer, the economist, and the political scientist. International trade and investment issues are no longer the arcane and obscure province of specialists; they are increasingly topics for lawyers in general practice. Perhaps because of the vastness of the field and the diversity of interests involved, every teacher has his or her own special approach to the topic, ranging from an emphasis on regulation of trade to an emphasis on structuring of an international investment. This is reflected by the variety of course offerings in the areas of international trade and investment.

Because of this variety of approaches, we have devised this book to permit and encourage flexibility. We place greatest emphasis on the basic body of international trade regulation, with appropriate background on the mechanics of the trade transaction itself. But we go on to cover procedures for and regulation of trade in technology, an area of growing importance. We conclude the book with explorations of the evolving legal issues surrounding international investment, ranging from portfolio investment, bank investment, and the associated debt crisis issues to direct investment, the multinational corporation, and the associated dispute settlement issues.

The book can thus be used for a full two-semester course on international business transactions, or a variety of one-semester courses. Chapters 1 through 10, together with chapter 12, provide a self-contained one-semester course on international trade law. The remaining chapters provide material for an advanced course on international technology, licensing, and investment law. Alternatively, by dropping several chapters and some of the specific cases within the chapters, a one-semester course can be assembled to follow the teacher's particular interest. One version, for example, might provide an overview. It would cover the trade system at work, in chapter 1, the trade transaction materials in chapter 2, the United States and GATT material in chapter 3, and selected cases in chapters 4 through 6 and chapter 9. This would be balanced with selected reading in chapters 13, 14, and 16 to provide insight into international licensing, lending, and direct investment.

This entire body of law is changing rapidly, and education most wisely respects the old principle of "learning how to learn." We believe that the key goals of any international business course are to help the student understand the vocabulary and institutions of international economic relations and gain a feel for the area's complex mixture of law, economics, and domestic and international politics. Accordingly, the materials are interdisciplinary in nature and attempt to provide an economic and political context for the regulatory problems that are considered.

The questions carry a significant share of the educational weight, and we have provided several types: (1) "reading" questions to emphasize important points in a case or statute that might be easily missed, (2) discussion questions to help explore the fundamental and often open-ended debates that underlie most policy choices in the area, and (3) prospective applications to new situations. Some of this last category of questions are accompanied by references to cases or articles dealing with the issues. Others are intended to encourage the student to integrate his or her thinking about different areas of law and to gain insight into emerging policy conflicts that may shape the law in the future.

We have sought consistency in dividing issues into the trade, technology, and investment areas. Rather than treating all international antitrust issues together, for example, we have broken up the antitrust materials by function, so that those most directly affecting trade, technology licensing, or investment are treated along with these topics. For the sake of brevity, we have avoided full-scale treatment of the investment act of state or sovereign immunity doctrines, assuming that those topics are more likely to be covered in a basic international law course (although we have given special attention to the act of state applications in the antitrust area, and we do not believe that a basic international law course is a necessary prerequisite to this course). We have also concentrated on United States materials, including a very few foreign examples to permit comparison of European Communities approaches with those of the United States and of GATT. Finally, we have compiled under separate cover a substantial documents volume to provide the student with easy access to the key legislative and treaty materials.

We wish to thank the many persons who have helped us in preparing these materials. Students at Georgetown, Michigan, Johns Hopkins, and Stanford have all studied from previous versions and have greatly helped us with their insights, as have teaching colleagues who have used the materials at other schools and provided their comments. Richard Heuser and Stephen St. Clair at Little, Brown have provided both constructive criticism and encouragement.

We have benefited from the work of a large number of student research assistants, including Anne Quigley at Georgetown, and Davis Goodman at Stanford. Thomas Graham, Esq., assisted in preparing the questions. A large number of persons reviewed particular chapters and provided constructive advice and criticism, including Dr. Charles Pearson, William Cline, Joel Davidow, Steven M. Schneebaum, and Frank R. Samolis.

Three persons especially deserve to be singled out. Robert Townsend, who contributed several semesters of research assistance at Stanford and also as a summer intern at Patton, Boggs & Blow, provided a great deal of original research along with thoughtful and helpful criticism of all the materials. And Mary Peabody at Stanford and Deborah Wharton at Patton, Boggs & Blow went far beyond the call of duty—to type innumerable revisions and modifications, to keep the manuscript in order, to bring in help as needed, to apply for permissions, and to provide cheerful and competent encouragement.

We thank them all.

Finally, we wish to acknowledge the support provided by our wives, Julie Barton and Margaret Fisher, who put up with the prolonged absences from home required to write this book. Their understanding strengthened our determination to bring what we consider to be a stimulating subject to the law school curriculum.

John H. Barton
Bart S. Fisher

April 1986

ACKNOWLEDGMENTS

We gratefully acknowledge the permission granted by the authors, publishers, and organizations to reprint portions of the following copyrighted materials.

Berman and Kaufman, The Law of International Commerical Transactions (Lex Mercatoria), 19 Harv. Intl. L.J. 221, 237-243 (1978).

Bill of exchange, reprinted with the permission of Barclays Bank International Limited.

Business Brief, The Economist, October 1, 1983. Copyright © The Economist Newspaper Ltd. Reprinted with permission.

S. Cohen, The Making of United States International Economic Policy 57-60. Copyright © 1977, Praeger Publishers. Reprinted with permission.

Erb and Fisher, U.S. Commodity Policy: What Response to Third World Initiatives?, 9 Law & Poly. Intl. Bus. 479. Copyright © 1977. Reprinted with the permission of the copyright holder and the authors.

Farnsworth, Tokyo's Car Curbs Hailed in U.S., But Japanese Makers Are Angered, May 2, 1981. Copyright © 1981 by The New York Times Company. Reprinted by permission.

P. Feller, U.S. Customs and International Trade Guide, Copyright © 1984 by Matthew Bender & Co., Inc., and reprinted with permission from U.S. Customs and International Trade Guide. Reprinted with permission of the copyright holder and the author.

Fisher, The Antidumping Law of the United States: A Legal and Economic Analysis, 5 Law & Poly. Intl. Bus. 85, 86-93. Copyright © 1973. Reprinted with permission of the copyright holder and the author.

Fisher, Making the World Trade Regime Work: An Agenda For GATT 4. SAIS Review (Winter/Spring 1986). Copyright © 1986 The Johns Hopkins University School of Advanced International Studies. Reprinted with permission of the copyright holder and the author.

GATT Panel Report on EEC Subsidies on Raisins and Canned Fruit, 20 U.S. Export Weekly 1028 (1984), reprinted by permission from U.S. Export Weekly, copyright © 1984 by the Bureau of National Affairs, Inc., Washington, D.C.

J. Gold, Financial Assistance by the International Monetary Fund: Law and Practice IMF Pamphlet Series No. 27, 2d Edition (1980). Reprinted with permission of the International Monetary Fund.

Jackson, The General Agreement on Tariffs and Trade, A Lawyer's Guide to International Business Transactions, Part I. Copyright © 1977 by The American Law Institute. Reprinted with permission of the American Law Institute-American Bar Association Committee on Continuing Professional Education.

Japan Agreement?, Washington Riceletter, April 25, 1980. Editor, Carlisle B. Morrison. Reprinted with permission.

Japanese Microchips: Envy and Success, The Economist, February 19, 1983. Copyright © The Economist Newspaper Ltd. Reprinted with permission.

Letter of credit, reprinted with the permission of Barclays Bank International Limited.

Lewis, U.S. and Third World at Odds over Patents, October 5, 1982. Copyright © 1982 by The New York Times Company. Reprinted by permission.

Lorenzen, Technical Analysis of the Antidumping Agreement and the Trade Agreements Act, 11 Law & Poly. Intl. Bus. 1405, 1406-1416. Copyright © 1979. Reprinted with permission.

Meier, Externality Law and Market Safeguards: Applications in the GATT Multilateral Trade Negotiations, 18 Harvard International Law Journal 491 (1971). Reprinted with permission.

Multinational Mummery, The Economist, June 26, 1976. Copyright © The Economist Newspaper Ltd. Reprinted with permission.

A Nightmare of Debt: A Survey of International Banking, The Economist, March 20, 1982. Copyright © The Economist Newspaper Ltd. Reprinted with permission.

Nimpoeno, The Banker's Song, from a letter to the editor, Far Eastern Economic Review, August 11, 1983. Reprinted with permission.

Pearson, Emergency Protection in the Footwear Industry 9-23, Thames Essay No. 36 (London: Trade Policy Research Centre, 1983). Reprinted with permission.

Restatement Second of Foreign Relations Law of the United States, Tentative Draft No. 4, dated April 1, 1983, §§801-804. Copyright © by the American Law Institute. Reprinted with the permission of the American Law Institute.

Rivers and Greenwald, The Negotiation of a Code on Subsidies and Countervailing Measures: Bridging Fundamental Differences, 11 Law & Poly. Intl. Bus. 1447, 1470-1474. Copyright © 1979. Reprinted with permission of the copyright holder and the author.

Smith, Badger Revisited, Implications for the Implementation of the Transfer of Technology Code, 1 Intl. Tax & Bus. Law. 117, 125-130. Permission to reprint granted by the International Tax & Business Lawyer, Boalt Hall School of Law, University of California, Berkeley.

Tharp, Auto Curb Hailed in U.S., May 2, 1981. Copyright © 1981 by The New York Times Company. Reprinted by permission.

Welt, Countertrade: Business Practices for Today's World Market, an American Management Briefing, 15-19, 21-23, © 1982 Leo G. B. Welt. Published by AMA Membership Publications Division, American Management Associations, New York. All rights reserved.

INTERNATIONAL TRADE AND
INVESTMENT

PART 1

REGULATION OF
INTERNATIONAL TRADE

Chapter I

Introduction

A. SCOPE OF THIS BOOK

International economic relations may fruitfully be viewed as including three discrete flows: (1) goods, (2) technology and services, and (3) capital.

The most visible and numerically significant flow is trade in goods. Finished goods produced domestically have to vie with imported products and may also be exported. Primary commodities raise different challenges—short-term price instability, long-term price trends, and supply access—and are accordingly regulated in different ways. Moreover, North-South trade poses difficult questions of the relations between the developing countries and the advanced industrial states.

The second trade flow we will consider in this book is trade in technology, chosen both because of its importance as a factor of production and because it is a form of trade in services. Trade in services of all types is becoming more important, as the United States evolves into a more service-oriented economy. Economic development in the United States, after moving from the agricultural to the industrial phase, has now entered a new service phase, resting on transactions in such areas as information, tourism, transportation, advertising, and technology.[1] More than 7 out of every 10 U.S. workers are employed in service industries, and services account for 66% of the U.S. Gross National Product (GNP).[2] Many of these service sectors are extremely complex and

---

[1] In 1900 50% of U.S. workers were employed in the agricultural sector; in 1984 4% of U.S. workers were earning their living on the farm. In recent years the proportion of our work force employed by manufacturing firms dropped from 27% in 1970 to 21% in 1983.

[2] As of May 1982, approximately 73% of the American work force was employed in the service sector. *See* Bureau of Economic Analysis, U.S. Dept. of Commerce, 62 Surv. of Current Bus. 7 at

specialized, especially when, as in such cases as transportation, the area is already subject to special domestic regulation. It is therefore impossible to deal with all these areas, a source of considerable frustration for the authors—but the example of technology transfer will provide a point of beginning.[3] Other services, such as telecommunications, are considered in more summary fashion.[4]

Finally, we consider trade in capital. Direct investment by a home-nation firm, portfolio investment by an investor in another nation, and capital flows through the banking system raise different economic and political considerations. These flows, along with the assistance provided by national governments, are the major source of capital for the developing world, and they are central to the stability of the international economic system. They are also likely to be one of the chief sources of future political dispute.

From a practical standpoint the most important implication of the international character of a business transaction is its inordinate complexity as compared to a domestic transaction, and one result is that legal counsel is more frequently needed for complicated international business than for parallel domestic transactions. Upon entering the international arena, traders immediately confront a welter of difficulties such as language and cultural barriers and differing national laws and regulations. Unpredictable geopolitical factors may be introduced that can jeopardize the sanctity of the proposed transaction.

Three different levels of regulation typically exist in the international trade transaction. The first level is private-party regulation through contractual relationships. The contract between the parties may "legislate" for the transaction with respect to arbitration, conflicts of laws, and other matters. This area is usually known as "private international law."

The second level of regulation includes national government laws that may bear on the transaction—those of the importing, exporting, or a third country. These materials emphasize the regulations and laws of the United States, because that is the authority most of us will have to deal with most frequently. The laws of other governments are considered, however, when appropriate and feasible.

The third level of regulation comprises international controls. The General Agreement on Tariffs and Trade (GATT), the European Community (EC),[5]

9-10 (1982). J. Carlson and H. Graham, The Economic Importance of Exports to the United States 47 (1980); Fisher and Steinhardt, Section 301 of the Trade Act of 1974: Protection for U.S. Exporters of Goods, Services, and Capital, 14 Law & Poly. Intl. Bus. 636 (1982).

[3] We use the term "technology transfer" as a form of shorthand for trade in proprietary rights, which mainly includes the sale of or use of intellectual property rights (i.e., patents, copyrights, or trademarks). "Business services" in international commerce include travel, passenger transportation, shipping and other transportation, and other types of business services (e.g., construction, engineering, banking, communications, advertising, financial), in addition to the use or sale of proprietary rights. We do *not* include in the term "business services" interest on loans, profit, and dividend remittances from foreign affiliates to parent firms, and services provided by governments.

[4] *See,* for example, Chapter IX, pp. 483-484.

[5] European Community regulatory activity is somewhat hybridized, as the EC acts through the national governmental level of regulation as well.

the Organization for Economic Cooperation and Development (OECD), and the United Nations are examples of the international organizations constantly spewing out rules and regulations for traders to worry about. The manager of a Belgian affiliate, for example, must worry whether his widget exports comport with EC export regulations or violate the GATT's subsidy rules. He must also worry about the increasing regulation of multinational enterprises by the OECD, the EC, and the United Nations. If he is exporting the widgets to Sweden he would have also to worry about the impact of the European Free Trade Area (EFTA), especially if he wishes to reexport the widgets to Finland.

B. TRADITIONAL TRADE THEORY AND ITS LIMITATIONS

The core of international economic relations is the international trade transaction, a sale from one nation into another. Questions exist at both the macroeconomic and microeconomic level about such transactions. The basic macroeconomic questions are: (1) why does international trade take place between two given countries; and (2) what are the effects of trade among nations? Microeconomic questions focus on the costs and benefits of the transaction for the importer and the exporter. The purchaser, for example, must ascertain whether it is cheaper to import than to buy domestically. The answer to this question will depend on tariff levels; nontariff barriers to international trade; the tax situation; the determination of who pays for freight, insurance, and financing charges; and the relative strengths of national currencies. This chapter examines the macroissues; traditional and revisionist views of the theory of international trade are considered. The "private law" of international commercial transactions is examined in the next chapter.

1. Why Does Trade Take Place?—A First Explanation[6]

To understand why trade takes place *between* countries it is useful to see why trade takes place *within* countries. In other words, using the United States as an example, why is steel produced in Pittsburgh, citrus fruit in California and Florida, and cars in Detroit? The phenomenon of *intracountry* regional specialization has traditionally been explained in terms of what are called "factor endowments." Thus, it would not make sense for the North to attempt to grow citrus fruits since states in the snowbelt do not have the climate that is ideal for their production; similarly, it would be inefficient for steel to be produced in

---

[6]This section draws on Fisher, The Multinationals and the Crisis in United States Trade and Investment Policy, 53 B.U.L. Rev. 308, 318-323 (1973).

an area that was distant from the iron ore, coal, and capital equipment needed in the steel industry. In other words, the traditional view is that the reason for interregional trade *within* countries is that each region is abundantly supplied, compared with other regions, with certain productive resources that render it especially well-suited for the production of a particular commodity. Under the traditional theory, it is assumed that each region possesses a *comparative advantage* in the production of some items, and a *comparative disadvantage* in the production of other items.

Turning to *international* trade, that is, trade between nation-states, the traditional economists such as Ricardo[7] hypothesized that trade takes place because substantial benefits are to be derived from countries specializing in the exportation of goods for which they are, relatively speaking, the lowest-priced producer. Some time later, Ohlin explained that the comparative advantage of different countries derives from differing relative endowments of such factors as labor, land, and capital.[8]

The traditional theory of trade can be demonstrated by the following two-product example of hypothetical price relationships prevailing in economic isolation, assuming that $1 U.S. equals $1 Canadian:

	Canada	*United States*
Cloth (per yard)	$1	$1
Wheat (per bushel)	$2	$3

Which goods will be exported when economic contacts between the two countries in the above example are opened? The traditional answer, proffered by Ricardo, was that the goods that are exported between the two countries could be predicted in advance by knowing the differences in the relative prices. Thus, cloth is relatively cheaper in the United States than in Canada; in the United States cloth is one-third the price of wheat, while in Canada it is one-half the price of wheat. Since the United States makes relatively cheaper cloth, it was argued, the United States would specialize in the production of cloth, and export it to Canada. A person could start with one bushel of wheat in Canada, take it to the United States and obtain three yards of cloth. Coming back to Canada, he could keep one yard as profit and use the other two to recover his original bushel of wheat.

This theory of trade was buttressed by the Heckscher-Ohlin principle of comparative costs, which states that

> a country tends to specialize in the production of, and to export, those commodities requiring in their production large amounts of productive factors in relatively abundant supply in that country, and to import [from abroad] those commodities requiring in their production large amounts of productive factors in relatively scarce supply at home.[9]

[7]See D. Ricardo, On the Principles of Political Economy and Taxation (1819).

[8]B. Ohlin, Interregional and International Trade (1933).

[9]D. Snider, Introduction to International Economics 35 (1963) (the theory of comparative costs was first articulated by the Swedish economist E. Heckscher and later developed in B. Ohlin).

2. The Effects of International Trade

The second major question discussed by the traditional economists was the gains to be derived from international trade. The prices described in the previous section would soon change into equilibrium prices, prices established when supply exactly equals demand. Suppose these equilibrium terms of trade turned out to be one bushel of wheat equals 2.5 yards of cloth. Domestically, Canadians could obtain two yards of cloth per bushel of wheat given up (not produced); with trade, they obtain 2.5 yards of cloth per bushel of wheat given up (exported), a net gain of 0.5 yards of cloth. In the United States, without trade, each bushel of wheat produced involves a sacrifice of three yards of cloth; with trade, cloth can be obtained at the rate of 2.5 yards per bushel, a net gain of 0.5 yards of cloth. The example demonstrates that with trade the world production is expanded, and each country has a greater volume of goods available to it as a result.

It does not follow, however, that each segment of society will be made better off by trade. For this to occur, each country's polity must redistribute the overall gains realized from trade among the various segments of the population; adjustment assistance might, for example, be granted to those in the disfavored factor sectors if maximum social welfare benefits are to be obtained. In the example, U.S. farmers and Canadian textile makers might seek assistance, for they would not benefit as much as Canadian farmers and U.S. textile makers. Any artificial interference with the allocation of scarce productive sources—through barriers to international trade—will, however, reduce the *world's* total real income (see *infra* pp. 13-15).

There are, nevertheless, several relatively technical cases in which free trade can disadvantage a nation and a tariff becomes actually beneficial to that nation. These technical cases, explained in the following section, are infrequently applicable. Moreover, they are all beggar-thy-neighbor situations. In free trade, national advantage is gained along with advantageous (or at worst indifferent) effects on other nations. In the special cases, the advantage is gained at another nation's expense, and that nation's effort to restore its position leaves all worse off.

3. A Diagrammatic Explanation of Trade Theory

It is possible to present the theory of free trade in a relatively simple graphic presentation that allows insight into its limitations as well as into the power of the theory.[10]

---

[10]The graphical approach is modeled on that of Haberler, Some Problems in the Pure Theory of International Trade in R. Caves & H. Johnson (eds.), Readings in International Economics 213 (1968).

a.   Single-Nation Equilibrium

Suppose that our attention can be focused on only one economy, so small that its trade with the rest of the world will not affect prices outside its borders. Suppose, also, that there are only two commodities to be traded: cotton (labor intensive) and steel (capital intensive). The first of these assumptions makes the presentation easier, and the possibility of price effects outside the nation can easily be brought into the analysis, as will be noted below. Neither does the two-commodity approach affect the result; more commodities could be included but at the cost of requiring a multidimensional graphic presentation.

Next, assume that our nation can produce a mix of cotton and steel products according to the "production possibility function," whose curve is shown in Figure 1-1. Such a curve, which shows the total production capability of the society, is also sometimes known as a "production frontier." Our nation can produce any combination of cotton and steel products shown on the line, but cannot produce any cotton or steel products outside its production frontier. (Of course, a nation can produce within its production frontier, as might happen during a recession or through plain inefficiency. We assume here that the economy is fully employed.) At point P along the curve, for example, the nation is producing amount OC of cotton and OS of steel. Production of one of the classes of products, cotton or steel, cannot be increased without decreasing the production of the other, moreover, as more of one product is produced, the corresponding decrease in the production of the other becomes that much more severe. That is, the nation must divert more and more resources from the production of the one to the production of the other product. This is known among economists as the law of diminishing returns or the law of variable proportions and accounts for the concave shape of the curve with respect to the origin. The assumption that a production function of the type shown in Figure 1-1 actually exists is unrealistic only in one respect—it assumes full employment, an assumption that will be lifted later.

Let us at this point introduce the economist's concept of utility. This will have to be done in a somewhat rough-and-ready way for, as we shall see, while the concept has a relatively clear application to an individual's behavior, it is very difficult to apply it to an entire society. With this caveat, then, let us define the utility of a good as the satisfaction the good yields to a particular consumer. Now one immediate problem with this is that there is no obvious standard of utility. It is difficult to understand what a consumer would mean if he were to say "this product gives me 2.75 times more utility than that one," i.e., that he is satisfied 2.75 times more by this product than by that. What he can say, though, and where the concept of utility becomes illuminating, is that he *prefers* this combination of products to that combination of the same products, or that between these two combinations, he is *indifferent*. We can imagine him saying, looking ahead a bit, that he prefers the combination of X amount of cotton plus Y amount of steel to the combination of R amount of cotton plus S amount of steel, or perhaps that he is indifferent to which of the two combi-

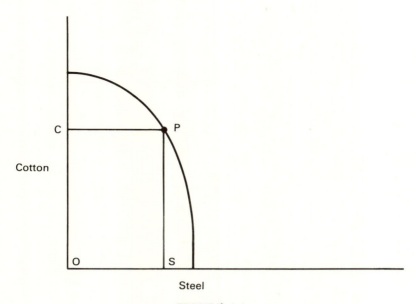

FIGURE 1-1
At point P on the production frontier the nation is producing
OC cotton and OS steel.

nations he chooses and that one combination will satisfy him as well as another.

This indifference concept underlies the curves in Figure 1-2. These curves are called "utility curves" (sometimes, "indifference curves"). Each curve represents, at a particular level of purchasing power, a series of combinations of cotton and steel products that might satisfy a buyer. For instance, while points A and B on curve U-2 represent different combinations of products, the individual purchasing combination A or B is indifferent to which he buys—each equally satisfies (hence, an "indifference curve"). Such curves are always convex with respect to the origin. Suppose we move up curve U-2 from A to B. As we move we are, in effect, passing through several different combinations of cotton and steel products, and as we move from A to B the amount of steel diminishes and greater quantities of cotton products are needed to offset the give-up on steel. A consumer must have very much clothing to give up the last bit of transportation and (say) kitchen utensils—and vice versa.

Each curve can be thought of as existing at a different level of purchasing power. All combinations on U-2 are equally appealing, as are all those on U-1, but each combination of U-2 is richer and more appealing than the combinations of U-1. Similarly, U-3 is preferable to U-2. For our individual buyer there is, in theory, a curve through each point in the diagram, although only three are shown. Economists call the totality of these curves the individual's "preference map."

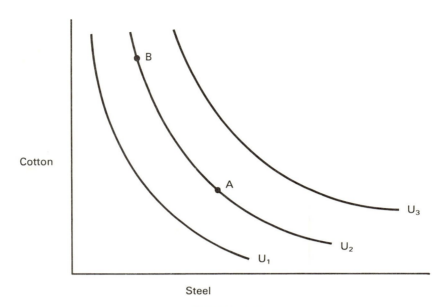

Cotton

Steel

FIGURE 1-2
All the combinations on U-1 are equally satisfying to a consumer, as are those on
U-2 and U-3, but the combinations on U-2 are preferable to those on U-1, and
those on U-3 to those on U-2 and U-1

As logical as these utility curves are for individuals, they become objects of controversy when it is claimed that they can be drawn for an entire society. If we hypothesize a *de minimis* society composed of just two consumers, one of whom likes cotton products relatively more than the other, then how should the two individual curves be added together to produce the utility curve for the society as a whole? If one of the consumers has quite a bit more money than the other, that person's curve will dominate the society's apparent behavior. On the other hand, what if relative income changes during an economic process? Given the absence of any absolute standard of utility that has the assent of all, it should come as no surprise that economic theory is unable to make interpersonal comparisons of utilities. Hence, although we will assume a constant set of utility curves in our analysis, this assumption hides a complex distribution problem: in any society, those helped by trade may not have the same consumer preferences as those hurt by trade. What follows, then, is an approximation, but a useful approximation.

It is now possible to put the concepts together in a combined figure, Figure 1-3, in which the society produces at the level corresponding to the highest utility curve that just touches (is tangent to) the production frontier. It produces OC amount of cotton and OS amount of steel.

To help understand why the society will reach this point—the equilibrium

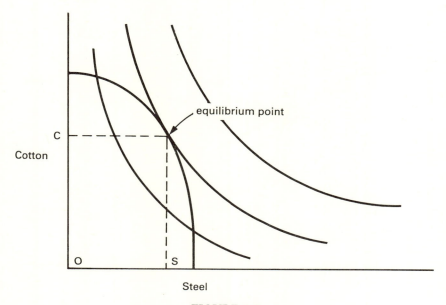

FIGURE 1-3
The nation reaches an equilibrium point when its production of commodities is just balanced by its demand for the commodities

point—it will be useful to amplify an idea adumbrated earlier: in our graphical representation of the situation a price can be viewed as a *slope*. Mathematically, the slope of a curve is the ratio of a vertical change to the corresponding horizontal change of a line tangent to the curve at a particular point. What this boils down to is displayed in Figure 1-4. At any point along the production frontier of that figure the two commodities can be traded off one for the other in a proportion corresponding to the slope of a line tangent at that point. Along AA, for instance, we see that by giving up a small amount of cotton production, the society can gain a great deal of steel. Here we would say that cotton is relatively valuable or high-priced, steel is relatively low-priced. Along BB, the relationship is reversed. With this concept in hand, and looking at Figure 1-5, we can see why and how our producer-nation reaches its equilibrium point.

Suppose the society were producing at point P, which differs from the optimum corresponding to P^1. What this means is that at any price relationship between that corresponding to the slope of AA on the first utility curve (as we said, a relatively high price for cotton) and the slope BB on the production frontier (a much lower price for cotton), producers and consumers find it desirable (maximizing) to shift toward more production and consumption of cotton and away from production and consumption of steel. This process is dynamic, and the nation works along the production frontier to the point of

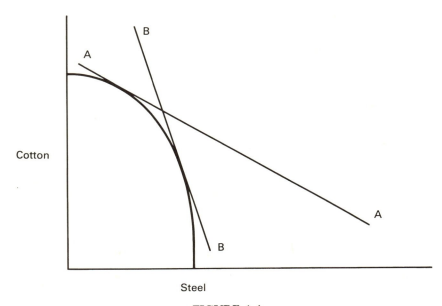

FIGURE 1-4
The commodities can be traded for one another according to a price determined
by the slope of line tangent to the production frontier

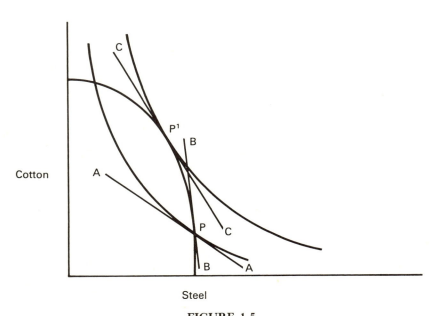

FIGURE 1-5
The nation will shift production towards the commodity having the most (relative)
utility, eventually reaching the equilibrium point

12

tangency P¹, that point, that is, where the production frontier is just tangent to the next highest utility curve. The price relationship at this point is the slope CC of the common tangent—the nation has achieved its equilibrium point.

b.   The Benefits of Trade and the Costs of Import Protection

The admittedly intimidating, but actually quite understandable, Figure 1-6 shows the benefit of trade for our small nation-producer. Under our assumptions, the economy—absent trade—achieves its equilibrium point P, producing exactly what it consumes, the price corresponding to the tangent common to its first utility curve and its production frontier. However, in the world beyond there is the world price, corresponding to the slope WW. It is our local producers' perception of this world price that provides a stimulus to trade. Why?

If we compare the equilibrium slope with WW, it is apparent that local producers of cotton are comparatively advantaged with respect to nonlocal producers, while local producers of steel are comparatively disadvantaged with respect to nonlocal producers. Steel producers, seeing their options, shift

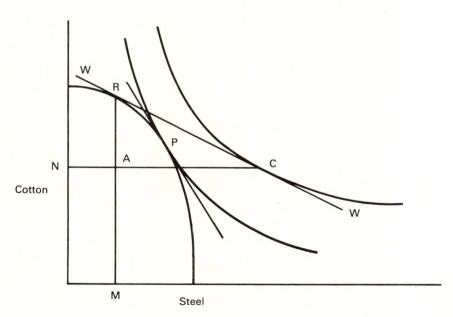

FIGURE 1-6
Producers will respond to the world price structure by devoting more resources to
their comparatively advantaged commodity. Trading this commodity on the world
market results in a net gain, moving the nation as a whole onto
a higher utility curve

their resources into the production of cotton and move the society to point R. MR represents now the total cotton production, with MA being the amount sufficient for the nation's internal needs. The extra amount, AR, can be traded on the world market for the amount AC of steel at the world price. (AN steel is produced locally.) There is, then, a net gain to the society because the consumers will consume on a higher utility curve than they would without the trade. Given the concave-convex relationship of the two sets of curves, and as long as there is a difference in the local price and the world price (which will favor one group of local producers and give them a comparative advantage), trade will be beneficial and will more than compensate for the lost production of the disadvantaged producers. Indeed, if we lift the assumption that our example economy is too small to affect the world economy, the opening of trade will affect prices there and produce benefits to other consumers. Let us now, though, introduce a next step into this account: what happens if, for whatever reason, a tariff is imposed on imported steel? As Figure 1-7 shows, the tariff will leave the nation's economy better off than in the absence of trade but not so well off as with free trade.

A tariff can be regarded as a way to create an artificial price. Without a tariff the initial higher-than-world price of steel will fall to the world price. Imposition of a tariff will arrest this fall to a point somewhere between the initial price and the world price. In effect, the tariff weakens the exporting nation's comparative advantage, i.e., the comparative advantage-disadvantage gap is narrowed in favor of the importing nation's steel producers. This will benefit the local producers. However, following the no-free-lunch principle, the artificially enhanced price is purchased only at a price.

Suppose the tariff-induced price corresponds to the slope AA of the production frontier at point T. Since producers will optimize at the price they perceive, regardless of how that price is set, this is the point at which production will occur. The local producers benefit. But what of the nation's consumers? How does the tariff affect them? The situation here is a bit more complicated.

Consumers, too, will react to the price they perceive. Note, though, that no matter what tariff legerdemain the nation engages in (at least for a hypothetically small nation), the world price remains unaffected. (An overstatement. For any nation, of course, the world price will be affected, and where a large nation is involved, it will be significantly affected. *See* p.16 *infra.*) Now, the consumers, perceiving the artificially induced price AA, will attempt to consume at that price on the world market. But their ability to acquire goods by trade is determined by the world price WW. Attempting to purchase at AA, they trade down the line TC, corresponding to WW, until a line parallel to AA becomes tangent to a utility curve, here U-2. Thus, the effect of the tariff on local consumers is to consign them to a lower utility curve than would be the case with free trade, here curve U-3 at point R. The tariff does protect the local steel industry, which does not have to reduce its production so much as it would with free trade, but the nation's consumers bear the costs of this.

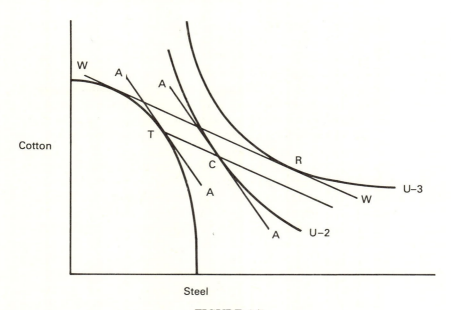

FIGURE 1-7
A tariff-induced price consigns the nation's consumers to a lower utility curve than
would be the case with free trade

In short, free trade theory implies the following effects for an economy such
as that of the United States:

(a) more goods are made available to the population;

(b) consumers benefit by moving to a higher consumer utility curve, obtaining a greater diversity of choice;

(c) vigorous foreign competition serves as a prod to innovation and adjustment by producers—such a development, while beneficial to the consumers, may cause severe unemployment in import-sensitive industries;

(d) trade serves as a deterrent to the creation of domestic monopolies and promotes a more competitive domestic marketplace; and

(e) freer trade acts as an antidote to inflation—the presence of foreign imports prevents the price of scarce local supplies from being bid up precipitously.

c. The Logical Limitations of the Free Trade Theory

The distribution problem goes beyond the formal problem of inability to make interpersonal comparisons of utilities. Free trade will, in the model just described, move jobs from the steel industry to the cotton industry. An economic analysis will show that it is generally better to accept that shift, subsidizing, if necessary, the retraining and movement accompanying the shift.[11] Yet, in the real world, political considerations often make that subsidy impossible while leaving the tariff misallocations politically tolerable. The subsidy is part of a government budget in a capital-scarce world; the effects of the tariff are disguised in relative prices. Moreover, distribution or national security concerns may lead one to hesitate to let completely free trade impose further costs on such depressed industries as steel and textiles for the sake of the nation's winners such as service-related industries, high-tech enterprises, and agriculture. There is a combination of taxes and subsidies that would accept free trade and leave everyone better off, but it is probably politically infeasible in light of the power of organized labor and particular industries.

In addition to this point, there are several more technical limitations to the free trade theory. All are proposed much more frequently than they are really applicable—yet they exist as arguments that may have a temporary validity—and, certainly, have a great political importance.

The first is commonly identified as the *terms of trade* argument.[12] To analyze this possibility, we must lift the assumption that trade with the nation we are analyzing has no effect on world prices. Suppose, in fact, that a buying nation is so powerful in the world market as to have significant effect on prices. As suggested in Figure 1-8, if it imposes a tariff, which will tend to reduce its own imports, that tariff will reduce world prices, corresponding to a flatter world price line. Conceivably, this price effect is so great as to leave the nation spending less for its imports than with free trade. Other nations will be less well off. As an example, consider the possibility that the United States is so major a global consumer of automobiles that a tariff on imports might significantly lower the global price of cars by decreasing global demand. The United States consumer would have to pay more for automobiles, but the proceeds of the tariff would be available to the government and fewer exports would be needed to purchase one automobile. As an argument for tariffs, the logic is only rarely applicable. It requires extensive market power—and if those affected by it can assemble comparably effective market power, they can take the benefit away from the first group, and all are worse off.

The second valid argument is the *infant industry* argument, developed by Alexander Hamilton and currently strongly urged on behalf of developing nations. The free trade logic is static and rests on the production possibilities and factor endowments of a particular time—but many nations would like much broader production possibilities for the future. Hence, they would like to use tariffs to affect the relative profitabilities of different industries and to ensure that their production frontier evolves in particular (generally high-tech) directions. Tariffs can certainly do this, efficiently or not. For a period,

---

[11]*See* W. Diebold, The United States and The Industrial World 185 (1972).

[12]The words "terms of trade" are often used more broadly to describe the exchange between exports and imports, for example, the price in agricultural products that a developing nation must pay for manufactured imports or the price in terms of manufactured goods that a developed nation must pay for oil.

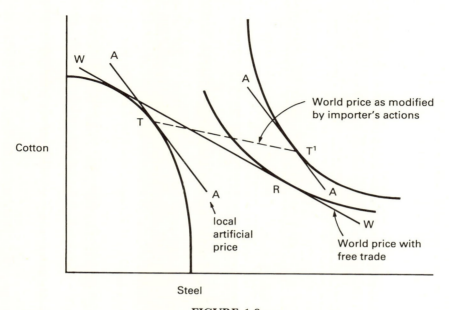

FIGURE 1-8
If a nation is economically so powerful that its buying practices affect world prices, a tariff imposed by that nation will depress world prices

for example, high tariffs on assembled automobiles led to the creation of small inefficient automobile assembly plants in many nations. Such a tariff can encourage the creation of an industry that would otherwise not be economical but can, after its start-up period, become economical. (There is doubt, of course, whether the political impulse will exist to remove the tariff at the later point.)

Finally, and crucially for a world marked globally by economic sluggishness, there are the *"Keynesian"* or *macroeconomic* questions of unemployment, imbalance of payments, and the monetary system. Few nations actually operate on their production frontier—most are operating well below it with significant unemployment. Governments therefore seek to increase employment.

Internationally, governments encourage their economies to export more than is imported, i.e., to run a balance-of-trade surplus, and gain the employment associated with manufacturing the extra exports. Thus, as United States wheat is sold to the Soviet Union, the Midwest (and the U.S. farm equipment industry, etc.) receive a boost from this injection of demand. In contrast, if the United States imports automobiles from Japan, it is the Japanese economy that receives the benefit of the direct and indirect employment.

As suggested by Figure 1-9, however, economies interact in such a way as to make it very difficult to pursue such policies. Most obviously, not all nations can run a surplus—one nation's surplus is another's deficit. More subtly, if a

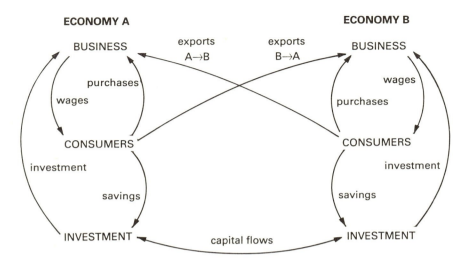

FIGURE 1-9
In a free trade environment national economies will tend
towards a balance of trade

nation maintains a continued balance-of-trade surplus, it is likely to suffer the inflation that seems automatically to accompany efforts to increase employment. Its citizens will receive income corresponding not only to what is made for domestic consumption but also corresponding to what is exported. This excess demand may thus bid up domestic prices. Moreover, the nation's currency will tend to rise in value in comparison with other currencies, as people in other nations seek to pay for the products they are buying from it. Both effects will make its products appear more expensive on world markets and tend to slow exports, increase imports, and bring the balance of trade back towards equilibrium.

Even more complicated effects arise when effects on savings are considered. A nation in a balance-of-trade deficit is manufacturing less than it is consuming, and is therefore, on net, decreasing its savings. Interest rates may, therefore, tend to rise. (They are also affected by the policy decisions, in the United States, of the Federal Reserve System and in other countries by its foreign analogues). And, as interest rates rise, foreign savings are likely to be attracted in order to gain the higher return.[13] To add to the complication, investors choosing among different national currencies will also attempt to take into

---

[13] In the early 1980s, for example, the effect of high U.S. interest rates, coupled with the desirability of the United States as a "safe haven" in which to invest, was the bidding up of its currency by foreigners seeking to take advantage of these high rates and U.S. political stability. The appreciation of the dollar vis-à-vis foreign currencies sharply reduced the competitiveness of U.S. export pricing; *see* Bergsten, The Cost of Reaganomics, 44 Foreign Poly. 24, 31 (1981).

account the prospects of inflation in different nations as well. In this world, clearly very complex and not yet well understood, it is possible that barriers to imports can help a single economy. Almost certainly, however, competition among nations to build such barriers will be harmful to all.

C.   OTHER THEORIES OF INTERNATIONAL TRADE[14]

The traditional theory of international trade is elegant. Unfortunately, it does not accurately describe observed world trading patterns in manufactures. The concern that comparative costs perhaps did not explain trade patterns in manufactures first appeared in 1953, when Leontief showed that United States export industries were heavily labor-intensive.[15] This finding dramatically undermined the Heckscher-Ohlin theory of comparative costs, since the United States was generally considered to have an abundance of capital, and to be poorly endowed with labor. More recently, it was also questioned why, for example, the United States was producing and exporting such products as optical crystals, when the comparative cost advantage of scientific personnel needed to produce such crystals was to be found in Israel.[16] To cope with these observed phenomena, a new theory called the "product life cycle" theory, which attempts to consolidate and address the questions of trade and investment within a coherent model, began to surface in the business schools of the United States.[17] It has been followed by other new theories.

The major assumptions of the product life cycle theory are:

(1) there is not an absolute flow of information across international boundaries—on the contrary, the information needed to make high-technology organizations run in high gear is drastically restricted through patents and other techniques;[18]

(2) corporations act in the world economy as Galbraith informs us they do in The New Industrial State—they not only react to domestic demand, but also have the capacity to shape it;[19] and

[14] Parts of this section draw heavily on Wells, International Trade: The Product Life Cycle Approach, The Product Life Cycle and International Trade 3-33 (1972) and on Barton, Technology Trade, Proc. of 77th Ann. Mtg. A.S.I.L. 130 (1985).

[15] Leontief, Domestic Production and Foreign Trade: The American Capital Position Re-examined, 97 Proc. Am. Phil. Socy. 332 (1953).

[16] Wells, supra note 14, at 11. See also S. Hirsch, Location of Industry and International Competitiveness (1967).

[17] It was perhaps logical that the business schools should be the first to isolate the impact of economic transnationalism on international trade, since they are typically closer than economics departments of universities to what international business is doing and how it relates to the international environment.

[18] Wells, supra note 14, at 5-6.

[19] Id. See J. Galbraith, The New Industrial State, 4th ed. (1985), for a trenchant analysis of the performance of large corporations in modern economic society.

(3) the management of the mature corporations is astute in increasing multinational profits in the long run by adjusting to changing national and international economic conditions such as the presence of tariffs abroad.[20]

The product life cycle model can be presented in a series of phases.[21]

(a) In the first phase, a corporation within the exporting market, such as the United States, produces items that are likely to appeal to high-income American citizens. Despite relatively more expensive American labor, the corporation will initially produce in the United States to be "near the market" and thus be able to translate market information into product changes—it is more important to know the market requirements of the new product than to maximize profits or save labor costs. The corporation will next export the product into foreign markets, "educating" them about the product, and in many instances, convincing foreigners that they need the product in question.

(b) As the foreign market becomes more familiar with the exported product, that is, "educated," local demand for local production also develops. The commencement of local production will tend to come sooner when local tariffs are high, local income elasticity of demand is low, and the size of the local market is large. Following the commencement of production in the "educated" foreign market, United States exports to that market will decline over time. Corporate transnational networks or local firms will preempt the local market in varying degrees from United States exports. Whether transnational firms or local entrepreneurs will play this role depends on the economies of integration, on the appeal of trademarks, on the transferability of the technology, and even on the firm's preferences for integration as opposed to licensing arrangements.

(c) The countries engaged in local production—whether with their own firms or with multinational enterprises—can typically soon undersell the American competitor due to the relatively higher American labor costs. First United States exports to nonproducing countries will be displaced to a degree by exports from other countries engaged in local production of the traded goods. Then, low-wage foreign production will increase its efficiency and maximize available economies of scale so that it is able to absorb United States tariffs and transport costs and still sell profitably in the American market. The United States will thus become a net importer of the product in question. Thus, certain electronic consumer goods produced in Hong Kong and Taiwan can successfully compete with American products.[22] It is this phase of the product life cycle that has given rise to organized labor's contention that

---

[20]The theory is almost Schumpeterian in its emphasis on the role of the innovative entrepreneur, *see* J. Schumpeter, Capitalism, Socialism, and Democracy (1950). *See* Wells, *supra* note 14, at 9.

[21]The leading description of the product life cycle has been offered in Vernon, International Investment and International Trade in the Product Cycle, 80 Q.J. Econ. 190 (1966). A five-phase model is offered in Wells, *supra* note 14, at 11-16.

[22]Wells, *supra* note 14, at 16-25.

multinational enterprises are setting up factories abroad merely to reimport products into the United States.[23]

The product life cycle theory is not the only one evolving to help explain the difference between the real world and the free trade theory. For example, theories based on Chamberlainian monopolistic competition are now being elaborated to explain international cross-trade in such product areas as automobiles and electronics.[24] Chamberlain's underlying work,[25] going back to the 1930s, was a theory of quasimonopolistic competition among differentiated products such as automobiles or cameras. Each brand has a quasimonopoly, for it is different from the other products. Yet, the products are substitutable enough that monopoly power is quite limited and new entry into the industry can drive profits to zero. Chamberlain's theory provided insight into these markets and into such factors as the number of semicompeting products that would be likely to emerge within a single industry.

When two such economies open trade, it is reasonable to assume that there will be cross-trade. For example, some Europeans will prefer U.S.-brand automobiles and vice-versa. It turns out that a strong and important statement can be made under fairly general conditions: the market that was bigger in the first place is likely to export more to the smaller market than vice-versa. "[C]ountries will tend to export those goods for which they have relatively large domestic markets."[26]

This is closely related to the "learning curve phenomenon"—the decrease in production cost as a firm gains experience. With semiconductor computer memories, for example, the cost per bit of storage has declined by about 30% for each doubling of production volume. Between 1973 and 1981, the cost of producing one bit of memory declined by about 97%.[27] The industry that first begins working down this learning curve has a continuing cost advantage over later competitors.

To the extent that these arguments are correct, the technical leader that is working from a larger market base can out-compete new entrants or those coming from smaller market bases. The law of diminishing returns is stood on its head. Under the high-tech arguments, the effect of a government subsidy "targeting" a particular industry or of an opportunity to develop a large protected market is thus to create an advantage that lasts "forever." With steel, a short-term advantage can be compensated for and everything will

[23] Jagar, The Foreign Trade and Investment Act of 1972: Three Points of View, 7 Colum. J. World Bus., Mar.-Apr. 1972, 16, 17.

[24] Ethier, National and International Returns to Scale in the Modern Theory of International Trade, 72 Am. Econ. Rev. 389 (1982). Krugman, Scale Economies, Product Differentiation, and the Pattern of Trade, 70 Am. Econ. Rev. 950 (1980).

[25] See E. Chamberlain, The Theory of Monopolistic Competition (1933).

[26] Krugman, supra Note 24 at 950.

[27] Hearings on Trade in Services and Trade in High Technology Products Before the Subcomm. on Trade of The House Comm. on Ways & Means, 97th Cong., 2d Sess. (1982) (statement of Charles E. Sporck on behalf of the Semiconductor Industry Association at 16).

arguably work out afterwards. With semiconductors, it is plausible to suppose, a short-term subsidy—or any other protective device—can confer a lasting advantage.

A far more sinister implication of the high-tech theories is that the situation of the developing nations is much more desperate than it would seem to be on the basis of the more traditional theories. Under traditional theories, the developing nations would have a chance to catch up if only other nations gave their exports a fair chance; under the high-tech theory, their position of technological inferiority is almost irreversible.

These high-tech theories thus directly contradict the more traditional economic theories. Free trade logic would have industry distribution reflect comparative advantage. Product cycle theory would have industries move down the wage ladder to lower and lower wage nations. These new theories, however, would have industries stay in the places that pioneer them, or subsidize them to a position of leadership.

These theories must not in every instance be accurate or the United States would have long been frozen in a position of superiority. Their current force is probably strongest for rapidly changing technologies whose production facilities are capital intensive rather than labor intensive. There are clearly ways to challenge such a leader, for example, through education and underlying basic research. Moreover, there are sometimes benefits in being *second* to develop a technology—being able to benefit from others' errors and even research, which can never be protected fully by patents. For example, it has been said that the French have much more successfully developed nuclear power for commercial purposes than the United States due to their ability to avoid errors already made by the United States. And the location of the next major technological breakthrough that brings a completely new learning curve and product is probably not predictable by any theory.

The product life cycle and high-tech theories are offered only to explain trade and investment in manufactures. For trade in agricultural products, and in "nonfootloose" industries, the Heckscher-Ohlin Theory would still appear to be valid. Even for manufacturing, alternate theories do not undermine the law of comparative advantage, but rather buttress it by recognizing that tariffs and other barriers to trade offer an artificial inducement for corporations to invest abroad. Moreover, the traditional goal of maximizing the marginal productivity of the factors of production still holds, despite the product life cycle theory.

D.   THE IMPORTANCE OF INTERNATIONAL ECONOMICS

During the 40 years since World War II, international trade has become increasingly important. Probably the critical measure is that international trade has grown significantly more rapidly than have economies as a whole. Between 1963 and 1982, world exports grew at an average rate of just under 6%, while world commodity output grew at a rate of just over 4%.[28] By 1980, exports had reached about $1.7 trillion, or over 15% of global GNP, up from about 7.5% in 1971.[29]

Figure 1-10 shows how unevenly this trade is distributed, in a reflection of the world's uneven distribution of income. Global trade is dominated by trade within the Western developed world (including Japan). Trade between these nations and any other group such as the developing world or even the oil exporting nations is only about one-fifth as big, or even smaller. Trade with the Eastern bloc, or within the developing world, is still smaller by a factor of two. Although these ratios are dramatic, they are not quite so dramatic as they were a decade or two ago—trade within the developing world and between developed and developing world has been growing more rapidly than other forms of trade, even after allowance for the effects of the 1973 oil price increase.

In the United States exports of goods and services for 1983 were about $334 billion, or over 15% of personal income. Of these exports, about 60% was merchandise, and about one-fifth of this was agricultural products. Imports were about the same as exports, but merchandise made up a larger share. By value, almost a third of that merchandise component was fuel, mainly oil.[30]

The proportion of U.S. goods produced that is exported rose from 14.3% in 1970 to 28.7% in 1980. Imports increased at a greater rate, from a volume equivalent of 14.4% of U.S. products in 1970 to 34.1% in 1980. Between 1960 and 1970 U.S. exports represented 4.4% of U.S. GNP. In the next decade, the share of U.S. output accounted for by exports nearly doubled, rising to 8.5%. In the 1970s, U.S. imports more than doubled, rising from 4.1% to 9.5% of GNP. In other words, almost 20% of the U.S. GNP is now involved in international trade, compared to 2% in 1950. By the end of the twentieth century, 40% of the U.S. GNP could be involved in international trade, reflecting not only the interdependence of the U.S. economy with the world economy, but also the expansion of trade as an engine of growth for the U.S. economy.

Apart from the absolute growth in size of U.S. trade is the shifting composition of U.S. exports and imports. The United States is now trading more with Asia and less with Europe; an economic shift that may also have significant political implications. Relative trade with Western Europe has declined sharply since 1962, when 46% of all the manufactures imported were from Europe, to 28% in 1980. Meanwhile, Asian countries dramatically increased their trade with the United States. Japan's share of manufactured imports to

[28]Calculated from General Agreement on Tariffs and Trade, Intl. Trade 1982/83 at p.1 (Geneva, 1983).

[29]Calculated from U.S. Arms Control and Disarmament Agency, World Military Expenditures and Arms Transfers 1971-1980 at 33, 75 (1983).

[30]These numbers are derived from United States Department of Commerce, 63 Surv. Current Bus. trade tables.

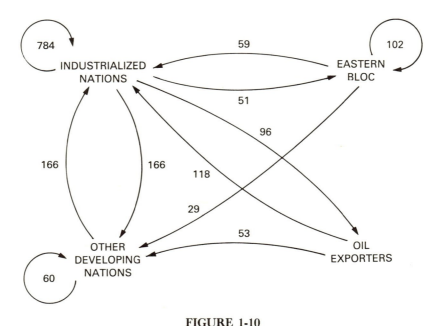

FIGURE 1-10
Uneven levels of income result in uneven levels of trade world-wide
Source: GATT, International Trade 1983/84 (1984). 1983 world exports in billions of dollars; amounts under $20 billion omitted

the United States moved from 16% in 1962 to 24% in 1980. The nations of East Asia, including Korea, Singapore, Hong Kong, and Taiwan, went up from 5% of U.S. imports in 1962 to 16% in 1980. Increasingly, U.S. traders can be expected to look to the Pacific Basin as the dynamic growth market for U.S. trade.

An important hidden trend is the growing role of U.S. trade with less-developed countries (LDCs). Imports from LDCs grew from 29% of total U.S. imports in 1973 to 48% in 1980. The LDCs purchased 37% of U.S. exports in 1980, up from 28% in 1973.

The flows of intangibles such as services, technology, and capital have taken on increasing importance. The imbalances that show up in Figure 1-10 are, at least in significant part, balanced out by flows of capital, ranging from bank loans to direct corporate investment and official government-to-government assistance. Private creditors loaned over $290 billion to non-oil-developing nations between the end of 1973 and the end of 1983,[31] and the total amount of funds deposited in foreign banks in the international Eurodollar market was over $700 billion in 1980.[32] This is greater than the total of demand and

[31]Calculated from World Bank, Debtor Reporting System as reproduced in IMF Surv., June 27, 1983, p.180.
[32]Source is the Bank for International Settlements, as reproduced in IMF Surv., January 12, 1981.

savings deposits in U.S. banks at the time. (The U.S. banks also had time deposits of just under the same amount.)[33]

Profits from foreign operations in 1983 amounted to about a fifth of all corporate profits. Similarly, investment abroad was about one-sixth of all manufacturing investment.[34]

Until recently the United States has relied on these new factors to maintain its own international payments situation in near balance. For 1983, it ran nearly a $60 billion deficit on merchandise trade, i.e., it bought that much more from foreign sellers than it exported to foreign buyers. The same year, it earned over $7 billion net on royalties (including those for licensed technology) and over $23 billion net on investment income.[35]

In 1985 the United States became a net debtor nation, a rapid change from its net creditor peak of $150 billion in 1982. This was due to a growth in the U.S. merchandise trade deficit to $150 billion, a sharp drop in the traditional U.S. surplus in international business services trade, and high levels of private capital inflows in response to higher rates of return by U.S. banks.

E.   THE POLITICS OF INTERNATIONAL ECONOMICS

Most of this text will reflect the politics that surrounds the economic phenomena just discussed. But a very brief review here at the beginning should help the student place the economic ideas in their political context.

1.   The Politics of Trade

Although it is properly subjected to minor adjustments and corrections, the free trade argument is nevertheless almost always correct in its general result: free trade is better for an economy than are trade restrictions. Yet, trade-restricting policies are frequently popular. Why?

The most obvious and important reason is that each import limitation benefits a specific industry, and national political systems in free societies are almost always better at responding to the sharp complaint of a specific industry than to the diffused complaints of consumers affected by higher prices.

In addition to the political appeal of job-related arguments, legislators will be tempted towards protectionist policies promoted by self-serving coalitions of import-impacted industries. Industries are scattered through many different regions of a developed nation, and practically every legislator is interested in

[33]Source is regular tables in 66 Fed. Reserve Bull. (1982).
[34]Data developed from 61 Surv. Current Bus. 33: international transactions table and finance part of regular statistics.
[35]Bach, U.S. International Transactions, Fourth Quarter and Year 1983, 64 Surv. Current Bus. 38, 41-44.

protecting some industry. The result, if tariff legislation comes to a vote, is a strong temptation toward log-rolling—toward trading votes to provide tariffs to help at least 51% of the legislators. In the United States this was one of the causes underlying the high Smoot-Hawley tariffs of 1930. Recognition of the risks of such a result are also one of the reasons why legislatures have delegated significant tariff establishment tasks to the administrative processes discussed later on in this book.

Sometimes, protectionism arises from opposition to what are perceived as unreasonable or "unfair" trade practices of other nations.[36] Moreover, as explained above, certain tariffs can benefit a nation at the expense of other nations, but the other nations can then retaliate. This is particularly serious when increased exports are sought in order to create employment at the expense of employment in the importing nation. And, when a nation subsidizes or otherwise favors its exports, other nations find it hard politically to resist the complaints of unfair competition and therefore impose retaliatory tariffs. In these situations, the avoidance of protectionism generally requires international agreement—nations are less likely to be taken advantage of if they obtain agreements with others that neither will take "unfair" action. Even these agreements may be politically difficult in time of recession, for they are, in a sense, a way to allocate unemployment among the various nations involved. Moreover, if a nation violates the accords, there are few effective sanctions available other than imposing new trade restrictions, which may hurt everyone.

Certain political approaches to trade go further and reject market solutions in the name of long-term goals, as global extensions of the infant industry argument. The developing world, fearful that it will always be but a supplier of raw materials, has sought to encourage industry and a "New International Economic Order" in order to expand its economic base. It argues that, as a matter of economic justice, the developed world should help in this process, and hopes, in imitation of the Organization of Petroleum Exporting Countries (OPEC), to impose higher prices on its exports to the developed world. And the developed world, seeing many of its traditional industries in decline in the face of lower cost imports from the developing world, has sought to intervene to protect these industries and to favor the expansion of new high-technology industries. An important question for students to contemplate as they read this textbook is to what degree *should* governments intervene to assist promising ("sunrise") or troubled ("sunset") industries. This is part of the "industrial policy" debate.

2.   *The Politics of Technology and Services*

Until recently, the international flow of technology was generally unregulated, but this has changed dramatically since World War II and is likely to change

---

[36]For example, the United States and the European Community have protested the import-limiting policies of Japan; the perception of Japan as an unfair trader has triggered protectionist sentiments against Japanese exports in these and other areas.

even more in the future. Nations receiving technology have generally been interested in acquiring as much technology as possible as inexpensively as possible. They once sent people abroad for foreign training. This is still extremely important, as is technology transfer through international institutions and foreign assistance programs. Recent attention, however, has focused heavily on business technology licensing and direct investment. Japan's Ministry of International Trade and Investment carefully reviewed technology licenses during the 1950s and 1960s to ensure that the Japanese recipient was obtaining as favorable an arrangement as possible; developing nations are today imitating this approach and seeking to impose more favorable terms on foreign investors who bring them technology. All these efforts take place against a backdrop of debates over the desirability of "appropriate technology," technology, typically less sophisticated, that seems more in keeping with a simpler and less sophisticated life style, and over the desirability of such advanced technologies as nuclear power or high-energy agriculture.

On the technology suppliers' side, there is more and more interest in legislation to prevent the export of technology and thus to protect the suppliers' competitive position. Most of the actual controls have covered only technologies of military significance. But, by the early 1980s these concerns were broadening. Some of the military arguments appeared to be excuses for economically motivated restrictions; labor unions were pushing governments to restrict the export of technologies that might carry employment with them; and nearly all governments sought to ensure that their own firms and economies were the primary beneficiaries of their subsidies for research in such areas as computers and bio-engineering.

Significant efforts have recently been made to enhance international access for other services, such as telecommunications, insurance, and shipping. Under pressure from the United States, the GATT signatories agreed in 1982 to undertake a survey of barriers to trade in services, with a view towards later negotiations on the growing proliferation of nontariff barriers throughout the world. It now appears likely that expansion of trade in services will be a central concern of the next round of GATT trade negotiations.[37]

3. *The Politics of Investment*

Attitudes toward international investment are much more ideological, and generally reflect either a free trade or liberal economic theory on the one hand or a *dependencia* theory on the other hand.[38]

[37] In November 1985, the members of the GATT agreed to include services as a topic for discussion in a new round, expected to begin by the end of 1986, despite the opposition of Brazil, India, and other developing countries. The Reagan administration has proposed that additional protection be provided for intellectual property rights in a new GATT round, including protection against trade in articles that infringe U.S. process patents, as well as other services such as banking, insurance, and telecommunications.

[38] For a general overview of the main competing theories of international investment, *see* Gilpin, Three Models of the Future in C. Bergsten and L. Krause (eds.), World Politics and International Economics, 29 Intl. Org. 37 (1975).

The arguments of the free trade theory in favor of the free flow of goods do not necessarily apply to the flow of capital. Indeed, within the neoclassical economic theory, the free flow of goods would make that of capital or technology or people unnecessary, and restrictions on the flow of goods are one of the explanations for the movement of capital and people. Ideologically and practically, however, free trade arguments are closely related to those for the free movement of capital. Both reflect a laissez-faire sense that government intervention in the economy is generally unwise and often counterproductive. And the free flow of capital will often produce much the same economic result as the free flow of goods. If it is pursuing its economic self-interest, even the multinational corporation is likely to invest in exactly the same locations and enterprises that would evolve independently under a free-trade regime. Beyond economics, many multinational theorists argue that, as a transnational institution, the multinational is a force that can help the world transcend the limits of the nation-state system.

The counterargument is equally multifaceted. It tends to begin with the actual experiences of host nations with branches of multinational corporations, experiences that are, in too many cases, an analogue of the injustices that drove the labor movement in the United States during the 1930s. There is no surprise in the fact that a Marxist-style class interest argument is often made against foreign investment—and is often persuasive in the developing world. Foreign investment frequently has produced no more than a small developed enclave within a society without creating opportunities for local business. To this, one can add more political arguments. The left often makes the *dependencia* point that foreign investment is a way for developed societies to gain power in developing societies. And in at least a few cases, the right may fear that the social changes associated with foreign investment are likely to break up the power of a traditional oligarchy.

4.   Other Political Themes

These central themes do not exhaust the politics of the international economic system. One much broader theme—whose force is extremely difficult to evaluate—should be mentioned: the question of how international political power and international economic power are linked.

In the one direction, it is abundantly clear that increased economic power brings a nation (or group of nations) increased political power. The obvious example is the Organization of Petroleum Exporting Nations, which, within less than a decade, went from obscurity to the central corridors of power at least for a period. This economic power perhaps transcends the power available from the weapons that the wealth can buy—the wealth itself is a form of power. If so, implications for the developing world—especially for a developing world sinking further and further into debt—are quite troublesome.

The other direction is much more ambiguous. Economic order *may* require political order. Many argue, for example, that the relative success of the liberal economic order of the 1950-1970 period rested in large part on the military dominance of the United States during that period, and that this military dominance was also essential to the dominance of the dollar during that period. For the new world, marked by greater relative Soviet and third-world power, liberal economic arrangements may no longer be possible. Whether or not such specific inferences are accurate, it does seem likely that the possibility of a specific type of international economic order depends on the character of the underlying military and political order.

QUESTIONS

1. Consider the shifting nature of power in the international economic system. What kinds of power are available to a country like Japan, which possesses a dynamic industrial system but only a small military and imports all its oil? In the European countries, which rely on Persian Gulf oil for 70% of their energy supplies and face military pressures from the U.S.S.R. on their eastern flank? In the United States, which relies on Persian Gulf oil supplies for part of its oil supplies, and which is unable to prevent U.S.S.R. military incursions such as the Afghanistan invasion? In Saudi Arabia, which possesses huge oil reserves, a fragile political system, and limited capacity for self-defense?

2. Is global interdependence a good thing? International business transactions bind nations more closely together in an economic sense, but doesn't this:

(a) make countries far more vulnerable to external economic disruptions, magnifying the possible effects of, for example, inflation or an "oil price shock"?

(b) create strong protectionist pressures due to intense foreign competition?

(c) circumscribe autonomy over national monetary and fiscal policies?

John Maynard Keynes wrote in 1933 that: "Ideas, knowledge, art, hospitality, travel, these are things which should of their nature be international. But let goods be homespun whenever it is reasonably and conveniently possible; and, above all, let finance be primarily national." Is Lord Keynes's advice relevant today? Would you support policies—perhaps a return to fixed exchange rates, or a system of "bands" limiting the upward movement of currencies—that might decouple economies from growing interdependence? If the interdependence of national economies is a reality from which there is no turning back, would you support stronger international institutions to keep national policy makers on a common track?

3. How should politicians react to the decline in "smokestack" industries in the United States? Employment has declined from 1979 through 1984 39% in the U.S. automobile industry, 19% in the shoe industry, 47% in steel, and 17%

in the apparel industry. Why do you suppose many Democratic Party candidates have sounded increasingly protectionist, while Republicans have, in a reversal of roles, appeared to support free trade?

Consider the words of former Vice-President Walter Mondale, a Democrat, in 1982:

> We've been running up the white flag when we should be running up the American flag. What do we want our kids to do? Sweep up around Japanese computers and spend a lifetime serving McDonald hamburgers?

Is "industrial policy" a viable alternative to protectionism, a complementary device to be used in tandem with protectionism, something to be rejected along with protectionism? Where are the constituencies for each of these positions? How are they likely to evolve in the future?

4. Consider the case of steel, where governments own raw steel products enterprises in 21 major countries. Should state ownership be encouraged or discouraged? How should the United States respond to the argument of the steel industry that it is somehow not "fair" for private U.S. companies to have to compete against state-owned enterprises?

5. How does commercial policy relate to foreign policy? Would you support quotas on steel or auto imports more (or less) readily if you were secretary of state than if you were the U.S. trade representative, the secretary of commerce, or the secretary of defense?

What would your position be if you were:

(a) president of the United Automobile Workers;
(b) president of the Consumers for World Trade;
(c) president of the American Farm Bureau;
(d) president of Ford Motor Company;
(e) president of Toyota Motor Company; and
(f) president of the American Association of Automobile Parts Producers.

6. Regulation is usually more acceptable if it rests on a theory, such as the "free market" efficiency analysis, the concept of "freedom of contract," or the idea of the "just price." What comparable theories might be applicable to an international trade issue such as the limitation—or not—of auto imports? What types of equity and justice arguments would the different parties make? What about the politician, eager to improve the relative status of his or her nation? Or the economist, interested in avoiding misallocation of resources?

7. What is the relationship between the U.S. budget deficit ($180 billion in 1984) and the U.S. trade deficit ($135 billion in 1984)? Would a reduction in the U.S. budget deficit automatically lead to a reduction in the U.S. trade deficit? What are the economic and political implications of the United States becoming a net debtor nation in 1985?

8. The Reagan administration has since 1981 sharply reduced the provision of adjustment assistance for firms and workers adversely affected by imports. Is this a wise policy?

Bibliographical Note

For further background on economics and international affairs, *see* R. Amacher, G. Haberler, and T. Willett (eds.), Challenges to a Liberal International Economic Order (1979); R. Baldwin, Non-Tariff Distortions of International Trade (1970); C. Bergsten, Toward a New International Economic Order (1975); R. Caves and H. Johnson, Readings in International Economics (1968); R. Cooper, The Economics of Interdependence: Economic Policy in the Atlantic Community (1968); Diebold, Multinational Corporations—Why Be Scared of Them?, 12 Foreign Poly. 79 (1973); I. Gossack, The International Economy and the National Interest (1979); P. Gray, International Trade, Investment and Payments (1979); P. Katzenstein, Between Power and Plenty: Foreign Economic Policies of Industrial States (1978); P. Kenen and R. Lubity, International Economics (1979); R. Shelp, Beyond Industrialization: Ascendancy of the Global Service Economy (1981); Sunkel, Big Business and "Dependencia": A Latin American View, 50 Foreign Affairs 517 (1972); R. Vernon, Sovereignty at Bay (1971); J. Viner, Studies in the Theory of International Trade (1937); and M. v. N. Whitman, International Trade and Investment: Two Perspectives (1981).

Chapter II

The Law of International Trade

A. THE TRADE TRANSACTION ITSELF

A trader faces a variety of special problems in carrying out business when that business is international. It is necessary to deal at long distance with people whom the trader may not know personally. If a conflict arises, the legal systems of the different parties may provide different answers. Moreover, each may regard the other's courts as likely to be unfair; even if a foreign court is fair, using it may be extremely expensive.

Those involved in transnational sales transactions, therefore, have developed a variety of special institutions to reduce their risks. For example, the London insurance companies, complete with global registers of ships, have long offered ways to deal with loss on the high seas. International arbitration has become available as a relatively neutral and inexpensive forum for the settlement of unavoidable disputes.

These institutions are beyond the scope of this text. Some of the special institutions, however, are central to the mechanisms of trade. These include ways to reduce the risks of contractual misunderstanding, to make sure that sellers actually ship goods, and to give sellers confidence that buyers will actually pay. Such arrangements are not always needed; in much international trade, a firm trades with its own subsidiary or a government undertakes the credit risks of an export. Yet, in another large portion of trade, the special institutions are used, and they are unfamiliar enough to deserve attention here.

1. The Trade Transaction and the Letters of Credit Procedure

The typical pattern for the transnational sales transaction between two strangers involves four institutions:

Internationally agreed standard trade contracts are detailed understandings, accepted throughout the world, that allocate the risks and costs of a transaction, and can easily be incorporated by reference in an international sales contract.

The bill of lading is a contract between the shippers and the shipping company that serves also as a receipt indicating that the shipping company has actually received the goods.

The letter of credit is a promise by a bank to make a specified payment under particular and well-defined circumstances.

The documentary draft is a negotiable instrument (a check is a simple example) by which payment can actually be accomplished.

Each of these institutions plays a role in reducing the risks of the transaction. The trader can use the standard trade contract to avoid misunderstandings with his or her foreign counterpart. The bill of lading becomes a way for the buyer to be able to rely on the shipping company, which will usually be easily accessible to all parties, for a guarantee that goods have actually been shipped. The letter of credit enables the seller to rely on a bank's international reputation for a guarantee that payment will actually be made. And, finally, although it is used in part for historical reasons only, the draft permits integration of the payment process into the regular bank clearing system and can also be used in extending short-term credit.

a.   The Sales Contract

The central issues in the contract itself are those surrounding the allocation of costs and risks. Insurance and freight costs are often large enough that it is very important to know whether or not a quoted price includes those costs. Moreover, the parties must be clear who is responsible for obtaining insurance and who is to bear the risk of an uncompensated loss.

The International Chamber of Commerce's "Incoterms"[1] are now the standard forms for international trade. The following two are among the most common of the 14 defined terms.

---

[1] *See* International Chamber of Commerce, Guide to Incoterms (1979). Note that the contract is itself subject to the domestic law (perhaps, for example, the Uniform Commercial Code) of the parties according to the conflict of law principles of the courts before which litigation might occur. In the near future, this law will probably be supplemented by the United Nations Convention on the International Sale of Goods, negotiated by the United Nations Commission for International Trade Law (UNCITRAL). Its text was approved at a diplomatic conference in 1980, and President Reagan submitted it to the Senate in 1983. For background on this convention, *see* Bonell, La nouvelle Convention des Nations-Unies sur les contrats de vente internationale de marchandises, 7 Droit et Pratique du Commerce Internationale 5 (1981); Uncitral Symposium, 27 A.J.C.L. 201 (1979); and Symposium on International Sale of Goods Convention, 18 Intl. Law. 3 (1984). Other new texts have also been or are being negotiated for bills of lading and for drafts and negotiable instruments.

FOB: FREE ON BOARD

International Chamber of Commerce Guide to Incoterms (1979)

FOB means "Free on Board." The goods are placed on board a ship by the seller at a port of shipment named in the sales contract. The risk of loss of or damage to the goods is transferred from the seller to the buyer when the goods pass the ship's rail.

A.   THE SELLER MUST:

1. Supply the goods in conformity with the contract of sale, together with such evidence of conformity as may be required by the contract.

2. Deliver the goods on board the vessel named by the buyer, at the named port of shipment, in the manner customary at the port, at the date or within the period stipulated, and notify the buyer, without delay, that the goods have been delivered on board.

3. At his own risk and expense obtain any export licence or other governmental authorization necessary for the export of the goods.

4. Subject to the provisions of articles B.3 and B.4 below, bear all costs and risks of the goods until such time as they shall have effectively passed the ship's rail at the named port of shipment, including any taxes, fees or charges levied because of exportation, as well as the costs of any formalities which he shall have to fulfil in order to load the goods on board.

5. Provide at his own expense the customary packing of the goods, unless it is the custom of the trade to ship the goods unpacked.

6. Pay the costs of any checking operations (such as checking quality, measuring, weighing, counting) which shall be necessary for the purpose of delivering the goods.

7. Provide at his own expense the customary clean document in proof of delivery of the goods on board the named vessel.

8. Provide the buyer, at the latter's request and expense (see B.6), with the certificate of origin.

9. Render the buyer, at the latter's request, risk and expense, every assistance in obtaining a bill of lading and any documents, other than that mentioned in the previous article, issued in the country of shipment and/or of origin and which the buyer may require for the importation of the goods into the country of destination (and, where necessary, for their passage in transit through another country).

B.   THE BUYER MUST:

1. At his own expense, charter a vessel or reserve the necessary space on board a vessel and give the seller due notice of the name, loading berth of and delivery dates to the vessel.

2. Bear all costs and risks of the goods from the time when they shall have effectively passed the ship's rail at the named port of shipment, and pay the price as provided in the contract.

3. Bear any additional costs incurred because the vessel named by him shall have failed to arrive on the stipulated date or by the end of the period specified, or shall be unable to take the goods or shall close for cargo earlier than the stipulated date or the end of the period specified and all the risks of the goods from the date of expiration of the period stipulated, provided, however, that the goods shall have been duly appropriated to the contract, that is to say, clearly set aside or otherwise identified as the contract goods.

4. Should he fail to name the vessel in time or, if he shall have reserved to himself a period within which to take delivery of the goods and/or the right to choose the port of shipment, should he fail to give detailed instructions in time, bear any additional costs incurred because of such failure, and all the risks of the goods from the date of expiration of the period stipulated for delivery, provided, however, that the goods shall have been duly appropriated to the contract, that is to say, clearly set aside or otherwise identified as the contract goods.

5. Pay any costs and charges for obtaining a bill of lading if incurred under article A.9 above.

6. Pay all costs and charges incurred in obtaining the documents mentioned in articles A.8 and A.9 above, including the costs of certificates of origin and consular documents.

CIF: COST, INSURANCE, AND FREIGHT

International Chamber of Commerce Guide to Incoterms (1979)

CIF means "Cost, Insurance and Freight." This term is the same as C & F but with the addition that the seller has to procure marine insurance against the risk of loss of or damage to the goods during the carriage. The seller contracts with the insurer and pays the insurance premium. The buyer should note that under the present term, unlike the term "Freight/Carriage and Insurance paid to," the seller is only required to cover insurance on minimum conditions (so-called FPA conditions).

A.   THE SELLER MUST:

1. Supply the goods in conformity with the contract of sale, together with such evidence of conformity as may be required by the contract.

2. Contract on usual terms at his own expense for the carriage of the goods to the agreed port of destination by the usual route, in a seagoing vessel (not being a sailing vessel) of the type normally used for the transport of goods of

the contract description, and pay freight charges and any charges for unloading at the port of discharge which may be levied by regular shipping lines at the time and port of shipment.

3. At his own risk and expense obtain any export licence or other governmental authorization necessary for the export of the goods.

4. Load the goods at his own expense on board the vessel at the port of shipment and at the date or within the period fixed or, if neither date nor time has been stipulated, within a reasonable time, and notify the buyer, without delay, that the goods have been loaded on board the vessel.

5. Procure, at his own cost and in a transferable form, a policy of marine insurance against the risks of carriage involved in the contract. The insurance shall be contracted with underwriters or insurance companies of good repute on FPA terms, and shall cover the CIF price plus ten per cent. The insurance shall be provided in the currency of the contract, if procurable.

Unless otherwise agreed, the risks of carriage shall not include special risks that are covered in specific trades or against which the buyer may wish individual protection. Among the special risks that should be considered and agreed upon between seller and buyer are theft, pilferage, leakage, breakage, chipping, sweat, contact with other cargoes and others peculiar to any particular trade.

When required by the buyer, the seller shall provide, at the buyer's expense, war risk insurance in the currency of the contract, if procurable.

6. Subject to the provisions of article B.4 below, bear all risks of the goods until such time as they shall have effectively passed the ship's rail at the port of shipment.

7. At his own expense furnish to the buyer without delay a clean negotiable bill of lading for the agreed port of destination, as well as the invoice of the goods shipped and the insurance policy or, should the insurance policy not be available at the time the documents are tendered, a certificate of insurance issued under the authority of the underwriters and conveying to the bearer the same rights as if he were in possession of the policy and reproducing the essential provisions thereof. The bill of lading must cover the contract goods, be dated within the period agreed for shipment, and provide by endorsement or otherwise for delivery to the order of the buyer or buyer's agreed representative. Such bill of lading must be a full set of "on board" or "shipped" bills of lading, or a "received for shipment" bill of lading duly endorsed by the shipping company to the effect that the goods are on board, such endorsement to be dated within the period agreed for shipment. If the bill of lading contains a reference to the charter-party, the seller must also provide a copy of this latter document.

Note: A clean bill of lading is one which bears no superimposed clauses expressly declaring a defective condition of the goods or packaging.

The following clauses do not convert a clean into an unclean bill of lading: (a) clauses which do not expressly state that the goods or packaging are unsatisfactory, e.g. "second-hand cases", "used drums", etc; (b) clauses which emphasize the carrier's non-liability for risks arising through the nature of the goods or the packaging; (c) clauses which disclaim on the part of the carrier knowledge of contents, weight, measurement, quality, or technical specification of the goods.

8. Provide at his own expense the customary packing of the goods, unless it is the custom of the trade to ship the goods unpacked.

9. Pay the costs of any checking operations (such as checking quality, measuring, weighing, counting) which shall be necessary for the purpose of loading the goods.

10. Pay any dues and taxes incurred in respect of the goods up to the time of their loading, including any taxes, fees or charges levied because of exportation, as well as the costs of any formalities which he shall have to fulfil in order to load the goods on board.

11. Provide the buyer, at the latter's request and expense (see B.5), with the certificate of origin and the consular invoice.

12. Render the buyer, at the latter's request, risk and expense, every assistance in obtaining any documents, other than those mentioned in the previous article, issued in the country of shipment and/or of origin and which the buyer may require for the importation of the goods into the country of destination (and, where necessary, for their passage in transit through another country).

B.   The Buyer Must:

1. Accept the documents when tendered by the seller, if they are in conformity with the contract of sale, and pay the price as provided in the contract.

2. Receive the goods at the agreed port of destination and bear, with the exception of the freight and marine insurance, all costs and charges incurred in respect of the goods in the course of their transit by sea until their arrival at the port of destination, as well as unloading costs, including lighterage and wharfage charges, unless such costs and charges shall have been included in the freight or collected by the steamship company at the time freight was paid.

If war insurance is provided, it shall be at the expense of the buyer (see A.5).

Note: If the goods are sold "CIF landed", unloading costs, including lighterage and wharfage charges, are borne by the seller.

3. Bear all risks of the goods from the time when they shall have effectively passed the ship's rail at the port of shipment.

4. In case he may have reserved to himself a period within which to have the goods shipped and/or the right to choose the port of destination, and he fails to give instructions in time, bear the additional costs thereby incurred and all risks of the goods from the date of the expiration of the period fixed for shipment, provided always that the goods shall have been duly appropriated

to the contract, that is to say, clearly set aside or otherwise identified as the contract goods.

5. Pay the costs and charges incurred in obtaining the certificate of origin and consular documents.

6. Pay all costs and charges incurred in obtaining the documents mentioned in article A.12 above.

7. Pay all customs duties as well as any other duties and taxes payable at the time of or by reason of the importation.

8. Procure and provide at his own risk and expense any import licence or permit or the like which he may require for the importation of the goods at destination.

QUESTIONS

1. The Brazilian Coffee Institute exports 100 bags of green coffee to the Beta Corporation in New York for roasting and grinding in its U.S. facilities. The bags are shipped from Brazil, on June 1, 1984, on an F.O.B. basis, pursuant to the F.O.B. definition cited at pp. 35-36. On June 3, 1984, due to heavy seas, the ship sinks en route to the United States. Who bears the loss in this instance, the Brazilian Coffee Institute or the Beta Corporation?

2. What if, due to leakage, water spoils the shipment of coffee, which arrives ruined in New York? What difference might this make in the outcome?

3. What if, following arrival of the coffee in New York, the coffee is stolen off the deck of the vessel while it is anchored in the harbor? What if the coffee is stolen off the dock after it is unloaded? Who bears the risk of loss here under (a) an F.O.B. sale or (b) a C.I.F. sale?

b. The Bill of Lading

Under either technique of shipment, the seller (or his or her agent) will receive a *bill of lading* from the carrier. This bill is in the form of a contract between the shipper (the person who wants the goods moved) and the carrier (the firm that actually transports them) and serves the standard form contract functions of allocating the various risks of carriage. But it also serves a very important additional function, that of being a receipt that becomes a document of title for the goods, and is frequently negotiable. After the seller receives the bill of lading in return for the goods, it can then sign it over to the buyer and give the latter the right to obtain the goods from the carrier at the destination. The negotiation can be thought of as similar to the negotiation or endorsement of a check—only it transfers the right to receive goods from a carrier rather than that to receive money from a bank. Thus, in form, the buyer can now think of buying the bill of lading—and the buyer's bank can confidently make payment to the seller when the bill of lading is received, rather than having to deal in the goods themselves or wait until they are received at the dock.

BERMAN AND KAUFMAN, THE LAW OF INTERNATIONAL COMMERCIAL TRANSACTIONS (LEX MERCATORIA)

19 Harv. Intl. L.J. 221, 237-243 (1978)

THE DOCUMENTARY CHARACTER OF AN INTERNATIONAL SALE

BILLS OF LADING

Under the typical c.i.f. or other "shipment" contract, the seller is required to select a vessel, to secure the necessary shipping space, and to see to it that the goods are placed on board. At that point the seller normally receives from the carrier a bill of lading. This document has a threefold character: (1) it is the carrier's acknowledgement of receipt of the goods; (2) it embodies the terms of the contract of carriage; and (3) it is a document of title, that is, the person rightfully in possession of it is entitled to possess, use, and dispose of the goods represented by it.

Two kinds of bills of lading should be distinguished: the straight (non-negotiable) bill and the order (negotiable) bill. A straight bill obliges the carrier to deliver the goods to the named consignee whether or not he surrenders the bill of lading. Transfer of a straight bill under the general principles of contract law gives the transferee no greater rights than those of his transferor. A negotiable bill, on the other hand, conveys greater rights, which are generally defined in special legislation.

In the United States, the Federal Bills of Lading Act of 1916 (Pomerene Act)[56] governs bills issued for shipments in interstate and foreign commerce which originate in the United States.[57] Bills of lading issued for shipments of goods to the United States from abroad would presumably be governed by foreign law. Under the Pomerene Act a negotiable bill of lading must be addressed "to the order of" the recipient or "to bearer" and is subject to transfer through due negotiation. The holder of a negotiable bill of lading, provided he has received it in good faith through due negotiation, has a claim to title and, upon surrender of the bill, to delivery of the goods from the carrier regardless of certain rights which the carrier or exporter may have against the

---

[56] 49 U.S.C. §§81-124 (1970). The act covers both straight and negotiable bills of lading, but the provisions on straight bills generally follow the normal rules of contract law and assignment. *See* 49 U.S.C. §112 (1970).

[57] 49 U.S.C. §81 (1970). The rights and obligations of carriers and shippers engaged in a foreign shipment which touches a port in the United States are also governed by the Carriage of Goods by Sea Act [COGSA] of 1936, 46 U.S.C. §§1300-1315 (1970). But COGSA deals mainly with the contract of carriage aspect of the bill of lading and not with its function as a document of title.

person to whom the bill of lading was originally issued or against some inter-vening party. In technical terms the order bill of lading is a negotiable docu-ment of title which may be transferred free of personal defenses.[58] . . .

PAYMENT AGAINST DOCUMENTS IN A C.I.F. CONTRACT . . .

The bill of lading makes the carrier liable for . . . loss or damage only under certain circumstances and only within certain financial limits.[61] Therefore, before an importer (or his bank) will pay for the goods, he (or it) will want to receive not only the bill of lading but also a policy or certificate of marine insurance naming the holder of the bill of lading as its beneficiary. He will also want an invoice as well as any other documents that may be required for exportation and importation, such as export license, import license, consular invoice, certificate of origin, and others. Under a typical c.i.f. contract, it is this entire package of documents that must be transferred by the seller to the buyer, or to the bank appointed by the buyer, before payment is made.[62] Indeed, the typical documentary transaction calls for multiple copies of the documents—the commercial invoice in triplicate, a "full set" of bills of lading (one to be sent by ocean mail, one by air, and perhaps one by land), and sometimes multiple copies of other documents as well.

Payment under a c.i.f. contract is to be made against documents only, unless otherwise agreed. The Uniform Commercial Code expressly forbids the seller to tender the goods themselves instead of the documents.[63] The reason for this is that banks normally play an important role in financing documentary transactions in international trade, and a bank that pays money to an exporter on behalf of an importer is better able to protect its security interest if the exporter is not permitted to avoid the tender of documents. Otherwise, possi-bilities of fraud may arise. For example, the importer who receives the goods may mortgage them to another lender, free of the bank's lien, or the exporter may supply goods of lower quality and value than the contract requires. With-out the disclosures provided by the documents, the bank will not be alerted to obtain the exporter's check to the importer for the difference in value or to take other measures to reduce its loan. Essentially, the requirement in a c.i.f. contract that documents be transferred meets the same need as the require-ment in a face-to-face transaction—for example, the sale of an automobile—that title documents go to the lender before the product goes to the buyer.

The documentary aspect of the c.i.f. transaction leads to the substitution of documents for goods in so many respects that it may also lead to the conclu-sion that the substitution is intended to be complete. Indeed, in one case, a great English commercial judge, Lord Scrutton, suggested that many of the difficulties arising from c.i.f. contracts could be resolved if the c.i.f. sale were

---

[58] Federal Bills of Lading Act, 49 U.S.C. §§111, 117 (1970).
[61] See 46 U.S.C. §§1302-1306 (1970).
[62] U.C.C. §2-320(2) (1962 version). . . .
[63] U.C.C. §2-320(4) (1962 version).

understood not as a sale of goods but as a sale of documents relating to the goods: "he [the buyer] buys the documents, not the goods."[64] This statement was sharply disputed in the same case by other English judges, who described the c.i.f. contract as "a contract for the sale of goods to be performed by the delivery of documents."[65] Yet in a later case, another English judge stated: "the obligation of the vendor is to deliver documents rather than goods—to transfer symbols rather than the physical property represented thereby."[66]

To say that the contract is for the sale of documents, not of goods, may be only a convenient metaphor.[67] Certainly the documents presuppose the shipment of the goods to which they refer. Yet there is at least one situation in which the seller may perform his c.i.f. contract by tendering documents although the goods have not been shipped—namely, where the buyer agrees to accept a received-for-shipment bill of lading which states that the goods are in the custody of the shipowner and awaiting shipment on a vessel which may or may not be named. Moreover, it is well established that if, after shipment, the goods are lost at sea, the seller may tender shipping documents and demand payment, even where he knows at the time of the transfer that the goods have been lost.[68] This makes sense because the buyer has agreed to accept the risk of loss of the goods and is protected by insurance.[69]

Figure 2-1 shows a contemporary international bill of lading (omitting the fine print on the reverse).

QUESTION

What problems might you expect in writing terms for a "through bill of lading," e.g., one evolving particularly for containerized goods, which is issued by an inland carrier, typically a railroad or trucking agency, to cover the entire voyage, including transshipment to a ship and perhaps carriage on

---

[64]Arnold Karberg & Co. v. Blythe, Green, Jourdain & Co., [1915] 2 K.B. 379, 388, *aff'd,* [1916] 1 K.B. 495 (C.A. 1915).

[65][1916] 1 K.B. at 510 (Bankes, L.J., dissenting); *id.* at 514 (Warrington, L.J., dissenting) (joining in the remarks of Bankes, L.J., as to the character of a c.i.f. contract).

[66]Manbre Saccharine Co. v. Corn Products Co., [1919] 1 K.B. 198, 203 (1918) (McCardie, J.).

[67]In Malmberg v. Evans & Co., [1924] 30 Com. Cas. 107, 112, Scrutton, L.J., replied to the rebuke of Bankes and Warrington, note 65 *supra,* stating: "I need not discuss, what perhaps is a mere question of words, whether that sale is a sale of goods or of documents. One of the features of a sale c.i.f. is that, in the absence of special terms, the seller claims payment against presentation of shipping documents."

[68]Smith Co. v. Marano, 267 Pa. 107, 110 A. 94 (1920); Manbre Saccharine Co. v. Corn Products Co., [1919] 1 K.B. 198 (1918).

[69]It is not wholly accurate to state that even if the goods are lost the buyer has nonetheless realized the object of his purchase, for the loss may have resulted from causes not covered by the insurance; and even if the loss or damage is attributable to risks covered by the policy, the buyer must bear the burdens and expense of recouping his loss and the risk that even after protracted litigation he may not in fact be effectively reimbursed.

SEA-LAND SERVICE, INC.

INTERNATIONAL BILL OF LADING
NOT NEGOTIABLE UNLESS CONSIGNED "TO ORDER"
(SPACES IMMEDIATELY BELOW FOR SHIPPERS' MEMORANDA)

(2) SHIPPER/EXPORTER (COMPLETE NAME AND ADDRESS)

(5) BOOKING NO.

(5A) BILL OF LADING NO.

(6) EXPORT REFERENCES

(3) CONSIGNEE (COMPLETE NAME AND ADDRESS)

(7) FORWARDING AGENT. F M C NO

(8) POINT AND COUNTRY OF ORIGIN

(4) NOTIFY PARTY (COMPLETE NAME AND ADDRESS)

(9) ALSO NOTIFY ROUTING & INSTRUCTIONS

(12) INITIAL CARRIAGE BY (MODE) ●

(13) PLACE OF INITIAL RECEIPT ●

(14) VESSEL   VOY   FLAG

(15) PORT OF LOADING

(10) LOADING PIER/TERMINAL

(10A) ORIGINAL(S) TO BE RELEASED AT

(16) PORT OF DISCHARGE

(17) PLACE OF DELIVERY BY ON CARRIER ●

(11) TYPE OF MOVE (IF MIXED USE BLOCK 20 AS APPROPRIATE)

PARTICULARS FURNISHED BY SHIPPER   SEA LAND U.S. CUSTOMS CONTAINER BOND IIT 145

MKS & NOS /CONTAINER NOS	NO OF PKGS	HM ●●	DESCRIPTION OF PACKAGES AND GOODS	GROSS WEIGHT	MEASUREMENT
(18)	(19)		(20)	(21)	(22)

(23) Declared Value $ _____ If shipper enters a value, carriers 'package'
limitation of liability does not apply and the ad valorem rate will be charged

RATE OF EXCHANGE

(24) FREIGHT PAYABLE AT/BY

ITEM NO		RATED AS	PER	RATE	PREPAID	COLLECT	LOCAL CURRENCY	

If this box is checked goods have been loaded stowed and counted by Shipper Carrier has NOT done so and is not responsible for accuracy of count condition or nature of goods described in PARTICULARS FURNISHED BY SHIPPER

THE RECEIPT. CUSTODY. CARRIAGE AND DELIVERY OF THE GOODS ARE SUBJECT TO THE TERMS APPEARING ON THE FACE AND BACK HEREOF AND TO CARRIER'S APPLICABLE TARIFF

in witness whereof three (3) original bills of lading all the same tenor and date one of which being accomplished the others to stand void have been issued by Sea-Land Service, Inc or its designated agent on behalf of itself other participating carriers, the vessel her master and owners or charterers

TOTAL CHARGES

● APPLICABLE ONLY WHEN USED FOR MULTIMODAL OR THROUGH TRANSPORTATION
●● INDICATE WHETHER ANY OF THE CARGO IS HAZARDOUS MATERIAL UNDER DOT, IMCO OR OTHER REGULATIONS AND INDICATE CORRECT COMMODITY NUMBER IN BOX 20

AT ....

BY ....

SL 2265 5/82   BILL OF LADING NO   DATE   **FOR SEA-LAND SERVICE, INC.**

FIGURE 2-1
An International Bill of Lading

43

another inland carrier at the destination? What about use of computers rather than paper? Note the problems of allocating responsibilities for damages, and also the possible problems of complying with different nations' internal laws. *See* Ramberg, The Vanishing Bill of Lading and the "Hamburg Rules Carrier," 27 A.J.C.L. 391 (1979), and the proposed United Nations Convention on the Carriage of Goods by Sea (1978) (id. at 421).

c.   The Letter of Credit

By the use of the bill of lading, the buyer can help protect itself against the risk that no goods were shipped. In essence, the shipping company—which is likely to be a plausible defendant in any jurisdiction that it serves—is relied upon for the accuracy of a statement that the goods really were loaded on board. Although that statement usually describes the goods in very general terms, or even uses language like "boxes said to contain," it helps resolve the buyer's central risk that no goods were shipped. It does not, however, solve the seller's central problem—that of being sure to be paid, a problem solved by the letter of credit procedure.

The letter of credit is a bank's commitment that it will, under certain circumstances, make a payment to the letter's beneficiary, typically the seller or its bank. The bank's statement is credible because of the bank's international reputation, a reputation that will generally be well understood in the international banking network. In the trade transaction, the stated condition of payment is that the bank will pay when it sights specified documents, including those evidencing title such as the bill of lading. It will then pay through a draft, a procedure to be discussed below.

It is already, however, possible to construct a simple case to show how the letter of credit and bill of lading concepts can be combined to protect the two parties against the most serious risks—that no goods were shipped or that no payment will be made. After entering a contract for sale of the goods, the buyer/importer would ask its bank to issue a letter of credit naming the seller/exporter as beneficiary, and promising to pay when a bill of lading for the goods is presented. The bank will send this letter to the seller/exporter, thus giving the seller enough confidence of payment to ship the goods. When the seller does so, it will receive a bill of lading in return, will negotiate the bill to the order of importer, and airmail it to the importer's bank. On seeing that the documents are correct, the bank will pay the exporter and give the documents to the importer, who can meet the ship and pick up the goods with them.

Only in minor detail is the real world more complicated. The letter of credit is governed by a combination of domestic law, particularly the Uniform Commercial Code in the United States, and of international principles stated in the Uniform Customs and Practice for Documentary Credits (*see* Selected Documents Supplement), and there are technical surprises in this law. The most important is that a credit is revocable unless actually labeled "Irrevocable."

This is a historical accident, permitting the exchange of draft letters of credit during negotiations, but implying the need to check for the language of irrevocability before relying on a credit.

Second, the parties to the paper work will sometimes be the banks, rather than the exporter and importer themselves. Thus, the beneficiary of the letter of credit will probably be the exporter's bank. Likewise, all the paper work will be transferred from bank to bank; the exporter or its agent will take the bill of lading to its bank for forwarding. Note that this bank is likely to be willing at that point to advance funds to the exporter, for a fee that represents little more than interest and administrative costs. With the bill of lading and the importing bank letter of credit in hand, it faces essentially no risk.

Third, the document list of the letter of credit will usually require more than a simple bill of lading and will generally also require insurance certificates and the various documents needed to clear customs in both the exporting and importing nations.

Finally, the bank issuing a letter of credit is undertaking to make a payment under certain circumstances and is thus exposed to risk of loss. It will understandably seek to protect itself against this risk. If its client's credit (the importer's credit) is good, it may simply accept the risk of giving the client what amounts to a line of credit, charge an appropriate fee, and, of course, protect itself by requiring the importer to promise to reimburse any payment, a promise typically found in the importer's application for a letter of credit. If the client's credit position is more questionable, the bank may require payment in advance or take a security interest in the goods and insist that the bill of lading be negotiated to it.

On occasion, a buyer who already has a contract to resell the goods may be able to use a letter of credit issued in its favor by the repurchaser's bank as security for a letter supporting its own purchase. Thus, a New York broker with a contract to buy coffee from Brazil and another contract to sell it to London, might use the London bank's letter of credit (which would name New York bank as beneficiary) as the basis on which New York bank would be willing to issue a letter of credit naming Sao Paulo bank as beneficiary. This is the concept of "back-to-back" letters of credit. For an example, *see* Asociacion de Azucareros de Guatemala v. U.S. Natl. Bank of Oregon, 423 F.2d 638 (9th Cir. 1970). This procedure evolved for historical reasons and as a way to help the person in the middle avoid revealing its markup to the ultimate buyer and seller. It takes the place of assignment of letters of credit, something relatively uncommon.

A bank may, however, be willing to "confirm" a letter of credit, i.e., to add its guarantee to that of the issuing bank. This is most likely when an inland exporter wishes to borrow against a foreign letter of credit and its local bank is unable to evaluate the foreign issuing bank but willing to rely on the promise of a domestic bank that does more international business. Not all forwarding of a letter of credit from bank to bank amounts to confirming; often a bank may simply "advise" its (exporting) client that another bank has issued a letter of credit in the client's favor, and even help with the paper work, but undertake no obligation to honor the letter.

Various provisions to protect banks dominate the fine print of the application for a letter of credit and are omitted here. The letter itself is quite simple, as Figure 2-2 shows.

d.   The Documentary Draft

Before recapitulating the typical use of the letter of credit and presenting cases showing the most common real problems, it is important to add one more concept, that of the "documentary draft," or "bill of exchange."

For historical reasons, and because of its negotiability, the "documentary draft" or "bill of exchange" is the usual instrument by which payment is signified in a letter of credit transaction.

A documentary draft is an instruction to pay money to the order of a named beneficiary. The person who writes and signs the instruction is called the "maker" or "drawer"; the person to whom instructions are given is the "drawee" or "addressee"; the person to whom payment is to be made is the "payee."

The normal check is a simple example of the draft, in which the bank is the drawee, the person signing the check the drawer, and the person to whom payment is to be made the payee. The draft, however, offers much more flexibility in that it need not be drawn on a bank but may be drawn on, for example, an importer directing payment to the exporter.

But the draft is like the check in that, by an appropriate endorsement, the payee may direct that payment be made instead to a third party (and will usually receive payment from that party when he or she does so). And, the transfer is a negotiation—the "holder in due course," basically a party who takes the instrument for value with no knowledge of problems, takes it free of many of the defenses that may be available against earlier holders. This means that drafts can relatively easily be transferred, deposited into accounts, or cleared like checks.

The draft can be a "time draft," rather than a "sight draft," and direct that payment be made a stated number of days, typically 60 or 90, after the instrument is seen by the drawee. Thus, it can evidence a debt, and may be purchased (by negotiation) as a short-term investment. The interest rate is defined implicitly by a discount in the price the investor pays; on maturity, the investor will receive the face value. Time drafts that have been accepted by the drawee bank are particularly likely subjects of investment. They are then relatively riskless assets, called "banker's acceptances"—and the final important source of law for the foreign trade transaction (beyond the provisions governing these negotiable instruments in the Uniform Commercial Code and its foreign analogues) is Federal Reserve Regulation C, defining

Barclays Bank International Limited
168 Fenchurch Street, London, EC3P 3HP.

date 20th May 19..

DOCUMENTARY CREDITS DEPARTMENT

SPECIMEN

IRREVOCABLE CREDIT No:- FDC/2/2345
To be quoted on all drafts and correspondence.

Beneficiary(ies)	Advised through
Smith, Jones and Robinson (Coventry) Ltd. Resin Works Market Street Coventry	

Accreditor	To be completed only if applicable
Carruthers & Cartwright Ltd. Mainland House King Street Kingston, Jamaica	Our cable of
	Advised through Refers

Dear Sir(s)

In accordance with instructions received from The Coconut Bank & Trust Co.
we hereby issue in your favour a Documentary Credit for £11180
(say) Eleven thousand one hundred and eighty pounds sterling
drawn on Carruthers & Cartwright Ltd.

available by your drafts

at sight
for the 100% c.i.f. invoice value, accompanied by the following documents:—

1. Invoice in triplicate, signed and marked Import Licence No. HDNL 64 19..

2. Full set of clean on board Shipping Company's Bills of Lading made out to order and blank endorsed, marked "Freight Paid" and "Notify Carruthers & Cartwright Ltd., Mainland House, King Street, Kingston, Jamaica."

3. Insurance Policy or Certificate in duplicate, covering Marine and War Risks up to buyer's warehouse, for invoice value of the goods plus 10%.

Covering the following goods:—

100 Drums Synthetic Resin

To be shipped from Liverpool	to	Kingston c.i.f.
not later than 23rd June 19..		
Partshipment not permitted	Transhipment	not permitted
The credit is available for presentation to us	until	14th July 19..

Drafts drawn hereunder must be marked "Drawn under Barclays Bank International Limited 168 Fenchurch Street, London branch, Credit number FDC/2/2345 ".
We undertake that drafts and documents drawn under and in strict conformity with the terms of this credit will be honoured upon presentation.

Yours faithfully,

Co-signed (Signature No. 9347)

Signed (Signature No. 10247)

CRE 202 (replacing CRE 83, 606 series)

PLEASE SEE REVERSE

Subject to Uniform Customs and Practice for Documentary Credits (1974 Revision,) I.C.C. Publication No. 290

FIGURE 2-2
A Letter of Credit
Reprinted with permission of Barclays Bank International Limited

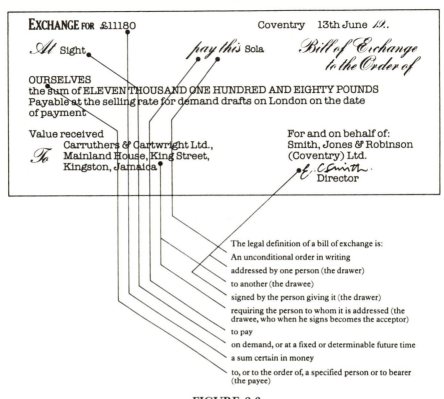

FIGURE 2-3
A Documentary Draft
Reprinted with permission of Barclays Bank International Limited

those foreign-trade derived assets that nationally chartered banks may hold as investments. Figure 2-3 shows a draft or bill of exchange.

e.   The Entire Transaction

It is now possible to work through the entire transaction. Assume that a Tokyo exporter and a Chicago importer wish to enter into a transnational sales transaction involving 50 television sets for $100 each:

(1) Tokyo exporter and Chicago importer enter a contract, perhaps by telex, quoting the prices, quantities, dates, and particular trade terms.

(2) Chicago importer obtains a letter of credit from its bank. It may have to pay in advance for this letter. Although the detailed form will be like that shown in the text, this letter will say in essence:

> Dear Tokyo Bank:
>
> On receipt of a bill of lading for 50 television sets, we will honor your sight draft in the amount of $5,000.
>
> [signed] *Chicago Bank*

This letter of credit would probably also require a number of insurance and customs certificates.

(3) Chicago importer (or bank) sends the letter of credit to Tokyo exporter (or bank).

(4) Tokyo exporter can now confidently deliver the goods to the carrier, who will provide a bill of lading, saying, in essence, that 50 television sets have been received on board. Exporter will negotiate this bill to the order of Chicago bank, and, through Tokyo bank, send it along with a draft and the other necessary documents to Chicago Bank. The draft, again in appropriate form, will say:

> Chicago Bank,
>
> On sight, pay to order of Tokyo Bank $5,000.
>
> [signed] *Tokyo Bank*

(5) On receiving the documents and seeing that they are all in proper form, Chicago Bank will make the payment to Tokyo bank and negotiate the bill of lading to its customer.

(6) Tokyo bank will pay its customer (if it has not done so already).

(7) Chicago importer, as holder of the bill of lading, will be able to obtain the television sets from the carrier.

The approach offers many mechanisms for credit. Importer's bank can simply offer credit to its client and permit the process to proceed as described above, paying exporter when the letter of credit is negotiated, but not receiving payment from its client until later. By using a time draft, under which importer bank (and presumably importer) is not required to pay for a specified number of days, the seller can extend short-term credit. This credit gives the buyer time to resell the goods and obtain the funds for their initial purchase; it is safe for the seller, who can rely on the bank's credit standing rather than on that of the buyer. Since importer's bank does face an exposure with this approach, it will probably not be willing to commit itself to honor such a time draft without taking a security interest in the goods at the time the documents are negotiated. And when the time draft is used, no matter what the arrangements at the importer's end, it need not be the seller who actually extends the credit from the exporter's end. Exporter may be able to discount the acceptance to its bank or a third party, as discussed above, and thus immediately obtain use of the money. The negotiated acceptance will eventually be presented to importer's bank for full payment at the appropriate time.

As the following case shows, the fundamental legal principle associated with the documentary sale concept is that the bank can and must ensure that the documents conform with the letter of credit—but is almost completely unconcerned with whether the goods conform to the underlying contract. The basic working assumption is that breach-of-warranty-style disputes should not be allowed to bar initial payment. It is assumed better to honor the letter of credit and bring breach-of-warranty problems to the exporter's courts if necessary; otherwise (real or bogus) quality disputes would render payment so uncertain as to be a barrier to trade.

MAURICE O'MEARA CO. v. NATIONAL PARK BANK OF NEW YORK

239 N.Y. 386, 146 N.E. 636 (N.Y. Ct. App. 1925)

McLaughlin, J. This action was brought to recover damages alleged to have been sustained by the plaintiff's assignor, Ronconi & Millar, by defendant's refusal to pay three sight drafts against a confirmed irrevocable letter of credit. The letter of credit was in the following form:

> The National Park Bank of New York.
> Our Credit No. 14956   October 28, 1920.
>
> Messrs. Ronconi & Millar, 49 Chambers Street, New York City, N.Y.—Dear Sirs: In accordance with instructions received from the Sun-Herald Corporation of this city, we open a confirmed or irrevocable credit in your favor for account of themselves, in amount of $224,853.30, covering the shipment of 1,322²/₃ tons of newsprint paper in 72¹/₂″ and 36¹/₂″ rolls to test 11-12, 32 lbs. at 8¹/₂¢ per pound net weight—delivery to be made in December, 1920, and January 1921.
>
> Drafts under this credit are to be drawn at sight on this bank, and are to be accompanied by the following documents of a character which must meet with our approval:
>
> Commercial invoice in triplicate.
>
> Weight returns.
>
> Negotiable dock delivery order actually carrying with it control of the goods.
>
> This is a confirmed or irrevocable credit, and will remain in force to and including February 15, 1921, subject to the conditions mentioned herein.
>
> When drawing drafts under this credit, or referring to it, please quote our number as above.
>
> > Very truly yours,
> > R. Stuart, Assistant Cashier.
> > (R. C.)

The complaint alleged the issuance of the letter of credit; the tender of three drafts, the first on the 17th of December, 1920, for $46,301.71, the second on January 7, 1921, for $41,416.34, and the third on January 13, 1921, for $32,968.35. Accompanying the first draft were the following documents:

1. Commercial invoice of the said firm of Ronconi & Millar in triplicate, covering three hundred (300) thirty-six and one-half (36½) inch rolls of newsprint paper and three hundred (300) seventy-two and one-half (72½) inch rolls of newsprint paper, aggregating a net weight of five hundred and forty-four thousand seven hundred and twenty-six pounds (544,726), to test eleven (11), twelve (12), thirty-two (32) pounds.

2. Affidavit of Elwin Walker, verified December 16, 1920, to which were annexed samples of newsprint paper, which the said affidavit stated to be representative of the shipment covered by the accompanying invoices and to test twelve (12) points, thirty-two (32) pounds.

3. Full weight returns in triplicate.

4. Negotiable dock delivery order on the Swedish American Line, directing delivery to the order of the National Park Bank of three hundred (300) rolls of newsprint paper seventy-two and one-half (72½) inches long and three hundred (300) half rolls of newsprint paper.

The documents accompanying the second draft were similar to those accompanying the first, except as to the number of rolls, weight of paper, omission of the affidavit of Walker, but with a statement: "Paper equal to original sample in test 11/12-32 pounds:" and a negotiable dock delivery order on the Seager Steamship Company, Inc. The complaint also alleged defendant's refusal to pay, a statement of the amount of loss upon the resale of the paper due to a fall in the market price, expenses for lighterage, cartage, storage, and insurance amounting to $3,045.02, an assignment of the cause of action by Ronconi & Millar to the plaintiff, and a demand for judgment.

The answer denied, upon information and belief, many of the allegations of the complaint, and set up (a) as an affirmative defense, that plaintiff's assignor was required by the letter of credit to furnish to the defendant "evidence reasonably satisfactory" to it that the paper shipped to the Sun-Herald Corporation was of a bursting or tensile strength of 11 to 12 points at a weight of paper of 32 pounds; that neither the plaintiff nor its assignor, at the time the drafts were presented, or at any time thereafter, furnished such evidence; (b) as a partial defense, that, when the draft for $46,301.71 was presented, the defendant notified the plaintiff there had not been presented "evidence reasonably satisfactory" to it, showing that the newsprint paper referred to in the documents accompanying said drafts was of the tensile or bursting strength specified in the letter of credit; that thereupon an agreement was entered into between plaintiff and defendant that the latter should cause a test to be made of the paper represented by the documents then presented, and, if such test showed that the paper was up to the specifications of the letter of credit, defendant would make payment of the draft; (c) for a third separate and distinct defense that the paper tendered was not, in fact, of the tensile or bursting strength specified in the letter of credit; . . .

After issue had been joined the plaintiff moved, upon the pleadings and affidavits, pursuant to rule 113 of the Rules of Civil Practice, to strike out the answer and for summary judgment. . . .

The motion for summary judgment was denied and the defendant appealed to the Appellate Division, where the order denying the same was unanimously affirmed, leave to appeal to this court granted, and the following question certified: "Should the motion of the plaintiff for summary judgment herein have been granted?" . . .

I am of the opinion that the order of the Appellate Division and the Special Term should be reversed and the motion granted. The facts set out in defendant's answer and in the affidavits used by it in opposition to the motion are not a defense to the action.

The bank issued to plaintiff's assignor an irrevocable letter of credit, a contract solely between the bank and plaintiff's assignor, in and by which the bank agreed to pay sight drafts to a certain amount on presentation to it of the documents specified in the letter of credit. This contract was in no way involved in or connected with, other than the presentation of the documents, the contract for the purchase and sale of the paper mentioned. That was a contract between buyer and seller, which in no way concerned the bank. The bank's obligation was to pay sight drafts when presented if accompanied by genuine documents specified in the letter of credit. If the paper when delivered did not correspond to what had been purchased, either in weight, kind or quality, then the purchaser had his remedy against the seller for damages. Whether the paper was what the purchaser contracted to purchase did not concern the bank and in no way affected its liability. It was under no obligation to ascertain, either by a personal examination or otherwise, whether the paper conformed to the contract between the buyer and seller. The bank was concerned only in the drafts and the documents accompanying them. This was the extent of its interest. If the drafts, when presented, were accompanied by the proper documents, then it was absolutely bound to make the payment under the letter of credit, irrespective of whether it knew, or had reason to believe, that the paper was not of the tensile strength contracted for. This view, I think, is the one generally entertained with reference to a bank's liability under an irrevocable letter of credit of the character of the one here under consideration. . . .

The defendant had no right to insist that a test of the tensile strength of the paper be made before paying the drafts; nor did it even have a right to inspect the paper before payment, to determine whether it in fact corresponded to the description contained in the documents. The letter of credit did not so provide. All that the letter of credit provided was that documents be presented which described the paper shipped as of a certain size, weight, and tensile strength. To hold otherwise is to read into the letter of credit something which is not there, and this the court ought not to do, since it would impose upon a bank a duty which in many cases would defeat the primary purpose of such letters of credit. This primary purpose is an assurance to the seller of merchandise of prompt payment against documents.

It has never been held, so far as I am able to discover, that a bank has the right or is under an obligation to see that the description of the merchandise contained in the documents presented is correct. A provision giving it such right, or imposing such obligation, might, of course, be provided for in the letter of credit. The letter under consideration contains no such provision. If the bank had the right to determine whether the paper was of the tensile strength stated, then it might be pertinent to inquire how much of the paper must it subject to the test. If it had to make a test as to tensile strength, then it was equally obligated to measure and weigh the paper. No such thing was intended by the parties and there was no such obligation upon the bank. The documents presented were sufficient. The only reason stated by defendant in its letter of December 18, 1920, for refusing to pay the draft, was that: "There has arisen a reasonable doubt regarding the quality of the newsprint paper. . . . Until such time as we can have a test made by an impartial and unprejudiced expert we shall be obliged to defer payment."

This being the sole objection, the only inference to be drawn therefrom is that otherwise the documents presented conformed to the requirements of the letter of credit. All other objections were thereby waived. . . .

The orders appealed from should therefore be reversed and the motion granted, with costs in all courts. The question certified is answered in the affirmative.

CARDOZO, J. (dissenting). I am unable to concur in the opinion of the court.

I assume that no duty is owing from the bank to its depositor which requires it to investigate the quality of the merchandise. Laudisi v. American Exchange Nat. Bank, 239 N. Y. 234, 146 N. E. 347. I dissent from the view that, if it chooses to investigate and discovers thereby that the merchandise tendered is not in truth the merchandise which the documents describe, it may be forced by the delinquent seller to make payment of the price irrespective of its knowledge. We are to bear in mind that this controversy is not one between the bank on the one side and on the other a holder of the drafts who has taken them without notice and for value. The controversy arises between the bank and a seller who has misrepresented the security upon which advances are demanded. Between parties so situated payment may be resisted if the documents are false.

I think we lose sight of the true nature of the transaction when we view the bank as acting upon the credit of its customer to the exclusion of all else. It acts not merely upon the credit of its customer, but upon the credit also of the merchandise which is to be tendered as security. The letter of credit is explicit in its provision that documents sufficient to give control of the goods shall be lodged with the bank when drafts are presented. I cannot accept the statement of the majority opinion that the bank was not concerned with any question as to the character of the paper. If that is so, the bales tendered might have been rags instead of paper, and still the bank would have been helpless, though it had knowledge of the truth, if the documents tendered by the seller were sufficient on their face. A different question would be here if the defects had no relation to the description in the documents. In such circumstances it would be proper to say that a departure from the terms of the contract between the vendor and the vendee was of no moment to the bank. That is not the case before us. If the paper was of the quality stated in the defendant's answer the documents were false.

I think the conclusion is inevitable that a bank which pays a draft upon a bill of lading misrepresenting the character of the merchandise may recover the payment when the misrepresentation is discovered, or at the very least, the difference between the value of the thing described and the value of the thing received. If payment might have been recovered the moment after it was made, the seller cannot coerce payment if the truth is earlier revealed.

We may find persuasive analogies in connection with the law of sales. One who promises to make payment in advance of delivery and inspection may be technically in default if he refuses the promised payment before inspection has been made. None the less, if the result of the inspection is to prove that the merchandise is defective, the seller must fail in an action for the recovery of the price. The reason is that "the buyer would have been entitled to recover back the price if he had paid it without inspection of the goods" 2 Williston on Sales (2d Ed.) §§479, 576.

I think the defendant's answer and the affidavits submitted in support of it are sufficient to permit a finding that the plaintiff's assignors misrepresented the nature of the shipment. The misrepresentation does not cease to be a defense, partial if not complete, though it was innocently made. . . .

The order should be affirmed and the question answered "No."

Hiscock, C. J., and Pound and Andrews, JJ., concur with McLaughlin, J. Cardozo, J., reads dissenting opinion, in which Crane, J., concurs. Lehman, J., not sitting.

The next case shows what happens to the *O'Meara* doctrine when the exporter pushes the situation too far. Note that, earlier in the litigation, the importer had sued the bank to enjoin it from honoring the letter of credit; this litigation pattern is typical of letter-of-credit disputes. Finally, in reading the case, be sure to consider both the policy issues underlying the U.C.C. rules, and the wisdom of applying these rules to Pakistani banks.

UNITED BANK LTD. v. CAMBRIDGE SPORTING GOODS CORP.

41 N.Y.2d 254, 360 N.E.2d 943 (1976)

GABRIELLI, Justice. . . .

In April, 1971 appellant Cambridge Sporting Goods Corporation (Cambridge) entered into a contract for the manufacture and sale of boxing gloves with Duke Sports (Duke), a Pakistani corporation. Duke committed itself to the manufacture of 27,936 pairs of boxing gloves at a sale price of $42,576.80; and arranged with its Pakistani bankers, United Bank Limited (United) and The Muslim Commercial Bank (Muslim), for the financing of the sale. Cambridge was requested by these banks to cover payment of the purchase price by opening an irrevocable letter of credit with its bank in New York, Manufacturers Hanover Trust Company (Manufacturers). Manufacturers issued an irrevocable letter of credit obligating it, upon the receipt of certain documents indicating shipment of the merchandise pursuant to the contract, to accept and pay, 90 days after acceptance, drafts drawn upon Manufacturers for the purchase price of the gloves. . . .

Despite the cancellation of the contract, Cambridge was informed on July 17, 1971 that documents had been received at Manufacturers from United purporting to evidence a shipment of the boxing gloves under the terms of the canceled contract. The documents were accompanied by a draft, dated July 16, 1971, drawn by Duke upon Manufacturers and made payable to United, for the amount of $21,288.40, one half of the contract price of the boxing gloves. A second set of documents was received by Manufacturers from Muslim, also accompanied by a draft, dated August 20, and drawn upon Manufacturers by Duke for the remaining amount of the contract price.

An inspection of the shipments upon their arrival revealed that Duke had shipped old, unpadded, ripped and mildewed gloves rather than the new gloves to be manufactured as agreed upon. Cambridge then commenced an action against Duke in Supreme Court, New York County, joining Manufacturers as a party, and obtained a preliminary injunction prohibiting the latter from paying drafts drawn under the letter of credit; subsequently, in November, 1971 Cambridge levied on the funds subject to the letter of credit and the draft, which were delivered by Manufacturers to the Sheriff in compliance therewith. Duke ultimately defaulted in the action and judgment against it was entered in the amount of the drafts, in March, 1972.

The present proceeding was instituted by the Pakistani banks to vacate the levy made by Cambridge and to obtain payment of the drafts on the letter of credit. . . .

This case does not come before us in the typical posture of a lawsuit between the bank issuing the letter of credit and presenters of drafts drawn under the credit seeking payment (see, generally, White and Summers, Uniform Commercial Code, §18-6, pp.619-628). Because Cambridge obtained an injunction against payment of the drafts and has levied against the proceeds of the drafts, it stands in the same position as the issuer, and, thus, the law of letters of credit governs the liability of Cambridge to the Pakistani banks.[1] Article 5 of the Uniform Commercial Code, dealing with letters of credit, and the Uniform

---

[1] Cambridge has no direct liability on the drafts because it is not a party to the drafts which were drawn on Manufacturers by Duke as drawer; its liability derives from the letter of credit which authorizes the drafts to be drawn on the issuing banks. Since Manufacturers has paid the proceeds of the drafts to the Sheriff pursuant to the levy obtained in the prior proceeding, it has discharged its obligation under the credit and is not involved in this proceeding.

Customs and Practice for Documentary Credits promulgated by the International Chamber of Commerce set forth the duties and obligations of the issuer of a letter of credit.[2] A letter of credit is a commitment on the part of the issuing bank that it will pay a draft presented to it under the terms of the credit, and if it is a documentary draft, upon presentation of the required documents of title (see Uniform Commercial Code, §5-103). Banks issuing letters of credit deal in documents and not in goods and are not responsible for any breach of warranty or nonconformity of the goods involved in the underlying sales contract (see Uniform Commercial Code, §5-114, subd. [1]; Uniform Customs and Practice, General Provisions and Definitions [c] and article 9; O'Meara Co. v. National Park Bank of N.Y., 239 N.Y. 386, 146 N.E. 636; . . . 1955 Report of N.Y. Law Rev. Comm., vol. 3, Study of Uniform Commercial Code, pp. 1654-1655). Subdivision (2) of section 5-114, however indicates certain limited circumstances in which an issuer *may* properly refuse to honor a draft drawn under a letter of credit or a customer may enjoin an issuer from honoring such a draft.[3] Thus, where "fraud in the transaction" has been shown and the holder has not taken the draft in circumstances that would make it a holder in due course, the customer may apply to enjoin the issuer from paying drafts drawn under the letter of credit (see 1955 Report of N.Y. Law Rev. Comm., vol. 3, pp. 1654-1659). This rule represents a codification of precode case law most eminently articulated in the landmark case of Sztejn v. Schroder Banking Corp., 177 Misc. 719, 31 N.Y.S.2d 631, Shientag, J., where it was held that the shipment of cowhair in place of bristles amounted to more than

---

[2] It should be noted that the Uniform Customs and Practice controls, in lieu of article 5 of the code, where, unless otherwise agreed by the parties, a letter of credit is made subject to the provisions of the Uniform Customs and Practice by its terms or by agreement, course of dealing or usage of trade (Uniform Commercial Code, §5-102, subd. [4]). No proof was offered that there was an agreement that the Uniform Customs and Practice should apply, nor does the credit so state (*cf.* Oriental Pacific [U.S.A.] v. Toronto Dominion Bank, 78 Misc. 2d 819, 357 N.Y.S.2d 957). Neither do the parties otherwise contend that their rights should be resolved under the Uniform Customs and Practice. However, even if the Uniform Customs and Practice were deemed applicable to this case, it would not, in the absence of a conflict, abrogate the precode case law (now codified in Uniform Commercial Code, §5-114) and that authority continues to govern even where article 5 is not controlling (see White and Summers, *op. cit.*, pp. 613-614, 624-625). Moreover, the Uniform Customs and Practice provisions are not in conflict nor do they treat with the subject matter of §5-114 which is dispositive of the issues presented on this appeal (*see* Banco Tornquist, S. A. v. American Bank & Trust Co., 71 Misc. 2d 874, 875, 337 N.Y.S.2d 489; Intraworld Ind. v. Girard Trust Bank, 461 Pa. 343, 336 A.2d 316, 322; Harfield, Practice Commentary, McKinney's Cons. Laws of N.Y., Book 62½, Uniform Commercial Code, §5-114, p. 686). Thus, we are of the opinion that the Uniform Customs and Practice, where applicable, does not bar the relief provided for in §5-114 of the code.

[3] Subdivision (2) of section 5-114 of the Uniform Commercial Code provides that,

[u]nless otherwise agreed when documents appear on their face to comply with the terms of a credit but . . . there is fraud in the transaction (a) the issuer must honor the draft or demand for payment if honor is demanded by a . . . holder of the draft . . . which has taken the draft . . . under the credit and under circumstances which would make it a holder in due course (Section 3-302) . . .; and

(b) in all other cases as against its customer, an issuer acting in good faith may honor the draft . . . . despite notification from the customer of fraud, forgery or other defect not apparent on the face of the documents but a court of appropriate jurisdiction may enjoin such honor.

mere breach of warranty but fraud sufficient to constitute grounds for enjoining payment of drafts to one not a holder in due course. . . . Even prior to the *Sztejn* case, forged or fraudulently procured documents were proper grounds for avoidance of payment of drafts drawn under a letter of credit (Finkelstein, Legal Aspects of Commercial Letters of Credit, pp. 231-236-247); and cases decided after the enactment of the code have cited *Sztejn* with approval. . . .

The history of the dispute between the various parties involved in this case reveals that Cambridge had in a prior, separate proceeding successfully enjoined Manufacturers from paying the drafts and has attached the proceeds of the drafts. It should be noted that the question of the availability and the propriety of this relief is not before us on this appeal. The petitioning banks do not dispute the validity of the prior injunction nor do they dispute the delivery of worthless merchandise. Rather, on this appeal they contend that as holders in due course they are entitled to the proceeds of the drafts irrespective of any fraud on the part of Duke (see Uniform Commercial Code, §5-114, subd. [2], par. [b]). Although precisely speaking there was no specific finding of fraud in the transaction by either of the courts below, their determinations were based on that assumption. The evidentiary facts are not disputed and we hold upon the facts as established, that the shipment of old, unpadded, ripped and mildewed gloves rather than the new boxing gloves as ordered by Cambridge, constituted fraud in the transaction within the meaning of subdivision (2) of section 5-114. It should be noted that the drafters of section 5-114, in their attempt to codify the *Sztejn* case and in utilizing the term "fraud in the transaction", have eschewed a dogmatic approach and adopted a flexible standard to be applied as the circumstances of a particular situation mandate.[5] It can be difficult to draw a precise line between cases involving breach of warranty (or a difference of opinion as to the quality of goods) and outright fraudulent practice on the part of the seller. To the extent, however, that Cambridge established that Duke was guilty of *fraud* in shipping, not merely nonconforming merchandise, but worthless fragments of boxing gloves, this case is similar to *Sztejn*.

If the petitioning banks are holders in due course they are entitled to recover the proceeds of the drafts but if such status cannot be demonstrated their petition must fail.[6] The parties are in agreement that section 3-307 of the code governs the pleading and proof of holder in due course status and that section provides:

---

[5] In its original version section 5-114 contained the language "fraud in a required document" (*see* 1955 Report of N.Y. Law Rev. Comm., pp 1655-1658).

[6] Although several commentators have expressed a contrary view, the weight of authority supports the proposition that fraud on the part of the seller-beneficiary may not be interposed as a defense to payment against a holder in due course to whom a draft has been negotiated (*see* Finkelstein, *op. cit.,* p. 246, Ward and Harfield, Bank Credits and Acceptances, pp. 94-98; 1955 Report of N.Y. Law Rev. Comm., pp. 1662-1663, and authorities cited therein). This approach represents the better view that as against two innocent parties (the buyer and the holder in due course) the former having chosen to deal with the fraudulent seller, should bear the risk of loss (*see* Harfield, Practice Commentary, McKinney's Cons. Laws of N.Y., Book 62½, Uniform Commercial Code, §5-114, pp. 686-687).

(1) Unless specifically denied in the pleadings each signature on an instrument is admitted. When the effectiveness of a signature is put in issue

(a) the burden of establishing it is on the party claiming under the signature; but

(b) the signature is presumed to be genuine or authorized except where the action is to enforce the obligation of a purported signer who has died or become incompetent before proof is required.

(2) When signatures are admitted or established, production of the instrument entitles a holder to recover on it unless the defendant establishes a defense.

(3) After it is shown that a defense exists a person claiming the rights of a holder in due course has the burden of establishing that he or some person under whom he claims is in all respects a holder in due course.

Even though section 3-307 is contained in article 3 of the code dealing with negotiable instruments rather than letters of credit, we agree that its provisions should control in the instant case. Section 5-114 (subd. [2], par. [a]) utilizes the holder in due course criteria of section 3-302 of the code to determine whether a presenter may recover on drafts despite fraud in the sale of goods transaction. It is logical, therefore, to apply the pleading and practice rules of section 3-307 in the situation where a presenter of drafts under a letter of credit claims to be a holder in due course. In the context of section 5-114 and the law of letters of credit, however, the "defense" referred to in section 3-307 should be deemed to include only those defenses available under subdivision (2) of section 5-114, i.e., noncompliance of required documents, forged or fraudulent documents or fraud in the transaction. In the context of a letter of credit transaction and, specifically subdivision (2) of section 5-114, it is these defenses which operate to shift the burden of proof of holder in due course status upon one asserting such status. . . . Thus, a presenter of drafts drawn under a letter of credit must prove that it took the drafts for value, in good faith and without notice of the underlying fraud in the transaction (Uniform Commercial Code, §3-302). . . .

In order to qualify as a holder in due course, a holder must have taken the instrument "without notice . . . of any defense against . . . it on the part of any person" (Uniform Commercial Code, §3-302, subd. [1], par. [c]). Pursuant to subdivision (2) of section 5-114 fraud in the transaction is a valid defense to payment of drafts drawn under a letter of credit. Since the defense of fraud in the transaction was shown, the burden shifted to the banks by operation of subdivision (3) of section 3-307 to prove that they were holders in due course and took the drafts without notice of Duke's alleged fraud. As indicated in the Official Comment to that subdivision, when it is shown that a defense exists, one seeking to cut off the defense by claiming the rights of a holder in due course "has the full burden of proof by a preponderance of the total evidence" on this issue. This burden must be sustained by "affirmative proof" of the requisites of holder in due course status (see Official Comment, McKinney's Cons. Laws of N.Y., Book 62½, Uniform Commercial Code, §3-307, p. 212). It was error for the trial court to direct a verdict in favor of the Pakistani banks because this determination rested upon a misallocation of the burden of proof; and we conclude that the banks have not satisfied the burden of proving that they qualified in all respects as holders in due course, by any affirmative proof. The only evidence introduced by the banks consisted of conclusory answers to the interrogatories which were improperly admitted by the Trial Judge. . . . The failure of the banks to meet their burden is fatal to their claim for recovery of the proceeds of the drafts and their petition must therefore be dismissed. . . .

Breitel, C. J., and Jasen, Jones, Wachtler, Fuchsberg and Cooke, JJ., concur.

NOTES AND QUESTIONS

1. Why is the law so clear that a bank must pay (and normally be entitled to receive reimbursement from its customer) even when the goods are clearly not satisfactory? Note that Cardozo's position in *O'Meara* has not been generally accepted. For general discussions of this body of law, *see* E. Ellinger, Documentary Letters of Credit (1970); L. Sarna, Letters of Credit (1984); W. Surrey & D. Wallace, A Lawyer's Guide to International Business Transactions (2d ed. 1978). Symposium, The Law of Letters of Credit and Standbys in the 1980's, 24 Ariz. L.R. 235 (1982); Berman & Kaufman, The Law of International Commercial Transactions (Lex Mercatoria), 19 Harv. Intl. L.J. 221 (1978); J. Honnold, Uniform Law for International Sales Under the 1980 UN Convention (1982); E. A. Farnsworth & J. Honnold, Cases and Materials on the Law of Sales and Sales Financing (1982).

2. What if the documents do not conform with the terms of the letter of credit? What practical solution might you negotiate if it appears likely that the discrepancy is technical only? *See* Banque de l'Indochine et de Suez S.A. v. J.H. Rayner (Mincing Lane) Ltd., [1983] 2 W.L.R. 841.

3. In a situation like *United Bank Limited* what can an importer do to protect itself? One approach, common in cases where a defect will reduce value only slightly, is to pay only, say, 90% of the purchase price through the letter of credit and the remainder after there has been a chance to inspect the goods. What new risks does this create? Another possibility is for the letter of credit to require an expert's inspection certificate as one of the documents. For an example, *see* Banco Espanol de Crédito v. State St. Bank & Trust Co., 385 F.2d 230 (1st Cir. 1967), *cert. denied*, 390 U.S. 1013 (1968). Under what circumstances will you expect international networks of trustworthy experts to evolve?

4. Are you troubled by the *United Bank* court's extraterritorial application of the Uniform Commercial Code? What about the special New York U.C.C. provision, discussed in footnote 2 of the case, explicitly allowing the parties to agree that the Uniform Customs rather than the U.C.C. should govern a letter of credit? For a British example of a court considering the U.C.C. and following the general theme of U.S. law on fraud in the letter of credit transaction,

but questioning the U.C.C.'s parallel treatment of fraud and forgery in certain contexts, *see* United City Merchants (Investments) Ltd. v. Royal Bank of Canada, [1982] 2 W.L.R. 1039.

f. Other Uses of the Letter of Credit

The next case is included to show a quite different role for the letter of credit, one in which it serves to guarantee a contractor's performance rather than a buyer's payment. Many of the Mideastern countries have insisted that foreign contractors maintain in force such "stand-by" letters of credit. This case is one of a number of similar cases arising out of the Iranian revolution.

AMERICAN BELL INTERNATIONAL, INC. v. THE ISLAMIC REPUBLIC OF IRAN

474 F. Supp. 420 (S.D.N.Y. 1979)

MacMahon, District Judge.

Plaintiff American Bell International Inc. ("Bell") moves for a preliminary injunction pursuant to Rule 65(a), Fed. R. Civ. P. and the All Writs Act, 28 U.S.C. §1651, enjoining defendant Manufacturers Hanover Trust Company ("Manufacturers") from making any payment under its Letter of Credit No. SC 170027 to defendants the Islamic Republic of Iran or Bank Iranshahr or their agents, instrumentalities, successors, employees and assigns. We held an evidentiary hearing and heard oral argument on August 3, 1979. The following facts appear from the evidence presented:

The action arises from the recent revolution in Iran and its impact upon contracts made with the ousted Imperial Government of Iran and upon banking arrangements incident to such contracts. Bell, a wholly-owned subsidiary of American Telephone & Telegraph Co. ("AT & T"), made a contract on July 23, 1978 (the "Contract") with the Imperial Government of Iran—Ministry of War ("Imperial Government") to provide consulting services and equipment to the Imperial Government as part of a program to improve Iran's international communications system.

The contract provides a complex mechanism for payment to Bell totalling approximately $280,000,000, including a down payment of $38,800,000. The Imperial Government had the right to demand return of the down payment at any time. The amount so callable, however, was to be reduced by 20% of the amounts invoiced by Bell to which the Imperial Government did not object. Bell's liability for return of the down payment was reduced by application of this mechanism as the Contract was performed, with the result that approximately $30,200,000 of the down payment now remains callable.

In order to secure the return of the down payment on demand, Bell was required to establish an unconditional and irrevocable Letter of Guaranty, to be issued by Bank Iranshahr in the amount of $38,800,000 in favor of the Imperial Government. The Contract provides that it is to be governed by the laws of Iran and that all disputes arising under it are to be resolved by the Iranian courts.

Bell obtained a Letter of Guaranty from Bank Iranshahr. In turn, as required by Bank Iranshahr, Bell obtained a standby Letter of Credit, No. SC 170027, issued by Manufacturers in favor of Bank Iranshahr in the amount of $38,800,000 to secure reimbursement to Bank Iranshahr should it be required to pay the Imperial Government under its Letter of Guaranty.

The standby Letter of Credit provided for payment by Manufacturers to Bank Iranshahr upon receipt of:

> Your [Bank Iranshahr's] dated statement purportedly signed by an officer indicating name and title or your Tested Telex Reading: (A) "Referring Manufacturers Hanover Trust Co. Credit No. SC170027, the amount of our claim $_____ represents funds due us as we have received a written request from the Imperial Government of Iran Ministry of War to pay them the sum of _____ under our Guarantee No._____ issued for the account of American Bell International Inc. covering advance payment under Contract No. 138 dated July 23, 1978 and, such payment has been made by us" . . .

In the application for the Letter of Credit, Bell agreed—guaranteed by AT & T—immediately to reimburse Manufacturers for all amounts paid by Manufacturers to Bank Iranshahr pursuant to the Letter of Credit.

Bell commenced performance of its Contract with the Imperial Government. It provided certain services and equipment to update Iran's communications system and submitted a number of invoices, some of which were paid.

In late 1978 and early 1979, Iran was wreaked with revolutionary turmoil culminating in the overthrow of the Iranian government and its replacement by the Islamic Republic. In the wake of this upheaval, Bell was left with substantial unpaid invoices and claims under the Contract and ceased its performance in January 1979. Bell claims that the Contract was breached by the Imperial Government, as well as repudiated by the Islamic Republic, in that it is owed substantial sums for services rendered under the Contract and its termination provisions.

On February 16, 1979, before a demand had been made by Bank Iranshahr for payment under the Letter of Credit, Bell and AT & T brought an action against Manufacturers in the Supreme Court, New York County, seeking a preliminary injunction prohibiting Manufacturers from honoring any demand for payment under the Letter of Credit. The motion for a preliminary injunction was denied in a thorough opinion by Justice Dontzin on March 26, 1979, and the denial was unanimously affirmed on appeal by the Appellate Division, First Department.

On July 25 and 29, 1979, Manufacturers received demands by Tested Telex from Bank Iranshahr for payment of $30,220,724 under the Letter of Credit, the remaining balance of the down payment. Asserting that the demand did not conform with the Letter of Credit, Manufacturers declined payment and so informed Bank Iranshahr. Informed of this, Bell responded by filing this action and an application by way of order to show cause for a temporary restraining order bringing on this motion for a preliminary injunction. Following argument, we granted a temporary restraining order on July 29 enjoining Manufacturers from making any payment to Bank Iranshahr until forty-eight hours after Manufacturers notified Bell of the receipt of a conforming demand, and this order has been extended pending decision of this motion.

On August 1, 1979, Manufacturers notified Bell that it had received a conforming demand from Bank Iranshahr. At the request of the parties, the court held an evidentiary hearing on August 3 on this motion for a preliminary injunction.

CRITERIA FOR PRELIMINARY INJUNCTIONS

The current criteria in this circuit for determining whether to grant the extraordinary remedy of a preliminary injunction are set forth in Caulfield v. Board of Education, 583 F.2d 605, 610 (2d Cir. 1978):

> [T]here must be a showing of possible irreparable injury *and* either (1) probable success on the merits *or* (2) sufficiently serious questions going to the merits to make them a fair ground for litigation *and* a balance of hardships tipping decidedly toward the party requesting the preliminary relief.

We are not persuaded that the plaintiff has met the criteria and therefore deny the motion.

A.   IRREPARABLE INJURY

Plaintiff has failed to show that irreparable injury may possibly ensue if a preliminary injunction is denied. Bell does not even claim, much less show, that it lacks an adequate remedy at law if Manufacturers makes a payment to Bank Iranshahr in violation of the Letter of Credit. It is too clear for argument that a suit for money damages could be based on any such violation, and surely Manufacturers would be able to pay any money judgment against it.

Bell falls back on a contention that it is without any effective remedy unless it can restrain payment. This contention is based on the fact that it agreed to be bound by the laws of Iran and to submit resolution of any disputes under the Contract to the courts of Iran. Bell claims that it now has no meaningful access to those courts.

There is credible evidence that the Islamic Republic is xenophobic and anti-American and that it has no regard for consulting service contracts such as the one here. Although Bell has made no effort to invoke the aid of the Iranian courts, we think the current situation in Iran, as shown by the evidence, warrants the conclusion that an attempt by Bell to resort to those courts would be futile. . . . However, Bell has not demonstrated that it is without adequate remedy in this court against the Iranian defendants under the Sovereign Immunity Act which it invokes in this very case. 28 U.S.C. §§1605(a)(2), 1610(b)(2) (Supp. 1979).

Accordingly, we conclude that Bell has failed to demonstrate irreparable injury.

B. PROBABLE SUCCESS ON THE MERITS

Even assuming that plaintiff has shown possible irreparable injury, it has failed to show probable success on the merits. *Caulfield, supra,* at 610.

In order to succeed on the merits, Bell must prove, by a preponderance of the evidence, that either (1) a demand for payment of the Manufacturers Letter of Credit conforming to the terms of that Letter has not yet been made, . . . or (2) a demand, even though in conformity, should not be honored because of fraud in the transaction, see, e.g., N.Y. UCC §5-114(2); *United Bank* [*supra,* p.54]. It is not probable, in the sense of a greater than 50% likelihood, that Bell will be able to prove either nonconformity or fraud.

As to nonconformity, the August 1 demand by Bank Iranshahr is identical to the terms of the Manufacturers Letter of Credit in every respect except one: it names as payee the "Government of Iran Ministry of Defense, Successor to the Imperial Government of Iran Ministry of War" rather than the "Imperial Government of Iran Ministry of War." *Compare* defendants' Exhibit A *with* Complaint Exhibit C. It is, of course, a bedrock principle of letter of credit law that a demand must strictly comply with the letter in order to justify payment. . . . Nevertheless, we deem it less than probable that a court, upon a full trial, would find nonconformity in the instant case. . . .

If conformity is established, as here, the issuer of an irrevocable, unconditional letter of credit, such as Manufacturers normally has an absolute duty to transfer the requisite funds. This duty is wholly independent of the underlying contractual relationship that gives rise to the letter of credit. . . . Nevertheless, both the Uniform Commercial Code of New York, which the parties concede governs here, and the courts state that payment is enjoinable where a germane document is forged or fraudulent or there is "fraud in the transaction." N.Y. UCC §5-114(2); *United Bank* [*supra*]. Bell does not contend that any documents are fraudulent by virtue of misstatements or omissions. Instead, it argues there is "fraud in the transaction."

The parties disagree over the scope to be given as a matter of law to the term "transaction." Manufacturers, citing voluminous authorities, argues that the term refers only to the Letter of Credit transaction, not to the underlying commercial transaction or to the totality of dealings among the banks, the Iranian government and Bell. On this view of the law, Bell must fail to establish a probability of success, for it does not claim that the Imperial Government or Bank Iranshahr induced Manufacturers to extend the Letter by lies or half-truths, that the Letter contained any false representations by the Imperial Government or Bank Iranshahr, or that they intended misdeeds with it. Nor does Bell claim that the demand contains any misstatements.

Bell argues, citing equally voluminous authorities, that the term "transaction" refers to the totality of circumstances. On this view, Bell has some chance of success on the merits, for a court can consider Bell's allegations that the Government of Iran's behavior in connection with the consulting contract suffices to make its demand on the Letter of Guaranty fraudulent and that the ensuing demand on the Letter of Credit by Bank Iranshahr is tainted with the fraud.

There is some question whether these divergent understandings of the law are wholly incompatible since it would seem impossible to keep the Letter of Credit transaction conceptually distinct. A demand which facially conforms to the Letter of Credit and which contains no misstatements may, nevertheless, be considered fraudulent if made with the goal of mulcting the party who caused the Letter of Credit to be issued. Be that as it may, we need not decide this thorny issue of law. For, even on the construction most favorable to Bell, we find that success on the merits is not probable. Many of the facts alleged, even if proven, would not constitute fraud. As to others, the proof is insufficient to indicate a probability of success on the merits.

Bell, while never delineating with precision the contours of the purported fraud, sets forth five contentions which, in its view, support the issuance of an injunction. Bell asserts that (1) both the old and new Governments failed to approve invoices for services fully performed; (2) both failed to fund contracted-for independent Letters of Credit in Bell's favor; (3) the new Government has taken steps to renounce altogether its obligations under the Contract; (4) the new Government has made it impossible to assert contract rights in Iranian courts; and (5) the new Government has caused Bank Iranshahr to demand payment on the Manufacturers Letter of Credit, thus asserting rights in a transaction it has otherwise repudiated. . . . Even if we accept the proposition that the evidence does show repudiation, plaintiff is still far from demonstrating the kind of evil intent necessary to support a claim of fraud. Surely, plaintiff cannot contend that every party who breaches or repudiates his contract is for that reason culpable of fraud. The law of contract damages is adequate to repay the economic harm caused by repudiation, and the law presumes that one who repudiates has done so because of a calculation that such damages are cheaper than performance. Absent any showing that Iran would refuse to pay damages upon a contract action here or in Iran, much less a showing that Bell has even attempted to obtain such a remedy, the evidence is ambivalent as to whether the purported repudiation results from non-fraudulent economic calculation or from fraudulent intent to mulct Bell.

Plaintiff contends that the alleged repudiation, viewed in connection with its demand for payment on the Letter of Credit, supplies the basis from which only one inference—fraud—can be drawn. Again, we remain unpersuaded.

Plaintiff's argument requires us to presume bad faith on the part of the Iranian government. It requires us further to hold that that government may not rely on the plain terms of the consulting contract and the Letter of Credit arrangements with Bank Iranshahr and Manufacturers providing for immediate repayment of the down payment upon demand, without regard to cause. On the evidence before us, fraud is no more inferable than an economically rational decision by the government to recoup its down payment, as it is entitled to do under the consulting contract and still dispute its liabilities under that Contract.

While fraud in the transaction is doubtless a possibility, plaintiff has not shown it to be a probability and thus fails to satisfy this branch of the *Caulfield* test.

C. SERIOUS QUESTIONS AND BALANCE OF HARDSHIPS

If plaintiff fails to demonstrate probable success, he may still obtain relief by showing, in addition to the possibility of irreparable injury, both (1) sufficiently serious questions going to the merits to make them a fair ground for litigation, and (2) a balance of hardships tipping decidedly toward plaintiff. *Caulfield, supra.* Both Bell and Manufacturers appear to concede the existence of serious questions, and the complexity and novelty of this matter lead us to find they exist. Nevertheless, we hold that plaintiff is not entitled to relief under this branch of the *Caulfield* test because the balance of hardships does not tip *decidedly* toward Bell, if indeed it tips that way at all.

To be sure, Bell faces substantial hardships upon denial of its motion. Should Manufacturers pay the demand, Bell will immediately become liable to Manufacturers for $30.2 million, with no assurance of recouping those funds from Iran for the services performed. While counsel represented in graphic detail the other losses Bell faces at the hands of the current Iranian government, these would flow regardless of whether we ordered the relief sought. The hardship imposed from a denial of relief is limited to the admittedly substantial sum of $30.2 million.

But Manufacturers would face at least as great a loss, and perhaps a greater one, were we to grant relief. Upon Manufacturers' failure to pay, Bank Iranshahr could initiate a suit on the Letter of Credit and attach $30.2 million of Manufacturers' assets in Iran. In addition, it could seek to hold Manufacturers liable for consequential damages beyond that sum resulting from the failure to make timely payment. Finally, there is no guarantee that Bank Iranshahr or the government, in retaliation for Manufacturers' recalcitrance, will not nationalize additional Manufacturers' assets in Iran in amounts which counsel, at oral argument, represented to be far in excess of the amount in controversy here.

Apart from a greater monetary exposure flowing from an adverse decision, Manufacturers faces a loss of credibility in the international banking community that could result from its failure to make good on a letter of credit.

CONCLUSION

Finally, apart from questions of relative hardship and the specific criteria of the *Caulfield* test, general considerations of equity counsel us to deny the motion for injunctive relief. Bell, a sophisticated multinational enterprise well advised by competent counsel, entered into these arrangements with its corporate eyes open. It knowingly and voluntarily signed a contract allowing the Iranian government to recoup its down payment on demand, without regard to cause. It caused Manufacturers to enter into an arrangement whereby Manufacturers became obligated to pay Bank Iranshahr the unamortized down payment balance upon receipt of conforming documents, again without regard to cause.

Both of these arrangements redounded tangibly to the benefit of Bell. The Contract with Iran, with its prospect of designing and installing from scratch a nationwide and international communications system, was certain to bring to Bell both monetary profit and prestige and good will in the global communications industry. The agreement to indemnify Manufacturers on its Letter of Credit provided the means by which these benefits could be achieved.

One who reaps the rewards of commercial arrangements must also accept their burdens. One such burden in this case, voluntarily accepted by Bell, was the risk that demand might be made without cause on the funds constituting the down payment. To be sure, the sequence of events that led up to that demand may well have been unforeseeable when the contracts were signed. To this extent, both Bell and Manufacturers have been made the unwitting and innocent victims of tumultuous events beyond their control. But, as between two innocents, the party who undertakes by contract the risk of political uncertainty and governmental caprice must bear the consequences when the risk comes home to roost.

Manufacturers also contends that, in view of the action apparently still pending in the state courts, we should abstain from deciding the issues before us and that Bell is engaging in forum-shopping which dirties its hands so as to require a denial of injunctive relief. In view of our findings and conclusions based on the *Caulfield* test, we find it unnecessary to consider these contentions.

The foregoing opinion constitutes this court's findings of fact and conclusions of law, pursuant to Rule 52(a), Fed. R. Civ. P.

Accordingly, plaintiff's motion for a preliminary injunction, pursuant to Rule 65(a), Fed. R. Civ. P., is denied. However, Manufacturers Hanover

Trust Company, its officers and agents are hereby enjoined from making any payments to Bank Iranshahr or the Islamic Republic of Iran, pursuant to the subject Letter of Credit, until August 6, 1979, at 3:00 P.M., to permit plaintiff to apply to the Court of Appeals for a stay pending appeal, if it is so advised. So ordered.

NOTES AND QUESTIONS

1. Why did the bank resist nonpayment in *American Bell*? Would you, as a banker's lawyer, ever advise nonpayment in such circumstances without a court injunction "against" you?

2. What commercial purposes did the letter of credit in *American Bell* serve? How are they different from those in the usual export/import transaction? For related cases and materials, *see* Harris Corp. v. National Iranian Radio and Television, 691 F.2d 1344 (11th Cir. 1982); KMW International v. Chase Manhattan Bank, 606 F.2d 10 (2d Cir. 1979); R. D. Harbottle (Merchantile) Ltd. v. National Westminster Bank, [1977] 2 All E.R. 862; Comment, Enjoining the International Standby Letter of Credit; The Iranian Letter of Credit Cases, 21 Harv. Intl. L.J. 189 (1980).

3. Is it understandable that U.S. banking law places severe restrictions on a bank's authority to issue letters of credit? *See* Murray, Letters of Credit in Nonsale of Goods Transactions, 30 Bus. Law. 1103 (1975); Verkuil, Bank Solvency and Guaranty Letters of Credit, 25 Stan. L. Rev. 716 (1973).

2. Banking Aspects

So far, the discussion has not explained how payment is actually made; neither has it faced the special problems of dealing in foreign currencies. In concept, both are relatively simple—in practice, dealing with large numbers of transactions, with increasingly electronic means, naturally becomes more complex.

The payment mechanism, as well as the mutual confidence of banks, depends heavily on a network of reciprocal deposits. Groups of correspondent banks typically collaborate by maintaining such deposits and also exchange market and credit information. These deposits or accounts permit easy transfer of funds.

Suppose that in the example developed in pp. 32-33 *supra,* Tokyo and Chicago banks each maintain a sizable dollar deposit with the other. Chicago bank can now transfer money to the Tokyo exporter simply by sending a draft or a cable transfer (essentially an electronic analogue of a draft) to Tokyo directing that bank to debit (take money from) Chicago bank's account and credit (put money in) the exporter's account. This works exactly like a check directing payment out of one's own account. In international banking parlance, the foreign bank will call its Tokyo account a *nostro* account ("our account with you"). As an alternative, the Chicago or *vostro* account ("your account with us" as seen from Chicago) can instead be used. Chicago bank credits this account with the payment and notifies Tokyo bank, which can now pay the exporter with its own funds and end up exactly even. For a description of these transfers, *see* Delbrueck & Co. v. Manufacturers Hanover Trust Co., 609 F.2d 1047 (2d Cir. 1979), especially footnote 1.

This approach can be supplemented to permit even greater flexibility. For example, the banks with whom the exporter and importer deal may not maintain a correspondent relation, but can still negotiate a draft through a series of banks that do maintain such relations. This is similar to the check clearing concept in domestic practice. In another form of flexibility, the transfer may be made through a third bank with whom both parties maintain relations: Australian bank directs London bank, with which it has an account, to pay Bahrain bank, which also has a London account. Only rarely, if ever, is it necessary for currency actually to be shipped from place to place.

As suggested above, mutual deposits also provide a basis for banking confidence in the letter of credit. The letter of credit cases showed that banks are quite eager to maintain their reputation; if a bank fails, however, its eagerness to honor its reputation is not enough. A bank, say in New York, can nevertheless recommend faith in a foreign bank's letters of credit if that bank has accounts in New York sufficient to cover the net obligations the foreign bank has outstanding on letters of credit to New York. The deposit serves as a sort of guarantee of payment, not very different from the deposit underlying a checking account. The international banks run daily balances of their relations with all major foreign banks, looking for risks arising from individual banks as well as from individual nations that might face a foreign exchange crisis.

The final issue to add to the routine trade transaction is that of foreign currency. A London buyer almost certainly wants to pay in sterling, while a U.S. seller wants payment in dollars. The contract of sale will have specified a currency and the drafts and letter of credit will almost certainly use the same currency. Under the assumption that that currency is dollars, the London bank will have to pay dollars while receiving payment from its customer in sterling. It will do so by going into the foreign exchange market—a telephone-based market to bring together those who wish to buy or sell foreign currency. In theory, the bank will find an individual who wishes to sell dollars and buy pounds and negotiate a price, which will be charged to its clients along with a transaction fee. In practice, the bank will follow daily market quotations in dealing with its client, will net out its own purchases and sales of specific currencies, and will enter the market to maintain or reach a desired overall balance of currency holdings.

The foreign trade transaction offers significant flexibility in dealing with currencies. Most of the examples used so far have involved transactions in dollars. But a transaction could easily be denominated in sterling and payment made to a New York bank (for a U.S. export) in that currency. That bank would then go into the New York foreign exchange market to obtain dollars and its customer would be the one immediately paying the conversion. If there is credit involved, the possible differences between sterling and dollar interest rates may affect the parties' choice of transaction format, as between, say, a draft denominated in dollars and one denominated in pounds.

The foreign exchange market operates like any other in that the price will shift to clear the market. As a very rough approximation, this means that a nation that is exporting more than it is importing and therefore running a balance-of-trade surplus will see the price of its currency rise as foreign purchasers compete to obtain the quantities needed to pay for their purchases. (Note that currency quotation figures are sometimes confusing. The dollar is rising if one dollar buys 50 pence instead of 40; but this can also be expressed as saying the dollar has *risen* from $2.50 = 1 £ to $2.00 = 1 £.) This price rise will generally cause the nation's exports to appear more expensive and be less competitive abroad. The nation will tend to sell less, thus restoring balance in the market.

The real world is not quite so simple, with capital flow, speculative, and political factors as well as trade-derived factors affecting the market. On the capital flow side, investors will seek to put their funds where interest rates are highest, making allowance of course for their expectations of changes in the relative currency prices. On the speculative side, investors will tend to invest in those currencies that they expect will rise. And most governments intervene in the foreign exchange market for economic and political reasons.

Moreover, the effect of currency price changes on exports and imports is less clear than one might expect. In general, as a nation's currency inflates, the competitiveness of its exports falls, and the competitiveness of foreign imports rises. These changes will tend to restore balance. But there is usually a significant time lag during which contracts that were made at the old exchange rate have still to be performed. Moreover, the cost of production of some exports may depend highly on the prices of imports, which will also be affected by an exchange rate change. In addition, some commodities are priced in currencies that may not be affected by the currency adjustment; almost all international oil transactions, for example, are priced in dollars, no matter what nations are involved.

Bibliographical Note

For additional—and easy to follow—information on fund transfer and foreign exchange, *see* A. R. Holmes & E. H. Schott, The New York Foreign Exchange Market, (1965); Lingl, Risk Allocation in International Interbank Electronic Fund Transfers: CHIPS & SWIFT, 22 Harv. J. Intl. Law 621 (1980); Hoffman and Giddy, Lessons from the Iranian Experience: National

Currencies as International Money, 3 Comp. Corp. Law & Sec. Reg. 271 (1980); S.W.I.F.T.: A Fast Method to Facilitate International Financial Transactions, 17 J.W.T.L. 458 (1983).

B.   EXPORT CREDIT ARRANGEMENTS

The letter of credit mechanism works well for exports to nations with relatively easy access to funds. Although the seller can easily extend short-term credit to the buyer, the latter must be able to pay within a few months. It is obviously difficult for private agencies in the exporting nation to extend long-term credit to the buyer when the goods, as the obvious collateral, are in another nation. In part for this reason, which restricts the ability of the regular banking system to help with sales to the developing world, but far more out of a desire to maintain exports and the consequent employment, most developed world governments have instituted a government export financing system. For background, *see* Duff, The Outlook for Official Export Credits, 13 Law & Poly. Intl. Bus. 891 (1981).

1.   The United States Version

The U.S. example is the Exim bank, described in the following excerpt from its own literature. This bank has a variety of programs for providing credit for exports. In some cases, it is itself the lender; in others, it guarantees a loan to make it easier for private lenders to make the loan.

EXIM BANK PROGRAM SUMMARY

The Export-Import Bank of the United States. Office of Public Affairs. July 1984

SUMMARY

The Export-Import Bank of the United States (Eximbank) was created in 1934, and established as an independent U.S. Government Agency in 1945. The purpose of the Bank is ". . . to aid in financing and to facilitate exports. . . ." Exim receives no appropriations from the U.S. Congress. Since inception, Exim has supported more than $160 billion in U.S. export sales, and has paid more than $1 billion in dividends to the U.S. Treasury. Eximbank is directed by statute (1) to offer financing for U.S. exporters that is competitive with the financing provided by foreign export credit agencies to assist sales by their nations' exporters, (2) to determine that the transactions supported provide for a reasonable assurance of repayment, (3) to supplement, but not compete with, private sources of export financing, and (4) to take into account the effect of its activities on small business, the domestic economy, and U.S. employment.

Foreign Credit Insurance Association (FCIA), a group of U.S. property, casualty and marine insurance companies, cooperates with Eximbank to cover repayment risks on short- and medium-term export credit transactions.

More than 350 commercial banks work with Eximbank to provide funding and participate in the commercial risks of medium-term export transactions. . . .

Program Selection Chart

Exports	*Appropriate Program*
SHORT-TERM (up to 180 days)	
Consumables	Export Credit Insurance
Small manufactured items	Working Capital Guarantee
Spare parts	
Raw materials	
MEDIUM-TERM (181 days to 5 years)	
Mining and refining equipment	Export Credit Insurance
Construction equipment	Commercial Bank Guarantees
Agricultural equipment	Small Business Credit Program
General aviation aircraft	Medium-Term Credit
Planning/feasibility studies	Working Capital Guarantee
LONG-TERM (5 years & longer)	
Power plants	Direct Loans
LNG and gas processing plants	Financial Guarantees
Other major projects	
Commercial jet aircraft or locomotives	
Other heavy capital goods	

DIRECT LOANS AND FINANCIAL GUARANTEES

The Export-Import Bank provides financing assistance for U.S. exports of heavy capital equipment and large-scale installations which are normally financed for a term of more than five years.

The Bank's long-term financing takes the form of either a direct credit to a public or private overseas buyer, or a financial guarantee assuring repayment of a private credit. This private credit may be denominated in either U.S. dollars or a foreign currency acceptable to Eximbank. Exim often blends these two forms of support in a single financing package. Review of requests for financing assistance includes appraisal of the financial, economic and technical aspects of the transaction, and also includes an analysis of the degree of foreign, publicly-supported export credit competition for the sale. The review also considers the effect which the transaction will have on the U.S. economy.

Eximbank will not provide credit support for transactions which will proceed without its assistance. Generally, the Bank will not provide lines of credit, credit support for sales to developed or rich countries, sales of military goods or services, or credit for sales of older generation aircraft.

In each transaction, the Bank will provide credit for up to 65 percent of the U.S. export value when such support is necessary. Eximbank requires a cash payment to the U.S. seller from the foreign buyer of at least 15 percent of the export value of the U.S. purchases. The balance of the financing is usually provided from private lenders, with such financing arranged by the borrower.

Repayment of principal and interest is scheduled in equal semiannual installments, normally beginning six months from the date of delivery of the products or completion of the project. Eximbank usually agrees to be repaid from the later installments, thereby encouraging financing by private banks which are repaid from the earlier maturities. Repayment terms normally range between five and ten years; however, Eximbank will, on a case-by-case basis, lengthen repayment terms to enable U.S. exporters to counter foreign publicly-supported export credit competition. . . .

REPAYMENT ASSURANCE

The Bank's statute requires Exim to find a reasonable assurance of repayment of its loans. To assure repayment, Exim often requires a repayment guarantee by a financial organization in the buyer's country. Frequently the central bank, finance ministry, or a government development bank will provide this guarantee. In some cases, larger commercial banks or parent firms are acceptable. . . .

SMALL BUSINESS CREDIT PROGRAM

This program enables U.S. commercial banks to extend fixed-rate, medium-term export loans by providing standby assurance that the bank can borrow from Eximbank against the outstanding value of a medium-term foreign debt obligation. Commercial banks are reluctant to provide fixed-rates on medium-term transactions because of the substantial fluctuations in their cost of funds. Often, however, fixed-rate financing is necessary for the U.S. exporter to obtain a foreign order.

Eximbank will follow the size guidelines set by the Small Business Administration (SBA) in determining eligibility for support under the Small Business Credit Program. The SBA definitions of small business are identified by four digit Standard Industrial Classification (SIC) codes. A size standard based on either sales volume or number of employees is set forth for each industrial classification. Regulations covering the SIC codes can be obtained from the nearest SBA office.

If a bank (as exporter of record) or supplier, agent, export management company, etc., is selling goods or services of a small business, the transaction is eligible.

Eximbank will issue advance commitments to make fixed-rate loans to eligible U.S. commercial banks when the applicant bank is not prepared to offer fixed-rate financing unless Eximbank provides a loan commitment.

Eximbank's loan commitment covers up to 85 percent of the contract price of an export sale financed by the U.S. bank on terms ranging from 366 days to 5 years. Eximbank will either commit to make a discount loan to the bank secured by the bank's promissory note to Eximbank or it will commit to purchase the foreign debt obligation from the U.S. bank. In either case, Eximbank will have full recourse on the U.S. bank for the amount of the loan. . . .

MEDIUM-TERM CREDIT PROGRAM

The Medium-Term Credit Program provides fixed interest rate support for those medium-term export sales that are facing subsidized, officially supported export credit competition from abroad.

Eximbank will make a fixed interest rate loan commitment to a U.S. bank that is financing the export sale and will lend its funds to the U.S. bank. The guidelines, fee rates, and internal administration of this program are nearly identical to the Small Business Program except as follows:

Evidence of Competition: Unlike the Small Business Credit Program, evidence of subsidized foreign officially supported export credit competition must accompany each request.

The U.S. suppliers and the applicant banks must submit the best information available regarding the existence of the subsidized foreign, officially supported export credit competition, preferably including the name of the foreign suppliers and the terms and interest rates they are offering. When specific identity of the foreign competitor, and/or its financing are not known, other means of indirectly establishing the reasonable likelihood of subsidized official export credit competition will be pursued by Eximbank. . . .

THE COMMERCIAL BANK GUARANTEE PROGRAM

Under the Commercial Bank Guarantee Program, the Export-Import Bank of the United States guarantees the repayment of medium-term export obligations acquired by U.S. financial institutions from U.S. exporters. The purpose of this program is to facilitate the export of U.S. capital and quasi-capital goods through the U.S. commercial banking system. Eximbank assumes commercial and political risks that U.S. exporters or private financial institutions are unwilling or unable to undertake.

Eximbank is able to accomplish its objective by working closely with the participating financial institutions. They are: U.S. commercial banks, Edge

Act Corporations, Agreement corporations operating under Section 25 and 25(a) of the Federal Reserve Act, and U.S. branches and agencies of foreign banks.

The foreign country in which the buyer is located must be mutually agreeable to the financial institution and Eximbank. Coverage is presently available in over 140 countries.

Eximbank requires a 15% cash payment from the buyer. For the financed portion, Eximbank's guarantee covers 100% of the political risk. For the commercial risk, after the exporter retains a 10% participation (5% for small business), the financing bank assumes a 5% or 15% participation and Eximbank covers the balance.

Repayment terms should not exceed those which are customary in international trade.

Eximbank's General Guidelines

Contract Value	Terms
Up to $50,000	181 days to 2 years
50,001 to 100,000	Up to 3 years
100,001 to 200,000	Up to 4 years
Over 200,000	Up to 5 years

Eximbank does not specify the rate of interest to be borne by the obligor, but interest guaranteed will be limited to the lower of either the interest rate of the note or one percent above the effective rate of interest at the date of default for Treasury borrowings having the same maturity as the remaining term of the note. In the event of a claim, Eximbank will pay interest accrued to the date of claim payment or 90 days beyond the required waiting period before a claim can be filed, whichever is earlier.

The commercial banks which use this program are experienced international lenders who are relied upon to submit credit-worthy applications. In recognition of this fact, when a bank has completed a number of satisfactory guaranteed export transactions, Eximbank will consider extending *Delegated Authority* subject to prescribed conditions, to the commercial bank, to commit Eximbank to specific transactions without obtaining prior Eximbank approval. Under Delegated Authority, commercial banks must retain 15% of the commercial risk. . . .

EXPORT CREDIT INSURANCE PROGRAM

The Export Credit Insurance Program is operated in cooperation with a private association, Foreign Credit Insurance Association. FCIA was created in 1961 to give U.S. exporters the means to become internationally competitive. It does this by insuring U.S. exports against commercial and political risks.

Such coverage helps the exporter to offer credit terms and to obtain financing of foreign receivables.

FCIA, a group of U.S. property, casualty and marine insurance companies, sells and services export credit insurance policies under an agency and reinsurance agreement with Eximbank. With FCIA insurance, the exporter obtains comprehensive protection against non-payment for its foreign receivables.

The benefits of FCIA coverage can be summarized as follows: (a) it protects the exporter against the failure of the buyer to pay his dollar obligation (or other currency, if so requested and approved) for commercial or political reasons, (b) it encourages the exporter to offer competitive terms of repayment to foreign buyers, (c) it supports the exporter's prudent penetration of higher risk foreign markets, and (d) it gives the exporter greater financial liquidity and flexibility in administering its foreign receivables portfolio.

LOSSES COVERED

The reasons for nonpayment are numerous. Commercial defaults may result from economic deterioration in the buyer's market area, fluctuations in demand, unanticipated competition, shifts in tariffs, or technological changes. One of the principals or key management members of the buyer's company may die or become inactive, causing the company to close. A buyer's own government or one of his major customers may alter purchasing patterns, or the buyer may be subjected to an unexpectedly sharp increase in operating expenses. Natural disasters, such as floods and earthquakes, can also affect the ability of a buyer to operate in a market.

Superimposed upon an exporter's commercial risks are those of a political or noncommercial nature. Political risks are beyond the control of either the buyer or seller. War, revolution, and insurrection are all legitimate fears of exporters. In the aftermath of political upheavals, the assets of a buyer may be confiscated, a shipment may be detained or licenses may be revoked. In a different vein, growing balance-of-payment strains can choke the capacity of a country's central bank to convert local currency into U.S. dollars.

Overall, the risks of extending credit to customers in other countries are typically much greater than the risks in granting credit to domestic buyers. The U.S. exporter needs to be insured against these risks, and FCIA helps. Policies offered are many and varied. Following appropriate consultation with FCIA and Eximbank, the exporter can expect to have a policy tailor-made to his needs. . . .

WORKING CAPITAL GUARANTEE PROGRAM

Program Objective: The Working Capital Guarantee program provides exporters with access to working capital loans that (1) would not be provided without Eximbank's assistance and, (2) without which, the exporter would not be able to export. Most of the working capital loans guaranteed by Eximbank are expected ultimately to support exports from small/medium-size/minority/ agricultural exporters. . . .

Exim has not been without its critics. In 1981 the Congressional Budget Office issued a particularly negative report on the Exim program, saying in its summary[2]:

> The Export-Import Bank of the United States (Eximbank) has outstanding about $13.8 billion in subsidized loans. The Administration has recently proposed curtailing the rate of new lending by about 12 percent from previously planned levels. This report examined the costs of and benefits from the operation of Eximbank. It finds that U.S. citizens pay additional costs of between $200 million and $1 billion annually (at current program levels and interest rates). These added costs are largely redistributed from nonbeneficiaries to U.S. exporters, foreign importers, and banks, with the remainder absorbed in efficiency losses. The report is unable to document any gains for the United States as a whole from the Eximbank program as it currently operates. The report notes, however, that Eximbank's lending policies could be redirected to combat foreign lending practices that are viewed as unfair or to foster U.S. foreign policy goals.

In its reply to the CBO's assessment, Exim vigorously defended itself, saying[3]:

> The Congressional Budget Office report addresses certain specific trade-related issues (such as employment, dollar exchange rates, and level of exports) according to theoretical concepts. Eximbank believes that the CBO analysis both assumes a macroeconomic world inconsistent with the reality around us and overlooks the microeconomic aspects that form the fundamental issues relating to Eximbank's economic value. Hence, Exim contends that the conclusions reached by CBO—that the benefits of Eximbank subsidized direct credit activity are minor, few, and worth much less than the subsidy cost—are unsubstantiated.
>
> In Eximbank's opinion, the real issue is whether the financial cost of subsidized Exim direct loans exceeds the economic benefit of maintaining an industrial structure which is the most efficient and productive for the U.S. over the long term. That is, the critical issue is not Exim's impact on overall employment, exchange rates, or export levels; rather, it is CBO's finding that Exim's direct loan program constitutes a net cost to the U.S. economy because it results in a transfer of resources from more efficient to less efficient uses or, as CBO states in its summary, ". . . a misdirection of resources."
>
> Eximbank takes issue with this finding and bases its rebuttal on the following two-step argument:
>
> (1) Foreign government export credit subsidies interfere with the market; international purchase decisions in certain capital goods sectors are not being

---

[2]Congressional Budget Office, The Benefits and Costs of the Export-Import Bank Loan Subsidy Program, in Hearings Before the Subcommittee on International Trade, Investment and Monetary Policy of the House Committee on Banking, Finance, and Urban Affairs on Export-Import Bank Budget Authorization, 97th Cong., 1st Sess. 1981.

[3]Hearings, note 2 *supra*.

based on market conditions, but rather on the extent to which another government will offer subsidized export credits.

(2) By neutralizing the effect of these foreign subsidies, Eximbank allows the market to once again operate freely. With the availability of *non-market related* financing no longer a decision element, the foreign purchaser must make a decision based on market-determined factors.

Hence, the fundamental economic rationale for a competitive Eximbank direct loan program is the benefit to the U.S. economy of allowing market forces to operate, which permits U.S. capital goods industries to achieve their "natural" level of output, including exports as well as domestic sales. This benefit prevents U.S. industrial resources from being continuously shifted from more efficient (market-determined) to less efficient (foreign-government-determined) uses—not vice versa, as CBO contends. By preventing such a shift, Exim credits help maintain the highest level of productivity possible, as presumably the market determines where resources can be used most productively.

The economic importance of Exim credit is due therefore, not to the *overall* level of exports which it facilitates, but to the fact that the exports supported represent those which the market would have achieved absent foreign government intervention—which, in turn, reflect the most efficient use of U.S. resources. Accordingly, U.S. productivity is higher, inflation lower, and real national income greater.

In addition, the magnitude of Eximbank's beneficial impact on U.S. national income could be much greater than the dollar value of the financial costs incurred in providing the competitive credit. For example, if those specific Exim-supported exports were not made, the lower productivity associated with the shift of those resources could cause the productivity of the entire industry sector losing the resources to decline—yielding a potential loss of billions of dollars of national income. Given the fact that Eximbank credits represent up to 10% of the total (domestic and export) output of some entire industry sectors, this "multiplier" potential would seem to be a valid concern.

NOTES AND QUESTIONS

1. Why does Exim offer so many different programs? Consider the service-oriented issues of convenience for different kinds of users, the financial issues of conserving capital, as well as the political questions of maintaining relations with different parts of the financial community.

2. Aircraft exporters have usually been the largest single users of Exim funds. Foreign airlines are, therefore, able to fly aircraft purchased at a lower interest rate than are U.S. airlines. Is this unfair to the U.S. airlines? What kinds of remedies might be appropriate for a firm affected this way?

3. Would you recommend that Exim grant foreign-currency loans and guarantees? It decided to do so in 1980. When it honors a foreign currency guarantee and the exchange rate varies between the times of guarantee, of default, and of actual payment, which should be used? For consideration of this issue in the British context, *see* Lucas v. Export Credits Guarantee Dept., 2 A.E.R. 889 (1974).

4. Is it wise to use Exim to offer relatively open-ended funding to nations in debt trouble to assist them in making purchases from the United States? (This was started in the 1980s.)

5. Exim has been marked by scandal more than have most federal agencies. *See*, e.g., Ann Crittenden, The Imbroglio Over the Export-Import Bank, The New York Times, Feb. 12, 1978, at C 1, col. 1, (allegations of inadequate economic review and possible favoritism to specific suppliers in sale of nuclear reactor to Philippines). Why might this be?

6. Part of the economic argument against the Exim concept is that subsidies to some exports raise the value of the dollar and therefore penalize other exports. Another part is that some of Exim's capital is effectively derived from an interest-free loan from the treasury, so that Exim is really not a profit-making venture. Does Exim successfully rebut these arguments?

7. Given the economic arguments against Exim, why is it regularly renewed?

2. International Responses

The United States is one of many nations with such export subsidy programs. Foreign programs are frequently much stronger in the sense of giving lower interest rates and a wider variety of services. This produces such bizarre situations as Great Britain loaning money to OPEC nations in order to be competitive in export terms. For broad, even if somewhat dated reviews of the programs, *see* Organization for Economic Cooperation and Development, The Export Credit Financing Systems in OECD Member Countries (1982); UK Adapts Its Export Credit Programs to Keep Them Comprehensive, Flexible, IMF Surv., July 3, 1978, at 194.

The response to this competition in credit terms has been to seek cartel-like agreement, partly to reduce the cost of the subsidies and partly to avoid the risk that this credit, like easy consumer credit in the domestic context, may encourage developing nations to spend beyond their means. The Berne Union, an organization of export credit granting agencies started in the 1930s, became more a data-exchange and credit-rating agency than a cartel.

During the 1970s the Organization for Economic Cooperation and Development (OECD) became the primary forum for negotiations on export credit terms, and a series of guidelines were developed. These guidelines, which often fell apart or required renegotiation, typically set interest rate floors and maturity ceilings for loans, often graduated to permit greater subsidies to poorer developing nations. Some stated interest rates; others were cast in terms of a specific market rate to make adjustment automatic. There were often special arrangements (or no agreement at all) for particularly competitive exports like aircraft or agricultural products.

NOTES AND QUESTIONS

1. Is it wise to give (or guarantee) easy export credit to the developing nations at a time when these nations are having trouble paying bank debts?

2. What are the comparable policy agreements about credit to the Soviet Union?

3. The existing export credit agreements are clearly weak and short-term. Why is agreement so hard to achieve in this area? For details of the Carter era negotiating history, *see* Statement of F. Bergsten, Hearings on the Export-Import Bank before the Subcomm. on International Trade, Investment and Monetary Policy of the House Comm. on Banking, Finance and Urban Affairs, 96th Cong. 2d Sess. 9 (1980).

4. Why aren't the GATT subsidy rules (to be discussed in Chapter VI) already an effective restriction on subsidized export credit? The legal answer is that these rules incorporate the "Gentlemen's Agreement" quoted above. The 1979 Subsidies Countervailing Measures Code, (Agreement on Interpretation and Application of Articles VI, XVI, and XXIII of the General Agreement on Tariffs and Trade, April 5, 1979), negotiated as part of the Tokyo Round, in general prohibits export subsidies, defined in Annex to include (footnotes omitted):

> (*j*) The provision by governments (or special institutions controlled by governments) of export credit guarantee or insurance programmes, of insurance or guarantee programmes against increases in the costs of exported products or of exchange risk programmes, at premium rates, which are manifestly inadequate to cover the long-term operating costs and losses of the programmes.
>
> (*k*) The grant by governments (or special institutions controlled by and/or acting under the authority of governments) of export credits at rates below those which they actually have to pay for the funds so employed (or would have to pay if they borrowed on international capital markets in order to obtain funds of the same maturity and denominated in the same currency as the export credit), or the payment by them of all or part of the costs incurred by exporters or financial institutions in obtaining credits, in so far as they are used to secure a material advantage in the field of export credit terms. Provided, however, that if a signatory is a party to an international undertaking on official export credits to which at least twelve original signatories to this Agreement are parties as of 1 January 1979 (or a successor undertaking which has been adopted by those original signatories), or if in practice a signatory applies the interest rates provisions of the relevant undertaking, an export credit practice which is in conformity with those provisions shall not be considered an export subsidy prohibited by this Agreement.

There is also a practical answer to the above question: the Subsidies Code is generally designed to protect the importing nation. A nation whose domestic industry is harmed by imports from a foreign subsidized industry may levy compensating ("countervailing") duties against those imports if the subsidies violate the Subsidies Code. The usual export credit problem, however, is that the importing nation is happy to receive the subsidy; it is competing exporters who are harmed—and there is no easy mechanism to protect these exporters. For additional information on the issue of officially supported export credits, *see* G. Hufbauer and G. Erb, Subsidies in International Trade 68-76 (Institute for International Economics: Washington, D.C.: 1984).

5. Given the difficulty of negotiating international arrangements, would the United States be wise to abandon any pretense that Exim is self-supporting and to make it into an open subsidy program? Note that the effort to match foreign credit terms in the high domestic interest rate period around 1980 significantly impaired Exim's financial position and caused it to cancel its "dividend" to the Treasury. *See* Comptroller General, To Be Self-Sufficient or Competitive? Eximbank Needs Congressional Guidance, Report ID-81-48 (June 24, 1981).

C.   BARTER AND COUNTERTRADE

The first part of this chapter outlined the conventional trade transaction involving the exchange of goods or services for money. Trade without money is becoming common, however, and may account for 20-30% of current international trade transactions.[4] One observer of the burgeoning nonmonetary trade scene described an instance of it in the following way[5]:

> *Countertrade made simple:* If you think it's tough selling cars and trucks in the U.S., this is what Chrysler went through to sell several hundred vehicles to credit-starved Jamaica. The American and Canadian mining companies, . . . which dig Jamaica's bauxite and refine it into alumina, hand over some 50,000 tons of alumina to the government's Bauxite & Alumina Trading Co. The trading company, in turn, gives the alumina to Metallgesellschaft, a German metals company. MG sells the alumina to a refiner, which converts it to aluminium. The money MG gets for the alumina goes to the European American Bank, Chrysler's adviser. EAB sends part of the money back to the Bauxite & Alumina Trading Co., which pays the mining companies. The balance goes to finance a letter of credit made out to Chrysler, which then ships trucks to Jamaica. Title is taken by another government firm, the Jamaican Commodity Trading Co., which sells the vehicles to Motors Sales & Services Co., Chrysler's local distributor. The dealer sells them to the public. The part you don't see—and the parties want to keep hidden—is what makes the convoluted deal click. Jamaica probably is shaving price to unload bauxite, while Chrysler is absorbing extra costs to make the sale.

[4]Barter is estimated to amount to $176 billion *within* the United States, or approximately 10% of the GNP. Gutman, The Subterranean Economy, Fin. Analysts J. at 27 (1977). *See also* Kaikati, Marketing Without Exchange of Money, 60 Harv. Bus. Rev. 72 (1982).

[5]Dizard, The Explosion of International Barter, Fortune, February 7, 1983, at pp. 88-89.

1. Definition of Terms

Barter, the oldest and simplest form of commercial transaction, consists of the direct exchange of goods or commodities of equal value without the use of currency. In the postwar era, barter has occupied a limited but defined sector of international trade, occurring until recently principally between the West and the nonmarket economies of Eastern Europe. Recently, a shortage of hard currency and of hard currency credits has contributed to an increased use of barter and related types of exchanges in trade with developing countries, who are often requiring barter or "counter-purchase" agreements as a precondition for sales.

The benefits of barter are mutual. For a less developed country, barter has the dual advantage of reducing or eliminating the need for hard currency to pay for the goods imported while creating an additional outlet for the goods exported. Continuing deficits in the balance of trade (caused in many instances by the demands for foreign exchange to pay for necessary oil imports), combined with the reduced availability of foreign aid and multilateral credit in the current world recession, has put many countries in the position of requiring exports to match imports on an agreement-by-agreement basis. Barter solves that problem.

For developed countries, such as the United States, the use of barter may be a necessary precondition for the export of goods for which the recipient is not in a position to pay cash. Barter thus represents an opportunity to expand sales into otherwise unavailable markets. Barter agreements may also provide assured supplies and allow long-term planning.

2. Typical Practices

L. WELT, COUNTERTRADE: BUSINESS PRACTICES FOR TODAY'S WORLD MARKET[6]

15-23 (1982)

FORMS OF COUNTERTRADE

BARTER

In recent years, pure barter—the exchange of goods under a single contract—has become rare, but not extinct. Barter is used most commonly today between

[6]Reprinted, by permission of publisher from Countertrade; Business Practices for Today's World Market, an AMA Management Briefing by Leo G. B. Welt, pp. 15-19, 21-23 © 1982 Leo G. B. Welt. Published by AMA Membership Publications Division, American Management Associations, New York. All rights reserved.

nonmarket countries and poor developing countries, although Western companies occasionally involve themselves when the circumstance arises that a Western firm and the trade organization of a less developed country (LDC) or a Council of Mutual Economic Assistance (CMEA) country have roughly equal values of goods that they desire from each other at the same time.

Problems such as determining and agreeing upon the relative value of traded goods discourage interest in barter transactions. Another crucial disincentive is the use of one contract to cover both deliveries and counterdeliveries. Western banks are rarely willing to finance or guarantee a transaction in which a creditor's proceeds are contingent upon another party's performance. Moreover, even if guarantees can be obtained from a willing financial institution, the complexity of covering contingency risks in a barter contract with guarantees is a disincentive in itself.

There are no letters of credit in barter transactions, but participants may obtain parallel bank guarantees in the form of standby letters of credit or performance bonds. These ensure that, in the case of default, the defaulting party would compensate the performing party in hard currency. In most cases, however, it is easier simply to employ two separate contracts: one for the delivery and one for the counterdelivery of goods, and to have each party pay for the goods in hard currency with payment guaranteed by a letter of credit. This type of transaction is referred to as *parallel barter* or, more commonly, *counterpurchase.*

COUNTERPURCHASE

Under a counterpurchase agreement, a Western company sells goods to a foreign trade organization in a communist or developing nation and contractually agrees to make reciprocal purchases from that organization, or from another commercial body in the same country, within a designated period of time. Counterdeliveries in these transactions are generally not resultant products (they are not produced by, derived from, or related to Western goods delivered in the original sale), but are chosen from among a range of products offered by the purchaser in the first contract. The duration of the entire transaction is relatively short—from one to three years, and the commitment for reciprocal purchase, stated in currency as a percentage of the original sale, varies from 10 percent to 100 percent, but is generally less than the full value of the original sale.

Counterpurchase is conducted under two separate contracts which may be linked by a protocol. Its financing can be organized in a fashion similar to that of standard trade, since each of the agreements is an exchange of goods for hard currency. Separating the contracts protects the original seller because payment for his goods cannot be legally withheld if problems arise in the execution of the second contract.

Unlike the first contract, which is a standard cash-for-goods agreement, the second contract is broader and more complex. Although it may call for the purchase of specific goods for a set price, usually it identifies a list of goods that may be chosen for purchase and the criteria for pricing rather than actual prices for the goods.

In East-West trade, it is often stipulated that reciprocal orders must be placed with the foreign trade organization . . . or, in China, with the foreign trade corporation (FTC) to which the original sale was made. In developing countries, the procedures vary. In many cases, however, goods may also be purchased from trade organizations other than that to which the sale had been made, or in the case of developing countries, from a different company. This practice of one entity purchasing the Western company's product and another providing the "counterpurchased material" is called "linkage."

Since counterpurchase is a short-term commercial arrangement for the exchange of goods, it does not typically involve significant technology transfer. Rather it is often employed by an Eastern or developing nation to acquire goods for which hard currency would not be otherwise allocated. In the case of CMEA countries, these are often products that are not included in the five- or ten-year plan, or hold a low priority in the plan. The amount of counterpurchase demanded on a sale is in inverse proportion to the importance of the good to the buyer's country.

Goods offered by East Bloc countries may be raw materials, manufactured goods, semimanufactured goods, machinery, and so on, but typically and increasingly they take the form of finished manufactured products. These are the products that have limited access to hard currency markets, often because of a lack of demand or low quality. Countertrade with developing countries in some respects resembles that with the nonmarket world, but the Western company is more likely to receive raw materials or oil in exchange for its products.

Normally, a counterpurchase agreement allows the seller in the first contract to assign his counterpurchase obligation to a third party—a trading house or other foreign buyer. If the Western company can find no products for counterdelivery that it can use in its own operations or that it can market through its organization, it often transfers its obligation to a trading house, which will dispose of the goods for a commission or "discount." These discounts range from under 5 percent for disposal of easily marketed goods such as raw materials, to as much as 40 percent for hard-to-market manufactured goods.

COMPENSATION

Compensation, often also called *buy back,* involves the sale of technology, equipment, or a plant with a contractual commitment on the part of the seller to purchase a certain quantity of products that are produced by or derived from the original sale. Because these transactions involve setting up entire production facilities, their values can run into hundreds of million of dollars. The duration of the transaction, accordingly, is far more lengthy than for counterpurchase arrangements owing not only to the magnitude of the projects, but also to the time necessary to complete projects before they come on stream to produce goods for counterdelivery. At a minimum, the period of the buy-back obligation runs 3 to 4 years, and it is not uncommon for a compensation arrangement to last 25 years or longer.

The commitment to buy back goods, as a proportion of the original sale, is also typically greater than for counterpurchase, with counterdeliveries often totaling 100 percent or more of the value of the original sale.

As in counterpurchase arrangements, compensation is conducted with the use of two separate contracts that may be linked by protocol. The separation of legal instruments for deliveries and counterdeliveries serves the same function as in counterpurchase, but both contracts gain added importance both because of the need to keep large payments for the transfer of technology and goods unencumbered, and because the innumerable variables and contingencies inherent in the establishment of full-scale facilities places an added risk in the second, buy-back contract of a deal. Similarly, the protocol that links the two contracts in a compensation deal takes on greater importance by ensuring that counterdeliveries are, in fact, produced with the technology and equipment delivered in the original sale.

Unlike counterpurchase, it is the first contract in compensation that is more complex and poses more problems. The Western seller in the deal is often setting up a potential competitor, and in the contract to transfer technology and equipment, he must pay special attention to clauses pertaining to the second party's right to transfer technology, its right to use the Western company's brand name, and its right to distribute in certain market territories. These considerations make compensation negotiations a complex business, often taking a number of years to complete.

Nevertheless, compensation is the fastest growing form of countertrade in terms of dollar value. The Organization for Economic Cooperation and Development (OECD) has estimated that the value of compensation deals in East-West trade could be as high as $30 to $35 billion for the years 1969-1979, with Soviet and Polish deals accounting for the greatest share. The use of compensation in major projects did not emerge until 1969, when it was employed by metallurgical firms of Austria and the Federal Republic of Germany to sell large-diameter steel pipes to the Soviet Union in exchange for subsequent deliveries of natural gas. It was not until 1974, however, that compensation began to flourish in East-West trade. In that year, according to the OECD, more compensation agreements were concluded by the Soviet Union and other CMEA nations than in all previous years combined.

These deals, referred to in the East as "industrial cooperation," are particularly attractive to the Soviet Union and other Eastern European nations because they involve a long-term participation on the part of the Western company. Through this long-term relationship, the Eastern party can obtain the technology, training, and capital goods by which to achieve their highest priority industrial projects, and to finance these projects, often entirely, by guaranteed exports to the West. China, in its recent modernization drive, has begun to place great emphasis on compensation for the same reasons, and the rest of the developing world may be expected increasingly to seek these arrangements as they aspire to obtain technology and capital imports for which they cannot afford to pay with hard currency.

Despite the complexity and risks, Western companies commit themselves to compensation agreements, particularly in these times of slack industrial development in the West, as a way to secure major plant, equipment, or licensing sales. In some cases, compensation can also offer guaranteed long-term supplies of energy products, raw materials, or manufactured goods that may be difficult to obtain and essential to the company's operation elsewhere. Manufactured goods may be less expensive in a compensation arrangement because of lower labor costs in a developing or communist country. . . .

EVIDENCE ACCOUNTS

Evidence accounts are commercial agreements between an exporter and one or more foreign trade organizations (FTOs) from the importing country. Under the agreement the exporter sells a pre-set volume of goods and services to one of the FTOs while simultaneously buying local products from the same or other FTO to balance the account. (The buying company has the right to sell the products anywhere else to realize its profits.) To ensure the balance, all transactions during the term of the agreement (commonly one or more years) are monitored by the country's bank of foreign trade, where the company maintains an evidence account, and a foreign bank designated by the Western firm. In this fashion, companies can find profitable business with FTOs of countries that don't have enough hard or transferable currencies on hand to make purchases. Because of this, the FTO can have access to certain goods it could not otherwise afford.

Eastern Bloc nations often find evidence accounts attractive because they fit well into their central economic-planning systems, and allow a great deal of flexibility in buying Western goods with guaranteed, offsetting, hard currency exports. Evidence accounts also hold certain advantages for Western firms. A broader range of goods is offered than in counterpurchase, protracted negotiations are not necessary on each transaction, and there is no need for the approval of one trade organization for purchase from another. Sales can be conducted on purely commercial considerations, and Eastern goods are not inflated with the knowledge that they are being taken as part of a countertrade arrangement.

In order to enter such an agreement, however, a Western firm must have a significant trade turnover with the importing country and must have reasonable expectations that bilateral trade will rise rather than decrease under the agreement. The Western party must also be certain that it can use products purchased under the account within its own operations or can dispose of them profitably.

BILATERAL CLEARING AGREEMENTS

When two countries wish to trade with one another without expending foreign currency, they may resort to a bilateral clearing agreement. Under this arrangement, the two governments agree to import a set volume of goods from the other over a specified period of time (usually one year).

Accounts are kept in artificial units bearing the denomination of one currency or another: clearing dollar, Swiss franc, rupee, and so on. By this accounting, the bilateral balance of trade can be monitored, and if too great an imbalance occurs, two-way exchange is stopped until accounts are brought back into line. The degree of trade imbalance allowed is referred to as the "swing." The swing is specified as a percentage of annual trade volume.

If, at the end of a term, one party has taken a greater value of goods than the other, the account must be brought into balance either by cash payment or by "switch trading." In a switch transaction, the party with trade credit left to its account may transfer this credit to a third party at a discount rate and may receive cash payment or other goods.

NOTES AND QUESTIONS

1. General Electric enters into an eight-year, $1 billion countertrade arrangement with Rumania, under which GE provides electric power to Rumania, in return for $1 billion in payment from Rumania. The money owed by Rumania, it is agreed, may be satisfied by countertrade, under which GE agrees to purchase $1 billion in goods from Rumania during the course of the next eight years.

a. What if GE does not fulfill its end of the bargain and purchase $1 billion in goods from Rumania? What is Rumania's recourse? If you were General Counsel for GE, would you prefer that this be handled through:

1. litigation;
2. arbitration; or
3. an agreed upon liquidated damages provision in the contract?

b. What if Rumania tenders goods of inferior quality to GE? Must GE accept the goods? How can this situation be avoided?

2. What if the Government of Mexico wanted to barter its excess flurospar (a fluxing agent used in the manufacture of steel, aluminum, and chemicals) for nonfat dry milk, corn, and wheat from the United States Commodity Credit Corporation (CCC) stockpile? Could such a transaction be consummated under U.S. laws? See 7 U.S.C. §1727; 15 U.S.C. §714, 50 U.S.C. §98; 41 C.F.R. §101-14.307(b). How would the CCC, which handles agricultural products, and the General Services Administration, which handles the strategic materials stockpiles, interact? Assuming that the legality of such a govern-

ment-to-government barter transaction could be assured, do you think the U.S. government should enter into such transactions? How might your answer differ if you were:

(a) the United States trade representative;
(b) the secretary of state;
(c) the secretary of agriculture;
(d) the administrator of the GSA stockpiles?

Do you think it would be preferable to handle such a proposed barter deal on a purely private basis? If so, why?

3. Boeing, a U.S. producer of aircraft, sells Happy Times a jet aircraft for $10 million. Happy Times, a manufacturer of confectionery products, leases the aircraft to Varig, Brazil's national airlines, for an annual fee of $1 million per year over a 10-year duration. Happy Times agrees in its contract with Varig to accept its $1 million annual payment for the lease in products such as cocoa and sugar at prevailing world prices. Why would Happy Times wish to enter into such a contract arrangement as a lessor, instead of merely purchasing the sugar and cocoa for use in its confectionery products? Why would Varig want to enter this transaction as a lessee? *See* Clouds on Boeing's Horizon, Forbes Magazine, July 2, 1984, at p.80.

4. Your client is an exporter of microcomputers, who has usually exported against a letter of credit denominated in dollars, issued by the importer's branch office of a major international bank, and advised by a U.S. office of the same bank. The U.S. bank office has just called the client's president to tell her that the Brazico government has directed the bank's Brazico office not to pay on the letter of credit arising from a recent sale. As a result of its debt crisis, the Brazico government had issued severe exchange control regulations that prohibit all payments in hard currency except for those authorized by its treasury, and the treasury has now announced that payment under letters of credit is covered by these rules and decided not to authorize payment at this time in connection with the specific import transaction.

The bank official told your client that he is very sorry but unfortunately expected other nations to issue similar rules in the future. Your client is especially concerned about this case, because the sale was large and the papers have long since been forwarded to the Brazico office of the bank. But she is also concerned about the future.

The legal issues governing the current situation are developed in Chapter 14: For an example case, *see* Banco de Vizcaya v. First Natl. Bank of Chicago, 524 F. Supp. 1280 (N.D. Ill. 1981). For now, please give her some suggestions for structuring future export transactions to avoid this problem.

5. How will the mechanics and economic feasibility of trade between the affiliates of a multinational differ from that between unrelated entities?

6. In May 1984, the Commerce Department authorized the following policy quotation:

POLICY GUIDELINES ON COUNTERTRADE

1. The U.S. government generally views countertrade as contrary to an open, free trading system. However, as a matter of policy, the U.S. Government will not oppose U.S. companies' participation in countertrade arrangements unless such action could have a negative impact on national security.

2. The U.S. government will provide advisory and market intelligence services to U.S. businesses, including information on the application of U.S. trade laws to countertrade goods.

3. The U.S. government will continue to review financing for projects containing countertrade/barter on a case-by-case basis, taking account of the distortions caused by these.

4. The U.S. government will continue to oppose government-mandated countertrade and will raise these concerns with the relevant governments.

5. The U.S. government will participate in reviews of countertrade in the International Monetary Fund (IMF), the Organization for Economic Cooperation & Development (OECD), and the General Agreement on Tariffs & Trade (GATT).

6. The U.S. Government will exercise caution in the use of its barter authority, reserving it for those situations which offer advantages not offered by conventional market operations.

Why is the government concerned? Are its guidelines wise?

Bibliographical Note

For more information on recent barter trends, *see* B. Fisher and K. Harte (eds.), Barter in the World Economy (1985); R. DeMarines, U.S. International Trade Commission Pub. No. 1237, Analysis of Recent Trends in U.S. Countertrade, March, 1982; D. Vogt, C. Jabara, and D. Linse, Barter of Agricultural Commodities, U.S. Department of Agriculture (April, 1982); P. Verzariu, Countertrade Practices in East Europe, the Soviet Union and China: An Introductory Guide to Business, Office of East-West Trade Development, ITA, U.S. Department of Commerce, April, 1980; McVey, Countertrade and Barter: Alternate Trade Financing by Third World Nations, 6 Intl. Trade L.J. 197 (1980-1981); OECD, East-West Trade: Recent Developments in Countertrade (1981); Ludlow, A Guide to Barter in the China Trade, 6 China Bus. Rev. 10-16, (1979); Shillinglaw & Stein, Doing Business in the Soviet Union, 13 Law & Poly. Intl. Bus. 1 (1981).

Chapter III

Regulation of International Trade: The Institutions

The last chapter explored the international trade transaction from a private law viewpoint. This chapter turns to the public regulation of the same transaction and concentrates on the national and international institutions that may be involved; later chapters will consider the substantive principles they employ.

International trade is regulated by a complex mixture of international agreement and domestic law; the latter may implement international accords or reflect purely domestic political processes. This chapter begins with a description of the overall structure, which will be observed in action in later chapters. The chapter then explores the constitutional issues that affect Congress's extensive delegations of power to the executive in the United States. The chapter next provides a parallel introduction to the central international institution, the General Agreement on Tariffs and Trade (GATT).[1] Finally, it explores the European Economic Community (EEC), an entity that not only trades extensively with the United States, but also exemplifies the political, legal, and constitutional difficulties of establishing and operating a common market, or customs union.

As you read this chapter, you should be asking questions about each institutional structure that is being described. What is the anatomy of each organization? What are the processes established within each institution for achieving a given result? Who are the main players in the bureaucratic structure of each administrative organization? How are disputes resolved within each system? What are the objectives of each institution? And how do differences in the systems described affect the making of international economic policy?

---

[1] The GATT dispute resolution process is considered in Chapter 9.

A. BACKGROUND AND INTRODUCTION

The Tariff Act of 1789 was the first substantive legislation passed by the first Congress.[2] It was supported, as are our tariffs today, by different people for different reasons. Alexander Hamilton argued, for example, much as do many of today's developing world leaders: that a tariff would help encourage industry and help U.S. society avoid being purely agrarian. Moreover, he contended that other nations gave an enormous array of subsidies and bounties to their industry; a tariff would help protect U.S. industry from the effects of these subsidies. Beyond these arguments, which one might expect, there was one that is now easy to forget—before the income tax was authorized by the Sixteenth Amendment in 1913 and became dominant in the early part of the twentieth century, the tariff was a key source of federal revenue.

As the nation moved toward the Civil War, the politics of the tariff became caught up in those of sectionalism. Northern manufacturers favored high tariffs; Southern planters, dependent on exports, favored free trade. One of the great efforts at compromise was tariff-based: Henry Clay's "American Plan." Under Clay's proposal, the manufacturers of the North would be protected by high tariffs to become a large market for the agricultural products of the West and the cotton of the South. Revenue from the tariff would support construction of the transportation system needed to make this internal trade possible. However, the North wanted the tariff without public works expenditures; the South wanted its food cheaper and was opposed to any tariff supporting the price of manufactured goods. Even though Clay's proposal failed, a high tariff did pass Congress in 1828, becoming known as the "Tariff of Abominations" and nearly sparking revolt at the time.

After the Civil War, domestic politics continued to favor a high-tariff policy—perhaps strengthened by the fact that industry was spreading through more of the nation and therefore broadening congressional support for high tariffs. By the 1890s, Congress was adding an important innovation to the legislation—a delegation of power to the executive to adjust tariffs in specific circumstances. An early example was what are now called "countervailing duties"—tariffs to be levied to correct for a foreign subsidy on a product exported to the United States. The executive was directed to measure the foreign subsidy and given authority to determine the countervailing duty without further congressional action. This became only one of a large number of

[2]This section is derived in part from Fisher, The Multinationals and the Crisis in United States Trade and Investment Policy, 53 B.U.L. Rev. 308, 309-316 (1973). For other sources on the history of trade policy, see J. Condliffe, The Commerce of Nations (1950); S. Metzger, Trade Agreements and the Kennedy Round (1964); E. Stanwood, American Tariff Controversies in the Nineteenth Century (1903); I. Tarbell, The Tariff in Our Times (1911). Although less historical, the Report and Appendices of the Williams Commission are extremely useful: The Commission on International Trade and Investment Policy, United States International Economic Policy in an Interdependent World, (Report to the President), Washington, D.C., July 1971.

such adjustment devices; other important ones include the antidumping duty, designed to respond to price discrimination between the United States and an exporter's home market, and the peril point or escape clause (*see* Chapter 4), designed to protect an industry suffering serious injury from competition by imports. The supporting procedures frequently relied on the United States Tariff Commission, an administrative agency created in 1916, as well as on officials in the bureaucracy (the Tariff Commission was renamed the United States International Trade Commission (ITC) in 1974).

President Woodrow Wilson, an ardent free trader, sought to reform the tariff, arguing against a "tariff which cuts us off from our proper part in the commerce of the world, violates the just principles of taxation, and makes the government a facile instrument in the hands of private interests."[3]

His efforts, which were only partially successful, were reversed by two bills: the Fordney-McCumber tariff of 1922 and the Smoot-Hawley tariff of 1930. The Fordney-McCumber tariff took the concept of delegation to an extreme through the "flexible clause," a clause empowering the president to alter tariff rates by up to 50% whenever he found, after investigation by the Tariff Commission, that the rates did not fairly equalize the costs of foreign production with those of domestic production. In essence, this was an effort to repeal the law of comparative advantage. The Smoot-Hawley tariff raised duties on more than 1,000 articles; by the end of 1931, 26 foreign nations had raised their tariffs against the United States in retaliation. The resulting harm to international trade undoubtedly contributed to the severity of the depression.

But the misery of the 1930s also brought a free-trade oriented innovation in tariff law: the "reciprocal trade agreement" concept. This was an application of the idea that nations trading with each other might agree reciprocally to reduce their tariffs. Provided the employment created by each nation's increase in exports was greater than that lost to new imports, such an agreement might be politically beneficial—and would almost certainly be economically desirable. Because there was already a network of "Most-Favored-Nation" (MFN) clauses in U.S. Friendship, Commerce, and Navigation treaties, a network deriving from the 18th century,[4] these reductions would also be effectively extended to all nations. It was Franklin D. Roosevelt's secretary of state from Tennessee, Cordell Hull, who succeeded in obtaining from Congress the delegation of authority needed to make this process easier. The Reciprocal Trade Agreements Act, passed in 1934, ultimately contributed to major reductions in tariffs through bilateral tariff-cutting negotiations, and by 1940 28 agreements had been concluded under the Trade Agreements Program.

These changes were roughly paralleled in other nations, and in the reconstruction period following World War II consideration was given to creating an International Trade Organization (ITO). At Bretton Woods, New Hamp-

[3] D. Muzzey, A History of Our Country 617 (1936).
[4] For the history of the Most-Favored-Nation clause, *see* R. Snyder, The Most-Favored-Nation Clause (1948).

shire, in 1944, the key negotiations took place to create the monetary and development organizations, the International Monetary Fund and the International Bank for Reconstruction and Development (the World Bank). The corresponding trade negotiations were slower and produced a charter at Havana in 1948—but it became apparent that the United States Congress would never approve the proposed trade organization. Then, as now, Congress was deeply suspicious of a supranational international organization that might infringe on U.S. sovereign powers in the regulation of international trade. Instead, the central principles of the ITO, as spelled out in an interim document, were presented and approved (by executive agreement in the United States) as the General Agreement on Tariffs and Trade (GATT), an agreement that has more and more become an organization, and to which the Congress has become increasingly receptive.[5] The text of the GATT agreement and its annexes appears as Appendix II.

The GATT provides a framework for tariff negotiations, includes specific rules and norms for trade regulation, and creates institutions for dispute settlement. The negotiations are an elaborated multipartite version of the reciprocal trade agreement pattern. These negotiations occur in rounds, each of which lasts several years (and is often effectively shaped by a specific congressional delegation of negotiation power to the United States executive). The most recent of the major rounds were the Kennedy Round of 1962 to 1967 and the Tokyo Round (or Multilateral Trade Negotiations (MTN)) of 1974 to 1979. Each produced significant reductions in tariffs, and the MTN succeeded in obtaining accords on some nontariff barriers (NTBs): devices such as quotas, import licensing, and restrictive technical standards that have much the same trade-restraining effects as tariffs. Preparations are under way for a new round that may extend the GATT's coverage beyond the traditional regulation of goods into new areas such as services, intellectual property, and, perhaps, trade-related investment requirements (see Fisher, Making the World Regime Work: An Agenda for GATT, at p.163 infra).

The rounds have tended increasingly to deal as well with rules. The rules in

---

[5] See Remaking the System of World Trade: A Proposal For Institutional Reform, Am. Soc. Int. Law Poly. No. 12 (1976). As the ASIL stated, "the centerpiece of the structure of international trade cooperation has been GATT, the General Agreement on Tariffs and Trade. It is in many ways an odd centerpiece. The GATT arose out of the tariff negotiations conducted in the late 1940s among the members of the Preparatory Committee for the International Trade Organization (ITO) and was concluded before the formal negotiations of the ITO charter began. The general provisions, that were a traditional part of any tariff negotiations, modified as the result of the preliminary drafting of the ITO, became the GATT. They were limited to those projected ITO provisions that the U.S. president could accept under his Trade Agreements authority. When the U.S. failed to ratify the ITO, the General Agreement remained. Subsequently, the GATT provided the framework for a series of tariff negotiations, the dismantling of wartime trade controls, and the handling of many other trade issues. Its organizational structure, however, remained rudimentary, and technically it is not even an 'organization.' "

For histories and background of GATT, see G. Curzon, Multilateral Commercial Diplomacy (1965). K. Dam, The GATT (1970); J. Jackson, World Trade and the Law of GATT (1969). J. Jackson, The General Agreement on Tariffs and Trade in W. Surrey & D. Wallace (eds.), A Lawyer's Guide to International Business Transactions (1977).

the GATT's initial text began with a reaffirmation of the Most-Favored-Nation principle. This principle is much more important than may appear at first glance, for it represents a commitment to nondiscrimination, globalism, and multilateralism as opposed to bilateralism, regionalism, or discriminatory trade arrangements. Moreover, it greatly reduces the opportunity to use trade arrangements as a way to obtain diplomatic advantage from specific nations, and thus tends to eliminate frictions that might otherwise exist between trading partners. Supplementing the MFN principle are many more specific rules covering, in particular, the circumstances in which tariff adjustments may be made. The more recent negotiating rounds have frequently further detailed and elaborated these principles. Thus, the work product of the Tokyo Round was not just a large number of specific tariff reductions, but also a book full of detailed codes covering such topics as the subsidies against which one might impose countervailing duties and the circumstances in which public agencies might favor their national suppliers over foreign bidders.

Finally, the GATT includes dispute-settlement mechanisms. These range from procedures by which a nation may be excepted from a provision that is raising severe economic and political problems, through consultation, to formal processes condemning a violation. The formal processes, however, have long been declining in importance. This is partly because the ultimate sanction available is the imposition of retaliatory duties,[6] something not usually desirable economically; it derives also from governments' unwillingness to accept the domestic political implications of free trade or cede significant sovereign decision-making power to an international trade forum.

The most recent trend, therefore, has been to bypass these formal procedures or to use them for symbolic purposes. Thus, Europe and the United States have frequently used the GATT dispute settlement process more to condemn each other's protectionism than to negotiate it away. And there have emerged an enormous number of side agreements, frequently on the edge of legality under GATT, governing issues ranging from trade in textiles to Japanese exports of automobiles to the United States. Both international and national law are reflecting the growth of protectionism in a depressed world economy.

B.   UNITED STATES TRADE INSTITUTIONS AND RELATED CONSTITUTIONAL ISSUES

It is now possible to describe briefly the institutional structure underlying U.S. trade law and to examine the relevant constitutional issues.

---

[6]Under some of the nontariff barrier codes we will encounter later, however, sanctions focus not on tariffs but instead on withdrawal of the privileges accorded to signatories who fail to live up to their obligations under the particular code.

1.   United States Trade Structure

The institutional structure administering the foreign trade laws of the United States involves all three branches of the federal government.

a.   Congress

The starting point for analysis is that the Congress, under Article I, Sec. 8 of the U.S. Constitution, possesses the plenary authority over the regulation of foreign commerce unless and until it delegates that authority in a permissible manner.[7] While the U.S. Constitution does not grant any right to import or export,[8] Congress has, since 1789, frequently addressed both sides of international trade transactions,[9] and there has been a progressive legalization of certain rights on both fronts by statute.

The following selection succinctly describes the role of Congress in U.S. trade policy.

S. COHEN, THE MAKING OF UNITED STATES INTERNATIONAL ECONOMIC POLICY

57-60 (1977)

THE CONGRESS

The principal source of the legislative branch's authority in the foreign commerce of the United States is Article 1, Section 8 of the Constitution, which specifically empowers Congress to "lay and collect Taxes, Duties, Imports and Excises" and to "regulate commerce with foreign Nations." Congress's specific duties include approving the budgets of the makers and managers of international economic policy, passing supplementary legislation (dealing with changes in the par value of the dollar, U.S. membership in international

---

[7] The U.S. Constitution empowers the Congress "to regulate Commerce with foreign Nations." U.S. Const. art. I, §8, cl.3. *See* Field v. Clark, 143 U.S. 649 (1891), where the Supreme Court upheld the delegation of broad powers to restrict trade to the president.

[8] The U.S. Constitution, however, prohibits Congress from levying a duty on exports. *See* U.S. Const. art. I, §9, cl.5. *See also* R. J. Reynolds Tobacco Co. v. Robertson, 14 F. Supp. 463 (M.D.N.C. 1935) (the clause shall be liberally construed and requires that the process of exportation shall not be obstructed by any burden of taxation).

[9] The fact that the first substantive piece of legislation passed by the new Congress, The Tariff Act of 1789, dealt with the imposition of customs duties was an early indication of the high priority trade policy has had with the U.S. Congress. Congressional preoccupation with U.S. trade policy has been due to many factors over the years, including the need for revenues, the desire for protection against "unfair" foreign trade advantages, the desire for national independence, and the desire to protect U.S. infant (as well as established) industries. *See* D. Muzzey, A History of Our Country (1936); Fisher, The Multinationals and the Crisis in United States Trade and Investment Policy, 53 B.U.L. Rev. 308, 309-311 (1973).

organizations, international taxation, and so on), and approval in the Senate of international economic treaties and political appointees.

The depth of Congress's imprint on American international economic relations has varied historically. Prior to 1934, it was very deep indeed; the executive branch was more administrator than policy formulator. But the growing volume of international trade and the growing burden of constituent pressures for tariff protection gave birth in 1934 to a transitory phase in which control over international economic policy began moving to the administration. By the early 1960s, Congress was doing the president's bidding. The complexity of the balance-of-payments problem and the paucity of grassroots interest channeled the average congressman's interest elsewhere. The politicization of international economics later in that decade marked the beginning of Congress's effort to redress the imbalance of influence. The overall post-Vietnam and post-Watergate reassertiveness marked the maturity of this effort. The Trade Act of 1974 is its first major offshoot.

No other national legislative body more extensively creates, revises, and offers critiques on a nation's international economic policy than does the Congress of the United States. To fulfill the duties of a separate and equal branch of government, it has an elaborate organizational structure to prepare legislation, challenge and reject administration proposals, evaluate existing policies, and suggest new ideas and approaches. The general reassertiveness of the Congress and specific statutory controls combine to assure that the legislative branch has become an active member of the policy-making process. That the executive branch must seriously consider congressional sentiment, the possibility of a congressional override of a trade action, means that an application of the bureaucratic politics model to international economic policy decision making may be specious if it concerns itself only with the clash of executive branch viewpoints and perspectives. Perhaps this is only a temporary situation. Nevertheless, at the present time, for specific policy decisions, the president may be forced to swallow hard—to the extent even of ignoring a State-Treasury Department consensus—and adapt U.S. policy to meet congressional demands.

At the heart of the congressional machinery are the committees. They are the vehicles for preparing legislation, confirming treaties, receiving briefings by executive branch policy makers, and exercising the oversight function. Relatively unknown outside of Washington, oversight hearings begin where the legislative function ends. . . . International economic legislation has begun to mandate tighter congressional scrutiny of policy. This fact, along with strengthened professional staff support for all committees, and increased scheduling of oversight hearings are the main manifestations of the new era of interest in international economics on Capitol Hill. Another symptom is the unofficial consultations that are becoming increasingly common on a personalized basis between international economic policy leaders in the two branches.

There are two striking features of the congressional committee structure in the international economic policy sphere: the large number of committees involved and the overlapping committee jurisdictions. The situation is, from an administrative point of view, strikingly similar to that which prevails in the executive branch. A major difference is the absence of any real attempts at coordination in Congress.

A reasonably complete, albeit nondefinitive, breakdown of committee responsibilities in international economic policy demonstrates that six legislative committees and one joint committee have jurisdictions involving the international economic relations of the United States:

Committee	*Function*
House Ways and Means, Senate Finance committees	Basic trade legislation and tariffs; international taxation
Banking committees	Export controls (Senate only); Export-Import Bank; exchange-rate and gold policy; international financial and monetary institutions (House only)
Foreign Relations, International Relations committees	General international economic policy; bilateral foreign aid; international financial institutions (Senate only); export controls (House only); multinational corporations
Commerce committees	Export promotion; foreign direct investment in the United States
Agriculture committees	Agricultural exports; international food stockpiles and food aid
Appropriations, Budget committees	Departmental, representational, and program budgets
Joint Economic Committee	Oversight on general international economic policy, especially in the international monetary and finance sectors

On hot and complex issues, such as energy, international commodity agreements, and the multinational corporation, jursidiction is fragmented ad nauseam. Aspects of the issues usually are parceled out on a narrow basis in response to initiatives and demands by several committees.

Most of the technical expertise is provided to members of Congress by the professional staffs retained by each committee. Since 1970, a rapid expansion of those staffs has taken place. Although the previously minuscule number of international economists working on Capitol Hill has increased geometrically, their numbers are still a small fraction of those employed in the executive branch. Additional expertise is provided on request by specialists in the Congressional Research Service, which is a part of the Library of Congress. The congressionally controlled General Accounting Office (GAO) undertakes investigations and evaluations of policies, practices, and programs maintained by the executive branch. The Congressional Budget Office, which provides analytic and research support for the budget committees who manage the Congress's newly adopted (1975) budget procedures, has the mandate, resources and influence to make it a further source of congressional ideas on international economic policy.

A final example of Congress's expanding involvement in this area has been the increased number of invitations by the executive branch to have congressional members serve as unofficial members of U.S. delegations to international economic conferences and negotiations.

b. The Executive Branch

The executive branch implements U.S. international economic policy on a daily basis. Congress may, from time to time, set the agenda and the broad contours of policy, but it lacks the expertise, resources, and flexibility to react to the daily events that are the stuff of the fast-moving world of international commerce.

Within the executive branch at least 20 different agencies have been the recipients of congressional delegations of authority, including the Office of the United States Trade Representative (USTR), the International Trade Commission (ITC), and the Departments of Commerce, Treasury, State, and Agriculture.

The multiplicity of agencies having something to do with trade regulation sharply limits the ability of the executive branch to implement a coordinated U.S. trade policy. Why has the centralization of U.S. trade policy not taken place, despite the recommendations of numerous academics and government officials? We will be in a better position to answer that difficult question after we have considered the material in the next six chapters; for starters we can note the importance of interest group politics, the reluctance of bureaucracies to yield jurisdictional turf, personalities, historical accident, and the pluralism inherent in the making of trade policy in a democratic society.

The most important mission of the executive branch in the making of U.S. international economic policy is its role in the U.S. tariff establishment process. This is really a form of shorthand for the administered protection provided for the segments of the U.S. economy that are injured by trade as well as the pursuit of liberal trade policies leading to a more rational allocation of resources. In summary, the U.S. tariff establishment process is a complicated mechanism providing for possible long-term duty reductions and short-term duty increases under certain limited circumstances (*see* Figure 3-1 *infra* p.102).

The current effective tariff rates are derived from the 1930 Smoot-Hawley Column 2 duty rates in the Tariff Schedules of the United States by a series of international negotiations (which generally lower the rates) and by various domestic adjustment processes (which generally raise the rates, albeit on a temporary basis). Figure 3-2, *infra* p.103, shows the average U.S. tariff rates since 1900. The ITC has prepared a chart, presented in Table 3-1, showing the processes in which it participates.

TABLE 3-1
The Foreign Trade Laws of the United States in Operation

Section	Statute	Common name, nickname	Issue to be decided	Usual basis for initiation	Hearing
201	Trade Act of 1974 (supersedes sec 301(b) of the Trade Expansion Act of 1962 and sec 7 of the Trade Agreements Extension Act of 1951)	Escape clause, industry	Is an article being imported in such increased quantities as to be a substantial cause of serious injury or threat thereof to the domestic industry producing a like or directly competitive article?	Petition by industry. But may be at request of the President, United States Trade Representative (USTR), House Ways and Means Committee, or Senate Finance Committee, or on Commission's own motion.	Required
203	Trade Act of 1974	Escape-clause review	Probable economic effect of the extension, reduction, or termination of import relief already granted.	Petition of industry at request of President or on Commission's own motion.	Required
733	Title VII, Tariff Act of 1930	Dumping	Preliminary investigation: Is there a reasonable indication of material injury, or threat thereof, by reason of imports allegedly sold at less than fair value (LTFV)?	Petition (filed concurrently at USITC and Commerce).	Conference conducted by the Director of Operations.
735	Title VII, Tariff Act of 1930	Dumping	Final investigation: Is an industry materially injured, or threatened with injury, by reason of LTFV imports?	Notification from Commerce of affirmative dumping determination.	At request of an interested party.
751	Title VII, Tariff Act of 1930	Dumping or countervail review.	Would an industry be injured, or threatened with injury, by reason of imports covered by an antidumping or countervailing duty order if that order were to be revoked?	Petition	At request of an interested party.
303 and 703	Tariff Act of 1930	Countervail	Preliminary investigation: Is there a reasonable indication of material injury, or threat thereof, by reason of subsidized imports?	Petition (filed concurrently at USITC and Commerce).	Conference conducted by the Director of Operations.
303 and 705	Tariff Act of 1930	Countervail	Final investigation: Is an industry materially injured, or threatened with injury, by reason of subsidized imports?	Notification from Commerce of affirmative subsidy determination.	At request of an interested party.
104	Trade Agreements Act of 1979	Countervail review.	Would an industry be materially injured, or threatened with injury, by reason of subsidized imports if certain countervailing duty orders were to be revoked? Applies only to orders issued before Jan. 1, 1980.	Request of foreign government.	Not required but usually held.
337	Tariff Act of 1930	Unfair import practices	Whether the effect or tendency of an unfair method of competition or unfair act in the importation of an article is to substantially injure an efficiently and economically operated industry, prevent the establishment of an industry, or restrain or monopolize U.S. trade and commerce.	Complaint	Trial conducted by administrative law judge (ALJ). Oral argument before the Commission.
603	Trade Act of 1974	Preliminary investigations	The Commission is specifically authorized to conduct preliminary investigations.	Various	Sometimes held; not required.

Usually voted on	Remedy vote required?	Appealable?	Investigation usually conducted by	Duration	Comments
In a Commission meeting	Yes, in tie or affirmative	No	Office of Investigations	6 months	Commission recommends relief to President. President makes final decision. If relief is provided, United States may have to compensate trade partners or face retaliation. If President does not follow USITC recommendation, Congress can direct President to do so.
No "vote," but nature of advice is usually made in a Commission meeting.	No	No	Office of Investigations	About 3 months	Advisory to the President. Of Commission recommends reduction or extension of relief, it usually sets forth specific recommendation.
In a Commission meeting	No	Yes	Director of Operations and Office of Investigations	45 days	If negative, no further action by USITC or Commerce. Investigation numbers begin with "731."
In a Commission meeting	No	Yes	Office of Investigations	75 or 120 days	If affirmative, dumping duties collectible. Investigation numbers begin with "731."
In a Commission meeting	No	Yes	Office of Investigations	Usually 3 months	On basis of Commission determination, Commerce can revoke previous dumping or subsidy order.
In a Commission meeting	No	Yes	Director of Operations and Office of Investigations	45 days	If negative, no further action by USITC or Commerce. Some investigation numbers begin with "701."
In a Commission meeting	No	Yes	Office of Investigations	75 or 120 days	If affirmative, countervailing duties collectible. Sec. 303 investigation conducted when imported article enters duty-free and is from country not a signatory to international subsidies code. Sec. 705 used when country is a signatory.
In a Commission meeting	No	Yes	Office of Investigations	Usually 3 months	On basis of affirmative Commission determination, Commerce revokes previous countervailing order.
In a Commission meeting (or terminated by circulation of an action jacket)	Yes	Yes	Unfair Import Investigations Division (UIID) and ALJ.	1 to 1 1/2 years	If violation found, Commission issues exclusion or cease and desist order which goes into effect unless disapproved by President for policy reasons. Most cases involve allegations of patent infringement.
In a Commission meeting (or terminated by circulation of an action jacket)	No	No	Depends on subject of investigation. If a sec. 337-type matter, UIID and Office of General Counsel.	Varies widely	In recent years such investigations generally have been conducted to gather information in order to determine whether a sec. 337 investigation should be instituted.

TABLE 3-1 *(continued)*
The Foreign Trade Laws of the United States in Operation

Section	Statute	Common name, nickname	Issue to be decided	Usual basis for initiation	Hearing
332	Tariff Act of 1930	General factfinding investigations	To investigate U.S. foreign trade and its effect on industries and labor or to provide assistance to the Congress and the President or USTR upon request.	Request of President, House Ways & Means Committee, Senate Finance Committee, either branch of Congress or on Commission's own motion.	Usually held; not required.
22	Agricultural Adjustment Act		Are imports of an article interfering with a program of the U.S. Department of Agriculture?	Request from the President.	Required
406	Trade Act of 1974	Market disruption	Whether market disruption exists as a result of imports from a Communist country.	Same as sec. 201 of Trade Act.	Required
131	Trade Act of 1974	PEC (probable effect of concessions)	What is the probable economic effect of modification of existing rules?	Request from the President or USTR.	Required
503	Trade Act of 1974	GSP (Generalized System of Preferences)	What is the probable economic effect of modification of existing rules?	Request from the President or USTR	Required

Source: International Trade Commission, Office of the Secretary

Who are the key players in the executive branch in the making of U.S. international economic policy? This also is a difficult question to answer, as the influence of agencies shifts due to particular personalities or events. In general, one may describe two sets of actors—the "superpowers" (the White House, the Departments of Commerce, Treasury, and State) and the "specialists" (a long list of departments and agencies with some international policy concern, including the Departments of Agriculture, Transportation, Justice, Energy, Labor, and Interior, and specialized agencies such as the Export-Import (Exim) bank, the Agency for International Development, the Federal Communications Commission, etc.).

The White House. As noted above, international negotiations covering the multilateral reduction of duties are conducted by the executive branch pursuant to authority delegated by Congress to the president. The most recent delegation of such authority was the Trade Act of 1974, which delegated negotiating authority for the Tokyo Round. The Trade Agreements Act of 1979 implemented that round's results. (These two acts appear, in edited form, as Appendices III and IV). Moreover, the Trade and Tariff Act of 1984 authorizes the president to undertake negotiations on a continuing basis to reduce or eliminate barriers to international trade in services, to reduce or eliminate trade-distorting effects of investment-related measures, and to improve foreign market access for the export of high technology industries (*see* Appendix V for relevant portions of the Trade and Tariff Act of 1984).

The Office of the United States Trade Representative (USTR) conducts international trade negotiations for the president. Due to the relatively small size of the agency (usually about 100 professionals), other, main-line agencies usually provide supporting personnel when a round of negotiations is in pro-

Usually voted on	Remedy vote required?	Appealable?	Investigation usually conducted by	Duration	Comments
By circulation of an action jacket	No	No	Office of Industries, Economics, General Counsel	Varies widely	A broad authority for the Commission to study and investigate trade-related matters.
In a Commission meeting	Yes	No	Office of Investigations	Varies	Advisory to the President.
In a Commission meeting	Yes	No	Office of Investigations	3 months	Similar to sec. 201 of Trade Act, but relief only applies to subject Communist country(ies).
By circulation of an action jacket	No	No	Office of Industries	Varies widely (6 months maximum)	Advisory to the President. Report submitted in confidence.
By circulation of an action jacket	No	No	Office of Industries	Varies widely (6 months maximum)	Advisory to the President. Report submitted in confidence.

gress. The USTR is legally and politically required to follow elaborate hearing and consultation procedures to ensure that the internationally negotiated package is acceptable to Congress.

A particularly interesting aspect of the USTR post is its highly politicized character. The trade-related issues of employment and resource allocation are of fundamental concern for the elected representatives in the political process. The appointments of two highly skilled politicians, the former chairman of the Democratic National Committee, Robert Strauss, as USTR by President Carter in 1977, and William Brock, the former chairman of the Republican National Committee, by President Reagan in 1981, were indications of how important it is for the White House to be able to "sell" any negotiated trade package to members of Congress. Both men were perceived as very successful Trade Representatives, due in large part to their political skills in dealing with the Congress.

The USTR is a cabinet-level position existing within the Executive Office of the President. As such, it is the chief White House actor on trade matters, although other bureaucratic players with an interest in trade policy also reside within the Executive Office of the President, including the Office of Management and Budget (OMB), the Council of Economic Advisors (CEA), the Central Intelligence Agency (CIA), and the National Security Council (NSC).

While some presidents in recent years have had White House coordinators involved in international economic policy in addition to the agencies listed above, the USTR over time has acquired the role of coordinator of U.S. trade policy. The USTR thus acts as:

(a)   the principal advisor to the president in trade relief actions of a discretionary character, including ITC §201 import relief actions (*see* Chap-

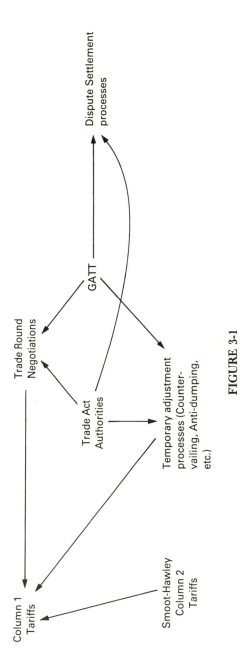

FIGURE 3-1
The Tariff Establishment Process

102

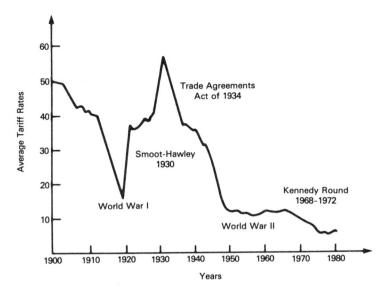

FIGURE 3-2
Average U.S. Tariff Rates Since 1900

ter IV) and actions under §301 of the Trade Act of 1974 to promote U.S. exports (*see* Chapter IX);

(b)   the U.S. representative and chief negotiator at all trade discussions in the GATT, the United Nations Conference on Trade and Development (UNCTAD), and other forums;

(c)   chairman of the Cabinet-level Trade Policy Committee; and

(d)   coordinator of all trade agreement programs and policy regarding export expansion, commodity agreements, unfair trade practices, bilateral trade issues, trade issues involving energy, and trade issues involving direct foreign investment (*see* Figure 3-3).

Department of Commerce. The Department of Commerce (DOC) was traditionally a weak participant in the formulation of trade policy. As part of the politics underlying the passage of the 1979 Act, however, the president transferred to the DOC from the Treasury Department the authority to make the evaluations relating to the price differences between foreign and U.S. markets (antidumping duty calculations) and foreign subsidies (countervailing duty calculations) (*see* Figure 3-4).

The Export Administration unit of the DOC is responsible for administering export controls imposed for reasons of national security, foreign policy, and short supply.

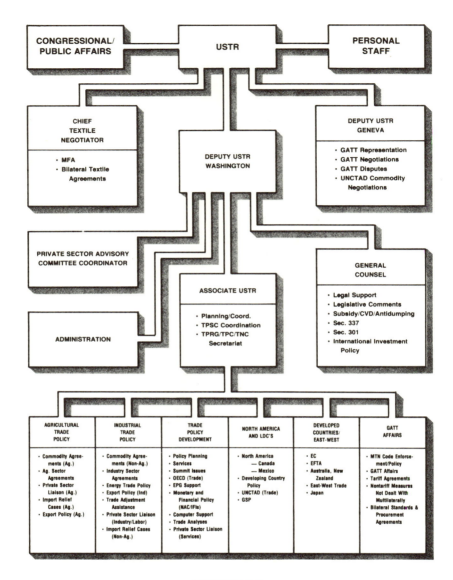

FIGURE 3-3
United States Trade Representative: Offices and Functions
Source: Department of Commerce, Foreign Relations Handbook, 17th ed. (1981)

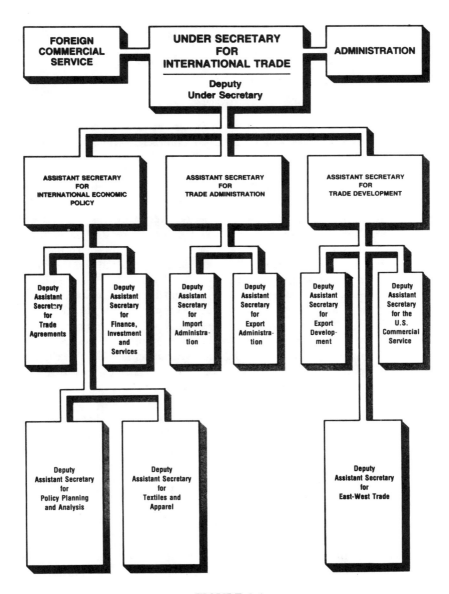

FIGURE 3-4
Department of Commerce: International Trade Representative
Source: Department of Commerce, Foreign Relations Handbook, 17th ed. (1981)

Third, the DOC has the responsibility for promoting U.S. exports through its Export Development unit.[10]

Pursuant to the reorganization plan of 1980, the primary *policymaking* responsibility for nonagricultural trade was placed in the USTR; the major responsibility for the *day-to-day operation of trade policy* was vested in the DOC.

Since the 1980 reorganization, the Commerce Department has continued to grow in power and stature in the trade area, due in large part to the warm personal relationship between the secretary of commerce, Malcolm Baldrige, and President Reagan.

Department of the Treasury. The third major executive branch actor in the formulation of U.S. trade policy is the Treasury Department. It administers the U.S. Customs Service, which has jurisdiction over tariff classification and valuation, international trade statistics, and Foreign Trade Zones. Treasury coordinates U.S. international financial policy by cooperating with the Federal Reserve System in intervening in the exchange market to counter disorderly conditions, authorizing positions to be taken by the United States in the International Monetary Fund (IMF), and by participating in international debt rescheduling negotiations. United States companies will also deal with Treasury's international tax regulatory role through the department's international tax regulations and rulings and participation in international tax treaty negotiations. Finally, the Treasury Department participates in the enforcement of trade policy through the Office of Foreign Assets Control (OFAC), which is currently administering, for example, the U.S. trade embargo against Nicaragua.

In a general sense, the influence of the Treasury Department has diminished since 1980, when its primary trade-related functions related to the administration of the dumping and countervailing duty laws were transferred to the Department of Commerce.

Department of State. The State Department has a broader mandate than trade policy—it is interested in promoting U.S. diplomatic and foreign policy objectives, and is thus a major player in the trade policy process, albeit frequently from the periphery. It occupies a strategic position in terms of location (overseas posts), communication (overseeing U.S. cable traffic), and personnel (a highly skilled Foreign Service). Yet the interest of the State Department in trade, viewed in terms of its zealousness in protecting U.S. commercial interests, was so low in the 1950s, that it was stripped of most of its formal trade authorities in 1962, when the Office of the United States Trade Representative (then called "Special Trade Representative") was established to promote U.S. commercial trade interests.[11] The clear intent of Congress in 1962 was to have

---

[10]*See* Exec. Order No. 12, 175, 3 C.F.R. 463.

[11]The deemphasis of trade was a reflection of the two-track system employed in formulating U.S. foreign policy until the mid-1970s. "High" foreign policy was traditionally defined almost

a separate agency devoted to the promotion and protection of U.S. trading interests.

The making of U.S. trade policy is frequently played out in terms of the clash between the State Department, interested in promoting overall U.S. foreign policy objectives, and the USTR and Commerce Department, whose primary mission is to promote U.S. commercial interests. This is not unhealthy if a referee exists to break up the predictable logjams that will result from these clashes.

The president, of course, should be the referee, acting through the institutional mechanism of his choosing. The National Security Council (NSC) frequently intrudes into the policy process as a clearinghouse, and a coordinator of the involved departments and agencies. Under President Nixon the Council on International Economic Policy (CIEP) played this role.

This formulation of U.S. trade policy within the executive branch is at present a messy process, and, in the opinion of many, places the U.S. government at a serious disadvantage in dealing with foreign governments in the international trade arena. It would perhaps be wise for the student to reserve judgment until additional materials are studied that describe the content of U.S. trade policy.

The judicial review processes for customs and trade-related matters have been assigned to the Court of International Trade, which sits in New York, with appeal to the Court of Appeals for the Federal Circuit (CAFC), which sits in Washington, D.C. The review of CAFC decisions by the Supreme Court is by certiorari, and not on an appeal basis.[12] Jurisdiction of the regular U.S. district court system is defined to exclude those areas within the jurisdiction of customs courts.[13] Nevertheless, the issue of choice of court has frequently been litigated and may still be controversial, in spite of congressional efforts at simplification.[14] Presumably, however, most trade-related cases will be brought in the first instance to the Court of International Trade, which has been provided with a "basket" grant of authorization encompassing all civil actions arising from import transactions. 28 U.S.C. §§1581-1585.

For additional information, see Strauss, The Difficult Politics of Trade Reorganization, 2 Intl. Tax & Bus. Law. 129, 138 (1984).

---

entirely in terms of national security matters; "low" foreign policy was considered within the foreign policy bureaucracy to encompass functional, economically-related issues, which were ascribed a lesser importance by the highest government officers. On the evolution of trade policy matters from "low" foreign policy in the post-war era to "high" foreign policy in the 1970s, see Cooper, Trade Policy Is Foreign Policy, 9 Foreign Poly. 18, 18-21 (1972). See also C. Bergsten, Toward a New International Economic Order 3-10 (1975).

[12]These procedures were reformed by the Customs Court Act of 1980, P.L. 96-419, 94 Stat. 1727. For discussion, see Re Litigation Before the United States Court of International Trade, 2 N.Y.L. Sch. L. Rev. 437 (1981).

[13]28 U.S.C. §1340.

[14]See, for example, Sneaker Circus v. Carter, 566 F.2d 396 (2d Cir. 1977); National Milk Producers Federation v. Shultz, 372 F. Supp. 745 (D.D.C. 1974).

2. *Delegation*

Under the legislation described above, Congress has transferred significant tariff-setting and NTB negotiating authority to the executive. This raises policy problems, as the extent of actual discretion delegated to the executive may be enormous. The fact that international business has drastically grown extends the effect of this discretion to nearly every major firm or industry in the nation, and the discretion certainly could be misused. At the same time, it is almost certain that these delegations of power have created a much less protectionist international trading system than would have resulted had Congress retained the powers.[15]

Delegation may transfer so much power as to distort the Constitution's separation of powers and become unconstitutional. The usual test has been whether Congress has provided an adequate standard to guide and restrict the executive's discretion. The two leading cases are United States v. Curtiss-Wright Export Corp., 299 U.S. 304 (1936) and Youngstown Sheet & Tube Co. v. Sawyer, 343 U.S. 579 (1952). The first, decided shortly after New Deal domestic legislation had been struck down on delegation grounds, held that the executive had enough inherent authority in the foreign policy area that a weaker delegation test was appropriate. The authority delegated was that needed to impose an embargo on export of arms to areas of warfare. In *Youngstown,* in contrast, the president's assertion of authority to seize steel mills during a war-time strike was held unconstitutional. This was going too far, for the president was clearly acting against congressional intent.

As the following cases show, however, the courts have become more and more willing to uphold delegation against constitutional attack. And when foreign policy concerns are involved, the courts are particularly ready to give the executive implied powers; the most important recent case in the foreign policy area is Dames & Moore v. Regan, 453 U.S. 654 (1981), upholding the Iranian hostage financial settlement (*see also* Haig v. Agee, 453 U.S. 280 (1981)). Courts have also become more and more willing to read congressional action broadly and to give the executive the benefit of the doubt as to whether specific authority was actually delegated. *See, for example,* The Florsheim Shoe Co. v. United States, 4 I.T.R.D. 1571 (Ct. Intl. Trade, 1983).

It is important to note that the trade act sequence discussed above is not the only major delegation of foreign economic policy power to the executive. There have been two other major lines, as shown in Table 3-2. The most far reaching are the Trading with the Enemy Acts (TWEA), a line of legislation going back to authority given to Abraham Lincoln to deal with Confederate assets during the Civil War. As a result of congressional concern about executive emergency powers, use of the power outside a wartime context is now

---

[15] For an excellent discussion of the delegation issues, *see* L. Jaffe, Judicial Control of Administrative Action (1965).

restated and made subject to congressional review under the International Economic Emergency Act (IEEA). Among the regulations supported by these acts are the Iranian asset freezes and restrictions on trading with Cuba and North Vietnam. The other major line is the Export Administration line, legislation empowering the president to prohibit the export of materials and information that might be militarily helpful to enemies, and to restrict exports on the grounds of short supply in the United States. This is the basis of regulations restricting export to the Soviet Union; other parts of the legislation authorize foreign policy embargos and related legislation attempts to restrict other forms of military exports that raise arms control concerns. During periods when Congress allows the Export Administration Act authority to lapse, the executive usually reissues these regulations under the Trading with the Enemy Acts line of authority.

The following lower court cases give the greatest available detail in this area. As you read through the cases you should be asking the following questions. What is the function that the legislative branch was trying to transfer to the president? What intelligible criteria are provided for executive action? Should the transfer of power in the international area be viewed differently than the domestic political arena? Finally, what are the alternatives to the

TABLE 3-2
Delegation Sequences

Trade Acts	Trading with the Enemy Acts	Export Control Acts
Reciprocal Trade Agreements Act of 1934	Trading with the Enemy Act of 1917 50 U.S.C. App. §§1 et seq.	Export Control Act of 1949
Trade Agreements Act of 1954		Export Administration Act of 1962
Trade Expansion Act of 1962	International Economic Emergency Act of 1977	Export Administration Act of 1969
Trade Act of 1974	50 U.S.C. §§1701-1706	Export Administration Act of 1979
Trade Agreements Act of 1979 19 U.S.C. assorted sections		50 U.S.C. App. §§2401 et seq.
Trade and Tariff Act of 1984		

delegation in each instance; is the power involved of a type that the legislature should not be allowed to transfer to the executive branch?

UNITED STATES v. YOSHIDA INTERNATIONAL, INC.

526 F.2d 560 (C.C.P.A. 1975)

MARKEY, Chief Judge.

This is an appeal from a judgment of the Customs Court, 73 Cust. Ct. 1, C.D. 4550, 378 F. Supp. 1155 (1974), granting Yoshida's motion for summary judgment, and declaring an import duty surcharge invalid. Presidential Proclamation 4074, because it imposed the surcharge, was held to have been beyond the President's delegated powers. The court stated that a delegation of sufficient breadth to encompass the proclamation would have been unconstitutional. We reverse.

FACTS

Yoshida's merchandise (zippers) was imported from Japan and entered the port of New York on August 17, 25, and 26, 1971. The government levied, in addition to the standard duty under TSUS item 745.72, an import duty surcharge of 10% in accordance with item 948.00, which was added to the TSUS [Tariff Schedules of the United States] by Presidential Proclamation 4074. Yoshida challenges only the validity of Proclamation 4074. . . .

PRESIDENT'S ACTIONS

During the summer of 1971, the United States was faced with an economic crisis. The nation suffered under an exceptionally severe and worsening balance of payments deficit. The gold reserve backing of the U.S. dollar had dropped from $17.8 billion in 1960 to less than $10.4 billion in June of 1971, reflecting a growing lack of confidence in the U.S. dollar abroad. Foreign exchange rates were being controlled by some of our major trading partners in such a way as to overvalue the U.S. dollar. That action, by stimulating U.S. imports and restraining U.S. exports, contributed substantially to the balance of payments deficit. As one step in a program designed to meet the economic crisis,[4] the President issued Proclamation 4074, which in relevant part stated:

WHEREAS, there has been a prolonged decline in the international monetary

[4]The Proclamation in suit was part of a "New Economic Policy," which involved suspension of the convertibility of foreign held dollars into gold, reductions in taxes, Federal spending and foreign aid, a 90-day wage-price freeze, and imposition of the surcharge "[a]s a temporary measure". Address to the Nation Outlining a New Economic Policy: "The Challenge of Peace," *Public Papers of the Presidents of the United States Richard Nixon 1971* 886 (1972), 65 *Dept. of State Bull.* 253 (1971), New York Times, Aug. 16, 1971, at 14, col. 1. The 90-day freeze, though challenged as

reserves of the United States, and our trade and international competitive position is seriously threatened and, as a result, our continued ability to assure our security could be impaired;

WHEREAS, the balance of payments position of the United States requires the imposition of a surcharge on dutiable imports; . . .

A. I hereby declare a national emergency during which I call upon the public and private sector to make the efforts necessary to strengthen the international economic position of the United States.

B. (1) I hereby terminate in part for such period as may be necessary and modify prior Presidential Proclamations which carry out trade agreements insofar as such proclamations are inconsistent with, or proclaim duties different from, those made effective pursuant to the terms of this Proclamation.

(2) Such proclamations are suspended only insofar as is required to assess a surcharge in the form of a supplemental duty amounting to 10 percent ad valorem. Such supplemental duty shall be imposed on all dutiable articles . . . provided, however, that if the imposition of an additional duty of 10 percent ad valorem would cause the total duty or charge payable to exceed the total duty or charge payable at the rate prescribed in column 2 of the Tariff Schedules of the United States, then the column 2 rate shall apply.

To implement the above language, Proclamation 4074 established the following item 948.00 of subpart C, part 2, of the TSUS Appendix:

Item	Article	Rates of duty	
		1	*2*
948.00	Articles, except as exempted under headnote 5 of this subpart, which are not free of duty under these schedules and which are the subject of tariff concessions granted by the United States in trade agreements	10% ad val. (See headnote 3 of this subpart.)	No change.

The referenced headnote 3 reads as follows:

3. *Limitation on additional duties*—The additional 10 percent rate of duty specified in rate of duty column numbered 1 of item 948.00 shall in no event exceed

---

based upon an unconstitutional delegation of legislative power, in violation of the separation of powers doctrine, was upheld in *Amalgamated Meat Cutters & Butcher Work v. Connally*, 337 F. Supp. 737 (D.D.C. 1971).

that rate which, when added to the column numbered 1 rate imposed on the imported article under the appropriate item in schedules 1 through 7 of these schedules, would result in an aggregated rate in excess of the rate provided for such article in rate of duty column numbered 2.

The President's authority for proclaiming the surcharge was stated in Proclamation 4074 to be:

> WHEREAS, pursuant to the authority vested in him by the Constitution and the statutes, including, but not limited to, the Tariff Act of 1930, as amended (hereinafter referred to as "the Tariff Act"), and the Trade Expansion Act of 1962 (hereinafter referred to as "the TEA"), the President entered into, and proclaimed tariff rates under, trade agreements with foreign countries;
> WHEREAS, under the Tariff Act, the TEA and other provisions of law, the President may, at any time, modify or terminate, in whole or in part, any proclamation made under his authority; . . .

Importers of products subject to the surcharge sought and obtained permission from the Cost of Living Council to pass the surcharge through to customers as a part of the price of the imported articles.

Within less than five months following imposition of the surcharge, a multilateral agreement (The "Smithsonian Agreement" of December 18, 1971) among the major industrial nations was reached which, inter alia, gave promise of ending the overvaluation of the U.S. dollar in relation to other major currencies. On December 20, 1971, the import duty surcharge was terminated. (Presidential Proclamation 4098, 36 Fed. Reg. 24201 (1971).)

CUSTOMS COURT

The main opinion below dealt extensively with the President's termination and emergency powers, finding that neither encompassed the tariff surcharge promulgated in Proclamation 4074.

The President's termination power, as expressed in the Tariff Act of 1930, as amended (Tariff Act) and the Trade Expansion Act of 1962 (TEA), was construed as follows:

> We conclude that the authority granted by statute to "terminate, in whole or in part, any proclamation" does not include the power to determine and fix unilaterally a rate of duty which has not been previously legally established. On the contrary, the "termination" authority, as statutorily granted, merely provides the President with a mechanical procedure of supplanting or replacing existing rates with rates which have been established by prior proclamations or by statute. Relevant thereto is United States v. American Bitumuls & Asphalt Co., 44 C.C.P.A. 199, C.A.D. 661, 246 F.2d 270 (1957), *cert. denied,* 355 U.S. 883, 78 S. Ct. 150, 2 L. Ed. 2d 113 (1957).

The power to "terminate, in whole or in part," existing proclaimed rates was characterized as twofold: the President may "nullify and bring to an end an entire proclamation" (whereupon the duty rate would revert to one previously established but not terminated), or he may "specify the extent to which a prior proclamation is terminated, thereby permitting a portion thereof to remain in effect." Thus, said the court, exercise of the termination power affects duty rates

> ... (1) to increase rates to the highest level, *i.e.*, the statutory rate, or (2) to raise or lower rates to conform to rates which have been established by a prior proclamation. In either of these instances, the rates, to which conformance may be sought, have been previously established either by the Congress (statutory rate) or by a bilateral negotiation embodied in a trade agreement pursuant to statutory authority. In short, the power to fix a new and independent rate requires a greater grant of power than that delegated to the President by the termination authority.

The Government's reliance on the phrase "unless otherwise provided" in general headnote 4(d) of the tariff schedules[8] was met with these words:

> In our view that phrase is nothing more than an exception to the provision contained in headnote 4(d) fixing the order of rate reversion resulting from a termination proclamation. More specifically, the phrase "unless otherwise provided" gives the President discretionary authority when terminating a proclamation to specify a rate established in a specific previous proclamation other than the next intervening proclamation and thus avoid an automatic reversion to the next intervening proclaimed rate. In other words, the phrase "unless otherwise provided" contemplates only the exercise of Presidential discretion to preclude the order of reversion set forth in general headnote 4(d).

ISSUE

The sole issue before us is whether the Customs Court erred, as a matter of law, in holding that Proclamation 4074 was an ultra vires Presidential act. Resolution of the issue requires determination of whether the surcharge imposed by Presidential Proclamation 4074 was within the delegated authority to be found in either (1) the termination provisions of §350(a)(6) of the Tariff Act of 1930, as amended (Tariff Act) (19 U.S.C. §1351(a)(6)) and §255(b) of the Trade Expansion Act of 1962 (TEA) (19 U.S.C. §1885(b)),[9] or (2) the

---

[8] General headnote 4(d) provides:

> whenever a proclaimed rate is terminated or suspended, the rate shall revert, unless otherwise provided, to the next intervening proclaimed rate previously superseded but not terminated or, if none, to the statutory rate.

[9] The Tariff Act and the TEA permit the President to enter foreign trade agreements and to implement them through modification of duties by proclamation. Each contains a termination provision:

> The President may at any time terminate, in whole or in part, any proclamation made pursuant to this section. (§350(a)(6), Tariff Act of 1930, as amended);
> The President may at any time terminate, in whole or in part, any proclamation made under this subchapter. (§255(b), Trade Expansion Act of 1962).

emergency powers granted by §5(b) of the Trading With the Enemy Act (TWEA), as amended (50 U.S.C. App. §5(b)),[10] and if so, whether such a delegation of authority was constitutional.

> (b)(1) During the time of war or during any other period of national emergency declared by the President, the President may, through any agency that he may designate, or otherwise, and under such rules and regulations as he may prescribe, by means of instructions, licenses, or otherwise—
> (A) investigate, regulate, or prohibit, any transactions in foreign exchange, transfers of credit or payments between, by through, or to any banking institution, and the importing, exporting, hording, melting, or earmarking of gold or silver coin or bullion, currency or securities, and
> (B) investigate, regulate, direct and compel, nullify, void, prevent or prohibit, any acquisition holding, withholding, use, transfer, withdrawal, transportation, importation or exportation of, or dealing in, or exercising any right, power, or privilege with respect to, or transactions involving, any property in which any foreign country or a national thereof has any interest, by any person, or with respect to any property, subject to the jurisdiction of the United States; . . .

OPINION

The people of the new United States, in adopting the Constitution, granted the power to "lay and collect duties" and to "regulate commerce" to the Congress, not to the Executive. U.S. Constitution, Art. I, Sec. 8, clauses 1 and 3. Nonetheless, as the Customs Court recognized in the opinion below, and as other courts and commentators have noted, Congress, beginning as early as 1794 and continuing into 1974, has delegated the exercise of much of the power to regulate foreign commerce to the Executive. As perhaps an inevitable result, "few areas of American constitutional law [are] more burdened with conflicting decisions and scholarly disagreement." Recent Decisions, 15 Va. J. Intl. L. 649 (1975).

As inferred in United States v. Curtiss-Wright Export Corp., 299 U.S. 304, 57 S. Ct. 216, 81 L. Ed. 255 (1936), the President has certain "inherent" powers in the conduct of foreign relations and foreign affairs. Some of the commentators referred to above have cited certain "concurrent" powers he shares with the Congress in those fields. The Supreme Court referred to "pooled" legislative and executive powers in foreign affairs, including delegations of power over foreign commerce, in Chicago & S. Air Lines, Inc. v. Waterman Steamship Corp., 333 U.S. 103, 110, 68 S. Ct. 431, 92 L. Ed. 568 (1948). It is nonetheless clear that no undelegated power to regulate *commerce,* or to set tariffs, inheres in the Presidency.

---

[10] TWEA §5(b), in pertinent part, follows:

TERMINATION PROVISIONS

[2] We are in basic agreement with the Customs Court's interpretation (quoted above) of the termination powers delegated by the Congress in the Tariff Act and in the TEA. United States v. American Bitumuls & Asphalt Co., 246 F.2d 270, 44 CCPA 199, C.A.D. 661 (1957), *cert. denied*, 355 U.S. 883, 78 S. Ct. 150, 2 L. Ed. 2d 113.

Having correctly found no delegation, in the acts or in their legislative histories, of the power to impose the surcharge here in question, the Customs Court nonetheless applied, and the parties have argued, the "separation of powers doctrine" and its corollary, the "delegation doctrine," in relation to the termination provisions of the Tariff Act and the TEA. But whether the limitations on Congress' power to delegate, as gleaned by the Customs Court from Schechter Poultry v. United States, 295 U.S. 495, 55 S. Ct. 837, 79 L. Ed. 1570 (1935) and Panama Refining Co. v. Ryan, 293 U.S. 388, 55 S. Ct. 241, 79 L. Ed. 446 (1935), are still viable, or whether they now rest on a rusted concept, are questions raisable only after it is determined that a particular delegation had been attempted. It is unnecessary to discuss the constitutional ramifications that might obtain if Congress *had* made such a delegation in the Tariff Act or in the TEA.

EMERGENCY POWERS

We are presented, in this case, with the first reliance upon the TWEA as authority for a Presidential imposition of a temporary surcharge on imports. There being nothing in the TWEA or in its history which specifically either authorizes or prohibits the imposition of a surcharge, and no judicial precedent involving the same, we tread new ground.[16]

---

[16]The TWEA has been considered by many different courts in hundreds of cases involving a variety of executive actions. Because it was hastily amended, the TWEA "has presented to the judiciary a collection of knotty problems which are probably not surpassed by those arising under any other statute of its size or weight." Bishop, Judicial Construction of the Trading With the Enemy Act, 62 Harv. L. Rev. 721 (1949). It has nonetheless survived every attack on its constitutionality: *See*, e.g., Veterans & Reserv. For Peace in Vietnam v. Regional Comr., 459 F.2d 676 (3d Cir.), *cert. denied*, 409 U.S. 933, 93 S. Ct. 232, 34 L. Ed. 2d 188 (1972) (literature detained under the Foreign Assets Control Regulations); Nielson v. Secretary of Treasury, 424 F.2d 833, 137 U.S. App. D.C. 345 (1970) (bank account blocked under the Cuban Assets Control Regulations); Teague v. Regional Commissioner of Customs, Region II, 404 F.2d 441 (2d Cir. 1968), *cert. denied*, 394 U.S. 977, 89 S. Ct. 1457, 22 L. Ed. 2d 756 (1969) (publications detained under the Foreign Assets Control Regulations); Sardino v. Federal Reserve Bank of New York, 361 F.2d 106 (2d Cir.), *cert. denied*, 385 U.S. 898, 87 S. Ct. 203, 17 L. Ed. 2d 130 (1966) . . .; Silesian-American Corp. v. Markham, 156 F.2d 793 (2d Cir. 1946), *aff'd sub nom.* Silesian-American Corp. v. Clark, 332 U.S. 469, 68 S. Ct. 179, 92 L. Ed. 81 (1947) (corporation stock vested in Alien Property Custodian); Draeger Shipping Co. v. Crowley, 55 F. Supp. 906 (S.D.N.Y. 1944) (corporation stock vested in Alien Property Custodian).

POWER DELEGATED . . .

It appears incontestable that §5(b) does in fact delegate to the President, for use during war or during national emergency only, the power to "regulate importation." The plain and unambiguous wording of the statute permits no other interpretation. As was said of a war power in Lichter v. United States, 334 U.S. 742, 782, 68 S. Ct. 1294, 92 L. Ed. 1694 (1948), the primary implication of an emergency power is that it should be effective to deal with a national emergency successfully. The delegation in §5(b) is broad and extensive; it could not have been otherwise if the President were to have, within constitutional boundaries, the flexibility required to meet problems surrounding a national emergency with the success desired by Congress.

A question remains, however, as to *how* the President may regulate importation in a national emergency, i.e., what means of execution of the delegated power are permissible. As appears below, we agree with the Customs Court that the delegation could not constitutionally have been of "the full and all-inclusive power to regulate foreign commerce." We do not believe, however, as the Customs Court apparently did, that only in such a sweeping delegation could authority be found for Proclamation 4074. The choice is not draconian.

MEANS OF EXECUTION

The Customs Court, considering a broad delegation unconstitutional in the absence of standards restricting the President's actions thereunder, found such standards in an interpretation of the words "by means of instructions, licenses or otherwise" as words of restriction. . . .

The opinion below states:

> The words "instructions, licenses, or otherwise" contained in section 5(b)(1) define the nature and mode of the regulatory authority intended to be delegated to the President. These words conform to the phraseology used through the history of the Act in the establishment of a system of *licenses and permits* for the control of property during a time of war and crisis and which have come to be recognized as the hallmark and distinguishing feature of the Act. [Emphasis added.]

We do not find, however, that the words "instructions, licenses, or otherwise," either "conform to the phraseology used throughout the history of the Act" or "have come to be recognized as the hallmark and distinguishing feature of the Act." . . .

Adhering to the analogy applied by the Customs Court, which found the roots of the TWEA in the Act of July 13, 1861 and the delegation in §5(b) a branch of the tree in which congressional power to regulate foreign commerce is lodged, we find, Mendel-like, a cross-breeding which produced an economic emergency branch. Only if the TWEA had remained limited to trading with the enemy in "time of war" would the "licensing" limitation and its historical background be controlling. . . .

We conclude, therefore, that Congress, in enacting §5(b) of the TWEA, authorized the President, during an emergency, to exercise the delegated substantive power, i.e., to "regulate importation," by imposing an import duty surcharge or by other means appropriately and reasonably related, as discussed below, to the particular nature of the emergency declared. Whether a delegation of such breadth as to have authorized Proclamation 4074 would be constitutionally embraced, is determined, however, by the nature of the particular surcharge herein and its relationship to other statutes, as well as by its relationship to the particular emergency confronted.

LIMITED NATURE OF PROCLAMATION 4074

In its proper concern for adherence to the Constitution, the Customs Court erred, we believe, in its expressed fear that, if Proclamation 4074 were upheld, the President, by "merely" declaring a national emergency, "could determine and fix rates of duty at will, without regard to statutory rates prescribed by Congress." . . .

Proclamation 4074, far from fixing rates in disregard of congressional will, specifically provided, as noted above, "that if the imposition of an additional duty of 10 percent ad valorem would cause the total duty or charge payable to exceed the total duty or charge payable at the rate prescribed in column 2 of the Tariff Schedules of the United States, then the column 2 rate shall apply."

Further, the surcharge was limited to articles which had been the subject of prior tariff concessions and, thus, to less than all United States imports. It resulted in a range of effective surcharge rates and duties. The surcharge rate on automobiles, for example, became 6.5% ad valorem. S. Rep. No. 92-437, 92d Cong., 1st Sess. 14 (1971) U.S. Code Cong. & Admin. News 1971, p. 1825. With respect to some articles the surcharge could result in the precise statutory duty set by the Congress. If a prior concession had reduced the statutory rate by 10% ad valorem, the imposition of the 10% ad valorem surcharge would produce the statutory rate of column 1 in the Tariff Schedules. As Proclamation 4074 recognized, the duty rate after the surcharge might become that of column 2 for other articles. With respect to some other articles, the surcharge might result in a duty set by one of a series of earlier concessions following presidentially negotiated trade agreements. In the case of still other articles, the total duty under Proclamation 4074 might be less than that resulting from a rate set by Congress and different from that resulting from prior tariff concessions.

With respect to those articles on which no concession had been granted, the congressionally established rates remained untouched. And the limitation to "dutiable" articles meant that no duties were created on goods entitled to free entry under the statute. Far from attempting, therefore, to tear down or supplant the entire tariff scheme of Congress, the President imposed a limited surcharge, as "a temporary measure" (see footnote 4, supra) calculated to help meet a particular national emergency, which is quite different from "imposing whatever tariff rates he deems desirable."[26]

RELATIONSHIP TO OTHER STATUTES

Reliance by the Customs Court on *Youngstown Sheet & Tube,* 343 U.S. 579 (1952) is misplaced. We do not have here, as was the case in *Youngstown,* what the Customs Court described as "legislative acts providing procedures prescribed by the Congress for the accomplishment of the very purpose sought to be obtained" by a Presidential Proclamation. The surcharge did not run counter to any explicit legislation. We know of no act, other than the TWEA, "providing procedures" for dealing with a national emergency involving a balance of payments problem such as that which existed in 1971. . . .

. . . We find it unreasonable to suppose that Congress passed the TWEA, delegating broad powers to the President for periodic use during national emergencies, while intending that the President, when faced with such an emergency, must follow limiting procedures prescribed in other acts designed for continuing use during normal times.

RELATION TO THE POWER DELEGATED AND THE EMERGENCY DECLARED

A standard inherently applicable to the exercise of delegated emergency powers is the extent to which the action taken bears a reasonable relation to the power delegated and to the emergency giving rise to the action. The nature of the power determines *what* may be done and the nature of the emergency restricts the *how* of its doing, i.e., the means of execution. Though courts will not normally review the essentially political questions surrounding the declaration or continuance of a national emergency, they will not hesitate to review the *actions* taken in response thereto or in reliance thereon. It is one thing for courts to review the judgment of a President that a national emergency exists. It is another for courts to review his acts arising from that judgment.

It is clear that the surcharge herein had, as its primary purpose, the curtailment, i.e., the regulation, of imports. What was sought was an offset to actions of our foreign trading partners which had led to loss of our favorable balance of trade and to a serious negative balance, as the President's address, supra note 4, made plain. Pressure exerted by the surcharge contributed to achievement of a multilateral agreement of major nations, which included a realignment of currency exchange rates. As was indicated in South Puerto Rico Sugar

---

[26] A charge on imports will inherently produce revenue. As stated by the President, however, "The surcharge was not imposed to raise revenue but to provide the U.S. external position with some temporary protection." Economic Report of the President 70 (1972).

Co. Trad. Corp. v. United States, 334 F.2d 622, 167 Ct. Cl. 236 (1964), it is purpose, not form, which should govern judicial characterization of a charge on imports. *Cf.* Moon v. Freeman, 379 F.2d 382, 391 (9th Cir. 1967). A principal function and necessary effect of the import surcharge in Proclamation 4074 was to regulate imports. Section 5(b) delegated power to "regulate importation." The relationship between the action taken and the power delegated was thus one of substantial identity.

The President's choice of means of execution must also bear a reasonable relation to the particular emergency confronted. In considering section 3 of the Tariff Act of 1890, which authorized the President, in non-emergency situations, to impose retaliatory measures at his discretion "for such time as he shall deem just," the Supreme Court, after noting the fact finding limitation normally involved in peacetime delegations, said in Field v. Clark, 143 U.S. 649, 691, 12 S. Ct. 495, 504, 36 L. Ed. 294 (1892):

> [I]n the judgment of the legislative branch of the government, it is often desirable, if not essential, for the protection of the interests of our people, against the unfriendly or discriminating regulations established by foreign governments, in the interests of their people, to invest the president with large discretion in matters arising out of the execution of statutes relating to trade and commerce with other nations.

The "discriminating regulations . . . in the interests of their people" referred to in *Field* may be likened to the "unfair exchange rates," "unfair treatment" and "the unfair edge" which the President described in his address, supra note 4, as causing the United States "to compete with one hand tied behind her back" and as the "major reason why our trade balance has eroded."

That the surcharge herein had overtones of foreign relations and foreign policy seems self-evident. As the world has grown smaller and trade more complex, foreign exchange rates, international monetary reserves, balances of payments, and trade barriers have become increasingly intertwined, with trade barriers being used as tools in furtherance of foreign policy. See the Congressional findings which appeared in §2 (50 U.S.C. App. §2401) of the Export Administration Act of 1969, 83 Stat. 841 (50 U.S.C. App. §2401-13). The Customs Court appreciated that the nature of the surcharge action converged with presidential representation of the United States in the "society of nations" and with the President's efforts to achieve "stability in the international trade position" of our country. The declared national emergency was premised on a prolonged decline in our country's international monetary reserves, the serious threat to our trade position, and our unfavorable balance of payments position. Unlike quotas and other forms of action, a surcharge can obviously be quickly imposed and removed, is not discriminatory among nations affected, and is administratively less complex. Through its impact on imports, the surcharge imposed by Proclamation 4074 had a direct effect on our nation's balance of trade and, in turn, on its balance of payments deficit and its international monetary reserves. We conclude, therefore, that the President's action in imposing the surcharge bore an eminently reasonable relationship to the emergency confronted.

CONSTITUTIONALITY

It should be understood, in considering the constitutionality of the TWEA as here interpreted, that the President's imposition of the surcharge could not violate any individual's constitutional rights in foreign trade. No one has a vested right to trade with foreign nations. . . . And no one has a legal right to the maintenance of an existing rate or duty. Norwegian Nitrogen Products Co. v. United States, 288 U.S. 294, 53 S. Ct. 350, 77 L. Ed. 796 (1933). Nor are we faced here with denial or infringement, even indirectly, of any right arising from any of the Amendments to the Constitution, as were the courts, for example, in Veterans & Reserv. For Peace In Vietnam v. Regional Comr., and Teague v. Regional Commissioner of Customs, *supra* note 16, wherein detention, under §5(b), of publications sent from North Vietnam was upheld against a claim of violation of First Amendment rights, or in Sardino v. Federal Reserve Bank of New York, *supra* note 16, wherein blocking of property, under §5(b), was found not to be a deprivation of property violative of the Fifth Amendment.

The Customs Court, as quoted above, perceived a constitutional flaw in §5(b) of the TWEA if it were interpreted as permitting the surcharge herein, viewing such interpretation as a denial of the people's right to a government of separated powers, i.e., that Congress' delegation in §5(b), unless restricted to "licensing," would be a violation of the "delegation doctrine." Whatever may be the current viability of that doctrine . . . , we find no conflict therewith in the TWEA as applied to Proclamation 4074. The Supreme Court in Hampton & Co. v. United States, 276 U.S. 394, 48 S. Ct. 348, 72 L. Ed. 624 (1928), dealing with non-emergency conditions, found those delegations proper which laid down an "intelligible principle" under which the President was to act. We find that principle, as did the court in Veterans & Reserv. For Peace In Vietnam v. Regional Comr., *supra,* in the express limitations that (1) §5(b) of the TWEA shall become operative only in "time of war" or "any other period of national emergency declared by the President" (i.e., a congressional requirement that the President, before acting in peacetime, must find and declare the fact that a national emergency exists), and (2) that the power delegated therein shall be applied only to "property in which any foreign country or a national thereof has any interest."

It cannot be lightly dismissed that the TWEA is operative only during (war or) national emergencies, which inherently preclude prior prescription of specific, detailed guidelines. . . .

That §5(b) and Proclamation 4074 deal only with *foreign* goods also is of significance. The Supreme Court, though dealing with international relations and the sale of arms rather than with imports, and with normal rather than national emergency conditions, in *Curtiss-Wright Export Corp., supra,* recognized the distinction between delegations of power in foreign and domestic affairs in these words (299 U.S. at 320, 57 S. Ct. at 221):

> It is quite apparent that if, in the maintenance of our international relations, embarrassment—perhaps serious embarrassment—is to be avoided and success for our aims achieved, congressional legislation which is to be made effective through negotiation and inquiry within the international field must often accord to the President a degree of discretion and freedom from statutory restriction which would not be admissible were domestic affairs alone involved.

Congress, by delegating to the President in §5(b) the power to regulate imports within the national emergency powers standard, has not succeeded in abdicating its constitutional power to regulate foreign commerce. It remains the ultimate decision maker and the fundamental reservoir of power to regulate commerce. It may, of course, recall or limit the delegated emergency power at any time. Throughout the 114 year life of the TWEA and its progenitors, Congress has repeatedly exercised its untrammeled plenary power over foreign commerce. . . .

The mere incantation of "national emergency" cannot, of course, sound the death-knell of the Constitution. Nor can it repeal prior statutes or enlarge the delegation in §5(b). The declaration of a national emergency is not a talisman enabling the President to rewrite the tariff schedules, as it was not in this case. We agree, also, with the statement of the court in Algonquin SNG, Inc. v. Federal Energy Administration, 518 F.2d 1051, 1062 (D.C. Cir. 1975), *cert. granted*, 423 U.S. 923, 96 S. Ct. 265, 46 L. Ed. 2d 249 (1975) (No. 75-382), that: "Our laws were not established merely to be followed only when times are tranquil." The TWEA, which is among "our laws" and is designed specifically for non-tranquil times, was not before the court in *Algonquin*. As we have noted, if *every* law applicable to tranquil times were required to be followed in emergencies, there would be no point in delegating emergency powers and no adequate, prompt means for dealing with emergencies.

The Executive does not here seek, nor would it receive, judicial approval of a wholesale delegation of legislative power. Nor do we find in §5(b) the grant of the "unrestrained and unbridled" authority feared by the Customs Court. The courts continue to sit and remain prepared . . . to impede an unreasonable or ultra vires exercise of the power granted in §5(b). We do not here sanction the exercise of an unlimited power, which, we agree with the Customs Court, would be to strike a blow to our Constitution. On the contrary, we find ourselves in agreement with this statement of the Court of Claims in *South Puerto Rico Sugar Co. Trad. Corp.* (334 F.2d at 632):

> [W]hen Congress uses far-reaching words in delegating authority to the President in the area of foreign relations, courts must assume, unless there is a specific contrary showing elsewhere in the statute or in the legislative history, that the legislators contemplate that the President may and will make full use of that power in any manner not inconsistent with the provisions or purposes of the Act. In a statute dealing with foreign affairs, a grant to the President which is expan-

sive to the reader's eye should not be hemmed in or "cabined, cribbed, confined" by anxious judicial blinders. [Footnote omitted.]

CONCLUSION

The broad and flexible construction given to §5(b) by the courts which have considered it is consistent with the intent of Congress and with the broad purposes of the Act. As was said by the Supreme Court in discussing the President's power to define "banking institution" under an earlier version of §5(b): "The power in peace and in war must be given generous scope to accomplish its purpose." Propper v. Clark, 337 U.S. 472, 481, 69 S. Ct. 1333, 1339, 93 L. Ed. 1480 (1949). Though such a broad grant may be considered unwise, or even dangerous, should it come into the hands of an unscrupulous, rampant President, willing to declare an emergency when none exists,[37] the wisdom of a congressional delegation is not for us to decide. As was said in Norman v. B. & O. R. Co., 294 U.S. 240, 297, 55 S. Ct. 407, 411, 79 L. Ed. 885 (1935), with respect to "gold clause" measures: "We are not concerned with their wisdom. The question before the Court is one of power, not of policy."

Congress, fully familiar with its own use of duties as a means of regulation, delegated to the President, in §5(b) of the TWEA, the power to regulate importation during declared national emergencies by means appropriate to the emergency involved. Interpreted as having authorized the President's imposition of the specific surcharge in Proclamation 4074, as a reasonable response to the particular national emergency declared therein, the delegation in §5(b) of the TWEA passes constitutional muster.

Accordingly, the President's action under review was within the power constitutionally delegated to him, and the judgment of the Customs Court that said action was ultra vires must be reversed.

Reversed.

STAR-KIST FOODS, INC. v. UNITED STATES

275 F.2d 472 (C.C.P.A. 1959)

MARTIN, Judge.

This appeal arose out of a protest filed by Star-Kist Foods, Inc., an American producer of canned tuna fish packed in oil and of tuna fish packed in

---

[37] The growth of power in the Executive has been phenomenal over the last 40 years. The risks inherent in a concentration of power in the Executive remain those feared by the Framers. The Federalist, Nos. 48-49 (Madison). Recent events have brought the question into wider public discourse. Whether Congress should devote more effort to defining, limiting or regaining powers previously delegated is not a matter within the jurisdiction of the courts. Whether the pendulum of power should now begin to swing further in the direction of the Congress is a matter of policy, reserved to the people and their elected representatives in the Congress. Absent a violation of the Constitution, or action contrary to statute, it is not grist for the mill of this court.

distilled water (a "dietetic pack"). The protest was filed pursuant to section 516(b) of the Tariff Act of 1930, as amended, 19 U.S.C.A. §1516(b), and attacked the assessment made by the Collector of Customs, Port of New York, of an import of tuna fish packed in brine at 12½ per centum ad valorem. The Collector assessed the imported merchandise in accordance with paragraph 718(b) of the Tariff Act of 1930, 19 U.S.C.A. §1001, par. 718(b), as modified by a trade agreement with Iceland, T.D. 50956.[1] Star-Kist asserted that the goods were dutiable at the rates imposed by Congress in paragraph 718(b). . . .

Appellant asserts two reasons for objecting to the Secretary's action refusing to disturb the collector's assessment of the imported tuna fish at the reduced duties under the trade agreement with Iceland. Each ground, it is asserted, requires a holding that the trade agreement, by virtue of which the duty on brine packed tuna fish was reduced from 25% to 12½% ad valorem, is null and void.

The first reason urged by appellant is that the Trade Agreements Act of 1934[2] by authority of which the trade agreement was negotiated, is null and void as being an unconstitutional delegation of legislative powers by the Congress to the President of the United States [enumerated in the U.S. Constitution as follows] . . .

---

[1] Paragraph 718(b) provides:
"Fish, prepared or preserved in any manner, when packed in air-tight containers weighing with their contents not more than fifteen pounds each (except fish packed in oil or in oil and other substances): . . . other fish, 25 per centum ad valorem."
The only change which T.D. 50956 has made, pertinent to this appeal, was the reduction of the dutiable rate to 12½ per centum ad valorem.

[2] Section 350(a) of the Tariff Act of 1930 as amended by the Act of June 12, 1934 entitled "An Act To amend the Tariff Act of 1930," 48 Stat. 943, 19 U.S.C. 1351 (1940 ed.) as further amended by the Joint Resolution of June 7, 1943, 57 Stat. 125, 19 U.S.C.A. §1351, and as it read at the time of the importation of the merchandise at bar, provided:

(a) For the purpose of expanding foreign markets for the products of the United States (as a means of assisting in the present emergency of restoring the American standard of living, in overcoming domestic unemployment and the present economic depression, in increasing the purchasing power of the American public, and in establishing and maintaining a better relationship among various branches of American agriculture, industry, mining, and commerce) by regulating the admission of foreign goods into the United States in accordance with characteristics and the needs of various branches of American production so that foreign markets will be made available to those branches of American production which require and are capable of developing such outlets by affording corresponding market opportunities for foreign products in the United States, the President, whenever he finds as a fact that any existing duties or other import restrictions of the United States or any foreign country are unduly burdening and restricting the foreign trade of the United States and that the purpose above declared will be promoted by the means hereinafter specified, is authorized from time to time—
(1) To enter into foreign trade agreements with foreign governments or instrumentalities thereof; and
(2) To proclaim such modifications of existing duties and other import restrictions, or such additional import restrictions, or such continuance, and for such minimum periods, of existing customs or excise treatment of any article covered by foreign trade agreements, as are required or appropriate to carry out any foreign trade agreement that the President has entered into hereunder. No proclamation shall be made increasing or decreasing by more than 50 per centum any existing rate of duty or transferring any article between the dutiable and free lists. The proclaimed duties and other import restrictions shall apply to

Article I, Sec. 1:

All legislative Powers herein granted shall be vested in a Congress of the United States, which shall consist of a Senate and House of Representatives.

Article I, Sec. 7:

All bills for raising Revenue shall originate in the House of Representatives; but the Senate may propose or concur with Amendments as on other Bills.

Article I, Sec. 8:

The Congress shall have Power To lay and collect Taxes, Duties, Imposts and Excises, to pay the Debts and provide for the common Defense and general Welfare of the United States; but all Duties, Imposts and Excises shall be uniform throughout the United States; . . .

To regulate Commerce with foreign Nations, and among the several States, and with the Indian Tribes; . . .

Second, appellant maintains that the trade agreement with Iceland, consummated under the provisions of the Trade Agreements Act of 1934, is a treaty and is therefore null and void because it was neither negotiated with the advice and consent of the Senate nor did two-thirds of the Senate concur in its execution as is required by Article II, Section 2, clause 2 of the Constitution, which reads as follows:

He [the President] shall have Power, by and with the Advice and Consent of the Senate, to make Treaties, provided two thirds of the Senators present concur; . . .

Appellant maintains further that the proclamation of the President pronounced in connection with this trade agreement is also null and void.

We shall treat these questions in the order in which we have outlined the contentions of appellant.

At the outset of this discussion it is well to bear in mind that this court has no authority to chart a new course in jurisprudence in a field in which precedents have been established by the Supreme Court. It behooves us, therefore, to endeavor to propound the principles governing the issues presented here as deduced from the pronouncements of that Court. . . .

Now we must endeavor to determine what principles of law can be adduced

---

articles the growth, produce, or manufacture of all foreign countries, whether imported directly, or indirectly: *Provided,* That the President may suspend the application to articles the growth, produce, or manufacture of any country because of its discriminatory treatment of American commerce or because of other acts (including the operation of international cartels) or policies which in his opinion tend to defeat the purposes set forth in this section; and the proclaimed duties and other import restrictions shall be in effect from and after such time as is specified in the proclamation. The President may at any time terminate any such proclamation in whole or in part.

from the cases just reviewed. It is apparent that the development of the concepts of law in this field has been accomplished by a process of evolution.

First, the delegation of authority to the President to proclaim the happening of an event as a condition precedent to the invocation of an embargo on imports was sanctioned. The Aurora v. United States, *supra*. Next, legislation was upheld wherein Congress pronounced a policy, but the President, in order to act, was required to make a finding by proclamation, in which event certain imported articles would be suspended from the free list and specified duties would be imposed thereon. The President was given discretion, not only with reference to the finding, but also as to the duration of the suspension. Field v. Clark, *supra*. Later, legislation was approved which established a policy and which empowered the President, after a required investigation by the Tariff Commission and findings by him, to proclaim increases or decreases in the duties on all imported articles within 50 percent of the established rates. The President was further authorized to modify and change the proclaimed rates of duty so long as he followed the same procedure. He was prohibited from transferring articles to and from the free list and from exceeding any maximum ad valorem rate of duty specified in Title I of the Tariff Act of 1922. J. W. Hampton, Jr., & Co. v. United States, *supra*. Again it should be noted that Congress can give the President much broader discretionary powers in legislation inherently bearing upon his conduct of foreign affairs, such as that here under consideration, than when purely domestic matters are involved. United States v. Curtiss-Wright Export Corp., *supra*.

The Court's decisions in those cases have followed a discernible pattern and have set out certain principles which are the guideposts of Congress in enacting legislation which enlists the assistance of the President, and which are the fundamental guides in ascertaining whether Congress has adhered to the constitutional limitations.

A constitutional delegation of powers requires that Congress enunciate a policy or objective or give reasons for seeking the aid of the President. In addition the act must specify when the powers conferred may be utilized by establishing a standard or "intelligible principle" which is sufficient to make it clear when action is proper. And because Congress cannot abdicate its legislative function and confer carte blanche authority on the President, it must circumscribe that power in some manner. This means that Congress must tell the President what he can do by prescribing a standard which confines his discretion and which will guarantee that any authorized action he takes will tend to promote rather than flout the legislative purpose. It is not necessary that the guides be precise or mathematical formulae to be satisfactory in a constitutional sense.

In the act before us the Congressional policy is pronounced very clearly. The stated objectives are to expand foreign markets for the products of the United States "by regulating the admission of foreign goods into the United States in accordance with the characteristics and needs of various branches of American production so that foreign markets will be made available to those branches of American production which require and are capable of developing such outlets by affording corresponding market opportunities for foreign products in the United States. . . . These objectives are in their nature no different than those of the Tariff Act of 1890 wherein the stated policy was to secure reciprocally equal trade with countries producing certain enumerated articles, and the Tariff Act of 1922 which was designed to enable domestic producers to compete on an equal basis with foreign producers in the marketplaces of the United States.

Pursuant to the 1934 act the presidential power can be invoked "whenever he [the President] finds as a fact that any existing duties or other import restrictions of the United States or any foreign country are *unduly burdening or restricting the foreign trade of the United States* and that the [purposes of the act] will be promoted. . . ." (Italics ours.) Under the 1890 act the President could invoke the statute when he was satisfied "that the Government of any country . . . imposes duties or other exactions upon . . . products of the United States . . . [which] he *may deem to be reciprocally unequal and unreasonable. . . .*" (Italics ours.) In this regard the 1922 act allowed the President to act if he found *"the duties prescribed in this Act do not equalize . . . differences in costs of production in the United States and the principal competing country. . . ."* (Italics ours.)

Now what could the President do under the several acts?

After making the requisite findings under the act of 1890, the President could suspend the free introduction of the articles specified for such time as he deemd *"just,"* and pursuant to the act of 1922, he could increase or decrease rates up to 50 per centum of those specified, but could not exceed any maximum stipulated in the act nor transfer any article between the dutiable and free lists.

Under the provisions of the 1934 act the President by proclamation can modify existing duties and other import restrictions but not by more than 50 percent of the specified duties nor can he place articles upon or take them off the free list. Furthermore, he must accomplish the purposes of the act through the medium of foreign trade agreements with other countries. However, he can suspend the operation of such agreements if he discovers discriminatory treatment of American commerce, and he can terminate, in whole or in part, any proclamation at any time.

Of course the acts of 1890, 1922, and 1934 are different, but we comprehend only a difference in degree. In each one Congress has allowed the President broad discretion, not only with respect to when he can act, but also in the exercise of the conferred powers. Under the act of 1890, he could suspend articles from the free list "for such time as he shall deem just." And under the Flexible Tariff Act of 1922, the President was authorized to modify duties to equalize the competitive opportunities of American and foreign producers in the markets of the United States. Although he was to be assisted by the Tariff Commission, and was to consider as far as was *"practicable"* certain enumerated factors, as well as any other factors he himself deemed to be relevant, the final decision as respected equalization was his and *his alone.* While it is true that under that act the President was required to seek the advice of the Tariff Commission before he could act, the Court in the Hampton case recognized that an advisory commission is not necessary. Consequently, the absence of such a provision in the Trade Agreements Act is inconsequential. Neither is the absence in the act of 1934 of a suggested list of factors to consider in applying the standard determinative of any of the issues. Under both the 1922 and the 1934 acts, the President was given the power to increase or decrease duties up to 50 per centum of the specified rates. The difference lies only in the procedure set out in the 1922 act to *assist* the Chief Executive in making *his* decision.

As has been earlier pointed out, appellant maintains that there is no limitation on the adjustment in duties which the Chief Executive is authorized to make. The argument leads to the conclusion, for example, that even if the President finds that duties should be increased 50 per centum to comply with the policy declaration of the act, he may arbitrarily decrease them 50 per centum instead. We do not so read the language which Congress has provided in the section we are considering.

After making the enabling finding, the President is authorized to act in a manner such "that the purpose above declared will be promoted by the means hereinafter specified." Those means are to enter into foreign trade agreements and to proclaim certain modifications in various import restrictions. It becomes immediately apparent, therefore, that the President is limited to action which will advance the policies of the act, and which will tend to secure the benefits considered desirable by the Congress. Not only must they advance the Congressional policy, but with respect to rate modifications, the problem with which appellant is most concerned, they must be "required or appropriate" to carrying out the trade-agreement as well. This additional language doubly emphasizes the fact that Congress limited the Presidential authority to modify duties strictly in accordance with the purposes for which the act was promulgated.

In view of the Supreme Court's recognition of the necessity of flexibility in the laws affecting foreign relations, and the many significant and limiting similarities between the 1934 act on the one hand, and the 1890 and 1922 acts on the other, which latter acts the Supreme Court has approved, we are of the opinion that the 1934 act does not grant an unconstitutional delegation of authority to the President.

Appellant has relied greatly upon Panama Refining Co. v. Ryan, 293 U.S. 388, 55 S. Ct. 241, 79 L. Ed. 446, and A. L. A. Schechter Poultry Corp. v. United States, 295 U.S. 495, 55 S. Ct. 839, 840, 79 L. Ed. 1570, to support its contention that the Trade Agreements Act of 1934 is unconstitutional in that it confers an "unfettered discretion" upon the President. We have considered those cases, but since we find that the Supreme Court cited approvingly Field and Hampton in the Panama case and Hampton in the Schechter case, and since we believe the decisions in Hampton and Field to be controlling of the issues at bar, we find it unnecessary to discuss those cases further.

We now come to the other contention of appellants, that the trade agreement with Iceland executed by the President pursuant to the Trade Agreements Act is null and void because it is, in fact, a treaty and lacks the concurrence of the Senate, required by Article II, §2 of the Constitution and, further, that since the agreement is illegal the proclamation which effectuated the agreement is also without legal effect.

This procedure was established by Congress so that its policy and the basic philosophy which motivated the passage of the Trade Agreements Act could be realized. From reading the act, it is apparent that Congress concluded that the promotion of foreign trade required that the tariff barriers in this and other countries be modified on a negotiated basis. Since the President has the responsibility of conducting the foreign affairs of this country generally, it gave to him the added responsibility of negotiating the agreements in pursuance of the spirit of the act. Such a procedure is not without precedent nor judicial approval. The Supreme Court in Altman & Co. v. United States, 224 U.S. 583, 601, 32 S. Ct. 593, 597, 56 L. Ed. 894, recognized that not all commercial compacts are treaties, saying:

> . . . While it may be true that this commercial agreement, made under authority of the Tariff Act of 1897, §3, was not a treaty possessing the dignity of one requiring ratification by the Senate of the United States, it was an international compact, negotiated between the representatives of two sovereign nations, and made in the name and on behalf of the contracting countries, and dealing with important commercial relations between the two countries, and was proclaimed by the President. If not technically a treaty requiring ratification, nevertheless it was a compact authorized by the Congress of the United States, negotiated and proclaimed under the authority of its President.

In United States v. Curtiss-Wright Export Corp., *supra,* 299 U.S. at page 318, 57 S. Ct. at page 220, the Court observed that "the power to make such international agreements as do not constitute treaties in the constitutional sense, . . . [although not] expressly affirmed by the Constitution, nevertheless exist[s] as inherently inseparable from the conception of nationality."

In United States v. Belmont, 301 U.S. 324, 57 S. Ct. 758, 81 L. Ed. 1134, which involved the assignment by the Soviet government to the petitioner of certain claims due to that government from American nationals, this question was again discussed. The assignment involved therein was effected by an exchange of diplomatic correspondence between the Soviet government and the United States coincident with the recognition of the Soviet government by the President of the United States. The purpose was to bring about a final settlement of the claims between those governments, it being agreed that the Soviet government would take no steps to enforce claims against American nationals and that all of such claims were released and assigned to the United States. The Supreme Court in upholding the transactions, stated:

That the negotiations, acceptance of the assignment and agreements and understandings in respect thereof were within the competence of the President may not be doubted. Governmental power over internal affairs is distributed between the national government and the several states. Governmental power over external affairs is not distributed, but is vested exclusively in the national government. And in respect of what was done here, the Executive had authority to speak as the sole organ of that government. The assignment and the agreements in connection therewith did not, as in the case of treaties, as that term is used in the treaty making clause of the Constitution (Article 2, §2), require the advice and consent of the Senate.

A treaty signifies "a compact made between two or more independent nations, with a view to the public welfare." Altman & Co. v. United States, 224 U.S. 583, 600, 32 S. Ct. 593, 596, 56 L. Ed. 894. But an international compact, as this was, is not always a treaty which requires the participation of the Senate. There are many such compacts, of which a protocol, a modus vivendi, a postal convention, and agreements like that now under consideration are illustrations. See 5 Moore, Int. Law Digest, 210-221. The distinction was pointed out by this court in the *Altman* case, *supra,* which arose under section 3 of the Tariff Act of 1897, (30 Stat. 151, 203), authorizing the President to conclude commercial agreements with foreign countries in certain specified matters. Id., 301 U.S. at pages 330-331, 57 S. Ct. at page 760.

In United States v. Pink, 315 U.S. 203, 62 S. Ct. 552, 86 L. Ed. 796, that Court approved the opinion in the Belmont case, *supra,* and reaffirmed the proposition that these may be international agreements and compacts which are not treaties within the meaning of the Constitution. We see no significant difference between the executive power exercised and approved in those cases and that in issue here.

This court had occasion to discuss this question in the case of Louis Wolf & Co. v. United States, 107 F.2d 819, 27 CCPA 188, C.A.D. 84. In that case a trade agreement with Cuba consummated under the provisions of the Trade Agreements Act of 1934 was involved. In upholding the agreement this court said:

We think that an agreement such as the one at bar relating to customs duties which may be levied upon articles of commerce between the two countries (when the agreement is authorized by Congress, although not ratified by the Senate) may be properly styled a commercial convention. We therefore hold that appellants' contentions with reference to the effect of the treaties with Austria and Norway are without merit. See E. & J. Burke, Ltd. v. United States, 26 CCPA, Customs, 374, 379, C.A.D. 44. Id., 107 F.2d at page 827, 27 CCPA at page 200.

We, therefore, hold that the trade agreement with Iceland and the accompanying proclamation are valid. In view of the above analysis of the issues herein and our conclusions with respect thereto, we affirm the judgment of the Customs Court.

Affirmed.

NOTES AND QUESTIONS

1. Are *Star-Kist* and *Yoshida* consistent?

2. Was the president's action in *Star-Kist* one expected by Congress when it made the delegation? That in *Yoshida?*

3. In *Yoshida,* what was the intelligible principle by which the TWEA delegation was limited? Are you convinced?

4. Does the lower court seem correct in its position (accepted by the appellate court) that the Trade Act series gives the president power to restore tariffs only to specific previous levels?

5. Are you troubled by the fact that the president stated that he was acting under the Trade Acts "and other provisions of law," while he was upheld under the TWEA? If you were president, do you think reference to the TWEA in the basic executive order would have posed any problems for you?

6. Should the fact that Congress later granted the president clear authority to do what he did in *Yoshida* affect the outcome of the case? Do you think the president will ever use this authority again?

7. Was President Nixon's imposition of an import surcharge, discussed in *Yoshida,* successful in limiting the U.S. trade imbalance? In 1971, when the import surcharge was imposed, U.S. citizens, for the first time in this century, purchased more goods from abroad than they sold. By the mid-1980s the trade deficit was running in excess of $130 billion per annum. What was the policy significance of Nixon's simultaneous decision to shut the U.S. gold window? Could the latter decision have been taken without the former? *Yoshida* permitted the president, for better or worse (some have suggested that the move had more to do with preelection politics than international economics) to take charge of a troublesome situation, whereas President Truman was prevented from seizing the steel mills in a difficult domestic situation in Youngstown Sheet and Tube Co. v. Sawyer, 343 U.S. 579, 72 S. Ct. 863 (1952). Can the distinction in the outcomes be adequately explained by the penumbra of the *Curtiss-Wright* decision granting a large measure of discretion to the president in the "vast external realm" of foreign affairs? *See* United States v. Curtiss-Wright Export Corp. 299 U.S. 304, 57 S. Ct. 216, 81 L. Ed. 255 (1936).

8. Does *Yoshida* adequately face the argument that delegated authority to impose a tariff, as opposed to other forms of regulation, amounts to taxation without representation? For other cases raising the issue, *see* South Puerto Rico Sugar Co. Trading Corp. v. United States, 334 F.2d 622 (Ct. Cl. 1964), *cert. denied,* 379 U.S. 964 (1965).

9. In what way does the international negotiation process of *Star-Kist* provide an intelligible standard on the delegated power? Is the standard stronger or weaker than that of Yoshida?

10. Would you hesitate to allow the President to impose a quota under one statute and a tariff under another on the same commodity? *See* United States Cane Sugar Refiners' Assn. v. Block, 544 F. Supp. 883 (Ct. Intl. Trade 1982).

11. Suppose the president attempted, without Japanese agreement or con-

gressional action, to restrict Japanese auto imports to the United States. Could he do this under the IEEA? Under §232 of the Trade Expansion Act of 1962 permitting import restraints to be imposed on national security grounds? Under §122 of the Trade Act of 1974? (*See* Selection Documents Supplement.) What does the section mean when it says that presidential actions should be "of broad and uniform application"? (Note that this request may derive from art. 1, §8, cl. 1 of the Constitution.)

12. Much of the delegation legislation in the trade area, (including §201— the "escape clause," §406, dealing with trade with communist countries, as well as the provision in the Trade Act of 1974 concerning the granting of most-favored-nation status) includes one or another form of congressional veto, i.e., a procedure under which one or more houses of Congress, or even a committee, may strike down executive action to which it objects. What will be the impact of Immigration and Naturalization Service v. Chadha, 103 S. Ct. 2764 (1983), on the "legislative override" provisions in the trade area? The Supreme Court held that the congressional veto procedure in that case violated the "presentment" clause of the Constitution, which requires that legislation must be passed by both houses and presented to the president for his signature or veto, *see* art. I, §7 of the U.S. Constitution. *See* the Trade and Tariff Act of 1984, §248 (Appendix X). How can you distinguish a joint resolution from a concurrent resolution of the Congress? What difference might a joint resolution make concerning the "presentment" clause of the Constitution?

In any event, do you think the congressional veto idea is wise or effective? On the legislative veto issue generally, *see* Bruff & Gellhorn, Congressional Control of Administrative Regulation: A Study of Legislative Vetoes, 90 Harv. L. Rev. 1369 (1977).

CONSUMERS UNION OF U.S. v. KISSINGER

506 F.2d 136 (D.C. Cir. 1974), *cert. denied*, 421 U.S. 1004 (1975)

McGOWAN, Circuit Judge:

These consolidated cross-appeals are directed respectively to two declarations made by the District Court in a suit challenging efforts by the Executive Branch of the United States Government to bring about reductions in steel imports by means of self-imposed limitations on foreign producers. Arrayed against each other are a complaining consumers organization, on the one side, and, on the other, the State Department, and foreign and domestic steel producers, individually and in association. In the form eventually taken by the litigation in the District Court, we consider that the only question before us is whether the actions of the Executive were a regulation of foreign commerce foreclosed to it generally by Article I, Section 8, Clause 3 of the Constitution, and in particular by the Trade Expansion Act of 1962, 19 U.S.C. §1801 et seq. To the extent that the District Court declared no such conflict to exist, we affirm its decision.

I

Steel imports into the United States increased more than tenfold over the period 1958-68, with the great bulk of imports coming from Japan and the countries of the European Communities. The effect of this development on the domestic steel industry, which is deemed to be of great importance to the nation's security as well as to its peacetime economy, became a matter of widespread concern. In 1968 bills with substantial backing were introduced in Congress to impose mandatory import quotas on steel.

The Executive Branch regarded the problem created by steel imports as temporary in nature and thus amenable to a short-term solution. It concluded, moreover, that unilaterally imposed mandatory quotas would pose a danger of retaliation under the General Agreement on Trade and Tariffs, prove inflexible and difficult to terminate, and have a seriously adverse impact on the foreign relations of the United States. Import limiting agreements negotiated with other governments were likewise rejected on the State Department's advice that negotiated official restrictions, if achievable, would have political consequences for the foreign governments that would also affect our external affairs adversely. Accordingly, the Executive Branch concluded in 1968 that voluntary import restraint undertakings by foreign producers offered the best hope of alleviating the domestic industry's temporary problems at the least cost to United States foreign, economic and trade policies.

After an initial showing of interest by the foreign producer associations, State Department officials entered into discussions that lasted from June to December, 1968, and resulted in letters being sent to the Secretary in which the Japanese and European producer associations stated their intentions to limit steel shipments to the United States to specified maximum tonnages for each of the years 1969, 1970, and 1971. During 1970, domestic industry and union representatives urged the State Department to seek renewal of the restraints beyond 1971 to provide greater time within which to achieve needed changes, and the House Ways and Means Committee issued a report to like effect. When various executive organs, such as the President's Council of Economic Advisors, had made the same recommendation, the President directed the Secretary to seek extensions of the limitation representations. Such extensions, covering 1972 through 1974, were forthcoming in letters dated early in May, 1972, and announced by the President on May 6.

The two 1972 letters are substantially alike. Each states the signatories' intention to limit exports of steel products to the United States both in aggregate tonnage and, within such limits, in terms of product mix. Each represents that the signatories "hold themselves [itself] ready to consult with representatives of the United States Government on any problem or question that may arise with respect to this voluntary restraint undertaking" and expect the United States Government so to hold itself ready.[6] In addition, each states that

---

[6]It is undisputed that "[i]n negotiating the arrangements and all of their specific terms, the State Department officers explained to the foreign producers that they were being asked to make

its undertaking is based on the assumptions that (1) the effect will not be to place the signatories at a disadvantage relative to each other, (2) the United States will take no unilateral actions to restrict exports by the signatories to the United States, and (3) the representations do not violate United States or international laws.

II

The original complaint in this action contained two separate and distinct claims. They were respectively denominated "FIRST CLAIM (Antitrust)" and "SECOND CLAIM (Unlawful Action by State Department Officials)." The first claim sought declaratory and injunctive relief with respect to what were said to be continuing violations of Section 1 of the Sherman Act, 15 U.S.C. §1. The court was asked to declare the 1972 letters of intent to be in violation of that statute, and to enjoin all of the named defendants from engaging in any act to effectuate the import reductions contemplated by those letters.

The second claim, as its title implies, sought relief only with respect to the State Department defendants, who were said to have violated the law by "facilitating, bringing about and negotiating" the limitations set forth in the 1972 letters of intent without compliance with Section 301 or Section 352 of the Trade Expansion Act of 1962. The relief sought was a declaration that the 1972 export limitations are illegal, and an injunction addressed to all the defendants, prohibiting acts in furtherance of the arrangement.

After answers had been filed by some of the defendants and a motion to dismiss or alternatively for summary judgment had been made by the State Department defendants, the parties stipulated that the first claim in the complaint be dismissed with prejudice, and an amended complaint was filed. The violation of law alleged in the amended complaint was that the State Department officials had acted to regulate foreign commerce within the meaning of Article 1, Section 8, Clause 3 of the Constitution, and of the laws relating to the regulation of foreign trade set forth in Title 19 of the U.S. Code, including Sections 301 and 352 of the Trade Expansion Act of 1962. The foreign producer defendants were said to be violating the same laws to the extent that they took steps to effectuate the limitations sought by the defendant State Department officials acting in excess of their authority. The relief sought was a declaration that the actions of the State Department officials in seeking the export limitations were *ultra vires,* and an injunction against the defendants from furthering the 1972 letters of intent in any way.

Answers to the amended complaint were filed by certain of the defendants and others moved for summary judgment, as did the plaintiff. The matter came on for hearing in the District Court on the cross-motions for summary

---

the requested commitments by the Executive Branch of the United States Government on the ground that they were in the national interest of the United States." JA 155a.

judgment. Its disposition was embodied in what is styled a "Memorandum Opinion, Declaration and Order." The court concluded its discussion of the issues by making two declarations. The first was that "the Executive has no authority under the Constitution or acts of Congress to exempt the Voluntary Restraint Arrangements on Steel from the antitrust laws and that such arrangements are not exempt." The second was that "the Executive is not preempted and may enter into agreements or diplomatic arrangements with private foreign steel concerns so long as these undertakings do not violate legislation regulating foreign commerce, such as the Sherman Act, and that there is no requirement that all such undertakings be first processed under the Trade Expansion Act of 1962."

The court then went on to say that, although the question of whether there was a violation of the Sherman Act was not before it by reason of the stipulated dismissal of the antitrust claim with prejudice, it was apparent to the court that "very serious questions can and should be raised as to the legality of the arrangements under the [Sherman] Act"; and the parties were "urged to reexamine their positions and premises in the light of this memorandum and the declarations made." The court characterized injunctive relief as inappropriate, and denied the respective motions for summary judgment to the extent that they were "inconsistent" with the declarations made by it. It concluded by saying that "no further proceedings are required," and "no costs will be awarded."

Appeals were filed by the State Department defendants and by the domestic and foreign producers. The plaintiff filed a cross-appeal "insofar as any declaration, or ruling on the relief requested, has been decided adversely to the plaintiff."

III

A substantial portion of the briefs and argument before us has been devoted to the Sherman Act. The defendant-appellants are, not surprisingly, perturbed by some of the comments made by the District Court with respect to possible Sherman Act liability. Although the court stated in terms that, by reason of the stipulation of dismissal, "the question of whether or not a violation of the Sherman Act is present is not before the Court to decide," it did not leave the matter at that. One of its declarations is that the Executive has no authority to exempt from the antitrust laws the arrangements here involved, and "that such arrangements are not exempt."

Since there is nothing in the record that shows the Executive as purporting to grant such an exemption, this observation by the court does not have the stature of a declaratory disposition of an actual controversy. The court's other comments in this connection are not couched in adjudicatory form, as indeed, so the court recognized, they could not be in the light of the abandonment by the plaintiff of its antitrust claim. With the declaration vacated, as we shall direct in our judgment, these expressions of the court's opinion are without judicial force or effect and are not appropriate for pursuit upon appeal.

We think that the Sherman Act issue, for all practical purposes, disappeared from this case when the plaintiff, for reasons best known to itself, stipulated its dismissal with prejudice. It is apparent from the face of the original complaint that the Sherman Act claim was originally conceived by the plaintiff as a vital aspect of its lawsuit. Its resolution would almost certainly have required the exploration by adversarial trial of a number of complex questions of fact and law, and the making of legal rulings in an area not distinguished for its simplicity. When the plaintiff, confronted by that formidable prospect, elected to abandon its antitrust claim, the Sherman Act could no longer play a significant part in this controversy, and we have no occasion to concern ourselves with the discussions by the parties of the precise reach of that statute.

IV

We turn, then, to the District Court's declaration that, in respect of the actions of the Executive culminating in the undertakings stated in the letters of intent, "the Executive is not preempted . . . and that there is no requirement that all such undertakings be first processed under the Trade Expansion Act of 1962." That statute, as its name suggests, had as its principal purpose the stimulation of the economic growth of the United States and the maintenance and enlargement of foreign markets for its products.

This was to be achieved through trade agreements reached by the President with foreign countries. Title II of the Act provided that, for a period of five years (1962-67), the President was authorized to enter into such agreements whenever he determined that any existing tariff duties or other import restrictions of either the United States or any foreign country were unduly burdening and restricting the foreign trade of the United States. Upon reaching any such trade agreement, the President was delegated the unmistakably legislative power to modify or continue existing tariffs or other import restrictions, to continue existing duty-free or excise treatment, or to impose additional import restrictions, as he determined to be necessary or appropriate to the carrying out of the agreement. 19 U.S.C. §1821. In connection with the first two of these powers, the Tariff Commission was given an advisory function, which included public hearings; and public hearings were also directed to be held, by an agency designated by the President, in connection with any proposed trade agreement. 19 U.S.C. §§1841, 1843.

Title III of the Trade Expansion Act of 1962, recognizing that domestic interests of various kinds may be adversely affected by concessions granted under trade agreements, authorizes the making of compensating adjustments of various kinds. Section 301 (19 U.S.C. §1901) provides that the Tariff Commission shall undertake investigations of injuries allegedly being done to domestic businesses or workers by such things as increased imports flowing from a trade agreement. After holding public hearings, the Tariff Commission shall make a report to the President. If it affirmatively finds injury to domestic industry, the President may under Section 351 increase or impose tariff duties or other import restrictions, 19 U.S.C. §1981, or alternatively he may under Section 352 negotiate agreements with foreign governments limiting the export from such countries to the United States of the article causing the injury. 19 U.S.C. §1981. If this latter option is taken, the Act provides that the President is authorized to issue regulations governing the entry or withdrawal from warehouse of the article covered by the agreement.

The foregoing description of the Trade Expansion Act of 1962 covers, among others, Sections 301 and 352. They are the only provisions expressly identified in the amended complaint as constituting the allegedly preemptive exercise by Congress of its constitutional power to regulate foreign commerce that, so it is said, forecloses the actions of the Executive challenged in this case. The description extends also to Sections 302 and 351, which are referred to in plaintiff-appellant Consumers Union's brief, as is also Section 232, 19 U.S.C. §1862. This last is the so-called national security clause which provides that the President shall not decrease or eliminate tariffs or other import restrictions if to do so would impair the national security. The Director of the Office of Emergency Planning is directed to investigate any situation where imports threaten to impair the national security; and if he finds such threat, and the President concurs, action shall be taken "to adjust the imports" of the article in question, which means that the article may by regulation be excluded from entry or withdrawal from warehouse.

What is clear from the foregoing is a purpose on the part of Congress to delegate legislative power to the President for use by him in certain defined circumstances and in furtherance of certain stated purposes. Without such a delegation, the President could not increase or decrease tariffs, issue commands to the customs service to refuse or delay entry of goods into the country, or impose mandatory import quotas. To make use of such delegated power, the President would of course be required to proceed strictly in accordance with the procedures specified in the statutes conferring the delegation. Where, as here, he does not pretend to the possession of such power, no such conformity is required.

The steel import restraints do not purport to be enforceable, either as contracts or as governmental actions with the force of law; and the Executive has no sanctions to invoke in order to compel observance by the foreign producers of their self-denying representations. They are a statement of intent on the part of the foreign producer associations. The signatories' expectations, not unreasonably in light of the reception given their undertakings by the Executive, are that the Executive will consult with them over mutual concerns about the steel import situation, and that it will not have sudden recourse to the unilateral steps available to it under the Trade Expansion Act to impose legal restrictions on importation. The President is not bound in any way to refrain from taking such steps if he later deems them to be in the national interest, or if consultation proves unavailing to meet unforeseen difficulties; and certainly the Congress is not inhibited from enacting any legislation it desires to regulate by law the importation of steel.

The formality and specificity with which the undertakings are expressed does not alter their essentially precatory nature insofar as the Executive Branch is concerned. In effect the President has said that he will not initiate steps to limit steel imports by law if the volume of such imports remains within tolerable bounds. Communicating, through the Secretary of State, what levels he considers tolerable merely enables the foreign producers to conform their actions accordingly, and to avoid the risk of guessing at what is acceptable. Regardless of whether the producers run afoul of the antitrust laws in the manner of their response, nothing in the process leading up to the voluntary undertakings or the process of consultation under them differentiates what the Executive has done here from what all Presidents, and to a lesser extent all high executive officers, do when they admonish an industry with the express or implicit warning that action, within either their existing powers or enlarged powers to be sought, will be taken if a desired course is not followed voluntarily.

The question of congressional preemption is simply not pertinent to executive action of this sort. Congress acts by making laws binding, if valid, on their objects and the President, whose duty it is faithfully to execute the laws. From the comprehensive pattern of its legislation regulating trade and governing the circumstances under and procedures by which the President is authorized to act to limit imports, it appears quite likely that Congress has by statute occupied the field of *enforceable* import restrictions, if it did not, indeed, have exclusive possession thereof by the terms of Article I of the Constitution. There is no potential for conflict, however, between exclusive congressional regulation of foreign commerce—regulation enforced ultimately by halting violative importations at the border—and assurances of voluntary restraint given to the Executive. Nor is there any warrant for creating such a conflict by straining to endow the voluntary undertakings with legally binding effect, contrary to the manifest understanding of all concerned and, indeed, to the manner in which departures from them have been treated.

In holding, as we do, that the District Court did not err in declining to characterize the conduct of the Executive here under attack as in conflict with the Trade Expansion Act of 1962, we are not to be understood as intimating any views as to the relationship of the Sherman Act to the events in issue here. The Sherman Act is not, as noted above, one of the regulatory statutes charged as preempting the field, and the question of its possible substantive applicability vanished from this case with the original complaint.

The declaration in the District Court's order with respect to antitrust exemption is vacated, and the declaratory aspect of that order is confined to the proposition that the State Department defendants were not precluded from following the course they did by anything in the Constitution or Title 19 of the U.S. Code. As so confined, the order appealed from is affirmed.

It is so ordered.

LEVENTHAL, Circuit Judge (dissenting):

With all respect, I must record my disagreement with the ruling of the majority that the President had the authority to negotiate detailed arrangements with foreign steel producers to limit their shipments of products to the United States. . . .

I am not persuaded by the majority's pronouncement that the statutes are not pertinent to the present case because the arrangements, incorporated in letters from foreign steel producers which describe themselves as "voluntary restraint undertakings," did not contemplate the mandate of judicial enforceability. These undertakings by the President and foreign steel producers were carefully structured in considerable detail, obviously after detailed consultation with American steel interests, without exposure to the kind of input by purchasers that would have been provided if the Congressional procedures had been followed. These undertakings are bilateral, and establish obligations. Their bite persists notwithstanding the majority's effort to coat them bland vanilla. The majority tolerates executive detours around the limits staked by Congress in the field it has occupied. Its concept that a different route is available for executive arrangements discerned as not intended for judicial enforcement is, in my view, unsound. . . .

The majority says that the steel import restraints are in harmony with the statutory program because they are not enforceable in courts of law; they are said to be mere precatory expressions which Congress never intended to circumscribe by the procedural requirements applicable to mandatory import controls.

This response presents an issue that focuses on the nature and effect of the undertakings before us. Turning first to effect, Presidents may engage in many activities that have a perceivable economic impact upon the volume of commodities imported. The effects vary in terms of their stability, their specificity, and their duration. At one pole would lie general Presidential exhortations— say, to consumers to "Buy American"—or general alarms, announcing that protective legislation will be sought if imports are not contained. Such appeals are valid even though they may have the effect of inhibiting some market behavior, and no one would view them as prohibited by even the strongest Congressional "free trade" legislation. At the other extreme is a Presidential proclamation that foreign-trade commodities will not be allowed to enter, which plainly cannot be reconciled with the existing statutory structure, or legitimated by reference to some aura of "inherent" Presidential authority. In between is a continuum of restrictions. In my view, the comprehensive statutory program constrains some but not all of the activities in this continuum. Here, the undertakings have an economic effect that parallels that of import quotas proclaimed by the President.

Turning to its nature, the Presidential action here goes far beyond a speech or announcement—even one preceded by "feelers" to foreign governments to ascertain how much they will tolerate. Far from being mere expressions of desire and intent, these are solemn negotiated bilateral understandings.

The arrangements are not unilateral announcements but the culmination of bilateral discussions that were not only participated in, but initiated by State Department officials. Although the final letters that embody the specific limitations are astutely couched in a litany of a "voluntary restraint undertaking" on the part of the foreign steel producers, the circumstances are instinct with bilateral undertaking.

Obviously, foreign firms that have vigorously marketed their products in the United States do not voluntarily withhold production without some reciprocal aspect indicating that forbearance is to their advantage. Here, the undertakings of the foreign producers rest on Government assurances that disadvantages would be equalized among producers; that the United States Government—or at least the not uninfluential Executive Branch—would not take or start other measures to limit steel imports or increase duties; and that the transaction would not violate any law of the United States.

The specificity of the limitations imposed by the undertakings also indicates that they were the result of bilateral bargaining and agreement.

Significantly, by the terms of the arrangements, the parties contemplate continuing consultations. The foreign steel producers "hold themselves ready to consult" on any question that may arise on the interpretation of their "undertaking." Does one accompany a unilateral declaration of intent with an offer to "consult" about what he has declared? When the foreign producers go on to say that their undertakings are based on their expectation that the United States Government will consult with them on questions that arise, and the White House releases these letters, along with a detailed Fact Sheet, as a "welcome development" that is the product of Executive negotiation can it be meaningfully denied that there is a reciprocal undertaking by the United States Government to engage in consultations with the producers? . . .

There is only local color, no legal significance, in the fact that in this case the Chairmen of key House and Senate Committees concerned with regulation of international trade voiced their approval on the occasion of the White House announcement of the undertakings. The Government does not contend, and I do not see how it could rightfully contend, that such participation by particular Congressmen can invest the President with executive authority not otherwise possessed, or constitute a legally decisive definition of the demarcation between the zone that belongs to Congress as a whole and that which belongs solely to the President. . . .

NOTES AND QUESTIONS

1. How could Consumers Union have "standing" to bring an action like this? Could a consumer of footwear challenge an Orderly Marketing Agreement (OMA) negotiated by the president on footwear outside the context of Section 201 of the Trade Act of 1974 (*see* Selected Documents Supplement). *See* Sneaker Circus v. Carter, 566 F.2d 396 (2d Cir. 1977). What about a competitor? What are the differences in the two situations?

2. How does the issue in this case differ from that in the preceding delegation cases? How should the court have come out if it held that the agreements were binding?

3. If the executive was acting in so informal a manner as not to gain the force of law, should its action have gained antitrust immunity?

4. Should the preceding argument really be defeated by the fact that plaintiff dropped its antitrust claim (probably to avoid costs and delays)?

5. Do you think that the plaintiff made a strategic error by dropping the antitrust claim? How would the antitrust claim come out today? *See* §607 of the Trade Act of 1974.

6. If one accepts Judge Leventhal's view that the agreements had significant force, does it follow that they are unconstitutional?

7. Is there a "right to import"? Is there a property right of some sort in the unhindered ability to import articles from other countries? *See* Norwegian Nitrogen Products v. United States, 288 U.S. 294 (1933). If there is no right to import, how can there be a right to be heard? How extensive are hearings rights under §201(c) of the Trade Act of 1974? Note that "military and foreign affairs functions" are exempted under the Administrative Procedure Act's rulemaking and adjudicating procedures. See 5 U.S.C. §§553(a)(1) and 554(a)(4). Is this an unfair deprivation for citizens of their right to be heard in trade-related controversies? If hearings rights are required as a matter of due process and fairness for welfare recipients (*see* Goldberg v. Kelly, 397 U.S. 254 (1970)) should U.S. citizens involved in trade have a lower degree of constitutional protection?

8. How do "voluntary" import restraints differ from OMAs? See §203 of the Trade Act of 1974. What are the antitrust questions raised by voluntary restraints that would not be raised by an OMA negotiated (or imposed) pursuant to §203 of the Trade Act of 1974? Do you see any foreign relations benefits to be obtained from going the "voluntary," as opposed to the OMA, or quota, route?

9. In congressional delegation of the power to modify tariffs through international agreement (the reciprocal trade negotiation power), where is the intelligible standard? Would you prefer to rest constitutionality on an argument that the negotiation process is an effective limit on discretion or on an argument that the agreement is a form of international settlement (as in *Dames & Moore*)?

10. At least 20 agencies (including some cabinet departments) apart from the Congress, have a major role in the formulation of U.S. trade and investment policy. Do you think it would be advisable to have one single cabinet-level department for U.S. trade and investment policy?

Note the comment of Sen. Lloyd Bentsen (D-Tex.):

Foreign economic policy in the United States is shaped not systematically, but almost by accident. It is a least common denominator, worked out, as some have so aptly put it, by a kind of guerilla warfare among the Departments of State,

Treasury, Agriculture, the Federal Reserve Board, and a whole host of other Executive Branch agencies.

Note also the proposals being floated by the Reagan administration to reorganize the international trade functions of the executive branch. Under the 1983 plan of the Reagan administration, a new cabinet-level Department of International Trade and Industry would be created, merging the U.S. Trade Representative's Office with Commerce's International Trade Administration. The plan also calls for abolishing the Commerce Department by merging those functions not subsumed in the new department into preexisting executive branch organizations. While it appears unlikely that the 1983 proposal will be implemented, there is no doubt that the organization of U.S. foreign policy will be a hotly discussed topic for years to come, given the increased political salience of U.S. trade policy. *See also* I. Destler, Making Foreign Economic Policy (1980); S. Cohen, The Making of United States International Economic Policy (1977); Green, Reorganization of Trade Policymaking, 13 Cornell Intl. L.J. 221 (1980); Note: Reorganization Plan No. 3 of 1979; Revamping U.S. Trade, 2 N.W. J. Intl. L. & Bus. 224 (1980); and Palmeter and Kossl, Restructuring Executive Branch Trade Responsibilities: A Half-Step Forward, 12 Law & Poly. Intl. Bus. 611 (1980).

How might your position on these issues differ if you represented:

(a)   a U.S. exporter?
(b)   a U.S. high-tech industry?
(c)   a U.S. industry threatened by foreign competition?
(d)   a U.S. labor union?
(e)   the State Department?
(f)   the European Economic Community?

11. Are you satisfied that the Congress should delegate large powers in the realm of international economic relations to the executive branch? How can you make the case that the executive branch will be superior to the legislature in carrying out trade and investment policy?

12. In order to limit the exportation of timber from the United States to Japan, due to a perceived short supply of timber in the United States, the president, pursuant to the Export Administration Act, imposes a duty on logs exported from the United States. Redwood, Inc., a major U.S. exporter of timber, seeks an injunction against the U.S. government on the ground that such a duty is unconstitutional. What result? *See* U.S. Constitution, art. I, §9, cl.5. Would the result differ if the export tax were assessed by the State of California? What if the president sought to restrain exports by the imposition of quantitative restraints?

13. In order to improve the position of its local producers, the State of Texas imposes a tariff on rice imported from other U.S. states as well as foreign countries. Husk, Inc., a Louisiana rice exporter, seeks to restrain this duty on the ground that such a duty against a U.S. "import" is unconstitu-

tional. What result? *See* U.S. Constitution, art. I, §10, cl.2. What if the products involved were beer, wine, or distilled spirits? How might your answer differ? *See* U.S. Constitution, amend. XXI, §2, and Note, State Control of Alcoholic Beverages in Interstate Commerce, 27 N.Y.U.L. Rev. 127 (1952).

C.   THE INTERNATIONAL SYSTEM: GATT

The emphasis of this chapter, up until now, has been on the U.S. process, but that process is embedded in the international framework of the GATT. The following materials highlight several of the key provisions of the GATT, and then focus on the GATT's negotiation process and the way that U.S. law relates to it. The GATT's dispute settlement procedures and the remainder of its substantive provisions are considered in more detail in later chapters.

1.   *Background*

The GATT's broadest obligations are stated in the first two articles. Article I incorporates the Most-Favored-Nation principle, a principle, as noted above, of enormous import in a world tempted toward bilateralism and regionalism. Article II adds the concept of a "tariff concession," a commitment to keep a tariff at a reduced level to reciprocate other nation's corresponding commitments on other tariffs. This helps make tariff negotiations effective. But these obligations are balanced by two kinds of broad exception. First, under certain conditions specified in Article XXIV there may be a custom union or free trade area like the European Economic Community (EEC). Second, a new part, consisting of Articles XXXVI through XXXVIII, was added in 1965 to cover the special problems of developing nations and permit some discrimination in their favor.

The second block of articles, Articles III through XXI, governs specific forms of discrimination against foreign goods and regulates the various processes of tariff adjustment. For example, Article III requires that foreign goods after clearing customs generally be treated the same as domestic goods—an effort to restrict hidden discrimination. Articles VI and XVI regulate subsidies, countervailing duties, and antidumping duties. Article XI governs quotas and XVII covers state trading. Article XIX deals with the escape clause—the political safety valve for a government to protect an industry being seriously harmed by imports. And Article XX deals, albeit weakly, with export restraints. Under the Protocol of Provisional Application, these provisions amount to goals rather than immediate requirements. A party is only required not to enact *new* trade barriers inconsistent with the GATT; preexisting trade barriers need not be removed.

Much of the remainder of the original text deals with dispute settlement. In reading it, one should remember an important interpretation that reflects the GATT's origin as a substitute for a full-fledged international trade organization: the words "Contracting Parties" mean "the contracting parties acting jointly."[16] Thus, under Article XXV, the Contracting Parties have the power to waive Gatt requirements. Article XXII creates a consultation procedure. And Article XXIII on "Nullification or Impairment" provides a mechanism to declare a party in violation of the agreement and authorizes sanctions under certain circumstances. These sanctions amount to the right to exclude certain exports from the offending trade partner.

JACKSON, THE GENERAL AGREEMENT ON TARIFFS AND TRADE

W. Surrey and D. Wallace (eds.), A Lawyer's Guide to International Business Transactions, Part I (1977)

THE SUBSTANTIVE OBLIGATIONS OF GATT

Although GATT was designed primarily as a tariff-reducing agreement, it was realized from the beginning that substantive obligations governing other ways in which countries could limit the inflow of goods were necessary; otherwise, the tariff reduction obligations would be meaningless. If countries could impose quotas, embargoes, special internal taxes on imports, and so forth, then an agreement by a country to lower the tariff on a particular item would not result in any more imports of that item. For this reason, GATT became a general code of conduct relating to international trade. . . .

.4(a) TARIFF CONCESSIONS (ARTICLE II)

The central obligation of GATT is the *tariff concession*, which is a commitment by a GATT contracting party to levy no more than a stated tariff on a particular item. Thousands of these commitments are contained in the *schedules*. Each member of GATT (with a few exceptions) has a schedule that lists the detailed item-by-item tariff concessions negotiated during the six major tariff negotiation rounds of GATT.

During the first five of these rounds, the tariff negotiating procedure was basically the same. Those countries which desired to participate in the new tariff round formed a *tariff negotiating committee* (TNC), and under the supervision of this committee each nation prepared a list of the tariff cuts that it desired from other participants. The basic rule was that any country which was the principal supplier of the commodity or article concerned could request a tariff cut from the importing country. These *request lists* were circulated. The

[16]GATT Article XXV, ¶1.

requesting countries would then prepare *offer lists*, indicating the tariff concessions or tariff bindings that they were willing to enter into in order to "pay for" their requested concessions.

Subsequently, countries would pair off and enter into bilateral discussions during the course of the conference, seeking to establish the exact concession that each would grant the other. Because of the most-favored-nation clause in GATT, it was understood that concessions granted to any participant would be available to all members of GATT. Consequently, when a pair of nations concluded a general framework for agreement between themselves, they would then go to other nations and continue negotiating to obtain the maximum concessions for their own offers. Toward the end of the tariff round or conference, all lists of offered concessions would be circulated, and every nation would judge whether the totality of offers during the conference sufficed to give it the required reciprocity for the totality of its own commitments or concessions.

This process was cumbersome, and partly as a consequence of difficulties which arose during the Dillon Round with the European Economic Community negotiating as an entity for the first time, it was decided during the initial stages of the Kennedy Round to conduct negotiations on a different basis. A "linear cut" was suggested, by which each nation would agree that its initial offer would be to cut all of its own tariffs by 50 percent. Each nation would be allowed to table a restricted list of *exceptions*. The negotiations would focus on allowance of an exception. Although this was the general procedure that was followed in the Kennedy Round, agriculture and certain basic commodities were exempted from the "linear cut," and a few nations were permitted to opt out of the "linear cut" and negotiate on an item-by-item basis.

A new GATT round of tariff and trade negotiations was launched by a ministerial meeting in Tokyo in September 1973. U.S. participation in this "Tokyo Round" was made definite by the passage of the Trade Act of 1974 (signed into law January 3, 1975). . . .

[Note that, under the terms of this Act, many of the resulting agreements had to be approved by Congress—as they were in the 1979 Trade Act.]

.4(b)   MOST-FAVORED-NATION (ARTICLE I)

By the twentieth century, treaty practice had already established the most-favored-nation (MFN) clause as a central obligation of international trade policy. MFN clauses, however, could be either conditional or unconditional. Conditional MFN signified that countries granting favors to a trading partner would also be required to grant it to their other trading partners if the latter gave something in return. Unconditional MFN required that when one country granted a favor to another country, it must also extend it to its other trading partners without receiving anything additional in return from them. The United States followed a conditional MFN policy until 1923 when it changed its policy to one of unconditional MFN. The unconditional MFN clause was written into a number of bilateral treaties and, by the time GATT was drafted in 1946-47, it was generally accepted among the participating countries that an unconditional MFN clause would be a central feature of GATT.

The first article of GATT now requires nondiscriminatory treatment in the importation and exportation of goods among all members of GATT. MFN has the advantage of generalizing the reduction in trade barriers much more quickly than might occur through conditional MFN or no MFN at all. On the other hand, MFN makes the negotiation of reductions in trade or tariff barriers more difficult because whenever a reduction is provided for one country, the country granting the reduction must consider the effect it will have on all its trading partners. There will be a natural reluctance to grant a tariff concession for the benefit of a country that has only a small percentage of the import trade in an item when such concession will benefit other countries who may not "pay" for it.

There are a variety of exceptions to the MFN principle in GATT. First, at the time GATT was drafted, there were a number of countries that had preferential arrangements with certain trading partners. This was particularly true of the British Commonwealth group of countries and of some of the other colonial relationships between European and African or Asian countries. Although the United States attempted to negotiate these away during the formation of GATT, the attempt did not entirely succeed and certain exceptions were engrafted in annexes of GATT, allowing these *historical preferences* to continue under a system that would generally see them reduced in importance over time.

In addition to these historical exceptions, there are various provisions of GATT, some of which will be discussed later, that can give rise to exceptions. For instance, the waiver provision of GATT can provide an exception to Article I of GATT, as was the case in the waiver for the generalized preference scheme for developing countries. Certain national security exceptions could depart from MFN (Article XXI), and there are possibilities for other exceptions under Articles XIV (balance of payments problems), XXIV (customs unions and free trade areas), XX (general health and welfare exceptions), and so forth.

.4(c)   NATIONAL TREATMENT (ARTICLE III)

Although the MFN clause provides for nondiscriminatory treatment among nations, the national treatment clause provides a somewhat more limited obligation of nondiscrimination as between domestic and foreign goods. Basically, the national treatment obligation requires a country to treat imports, once they have crossed the border and cleared customs, the same as domestic goods. Thus, internal taxes cannot discriminate against imported goods. Likewise, governmental regulations are not allowed to apply in a more onerous fashion to imported goods. An explicit exception is made for government procurement or government purchases (an exception that is becoming increasingly significant).

.4(d)   QUOTAS (ARTICLE XI)

The importance of nontariff barriers can be easily illustrated if one remembers that, despite a commitment to impose a low or zero tariff on an item, quotas can limit or prevent any imports of that item. This result would deny the country to whom a concession had been made the full or partial benefit that it had sought by the concession. Quotas are nontariff barriers occurring at the border. During the depression of the 1930's, quotas were heavily relied upon and are thought to have been a major cause of the reduction of international trade. If border protection is to be used, economists and other policy makers generally prefer tariffs to quotas, since in the case of tariffs some of the monopoly profits attributed to import protection are captured by the government through the revenue from the tariffs; and the extent of protection granted by a tariff is limited since some firms may be able to produce cheaply enough to "hurdle" the tariff and sell imported goods anyway. Tariffs are also more "visible"—the consumer can see their effect on the price he pays.

One of the most troublesome situations to arise under Article III concerns "latent" discrimination. In some cases, regulations on their face appear to apply equally to domestic and imported goods, but, because of certain factual circumstances, they have the effect of applying more onerously to imported goods. For instance, a safety regulation that requires in-plant inspection of the manufacturing process, coupled with the lack of funds for personnel to take inspection trips abroad, can effectively prohibit the use of imported articles of certain types, such as gas cylinders. A number of the official disputes that have arisen through the dispute settlement procedure in GATT have dealt with the national treatment clause of GATT.

A particularly significant problem with the national treatment clause has been tied to border tax adjustments. The national treatment clause explicitly provides that goods that enter a country can be taxed to the extent that domestic goods are also taxed. It likewise provides that the tax on domestic goods can be remitted at the border when the domestic goods are exported. This exception applies to a *tax on products*—that is, a so-called indirect tax—whereas it does not apply to a tax that is imposed upon a firm or unit of production, such as domestic personal or corporate income taxes. Consequently, when a country relies more heavily on a system of indirect taxation, for example, a value added tax or national sales tax for its governmental revenues, it may have an international trade advantage over a country that places greater reliance on income taxes. The actual difference in effect of these two types of taxes is disputed by economists and lawyers, and the situation is anything but clear. In an era of floating exchange rates, it has been argued that once the initial impact of the imposition of a border tax adjustment has occurred, and the exchange rate adjusted to that impact, there is no further advantage to the border tax adjustment country.

RESTATEMENT OF FOREIGN RELATIONS LAW OF THE UNITED STATES, TENTATIVE DRAFT NO. 4

§§801-804 (1983)

CHAPTER 1

LAW OF INTERNATIONAL TRADE

§801. Definitions

As used in this Restatement:

(1) "Most-favored-nation" treatment by a state means according to another state or its nationals or goods treatment no less favorable than is accorded to any other state, its nationals or goods.

(2) "National treatment" by a state means according to the nationals of another state treatment equivalent to that which the state accords to its own nationals.

(3) "Reciprocity" means according to another state or to its nationals or goods treatment equivalent to that which the other state accords to the first state or to its nationals or goods.

(4) A "preference" means a grant by a state to another state of a benefit not accorded to all other states. . . .

§802. Most-Favored-Nation Treatment as to Imports

(1) A state party to the General Agreement on Tariffs and Trade or a comparable international agreement is obligated, subject to specified exceptions, to accord to products imported from other states parties treatment that is no less favorable than that accorded to like products from any other state.

(2) Under the law of the United States, imports from all states are entitled to most-favored-nation treatment, except as otherwise provided by law.

§803. Commitment to Tariffs Bound by
International Agreement

(1) A state party to the General Agreement on Tariffs and Trade is obligated not to increase a tariff to a level above the rate to which it is bound by its inclusion in a schedule to which the state is committed.

(2) Subject to limitations specified in the General Agreement on Tariffs and Trade, a state may withdraw a binding on a product if it negotiates substantially equivalent concessions on other products of trade interest to the principal beneficiaries of the original binding.

(3) Under the law of the United States, the President may proclaim modification of tariffs in implementation of international agreements, under authority delegated to him by Congress. . . .

REPORTERS' NOTES

1. *The binding process.* The binding process takes place largely at the successive meetings of the Contracting Parties of the GATT, referred to as "rounds". Past

"rounds" have taken place as follows: Geneva, 1947; Annecy, 1948; Torquay, 1950; Geneva, 1956; Geneva, 1960-61 ("Dillon"); Geneva, 1964-67 ("Kennedy"); and Geneva, 1973-79 ("Tokyo").

The presence of all the Contracting Parties makes it possible for State X to make a concession that benefits exports from State Y even though it receives no corresponding concessions from that state, because it simultaneously receives one from State Z. As a result of the most-favored-nation element any concession benefits not only the state that sought or negotiated for the concession but all other states as well. Negotiating rules are established prior to each round. In the earlier rounds, the rules provided for negotiation item-by-item with the principal supplier; when that proved cumbersome a "linear technique" was used under which states were expected to offer a flat percentage cut on all tariffs and to negotiate about exceptions.

2. *Definition of "Principal supplier"*. The determination of who has a "principal supplying interest" (Comment *b*) affects both negotiations of concessions and renegotiations after withdrawal of concessions. Note 4 ad Article XXVIII provides that a party should only be found to have such an interest if it "had, over a reasonable period of time prior to the negotiations, a larger share in the market of the applicant contracting party than a contracting party with which the concession was initially negotiated". The note also provides for situations in which discriminatory quantitative restrictions prevented a party from achieving such a share. The United States was in such a situation with respect to poultry following Germany's inclusion in the European Economic Community. Germany had become bound as a result of negotiations with Denmark. In 1958, the United States sold only one-third as much poultry to Germany as did Denmark, moved to approximate equality with Denmark in 1959 and exceeded it in 1960, the year the negotiations began. On Germany's joining the European Community, European poultry displaced imports from the United States. In the ensuing procedures it was assumed the United States was a principal supplier. See Walker, "Dispute Resolution: The Chicken War", 58 Am. J. Intl. L. 671 (1964); 1 Chayes, Ehrlich & Lowenfeld, International Legal Process 240-305 (1968). When the United States, as compensation, applied higher duties to various products of which the European Economic Community was the principal supplier, those higher duties were applied also to like products coming from other states. See Star Indus. Inc. v. United States, 462 F.2d 557 (C.C.P.A. 1972); Lowenfeld, "Doing Unto Others, The Chicken War Ten Years After," 4 J. Mar. L. & C. 599 (1973).

3. *Measurement of "substantially equivalent concessions"*. The simplest measure of substantial equivalence is the amount of trade in the period before the unbinding, perhaps adjusted to reflect trends. Thus, if country X withdraws a concession covering $25 million of exports from Y, Y may levy a burden on $25 million of X's exports. A more sophisticated measure would be the change in the rate of the tariff, or the potential trade effect of such change, but such calculations are generally regarded as too complex to be administratively fea-

sible. See the decision, dated Nov. 21, 1963, of the panel on poultry established in connection with the United States-European Economic Community poultry dispute referred to in Reporters' Note 2, reprinted in 3 Intl. Leg. Mat. 116. . . .

§804. *Quantitative Restrictions on Imports*

(1) A state party to the General Agreement on Tariffs and Trade may not impose quantitative restrictions on imports from other states parties, except such as are imposed for reasons of national security, for balance of payments purposes or as part of an agricultural commodity support, or as a measure of general law enforcement.

(2) Under the law of the United States, quantitative restrictions on imports are authorized only in situations of emergency import relief (§808) and for particular products expressly authorized by statute. . . .

NOTES AND QUESTIONS

1. What does "nullification and impairment," as used in Article XXIII, mean? Can there be a nullification and impairment due to an action that does not violate the GATT? *See* Hudec, Retaliation Against "Unreasonable" Foreign Trade Practices: The New Section 301 and GATT Nullification and Impairment, 59 Minn. L. Rev. 461 (1975); R. Hudec, The GATT Legal System and World Trade Diplomacy, Chapters 4 and 14 (1975); and J. Jackson, World Trade and the Law of GATT, Chapter 8 (1969).

2. Is the binding of a concession something in addition to the original concession so that a negotiating party must pay for it with an additional reciprocal concession? *See generally* J. Jackson, World Trade and the Law of GATT, Chapter 10 (1969).

3. What is the principle behind the Most-Favored-Nation (MFN) concept? Why do you imagine the MFN concept came into being? What are the exceptions to MFN treatment? Why might MFN be more appropriate in a tariff than a nontariff context? How might MFN make trade negotiations easier or harder? *See* J. Jackson, World Trade and the Law of GATT, Chapter 11 (1969); and Hufbauer, Erb, and Starr, The GATT Codes and the Unconditional Most-Favored-Nation Principle, 12 Law & Poly. Intl. Bus. 59 (1980).

4. What is the rationale of the "customs union" exception of Article XXIV? What distinction is there between a customs union and a free trade area? How would you decide whether or not a specific customs union is consistent with the GATT? For more information on economic integration, *see* B. Balassa, The Theory of Economic Integration (1961), and S. Dell, Trade Blocs and Common Markets (1963).

5. Is a mandated governmental counterpurchasing requirement for private or public entities consistent with the letter of GATT? The spirit? Consider the

application to counterpurchase requirements of the GATT Articles XVII, XXIII, I, II, III. *See* Gadbaw, The Implications of Countertrade under the General Agreement on Tariffs and Trade, in B. Fisher and K. Harte (eds.) Barter in the World Economy (1985).

6. Canada permits advertisers who place commercials on Canadian television stations to deduct the cost of such commercials as a business expense. It denies deductibility for cross-border advertising placed on U.S. television stations whose services are received in Canada on cable systems and out-of-the-air. What GATT obligations, if any, does this violate? *See* Articles I, III, and IV of the GATT. *See* Fisher and Steinhardt, Section 301 of the Trade Act of 1974: Protection from U.S. Exporters of Goods, Services and Capital, 14 Law & Poly. Intl. Bus. 569, 641, 652 (1982); Comment: Purging Madison Avenue from Canadian Cable Television, 7 Law & Poly. Intl. Bus. 655 (1975); Stoler, The Border Broadcasting Dispute, 6 Intl. Trade L.J. 39 (1980-1981).

7. Why do you suppose the GATT, in Article XI, expresses a bias against quantitative restrictions and a stated preference for tariffs if import restraints are found to be necessary? Does this make sense as a matter of economics or is this bias political in nature? Why is there an exception permitting quantitative restraints on agricultural products under certain circumstances?

8. Title IV of the Trade and Tariff Act of 1984 authorizes the president to enter into a free trade agreement with Israel on behalf of the United States provided appropriate approval is given by the Congress. Is this bilateral type of agreement consistent with Article I of the GATT? How would the United States assure its conformity with the GATT? As a matter of trade policy, is it wise for the United States to act on a bilateral, as opposed to a multilateral, basis?

9. What if the United States were to enter a sectoral free trade area agreement with Canada covering only petrochemicals. Would this be consistent with Article XXIV of the GATT? How could the United States assure its conformity with the GATT? *See* GATT Article XXV.

10. Suppose the automobile industry proposed the following "tax equalizer" scheme, arguing that under the current U.S. tax system, with its emphasis on payroll taxes and income taxes, foreign automobile companies or their U.S. subsidiaries pay relatively lower taxes than do U.S. automobile manufacturers. The industry also argues that the scheme would raise at least $1 billion annually in terms of additional revenue for the U.S. government at the expense of foreign automobile manufacturers, would not increase the cost of U.S. vehicles, and would increase U.S. employment by inducing foreign automobile companies to locate in the United States.

Consider the proposal and answer these questions:

(a) Is the excise tax proposal compatible with the national treatment obligation of Article III of the GATT? Other provisions of the GATT? The non-tariff barrier codes adopted in The Multilateral Trade Negotiations?

(b) What possible defenses of the proposal might be raised?

(c) Would you support this proposal if you were president of the United Automobile Workers? Why or why not?

PROPOSAL TO NEUTRALIZE JAPANESE TAX COST ADVANTAGE

1. A 5% excise tax should be imposed on the invoice price of all vehicles sold in the country. The tax would be imposed when a vehicle is sold or consigned by the automobile manufacturer or its U.S. distributor/importer subsidiary to an independent dealer or other concern. If the automobile manufacturer or its U.S. distributor/importer subsidiary fails to pay the tax, the independent dealer becomes liable for the tax. . . .

2. The automobile manufacturer or its U.S. distributor/importer subsidiary could use the following taxes as a credit against the excise tax:

(1) The employers' share of Social Security taxes paid by the automobile manufacturer or its U.S. distributor/importer subsidiary for the current year and for the five previous years;

(2) The employees' share of Social Security taxes paid by the automobile manufacturer or its U.S. distributor/importer subsidiary for the current year and for the five previous years; and

(3) Beginning in 1985, one dollar of federal income tax paid by the automobile manufacturer or its U.S. distributor/importer subsidiary could be used as a credit to eliminate two dollars of excise tax.

Bibliographical Note

The classic treatise on the GATT is J. Jackson, World Trade and the Law of GATT (1969). Also of particular interest is K. Dam, The GATT: Law and International Economic Organization (1970), and R. Hudec, The GATT Legal System and World Trade Diplomacy (1975), which contain a number of case studies of GATT law in operation. For consideration of the GATT in the post-MTN era, *see* Wolff, The Larger Political and Economic Role of the Tokyo Round, 12 Law & Poly. Intl. Bus. 1 (1980), and Jackson, The Birth of the GATT-MTN System, 12 Law & Poly. Intl. Bus. 21 (1980).

For an analysis of the substantive side of the MTN in terms of economic results, *see* W. Cline, Trade Negotiations in the Tokyo Round: A Quantitative Assessment (1978).

For a fascinating analysis of the politics of the Kennedy Round, *see* E. Preeg, Traders and Diplomats (1970).

2. The Negotiation Process

One of the most important values of the GATT is as a framework for negotiating trade agreements. Consider the following report of the most recent of these negotiations.

THE TOKYO ROUND OF MULTILATERAL TRADE NEGOTIATIONS, GENERAL AGREEMENT ON TARIFFS AND TRADE: REPORT BY THE DIRECTOR-GENERAL OF GATT

1-16, 40-52 (1977)

PART I: THE NEGOTIATIONS

CHAPTER I: INTRODUCTION

The Multilateral Trade Negotiations under the auspices of the General Agreement on Tariffs and Trade (GATT) were opened in September 1973 at a Meeting of Ministers in Tokyo.

Ninety-nine countries of widely differing levels of development and economic systems, both GATT and non-GATT members, have been involved in the Negotiations: the industrialized countries of Western Europe and North America; less-industrialized countries, such as Australia and New Zealand; countries of Eastern Europe; and the whole range of developing countries from the least developed to the most advanced. . . .

In the period between the Kennedy Round and the Tokyo Round there had been a significant shift in the relative weight of the major economic powers in international trade. The European Communities had grown to become the world's largest trading entity, while Japan's economic progress had been such that it was now among the top three trading nations. The result was that in the Tokyo Round three economic powers—the United States, the European Communities and Japan—would together take the lead and largely govern the direction, pace and content of the Negotiations.

The other outstanding difference concerned the developing countries. For the first time in GATT multilateral trade negotiations the problems of these countries assumed a prominent place, reflecting their increased economic and political significance in international affairs, and the importance and weight of their participation in the Negotiations themselves. . . .

CHAPTER III: OPENING OF THE MULTILATERAL TRADE NEGOTIATIONS

The Meeting of Ministers took place in Tokyo from 12 to 14 September 1973. At its conclusion, the representatives of the 102 countries present unanimously adopted the Tokyo Declaration and launched the Multilateral Trade Negotiations, participation in which would be open to GATT members and non-members alike.

Two specific issues had been left by the Preparatory Committee for decision by the Ministers. A major issue concerned differences between the European Economic Community and the United States over the monetary-trade link. A compromise formula was finally agreed and was subsequently approved by the full Ministerial meeting. The language of the relevant paragraph in the Tokyo Declaration—paragraph 7—reflects both the concerns of the Community and the position of the United States, while avoiding a contradiction between the two. Discussions under the aegis of the International Monetary Fund on the reform of the international monetary system were being pressed forward at that time.

A second issue concerned the least developed countries and the question of the extent to which special treatment could be extended to these countries without the same treatment being accorded to other developing countries. The difficulties that had arisen—particularly with certain developing countries— were eventually overcome and paragraph 6 of the Declaration approved.

The Tokyo Declaration was a political act of considerable significance. It involved important new commitments, particularly as regards the developing countries. . . .

B.   Establishment of Machinery

1.   **The Trade Negotiations Committee.** A Trade Negotiations Committee, consisting of all the countries participating in the Negotiations, was set up under the Tokyo Declaration. Its task was to elaborate and put into effect detailed trade negotiating plans and establish appropriate negotiating procedures, and to supervise the progress of the Negotiations. The Director-General of GATT, Mr. Olivier Long, was Chairman of the Committee. The Committee was not intended to be the place where substantive negotiations would take place. It would be impossible to negotiate in a forum in which almost a hundred countries were represented and where up to some three hundred delegates—and on occasions more—would be present.

The Committee met toward the end of October 1973 and, in February 1974, set up six specialized sub-groups, which were to concern themselves with the subjects set out in (a) to (f) of paragraph 3 of the Tokyo Declaration [listed below].

The tasks to be undertaken in 1974 would essentially be technical in character and largely a continuation of the kind of work that had been going on over the past several years. Despite the expectations created first by the Declarations of early 1972, and more importantly by the Tokyo Declaration, the fact remained that the engagements undertaken still lacked the backing of the necessary constitutional or legislative authority.

With the entry into force of the United States Trade Act at the beginning of 1975, and approval of an agreed negotiating mandate for the Commission of the European Communities shortly afterwards, the Negotiations were moved a major step forward. In February 1975, the Trade Negotiations Committee established six groups to conduct the various parts of the Negotiations.

2.   **The negotiating groups and sub-groups.** The machinery for the Tokyo Round comprising the six Groups and a number of Sub-Groups, and including also certain additions made to the machinery at a later stage, was the following. These were the bodies within the framework of which, under the overall supervision of the Trade Negotiations Committee, the Negotiations were to be conducted.

(a)   Group: Tropical Products (Chairman, Ambassador G. Martinez, Argentina);
(b)   Group: Tariffs (Chairman, Mr. G. Patterson, Deputy Director-General, GATT secretariat);
(c)   Group: Non-Tariff Measures (Chairman, Mr. M. G. Mathur, Deputy Director-General, GATT secretariat);
    (i)   Sub-Group: Quantitative Restrictions (Chairman, Mr. Chadha (India) followed by Mr. Mathur);
    (ii) Sub-Group: Technical Barriers to Trade (Chairman, Mr. P. Williams, GATT secretariat);
    (iii) Sub-Group: Customs Matters (Chairman, Mr. K. Kautzor-Schröder, GATT secretariat);
    (iv) Sub-Group: Subsidies and Countervailing Duties (Chairman, Mr. A. Lindén, GATT secretariat);
    (v)   Sub-Group: Government Procurement (Chairman, Mr. R. Tooker, GATT secretariat);
(d)   Group: Agriculture (Chairman, Mr. G. Patterson);
    (i)   Sub-Group: Grains (Chairman, Mr. G. Patterson);
    (ii) Sub-Group: Meat (Chairman, Mr. J.-M. Lucq, GATT secretariat);
    (iii) Sub-Group: Dairy Products (Chairman, Mr. J.-M. Lucq);
(e)   Group: Sector Approach (Chairman, Dr. P. Tomić, Yugoslavia);
(f)   Group: Safeguards (Chairman, Mr. H. Colliander (Sweden) followed by Mr. K. Kautzor-Schröder).

A seventh Group, described as the Framework Group, was established in November 1976, under the Chairmanship of the Director-General of GATT, with the task of considering "improvements in the international framework for the conduct of world trade which might be desirable in the light of progress in the negotiations."

CHAPTER IV: PRINCIPAL DEVELOPMENTS

The story of the Tokyo Round covers a period of over five years. It is one of vicissitudes and "stop and go" with delays—sometimes long—alternating with renewed impetus and progress, depending on developments in the international economic situation, on political factors, and on the speed of governments' constitutional and legislative processes. . . .

C.   *Later Developments in the Negotiations*

The substantive issue in the Tokyo Round that most slowed down progress arose from differences in approach between the United States and the European Economic Community to the agricultural negotiations. . . . There was little or no narrowing of the gap between the two approaches during the early years of the Negotiations. As an essential aspect of the differences of view related to where, and how, within the overall framework of the Negotiations, agriculture should be dealt with, the deadlock spilled over into the rest of the Negotiations and held up progress.

A new attempt to inject life into the Negotiations was made early in 1976 when the United States and the European Economic Community proposed, and other countries agreed, on a procedure for the exchange of information, consultation, and dialogue between participants on agricultural products other than grains, dairy products and meat, for which separate sub-groups had been set up. No substantive negotiation followed this move, however, and things relapsed into a state of relative inactivity.

The consequences of the substantive difficulties in the agricultural negotiations, and the effects of the economic and political factors that have been referred to, are evident in the status of the Negotiations early in 1977. Very little substantive progress had been made and all crucial issues remained outstanding. In several key areas the Negotiations were still at the stage of identification of the areas to be dealt with, the bodies to deal with them and the specific positions of governments. Except in the case of tropical products and standards, the Negotiations were not yet off the ground, although a lot of the work that had been done could be described as pre-negotiation.

It was urgent for the Negotiations to move forward for a number of reasons. Under the US Trade Act, 1974, the negotiating authority of the President would expire on 3 January 1980. This meant that the negotiations on non-tariff measures and other distortions of trade would have to be completed sufficiently in advance of that date to make it possible for the procedures laid down in Section 102 of the Trade Act to be completed within the time periods prescribed in that Section. . . .

In July 1977 came the breakthrough that had been awaited and which, as will be seen from the following chapters, had its effects in every area of the Tokyo Round. At a meeting in Brussels between Mr. Robert Strauss, the recently appointed United States Special Trade Representative, and Mr. Wilhelm Haferkamp, the European Communities' Commissioner for External Relations, it proved possible to resolve certain major differences of policy and procedure, including in the agricultural sector.

Specifically, agreement was reached on an accelerated time-table for the Tokyo Round. This involved action on the following:

> *First phase.* A general tariff plan: to include a tariff-cutting formula; specific directives for treatment of agriculture; method of dealing with countries not subscribing to the tariff-cutting formula; specific statement on treatment of developing countries.
>
> *Second phase.* Tabling of requests for: tariff cuts on agricultural goods; nontariff measures not the subject of codes; tariff cuts by countries not subscribing to the tariff-cutting formula.
>
> *Third phase.* Tabling of draft texts for non-tariff measure codes.
>
> *Fourth phase.* Tabling of offers by participants in response to requests received.

These four phases were to be completed by January 1978. Requests were to be submitted in November 1977 and offers in January 1978. This was an important development. The aim was to have the whole pattern and material of the Negotiations laid out by the spring of 1978 and the final phase of substantive negotiations embarked upon.

There followed much negotiating activity at a high political level during the first half of 1978. Over the period 3 to 13 July 1978 in particular, there were intensive bilateral and plurilateral negotiations in Geneva involving a number of personalities from capitals with responsibilities in connexion with the Tokyo Round.

The aim was to have, by the time of a further summit meeting of Heads of States and Governments to be held in Bonn on 16 and 17 July 1978, the political outlines of an agreed package, leaving the autumn for clearing up the details.

In the meanwhile, there had been two multilateral meetings, at which countries had the opportunity to make known their points of view. One was a meeting of the Trade Negotiations Committee on 3 July 1978 and the other an informal meeting of countries participating in the Tokyo Round on 10 July.

On 13 July 1978 an agreed "Framework of Understanding", covering all the main issues in the Tokyo Round, was tabled. It represented an agreement reached by the European Economic Community, the United States, Japan, Switzerland, New Zealand, Canada, the Nordic countries and Austria and set out the principal elements they considered necessary for a balanced package at the end of the Tokyo Round. It was the hope of the countries subscribing to the "Framework of Understanding" that other countries would see in the memorandum a solid basis for conclusion of the Tokyo Round.

The developing countries, however, were far from happy about the way in which, as they saw it, they had been left on the periphery of the negotiations. A strong statement on their behalf on 14 July made this clear. It stated that the developing countries had not been consulted on the "Framework of Understanding", and stressed that a balanced assessment of the current status of the negotiations could only be made with the participation of all the countries involved.

At the same time the Director-General, Mr. Long, gave in a statement an overall view of the situation in the Negotiations, stressing the substantial progress that had been made and his belief that the Negotiations could be completed by the end of 1978.

The Heads of State and Government, at the Bonn summit, in the communiqué issued at the end of the meeting on 17 July 1978, charged their negotiators in Geneva, in co-operation with the other participants, to resolve the outstanding issues and to conclude the negotiations successfully by 15 December 1978.

Following the summer recess, the Negotiations were energetically moved forward with the firm intention and will on all sides to complete them by the end of the year. There were intensive bilateral and plurilateral consultations and negotiations among delegations. Texts were further refined. Critical decisions however, for example on agriculture, safeguards and subsidies and countervailing duties, had still to be taken. The aim was to limit and clearly define the outstanding issues in advance of a further high-level meeting envisaged for mid-November. . . .

. . . Continuous intensive bilateral and plurilateral negotiations among delegations, and meetings of the various Groups and Sub-Groups over the following few weeks, led up to a meeting of the Trade Negotiations Committee on 11 and 12 April 1979.

At its meeting, the Committee had before it the texts on all elements in the Negotiations that had emerged . . . together with the summings-up of the Chairmen of the negotiating Groups and Sub-Groups.

A large number of representatives made statements on their positions in relation to the various texts before the Committee.

At the end of the meeting the Chairman proposed the text of a Procès-Verbal which met the approval of all the participants and was subsequently opened for signature as from 12 April 1979 without time-limit. . . .

CHAPTER VII: TARIFFS

A. Issues

Although in all previous GATT multilateral negotiations tariffs had been the principal target and substantial reductions had been made, there was still considerable scope for further cuts.

An overriding issue—the implications of which went well beyond the tariff field—was whether tariff cuts applied to industrial goods should likewise be applicable to agricultural products. This was part of the general question as to how and where within the overall framework of the Negotiations agriculture should be dealt with.

The alternative techniques for tariff reduction had been thoroughly investigated in the course of the preparatory work in the years preceding the Tokyo meeting. Two approaches were the most favoured: the technique of harmonization, whereby the higher the tariff the greater would be the cut, and the linear technique which would involve equal percentage cuts on all tariffs.

A country's preference would be influenced by its tariff structure. The linear approach would still leave a country having peaks in its tariff with some relatively high duties, whereas a country with a fairly uniform tariff might favour the harmonization technique. Other issues would be of particular concern to individual countries, whatever general formula they were likely to support once the negotiations got under way. For some countries low tariffs—particularly if these were in a principal market—could be a barrier. Others were likely to resist an elimination of tariffs on the grounds that this would reduce their future negotiating possibilities.

An issue of considerable difficulty and sensitivity would concern exceptions from the general formula. This would involve both countries and products. It was recognized that developing countries would be excepted from the formula, although some contributions would be expected from these countries. Problems would, however, arise in the case of developed countries such as Australia and New Zealand which, although at a certain stage of industrialization, rely mainly on exports of agricultural products.

The products to be excepted would also pose difficult problems for governments. Great pressure for exemption would be exerted by industries—such as steel, textiles and shoes for example—that were in difficulties. In a situation of high unemployment and under persistent protectionist pressures governments, particularly those with minimal parliamentary majorities, would not find it easy to resist these demands. The more the exceptions, the more likely the withdrawal of offers or the addition of exceptions by others, and a general decline in the extent and value of the tariff-cutting exercise. Moreover, there would be the probability that products of considerable export interest to developing countries—often the target of the protectionists—would be prominent in exception lists; this would create a situation difficult to reconcile with the spirit and letter of important objectives of the Tokyo Declaration.

A fundamental issue would be how to provide, in terms of the Tokyo Declaration, differential and more favourable treatment for developing countries. The sort of questions to which answers would be required included whether the preferential duties existing in the Generalized System of Preferences should be bound in accordance with the wishes of the developing countries; whether deeper cuts than the general formula could be given to products of special export interest to these countries; whether products on which developing countries enjoyed preferences should be exempted from the [MFN] cuts of the general formula and so maintain the margin of preferences; whether new subcategories in the tariff classification should be created in order to provide opportunity for more favourable treatment for their exports; and whether there should be advance implementation of tariff cuts in the case of products of special export interest to developing countries. . . .

While governments were not committed to any particular approach at that time, attention was mainly focussed on three possibilities: tariff elimination, linear reduction of tariffs, and harmonization techniques. However, no possible technique was excluded. . . .

C.   The Negotiations on Tariffs

1. **Lack of Substantive Negotiations: 1975-1977.** The mandate of the Group on Tariffs set up in February 1975 was "to draw up a tariff negotiating plan of as general application as possible, taking due account of the views of the developing countries, particularly as regards the Generalized System of Preferences."

The Group held a number of meetings in 1975 and 1976 but, because of the deadlock in the Tokyo Round generally at that time, it was not possible for substantive negotiations to be engaged.

Nevertheless, considerable progress was made in a number of important areas. There were wide-ranging discussions in the Group on issues that would predominate once the tariff negotiations got under way. These were mainly concerned with the elements that might be included in a tariff-negotiating plan such as the tariff-cutting formula, base rates and base dates, special and more favourable treatment for developing countries, and staging of cuts.

It was during this period that all the tariff cutting proposals were made. Canada was the first to suggest a hypothesis for a possible tariff-cutting formula in 1975. During 1976 the United States, the European Economic Community, Japan and Switzerland put forward proposals, adding to those already made by Canada. The European Economic Community favoured the harmonization approach, as did Japan and Switzerland. The United States favoured the linear reduction technique.

Activity in the Group slowed down considerably for some time after the autumn of 1976 during the later stages of the Presidential elections in the United States and, thereafter, pending the appointment by the President of the new Special Trade Representative.

2. **Negotiations Engaged: 1977-1979.** The deadlock in the Tokyo Round was broken at the meeting in July 1977 between Mr. Strauss and Mr. Haferkamp in Brussels. As regards the negotiations on tariffs, it was agreed that a negotiating plan, including a tariff-cutting formula, should be established by 15 January 1978.

At a further meeting in Brussels between Mr. Strauss and Mr. Haferkamp in September 1977, there was agreement that the "working hypothesis" for the tariff-cutting exercise should be established along the lines of the proposal put forward by Switzerland. In the weeks thereafter most developed countries accepted the Swiss proposal as a working hypothesis and agreed to table their detailed tariff offers by 15 January 1978.

Expressed algebraically, with X representing the initial rate of import duty applied, A a coefficient to be agreed upon, and Z the resulting reduced rate of duty, the formula proposed by Switzerland was:

$$Z = \frac{A\,X}{A + X}$$

On the basis of a proposed coefficient 16, for instance, an initial 10 per cent tariff would be reduced to $(16 \times 10) \div (16 + 10) = 160 \div 26 =$ about 6.15 per cent. A higher tariff would be reduced by a greater proportion, a lower by a less one. If applied without exceptions, this formula would have the effect of reducing the average tariff level of the main industrialized countries by about 40 per cent. The new tariff levels would, in accordance with normal GATT practice, be "bound" against subsequent increase.

The autumn of 1977 was devoted to the preparation of detailed tariff offers in capitals. In mid-January 1978 the tabling of offers on industrial products and the submission of bilateral requests for tariff concessions began. Copies of these initial requests and offers were made available to all countries participating in the Tokyo Round.

By the middle of 1978 countries were proceeding to reciprocal adjustments in their initial offers, involving both improvements and exceptions. A high level of binding of duties by all participants continued to be an important objective. There still remained certain technical problems to be dealt with, such as how to treat specific duties, how to take account of the fact that some tariffs are levied on a c.i.f. and others on an f.o.b. basis, etc. . . .

(a) *Tariff-cutting formula.* Although the Swiss formula had been generally accepted by the main industrialized countries as a working hypothesis, there were considerable variations in its application. The European Economic Community and the Nordic countries—followed later by Australia—used the coefficient 16, whereas the coefficient 14 was used by the United States, Japan and Switzerland. Canada employed its own formula. These variations were designed to yield an approximately equal average cut in each country's overall tariff. Certain other countries, New Zealand for example, resorted to the item-by-item technique.

CHAPTER VIII: NON-TARIFF MEASURES

1. **Background.** The negotiations on a wide range of non-tariff measures were what most distinguished the Tokyo Round from earlier GATT multilateral negotiations, which had been concerned primarily with tariffs.

In the extensive preparatory work undertaken in the years before the Tokyo Meeting of Ministers, the characteristics of non-tariff measures, and the difficulties that would be involved in negotiating in this area, became clearer. There had been very little experience in GATT of negotiating multilaterally on these measures. Although it had been provided in the procedures for the Kennedy Round that all non-tariff barriers were negotiable, concrete results were negligible, with the important exception of the Anti-Dumping Code. The Code was important in itself. It was also a demonstration that non-tariff measures were negotiable.

Negotiating on non-tariff measures would obviously present problems. They were more diversified and changeable than tariffs. Similar negotiating techniques could not be applied to them. There was little, or no, uniformity between them as to their purpose. Many of those in national administrations dealing with such measures had little experience in international negotiations. A quantitative assessment of the impact of a non-tariff measure on trade, or of the value to be put on its reduction or elimination, was practically impossible. Some measures justified as being in the national interest—for example on grounds of security, health or safety—can have trade-distorting effects incidental to their main purpose.

There could also develop juridical complications. Many non-tariff measures are contrary to the GATT. Would these be considered negotiable and, if so, should they attract reciprocal concessions? A number of the modifications to the GATT rules would take the form of codes or agreements. Would the provisions of these instruments be applied only between those countries subscribing to them or to all GATT member countries in accordance with the most-favoured-nation clause? These were the sort of questions to which answers would have to be sought in the course of the negotiations.

2. **The Material Base.** Unlike tariffs, non-tariff measures were unfamiliar territory and a great deal of exploration in this complex field would obviously be necessary.

As a first step, a comprehensive inventory was drawn up in 1968 and subsequently kept up to date based on measures—some 800 in all—notified by exporting countries as adversely affecting their trade.

It was found that the approximately thirty categories of measures notified could be classified under five broad headings: government participation in trade; customs and administrative entry procedures; standards applicable to imported and domestic products; specific limitations on imports and exports; and limitations on imports and exports through price mechanisms.

On examination, it was considered that some of these measures might be dealt with through multilateral action. At the time, however, governments did not have the authority to negotiate substantive and binding solutions and it was therefore decided that the best way to proceed would be to elaborate solutions on an *ad referendum* basis—in other words solutions that would be submitted to governments for consideration, but which would, in the meanwhile, be without commitment on their part.

By the time of the Tokyo meeting in September 1973, *ad referendum* solutions had been elaborated for Valuation for Customs Purposes, Automatic Licensing and Licensing to Administer Import Restrictions, and Standards.

In addition, solutions were being sought to problems in the following areas: export subsidies, domestic subsidies that stimulate exports, subsidies that have import substitution effects and countervailing duties; import documentation including consular formalities, packaging and labelling; and quantitative restrictions, including embargoes and export restraints.

A number of other subjects were discussed but were not at that time being examined for *ad referendum* solutions. They included government procurement; State-trading enterprises in market economy countries; anti-dumping duties; customs classification; certificates of origin; samples requirements; marks of origin; minimum price regulations; motion picture restrictions; prior deposits; credit restrictions for importers; fiscal adjustments either at the border or otherwise; restrictions on foreign wines and spirits; discriminatory taxes on motorcars; statistical and administrative duties; and special duties on imports.

The list is quoted as a good indication of the extent, variety and complexity of non-tariff measures. It clearly shows the difficulty of putting a limitation on the type and number that can reasonably be described as "non-tariff measures".

At the meeting of the Preparatory Committee in 1973 the following common list of priorities was proposed:

  (i)   export subsidies and domestic subsidies that distort trade;
  (ii)   anti-dumping duties and countervailing duties;
  (iii) government procurement;
  (iv)   valuation for customs purposes;
  (v)   standards, including packaging and labelling;
  (vi)   quantitative restrictions including embargoes and export restraints and licensing systems;
  (vii) import documentation and consular formalities.

Although, strictly speaking, all non-tariff measures remained on the table, attention in the forthcoming negotiations would be mainly concentrated on this priority list.

3.   **The Negotiations.** The aim of the negotiations was to reduce or eliminate those non-tariff measures that are barriers to international trade, or, where this was not appropriate, to reduce or eliminate their trade-distorting effects and bring them under more effective international discipline.

(a) *Machinery.* A group to oversee the negotiations was set up by the Trade Negotiations Committee in February 1975. It established four Sub-Groups to deal respectively with the following subjects:

quantitative restrictions (including import prohibitions and so-called voluntary export restraints) and import licensing procedures;
subsidies and countervailing duties;
technical barriers to trade, to include standards, packaging and labelling requirements, and marks of origin;
customs matters, including customs valuation, import documentation (including consular formalities) customs nomenclature, and customs procedures.

A fifth Sub-Group—on government procurement—was set up in July 1976.

(b) *Developments in the negotiations.* The most important part of the work on non-tariff measures in the Tokyo Round concerned the negotiation of agreements on issues considered appropriate for multilateral solutions. These were subsidies and countervailing duties; technical barriers to trade; customs valuation; government procurement; and import licensing procedures. For each of these, agreements were negotiated.

There was uneven progress in the work of the Sub-Groups in the early years but the breakthrough in the deadlock in the Tokyo Round generally in July

1977 gave added impetus to this work. Thereafter negotiations went on, at differing rates of progress, right up to the final stages of the Tokyo Round in March and April 1979. The various agreements were before the Trade Negotiations Committee at its meeting on 11-12 April 1979, following which they were opened for acceptance by governments. . . .

FISHER, MAKING THE WORLD TRADE REGIME WORK: AN AGENDA FOR GATT[17]

6 SAIS Review 53-60 (Winter-Spring 1986)

The United States has tried to expand the ambit of the GATT to include services and investments, as well as trade in goods; to have further negotiations on the codes left unfinished in the MTN, including safeguards and counterfeiting; to develop approaches to high-technology trade and to press for a round of North-South negotiations focusing on preferential arrangements and high tariff levels in major LDC markets.

On November 27, 1985, following three years of intense U.S. pressure, the 90 member countries of the GATT unanimously agreed to embark on a new round of multilateral trade negotiations, the eighth since World War II. Meeting in Geneva, the seat of the GATT Secretariat, officials from the member countries appointed a working party to devise a detailed program for the negotiations. The working party is to conclude its deliberations in July, 1986, to permit its recommendations to be adopted at the meeting of trade ministers scheduled for September, 1986. The negotiations are expected to begin in earnest shortly thereafter. This will mark the first time that GATT signatories have assembled in the multilateral trade negotiations format since the close of the Tokyo Round in 1979. The issues the next GATT round will address are outlined in summary fashion below.

1. Strengthening the GATT. As the earlier materials indicate, the failure of the international community to establish the International Trade Organization (ITO) after World War II left an institutional vacuum in international decision-making in the trade area. The GATT was created not as a permanent international organization but as an agreement among nations to uphold certain principles. More than 35 years later, the GATT remains a contract supported by an extremely weak organizational infrastructure. Members agree to meet only periodically to address matters as they arise.[18] In an increasingly

---

[17]Some alterations have been made in the original text. For further details, *see* C. Ako and J. Aronson, Trade Talks: America Better Listen! (1985).

[18]The GATT, Article XXV, para. 1: "Representatives of the contracting parties shall meet from time to time for the purpose of giving effect to those provisions of this Agreement which involve joint action and, generally, with a view to facilitating the operation and furthering the objectives of this Agreement."

conflictual international trading system, these irregular and infrequent negotiations are insufficient.

A permanent mechanism is needed to ensure continuity in the formulation
and enforcement of trade rules. We need to transcend the idea of trade regulation as a "movable feast" that occurs whenever the international trading
system faces a crisis.

It matters little whether the GATT itself is transmogrified from a contract
to an institution, or whether a completely new international trade organization is established. What is crucial, however, is the creation of an entity to
which enough power has been ceded by the signatory nations to solve international trade problems as they arise, rather than in response to long-festering
crises.

The need for longer, more intensive trade negotiations presents a difficult
issue of U.S. constitutional law. Under Article I, §8 of the Constitution, as we
saw earlier in this chapter in the *Starkist, Yoshida,* and *Consumers Union* cases,
Congress possesses plenary authority over the regulation of foreign commerce
unless and until it delegates its powers to the Executive Branch. For the
United States to commit itself to a stronger GATT formed by lengthier, more
extensive trade negotiations, Congress must be willing to make a long-term, if
not permanent, delegation of authority to the president to enter into these
discussions.

Strengthening the GATT implies reforms not only in the formulation of
trade rules but also in their enforcement. It is clear that the GATT process of
dispute settlement must be improved if the organization is to remain viable. As
we will see in Chapter 9 consideration of the GATT, one lesson of recent
GATT cases is that they take too long to adjudicate and are overly politicized
by member countries. Even when decisions are finally reached, they may be
ignored by the affected parties. The core of the problem is whether more
weight should be given to the juridical or the political approach to trade
disputes. The juridical approach is more consistent with the goal of a stronger
international trade organization to which a degree of sovereignty is ceded by
members, as is the case in the International Monetary Fund. For a stronger
trade organization to become a reality, the contracting nations must similarly
devolve certain of their sovereign rights to the GATT.

Apart from strengthening the GATT as an institution, reforms will be
needed to allow it to relate more effectively to other international institutions,
such as the International Monetary Fund (IMF) (which we will consider in
detail in Chapter 15), the Organization for Economic Cooperation and Development (OECD), the International Bank for Reconstruction and Development (better known as the World Bank), and the United Nations Conference
on Trade and Development (UNCTAD). The need for closer cooperation
among international economic institutions is based on three realities that must
be taken into account in the coming round of trade negotiations.

First, in the next decade the United States will be as concerned with the
problems of currency misalignment and the relatively strong dollar as with

particular measures for trade liberalization.[19] Pressures will intensify to adapt the GATT, which was created in a period of fixed exchange rates, to the special problems that floating exchange rates pose for the trading system. A parallel negotiation under IMF supervision might be conducted on how to implement a realistic realignment of exchange rates. This much discussed "new Bretton Woods" conference should be closely coordinated with overall efforts at trade liberalization, as concessions made in one set of negotiations may have to be factored into the other.

Second, a closer interaction between international financial and trade institutions needs to be forged in order to avoid conflicting pressures on developing countries. If the IMF, World Bank, or regional development banks continue to pressure less developed countries (LDCs) to run balance of trade surpluses, the international trading system may be seriously strained.

Finally, the next round of trade negotiations will have to consider cooperation between the GATT and the OECD on the implementation of new rules on trade in services, an area of increasing importance to international commerce. The OECD has done exhaustive research on this subject; its findings and recommendations could be incorporated into a GATT accord on trade liberalization in services analogous to the subsidies and dumping codes adopted in the Tokyo Round. Such an agreement may be easier to sell to OECD nations than the GATT's imposition of rules liberalizing trade in services.

2. *The Role of the Developing Countries.* Since the end of the last round of multilateral trade negotiations in 1979 the economic situation of much of the Third World has worsened dramatically. We will consider the regulation of trade as it affects the developing countries in Chapter 10. This is the single factor that most distinguishes the circumstances surrounding the next round from the last. The $500 billion "debt bomb" of the Third World, considered in the context of an overall decline in the price of oil and other primary commodities, calls for an imaginative and humanitarian response from the developed country members of the GATT.[20] To assist LCDs in the next round, the following trade-related measures might be undertaken: roll back recent re-

---

[19] An indication of this is the 22 September 1985 announcement of the Ministry of Finance and Central Bank Governors of France, Germany, Japan, the United Kingdom, and the United States, in which it was stated:

> The Ministers and Governors agreed that exchange rates should play a role in adjusting external imbalances. In order to do this, exchange rates should better reflect fundamental economic conditions than has been the case. They believe that agreed policy actions must be implemented and reinforced to improve the fundamentals further, and that in view of the present and prospective changes in fundamentals, some further orderly appreciation of the main non-dollar currencies against the dollar is desirable. They stand ready to cooperate more closely to encourage this when to do so would be helpful.

[20] For a description of the magnitude of the problems confronting developing countries, *see* The Brandt Commission Report, which refers to "North-South relations as the great social challenge of our time." North-South: A Program for Survival 7 (1980).

strictions on exports by developing countries; expand trade preference schemes; and allow special and differential treatment in favor of developing countries in any new tariff and non-tariff barrier arrangements that might be concluded regarding goods and services. In addition, the next round might be broadened to include more agenda items of interest to developing countries, such as stabilizing international commodity prices and improving the transfer of technology from developed to developing countries.

3. Application of the Most-Favored-Nation Principle. As is noted in the Jackson selection earlier in this chapter, the unconditional most-favored-nation (MFN) principle is a key provision of the GATT.

The trend in the international community has been to ignore the restrictive MFN rule, creating a gray zone of measures arguably in conformance with the letter of the GATT but not its spirit. Some of these industry to industry agreements or "voluntary" export restraints such as in the U.S.-EEC and U.S.-Japan steel arrangements described in Consumers Union v. Kissinger, *infra,* or the Japanese auto restraints discussed in Chapter 4, may be more trade-restricting than formal governmental import restraints. Of the 20.8 percent of total imports covered by quantitative restraints in developed countries in 1985, only 7.6 percent were reported by members to come under GATT rules.[21]

What may be required is a new "safeguards" code to regulate the means by which GATT members can lawfully limit imports. As we will see in Chapter IV, this is a key bit of unfinished business from the 1974-79 Multilateral Trade Negotiations. A new safeguards code would have to address not only the MFN-related issues of geographical selectivity and special and differential treatment of developing countries, but also the appropriate injury standards for the granting of escape clause relief, compensation for affected exporters, more transparent procedures, time limits, and consultation procedures.

Some relaxation of the MFN principle may be necessary in order to preserve the GATT trading system. The constant deviations from the norm that we see today suggest that the current system is not working and may need to be modified.

4. The Scope of Trade Institution Coverage. The GATT currently regulates trade in goods but does not reach services or investments. Bringing the services sector under the jurisdiction of the GATT is a high U.S. priority in the next round. Negotiations on investment issues raise more difficult conceptual and practical problems.

With regard to services, the goal should be an umbrella code that sets forth general principles for trade in that sector. In addition, specific accords on particular service areas could be negotiated, as appropriate. It is inconceivable

---

[21] A. Winters, Negotiating the Removal of Non-Tariff Barriers, International Economic Research Division, Development Research Department, The World Bank, Washington, D.C., 1985.

that the United States, whose GNP is 66% services,[22] could walk away from a new round without rules covering services as well as goods. It is also clear that the developed countries will have to be particularly sensitive to the "infant" service industries in many developing countries.

What might a new services code look like? The following interests would need to be recognized: the right to market access, i.e., the right to establish a business in a given country; the right to non-discriminatory national treatment; fair rules for competition between private corporations and government monopolies; and guarantees of transparency and a fair international dispute-settlement mechanism.

Expanding the scope of the GATT to include the full set of investment issues would probably not be a wise strategy for the next round. The United States is virtually alone in its desire to have investments covered by the GATT, and to plunge headlong into uncharted seas as a party of one is not an advisable course. It would be far wiser to expand the scope of GATT coverage incrementally, first into the service area, and possibly into investments at a later date. Moreover, it should be recognized that many so-called service issues, such as establishment rights for U.S. insurance companies in foreign countries, are really investment issues as well. The safest course for all concerned may be to write an umbrella services code that covers some investment issues. The final point here is that requiring the elimination of trade-related investment requirements (such as domestic content rules) and export requirements may in some cases impair the ability of the developing countries to pay back their large debts through export-led growth. Many of these trade-related investment barriers may also be reached under current GATT rules as illegal trade restraints.

5.   *Reduction of Barriers to Trade.* The great success of the Tokyo Round was its codification of a host of rules on nontariff barriers to trade, such as standards (*see* Chapter 8), subsidies (*see* Chapter 6), customs valuation (*see* Chapter 7), licensing, and government procurement (*see* Chapter 8). These codes need to be analyzed and refined to remedy their perceived inadequacies. For example, improved definitions of acceptable forms of public assistance are required for the subsidies code; clearer definitions are required to delimit permissible subsidies for agricultural exports; services need to be included under the government procurement code; and the number of governmental entities purchasing goods or services subject to the government procurement codes needs to be expanded.

The key new nontariff barrier code that needs to be considered is an accord on intellectual property rights. U.S. producers are becoming increasingly concerned about the attitude of foreign governments and companies toward intellectual property rights and agree that legal protections for patents, copyrights,

---

[22] As of May 1982 approximately 73% of the American work force was employed in the service sector. Survey of Current Business 62:7, at pp.9, 10 (1982).

and trademarks currently in place are inadequate. As the level of technical innovation grows, so will U.S. sensitivities on this issue. The GATT might thus supplement the technical work of the World Intellectual Property Organization (WIPO) by providing an effective dispute settlement mechanism. In addition, a new GATT International Counterfeiting Code providing effective unilateral methods of enforcing intellectual property rights could be considered.

Despite the increased importance of nontariff barriers, tariffs remain as an important obstacle to trade in the industrial and developing countries. Buried within Japan's relatively low overall tariff schedule, for example, are a 30.4% duty on bottled wine, a 20% duty on chocolate confectionery, and a 15% duty on plywood. The U.S. average duty rate of 8% includes many high duties on items such as textiles and tuna packed in oil (35%), and the EEC has still more high-tariff items.

The developed countries will probably not be expected to eliminate their tariffs to the maximum extent in the next round. The developed countries will probably seek full tariff reciprocity with the less developed countries; in fact they may want to continue meaningful preferences in favor of LDCs. For their part, the developing countries might agree to liberalize the quantitative restraint and import licensing schemes that have precluded market entry by the developed countries.

The agenda for the next round of GATT trade negotiations is daunting. But the price of failure would be very high. Failure to move ahead on the problems of institutional reform described above would play directly into the hands of protectionists, who claim that the United States is being unfairly discriminated against by the trading system and its major players. The current euphemism used by many is that the United States seeks only a "level playing field."

For the next round of trade negotiations to be deemed a success from the American perspective the "fairness issue" must be addressed. If many influential American economic interests continue to believe that the international trading system is slanted against U.S. interests, support for the GATT will be hard to muster. How these GATT negotiations unfold will, then, profoundly affect the shape of the U.S. debate on the degree to which imports should be restricted.

NOTES AND QUESTIONS

1. What are the political requirements for the GATT negotiating process to succeed? What would you expect about the relation between new exports and new imports that each nation expects to result from the agreement?

2. Consider the detailed prenegotiation provisions in Title I, Chapter 3 of the 1974 Trade Act. What interests are they designed to serve? Would you expect them to be effective?

3. What about the approval provisions of Chapter 5 of the same title? What are the arguments for and against this special process and who gains power under it? Would you expect to see more such provisions as a result of *Chadha*? Are there constitutional problems with these provisions as well? For interesting background on the 1979 approval, *see* Winham, Robert Strauss, the MTN and the Control of Faction (Multilateral Trade Negotiations), 14 J.W.T.L. 377 (1980).

4. Do you think it likely that there will ever be another round in the Kennedy and Tokyo tradition? Under what circumstances might it become more likely? For background on the negotiation generally, *see* McRae & Thomas, The GATT and Multilateral Treaty Making: The Tokyo Round, 77 A.J.I.L. 51 (1983), and Symposium—The Tokyo Round; Its Meaning and Effect, 9 Ga. J. Intl. & Comp. Law 151 (1979).

5. Assume that the USTR, although pleased at the successes of the Tokyo round, is troubled by the overall course of GATT, the international trade system, and related U.S. law. He is particularly concerned by (1) the growing tide of protectionism (although he notes that the ITC is now proving substantially less protectionist than many expected); (2) the move toward discretionary, ad hoc arrangements (such as the "voluntary" export limitation systems in *Consumers' Union;* (3) the weakness of GATT dispute settlement mechanisms; and (4) the technicality of U.S. law in the area, a technicality reinforced by the existence of a specialized bar.

He would like to create a national or international working group to consider these issues, believing that, even though no one has the heart for a new negotiating round, the world may need a "great leap forward."

Please tell him (a) plausible outcomes of and tasks for such a working group, and (b) (by title or role) who should be included at what stages in the negotiations.

6. In 1984, Congress passed legislation to limit the investment tax credit for luxury automobiles purchased for business use. A large portion of these automobiles were imports. If you represented a foreign manufacturer such as Mercedes-Benz, what GATT arguments would you make? What would be the counterarguments? Note that in Senate debate, Senator Moynihan (D-New York) quoted a Congressional Research Service report that the articles of the GATT do not apply to income tax laws and Senator Baucus (D-Montana) said that he thought any GATT argument was "specious," for the provision was designed to solve a tax problem, not a trade problem. 130 Cong. Rec. S4467, 4469 (daily ed. April 12, 1984).

7. The United States shipbuilding industry is currently facing severe economic problems. Japanese and other shipbuilders have been able to significantly undercut U.S. sale of vessels due to lower labor and other production costs.

Widespread sentiment appears to exist in the Congress for legislation that will remedy the economic distress of the U.S. shipbuilding industry.

The U.S. shipbuilders have developed a legislative proposal that would permit purchasers of U.S. vessels to depreciate these vessels in five years. Foreign-built vessels would continue to be depreciated over a 14-year period.

You are Counsel to the Senate Finance Committee. Several members of the Committee have asked your opinion on the compatibility of the shipbuilders' proposal with U.S. international obligations under the GATT. In your memorandum for the Committee members, which analyzes the depreciation proposal from the standpoint of U.S. domestic law and other U.S. international obligations, what points would you raise for consideration of the members of the Committee?

D.   THE EUROPEAN ECONOMIC COMMUNITY

Materials on the European Economic Community (EEC) are included here for two purposes. First, they provide background information and an example to compare with the United States—the EEC is an important trading partner and has its own elaborate set of procedures for trade negotiations. Second, the EEC reflects an effort to establish completely free trade within a single region. In a sense, it is a much more fully successful GATT, and helps suggest what would be needed to create a fully free-trade oriented international trading system.

1.   *Background*

The European Economic Community (the Common Market) is but one (but for international trade, the most important) of the three communities of nations composing the European Community. In the following, the overall structure of the European Community is set out.

THE INSTITUTIONS OF THE EUROPEAN COMMUNITY

Information Office of the European Community (1982)

25 March 1982—the 25th Anniversary of the European Community (EEC) and the European Atomic Energy Community (EAEC or Euratom). The two Treaties of Rome founding the Communities were signed on 25 March 1957. The Member States of that period decided to jointly deepen and extend their economic relations—an experiment which proved largely beneficial with the

signature of the Treaty of Paris and the setting up of the European Coal and Steel Community, which took place on 18 April 1951 and marked the first major step in the construction of Europe.

Consisting initially of six countries—Belgium, Germany, France, Italy, Luxembourg and the Netherlands—joined on 1 January 1973 by Denmark, Ireland and the United Kingdom and on 1 January 1981 by Greece, the European Communities are managed by common institutions. [Negotiations have since led to the admission of Portugal and Spain.]

THE EUROPEAN COMMISSION—INITIATOR AND EXECUTIVE

The Commission of the European Communities is composed of 14 Members—two British, two French, two German, two Italian and one from each of the other countries—appointed for a four-year period by mutual agreement of the governments of the ten countries. The Members of the European Commission act only in the interests of the Community; they may not receive instructions from any national government and are subject only to the supervision of the European Parliament which alone can force them collectively to resign their responsibilities. Commission decisions are taken collegiately, even though each Commissioner is directly responsible for one or more portfolios.

The Commission's tasks are:

to ensure that Community rules and the principles of the Common Market are respected. As guardian of the Treaties the Commission is responsible for seeing that they are observed and that decisions of the Community institutions deriving from the Treaties are correctly applied. The Commission decides on requests from Member States to apply safeguard clauses and can, in exceptional cases, authorize temporary waivers (derogations) from the rules of the Treaties. It has investigative powers and can impose fines on individuals, particularly regarding violations of Community competition rules. States which do not respect their obligations can also be taken to the European Court of Justice by the Commission;

to propose to the Community's Council of Ministers all measures likely to advance Community policies (in the fields of agriculture, energy, industry, research, e ivironment, social and regional problems, external trade, economic and monetar union, etc.). In 1981 the Commission transmitted 651 proposals to the Council of Ministers;

to implement Community policies on the basis of Council decisions or derived directly from the provisions of the Treaties;

The Commission thereby has particularly extensive powers in the fields of coal and steel (investment coordination, price control, etc.), competition (control of monopolies and public aid), nuclear energy (supply of fissile materials, control of nuclear installations, etc.);

In other cases the Commission operates upon a mandate from the Council, e.g. to negotiate trade agreements with third countries or to manage the agricultural markets;

The Commission also administers the funds of the common programmes which account for most of the Community budget and which aim in particular to support and modernize agriculture (European Agricultural Guidance and Guarantee Fund), to encourage industrial, vocational and regional change (ECSC [European Coal and Steel Community] appropriations, Social Fund, European Regional Development Fund), to promote scientific research (the Joint Research Centres and other services employ 2,700 people), to affirm European solidarity towards the Third World (European Development Fund, food-aid programmes, etc.).

The Commission has an administrative staff—concentrated mostly in Brussels and, to a lesser extent, in Luxembourg—of about 9,000 officials working in some 20 directorates-general (this is less than the staff of a good number of national ministries). One-third of the personnel is employed on linguistic work to ensure the equal recognition of the seven Community languages.

COUNCIL OF MINISTERS—DECISION-MAKER

The Community's Council of Ministers, which meets in Brussels and, less often, in Luxembourg, is composed of ministers from each Member State and decides on the principal Community policies. Each country acts as president of the Council for a six-month period on a rotation basis. Attendance at meetings is determined by the agenda; national agriculture ministers, for example, deal with agricultural prices, economics and employment ministers deal with unemployment problems. The Ten's ministers for foreign affairs are responsible for coordinating the specialized work of their colleagues. The Council is assisted by:

a Committee of Permanent Representatives (COREPER) which coordinates the preparatory work of Community decisions and is assisted by numerous working groups of senior officials from Member States;

a general secretariat with a staff of some 1,900 people.

The European Councils which have met three times a year since 1975 (before this they were only occasional) bring together the Heads of State or Government and provide political guidance and impetus—a role which should not be underestimated even if the meetings do not directly produce legislative measures.

The Council of Ministers held 63 sessions in 1981. All the proposals it deals with come without exception from the Commission, and the Council can only reject them by a unanimous vote.

Unanimity in the Council is also required for certain important decisions. In practice it is frequently demanded by ministers even when not strictly necessary, which tends to slow down the Community's decision-making process. In recent times, there has been more frequent recourse to the use of the qualified majority—45 out of 63 votes—as instituted by the Treaties. France, Germany, Italy and the United Kingdom each have ten votes under this procedure. Belgium, Greece and the Netherlands have five, Denmark and Ireland three and Luxembourg two.

In the agriculture sector, procedures have been accelerated by the creation of 'Management Committees' composed of representatives from the Commission and national governments: Commission decisions have to be submitted for Council approval only if a qualified majority within the Committee disagree with them.

COURT OF JUSTICE AND COMMUNITY LAW

The Community's Luxembourg-based Court of Justice is composed of eleven judges assisted by five advocates-general who are appointed for a six-year period by mutual agreement of Member States and who work independently of them. The Court's function is:

> to annul any measures taken by the Commission, the Council of Ministers, or national governments which are incompatible with the Treaties. This can be done at the request either of a Community institution, a Member State, or an individual directly concerned;

> to pass judgment at the request of national courts on the interpretation or the validity of the provisions of Community law. Whenever a case cannot be resolved by national courts they can request an interlocutory decision from the Court. Where a national court is the highest court of appeal it must submit an issue involving Community law to the Court of Justice for a ruling.

In 1981 the Court dealt with 323 cases (of which 99 were interlocutory) and passed 149 judgments. The Court can also be invited to give its opinion—which is then binding—on agreements which the Community envisages concluding with third countries.

Through its judgments and interpretations, the Court of Justice is contributing to the emergence of a veritable European law applicable to all: Community institutions, Member States, national courts and individuals. The authority of the Court's judgments in the field of Community law surpasses that of national courts. In cases of nonapplication of Community law by the Council, or Member States, the Court has been approached by individuals and upheld the direct applicability of principles contained in the Treaties relating to equal pay for men and women and the free exercise of the liberal professions throughout the Community.

EUROPEAN PARLIAMENT AND PARTICIPATION

Since June 1979, the date of the first European elections, the European Parliament has been composed of members elected every five years through universal suffrage instead of members delegated from national parliaments. The European Parliament has 434 members: 81 from each of the countries with the largest populations, 25 from the Netherlands, 24 from Belgium, 24 from Greece, 16 from Denmark, 15 from Ireland and 6 from Luxembourg.

The members of the Parliament form political rather than national groups. . . .

The European Parliament has a secretariat of some 2,900 officials based in Luxembourg. It has 18 parliamentary committees and its plenary and public sessions are held in Strasbourg or Luxembourg (though a vote gave preference to Strasbourg) in the presence of representatives from the European Commission and the Council of Ministers. This enables the Parliament to make fully-informed pronouncements on the problems of building Europe.

The European Parliament does not have the same legislative power as national assemblies. In the current Community system, it is the Commission which takes the initiatives and the Council which passes most Community legislation. Nevertheless, the Parliament:

has the power to remove the Commission by a two-thirds majority;

supervises the Commission and the Council, and often addresses incisive written and oral questions to them (there were 2,946 in 1981);

is called upon to give its opinion on Commission proposals before the Council can make its decision;

has budgetary powers which enable it to participate in all major decisions involving expenditure. It is effectively the Parliament which accepts or rejects the draft budget prepared by the Commission and agreed by the Council following consultation procedures with the Council:

For expenditure (mainly agricultural) arising from the Treaties and decisions taken as a consequence of these, the Council can reject the modifications introduced by the Parliament if it increases the total size of the budget:

For non-obligatory expenditure, resulting in new developments in European construction, the Parliament has discretionary power over the limits of a margin of manœuvre which is dependent on the economic situation in the Community and which can be modified by mutual agreement with the Council. . . .

THE BUDGET AND THE COURT OF AUDITORS

The Community budget stands at around 23 billion ECU for 1982 which represents about 3% of the expenditure of the governments of its Member States and about 85 ECU for each citizen.[1]

[1] 1 ECU (European currency unit)=about £0.56 or Ir.£0.70 (at exchange rates current on 12 February 1982). [It was equal to about $0.64 in March, 1985. Eds.]

The budget is no longer financed by national contributions, but by the Community's own resources:

duties and taxes on imports from the rest of the world;

a proportion of VAT not exceeding 1% of a uniform assessment basis.

As a percentage of the total, the principal expenditures contained in the 1982 budget were as follows:

support for agricultural prices, modernization in agriculture and fishing: 62.5%;

aid for industrial and infrastructure investment in the poorest regions: 8.5%;

social measures, particularly employment, vocational training and retraining, education, culture, environment and consumer affairs: 5.8%;

aid to Third World countries: 4.1% (plus non-budgetary expenditures arising from the Lomé Convention);

joint action in research, energy, industry and transport: 2.4%;

operating expenses: 4.7% covering the salaries of the 18,000 officials and operatives in all the various Community institutions, and including buildings, administrative costs, information expenditure, etc.;

supplementary regional aid measures and financial arrangements aimed at reducing the gap between the United Kingdom's income from the Community and what it pays in: 7.1%. A new agreement on this problem is currently being discussed. Such imbalances will eventually be avoided through improved sectoral distribution of expenditure: a relative reduction in agricultural expenditure, increased social, regional, and industrial expenditure, etc. But such a reorientation will not be painless as the Community's total resources are limited.

The operation of the budget is supervised by a Court of Auditors. The Court is composed of ten members appointed by the mutual agreement of the Council of Ministers for a six-year period. The Court of Auditors has extensive powers to verify the legality and the regularity of Community revenue and expenditures. . . .

CONCLUSION

Throughout the world there are a large number of international organizations to bring together the States that wish to cooperate with each other. The European Community goes much further than this:

in its aim: to build over a period of time a veritable European Union, the shape of which is still subject to considerable debate;

in its methods: the operation of the Community is not purely inter-governmental—Community institutions have their own powers and the organization of their relationships aims to promote the general interest of Europeans;

in its results: the Council of Ministers and the Commission, wherever it has autonomous decision-making powers, takes action with the force of law and which in many cases is applied directly to European citizens.

Their actions are termed:

regulations, which are applied directly;

decisions, which are binding only on the Member States, companies or individuals to whom they are addressed;

directives, which set down compulsory objectives but leave it to the discretion of Member States to translate them into their national legislation;

recommendations and opinions which are not binding (except for recommendations in the ECSC sector where they are equivalent to directives).

Concerned with strengthening the Community's effectiveness, the European Commission has taken a stand in favour of rebalancing the institutions. This implies: full recognition of the initiating, executive and management role of the Commission; recourse, when needed, to a qualified majority in the Council; strengthening the influence of the Parliament, particularly through greater cooperation with the Commission and the Council.

2.   The EEC in Operation: The Case of Agriculture

Although the EEC's programs, once defined, are carried out with a high degree of supranationalism, the negotiation of these programs is very much an exercise in nationalism—an exercise in which each nation calculates its gains and losses quite precisely. The result is frequently an elaborate package negotiation in which each nation's losses in some areas are compensated by gains in others.

Probably the central EEC program is the agricultural price support system, initially a benefit to French agriculture that balanced the benefits of the free trade zone to German manufacturing. Today, the politics and the program are both much more complicated. The Common Agricultural Policy (CAP) has been referred to as the "glue" or "cement" holding the EEC together.

The agricultural system seeks to benefit the farmer by maintaining high farm prices (as opposed to direct subsidies). There is a Community fund, the "European Agricultural Guidance and Guarantee Fund" (EAGGF) that intervenes in the agricultural markets to buy specific commodities should the price fall below levels that are renegotiated each year. The prices and sometimes the allocation of the intervention costs are revised annually in a marathon negotiation.

This was complicated enough when the only price differences within the Community were those deriving from transportation and local supply and demand differences. When EEC currencies began to vary against one another in the 1970s the task became even more complicated because currency fluctuations would modify effective prices. The Community responded with a detailed system of border adjustments (monetary compensation amounts or MCAs) and assumed exchange rates. The latter were actually politically negotiated as part of the overall balance and typically diverged from the real exchange rate, so that the value of the "Green Pound" might be different from that of the real pound.

The following excerpt provides a view of the Common Agricultural Policy, as well as a sense of Community documentation. The excerpt is from the Commission's defense of the agricultural program, which has come under increasing attack because of its cost to both the consumer and the Community budget. The student should closely analyze the justifications given by the Commission for its high domestic support prices and export restitutions (subsidies). The problems posed by the CAP for U.S. agricultural exporters continue, and have been the subject of several GATT panels. (See Chapter 9, which considers dispute resolution within the GATT).

REFLECTIONS ON THE COMMON AGRICULTURAL POLICY

Commission of the European Communities, ¶¶1-18 (1980)

GENERAL CONSIDERATIONS . . .

THE REASONS FOR THE CAP, ITS PRINCIPLES AND ITS RESULTS

Reasons

2. The common agricultural policy was set up with the objective of permitting free trade in agricultural produce within the newly-created common market. While the freeing of trade in industrial products was to be based essentially on the removal of customs barriers and quantitative restrictions, for agricultural products it was necessary to put an end to the multiplicity of State aids, market organizations and income support systems which existed in all Member States.

Furthermore, the maintenance of different agricultural systems would have led to distortions of competition which would have impeded trade and produced differences in the cost of food, and hence in the cost of living and in wage costs, which would have been prejudicial to true economic integration.

For the above reasons the founding Member States considered that there should be free trade in agricultural products as well as a common market in industrial products and that therefore there should be a common policy for agriculture. Agricultural policy and free trade in industrial products thus remain indissolubly linked and together constitute the very basis of the Community.

Principles

3. The common agricultural policy has been based since its inception on three principles:

freedom of trade and Community preference;

the creation of market organizations based on common prices;

the sharing of the cost of this common policy.

These three principles are interdependent and cannot be dissociated from the objective to be achieved. In order for there to be free trade, it is necessary to have a common support policy and a single price level. Once prices are decided on in common it is not only natural but essential for the financial consequences of that common agricultural policy to be borne jointly.

Single price. The experience of the last ten years since the introduction of compensatory amounts has shown how difficult it is to avoid distortions of production and distortions of trade once the concept of price unity is set aside. The introduction of the European Monetary System in 1979 and the close relationship between the currencies maintained since then have caused this 'sickness' of compensatory amounts to recede. It was high time, because their continuation and their increase would certainly have led to the break-up of the common agricultural policy.

Cost-sharing. Once there is a Community decision on the fixing of prices, and hence indirectly on the development of budgetary expenditure, it is only natural for the consequences to be borne by the budget of the Community.

Without a common system of financing there can be no certainty about the fixing of single prices. We need only consider the following examples, which are not exhaustive but will serve as illustrations for readers who are acquainted with the nature of discussions in the Council of Agriculture Ministers: Would Ireland accept high prices for beef and veal if it had to bear the consequences from its own budget? Would France have agreed to high prices for cereals and sugar for fifteen years if it had to meet the expenditure itself? Would Italy have subsidized olive oil or processed fruit and vegetables to the same extent if the Italian Parliament had had to vote the necessary appropriations each year?

The answer is clearly no.

4. If we look closely at the internal structure of the common agricultural policy it is evident that these three principles, or pillars erected by the architects of the policy, are not merely decorative features. They are essential foundations for the insertion of any common agricultural policy into a common market based on freedom of trade. Calling these principles into question would affect the balance between the agricultural policy and the free circulation of industrial products and could thus lead to a change or a weakening in the rules applicable to the latter.

The common agricultural policy may be characterized as a system of support of farmers' incomes mainly through support of market prices with certain elements of direct aid to incomes. For political, financial and administrative reasons, one could not envisage a radically different model for the Community's agricultural policy than the support of market prices. But this does not mean that, in future, problems of a special regional nature or concerning particular commodities cannot be solved by Community measures involving direct income support, as indeed has already been done in certain specific cases.

Results

5. If we are to judge the results of the common agricultural policy after fifteen years of existence, we should look to see, objectively and on the basis of statistics, whether the objectives set have been attained.

6. Since the creation of the common market the consumption of foodstuffs has improved in both quantity and quality to an extent never before known. This development, to the advantage of consumers, was helped by the spectacular development of agriculture and of intra-Community trade in agricultural produce.

7. Similarly, if we look at agricultural production, which has increased by 2.5% a year over the last twenty years, the growth in productivity and the optimum use made of production factors, we can see that the common agricultural policy has encouraged the modernization of European agriculture.

The growth in productivity revealed by the figures shows the extent to which agriculture, supported by the common policy, contributed in the 1960s and 1970s to the remarkable boom in the industrial and tertiary sectors by providing them with the necessary labour: between 1958 and 1979 more than 10 million members of the working population left agriculture, i.e. at the rate of one a minute.

In 1980 the agricultural policy enables 8 million persons to be directly employed in agriculture. If we add the employment 'upstream' (fertilizers, equipment) and 'downstream' (foodstuffs processing), agriculture and agri-business form one of the major branches of economic activity in the Community.

8. The common policy has enabled agricultural income to keep on growing and at the same time it has protected the sector from the recessions which have affected the economy since 1974. Since 1968 real income in agriculture has on average increased by 2.8% a year, a rate equal to the increase in the other branches of the economy over the period 1968-76.

9. As regards security of supply, Europe has not only been shielded from any physical shortage of foodstuffs but it has also been protected from the speculative movements which sometimes affect the world markets in raw materials. We need only think of the dependence of Europe as regards energy and of the vulnerability of supplies from overseas in order to understand that an

entity such as Europe, with a population of 260 and perhaps soon more than 300 million, cannot afford to rely on others for its food supplies and has the duty to exploit the richness of its soil.

10. On the subject of exports, it should not be forgotten that the CAP has facilitated the export of agricultural products both within the Community and to non-member countries and has thus had important consequences for the trade balance of the Member States. Neither should we forget the contribution of European agriculture to satisfying world demand for food, including the demand from those parts of the world unable to pay for it. If the FAO's [Food and Agriculture Organization of the United Nations] forecasts are correct, the world will need all its available resources in order to meet its future food requirements.

Any change in the CAP which substantially disturbed these trade flows would seriously upset the balance which has existed within the common market since its inception. One cannot expect to have a common market for the sale of one's industrial goods, or to take advantage of the free movement of capital and services, and at the same time refuse to provide the instrument which is essential to the free movement of agricultural produce.

DIFFICULTIES ENCOUNTERED BY THE CAP: POSSIBLE SOLUTIONS

Criticisms

11. The main difficulty encountered by the common agricultural policy, after fifteen years of operation, is the lack of sufficiently effective regulatory mechanisms whereby the development of production is geared to the needs of the internal and external markets. As the common agricultural policy is based essentially on mechanisms which support farmers' incomes by means of guaranteed prices or direct product subsidies, the continual increase in production engenders an uncontrollable rise in expenditure.

Of the EAGGF chapters which have shown rapid increases over the last three years, it is evident that those for milk, beef and processed fruit and vegetables represent rises in expenditure which can no longer be kept under control as the rules stand at present. For wine, although the development of expenditure from year to year is strongly influenced by the ups and downs of the harvest, the trend is for output to rise while consumption continues to fall. Similarly for cereals and sugar, despite annual variations, the trend has been for Community production to increase rather faster than consumption. The difficulty with regard to the milk surpluses stems from the fact that there is no internal market or external market that can pay where disposal is possible at a reasonable cost, and that the scope for increasing food aid is limited. To get rid of stocks it has proved necessary to grant even higher export refunds or subsidies for internal disposal, sometimes equivalent to 80% of the product's value.

Similarly, the aid for processed fruit and vegetables may exceed the price received by agricultural producers, since the aid is in fact a deficiency payment to cover the difference between the production cost of the European industry and the world market price.

This being the case, it is clear that, unless prices are drastically readjusted, any guarantee arrangements applicable to unlimited quantities are bound to result in further increases in production. This is only common sense: without physical or economic control, no system can function properly in the long term.

12. The second criticism which may be directed at the common agricultural policy concerns the way in which the common market organizations, based as they are on price guarantees or product subsidies, work to the advantage of the largest producers, who already have the most favourable production structures.

It is not really surprising that, in a market economy, farms should tend to become larger and larger. In the long term, there is no valid reason why agricultural production should not follow industry in the trend towards larger and more rational economic units with better allocation of resources and economies of scale.

Criticism centres round those situations where prices (i.e. incomes, to a great extent) receive direct support from public funds. In other words, in a Europe facing, because of the energy crisis, a long slowdown in its economic growth, voices are being raised in protest against public money being used, for the most part, to support the incomes of the richest farmers.

13. The view that this system whereby incomes are supported by prices is a source of social inequality, under the cloak of economic equality, is akin to a third criticism, namely that the common agricultural policy has been of greater assistance to the regions which were already rich than it has been to the least-favoured areas of the Community.

This criticism is clearly connected with the differences in natural resources and the structural disparities which already existed when the Community was set up. However, it must be recognized that there are large differences in income and productivity between the Community agricultural regions, and, worse still, in spite of some closing of the gap in some regions in Ireland and north-eastern Italy, these differences have increased during the 1970s. There are two basic reasons why the price and markets policies are connected with this growth in regional disparities. Firstly, the richer Community regions, on account of the type of their production (cereals, milk and sugar), receive more substantial support than the less-favoured regions, which are largely in the Mediterranean area and mainly produce fruit and vegetables and wine. Secondly, it should be borne in mind that the common market organizations tend to favour the more well-to-do producers, who are mainly concentrated in the richer regions. Only in recent years has more sustained attention been given to the Mediterranean production sector or, more generally speaking, to areas with economic or natural handicaps. Special consideration must be given to this aspect now that the Community is to take in three Mediterranean countries whose agricultural structures are very disparate and, in most cases, extremely weak and now that consideration is being given to recasting the CAP.

It is true that the prices fixed at the outset by the Community are generally higher than world prices, but they are not necessarily higher than the prices on other major markets, such as the USA or Japan. The price of milk, for instance, is at present higher in the USA than in the Community. Also, everybody knows that world prices relate only to limited, often marginal quantities and that it would be wrong to think that European consumers could be supplied for long at low and stable world prices. But on the other side it is the world market price on which exports have to be based as far as the financial aspects are concerned.

The common price level reflects Europe's stage of industrial and social development. However, more important than price levels is the trend of agricultural prices. This trend has been particularly prudent in recent years and European agriculture has thus made a highly effective contribution to the fight against inflation. Common agricultural prices have been falling by about 4% per annum in real terms.

If since 1972 agricultural price support in national currencies (common prices translated into national currencies via green rates) has increased in the Community slightly faster than the general price index, it is because until 1976/77 prices increased in real terms. Since then they have decreased owing to the prudent price policy. This prudent price policy is one of the reasons why—after a satisfactory evolution for a number of years—real farm incomes decreased in 1980 for the second successive year.

14. The fourth and last criticism, which is of a financial and budgetary nature, has given rise to differences over the budget not only between the Member States but also between the European institutions, particularly where Parliament was concerned.

This criticism falls under four distinct headings:

15. Some take the view that the overall burden which agriculture imposes on public funds is too high in absolute terms. . . .

16. Others consider that agriculture's share of the Community budget is disproportionately large and retarding the development of other common policies. . . .

17. Another reason for criticism relating to the budget has been the way in which the financial burden is shared among the Member States. Some are net contributors because of the structure, type and volume of their agricultural production, while others are substantial net beneficiaries.

This criticism cannot be rebutted, but it should be said that this disparity results from the very structure of the Community and its external trade and from the different degrees to which its common policies have been developed. It does not, by itself, justify a reconsideration of the single common policy—agriculture. If the principle of equal burdens and equal benefits, i.e. the principle of a fair return, is to be introduced, how shall we assess what is a fair economic return from the common market in industrial products?

Let this be quite clear: the principle of a fair return is incompatible with the notions of financial solidarity and common policy, whether on agriculture or on anything else. No State, unitary or federal, has been able to achieve unity or integration by applying it. The same will hold true for the Community.

A discussion paper on the common agricultural policy is not the place for an 'assessment' of the mechanisms of the Financial Regulation. It should be pointed out, however, that from the strictly agricultural point of view any reform of these mechanisms should maintain effective solidarity and ensure that the agricultural levies and customs duties are used for their proper purpose in a customs union, i.e. as own [community] resources.

18. Lastly, the criticism on budgetary and financial counts is also directed against the way in which the agricultural appropriations are spent for ever-larger structural surpluses without reducing the income disparities in the agricultural sector and with the criticism that agricultural expenditure has an anti-social facet.

In plain terms, then, what is being criticized is not so much the total expenditure of 1000 million units of account against the EAGGF Guarantee Section as the expenditure of 4500 million units of account on milk products for which the market outlook is unlikely to improve in the near future, or the fact that, the richer you are, the larger your share of this bounty.

A very close correlation can be discerned between the regional agricultural income level and of the level of support expenditure per unit. Expressed on the basis of an average index for the Community of 100, agricultural expenditure per labour unit exceeds 150 in most regions in the Paris basin, Belgium, northern Germany, the Netherlands and Denmark, but is generally below 50 in one out of three regions in Italy and lower than 80 in most other Italian regions and in the mountain regions and in south-west France. The regions with the highest agricultural incomes are those which incur the most expenditure.

It is this fourth aspect of the financial criticism which we see as most pertinent and which calls for certain amendments to the common agricultural policy. The Commission believes that it is wrong to assess the common agricultural policy solely in terms of budgetary implications, although a rigorous approach to the growth of agricultural expenditure, as for other items, is of course indispensible. The common policy has assumed responsibility, by substitution, for expenditure formerly borne by the governments, and there is in fact no evidence that this has led to an increase—if anything, there has been a decrease in Member States' total transfers of public funds to agriculture. It should also be remembered that the Community's agricultural budget includes expenditure which could just as well be assigned to other policies (social, regional, external policy). . . .

QUESTIONS

1. What would you regard as success for your nation in the EEC's annual agricultural negotiation? How would your views differ if you were Minister of

Agriculture? Finance? Consumer Affairs? In what ways might your position depend on your political party?

2. As suggested in the introduction, arrangements in the EEC are negotiated in elaborate packages, with trade-offs being made across different areas. Is that different from the GATT? From any national legislature?

3. What does the description of the CAP tell you about the role of special interests in the EEC? If you were a European citizen, would you support the CAP? Which constituencies would support it?

4. Is the Common Agricultural Policy consistent with the GATT? Consider GATT Articles I, VII, XI, XXIII, XXIV and XXVIII. Are the export restitutions under the CAP consistent with the GATT? *See* GATT Article XVI and the MTN Code on Subsidies discussed in Chapter 6. For a description of the status of the CAP *see* Marsh, European Agriculture in an Uncertain World in J. Marsh, W. Hager, F. Basagni, F. Sauzey, and M. Camps (eds.), European Economic Issues: Agriculture, Economic Security, Industrial Democracy, the OECD (1977).

3.   *European Economic Community Constitutional Issues Affecting the EEC Approach to Trade Negotiations*

The European Economic Community was established by the Treaty of Rome in 1957[23] for, among other things, the coordination of economic policy among the signatories. The treaty also contains provisions for the conduct of economic relations between the EEC and nonsignatory nations:

ARTICLE 113

1. After the end of the transitional period, the common commercial policy shall be based on uniform principles, particularly in regard to tariff modifications, the conclusion of tariff and trade agreements, the establishment of uniformity as regards measures of liberalization, export policy and protective commercial measures including measures to be taken in cases of dumping or subsidies.

2. The Commission shall submit proposals to the Council for putting into effect this common commercial policy.

3. Where agreements with third countries require to be negotiated, the Commission shall make recommendations to the Council, which will authorize the Commission to open the necessary negotiations.

The Commission shall conduct these negotiations in consultation with a special Committee appointed by the Council to assist the Commission in this task and within the framework of such directives as the Council may issue to it.

4. The Council shall, when exercising the powers conferred upon it by this Article, act by a qualified majority vote. . . .

ARTICLE 116

From the end of the transitional period, Member States shall, in respect of all matters of particular interest in regard to the Common Market, proceed only by

[23] March 25, 1957, 298 U.N.T.S. 11 (effective Jan. 1, 1958).

common action within the framework of any international organizations of an economic character. The Commission shall for this purpose submit to the Council, which shall act by a qualified majority vote, proposals concerning the scope and implementation of such common action.

During the transitional period, Member States shall consult with each other with a view to concerting their action and, as far as possible, adopting a uniform attitude. . . .

ARTICLE 177

The Court of Justice shall have jurisdiction to make a preliminary ruling concerning:

(a) the interpretation of this Treaty;

(b) the validity and interpretation of acts of the institutions of the Community;

(c) the interpretation of the statutes of any bodies set up by an act of the Council, where such statutes so provide.

Where any such question is raised before a court of one of the Member States, such court may, if it considers that a decision on this point is necessary in order to deliver its judgment, request the Court of Justice to rule on this question.

Where any such question is raised in a case pending before a national court from whose decisions no appeal lies under municipal law, such court is required to refer the matter to the Court of Justice. . . .

ARTICLE 228

1. Where this Treaty provides for the conclusion of agreements between the Community and one or more States or an international organization, such agreements shall be negotiated by the Commission. Subject to the powers conferred upon the Commission in this field, such agreements shall be concluded by the Council after the Assembly has been consulted in the cases provided for by this Treaty.

The Council, the Commission or a Member State may, as a preliminary, obtain the opinion of the Court of Justice as to the compatibility of the contemplated agreements with the provisions of this Treaty. An agreement which is the subject of an adverse opinion of the Court of Justice may only enter into force under the conditions laid down, in Article 236.

2. Agreements concluded under the conditions laid down above shall be binding on the institutions of the Community and on Member States.

ARTICLE 236

The Government of any Member State or the Commission may submit to the Council proposals for the revision of this Treaty.

If the Council, after consulting the Assembly and, where appropriate, the Commission, expresses an opinion in favor of the calling of a conference of representatives of the Governments of Member States, such conference shall be convened by the President of the Council for the purpose of determining in common agreement the amendments to be made to this Treaty.

Such amendments shall enter into force after being ratified by all Member States in accordance with their respective constitutional rules.

The following three cases were selected to show the way the EEC defines a negotiating position and applies international trade law. They also show the intensely legal facets of the Community that balance the political facets just emphasized. The first case arises from a conflict over the Community's approach to negotiation of the International Rubber Agreement, a commodity agreement of a type that will be explored more fully in Chapter 10. The case contrasts the internationalism of the Community with the nationalism of the individual governments, and poses issues parallel to those posed by the United States delegation cases presented earlier in the chapter.

The second and third cases show the problems of an individual trader who seeks to argue international law principles against Community actions—problems that, in United States law, would be treated by analyzing whether the principles are "self-executing." In the first of these cases, the court makes the GATT applicable to the Community even though only the national members of the Community ever signed the GATT; it then goes on to deny an individual the right to rely upon the provision. In the second, the court resists an effort to base the equivalent of Most-Favored-Nation protection on traditional Community law principles.

Although the cases are basically self-explanatory, two background points may help in understanding the European law aspects of the cases. First, the two cases arise under different heads of European Court of Justice jurisdiction. The first case arises under Treaty Article 228, a special advisory jurisdiction procedure, under which one EEC institution can bring certain disputes with another EEC institution to the court. The other two arise under Treaty Article 177 by reference from a national court; when such a court faces an issue involving the interpretation of EEC actions it may, and in some cases must, refer the issue (not the entire case) to the European Court for resolution.

The second point is that the second of the court's decisions is accompanied by the recommendation of the Advocate General, a civil law institution. His or her responsibility is to prepare the case for the court with a careful memorandum. The advocate general's position is a career position and is essentially as prestigious as membership on the court.

RE THE DRAFT INTERNATIONAL AGREEMENT ON NATURAL RUBBER

[1979] 3 E.C.R. 2871, [1979] 3 C.M.L.R. 639

[1] By a request dated 13 November 1978 the Commission has asked the Court to give its opinion in pursuance of the second subparagraph of Article 228 (1) of the EEC Treaty on the compatibility with the Treaty of the draft International Agreement on Natural Rubber which is the subject of negotiations in the United Nations Conference on Trade and Development (hereinafter referred to as "UNCTAD"), and, more particularly, whether the Community is competent to conclude the agreement in question.

[2] The Commission has taken this step following a divergence of view

which has become apparent between itself and the Council on the question of the delimitation of the respective powers of the Community and of the member-States to negotiate and conclude the agreement in question. The views for which the Commission and the Council contend on this subject may be summarised as follows:

According to the Commission, the agreement envisaged comes entirely, or at least in essentials, within the context of Article 113 of the EEC Treaty relating to the common commercial policy. On that basis the negotiation and conclusion of the agreement come within the Community's exclusive powers; consequently the Community must assume, through the intermediary of its own institutions, the whole of the rights and obligations attached to its status as a Contracting Party to the agreement, must participate on the same footing as the other parties in the institutions to be set up within that framework and be entitled to vote there in its own right and to exercise such right by its own representatives alone.

According to the Council the subject-matter of the agreement falls outside the framework of commercial policy and thus calls for a division of powers between the Community and the member-States so that the agreement must be concluded, following the pattern of other similar agreements, according to the technique of the so-called "mixed-type" agreement, that is to say, by the Community and the member-States jointly. The Council takes the view that that formula, well tried in the context of association agreements, negotiations entered into in the context of the 'North-South dialogue' and the commodity agreements previously concluded, have made it possible to assert the unity of the Community in a fully satisfactory manner on the international scene.

[3] It appears from the foregoing that the right of the Community to participate in the agreement envisaged is not in itself contested. The only point of disagreement consists in determining whether the subject-matter of the agreement comes entirely within the powers of the Community or whether it may possibly give rise to a division of powers in such a way as to justify the joint participation in the agreement of the Community and of the member-States.

I

HISTORY AND STATE OF THE PROCEEDINGS . . .

[5] As the negotiations which are in progress on natural rubber were undertaken within the framework of UNCTAD, it is appropriate to recall, first, certain features of the constitution of that body which was laid down by Resolution 1995 (XIX) of 30 December 1964 of the United Nations General Assembly. In the wording of that resolution the functions of UNCTAD are to "promote international trade, especially with a view to accelerating economic development, particularly trade between countries at different stages of development, between developing countries and between countries with different

systems of economic and social organization," and to "formulate principles and policies on international trade and related problems of economic development." In this respect it is charged to "initiate action . . . for the negotiation and adoption of multilateral legal instruments in the field of trade."

[6] On the basis of those provisions the General Assembly adopted on 1 May 1974 a Declaration and Programme of Action on the Establishment of a "New International Economic Order" and, on 12 December 1974, the "Charter of the Economic Rights and Duties of States." Amongst the principles of the "New International Economic Order" Resolution 3281 (S-VI) mentions the "just and equitable relationship between the prices of raw materials, primary commodities, manufactured and semi-manufactured goods exported by developing countries and the prices of raw materials, primary commodities, manufactures, capital goods and equipment imported by them with the aim of bringing about sustained improvement in their unsatisfactory terms of trade and the expansion of the world economy." Resolution 3202 (S-VI) requires all efforts to be made "to take measures to reverse the continued trend of stagnation or decline in the real price of several commodities exported by developing countries, despite a general rise in commodity prices, resulting in a decline in the export earnings of these developing countries." The same resolution recommends the "expeditious formulation of commodity agreements where appropriate, in order to regulate as necessary and to stabilise the world markets for raw materials and primary commodities" and the "preparation of an overall integrated programme, setting out guidelines and taking into account the current work in this field, for a comprehensive range of commodities of export interest to developing countries." On the basis of those resolutions UNCTAD adopted on 30 May 1976, at the time of the Nairobi session, Resolution 93 (IV) which bears the title "Integrated Programme for Commodities" (hereinafter referred to as the "Nairobi Resolution"). . . .

[11] At the beginning of 1978, following a number of preparatory meetings, UNCTAD decided to open negotiations for the conclusion of an International Agreement on Natural Rubber. These were the first negotiations undertaken under the Nairobi Resolution on the "Integrated Programme."

[12] For the purposes of these negotiations the Commission sent to the Council on 22 November 1977 and 24 May 1978 communications concerning guidelines for a Community position. These documents take stock of the preparatory work performed within UNCTAD, in which the Commission had taken part, and put forward certain guidelines for the preparation of the negotiations still to be accomplished. As it was expected that the negotiations would start on 13 November 1978 the Commission on 5 October 1978 put to the Council a "recommendation" under Article 113 (3) of the Treaty, including the draft of a "Decision on the negotiation of an international agreement on rubber" and a draft of "Directives for negotiation." Under the draft decision, the Commission was to be "authorised to conduct, on behalf of the Community, . . . negotiations in accordance with the directives" laid down by the Council and "in consultation with the special committee provided for in Article 113 of the Treaty."

[13] In the statement of the reasons on which its recommendation was based, the Commission put forward the following grounds for the participation of the Community in the agreement: "All the instruments of the agreement directly and substantially affect the volume and conditions of international trade in natural rubber and will therefore fall within the Community's competence on the basis of Article 113 of the Treaty of Rome. As a consequence the financial implementation of the agreement on natural rubber shall be assumed by the Community itself through a direct contribution from the Community budget."

[14] After considering that recommendation the Council examined the questions relating to the participation of the Community in the agreement envisaged. At its meeting on 17 October 1978 it approved a procedural decision prepared by the Committee of Permanent Representatives entitled "Procedures for the Committee's Participation in the Conference" and worded as follows:

> The Community and its member-States must be represented in the negotiations on natural rubber by a Community delegation and by nine national delegations. As is customary, the Community delegation will be a joint one (Commission and a representative of the President of the Council, plus one official from each member-State).
>
> Negotiations will be conducted from a common standpoint agreed in advance.
>
> With regard to matters which come within the scope of the Community's powers, the Commission is responsible for negotiating on behalf of the Community.
>
> With regard to other matters of particular interest to the Community, joint action will be taken throughout the negotiations.
>
> The Commission representative will usually act as joint spokesman in accordance with the procedure laid down in the case of joint delegations. The views expressed by the member-States must be in line with the common standpoint defined in advance and must support and develop the latter.
>
> Should difficulties arise at the Conference, the delegations must refer them to the Council in Brussels.

[15] In the report submitted on this matter to the Council by the Committee of Permanent Representatives there is a statement to the effect that this is a pragmatic formula based on the detailed arrangements already laid down for other negotiations on commodities and that it is to be understood that that formula in no way pre-judges the legal positions in this matter put forward by the various delegations and more particularly by the Commission. A note to that report states that in the Commission's view the negotiation of the agreement in question comes within the Community's exclusive powers under Article 113 of the EEC Treaty. On the other hand the delegations take the view that the negotiations occupy a wider framework than that envisaged by Article 113 and some of the delegations consider that Articles 113 and 116 apply.

[16] It was by virtue of the above-mentioned decision of the Council that negotiations were undertaken within UNCTAD on the date arranged. It

should be added that on 15 November 1978 the Council, still following proposals from the Commission, adopted a "common position" for the negotiation of the agreement and it was understood that the work for the final formulation of that position would be pursued on the basis of co-ordination on the spot in Geneva and that in the event of difficulties the officers of the Council in Brussels would be apprised of the situation.

[17] The recommendation presented by the Commission under Article 113 on the negotiating procedures was thus by implication rejected by the effect of the decision of 17 October 1978 and the Commission therefore immediately lodged with the Court a request for an opinion in pursuance of Article 228 so as to clarify the divergence of views between the Commission and the Council. The Council lodged its written observations on 19 February 1979. At the same time statements of case were lodged in support of the Council's observations by the Government of the French Republic and the Government of the United Kingdom. The Court invited the Commission and the Council to attend a hearing in closed session, which took place on 9 May 1979, at which the two institutions were enabled to give explanations with regard to their position and reply to questions put by a number of members of the Court. The Governments of the member-States had also been informed of this hearing but none of them submitted observations on that occasion. The Advocates General were heard by the Court in closed session in accordance with Article 108 of the Rules of Procedure. . . .

(a) The economic objectives of the Agreement

[20] The essential purpose of the International Agreement on Rubber is to achieve a balanced growth between the supply and demand for natural rubber with a view to stabilising its prices around their long-term trend. The function of these prices is to guarantee stable export earnings for the exporting countries whilst ensuring reliability of supplies for the importing countries at a fair price level. Whilst improving by means of this price policy the competitiveness of natural rubber as against artificial rubber and substitutes, the agreement is intended to lead to a harmonisation in importing countries of production of synthetic rubber and substitutes with the importation of natural rubber. The agreement as a whole is thus intended to encourage a balanced increase both of production and consumption of natural rubber with a view to alleviating the serious difficulties arising, for the parties concerned, according to the economic outlook, either from surpluses or shortages of the product.

[21] The objective thus described is to be realised by building up a buffer stock, the purpose of which is to purchase surpluses of rubber at a time when prices are declining and to sell the stocked rubber when prices are rising so as to contain the price within a margin of fluctuation determined in advance. One of the essential stakes in the negotiations is to determine the central reference price and the margins of fluctuation upwards or downwards, the exceeding of which will make possible or compulsory, as the case may be, the intervention of the buffer stock. The reference prices envisaged are not guaranteed prices, either minimum or maximum, but thresholds for triggering the

operations of the buffer stock, the market price being determined by the operation of supply and demand. Apart from the normal buffer stock, the aggregate amount of which is fixed at 400,000 tonnes, there is envisaged the creation of a supplementary contingency stock of 150,000 tonnes, intended for intervention where the normal operations of the buffer stock prove to be insufficient to cope with an exceptional price depression. . . .

III

PRELIMINARY OBJECTIONS TO THE ADMISSIBILITY OF THE REQUEST

[28] The Council has expressed doubts as to whether the request made by the Commission is not premature and does not, further, constitute an incorrect use of the procedure of Article 228 inasmuch as its aim is to obtain from the Court a solution of questions which lie outside that procedure. This view was supported by the Government of the French Republic and the Government of the United Kingdom. The French Government in particular expressed the opinion that the Commission's request was inadmissible and that it amounted to a misuse of procedure under Article 228.

As a subsidiary issue the Council has suggested that the Court should in any case stay proceedings until such time as the negotiations have reached a more advanced stage.

(a) The recourse to Article 228

[29] According to the Council the request for an opinion lodged by the Commission is not of the type envisaged by Article 228. The opinion on which this view seems to be based is that that procedure does not lend itself to the settling of questions relating to the division of powers in matters of external relations or in particular to resolving questions of a general scope relating to the interpretation of Article 113 and to the legitimacy in the light of that provision of the practice of so-called 'mixed-type' agreements. . . .

[Discussion omitted—the Court decided this issue favorably to the Commission.]

(b) The question whether the request is premature

[32] The objection as to the premature nature of the reference to the Court derives from the fact that at the time when the Commission lodged its request for an opinion the negotiations were still not in an advanced state. . . .

[Details of decision on point favorable to Commission omitted.]

IV

THE SUBJECT-MATTER AND OBJECTIVES OF THE AGREEMENT ENVISAGED

[36] As the Council has indicated, the problem of competence which has been submitted to the Court must be examined from two aspects. The first

question is whether the agreement envisaged, by reason of its subject-matter and objectives, comes within the concept of common commercial policy referred to in Article 113 of the Treaty. The second question—but only if the first question is answered in the affirmative—is whether, by reason of certain specific arrangements or special provisions of the agreement concerning matters coming within the powers of the member-States, the participation of the latter in the agreement is necessary.

The Court will consider first the general aspects concerning the subject-matter and objectives of the agreement.

[37] The central question raised by the Commission's request is whether the international agreement on rubber comes as a whole or at least in essentials within the sphere of the "common commercial policy" referred to in Article 113 of the Treaty. It is common ground that the agreement envisaged is closely connected with commercial policy. The difference of views relates to the extent of the sphere of application of Article 113 so that it remains uncertain whether that provision entirely covers the subject-matter of the agreement in question.

[38] The Commission is fully aware that the provisions of the Treaty relating to the common commercial policy are brief. However, it recalls that in several decisions the case law of the Court has contributed towards interpreting those provisions; it mentions in this respect the judgments in *Massey-Ferguson* (8/73)[14] and *Donckerwolcke* (41/76),[15] in which the Court emphasised the necessity for a complete and consistent management of the Community's international trade, and Opinion 1/75,[16] where the Court emphasised on the one hand that the concept of commercial policy cannot have for the Community a more restricted meaning than for the States and, on the other hand, the exclusive nature of Community powers in the sphere thus defined. Having regard to these guidelines the Commission considers that a measure of commercial policy must be assessed primarily by reference to its specific character as an instrument regulating international trade, having regard to the links established by the Treaty between the removal of barriers to trade between member-States and the implementation of a common commercial policy. Any restrictive conception of the common commercial policy might, by reason of the disparity as between member-States in the use of instruments for regulating external trade from one member-State to another, entail the maintenance of some barriers to intra-Community trade. Having regard to the fact that the essential object of the agreement envisaged is to stabilise prices for natural rubber, this appears to be a characteristic measure for regulating external trade and thus an instrument of commercial policy.

[39] The Council, after recalling that the exclusive nature of Community powers in the matter of commercial policy is not in question and that it does

---

[14][1973] E.C.R. 897, 908.
[15][1976] E.C.R. 1921; [1977] 2 C.M.L.R. 535.
[16][1975] E.C.R. 1355; [1976] 1 C.M.L.R. 85.

not reject the idea of a gradual evolution in this sphere, emphasises that the common commercial policy nevertheless fulfils a function of its own in the context of the structure of the Treaty inasmuch as it applies to "any measure the aim of which is to influence the volume or flow of trade." Thus Article 113 should be interpreted so as not to render meaningless other provisions of the Treaty, in particular those dealing with general economic policy, including the supply policy for raw materials which remains within the powers of member-States and for which the Council has only, under Article 145, a power of "co-ordination." According to the Council there is here a close interrelation between the powers of the Community and those of the member-States, since it is difficult to distinguish between international economic relations and international political relations. In this connection the Council once again draws attention to the fact that rubber is a "strategic product" so that the agreement in question impinges also on the defence policy of member-States. In these circumstances the Council takes the view that the negotiation of the agreement envisaged comes not only under Article 113 of the Treaty but also under Article 116 relating to common action by member-States within the framework of international organisations of an economic character to which they belong.

[40] The Council also mentions that the negotiations undertaken within UNCTAD with a view to arriving at agreements on a number of commodities must be seen against "the general political background of North-South relations between the industrialised world and the developing countries." According to the Council it is obvious from the very nature of such agreements that, notwithstanding the aim of the negotiators from the consumer countries to obtain a balanced agreement, such agreements contain elements of "non-reciprocity" which are typical of "development aid." This is particularly the case with the price-fixing system provided for in the context of the buffer stock mechanism. These development aid features, which are inherent in the agreement, do not come within the field of commercial policy. The French Government has particularly emphasised this aspect in its observations. It declares that it cannot accept the statement that the whole of the substance of the rubber agreement constitutes commercial policy because, in its opinion, it is a matter of "the performance of a duty of international solidarity excluding commercial considerations."

(a) Consideration of the Agreement's Links with Commercial Policy and Development Problems

[41] By its special machinery as much as by certain aspects of its legal structure, the International Agreement on Natural Rubber which it is proposed to conclude stands apart from ordinary commercial and tariff agreements which are based primarily on the operation of customs duties and quantitative restrictions. The agreement in question is a more structured instrument in the form of an organisation of the market on a world scale and in this way it is distinguished from classical commercial agreements. An answer

to the question which is the subject of the request for an opinion requires a reference to the scope and consequences of these specific characteristics in relation to the concept of common commercial policy as referred to in Article 113 of the Treaty. At the same time consideration must be given to the question whether the link which exists between the agreement envisaged and the development problems to which the Council refers may perhaps exclude the agreement from the sphere of the common agricultural policy as defined by the Treaty.

[42] The Nairobi Resolution, which is the basis of the negotiations in progress on natural rubber, shows that commodity agreements have complex objectives. Whilst stressing the needs of the developing countries the resolution includes many references to mechanisms of a commercial nature and does not overlook the needs of the industrialized countries. As regards, more particularly, the interests of the developing countries, it is true that commodity agreements may involve the granting of advantages which are characteristic of development aid; it must however be acknowledged also that for those countries such agreements respond more fundamentally to the preoccupation of bringing about an improvement in the "terms of trade" and thus of increasing their export earnings. This characteristic is particularly brought out in the agreement in question, which seeks to establish a fair balance between the interests of the producer countries and those of the consumer countries. It is natural that, in negotiating an agreement of this type, the industrialised countries, whilst seeking to defend their own interests, should be obliged to recognise the situation of the producer countries which are negotiating from an economic standpoint which is very different from their own and that a reasonable compromise must be found between these points of view so as to make an agreement possible.

[43] The link between the various agreements on commodities which was emphasised by the Nairobi Resolution must also be taken into account. As an increasing number of products which are particularly important from the economic point of view are concerned, it is clear that a coherent commercial policy would no longer be practicable if the Community were not in a position to exercise its powers also in connection with a category of agreements which are becoming, alongside traditional commercial agreements, one of the major factors in the regulation of international trade.

[44] Following the impulse given by UNCTAD to the development of this type of control it seems that it would no longer be possible to carry on any worthwhile common commercial policy if the Community were not in a position to avail itself also of more elaborate means devised with a view to furthering the development of international trade. It is therefore not possible to lay down, for Article 113 of the EEC Treaty, an interpretation the effect of which would be to restrict the common commercial policy to the use of instruments intended to have an effect only on the traditional aspects of external trade to the exclusion of more highly developed mechanisms such as appear in the agreement envisaged. A "commercial policy" understood in that sense would

be destined to become nugatory in the course of time. Although it may be thought that at the time when the Treaty was drafted, liberalisation of trade was the dominant idea, the Treaty nevertheless does not form a barrier to the possibility of the Community's developing a commercial policy aiming at a regulation of the world market for certain products rather than at a mere liberalisation of trade.

[45] Article 113 empowers the Community to formulate a commercial "policy" based on "uniform principles" thus showing that the question of external trade must be governed from a wide point of view and not only having regard to the administration of precise systems such as customs and quantitative restrictions. The same conclusion may be deduced from the fact that the enumeration in Article 113 of the subjects covered by commercial policy (changes in tariff rates, the conclusion of tariff and trade agreements, the achievement of uniformity in measures of liberalisation, export policy and measures to protect trade) is conceived as a non-exhaustive enumeration which must not, as such, close the door to the application in a Community context of any other process intended to regulate external trade. A restrictive interpretation of the concept of common commercial policy would risk causing disturbances in intra-Community trade by reason of the disparities which would then exist in certain sectors of economic relations with non-member countries.

[46] Moreover, when the whole canvas of existing and planned agreements is considered, it appears that as far as the Community is concerned a wide range of interests is involved in the negotiation of those agreements and that there are connections with the most varied spheres in which the Community has undertaken responsibilities. Thus, alongside agreements dealing, like the rubber agreement, with products with regard to which (always excepting of course the problem of substitution products) the Community appears only in the position of a consumer, there are other agreements, for example those concerning products such as wheat, oils and fats and sugar, in which the Community is interested also as a producer and by which its export policy, expressly mentioned in Article 113 as being amongst the objectives of the common commercial policy, is affected at the same time as import policy. Several of the agreements belonging to this category are furthermore directly related to the execution of the Common Agricultural Policy.

(b) The Agreement's Links with General Economic Policy

[47] In its arguments the Council has raised the problem of the interrelation within the structure of the Treaty of the concepts of "economic policy" and "commercial policy." In certain provisions economic policy is indeed considered primarily as a question of national interest; such is the meaning of that concept in Articles 6 and 145 which, for that reason, prescribe for the member-States nothing more than a duty to ensure co-ordination. In other provisions economic policy is envisaged as being a matter of common interest as is the case with Articles 103 to 116, which are grouped together in a title devoted to

the "economic policy" of the Community. The chapter devoted to the common commercial policy forms part of that title.

[48] The considerations set out above already form to some extent an answer to the arguments relating to the distinction to be drawn between the spheres of general economic policy and those of the common commercial policy since international co-operation, inasmuch as it does not belong to commercial policy, would be confused with the domain of general economic policy. If it appears that it comes, at least in part, under the common commercial policy, as has been indicated above, it follows clearly that it could not, under the name of general economic policy, be withdrawn from the competence of the Community.

[49] Having regard to the specific nature of the provisions relating to commercial policy in so far as they concern relations with nonmember countries and are founded, according to Article 113, on the concept of a common policy, their scope cannot be restricted in the light of more general provisions relating to economic policy and based on the idea of mere co-ordination. Consequently, where the organisation of the Community's economic links with nonmember countries may have repercussions on certain sectors of economic policy such as the supply of raw materials to the Community or price policy, as is precisely the case with the regulation of international trade in commodities, that consideration does not constitute a reason for excluding such objectives from the field of application of the rules relating to the common commercial policy. Similarly, the fact that a product may have a political importance by reason of the building up of security stocks is not a reason for excluding that product from the domain of the common commercial policy.

[50] It is in the light of the same considerations that the connection between Article 113 and Article 116 must be determined in the context of the chapter of the Treaty devoted to the common commercial policy. Whilst those two provisions contribute to the same end inasmuch as their objective is the realization of a common policy in international economic relationships, as a basis for action the two Articles are founded on different premises and consequently apply different ideas. According to Article 113 the common commercial policy is determined by the Community, independently, that is to say, acting as such, by the intervention of its own institutions; in particular, agreements entered into under that provision are, in the terms of Article 114, "concluded . . . on behalf of the Community" and accordingly negotiated according to the procedures set out in those provisions and in Article 228. Article 116 on the other hand was conceived with a view to evolving common action by the member-States in international organisations of which the Community is not part; in such a situation the only appropriate means is concerted, joint action by the member-States as members of the said organisations.

[51] In this case a problem relating to the demarcation of the sphere of application of Articles 113 and 114 on the one hand and 116 on the other hand arises from the fact that the agreements on commodities are at present

being negotiated within UNCTAD. The Court has already given its views on this problem in its Opinion 1/75, which itself concerned an international agreement arrived at within the framework of an international organisation (the OECD). In that opinion the Court stressed that what counts with regard to the application of the Treaty is the question whether negotiations undertaken within the framework of an international organisation are intended to lead to an "undertaking entered into by entities subject to international law which has binding force." In such a case it is the provisions of the Treaty relating to the negotiation and conclusion of agreements, in other words Articles 113, 114 and 228, which apply and not Article 116.

V

PROBLEMS RAISED BY THE FINANCING OF THE AGREEMENT AND BY OTHER SPECIFIC PROVISIONS

[52] Consideration must still be given, having regard to what has been stated above as regards correspondence between the objective and purposes of the agreement envisaged and the concept of common commercial policy, to whether the detailed arrangements for financing the buffer stock, or certain specific clauses of the agreement, concerning technological assistance, research programmes, the maintenance of fair conditions of labour in the rubber industry and consultations relating to national tax policies which may have an effect on the price of rubber lead to a negation of the Community's exclusive competence.

[53] As regards the question of financing, the Council and those of the governments which have supported its views state that since those negotiating the agreement have opted for financing by means of public funds, the finances of the member-States will be involved in the execution of the agreement so that it cannot be accepted that such undertakings should be entered into without their participation. The Commission, for its part, takes the view that the question of competence precedes that of financing and that the question of Community powers cannot therefore be made dependent on the choice of financial arrangements.

[54] As regards the specific clauses mentioned above, the Council states that provisions of this kind lie in any case outside the sphere of commercial policy, with the consequence that the negotiation of the agreement envisaged comes from this point of view also under Article 116 relating to common action by member-States within international organisations.

[55] The Court feels that a distinction should be made in this respect between the specific clauses referred to by the Council and the financial provisions which occupy a central position in the structure of the agreement and which, for that reason, raise a more fundamental difficulty as regards the demarcation between the powers of the Community and those of the member-States.

[56] The Court takes the view that the fact that the agreement may cover subjects such as technological assistance, research programmes, labour conditions in the industry concerned or consultations relating to national tax policies which may have an effect on the price of rubber cannot modify the description of the agreement which must be assessed having regard to its essential objective rather than in terms of individual clauses of an altogether subsidiary or ancillary nature. This is the more true because the clauses under consideration are in fact closely connected with the objective of the agreement and the duties of the bodies which are to operate in the framework of the International Natural Rubber Organisation which it is planned to set up. The negotiation and execution of these clauses must therefore follow the system applicable to the agreement considered as a whole.

[57] With regard to the system of financing it should be borne in mind in the first place that, in its recommendation to the Council on 5 October 1978 under Article 113, the Commission had proposed that the application of the financial clauses of the agreement on natural rubber should be effected by the Community itself with a direct contribution from the Community budget. Whilst accepting that this method of financing would be possible having regard to the financial provisions of the EEC Treaty, the Council expressed its preference for financing by the member-States. However, no formal decision has yet been taken on this question. Moreover, there is no certainty as regards the attitude of the various member-States on this particular question and its implications for the apportionment of the financial burdens.

[58] Having regard to the uncertainty which exists as regards the final solution to be adopted for this problem, the Court feels bound to have regard to two possible situations: one in which the financial burdens envisaged by the agreement would be entered in the Community budget and one in which the burdens would be directly charged to the budgets of the member-States. The Court itself is in no position, within the limits of the present proceedings, to make any choice between the two alternatives.

[59] In the first case no problem would arise as regards the exclusive powers of the Community to conclude the agreement in question. As has been indicated above, the mechanism of the buffer stock has the purpose of regulating trade and from this point of view constitutes an instrument of the common commercial policy. It follows that Community financing of the charges arising would have to be regarded as a solution in conformity with the Treaty.

[60] The facts of the problem would be different if the second alternative were to be preferred. It cannot in fact be denied that the financing of the buffer stock constitutes an essential feature of the scheme for regulating the market which it is proposed to set up. The extent of and the detailed arrangements for the financial undertakings which the member-States will be required to satisfy will directly condition the possibilities and the degree of efficiency of intervention by the buffer mechanism whilst the decisions to be taken as regards the level of the central reference price and the margins of fluctuation to be permitted either upwards or downwards will have immediate repercussions

on the use of the financial means put at the disposal of the International Rubber Council which is to be set up and on the extent of the financial means to be put at its disposal. Furthermore sight must not be lost of the fact that the financial structure which it is proposed to set up will make necessary, as is mentioned in the documents submitted to the Court and reflecting the most recent stage of negotiations, co-ordination between the use of the specific financial means put at the disposal of the future International Rubber Council and those which it might find in the Common Fund which is to be set up. If the financing of the agreement is a matter for the Community, the necessary decisions will be taken according to the appropriate Community procedures. If on the other hand the financing is to be by the member-States that will imply the participation of those States in the decision-making machinery or, at least, their agreement with regard to the arrangements for financing envisaged and consequently their participation in the agreement together with the Community. The exclusive competence of the Community could not be envisaged in such a case.

VII

CONCLUDING REMARKS

[63] It follows from all the foregoing considerations that the envisaged International Natural Rubber Agreement, in spite of the special features which distinguish it from classical trade and tariff agreements, comes under the commercial policy as it is envisaged in Article 113 of the EEC Treaty.

The consequences of that finding as regards the exclusive powers of the Community to negotiate and conclude the agreement envisaged might nevertheless be modified having regard to the option still to be exercised with regard to the arrangements for financing the machinery of the buffer stock in the event of the financial burden's being directly assumed by the member-States.

In conclusion, The Court gives the following opinion:

1. The Community's powers relating to commercial policy within the meaning of Article 113 of the Treaty establishing the European Economic Community extend to the International Agreement on Natural Rubber which is in the course of negotiation within the United Nations Conference on Trade and Development.

2. The question of the exclusive nature of the Community's powers depends in this case on the arrangements for financing the operations of the buffer stock which it is proposed to set up under that agreement. If the burden of financing the stock falls upon the Community budget the Community will have exclusive powers. If on the other hand the charges are to be borne directly by the member-States that will imply the participation of those States in the agreement together with the Community.

3. As long as that question has not been settled by the competent Community authorities the member-States must be allowed to participate in the negotiation of the agreement.

INTERNATIONAL FRUIT COMPANY N.V. AND OTHERS v. PRODUKTSCHAP VOOR GROENTEN EN FRUIT (NO. 3)

18 Recueil 1219 (1972), [1975] 2 C.M.L.R. 1

SUBMISSIONS OF THE ADVOCATE-GENERAL . . .

In May 1970, four Rotterdam undertakings involved in the import of fruit, the firms International Fruit Company, Kooy Rotterdam, Velleman en Tas and Jan van den Brinks-Im- en Exporthandel, applied to the Produktschap voor Groenten en Fruit, the competent Dutch office, charged in particular with applying the rules relating to the import of fruit and vegetables, for the issue of import licences for eating apples originating from non-member States. The Produktschap having informed them that these applications "must be rejected" or that it "had been decided to reject them," these companies on the one hand brought the matter before your Court, with a view to obtaining, by means of a direct appeal, the annulment of the acts of the E.C. Commission regarded as underlying the refusal with which they were met; on the other hand, they brought before the competent national jurisdiction, the Appeal Tribunal of the Netherlands for economic matters, applications aimed at securing annulment of the decisions to reject notified by the Produktschap. . . .

The Economic Appeal Tribunal, considering, rightly in my opinion, that it was not competent to pronounce on the validity of Community regulations with regard to an international agreement in view of the powers conferred in this domain on the Community in relations with non-member States, decided on 5 May 1972 to have recourse for the second time to the Article 177 procedure, and submits the following questions to you:

1. Does the "validity" of acts taken by institutions of the Community referred to in Article 177 of the EEC Treaty also cover the validity of these acts *with regard to international law other than Community law?*

2. If so, are EEC Regulations 459/70, 565/70 and 686/70 invalid as being at variance with Article XI of the General Agreement on Tariffs and Trade?

II.   POSITION OF THE PROBLEM

The Dutch economic court has intentionally given the first of these questions as general a formulation as possible by asking you to choose between the following alternatives:

—Can the validity of acts emanating from Community organs only be assessed with regard to the provisions of the Treaty of Rome or, additionally, to norms of derived Community law, standing higher in the hierarchy of juridical acts than those whose validity is in dispute?

or

—In appropriate cases, must this assessment of validity be operated by the Court of Justice according to rules external to Community law, both original and derived, rules dependent—to borrow the formula used—on international law other than the law of the Community? . . .

I submit that you should declare:

1. that, within the meaning of Article 177 of the EEC Treaty, the validity of acts taken by Community institutions must be assessed with regard to a rule of international law other than Community law if this rule binds the Community and is directly applicable in its legal order;

2. that, since the provisions of Article XI of the General Agreement on Tariffs and Trade are not directly applicable in the Community legal order, the validity of Commission Regulations 459/70, 565/70 and 686/70 cannot be put in issue with regard to these provisions.

JUDGMENT

[1] By a decision of 5 May 1972, which reached the Court on 8 May 1972, the College van Beroep voor het Bedrijfsleven submitted to the Court, under Article 177 of the EEC Treaty, two questions involving the interpretation of that Article and the validity of certain regulations adopted by the Commission.

[2] By the first question, the Court is asked to say whether the validity of acts taken by institutions of the Community also covers, in the sense of Article 177, their validity with regard to international law.

[3] The second question, raised in case the first is answered in the affirmative, is aimed at discovering whether Commission Regulations 459/70, 465/70 and 686/70—which provided, as safeguard measures, for restrictions on the import of apples originating from non-member States—"are invalid as being at variance with Article XI of the General Agreement on Tariffs and Trade (GATT)," hereinafter referred to as the "General Agreement."

[4] In the terms of Article 177 (1) of the EEC Treaty, "the Court of Justice is competent to pronounce, on the basis of a preliminary ruling, . . . on the validity . . . of acts taken by institutions of the Community."

[5] The competence of the Court thus formulated implies no limit on the reasons for which the validity of these acts might be contested.

[6] Since this competence extends to all reasons for invalidity capable of marring these acts, the Court is obliged to examine whether their validity could be affected by their being at variance with a rule of international law.

[7] For the incompatibility of a Community act with a provision of interna-

tional law to be able to affect the validity of such act, the Community must first be bound by the provision.

[8] Where the invalidity is invoked before a national Court, it is additionally necessary that the provision should be such as to create, for those subject to the Community's jurisdiction, the right to rely on it in a court of law.

[9] One must therefore examine whether both these two conditions are fulfilled with regard to the General Agreement.

[10] It is settled that, at the time of concluding the Treaty instituting the European Economic Community, the member-States were bound by the undertakings of the General Agreement.

[11] They could not disengage themselves, by an act passed among themselves, from the obligations existing with regard to non-member-States.

[12] On the contrary, their readiness to respect the undertakings of the General Agreement results as much from the provisions of the EEC Treaty itself as from the declarations made by the member-States when they presented the Treaty to the Contracting Parties of the General Agreement in accordance with Article XXIV of the latter.

[13] This intention was manifested in particular in Article 110 of the EEC Treaty, which contains a statement of adherence by the Community to the objectives pursued by the General Agreement, as well as in Article 234 (1), which provides that rights and obligations resulting from agreements concluded prior to the coming into force of the Treaty, and in particular from multilateral conventions concluded with the participation of the member-States, are not affected by the provisions of the Treaty.

[14] The Community assumed the functions inherent in the tariff and trade policy—gradually during the period of transition, and in their entirety on the expiry of that period, under Articles 111 and 113 of the Treaty.

[15] By conferring these competences on the Community, the member-States marked their readiness to bind it by the obligations contracted under the General Agreement.

[16] Since the coming into force of the EEC Treaty and, more particularly, since the establishment of the common external tariff, the transfer of competences arising in the relations between the member-States and the Community was given concrete expression in various ways in the framework of the General Agreement and recognised by the other Contracting Parties.

[17] In particular, since that time, the Community, acting through its institutions, has appeared as a participant in the tariff negotiations and as a party to the agreements of all kinds concluded within the framework of the General Agreement, in accordance with the provisions of Article 114 of the EEC Treaty, which provides that tariff and trade agreements "shall be concluded . . . on behalf of the Community."

[18] It therefore appears that, in so far as, under the EEC Treaty, the Community has assumed competences previously exercised by the member-States in the sphere of application of the General Agreement, the provisions of this Agreement have the effect of binding the Community.

[19] One must furthermore examine whether the provisions of the General

Agreement create, for those subject to the Community jurisdiction, the right to rely on them in a court of law, with a view to contesting the validity of a Community act.

[20] In order to do so, one must view together the spirit, the structure and the terms of the General Agreement.

[21] This Agreement, which, according to its preamble, is based on the principle of negotiations entered into on 'a basis of reciprocity and mutual advantage', is characterised by the great flexibility of its provisions, particularly of those which concern the possibilities of derogation, the measures which may be taken in the face of exceptional difficulties, and the settlement of differences between the contracting parties.

[22] Thus, in the terms of Article XXII (1), "each contracting party will examine with comprehension the representations which may be addressed to it by any other contracting party and must make itself available for consultations about these representations when they relate to a question concerning the application of the present agreement."

[23] Under Article XXII (2), "the Contracting Parties"—this term designating "the contracting parties acting collectively," as stated in Article XXV (1)—"may enter into consultation with one or more contracting parties on a question for which no satisfactory solution has been able to be found through the consultations provided for in the paragraph (1) above."

[24] Where a contracting party considers "that an advantage resulting for it directly or indirectly from the present agreement is annulled or compromised, or that the achievement of one of the objectives of the agreement is compromised because," in particular, "another contracting party is not fulfilling the obligations which it has entered into under the present agreement," Article XXIII regulates in detail the measures which the parties concerned, or the contracting parties acting collectively, may or must take when faced with such a situation.

[25] For the regulation of differences, these measures include, according to the case, written representations or proposals, to be "examined with comprehension," inquiries possibly followed by recommendations, consultations or decisions of the Contracting Parties, including the decision to authorise certain Contracting Parties to suspend, with regard to others, the application of any concession or other obligation resulting from the General Agreement, and, finally, in the case of such a suspension, the option for the party concerned of denouncing this agreement.

[26] Finally, where, because of an undertaking assumed under the General Agreement or because of a concession relating to a preference, certain producers suffer or risk suffering grave damage, Article XIX provides for the option for a contracting party of unilaterally suspending the undertaking, and of withdrawing or modifying the concession, either after consultation of the Contracting Parties collectively and, in default of agreement, among the contracting parties concerned, or even without prior consultation, on a provisional basis, if the matter is urgent.

[27] These elements suffice to show that, put in such a context, Article XI

of the General Agreement is not such as to create, for those subject to the Community's jurisdiction, the right to rely on it in a court of law.

[28] Therefore, the validity of Commission Regulations 459/70, 565/70 and 686/70 cannot be affected by Article XI of the General Agreement.

[29] The costs incurred by the Government of the Kingdom of the Netherlands and by the E.C. Commission, which submitted observations to the Court, cannot form the object of reimbursement, and since, with regard to the parties in the original cases, the proceedings bear the character of an incident raised before the national jurisdiction, it falls to the latter to decide on the costs.

The court, for these reasons, ruling on the question referred to it by the College van Beroep voor het Bedrijfsleven in accordance with the latter's decision of 5 May 1972, hereby declares:

1. The validity, in the sense of Article 177 of the EEC Treaty, of acts taken by the institutions can be assessed with regard to a provision of international law when such provision binds the Community and is such as to create, for those subject to the Community's jurisdiction, the right to rely on them in a court of law.

2. Since Article XI of the General Agreement does not produce such an effect, the validity of Commission Regulations 459/70, 565/70 and 686/70 cannot be affected by this provision.

EDEKA ZENTRALE AG v. FEDERAL REPUBLIC OF GERMANY

[1982] E.C.R. 2745

In an order dated August 17, 1981, which was received at the Court of Justice on September 9, 1981, the Hessischer Verwaltungsgerichtshof [Superior Administrative Court, Hesse] referred to the Court for a preliminary ruling pursuant to Article 177 of the EEC Treaty a question relating to the validity of Commission Regulation No. 1102/78 of May 25, 1978, adopting protective measures applicable to the importation of preserved mushrooms (Official Journal 1978, No. L. 139, page 26).

That question was raised in the context of administrative proceedings between Edeka Zentrale AG, Hamburg (hereinafter referred to as "Edeka"), and the Federal Republic of Germany, represented by the Bundesamt für Ernährung und Forstwirtschaft [Federal Office for Nutrition and Forestry Management] (hereinafter referred to as the "Bundesamt"). Edeka, an importer of preserved mushrooms from Taiwan and South Korea, on September 25, 1979, applied to the Bundesamt for import licenses for two consignments of mushrooms originating in those countries. The applications were refused on the ground that the issue of import licenses in respect of preserved mushrooms originating in Taiwan and South Korea had been suspended in pursuance of Commission Regulation No. 1102/78.

That regulation, which was adopted following a commercial agreement entered into on April 3, 1978, between the European Economic Community and the People's Republic of China (Official Journal 1978, No. L 123, page 2), states in Article 1 that the issue of import licenses for preserved mushrooms is suspended from May 26, 1978. Article 2(1), however, exempts from the application of that measure products from non-member countries "which the Commission accepts as being able to ensure that their exports to the Community do not exceed a level agreed by the Commission." Article 3 lays down that the People's Republic of China is to benefit under the terms of Article 2.

The benefit of that exemption was extended to products originating in Taiwan by Commission Regulation No. 1213/78 of June 5, 1978, on the non-application of protective measures applicable to preserved mushrooms (Official Journal 1978, No. L 150, page 5), but that measure was repealed by Commission Regulation No. 1449/78 of June 28, 1978 (Official Journal 1978, No. L 173, page 25). . . .

VALIDITY OF REGULATION CHALLENGED

Edeka took the view that Regulation No. 1102/78 contravened principles of Community law and in particular that it was in breach of the prohibition of discrimination contained in the second subparagraph of Article 40(3) of the EEC Treaty and was therefore invalid. It accordingly brought an action in the administrative court seeking a declaration that the Bundesamt was obliged to issue to it the import certificates applied for.

In order to enable it to adjudicate upon that application, the Hessischer Verwaltungsgerichtshof, before which the case came on appeal, referred the following question to the Court of Justice:

> Was Commission Regulation (EEC) No. 1102/78 of May 25, 1978, adopting protective measures applicable to imports of preserved mushrooms (Official Journal No. L 139 of May 26, 1978, page 26) valid, or was it in breach of the prohibition of discrimination because, as the plaintiff believes, certain importers were in practice generally debarred thereby from effecting imports from non-member countries? . . .

THE PRINCIPLE OF NON-DISCRIMINATION

As the Court held in its judgments of October 19, 1977, in Joined Cases Nos. 117/76 and 16/77, Ruckdeschel v. Hauptzollamt Hamburg-St. Annen [1977] E.C.R. 1753 . . . and in Joined Cases Nos. 124/76 and 20/77, Moulins et Huileries de Pont-à-Mouson [1977] E.C.R. 1795 . . . the prohibition of discrimination contained in the second subparagraph of Article 40(3) of the Treaty is merely a specific enunciation of the general principle of equality, which is one of the fundamental principles of Community law. This principle means that like situations should not be treated differently unless such different treatment is objectively justified.

Since the discriminatory treatment alleged as between importers results from the different treatment that Regulation No. 1102/78 applies as between the supplier countries concerned and that is based on the fact that only the People's Republic of China and not Taiwan or South Korea agreed voluntarily to restrict its exports to the Community, the allegation made against the regulation in question is in truth directed at the policy, pursued by the Commission at the time of its negotiations with those countries, with a view to obtaining from them an assurance of voluntary restraint.

The Court of Justice must therefore consider whether that policy is arbitrary in nature, in particular whether the quantities of imports proposed by the Commission to the non-member countries concerned as the basis for an agreement of voluntary restraint were in accordance with the needs of the Community market.

With regard, first of all, to the year 1978 it appears from the information supplied by the Commission that both the quantities of preserved mushrooms offered to each of the three countries in question and the quantities actually exported by each of those countries to the Community were fixed on the basis of the average annual tonnage exported during the preceding years and that no preferential treatment was granted to any of those countries. Therefore, as far as 1978 is concerned, Regulation No. 1102/78 is not of such a nature as to provide the appellant in the main proceedings with grounds for complaint.

This conclusion is not affected by the fact that the regulation in question concerns only imports originating in Taiwan and South Korea, to the exclusion of those originating in the People's Republic of China. In fact, the reason that regulation exempted from its sphere of application only the People's Republic of China was that only that country had actually restricted its exports to the Community on the basis of the quantities offered.

As far as Taiwan is concerned, the Commission, in adopting the regulation on May 25, 1978, cannot be criticized for not having taken account of a telex message from the Taiwanese authorities on May 23, 1978, in which they stated their readiness to restrict exports to an amount closely corresponding to that offered. In view of the urgency of the measures to be taken, the Commission was entitled to conclude the procedure initiated and then within a reasonable period of time to carry out the investigation necessary before also exempting Taiwan from the application of the protective measures, which it did by means of Regulation No. 1213/78 of June 5, 1978. The Commission later discovered that Taiwan had already sold and was continuing to sell preserved mushrooms in excess of the quantities agreed and was therefore justified in putting an end to that exemption by Regulation No. 1449/78 of June 28, 1978.

PREFERENTIAL TREATMENT FOR CHINA

On the other hand, as far as the year 1979 is concerned, a comparison between the quantities offered to each of the three countries in question and those imported from those countries reveals preferential treatment in favor of the People's Republic of China at the expense of Taiwan and South Korea such as to provide the appellant in the main proceedings with grounds for complaint.

However, it is clear from the explanations given by the Commission that it maintained Regulation No. 1102/78 in force unchanged for 1979, that is to say, by excluding from its sphere of application merely the People's Republic of China and not Taiwan and South Korea since initially only the People's Republic of China had accepted an agreement of voluntary restraint while South Korea agreed to restrict its exports to the Community only as late as September 1979, but, in actual fact, did not avail itself of the quota allocated, and negotiations with Taiwan did not result in an agreement of voluntary restraint before February 1980. The Commission increased the quota initially fixed for the people's Republic of China in July and August 1979, having regard to the state of negotiations with those three countries and after it had found that the Community market was capable of absorbing supplementary quantities.

It is well established that the Community institutions enjoy discretion in the sphere of commercial policy and, as the Court stated in its judgment of January 22, 1976, in Case No. 55/75, Balkan-Import Export GmbH v. Hauptzollamt Berlin-Packhof [1976] E.C.R. 19 . . . the Treaty contains no general principle that may be relied upon by traders, compelling the Community in its external relations to accord equal treatment in all respects to non-member countries. Therefore, the fact that the Commission's regulations give rise to a deflection in the flow of imports from Taiwan and South Korea toward the People's Republic of China does not provide any ground for criticism.

In those circumstances and in the light of the factors mentioned above, Regulation No. 1102/78 answered the needs of the Community market in respect of both 1978 and 1979 and thus the different treatment which it accords to the supplier countries in question and consequently to the traders importing from those countries must be considered to be objectively justified, so that the submission relating to an infringement of the second subparagraph of Article 40(3) of the Treaty must be rejected.

THE PRINCIPLE OF PROPORTIONALITY

The appellant in the main proceedings further claims that, even if the discriminatory treatment accorded by the regulation in question may be considered justified, the regulation contravenes the principle of proportionality underlying the Community legal order since it amounts to an almost total ban on imports from Taiwan and South Korea, thus making importers bear an excessive proportion of the consequences of that prohibition.

As the Court acknowledged in its judgment of May 5, 1981, in Case No. 112/80, Dürbeck v. Hauptzollamt Frankfurt am Main [1981] E.C.R. 1095, the Commission's attempt, before adopting coercive measures, to obtain the agreement of supplier countries on a voluntary restriction of their exports to the Community cannot be regarded as being unacceptable from the stand-point of Community law since it demonstrates the Community's effort to re-frain from adopting coercive measures unless all else fails. That attempt was all the more acceptable in the present case since both the basic Regulation No. 516/77 adopted by the Council on March 14, 1977, and the implementing Regulation No. 521/77 adopted by the Council on the same date state that the protective measures must be limited to that which is strictly necessary.

COMMISSION'S DISCRETION NOT EXCEEDED

It follows that the Commission is justified, when adopting protective measures, in taking account of whether or not a non-member country is ready to accept a voluntary restriction of its exports to the Community. It cannot therefore be said that it exceeded the limits of its discretionary power by almost totally prohibiting imports from Taiwan and South Korea, countries which did not agree to such a voluntary restraint, in favor of imports originating in the People's Republic of China, which did accept an agreement of voluntary re-straint, even though such a prohibition is capable of bringing about a deflec-tion in the flow of imports from Taiwan and South Korea to the People's Republic of China.

In that connection the appellant in the main proceedings refers to Article 110 of the Treaty, which is also relied on as precluding a total prohibition of imports from Taiwan and South Korea. However, in this respect it is necessary merely to call to mind the Court's judgment of May 5, 1981, in the previously mentioned *Dürbeck* case, in which it was held that Article 110 of the Treaty could not be interpreted as prohibiting the Community from enacting, upon pain of committing an infringement of the Treaty, any measure liable to affect trade with non-member countries, in particular where, as in the present case, the adoption of such a measure is made necessary by the risk of a serious disturbance which might endanger the objectives set out in Article 39 of the Treaty and where the measure is legally justified by provisions of Community law.

Therefore, the argument relating to a breach of the principle of proportion-ality must also be rejected.

THE PRINCIPLE OF THE PROTECTION OF LEGITIMATE EXPECTATION

The appellant in the main proceedings finally claims that the almost total prohibition of imports from Taiwan and South Korea was contrary to the principle of the protection of legitimate expectation which, in the present case, required traditional trading relations to be maintained. That requirement found recognition in Article 12(2) of Council Regulation No. 926/79 of May 8, 1979, on common rules for imports (Official Journal No. L 131, page 15), and in Article XIII (2) of the General Agreement on Tariffs and Trade.

That argument must also be rejected. Since Community institutions enjoy a margin of discretion in the choice of the means needed to achieve their policies, traders are unable to claim that they have a legitimate expectation that an existing situation which is capable of being altered by decisions taken by those institutions within the limits of their discretionary power will be maintained. In the present case, there can be no question of a breach of the principle of the protection of legitimate expectation, particularly since the commercial agreement entered into on April 3, 1978, between the Community and the People's Republic of China, published in the Official Journal of May 11, 1978 (Official Journal No. L 123, page 2), was of such a nature as to alert traders to an imminent change of direction in the Community's commercial policy.

For all those reasons, the reply to be given to the Hessischer Verwaltungsgerichtshof should be that consideration of the question submitted by it has disclosed no factor of such a kind as to affect the validity of Commission Regulation No. 1102/78 of May 25, 1978.

COSTS

The costs incurred by the Commission, which submitted observations to the Court, are not recoverable. Since these proceedings are, for the parties to the main action, in the nature of a step in the action pending before the national court, costs are a matter for that court.

RULING

For these reasons, the Court of Justice (Third Chamber), in answer to the question referred to it by the Hessischer Verwaltungsgerichtshof in an order of August 17, 1981, hereby rules:

Consideration of the question raised has disclosed no factor of such kind as to affect the validity of Commission Regulation No. 1102/78 of May 25, 1978.

NOTES AND QUESTIONS

1. How do the process and the underlying issues described in the preceding cases differ from those in the U.S. delegation law cases, *Yoshida* and *Starkist, supra*? Note that the EC Council/Commission relation is only in part parallel to the U.S. Executive/Congress relation. For another example of similar issues, *see* Re the Draft Convention on the Physical Protection of Nuclear Materials, Facilities and Transport (Opinion 1/78), [1979] 1 C.M.L.R. 131.

2. Does *International Fruit* hold that the EEC is not bound by GATT in the case? Why does it not give relief to plaintiff? For another case raising similar issues, *see* Polydor Ltd. v. Harlequin Record Shops Ltd., [1982] 1 C.M.L.R. 677.

3. Does it appear likely that the EEC did violate GATT in the case?

4. How would a case like *International Fruit* come out in the United States? For a general discussion, *see* Jackson, The General Agreement on Tariffs and Trade in United States Domestic Law, 66 Mich. L. Rev. 249 (1967).

5. Why didn't the importer in *Edeka* seek relief under a GATT provision? Did the Regulation at issue in that case violate GATT?

6. Would an importer in a position parallel to that of *Edeka* have been able to obtain relief in the United States? Would the principles considered in *Edeka* be helpful in *Consumers Union*?

7. Why do you suppose the United States supported the creation of the Common Market? For an analysis of the economic effects of the EC on the United States *see* L. Krause, European Economic Integration and the United States (1968); and H. Jacobsen, Trade Between the European Community and the United States: The Diminishing Asymmetry in W. Feld (ed.), Western Europe's Global Reach: Regional Cooperation and Worldwide Aspirations (1979).

Chapter IV

Relief from Fairly Priced Foreign Competition

This chapter examines regulatory responses that can be used to limit fairly priced foreign imports. We begin to ask in this chapter a question that reappears constantly throughout the text: what is "unfair" foreign competition? Why should the U.S. government respond more favorably to limitations on "unfair" import competition than to an industry that seeks protection when it is badly hurt by imports, regardless of their cause?

The relief discussed in this chapter hinges primarily upon harm to the domestic industry, rather than any specific foreign "unfair" practice. The concept of and plausible standard for injury to an industry are difficult to grasp. Moreover, since the import-limiting approach can be so easily misused, there are equally complicated international efforts to define standards for such relief—and the choice of specific relief itself becomes a serious political problem.

This chapter considers six different U.S. statutory responses to fairly priced foreign competition:

1. the escape clause, contained in §201 of the Trade Act of 1974, once known as the "peril point" provision, and treated in the GATT under Article XIX, the "safeguard" provision;
2. adjustment assistance to help firms, workers, and communities harmed by foreign imports;
3. Section 22 of the Agricultural Adjustment Act, which is designed to deal with problems caused by agricultural imports;
4. Section 406 of the Trade Act of 1974, which specifically addresses the issue of market disruption created by nonmarket economies;
5. Section 232 of the Trade Expansion Act of 1962, which is designed to limit imports that may impair U.S. national security; and

6. the import restraints on textiles permitted under the Multifiber Arrangement (MFA) and the bilateral agreements negotiated by the United States pursuant to the MFA.

A.   THE FRAMEWORK FOR RELIEF FROM FAIRLY PRICED IMPORTS

1.   *The Escape Clause: §201 of the Trade Act of 1974*

The foreign trade laws of the United States should be approached in terms of the elements that must be established before a petitioner can prevail under a particular trade action. In the case of the escape clause, §201(b)(1), U.S.C. §2251(b)(1), four conditions must be satisfied before the International Trade Commission (ITC) can grant relief on the grounds that imports are causing injury to a U.S. industry (*See* Selected Documents Supplement):

1. *Imports:* an article must be imported in increased quantities, either in actual terms or relative to domestic production (in making this calculation the ITC may exclude "captive imports" of overseas affiliates of U.S. companies);
2. *Industry:* the petition must denominate an industry that produces an article domestically that is like or directly competitive with the imported article;
3. *Injury:* the industry that is the subject of the investigation must be experiencing serious injury or the threat thereof; and
4. *Causation:* the increased imports must be a substantial cause of serious injury to the U.S. industry; for this purpose, "substantial cause" means a cause that is important and not less than any other cause.

If the International Trade Commission decides that relief should be provided to an industry, the following import restraints are available to the president: (1) an increase in, or the imposition of, duties; (2) tariff-rate quotas; (3) quantitative restrictions; (4) orderly marketing agreements; or (5) any combination of such actions. The term of import relief, including any combination of the foregoing, may not exceed five years, but may be extended for an additional three-year period.

Under the Trade Act, the president has the discretion to refuse to accept the recommendation of the International Trade Commission to provide import relief if he determines that it would not be in the national economic interest. Under the revisions to §201 in 1984, following the *Chadha* decision, both houses of Congress, by an affirmative vote of a majority of those present and voting, are now permitted to pass a joint resolution within 90 days requiring the president to implement the relief recommended by the Commission. This joint resolution is subject to a presidential veto, but Congress can override such a veto if both houses can muster a two-thirds majority vote.

Relief may be granted by tariff increases to a rate up to 50% *ad valorem* above the rate existing at the time of presidential action. Quantitative restrictions must be limited to the quantity or value of the article imported during the "most recent period which the President determines is representative of imports of such article."

The impact of the 1974 Trade Act on the "escape clause" cannot fully be appreciated without a look back at the Trade Expansion Act of 1962. That act provided that to meet the causation requirement, it had to be determined that increased imports were due "in major part" to trade agreement concessions, and were the "major factor" in causing or threatening serious injury. Three basic changes in the escape clause were effected by the 1974 Trade Act. First, the linkage of prior tariff concessions to the increased imports was cut. Second, the increased imports formerly had to be the "major factor," which was often interpreted as the cause greater than all the others combined. As noted above, "substantial" cause is now the Trade Act's criterion—which means a cause that is important and not less than any other cause. And, finally, the choice of remedies was broadened under the Trade Act. Formerly, the president had only tariff remedies under the escape clause. The Trade Act gives flexibility to the president by permitting him to use tariffs, tariff quotas, or orderly marketing agreements as remedies for the distress of a domestic industry.

a. Objectives of §201 Enforcement

The enforcement of §201 has distinct juridical, political, and economic objectives. From a juridical point of view, it is important that U.S. citizens perceive that §201 protects their legal "rights." The "right" at stake is the expectation of protection from foreign competition when serious injury is being sustained by a U.S. industry. If the prior sentence sounds like it is describing an anti-competitive statute, the student has obtained the correct impression. Section 201 is the most protectionist of the U.S. trade laws, because it is not predicated upon the existence of a specific unfair foreign trade practice. It has no domestic analogue, as U.S. enterprises folding under the pressure of *domestic* U.S. competition simply go out of business, and cannot petition the government for any relief outside of the protection offered by the bankruptcy laws.

Section 201, like the other U.S. foreign trade laws, has an independent political significance. Its enforcement can vitiate protectionist sentiments that may not serve the interests of the overall polity. Section 201 can serve as a safety valve in the formulation of trade policy in a democratic society by relieving pressures that might result in even more extreme solutions from Congress. If §201 were not present Congress would be much more active in formulating U.S. tariffs and quotas on a product by product basis in response to specific pressures. Section 201 permits the executive branch to set trade policy when a U.S. industry is seriously injured; Congress has made this delegation of authority in recognition of the greater resources and expertise available in the executive branch for this type of decision-making.

Perhaps most important, §201 is of major economic significance. With the United States running a serious trade deficit (the United States had a $150 billion trade deficit in 1985), less competitive U.S. industries will be increasingly looking to §201 for protection from foreign competition. It is appropriate that the president be the final authority in §201 cases, since the decisions made have to take into account the national interest as well as the particular interest of each petitioning industry. A selection later in this chapter from former International Trade Commission (ITC) Chairman Alfred E. Eckes shows the defensiveness of the Commission regarding its enforcement of §201. Eckes contends that §201 is merely a temporary relief and adjustment mechanism, and not a form of permanent industrial policy designed to save U.S. industrial "dinosaurs."

The reality is that each time the president decides to impose import limitations pursuant to §201, a political decision is being made to reverse the economic effects of comparative advantage discussed in Chapter 1.[1] The executive branch has understandably been reluctant to provide import relief under §201, in order to avoid provoking U.S. trading partners from responding in kind.

As imports continue to exceed exports and U.S. trade policy edges further into the winter of its discontent, an increasing number of U.S. industries will probably be reluctant to face the cold winds of foreign competition and will instead seek shelter under §201 and its import restraint remedies.

QUESTIONS

1. Would there be any difference between damage by socialist imports and damage by free-market imports? Might there be a difference in the international politics of applying a remedy?

2. Which is economically preferable—adjustment assistance or import restraint? Which is preferable from the viewpoint of domestic politics?

3. How might your perception of the relative value of adjustment assistance and import quotas differ if you represented a craft union? An industrial union? Management? A business trade association?

4. Why does the escape clause procedure leave the president so much flexibility in the choice of remedy?

5. Why do you think an inordinate number of escape clause petitions are filed around February of presidential election years? In early 1984, for exam-

---

[1] This presumes that if subsidies or dumping are involved, the affected U.S. industries would seek "a level playing field" under the countervailing duty or dumping laws.

ple, escape clause provisions were filed for the carbon steel, copper, nonrubber footwear, flatware, and canned tuna industries.

6. Should §201 require enterprises to submit detailed plans for recovery before relief is granted?

b. The Escape Clause in Action: The Automobile Example

The framework of international trade determines many important economic issues in our lives, such as the food we eat, the clothes we wear, and the automobiles we drive. This section focuses on the most famous of the recent ITC escape clause cases, the 1980 ITC automobile decision, which still has important repercussions.

The automobile case highlights the importance of understanding the economics of the product under investigation. Since the early 1970s many questions have been raised concerning the long-term prospects for the automobile industry.[2] Three pressing structural problems in the 1970s were compounded by economic difficulties. From 1950 to 1980 world gasoline consumption increased from 1.29 to 5.32 billion barrels per annum—against the backdrop of a finite and declining world supply of petroleum. As a result gasoline prices were being ratcheted upwards in a seemingly endless spiral. Simultaneously, the absorptive capacity of the earth's atmosphere was stable or, perhaps, declining. Also troubling were the implications of automobiles and ever-growing traffic for the world's urban environments, with worldwide automobile fatalities running at more than 250,000 per year in the late 1970s.

The second severe energy shock of the 1970s swiftly followed the fall of the Shah of Iran in the spring of 1979. The fall of the Shah, and the revolution in Iran, triggered a sharp increase in the price of oil and long lines at U.S. gasoline stations, as many will painfully remember. The "scarcity" mentality affecting consumers seeking fuel-efficient vehicles led to a consumer rush for small automobiles in 1979, a demand that Japan was happy to satisfy.

Imports as a Percentage of
Total U.S. Auto Sales

Year	All imports	Of which Japanese
1970	15.2%	24.4%
1975	18.3%	52.0%
1979	22.0%	76.0%
1980	26.7%	80.6%

Compounding Detroit's difficulties in 1980 was the onset of a prolonged worldwide recession that drained the ability of U.S. consumers to buy *any* cars, not just the traditional U.S. large car models.

[2]The information in this paragraph is from D. Roos and A. Altshuler, The Future of the Automobile (1984).

"Engine" Charlie Wilson, the President of General Motors, had said in 1952 that what was good for General Motors was good for the U.S.A. One might doubt the axiomatic status of this utterance, but it is true that a depression in Detroit sends major shock waves through the United States, the country with the highest degree of motorization. In 1979 9.1% of the U.S. work force was employed in motor-vehicle-related occupations: 1.2% in manufacturing vehicles, 2.8% in selling and servicing them, 1.0% in building and maintaining the highway network, and 4.1% in hauling freight or passengers by means of motor vehicles.

In 1972 Henry Ford had said: "Minicars, mini-profits." In the eyes of many, Detroit was paying the price in 1979 for its neglect of the small car market. The mistakes of the managers of the manufacturers, however, were being paid for by their workers as well, as by the spring of 1979 more than 200,000 unemployed automobile workers created a social, economic, and political problem that could not be ignored. The Ford Motor Company suggested in its import relief petition that over 40% of all U.S. automobile workers were laid off or furloughed.

Against that background the Ford Motor Company and the United Automobile Workers (UAW) filed petitions at the ITC under §201 of the Trade Act of 1974 for import relief. Interestingly, the petitions sought different forms of relief. The UAW sought five years of import protection through a 20% *ad valorem* tariff; Ford requested a quota of 1.7 million automobiles for the same length of time.

The importers and foreign manufacturers contended that the requested remedies would amount to an onerous tax on consumers and severely limit freedom of choice in selecting automobiles.

The ITC had before it two unassailable facts: the U.S. automobile industry was in a shambles, and Japanese automobile imports had dramatically increased. The issue it had to consider was whether Detroit's distress was due to imports or to other factors. The ITC decision followed 46 hours of public testimony from 27 different groups over a one-week period. Its conclusions surprised many industry observers and posed thorny issues for the newly installed Reagan administration in 1981.

REPORT TO THE PRESIDENT ON CERTAIN MOTOR VEHICLES AND CERTAIN CHASSIS AND BODIES THEREFOR

United States International Trade Commission Investigation No. TA-201-44 (Dec. 3, 1980)

DETERMINATION

On the basis of the information developed in the course of the investigation, the Commission has determined (Commissioners Moore and Bedell dissenting in part) that automobile trucks, on-the-highway passenger automobiles, and bodies (including cabs) and chassis for automobile trucks, provided for in items 692.02, 692.03, 692.10, 692.11, 692.20, and 692.21 of the Tariff Schedules of the United States (TSUS), are not being imported into the United States in such increased quantities as to be a substantial cause of serious injury, or the threat thereof, to the domestic industries producing articles like or directly competitive with the imported articles.

BACKGROUND

The Commission instituted the present investigation, No. TA-201-44, on June 30, 1980, following the receipt, on June 12, 1980, of a petition for import relief filed by the International Union, United Automobile, Aerospace, and Agricultural Implement Workers of America (UAW). The investigation was instituted pursuant to section 201(b)(1) of the Trade Act of 1974 (19 U.S.C. 2251(b)(1)) in order to determine whether—

> automobile trucks (except automobile truck tractors and truck trailers imported together); on-the-highway passenger automobiles; and bodies (including cabs) and chassis for automobile trucks (except truck tractors); provided for in items 692.02 and 692.03; 692.10 and 692.11; and 692.20 and 692.21 of the TSUS;

are being imported into the United States in such increased quantities as to be a substantial cause of serious injury, or the threat thereof, to the domestic industry producing an article like or directly competitive with the imported article. . . .

VIEWS OF CHAIRMAN BILL ALBERGER

Section 201(b) of the Trade Act of 1974 requires that each of the following conditions be met before an affirmative determination can be made:

> (1) There are increased imports (either actual or relative to domestic production) of an article into the United States;
> (2) The domestic industry producing an article like or directly competitive with the imported article is being seriously injured, or threatened with serious injury; and
> (3) Such increased imports of an article are a substantial cause of serious injury, or the threat thereof, to the domestic industry producing an article like or directly competitive with the imported article.

While I find the first two conditions met for both passenger automobiles and light trucks, I do not find the third to be satisfied, and therefore my determination with respect to these items is in the negative. Medium and heavy trucks do not satisfy the first criterion, and therefore also mandate a negative determination.

In analyzing the above criteria, it is first necessary to define the scope of the domestic industries against which each imported article should be assessed. The issue raised by petitioners of how to treat Canadian imports must then be resolved. Finally, it is possible to analyze whether imports of each particular article have increased within the meaning of the statute, whether the corresponding industry is being seriously injured and whether such increased imports constitute a substantial cause of such harm.

THE DOMESTIC INDUSTRY

This case raises a number of issues with respect to the scope of the industry or industries to be analyzed. The judgment of how to define an industry depends largely upon the nature of the imported products, the competitive conditions in the domestic market, and the nature of U.S. production. It is therefore difficult to rely exclusively on general legal prescriptions for ascertaining the appropriate industry definition; rather, each determination will necessarily depend heavily on our perceptions of the particular facts of each case. The definition of industry can have a major impact on the question of serious injury, however, and must be made with a clear understanding of both the statutory scheme and Commission precedent relating to the particular fact situation.

The methodology which I believe to be appropriate for delimiting the relevant industries was fully described in TA-201-43 (Mushrooms) [US ITC Pub. 1089 (1980)]. Briefly stated, it is as follows:

Since the phrase "like or directly competitive" is clearly expressed in the disjunctive, and since the adjectives "like" and "directly competitive" were not intended to be synonymous or explanatory of each other, the escape clause may be invoked where either type of producers satisfies the statutory requirements of injury under section 201. Thus, our initial task is to draw distinctions where possible between the "like product" to the imported article (i.e., that which is "the same or nearly the same in inherent or intrinsic characteristics") and those which are "directly competitive" with it (i.e., "substantially equivalent for commercial purposes, that is, . . . adapted to the same uses and . . . essentially interchangeable therefor"). If these groups of producers can clearly be treated as separate and distinct industries in terms of production, sales, employment, etc., and if such action is consistent with the realities of the marketplace, then a showing of serious injury to either group (assuming increased imports were a substantial cause of such injury) will satisfy the criteria for relief and mandate an affirmative result.

Applying these principles to the facts at hand, I believe we are faced with three separate and distinct industries—in essence any combination of groupings with respect to products either "like" or "directly competitive" with the imported articles yields only three possibilities. These industries could be defined as firms and facilities devoted to the production of (1) all passenger automobiles of the type classified under items 692.10 and 692.11 of the TSUS, (2) light trucks of under 10,000 lbs. gvw [gross vehicle weight] (of the type classified as automobile trucks under items 692.02 and 692.03 of the TSUS) and (3) medium and heavy trucks (also of the type classified under 692.02 and 692.03) but not truck tractors and trailers imported together, which we specifically excluded from the scope of our investigation. Since our report covers bodies (including chassis) for automobile trucks, it is also important to point out that we would consider domestic producers of these articles to fall within the same general industry definition (either light trucks or medium/heavy trucks) as the assembled product. I reach this industry segmentation on the basis of the following rationale:

1. There is no persuasive basis on which to segment passenger automobiles into more than one industry, as requested by several importers. While there may be an endless variety of sizes and characteristics, there is no clear dividing line between "large autos" and "small autos" for example. Furthermore, all passenger automobiles have substantially similar uses, and there is certainly ample evidence that all are—to a greater or lesser extent—directly competitive. While various government bodies, industry groups and trade publications do subdivide cars into different groups, these classifications are somewhat arbitrary and vary considerably.

2. Light trucks are inherently distinct from passenger vehicles in terms of their characteristics and principal uses. All types are, to some extent, able to carry substantial quantities of freight, materials or supplies. While many are also adapted to passenger transport, they are purchased by a wide variety of consumers for utilitarian purposes. I believe this is enough of a qualitative difference to make them unlike passenger vehicles. Moreover, there is insufficient evidence to conclude that they compete "directly" with passenger vehicles, although they are produced by the major auto manufacturers and sold through automobile dealerships.

3. Medium and heavy trucks, which are not the main focus of this investigation, are essentially distinct from either passenger vehicles or light trucks. The vast majority are commercial vehicles designed for specific commercial purposes. They are produced by a different group of firms and marketed separately (although the major auto companies do have heavy truck divisions).

The testimony and written submissions extensively discussed the question of whether large cars, small cars and various types of light trucks should be classified in separate industries. Some European importers even contend that their products are unique and do not compete with domestic products of any sort. The importers point to the great number of differences between "large" and "small" passenger vehicles. Most propose a classification based upon weight, size, engine specifications, wheelbase and other factors. They contend that it is logical to draw a line somewhere between "large" and "small" cars on this basis—that the auto industry itself draws several classifications based upon these criteria. Furthermore, they purport to demonstrate through consumer surveys and other cross-elasticity studies how demand for these two basic vehicle types differs, thus suggesting that they are not "directly competitive."

I believe that the reasoning which would lead to a subdivision of passenger autos into two or more industries is flawed in many respects. First, the very uncertainty about where to draw the dividing line illustrates vividly that what really exists is a full continuum of products. There is an endless choice of sizes and features. The same basic car body can be given a larger engine and a few optional features, thereby transforming it into a substantially larger car than the stripped-down model. Most domestic producers offer a "full line" of products, from subcompact to large and luxury cars, and all have a range of options that might change their classification. In reviewing the classification of "small" versus "large" autos suggested by one importer [Toyota], it becomes obvious that one can find more similarity between the largest small car and the smallest large car than between products at either end of the small car spectrum.

Another factor which militates against the segmentation of large and small cars is that all are designed as private vehicles for the principal purpose of transporting passengers. The fact that some might be faster, hold more passengers, or consume less fuel is not something which alters their basic similarity of uses.

Importers also seek to create meaningful distinctions between small and large cars in terms of competitiveness, arguing essentially that consumer surveys show a marked lack of direct competitiveness between these classes. There appears to be an inherent contradiction here, because the same parties cite the shift in demand from large to small cars as an important cause of injury. This shift merely demonstrates why these goods are "directly competitive." In essence, an increase in the cost of owning one size car—brought on by rising fuel costs—has led to increased demand for the other. This suggests a high degree of cross-elasticity. It is true that importers have focused primarily on the "small" end of the market while domestic producers previously seemed content with concentrating primarily on large autos, but this does not alter the fact that these products are "substantially equivalent for commercial purposes" and are "essentially interchangeable."[3] Both importers and domestic producers serve a single—admittedly heterogeneous but nevertheless unitary—domestic market.

A final argument in favor of treating passenger autos as one industry is the notion, referred to in our last decision [mushrooms], that it is difficult to analyze profit and loss data, employment, costs and other factors on a model-by-model basis. While few production lines turn out more than one type of vehicle, some produce a particular type with different options that may lead to different classifications. As already noted, the major domestic firms produce a full line, and this leads to nightmarish problems in attempting to

---

[3]S. Rep. 93-1298, 93d Cong. 2d Sess. 122 (1974).

allocate profits, production costs and employment data (many of the executive and product development personnel work on both groups of products). Given that no other factors argue in favor of further segmentation, this practical difficulty merely emphasizes the inappropriateness of such a recommendation.

With respect to trucks, I am not persuaded by the petitioners' arguments regarding the likeness of small trucks, vans and light utility vehicles to passenger automobiles. Not only do they differ from passenger autos in design, shape and engineering, but most of these vehicles have as a primary use the transportation of materials. While they may also be used quite frequently for the sole purpose of carrying passengers, the capacity for use in carrying supplies or equipment is the obvious feature which prompts ordinary consumers to purchase a truck-like vehicle. A dealer with experience in truck sales acknowledged in our hearings that light trucks and passenger vehicles had little if any interchangeability. Moreover, the record before us is insufficient to conclude that there is high cross-elasticity of demand between cars and light trucks or that the products are "commercially equivalent." Therefore, I cannot find them to be "like or directly competitive" with passenger autos.

Medium and heavy trucks are overwhelmingly used as commercial vehicles, sold through separate outlets and purchased by an entirely different class of consumers than light trucks. I find them to constitute a separate industry, although the precise scope and definition are not essential in this case because they are not alleged to be the recipient of any injury. . . .

INCREASED IMPORTS . . .

Clearly, imports of automobiles and light trucks (including cab chassis) are each increasing in terms of the statute. Imports of medium and heavy trucks, on the other hand, have declined significantly throughout the period of investigation, both absolutely and relative to domestic production. The market share of imports has steadily declined from about 18 percent in 1976 to below 8 percent in 1979. Thus, with respect to this industry, the first criterion is not met.

SERIOUS INJURY

To determine serious injury, Section 201(b)(2) of the Trade Act requires that "the Commission shall take into account all economic factors which it considers relevant, including (but not limited to)—

the significant idling of productive facilities in the industry, the inability of a significant number of firms to operate at a reasonable level of profit, and significant unemployment or underemployment within the industry.

We have also considered the decline in domestic sales and the increases in inventories.

There can be little argument that the two domestic industries under primary investigation (passenger autos and light trucks) manifest serious injury when all of these factors are analyzed. While most importers argued that only the "large car" segment is being injured, the facts and testimony before us overwhelmingly demonstrate that the passenger automobile industry in the aggregate is in serious difficulty. Data for light truck production yields a similar analysis. The injury which I find to exist commenced in early 1979, but has become most pronounced in the first six months of 1980. When this latter period is examined, the declines in production, employment, profitability and sales are devastating. While sales have rebounded slightly in the most recent quarter, third quarter losses are reported to be of record proportions. Thus, I find both industries to be suffering "serious injury" within the meaning of the statute. The following facts lend support to this finding:

In the aggregate most of the indices of the U.S. automobile producers' performance during the period of investigation reveal a healthy picture from 1976 through 1978 and rapidly declining trends thereafter. Domestic production of passenger automobiles reached a peak of slightly over 9.1 million units in 1978, but by 1979 production had declined to 8.4 million units and continued to decline during January-June 1980. Domestic production of light trucks declined from 3.3 million units in 1978 to 2.7 million units in 1979, or by 17 percent, and further declined by 60 percent in January-June 1980. Domestic sales, as reflected in data on total shipments, followed the trends in production—increasing substantially until 1978 and then declining. The decline in shipments for passenger autos was almost entirely due to the drop in sales of large cars. Subcompact and compact car shipments actually increased throughout 1979-80.

Trends in domestic capacity to produce passenger automobiles as compared to those for light trucks differed somewhat during the period of investigation. Domestic capacity to produce passenger automobiles of all sizes fluctuated very little from 1975 through January-June 1980. Capacity to produce automobiles increased slightly from 10.7 million units in 1975 to a peak of 10.8 million units in 1977, but then declined slightly in every period through the first half of 1980. During the period of investigation there were notable shifts in capacity to produce different sizes of automobiles. The capacity of domestic producers to build larger-size cars declined, while their ability to produce smaller-size cars, especially subcompacts, increased in response to the shift in demand toward smaller, more fuel-efficient cars. Domestic capacity to produce light trucks increased steadily from 2.7 million units in 1975 to 3.2 million units in 1979. However, during January-June 1980, capacity to produce such vehicles declined by about 9.3 percent from the corresponding period of 1979.

Capacity utilization figures indicate significant idling of productive facilities during the period of investigation. Utilization of domestic capacity to produce passenger automobiles reached a high of 86.2 percent in 1978, declined to 79.5 percent in 1979, and continued to fall to 66.5 percent during January-June 1980. Utilization of domestic capacity to produce light trucks followed a trend similar to that for automobiles, but the downturn in utilization of light truck facilities after 1977 is even more pronounced than for automobiles. Capacity utilization of domestic light truck facilities was over 100 percent as recently as 1977, but by January-June 1980 had dropped markedly to 41.5 percent.

Since most U.S. producers do not maintain inventories, it is necessary to look at dealers' inventories of new vehicles if this factor is to be assessed. While the absolute figures do not reveal any particular trend, the ratio of inventories to annual shipments has been increasing since 1978. This is particularly true of large cars, the vehicles which cost the most to carry on inventory because of their higher sales prices.

Financial data provided by domestic firms clearly reveal the inability of a significant number of firms to operate at a reasonable level of profit. From 1978 to 1979, the net operating profit for U.S. producers on their U.S. automotive operations fell by 76 percent from $5.6 billion to $1.3 billion, and continued to fall to a net loss of $2.9 billion in January-June 1980. The major losses recorded in these recent periods are indicative of the financial status of most of the producers of passenger automobiles and light trucks. During January-June 1980 the only U.S. producer to report a profit was Volkswagen of America. The declining financial position of the U.S. motor vehicle manufacturers is also revealed in the substantial drop in cash flow. U.S. producers' cash flow from operations declined from $8.9 billion in 1978 to $5.1 billion in 1979, and then to a negative $356 million in January-June 1980.

Similarly, employment patterns declined during 1979 and the first half of 1980. The average number of all employees in U.S. establishments producing passenger automobiles and light trucks declined from 1,003,430 in 1978 to 971,929 in 1979 and then in January-June 1980 declined again by about 22 percent below the level recorded for the corresponding period of 1979. Other employment indices, including the average number of production workers, man-hours worked, and output per 1,000 man-hours, mirror trends for all employees.

In April 1980, the U.S. Department of Transportation issued projections of employment changes in the auto industry based on several assumptions, including peak consumption levels of 11 million units per year, employment levels reached in 1978/79, and a return to a 15 percent import penetration level. Based on these assumptions, the report indicates that a decline in employment of auto manufacturers due to productivity gains could be as great as 150,000 by 1985. Employment gains of about 48,000 jobs due to changes in the market by 1985 offset somewhat the 150,000 loss related to increased productivity, indicating a total projected decline in employment resulting from both productivity gains and changes in the market of about 100,000 from 1978/79 levels. Thus, with increased demand for automobiles and light trucks and substantially reduced imports, employment in these industries would still not return to previous levels.

There is no doubt that both the passenger automobile and light truck industries are seriously injured.

SUBSTANTIAL CAUSE

While I find the domestic industries producing passenger automobiles and light trucks to be suffering serious injury within the meaning of Section 201(b)(1), I do not find that increased imports are a substantial cause of such injury. The statute defines the term "substantial cause" as "a cause which is important and not less than any other cause."[4] Applying this test, I have found the decline in demand for new automobiles and light trucks owing to the general recessionary conditions in the United States economy to be a far greater cause of the domestic industries' plight than the increase in imports. While I also believe that the rapid change in product mix necessitated by the shift of consumer preference away from large, less fuel-efficient vehicles is an important cause of the present injury, I do not view this factor to be a more important cause than increased imports.

The Decline in Overall Demand

One noticeable factor in this case is the apparent lack of correlation between the growth in import volume and the state of health of domestic producers. Our investigation reveals that the period 1976-78 was characterized by strong domestic sales and record profits. Yet it was during this period that the largest increase in total imports occurred. (Passenger automobile imports increased from 2 million units in 1975 to 2.9 million in 1978, while light truck imports grew from 375,000 in 1975 to 859,000 in 1978.) Imports actually declined in 1979, when the recession began in earnest. Even Japanese imports grew most dramatically in the prior period, and remained about steady in 1979. While Japanese imports have increased by a more alarming rate in the first 6 months of 1980 (by about 200,000 units over the comparable period of 1979), imports from other sources have declined. This juxtaposition of events becomes even more curious when we consider the testimony of petitioners that the injury began in early 1979 and has deepened over the past 18 months. Given the relatively slight import growth in that period, and considering how healthy the monthly sales figures were before 1979, one obviously begins to look for other explanations of the current injury.

One figure that stands out in stark contrast to the rather marginal import increases for 1979-80 is the very large decline in overall consumption of both passenger autos and light trucks. Consumption of passenger autos fell by almost 1 million units in 1979, a decline of 7.8 percent. Moreover, consumption in January-June 1980 was 1.1 million units or 18.5 percent below the figure for January-June 1979. For light trucks the decline in 1980 was over 700,000 units or 19.3 percent, and the January-June 1980 figure was 47 percent below the comparable figure in 1979. It is therefore clear that domestic producers faced seriously declining demand in the period January 1979-June 1980. While imports did improve their market share substantially during this period by maintaining constant or slightly increasing volume in the face of falling

---

[4]Trade Act of 1975, Section 201(b)(4), 19 U.S.C. 2251(b)(4).

demand, the downturn in demand itself is obviously a variable factor which must be independently assessed for its impact on U.S. producers.

At the most fundamental level, then, it is useful to allocate the decline in domestic producers' shipments in 1979 and 1980 into two basic components: that portion accounted for by the reduced overall consumption of autos and light trucks because of general economic conditions, and that portion attributable to the increasing market share of import vehicles. The relative magnitude of these two causes can be assessed by comparing the actual decline in domestic shipments to the decline that might have occurred if imports had not increased their market share in 1979-80, i.e., if imports and domestic vehicles had shared equally in the overall decline in sales. The difference between these two figures represents the maximum potential loss in sales due to increased imports. This amount can then be compared to the volume of loss attributable *solely* to reduced demand. The following tables, based upon data available in the Commission's report, reveal the results of this exercise for 1979 and for January-June 1980 [only the first is reproduced here]:

I believe that [the table demonstrates] graphically why imports are not a "substantial cause" of either industry's present malaise. [It suggests] that declining demand accounted for over 80 percent of the net decline in U.S. producers' domestic shipments of both automobiles and trucks from 1978 to 1979, as compared with less than 20 percent of the decline in U.S. producers' domestic shipments being attributable to imports' increasing share of U.S. consumption. Between January-June 1979 and January-June 1980, about two-thirds of the decline in U.S. producers' domestic shipments was attributable to declining demand and only a third was due to the increased share of the U.S. market accounted for by imports. Thus, even if the import share had been held constant during these critical 18 months, and even if all of those sales which went into the increased import share had instead gone to U.S. producers, domestic firms' sales still would have fallen by over 80 percent of their actual decline in 1979 and by over 60 percent of their actual decline in January-June 1980. While the legislative history cautions against the application of a pure mathematical test, it is necessary to assess the relative impact of these factors, and I think these percentages reveal why one is so overwhelmingly greater than the other.

Petitioners would perhaps dispute the conclusions I draw from the above [table] because the [table fails] to allow for the theory that an import increase in the earlier period of 1976-78 could be accountable for injury which did not become manifest until 1979. However, even if average imports, consumption and domestic shipments for 1976-78 are compared to the 1979 figures, the decline in demand is still greater than the import factor. Moreover, the above tables really account for the overall import increase since 1975, because they postulate the overall effect of the increased *market share* of imports caused by a drop in domestic sales after three years of steady import growth. Thus, the above analysis gives an accurate picture of the demand *and* import factors since 1975.

It has been argued in this case that the downturn in demand is itself a result

TABLE 1

Passenger automobiles: U.S. apparent consumption, U.S. producers' domestic shipments, imports for consumption, imports' share of consumption, 1978 and 1979, and relative increases or declines in imports and producers' shipments in 1979, if the share of imports is held constant at the 1978 level

Item		1978	1979
Actual 1978 and 1979 data:			
Apparent consumption	1,000 units	11,185.0	10,315.3
U.S. producers' domestic shipments	do	8,256.9	7,518.2
Imports for consumption	do	2,928.1	2,797.1
Ratio of imports to consumption	percent	26.2	27.1
Estimated data for 1979, holding import share of consumption constant at 1978 level and using actual 1979 consumption data:			
Imports, if held at 1978 share of consumption	1,000 units	[1]	2,702.6
U.S. producers' domestic shipments, if held at 1978 share of consumption	1,000 units	[1]	7,612.7
Net change from 1978 to 1979:			
Total actual decline in U.S. producers' shipments	1,000 units	[1]	738.7
Net decline due to increasing import share	do	[1]	94.5
Net decline due to declining demand	do	[1]	644.2
Share of declining shipments due to declining demand	percent	[1]	87.2

[1] Not applicable.

Source: Compiled from data presented in table 19 of the staff report.

of several factors, and that each should be assessed individually to determine whether any single factor is greater than increasing imports. To consider demand in the aggregate, the argument goes, is to cumulate artificially what are clearly separate causal elements in a manner inconsistent with the purposes or legislative history of Section 201. Among the separate and identifiable causes mentioned in this case are inflation, unemployment, rising interest rates, and higher energy costs. Undoubtedly, all of these factors played a part in bringing about the present recession in new vehicle sales. Supporters of the petition contend that none of these factors *alone* played as great a role in bringing about the injury as increasing imports. In fact, the UAW brief contends that increasing imports brought on much of the recession, and so the recession should be viewed as an effect rather than a cause.

All of these contentions seek to isolate and weigh separately the various components of a general economic downturn. In reality, most of the factors mentioned above have worked in unison to bring about what is commonly termed a "recession." Inflation in new vehicle prices coupled with higher credit rates have acted together to drive up the total costs of new motor vehicles. Interest rates have played a particularly important part in the volume of auto sales, because these are long-term consumer durable purchases where credit financing is the norm. Not only have transaction prices for new vehicles and monthly payments for loans increased, but credit has become "tighter," and the refusal rate on auto credit applications has grown. Unemployment and general inflation have acted to reduce the real disposable income of the average consumer, and a normal reaction has been to delay many long-term capital outlays.

All of these phenomena are part and parcel of a generalized recession, which is normally defined as a period of reduced economic activity, and which can be brought on by a multitude of factors. Recessions are often characterized by rising prices, high interest rates and unemployment. But to say they are comprised of a multitude of causes is not to say that reduced demand in a recession cannot be cited as a single cause for purposes of section 201. In fact, I have cited this very factor in several past cases, particularly where we were considering highly cyclical industries which fluctuate with the general economy. The reason for such a policy is readily apparent; if decline in demand for the product is a consequence of a general economic downturn, then the inevitable recovery from the recession will restore health to the industry. This is precisely what happened to the automobile industry after the downturn in 1974-75. Cyclical downturns in the economy are to be expected, and must not force a reliance on unnecessary import remedies. The problem which auto producers confront is one which confronts many sectors of the economy (the building industry, for example), and it cannot be solved by import relief.

Of course, it is possible for imports to be a "substantial cause" of serious injury or threat thereof during a recession, but only where the absolute or relative increase is of sufficient magnitude to outweigh or equal the effects of the recession itself. As the previously cited [table] [demonstrates], that is not the case in the present investigation.

The Shift In Demand

A general understanding of how purchasers are reacting to changes in the marketplace is helpful in assessing the significance of the shift in demand and Detroit's reaction to it. With the high cost of new cars and high interest rates seriously affecting consumer confidence, it appears that a number of would-be purchasers are keeping their vehicles longer. This is verified by our information regarding the average age of motor vehicles. Such data shows a substantial change in buying habits from the days when trade-ins were encouraged every 2 or 3 years. At the same time, the rising cost of fuel creates a shift in demand, so that consumers who do have the economic means to make purchases want a more fuel-efficient model. Some consumers perhaps see the rapid improvements in fuel economy and decide to delay purchases another year or two until their favorite models have substantially better mileage ratings. In short, the rapid changes in product mix may be creating some of the buying uncertainty. The shift to smaller cars also affects the trade-in value of used cars, which in turn increases the cost of purchasing a new model. All of these problems result in a general reluctance to enter the market until prices and credit rates stabilize, general economic conditions improve, and buyers become convinced that the new generation of products are sufficiently fuel-efficient and well made.

This theory of consumer behavior explains much of the current recessionary difficulty, but it also raises the inevitable question of whether shift in demand to smaller cars is itself a more important cause of serious injury than increased imports. The facts speak for themselves about the size of this change in consumer preference. One of the difficulties in assessing such a factor quantitatively is that it is inextricably bound together with the increase in imports. While a shift from big to small is conceptually different than a change from domestic to imported, the fact is that two-thirds of the recent increase in small car sales has accrued to the benefit of importers. Ultimately, one becomes involved in a tautological debate about whether increased imports of small cars are an effect of the shift in demand or the explanation for it. Thus, it is only possible to make certain qualitative judgments about the shifting product mix within the domestic industry itself.

Ordinarily, the shift to another product within the same industry should not necessarily be injurious to that industry. However, the lead times associated with introducing new models and the magnitude of capital investments required make the auto industry unique. In order to be able to accommodate a shift, they must anticipate it by 3 to 5 years. Industry estimates of the need to alter production between 1975 and 1980 did not accurately predict how fast Americans would abandon their large cars. Due largely to unforseen events such as the Iranian revolution and subsequent oil shortage, and because of the lead-time problem associated with auto production, U.S. producers' plans for expanding small car output lagged far behind the market and its needs. In fact, Ford Motor Co. had made a conscious decision not to downsize its entire fleet as far back as 1976, and instead concentrated on creating the entirely new Escort/Lynx model. Thus, Ford found itself with little flexibility to expand small car production when market forces changed, and in addition found itself needing to accelerate capital expenditures and squeeze them into a shorter time-frame in order to react to sweeping changes in consumer preference. Chrysler found itself in much the same situation, but it received substantial federal support which helped to offset some of its capital expenditures. Moreover, its small car plans were further along than Ford's, although Chrysler still had excess large car capacity. Only General Motors, with superior capital resources, was in a position to face the trend toward smaller cars. Its downsizing was well along, and it had substantial numbers of small car models in production.

Clearly then, the rapid transition to smaller autos and trucks disturbed U.S. producers' plans for a slow, orderly transition. They had hoped to finance their plans for new, fuel-efficient models through the profits on large autos. Without these profits being generated, they found themselves incurring huge capital costs when they could least afford them. Our investigation also reveals that the profit margin on small cars has traditionally been much less, so the industry found itself shifting into a product line which resulted in a lower ratio of net profits to sales. Yet they were not producing such models on sufficient economies of scale to yield the type of profits that sales of large cars—loaded with expensive "extras"—could produce.

All of these factors unquestionably affected the profit picture of U.S. firms. Moreover, the carrying costs to dealers incurred from having high inventories of large cars has also been injurious, especially with the higher interest rates. A record number of dealers have gone out of business since 1979. Thus, the shift in demand must be viewed as an "important cause" of injury separate and apart from the shift to imports. Many of the industries' costs would have been incurred even if import competition had not existed, because simple economics dictated the change in consumer preference. However, I do not believe that the problems associated with this shift in demand should be considered more important than the relative increase in imported products. First, there is the previously mentioned fact that two-thirds of the growth in small cars has accrued to the benefit of imports. Some have suggested that this merely means imports, particularly Japanese vehicles, were better situated to capitalize on the shift in demand. While this is certainly true, it does not alter the fact that the transition of domestic producers to smaller vehicles was much less profitable in the short run because a disproportionate number of small car sales were going to importers. Were it not for the growing volume of imported small cars, Detroit could have undergone its present transformation more profitably and perhaps more dramatically. But the awareness that expanding small car output might not have expanded new car sales certainly impacted upon corporate decision-making regarding small vehicles. Also, U.S. firms have found themselves unable to charge sufficient markups on their small models because of import competition. Thus, I believe imports were an equal or greater problem for the industry to confront than the mere transition to small cars.

Summary

I find the overall decline in consumption brought about by the current recession to be a greater cause of serious injury than increased imports. I also find that the shift in consumer demand is an important cause of the present injury, but it is not in and of itself a greater cause than the relative import increase. Increased imports made it difficult for U.S. firms to conduct the transition to smaller vehicles, thus impairing their competitiveness and inhibiting a faster shift to meet changing demand. But by far the greatest explanation of the damage suffered in the past 18 months has been the recession itself. Without it, there would be no serious injury today.

Undoubtedly, there will be debate about the appropriateness of the majority's causation determination. This is an area of legal policy that is by its very nature controversial and subjective. There are those who might disagree with the policy of treating demand as a separate cause, but I believe this policy makes good sense. It is our task under the statute to find "substantial cause," and despite the fact that I realize imports are an "important" cause of the problem, they do not satisfy the strict criteria of Section 201. Perhaps the dilemma which this determination posed for me was best summed up by the court in the famous case of *Palsgraf v. Long Island Railway.*[5]

> The proximate cause, involved as it may be with many other causes, must be, at the least, something without which the event would not happen. The court must ask itself whether there was a natural and continuous sequence between cause and effect. Was the one a substantial factor in producing the other? Was there a direct connection between them, without too many intervening causes? Is the effect of cause on result not too attenuated? Is the cause likely, in the usual judgment of mankind, to produce the result? Or, by the exercise of prudent foresight, could the result be foreseen? Is the result too remote from the cause, and here we consider remoteness in time and space? . . . *We draw an uncertain line, but draw it we must as best we can.*

In addition to concluding that increased imports are not a substantial cause of the serious injury which presently exists, I also believe they could not be a substantial cause of any threat thereof. U.S. small car production is steadily increasing. The three major manufacturers have begun introducing their new generation of front wheel drive, fuel efficient vehicles. We received extensive testimony that such products were fully competitive and would revolutionize the automobile industry. As such products come on stream the import share of the small car market should decline, particularly if demand picks up. Of course, if we remain in a deep recession with high interest rates it is probable that the present critical state of the industry will continue for some time. However, the adjustment already made by domestic firms to changing consumer demand should act to reduce the import share. Thus, imports should not become a greater causal factor in the next year or two. It is also worth noting that monthly import sales have actually declined since August, 1980. This seems to suggest that import volume has peaked, and that there would only be a noticeably higher import market share if demand for automobiles continued to decline. Such a decline in demand would only dramatize the causal link to recessionary factors which I have already cited as the major problem. . . .

[Commissioner Stern's opinion is omitted. It is closely parallel to that of Chairman Alberger except on the issue of Canadian imports. The critical paragraphs of the dissenting opinion follow.]

SUBSTANTIAL CAUSE OF SERIOUS INJURY

Section 201(b)(4) of the Trade Act defines the term "substantial cause" to mean "a cause which is important and not less than any other cause." Thus,

---

[5]248 N.Y. 339, 162 N.E. 99 (1928) (Andrews, J., dissenting) (emphasis supplied).

increased imports, to be a substantial cause of serious injury, must be both an "important" cause of injury and not less important than any other cause. If another single cause is more important, increased imports cannot be a "substantial cause." In addition, section 201(b)(2) directs the Commission, in determining whether increased imports are a substantial cause of injury, to take into account all economic factors which it considers relevant, including (but not limited to) "an increase in imports (either actual or relative to domestic production) and a decline in the proportion of the domestic market supplied by domestic producers" (sec. 201(b)(2)(C)).

As discussed above, imports have increased significantly, in both actual and relative terms. More important, however, imports have captured an ever larger share of the domestic passenger automobile market during the last 3 years. The ratio of automobile imports to domestic automobile consumption increased from 25 percent in 1976 and 1977 to 26 percent in 1978 and 27 percent in 1979, and from 25 percent in the first 6 months of 1979 to 34 percent in the first 6 months of 1980.

Section 201(b)(2) does not limit us to consideration of only certain economic factors in determining whether increased imports are a substantial cause of serious injury. We are to take into account "all" relevant economic factors. We believe that there are a number of other individual causes of injury, such as increased costs of passenger automobiles, the shift in consumer preferences from large to small cars, high interest rates, a shortage of consumer credit, increased gasoline prices, shortages of gasoline (in 1979), the failure of domestic corporate management to anticipate current conditions, and costly Government regulations. We find that none of these other causes, even if considered an important cause of injury, are a more important cause of serious injury to the domestic industry than increased imports.

It is clear that our determination differs from the majority in the interpretation given to the provisions in section 201 of the Trade Act relating to the weighing and comparison of the relevant economic factors contributing to the serious injury experienced by the domestic industry. We believe that the law clearly and unequivocally provides that the Commission shall, to the extent practicable, isolate each of the economic factors relevant to the matter of serious injury for the purpose of comparing each of them with the factor of increased imports. If we were to do otherwise—that is, to aggregate the negative economic factors in comparing them with increased imports—there would be few, if any, Commission decisions favorable to a domestic industry in section 201 cases in times of recession or economic downturn.

In this regard, we refer specifically to the prepared statements read by two of our colleagues at the open Commission meeting of November 10, 1980, at the time of the vote on this matter. Commissioner Stern, in voting in the negative, stated "I find the downturn in economic demand due to general economic conditions, recession, credit crunch, rising costs of car ownership and a major unprecedented shift in demand from large to small cars, brought the domestic industry to its present weakened state." Supporting this point of view was Commissioner Calhoun, who, in voting in the negative, said "My analysis reveals that the general decline in purchases of automobiles and light trucks owing to the downturn of the economy has contributed more so than imports to the serious injury suffered by the automobile industry."

We reject the notion that the statute permits the Commission to aggregate a number of economic factors which in combination are to be weighed against increased imports to find the substantial cause of serious injury. Further, we believe that economic downturns represent the concurrence of a number of adverse factors. We do not believe that Congress envisioned that the Commission would consider an economic downturn per se to be a single economic factor in determining injury in section 201 investigations. Instead, we believe that Congress intended the Commission to examine imports and their impact on the domestic industry over the course of the business cycle—during both good and bad years—in order to ascertain whether import penetration is increasing and, if so, whether the increasing penetration is seriously injuring the domestic industry. This is the approach we have followed in past section 201 cases. . . .

NOTES AND QUESTIONS

1. How might the UAW's interest in filing the §201 petition differ from those of Ford? Why didn't General Motors or Chrysler file a petition for relief?

2. What are the factors relevant to defining the market in this case? Consumer perceptions? Cross-elasticity of demand? What is the relevance of the market definition to the issue of causation?

The Senate Finance Committee Report on the Trade Act provides guidance as to what the phrase "like or directly competitive with" means:

> The words "like" and "directly competitive," as used previously and in this bill, are not to be regarded as synonymous or explanatory of each other, but rather to distinguish between "like" articles and articles which, although not "like" are nevertheless "directly competitive." In such context, "like" articles are those which are substantially identical in inherent or intrinsic characteristics (i.e., materials from which made, appearance, quality, texture, etc.), and "directly competitive" articles are those which, although not substantially identical in their inherent or intrinsic characteristics, are substantially equivalent for commercial purposes, that is, are adapted to the same uses and are essentially interchangeable therefor." [S. Rep. No. 98-1298, 93d Cong. 2d Sess. 122 (1974)]

3. Why do you suppose the petitioners are seeking to have all the vehicles "viewed as a single industry"? Why would respondents seek to have such vehicles treated as separate markets? Why would respondents seek to have the investigation limited to injury to the large-car segment of the domestic automobile industry? (Note that in most cases the party seeking relief from imports will seek to define the market as narrowly as possible, in order to emphasize the harm.)

4. In evaluating the market, did the majority opinion follow the principles it laid down for itself?

5. Why do you think the UAW and Ford wanted Canadian auto imports to be excluded from the case? Does the ITC have the power to discriminate in favor of Canadian imports? Does the president? *See* §203(k)(1) of the Trade Act of 1974.

6. Are you impressed with the way the various opinions handled the causation issue? What in your opinion was the most serious cause of the industry's distress? Is the ITC's interpretation sensitive to the policy issues? The international relations issues?

7. How might the *threat* of serious injury be measured (as distinguished from serious injury itself)? In considering the situation regarding imported automobiles, how relevant should be:

(a)   substantial overcapacity in Japan;
(b)   the new "world cars" to be produced by the U.S. manufacturers;
(c)   Japanese investment in U.S. automobile facilities?

8. What types of expertise and evidence would you want in order to prove or disprove injury? How confident are you of such evidence?

9. Was the ITC wise to wait until after the 1980 presidential election to issue its opinion? Did the ITC decision appear likely to defuse the issue politically? Is the delay of waiting for the ITC very often likely to help a free-trade president deflect political pressure?

10. Had the ITC decided the other way, what would you have done had you been in President Carter's shoes?

11. Between 1978 and 1982, total imports of tuna packed in airtight containers from all sources increased from 51,781 pounds to 87,579 pounds, a 69% increase. The rate of increase picked up markedly in the year 1981-1982, from 70,852 pounds to 87,579 pounds, or 24% in that one year alone. Moreover, the ratio of imports to consumption increased from 6.9% in 1978 to 10.1% in 1981, and then vaulted to 14.1% in 1982.

During that same period, domestic production decreased from 704,793 pounds to 539,397 pounds, or 23%, and apparent domestic consumption fell from 749,900 pounds to 619,200 pounds. In addition, the U.S. tuna fleet fishing in U.S. waters was extremely depressed, with many vessel owners claiming bankruptcy. Both profits and employment were off in the domestic tuna industry.

Do these facts provide a firm foundation for a successful action under §201 of the Trade Act of 1974? How would you correlate these facts with the criteria for relief described in §201(b) of the Trade Act of 1974, 19 U.S.C. §2251(b)(1)? What additional evidence would you attempt to develop as a litigant representing the domestic industry? One representing the foreign industry? If the ITC were to grant relief, do you think the president should follow the ITC lead? (ITC decision pending in July 84.) *See* Certain Canned Tuna Fish, U.S.I.T.C. Pub. No. 1558, August, 1984.

———————————————

The political fallout from the automobile decision was substantial. Candidate Reagan described himself as a free trader, but during the course of the 1980 presidential campaign he had promised to take steps to assist the U.S. automobile industry.[6] The failure of the ITC to provide import relief for the U.S. automobile industry thus placed the president in the difficult position of having to live up to his campaign rhetoric despite the negative ITC decision. The following articles and excerpts describe the "voluntary restraint agreement" (VRA) negotiated in 1981 with Japan limiting automobile imports. A stricter quota bill or domestic content legislation mandating that a large percentage of each automobile sold in the United States be produced in the United States[7] may well have passed the Congress had President Reagan not induced Japan to accept the VRA.

Tokyo's Car Curbs Hailed in U.S., But Japanese Makers Are Angered

Congress Move Now Unlikely

By CLYDE H. FARNSWORTH
[N.Y. Times, May 2, 1981]

WASHINGTON, May 1—The White House, Congressional leaders and the domestic auto industry today welcomed the Japanese Govern-

———————————————

[6]On September 3, 1980, while campaigning in a Chrysler Corporation plant, candidate Reagan declared that:

> There is a place where government can legitimately be involved—and this is where I think government has a role it has shirked so far—and that is to convince the Japanese one way or another, and in their own best interest, the deluge of cars must be slowed while our industry gets back on its feet. [Cannon and Lescaze, Auto-Import Compromise Bore Meese's Subtle Mark, Washington Post, May 26, 1981, at p. A2.]

[7]*See*, for example, H.R. 5133 (Sept. 21, 1982), which would have required foreign producers selling over 900,000 units in the U.S. market to have a minimum domestic content of 90%. A sliding domestic content scale for foreign producers selling fewer than 900,000 units in the United States was also provided.

ment's three-year plan to limit car shipments to the United States and said it should deflect moves in Congress to legislate import quotas.

But Government officials and representatives of the 4,000 dealers who sell Japanese cars in this country warned that the action could add to inflation through higher automobile prices resulting from a reduced Japanese supply.

Robert M. McElwaine, president of the American International Automobile Dealers Association, said that a Japanese car on which a consumer might have received a discount yesterday would no longer be discounted today and that, "by next week, you might be paying over list for certain attractive models."

Reagan Depicted as 'Pleased'

Larry Speakes, the acting White House press secretary, said that President Reagan was "pleased" with the accord and that it should give the auto industry "time to retool and become competitive," a point echoed by Philip Caldwell, chairman of the Ford Motor Company, who said the Japanese "will doubtless cut back on their least profitable models.

The three-year agreement, reached in Tokyo early today, limits auto exports to this country to 1.68 million during Japan's fiscal year, from last April 1 to March 31, 1982. That is a decline of 7.7 percent from the 1.82 million Japanese cars sold in the United States in 1980, representing 21.3 percent of the total American market.

The American auto industry has argued for import quotas so that it can sell more cars and thus raise the billions of dollars needed to retool for the manufacture of smaller, fuel-efficient vehicles, such as the Japanese sell. In the second year of the agreement, Japanese car imports would rise from the 1.68 million level if total American sales rose. No quota was set for the third year.

Mr. Caldwell said that the agreement would prompt the Japanese to sell more high-priced luxury models and fewer of the low-cost economy models. Currently, the most popular Japanese cars in this country, according to this week's Automotive News, a trade publication, are the Datsun 210, a standard two-door sedan, which lists for $4,599; the Honda Accord, a three-door hatchback listing at $6,999, and the Toyota Corolla, a two-door sedan, at $5,178. All are small cars.

One Government analyst said it would be "reasonable" to expect that the American buyer of a small car, whether an imported or domestic model, would now have to pay an extra $200 to $400.

Roger B. Smith, chairman of the General Motors Corporation, and Lee A. Iacocca, chairman of the Chrysler Corporation, joined Mr. Caldwell in welcoming the import agreement, although Mr. Iacocca noted that the program "might not be as extensive as some would like."

Price Rise Tied to Accord

Mr. McElwaine of the dealers association contended that last week's 3½ percent auto price increases announced by General Motors and the 2.8 percent rises announced by both Chrysler and Ford this week were "in anticipation of this agreement."

One of the chief authors of a bill to legislate import quotas, Senator John C. Danforth, Republican of Missouri, said he did not expect to proceed with the legislation at this time.

"This isn't all that we wanted," added Senator Lloyd Bentsen, Democrat of Texas, co-sponsor of the bill, "but it is helpful and we will be watching to make sure" the Japanese "are complying."

Senator Danforth said the agreement meant that, over the next 12 months, imports should be reduced by about 250,000 to 300,000 cars below what would have occurred without curbs. It should reduce imports the following year by 300,000 to 400,000 depending on the size of the American market.

"The numbers are so small," said Arvid Jouppi, an auto analyst with John Muir & Company in Detroit, "far less than the number of new energy-efficient vehicles that the United States would throw against the Japanese this year anyway."

The Danforth-Bentsen bill, which had been scheduled to be voted on by the Senate Finance Committee on May 12, would have limited Japanese shipments to 1.6 million vehicles a year over three years, representing deeper and longer-term cuts than those agreed to by Japan.

Senator Donald W. Riegle Jr., Democrat of Michigan, who had backed more restrictive quota legislation, said the agreement had "some positive aspects," but added that the Government "could have achieved a tougher agreement."

Unanswered Questions Seen

There were still many unanswered questions, according to Senator Riegle, over the way the agreement would be put into effect. He said he was troubled, for instance, by reports that the Japanese have more than 400,000 vehicles in inventory in the United States and that these may not be counted under the new import ceilings.

The agreement, the Senator said, apparently only covered shipments into the 50 states, leaving open the question of transshipments from Guam, the Virgin Islands and Puerto Rico. Some 62,000 Japanese cars were shipped into Puerto Rico last year.

Douglas A. Fraser, president of the United Automobile Workers union, who has been pressing for restraints for the last two years, was somewhat more tempered in his reaction, calling the agreement "a modest, but positive, step that we hope will improve the job prospects of American workers in the months ahead."

Like Senator Riegle, Mr. Fraser said he believed the numerical limit of 1.68 million Japanese cars to be imported over the next 12 months was "too high" and that specific limits should have been made mandatory for three full years.

Auto Curb Hailed in U.S.

Toyota Chief Cites Politics

By MIKE THARP
[N.Y. Times, May 2, 1981]

TOKYO, May 1—Japanese auto industry officials were uncommonly critical today of their Government's agreement to restrict car shipments to the United States.

The agreement, said Eiji Toyoda, president of the Toyota Motor Company, was made "with undue haste and insufficient appreciation of the real situation."

Japanese businessmen seldom speak critically in public, and the auto makers' statements today reflected their intense objections to any restrictions on winning a healthy share of the big American market.

Economist Critical

Mr. Toyoda said American consumers and the Japanese economy would suffer as a result of the package. "It is extremely regrettable that what is essentially an economic issue has been politicized in this way," he said.

Ryoichi Hirono, professor of economics at Seikei University in Tokyo, had still harsher words. The agreement "benefits only a handful of politicians, some lazy managers and certain irresponsible trade officials," he said.

Takashi Ishihara, president of the Japan Automobile Manufacturers Association and the Nissan Motor Company, said he was concerned about the impact of the measures on the auto and parts industries here. "This measure will weaken our dealer networks in the United States and will bring our competitive position with the United States auto makers into question," he said.

In opposing any trade restrictions, the automakers had argued that their share of a growing

American auto market should be at least equal to the 1.82 million Japanese vehicles sold to Americans in 1980.

The agreement, which reduces shipments to 1.68 million in the first year, came after two days of negotiations here between Bill Brock, the United States trade representative, and Japanese Cabinet officials.

7.7% Export Reduction

For the period between April 1, 1981, and March 31, 1982, it calls for a 7.7 percent decline in Japanese exports to the United States from the 1.82 million Japanese cars sold there last year. That represents a drop of 140,000 vehicle sales.

In the second year of the plan, which coincides with Japan's fiscal year, exports would be limited initially to the same level as the previous year, 1.68 million, plus 16.5 percent of a projected increase in the American passenger car market. A recent United States mission here projected this calendar year's auto sales in the United States at 9.5 million, and forecast sales between 11 million and 13 million in 1982.

Finally, the Japanese Government said it would closely watch exports during the third year and would apply controls, if necessary.

The automobile agreement apparently resolves the thorniest trade issue between the two countries. It also bodes well for Prime Minister Zenko Suzuki's scheduled visit with President Reagan next week in Washington.

Agreement Called 'Temporary'

Rokusuke Tanaka, Minister of International Trade and Industry, called the agreement "temporary and extraordinary," and said that, in any case, the curbs would end by March 1984.

Japanese trade officials said they would put the agreement into effect by asking auto makers to provide monthly reports of their car exports to the United States. Enforcement of the measures would include a combination of the trade ministry's informal administrative guidance—a kind of jawboning—and possible reliance on Japan's export control law.

"It is rather complicated," one trade ministry official said, "and it is more of a directive than background persuasion." He added that the three Japanese partners of American companies—Isuzu Motors with the General Motors Corporation, the Toyo Kogyo Company with the Ford Motor Company and Mitsubishi Motors with the Chrysler Corporation—would not receive preferential treatment under the restrictions. Their American partners have been encouraging the Japanese companies to ship more cars to the United States to meet the demand for fuel-efficient, reliable vehicles.

Note on the Automobile Case and the Politics of U.S. Trade Policy

The automobile case is a good introduction for the student to the politics of U.S. trade policy.[8] In domestic terms the automobile case demonstrated the crucial role of Congress in the making of U.S. trade policy, and the increasing political salience of international trade issues. In 1979 the UAW had requested Congress to provide trade relief. Following congressional hearings it was clear that §201 was the appropriate statute to utilize since the Japanese were not being accused of any particular "unfair" trading practice. After the negative ITC decision in 1980 the UAW took its case back to the Congress, and found sympathy for its position. Senator Dan Riegle (D.-Mich.), for example, described the ITC decision as a "monumental error," and Sen. John Danforth (R.-Mo.) was determined to obtain import quotas against Japanese automobiles.

Prodded by Congress, and saddled with his 1980 campaign promises, President Reagan felt compelled to "do something" to assist the U.S. automobile industry, despite the administration's strong preference for free market policies. The "something" was a "voluntary" agreement with Japan that relieved Reagan's domestic political pressure, but set an unfortunate policy precedent for other U.S. industries seeking an "end run" around negative ITC decisions. The unanswered political question is whether any other U.S. industry will have the political clout to force presidential action in the face of a negative ITC decision. To date no other U.S. industry has been able to force the president's hand in this manner.

In terms of U.S. international trade policy the automobile case has had

---

[8]For a detailed description of the politics of the automobile case, *see* S. Cohen and R. Meltzer, United States International Economic Policy in Action: Diversity of Decision Making, Chapter 2 (1982).

extremely important ramifications. Of the $150 billion U.S. trade deficit in 1985, about $50 billion was with Japan. U.S.-Japan frictions over trade have threatened to spill over to the political and national security aspects of the bilateral relationship. The continued increase in Japanese imports has come as a considerable assault to the U.S. national ego, and a great deal of frustration and anger have poured forth as to what to do about Japanese imports.[9]

Approximately half of the U.S. trade deficit with Japan is accounted for by the automobile trade deficit, and in 1980 the United States imported nearly 13 times as many vehicles as it exported (2.76 million versus 0.22 million). A solution to the U.S.-Japan trade deficit thus revolves in large part around U.S. policy on Japanese automobile imports.

What is not clear at this writing is how auto trade policy will be used to sustain what is now (in 1986) a healthy U.S. automobile industry. Japan announced its intention on February 12, 1986, to continue the VRA for one more year, albeit at a higher export ceiling of 2.3 million cars.[10]

Finally, the ITC decision in the automobile case raised serious legal questions about the need for reform of the escape clause. Representatives of domestic industries contended that the causation criteria of §201 were too difficult, and should be relaxed. It was argued that under the current wording, and its interpretation by the ITC, it would be very difficult to win a case during a recession, if the ITC were permitted to aggregate a variety of different factors into one "decline in demand." Behind this debate is the continuing controversy whether the United States should adopt an "open trade" or "interventionist" trade policy (here defined as a policy that discriminates between domestic and foreign enterprises to shape international trade flows).[11] The protectionist-versus-free-trade policy debate continues unabated, with intense pressure for an import surcharge or quantitative restraints to relieve the pressure from foreign imports in general and Japan in particular.

NOTES AND QUESTIONS

1. Why, do you think, did President Reagan accept the "voluntary" restraint? What about the Japanese government? For additional background on this agreement, see Note: Regulating Japanese Automobile Imports: Some Implications of the Voluntary Quota System, 5 B.C. Intl. & Comp. L. Rev. 431 (1982); Comment: Imposing Import Restrictions Under Escape Clause Provisions: A Case Study of the Automobile Industry, 12 Cal. W. Intl. L.J. 325 (1982).

[9] See W. Watts, The United States and Japan (1984).
[10] See A Review of Recent Developments in the U.S. Automobile Industry Including an Assessment of the Japanese Voluntary Restraint Agreements, U.S.I.T.C. Pub. No. 1648 (February, 1985). The Wall Street Journal, Feb. 13, 1986, at 3, col. 1.
[11] See D. Roos and A. Altshuler, The Future of the Automobile, Chapter 10 (1984).

2. In fact, the "Voluntary Restraint Agreement" (VRA) with Japan on automobiles was neither "voluntary" nor an "agreement"—it was, in effect, a coerced unilateral export restraint. Do you think this VRA was legally obtained under the U.S. trade laws? How might you attack the lawfulness of this restraint following the negative determination of the ITC and absence of congressional action?

See Consumers Union of the United States v. Kissinger, 506 F.2d 136 (D.C. Cir. 1974), *cert. denied,* 421 U.S. 1004 (1975); Sneaker Circus v. Carter, 566 F.2d 396 (2d Cir. 1977) and 457 F. Supp. 771 *on remand* (E.D.N.Y., 1978), *aff'd. without op.* 614 F.2d 1290 (Ct. App. N.Y. 1979). United States v. Guy W. Capps, Inc., 204 F.2d 655 (4th Cir. 1953), *aff'd,* 348 U.S. 296 (1955). Consider the following excerpt from the Senate Finance Committee Report on Trade Act of 1974 (§§201-203) (S. Rep. No. 98-1298, 93d Cong., 2d Sess. (1974)) explaining the escape clause mechanism:

> For many years, the Congress has required that an "escape clause" be included in each trade agreement. The rationale for the "escape clause" has been, and remains, that as barriers to international trade are lowered, some industries and workers inevitably face serious injury, dislocation and perhaps economic extinction. The "escape clause" is aimed at providing temporary relief for an industry suffering from serious injury, or the threat thereof, so that the industry will have sufficient time to adjust to the freer international competition.
>
> By reason of the Congressional requirement, the trade agreements to which the United States is a party contain an escape clause or equivalent provision. Typical and of most general effect is Article XIX.1.(a) of the General Agreement on Tariffs and Trade.*
>
> From 1951 through 1962 the escape clause worked reasonably well. The criteria were fair and equitable, and relief was occasionally granted. However, in 1962 the Administration proposed and the Congress adopted rigid and stringent tests of injury and causal relationships between tariff concessions, increased imports and serious injury.
>
> As a result, the provisions of the Trade Expansion Act of 1962 for invoking the escape clause (like the adjustment assistance provisions also adopted in that Act, which contained similar injury tests) have proven to be an inadequate mechanism for providing relief to domestic industries injured by import competition. One result of this inadequacy has been a number of special "voluntary" agreements for industries deemed by the Congress or the Executive to be suffering from excessive imports. The Committee believes it is better to provide a fair and reasonable test for any industry which is being injured by imports—a determination made by an independent factfinding body, such as the International Trade Commission—than to rely on ad hoc agreements for a few select industries. . . .

---

*"If, as a result of unforeseen developments and of the effect of the obligations incurred by a contracting party under this Agreement, including tariff concessions, any product is being imported into the territory of that contracting party in such increased quantities and under such conditions as to cause or threaten serious injury to domestic producers in that territory of like or directly competitive products, the contracting party shall be free, in respect of such product, and to the extent and for such time as may be necessary to prevent or remedy such injury, to suspend the obligation in whole or in part or to withdraw or modify the concession."

Section 607 would provide that no person shall be liable for damages, penalties, or other sanctions under the Federal Trade Commission Act or the Antitrust Acts (as defined in section 4 of the Federal Trade Commission Act), or under any similar State law on account of his negotiating, entering into, participating in, or implementing an arrangement providing for the voluntary limitation on exports of steel and steel products to the United States. This provision would be limited to such participation in any such arrangement, or modification or renewal thereof that was undertaken at the request of the Secretary of State or his delegate prior to the enactment of this bill, which ceases to be effective no later than January 1, 1975. This section is not intended to modify the application of the aforementioned laws except to the extent that they may have applicability to the voluntary arrangement described. This section of the Committee's bill is deliberately limited in scope and purpose, and is not intended to be a precedent for the future.

3. What about attack under the antitrust laws? Although the formal logic of *Consumer's Union* is certainly applicable to both this question and the preceding one, are you convinced? Consider also United States v. Watchmakers of Switzerland Information Center, 1963 Tr. Cas. ¶70,600 at 77,456 ("If, of course, defendants' activities had been required by Swiss law, this court could indeed do nothing."); Continental Ore v. Union Carbide and Carbon, 370 U.S. 690 (1962); United States v. Aluminum Corp. of America, 148 F.2d 416 (2d Cir. 1945); Timken Roller Bearing v. United States, 341 U.S. 593 (1951). Does "administrative guidance" under Japanese law amount to an act of state or sovereign compulsion? (This question will be easier to handle after the antitrust chapter.)

4. Is the "voluntary" quota legal under the GATT? Consider Articles I, XI, XIX.

5. Would a domestic content bill designed to force foreign automobile producers to invest in the United States be legal under the GATT? Consider Articles I, III, XI, XIII, and XXVIII.

6. As president or ITC member, what would you have done in the automobile context if it had appeared to you that a steel import restraint like that of *Consumer's Union* were a major cause of the automobile industry's problems?

7. In the 1983-1984 model year, the U.S. auto industry did much better and the executives received large bonuses. This angered the administration, which indicated that it would not seek renewal of the arrangements in 1985. What would you do if you represented a Japanese auto manufacturer?

8. The later success of the automobile industry suggests that the problem was, so to speak, a short-term import surge. If such surges were common, and there is some evidence that they are (*see, e.g.,* Pearson and Ellyne, Surges of Imports: Perception Versus Evidence, 8 World Economy 3 (Sept. 1985)), what are the implications for §201 policy?

9. What about cases like color television and textiles, where the restriction attempts to slow a long-term shift in optimal location of production facilities?

10. What if the Japanese government selected out a special "basket" of 300,000 cars for export to General Motors, as part of its agreement to renew

the "voluntary" quota arrangement with the United States? Would Chrysler or Ford have a valid argument in contesting this action under the antitrust laws of the United States? Would Japan's action be "state action" protected by sovereign immunity?

11. A wag once remarked that the practice of trade law is so frustrating because the attorney always has the feeling that someone has his thumb on the scale of justice. Isn't this particularly true in the "escape clause" area, where the ultimate result is so colored by political, as opposed to legal and economic, concerns? Is it a good or bad thing that policymaking under §201 is politicized? Can this aspect of trade policy ever be depoliticized?

12. The "safeguard" area focuses on "fair" as opposed to "unfair" competition such as that which is subsidized by a foreign government. What is the difference between the two? Is this distinction meaningful to the U.S. worker put out of a job by imports? Why do the U.S. trade laws distinguish between the two types of foreign competition?

13. Should the United States have different standards in applying §201 to less developed countries?

14. Should the Most-Favored-Nation principle apply to safeguard remedies, or should trade restraints be applied on a selective (discriminatory) basis?

15. How could you argue that trade restraints, such as those that could be imposed under §201, are far less effective at protecting jobs than is generally supposed? Discuss the relevance of higher prices, higher input costs, and exchange rate effects.

16. Do you think it is profitable to approach the automobile case with "long-run" or "immediate" explanations for the difficulties of the U.S. automobile industry? To what extent does increased automobile import competition reflect lagging productivity and high wages in the United States? Is that relevant under the §201 causation criteria? Have U.S. government regulations in areas such as safety and emission control, and the policy of controlling prices contributed? How does one apportion responsibility for the decline in the U.S. automobile industry between labor, management, and the federal government? *See* L. White, The Automobile Industry Since 1945 (1971); B. Yates, The Decline and Fall of the American Automobile Industry (1983); R. Sobel, Car Wars (1984).

17. After the Japan-U.S. auto quota agreement described in the text, what would be your concern if you represented the European auto industry?

18. Is §201 effectively an industrial policy that picks winners and losers? If so, what are its biases and is the ITC the proper form for this type of government intervention? In 1984, in a speech before the National Press Club, ITC Chairman Alfred E. Eckes, made the following remarks concerning import protection:

> Is Section 201 really buying time for adjustment, or is it simply building walls to shield noncompetitive industries? How protectionist is the escape clause in

practice? Examination of the record shows that relief is not automatic, either from the Commission or the President. Between 1975 when the current version of Section 201 became law and the conclusion of the nonrubber footwear case, the ITC has completed 50 escape clause investigations. In 29 cases (58 percent) the Commission found injury and recommended relief. In 19 of these 29 cases, (less than 40 percent of the total) the President provided relief. Even in those cases where relief was provided, the President's remedy often differed from the Commission's recommendation; and quite frequently, he provided relief for less than a full five years.

Looking at these 50 cases from another angle, it is clear that the ITC has not favored big industries and turned aside the claims of small domestic petitioners. For instance, the ITC ruled negatively on big industries like automobiles, footwear and cattle. On the other hand, it made relief recommendations for large industries, like specialty steel, and for smaller ones like clothespins, and mushrooms. There is nothing in this record that indicates Section 201 has become a permanent shield for industrial dinosaurs.

It is my personal view that Section 201 provides a constructive approach to assisting import-jolted industries of any size or composition. It offers a formula for temporary protection, which is authorized under the General Agreement on Tariffs and Trade, to facilitate adjustment. It is not a prescription for permanent protectionism. Moreover, it does not involve government deeply in the marketplace with subsidies and loans, or in the managerial decision-making process. Rather use of escape clause relief temporarily protects the domestic market from emerging foreign competition and thus enables firms with sound adjustment plans, determined leadership, and committed employees to adapt. Domestic law, and international trade law, thus provide a procedure so that private industry can help itself. It involves a temporary escape from global competition.

In contrast, I resist the enthusiasm in some quarters for having government pick industrial winners and losers. Well-intentioned public officials, for example, might conclude that labor-intensive industries, such as tableware and even footwear, are phase-out industries. They might presume that, because production technology is relatively uniform around the world, American firms with higher labor costs lack comparative advantages and should "adjust out."

Consider Commissioner Eckes' remarks in light of Table 4-1, which describes the results in §201 cases in the 1976-1983 time period.

2. The Adjustment Assistance Alternative

As an alternative to §201 the executive branch can bring into play the adjustment assistance program, which, as opposed to §201, has purely domestic ramifications. The problem with adjustment assistance is not only budgetary (inadequate fiscal resources) but political—large U.S. industries would in practically all cases prefer to continue doing what they are already doing, rather than adjust to a new type of endeavor. Adjustment assistance may be sought by a domestic firm or workers before a §201 escape clause action or in tandem with a §201 action.

TABLE 4-1
Section 201 Cases in Years 1976–1983

Investigation	Product	Date of investigation	Duty on product in effect in year of investigation		Existing quantitative restriction on product	Determination of ITC	Recommended Relief of ITC	Relief granted by president
			Col. 1	*Col. 2*				
TA–201–4	Asparagus	Jan. 76	Fresh: 25% ad val. Canned: 17.5% ad val.	50% ad val. 35% ad val.	None	Commission equally divided	5-year quantitive restriction declining after third year	None
TA–201–10	Mushrooms	March 76	3.2 cts ad val. per lb (rate fluctuated periodically from June 18, 1930)	+ 10%	None	Affirmative	Adjustment Assistance (3 commissioners) Quota, allocated on country by country basis; 3.2 cts/lb & +35% ad val. duty on over quota imports in first 3 years, +25% ad val. in 4th year, +15% + in 5th year (1 commissioner)	Expedited Adjustment Assistance
TA–201–12	Shrimp	May 76	Duty free		None	Affirmative as to shrimp fishing industry (negative as to shrimp processing industry)	Adjustment Assistance	Expedited Adjustment Assistance

TA-201-17	Mushrooms	Jan. 77	3.2 ct/lb +10% ad val.	10ct/lb +45% ad val.	None	Affirmative	Tariff-rate-quota system for 5-year period: Quota allocated in country-by-country basis-Tariff over quota decreasing in 4th & 5th years (3 Commissioners Adjustment Assistance (2 Commissioners))	Monitored imports; ITC Quarterly Reports
TA-201-22	Fresh Cut Flowers	Aug. 77	10% ad val.	40% ad val.	None	Negative	None	None
TA-201-25	Live Cattle & Certain Edible Meat Products of Cattle	Sept. 77	Between 1.5 ct/lb and 2.5 ct/lb depending on weight	Between 2.5 ct/lb and 3.0 ct/lb depending on weight	None	Negative	None	None
TA-201-40	Leather Wearing Apparel	Jan. 80	Duty Free: On GSP list of eligible products Jan. 1, 1976-March 1, 1979		None	Affirmative (as to costs and jackets only)	Increased tariff 25% ad val. 1st year 20% ad val. 2d year 15% ad val. 3d year	Adjustment Assistance
TA-201-41	Certain Fish	Jan. 80	N.A.		None	Negative	None	None
TA-406-6	Anhydrous Ammonia	April 80	Duty Free (except small quantities: 6.4% ad val. (col. 1); 28% ad val. (col. 2); (GSP eligible)		None	Negative	None	None

TABLE 4-1 (continued)
Section 201 Cases in Years 1976–1983

Investigation	Product	Date of investigation	Duty on product in effect in year of investigation		Existing quantitative restriction on product	Determination of ITC	Recommended Relief of ITC	Relief granted by president
			Col. 1	Col. 2				
TA–201–42	Fresh cut Roses	April 80	8% ad val. (not GSP eligible)	40% ad val.	None	Negative	None	None
TA–201–43	Mushrooms	August 80	3.2 ct/lb + 10% ad val.	10 ct/lb + 45% ad val.	None	Affirmative	3-year quantitive restriction; decreasing in 2d and 3d years	Additional tariffs for 3 years: 20%, 15% and 10% ad val. in 1st, 2d & 3d years respectively
TA–201–44	Motor Vehicles	Dec. 80	2.9% ad val. to 8.5% ad val. depending on type and weight	10% ad val. to 25% ad val.	None	Negative	None	None
TA–201–45	Fishing Rods & Parts thereof	Nov. 81	14.3 ad val. (decreasing to 7.6% ad val. by 1987)	55% ad val.	None	Negative	None	None
TA–201–46	Tubeless Valves	Sept. 82	3.7% ad val. (decreasing to 3.1% ad val. by 1987 (GSP eligible)	25% ad val.	None	Negative	None	None

TA-406-9	Mushrooms from PRC	Sept. 82	3.2 ct/lb & 20% ad val. (decreasing to +15% ad val. in 1981 and to +10% ad val. in 1982)	10 ct/lb + 45% ad val.	Quantitative restrictions for a 3-year period	Commission equally divided	None	None
TA-201-47	Heavyweight Motorcycles	Feb. 82	Decreasing between 1983-1987 from 4.4% to 3.7% ad val., 2.0% ad val. to free; 3.6% to 3.1% ad val., or 52% ad val. to 4.2 ad val., depending upon type and weight		None	Affirmative	5-year tariff increase, decreasing from 45% ad val. in 1st year to 10% ad val. in 5th year	ITC relief adopted and tariff rate quotas adopted in addition
TA-201-48	Stainless Steel & Tool Steel	May 83	Between 4.2% ad val. and 11.5% ad val. depending upon type (+ additional duties of up to .4% ad val. depending upon alloy content)	Between 11% ad val. and 33% ad val. depending upon type (+ additional duties of up to 1% ad val. depending upon alloy content)	None	Affirmative	Quantitative restrictions for 3-year period; added duties for other products	Additional tariffs for 4 years, declining each year on some products; global quotas on other products

a.   The Theory of Adjustment Assistance

The theory of adjustment assistance, as its title suggests, is premised on the concept of adjustment to a dynamic world economy.[12] Moves toward a freer trade regime—especially for the developed countries[13]—will tend to increase each country's overall national income under the law of comparative advantage.[14] Those individuals in disfavored factor sectors of the economy will, however, be rendered worse off, since a reduction in import barriers will lead to an increase in competing imports and a decrease in the domestic output of the "liberalized" industry.[15]

Familiar general principles of loss allocation lie behind the notion that the government should recompense "victims" of trade liberalization by redistributing part of the gains from expanded trade. The first is the principle of enterprise liability, by which enterprises giving rise to a loss bear the burden of that loss.[16] It could be argued that the government is frequently "causing" the "injury" to the industry or its workers by removing the protection it has given them. It thus seems equitable to recompense the reliance interests that have grown up over time. Second, adjustment assistance spreads the loss from the removal of trade restrictions, causing fewer severe economic dislocations.[17] A third justification for adjustment assistance can be found in the deep pocket theory of loss allocation.[18] This rationale would apply to *all* imports, not just those resulting from trade liberalization; it would treat all imports as an "accident," the costs of which must be equitably distributed. The industries that are candidates for adjustment assistance are typically the sick and the dying, the marginal industries relying on static technologies and homogeneous product lines. It seems reasonable to finance their adjustments through our progressive tax system, as other expenditures considered necessary by the government are financed.

b.   The Statutory Framework of Adjustment Assistance

Sections 222-283 of Title II of the Trade Act of 1974 (see Selected Documents Supplement) provide a framework for direct financial aid in the form of

[12]This section is drawn from Fisher, The Multinationals and the Crisis in United States Trade and Investment Policy, 53 B.U.L. Rev. 308 (1973).

[13]For the view that free trade does not tend to benefit the developing countries, see the writings of Prebisch, Myrdal, & Singer, analyzed in P. Pincus, Trade, Aid and Development: The Rich and Poor Nations 126-134 (1967).

[14]*See supra* p.6.

[15]W. Salant & B. Vaccara, Import Liberalization and Employment 15 (1961).

[16]*See* G. Calabresi, The Costs of Accidents: A Legal and Economic Analysis 21 (1970); and Calabresi, Some Thoughts on Risk Distribution and the Law of Torts, 70 Yale L.J. 499 (1961).

[17]G. Calabresi, The Costs of Accidents: A Legal and Economic Analysis 21 (1970).

[18]Calabresi, Some Thoughts on Risk Distribution and the Law of Torts, 70 Yale L.J. 499, 518 (1961).

adjustment assistance for workers, firms, and communities. An affirmative determination of eligibility for adjustment assistance for firms and workers may be made if it is found that increased imports have contributed importantly (rather than being the major factor) to a decline in sales or production and to the total or partial separation of a significant number or proportion of the workers in question. Eligibility determinations for workers and firms are made, respectively, by the secretary of labor and the secretary of commerce, rather than the International Trade Commission.

Eligible workers have been entitled to up to 52 weeks of cash allowances, amounting initially to 70% of the workers' average wage rate, but revised in 1981 to an amount beyond unemployment insurance levels. Workers could also obtain job search allowances of up to $500 (later $600) per worker, and relocation allowances of up to $500 plus 80% of the expenses of relocation (later $600 and 90%).

The assistance program for eligible firms includes technical assistance and financial assistance. As of early 1984, the limit on loans to any one firm was $1 million in direct loans and $3 million in government guaranteed loans. Technical assistance may be furnished for the purpose of developing a program for economic adjustment, assistance in implementing a proposal, or both.

NOTE AND QUESTION

How effective would you expect adjustment assistance to be? It has generally been criticized. For a sample of the literature, see Comptroller General, Report to Congress, Adjustment Assistance to Firms Under the Trade Act of 1974—Income Maintenance or Successful Adjustment? (Report ID-78-53, December 21, 1978). And for discussion of other nations' programs, see Comptroller General, Report to Congress, Considerations for Adjustment Assistance Under the 1974 Trade Act: A Summary of Techniques Used in Other Countries (Report ID-78-43, January 18, 1979).

3.   Imports of Agricultural Products

Section 22 of the Agricultural Adjustment Act provides in pertinent part:

(a) Whenever the Secretary of Agriculture has reason to believe that any article or articles *are being* or are *practically certain to be* imported into the United States under such conditions and in such quantities *as to render* or *tend to render ineffective, or materially* interfere with . . . any loan, purchase, *or other program* or operation *undertaken by the Department of Agriculture,* or any agency operating under its direction, *with respect to any agricultural commodity or product thereof,* or to reduce substantially the amount of any product processed in the United States from any agricultural commodity or product thereof with respect to which any such program or operation is being undertaken, *he shall so advise the President,* and, *if the President agrees* that there is reason for such belief, the President shall cause an immediate investigation to be made *by the United States International Trade Commission,* which shall give precedence to investigations under this section to determine such facts.

7 U.S.C. §624(a) (emphasis added).[19] There have been 46 investigations conducted under §22, most recently involving dried milk mixtures, sugar, peanuts, tobacco, casein, and lactalbumin, and articles containing sugar.[20]

In carrying out its investigatory and reporting role in a §22 investigation, the Commission has listed as the factors to be examined: (1) import levels, (2) inventories held by the Commodity Credit Corporation under the particular program, (3) changes in the cost to the government of running the program (4) price differences between the domestic and imported products, (5) world stocks of the imported product, (6) the ability of foreign producers to ship significant quantities of the subject article to the United States, and (7) whether the objectives of the program are being met. Sugar, No. 22-45 USITC Pub. No. 1253 (June 1982) at 7, Certain Articles Containing Sugar, No. 22-46 USITC Pub. No. 1462 (December 1983) at 11.

Section 201(b) of the Trade Act of 1974 provides on the other hand that upon request of the president or the United States Trade Representative, or upon resolution of either the House Ways and Means Committee or the Senate Finance Committee, the Commission shall undertake an investigation

---

[19] The statute thus provides for four phases in a §22 action: (1) "reason to believe" determination by the secretary of agriculture, (2) agreement by the president that there is such reason for belief, (3) investigation and report by the Commission, and (4), as provided in §22(b), agreement by the president with the commission and attendant determination and proclamation of relief.

[20] Dried Milk Mixtures, No. 22-40, USITC Pub. No. 783 (July 1976); Sugar, No. 22-41, USITC Pub. No. 881 (April 1978); Peanuts, No. 22-42, USITC Pub. No. 1124 (January 1981); Certain Tobacco, No. 22-43, USITC Pub. No. 1174 (August 1981); Casein, Mixtures in Chief Value of Casein, and Lactalbumin, No. 22-44, USITC Pub. No. 1217 (January 1982); Sugar, No. 22-45, USITC Pub. No. 1253 (June 1982); Certain Articles Containing Sugar, No. 22-46, USITC Pub. No. 1462 (December 1983).

In Dried Milk Mixtures, the Commission found in the affirmative based upon market prices declining towards the support price, increases in government stocks and recent heavy purchasing by the Commodity Credit Corporation (CCC), growing stocks of milk in the major foreign producing countries (a doubling to 3 billion pounds between December 1974 and December 1975), and the efforts of importers to circumvent existing quotas by mixing sugar into the dried milk mixtures, etc.

In the April 1978 and the June 1982 §22 sugar investigations, the Commission found in the affirmative on both occasions, noting that world production far exceeded world consumption, that there exists a likelihood that foreign sugar would undersell the domestic product, that as of 1982 the U.S. imported 51% of its sugar needs, that use of sugar substitutes had increased, that prices continued to fall and that a large amount of stock had been recently purchased by CCC.

In Casein, the Commission's finding was in the negative, as there had been no U.S. production of casein since 1968, and the Commission considered any indirect effects of casein imports upon the dairy program to be too speculative to justify §22 relief.

Most recently, in Certain Articles Containing Sugar, the Commission found in the affirmative as to certain products, pointing out that it placed great reliance upon the opinion of the USDA, and citing in particular the continued great increases in imports, fluctuating world prices, bulging world inventories, foreign ability to ship and production continuously outstripping consumption.

to determine whether an article is being imported into the United States in such *increased quantities* as to be a *substantial cause* of *serious injury*, or the *threat thereof*, to the *domestic industry* producing an article *like or directly competitive with the foreign article*.

19 U.S.C. §2251(b)(1) (emphasis added).

Thus the two statutes require different showings in order to obtain relief. Whereas §22 calls for an inquiry into (1) the quantity of imports and (2) the effect of such imports, either currently or prospectively, in "materially interfering" with a price support program,[11] §201 looks to (1) the nature of the industry and the product, (2) the magnitude of the increase in imports, (3) the seriousness of the injury to a domestic industry, and (4) the nexus between the imports and the injury. In evaluating the seriousness of the injury, the Commission examines, inter alia, trends in domestic production, consumption, sales, inventories, net profits, wages, employment, exports, and capacity utilization.

QUESTIONS

1. U.S. imports of flue-cured tobacco increase from 5% of U.S. comsumption in 1980 to 30% in 1984. During the period U.S. stockpiles of flue-cured tobacco retained by the Commodity Credit Corporation (CCC) of the U.S. Department of Agriculture increase sharply, from a value of $750 million to $1.5 billion. Should the U.S. tobacco industry file for relief from foreign imports under §201 of the Trade Act of 1974, or under §22 of the Agricultural Adjustment Act (7 U.S.C. §624)?

2. In 1985 the president asks the ITC to investigate whether candy bar imports are undermining the U.S. sugar program. EC confectionery exporters base their case on the high value of the U.S. dollar compared to the members of the European Community, arguing that the increase in confectionery imports is due to the changes in exchange rates rather than to a desire to circumvent the import restrictions on sugar. What result?

4.   Imports from Nonmarket Economies

Imports from nonmarket economies[21] are treated differently from other imports. First, when the allegation is an excessive volume of imports, Section 406 of the Trade Act of 1974 (*see* Selected Documents Supplement), with its lower injury standard, is employed instead of §201. Pursuant to §201 the petitioner

---

[21] The terms "nonmarket economies," "controlled economies," and "communist countries," are used interchangeably in this section, although it is, of course, possible that parts of a market economy may be controlled, or vice versa.

must establish that the increased imports are a substantial cause of serious injury, while under §406 the president may limit nonmarket economy imports following an ITC finding of "market disruption," which has much lower injury and causation criteria than §201.[22] The 1979 and 1980 anhydrous ammonia cases involving U.S.S.R. imports[23] demonstrate the political sensitivities to imports from non-market economies, and it is fair to say that §406 is a highly politicized statute. Those wishing to import into the United States from nonmarket economies would be well advised to move slowly and incrementally, and to enter a U.S. market in carefully phased stages. Section 406 stands as a ready watchguard to keep out excessive nonmarket economy imports, even if they are fairly competing in the U.S. marketplace.

The second distinction involving nonmarket economy imports occurs with respect to unfairly traded goods that are either dumped or subsidized. As the student will learn in Chapter 5, dumping is a term of art, with specific legal connotations and definitions, although the term is frequently used loosely by non-lawyers to mean merely a lot of imports. Dumping is generally defined in the U.S. statutes to mean sales in the U.S. market at a price lower than in the home market. But with goods from nonmarket economies, a different test is used. Commerce Department officials will instead calculate a constructed value based on the third country price of a market economy at a comparable stage of economic development. The application of this third-country test can lead to the imposition of very high levels of additional antidumping duties equal to the margin of dumping, which is defined as the difference between the "fair value" and the U.S. price. Again, those importing from nonmarket economies should be totally aware of the U.S. price situation prevailing in the marketplace before launching any import campaign, and avoid low-priced sales that substantially undercut the sales prices of U.S. competitors. The petitioner confronting rapidly increasing, low-priced sales from a nonmarket economy has an election of remedies between Section 406 and the U.S. dumping laws; the former leads to quantitative restraints as the remedy, while the latter leads to the imposition of additional antidumping duties as the solution.

A second form of unfair competition is the subsidization of foreign goods entering the U.S. marketplace, an issue we will consider in some detail in Chapter 6. If exports are subsidized by what is deemed by Commerce Department officials to be a bounty or grant, and they are causing material injury to a U.S. industry, a special additional countervailing duty may be assessed equal to the amount of the export subsidy. In 1985 the Court of International Trade held that the U.S. countervailing duty law applies to nonmarket econ-

[22] Section 406(e)(2) defines market disruption as follows: "Market disruption exists within a domestic industry whenever imports of an article, like or directly competitive with an article produced by such domestic industry, are increasing rapidly, either absolutely or relatively, so as to be a significant cause of material injury, or threat thereof, to such domestic industry."

[23] Anhydrous Ammonia from the U.S.S.R., determination of no market disruption, 45 Fed. Reg. 27,570 (1980) (Investigation No. TA-406-6, U.S.I.T.C. Pub. No. 1051); Anhydrous Ammonia from the U.S.S.R., determination of market disruption 44 Fed. Reg. 61,269 (1979) (Investigation No. TA-406-5, U.S.I.T.C. Pub. No. 1006).

omies as well as market economies. The 1985 case involved the importation of wire rod, a steel product, from Poland and Czechoslovakia.[24] The court found that the Congress had had many opportunities to make it clear that the countervailing duty laws were not intended to reach planned economy imports but had never done so. The Commerce Department had initially refused to extend the countervailing duty law to communist country imports, but it has now been mandated to undertake the task. But the following question now presents itself: what is an export subsidy in a nonmarket economy run on the basis of five-year plans where decisions that in market economies that would normally be made by the market are instead made by governmental officials?

The core of the current problem with respect to imports from nonmarket economies revolves around the fact that the U.S.S.R. and certain other communist countries, Most-Favored-Nation (MFN) duty treatment has been denied, due to the failure to meet freedom of emigration conditions established by the Congress.[25]

The linkage between freedom of emigration and MFN trade privileges was established by Sen. Henry Jackson (D.-Wash.) and Rep. Charles Vanik (D.-Ohio), and has come to be known as the Jackson-Vanik Amendment. A few examples indicate how profoundly the Jackson-Vanik Amendment has worked to limit imports from nonmarket economies that do not permit free emigration. Automobiles from non-MFN recipient countries, for example, instead of confronting a nominal 2.6% duty, must pay a U.S. tariff of 25%, about 10 times the level of those U.S. trading partners receiving MFN treatment. The duty on machine tools similarly rises from 10% to 35%; the duty on chemicals from 15% to 75%; and the duty on jewelry from 30% to 100%. So there can be no doubt that the denial of MFN treatment has been a key reason for the very low level of U.S.S.R. imports, for example, into the United States, $600 million in 1984, compared with $3.3 billion in U.S. exports in 1984 to the U.S.S.R.

Why is communist country trade discriminated against by the United States? The answer to this question has pervasive political overtones. Whereas trade policy with market economies is typically controlled by economic motivations, trade with nonmarket economies tends to be dominated by political considerations. Thus, when the U.S.S.R. invaded Afghanistan in 1979, President Carter's immediate reaction was to announce a partial embargo on U.S. grain sales to the U.S.S.R. and a ban on the licensing of high technology to the U.S.S.R. Similarly, in 1985, when President Reagan sought to demonstrate U.S. displeasure with the perceived trend towards Marxism in Nicaragua, he imposed a trade embargo on that country. Realistically, U.S.-U.S.S.R. trade will continue to be a function of the political relationship existing between the two countries, and the extent of discrimination against imports from the

---

[24]Continental Steel Corp. v. United States, Slip Op. 85-77 7 I.T.R.D. 1001 (C.I.T. 1985).
[25]*See* §402 of the Trade Act of 1974. Rumania, Hungary, Yugoslavia, and the People's Republic of China are the only communist countries currently receiving MFN treatment. Poland's MFN grant was suspended in 1984.

U.S.S.R. and other communist countries will, correspondingly, be linked to external political variables as well.

East-West trade policy is where law and diplomacy meet. What is perceived as blatant, hostile discrimination against imports from the U.S.S.R. and other communist countries by those countries, is seen by the U.S. government as a mechanism to promote the enforcement of human rights, the free emigration of peoples, and a technique to limit the difficulties inherent in competing with a nonmarket economy. Whether or not the linkage between trade and politics should have been made is less important now than the reality that it exists as a political fact of life.

Apart from the use of trade policy as an instrument of foreign policy, there have in the past been special economic factors inducing the movement of excessive nonmarket economy goods into the United States, including: (1) the need for foreign exchange to finance the importation of needed goods; (2) simple errors of judgment by state planners; and (3) a tendency to use foreign markets as a cushion to absorb the oversupplies resulting from unexpectedly good harvests.

United States trade with communist countries is statistically insignificant (imports plus exports typically amount to less than 2 percent of total U.S. trade). It is thus easy to make trade policy a hostage to foreign policy considerations, as relatively few U.S. interests will protest the trade discriminations employed.

The most recent exception to the generalizations made above is the People's Republic of China (PRC). With two-way trade running above $5 billion per annum, all U.S. administrations have, since 1972, encouraged trade with the PRC. Finally, on February 1, 1980, MFN status was accorded to the PRC.

5.   Import Restraints for National Security Reasons

Section 232 of the Trade Expansion Act of 1962 provides that if the secretary of the treasury finds that an "article is being imported into the United States in such quantities or under such circumstances as to threaten the national security," the president is authorized to "take such action, and for such time, as he deems necessary to adjust the imports of [the] article and its derivations so that imports [of the article] will not threaten to impair the national security."[45]

---

[45] Section 232(b) provides in full:

Upon request of the head of any department or agency, upon application of an interested party, or upon his own motion, the Secretary of the Treasury (hereinafter referred to as the "Secretary") shall immediately make an appropriate investigation, in the course of which he shall seek information and advice from, and shall consult with, the Secretary of Defense, the Secretary of Commerce, and other appropriate officers of the United States, to determine the effects on the national security of imports of the article which is the subject of such request, application, or motion. The Secretary shall, if it is appropriate and after reasonable notice, hold public hearings or otherwise afford interested parties an opportu-

6. Textiles and Apparel: A "Managed Trade" Approach

The preceding sections described a procedure for government to intervene in trade on a case-by-case basis at the request of individual parties. Textiles and apparel present a contrasting pattern of "managed trade," in which the government plays a much larger role.

The textile and apparel sector is significant both economically and politically. It directly employs about 1.9 million workers or over 10% of the manufacturing sector; about another million workers are employed in related sectors.[26] Together with corresponding industries in Europe and even Japan, this sector is highly subject to competition, especially from developing nations, and is thus often troubled economically. At the same time, it is extremely important politically to many in the House and the Senate. It is not surprising then that it is subject to a special arrangement: the Multifiber Arrangement (MFA) of 1974, done December 20, 1973, 25 U.S.T. 1001, T.I.A.S. 7840, a

---

nity to present information and advice relevant to such investigation. The Secretary shall report the findings of his investigation under this subsection with respect to the effect of the importation of such article in such quantities or under such circumstances upon the national security and, based on such findings, his recommendation for action or inaction under this section to the President within one year after receiving an application from an interested party or otherwise beginning an investigation under this subsection. If the Secretary finds that such article is being imported into the United States in such quantities or under such circumstances as to threaten to impair the national security, he shall so advise the President and the President shall take such action, and for such time, as he deems necessary to adjust the imports of such article and its derivatives so that such imports will not threaten to impair the national security, unless the President determines that the article is not being imported into the United States in such quantities or under such circumstances as to threaten to impair the national security.

Section 232(c) of the Act, 19 U.S.C. §1862(c) (1970 ed. Supp. IV) [19 U.S.C.S. §1862(c)] provides the President and the Secretary of the Treasury with guidance as to some of the factors to be considered in implementing §232(b). It provides:

For the purposes of this section, the Secretary and the President shall, in the light of the requirements of national security and without excluding other relevant factors, give consideration to domestic production needed for projected national defense requirements, the capacity of domestic industries to meet such requirements, existing and anticipated availabilities of the human resources, products, raw materials, and other supplies and services essential to the national defense, the requirements of growth of such industries and such supplies and services including the investment, exploration, and development necessary to assure such growth, and the importation of goods in terms of their quantities, availabilities, character, and use as those affect such industries and the capacity of the United States to meet national security requirements. In the administration of this section, the Secretary and the President shall further recognize the close relation of the economic welfare of the Nation to our national security, and shall take into consideration the impact of foreign competition on the economic welfare of individual domestic industries; and any substantial unemployment, decrease in revenues of government, loss of skills or investment, or other serious effects resulting from the displacement of any domestic products by excessive imports shall be considered, without excluding other factors, in determining whether such weakening of our internal economy may impair the national security.

[26]Data derived from Nehmer and Lore, Textiles and Apparel: A Negotiated Approach to International Competition, in B. Scott and G. Lodge (eds.), U.S. Competitiveness in the World Economy (1985).

global agreement whose key predecessors were negotiated by President Kennedy, who had promised southern voters to limit textile imports if elected president.

The fundamental concept of the MFA, which has been renewed twice, and is up for renewal in 1986, is that each textile or apparel importing nation will accept at least a 6% increase in imports each year from each exporting nation. This would provide both protection for threatened industries and opportunity for new exporters. There has, however, evolved a practice, formalized in the 1977 renewal, that nations could sign bilateral agreements, providing for deviations from this 6% norm. These bilaterals are usually much more restrictive; they also often provide specific ceilings for particular categories (e.g. manmade fiber gloves). They may further include detailed provisions setting ceilings that can be modified by consultation and governing whether unfilled quotas can be transferred from one year to another. The result is an elaborate global network of detailed specific quotas (although not all quotas have actually been filled, nor have quotas been set on all exporter-importer-product combinations).

United States implementation, authorized by §204 of the Agricultural Act of 1956, 7 U.S.C. §1854, involves an interdepartmental Committee for the Implementation of Textile Agreements (CITA) and a Commerce Department Office of Textiles and Apparel (OTEXA). OTEXA, together with the Customs Service, monitors imports by category; CITA negotiates agreements and conducts the consultations. In addition, there are advisory committees reflecting the interests of United States manufacturers, of importers, and of exporters.

In some cases, exporting nations apply the restraints; they may even require a manufacturer to purchase the right to use a portion of the quota, thus ensuring that the product price reflects the artificial scarcity. The exporters have also responded with elaborate programs that spread production of a specific item of clothing across several nations. Thus, the body and arms of a sweater may be made in different nations, and the pieces assembled in a third nation in order to reduce costs while shipping the product from a nation with an otherwise unused sweater quota. The United States has developed elaborate rules to respond to this practice.

Predictably, the industries of importing nations believe that the MFA is effectively too liberal; those of exporting nations believe that it is too restrictive. Whether the approach has really avoided still more severe trade restraints is difficult to say. In 1985, both Houses of Congress passed bills that would have imposed quota rollbacks on textile imports from major exporting countries, based on a 6% per year increase between 1980 and 1984 and 1% per year thereafter. Imports from these nations had grown more rapidly than this baseline, so the bill would have produced about a 30% decrease in imports. The president, however, vetoed the bill on December 17, 1985, citing the existing level of protection for the textile industry and the costs to the consumer.

Bibliographical Note

For more information, *see* Background Material on the Multifiber Arrangement, Subcomm. on Trade of the House Ways and Means Comm., 96th Cong., 1st Sess. (1979); The Multifiber Arrangement: 1973 to 1980, U.S.I.T.C. Pub. No. 1131 (March, 1981); G. Perlow, The Multilateral Supervision of International Trade: Has the Textile Agreement Worked? 75 Am. J. Intl. L. 93 (1981); Symposium in 37 Intl. Org. 551 (1983).

QUESTIONS

1. In what way is this approach better than the more ad hoc procedure of §201? In what ways worse? How would your evaluation differ if you represented the United States industry? The developing world industry? The United States consumer?

2. To what extent is your answer to the previous question affected by the fact that the major affected exporters are developing nations? The fact that other major developed nation importers are parties to the MFA? Can you imagine the MFA approach being used for other examples of adjustment to developing nation competition (steel, footwear, etc.)?

3. Considering the wide use of voluntary restraint agreements, is the MFA approach really all that different from §201?

4. How could the consumer interest be represented in a procedure like that of the MFA?

5. (As a review question) Is the MFA, as it has evolved, consistent with the Generalized System of Preferences described in Chapter 10?

B. THE ECONOMICS OF IMPORT RESTRAINTS

A bewildering array of possible government responses to fairly traded goods has been presented in this chapter, including tariffs, quotas, orderly marketing agreements (OMAs), voluntary export restraints (VERs), congressional "signals", and negotiated shares of the U.S. market.

The political imperatives for protection need to be tempered by the economics of import restraints. Once import protection for an industry has been decided upon, the issue becomes one of allocating the domestic costs of protection for the U.S. industry. The following excerpt demonstrates that the Federal Trade Commission and the International Trade Commission have very different philosophies, in spite of the similarity of their names.

M. MORKRE AND D. TARR, FEDERAL TRADE COMMISSION (BUREAU OF ECONOMICS) STAFF REPORT ON EFFECTS OF RESTRICTIONS ON UNITED STATES IMPORTS: FIVE CASE STUDIES AND THEORY

34-51 (1980)

TARIFFS VS. QUANTITATIVE RESTRAINTS

The traditional preference of tariffs to QR's [Quantitative Restraints] is primarily based on two arguments. The first involves international distribution effects. A QR generates scarcity rents that need not accrue to the importing country, but a tariff yields customs revenue. . . . [T]he "Voluntary Export Restraints" (VER's, and the newer Orderly Marketing Agreements (OMA's) are similar to quotas and do not yield customs revenue. The second argument concerns flexibility when underlying demand/cost conditions change. . . .

. . . [S]econdary features should also be noted. Because of the fixity of QR's they tend to sponsor wasteful (resource consuming) efforts to obtain permission to export or import the restricted product. An example might be the old sugar quota arrangements. In the mid-1950's it was alleged that there was a "sugar subgovernment." As reported by Gerber,[49] Washington was ". . . literally throbbing with (sugar) lobbyists and lawyers, jockeying to secure for their client countries a larger share of the sugar quota pie." QR's however offer an advantage to domestic firms and workers precisely because they are fixed. . . . QR's impose greater administrative costs, on the U.S. or foreign countries, or possibly both. Finally, there are the issues of discrimination and political repercussions. Tariff rates for particular products are the same for nearly all important foreign suppliers and, therefore, are much less discriminatory than QR's which tend to be imposed only on a few specific countries.

COMPARISON OF QUOTAS AND OMA-VER'S

DEADWEIGHT LOSSES

In terms of ranking, OMA's and VER's will be lumped together and contrasted with quotas. The first issue to consider is the degree of restrictiveness of imports, which means assessing the likely deadweight losses produced by quotas and OMA-VER's. Bergsten[50] argues that quotas are expected to be more restrictive. First, OMA-VER's usually do not cover all suppliers. The admin-

---

[49]The United States Sugar Quota Program: A Study in the Direct Congressional Control of Imports, 19 J. Law & Econ. 103, 120 (1976).

[50]On the Equivalence of Import Quotas and "Voluntary" Export Restraints, in C. Bergsten (ed.), Toward a New World Trade Policy: The Maidenhead Papers, 239, 241-45 (1975).

istration typically looks to the countries which have most recently been very successful in increasing their exports to the U.S. and whose share of the market has become significant. Second, imports from noncovered suppliers typically increase to partly offset the initial import reduction. This has been a prominent feature, for example, in textiles, nonrubber footwear, and color TV's. Finally, since OMA-VER's involve negotiation between the U.S. and a foreign supplier there is some opportunity for the supplier to lessen the severity of the quantity limits and introduce provisions which enhance flexibility. Flexibility is particularly important for goods like textiles, which are subject to abrupt demand shifts in response to changes in fashion, and durables and semi-durables, the purchase of which is postponable during general economic downswings.

To sum up, the deadweight losses of a quota are expected to be larger than those for an OMA-VER in a particular situation. Overall losses, deadweight plus rent losses may, however, be larger for the OMA-VER as this depends on how the quota arrangement deals with the disposition of the scarcity premium. If the premium goes to exporters the overall loss of the quota will be larger than that of an OMA-VER. But, if rents are retained by the U.S., the ranking may be reversed. . . .

An advantage of OMA-VER's is that the foreign country undertakes the task of regulating its exports leaving U.S. officials with the less onerous chore of monitoring the agreement. The U.S. Government, therefore, escapes the problems of administering a quota program and granting (or auctioning) import licenses to domestic interests. However, the OMA-VER surrenders the scarcity rents to foreigners. A complete assessment of the two policy alternatives must, therefore, estimate (marginal) U.S. administrative costs of a quota but it is unlikely this would significantly alter quota costs. However, it would raise distributive questions (e.g. which U.S. individuals/firms obtain import quota entitlements and on what terms) which are politically delicate.

A major premise in the foregoing discussion is that supplying countries capture the scarcity rents created by OMA-VER's. Empirical evidence on the issue is scanty, primarily because recipients of export licenses are, not surprisingly, reluctant to reveal the value of the surplus involved. After a review of available pieces of information, Bergsten concludes that the VER quota premium is captured by exporters, except where the U.S. has raised a tariff on the imported articles which recaptures a portion of the rent.

Note: The Auctioning of Import Relief?

Morkre and Tarr suggest that the OMA-VER model surrenders scarcity rents to foreigners. Should import relief in the form of quota shares be auctioned domestically? As the authors suggest, it would be possible to auction import licenses and keep some of the "rents" from protection in the United States. In 1985 the International Trade Commission proposed, for the first time, the auctioning of import licenses as part of its relief for the footwear industry in a §201 proceeding.

QUESTIONS

1. Given all the arguments just presented for the economic superiority of a tariff to a quota, why, do you think, have quantitative restrictions of various forms become so popular in the last few years?

2. How would a domestic content approach requiring a certain amount of internal production compare economically with tariffs and quotas?

3. Suppose the automobile industry has reached the point at which individual firms find that the returns to scale are achieved only at the global level— in other words, each firm finds it economical to have only one transmission plant and only one engine plant, etc., each of which can be located *somewhere* to serve the entire world. Would you be more sympathetic with a domestic content approach in such a case?

C.   THE GATT

Within the GATT, the escape clause is governed by Article XIX (*see* Selected Documents Supplement), whose interpretation and reform was a leading issue during the Tokyo Round. The underlying concern was that developed nations would be particularly tempted to use this clause to protect their older industries from the competition of new developing nation industries. This concern led to disputes over whether escape clause duties should be applied on an MFN basis or a selective basis. Some nations feared the effect on their exports if such duties were applied on an MFN basis in response to exports from other nations; other nations feared that a derogation of MFN principles would make it easier to target restrictions against their own exports. Compromises were sought, based on such approaches as international reviews of the application of the escape clause protection in each case, but the efforts failed.

The following two excerpts provide more detail on these concerns and on the politics of the escape clause.

MEIER, EXTERNALITY LAW AND MARKET SAFEGUARDS: APPLICATIONS IN THE GATT MULTILATERAL TRADE NEGOTIATIONS

18 Harv. Intl. L.J. 491 (1977)

As one observer has said,

> It is worth noting that the dominant place accorded to the MFN principle in postwar international trade relations tended to make them even more fragile and

subject to the accidents of bargaining than they had been before. MFN is in fact a ready-made instrument for setting in motion a downward spiral in the process of bargaining, once nations begin to adopt an adversary posture towards one another; for a dispute between two countries which leads one of them to withdraw a trade concession originally made as part of a general bargain between them is almost bound to inflict some injury on the trading interests of other countries who happen to be exporters of the products affected. Assuming that everyone insists on precise reciprocity, there is no end to the series of consequent adjustments that may have to be made.[73]

The nondiscriminatory basis of article XIX may appear particularly inequitable to developing countries who are small suppliers or new entrants but are denied access to the safeguard-invoking country's market even though the safeguard was initially invoked because of injury from another large developed-country supplier. In most cases in which article XIX action has been taken by GATT members, only a limited number of large suppliers were responsible for injurious imports, but all sources suffered from the MFN provision.

On the other hand, the only contracting party injured by a retaliatory suspension if the MFN clause is not applied is the party invoking article XIX. If the purpose of retaliation is punitive, then the MFN clause should be inapplicable for retaliatory increases. Even if it is meant only to pressure the invoking party to complete speedily its adjustment process, there is no reason to injure other contracting parties unnecessarily. Furthermore, the application of the MFN clause to retaliatory increases also carries with it the danger of chain reactions of further tariff increases by third countries. This dilemma can be avoided by eliminating the principles of most-favored-nation treatment and reciprocity from the regulation of emergency protection.

The waiver of the MFN rule and reciprocity does not mean, however, that there should be no international discipline with respect to the use of article XIX. On the contrary, the principle of multilaterality might be strengthened without a MFN principle.

> The principle of multilaterality would stand for common responsibilities, joint decisions and international surveillance—the continuous presence of a concerned forum in which a country can complain and seek mediation for its grievance against another country, or even seek adjudication. . . . [E]xperience . . . suggests that this principle is more important than non-discrimination pure and simple for ensuring that emergency protection will be limited to real emergencies, where there would be a right to protect and no need to compensate, and that the protective measures will be eventually lifted. The pragmatic course would be to seek ways of compromising with the MFN principle without sacrificing multilaterality.[76]

---

[73]Shonfield, International Economic Relations of the Western World: An Overall View, in I International Economic Relations of the Western World 1959-1971, 47-48 (1976).

[76]Tumlir, [Emergency Protection Against Sharp Increases in Imports, in J. Tumlir, In Search of a New World Economic Order (1974)] at 266.

The provision that under article XIX a concession may be suspended, withdrawn, or modified "to the extent and for such time as may be necessary to prevent or remedy" the injury resulting from the concession has allowed the invoking country to make emergency protection in essence permanent. A working party long ago stated that "action under Article XIX is essentially of an emergency character and should be of limited duration. A government taking action under that Article should keep the position under review and be prepared to reconsider the matter as soon as this section is no longer necessary to prevent or remedy a serious injury."

Most of the tariff increases made under article XIX have not, however, been rescinded. Reform of this article should therefore also involve some commitment, and a procedure, giving other countries an effective assurance of a continually growing access to the protected market and of a foreseeable removal of the market safeguard. This is especially important for LDCs that are entering new export markets. To this end, the right to invoke the article might be conditioned by requirements that (a) the protection afforded by the safeguard measure be degressive over a certain number of years, and terminal within some designated time period; (b) the invoking country is obligated to promote adjustments that will reduce the dislocation costs; and (c) the use of the safeguard measures and the adjustment efforts must be open to multilateral surveillance.

If the situation of "serious injury" is to be ameliorated, and dislocation costs reduced, governments must give special attention to adjustment policies. Otherwise industries that prefer protection to adjustment will continue the pressure for retention of the market safeguard.

It must be emphasized, as Johnson has, that

> from the standpoint of the advanced countries, adjustment assistance and safeguards against market disruption need to be considered as complementary and not as substitute policies. Adjustment assistance is designed to increase the speed with which change can be absorbed and digested; safeguards against market disruption are designed to slow down the speed of the change that has to be absorbed and digested. Optimum policy with respect to change associated with shifting comparative advantage in response to the development and diffusion of technology requires joint optimization with respect to both types of policy, not prior choice of one line or other of policy and subsequent optimization with respect to it alone. Both policies also require drawing a fine line between optimal pacing of change and protectionist resistance to change, a line which is probably significantly easier to draw and maintain where the two policies are considered jointly than when the full weight of responsibility for controlling the rate of change and absorption of it is placed on one type of policy only.[80]

The adjustment assistance must ensure adjustment out of the industry that is losing its comparative advantage: it cannot merely perpetuate the retention

[80] Johnson, Technological Change and Comparative Advantage: An Advanced Country's Viewpoint, 9 J.W.T.L. 1, 13 (1975).

of inefficient resources in the depressed industry. It must either promote measures to increase productivity or stimulate an exodus of factors from the industry. No matter what their particular form, adjustment measures must avoid trade-distorting effects: an inefficient adjustment-assistance measure has no more merit than does an inefficient VER or tariff or QR.

Not only should assistance facilitate the conversion of resources to higher productivity uses, but it should do so as early as possible. Instead of delaying an investigation and an adjustment assistance program until "serious injury" has been determined, it may be more sensible to shift to an "early warning" approach that makes it possible both to anticipate probable difficulties and to deal with these at an earlier stage. In essence, the problem is to devise an anticipatory, comprehensive approach that will be harmonious with the changing character of the international division of labor and facilitate the movement of resources in the direction of more efficient international resource allocation. This problem of dislocation will become more acute—and the time for adjustment shorter—as technology is diffused more rapidly to the LDCs, transnational corporations expand, and the developing countries accelerate their industrialization process. As these countries acquire a wider comparative advantage in the well-standardized, labor-intensive manufacturing industries they will become increasingly competitive with the older labor-intensive, import-sensitive industries of the more developed countries. . . .

4. DIFFERENTIAL TREATMENT FOR LDCs

This leads to the question implicit throughout this paper, and that should now be examined directly: is there a case for differential treatment for LDCs in the application of market safeguards? While advocating financial compensation only for LDCs, Bhagwati devotes only one short paragraph in justification of such differential treatment. He merely states that

> They [LDCs] are, after all, the countries which have been seriously affected by the textiles restrictions and by VER's. . . . Further, there is greater willingness, as part of the new international economic order, to grant LDCs reasonable accommodation via framing new rules regarding their trade. Moreover, the flow of funds to be so generated are far more likely to be significant, relative to their needs, for LDCs than for DCs. Finally, discriminatory adjustment of trade rules, in favor of LDCs, is well-embedded in GATT reform, as in the enactment of Article XXIII for them at GATT.[91]

Can more be said? From a sense of distributive justice or redistributive justice, one might maintain that the poorer party should not be made to stand a loss which the richer party could stand better. Indeed, it has been submitted that "the idea of need as a basis for entitlement" is

[91] Bhagwati, [Market Disruption, Export Market Disruption, Compensation and GATT Reform, 4 World Dev. 989 (1976)] at 1009.

the central feature of the contemporary international law of development. When we reflect on it, it may seem extraordinary how we have come to accept it and how far-reaching its implications may extend. Can we reconcile need as a basis of entitlement with other fundamental legal principles such as equality among states or their established rights? How can need fit into the still prevailing conception of a world market economy based on principles of comparative advantage and non-discriminatory trade? We have in fact already experienced the conflicts and dilemmas which these general questions suggest. It is clear enough that in treating need as a basis of entitlement, states have to diverge from other principles. And to a considerable extent, that is exactly what is being done. . . . The present rationale for international assistance and preferential treatment on the basis of need is more in keeping with the premises of the modern welfare state—that is, to provide for the minimal human needs of the most disadvantaged segments of society. For this reason, it does not seem so utopian or so revolutionary as the abstract formulation may suggest. Yet we should not underestimate its impact in international affairs.[92]

Although most international lawyers would consider a doctrine that "needs are right" to be too revolutionary, many might nonetheless recognize the inappropriateness of formal equality and reciprocity as governing principles of the relations between DCs and LDCs on the basis of an attempt to counterbalance existing inequalities. This principle has been variously termed the "welfare" principle, the principle of "the double standard," or the principle of "capability." Alternatively, one may admit to the reality of discrimination, and recognize special treatment for the LDCs on the basis that law must accurately reflect community expectations, rather than consist of a mere statement of often unheeded rules.

It can not be maintained that an LDC is "at fault" in exporting to a DC. A country has a reasonable expectation to improve its standard of living by following its comparative advantage. This is especially relevant for a developing country which is entering an "infant trade" of manufacturing. Other provisions of GATT allow preferential treatment for infant industries, and the same may be extended to "infant trade."

On the negative side, the invocation of market safeguards weighs more heavily on less developed than on developed countries. The capacity to transform from one industry to another within the LDC is limited because of compartmentalized markets, factor immobility, and absence of a well-defined integrated price system, so that resources are much more specific to the export industry and less transferable to another sector than in a developed country. The element of uncertainty is therefore especially deleterious to an LDC, as the LDC is less capable than a DC of bearing the uncertainty of having its exports encounter trade barriers.

Another reason for special differential treatment for LDCs is that in return for improved access for their exports in advanced country markets, the LDCs

---

[92]Schachter, The Evolving International Law of Development, 15 Colum. J. Transnatl. L. 1, 10 (1976). *See also* O. Schachter, Sharing the World's Resources at pt. I (1977).

might commit themselves to refrain from organizing commodity markets with price-raising objectives and might guarantee stable supplies of primary commodities. Both LDCs and DCs may gain if in the negotiating process the issue of market access for LDCs were linked with the issue of supply access to primary commodities for DCs.

C. PEARSON, EMERGENCY PROTECTION IN THE FOOTWEAR INDUSTRY

9-13 (1983)

PURPOSE OF PROPOSED SAFEGUARDS

A principal reason why safeguard actions remain contentious is that there is no universal agreement as to their purpose. Indeed, the differing views on purpose imply quite different features with respect to eligibility criteria, time limit and type of trade restraint employed. Features that promote one purpose can be inconsistent with others.

Four views on purpose can be identified. The first, generally held by the domestic industry, is that trade relief offers a temporary breathing spell from intense import competition, during which the domestic industry can regain its competitive position in essentially the same product lines. The second view, often held by economists, is that temporary import restraint following a sudden surge in imports allows an orderly transfer of domestic resources, both labour and capital, to more productive activity. The premise is that social adjustment costs, mainly due to unemployed resources, can be reduced by slowing the pace of the industry's decline and relying on attrition rather than involuntary unemployment to reduce the workforce. The third view is based on consideration of equity or fairness. It holds that trade relief is a method for preventing concentrated injury to specific groups (the industry and its workers) when the general interest is served by a liberal trade policy. The fourth view is pragmatic; it argues that a government can "buy" a more liberal trade policy if it has a credible method for compensating politically important groups that perceive the possibility of injury from trade. In other words, the safeguard mechanism is a price to be paid to secure liberal trade legislation or to forestall more severe trade restrictions.

These four views on purpose have internal weaknesses and inconsistent features. For example, the first view would require a government granting import relief to determine that a domestic industry has not permanently lost comparative advantage and that its decline is reversible. This is an extraordinarily difficult determination to make. The second view would require that an industry use its period of relief to shed resources in an orderly fashion. Trade measures by their nature, however, raise prices and profits in the protected industry, quite possibly attracting additional resources to the industry. The third view of purpose, that trade restraints can remedy injury by maintaining employment, offers protection to all firms and workers in the industry and thus cannot target benefits to those firms and workers actually injured by import competition. The pragmatic view, by promoting safeguard actions, threatens the underlying objective of freeing trade. Textile restraints, originally justified to forestall more severe import restrictions, are a case in point.

The inconsistencies among these views on purpose are equally troubling. For example, the first view would limit trade relief to industries that have a fair chance of regaining competitiveness, and would encourage new resources to flow into the industry, especially capital and technology, whereas the second view would make orderly contraction of the industry a criterion for temporary trade relief. The first view would welcome price increases from trade restraints as a source of financing for new investment, whereas the second view would consider price increases as a cost, to be set against the benefit of avoiding unemployed resources. The confusion centres on what is meant by adjustment to imports—regaining competitiveness in the same products or re-employing resources elsewhere in the economy.

The third view of purpose, to compensate for injury, is generally inconsistent with both types of adjustment. Rationalising existing productive capacity to become more competitive involves substitution of capital and technology for labour and often increases concentration of domestic production among fewer firms. Both effects displace labour and undercut the equity purpose. Also, trade relief that simply maintains employment in the affected industry frustrates and delays the adjustment of resources to other activities, the principal purpose of adjustment according to the second view. Finally, for credibility, the pragmatic view of purpose requires that the safeguard mechanism be readily available as political needs dictate, without much attention to the adjustment prospects of the industry. The more credible the safeguard mechanism, the less likely that it will be used in a discriminating fashion to further adjustment.

If this confusion of purpose is not enough, the availability of trade adjustment assistance (TAA) programmes as an alternative to trade relief ensures a problem. TAA programmes have exactly the same divergence of views as to purpose, and thus the same inconsistencies. Trade adjustment assistance is designed to: (i) make the domestic industry more competitive through technical assistance and financing; (ii) retrain and relocate workers in more productive activity (shorten unemployment); (iii) compensate labour through more generous unemployment benefits than are generally available; and (iv) "buy" more liberal trade legislation. These are clearly inconsistent objectives for the reasons given above, and the record of the United States TAA programme documents the resulting problems. The main difficulties are that generous assistance for equity purposes delays adjustment, as workers have less incentive to seek other jobs, and that attempts to salvage a declining industry, through government infusion of financing and technical assistance, cannot succeed if the loss of comparative advantage is permanent.

American trade legislation does not help in resolving the divergent views as to purpose. Section 201 of the Trade Act of 1974 allows a petition to be filed for import relief "for the purpose of facilitating orderly adjustment to import competition" where purpose "may include such objectives as facilitating the orderly transfer of resources to alternative uses and other means of adjustment to new conditions of competition." Once a petition is filed, the main responsibility of the International Trade Commission in escape clause cases is to determine if there is serious injury due to imports and to recommend a duty or other import restriction that will "prevent or remedy" such injury or to recommend adjustment assistance.

There are three ambiguities in this formulation. First, it gives no guidance as to when trade adjustment assistance is to be recommended in lieu of trade relief. Second, the language does not specify whether the principal purpose of trade relief is to make the industry more competitive or to transfer resources to other economic activities (the two divergent views on adjustment). Finally, the injunction to recommend a trade restriction that will prevent or remedy injury is especially vague. Is injury remedied by adjustment or by compensation? Is it even possible to remedy injury by restricting trade?

NOTES AND QUESTIONS

1. Why, do you think, was Congress interested in Article XIX in 1974?

2. As between the U.S., the European, and the developing countries' positions on the linkage of MFN and Article XIX, which do you think is right? Is it the long-term interest of those who propound it? For a good discussion from the European viewpoint, see Bronckers, The Non-Discriminatory Application of Article XIX GATT: Tradition or Fiction?, 1981/82 Legal Issues of European Integration 35 (1982).

3. Do you see any chance of the more substantial reforms that Professor Meier proposes? Note that multilateral surveillance has been used, even leading to a finding against the United States, in the context of the Multifibre Arrangement. See 9 Intl. Trade & Invest. Mgmt. 1035 (I.T.A. May 23, 1984).

4. Would you favor a code governing adjustment assistance? What would you include? How would it help?

5. Suppose the president applies an import restriction to all nations *except* a defined one? For an example, see Farr Mgmt. & Co. v. United States, 544 F. Supp. 908 (Ct. Intl. Trade 1982) (Agricultural Adjustment Act §22 restraint on sugar from everywhere by Malaysia).

6. Suppose a U.S. president, interested in protecting the U.S. steel industry, but also concerned about developing nations, considered imposing import restrictions that, in effect, would force steel imports from Japan and Europe to fall by, say, 10% each year and permit those from developing nations to rise by, say, 15% each year. Under what conditions might the president have the legal authority to do this? Would it violate the GATT? What international repercussions would be likely? Would the action be wise?

7. In the automobile case, the ITC decision against the U.S. industry had

little effect on the political move toward protectionism. The result is, perhaps, that politically powerful industries can gain protection any time they want it, while weaker industries are restricted to the statutory procedures. What reforms, if any, might help alleviate this imbalance?

8. Suppose the following international agreement concept were proposed:

(a) Each major firm selling manufactured products in several nations shall locate its manufacturing facilities in such a way that the employment it generates in each nation shall be proportional to the sales of its products in that nation. The agreement would fill in details so this requirement would not be triggered below some reasonable level of sales (correlated with the rational size of a specific plant in different industries), so that it would give firms a reasonable time to adapt to market changes, and so that the required proportions of production in different nations would not add up to more than 100%.

(b) No nation shall impose domestic content requirements other than those spelled out internationally in paragraph (a).

Would you recommend U.S. adherence? If U.S. adherence appeared likely, what special features and modifications might you urge?

9. The manufactures readily exportable from developing nations and often heavily protected in developed nations—shoes, textiles, etc.—pose very sensitive issues in both trade and development. It would be very desirable if there were ways that the developed nations could shift their production emphasis away from these sensitive areas and maintain employment instead in less sensitive areas. Having seen the political and institutional problems of international trade institutions, please outline as effective a way as you can of internationally encouraging such a shift, and then step back and evaluate the proposal you have made. Do the ideas in the Pearson article help you here?

10. What are the implications of the failure to date to achieve multilateral agreement on the implementation of Article XIX of the GATT? Is the lack of transparency with respect to foreign restrictions taken pursuant to Article XIX healthy for the international trading system?

Bibliographical Note

For general background on safeguards, §201 of the Trade Act of 1974, and the GATT, see A. Lowenfeld, Public Controls on International Trade (1979) 197-254; Adams & Dirlam, Import Competition and the Trade Act of 1974: A Case Study of Section 201 and Its Interpretation by the International Trade Commission, 52 Indiana L.J. 544 (1977); Note: Title II of the Trade Act of 1974: What Changes Hath Congress Wrought to Relief from Injury Caused by Import Competition, 10 J. of Intl. Law & Econ. 197 (1975); Pearson, Protection by Tariff Quota: Case Study of Stainless Steel Flatware, 13 J. of World Trade L. 311 (1979); Note: The Harley-Davidson Case: Escaping the Escape Clause, 16 Law & Pol. Intl. Bus. No. 1, 325 (1984); C. Fulda and W.

Schwartz, Regulation of International Trade and Investment, Chapter 5, Section 4 (1970); J. Jackson, Legal Problems of International Economic Relations Chapters. 8, 9, 11 (1977); C. Bergsten, Toward a New International Economic Order Chapter 11 (1975); Commission on International Trade and Investment Policy, Papers, Vol. I, pp.167-394; Judicial Conference, Reform of the International Trading System (Safeguards), 84 F.R.D. 554 (1980); H. Malmgren, International Economic Peacekeeping in Phase II, Chapter 7 (1972).

For additional information on §406, see P. Feller, U.S. Customs and International Trade Guide (1979) 20-13 through 20-16; and Erlick, Relief from Imports from Communist Countries: The Trials and Tribulations of Section 406, 13 Law & Pol. Intl. Bus. 617 (1981).

Chapter V

Antidumping Duties

Chapters V and VI consider responses to foreign trade practices deemed to be "unfair." Chapter V covers the imposition of antidumping duties designed to counter price discrimination by a foreign firm. For a number of reasons, such a manufacturer may export goods at substantially lower prices than those it charges at home; this will sometimes hurt an industry in the importing nation, which may then respond with an antidumping duty.[1]

Chapter VI covers the imposition of countervailing devices aimed at equalizing the benefit of subsidies given by foreign governments. Antidumping and countervailing duties are frequently linked; the presence of subsidies may permit exports to take place at a lower price than would be justified if competition was proceeding solely on the economic merits of the product in question. The domestic petitioner may face a choice-of-remedies question ab initio: should he take action first against foreign dumping or foreign subsidies?

A. THE ECONOMICS

Price discrimination arises in the domestic context as well as in the international one. Alcohol, for example, has two radically different prices, one for drinking alcohol and one for alcohol used in industry and as a fuel or an antifreeze. Both to enforce the taxes on drinking alcohol and to protect the distiller's profits, the markets are kept separate by denaturing publicly avail-

---

[1] For general background on antidumping law, see J. Pattison, Antidumping and Countervailing Duties (1984); G. Bryan, Taxing Unfair International Trade Practices (1980); Antidumping Law: Policy and Implementation, 1 Mich. Y.B. Intl. Legal Stud. (1979).

able industrial alcohol so as to make it unfit to drink. (Advertising campaigns emphasizing the importance of specific liquor brands also help.) In another example, airlines offer a range of possible prices. The lower fares are available only to those who are able to plan far ahead and willing to travel at hours that are inconvenient for business traffic. The higher fare is thus charged to the "less elastic" business market—those who tend to travel anyway, regardless of the high price. The lower fare goes to the "more elastic" tourist market—those who may not travel at all unless the price is right. And the airline will fill more seats as a result of the dual pricing practice, thus maximizing its profits.

Figure 5-1 shows the principle graphically. Here L is the lower price—that for industrial alcohol or for tourist class airfares. In contrast, H is the higher price, that for drinking alcohol or for business class fares. By price discrimination, the firm is able to add the shaded area of profits, LHQhB, to the profits available if just the lower price option is offered. And the profits with price discrimination are also greater than those available through offering just the higher price. This form of price discrimination permits the firm to appropriate some of the "consumer surplus," the triangle above the line LBQ$_L$ in Figure 5-1. In this area, the consumer is in fact willing to pay more than he or she has to at a single price—to pay, for example, $10 per bottle for gin that, absent

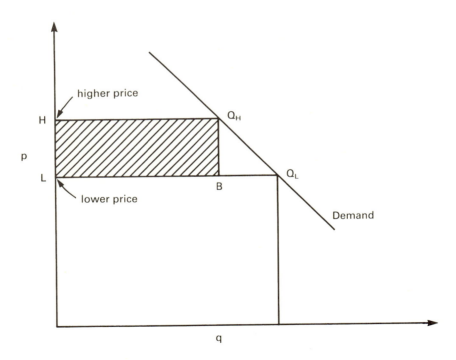

FIGURE 5-1
By discriminating in its pricing structure a firm can reap higher profits than would be the case with a uniformly high price

price discrimination, might be available for $1 per bottle. Permitting the industry to recoup the $9 contributes not just to profits but to the level of investment and may move toward optimality. Or, looking at essentially the same phenomenon a little differently, the airline's multiple fare schedule permits it to recover a large portion of the fixed cost of a flight from the business travelers. By filling the otherwise empty seats—which would have to be flown anyway—at any price above the costs of the meal and similar individual passenger handling costs, the airline is able to recoup part of the fixed trip cost, and offer transportation and probably more flights for the benefit of both groups of passengers.

The international aspects are described in the following articles.

FISHER, THE ANTIDUMPING LAW OF THE UNITED STATES: A LEGAL AND ECONOMIC ANALYSIS*

5 Law & Poly. Intl. Bus. 85, 86-93 (1973)

I. THE ECONOMICS OF DUMPING

A. THE DEFINITION OF DUMPING

Dumping is traditionally defined as selling at a lower price in one national market than in another. Accordingly, Viner, in his classic study of dumping, concluded that dumping should be confined to "price discrimination between national markets." Theoretically, the definition of dumping includes "reverse dumping," i.e., selling at a lower price in the home market than abroad, but this practice typically does not create international tensions. The prototype dumping case is that in which a country sells goods abroad at a price lower than that price prevailing in its home market. The "dumping" referred to in this article is solely of the latter type.

B. THE ECONOMIC MOTIVATION FOR DUMPING

The rationale for dumping products in a foreign market is analogous to that for price discrimination within a domestic market: the discriminating firm can maximize its profits by charging different customers different prices for essentially identical products. For example, if some customers are willing to pay no more than $7, when others will pay $15, for an item, it would be advantageous for the seller to be able to charge the higher price to those customers prepared to pay more. Only when sectorization of markets obtains, however, can goods be sold to the low-price customers without sacrificing the benefits to be obtained from the high-price customers.

The opportunities for profits from dumping will depend upon the interaction of three variables: the demand for the firm's product in its own country

*Reprinted with permission of 5 Law & Poly. Intl. Bus., © 1973.

and abroad, the barriers to reentry into the exporting market, and the nature of the firm's cost structure. These variables are considered below.

1.   Demand in the Exporting and Importing Countries

The firm will be more likely to profit from dumping if the home demand for the dumped goods is inelastic. If demand does not slacken in the home market when the dumping firm raises its prices initially (or raises its prices later, if the dumped good is one that can be produced only at increasing costs), then the overall net revenue of the dumping firm will be increased. Profitability of the dumping firm will also be increased if there is high price elasticity abroad for the dumped goods. If foreigners respond sharply to lower prices, more goods will be sold and the firm's revenues will be increased.

2.   Reentry into the Exporting Country

Internal price discrimination, i.e., within the same country, is difficult to sustain over a long period of time because there are no barriers to reimportation. In international transactions, the seller will find it far easier to engage in price discrimination between the home market and foreign markets, as he can avail himself of barriers to reimportation in the form of tariffs, quotas, and nontariff barriers to trade. A condition precedent for a successful dumping scheme is, therefore, the effective insulation of the home market from the world market for the dumped goods. Otherwise, the dumped goods would reenter the domestic market, equalize the home and export prices, and "ruin" the home market for the discriminating firm.

3.   The Cost Structure of the Firm

The final variable in the dynamics of international dumping is the cost function under which the firm must operate. In general, a firm will not dump unless the marginal revenue that it derives from abroad is substantially greater than its marginal costs of production for the dumped goods. Generally, this can be achieved at a lower foreign price only where the cost curve is descending at the margin, i.e., where there is a declining-cost industry involving economies of scale.

The concept of marginal costs helps to explain the three customary subdivisions of dumping—sporadic, intermittent, and continuous (or persistent). Sporadic dumping is of relatively minor concern to the country dumped on, since, typically, it is an unloading of overstock by a foreign producer who prefers to dump his goods in a foreign market rather than endanger his domestic price structure. The firm will ordinarily regard its costs as fixed, its marginal cost as zero, and accept virtually *any* price that can be obtained for the goods abroad.

Generally, intermittent dumping is an element of a larger scheme to secure a foothold in a foreign market. Consequently, the motives here are much more pernicious than those associated with sporadic dumping. The foreign producer seeks to forestall the development of competition, or eliminate it entirely, in the market he selects for the dumping. A frequent technique of such predatory, intermittent dumping is to sell abroad for brief periods at prices below marginal (but not necessarily average) cost. After the foreign competitor is eliminated, the predatory dumper may then raise his prices above marginal costs.

Continuous dumping may be predicated upon an assumption by the foreign producer that its costs over the long term will be cheaper if it manufactures a large number of items in order to realize maximum economies of scale. Since the overproduction might be a burden upon domestic prices, the foreign producer may wish to dump abroad permanently in order to maintain its domestic price structure. A sustained profit from the firm's overall sales will thus be ensured for as long as the average prices charged customers exceed the average cost of production. If the firm desires to pass along the benefits of the dumping to its home customers, lower prices may be made available for the home market. There is no guarantee, however, that the discriminating firm will shift the benefits resulting from dumping to its local customers. Indeed, the interests of the firm and the consumers of the dumping country may be antithetical, i.e., the firm may choose to retain all its profits.

C. THE EFFECTS OF DUMPING ON NATIONAL ECONOMIES

1. The Exporting Country

As noted above, the *firm* in the exporting country can profit from dumping under certain demand, reentry, and cost conditions. Whether or not a net benefit will accrue to the exporting *country* is, however, another matter. First, other firms in the dumping country may not benefit from the dumping situation, as foreign fabricators having received dumped goods can undersell the home price for finished goods and, thus, underbid home producers in third-country export markets. The effect of the dumping on consumer prices in the dumping country is more complex. If the dumped goods are being produced at declining marginal costs, then consumer prices may fall in the dumping country if the firm chooses to "pass along" the benefits of the dumping to the local consumers. If the goods are produced at rising marginal costs, then the equilibrium home price after dumping will tend to rise, as the dumping firm must "cover" its relatively unprofitable dumping. In the rising cost situation, then, the dumping firm may obtain higher profits; the user industries in the home market, which must compete with foreign goods containing the dumped items, are harmed; and the consumers, facing rising prices, will suffer.

There is, in any case, a misallocation of resources in the exporting country when intermittent or continuous dumping takes place. Such dumping cannot be successful without the artificial conditions of barriers to reentry into the domestic market and some monopolistic control of the home market. These facts, as de Jong notes,

> [c]ondemn the existing economic situation in the exporting country as an inefficient one, because of the misallocation of its productive resources. This country

could raise its economic welfare by reducing the output of the dumped article, stop dumping abroad, and expand production of something else.[21]

2.   The Importing Country

In the importing country, the most obvious problem caused by dumping is the harm inflicted upon competing producers of the dumped goods. The degree of harm will depend largely upon the quantity of dumped goods and the margin of dumping involved, i.e., the amount by which the dumped goods were underselling the home-market goods. Under the traditional Commission analysis, if a foreigner increased his U.S. market share by 5 percent through his less-than-fair-value (LTFV) exports, the domestic competitors normally would suffer a corresponding loss.

There are also at least three types of "implied injuries" to domestic producers that result from dumping. The first is the amount of growth that would have taken place in the competing industry in the absence of dumping. For example, assume that country X, prior to the sale of LTFV imports, holds 15 percent of the U.S. market in widgets. After the sale of a given amount of LTFV imports, country X still holds 15 percent of the U.S. market in widgets. Has "injury" to competing industries in the United States occurred? The answer is yes: in the absence of LTFV imports, U.S. widget manufacturers would have gained a portion of country X's market share (if the foreign margin of underselling is not substantially greater than the margin of dumping). With LTFV imports, U.S. manufacturers have lost that market opportunity. Thus, while no actual "present" injury has occurred, there is implied injury to U.S. competitors to the extent of lost market opportunities.

The second type of implied injury is the harm suffered by domestic industries with products that are not directly competitive with the dumped imports. Harm to such industries arises because U.S. consumers are tempted to purchase the dumped goods rather than the nondirectly competitive domestic goods. For example, assume that the exporting country dumps television sets but not radios. The LTFV television sets will deflect consumer preferences away from radios in many instances (the degree depending upon the relevant cross elasticities of demand), and thus harm the radio industry in the United States as well as the television industry.

The third type of implied injury is that occurring to user industries in the importing country. Unaware of the source of their low-priced imports, these industries might undertake expansion programs in reliance upon a continued source of supply. If the dumping country terminates the flow of dumped goods, however, the additional facilities would be economically dysfunctional and would represent a misallocation of resources caused by faulty signals from the price system.

The key benefit for the importing country is the lower prices that the dumped goods bring to its consumers. When dumping is sporadic, the benefit

---

[21] De Jong, [The Significance of Dumping in International Trade, 2 J.W.T.L. 162] at 173.

of lower prices would appear to outweigh the marginal harm suffered by local producers. When dumping is intermittent or predatory, however, the substantial injury suffered by local industries would appear to outweigh any benefits resulting from lower consumer prices. The most controversial area is that of continuous (or persistent dumping), which may or may not be economically desirable. If there is a smoothly functioning system of adjustment from import-impacted industries, then the importing country can realize a net benefit from the increased efficiency and lower prices provided by the continuous dumping. If, however, the continuous dumping creates large pools of unemployed manpower, then it can effect a hardship upon the receiving country in excess of the benefits consumers will realize. . . .

3. Competing Third Countries

Competing producers in third countries will be injured by dumping in the same manner as suppliers in the importing country. As the demand for their goods declines, so will their profits. In contrast to importing countries, however, competing third countries receive none of the potential benefits of dumping, such as lower consumer prices and increased efficiency in the operations of domestic manufacturers. Indeed, it would appear that it is the competing third countries that bear the brunt of the disadvantages caused by dumping.

FISHER, DUMPING: CONFRONTING THE PARADOX OF INTERNAL WEAKNESS AND EXTERNAL CHALLENGE, ANTIDUMPING LAW: POLICY AND IMPLEMENTATION

1 Mich. Y.B. Intl. Legal Stud. 11, 22-23 (1979)

THE IMPLEMENTATION OF FOREIGN DUMPING: THE ENIGMATIC ROLE OF THE STATE

With the exception of market entry, . . . lower unemployment, reduced balance of trade deficits, and use of overcapacity are *national* objectives superimposed on the objectives of individual enterprises. While an individual firm may be willing to lay off workers and idle capacity, the government may not be willing to do so for political reasons. Conversely, the government may desire to rationalize an inefficient sector of the economy but be unable to stand up to powerful trade unions wishing to avoid economic dislocations. In each case the result is the same: labor becomes a fixed cost that needs to be covered by the domestic enterprise. It is the thesis of this article that dumping policies are increasingly state-led or state-supported efforts to improve national economic postures.

In 1900 Brooks Adams said that nation-states were behaving more and more like huge corporations in competition. Today nation-states frequently are huge corporations in competition. This is especially true in such dumping-prone sectors as steel. For example, governments owned raw steel products enterprises in twenty-one major countries in 1975. Government-owned exports to the United States from these twenty-one countries accounted for 11.1 percent of total United States steel imports in 1974.

In Japan, the state has played a crucial role in the generation and implementation of foreign economic policy. As early as 1950 the government in Japan emphasized the development of the steel industry. Furthermore, the government facilitates the steel industry development by acting, in effect, as a well-controlled revolving door providing entrance to and exit from Japan.

In Italy, state-controlled enterprises have become as significant in domestic and international economic affairs as the large private corporations. The Institute for the Reconstruction of Italy (hereinafter IRI), the Ente Nazionale Idrocarburi, and other state-owned enterprises are responsible to the Ministry for State Holdings, and the Foreign Ministry. Finsider, the steel state-participation enterprise run by IRI, has, like its British counterpart, British Steel Corporation, lost enormous sums in recent years.

The list could continue, but, hopefully, the point has been made. United States industries which are particularly vulnerable to dumping, such as the steel industry, are private firms in which shareholders hold management responsible for making a profit, and these private firms are increasingly competing in a world of profitless enterprises with markets insulated by governmental tariff and nontariff barriers to trade. Dumping has thus become transmogrified from the classical profit-maximizing action of a private firm to a concealed partial devaluation of the currency of the exporting country carried out by the national government for national objectives. Instead of its traditional role as a micro-economic industry problem, dumping is increasingly a reflection of the macroeconomic problems of central government authorities.

Without the ability to implement the decision to dump for the reasons enumerated earlier, the objectives of national policy would remain objectives, and not national policies implemented by the government. . . .

NOTES AND QUESTIONS

1. Are you convinced that a nation should have an antidumping law? Is international price discrimination any different from its domestic analogue?

2. How (for those of you with antitrust background) does the wisdom of an antidumping law compare with that of the Robinson-Patman Act?

3. What about a law that applied just to predatory dumping? Note that some economists contend that predatory pricing is no more likely or serious than any other form of price discrimination.

4. How important economically is the distinction between intermittent and continuous dumping?

5. What about the practical implications of this intermittent versus continu-

ous distinction for the design of a remedy? Note that litigation delays are so great that an episode of intermittent dumping could be long finished before the merits of a specific case could be evaluated; hence provisional, interim, and retroactive arrangements become crucial. *See, for example,* the retroactive dumping duty levied in Cell Site Transceivers From Japan, 49 Fed. Reg. 24, 155 (1984).

6. What other special features of dumping might make the design of a remedy for dumping different from that of one for subsidies? What about the fact that it is usually a *firm* that dumps but a *government* that subsidizes? What about relative ease of access to data? For an example of the problem of dealing with data that a firm in an antidumping proceeding hopes to keep confidential, *see* Arbed, S.A. v. United States, 4 Ct. Intl. Trade 132 (1982).

7. Is there any justification for A to impose an antidumping duty on B's exports to A if A's firms have access to the higher-price market in B?

B.   THE UNITED STATES LAW

The dumping laws of the United States are administered by two different agencies, the Commerce Department and the International Trade Commission (ITC). Each agency has a different mandate. The ITC must find material injury, or the threat thereof, to the U.S. industry (or material retardation in its establishment); the Commerce Department is responsible for determining whether goods are being sold, or are likely to be sold, in the United States at less than their fair value. The difference between the "fair value," typically the home market price, and the United States sales price, is known as the margin of dumping. This amount is assessed as a separate antidumping duty, and is added to any other duties or import restraints already existing.

Dumping has been condemned by U.S. law since 1916 and by the GATT since 1947. The following article by Lorenzen traces some of the historical background of the U.S. antidumping law.

LORENZEN, TECHNICAL ANALYSIS OF THE ANTIDUMPING AGREEMENT AND THE TRADE AGREEMENTS ACT*

11 Law & Poly. Intl. Bus. 1405, 1406-1416 (1979)

This article will examine the most recent international agreement and U.S. legislation pertaining to dumping—the Agreement on Implementation of Article VI of the General Agreement on Tariffs and Trade and the Trade Agree-

*Reprinted with permission of 11 Law & Poly. Intl. Bus., © 1979.

ments Act of 1979. To understand the competitive and protectionist strains in the new international Code and the U.S. implementing legislation, it is essential to examine previous international efforts to curb the protectionist potential of domestic antidumping laws, as well as the statutory histories of several U.S. antidumping laws.

BACKGROUND

THE ANTIDUMPING ACT OF 1916

Widespread fear during World War I that emerging U.S. industries would be harmed by the dumping of merchandise stockpiled by the great European cartels prompted Congress to enact the first federal statute aimed specifically at dumping. There was no concensus, however, as to the focus of the new bill: the Republicans strongly supported a protectionist policy, believing that imports should not undermine domestic industry; the Democrats adamantly argued for relatively free international competition.

In 1916, the free-trade-oriented Democratic Congress prevailed. The Antidumping Act of 1916 took the form of an unfair competition law and condemned only predatory dumping. The Act made it unlawful for persons to import articles into the United States:

> at a price substantially less than the actual market value or wholesale price . . . Provided, That such act . . . be done with the intent of destroying or injuring an industry in the United States, or of preventing the establishment of an industry in the United States, or of restraining or monopolizing any part of trade and commerce in such articles in the United States.

The Act provided for federal criminal sanctions (including fines of up to $5000 or imprisonment for up to one year, or both) as well as for private treble damage actions. . . .

THE ANTIDUMPING ACT OF 1921

In 1921, Congress passed a second antidumping statute to remedy the inadequacies of the 1916 Act. The new legislation embodied (1) a broad "injury to industry" standard (instead of a narrow "injury to competition" standard) to measure the adverse impact of dumping, and (2) administrative, rather than judicial, enforcement of the Act.

1.   Injury to Competition versus Injury to Industry

The proposed House version of the 1921 Act was modeled on the Canadian Antidumping Act, which provides that dumping at less than fair value is per se subject to an antidumping duty. Like its Canadian counterpart, the House bill would have imposed a special dumping duty on merchandise "like" that produced in the United States whenever the merchandise was imported at less than the foreign market value, regardless of predatory intent on the part of the seller or the effect of the dumped sales on domestic businesses. The Senate, however, added a provision requiring a finding that an industry in the United States is being or is likely to be injured, or is prevented from being established by reason of the dumped merchandise, before dumping duties could be assessed.

It is not clear why the Senate added the "injury to industry" requirement to the House bill. The legislative history alludes to the Sherman Act and the need to protect competitors from unfair trade practices, but there are also strong suggestions that the purpose of the 1921 Act was to protect U.S. labor and capital from foreign competition. The latter view of bolstered by the fact that the Act was enacted as title II of the Emergency Tariff Act of 1921, which was designed to impose protective tariffs on specific imports in the hope of reducing unemployment in key U.S. industries.

The Antidumping Act of 1921 manifested a trade policy more protectionist than that of its 1916 predecessor. It did not discriminate between injury caused by predatory pricing and that caused by competitive pricing. Any injury to a domestic business, such as loss of sales or lower profits, triggered application of the statute; the fact that such injury resulted from competitive pricing was not a defense against the imposition of a dumping duty. The statute thus furnished not only the power to deter predatory pricing, but also the opportunity to chill international price competition with U.S. producers. . . .

INTERNATIONAL AGREEMENTS

The international community has long opposed dumping. In 1927, the World Economic Conference in Geneva adopted a resolution stating that "dumping creates a state of insecurity in production and commerce, and can therefore exercise a harmful influence quite out of proportion to the temporary advantage resulting from cheap imports." By the 1930s, at least 25 countries had enacted antidumping legislation in some form. In 1947, the Western trading nations adopted the General Agreement on Tariffs and Trade (GATT) with the general purpose of encouraging freer international competition and discouraging nationalistic economic policies.

GATT article VI, which governs antidumping, condemns dumping only if it "causes or threatens material injury to an established industry in the territory of a contracting party or materially retards the establishment of a domestic industry." Although the GATT uses the broader "injury to industry" language instead of condemning only dumping that injures competition, the standards that must be met before a dumping duty may be imposed suggest that the Agreement adopts a competitive rather than a protectionist stance. First, in order to constitute dumping, import sales must be below "normal value," which is expressly defined as the home market price, or in the absence of such, the highest export price to any third country, or the cost of production in the country of origin plus a "reasonable addition for selling cost and profit." In making these calculations, GATT countries are required to make "[d]ue allowance . . . for differences in conditions and terms of sale. . . ." Second, the injury to or retardation of a domestic industry must be "material."

The United States, however, is not bound by article VI due to a provision exempting from compliance with part II of the GATT countries with prior conflicting legislation. The United States thus was able to apply a less stringent injury standard in enforcing its own antidumping law. Accordingly, anything more than *de minimis* injury to an industry has been held sufficient to satisfy the 1921 Act requirements.

THE INTERNATIONAL DUMPING CODE OF 1967

By the opening of the Kennedy Round of negotiations in 1963, GATT members had begun to attack nontariff barriers to trade, including the U.S. antidumping law. In addition to the fact that article VI was not binding on the United States, there was increasing concern among European countries regarding the administration of the U.S. antidumping law. The United States, on the other hand, objected to the absence of an injury requirement in the Canadian statute and the failure of European nations to prescribe adequate procedural protections in processing antidumping cases.

The 1967 Code that resulted from the Kennedy Round was aimed principally at establishing uniform antidumping standards and procedures and tightening restrictions against the use of such measures for protectionist ends. In an effort to encourage uniform dumping laws, the 1967 Code outlined in greater detail the basic concepts of "industry," "injury" and "causation.". . .

Implementation of the International Antidumping Code

The International Code was signed on June 30, 1967 by 17 countries in addition to the United States; within a short time, the Code was implemented by every signatory except the United States. The U.S. Congress, however, vehemently opposed the Code for two basic reasons. First, Congress found "sharp and unreconcilable differences" between the 1967 Code and the Antidumping Act of 1921. Congress was particularly unhappy with the provision concerning the degree of injury required for a finding of dumping. It was feared that the differences on this point between the 1967 Code and the 1921 Act would make the domestic law less effective as a defense against predatory pricefixing by foreign producers and that adoption of the 1967 Code thus would result in fewer instances of dumping duties actually being assessed. Second, Congress took umbrage at being excluded from the process of formulation of U.S. trade policy when the problem (by its conception) was essentially a matter of the domestic economic effects of "unfair trade practices." Accordingly, the Senate Finance Committee concluded that the Executive branch, acting without the Congress, lacked constitutional authority to alter the Antidumping Act of 1921.

Ultimately, however, an act of Congress accommodated the conflicting interests of the two branches of government. Title II of the Act assured the supremacy of the 1921 Act over the 1967 Code, but allowed the Treasury and the Tariff Commission to effectuate the 1967 Code as long as basic consistency with the 1921 Act was maintained. . . .

THE INTERNATIONAL DUMPING CODE OF 1979[2]

The Tokyo Round of Multilateral Trade Negotiations, officially opened in September 1973, has been proclaimed the most ambitious effort undertaken by the international trading community since World War II to revise the rules of international trade. For five years, representatives of 99 nations worked to reduce or remove barriers to international trade and to develop new rules to govern the international trading system in the future. On April 12, 1979, the negotiations culminated in a comprehensive set of trade agreements between the participating nations, one of the most important of which is the code of conduct regulating antidumping practices. The principal objectives of the International Dumping Code of 1979 are (1) to harmonize world antidumping laws, and (2) to provide for open procedures and speedy and equitable resolution of antidumping disputes.

To achieve the first goal, the Code provides uniform definitions of the basic concepts of "industry," "injury," and "causation," and details the factors that must be considered in a dumping determination. In this respect, the 1979 Code is very similar to the 1967 International Dumping Code. Although the 1979 Code eliminates the requirement that the dumped imports be the "principal cause" of domestic injury, the new Code retains the requirement that the dumped imports cause "material" injury and provides that a finding of such injury is a sufficient basis for a determination of dumping. The definitions of the terms "injury" and "industry," as well as the factors that must be analyzed in determining whether these terms apply to a given case, are substantially identical in the 1967 and 1979 Codes.

The 1979 Code pursues the objective of speedy and equitable resolution of dumping disputes by reducing the harassment potential of the dumping proceeding and promoting procedural fairness. The Code requires that there be evidence of both dumping and injury, and of a causal link between the two before an investigation proceeding is initiated. This prevents domestic complainants from harassing foreign competitors with a steady barrage of dumping complaints based solely on evidence of price discrimination or solely on evidence of injury. The 1979 Code mandates simultaneous consideration of evidence of both price discrimination and injury in the preliminary decision whether to initiate an investigation, as well as in the later decision whether to

---

[2]Included in the Selected Documents Supplement, as are the provisions of U.S. domestic law implementing the 1979 Code, Title I of the Trade Agreements Act of 1979.—EDS.

apply provisional measures. This not only shortens the entire proceeding but discourages the filing of frivolous complaints. The proceeding is further expedited by the requirement that, except in "special circumstances" undefined by the 1979 Code, investigations be concluded within one year after their initiation.

The 1979 Code promotes procedural fairness by requiring the domestic authorities to notify the parties whose products are subject to the investigation, exporters and importers known to have an interest in the proceeding, the complainants and the public of the initiation of an antidumping proceeding. All interested parties must be given an opportunity to submit written evidence, in all cases, and oral evidence if justified. The complainant, concerned exporters and importers, and the governments of the exporting countries must be afforded an opportunity to see all relevant, nonconfidential information. When an antidumping investigation is suspended or terminated, or a preliminary or final determination is arrived at or revoked, the decision and findings, and the conclusions and reasons therefor must be published in the Federal Register.

The 1979 Code provides for provisional remedies to be invoked against goods under investigation only if there has been an affirmative preliminary finding of dumping and sufficient evidence of injury. The purpose of such interim remedies, which may be in the form of special provisional duties, a security deposit or bond for the estimated provisional duty, is to prevent continuing injury during the investigation period. Provisional measures may not exceed the estimated margin of dumping, and are to be limited to "as short a [time] period as possible," not to exceed four months or, where the exporters comprising a significant percentage of the trade involved request, six months.

Antidumping duties may be assessed retroactively in four circumstances: (1) where a final finding of *injury* (not including material retardation of the establishment of an industry) is made; (2) where a final finding of *threat of injury* is made and the effect of the dumped imports is such as would have led to a finding of injury in the absence of provisional measures; (3) where there is a history of injury-causing dumping or the importer was or should have been aware that the exporter has practiced such dumping; or (4) where retroactive application of the duty is necessary to preclude the recurrence of injury-causing sporadic dumping.

Note

Figure 5-2 outlines the investigatory time table embedded in the 1979 statute. As the previous piece makes clear, interim procedures and the possibility of retroactivity are extremely important, for they affect the possibility of trade during the litigation. *See also,* on this point, Zenith Radio Corp. v. United States, 710 F.2d 806 (Fed. Cir. 1983).

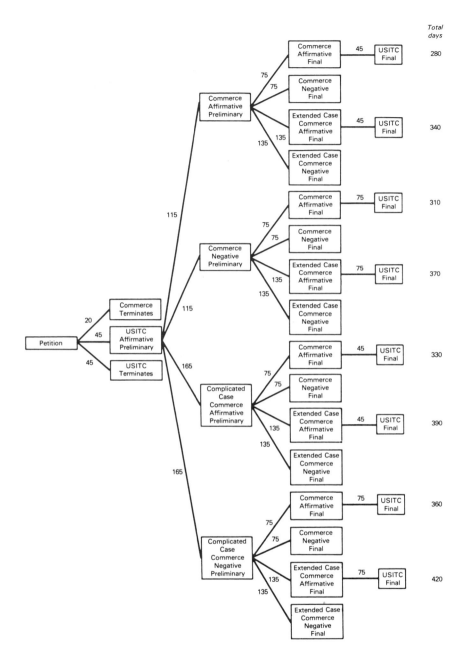

FIGURE 5-2
Statutory Timetable for Antidumping Investigations (in days)
Source: International Trade Commission, Annual Report (1982)

287

For an extremely valuable statistical analysis of the U.S. procedure that explores these economic underpinnings and political roles, *see* Finger, et al, The Political Economy of Administered Protection, 72 Am. Econ. Rev. 452 (1980).

On the parallel European procedures, *see* Pitt & Moncraft, The Anti-Dumping and Anti-Subsidy Rules and Practices of the EEC, 11 Intl. Bus. Law. 333 (Nov. 1982).

1.   *The LTFV Analysis*

Sales in the United States at less than fair value (LTFV) are proscribed under the U.S. antidumping law. But what is the basis for this LTFV determination? The answer is not a simple one, *see* Figure 5-3. The preferred valuation for comparison of prices between national markets is the "home market price," i.e., the price, at the time of exportation to the United States, at which such or similar merchandise is sold in the principal markets of the exporting country. The prices are compared at the ex-factory level and appropriate allowances are made for differences in circumstances of sale that might account for price differentials. On a given sewing machine, for example, the Commerce Department would strip off transport costs to reach the ex-factory prices in the home market, and would subtract an appropriate amount from that price if a guar-

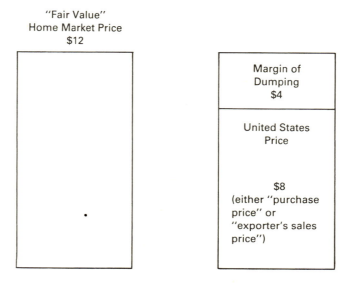

FIGURE 5-3
The LTFV Analysis

antee were given on the machine in the home market and not in the United States.

The "circumstances of sale" adjustment is generally limited to differences in selling expenses that are directly related to the sales under consideration. The purpose of the adjustments for "circumstances of sale" is to make sure that apples are being compared with apples, and not oranges.

For purposes of the LTFV analysis an initial, and crucial, distinction is whether or not the sale by the foreign party is to a related party, e.g., an affiliate, or to an unrelated party. The intent of the U.S. antidumping law is to establish value on the basis of arm's length transactions, thereby assuring the use of unbiased numbers in the final LTFV calculations.

In the normal course, the foreign producer sells to an unrelated importer in the United States. In this type of transaction the Commerce Department will use the "purchase price" as the basis for the LTFV calculation (i.e., deduct the U.S. purchase price from the home market price to ascertain the margin of dumping). The statute defines purchase price as the price at which "merchandise is purchased, or agreed to be purchased, prior to the date of importation, from the manufacturer or producer of the merchandise for exportation to the United States." 19 U.S.C. §1677a(b) (1982). *See also* 19 C.F.R. §353.10(b) (1983).

An increasing amount of international commerce, however, revolves around interaffiliate trade, involving transactions between related parties. From the importing standpoint the normal transaction here is for a foreign manufacturer to ship goods to a U.S. subsidiary, which then keeps the goods in its inventory until it sells them to an unrelated U.S. purchaser. In this case the Commerce Department will use what is known as the "exporter's sales price" (ESP), which is defined as the price "at which merchandise is sold or agreed to be sold in the United States, before or after the time of importation, by or for the account of the exporter." 19 U.S.C. §1677(a)(c) (1982). *See also* 19 C.F.R. 353.10(c) (1983). The ultimate transaction between the subsidiary and the independent U.S. customer becomes the exporter's sales price, which will be used as the U.S. price for purposes of the LTFV calculations.

The *Brother Industries* case, which follows, deals with the problem of making price comparisons when the U.S. price is based on the ESP technique. When the ESP is calculated, the Commerce Department must deduct from it "expenses generally incurred by or for the account of the exporter in the United States in selling identical or substantially identical merchandise." 19 U.S.C. §1677(a)(e)(2). To make sure that we are comparing "apples to apples," an equal amount should be deducted from the foreign market value (FMV) as well.

An example may help to clarify the point. Let us assume that a foreign manufacturer sells a sewing machine in its home market for $100, and, through its U.S. subsidiary, sells the same sewing machine in the United States for $100. Assume further that the foreign parent has $10 in direct and $10 in indirect selling expenses in the home market, and that the subsidiary has the same expenses in selling in the United States. What is the margin of dumping? Although the manufacturer is selling at the same price in both markets there is an initial dumping margin of $20, because the ESP, due to the mandatory deduction for selling expenses, is $80: $100 (FMV) − [$100(ESP) − ($10 + $10)]. As noted above, the Commerce Department can adjust the foreign market value for $10 of direct selling expenses under the circumstances of sale doctrine. This reduces the margin to $10: ($100 − $10) − $80. This leaves us with an unfair result, as the margin of dumping ($10) is due to the fact that we have deducted $10 in indirect selling expenses from ESP without making a comparable deduction from the foreign market value.

The Commerce Department's solution to that problem is the "ESP offset," under which an amount is deducted from FMV for indirect selling expenses up to the amount of indirect selling expenses deducted from ESP. According to the Commerce Department, the "ESP offset" permits it to compare apples with apples and oranges with oranges. What do you think?

BROTHER INDUSTRIES, LTD. v. UNITED STATES

540 F. Supp. 1341 (Ct. Intl. Trade), *cert. denied,* 4 I.T.R.D. 2297 (S. Ct. 1984)

NEWMAN, J.

We are faced in this consolidated action with a number of highly complex issues which are of novel impression, and undoubtedly are of great significance in the administration of the nation's antidumping laws. The above-captioned cases arose out of the same determination by the Department of Commerce, thus are largely interrelated and consequently—for the sake of expedition— were consolidated by this Court for review.

I. BACKGROUND

Smith-Corona Group, Consumer Products Division, SCM Corporation ("SCM"), and the related companies of Brother Industries, Ltd., of Nagoya, Japan and Brother International Corporation, of Piscataway, New Jersey (collectively "Brother"), challenge the "Early Determination of Antidumping Duties" by the International Trade Administration, United States Department of Commerce ("Commerce") in Portable Electric Typewriters from Japan; Determination of Duty, published in the Federal Register on August 13, 1980, 45 F.R. 53853-56, as clarified and corrected in 46 F.R. 14006 (1980).

SCM is the sole domestic manufacturer of portable electric typewriters ("PETs"). Brother Industries, Ltd. is a Japanese manufacturer of PETs and Brother International Corporation is an importer of such merchandise from Japan. Silver Seiko, Ltd. and Silver Reed America, Inc. (collectively "Silver") have intervened in these proceedings. The former is a Japanese manufacturer of PETs, and the latter is an importer of such merchandise from Japan. . . .

In its early determination of antidumping duties, Commerce granted Brother and Silver a wide range of adjustments or deductions in determining the foreign market value of their PETs sold in Japan in the four-month period investigated that resulted in findings of various weighted average dumping margins. The gravamen of SCM's action is that certain of these adjustments or deductions are contrary to law and unsupported by substantial evidence in the administrative record.

Specifically, the adjustments to foreign market value made by Commerce which are challenged by SCM are:

> (1) Adjustment of the foreign market value of each typewriter model for differences in packing costs and in Japanese inland freight incurred in sales in the home market and to the United States.
> (2) Adjustment of the foreign market value of each typewriter model by the amount of certain types of rebates in connection with sales in Japan.
> (3) Adjustment of the foreign market value of each typewriter model pursuant to 19 C.F.R. §353.15(c), for the exporter's sales price offset ("ESP offset") in those instances where foreign market value was compared with the exporter's sales price.
> (4) Adjustment of the foreign market value of each Brother typewriter model for differences in physical characteristics by an amount that was equal to the difference in the costs of certain accessories and printed materials provided in connection with sales in Japan and to the United States.
> (5) Adjustment to the foreign market value of each typewriter model by an amount for certain advertising expenses incurred in sales in Japan.

As is evident from the above, SCM has mounted a broad and multifaceted challenge to Commerce's early determination of antidumping duties.

Brother's action contests the denial by Commerce of an additional adjustment to foreign market value for the cost of a promotional campaign conducted in Japan, namely the give-away of transistor radios in connection with the sale of portable typewriters (including PETs). Brother contends that the disallowance was arbitrary and capricious or otherwise not in accordance with law. In all other respects, Brother supports the adjustments made by Commerce and challenged by SCM.

Presently before the Court are SCM's motion for summary judgment and cross-motions for summary judgment by the Government, Brother and Silver. Silver takes no position on that aspect of Commerce's determination challenged by Brother.

II. "CAUSAL LINK" ISSUE

We first consider SCM's argument that Commerce erred as a matter of law in granting the contested adjustments to foreign market value because no "causal link" was established between the differences in circumstances of sale and the differential between United States price and the foreign market value, as required by 19 U.S.C. §1677b(a)(4). In this connection, SCM argues that the Court must hold invalid the administering authority's regulation 19 C.F.R. §353.15(d) as being inconsistent with and in violation of the antidumping law. The "causal link" issue is the centerpiece of SCM's challenge to all of the contested adjustments.

SCM complains that Commerce in its early determination of antidumping duties made no finding of a causal link between the differences in circumstances of sale and the difference in the United States price and the foreign market value. Further, SCM contends that no information concerning a causal link was submitted by Brother or Silver to Commerce, nor was any such information requested by the administering authority.

The "causal link" issue presented by SCM arises from 19 U.S.C. §1677b(a)(4), which so far as pertinent, reads:

> (4) Other adjustments.—In determining foreign market value, *if it is established to the satisfaction of the administering authority that the amount of any difference between the United States price and the foreign market value* (or that the fact that the United States price is the same as the foreign market value) *is wholly or partly due to—*
>
> (A) the fact that the wholesale quantities, in which such or similar merchandise is sold or, in the absence of sales, offered for sale, for exportation to, or in the principal markets of, the United States, as appropriate, in the ordinary course of trade, are less or are greater than the wholesale quantities in which such or similar merchandise is sold or, in the absence of sales, offered for sale, in the principal markets of the country of exportation in the ordinary course of trade for home consumption (or, if not so sold for home consumption, then for exportation to countries other than the United States);
>
> (B) *other differences in circumstances of sales;* or
>
> (C) the fact that merchandise described in paragraph (B) or (C) of section 1677(16) of this title is used in determining foreign market value.
>
> *then due allowance shall be made therefor.* [Emphasis added.]

From a reading of the statute, it is clear that the party claiming entitlement to an adjustment of foreign market value must prove: (1) the existence of "other differences in circumstances of sales" within the meaning of the statute; (2) that the difference in United States price and foreign market value is wholly or partly *due to* other differences in circumstances of sale; and (3) the monetary value of the differences for which adjustments are claimed.

Focusing on the second requirement above, and particularly the language "due to" (denominated by SCM as the "causal link" requirement), it must be stressed that the statute requires only that a causal link be established to the *satisfaction of the administering authority*. But the statute provides no standards or guidelines as to how the administering authority is to determine whether the price differential is wholly or partly "due to" other circumstances of sale. Manifestly, then, since the statute sets forth no definitive criterion, Congress intended to rely upon the expertise and judgment of the administering authority to determine the criterion which will establish the existence of the necessary causal link between the difference in prices and differences in circumstances of sale. In granting adjustments to the foreign market value of the Brother and Silver typewriters, the administering authority was presumptively satisfied from the evidence submitted that the requisite causal link between the differentials in price and the differences in circumstances of sale existed in this case.

While 19 U.S.C. §1677b(a)(4) does not define "other differences in circumstances of sales" or prescribe the method for determining allowances, 19 C.F.R. §353.15 has been promulgated for that purpose. That regulation reads:

§353.15 DIFFERENCES IN CIRCUMSTANCES OF SALE.

(a) *In general.* In comparing the United States price with the sales, or other criteria applicable, on which a determination of foreign market value is to be based, reasonable allowances will be made for bona fide differences in the circumstances of the sales compared to the extent that it is established to the satisfaction of the Secretary that the amount of any price differential is wholly or partly due to such differences. Differences in circumstances of sale for which such allowances will be made are limited, in general, to those circumstances which bear a direct relationship to the sales which are under consideration.

(b) *Examples.* Examples of differences in circumstances of sale for which reasonable allowances generally will be made are those involving differences in credit terms, guarantees, warranties, technical assistance, servicing, and assumption by a seller of a purchaser's advertising or other selling costs. Reasonable allowances also generally will be made for differences in commissions. Allowances generally will not be made for differences in advertising and other selling costs of a seller, unless such costs are attributable to a later sale of the merchandise by a purchaser.

(c) *Special rule.* Notwithstanding the criteria for adjustments for differences in circumstances of sale set forth in paragraphs (a) and (b) of this section, reasonable allowances for other selling expenses generally will be made in cases where a reasonable allowance is made for commissions in one of the markets under consideration and no commission is paid in the other market under consideration, the amount of such allowance being limited to the actual other selling expenses incurred in the one market, or the total amount of the commission allowed in such other market, whichever is less. In making comparisons using exporter's sales price, reasonable allowance will be made for all actual selling expenses incurred in the home market up to the amount of the selling expenses incurred in the United States market.

(d) *Determination of allowances.* In determining the amount of the reasonable allowances for any differences in circumstances of sale, the Secretary will be guided primarily by the cost of such differences to the seller, but, where appropriate, he may also consider the effect of such differences upon the market value of the merchandise.

It is evident that section 353.15(d) assumes a causal link exists between differences in circumstances of sale and price differentials primarily where there are cost differences to the seller or, where appropriate, the differences in circumstances of sale have an effect upon the market value of the merchandise. . . .

But in determining the validity of regulation 353.15(d), it must be emphasized that under the *statute* whether a price differential is due to differences in circumstances of sale need only be established *to satisfaction of the administering authority.* . . .

Aside from suggesting the possibility that factors other than a difference in costs for sales in the home market versus sales for export to the United States may account for a difference in selling prices, SCM cites no authority for its contention that the costs bear no rational relationship to the selling prices of merchandise. . . .

In the final analysis, one need not be an economist to recognize that under normal market conditions prices directly reflect costs. . . .

Moreover, as a familiar matter of well-established principles of administrative law, a long-standing construction of a statute by an agency charged with its administration is afforded great weight by a reviewing court. . . .

III.   ESP OFFSET

In determining foreign market value, Commerce allowed certain adjustments to the home market selling prices of the Brother and Silver typewriters as "other differences in circumstances of sale" in accordance with its "Special Rule" set forth in 19 C.F.R. §353.15(c), which provides for the so-called exporter's sales price offset ("ESP offset"). *See* 45 F.R. 53855. Section 353.15(c) provides:

> (c) *Special rule.* Notwithstanding the criteria for adjustments for differences in circumstances of sale set forth in paragraphs (a) and (b) of this section, reasonable allowances for other selling expenses generally will be made in cases where a reasonable allowance is made for commissions in one of the markets under consideration and no commission is paid in the other market under consideration, the amount of such allowance being limited to the actual other selling expenses incurred in the one market, or the total amount of the commission allowed in such other market, whichever is less. *In making comparisons using exporter's sales price, reasonable allowance will be made for all actual selling expenses incurred in the home market up to the amount of the selling expenses incurred in the United States market.* [Emphasis added.]

Following the authority of the last sentence of paragraph (c) (the so-called "exporter's sales price offset" or "ESP offset") Commerce adjusted the foreign market value of Silver's PETs for various advertising expenses incurred in Japan up to the amount of the selling expenses incurred in the United States, and of Brother's PETs for certain home market selling expenses (payroll and payroll-related expenses, depreciation, other operating expenses, indirect advertising and promotional premiums). The ESP offset adjustments were made on the basis of evidence of the various *costs* involved. . . .

By stripping all of the selling expenses incurred in the United States from the exporter's sales price, Congress made it plain that it did not want a comparison between a price in the home market and a price in the United States market (which prices would then properly reflect all selling expenses incurred), but rather between a price in the home market and a price for export to the United States. Accordingly, then, the intent of the exporter's sales price adjustment is to permit an estimation of the "true" *f.o.b.* foreign, port price for the merchandise under consideration in an arms-length transaction regarding an importation made by a party related to the exporter. The explanation in Senate Finance Committee Report No. 1619 at 10, makes it clear that the 1958 amendment to the Antidumping Act, which first added the provision for other differences in circumstances of sale, was "designed to facilitate efficient and fair comparison between foreign market value and price to the United States market". Obviously, it would have been unfair to continue comparing an unadjusted foreign market value with an adjusted exporter's sales price from which all selling costs have been deducted in circumstances where the foreign market value represented a price higher because of inclusion of the manufacturer's selling costs in the home market.

In 1976, Treasury amended the Customs regulations and acknowledged its long-existing practice to permit the ESP offset. . . . Interestingly, Congress took no steps concerning the Trade Agreements Act of 1979 to eliminate this long-established administrative practice, as codified in the 1976 regulation, while reenacting without change the statutory circumstances of sale provision. . . .

I have carefully considered SCM's contentions that Commerce's "Special rule" providing for the ESP offset is invalid because: (1) the rule allows adjustments that are not directly related to the sales under consideration; (2) the rule allows "unilateral" adjustments for home market selling expenses that are not compared with similar expenses incurred by the foreign producer in its export sales, and thus permits allowances that are not adjustments for "other *differences* in circumstances of sale" (emphasis by SCM); and (3) the rule permits adjustments that are not available equally in "purchase price" and "exporter's sales price" transactions.

With reference to point (1), I see nothing in the language of the statute or its legislative history or in *F. W. Myers* [72 Cust. Ct. 219, 376 F. Supp. 868 (1974)] that compels the conclusion that adjustments for differences in circumstances of sale be directly related to the sales under consideration *in ESP transactions*. While it is true that under 19 C.F.R. §353.15 adjustments are limited, "in general", to circumstances of sale having a "direct relationship to the sales which are under consideration", the provision for the ESP offset is expressly deemed a "[s]pecial rule".

Second, the legislative history of the Trade Agreements Act of 1979 strongly indicates that Congress regarded the ESP offset as an adjustment for differences in circumstances of sale. On this score, the ESP offset regulation was specifically called to the attention of Congress by the Comptroller General in the G.A.O. report of March 15, 1979. . . . Significantly, both the G.A.O. report and the regulation directed the ESP offset to Congress's attention as a *circumstances of sales adjustment.*

Third, although the legislative history of the Trade Agreements Act of 1979 reveals that the new term "United States price" was utilized to incorporate the existing terms "purchase price" and "exporter's sales price" (S. Rep. No. 96-249, 96th Cong., 1st Sess. 93 (1979), I see nothing in the legislative history cited by SCM that indicates Congress thereby intended to preclude the ESP offset practice (which had been called to its attention) because a similar offset was not permissible in purchase price transactions. Had Congress intended to devitalize the "Special rule" granting an ESP offset, it surely would not have contemplated that "Regulations will establish groups of adjustments based on types of adjustments currently recognized, that is differences in circumstances of sale . . . ". H. R. Rep. No. 96-317, 96th Cong., 1st Sess. at 76 (1979).

IV.   ADJUSTMENTS FOR INLAND FREIGHT AND PACKING COSTS

Commerce's early determination of antidumping duties made allowances in determining the foreign market value of the PETs imported by Brother and Silver for differences in Japanese inland freight charges and differences in packing costs incurred in sales in the home market and for export to the United States. 45 F.R. 53853-55. SCM contends that these adjustments are contrary to the statutory definition of foreign market value in section 773(a) of the Act, the legislative history, basic rules of statutory construction and regulatory practice of the Treasury, and are unsupported by substantial evidence.

I conclude, however, that SCM's contentions have no merit because the allowances for inland freight and packing cost differentials were properly granted in determining the foreign market value as differences in circumstances of sale.

V.   ADJUSTMENT FOR AFTER-SALE REBATES

In its early determination of antidumping duties, Commerce made adjustments to the foreign market value of PETs sold in Japan by Brother and Silver for certain after-sale rebates. 45 F.R. 53854, 53855. SCM contests the allowance of these rebates as adjustments for differences in circumstances of sale. Specifically, SCM identifies Silver's after-sale volume rebates and Brother's monthly and periodic after-sale rebates as the subject of its attack upon Commerce's allowances for rebates.

SCM contends: first, that the rebates given by Brother and Silver are not "directly related" to the sales under consideration; second, that the values of the various rebates, even if directly related, are not quantifiable; third, that the values upon which the adjustments were granted to Brother and Silver were not based upon actual values, but rather upon "estimates, approximations, or averages," contrary to the holding in *F. W. Myers*; and finally, that the adjustments for rebates constituted a misapplication of statutory requirements rendering them contrary to law.

We first summarize the pertinent facts established by the administrative record. Silver granted volume rebates to Japanese customers for purchases of targeted quantities of certain Silver typewriters. Commerce's adjustment to foreign market value was calculated on the basis of the expense to Silver in granting these after-sale volume rebates to two domestic purchasers—Company A and Company B.

The rebates granted by Silver to Company A and Company B were for the sale of manual and electric typewriters, and as to Company B, included an additional rebate for the sale of cash registers. In order to determine the rebate expenses attributable to sales of PETs, Commerce initially computed the ratio of total PET sales in yen to the total yen amount of all sales subject to the rebate program for Company A and Company B. Multiplying this percentage by the total rebate amount granted to companies A and B individually resulted in the two "total-volume amount" figures (one for Company A and one for Company B), representing total PET rebates paid each. Commerce then computed the percentage of PET sales attributable to each relevant model on the basis of volume of sales in yen, and multiplied each of these percentages by the yen amount of rebates granted to each company for PETs. This calculation gives the yen amount of rebates for all sales of each particular model PET which, when divided by quantity sold, gives the rebate per unit allowed as an adjustment to foreign market value. . . .

The second rebate program challenged by SCM involves the periodic rebate, granted only to the Franchised Dealers. That rebate was a fixed yen amount, determined by the total number of typewriters (manual and electric) purchased during a six-month period; and the per unit expense was calculated by dividing the total amount incurred for this program by the number of units sold during the six-month time period.

SCM's argument that Silver's rebates were not directly related to the sales under consideration is premised upon three grounds: (1) the rebate program was not based upon "particular sales", but total sales, and hence the payments were not "rebates" but rather general "goodwill expenditures"; (2) the rebate program was conducted over a period of time which did not exactly coincide with the time period of the investigation, and therefore, sales other than those under consideration were included in the calculation, thus negating any direct relationship; and, (3) the statute requires that foreign market value shall reflect home market prices at the time of exportation of the merchandise to the United States so that after-sales volume rebates do not qualify as an adjustment.

I am unable to agree with SCM's position. The fact that rebates were granted on the predicate of total sales of PETs, manual typewriters and cash registers does not negate the direct relationship of the rebates to sales of any one line of Silver products. The amount of rebates attributable to each of the different products was accurately quantifiable as a percentage of the total yen volume amount of all of the involved products, and the per unit (by model) rebate amount was just a matter of simple arithmetical calculation.

Congress intended that adjustments to "foreign market value" should be permitted if they are reasonably quantifiable and directly related to the sales under consideration. Thus, the *House Report* states:

"The Committee intends that adjustments should be permitted if they are reasonably identifiable, quantifiable, and directly related to the sales under consideration and if there is clear and reasonable evidence of their existence and amount." H. Rep. No. 96-317, 96th Cong., 1st Sess., p. 76 (1979). Here, the challenged rebates for PETs are clearly identifiable, easily quantifiable, and there is substantial evidence of their existence and amount. . . .

In brief, the rebate adjustments were not approximations or estimates, but allocations derived from an actual total rebate amount. So long as the foreign market value reflects actual net selling prices to the purchasers on the date of exportation to the United States, which are known at the time Commerce conducts its antidumping duty investigation, the objectives of 19 U.S.C. §1677b(a)(4) are satisfied. Hence, the adjustments for rebates granted to Brother and Silver are in compliance with the statutory criteria, Congressional intent, and are supported by substantial evidence. . . .

IX.   CONCLUSION

In summary, I have carefully considered the excellent briefs and oral arguments of counsel for the parties and have concluded that the regulations followed by Commerce in making the adjustments to foreign market value challenged by SCM do not frustrate the Congressional policy underlying the antidumping law. If, as this Court believes, a fair and equitable comparison of the United States price and the foreign market value is the ultimate goal of the statutory adjustment for differences in circumstances of sale, the regulations attacked by SCM are reasonable, effectuate the Congressional scheme, and were properly applied by Commerce, the administering authority, under the facts and circumstances in this case.

Brother's claimed adjustment for the promotional give-away program must fail for lack of the necessary proof of entitlement.

I find no issue of material fact as to which there is a genuine dispute, and conclude that the Government is entitled to summary judgment as a matter of law with respect to all claims asserted by SCM and Brother. Accordingly, it is hereby ordered:

1. that the early determination of antidumping duties by Commerce published on August 13, 1980 is affirmed in all respects;

2. that SCM's motion for summary judgment is denied;

3. that the Government's cross-motion for summary judgment is granted;

4. that Brother's cross-motion for summary judgment is denied insofar as it challenges Commerce's disallowance of an adjustment to foreign market value for Brother's promotional give-away expenses; Brother's cross-motion for summary judgment is granted insofar as Brother seeks to sustain the early determination of antidumping duties, as that determination relates to Brother's PETs;

5. that Silver's cross-motion for summary judgment sustaining the early determination of antidumping duties as that determination relates to Silver's PETs is granted.

It is further ordered that the United States Customs Service shall liquidate all entries, the liquidation of which have been suspended pursuant to this Court's order of December 30, 1980, 1 C.I.T.—, Slip Op. 80-17, 507 F. Supp. 1015 (1980), in the amounts specified in Commerce's early determination of antidumping duties.

The foregoing constitutes the decision and order of the Court.

Note on Sales at Less than the Cost of Production

The primary means of determining dumping is the price comparison. Sales at prices below the cost of production may negate the utility of the price test, and force the Commerce Department to use a constructed value as the LTFV referent, i.e., as a surrogate for the home market price. Consider 19 U.S.C. §164(b), "Home market sales at less than cost of production":

> (b) Whenever the Secretary has reasonable grounds to believe or suspect that sales in the home market of the country of exportation, or, as appropriate, to countries other than the United States, have been made at prices which represent less than the cost of producing the merchandise in question, he shall determine whether, in fact, such sales were made at less than the cost of producing the merchandise. If the Secretary determines that sales made at less than cost of production (1) have been made over an extended period of time and in substantial quantities, and (2) are not at prices which permit recovery of all costs within a reasonable period of time in the normal course of trade, such sales shall be disregarded in the determination of foreign market value. Whenever sales are disregarded by virtue of having been made at less than the cost of production and the remaining sales, made at not less than cost of production, are determined to be inadequate as a basis for the determination of foreign market value, the Secretary shall determine that no foreign market value exists and employ the constructed value of the merchandise in question.

Compare 19 U.S.C. §164(b) with Article VI(1) of the GATT:

> For the purposes of this Article, a product is to be considered as being introduced into the commerce of an importing country at less than its normal value, if the price of the product exported from one country to another

(a) is less than the comparable price, ordinary course of trade, for the like product when destined for consumption in the exporting country, or,

(b)   in the absence of such domestic price, is less than either

(i)   The highest comparable price for the like product for export to any third country in the ordinary course of trade, or

(ii)   the cost of production of the product in the country of origin plus a reasonable addition for selling cost and profit.

Article 2(d) of the [1979] Antidumping Code permits determination of the dumping margin by comparison to a third country price or cost of production "[w]hen there are no sales of the like product in the ordinary course of trade in the domestic market of the exporting country or when, because of the particular market situation, such sales do not permit a proper comparison."

If it appears that sales are taking place at less than the cost of production, 19 U.S.C. §165(a) comes into play; it describes the means by which the Commerce Department may calculate the constructed value of the goods in question.

§165.   CONSTRUCTED VALUE

DETERMINATION

(a) For the purposes of sections 160 to 171 of this title, the constructed value of imported merchandise shall be the sum of—

(1) the cost of materials (exclusive of any internal tax applicable in the country of exportation directly to such materials or their disposition, but remitted or refunded upon the exportation of the article in the production of which such materials are used) and of fabrication or other processing of any kind employed in producing such or similar merchandise, at a time preceding the date of exportation of the merchandise under consideration which would ordinarily permit the production of that particular merchandise in the ordinary course of business;

(2) an amount for general expenses and profit equal to that usually reflected in sales of merchandise of the same general class or kind as the merchandise under consideration which are made by producers in the country of exportation, in the usual wholesale quantities and in the ordinary course of trade, except that (A) the amount for general expenses shall not be less than 10 per centum of the cost as defined in paragraph (1), and (B) the amount for profit shall not be less than 8 per centum of the sum of such general expenses and cost; and

(3) the cost of all containers and coverings of whatever nature, and all other expenses incidental to placing the merchandise under consideration in condition, packed ready for shipment to the United States.

NOTES AND QUESTIONS

1. In whose interest is it to minimize the various adjustments to the quoted foreign price? For a more recent decision focusing on the adjustment procedure, *see* Silver Reed America and Silver Seiko v. U.S., 5 I.T.R.D. 1673 (Ct. Intl. Trade 1984).

2.(a) Steelco, a Canadian steel producer, sells steel sheet in Canada for $100 per metric ton on an *ex-factory "netback" basis* (i.e., the price of the goods as they leave the factory). The product is sold in the United States for $140 per ton. The U.S. price includes:

(1) $10 freight charges in Canada;
(2) $10 inland freight charges in the United States;
(3) $20 for the U.S. tariff applied to the imported product; and
(4) $10 for other miscellaneous charges, including insurance, custom charges, commissions and selling expenses.

What is the margin of dumping?

(b) Suppose Steelco produced steel only for export, and had no sales of any steel products in Canada but had sales of steel sheet to third countries that averaged $120 ex-factory netback in price? Assuming the same facts with regard to U.S. price in (a) above, what would the margin of dumping be? *See* Antidumping Code, Article 2; 19 U.S.C. §1677(a) and (b).

(c) Assume the same facts as in (a) above, and, as an additional fact, the knowledge by the petitioner that the cost of production in Canada for the steel sheet is $130 per ton?

3. The Canadian Saltfish Corporation (CSC) has no home market sales of dried codfish, and a cost of production of $1.00 per lb. Over an extended period of time CSC sells dried codfish to the United States for $0.85 per lb., to France for $0.80 per lb., and to Nigeria for $0.78 per lb. CSC supplies 80% of the U.S. market for dried codfish.

Codfish Corp., the sole U.S. producer of dried codfish, files an antidumping petition alleging that the margin of dumping in the case should be $0.15 per lb. CSC responds that it could not possibly be dumping in the United States since it receives its highest export prices for dried codfish in the U.S. marketplace.

What result? *See* Certain Dried Salted Codfish from Canada, Inv. No. 731-TA-199 (Preliminary), U.S.I.T.C. Pub. No. 1571 (1984), and Final Decision (1985), U.S.I.T.C. Pub. No. 1711. *See* Connors Steel v. United States, 527 F. Supp. 350, *modified on reh.,* 566 F. Supp. 1521 (Ct. Intl. Trade 1982). For International Trade Administration (ITA) methodology for calculating the constructed foreign market value and the United States price when the foreign producer uses a U.S. subsidiary as its marketing agent, *see* High Power Microwave Amplifiers from Japan, 47 Fed. Reg. 22,134, 4 I.T.R.D. 1110 (1982).

4. The People's Republic of China (PRC), a nonmarket economy, sells canned mushrooms to the United States for $3.00 per 64-ounce institutional-size container. The American Mushroom Institute (AMI) files a dumping complaint against the PRC, alleging that the fair value for canned mushrooms is $4.00 per 64-ounce container. In support of its case the Institute points out that the home market and export price for canned mushrooms in Taiwan is $4.00 per container.

Suppose a U.S. importer of PRC mushrooms asks you, as counsel to the company, if the AMI has a valid complaint? AMI's president points out that Thailand and India, which also grow mushrooms, have home market prices of $2.90. (*See* Antidumping Code, Article 2(e); 19 U.S.C. §1677(b); and Menthol from People's Republic of China, 46 Fed. Reg. 3,258, 2 I.T.R.D. (preliminary) (1981) and 46 Fed. Reg. 24,614, 2 I.T.R.D. 5,661 (final) (1981).

5. Suppose the foreign price is not competitive but is set by a monopoly or oligopoly, or even by government action. Under the statute, what foreign price should be used in the LTFV calculation? Under economic common sense, what foreign price should be used?

6. Can a firm manufacturing and selling in a higher-price market ever export competitively to a lower-price market without triggering antidumping duties? *See* Connors Steel v. United States, 527 F. Supp. 350 (Ct. Intl. Trade 1981) (sale below cost of production is dumping, even though price was set at competitive level).

7. Is antidumping policy consistent with antitrust policy? What if the Robinson-Patman Act is included as part of antitrust policy? (Note that this set of issues will also be posed in Chapter XI in connection with the Antidumping Act of 1916, an act that provides an antitrust-style remedy to a manufacturer harmed by predatory dumping.)

8. What about the settlement procedures of §734 of the 1979 Act (19 U.S.C. §1673(a))? Do you see any antitrust problems there? For examples of the difficulty of contesting a settlement, *see* Montgomery Ward v. Zenith Radio, 673 F.2d 1254 (C.C.P.A., 1982) *cert. denied,* 459 U.S. 943 (1983); and Committee to Preserve American Color TV v. United States, 527 F. Supp. 341 (Ct. Intl. Trade 1980). And for general background, *see* the General Accounting Office report, Administration of Suspension Agreements by the Department of Commerce, GAO/NSIAD-84-125 (June 15, 1984).

9. What exchange rate should be used to compare the foreign and the domestic prices? Can changes in the exchange rate alone create dumping where before there was none? *See* Dickey, Antidumping: Currency Fluctuations as a Cause of Dumping Margins, 1 Intl. Trade L.J. 66 (1982).

10. According to the statute, when can (or must) the LTFV calculation be based on prices in other markets or on constructed prices? *See generally* Alberta Gas Chemicals v. United States, 515 F. Supp. 780 (Ct. Intl. Trade 1981); Rodriguez, Gilmore: An Antidumping Proceeding as Cost-Price Comparison, Antidumping Law: Policy and Implementation, 1 Mich. Y.B. Intl. Legal Stud. 186 (1979).

11. Suppose you wanted to bring suit contesting a Commerce Department procedure. What court would you use? For an example of the issue, which ended up on the District Court side before the 1979 Act, *See* Flintkote v. Blumenthal, 596 F.2d 51 (2d Cir. 1979) (Secretary of Treasury held not in accord with U.S. law in effort to interpret retroactivity provisions of antidumping law to accord with International Antidumping Code). For another typical jurisdictional issue, *see* SCM v. ITC, 549 F.2d 812 (D.C. Cir. 1977).

12. What is the best economic definition of dumping, or LTFV sales:

(a) sales below home-market price;
(b) sales below the cost of production;
(c) sales below third-country export sales price?

Would your answer to this question differ if the exporting country in question were a communist country? *See* Meuser, Dumping from "Controlled Economy" Countries: The Polish Golf Car Case, 11 Law & Pol. Intl. Bus. (1979), at pp. 777-803. *See also* Truck Trailer Axle-and-Brake Assemblies from Hungary, 3 I.R.T.D. 1969 (I.T.A. Sept. 17, 1981); the case involving natural menthol imports from China, 61 Intl. Trade & Invest. Mngmt. A-1 (I.T.A. June 21, 1981); and Canned Mushrooms From the People's Republic of China, 48 Fed. Reg. 45,445 (1983), terminated in 1983 due to "de minimis" dumping margins after a preliminary affirmative determination of dumping (48 Fed. Reg. 22,768 (1983)).

See also Wilczynski, Dumping and Control Planning, 74 J. Pol. Econ. 254 (1966) and Feller, The Antidumping Act and the Future of East-West Trade, 66 Mich. L. Rev. 115, 126 (1967).

13. What problems might be encountered in trying to apply the U.S. antidumping laws to fresh winter vegetables from Mexico? *See* Southwest Florida Winter Vegetable Growers' Assn. v. United States, 85 Cust. Ct. 107, C.R.D. 80-7 (1980). *See also* Note, Applying Antidumping Law to Perishable Agricultural Goods, 80 Mich. L. Rev. 524 (1982).

14. Must a dumping action relate only to imports that have already entered the United States? What about future sales, irrevocable offers to sell, or "likely" sales? See Title VI of the Omnibus Tariff and Trade Act of 1984 in Appendix X.

15. Suppose the home market price of a sewing machine is $10 and the U.S. price of an identical sewing machine is $10. Suppose also that the home market sewing machine is subject to a 10% indirect tax, paid by the manufacturer. Assuming that there is a full pass-through of the tax to the purchaser in the home market, the price for the sewing machine in the home market would be $11. What is the dumping margin, if any, in this case? *See* 19 U.S.C. §1677a(d)(1)(c), and Color Television Receivers from Korea, 49 Fed. Reg. 7,620 (1984) and Color Television Receivers from Taiwan, 49 Fed. Reg. 7,628 (1984).

2. The Injury Evaluation

Apart from LTFV sales the petitioner must also demonstrate the presence of injury to a domestic industry. The ITC must find that

(1)   An industry in the United States is
    (a)   materially injured or
    (b)   threatened with material injury; or
(2)   the establishment of an industry in the United States is materially retarded. 19 U.S.C. §§1671b(a), 1673b(a) (1982).

The "material injury" standard now embedded in U.S. dumping law is in accordance with GATT's Article VI and the International Dumping Code of 1979, which also requires material injury to be found before antidumping duties can be imposed.

How is "material injury" to be defined? The statute defines it as "harm which is not inconsequential, immaterial, or unimportant." 19 U.S.C. §1677(7)(A) (1982). *See also* 19 C.F.R. §207.27 (1983). The statute directs the Commission to consider three key economic aspects in its application of the injury standard:

(1)   the volume of imports of the merchandise which is the subject of the investigation;
(2)   the effect of the imported merchandise on prices in the United States for like products; and
(3)   the impact of imports of the subject merchandise on domestic producers of like products. 19 U.S.C. §1677(7)(B) (1982). *See also* 19 C.F.R., §207.26(a) (1983).

The statute directs the ITC to "evaluate all relevant economic factors which have a bearing on the state of the industry," and specifies that the ITC's evaluation should include, but not be limited to, three sets of factors:

(i)   actual and potential decline in output, sales, market share, profits, productivity, return on investments, and utilization of capacity;
(ii)   factors affecting domestic prices; and
(iii)   actual and potential negative effects on cash flow, inventories, employment, wages, growth, ability to raise capital and investment.

As a practical matter the definition of the basic term "industry" may spell the difference between victory and defeat in a dumping case. For example, the ability to limit a case to electric golf cars could result in an affirmative determination of injury, whereas a negative determination might result if gasoline-powered golf cars are also deemed to be a "like product" and included in the scope of an injury investigation involving imported electric golf cars. Typically, petitioners will be seeking to limit the scope of the investigation to a relatively narrow segment, thus permitting the calculation of a higher import penetration ratio.

The *Babcock & Wilcox* case, which follows, demonstrates the difficulty of trying to define the appropriate range of products for the injury investigation.

BABCOCK & WILCOX CO. v. UNITED STATES

521 F. Supp. 479 (Ct. Intl. Trade 1981)

RICHARDSON, J. . . .

It appears from the record that on February 28, 1980, plaintiff, a domestic producer of steel pipes and boiler tubes, among other things, filed a petition simultaneously with the Department of Commerce ["Commerce"] and the Commission alleging that Japanese producers of certain pipes and tubes of steel were selling their products at less than fair value ["LTFV"] in contravention of the antidumping provisions of the Trade Agreements Act of 1979 [Pub. L. No. 96-39, 93 Stat. 144 (July 26, 1979)]. LTFV sales were alleged with respect to the following products:

(1) welded carbon steel boiler tubes (TSUS item 610.3205); [Tariff Schedules of United States]
(2) seamless carbon steel boiler tubes (TSUS item 610.4920);
(3) seamless stainless and heat resisting steel boiler tubes and process pipes (TSUS items 610.5210 and 610.5215);
(4) seamless alloy steel tubes for bearings (TSUS item 610.4600); and
(5) seamless alloy steel boiler tubes and process pipes (TSUS item 610.5270).

On March 25, 1980, Commerce determined that plaintiff's petition was sufficient to initiate an investigation which it then commenced.

On April 9, 1980, by a vote of 3-2, the Commission made an affirmative determination of *reasonable indication* of material injury or threat thereof to the welded carbon boiler tube industry (TSUS item 610.3205), and a negative injury determination with respect to the seamless boiler tube and process pipe industry (TSUS items 610.4920, 610.5210, 610.5215, and 610.5270).

Thereafter, and on June 18, 1980, the Commission reopened Investigation No. 731-TA-15 (Preliminary) to *reconsider* import statistics relating to welded carbon boiler tubes (TSUS item 610.3205) which was said to be erroneous [45 Fed. Reg. 42898 (1980)]. And, after *reconsidering* corrected statistical data regarding TSUS item 610.3205, the Commission, by a vote of 4-1 made a negative injury determination on June 24, 1980, with respect to the welded carbon boiler tube industry [45 Fed. Reg. 47769 (1980)].

Plaintiff contends that the Commission's negative injury determinations in its preliminary investigation were arbitrary, capricious, an abuse of discretion, and otherwise not in accordance with law. Plaintiff argues that the Commission's concept of the relevant industries is at variance with the mandatory requirements of the Trade Agreements Act of 1979, which has resulted in the Commission's utilization of overbroad and irrelevant injury data at the expense of pertinent injury data from domestic producers not addressed by the Commission. Plaintiff also argues that the Commission was without statutory authority to reopen the preliminary investigation for reconsideration of its determination upon additional evidence.

Defendant contends that the record supports the Commission's findings as to the absence of a *reasonable indication* of material injury or the threat thereof to the domestic industries assessed by the Commission, in which contention it is joined by *Amicus Curiae* Sumitomo Metal Industries, Ltd. and Nippon Steel Corp., foreign producers and exporters of the pipe and tube products investigated. Defendant argues that the best information available to the Commission indicated that the several products plaintiff sought to have investigated had no separable identities, and that the only distinction between products which industry practice allowed was as between seamless and welded pipe and tube products.

Defendant also contends that the Commission possesses discretionary and inherent authority to reopen proceedings and reconsider its decisions. In this contention defendant is joined by *Amicus Curiae* Nippon Steel Corporation, a foreign producer of the pipe and tube products covered by the investigation. Defendant argues that, given the posture of this case, especially in view of the "egregiously erroneous" information relied upon, this court would have had little choice but to remand the case to the Commission; and the Commission's actions merely obviated this circuitous procedure, and attained the mandated corrected result without adversely affecting plaintiff's right of judicial review.

The views of the Commissioners on these issues are diverse. First, with respect to scope of the industry, Chairman Bedell and Commissioner Moore stated:

> The three seamless products—are all produced by essentially the same production methods, on the same machinery, and by the same workers. For these reasons, we have assessed the effect of the allegedly dumped imports on the U.S. industry . . . in relation to the aggregate U. S. production of the three seamless pipe and tube items. (Pub. Doc. 57, p. 5)

Commissioner Stern stated:

> In this case, where there is no absolutely clear answer to the question of scope of the domestic industry impacted by imports, it is my judgment that the information on the record in this investigation does not permit assessment by separate and identifiable product lines. Therefore, guided by the law's directive to make my findings on the basis of the best information available to the Commission at this time, I have determined that reasonable indication of injury to the domestic industry must be assessed with respect to boiler tubes and process pipes. (Pub. Doc. 57, p. 21)

Commissioner Alberger stated:

> I am uncertain whether it is feasible for a product such as seamless stainless boiler tubes . . . to be analyzed as a separate "product line" as defined by Section

771(4)(D) of the Trade Agreements Act of 1979. . . . Specific data are available on shipments, exports, and imports for each of the three categories of seamless pipe and tube and the one welded pipe and tube product under investigation. Only the petitioner was able to provide profit and loss data on each of these four products. Other manufacturers were apparently unable to provide such data, due to difficulty in allocating profits between products made on essentially the same machinery by the same employees. . . .

And Commissioner Calhoun stated:

That the petitioner was able to supply data on four separate products implies the possibility of four distinct product lines against which the Commission must apply section 771(4)(D). In the time available, however, none of the other domestic producers was able to provide similar disaggregated data. This inability of the other domestic producers to provide similar disaggregated data results in confusion as to the precise character of the industry. (Pub. Doc. 57, p 27)

Secondly, with respect to reconsideration of the Commission's affirmative preliminary injury determination of April 14, 1980, only two of the Commissioners made significant comment at the time of voting on June 24, 1980. Commissioner Stern, who voted for reversal, stated:

I think that I should just briefly say that as far as I'm concerned that we are conserving a great deal of Commission energy in expressing our concern for the public because we are not, in fact, dealing with new facts. In other words, this is not a further fact finding for which we are reopening the vote, but we're dealing with the same old facts. The problem was that the facts that were given were inaccurate and we are simply responding quite immediate to what was immediately recognized upon publication of our report that there were inaccuracies there. I don't believe that this is setting any precedence that we will open a case after 45 days for new facts and go into future fact finding exercises. . . .

Turning first to the issue of industry scope, it is to be noted that prior to the enactment of the Trade Agreements Act of 1979 the Commission had a broad grant of discretion in delineating the relevant domestic industry against which it was required to assess the effects of LTFV imports. Neither the Anti-dumping Act of 1921, nor section 303 of the Tariff Act of 1930 defined the term "industry". See S. Rept. No. 96–249 to accompany HR. 4537, 96th Cong., 1st Sess., p. 82 (1979), U.S. Code Cong. & Admin. News 1978, p. 381. The Trade Agreements Act of 1979 contains specific guidelines for the determination of the relevant "industry" or "industries", as the case may be.

Section 771(4)(A) of the Tariff Act of 1930, as amended (19 U.S.C. §1677(4)(A)) defines the term "industry" as

the domestic producers as a whole of a like product, or those producers whose collective output of the like product constitutes a major proportion of the total domestic production of that product.

And the term "like product" mentioned in section 771(4)(A) is defined in section 771(10) of the Tariff Act of 1930, as amended (19 U.S.C. §1677(10)) as

> a product which is like or in the absence of like, most similar in characteristics and uses with, the article subject to investigation under this title.

Also, Congress has provided guidelines for the application of these terms by the Commission in connection with product line assessments. Section 771(4)(D) of the Tariff Act of 1930, as amended (19 U.S.C. §1677(4)(D)) states in relevant part

> The effect of . . . dumped imports shall be assessed in relation to the United States production of a like product if available data permit the separate identification of production in terms of such criteria as *the production process or the producer's profits*. If the domestic production of the like product has no separate identity in terms of such criteria, then the effect of the . . . dumped imports shall be assessed by the examination of the production of the narrowest group or range of products, which includes a like product for which the necessary information can be provided. (Emphasis added.)

It will be observed that section 771(4)(D) stresses the utilization of the applicable criteria *alternatively,* i.e., production process or the producer's profits. And profits, it would appear, heads the list of economic factors which Congress intended the Commission to examine in ascertaining the impact of LTFV imports on the domestic producers comprising the "industry". See: S. Rept. 96–249 to accompany H.R. 4537, 96th Cong., 1st Sess., p. 83 (1979).

Although the producer's questionnaires distributed by the Commission did not solicit profit information from the domestic producers of the subject boiler tubes and pipes (Conf. Doc. 18–25), the Commission's findings for the most part seem to indicate that all but one of the domestic producers of these products were unable to furnish the Commission with profit information. The court is unable to find that fact documented in the records before it. What does appear in the record, however, is that profit data was voluntarily supplied by plaintiff to the Commission covering each of the products under investigation, which generated the Commission's comments about profit data as noted above. There is nothing in the record to indicate that the Commission ever solicited profit data pertaining to the investigated products from the domestic producers who, together with plaintiff, were responsible for 90 percent of the total domestic output of boiler tubes and pipes.

There is no question but that section 771(4)(D) must be read as permitting the separate assessment of products for which profit can be identified even if multiple products are produced by the same production force. The key is profit *accountability.*

The Commission's practice of rigidly adhering to a preference for isolation of all production factors supporting a product as a predicate for ascertaining the scope of an "industry" is not in step with the more flexible standard devised by Congress in section 771(4)(D). But, in any case, it is clear that Congress intended that petitioners in antidumping proceedings should have a choice. In this regard the Senate Finance Committee report states:

> In examining the impact of imports on the domestic producers comprising the domestic industry, the ITC should examine the relevant economic factors (such as profits, productivity, employment, cash flow, capacity utilization, etc.), as they relate to the production of only the like product, if available data permits a reasonably separate consideration of the factors with respect to production of only the like product. If this is not possible *because,* for example, *of the accounting procedures in use* or practical problems in distinguishing or separating the operations of product lines, then the impact of the imports should be examined by considering the relevant economic factors as they relate to the production of the narrowest group or range of products which includes the like product and for which available data permits separate consideration. (Emphasis added.)

It appears that plaintiff's profit data was disregarded by the Commission because of its self-serving nature. However, the self-serving nature of the data should not be defeating, given the Commission's investigatory function to verify data received. Congress anticipated that petitioners in antidumping proceedings would have a stake or interest in developing the relevant facts supporting a dumping finding. Not only should the Commission have considered plaintiff's profit data in connection with its determination as to the scope of the "industry", it should have sought such data from the other domestic producers comprising the boiler tube and pipe industry before moving to the broader industry which even the Commission's own staff acknowledges to have been a mistake. (Pub. Doc. 50, p.7) That such other domestic producers might also have been able to isolate profit on a product-by-product basis is indicated in the Quanex Corporation's response to the Commission's questionnaire wherein it is stated, "The boiler tube market erosion caused by Japanese has taken place over a period of time and the displacement of this business has been offset by a change in product mix." (Conf. Doc. 22, p.8)

Expansion of the Commission's inquiry to other domestic producers' profits on a product-by-product basis would have given the Commission a better overview of the impact of LTFV imports on domestic producers. It is not enough for the Commission to have singled out plaintiff's ability to increase prices in the face of a shrinking market share as being indicative of the state of good health of the industry, given plaintiff's position as the acknowledged price leader, without knowing what experiences the other domestic producers were having in the face of import penetration attributable to LTFV sales. In this connection, it is noteworthy that Republic Steel declined to bid against the LTFV sales, noting "Customers are reluctant to give us lost sales to Japanese competitors in detail. However, we are attaching documentation of actual quotations made to our customers which we chose not to meet." (Conf. Doc. 23, p.8)

Moreover, such a stalwart in the steel industry as United States Steel had withdrawn from the boiler tube market, stating, "The reason U.S. Steel discontinued producing welded and seamless boiler tubes was due in part to foreign imports. It was not feasible for U. S. Steel in the face of rising production costs and depressed prices from imports to make capital investment to continue to participate profitably in this market." (Conf. Doc. 25, p.2)

On the record in this case the court agrees with plaintiff that the Commission erred as a matter of law in failing to properly apply the directives of section 771(4)(D) in determining the scope of the "industry" or "industries" against which to assess the effects of LTFV imports upon the like products being investigated, in consequence of which, the Commission's determination of April 14, 1980, is not in accordance with law.

The court also agrees with plaintiff that the Commission's determination of June 24, 1980, is unlawful. It is not denied by defendant that there is no statutory authorization for the Commission to reopen a terminated preliminary investigation and reconsider its determination in the light of additional evidence. What authority there is to support this course of action is said by defendant to rest in inherent agency authority to modify or correct its decisions. However, it is a well settled principle of administrative law that a governmental agency has only those powers which are granted to it by statute. 73 C.J.S. §48 (1951).

In any case, whatever may be the extent of the Commission's inherent authority to reconsider its decisions in the light of additional evidence, it is clear that the exercise of such authority must yield to a contrary legislative policy manifest in the governing statutes. Section 733(a) of the Tariff Act of 1930, as amended (19 U.S.C. §1673b(a)) specifically limits the Commission to making a preliminary determination on the basis of the best information available within 45 days. And the Senate Finance Committee report emphasizes that "This determination would have to be made within 45 calendar days. . . ." *See:* S. Rept. 96-249 to accompany H.R. 4537, 96th Cong., 1st Sess., p. 64 (1979), U.S. Code Cong. & Admin. News 1979, p. 450. Other passages in the legislative history indicate that a major objective of the revision is to reduce the length of the investigations undertaken by the Commission (Id., 66), and also to discourage the practice of time-consuming verification of data furnished as a preliminary matter (H. Rept. 96-317 to accompany H.R. 4537, 96th Cong., 1st Sess., p.62 (1979))—both of which circumstances are involved in the *reconsideration* undertaken by the Commission in this case. . . .

In view of the foregoing legislative history, it is clear that the 45-day time period is *mandatory* and not *directory.* And to the extent that the Committee reopened the preliminary investigation to receive additional evidence and to verify information it had previously acted upon without verification, the reconsideration extends the statutory time period, and as such, is void.

Inasmuch as the ITC did not give proper consideration to product lines nor seek to obtain profit factors in the domestic industry in making its preliminary determination, its finding was unsupported by substantial evidence and not in accordance with law. Also, its reopening a terminated preliminary investigation and reconsidering its determination in the light of additional evidence, after the expiration of the 45 day statutory limit for making its preliminary determination, such action was also not in accordance with law. The motion of plaintiff is granted and defendant's cross-motion is denied.

This matter is remanded to the ITC for disposition consistent with the decision of this court.

NOTES AND QUESTIONS

1. Is the case reading the statute's definition of an industry in a helpful way? In an economically reasonable way? In a way compelled by the text?

2. As a lawyer for a firm alleging injury, could you shape the result by careful accounting procedures?

3. What about the legislative history's focus on declining profits? Is this an accurate and appropriate alternative to a focus on prices? (Note the Commission's intitial determination in this case that there was no harm because the U.S. industry was raising prices in the face of a declining market share.)

4. Limerock, a Canadian producer of limestone, sells limestone into the Great Lakes region of five states surrounding the Great Lakes. Collectively, firms in these states sell 90% of their production of limestone to users (municipal water facilities and steel factories) in the Great Lakes region, and only about 20% of the total usage of limestone is supplied by producers outside of the five-state area.

Gravel, Inc., a Michigan producer of limestone, seeks your counsel on whether it would be possible to sustain an antidumping action against Limerock. Gravel's president cites the facts that import penetration in the Great Lakes area has increased from 20% to 40% in the last three years; Gravel's profits have declined; and it has been forced to lower its prices as a result of the "dumping" of Canadian limestone.

Could an antidumping case lie on a "regional injury" theory? (*See* Antidumping Code, Art. 4; 19 U.S.C. §1677(4)(c) and Atlantic Sugar. v. United States, 519 F. Supp. 916 (Ct. Intl. Trade 1981).

Could antidumping duties in the United States be imposed on a regional basis? What constitutional infirmity might exist?

5. Is it consistent with the GATT for the ITC to consider the effect of dumped merchandise on agricultural price support programs? *Note* §1677(7)(D)(ii)). *See also* §22 of the U.S. Agricultural Adjustment Act of 1933, as amended, and the GATT waiver permitting the imposition of U.S. import restraints (which is excerpted in Chapter 9).

6. A, B, C, D, E, and F are all television producers in Japan providing TV sets for the United States as well as other foreign markets. A, B, C, and D are selling television sets in the United States at less than fair value. E and F are not. On whom are the U.S. antidumping duties imposed? What if G and H

from Taiwan are also dumping TV sets? Are antidumping duties imposed on all sellers of TV's from Japan and Taiwan? (*See* Antidumping Code, Article 8; 189 U.S.C. §1673(e).) For a case sustaining an injury finding in such a situation, based on the concept of a "hammering effect," *see* City Lumber v. United States, 457 F.2d 991 (C.C.P.A. 1972).

7. The American Paper Institute files an antidumping case against the exporters of pulp from Canada. It then reconsiders and decides to withdraw its petition. What result?

Note that the current antidumping and countervailing duty statute provides the Department of Commerce with the authority to terminate cases once the petition has been withdrawn, *if* Commerce determines that it would not be in the public interest to continue the investigation.

The Omnibus Tariff and Trade Act of 1984 provides a "public interest" test which any suspension agreement must pass following the withdrawal of a petition;[3] if the test's requirements are not met, Commerce must continue with the investigation. The following considerations must be taken into account:

(i)   whether, based upon the relative impact on consumer prices and the availability of supplies of the merchandise, the agreement would have a greater adverse impact on United States consumers than the imposition of [countervailing or antidumping] duties;
(ii) the relative impact on the international economic interests of the United States; and
(iii) the relative impact on the competitiveness of the domestic industry producing the like merchandise, including any such impact on employment and investment in that industry.

The act further provides that in reaching this determination, the department must consult with (i) potentially affected consuming industries, and (ii) potentially affected producers and workers in the domestic industry producing the like merchandise, including producers and workers who are not parties to the investigation.

The provision was included because of concern that the present law encourages firms to make private deals with their adversaries, and that these deals may not be in the public interest.

8. How long does an antidumping duty remain in effect? See Bello and Holmer, Import Law and Policy Series: Review and Revocation of Antidumping and Countervailing Duty Orders, 19 Intl. Law No. 4 (Fall 1985).

---

[3] *See* Holmer and Bello, Import Law and Policy Series: Suspension and Settlement Agreements in Unfair Trade Cases, 18 Intl. Law. No. 3 (Summer 1984).

This test only applies in cases where the petition is withdrawn as a consequence of a quantitative restraint agreement concluded by the Commerce Department with the foreign supplier. If the petition is withdrawn for some other reason, this specific test would not be required. Because quantitative restraint agreements are not the principal reason for most withdrawals, this provision may prove to be less significant than it appears on the surface.

C. THE STEEL EXAMPLE

The most politically charged recent example of the antidumping law—and of a variety of special applications and evolutions of that law—is posed by the steel industry.[4] This industry, often in economic difficulty, has several times benefited from special arrangements such as a voluntary quota on Japanese imports in the 1969 to 1974 period. *See* Consumers Union v. Kissinger case in Chapter III at p.131. Recent developments began with the "trigger price mechanism" (TPM), a procedure designed and recommended by a panel chaired by the then undersecretary of the treasury, W. Michael Blumenthal.[5] The procedure is described in the following case.

DAVIS-WALKER CORP. v. BLUMENTHAL

460 F. Supp. 283 (D.D.C. 1978)

GASCH, J.

Plaintiffs Davis Walter Corporation and United International Corporation seek declaratory and injunctive relief with respect to the "trigger price mechanism" (TPM). Plaintiffs claim that the adoption by the Department of the Treasury (Treasury) of the TPM insofar as it pertains to steel wire rod contravenes the Antidumping Act, 19 U.S.C. §§160 173 (1970), *as amended,* (Supp. V 1975), is arbitrary and capricious in violation of section 10(e) of the Administrative Procedure Act (APA), 5 U.S.C. §706(2)(A), and is invalid for failure to comply with the rulemaking requirements of the APA, 5 U.S.C. §553 (1976).

Davis Walker Corporation (Davis Walker) is a manufacturer of wire and wire products, such as barbed wire, chain link fence, and welded wire fabric. Plaintiff United International Corporation, a wholly-owned subsidiary of Davis Walker, purchases steel wire rod, the principal raw material used in the manufacture of wire and wire products, from foreign suppliers and then sells the wire rod to Davis Walker. Defendants are the United States and five officials of the Department of the Treasury. . . .

The efficacy of the Antidumping Act procedures is one of the topics addressed in the Solomon Report, which was prepared by a task force formed in response to concern over the economic problems of the steel industry.[3] The

---

[4]*See* A. Harris, U.S. Trade Problems in Steel: Japan, West Germany, and Italy (1983); and C. MacPhee, Restrictions on International Trade in Steel (1974).

[5]A. Solomon, Report to the President: A Comprehensive Program for the Steel Industry (1977).

[3]The Report cites the following problems confronting the United States steel industry:

its competitive position has eroded over time, and its traditional market is being encroached upon by substitute materials and by imports of steel;

its competition from imports, often at dramatically reduced prices, has increased as the world steel industry has stagnated;

Solomon Report traces the factors leading to the recent aggressive exporting by foreign steel producers and antidumping complaints. It noted that nineteen separate antidumping petitions involving steel products, an unprecedented number for a single industry in such a short period of time, were pending before the Treasury. *See* A. Solomon, Report to the President: A Comprehensive Program for the Steel Industry (Dec. 6, 1977) (Solomon Report).

The Report next described and evaluated the procedures and remedy under the Antidumping Act. The Task Force concluded that the statutory "procedure is too cumbersome to provide relief quickly from sudden surges of imports that may cause injury to an American industry." *Id.* at 12. The Task Force estimated that the entire statutory procedure, from the date a complaint was filed to the publication of a dumping duty, would take approximately thirteen months in addition to the time it takes the complainant industry to prepare the petition. It also noted the limitations imposed by the "specific product orientation of individual investigations and findings." *Id.* at 13.

The Task Force recommended that:

> *the Department of the Treasury, in administering the Antidumping Act, set up a system of trigger prices, based on the full costs of production including appropriate capital charges of steel mill products by the most efficient foreign steel producers (currently the Japanese steel industry), which would be used as a basis for monitoring imports of steel into the United States and for initiating accelerated antidumping investigations with respect to imports priced below the trigger prices.*

Id. at 13-14 (emphasis in original). The President approved the Report on December 6, 1977.

On December 30, 1977, the Treasury published in the Federal Register a notice of proposed rulemaking relating to a new Customs invoice, the Special Summary Steel Invoice (SSSI), for certain steel mill products. In the introductory comments to this notice, the Treasury, characterizing the SSSI as one aspect of the TPM, announced its intention to implement the TPM. It described the TPM as a four-part system:

> (1) The establishment of trigger prices for steel mill products imported into the United States; (2) adoption of a new Special Summary Steel Invoice ("SSSI")

---

its earnings have dropped sharply and are considerably below historic levels;

it must invest heavily to modernize and increase efficiency in order to remain competitive;

it must make substantial expenditures to meet environmental regulations; but

it has had difficulty in raising the necessary capital for these expenditures under present market conditions.

Solomon Report, at A-1. Moreover, the Treasury has represented to the Court that sixteen steel plants closed or suffered permanent cutbacks in 1977, and employment in the industry dropped from 472,000 to 437,000 within four months in 1977. Defendants' Response to Plaintiffs' Memorandum of Points and Authorities at 8.

applicable to imports of all steel mill products; (3) the continuous collection and analysis of data concerning (a) the cost of production and prices of steel mill products in the countries that are the principal exporters of such products to the United States, and (b) the condition of the domestic steel industry; and (4) where appropriate, the expedited initiation and disposition of proceedings under the Antidumping Act of 1921 with respect to imports below the trigger prices. . . .

On January 3, 1978, the Treasury announced trigger prices for certain steel mill products, including steel wire rod. These trigger prices were published in the Federal Register on January 9, 1978, and became effective on that date to all goods entering the United States on or after February 21, 1978. 43 Fed. Reg. 1464 (1978). . . .

Plaintiffs assert three legal theories in this lawsuit. First, plaintiffs claim that the TPM circumvents the procedures prescribed in the Antidumping Act by establishing a minimum price system that will deter imports of steel mill products at prices below the published prices, without regard to the fair value of such imports or whether such imports are likely to injure an American industry. Second, plaintiffs contend that the TPM is a substantive rule subject to the rulemaking requirements of the APA, 5 U.S.C. §553 (1976), and is therefore invalid for failure to comply with these requirements. Finally, plaintiffs assert that the TPM insofar as it pertains to steel wire rod is arbitrary and capricious. In response, defendants filed a motion to dismiss or, in the alternative, for summary judgment. . . .

A. WHETHER THE TPM VIOLATES THE ANTIDUMPING ACT

Plantiffs argue that the TPM, by deterring the importation of goods at less than the trigger price and thereby establishing the trigger price as the minimum price for the affected goods, was intended and has had the effect of circumventing the elaborate statutory Antidumping Act procedures. Plaintiffs contend that virtually every foreign supplier of steel wire rod will refuse to offer steel wire rod at less than the trigger price, if the trigger price mechanism operates with respect to steel wire rod. They further contend that, because steel wire rod will not be imported at less than the trigger price, antidumping investigations will never be initiated. They finally argue that the TPM in effect imposes a dumping duty with respect to all goods for which trigger prices have been set without following the Antidumping Act procedures.

The Court finds that this claim may appropriately be resolved on summary judgment, since no issues of material fact remain in dispute. The Court holds, upon review of the Solomon Report, announcements in the Federal Register and other information concerning the TPM released by the Treasury, the Antidumping Act, and the legislative history, that the adoption of the TPM is within the Treasury's authority to administer the Antidumping Act.

As noted earlier, the TPM is described in the Solomon Report as

a system of trigger prices, based on the full costs of production including appropriate capital charges of steel mill products by the most efficient foreign steel
producers (currently the Japanese steel industry), which would be used as a basis
for monitoring imports of steel into the United States and for initiating accelerated antidumping investigations with respect to imports priced below the trigger
prices.

The trigger price mechanism is intended to provide the Secretary of the Treasury with a basis for initiating antidumping investigations without any prior
industry complaint. Such authority exists under the Antidumping Act although
it has not been used in recent years. As such it does not detract from any of the
legal rights that foreign producers or the domestic industry presently enjoy under
the Act. The trigger price is also a device for applying the resources of the
Treasury Department to a constant monitoring of imports affecting a particularly sensitive industry viewed as a whole, instead of focusing on the investigation
of individual complaints with respect to specified products—and then taking
expedited action under the law.

Solomon Report, at 13-14. The extent of coverage of the TPM, the methodology to be used in calculating trigger prices, and the Treasury's procedures for
implementing the system are discussed in the notice of proposed rulemaking
concerning the adoption of the special invoice in the Federal Register, and
other press releases issued by the Treasury as well as in the Solomon Report.
The Treasury stated that the TPM would cover only "steel mill products" as
defined by the American Iron and Steel Institute (AISI) and therefore would
not extend to fabricated articles. However, the Treasury noted that it would
consider including additional products should circumstances warrant it. The
Treasury indicated that it would also establish trigger prices for the "extras"
for those steel mill products for which trigger prices had been set.

The Treasury announced that, in developing trigger prices, it would utilize
and adjust information reflecting the cost of production of the particular product supplied by the Japanese steel industry, which is considered to be the most
efficient steel industry in the world. The information was to be collected from
the six major integrated steel companies as well as several smaller noninte-
grated steel makers in Japan. . . .

The evidence submitted by plaintiffs, particularly the Treasury materials
that describe the trigger price system, reveals that the TPM is merely a device
to monitor imports and to provide the Secretary with sufficient information to
enable him to determine whether to self-initiate an investigation. The TPM
itself does not establish any restrictions upon the affected industry; rather it
serves to aid the Treasury in its administration of the Antidumping Act. The
implementation of the TPM does not *by its terms* set trigger prices as minimum
import prices or preclude the importation of goods at less than trigger prices.
Plaintiffs have not and could not so argue.

The main thrust of plaintiff's argument is that the effect of the trigger price
system is to circumvent the Antidumping Act procedures. Plaintiffs claim that
the implementation of the TPM with respect to steel wire rod has caused

foreign manufacturers to raise prices to the trigger price level and that such a uniform price increase is tantamount to an across-the-board imposition of a dumping duty. The Court rejects plaintiff's interpretation: The decision by foreign manufacturers to increase prices to the trigger price level is not the legal equivalent of the imposition of dumping duties with respect to all such goods imported at the trigger price level. Moreover, the decision of foreign steel wire rod manufacturers to increase prices does not allow the Secretary to avoid the statutory procedures. Thus, the Court concludes that, even if plaintiff's allegations concerning the factual effects of the TPM (*i.e.,* foreign manufacturers' refusal to sell steel wire rod at less than trigger prices) were true, the TPM would not be contrary to the Antidumping Act.

The only direct effect of the TPM is a greater probability that antidumping investigations will be initiated for imports below trigger prices. Significantly as the Treasury has repeatedly stated, the importation of goods at below trigger prices "will not, by itself, result in any action by the Department." 42 Fed. Reg. 65,215 (1977). The Treasury explains that in those cases

> in which a shipment is found to be at prices below applicable trigger prices, the Customs Service may initiate immediate, informal inquiries of the importer to determine whether such sale is less than fair value within the meaning of the Antidumping Act. Unless the Secretary is satisfied within the time to be allotted therefor, that no reasonable possibility of sales at less than fair value may be found, an antidumping proceeding notice will promptly be published with respect to that shipment and other shipments of such or similar merchandise from the same exporter or from the same country of exportation as he deems appropriate.

43 Fed. Reg. 1468 (1978). Conversely, importation at prices above trigger prices will not necessarily foreclose the possibility of investigation, since an investigation by the Secretary may be triggered by a private industry complaint.

Regardless of whether an investigation is self-initiated by the Secretary on the basis of TPM information or is prompted by an industry complaint, *all* the statutory procedures must be followed before a dumping duty may be imposed. . . .

Having ascertained that the TPM is a guide to aid the Secretary in determining whether to self-initiate an antidumping investigation, the only remaining question is whether the Secretary has authority to monitor information and self-initiate an investigation. The statute does not expressly address the Secretary's authority to self-initiate an investigation. However, it does give the Secretary authority to "make rules and regulations necessary for the enforcement [of the Act]." 19 U.S.C. §173. More specifically, the Act does not specify or restrict the means by which the Secretary obtains the information upon which he bases the decision to initiate an investigation; it merely provides that the Secretary shall determine whether to initiate an investigation after receipt of information alleging an Antidumping Act violation. 19 U.S.C. §160(c)(1). . . .

B.   WHETHER THE TPM IS INVALID FOR FAILURE TO COMPLY WITH APA RULEMAKING REQUIREMENTS

Plaintiffs characterize the TPM as a substantive rule to which the APA rule-making requirements, 5 U.S.C. §553, apply. Plaintiffs primarily rely on a line of cases that utilize the so-called "substantial impact" test to determine whether the agency action is a substantive rule subject to the APA notice and comment procedures or is an interpretative rule, policy statement, or agency practice or procedure specifically exempted from APA rulemaking requirements. . . .

. . . the Court concludes that the TPM is a policy statement. The TPM clearly falls within the definition of policy statement in the Attorney General's Manual, since it serves to apprise the public and guide the Treasury in the administration and enforcement of the Antidumping Act. The TPM appears to be similar in nature to guidelines adopted without prior rulemaking by other agency or Executive Branch officials in the exercise of their discretionary authority. For example, the Department of Justice Merger Guidelines (1968), which set forth the market conditions under which the Antitrust Division will ordinarily challenge a merger as being a violation of section 7 of the Clayton Act, 15 U.S.C. §18 (1976), were adopted without rulemaking. Although these guidelines, like the TPM, definitely affect behavior in the business community, they serve "to insure that the business community, the legal profession and other interested persons are informed of the Department's policy of enforcing [the Act.]" Department of Justice Merger Guidelines §1.

. . . [T]he TPM does not impose rules or restrictions on the regulated industry or the public, and the Treasury consistently characterized it as a guide to aid the Secretary in the administration and enforcement of the Antidumping Act, *see, e.g.,* 43 Fed. Reg. 6065 (1978); 42 Fed. Reg. 65,214 (1977), rather than a substantive rule. Moreover, the TPM does not lead directly to final agency action but merely to the possibility of initiation of an antidumping investigation. Indeed, as the Treasury has reiterated, importation of goods below trigger prices will not in itself result in a decision to initiate an investigation. . . .

The Court concludes that the TPM is not invalid for failure to follow the APA notice and comment procedures. Accordingly, the Court will grant summary judgment in favor of defendants on this issue.

C.   WHETHER THE TPM INSOFAR AS IT PERTAINS TO STEEL WIRE ROD IS ARBITRARY AND CAPRICIOUS

Plaintiffs claim that the adoption of the TPM insofar as it pertains to steel wire rod is arbitrary and capricious in violation of section 10(e) of the APA, 5

U.S.C. §706(2)(A), for two reasons. First, they claim that the decision to limit the TPM to AISI steel mill products only, which includes steel wire rod but excludes many wire and wire products from TPM coverage, was arbitrary. Second, they contend that the trigger prices for steel wire rod were arbitrarily set too high. . . .

The Treasury has adopted and intends to adopt trigger prices only for those goods classified as steel mill products by the American Iron and Steel Institute (AISI). This list consists of 32 product categories; the products that fall within these categories historically have been produced in steel mills.

The Court finds the decision to limit the TPM to AISI steel mill products, even though many wire and wire products are not covered, was rational. The AISI is well recognized within the steel industry. The Treasury, by limiting the TPM to these 32 product categories, can more effectively deal with the most serious problems in the basic steel industry. As defendant Peter D. Ehrenhaft, Deputy Assistant Secretary of the Treasury for Tariff Affairs, observed, if the Treasury departed from the AISI list and attempted to include other fabricated articles, "the task of developing trigger prices would be enormously expanded because of the infinite range, diversity and complexity of such fabricated items." Deposition of Peter D. Ehrenhaft at 247. Indeed, a great deal of work is required to develop trigger prices for one additional category, which often encompasses a number of different products. Moreover, it would be extremely difficult to develop a rationale for limiting the categories of fabricated products that should be added.

The gist of plaintiffs' complaint is that the coverage by the TPM of the semifinished product, steel wire rod, but not all finished wire and wire products is arbitrary and capricious. While it may appear rational to include steel wire rod and all wire and wire products in the TPM, it is not irrational to exclude some of the wire products. Indeed, if the Treasury expanded the TPM to include all fabricated steel products on the same theory that plaintiffs present, the Treasury would be unable to devote sufficient enforcement resources to the basic steel mill industry. Thus, the decision to limit the TPM to AISI steel mill products has a rational basis, as it allows the Treasury to focus its enforcement energies on the area most urgently needing attention, the basic steel mill industry.

Finally, the Court will consider plaintiffs' claim that the trigger prices were arbitrarily set too high. The Court notes at the outset that it must affirm the Treasury if the Court finds a rational basis for the Treasury's calculations. It is not necessary that the Court find the Treasury's method and price to be "the only reasonable one, or even that this Court would have reached the same result." Jennings v. Shultz, 355 F. Supp. 1198, 1207 (D.D.C. 1973).

The theory underlying the Treasury's calculations of trigger prices is that "the 'fair value' of imported products is unlikely to be lower than the costs of production by the world's most efficient producer." Findings of the Department of the Treasury at 13. Since the Japanese steel industry is generally considered to be the most efficient, the Treasury based the trigger prices on the production costs of six Japanese integrated steel producers supplied by the Japanese Ministry of International Trade.

In setting trigger prices for steel wire rod, the Treasury utilized data from the six largest Japanese integrated steel companies on the model cost per ton of finished steel. The Treasury, after careful review of the available evidence, made adjustments to the Japanese data for yield per ton, labor productivity, exchange rate, and profit rate. The Treasury then multiplied this adjusted figure for the average cost of production of a net ton of finished steel by a coefficient supplied by the Japanese that reflects the portion of the cost of steel wire rod to the average cost of finished steel. Deposition of Robert W. Crandall at 100.

Plaintiffs challenge every step of the Treasury's calculations. First, plaintiffs contend that it was inappropriate to base calculations solely on the production costs of Japanese integrated steel companies, particularly since the cost of production of Japanese mini-mills is lower. In light of the fact that Japanese mini-mills do not currently export steel wire rod, *see* Findings of the Department of the Treasury at 17, the Treasury's reliance upon data from the integrated steel companies was reasonable.

Plaintiffs complain that the "Japanese costs do not form the basis of the trigger price system because Treasury made various adjustments in the Japanese Data." Plaintiffs' Summary of Evidence in the Record at 13. However, the Treasury clearly has authority to evaluate raw data and make adjustments upon careful consideration of all the information available. It appears to the Court that Robert W. Crandall and William J. Vaughn, the economists primarily responsible for developing these prices and, in particular, for making these adjustments, made such a careful study.

Plaintiffs also argue that these adjustments were based on an improper interpretation of the method for ascertaining "fair value" set forth in the Antidumping Act. This argument is totally erroneous. The trigger price is not the equivalent of "fair value" under the Antidumping Act. Indeed, the TPM does not even set minimum prices. The trigger prices merely serve as enforcement guidelines for the Treasury.

For the reasons stated above, the Court finds the calculations utilized by the Treasury to set trigger prices for wire rod were reasonable. Thus, the Court holds that the adoption of the TPM is not arbitrary and capricious within the meaning of section 10(e) of the APA for either of the reasons asserted by plaintiffs. Accordingly, the Court concludes that defendants are entitled to summary judgment on this issue.

CONCLUSION

Upon review of the Secretary's findings and the entire record herein, the Court will dissolve the preliminary injunction entered on March 24, 1978. The Court will grant summary judgment in favor of defendants on all of the claims presented. Accordingly, the entire action is dismissed with prejudice.

NOTES AND QUESTIONS

1. Are you impressed with Judge Gasch's handling of the jurisdiction question? How did this case differ—if at all—from a decision with respect to the imposition of an antidumping duty? Why didn't an adequate remedy exist in the Customs Court for Davis-Walker?

2. Could a consumer of Davis-Walker's wire products, e.g., a purchaser of barbed wire fence from the company, also have brought this case before Judge Gasch with the same result on jurisdiction? What is the difference between jurisdiction over the subject matter and standing in this type of case?

3. Is Judge Gasch correct in stating that: "The implementation of the TPM does not by its terms set trigger prices as minimum import prices or preclude the importation of goods at less than trigger prices"?

4. Is the TPM a policy statement or a rule? What does Judge Gasch say? Do you agree? What are the implications of this determination in terms of the Administrative Procedure Act?

5. Isn't the decision to have the TPM cover wire rod, but not cover products fabricated from wire rod, arbitrary? What does the court say? Should our decisions about what is arbitrary be based on the amount of work that is being created for Washington bureaucrats?

6. Should it have made any difference in the calculation of the cost of production in Japan whether Japanese mini-mills currently export wire rod?

7. What would induce Japan to collaborate with Treasury in setting the TPM? What about Japanese industry?

8. What would you expect the TPM to do to the price of steel in the United States? In the world? Would the U.S. Treasury become the price leader? For an argument that the TPM created a global floor price for steel, see Whitman, A Year of Travail: The United States and the International Economy, 57 Foreign Affairs 527, 543-544 (1978).

9. Suppose, as a U.S. steel firm, you learned of a steel import at a price below the TPM. What about one by, say, a less-efficient European firm, at a price below the exporter's home price but above the trigger price? What would you do? For arguments that there were many such imports of both types, see Comptroller General of the United States, Administration of the Steel Trigger Price Mechanism (Report ID-80-15, July 23, 1980).

United States Steel, precisely concerned that European exporters were dumping by selling at the trigger price, which was below their home price, filed an antidumping proceeding against these imports on March 21, 1980, and six hours later the Department of Commerce suspended the TPM. Now the shoe was on the other foot—at least one U.S. firm unsuccessfully brought suit against the suspension, Korf Indus. et al. v. Philip M. Klutznick et al., 2. I.T.R.D. 1131 (D.D.C. 1980).

Moreover, the Europeans protested. The TPM's trigger price had been defined quarterly on the basis of Japanese production costs in yen. The yen was rising through the period so the Europeans, along with exporters such as

Brazil, Korea, and Taiwan, had found it relatively easy to compete with Japan in exports to the United States. When the TPM was terminated, European exports to the United States abruptly fell.

The U.S. industry continued to have difficulty, and both the United States and Europe patched up their systems just before the 1980 U.S. election— denying that there was any deal between them. The U.S. package, which also included proposals for domestic assistance, reinstated the TPM at a price level about 13% higher, with special rolling averaging computations to cope with variable exchange rates.[6] In return, the U.S. firms dropped their antidumping actions.

Once again, the U.S. industry, its economic situation worsening in the global economic slow-down, soon sought protection against European imports at prices at the trigger price, but below actual European costs. The U.S. industry argued that it was simply attempting to enforce the law. And the Reagan administration responded to the initiation of law suits, as had the Carter administration earlier, by terminating the TPM in January, 1982. The antidumping actions, along with a number of countervailing duty actions, proceeded through the Department of Commerce and the ITC, generally with findings in favor of import relief.

Ultimately, after one compromise plan was rejected by the U.S. industry, the United States and Europe reached the following agreement, 47 Fed. Reg. 49,060 (1982):

ARRANGEMENT

Concerning trade in certain steel products between the European Coal and Steel Community (hereinafter called "the ECSC") and the United States (hereinafter called "the U.S.").

1. BASIS OF THE ARRANGEMENT

Recognizing the policy of the ECSC of restructuring its steel industry including the progressive elimination of state aids pursuant to the ECSC State Aids Code; recognizing also the process of modernization and structural change in the United States of America (hereinafter called the "USA"); recognizing the importance as concluded by the OECD of restoring the competitiveness of OECD steel industries; and recognizing, therefore, the importance of stability in trade in certain steel products between the European Community (hereinafter called "the Community") and the USA;

The objective of this Arrangement is to give time to permit restructuring and therefore to create a period of trade stability. To this effect the ECSC shall restrain exports to or destined for consumption in the USA of products described in Article 3(a) originating in the Community (such exports hereinafter called "the Arrangement products") for the period 1st November 1982 to 31st December 1985.

The ECSC shall ensure that in regard to exports effected between 1st August and 31st October 1982, aberrations from seasonal trade patterns of Arrangement products will be accommodated in the ensuing licensing period.

---

[6]45 Fed. Reg. 66,833 (1980).

2. CONDITION—WITHDRAWAL OF PETITIONS; NEW PETITIONS

(a) The entry into effect of this Arrangement is conditional upon:

(1) The withdrawal of the petitions and termination of all investigations concerning all countervailing duty and antidumping duty petitions listed in Appendix A at the latest by 21st October 1982; and

(2) Receipt by the U.S. at the same time of an undertaking from all such petitioners not to file any petitions seeking import relief under U.S. law, including countervailing duty, antidumping duty, Section 301 of the Trade Act of 1974 (other than Section 301 petitions relating to third country sales by U.S. exporters) or Section 337 of the Tariff Act of 1930, on the Arrangement products during the period in which this Arrangement is in effect.

(b) If during the period in which the Arrangement is in effect, any such investigations or investigations under Section 201 of the Trade Act of 1974, Section 232 of the Trade Expansion Act of 1962, or Section 301 of the Trade Act of 1974 (other than Section 301 petitions relating to third country sales by U.S. exporters) are initiated or petitions filed or litigation (including antitrust litigation) instituted with respect to the Arrangement products, and the petitioner of litigant is one of those referred to in article 2a), the ECSC shall be entitled to terminate the Arrangement with respect to some or all of the Arrangement products after consultations with the U.S., at the earliest 15 days after such consultations.

If such petitions are filed or litigation commenced by petitioners or litigants other than those referred to in the previous paragraph, or investigations initiated, on any of the Arrangement products, the ECSC shall be entitled to terminate the Arrangement with respect to the Arrangement product which is the subject of the petition, litigation or investigation after consultations with the U.S., at the earliest 15 days after such consultations. In addition, if during the consultations it is determined that the petition, litigation or investigation threatens to impair the attainment of the objectives of the Arrangement, then the ECSC shall be entitled to terminate the Arrangement with respect to some or all Arrangement products, at the earliest 15 days after such consultations.

These consultations will take into account the nature of the petitions or litigation, the identity of the petitioner or litigant, the amount of trade involved, the scope of relief sought, and other relevant factors.

(c) If, during the term of this Arrangement, any of the above mentioned proceedings of litigation is instituted in the USA against certain steel products as defined in Article 3(b) imported from the Community which are not Arrangement products and which substantially threaten its objective, then the ECSC and the U.S., before taking any other measure, shall consult to consider appropriate remedial measures.

3. PRODUCT DESCRIPTION

(a) The products are:

Hot-rolled sheet and strip
Cold-rolled sheet
Plate
Structurals
Wire rods
Hot-rolled bars

Coated sheet
Tin plate
Rails
Sheet piling
as described and classified in Appendix B [omitted] by reference to corresponding Tariff Schedules of the United States Annotated (TSUSA) item numbers and EC NIMEXE classification numbers.

(b) For purposes of this Arrangement, the term "certain steel products" refers to the products described in Appendix E [omitted].

4. EXPORT LIMITS

(a) For the period 1st November 1982 to 31 December 1983 (hereinafter called "the Initial Period") and thereafter for each of the years 1984 and 1985 export licenses shall be required for the Arrangement products. Such licenses shall be issued to Community exporters for each product in quantities no greater than the following percentages of the projected U.S. Apparent Consumption (hereinafter called "export ceilings") for the relevant period:

Product	Percentage
Hot-rolled sheet and strip	6.81
Cold-rolled sheet	5.11
Plate	5.36
Structurals	9.91
Wire rods	4.29
Hot-rolled bars	2.38
Coated sheet	3.27
Tin plate	2.20
Rails	8.90
Sheet piling	21.85

6. EXPORT LICENCES AND CERTIFICATES

(a) By Decisions and Regulations to be published in the Official Journal of the European Communities the ECSC will require an export licence for all Arrangement products. Such export licences will be issued in a manner that will avoid abnormal concentrations in exports of Arrangement products to the USA taking into account seasonal trade patterns. The ECSC shall take such action, including the imposition of penalties, as may be necessary to make effective the obligations resulting from the export licences. The ECSC will inform the U.S. of any violations concerning the export licences which come to its attention and the action taken with respect thereto.

APPENDIX A.—LIST OF COUNTERVAILING DUTY (CVD) AND ANTIDUMPING DUTY (AD) PETITIONS TO BE WITHDRAWN

CVD petitions, filed on January 11, 1982, by (1) United States Steel Corporation, (2) Bethlehem Steel Corporation, and (3) Republic Steel Corporation, Inland Steel Company, Jones & Laughlin Steel, Inc., National Steel Corporation, and Cyclops Corporation concerning certain steel products from Belgium,

France, the Federal Republic of Germany, Italy, Luxembourg, the Netherlands, the United Kingdom, and the European Communities.

AD petitions, filed on January 11, 1982, by (1) United States Steel Corporation, and (2) Bethlehem Steel Corporation concerning certain steel products from Belgium, France, the Federal Republic of Germany, Italy, Luxembourg, the Netherlands, and the United Kingdom.

CVD petitions, filed on February 8, 1982, by Atlantic Steel Corporation, Georgetown Steel Corporation, Georgetown Texas Steel Corporation, Keystone Consolidated, Inc., Korf Industries, Inc., Penn Dixie Steel Corporation and Raritan River Steel Company concerning carbon steel wire rod from Belgium and France.

CVD petitions, filed on May 7, 1982, by United States Steel Corporation concerning carbon steel welded pipe from France, the Federal Republic of Germany and Italy.

CVD petition, filed on September 3, 1982, by CF & I Steel Corporation concerning steel rails from the European Communities.

AD petitions, filed on September 3, 1982, by CF & I Steel Corporation concerning steel rails from France, the Federal Republic of Germany and the United Kingdom.

The essence of the arrangement between the United States and the European Community was that, in return for the withdrawal of a host of dumping and countervailing duty petitions by the United States, the EC would limit its steel exports to the United States. The "export ceilings" were "de facto" quotas, but the EC sought assurances that its exporters would not be subject to the penalties of the U.S. antitrust laws if export shipments were limited. The following letter from William Baxter provided the assurances sought by the EC. Contrast the implementation of the EC export restraints on steel outlined in this chapter with those discussed in the *Consumer's Union* case in Chapter 3, and the Japanese "voluntary" restraints on automobiles in Chapter 4.

U.S. DEPARTMENT OF JUSTICE
Antitrust Division
Office of the Assistant Attorney General

Oct 21, 1982

Sir Roy Denman
The Head of the Delegation
Delegation of the Commission
   of the European Community
2100 M Street
Suite 707
Washington, D.C. 20037

Dear Sir Roy:

This letter is in response to the request of the Commission of the European Communities (the Commission), set forth in its letter of October 21, 1982, for the views of the Department of Justice on antitrust questions regarding measures now being considered by the Communities, pursuant to discussions with the United States Government, to restrain the export of certain steel products to the United States.

The Commission has advised us that, pursuant to a Decision of the Commission acting under Article 95 of the Treaty establishing the European Coal and Steel Community and a Regulation of the Council under Article 113 of the Treaty establishing the European Economic Community, it will set up a system of export restrictions and controls for certain steel products destined for export to the United States. The Communities will permit companies to export to the United States only with a valid export license and will establish or provide for the establishment by the Commission of quantitative export limits for each covered steel product. The export licenses will be allocated to individual companies by each Member State according to criteria specified in the Decision and Regulation, in accordance with the Member States' obligations under Community law. The Member States will apply legal sanctions for violations of the system of export restrictions; typical sanctions include fines, forfeiture of goods, and imprisonment, the specifics of which vary from Member State to Member State. The Commission asserts that the Communities have authority to establish such a system of mandatory export restrictions and to cause the supporting sanctions to be enforced. The Commission further asserts that the system will be binding under Community law both on Member States and the enterprises concerned.

We understand the above advice regarding proposed actions by the Communities and Member States to constitute your representation that the proposed quantitative restrictions on the export of steel to the United States, and the allocation of those quantities among individual firms, will be imposed as mandatory controls by governmental entities acting within their sovereign powers. In such circumstances, the foreign sovereign compulsion doctrine would preclude liability under United States antitrust law for conduct compelled by those controls. We believe that U.S. courts interpreting the antitrust laws in such a situation would likely so hold.

Sincerely,

William F. Baxter
Assistant Attorney General
Antitrust Division

Even after the 1982 quotas, the specialty steel industry sought and obtained further import relief under §201 (Proc. 5074, July 19, 1983), leading to further

European concern, and retaliation against unrelated U.S. industries. In June, 1984, the ITC found injury in a much broader §201 steel proceeding triggered by a petition from the Bethlehem Steel Corporation. In response to the ITC's affirmative injury determination, President Reagan set a "target" of 18.5% for imports to be permitted in the U.S. market. This "target" was to be reached by government-to-government agreements, but the U.S.-EC quota arrangement described above was left in place.

September 25, 1984
THE WHITE HOUSE
Office of the Press Secretary

For Immediate Release

MEMORANDUM FOR THE UNITED STATES
TRADE REPRESENTATIVE
SUBJECT: Steel Import Relief Determination

Pursuant to Section 202(b)(1) of the Trade Act of 1974, (P.L. 93-618, 88 Stat. 1978), I have determined the actions I will take with respect to the report of the United States International Trade Commission (USITC) dated July 24, 1984 concerning carbon and alloy steel.

I have determined today under Section 203 of the Trade Act that import relief is not in the national economic interest for the following reasons:

1. In responding to this pressing import problem, we must do all we can to avoid protectionism, to keep our market open to free and fair competition, and to provide certainty of access for our trading partners. This Administration has repeatedly, and most recently at the London Economic Summit, committed itself to "resist" continuing protectionist pressures, to reduce barriers to trade, and to make renewed efforts to liberalize and expand trade in manufactures, commodities and services."

2. It is not in the national economic interest to take actions which put at risk thousands of jobs in steel fabricating and other consuming industries or in the other sectors of the U.S. economy that might be affected by compensation or retaliation measures to which our trading partners would be entitled.

3. This Administration has already taken many steps to deal with the steel import problem. In 1982, a comprehensive arrangement restraining steel imports from the European Community was negotiated. This Administration has also conducted an unprecedented number of antidumping and countervailing duty investigations of steel imports, in most cases resulting in the imposition of duties or a negotiated settlement. In addition, the governments of Mexico and South Africa have unilaterally imposed

voluntary restraint on exports, leading to the termination of unfair trade complaints.

However, I have decided to establish a government policy for the steel
industry. I believe that this new policy is the best way to respond to the
legitimate concerns of the domestic industry while maintaining access to
our market for those who trade fairly.

I am directing you to coordinate and direct the implementation of this
policy for the U.S. steel industry which includes the following elements:

1. The United States Trade Representative (USTR) will negotiate
    "surge control" arrangements or understandings and, where ap-
    propriate, suspension agreements with countries whose exports to
    the United States have increased significantly in recent years due
    to an unfair surge in imports—unfair because of dumping subsidi-
    zation, or diversion from other importing countries who have re-
    stricted access to their markets. The USTR will negotiate
    additional such arrangements and understandings, if necessary, to
    control new surges of imports that result from subsidizing, dump-
    ing or other unfair or restrictive trade practices during the next
    five years. If agreements cannot be reached to control new surges
    from countries that are guilty of unfair practices, the President
    will use his authority under the unfair trade laws including Sec-
    tion 301 of the Trade Act of 1974 to assure that these countries do
    not maintain unrestricted access to the United States market.

2. The United States Trade Representative will reaffirm existing
    measures with countries that have voluntarily restrained their ex-
    ports to our market, and will take necessary steps to ensure the
    effectiveness of these measures. Specifically the Administration
    will support legislation in the Congress to make enforceable at our
    borders all voluntary agreements and "surge control" arrange-
    ments.

3. The United States Trade Representative will consult with our
    trading partners to seek the elimination of trade distortive and
    trade restraining practices in other markets to lead to the liberal-
    ization of steel trade around the world.

4. The Department of Commerce will continue to rigorously enforce
    our unfair trade laws. Further, the Department of Commerce and
    the United States Trade Representative will self-initiate unfair
    trade cases including antidumping, countervailing duty and Sec-
    tion 301 actions when appropriate.

5. The United States International Trade Commission will be asked
    to monitor the efforts of the steel industry to adjust and modern-
    ize, and to prepare an annual report for the President on those
    efforts.

6. The Secretary of Commerce will establish an interagency group
    to analyze all U.S. government domestic tax, regulatory and an-

titrust laws and policies which could hinder the ability of the steel industry to modernize.

7. The Secretary of Defense and the Federal Emergency Management Agency will analyze domestic steel plate rolling capacity in relationship to emergency needs, and to recommend to the President appropriate actions if deficiencies are found to exist.

8. The Secretary of Labor will work with state and local governments to develop a program to assist workers in communities adversely affected by steel imports.

9. The United States Trade Representative will closely monitor the trade elements of this program and the resultant import trends and report them to the President on a quarterly basis.

The Administration's hope is that this combination of actions, taken without protectionist intention or effect would enable one of the United States' most basic and vital industries to return to a level playing field, one in which steel is traded on the basis of market forces, not government intervention, and one in which the market would seek a return to a more normal level of steel imports, or approximately 18.5 percent, excluding semi-finished steel.

This determination is to be published in the *Federal Register.*

RONALD REAGAN

NOTES AND QUESTIONS

1. Is the U.S.-EC quota arrangement legal under the trade laws and *Yoshida?* What about regarding it as a compromise of disputed antidumping and countervailing duty claims?

2. Is the U.S.-EC arrangement legal under *Consumer's Union?* Is Assistant Attorney General Baxter's approach persuasive? You will want to come back to this antitrust question after Chapter XI.

3. Are you pleased or troubled at the ability of the industry to veto such an agreement?

4. Compare this agreement with a trigger price designed to let in about the same quantity of steel from Europe. As a U.S. consumer and citizen, which do you prefer economically? Administratively? Legally?

5. How would you answer the same questions if you were associated with the U.S. steel industry?

6. What if you were a European producer? How about a Japanese or Mexican steel producer?

7. Would it be wise to extend this quota concept globally so as to provide international political agreements controlling all steel flows? (This was being

seriously considered in early 1983, and similar global quotas have long applied to textiles.)

8. Do you agree with President Reagan's assertion that the September 25, 1984, 18.5% "target" decision was "taken without protectionist intention or effect"?

9. How might we go back and face the steel issue differently? Consider the following excerpts from the Business Brief section of The Economist, October 1, 1983, p.74.

Business Brief

Steelmakers of the world, repent . . .

Leaders of the world's steel industry are meeting in Vienna for the 17th annual conference of the International Iron and Steel Institute (IISI) from October 2nd to October 5th. When they met last year in Tokyo, the steel companies of all but the super-efficient host country were flat on their backs. This year, sustained by government subsidies, they are back up on their knees, wondering which of them will struggle to their feet.

The steelmakers' problems boil down to (a) the drift of steel production to (mostly newly industrialising) countries with low labour costs and few inhibitions about subsidising industries that earn foreign exchange; (b) the slowness of the steel industries in Europe and America to adapt to change because governments are loth to allow unemployment to increase; and (c) the uncoupling of the steel industry from the engine of economic growth.

Despite a modest world economic recovery this year and next, steelmen's prospects are no better than they have been since the rapid expansion of demand for steel petered out in the mid-1970s. Since October, 1982, IISI predictions of the growth in steel consumption in 1983 in the non-communist world have been revised downwards. An original forecast of a 3.3% increase in demand in 1983 was pared in April to 1.3%, or 407.8 tonnes.

Even this depends mightily on revived demand in America, where the car and white goods industries are buying more steel than in an awful 1982 (when many American steel mills were running at a third of capacity). Though the American steel industry is now operating at 54% of capacity and its industry-wide losses, at around $2 billion, will be a third lower than at the bottom of the 1982 slump, its hopes of good times to come are fading.

Rapid economic growth used to work wonders for steel because the industry benefited from construction work and from factory building and extensions by industry. But periods of episodic, fast growth that interrupt a general pattern of no or slow growth are now failing to persuade business to build new plants. Companies are not convinced that this recovery is better than episodic. So firms tend to spend money instead on replacing and modernising existing equipment. Such tinkering calls for less steel.

For many years in industrial countries increases in industrial output have not required equivalent increases in steel consumption. That relationship is not likely to change (see chart below).

Pessimists in this industry call themselves realists. They say that only a sustained return to fast economic growth can put an end to the industry's troubles. They are made glummer by the many varieties of government intervention: eg, schemes to subsidise old steel mills in Europe; tariffs and quotas that protect American steelmakers from foreign competition; cheap state money in third-world countries (often via international loans) for steel mills aimed at export markets.

Occasionally, an optimistic jack-in-the-box pops up to forecast a steel shortage in 1985 or 1986, with prices soaring to levels that will rub the red off American steel companies' books. One such is Mr Peter Marcus, a steel analyst at Paine Webber, Mitchell Hutchins, a Wall Street brokerage house. His thesis is that things have got so bad they can only get better: years of losses and low investment in the steel industry should wipe out capacity and lead to better utilisation of the surviving plants.

In a free-market world bereft of subsidies, but full of profit seekers, Mr Marcus would be right. In the real world, the industry and its government backers are slow to adapt to a complex change, both in steel production and in world steel demand. And each time an influential analyst promises a renaissance, some company in America or a government in Europe is tempted to postpone a mill closure.

All the same, the challenges that confront the non-communist world's big steelmaking regions are plain:

• America must decide what size of steel industry it wants or needs. Can it afford to haul its nineteenth-century furnaces into the late twentieth century at great cost (eg, some $1.5 billion to modernise a single plant of the US Steel Corporation at Fairless, Pennsylvania)? Is it prepared to import semi-finished steel from Europe (eg, the British Steel plant at Ravenscraig in Scotland that is party to a controversial plan to supply slabs for Fairless's rolling mill), or steel from the spanking new plants in Latin America and other developing countries?

• Europe must decide whether its "temporary" aids for steel are permanent. It has been cartelising its steelmakers for eight years without cutting enough capacity to remove the need for rigged production shares and prices, despite the disappearance of some 300,000 jobs. Few believe that the EEC commission in Brussels can really phase out subsidies by the end of 1985. The Europeans will eventually have to decide whether to continue to throw millions at loss makers to stave off unemployment; or to let the markets sort out the surplus capacity; or to attempt a grand *dirigiste* scheme to reshape the whole of the common market's steel industry with Brussels specifying the plants that can stay and those that must go.

• Japan has to prepare itself for larger imports of steel from the "new Japans": South Korea, Taiwan and even Indonesia. Its steel industry has adjusted best so far, but its huge favourable trade

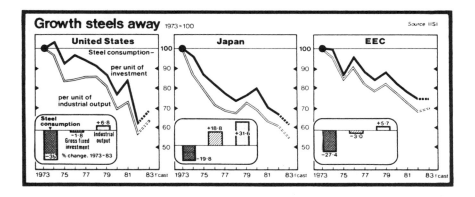

imbalance—exports of 30m tonnes a year and domestic consumption of 93m tonnes a year versus imports of 450,000 tonnes—will increasingly come under challenge from the new, efficient steel producers it has helped nurture in the far east

• The fast growing end of world steel consumption and production—the newly industrialising countries and those aspiring to that elite of the third world—will have to judge what share of the world steel trade market it can win before provoking even fiercer trade restrictions like the imminent barrage of American anti-dumping actions against Brazil, Mexico and others.

See also, on steel, Canto, Eastin, and Laffer, Failure of Protection: A Study of the Steel Industry, 11 Colum. J. W. Bus. 43 (1982); R. Crandall, The U.S. Steel Industry in Recurrent Crisis (1981); Note, Cyclical Dumping: The Case of Steel Products, 9 J. Intl. Econ. 57 (1979).

Chapter VI

Subsidies and Countervailing Duties

The next tariff adjustment process to be considered is the countervailing duty, a tariff levied in response to and designed to counterbalance a foreign export subsidy.

When actually equal to the subsidy, the countervailing duty produces allocative neutrality between the foreign product and competing domestic products. The combination of subsidy and countervailing duty produces a financial flow from the exporting nation's treasury (which is subsidizing the export) to the importing nation's treasury (which is gaining from the duty). If the subsidy were not countervailed, the importing nation's consumers would benefit at the expense of the exporting nation's treasury and of the sales of the importing nation's competing industry.

As will be seen below, it is not, however, that easy to distinguish between a subsidy that is specific to exports and is clearly countervailable under both national and GATT principles, as compared with the broader economic assistance that a government grants to its industries. The distinction has become even more difficult to make as nations subsidize their industries more and more during a period of slow economic growth.

Table 6-1 suggests the upward drift in subsidies since 1952, and the relatively lower incidence of subsidies in the United States compared to its major trading partners. Of particular interest from the U.S. perspective is the decline in U.S. governmental subsidies since the late 1960s; this may partially explain the constant stream of grievances expressed by U.S. industries against subsidized trading practices by other countries.

TABLE 6-1

Subsidies as shown in national account statistics as a percentage of GDP[a]

Country	1952	1956	1960	1964	1968	1972	1976	1980
Italy	0.89	1.30	1.51	1.23	1.67	2.29	2.60	3.01
France	1.71	2.71	1.62	2.03	2.62	1.99	2.68	2.51
Canada	0.41	0.39	0.81	0.85	0.87	0.83	1.73	2.34
United Kingdom	2.68	1.76	1.93	1.56	2.06	1.82	2.78	2.32
Germany	0.65	0.20	0.79	0.99	1.44	1.48	1.49	1.59
Japan	0.79	0.26	0.34	0.65	1.11	1.12	1.32	1.32
United States	0.11	0.20	0.25	0.44	0.50	0.59	0.34	0.43

Source: OCED, National Accounts 1951-1980, vol. 1, Main Aggregates, 1982, in G. Hufbauer and J. Erb, Subsidies in International Trade (1984) at p. 3.

[a]Countries listed in order of amount of subsidies as a percentage of GDP in 1980.

A.   THE FRAMEWORK OF UNITED STATES LAW

1.   The Requirement to Countervail

United States law has long required the relevant secretary (once Treasury, now Commerce) to countervail when he or she finds that a foreign nation is extending a "bounty or grant" on exported goods. (*See* the Trade Act of 1974, §331, and the Trade Agreements Act of 1979, §§101-107.) Before 1974, the provision applied only to goods that already carried a duty and it applied whether or not a U.S. industry was harmed. This was acceptable under GATT Articles VI and XVI only because it was grandfathered under the Protocol of Provisional Application.

In 1974, when Congress extended the coverage of the act to goods that had not previously carried a duty, it therefore created a two-track procedure to comply with the GATT: where a good did not carry a duty, an International Trade Commission injury determination would be necessary because this was a new application of the duty and therefore not grandfathered. Congress took another step in 1974, based on the 1974 act's role in shaping the Multilateral Trade Negotiations (MTN): the president was given power to waive application of a countervailing duty for the expected term of the MTN—but the exercise of this power was subjected to a one-house congressional veto. (As it turned out, the MTN lasted a few months longer than this waiver authority, and the politics of extending it—retroactively—proved particularly complex in the 1979 negotiations between the president and Congress.)

More changes came in 1979 with the MTN, which included a new international code on subsidies and countervailing duties (already noted in the Exim bank discussion of Chapter II). This agreement was essentially a commitment to use an injury requirement, plus an elaborate—but often ambiguous—definition of "subsidy." Congress legislated the appropriate changes in the 1979 act, but left the old provisions in force for countervailing against subsidies by those nations that did not accept the new code. Thus, countries that have not signed the subsidies code, or entered into obligations that are substantially equivalent to obligations under the agreement, are *not* entitled to an "injury" determination in a countervailing duty action with respect to dutiable articles, and a countervailing duty may be obtained merely upon a demonstration of a subsidy. The benefits of the Subsidies Code, in other words, flow only to those countries that have accepted its obligations. 19 U.S.C. §1303(b) (1982). The statutory timetable for countervailing duty actions is shown in Figure 6-1.

2. Border Tax Adjustments

The definitional issue that evoked the leading Supreme Court interpretation of the countervailing duty statutes is that of border rebates of "direct" and "indirect" taxes. The idea, reflected in the notes in Article VI of Annex 1 to the GATT, is that a direct tax, such as the income tax, is absorbed directly by the person taxed. Should such a tax be rebated on export, the rebate would be a subsidy to the exporter, and would therefore be countervailable. In contrast, an indirect tax, such as the sales tax, is one paid indirectly—it may be levied

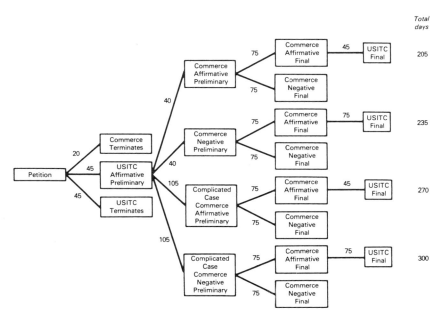

FIGURE 6-1
Statutory Timetable for Countervailing Duty Investigations (in days)
Source: International Trade Commission, Annual Report (1982)

by the seller, but would in fact be absorbed by the consumer. Rebate of such a tax on export is therefore simply a recognition that the tax is not really part of the price of the goods, in the way the seller's income tax is part of the price of the goods. Such a rebate therefore is assumed not to constitute a subsidy.

DEPARTMENT OF THE TREASURY, COUNTERVAILING DUTIES

United States International Economic Policy in an Interdependent World, Supplement 1 (The Williams Report, 1971) at 409-410

II.   Treasury Administrative Interpretations of "Bounty or Grant"

DIRECT SUBSIDY

Where a foreign government pays a direct subsidy on its exports to the United States, this clearly constitutes a "bounty or grant". Thus, for example, if country A pays $1 a dozen subsidy on all widget exports, and widgets are dutiable under the provisions of the Tariff Schedules, the Treasury would, in accordance with past administrative and judicial precedents, impose a countervailing duty of $1 a dozen on widgets, in addition to all other duties normally payable. As in the case of the Antidumping Act, it is the importer who is liable for payment of the countervailing duty.

REBATES OF TAXES

Under past administrative precedents of the Treasury Department, non-excessive rebates of ordinary indirect taxes and drawbacks of duty do not constitute a "bounty or grant". On the other hand, rebates of direct taxes do constitute a "bounty or grant". Typical of direct taxes under these precedents are income and social security taxes. Typical of indirect taxes are excise and sales taxes. The Treasury's interpretation of the applicability of the Countervailing Duty Law to rebates of direct and indirect taxes is consistent with Article VI 4 of the GATT.

The exemption of rebates of indirect taxes from the term "bounty or grant" does not apply to over-rebates. If for example an exporter in country A has paid $1 in excise taxes on a product he exports to the United States, and he receives a rebate of $1.20 on exportation, under past administrative precedents of the Treasury Department, the imported merchandise would be subject to a countervailing duty of $.20.

III.   Judicial Interpretations of "Bounty or Grant"

Considerable confusion has arisen in the countervailing duty field over the interpretation of two early Supreme Court opinions, the dicta of which refer to the term "bounty or grant" as applying to all tax rebates, including rebates of indirect taxes. These opinions were rendered in the *Downs* and *Nicholas* cases (Downs v. United States, 113 F. 144 (1902) *aff'd* 187 U.S. 496 (1903); Nicholas & Co. v. United States, 7 Ct. Cust. Appls. 97 (1916), *aff'd* 249 U.S. 34 (1919). However, the holdings of the Supreme Court in these two decisions, as distinguished from the dicta, were that over-rebates constitute a "bounty or grant" to the extent of the over-rebate. The Treasury Department has for more than a half century, in its administrative decisions, consistently construed the *Downs* and *Nicholas* opinions in accordance with the holdings rather than the dicta. The Congress has been aware of the Treasury's construction of the *Downs* and *Nicholas* opinions and has not seen fit to require the Treasury to alter its administrative interpretations by revising the statute.

The issue was recently reopened in a decision of the Customs Court in Hammond Lead Products, Inc. v. United States, C.D. 3915 (Cust. Ct., November 7, 1969). The Mexican Government imposes export taxes on numerous products including various types of lead. However, the Mexican Government has chosen not to impose an export tax on litharge, a substance produced primarily of lead and used for fabricating batteries. The Hammond Lead Company, an American litharge manufacturer, filed a countervailing duty "complaint" with the Treasury Department charging that the exclusion of litharge from the Mexican Government's program of collecting revenues on tax exports constituted the payment or bestowal of a "bounty or grant" on litharge within the meaning of the Countervailing Duty Law.

The Treasury Department rejected this contention on the ground that foreign governments are free to decide for themselves on what particular products they may, or may not, see fit to assess export taxes. Hammond Lead Company petitioned the Customs Court for redress. The latter reversed the Treasury's position, holding that the failure of the Mexican Government to tax litharge exports constituted, under the circumstances outlined, the payment or bestowal of a "bounty or grant." In reaching this decision, the Customs Court quoted liberally from the previously cited dicta of the *Downs* and *Nicholas* cases. This is the first time in many years that the *Downs* and *Nicholas* dicta have been relied upon in a court opinion. The *Hammond Lead* decision is currently being appealed by the United States to the Court of Customs and Patent Appeals.

The *Hammond Lead* case, ultimately United States v. Hammond Lead Products, 440 F.2d 1024 (C.C.P.A., 1971), was decided on procedural grounds. The appellate court held that the Customs Court, which clearly had jurisdiction to consider an importer's protest that a countervailing duty had been improperly levied, lacked jurisdiction to consider a U.S. manufacturer's protest that a countervailing duty had incorrectly *not* been levied. The result was a barrier to bringing a legal test of the Treasury Secretary's discretion. *Hammond Lead,* however, implied that there would be jurisdiction in the regular courts, which had jurisdiction over issues not within Customs Court jurisdiction. These courts were stepping in, *see, e.g.,* National Milk Producers Federation v. Shultz, 372 F. Supp. 745 (D.D.C. 1974), at the same time that Congress responded legislatively in §331 of the 1974 Act, amending 19 U.S.C. §161.

The substantive issue reached the Supreme Court in the following case.

ZENITH RADIO CORP. v. UNITED STATES

437 U.S. 443 (1978)

Mr. Justice MARSHALL delivered the opinion of the Court.

Under §303(a) of the Tariff Act of 1930, 46 Stat. 687, as amended, 19 U.S.C. §1303(a) (Supp. V, 1975), whenever a foreign country pays a "bounty or grant" upon the exportation of a product from that country, the Secretary of the Treasury is required to levy a countervailing duty, "equal to the net amount of such bounty or grant," upon importation of the product into the United States. The issue in this case is whether Japan confers a "bounty" or "grant" on certain consumer electronic products by failing to impose a commodity tax on those products when they are exported, while imposing the tax on the products when they are sold in Japan.

I

Under the Commodity Tax Law of Japan, Law No. 48 of 1962, see App. 44-48, a variety of consumer goods, including the electronic products at issue here, are subject to an "indirect" tax—a tax levied on the goods themselves, and computed as a percentage of the manufacturer's sales price rather than the income or wealth of the purchaser or seller. The Japanese tax applies both to products manufactured in Japan and to those imported into Japan. On goods manufactured in Japan, the tax is levied upon shipment from the factory; imported products are taxed when they are withdrawn from the customs warehouse. Only goods destined for consumption in Japan are subject to the tax, however. Products shipped for export are exempt, and any tax paid upon the shipment of a product is refunded if the product is subsequently exported. Thus the tax is "remitted" on exports.

In April 1970 petitioner, an American manufacturer of consumer electronic products, filed a petition with the Commissioner of Customs, requesting assessment of countervailing duties on a number of consumer electronic products exported from Japan to this country. Petitioner alleged that Japan had bestowed a "bounty or grant" upon exportation of these products by, inter alia, remitting the Japanese Commodity Tax that would have been imposed had the products been sold within Japan. In January 1976, after soliciting the views of interested parties and conducting an investigation pursuant to Treasury Department regulations, see 19 CFR §159.47(c) (1977), the Acting Commissioner of Customs published a notice of final determination, rejecting petitioner's request. 41 Fed. Reg. 1298 (1976).

Petitioner then filed suit in the Customs Court, claiming that the Treasury Department had erred in concluding that remission of the Japanese Commodity Tax was not a bounty or grant within the purview of the countervailing duty statute. The Department defended on the ground that, since the remission of indirect taxes was "nonexcessive," the statute did not require assessment of a countervailing duty. In the Department's terminology, a remission of taxes is "nonexcessive" if it does not exceed the amount of tax paid or otherwise due; thus, for example, if a tax of $5 is levied on goods at the factory, the return of the $5 upon exportation would be "nonexcessive," whereas a payment of $8 from the government to the manufacturer upon exportation would be "excessive" by $3. The Department pointed out that the current version of §303 is in all relevant respects unchanged from the countervailing duty statute enacted by Congress in 1897, and that the Secretary—in decisions dating back to 1898—has always taken the position that the nonexcessive remission of an indirect tax is not a bounty or grant within the meaning of the statute.

On cross-motions for summary judgment, the Customs Court ruled in favor of petitioner and ordered the Secretary to assess countervailing duties on all Japanese consumer electronic products specified in petitioner's complaint. 430 F. Supp. 242 (1977). The court acknowledged the Secretary's longstanding interpretation of the statute. It concluded, however, that this administrative practice could not be sustained in light of this Court's decision in Downs v. United States, 187 U.S. 496, 23 S. Ct. 222, 47 L. Ed. 275 (1903), which held that an export bounty had been conferred by a complicated Russian scheme for the regulation of sugar production and sale, involving, among other elements, remission of excise taxes in the event of exportation.

On appeal by the Government, the Court of Customs and Patent Appeals, dividing 3-2, reversed the judgment of the Customs Court and remanded for entry of summary judgment in favor of the United States. 562 F.2d 1209 (1977). . . .

We granted certiorari . . . and we now affirm.

II

It is undisputed that the Treasury Department adopted the statutory interpretation at issue here less than a year after passage of the basic countervailing duty statute in 1897, see T.D. 19321, 1 Synopsis of [Treasury] Decisions 696 (1898), and that the Department has uniformly maintained this position for over 80 years. This longstanding and consistent administrative interpretation is entitled to considerable weight.

When faced with a problem of statutory construction, this Court shows great deference to the interpretation given the statute by the officers or agency charged with its administration. "To sustain [an agency's] application of [a] statutory term, we need not find that its construction is the only reasonable one, or even that it is the result we would have reached had the question arisen in the first instance in judicial proceedings." Udall v. Tallman, 380 U.S. 1, 16, 85 S. Ct. 792, 801, 13 L. Ed. 2d 616 (1965), quoting Unemployment Compensation Commission v. Aragon, 329 U.S. 143, 153, 67 S. Ct. 245, 250, 91 L. Ed. 136 (1946).

Moreover, an administrative "practice has peculiar weight when it involves a contemporaneous construction of a statute by the [persons] charged with the responsibility of setting its machinery in motion, of making the parts work efficiently and smoothly while they are yet untried and new." Norwegian Nitrogen Products Co. v. United States, 288 U.S. 294, 315, 53 S. Ct. 350, 358, 77 L. Ed. 796 (1933); *see* e.g., Power Reactor Co. v. Electricians, 367 U.S. 396, 408, 81 S. Ct. 1529, 1535, 6 L. Ed. 2d 924 (1961).

The question is thus whether, in light of the normal aids to statutory construction, the Department's interpretation is "sufficiently reasonable" to be accepted by a reviewing court. Train v. Natural Resources Defense Council, 421 U.S. 60, 75, 95 S. Ct. 1470, 1479, 43 L. Ed. 2d 731 (1975). Our examination of the language, the legislative history, and the overall purpose of the 1897 provision persuades us that the Department's initial construction of the statute was far from unreasonable; and we are unable to find anything in the events subsequent to that time that convinces us that the Department was required to abandon this interpretation.

A

The language of the 1897 statute evolved out of two earlier countervailing duty provisions that had been applicable only to sugar imports. The first provision was enacted in 1890, apparently for the purpose of protecting domestic sugar refiners from unfair foreign competition; it provided for a fixed countervailing duty on refined sugar imported from countries that "pay . . . , directly or indirectly, a [greater] bounty on the exportation of" refined sugar than on raw sugar. Tariff Act of 1890, ¶237, 26 Stat. 584. Although the congressional debates did not focus sharply on the meaning of the word "bounty," what evidence there is suggests that the term was not intended to encompass the nonexcessive remission of an indirect tax. Thus, one strong supporter of increased protection for American sugar producers heavily criticized the export "bounties" conferred by several European governments, and attached a concise description of "The Bounty Systems in Europe"; both the remarks and the description indicated that the "bounties" consisted of the amounts by which government payments exceeded the excise taxes that had been paid upon the beets from which the sugar was produced. See 21 Cong. Rec. 9529, 9532 (1890) (remarks of Sen. Gibson); *id.,* at 9537 (description).

According to the description, for example, French sugar manufacturers paid an "excise tax [of] $97.06 per gross ton[,] [b]ut upon the export of a ton of sugar . . . received back as a drawback $117.60, making a clear bounty of $20.54 per gross ton of sugar exported." *Id.*, at 9537.

This concept of a "net" bounty—that is, a remission in excess of taxes paid or otherwise due—as the trigger for a countervailing duty requirement emerged more clearly in the second sugar provision, enacted in 1894. Tariff Act of 1894, ¶182½, 28 Stat. 521. The 1894 statute extended the countervailing duty requirement to all imported sugar, raw as well as refined, and provided for payment of a fixed duty on all sugar coming from a country which "pays, directly or indirectly, a bounty on the export thereof." A proviso to the statute made clear, however, that no duties were to be assessed in the event that the "bounty" did not exceed the amount of taxes already paid. The author of the 1894 provision, Senator Jones, expressly characterized this difference between the amounts received upon exportation and the amounts already paid in taxes as the "net bounty" on exportation. 26 Cong. Rec. 5705 (1894) (discussing German export bounty system).

The 1897 statute greatly expanded upon the coverage of the 1894 provision by making the countervailing duty requirement applicable to all imported products. Tariff Act of 1897, §5, 30 Stat. 205, . . . There are strong indications, however, that Congress intended to retain the "net bounty" concept of the 1894 provision as the criterion for determining when a countervailing duty was to be imposed. Although the proviso in the 1894 law was deleted, the 1897 statute did provide for levying of duties equal to the "net amount" of any export bounty or grant. And the legislative history suggests that this language, in addition to establishing a responsive mechanism for determining the appropriate amount of countervailing duty, was intended to incorporate the prior rule that nonexcessive remission of indirect taxes would not trigger the countervailing requirement at all. . . .

B

Regardless of whether this legislative history absolutely compelled the Secretary to interpret "bounty or grant" so as not to encompass any nonexcessive remission of an indirect tax, there can be no doubt that such a construction was reasonable in light of the statutory purpose. *Cf.* Mourning v. Family Publications Service, Inc., 411 U.S. 356, 374, 93 S. Ct. 1652, 1663, 36 L. Ed. 2d 318 (1973). This purpose is relatively clear from the face of the statute and is confirmed by the congressional debates: the countervailing duty was intended to offset the unfair competitive advantage that foreign producers would otherwise enjoy from export subsidies paid by their governments. *See*, e.g., 30 Cong. Rec., at 1674 (remarks of Sen. Allison), 2205 (Sen. Caffery), 2225 (Sen. Lindsay). The Treasury Department was well-positioned to establish rules of decision that would accurately carry out this purpose, particularly since it had contributed the very figures relied upon by Congress in enacting the statute.

See Zuber v. Allen, 396 U.S. 168, 192, 90 S. Ct. 314, 327, 24 L. Ed. 2d 345 (1969).

In deciding in 1898 that a nonexcessive remission of indirect taxes did not result in the type of competitive advantage that Congress intended to counter- act, the Department was clearly acting in accordance with the shared assump- tions of the day as to the fairness and economic effect of that practice. The theory underlying the Department's position was that a foreign country's re- mission of indirect taxes did not constitute subsidization of that country's ex- ports. Rather, such remission was viewed as a reasonable measure for avoiding double taxation of exports—once by the foreign country and once upon sale in this country. As explained in a recent study prepared by the Department for the Senate Committee on Finance,

> [the Department's construction was] based on the principle that, since exports are not consumed in the country of production, they should not be subject to consumption taxes in that country. The theory has been that the application of countervailing duties to the rebate of consumption [and other indirect] taxes would have the effect of double taxation of the product, since the United States would not only impose its own indirect taxes, such as Federal and state excise taxes and state and local sales taxes, but would also collect, through the use of the countervailing duty, the indirect tax imposed by the exporting country on domestically consumed goods." (Executive Branch GATT Studies, Senate Com- mittee on Finance, 93d Cong., 2d Sess., 17-18 (1974)).

This intuitively appealing principle regarding double taxation had been widely accepted both in this country and abroad for many years prior to enactment of the 1897 statute. *See,* e.g., Act of July 4, 1789 §3, 1 Stat. 26 (remission of import duties upon exportation of products); 4 D. Ricardo, Works and Correspondence 216-217 (P. Sraffa ed. 1951) (first published in 1822); A. Smith, An Inquiry Into the Nature and Causes of the Wealth of Nations, Book Four, ch. IV (1776).

C

The Secretary's interpretation of the countervailing duty statute is as permis- sible today as it was in 1898. The statute has been re-enacted five times by Congress without any modification of the relevant language, . . . and, whether or not Congress can be said to have "acquiesced" in the administrative prac- tice, it certainly has not acted to change it. At the same time, the Secretary's position has been incorporated into the General Agreement on Tariffs and Trade (GATT), which is followed by every major trading nation in the world; foreign tax systems as well as private expectations thus have been built on the assumption that countervailing duties would not be imposed on nonexcessive remissions of indirect taxes. In light of these substantial reliance interests, the longstanding administrative construction of the statute should "not be dis- turbed except for cogent reasons." McLaren v. Fleischer, 256 U.S. 477, 481,

41 S. Ct. 577, 578, 65 L. Ed. 2d 1052 (1921); *see* Udall v. Tallman, *supra,* 380 U.S., at 18, 85 S. Ct., at 802.

Aside from the contention, discussed in Part III, *infra,* that the Department's construction is inconsistent with this Court's decisions, petitioner's sole argument is that the Department's position is premised on false economic assumptions that should be rejected by the courts. In particular, petitioner points to "modern" economic theory suggesting that remission of indirect taxes may create an incentive to export in some circumstances, and to recent criticism of the GATT rules as favoring producers in countries that rely more heavily on indirect than on direct taxes.[14] But, even assuming that these arguments are at all relevant in view of the legislative history of the 1897 provision and the longstanding administrative construction of the statute, they do not demonstrate the unreasonableness of the Secretary's current position. Even "modern" economists do not agree on the ultimate economic effect of remitting indirect taxes, and—given the present state of economic knowledge—it may be difficult, if not impossible, to measure the precise effect in any particular case. *See* e.g., . . . Marks & Malmgren, *supra,* n. 1 at 351. More fundamentally, as the Senate Committee with responsibility in this area recently stated, "the issues involved in applying the countervailing duty law are complex, and . . . internationally, there is [a] lack of any satisfactory agreement on what constitutes a fair, as opposed to an 'unfair,' subsidy." S. Rep. No. 93-1298, p. 183 (1974). In this situation, it is not the task of the judiciary to substitute its views as to fairness and economic effect for those of the Secretary.

III

Notwithstanding all of the foregoing considerations, this would be a very different case if, as petitioner contends, the Secretary's practice were contrary to this Court's decision in Downs v. United States, *supra,* 187 U.S. 496, 23 S. Ct. 222, 47 L. Ed. 275. Upon close examination of the admittedly opaque opinion in that case, however, we do not believe that *Downs* is controlling on the question presented here.

The Russian sugar laws at issue in *Downs* were, as the Court noted, "very complicated." *Id.,* at 502, 23 S. Ct., at 223. Much of the Court's opinion was devoted to an exposition of these provisions, *see id.,* at 502-512, 23 S. Ct., at 223-227, but for present purposes only two features are relevant: (1) excise taxes imposed on sugar sales within Russia were remitted on exports; and (2)

---

[14]*See* Marks & Malmgren, Negotiating Nontariff Distortions to Trade, 7 Law & Poly. Intl. Bus. 327, 351-355 (1975); The United States Submission on Border Tax Adjustments to Working Party No. 4 of the Council on Border Tax Adjustments, Organization for Economic Cooperation and Development (1966), reprinted in App. 93-116; Paper Submitted by John R. Petty, Assn't Secy. of the Treasury, Twenty-First Annual Conference of the Canadian Tax Foundation (1968), reprinted in App. 117-138. Both the Secretary and GATT apparently consider remissions of direct taxes (e.g., income taxes) to be countervailable export subsidies. See Brief for the United States 18 n. 10, 37-38; GATT, Basic Instruments and Selected Documents, 9th Supp., at 186-187 (1961).

the exporter received, in addition, a certificate entitling its bearer to sell an amount of sugar in Russia, equal to the quantity exported, without paying the full excise tax otherwise due. This certificate was transferable and had a substantial market value related to the amount of tax forgiveness that it carried with it.

The Secretary, following the same interpretation of the statute that he followed here, imposed a countervailing duty based on the value of the certificates alone, and not on the excise taxes remitted on the exports themselves. Downs, the importer, sought review, claiming that the Russian system did not confer any countervailable bounty or grant within the meaning of the 1897 statute. He did not otherwise challenge the amount of the duty assessed by the Secretary.

The issue as it came before this Court, therefore, was whether a nonexcessive remission of an indirect tax, together with the granting of an additional benefit represented by the value of the certificate, constituted a "bounty or grant." Since the amount of the bounty was not in question, neither the parties nor this Court focused carefully on the distinction between remission of the excise tax and conferral of the certificate. . . .

The judgment of the Court of Customs and Patent Appeals is, accordingly, affirmed.

QUESTIONS

1. Is the statutory interpretation approach to *Zenith* persuasive? Is the 1897 history really relevant?

2. What about the fact that Congress was silent on the issue in 1974 when the issue was clearly going to be presented to the Court? Why, do you think, did not Congress attempt to resolve it? What are the implications?

3. Is *Zenith* persuasive as a matter of administrative delegation? In the face of the mandatory statutory language, would the Court have been wise to rest its position more upon congressional acquiescence and less upon executive expertise?

4. What about the Court's "promissory estoppel" approach to the GATT, especially in light of Congress' traditional (but diminishing) dislike of this executive agreement?

5. What should have been done in *Zenith* if Japan's remission to the exporter had exceeded the commodity tax on consumer electronic products?

6. What economic basis is there for distinguishing between direct and indirect taxes? Is it persuasive? Suppose a careful economic analysis were to show that 70% of a sales tax were borne by the consumer and 30% by the manufacturer while different numbers were to apply to an income tax. Would you support countervailing at the appropriate ratio in each case? In short, might the direct/indirect distinction be a useful rough and ready approximation?

7. Beyond quirks of statutory construction, what is there to be said for the *Hammond Lead* result? Note that part of the traditional logic for this result is a general dislike of suits by A to persuade the government that B is not paying enough taxes.

8. How would *Zenith* be decided under the 1979 act and the MTN Subsidies Code? See Annex A(g) of the code (*infra*) and §101 of the act.

9. Why didn't Congress just make the new rules applicable to all countervailing duty cases?

10. What if a country rebates import duties upon the exportation of a product? For example, Sacilor of France produces steel platforms, but it imports the steel used to make the platforms. France imposes a $10 tariff on the steel imported to make the platform, but when Sacilor exports the platform, France pays the company the equivalent of $11. In this situation there is a subsidy of $1, because the rebate is in excess of the actual duties paid on the imported steel. This is known as an "excessive customs drawback," and is countervailable. Is this consistent with the *Zenith* decision on the countervailability of excessive rebates of indirect taxes? We will study customs practices in Chapter VII. *See in general* 19 C.F.R. 355, Annex I, 1.3. For examples of cases holding that the nonexcessive rebate of customs duties is not a subsidy, *see, e.g.,* Frozen Potato Products From Canada, 44 Fed. Reg. 30,496 (1979); Glazed Ceramic Wall Tiles from the Philippines, 40 Fed. Reg. 37,239 (1975).

WONNACOTT, TAX ADJUSTMENTS ON INTERNATIONALLY TRADED GOODS

United States Economic Policy in an Interdependent World, Supp. 1 (The Williams Report, 1971) at 729-731

The tax treatment of goods entering into international trade has been a continuing source of dissatisfaction in the United States. When American goods are exported to Germany, for example, they are subjected not only to the regular customs duties, but also to a levy equivalent to the German internal tax on value added (11%). On the other hand, when goods are exported from Germany to the United States, the German Government provides tax credit or rebates for the tax on value added (TVA) already paid on these exports, while tax levies are made by the United States Government only on the relatively few products on which there are federal excise taxes. Furthermore, the United States exporter sees himself at a disadvantage in exporting to third markets, since the German exporter is granted tax credit for the TVA already paid on exports, while the U.S. exporter receives no such credit for the predominant tax which he pays, i.e., the corporation income tax.

This tax treatment is consistent with the rules of the General Agreement on Tariffs and Trade (GATT), which, broadly speaking, require the application of the origin principle of taxes for direct (income-type) taxation, while permitting the application of the destination principle for indirect (sales-type) taxation. That is, income taxes are generally imposed according to the location of the origin of the income, while sales-type taxes are imposed on goods according to the location of their consumption rather than the location of their production. While U.S. complaints have centered on the indirect taxes of the countries of the European Economic Community, similar treatment is generally applied to indirect taxes—including the federal excise taxes and the state sales taxes in the United States. These taxes are imposed on imported goods sold in the United States, and are not levied on goods produced in the United States for export.

Because the present practices are consistent with GATT provisions, U.S. dissatisfaction over the tax treatment of exports to the EEC has been expressed in the form of a recommendation that the GATT rules be changed. This recommendation gained its most conspicuous expression in the January 1, 1968 balance-of-payments message of President Johnson:

> American commerce is at a disadvantage because of the tax systems of some of our trading partners. Some nations give across-the-board tax rebates on exports which leave their ports and impose special border tax charges on our goods entering their country.
>
> International rules govern these special taxes under the General Agreement on Tariffs and Trade. These rules must be adjusted to expand international trade further.

The questions which this raises are really two: what are the implications of the present GATT arrangements, and what are the merits and feasibility of alternative arrangements. These two questions will be the focus of the discussion below.

I.   Internal Taxes and Adjustments at the Border

Before attention turned to a detailed consideration of U.S. complaints regarding the GATT rules on the treatment of taxes at the border, it is appropriate to look at these arrangements in some detail.

It is a useful shorthand to classify indirect or sales-type taxes as being eligible for treatment according to the destination principle; that is, exports may be exempted from taxation and rebates provided for indirect taxes already applied to exports, while levies may be made on imports equivalent to the taxes applied to domestically produced goods destined for domestic consumption. For direct or income-type taxes, the origin principle must be used, and therefore no rebates are permitted to exports on account of direct taxes paid domestically.

The taxes which are generally regarded as eligible for treatment according to the destination principle, and for which, consequently, tax adjustments may be made on goods entering international trade, are: single-stage general sales taxes; cascade (multi-stage cumulative) taxes; value added taxes; and excise taxes. On the other hand, the following are generally accepted as direct taxes which are ineligible for border adjustments; that is, they are taxed according to the origin principle: personal and corporate income taxes; capital gains taxes; wealth taxes; and estate duties.

There are a number of other taxes which are not normally considered eligible for border adjustment, but for which border adjustments have sometimes been made, namely: property taxes, employers' contributions to social security, payroll taxes, and stamp duties (e.g., taxes on transfers of certain documents).

While these ambiguous cases have from time to time been an irritant, much of the United States resentment has centered on the Tax On Value Added. This is a multi-stage tax which is broadly equivalent to a single-stage sales tax, but is collected at each step of the productive process at which sales take place.

Under the TVA as it is applied, say, in Germany, the businessman is required to apply the tax (11%) on the sales to his customers. He is then required to remit to the government the 11% tax, less any tax which he has paid to his suppliers. For example, suppose a manufacturer buys $100,000 worth of raw materials, with $11,000 in taxes being added to the price of these materials. Suppose, also, that his costs (excluding taxed inputs) and profits are $50,000. He will now sell the product for $150,000 plus the 11% tax which he is required to charge his (domestic) purchaser. His tax liability to the government will not, however, be the total 11% collected on his sales, or $16,500. Rather, from these taxes collected he may subtract the taxes of $11,000 paid on his inputs. As a result, his net tax bill will be $5,500, or 11% on the value which he has added to production. The consequences of the TVA are similar to those of a single-stage sales tax on the final product, except that part of the tax is collected at an earlier time, and there is therefore an advantage to the government and a disadvantage to the producer arising from the earlier timing of tax payments.

Because of the fundamental similarity between the TVA and a single-stage sales tax, the TVA has sometimes been characterized as analogous to counting sheep by counting their legs and dividing by four. The basic advantage to the government in the TVA—apart from the timing of tax collections—is the reduction in enforcement problems. If a seller escapes the tax collection machinery, not all the tax on his sales is lost (as would be the case with a single-stage tax); rather, the tax is lost only on the value which he has added. On the other hand, since the tax is being collected at all stages, the administrative costs tend to be high. This is particularly true where the TVA is collected at different rates on different products. (The Dutch, for example, have two rates, while the French have four.)

When goods are imported, taxes are imposed on them at the domestic rate; in this example, at 11%. At following stages of production, this 11% collected on imported inputs can be subtracted from the total tax liability, just like the tax paid on domestic inputs. Because imports are thus caught up in the whole process, an exemption of imports per se would not encourage imports (except insofar as it slightly changed the timing of tax collections, or except insofar as imports going directly to the final purchaser escaped taxation altogether.) This is so because, with a tax unpaid on imports, there would be no credit available at the next round of the productive process. The exemption of imports itself is therefore a relatively minor concession, affecting the timing of collections; it was partially practiced for a time in Denmark, with a 9% levy being made on imports compared to a standard TVA rate of 12.5%. Rather, if a significant favorable change is to be made in the treatment of imports, they must either be overtly subsidized, or, what amounts to the same thing, the producer employing imported inputs must be given credit for taxes not actually paid on imports. Such a subsidization of imports (together with taxes on exports) was used by Germany from November 29, 1968, until the float of the German mark in the fall of 1969.

On exports, no tax is collected; in this respect, the TVA is like ordinary single-stage taxes. There is no refund on exports as such. However, credit is granted for taxes paid on inputs used in the production of exports, just as it is granted for taxes paid on other inputs.

QUESTIONS

1. Had *Zenith* come out the other way, what would have been the effects for international trade?

2. Are you persuaded by the difference between the Value Added Tax (VAT) and the income tax? Note that, in essence, the VAT is a tax on gross profits, before subtraction of wages, salaries, interest, etc.

3. From an international trade viewpoint would it be desirable for the United States to replace its income tax with a VAT or deny the income tax deduction for sales taxes, excise taxes, or tariffs?

4. What is the impact of the current floating exchange rate system on the outcome of the *Zenith* case? Is it possible that exchange rate adjustments can compensate for the disadvantage of a heavier reliance on direct taxation? If so, isn't the entire border tax adjustment issue a tempest in a teapot? See G. Hufbauer and J. Erb, Subsidies in International Trade (1984) at 51-56.

5. Do you agree with the observation of William Gladstone in 1861:

> I can never think of direct and indirect taxation except that I should think of two attractive sisters . . . differing only as sisters may differ. I cannot conceive any reason why there should be unfriendly rivalry between the admirers of two such damsels. (Speech on the floor of the House of Commons, 1861).

Is there a reason for the "unfriendly rivalry" of these two systems of taxation in the context of a heavily interdependent world economy? If so, what is the answer for this rivalry on a unilateral, bilateral, or multilateral basis?

B. THE PURSUIT OF INTERNATIONAL REGULATION—AND THE GROWING SCOPE OF COUNTERVAILABILITY

1. The MTN Subsidies Code

The Multilateral Trade Negotiations produced a host of codes addressing the issues of nontariff barriers. No code was more controversial than the negotiation of an accord governing subsidies and countervailing measures.

Two issues were particularly contentious in the subsidies code negotiations—the problem of domestic (sometimes called "internal" or "production") subsidies and subsidies for agricultural exports. The materials that follow in this chapter emphasize these two problems. The Rivers and Greenwald selection describes, from the U.S. negotiators' perspective, the difficulty of trying to obtain international agreement on the domestic subsidy issue. From the U.S. standpoint domestic subsidies were a matter of legitimate international concern, as the interdependence of national economics and policies continued to grow. The excerpts from the Subsidies Code (included in the Selected Documents Supplements) and the annex to the code that follow the Rivers and Greenwald selection, should be read carefully and then compared with the U.S. legislation implementing the code, Title I of the Trade Agreements Act of 1979 (*see* Selected Documents Supplement). European governments in particular have contended that the Congress went beyond the Subsidies Code and included several areas of countervailability not covered by the code itself.

RIVERS AND GREENWALD, THE NEGOTIATION OF A CODE ON SUBSIDIES AND COUNTERVAILING MEASURES: BRIDGING FUNDAMENTAL POLICY DIFFERENCES*

11 Law & Poly. Intl. Bus. 1447, 1470-1474 (1979)

DOMESTIC SUBSIDIES

In political terms, U.S. insistence on developing agreed-upon rules governing the use of domestic or internal subsidies was perhaps the most sensitive issue raised in the MTN. Domestic subsidy programs are often at the heart of government social/economic planning. When the Italian, Canadian or Israeli government decides to encourage business to locate in a depressed region, the effects of such regional development programs on international trade are not likely to dictate government policy. Similarly, aid by the British to a nationalized steel or automobile company is not influenced by trade considerations.

* Reprinted by permission of Law & Poly. Intl. Bus. © 1979.

Nevertheless, such programs can have as serious an impact on trade and production in other countries as any direct export subsidy. In the U.S. business community, the trend toward greater government involvement in, and aid to, foreign industry has been a major concern. This was particularly so for the capital intensive industries such as steel, chemicals, computers and aircraft. In the U.S. view, unless the MTN could provide some reasonable basis for coping with the trade problems likely to arise in the coming years from such government involvement, there would be no basis for a subsidies/countervailing measures Agreement.

As mentioned before, existing GATT rules on domestic subsidies fell far short of providing a useful framework for resolving such problems. Europeans and, for that matter just about everybody else involved in the negotiations, were of course quite happy with the status quo. Any attempt at stringent international regulation of domestic subsidies would, the United States was told, amount to intolerable interference in internal policy matters.

Rhetoric aside, there were obvious limitations on the extent to which rules on domestic subsidies could be agreed to. The notion that the British government would get out of the steel business or that the Italian government would abandon, or accept fixed limits on, its programs to develop the economically-depressed MezzoGiorno was fantasy. Even the United States could not go beyond a certain point. For example, it would have been impossible for the United States to agree to a hard cap on research and development aids to industry.

The United States did believe however that there was scope to identify the types of subsidies that were most likely to have an adverse effect on the trade interests of other countries and to provide for a procedure under which any country adversely affected could first consult to see whether the problem could be worked out, and, failing resolution, be authorized to remedy the situation through the imposition of countermeasures. While the United States was not after a hard obligation limiting a country's right to use domestic subsidies, it did seek a remedy, even absent a corresponding obligation. To this end, the United States proposed a Supplementary Understanding to the subsidies/countervailing measures Code on domestic subsidies. It provided as follows:

1. Internal subsidies have a proper role in promoting important objectives of national policy. They are used by governments to, inter alia, aid economic development, facilitate structural adjustment of the economy, and avoid unemployment. Yet, in certain circumstances, such subsidy practices can have a significant impact on the economic interests of other countries.

2. Signatories agree that they will seek to avoid the use of subsidy practices in a manner which causes serious prejudice to the interests of other signatories. To the extent that a particular practice causes or is likely to cause such serious prejudice, signatories reaffirm their commitment to consult with the signatory or signatories affected with a view towards developing a mutually satisfactory solution to the problem under which the adverse effects of the particular practice would be substantially reduced or eliminated.

3. Below is a list of specific internal subsidy practices to which the foregoing

applies. The list is illustrative, not exhaustive. Further it is not intended to create any presumption—either by inclusion or by omission—that a particular practice either causes or does not cause or threaten or does not threaten serious prejudice.

(a) Government financing of commercial enterprises on terms significantly more favorable than the terms of available non-government financing. Such government financing can conclude [*sic*]:

    (i) the subscription or provision of equity capital on terms significantly more favorable to the recipient than those at which private investors would invest;

    (ii) the subscription to, or provision of, equity capital to cover significant operating losses sustained over a period of at least two successive years and in the absence of reasonable grounds to believe that such losses will cease within a reasonable period;

    (iii) the loan of funds on terms significantly more favorable to the recipient than those at which the recipient could then borrow comparable amounts from private sources, such terms to include the rate of interest due, the period of repayment, and the security provided to the lender;

    (iv) The guarantee of indebtedness incurred on terms that would, in the absence of such guarantee, be more favorable to the recipient than those at which the recipient could borrow comparable amounts, if such guarantee is provided without appropriate cost or without the existence of an actuarially-based fund from which such guarantee could be paid; and

    (v) the grant of funds without concurrent creation of a debt obligation or dilution of equity interests;

(b) Government regional development programs that provide financial assistance to enterprises locating in such regions on terms significantly more favorable than necessary to overcome the financial disadvantage of locating in such regions as compared to other geographic regions of the same country;

(c) Government financed provision of utility, supply distribution and other operational services on terms significantly more favorable than those offered to privately owned enterprises in the same country;

(d) Government benefits in such forms as reductions in or exemptions from taxation or other obligations that are available solely to specified enterprises and not generally available in that country or region of that country.

The proposal ultimately proved too ambitious for other delegations. Even though there was an express disavowal of any intention to create a presumption that the practices listed would cause serious prejudice to the trade or production interests of others, there was general concern that so detailed a listing of domestic subsidies would inevitably become the standard for acceptable or unacceptable behavior. And, in truth, the creation of such a standard was one of the U.S. objectives in fashioning the proposed Supplementary Understanding.

The U.S. proposal, however, did generate serious discussion, and out of that discussion came agreement on a number of points. First, there was recognition that widely used forms of domestic subsidies should be identified. The purpose would be to limit the scope of debate over whether a practice is a subsidy within the meaning of the Code. Second, there was general acceptance that where a domestic subsidy caused or threatened serious prejudice to the trade or production interests of another Code signatory, there should be consultations with a view to modifying the practice so as to cure the adverse effects and, should such consultations fail, a procedure under which countermeasures by the adversely affected country could be authorized. Agreement on this point would create, for the first time under GATT, an express right to take action against problems caused by domestic subsidies. Third, there was agreement that the concept of serious prejudice should be clarified. Delegations accepted the premise that serious prejudice could arise through adverse effects caused by competition in one's home market, by import substitution (i.e., reduction of imports into the subsidizing country's market) or through competition in third markets.

These points were all included in the final Agreement and constitute the heart of the new rules on domestic subsidies. They have been packaged in a manner designed to minimize the potential problems for other countries; there is recognition for example that domestic subsidies are "widely used as important instruments for the promotion of social and economic policy objectives," and a number of such objectives are listed. But when one unwraps the package, it should be clear that, while hard international rules on domestic subsidies are still some way off, we have for the first time a set of rules and procedures that offers some hope for resolving trade problems that domestic subsidies may cause.

MULTILATERAL TRADE NEGOTIATIONS SUBSIDIES CODE

Articles 1, 6, 9-11 (1979)

PART I

ARTICLE 1—APPLICATION OF ARTICLE VI OF THE GENERAL AGREEMENT

Signatories shall take all necessary steps to ensure that the imposition of a countervailing duty on any product of the territory of any signatory imported into the territory of another signatory is in accordance with the provisions of Article VI of the General Agreement and the terms of this Agreement. . . .

ARTICLE 6—DETERMINATION OF INJURY

1. A determination of injury for purposes of Article VI of the General Agreement shall involve an objective examination of both (a) the volume of subsi-

dized imports and their effect on prices in the domestic market for like products and (b) the consequent impact of these imports on domestic producers of such products. . . .

2. With regard to volume of subsidized imports the investigating authorities shall consider whether there has been a significant increase in subsidized imports, either in absolute terms or relative to production or consumption in the importing country. With regard to the effect of the subsidized imports on prices, the investigating authorities shall consider whether there has been a significant price undercutting by the subsidized imports as compared with the price of a like product of the importing country, or whether the effects of such imports is otherwise to depress prices to a significant degree or prevent price increases, which otherwise would have occurred, to a significant degree. No one or several of these factors can necessarily give decisive guidance.

3. The examination of the impact on the industry concerned shall include an evaluation of all relevant economic factors and indices having a bearing on the state of the industry such as actual and potential decline in output, sales, market share, profits, productivity, return on investments, or utilization of capacity; factors affecting domestic prices; actual and potential negative effects on cash flow, inventories, employment, wages, growth, ability to raise capital or investment and, in the case of agriculture, whether there has been an increased burden on government support programs. This list is not exhaustive, nor can one or several of these factors necessarily give decisive guidance. . . .

7. In exceptional circumstances the territory of a signatory may, for the production in question, be divided into two or more competitive markets and the producers within each market may be regarded as a separate industry if (a) the producers within such market sell all or almost all of their production of the product in question in that market, and (b) the demand in that market is not to any substantial degree supplied by producers of the product in question located elsewhere in the territory. In such circumstances, injury may be found to exist even where a major portion of the total domestic industry is not injured, provided there is a concentration of subsidized imports into such an isolated market and provided further that the subsidized imports are causing injury to the producers of all or almost all of the production within such market.

8. When the industry has been interpreted as referring to the producers in a certain area, as defined in paragraph 7 above, countervailing duties shall be levied only on the products in question consigned for final consumption to that area. When the constitutional law of the importing country does not permit the levying of countervailing duties on such a basis, the importing signatory may levy the countervailing duties without limitation, only if (1) the exporters shall have been given an opportunity to cease exporting at subsidized prices to the area concerned or otherwise give assurances . . . and adequate assurances in this regard have not been promptly given, and (2) such duties cannot be levied only on products of specific producers which supply the area in question. . . .

ARTICLE 9—EXPORT SUBSIDIES ON PRODUCTS OTHER THAN CERTAIN PRIMARY PRODUCTS

1. Signatories shall not grant export subsidies on products other than certain primary products.

2. The practices listed in points (a) to (1) in the Annex are illustrative of export subsidies.

ARTICLE 10—EXPORT SUBSIDIES ON CERTAIN PRIMARY PRODUCTS

1. In accordance with the provisions of Article XVI:3 of the General Agreement, signatories agree not to grant directly or indirectly any export subsidy on certain primary products in a manner which results in the signatory granting such subsidy having more than an equitable share of world export trade in such product, account being taken of the shares of the signatories in trade in the product concerned during a previous representative period, and any special factors which may have affected or may be affecting trade in such product.

2. For purposes of Article XVI:3 of the General Agreement and paragraph 1 above:

(a) "more than an equitable share of world export trade" shall include any case in which the effect of an export subsidy granted by a signatory is to displace the exports of another signatory bearing in mind the developments on world markets;

(b) with regard to new markets, traditional patterns of supply of the product concerned to the world market, region or country, in which the new market is situated shall be taken into account in determining "equitable share of world export trade";

(c) "a previous representative period" shall normally be the three most recent calendar years in which normal market conditions existed.

3. Signatories further agree not to grant export subsidies on exports of certain primary products to a particular market in a manner which results in prices materially below those of other suppliers to the same market.

ARTICLE 11—SUBSIDIES OTHER THAN EXPORT SUBSIDIES

1. Signatories recognize that subsidies other than export subsidies are widely used as important instruments for the promotion of social and economic policy objectives and do not intend to restrict the right of signatories to use such subsidies to achieve these and other important policy objectives which they consider desirable. Signatories note that among such objectives are:

—the elimination of industrial, economic and social disadvantages of specific regions;

—to facilitate the restructuring, under socially acceptable conditions, of certain sectors, especially where this has become necessary by reason of changes in trade and economic policies, including international agreements resulting in lower barriers to trade;

—generally to sustain employment and to encourage re-training and change in employment;

—to encourage research and development programs, especially in the field of high-technology industries;

—the implementation of economic programs and policies to promote the economic and social development of developing countries;

—redeployment of industry in order to avoid congestion and environmental problems.

2. Signatories recognize, however, that subsidies other than export subsidies, certain objectives and possible forms of which are described, respectively, in paragraphs 1 and 3 of this Article, may cause or threaten to cause injury to a domestic industry of another signatory or serious prejudice to the interests of another signatory or may nullify or impair benefits accruing to another signatory under the General Agreement, in particular where such subsidies would adversely affect the conditions of normal competition. Signatories shall therefore seek to avoid causing such effects through the use of subsidies. In particular, signatories, when drawing up their policies and practices in this field, in addition to evaluating the essential internal objectives to be achieved, shall also weigh, as far as practicable, taking account of the nature of the particular case, possible adverse effects on trade. They shall also consider the conditions of world trade, production (e.g. price, capacity utilization etc.) and supply in the product concerned.

3. Signatories recognize that the objectives mentioned in paragraph 1 above may be achieved, inter alia, by means of subsidies granted with the aim of giving an advantage to certain enterprises. Examples of possible forms of such subsidies are: government financing of commercial enterprises, including grants, loans or guarantees; government provision or government financed provision of utility, supply distribution and other operational or support services or facilities; government financing of research and development programs; fiscal incentives; and government subscription to, or provision of, equity capital.

The signatories note that the above forms of subsidy are normally granted either regionally or by sector. The enumeration of forms of subsidy set out above is illustrative and non-exhaustive, and reflects these currently granted by a number of signatories to this Agreement.

Signatories recognize, nevertheless, that the enumeration of forms of subsidy set out above should be reviewed periodically and that this should be done, through consultations, in conformity with the spirit of Article XVI:5 of the General Agreement.

4. The signatories recognize further that, without prejudice to their rights under this Agreement, nothing in paragraphs 1-3 above and in particular the enumeration of forms of subsidy creates, in itself, any basis for action under the General Agreement, as interpreted by this Agreement.

━━━━━━━━━━━━━━━━

MULTILATERAL TRADE NEGOTIATIONS SUBSIDIES CODE ANNEX

¶¶a-1 (1979)

ILLUSTRATIVE LIST OF EXPORT SUBSIDIES

(a) The provision by governments of direct subsidies to a firm or an industry contingent upon export performance.

(b) Currency retention schemes or any similar practices which involve a bonus on exports.

(c) Internal transport and freight charges on export shipments, provided or mandated by governments, on terms more favourable than for domestic shipments.

(d) The delivery by governments or their agencies of imported or domestic products or services for use in the production of exported goods, on terms or conditions more favourable than for delivery of like or directly competitive products or services for use on the production of goods for domestic consumption, if (in the case of products) such terms or conditions are more favourable than those commercially available on world markets to its exporters.

(e) The full or partial exemption, remission, or deferral specifically related to exports, of direct taxes[1] or social welfare charges paid or payable by industrial or commercial enterprises.

(f) The allowance of special deductions directly related to exports or export performance, over and above those granted in respect to production for domestic consumption, in the calculation of the base on which direct taxes are charged.

(g) The exemption or remission in respect of the production and distribution of exported products, of indirect taxes[1] in excess of those levied in respect of the production and distribution of like products when sold for domestic consumption.

---

[1] For the purpose of this Agreement:

The term "direct taxes" shall mean taxes on wages, profits, interest, rent, royalties, and all other forms of income, and taxes on the ownership of real property.

The term "import charges" shall mean tariffs, duties, and other fiscal charges not elsewhere enumerated in this note that are levied on imports.

The term "indirect taxes" shall mean sales, excise, turnover, value added, franchise, stamp, transfer, inventory and equipment taxes, border taxes, and all taxes other than direct taxes and import charges.

(h) The exemption, remission or deferral of prior stage cumulative indirect taxes[1] on goods or services used in the production of exported products in excess of the exemption, remission or deferral of like prior stage cumulative indirect taxes on goods or services used in the production of like products when sold for domestic consumption; provided, however, that prior stage cumulative indirect taxes may be exempted, remitted or deferred on exported products even when not exempted, remitted or deferred on like products when sold for domestic consumption, if the prior stage cumulative indirect taxes are levied on goods that are physically incorporated (making normal allowance for waste) in the exported product.

(i) The remission or drawback of import charges in excess of those levied on imported goods that are physically incorporated (making normal allowance for waste) in the exported product; provided, however, that in particular cases a firm may use a quantity of home market goods equal to, and having the same quality and characteristics as, the imported goods as a substitute for them in order to benefit from this provision if the import and the corresponding export operations both occur within a reasonable time period, normally not to exceed two years.

(j) The provision by governments (or special institutions controlled by governments) of export credit guarantee or insurance programs, of insurance or guarantee programs against increases in the costs of exported products or of exchange risk programmes, at premium rates, which are manifestly inadequate to cover the long-term operating costs and losses of the programmes.

(k) The grant by governments (or special institutions controlled by and/or acting under the authority of governments) of export credits at rates below those which they actually have to pay for the funds so employed (or would have to pay if they borrowed on international capital markets in order to obtain funds of the same maturity and denominated in the same currency as the export credit), or the payment by them of all or part of the costs incurred by exporters or financial institutions in obtaining credits, in so far as they are used to secure a material advantage in the field of export credit terms.

Provided, however, that if a signatory is a party to an international undertaking on official export credits to which at least twelve original signatories to this Agreement are parties as of 1 January 1979 (or a successor undertaking which has been adopted by those original signatories), or if in practice a signatory applies the interest rates provisions of the relevant undertaking, an export credit practice which is in conformity with those provisions shall not be considered an export subsidy prohibited by this Agreement.

(l) Any other charge on the public account constituting an export subsidy in the sense of Article XVI of the General Agreement.

"Prior stage" indirect taxes are those levied on goods or services used directly or indirectly in making the product.

"Cumulative" indirect taxes are multi-staged taxes levied where there is no mechanism for subsequent crediting of the tax if the goods or services subject to tax at one stage of production are used in a succeeding stage of production.

"Remission" of taxes includes the refund or rebate of taxes.

Note on the MFN Principle, Conditionality, the MTN Subsidies Code, and the Concept of Special and Differential Treatment for Developing Countries

A cardinal principle of the GATT (in Article I(1)), and U.S. trade policy, has been the application of tariff schedules on an unconditional Most-Favored-Nation (MFN) basis. Separate rationales exist for the MFN principle and the idea of unconditionality. The MFN rule was installed to avoid bilateral favoritism, maximize the welfare benefits from duty concessions, and reduce trade distortions that might induce trade wars. But does it follow that the MFN principle should be applied unconditionally, i.e., to all third countries, or should any benefits obtained be made conditional on the reciprocal acceptance of obligations?

Long ago countries began to apply countervailing duties against a single country without violating the MFN clauses in bilateral Friendship, Commerce and Navigation (FCN) treaties. Thus, it is well established that the MFN principle does not preclude retaliation against a single country for its illegal subsidies.

Moreover, the MTN Subsidies Code, along with other MTN codes covering government procurement, technical barriers to trade (standards) and customs valuation does *not* apply on an unconditional basis. As with these other accords affecting nontariff barriers to trade (NTBs), the benefits from the Subsidies Code flow only to those who have accepted its obligations. The key "benefit" to be obtained by a country exporting to the United States from being a Subsidies Code signatory is the requirement that the ITC must find material injury to a U.S. industry before countervailing duties can be imposed. A nonsignatory would instead be subject to the "old" U.S. countervailing duty law, §303 of the Tariff Act of 1930, which had no injury requirement.

Layered onto the concept of conditionality is the issue of differential treatment for less developed countries (LDCs) under the Subsidies Code. Developed countries had to decide in the MTN whether LDCs should be permitted to have export subsidy regimes that would otherwise be denied to the more developed countries. Article 14 of the Subsidies Code addresses the vexing problem of LDC treatment. It provides for "commitments" to be entered into by developing country signatories to reduce or eliminate export subsidies when the use of such export subsidies is inconsistent with competitive and development needs. When a satisfactory commitment has been entered into, countermeasures against any export subsidies of such LDC signatory are not authorized by the code. Moreover, LDC signatories are granted the advantage that there shall be no presumption that their export subsidies result in adverse effects to signatories. Such adverse effects must be demonstrated by positive evidence related to the impact on trade or production of another signatory. These dual buffers make it likely that there will be relatively few cases brought by developed country signatories against developing country export subsidies under Track II of the code (multilateral authorization of relief).

Out of this confusing statutory labyrinth you should consider these important questions. Should deviations from the principle of unconditionality be encouraged, even for NTB agreements? Does it make any sense to treat developing countries in a different fashion than developed countries? If so, what are the appropriate institutional arrangements needed to carry on the developed country-LDC dialogue in the context of the MTN Codes, the GATT, and the United Nations Conference on Trade and Development (UNCTAD)?

NOTES AND QUESTIONS

1. Which of the following subsidies are countervailable under the MTN Subsidies Code? Under U.S. legislation?

    a.   An income tax credit for R&D or for investment?

    b.   Such a credit for just those industries that happen to be major exporters?

    c.   A free-trade zone?

    d.   A subsidy to a specific depressed industry or to the firms in a particular depressed region (e.g., Appalachia, Nova Scotia, Merseyside)?

    e.   Improved public educational facilities, including the institution of innovative vocational training programs (see Fresh Cut Roses from Israel, 45 Fed. Reg. 58,516 (1980)?

    f.   Modernization of a port facility, and the construction of roads to a port (see Certain Fish from Canada, 43 Fed. Reg. 25,997 (1978); 44 Fed. Reg. 1372 (1979))?

    g.   Suspension of applicable environmental regulations for all manufacturing facilities (MX-Radial Steel Belted Tires from Canada, 38 Fed. Reg. 1018 (1973); 44 F.R. 22,052 (1979); 44 Fed. Reg. 58,517 (1979))?

2. Is the United States in conformity with the subsidy definitions of the MTN Subsidies Code? With the injury standards? On the latter point, see Note; Implementing "Tokyo Round" Commitments: The New Injury Standard in Antidumping and Countervailing Duty Laws, 32 Stan. L. Rev. 1183 (1980). For additional data on the agreement, see GAO, Benefits of International Agreement of Trade-Distorting Subsidies Not Yet Realized (GAO/NS1AD-83-10, Aug. 15, 1983).

3. Does the code appear to reflect a meeting of the minds with respect to subsidies?

4. Is such a meeting possible without fundamental agreement on political subsidy strategies (e.g., international agreement on such choices as those between "trickle-down," government ownership of industries, extended social security, etc.)?

5. What is meant within the context of the MTN Subsidies Code by:

    (a)   injury;

    (b)   serious prejudice;

    (c)   nullification; and

    (d)   adverse effects?

Are these distinctive tests or overlapping terms? What is the relationship between Article 11(2) of the code and the "nullification and impairment" concept of Article XXIII of the GATT? *See* Hudec, Regulation of Domestic Subsidies under the MTN Subsidies Code, in D. Wallace, F. Loftus, and V. Krikorian (eds.), Interface Three: Legal Treatment of Domestic Subsidies.

6. Are you persuaded that the countervailing duty law is needed, given the presence of §201 of the 1974 Act and the antidumping laws for import relief? Assuming *arguendo* that retaliatory actions by the United States to counter foreign subsidies are desirable, should harm to U.S. exports displaced by foreign subsidies be treated differently than harm to U.S. industry caused by subsidized imports entering the U.S. marketplace? What are the counterbalancing welfare benefits in each instance? *See* Barcelo, An "Injury-Only" Regime (For Imports) and Actionable Subsidies in Wallace, Loftus, and Krikorian, *supra* question 5.

2.   *Treatment of General Purpose Subsidies*

Following is the leading U.S. countervailing duty case on general economic subsidies. There are related procedural cases, e.g., ASG Industries v. United States, 657 F.2d 1226 (C.C.P.A. 1981) (remand on basis that C.C.P.A. decision at 610 F.2d 770 not followed by lower court), but the case's substantive doctrine remains solid. The case is an appeal of one of four brought by ASG challenging the secretary's determination that a range of general-purpose subsidies to foreign float-glass manufacturers were not "bounties or grants" under the statute. The others—some decided by different judges—were: ASG Industries v. United States, 467 F. Supp. 1187 (Ct. Cl. 1979) (Great Britain, secretary upheld on presumption that he was correct and on his finding that the subsidies did not distort international trade); ASG Industries v. United States, 467 U.S. 1200 (Ct. Cl. 1979) (Italy, secretary's decision struck down); and ASG Industries v. United States, 495 F. Supp. 904 (Ct. Cl. 1980) (Belgium, decision in accord with the following appellate case). For other recent interpretations, *see* Carlisle Tire and Rubber v. United States, 517 F. Supp. 704 (Ct. Intl. Trade 1981) (Taiwan, *de minimis* bicycle tire subsidies); Industrial Fasteners Group v. United States, 710 F.2d 1576 (Fed. Cir. 1983) (India, "cash compensatory support" export payments).

ASG INDUSTRIES, INC. v. UNITED STATES

610 F.2d 770 (C.C.P.A. 1979)

MILLER, J.

This is an appeal from the judgment of the United States Customs Court, 82 Cust. Ct.—, C.D. 4782 (1979), which upheld the decision of the Secretary of the Treasury ("Secretary") that float glass manufactured in West Germany did not benefit from the payment or bestowal of a bounty or grant within the meaning of section 303 of the Tariff Act of 1930, as amended (19 U.S.C. §1303). We reverse and remand.

BACKGROUND

Appellants, domestic manufacturers and wholesalers of float glass, petitioned the Commissioner of Customs for imposition of a countervailing duty on float glass manufactured in West Germany. They alleged that benefits received by float glass manufacturers in West Germany under various regional development programs, which included low-interest loans and investment subsidies in the form of cash grants and tax credits, were bounties or grants within the countervailing duty law.

The Treasury Department ("Treasury") preliminarily determined that imports of float glass from West Germany benefit from the payment or bestowal of a bounty or grant within the meaning of 19 U.S.C. §1303 by reason of the payments made under the regional development programs. After further study based on additional information, Treasury changed its position giving the following reasons:

> The German Government has advised the Treasury Department that these benefits have the effect of offsetting disadvantages which would discourage industry from moving to and expanding in less prosperous regions. Inasmuch as the recipient glass producers sell a preponderance of their production in the West German home market (not less than 80 percent and up to 99%), the level of exports to the United States is a small percentage of the amount exported, and the amount of assistance provided by the regional incentive programs is less than 2 percent of the value of float glass produced, these benefits are not regarded as bounties or grants within the meaning of section 303 of the Tariff Act of 1930, as amended (19 U.S.C. §1303).

Appellants then brought an action in the Customs Court, under 19 U.S.C. §1516(d), contesting this negative countervailing duty determination. Both sides moved for summary judgment. Appellants alleged that the payments are countervailable; the Government contended that appellants failed to establish that the alleged bounties or grants possess the requisite effect upon international trade that is necessary before countervailing duties will be imposed.

THE CUSTOMS COURT

. . . Because only up to 20 percent of the float glass manufactured by the participants in the regional development programs was sold outside the West German home market, and because the ad valorem size of the assistance provided by these programs was less than 2 percent of the value of the float glass produced, the Customs court found that, although such assistance was more than *de minimis,* "the *bounties* do not appear to have induced the sale of merchandise in such quantities or value *as would tend to distort international trade.*" (Emphasis added.) The Customs Court cited trade statistics showing increases in the United States production and exports (especially to West Germany) of float glass, and decreases in importations of West German float glass, for support of the Secretary's decision to not impose countervailing duties. Having determined that appellants "failed to overcome the presumption of correctness attaching to the action of the Secretary," the Customs Court denied appellants' motion and granted the Government's motion for summary judgment.

OPINION

Essentially, appellants argue that, since the countervailing duty statute is mandatory, once the Secretary has determined that foreign manufacturers are receiving any benefit from their government, a countervailing duty must be imposed. The Government, agreeing with the Customs Court, argues that the legislative history and case law show that Congress intended countervailing duties to be imposed only against those programs and actions of a foreign government that have been shown to distort international trade and that the following factors involved in international trade distortion must be considered in determining the existence of a bounty or grant: (1) the ad valorem size of the benefits; (2) the level of exports from the foreign country of goods receiving the benefits; and (3) whether the benefit programs had a positive effect on these exports.

With respect to the ad valorem size of the benefits, the Government's concession that the benefits under the regional development programs are not *de minimis* establishes, prima facie, that this factor is met. The finding by Treasury that up to 20 percent of the goods are exported likewise establishes that the second factor is met. As to whether the benefit programs had a positive effect on exports, Treasury's finding that "the amount of assistance provided by the regional incentive programs is less than 2 percent of the value of float glass produced" does not, without more, overcome a presumption that such benefits had a positive effect, or would have a potentially positive effect, on exports, particularly when compared to the average ad valorem rate of duty of 8.2 percent during the year involved (1974), as pointed out by appellant. *See* 42 Fed. Reg. 23146-47 (1977), where Treasury determined that "bounties or grants were being paid or bestowed, directly or indirectly on exports of certain fasteners [nuts, bolts, and cap screws] from Japan," the benefits being .20 percent ad valorem. It said that, ordinarily, benefits of this size might be considered *de minimis* in relation to the value of the merchandise, but that they were "significant" when compared to the regular duty rate (up to .75 percent on an ad valorem basis.) *See also* 42 Fed. Reg. 28531 (1977) (aggregate benefits of eight tenths of one percent under a preferential loan program were greater than *de minimis* and it was, therefore, determined that the involved goods received bounties or grants within the meaning of section 303 of the Tariff Act of 1930, as amended). . . .

Congress also made clear its understanding that "the present [countervailing duty] statute is mandatory in terms." H.R. Rep. No. 93-571, 93d Cong., 1st Sess. 73 (1973). This demonstrates that, except for the waiver provision in the 1974 Act, the Secretary has not had any discretion to not impose a countervailing duty once it has been determined that a bounty or grant is being paid or bestowed. American Express Co. v. United States, 60 C.C.P.A. 86, 93, 472 F.2d 1050, 1056 (1973). Also, by including a requirement that the Secretary reach a final countervailing duty determination within one year of the filing of a petition (19 U.S.C. §1303(a)(4)), Congress indicated its intent to put an end to Treasury Department practice calculated "to stretch out or even shelve countervailing duty investigations for reasons which have nothing to do with the clear and mandatory nature of the countervailing duty law." S. Rep. No. 93-1298, *supra* at 183, *reprinted in* [1974] U.S. Code Cong. & Admin. News, *supra* at 7318. To permit the Secretary to place a narrow or restricted interpretation on "bounty" or "grant" as a basis for a negative countervailing duty determination would clearly frustrate the Congressional purpose of "assuring effective protection of domestic interests from foreign subsidies. . . ." *Id.* . . .

Accordingly, we conclude that it was error to employ an injury (to United States trade) test in determining whether a bounty or grant was paid upon the manufacture or production of the involved merchandise. Also, we hold that, for purposes of the countervailing duty law, the benefits (as analyzed above) bestowed by West Germany upon float glass manufacturers under the regional development programs were bounties or grants.

At the same time, it must also be pointed out that appellants' proposed test (any benefit, that is not *de minimis,* bestowed by a foreign government in connection with the production of merchandise requires a countervailing duty) ignores the clear wording of the statute. Once it has been determined that a bounty or grant is being paid or bestowed, 19 U.S.C. §1303(a)(1) provides that "there shall be levied . . . a duty equal to the *net amount* of such bounty or grant." (Emphasis supplied.) Such language implies that certain deductions may be made from the actual payments to calculate the net bounty or grant and that all relevant circumstances are to be taken into account. . . .

Although the Secretary apparently made a feeble attempt to calculate the amount of the net bounty or grant involved here, the statement that "[t]he German Government has advised the Treasury Department that these benefits have the effect of offsetting disadvantages which would discourage industry from moving to and expanding in less prosperous regions" is totally inadequate. If a *factual basis* were shown for such an assertion, it might be concluded that no net bounty or grant was involved. However, contrary to the dissenting opinion, the statement that Treasury was "advised" is hardly a factual basis supporting the conclusion that there was no bounty or grant. *See*

Yale University v. Department of Commerce, 65 C.C.P.A. 97, 104, 579 F.2d 626, 632-33 (1977). Once it is established that a foreign manufacturer is receiving payments *such as those here involved* (*not* "every payment," as the dissenting opinion imagines) from its government, a countervailing duty *must,* absent a waiver by the Secretary, be imposed unless, in considering all circumstances surrounding the payment, certain deductions can be established resulting in no net benefit to that manufacturer. These deductions must be established by facts—not by mere allegations of the foreign government or of the enterprises receiving the bounty or grant. Needless to say, without an adequate factual record, neither this court nor the Customs Court can perform a meaningful judicial review of countervailing duty determinations. . . .

In view of all the foregoing, we reverse the judgment of the Customs Court and remand for further proceedings consistent with this opinion.

MARKEY, Chief Judge, with whom RICH, Judge, joins, dissenting. . . .

If the presumption and burden application of 28 U.S.C. §2635(a) means anything,[1] it means that only after a domestic manufacturer has submitted evidence that a payment constituted a bounty, i.e., some evidence that the Secretary's negative decision was incorrect, need the Secretary be required to go forward with evidence in support of his decision. Even then, the ultimate burden of proving the Secretary's decision incorrect remains with the domestic manufacturer. In the present record, I find no evidence submitted by appellants that the payments here involved constituted a bounty, and the majority opinion cites none. Absent that proof, the question of whether the Secretary's bases for his decision would appear adequate to this court is simply not, and should not be, reached.

I agree that American manufacturers carry a burden most heavy and probably unfair. They are faced with a presumption of correctness favoring the Secretary's negative finding, and have limited access to foreign data more readily available to the Secretary and to an importer. But the cure is for Congress to devise. No judge is and none ever truly was, an oracle. That judges do make law, however, argues for reasoned restraint, and for limitation of that institutional imperative to cases of clear necessity. Concerning the design and placement of the present burden of proof, Congress has spoken, leaving no room in this case for the courtroom creativity reflected in the majority opinion.

---

[1] The court may be referring to 28 U.S.C. §2639, Burden of proof; evidence of value, subsection (a):

> (a)(1) Except as provided in paragraph (2) of this subsection, in any civil action commenced in the Court of International Trade under section 515, 516, or 516A of the Tariff Act of 1930, the decision of the Secretary of the Treasury, the administering authority, or the International Trade Commission is presumed to be correct. The burden of proving otherwise shall rest upon the party challenging such decision.
> (2) The provisions of paragraph (1) of this subsection shall not apply to any civil action commenced in the Court of International Trade under section 1582 of this title.
>   —EDS.

THE MERITS

Assuming the existence of a basis for disregarding Congress' placement of the burden of proof, and for thereby opening the door to judicial probing of the Secretary's reasoning in this case, I would nonetheless affirm the judgment below.

Concerning the determination of the existence or nonexistence of a bounty, the Congress unquestionably left to the Secretary the clear discretion to decide. Congress has, moreover, consistently refused to impede or guide that discretion by statutory definition or guidelines to be used in its exercise.[5] Absent violation of the Constitution, or a concern of virtually equal dimension, the courts should not rush in where the people's representatives have refused to tread.

Naked of guidance, and faced with provisions for judicial review, the Secretary has assertedly employed a guideline of his own devising, i.e., the presence or absence of distortions and of barriers to trade caused by the challenged payments. Though "distortions" and "barriers" are terms undefined, the Secretary's references to sales of float glass in various locales were apparently meant to show absence of distortion or of erected barriers. The Secretary's approach to the exercise of his discretion is in my view perfectly reasonable.

In all events, the Secretary's approach appears far more reasonable than that set forth in the majority opinion. Reasonableness resides in equating the absence of a bounty with failure of a payment to produce adverse trade effects. The majority opinion's effective equation of every payment to a foreign manufacturer (by a government, person, partnership, association, cartel, or corporation) with a bounty is an approach not recommended by reason. It is creative of chaos. Administrative, diplomatic, and judicial channels would be clogged if every payment to every manufacturer were presumptively a bounty and subject to judicial review for its "net" amount, and if that review were available to every manufacturer upon a mere showing that a payment had been

---

[5] The majority opinion appears oblivious to the Secretary's discretion to determine what is or is not a bounty or grant. This court has stated, "Congress' intent to provide a wide latitude, within which the [Secretary] may determine the existence or nonexistence of a bounty or grant, is clear from the statute itself, and from the congressional refusal to define the words 'bounty,' 'grant' . . . in the statute or anywhere else, for almost 80 years." United States v. Zenith Radio Corp., 562 F.2d 1209, 1216 (C.C.P.A. 1977), aff'd, 437 U.S. 443, 98 S. Ct. 2441, 57 L. Ed. 2d 337 (1978). In reporting the Trade Agreements Act of 1979, Congress acknowledged that, under the provision here at issue, "The Secretary of the Treasury has discretion in determining what is a bounty or a grant." Report of the Committee on Finance of the United States Senate on H.R. 4537, S. Rep. No. 96-249, 96th Cong., 1st Sess. 84 (1979). See also Berger, Judicial Review of Countervailing Duty Determinations, 19 Harv. Intl. L.J. 593, 604-606 (1978); O'Neill, United States Countervailing Duty Law: Renewed, Revamped and Revisited—Trade Act of 1974, 17 B.C. Indust. & Comm. L. Rev. 832, 864 (1976); Butler, Countervailing Duties and Export Subsidization: A Reemerging Issue in International Trade, 9 Va. J. Intl. L. 82, 125 (1969). As this court has repeatedly stated, countervailing duty determinations involve complex economic and foreign policy decisions of a delicate nature, for which the courts are woefully ill-equipped. United States v. Hammond Lead Products, Inc., 58 C.C.P.A. 129, C.A.D. 1017, 440 F.2d 1024, cert. denied, 404 U.S. 1005, 92 S. Ct. 565, 30 L. Ed. 2d 558 (1971); United States v. Zenith Radio Corp., supra.

made. The law is not, and should not be made, an adversary of common, practical sense. . . .

Moreover, if a bounty could exist without adverse effect on international trade, who cares? What would there be to shout about on the international stage? And, absent adverse effects and distortions to be reduced and eliminated, whence the bases for waiver? . . .

QUESTIONS

1. Does the majority's interpretation leave a foreign nation or industry in economic difficulty any possibility of subsidy without triggering rights to countervail? Is this healthy?

2. Is the information needed to carry out this court's interpretation of the statute likely to be sensitive? What might lead a foreign government to provide the necessary data?

3. In light of the statute, could the court have reached any other conclusion?

4. How much should the court let its review of the secretary's determination amount to a *de novo* factual determination? *See* Michelin Tire v. United States, 469 F. Supp. 270 (Ct. Cl. 1979) (Canadian provisions for depressed areas).

3. Calculating the Valuation of Subsidies

The materials in this chapter have emphasized the identification of countervailable subsidies under the MTN Subsidies Code and U.S. law. An equally important issue is the technique that is employed to calculate the value of the subsidy. Three issues need to be addressed during the course of the valuation allocation calculation: shape, length, and discount rate.

"Shape" describes the flow in the benefit stream, and when the subsidy benefits arise. Three shapes form heuristic models for analysis:

(1) if equal benefits arise each year, the shape is flat, or horizontal:

_____

This is also known as an annuity-style schedule;

(2) if higher benefits arise in earlier years, "front loading" of subsidy benefits will occur under the following schedule; and

_____

(3) a shape could be fashioned that would provide greater benefits over time, increasing as production comes on stream:

_____

By 1984 the Commerce Department had shifted to a declining balance schedule (model 2), effectively "front loading" the benefit stream in both nominal and effective terms.

"Length" involves the problem of calculating the number of years a given subsidy is determined to last. In other words, when does the benefit begin and when does it end? Although the Commerce Department has in the past distinguished between "large" and "small" grants, and grants "tied" to the purchase of capital equipment and "untied" grants, its current practice is to allocate larger grants over the average useful life of the company's renewable capital assets (when the sum of grants received in one year exceeds 0.5% of the company's gross revenue in that year). Smaller grants are allocated to the year of receipt.

The "discount rate" is a reflection of what a firm could do with the subsidy provided over time. A firm, as a consumer of a subsidy, may be indifferent whether it receives $1.00 today or $1.20 one year from now. If so, its discount rate for the intervening year would be 20%.

Another way of viewing the "discount rate" is the concept of the time value of money, or a company's time preference for money. The discount rate used by the Commerce Department prior to 1982 was zero. This reflected a degree of naivete about the real world, in which money has a changing value over time. The following selection describes the methodology used in the 1982 steel cases that reflected a conscious determination that the prior calculations substantially understated the value of the money that was being received.

A key issue left unresolved by the 1982 steel decisions was the appropriate level for the discount rate. In the 1982 decisions the national cost of long-term corporate debt was used as the appropriate referent. In 1984 Commerce established a firm-specific discount rate based on each firm's weighted cost of capital (WCC). The formula currently applied by Commerce is:

$$WCC = K_d\,(D/D+E) \;+\; K_e\,(E/D+E)$$

Where

D = value of outstanding debt,
E = value of outstanding equity,
K_d = marginal cost of debt,
K_e = K_d + (national average rate of return on equity = national average cost of debt, if this is greater than 0)

See 49 Fed. Reg. at 18,017 (April 26, 1984).

In the 1979 Act (§771(5)), Congress detailed the meaning of "subsidy," and clearly sought to countervail both against export subsidies and against those domestic subsidies that are particular to specific industries. The following excerpt shows the difficulty of applying the concepts of shape, length, and discount rates to domestic subsidies.

RE PRELIMINARY COUNTERVAILING DUTY DETERMINATIONS CONCERNING CERTAIN STEEL PRODUCTS ORIGINATING IN BELGIUM

2 C.M.L.R. 550 (1982)

APPENDIX B

[1] Several basic issues are common to many of the countervailing duty investigations of certain steel products, initiated by the Department of Commerce (the "Department") on 1 February 1982, e.g. government assistance through grants, loans, equity infusions, and research and development projects. This Appendix describes in some detail the general principles applied by the Department when dealing with these issues as they arise within the factual contexts of these cases.

GRANTS

[2] Petitioners allege that respondent foreign steel companies have received numerous grants for various purposes. Under section 771(5)(B) of the Tariff Act of 1930, as amended ("the Act") (19 U.S.C. 1677(5)(B)), domestic subsidies are countervailable where they are "provided or required by government action to a *specific* enterprise or industry, or group of enterprises or industries" (emphasis added).

[3] The legislative history of Title VII of the Act states that where a grant is "tied" to—that is, bestowed expressly to purchase—costly pieces of capital equipment, the benefit flowing from the grant should be allocated over the useful life of that equipment. A subsidy for capital equipment should also be "front loaded" in these circumstances; that is, allocated more heavily to the earlier years of the equipment's useful life, reflecting its greater commercial impact and benefit in those years.

[4] In the past we have allocated the face value of the grant, in equal increments, over the appropriate time period. For large capital equipment, we used a period of half the useful life of the equipment purchased with the grant. In each year we countervailed only that year's allocated portion of the total grant. For example, a hypothetical grant of $100 million used to purchase a machine with a 20-year life would have been countervailed at a rate of $10 million per year (allocated over the appropriate product group) for 10 years, beginning in the year of receipt.

[5] This allocation technique has often been criticised for not capturing the entire subsidy by ignoring the time value of money. It has been argued that $100 million today is much more valuable to a grant recipient than $10 million per year for the next 10 years, since the present value of the latter is considerably less than $100 million. We agree, and are now changing our methodology of grant subsidy calculation to reflect this agreement. So long as

the present value (in the year of grant receipt) of the amounts allocated over time does not exceed the face value of the grant, we are consistent with both our domestic law and international obligations because the amount countervailed will not exceed the total net subsidy.

[6] Present value is calculated using a discount rate. We considered using each company's weighted cost of capital at the time of the grant receipt as the appropriate measure of the time value of its funds. However, we lacked sufficient information to do so for these preliminary determinations. Instead we used the national cost of long-term corporate debt as a substitute measure of a company's discount rate. We welcome additional information or comments on this estimate between the preliminary and final determinations.

[7] For costly pieces of capital equipment, we believe that the appropriate time period over which to allocate the subsidy is its entire useful life. In the past, we allocated the subsidy over only half the useful life in order to front load the countervailing duties in order to comply with the legislative intent of the Act. However, so long as we allocate the subsidy in equal nominal increments over the entire useful life, it will still be effectively front loaded in real terms since money tomorrow is less valuable than money today.

[8] For these steel investigations we have allocated a grant over the useful life of equipment purchased with it when the value of that grant was large (in these investigations, greater than $50 million), and specifically "tied" to pieces of capital equipment.

[9] Where the grant was small (less than one percent of the company's gross revenues or, where we do not know gross revenues, less than one percent of the company's total value of 1981 steel production) and 'tied' to items generally expended in the year purchased (e.g. wages, purchases of materials), we have allocated the subsidy solely to the year of the grant receipt.

[10] All other grants—the vast majority of those involved in these investigations—will be allocated over 15 years, a period of time reflecting the average life of capital assets in integrated steel mills in the United States. The 15-year figure is based on Internal Revenue Service studies of actual experience in integrated mills in the United States. Furthermore, we understand that a 15-year period is also used in some of the countries involved in these investigations. We are using this time period as the best available estimate of the average steel asset life worldwide. We could not calculate the average life of capital assets on a company-by-company basis, since different accounting principles, extraordinary write-offs, and corporate reorganisations yielded extremely inconsistent results. For example, the average life of one steel company's assets, as indicated on its books, increased from three years to 22 years within three years.

[11] We do not distinguish grants bestowed expressly to cover operating losses from other "untied" grants. Since grants used to cover operating losses often keep the company in business and are frequently quite large, their real effects extend for a considerable period of time. It is appropriate to allocate them over a number of years.

LOANS AND LOAN GUARANTEES FOR COMPANIES CONSIDERED CREDITWORTHY

[12] In these investigations, various loan activities give rise to subsidies. The most common practice is the extension of a loan at a preferential interest rate where the government is either the actual lender or directs a private bank to lend at a preferential rate. The subsidy is computed by comparing what a company would pay a normal commercial lender in principal and interest in any given year with what the company actually pays on the preferential loan in that year. We determine what a company would pay a normal commercial lender by constructing a comparable commercial loan at the appropriate market rate (the "benchmark"). If the preferential loan is part of a broad, national lending programme, we use a national average commercial interest rate as our benchmark. If the loan programme is not generally available—like most large loans to respondent steel companies—the benchmark used instead, where available, is the company's actual commercial credit experience (e.g. a contemporaneous loan to the company from a private commercial lender). If there were no similar loans, the national commercial rate is used as a second-best alternative. . . .

LOANS AND LOAN GUARANTEES FOR COMPANIES CONSIDERED UNCREDITWORTHY

[18] In a number of cases petitioners have alleged that certain respondent steel companies were uncreditworthy at the time they received preferential loans or guarantees, and that they could not have obtained any commercial loan without government intervention.

[19] Where the company under investigation has a history of deep or significant continuing losses, and diminishing (if any) access to private lenders, we generally agree with petitioners. In these situations neither national nor company-specific market interest rates provide an appropriate benchmark since, by definition, an uncreditworthy company could not receive loans on these terms without government intervention. Nor have we been able to find any reasonable and practical basis for selecting a risk premium to be added to a national interest rate in order to establish an appropriate benchmark for companies considered uncreditworthy. Therefore, we have treated loans to an uncreditworthy company as an equity infusion by the government. We believe this treatment is justified by the great risk, very junior status, and low probability of repayment of these loans. To the extent that principal and/or interest is actually paid on these loans, however, the subsidy (which is calculated using our equity methodology, *infra*) is reduced dollar for dollar in the year of repayment. Moreover, in no case do we countervail a loan subsidy to a creditworthy or uncreditworthy company more than if the government gave the principal as an outright grant.

EQUITY

[20] Petitioners allege that government purchases of equity in respondent steel companies constitute a countervailable subsidy equal to the entire

amount of the equity purchased. Many respondents claim that such equity purchases are investments on commercial terms, and thus are not subsidies to these companies.

[21] It is well settled that government equity ownership per se is not a subsidy. Such ownership is a subsidy only when it is on terms inconsistent with commercial considerations. An equity subsidy potentially arises when the government makes equity infusions into a company which is sustaining deep or significant continuing losses. If such losses have been incurred, then we consider from whom the equity was purchased and at what price.

[22] If the government buys previously issued shares on the market and not directly from the company, there is no subsidy to the company. This is true no matter what price the government pays, since any overpayment benefits only the prior shareholders and not the company.

[23] If the government buys shares directly from the company (either a new issue or corporate treasury stock) and similar shares are traded in a market, a subsidy arises if the government pays more than the prevailing market price. To avoid any effect on the market price resulting from the government's purchase or speculation in anticipation of such purchase, we used for comparison a market price on a date sufficiently preceding the government's action. Any amount of overpayment is treated as a grant to the company.

[24] It is more difficult to judge the possible subsidy effects of direct government infusions of equity where there is no market price for the shares since they were untraded (as where, for example, the government is already sole owner of the company). As a matter of principle, government equity participation can be a legitimate commercial venture. Often, however, as in many of these steel cases, equity infusions follow massive or sustained losses and are part of national government programmes to sustain or rationalise an industry which otherwise would be non-competitive. We respect the government's characterisation of its infusion as equity in a commercial venture. However, to the extent in any year that the government realises a rate of return on its equity investment less than the average rate of return on equity investment for the country as a whole (thus including returns on both successful and unsuccessful investments), its equity infusion is considered a subsidy. Under no circumstances do we countervail an amount greater than that which is calculated treating the government's equity infusion as an outright grant.

FORGIVENESS OF DEBT

[25] Where we have found that the government has forgiven an outstanding debt obligation, we have treated this as a grant to the company equal to the outstanding principal at the time of forgiveness. Where outstanding debt has been converted into equity (i.e. the government receives shares in the company in return for eliminating debt obligations of the company), a subsidy may result. The existence and extent of such subsidies are determined by treating the conversions as an equity infusion in the amount of the remaining principal of the debt. We then calculate the value of the subsidy by using our equity methodology, *supra*. . . .

RESEARCH AND DEVELOPMENT GRANTS AND LOANS

[30] Grants and preferential loans awarded by a government to finance research that has broad application and yields results which are made publicly available are not subsidies. Programmes of organisations or institutions established to finance research on problems affecting only a particular industry or group of industries (e.g. metallurgical testing to find ways to make cold-rolled sheet easier to galvanise) and which yield results that are available only to producers in that country (or a limited number of countries) confer a subsidy on the products which benefit from the results of the research and development ("R & D"). On the other hand, programmes which provide funds for R & D in a wide range of industries are not countervailable even when a portion of the funds is provided to the steel sector.

[31] Once we determine that a particular programme is countervailable, we calculate the value of the subsidy by reference to the form in which the R & D was funded. An R & D grant is treated as an "untied" grant; a loan for R & D is treated as any other preferential loan.

LABOUR SUBSIDIES

[32] To be countervailable, a benefit programme for workers must give preferential benefits to workers in a particular industry or in a particular region. Whether or not the programme benefits specifically some workers and not others is determined by looking at both programme eligibility and participation. Even where provided to workers in specific industries, social welfare programmes are countervailable only to the extent that they relieve the firm of costs it would ordinarily incur—for example, the government's assumption of a firm's obligation partially to fund worker pensions.

Note Herein of Subsidies, Targeting, and Industrial Policy

Custodial governmental actions that directly affect the structure of an economy may be described alternatively as "subsidies," "targeting," or "industrial policy." Fundamentally, governments will try to shore up employment in depressed ("sunset") industries or shift employment to emerging, winner ("sunrise") industries. Industrial policy connotes an active *governmental* effort to shift domestic *economic* gears.

How active governmental intervention should be is controversial. Much current U.S. infatuation with the notion of industrial policy stems from the association made by many with the extent to which the Ministry of International Trade and Investment (MITI) or other governmental agencies in Japan deserve credit for the spectacular growth of the Japanese economy. Given the enormous energy and intelligence of the Japanese people, its probable economic success would have resulted in Japan in any event at some point absent

MITI. Does the experience of Japan have any relevance for the United States, anyway, given the differing cultural contexts? Among the industries said to have been targeted by Japan and other countries are computers, microelectronics, robotics, machine tools, and aerospace.

Assessments of industrial policy in Western Europe and Japan suggest that its core is use of the *political system* to direct capital and labor into areas that would otherwise be neglected if reliance were placed solely on *market forces*. "Industrial policy" is such a broad term that it could encompass Italy's efforts to shore up its depressed Mezzogiorno, the efforts of the British, French, and Belgian governments to rescue failing steel industries, the creation of emergency cartels in Japan to bail out particular industries, or U.S. federally sponsored research in high-tech industries.

From a trade policy perspective, the issue is whether targeting should be considered as a form of governmental export subsidy, or some other type of unfair foreign trade practice that should be moved against. To date, efforts to make targeting an unfair foreign trade practice have been unsuccessful. The analytical problem is whether a particular *domestic* program with *domestic* objectives should be moved against if it has broader *international* effects and implications. For example, Canada provides government assistance for fishermen in its depressed maritime provinces of Nova Scotia and Newfoundland for social and political reasons. Yet over 80 percent of the fish caught in Canada are exported, and the majority of those exports come to the United States. From the standpoint of the U.S. fishing industry, Canada has given an export subsidy designed to provide a competitive advantage. From the perspective of the Canadian government, it has provided a domestic industry with assistance to continue a "way of life" that is important to the fabric of the nation and has helped it stay in power. Where one stands on this issue may depend on where one sits.

In terms of U.S. domestic politics, Democrats in the 1980s have been particularly enamored of the alleged need to pursue an "active" industrial policy to counter the governmental assistance policies of other nations, while the Republican party has tended to favor a more unfettered capitalism. In the trade policy context, industrial policy may be protectionism. Import restraints on steel may be described as an industrial policy designed to promote the U.S. steel industry.

In considering what is "unfair" you should bear in mind the increasing interdependence in the world economy. As trade and investment increase internationally, the relevance of governmental actions of all types for other countries also increases.

Bibliographical Note

For more on targeting, *see* ITC, Foreign Industrial Targeting and Its Effects on U.S. Industries: Phase I—Japan (U.S.I.T.C. Pub. No. 1437) (1983). On industrial policy, *see* I. Magaziner and R. Reich, Minding America's Business (1982); J. Pinder (ed.), National Industrial Strategies and the World Economy (1982); C. Johnson (ed.), The Industrial Policy Debate (1984); and B. Hindley (ed.), State Investment Companies in Western Europe: Picking Winners or Backing Losers? (1984).

NOTES AND QUESTIONS

1. Is the Commerce analysis consistent with the statute? With *ASG?*

2. Would the European steel arrangement described in Chapter III trigger countervailing duties? What about subsidies to help the industry's workers prepare for and find new jobs?

3. In light of Table 6-1, *supra* p. 336, and the Featherbedders chart from The Economist, Dec. 25, 1982, at p. 76, what alternative is there to the U.S. legislative position?

4. Suppose that U.S. steel firms have initiated countervailing duty proceedings against Brazil, on the theory that (a) U.S. Exim bank loans to Brazil (at low interest rates) to purchase U.S. steel mill equipment and (b) World Bank loans (again at low interest rates) to build the mills constitute subsidies.

Suppose the ITA is facing the question of whether these actions constitute subsidies for the purposes of countervailing. As the U.S. lawyer hired by the Brazilian government to resolve this situation, you have been asked to prepare a briefing for the Brazilian president on the likely outcome of the situation and on the various responses that his nation may make. Please do so.

You may assume that Brazil has *not* accepted the MTN Subsidy Code, but that it might do so if that would help it in the current situation. As further information that you may want, the World Bank is a public, international organization dedicated to international economic development. The United States plays a leading role in it. Also, you may assume that the Exim bank's loan was not in violation of any regulations or procedures implemented under the following provision (12 U.S.C. §635a-2):

Implementation of regulations and procedures to lessen adverse effect of loans and guarantees on industries in United States; report by United States International Trade Commission

The Bank shall implement such regulations and procedures as may be appropriate to insure—that full consideration is given to the extent to which any loan or financial guarantee is likely to have an adverse effect on industries, including agriculture, and employment in the United States, either by reducing demand for goods produced in the United States or by increasing imports to the United States. To carry out the purposes of this subsection, the Bank shall request, and the United States International Trade Commission shall furnish, a report assessing the impact of the Bank's activities on industries and employment in the United States. Such report shall include an assessment of previous loans or financial guarantees and shall provide recommendations concerning general areas

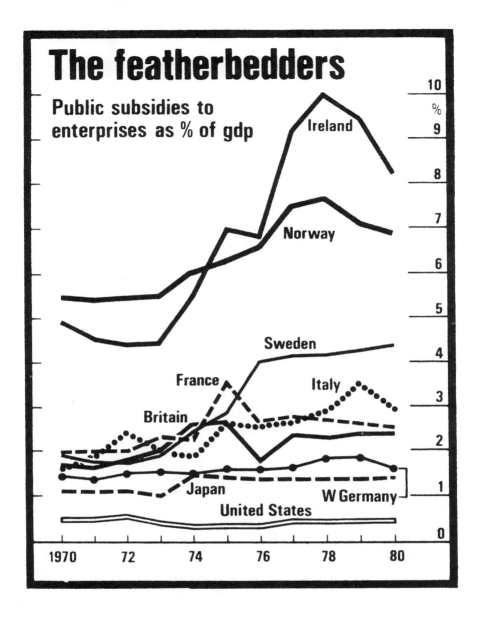

The featherbedders

Public subsidies to enterprises as % of gdp

Ireland

Norway

Sweden

France

Italy

Britain

Japan

W Germany

United States

10
%
9
8
7
6
5
4
3
2
1
0

1970   72   74   76   78   80

which may adversely affect domestic industries, including agriculture, and employment.

5. Would you favor an agreement among developed nations to restrict export credits for the construction of steel mills in developing countries? The United States proposed such an agreement in December, 1983.

6. The U.S. producers of expendable launch vehicles (ELVs) complain that the Member States of the European Space Agency (ESA) are subsidizing the activities of a French company, Arianespace, S.A., in the following manner:

(a) Member States of ESA have agreed to pay 25% to 33% per launch more than is charged on the export market for the same services;

(b) the French national space agency provides launch and range facilities and services and/or personnel, at no charge, or unreasonably low cost, to Arianespace.

What results under:

(1) the MTN subsidies code
(2) the U.S. countervailing duty law?

See Petition filed on May 25, 1984, before the Office of the U.S. Trade Representative by Transpace Carriers, Inc.

7. Assume that U.S. Steel files a countervailing duty petition against British Steel on the grounds that the government of the United Kingdom, by underwriting British Steel's huge operating losses for the three previous years, had provided an "export subsidy" within the meaning of the MTA on subsidies and the 1979 Act.

British Steel counters by citing the earlier refusal of the U.S. government in 1978 to countervail against steel imports from Italy's Terni Steel, 98.6% of whose shares are owned by Finsider, which is the financial holding company for the Italian state steel industry. *See* Grain Oriented Silicon Electrical Steel from Italy, 44 Fed. Reg. 9, 638 (1970). *Contrast with* Certain Steel Powders from Italy, 47 Fed. Reg. 39,356, 39,357 (1982). What result? *See* MTN Subsidies Code, Article 11; *see* 1979 Act, §101, and Certain Steel Structural Shapes, Hot-Rolled Carbon Steel Plate, and Hot-Rolled Carbon Steel Bar from the United Kingdom, 47 Fed. Reg. 39,384, 39,386 (1982).

8. Suppose that the People's Republic of China (PRC), to earn badly needed foreign exchange, has begun to export a vehicle known as the "Beijing Tiger" to the United States. Unexpectedly, the automobile "takes off" in the U.S. marketplace, rising from 0% of the U.S. market in the early 1980s to 6% of the U.S. market (in terms of volume) in the mid-1980s.

If the U.S. auto industry comes to you asking about countervailing duty relief, what special problems do you see?

What would be the implication of the following hypothetical facts?

(1) The Beijing Tiger, which is a cross between a bulky four-wheel drive vehicle and a light truck, sells for $8,000 in the U.S. marketplace, while the

vehicle it most nearly resembles in the United States, the Jeep Waggoneer, sells for $10,000. A comparable model of the Beijing Tiger is apparently produced in Taiwan for $11,000, and in Thailand for $8,000. The cost of production of the Jeep Waggoneer is $9,000. The PRC exports the vehicle to Taiwan and India as well as the United States;

(2) The size of the U.S. automobile market has remained static in terms of volume, while overall import penetration has remained constant in the 1982-1984 period at approximately 27%;

(3) The U.S.-Japan VRA is not renewed by Japan;

(4) The Beijing Tigers are paid for by U.S. importers through a complicated barter transaction;

(5) No U.S., or other, automobiles are permitted to be imported into the PRC;

(6) The Beijing Tigers are produced in a joint venture with AMC Jeep of Kenosha, Wisconsin, in Fujian province, PRC, on a 50-50 equity split basis;

(7) The national and provincial authorities in the PRC have "targeted" the vehicle industry for special assistance, by providing accelerated depreciation, direct cash grants, and duty-free treatment for imports of the capital equipment used in the manufacture of the products;

(8) The vehicle has an expandable rear portion that may be "pulled out" in stretch fashion and used as a cab to carry equipment, in the same fashion as a light truck.

On the issues of subsidies in a socialist economy, *see* Continental Steel v. United States, Slip. Op. 85-77, 7 I.T.R.D. 1001 (C.I.T. 1985), which holds that the U.S. countervailing duty laws may reach exports from communist countries that are subsidized.

9. On January 1, 1981, the PRC introduced a system under which the Bank of China gives an exchange rate of 2.8 yuan to the dollar to Chinese enterprises engaged in foreign trade. This internal settlement rate contrasts with an official foreign exchange rate, pegged to a basket of currencies, which on May 31, 1983, was 1.9939 yuan to the dollar. National enterprises engaged in foreign trade are allowed to retain 10-15% of their foreign exchange earnings, which can be traded at the internal settlement rate to other national enterprises. Is this system of multiple exchange rates the proper subject of a countervailing duty action under U.S. law? *See* Countervailing Duty Petition of the American Textile Manufacturers Institute et al., September 12, 1983; and F. W. Woolworth Co. v. United States, 115 F.2d 348 (C.C.P.A. 1940).

How could you argue that the U.S. countervailing duty laws should not reach the Chinese exchange rate scheme? *See* briefs on this subject filed pursuant to the Commerce Dept. investigation on the alleged PRC export rate subsidy, (48 Fed. Reg. 46,600, October 13, 1983).

10. Should "industrial policy" or "targeting"—efforts to combine subsidized research, antitrust exemptions, market protection, and the like to help specific industries—be regarded as a basis for countervailing? Under GATT? Under U.S. law? Under wise policy?

11. Consider situations such as the following:

(a) the government of Canada provides free "stumpage" (timber) to Canadian log producers (*see* Certain Softwood Lumber from Canada, 48 Fed. Reg. 24,159 (1983));

(b) the government of Mexico provides free gravel to the producers of concrete blocks in Mexico;

(c) the government of Mexico provides low-cost feedstock to the petrochemicals industry (*see* Anhydrous and Aqua Ammonia from Mexico, 47 Fed. Reg. 28,522 (1983)).

Should these "upstream" subsidies be countervailable under U.S. law? Under what theory? *See* Trade and Tariff Act of 1984, Section 613 (Appendix X).

12. What about alternative remedies for foreign subsidies such as

(a) U.S. tax penalties such as the denial of the investment tax credit for offending countries—considered under the Houdaille petition, excerpted at 15 Tax Notes 777 (May 31, 1982). (This relief was denied by the U.S. Trade Representative on April 22, 1982); or

(b) counter subsidies on exports to the foreign nations?

13. What if country A subsidizes widget exports to the United States and accounts for 60% of all imports of widgets to the United States. Country B subsidizes widget exports and accounts for 30% of the U.S. widget imports, while C also subsidizes widget exports and has 10% of the U.S. widget import market. May X, a U.S. widget producer, file a countervailing duty complaint collectively against A, B, and C and cumulate the total injury sustained? On the issue of cumulation *see* the Tariff and Trade Act of 1984, §612(a)(2)(A).

14. The U.S. fishing industry files a countervailing duty case against the exporters of fish from Canada. Seeing that it is likely to lose, the government of Canada offers to limit the volume of fish imports that could enter the United States. Would such a quantitative restriction agreement between Canada and the United States in lieu of a countervailing duty determination be permissible? See the Tariff and Trade Act of 1984, §604. Is the inclusion of consumer considerations in the "public interest" criteria of §604 an adequate means of protecting U.S. consumers from implementation of the countervailing duty law?

15. Subsidy calculations may be relatively straightforward if the investigation deals with a firm that produces only one product, or if the relevant subsidy applies only to the product subject to a countervailing duty proceeding.

Consider, however, how this situation might be handled. Respondent A:

(a) has total annual revenues of $10 million;

(b) produces three products, X, Y, and Z; and

(c) receives $1 million in countervailable export loans.

Only product X is under investigation; product X receives $100,000 of the countervailable benefit but provides one half, or $5 million, of A's revenues. If a *product specific* methodology were employed, the countervailing duty would only be equal to 2% ($100,000 in benefits divided by $5 million in revenues). If a *corporate wide allocation* were utilized, however, a dramatically different result—10%—would occur ($1 million in benefits divided by $10 million in revenues).

What result? *See* Certain Steel Products from Belgium, 47 Fed. Reg. 39,304, 39,320 (1982).

16. Is it fair to describe the Commerce Department's position as considering a subsidy to exist when there is: (a) selective government treatment; and (b) the selective government treatment is different from the treatment that the recipient would otherwise receive in a competitive, unfettered marketplace?

If so, how is one to define the term "selective" treatment—to include exports, a specific enterprise, an industry, or a group of enterprises or industries? What do you make of the "specificity" language in §771(5)(B) of the 1979 Act?

17. Section 771(5)(B) of the 1979 Act provides that the provision of capital, loans, or loan guarantees on terms inconsistent with commercial considerations constitutes a subsidy. What does the phrase "inconsistent with commercial considerations" mean? How relevant would a "private investor" standard be? Or the prevailing market price of stock if we are dealing with a government equity infusion via a stock acquisition? When should a particular enterprise be deemed to be uncreditworthy? What external indicia might be relevant in making this judgment?

18. Assume that the government of Canada provides unemployment insurance to fishermen in its maritime provinces for 40 weeks of the year, at a rate equal to 80% of the average annual wage for fishermen. Is this countervailable under the MTN Subsidies Code or U.S. law? What if the government of Canada were to provide severance allowances for employees of steel companies that would otherwise be owed by the companies pursuant to contractual labor obligations? *See* Certain Steel Products from Belgium, 47 Fed. Reg. 39,304 (1982).

C.   THE SPECIAL PROBLEM OF AGRICULTURAL SUBSIDIES

Agricultural subsidies pose special problems. They are very common and their measurement is very complex. In Europe, for example, agricultural prices are kept high, leading to production beyond domestic needs. Some of this production is exported—and the European Community bears the cost of meeting the world price. Arguably, the amount of the subsidy is the difference between the domestic and the export price—yet the first is a politically determined price and the second is influenced by the subsidy programs of other nations.

Another problem is emphasized by the fact that the subsidy generally affects competition in third markets as well as home markets. Thus, the European or Japanese export subsidy is more likely to take away U.S. markets in third nations than to penetrate the United States and take away home sales. Countervailing duties are therefore not helpful; and the available trade devices depend on diplomatic and commercial pressure against the subsidizing nation. In the United States, this procedure is spelled out in §301 of the 1974 Act (which will be presented more fully in Chapter IX).

PETITION OF THE RICE MILLERS' ASSOCIATION REQUESTING THE PRESIDENT TO TAKE ACTION UNDER §301 OF THE TRADE ACT OF 1974

Before the §301 Committee Office of the United States Trade Representative, April 4, 1980

On behalf of The Rice Millers' Association, the undersigned hereby respectfully request that the President take action against Japan pursuant to Title III of the Trade Act of 1974, as amended ("the Act"). For the reasons set out in detail below, Petitioners allege that certain actions, policies, and practices of the Government of Japan with respect to the production, procurement, and exportation of rice are inconsistent with the provisions of trade agreements, are unjustifiable and unreasonable, and burden and restrict United States commerce, all within the meaning of section 301 of the Act, 19 U.S.C. §2411.

The Rice Millers' Association, whose members are the millers of virtually all of the milled rice exported from the United States, is an "interested party" as required by 15 C.F.R. §2006.0(a).

I.   FACTS

A.   THE JAPANESE SUBSIDY ON RICE

1. The Japanese Government, through the maintenance of artificially high farm prices, has brought about a massive domestic surplus of rice. It is currently disposing of this surplus by selling rice on the world market at prices below the world price and far below cost.

2. During 1979 the Government of Japan announced a five-year plan aimed at disposing of 4.8 million metric tons of surplus rice. Exports were initially intended to absorb 1.0 million metric tons during the full course of the plan, or about 200,000 metric tons per year. Nevertheless, Japanese rice exports in 1979 reached almost 900,000 metric tons—far beyond the annual export allocations outlined in the 1979-1983 rice surplus disposal program.

3. The Government of Japan has long encouraged domestic rice production

by purchasing Japanese-produced rice at several times the world price. In 1960, this purchase price was twice world levels, in 1970 three times the world price, and in 1976 almost four times the world price. In January, 1980, producers were receiving 286,267 yen per metric ton, or $1192.78, while the world price for comparable rice was approximately $375.00 per metric ton (90,000 [yen]). The mid-1979 producer price was as high as $1450 per metric ton. Japanese producers have thus been receiving from three to five times the world price for their rice. This support program has maintained the average annual level of Japanese rice production at over twelve million metric tons, which is far more than necessary to meet the declining domestic demand for rice.

4. Faced with rice stocks of approximately 6.5 million metric tons, which are expected to grow to 7.1 million metric tons by October, 1980, the Government of Japan began in 1979 to export large supplies of rice, often at below world prices. The Japanese have sold rice for export within a range of $228-305 per metric ton over the last ten months, as compared with world prices of approximately $300-375 per metric ton, for comparable quality rice.

5. Japanese export prices are well below the Japanese domestic retail price for rice, which is also set by the Government of Japan. During the summer of 1979, while rice was being sold for export at 49,680 [yen] ($227.89) per metric ton, the domestic retail price was maintained at 256,517 [yen] ($1176.68) per metric ton. This domestic price has been set at 264,850 [yen] ($1103.54) for 1980. . . .

7. With production continuing to exceed consumption, the Japanese rice surplus will continue to grow by as much as 1.5 million metric tons each year. The October, 1980, estimate of 7.1 million metric tons represents the highest level since Japan has record surplus stocks of 7.2 million metric tons in 1970. There is no relief in sight.

B. THE INJURY TO UNITED STATES COMMERCE

8. The United States expects in 1980 to be the largest exporter of rice in the world. Since 1962, United States exports of rice have consistently outpaced domestic utilization. During the last three years the United States has exported approximately 2.1-2.3 million metric tons per year, representing 20 to 30% of world trade in rice. Over 80% of those exports were on commercial terms. The Department of Agriculture projects that 1979-80 marketing year exports will reach 2.6 million metric tons, with 85% commercial.

9. Japan's sales and grants of rice in its fiscal year 1979 amounted to over 870,000 metric tons. The addition of this subsidized supply to the marketplace lowered prices generally, and displaced sales that would otherwise have been made.

10. A large portion of United States rice exports is destined for the major rice-consuming nations in Asia, including in particular Korea and Indonesia. U.S. sales in these markets have been reduced by sales of Japanese rice offered at subsidized prices.

11. *Korea.*

(a) In 1975, 1976 and 1977, Korea obtained 100 percent of its rice imports from the United States. Although in 1978 Korea achieved self-sufficiency and did not import rice at all, Korean rice imports from the United States prior to 1978 and in 1979 were substantial. During the period 1967-1977, Korea imported about 3.4 million metric tons of rice from the United States. In the marketing year 1979-80, Korea will be the single largest purchaser of U.S. rice. . . .

(c) The sale of 250,000 metric tons of subsidized Japanese rice to Korea in the spring of 1979 directly displaced a United States commercial sale. In late April 1979, an American company contracted to sell 55,000 metric tons of rice to Korea at a price of $274.50 per ton, f.o.b. This purchase was part of a planned importation of 500,000 metric tons of rice from the United States for an emergency stockpile. Soon thereafter, however, Korea cancelled the sale and purchased 250,000 metric tons of subsidized Japanese rice at a lower price than the United States price previously accepted. . . .

17. The Japanese export subsidization program serves to perpetuate the surplus problem. It enables Japan to avoid taking the strong measures needed to correct its supply-demand imbalance without harming the world rice export market. It insulates the Japanese rice farmer from the price consequences of the domestic surplus, and forces those consequences upon rice farmers elsewhere in the world, who must market their production without the benefit of export subsidies.

II.   THE JAPANESE POLICIES AND PRACTICES ARE UNJUSTIFIABLE AND ARE INCONSISTENT WITH THE PROVISIONS OF TRADE AGREEMENTS

18. The Japanese policies and practices of buying domestic rice at a price far higher than the world market level, and then reselling it at artificially low prices in third country markets, constitute violations of Article XVI of the GATT, of the Subsidies Code concluded in the "Tokyo Round" of Multilateral Trade Negotiations, and of the Principles of Surplus Disposal of the United Nations Food and Agriculture Organization.

19. *Article XVI of the GATT.*

(a) Section A of GATT Article XVI applies to subsidies in general, specifically including any subsidy which maintains exports at a level higher than would obtain in the absence of the subsidy.

(b) The Japanese Government's purchase of domestic rice at a price substantially above the world market price, and its subsequent resale of the rice at or below the world price, come within the language of Section A. These Government policies constitute dumping of Japanese rice in the world market and inevitably increase exports beyond the level they would attain without the subsidy.

(c) Japan has not notified the other Contracting Parties to the GATT of its subsidy programs, as required by Section A.

(d) Section B of Article XVI obliges Contracting Parties to "seek to avoid the use of subsidies on the export of primary products." The expression "primary products" includes rice.

(e) When, as here, products that are price-maintained are exported at prices below those of the domestic market, there is a direct subsidy on exports. That is, the difference between the Japanese export resale price and the domestic support price represents a subsidy on Japanese exports, exactly as if Japan had provided a cash payment to Japanese producers as an incentive to export.

(f) Even if the Japanese subsidy practices do not themselves violate the GATT, the application of a subsidy "in a manner which results in that Contracting Party having more than an equitable share of world export trade" in a product constitutes a violation of Article XVI(3). In 1979, the Japanese sold 870,000 metric tons of rice to Korea, Indonesia, and other countries. They reportedly plan to sell additional large quantities of rice in 1980.

(g) Taking into account the shares of the relevant Contracting Parties in world rice trade during the last few years, and particularly Japan's recent entry into the market as an exporter, as required by Article XVI(3), the dramatic increase in Japanese rice exports has resulted in the development of a Japanese market share that is far more than equitable.

20. *The Subsidies Code.*

(a) Article 3 of the Subsidies Code states that both the United States and Japan as signatories recognize "that subsidies may cause adverse effects to the interests of other signatories." The signatories agreed "not to use export subsidies in a manner inconsistent with the provisions of [the Code]."

(b) More specifically, Japan agreed that it would seek to avoid causing "serious prejudice" or a "threat of serious prejudice" to the interests of another signatory, arising through, inter alia, "the effects of the subsidized exports in displacing the exports of like products of another signatory from a third country market."

(c) Japan's subsidy program has already displaced United States commercial sales to Korea. In addition, the subsidy is certain to affect U.S. sales to Indonesia and other countries. Displacement of sales of this magnitude is "serious prejudice" within the meaning of Article 3.

(d) In Article 10 of the Subsidies Code, the signatories reaffirmed their commitment under GATT Article XVI not to apply subsidies which result in the subsidizing Party having more than an equitable share of the world market. The Article specifically includes "any case in which the effect of an export subsidy . . . is to displace the exports of another signatory." The Parties also agreed that the relevant period for determining an equitable share of the market would normally be the three previous calendar years.

(e) . . . Japanese subsidized rice sales in foreign markets this year represent an unjustifiable increase over Japan's market share during the last three calendar years. The effect of this increase is to displace United States exports to those markets. The Japanese practices therefore constitute violations of Article 10 of the Subsidies Code.

(f) Article 11 of the Subsidies Code formally recognizes the right of signatories to employ subsidies other than export subsidies to achieve certain policy objectives. However, Article 11 repeats the commitment of the signatories in Article 3 to avoid causing or threatening to cause injury to, or serious prejudice to the interests of, another signatory.

(g) Thus even were the Japanese subsidy to be characterized as other than an export subsidy, Japan would be in violation of its obligations under Article 11 to avoid causing injury to the United States.

21. *The FAO Principles.*

(a) The United Nations Food and Agriculture Organization (FAO) Principles for Disposal of Agricultural Surpluses provide (in Conference Resolution 14(53) and Council Resolution 2/20) that surpluses should be moved into consumption "without harmful interference with the normal patterns of production and international trade."

(b) Japan's subsidized disposal of large quantities of surplus rice in the export market is likely to interfere seriously with normal patterns of production and trade, and will cause a significant reduction in exports from the United States. This disposal program violates the Japanese obligation not to cause harmful interference with international trade.

(c) The FAO Principles provide more specifically that to the extent that surplus sales on concessional terms "may constitute some danger of displacement of commercial sales," such factors as other exporters' shares in the import markets must be considered.

(d) The documented displacement of United States commercial rice exports, and the effect of the Japanese program on both countries' market shares, suggest that Japan is in violation of its obligation to dispose of its surplus in an orderly fashion.

(e) Large quantities of a commodity sold over a short period of time can be particularly disruptive of normal patterns of trade. The FAO Principles specifically state that "the quantity of the commodity sold, and/or the rate at which it is moved" may cause harmful interference with trade.

(f) Japan's export of massive quantities of surplus rice in a very short period of time threatens to cause harmful interference with trade in violation of Japan's obligations under the FAO Principles.

(g) In addition, Japan has violated its obligation under the FAO Principles "whenever practicable, [to] consult with other countries interested in the possible effects of such transactions." In particular, Japan has not engaged in true and meaningful consultations with the United States.

(h) Japan has also violated its general obligations under the FAO Principles to "undertake bilateral consultations with countries substantially interested by reason of their exports of the commodity concerned to the recipient country" and to "notify [the Consultative Subcommittee on Surplus Disposal] of the main features of the proposed transaction in order to provide other countries directly interested in exports of the commodity an opportunity for bilateral consultations."

(i) Japan has not undertaken such bilateral consultations with the United States. Nor has Japan proposed "Usual Marketing Requirements," agreements by recipient countries to maintain at least a specified level of commercial imports (established on an historical basis) in addition to any purchases of surplus rice from Japan.

III. THE JAPANESE POLICIES AND PRACTICES ARE UNJUSTIFIABLE AND UNREASONABLE, AND BURDEN AND RESTRICT UNITED STATES COMMERCE

22. Even if the Japanese subsidy were not a violation of Japan's international obligations discussed above, it would nevertheless give rise to a remedy under §301 of the Act. Section 301 is not coterminous with any international agreement. Rather, it is designed to prevent all unfair and unreasonable foreign trade practices that adversely affect United States commerce.

23. In particular, §301(a)(3) of the Act before its 1979 amendment listed as illustrative of the practices justifying Presidential action the granting of subsidies on exports "to other foreign markets which have the effect of substantially reducing sales of the competitive United States product . . . in those other foreign markets."

24. Subsidies distort international trade by breaking the normal market link between price and the cost of production. Subsidies insulate producers from the need to be efficient and competitive.

25. The Japanese subsidy practices complained of herein allow the sale of Japanese rice in foreign markets at prices that are in no way related to the economics of production. Japanese rice is offered for export sale at or below the world market price regardless of the fact that the Government paid producers many times the export price for the rice.

26. Both the text and the legislative history of §301 and its recent amendments suggest that such a practice is unreasonable within the terms of the section.

27. Japan has used its subsidy in connection with export sales made on both commercial and concessional terms. Japan's concessional sales provide for deferred repayment of principal and low interest rates. By also employing subsidies in concessional sales, the terms of which are already exceedingly favorable to the recipient counting, Japan exacerbates the subsidy's injurious impact on the world rice market.

28. The Japanese subsidy on commercial and concessional sales also distorts free trade by artificially depressing the world price for rice. This sharply reduces the ability of other rice exporting nations, principally the United States, to maintain efficient, unsubsidized rice production and exportation.

29. The Japanese subsidy practices have burdened or restricted United States commerce by causing tremendous increases in sales by Japan to Korea, Indonesia, and other markets for U.S. rice, and by bringing about a serious instability in world rice trade as a whole.

PRAYER FOR RELIEF

30. WHEREFORE, Petitioners respectfully seek relief, as follows:

(a) The President is requested to take all appropriate and feasible action within his power to obtain the elimination of the policies and practices that are the subjects of the instant Petition;

(b) the President is requested, in default of obtaining the elimination of such policies and practices, to impose duties or other import restrictions on the products of Japan for such time as he deems appropriate; and

(c) the United States Trade Representative is requested to initiate forthwith an investigation of the policies and practices complained of herein.

31. Petitioners hereby request a public hearing on all matters contained herein, as provided by §302(b)(2) of the Act as amended and 15 C.F.R. §2006.6(a).

32. Petitioners aver that no other relief has been sought by The Rice Millers' Association concerning the Japanese policies and practices described herein, under the Trade Act of 1974 as amended, or any other Act.

On April 12, 1980, the Government of Japan agreed to limit its exports of rice to third countries for a four-year period. The Rice Millers' Association withdrew its §301 petition in May, 1980, in consideration of the proposed accord.

Washington Riceletter

April 25, 1980

Japan Agreement?

One of the "ifs" that is going to affect your prices next year is the big rice surplus in Japan, and the efforts of the Japanese Government to move that surplus out to world markets (our markets) at subsidized prices.

A negotiating team from USDA was in Tokyo for three days earlier in the month, accompanied by representatives of the Congress and the U.S. rice industry. An agreement was finally hammered out and agreed to by the Japanese.

Basically, the Japanese agreed to limit shipments of their surplus rice stock to 1.6 million tons over the next four years, or 400,000 metric tons per year. That is all well and good. One industry spokesman closely involved in trying to deal with this problem over the last several months called it a "significant first step."

The agreement does not get to the heart of the problem, however. It does not speak to the high subsidized price the Japanese Government pays to its growers to produce far more rice than the country needs. And it does not speak to the problem of how this production could be reduced in future years.

More important, the document that our officials agreed to (or so we are informed) sanctions soft-loan sales of rice to Indonesia, by Japan, *while our Government is saying at the same time that Indonesia does not qualify for soft-loan food aid from the United States.* That means our Government, or parts of it, is saying that Indonesia should be able to get terms for the purchase of rice from Japanese bins, but not from U.S. farmers (who are not subsidized).

It makes no sense, especially when the Indonesians can be expected to begin buying U.S. rice for cash, if they can be assured of getting additional supplies under the terms of the Food for Peace program (PL-480).

In any event, it now begins to appear that the agreement may start falling apart before the ink is dry on the signatures. We are informed that the South Korean representatives are already knocking down the doors, saying that more rice is needed by their country on an emergency basis, and they say Japan is willing to supply it cheaply. (The agreement calls for Japan to supply South Korea with 50,000 tons annually, and the South Koreans have expressed the need for five times that amount, immediately.)

There is U.S. rice available in West Coast bins, ready to go, held as part of the stocks owned by the Commodity Credit Corporation and the USDA. And we have heard of no efforts to speed up the shipments to Korea of the supplies purchased here several weeks ago.

Something is wrong somewhere. It is very plain that if our Government agrees to the South Korean-Japanese request, it will blow the agreement of this month out of the water entirely. Our farmers and millers will soon be faced once again with the prospect of the Japanese Government flooding world markets with subsidized rice simply to get rid of it.

We suggest you let your Congressman know how you feel about this, and in no uncertain terms.

Regards,

RICELETTER Editors

Note on the International Trade Regime for Agricultural Products

The international trade regime for agricultural products reflects the political strength of farmers in the developed and developing countries. As we saw in Chapter 5, the GATT permits a more restrictive regulation of imports on the agricultural than the industrial side. Article XI(1) of the GATT proscribes import quotas for industrial products, but Article XI(2) permits them for agricultural and fisheries products in order to allow domestic price support programs to be maintained.

Section 22 of the U.S. Agricultural Adjustment Act, discussed in Chapter 4, is the U.S. mechanism for establishing quantitative or other restraints on U.S. agricultural imports.

On the export side of the equation, Article 9 of the MTN Subsidies Code proscribes export subsidies for industrial products, but Article 10 of the code, like Article XVI(3) of the GATT, permits export subsidies for agricultural products so long as such subsidies do not result in the exporter obtaining "more than an equitable share of the world market."

The interest of developing countries in agriculture is twofold: first, to protect domestic markets, and, second, to maximize the export earnings of primary product exports through particularized commodity arrangements. In Chapter X we consider the efforts within the United Nations Conference on Trade and Development (UNCTAD) to provide a network of commodity agreements to support prices. In the last 25 years commodity agreements have been negotiated for agricultural products such as coffee, cocoa, sugar, olive oil, and wheat.

In developed countries such as Japan, those of the European Community, and the United States, farmers are a key interest group that is not easily denied, although the rationales for agricultural protection may vary. Agricultural protectionism is defended in Japan under the guise of "food security." Government officials and the general public rationalize agricultural protectionism as vital for an island that could be cut off from foreign food supplies. Memories of pre-World War II efforts by foreign countries to curtail Japanese expansionism through economic measures still rankle, as do the memories of starvation conditions in Japan in the immediate post-World War II years. The political reality of the 1980 U.S.-Japan rice dispute was that farmers were politically crucial in both countries. In Japan the ruling Liberal Democratic Party (LDP) relies on farmers as a primary base of rural support, and makes relatively few concessions regarding agricultural imports such as beef and citrus products for that reason. *See* E. Castle, K. Hemmi, & S. Skillings (eds.), U.S.-Japanese Agricultural Trade Relations (1982).

In the EC, as we saw in Chapter 3, the Common Agricultural Policy (CAP) limits imports through its restrictive variable levy system, and promotes exports through export restitutions. The rationale for agricultural mercantilism in the EC hinges on the role of agriculture in promoting European economic integration, with the CAP frequently being described as the glue holding the EC together.

From the standpoint of the United States, export subsidies are being defended by some as necessary to counter the subsidies of U.S. trading partners, compensate for the high value of the dollar relative to other currencies, and ease the structural shake-out now going on in U.S. agriculture. As the world's most efficient producer, the United States has the greatest interest in promoting freer trade in agricultural products. The regulation of agricultural trade will be a crucial topic in the next round of international trade negotiations, but, realistically, free trade in agriculture will be an extremely difficult, if not impossible, goal to realize. On the evolution of U.S. farm policy *see* D. Paarlberg, *Farm and Food Policy: Issues of the 1980's* (1980).

QUESTIONS

1. Why won't countervailing duties solve the rice problem? What could the U.S. exporter do if Japan were less cooperative? (The §301 procedures will be developed more fully in Chapter IX.)

2. As a representative of Korea or any other similarly affected nation, how would you feel about the U.S.-Japanese arrangement? Would you have any way to participate in the decisionmaking or to attack it legally?

3. How would the §301 procedure work if the exporter's complaint were that a subsidy program in, say, the EC were destroying its *EC* market?

4. Would any domestic agricultural price-support program be enough to trigger a §301 response? What are the differences in standard between §301 and regular countervailing duties?

5. Does the existence of a subsidy on a U.S. product bar relief when its export market is hurt by another nation's subsidy program? Under §301? Under GATT?

6. The Common Agricultural Policy (CAP) of the European Economic Community (EEC) provides both internal support to domestic producers and export subsidies. In the case of rice, export restitutions equal to the difference

between the EEC price and the world market price are provided to EEC exporters in order to make EEC rice (primarily from Italy) competitive on the world market.

Citing Article XVI of the GATT, the MTA on subsidies (Article 10), The Rice Millers' Association files a complaint under §301 of the Trade Act of 1974. What result? What other facts do you need to know in order to answer this question? For other examples in the agricultural area, *see* Bishop, The Multilateral Trade Negotiations, Subsidies, and the *Great Plains Wheat* Case, 16 Intl. Law. 339 (1982).

7. For highly subsidized commodities, as are many agricultural commodities, are there any plausible alternatives to multilateralizing the entire subsidy structure? In thinking about this question, consider the EC's agricultural subsidy program, Chapter III, *supra*, both as an example of how heavily-subsidized agriculture really is and as an example of an effort to multilateralize a subsidy.

Bibliographical Note

For additional information on subsidies and countervailing duties *see* Jackson, The Jurisprudence of International Trade: The Disc Case in GATT, 72 Am. J. Law 747 (1978); Anninger, Disc and GATT, 13 Harv. Intl. L.J. 391 (1972); Barcelo, Subsidies and Countervailing Duties—Analysis and a Proposal, 9 Law & Poly. Intl. Bus. 779 (1977); G. Bryan, Taxing Unfair International Trade Practices (1981); Ehrenhaft, What the Antidumping and Countervailing Duty Provisions (Can) (Will) (Should) Mean for U.S. Trade Policy, 11 Law & Poly. Intl. Bus. 1439 (1979); Practicing Law Institute, The Commerce Department Speaks on Import Administration and Export Administration 1984 (1984); Practising Law Institute, The Trade Agreements Act of 1979—Four Years Later (1983); J. Pattison, Antidumping and Countervailing Duties (1984); Barcelo, Subsidies, Countervailing Duties and Antidumping After the Tokyo Round, 13 Cornell L.J. 257 (1980); de Kieffer, When, Why and How to Bring a Countervailing Duty Proceeding: A Complainant's Perspective, 6 N.C. J. Intl. C. & Law Reg. 363 (1981).

Chapter VII

Customs: Classification and Valuation

This chapter addresses the legal difficulties—and commercial opportunities—involved when articles enter the customs territory of the United States. The materials deal primarily with the customs-related problems of tariff classification and of appraising the valuation of a product.

Choosing the appropriate tariff classification is crucial for the importer, as the enumeration selected will determine the duty rate that will be assessed. The importer will typically argue for the classification providing the lowest duty rate.

The question of valuation is the other half of the equation as this determines the multiplicand for the duty rate. For example, if the duty rate on widgets is 10% ad valorem, and they are valued at $10 each instead of $20 each, the total amount paid will be only half as large.

A. TYPES OF CUSTOMS TRANSACTIONS

Customs laws and procedures are a necessary part of any national system seeking to regulate the flow of international trade. Imports do not just "arrive" in a national economy—they must be properly entered for home use by customs officials, and assessed the appropriate level of duty.

Businessmen seeking to cut costs should focus on ways to reduce tariff expenditures through tariff classifications, valuation, and entry techniques. The world of customs is not difficult, but it is arcane, and the student should first master the terminology associated with the type of customs transactions in the United States:

1. Entry for Home Use

The primary function of customs operations is the clearance of goods for home use or consumption.[1] This is the procedure employed by customs officials regarding goods that will remain permanently in the customs territory of the entering country. The administering authority for this procedure in the United States is the U.S. Customs Service, which is an agency of the U.S. Treasury Department. "Entry" refers to the filing of appropriate documents with the U.S. Customs Service to secure the release of imported merchandise from custody.

In the normal case, goods[2] manufactured wholly outside the United States are "entered for consumption," and duties are paid as the articles enter the flow of commerce in the United States.[3] 19 C.F.R. §141.0a(f). The "entry documentation" required for a common carrier is either a bill of lading, air waybill, or a carrier's certificate, 19 C.F.R. §141.11; for entries not imported by a common carrier possession of the merchandise at the time of arrival in the United States is sufficient evidence of the right to make entry, 19 C.F.R. §141.12.

Estimated duties are deposited with the U.S. Customs Service at the time of the filing of the entry documentation. The first step in the calculation of the duties is the classification of the imported article in the appropriate line item in the Tariff Schedules of the United States (TSUS), 19 C.F.R. §152.11. The valuation of the goods must then be appraised by the Customs Service, 19 C.F.R. §152.101.

Items 806.30 and 807.00 of the TSUS provide for the exemption from customs duties of goods that are exported from the United States and then entered for consumption in the United States. This exemption is of particular advantage to U.S. multinational enterprises. Thus, for example, a Mexican affiliate could, pursuant to item 807.00, make a television set with certain American-made parts and the duty paid on reentry into the United States would be imposed only on the value added overseas.

The tariff treatment of item 806.30 should be distinguished from that of

---

[1] *See* Annex B.1 of the Kyoto Convention, in force July 13, 1977, C.C.C. Kyoto Convention Handbook.

[2] Certain "intangibles" are deemed in General Headnote 5 of the TSUS not to be "articles" subject to the entry provisions, including:

  (a) corpses, together with their coffins and accompanying flowers;
  (b) currency (metal or paper) in current circulation in any country and imported for monetary purposes;
  (c) electricity;
  (d) securities and similar evidence of value; and
  (e) vessels that are not "yachts or pleasure boats".

[3] For customs purposes, the territory of the United States includes the District of Columbia and Puerto Rico as well as the 50 states. Guam, Wake Island, Midway Islands, Kingman Reef, Johnston Island, and American Samoa are American territory but not within the customs territory of the United States.

807.00. Under item 806.30, articles of metal other than precious metal that have been subjected to a process of manufacture in the United States and exported for processing and return to the United States are subject to duty only on the value of the foreign processing. Under item 807.00, imported items assembled in foreign countries with fabricated components that have been manufactured in the United States are subject to duty on the full value of the imported product less the value of the components fabricated in the United States. No further processing is required in the United States for preferential treatment under item 807.00.

Proposals have been made by organized labor to repeal these items, which are perceived as unfair advantages for multinational enterprises. In addition, the principle of tax neutrality would suggest an equal application of the tariff to all imports regardless of origin. Nevertheless, these items have remained in the TSUS, in recognition of the impact that repeal would have on U.S. exporters of component parts and the consequent negative impact on the U.S. balance of trade.[4]

2. Alternative Forms of Entry

There are alternative means of customs entry into the United States that may be designed to serve the particular needs of the importer. Comprehending these forms of entry requires distinguishing the "admission" of goods into the United States as a physical fact from the "entry" of goods into the United States territory for consumption. Accordingly, goods may be admitted into the United States but entered for "warehousing," for "transportation" within the United States, or for further entry into a Foreign Trade Zone or a Foreign Trade Fair. The theory behind these types of importations is that the articles involved will not enter the flow of commerce in the United States, and will in effect be isolated from the rest of the U.S. economy.

Bonded Warehouse. Entry may be permitted on a duty-free basis (under bond) into a bonded warehouse, where the goods may be stored, repacked, or further transformed. The imported goods, which may remain in the bonded warehouse for a period up to five years, become dutiable when they are withdrawn from consumption in the United States during this period. *See* 19 C.F.R. §§113, 114 (1984).

---

[4]*See* Tariff Commission Report No. 332-619 (1970); Comment, The Approaching Confrontation over Item 807.00 of the Tariff Schedule, 4 Law & Pol. Intl. Bus. 628, 629 (1972); Einhorn, Special Classification under the U.S. Tariff Schedules: U.S. Goods Returned (806.30, 807.00), 9 Law & Pol. Intl. Bus. 681 (1977); Background Material on Selected Trade Legislation Introduced in the House of Representatives, Committee on Ways and Means, 91st Cong., 2d Sess. 75-83 (1970). For a treatment of articles 806.30 and 807.00, from which much of this paragraph is drawn, *see* Fisher, The Multinationals and the Crisis in United States Trade and Investment Policy, 53 B.U.L. Rev. 308 (1973). For a discussion of international analogues to items 806.30 and 807.00, *see* D. McGovern, International Trade Regulation (1982), Chapter 3.

Temporary Importation in Bond (TIB). Entry of certain articles may be permitted on a TIB basis, if it is planned to move the goods out of the United States within one year after the date of importation (this period may be extended up to two years); again, no duty is paid by the importer. *See* 19 C.F.R. §§10.31-10.40 (1984).

Foreign Trade Zone. If goods are entered into a Foreign Trade Zone no duty is paid. *See* 19 U.S.C. §81 a-v; Armco Steel v. Stans, 431 F.2d 779 (2d Cir. 1970). Foreign Trade Zones are treated as being outside the customs territory of the United States.[5]

Foreign Trade Fair. Deferral of duties may be obtained by receiving designation as a Foreign Trade Fair. Duties need not be paid upon entry but as goods are sold out of the "Fair."

All the alternative forms of entry, except entry on a TIB basis, share one common characteristic—deferral of U.S. customs duties. Although U.S. customs duties will eventually have to be paid when the goods enter the customs territory of the United States, the deferral of the duties may greatly assist the cash flow position of the importer.

The TIB will result in exemption from U.S. duties, as would exports from Foreign Trade Zones or bonded warehouses not entering the customs territory of the United States.

You should focus on methods that can legally minimize the costs of the international business transaction, including the deferral, whenever possible, of all taxes that might be levied. The net effect of deferral of customs duties is that the importer grants himself an interest-free loan from the federal government for the period of the tax deferral. Over a period of years this "loan" can amount to a substantial sum of money.

B. CLASSIFICATION

The first decision that must be made by the importer in the customs entry process is to choose the proper "line item" in the TSUS in which to classify the imported article. The importer or his customs broker will, of course, be seeking the category with the lowest duty.

In the following selection, Feller describes the TSUS. If the importer is uncertain where to place his entry he may seek a letter ruling from the U.S.

---

[5]On Foreign Trade Zones, *see* Clasea, U.S. Foreign Trade Zone Manufacturing and Assembly: Overview and Update, 13 Law & Pol. Intl. Bus. 339 (1981).

Customs Service on the appropriate classification. The other device frequently used by the U.S. Customs Service is an "advice" to the ports instructing them on how to classify particular merchandise.

1. General Matters

P. FELLER, U.S. CUSTOMS AND INTERNATIONAL TRADE GUIDE

6-2—6-6 (1979)

The Tariff Schedules of the United States went into effect in August 1963. They currently contain over 6,700 separate product categories, each presented in a format that includes a five-digit identifying number, product description, and applicable tariff rates. The Tariff Schedules are contained in 19 U.S.C. 1202. They are also contained in the Tariff Schedules of the United States Annotated (TSUSA), published by the United States International Trade Commission pursuant to section 201 of the Tariff Classification Act of 1962. . . .

Two sets of duty rates are subsumed under the heading "Rates of Duty." The rates listed in column 1 [MFN rates] are the trade agreement rates or most favored nation (MFN) rates. They reflect successive rate reductions made pursuant to the U.S. trade agreements program since 1934. These rates apply to the vast majority of products imported into the United States. The rates listed in column 2 under that heading are generally the statutory rates established by the Tariff Act of 1930—the so-called Smoot-Hawley tariff. These high tariff rates apply to imports from most communist countries.

The Tariff Schedules provide for three different types of rates. The majority of rates are ad valorem rates (a stated percentage of the value of the article). There are also specific rates (a stated amount per unit of the article) and compound rates (a combination of specific and ad valorem rates).

The Tariff Schedules are comprised of eight separate schedules, plus an appendix which is essentially a ninth schedule. The Tariff Schedules are applicable in accordance with the provisions set forth in an introductory section called General Headnotes and Rules of Interpretation (hereinafter cited as the "General Headnotes"). The first six schedules are organized along generic lines as follows:

Schedule 1 (Animal & Vegetable Products)
Schedule 2 (Wood & Paper; Printed Matter)
Schedule 3 (Textile Fibers & Textile Products)
Schedule 4 (Chemicals & Related Products)
Schedule 5 (Nonmetallic & Mineral Products)
Schedule 6 (Metals & Metal Products).

The product categories within each of the first six schedules are, for the most part, arranged sequentially according to the degree of processing performed on the basic raw material. This parallels the U.S. tariff rate structure under which raw material imports are generally duty-free or dutiable at low rates, while progressively upgraded forms of the product are subject to progressively higher rates of duty. For example, most categories of lumber are duty free, while certain pine wood moldings are dutiable at 1.5 percent, cigar boxes and wood doors at 7.5 percent, and certain wood shutters at $16^{2}/_{3}$ percent.

Schedule 7 (Specified Products; Miscellaneous and Nonenumerated Products) covers all other products, either specified by name or described in "basket categories." Every product entering the Customs territory of the United States is classifiable somewhere within the first seven schedules. Some products, however, may be subject to a dual classification. That is, in addition to the ordinary tariff classification they may be subject to one of the special provisions set forth in Schedule 8 or the appendix.

Schedule 8 (Special Classification Provisions) generally classifies merchandise on the basis of factors other than their intrinsic characteristics or commercial significance. A number of these provisions implement national policies unrelated to ordinary trade policy considerations. Schedule 8 provisions include, for example, the baggage and effects of personnel of foreign governments and international organizations; household articles accompanying returning American residents; and importations of religious, educational, or scientific paraphernalia. Schedule 8 items also provide for duty-free or preferential duty treatment under certain conditions. . . .

The appendix contains tariff and quota provisions of limited duration, such as temporary increased duties under presidential escape clause actions and temporary duty suspensions on specific products.

During the development of the Tariff Schedules it was recognized that the great number and range of product categories created problems of definition, differentiation, and precedence. Thus, the United States Tariff Commission in its 1960 "Tariff Classification Study Submitting Report" to the Congress observed that it was "inevitable that any tariff structure geared to a highly diversified economy such as that of the United States will frequently become involved in hair-splitting administrative and judicial interpretations." For that reason the Tariff Schedules provide elaborate rules of interpretation to deal with such inherent difficulties. These interpretive rules (including definitions) are contained in "headnotes" prefacing various organizational segments of the Tariff Schedules (such as an individual schedule, a "part" thereof, or a "subpart") or prefacing the Tariff Schedules as a whole (i.e., the General Headnotes).

Note on the Proposed Harmonized System of Tariff Classification

A new international commodity classification system designated as the Harmonized Commodity Description and Coding System, or "Harmonized System" or "Harmonized Code," is nearing completion under the auspices of the Customs Cooperation Council (which is headquartered in Brussels). It is hoped that this system can serve as a common basis for the customs tariffs and foreign trade statistical systems of the United States and its major trading partners; being designed for adoption on an international basis, it would serve as a uniform basis for classifying merchandise in international trade. Adoption of the Harmonized System by the United States would entail the replacement of the current Tariff Schedules of the United States. Under the current time-table, it is expected that the necessary implementing legislation will be intro-duced in the Congress in 1986. In the meantime, all potential signatories to the Harmonized System have been presenting their new GATT schedules in Har-monized System format for negotiation under GATT Article XXVIII. The GATT Tariff Concessions Committee has developed guidelines for this process that state that countries should avoid modifying tariffs at this time for reasons other than those associated with the Harmonized System.

In 1983, the International Trade Commission issued a draft tariff schedule that "converted" the TSUS into the format of the new Harmonized System. Hearings were held on this draft schedule in late 1983. Thereafter, a separate review was undertaken by the Trade Policy Staff Committee, an interagency body chaired by the U.S. Trade Representative. This committee issued a new draft schedule in September 1984.

Since the United States has followed a tariff classification system (the TSUS) different from the systems adopted by its major trading partners (based on the Brussels Tariff Nomenclature), the many differences in classifi-cation and documentation have created an ongoing stream of disputes con-cerning the proper classification of imported articles. The proposed Harmonized System would revise not only the TSUS but the present interna-tional classification system known as the Customs Cooperation Council No-menclature (CCCN). A new harmonized international custom classification system would facilitate trade, commercial shipments, and customs administra-tion, and should lower the costs of international trade.

2. Forms of Product Description

Four principal descriptive forms are used to classify merchandise in the TSUS: (a) general description; (b) *eo nomine* description; (c) physical characteristics; and (d) use. The courts have formulated general guidelines based on these descriptive forms to determine the legislative intent of tariff statutes and the proper classification in the Tariff Schedules.

a. Designation by General Description

This designation uses generic terms or words of general description and constitutes the broadest type of classification, e.g., fish, fruit, beans, wheat, manufactures of a material.

b. *Eo Nomine* Designation

An *eo nomine* description identifies a product by its commonly used name, especially in trade and in commerce. Many products are sufficiently identified by their common names and require no further description to enable an importer or customs official to determine their proper classification, e.g., oranges, lacrosse sticks, parachutes.

Eo nomine descriptions are based on a recognition by courts that tariff statutes are drafted in the language of trade and commerce, which is generally that of common usage. For some products, however, general usage may be a technical or scientific name and courts would rely on the technical or scientific definition of the term. Also, definitions of certain products are provided in the headnotes preceding individual schedule parts and subparts. These definitions are statutorily prescribed and have binding effect.

Courts have developed a "dedicated to single use" test to determine whether an article should be included in an *eo nomine* designation even if, for example, it is in unfinished form. Thus, if an article is so advanced in the processing stage that it cannot be used for any purpose other than final processing of the product within the *eo nomine* designation, it will be included in that product category. For example, in Acme Shear v. United States, 365 F. Supp. 513 (Cust. Ct. 1974), *aff'd,* 524 F.2d 1212 (C.C.P.A. 1975), the court held that rough iron castings in the shape of blades could be used only in the manufacture of scissors or shears.

c. Designation by Description of Physical Characteristics

The descriptive form most commonly used is based on the physical characteristics or composition of a product, i.e., "of wood," "of cotton," "wholly of silk fiber," "in part of bamboo," "wholly or in chief value of earthy or mineral substances," "with stainless steel handles," "wholly or almost wholly of rubber or plastics," "wholly or in part of braid."

The determination of the chief value of a product, as required by the use of "of," is prescribed by General Headnote 10 of the TSUS, which provides:

> (f)   an article is in chief value of a material if such material exceeds in value each other single component material of the article; . . .

The value of each component includes the cost of processing as well as the cost of the raw material. However, labor costs incurred in combining or assembling the completed product are not included as costs of components.

d. Designation by Description of Use or Function

The fourth principal descriptive form of product categories is based on the use or function of the imported article.

The General Interpretive Rules of the Tariff Schedules define classification by use as follows:

> 10. General Interpretive Rules. For the purposes of these schedules—
>
> (e)   in the absence of special language or context which otherwise requires—
>
> > (i)   a tariff classification controlled by use (other than actual use) is to be determined in accordance with the use in the United States at, or immediately prior to, the date of importation, of articles of that class or kind to which the imported articles belong, and the controlling use is the chief use, i.e., the use which exceeds all other uses (if any) combined; . . .

Chief use. The majority of classifications by use depend on the principal or predominant use of the class of articles to which the imported article belongs. Chief use has been interpreted to mean usual or common use or the one which exceeds all other uses combined, as defined by the General Interpretative Rules.

Fugitive use. An alternative use of lesser importance than the chief use is known as a "fugitive" use. As the case of United States v. Baltimore & Ohio R.R. A/C United China & Glass, 17 C.C.P.A. 1 (1959) held:

> Merely because one *can* drink from the imported cups and saucers does not establish the chief use thereof. A fugitive use or a mere susceptibility or capability of use is not controlling as to such chief use.

Note that a designation by specific use will be considered more specific than either an *eo nomine* designation or a general description.

3.   The Rule of Relative Specificity

The principal interpretive rule for classifying items under the TSUS is the rule of relative specificity found in General Headnote 10:

> (c)   an imported article which is described in two or more provisions of the schedules is classifiable in the provision which most specifically describes it; but, in applying this rule of interpretation, the following considerations shall govern:
>
> > (i)   a superior heading cannot be enlarged by inferior headings indented under it but can be limited thereby;
>
> > (ii) comparisons are to be made only between provisions of coordinate or equal status, i.e., between the primary or main superior headings of the schedules or between coordinate inferior headings which are subordinates to the same superior heading.

Several guidelines based on the descriptive forms discussed above have also been developed by the courts to facilitate application of the rule of relative specificity. By far the most important interpretive principle is that an *eo nomine* designation will generally prevail over a general description of the product, unless a contrary legislative intent appears.

Consider the following decisions dealing with the application of *eo nomine* provisions.

W & J SLOANE, INC. v. UNITED STATES

408 F. Supp. 1392 (Cust. Ct. 1976)

RE, J.

The question presented in this case pertains to the proper classification, for customs duty purposes, of certain merchandise imported from Hong Kong between 1967 and 1969. The merchandise, consisting of hand carved wooden panels in configurations of four, six, eight and twelve panels of various heights and weights, is known as "Coromandel screens."

The Customs Service classified the merchandise under item 206.67 of the Tariff Schedules of the United States [TSUS], as modified by T.D. 68-9, as "[w]ood . . . screens," and imposed a duty at the rate of 40, 36 or 32 percent ad valorem, depending upon the date of entry.

Plaintiff contests that classification and claims that the merchandise is properly classifiable under item 207.00, TSUS, as modified by T.D. 68-9, as "[a]rticles not specially provided for, of wood," and that the duty rate should therefore have been only $16\frac{2}{3}$, 15 or 13 percent ad valorem, depending upon the date of entry. In essence, it is plaintiff's contention that, since the Coromandel screens are not used to "shield light, heat, or wind, or to effect privacy," they are not screens within the meaning of item 206.67 of the tariff schedules. Maintaining that they are not "screens," plaintiff, in its brief, refers to the merchandise as "Coromandel wall panels." It succinctly describes their use as follows:

> . . . Coromandel wall panels are highly decorative articles used to beautify and enrich the surroundings in which they are installed. In this respect, they resemble or take the place of paintings, wall hangings, or other non-utilitarian articles of admiration and contemplation and are used in the same manner as paintings, wall hangings, or other non-utilitarian articles of admiration and contemplation which enhance the esthetic appeal of any room.

It is axiomatic in the law to state that the legal conclusion is dictated by the facts of the particular case. The thought is expressed well by the latin maxim *ex facto jus oritur*. In customs classification cases it is equally fundamental to state that the proper classification of imported merchandise also depends upon the competing tariff provisions. . . .

Although elementary, it is pertinent to state that, in customs classification cases, plaintiff bears the dual burden of proving that the classification ascribed to the merchandise by the customs officials is wrong, and that the claimed classification is correct. The facts and the competing tariff provisions of the present case highlight the reason and purpose which impose this dual burden upon the plaintiff. Specifically, plaintiff will not succeed simply by showing that the uses of the Coromandel screens do not necessarily conform to the traditional or usual uses of screens. Rather, to prevail plaintiff must also prove that, in accordance with principles of customs law, its claimed classification is correct, i.e., it more specifically or more appropriately describes the merchandise.

Notwithstanding the excellence of its presentation, plaintiff, for a variety of reasons, could not and did not succeed in meeting this dual burden. Its claim must, therefore, fail.

It is basic in customs law that an *eo nomine* provision for an article, without limitation or contrary legislative intent, judicial decision, or administrative practice, includes all forms of the article. Nootka Packing Co. et al. v. United States, 22 C.C.P.A. 464, 470, T.D. 47464 (1935). The parties are in agreement that tariff item 206.67 for wood screens is an *eo nomine* provision. Clearly, therefore, if the Coromandel screens are indeed screens, within the legislative intendment of the provision for wood screens, they have been correctly classified, and plaintiff's protest must be overruled. . . .

The defendant, in support of its contention that the Coromandel screens are screens within the meaning of item 206.67, has submitted lexicographic definitions found in Webster's Third New International Dictionary of the English Language, Unabridged (1963) at page 2040:

> screen 1: a device used as a protection from the heat of a fireplace or from drafts or as an ornamental piece: as a: a folding temporary partition consisting of hinged leaves usu. made of wood or metal framework covered with cloth, leather, or paper. . . .
>
> 2a: a nonbearing partition that may be solid or pierced, is often ornamental, and is carried up to a height necessary for separation and protection.

It has also quoted extensively from the discussion of "screen" found in the Encyclopaedia Britannica, Volume 20, 14th edition, 1929. This treatment, under the heading of "Screens of China and Japan," deals specifically with "Coromandel screens," and is helpful in understanding the nature of the merchandise in issue.

More significant, however, are the following quotations from the 1948 Summaries of Tariff Information, and the 1968 Summaries of Trade and Tariff Information:

1948 Summaries of Tariff Information, Volume 4, page 80 (with reference to paragraph 411, Tariff Act of 1930):

> The products covered by this summary include woven roll shades, venetian blinds, 2-, 3-, or 4-section folding screens, *ornamental screens,* and various other

types of utility and *ornamental* blinds, curtains, shades, and screens. These are generally, made of wood, bamboo, straw, papier mâche, palm leaf, or compositions of wood. (Emphasis added.)

1968 Summaries of Trade and Tariff Information, Schedule 2, Volume 2, pages 85-87 (with reference to the provision for wood screens):

> The articles include here ordinarily are completely assembled wood shutters, blinds, shades, and screens, with or without their hardware. . . .
> Utility or *decorative* screens usually consist of rectangular wooden frames in sizes comparable to those of shutters. Each frame encloses a thin panel of wood, cloth, plastic, paper, or other material, which may be plainly finished or *highly decorated.* Each frame may have leg members or a supporting stand, and generally three or four frames of the same size are hinged together to make a complete screen. Such movable screens are used to separate, conceal, shelter, or protect room and porch areas. . . .
> The use of wood *decorative* screens has also been rising. Such screens, which have frames of wood, but may have panels of plastics or textile material, are increasingly used as *ornamental* screens and interior room dividers in modern homes. (Emphasis added.)

The quoted sources leave no doubt that the term "screens," includes screens that are "highly decorated," "decorative" and "ornamental"; i. e., decorative screens. As stated in the 1968 *Summaries,* screens may be either "utility or decorative."

It is often stated in customs classification cases that the controverted articles themselves are potent witnesses. Indeed, their careful examination may dictate a classification within a particular tariff provision. . . .

A viewing of the Coromandel screen exhibited during the trial, and a study of the various exhibits submitted by the parties, indicate that the Coromandel screens or Coromandel "wall panels" are *decorative screens.*

Several features may be stated for the conclusion that Coromandel screens are decorative screens. First, it is not disputed that they are decorative. Indeed, plaintiff has taken great pains to prove that a "Coromandel is not a simple screen," but is an artistic creation having artistic merit, and is "installed in rooms for decorative purposes." Second, Coromandel screens have legs so that they may stand or be affixed to the floor in accordion fashion. Third, they have design, decoration or decor on both sides, so that when used as a room divider, the decoration is present on both sides of the divided area. Fourth, the Coromandel screens are sufficiently large and tall to perform the functions of screens. . . .

On the facts and competing tariff provisions of the present case, the successful blending of a utilitarian and decorative function in an imported article does not remove that article from the tariff category which describes it *eo nomine.* . . .

Plaintiff's testimony at the trial concentrated on the use of the Coromandel screens. The emphasis upon use was obviously an attempt to bring the case within the reasoning of Sanji Kobata et al. v. United States, 66 Cust. Ct. 341, C.D. 4213, 326 F. Supp. 1397 (1971). In *Sanji Kobata* certain Japanese "byobu" screens had been classified as "wood screens" under item 206.67 of the tariff schedules. Plaintiffs therein claimed that they were properly classifiable under item 765.03 of the tariff schedules which provided for "[p]aintings . . . executed wholly by hand." The question presented was whether plaintiffs succeeded in establishing that the byobu *screens* were not screens, as classified, but rather *paintings*, as claimed. On the facts, and the competing tariff provisions, this court held that they were paintings for tariff purposes. . . .

A careful examination of the byobu screens and their use in *Sanji Kobata* persuaded the court that they were *paintings* within the claimed tariff provision. This examination caused the court to observe that the screen was merely the surface, comparable to a canvas, upon which the artist painted the landscape or other picture. Indeed, the court noted that the finished artistic creation was embraced in the dictionary definitions of a "painting" as a "decoration achieved by applying paint to a surface."

In addition to the testimony as to use, other factors warranted the classification of the byobu screens as "paintings." For example, it was clear that the byobu screens were designed to satisfy the demand in the United States for wall hangings. Unlike the Coromandel screens, only one side was decorated or adorned with the painting. Moreover, the byobu screens were smaller "and are not the larger size screens that are furniture and serve the function of screens." *Sanji Kobata* at 353. Proof of use in *Sanji Kobata,* as confirmed by the physical characteristics of the byobu screens themselves, not only indicated that they were not used as screens, but also proved that they were used as paintings. Proof of use was helpful in identifying the article in order to determine whether they were "screens," as classified, or more appropriately, "paintings," as claimed. The court in *Sanji Kobata* held that as between those two tariff provisions, "paintings" was more appropriate.

The *Sanji Kobata* case is clearly distinguishable from the case at bar. On the facts, the byobu screens of *Sanji Kobata* differed from the Coromandel screens presently before the court. At the trial of the case at bar, plaintiff brought into the courtroom a seven foot high, eight panel Coromandel screen, a photograph of which was admitted into evidence as plaintiff's illustrative exhibit 1. The byobu screens were considerably smaller, had no legs and contained no painting on the back. The byobu screens were merely the canvas that contained the oriental hand painting and were hung on walls precisely as paintings. More important, in *Sanji Kobata* the competing provisions were *wood screens,* under item 206.67 of the tariff schedules, and *paintings,* under item 765.03 of the schedules. A thorough examination of the byobu screens, the testimony as to use and the exhibits in that case, led to the conclusion that the articles were *paintings,* as claimed.

However obvious, perhaps it is well to repeat that in *Sanji Kobata* plaintiffs succeeded in showing that the merchandise was described in an existing tariff provision for "paintings." In the case at bar, plaintiff has emphasized the artistic nature of the Coromandel screens and, by the careful introduction of testimony as to use, attempted to show that they are creations, and works of art of wood. Unfortunately for plaintiff, it labored mightily to fit the imported merchandise into a customs classification that does not exist in the tariff schedules.

Plaintiff correctly points out that the "competing tariff provisions in this action both cover merchandise 'of wood'." It is an error, however, when it asserts that the Coromandel screens are "not provided for elsewhere in the tariff schedules."

Defendant concedes that item 207.00 of the tariff schedules describes the Coromandel screens, since, clearly, they are articles of wood. It points out, however, that item 207.00 is a general or "basket" provision for articles of wood. Item 206.67 of the tariff schedules is more specific, being an *eo nomine* provision for wood screens. Defendant, therefore, indicates the applicability of General Interpretative Rule 10(c) which provides that: "an imported article which is described in two or more provisions of the schedules is classifiable in the provision which most specifically describes it; . . ."

Rule 10(c), in effect, codifies a rule of eminent good sense that if an imported article is described in two or more tariff provisions it is to be classified under the provision which describes it more specifically.

This rule of relative specificity, as it is known in customs law, is applicable to the case at bar since the Coromandel screens are more specifically provided for under the tariff provision for wood screens. As stated by the Supreme Court: " . . . the designation of an article, *eo nomine*, . . . must prevail over words of a general description which might otherwise include the article specially designated." Chew Hing Lung v. Wise, 176 U.S. 156, 160, 20 S. Ct. 320, 322, 44 L. Ed. 412, 414 (1900). . . .

In view of the foregoing, the tariff classification of the imported merchandise by the customs officials is sustained, and the protests are hereby overruled.

Judgment will issue accordingly.

ATALANTA TRADING CORP. v. UNITED STATES

42 C.C.P.A. 90, C.A.D. 559-599 (1954)

Worley, J.:

This appeal is from a judgment of the United States Customs Court, Third Division, rendered pursuant to its decision, C.D. 1574, overruling appellant's protest involving the classification of certain frog legs imported from Cuba. The Collector of Customs classified and assessed duty on the merchandise at 8 per centum ad valorem under paragraph 1558 of the Tariff Act of 1930, as modified by the Exclusive Trade Agreement with Cuba, T.D. 51819.

The importer claimed the merchandise to be properly dutiable by similitude as "Other" fish provided for in paragraph 717 (b) of the Tariff Act of

1930, as modified by the General Agreement on Tariffs and Trade, T.D. 51802, by virtue of paragraph 1559 of the Tariff Act of 1930, at 1½ cents per pound, or as "Other game" either directly under paragraph 704 of the Tariff Act of 1930, as modified by the General Agreement on Tariffs and Trade, T.D. 51802, or by virtue of the similitude clause in paragraph 1559, at 3 cents per pound.

The pertinent provisions of the paragraphs referred to above read as follows:

Exclusive Trade Agreement with Cuba, T.D. 51819:

Tariff Act of 1930 paragraph	*Description of products*	*Rate of duty*
1558	Frog legs, fresh, chilled, frozen, prepared, or preserved.	8% ad val.

Tariff Act of 1930:

Par. 1558.   That there shall be levied, collected, and paid on the importation of all raw or unmanufactured articles not enumerated or provided for, a duty of 10 per centum ad valorem. and on all articles manufactured, in whole or in part, not specially provided for, a duty of 20 per centum ad valorem.

Par. 1559.   That each and every imported article, not enumerated in this Act, which is similar either in material, quality, texture, or the use to which it may be applied to any article enumerated in this Act as chargeable with duty, shall be subject to the same rate of duty which is levied on the enumerated article which it most resembles in any of the particulars before mentioned: . . .

General Agreement on Tariffs and Trade, T.D. 51802:

Tariff Act of 1930 paragraph	*Description of products*	*Rate of duty*
717 (b)	Fish, fresh or frozen, (whether or not packed in ice), filleted, skinned, boned, sliced, or divided into portions, not specially provided for:	
	Other	1½¢ per lb.
704	Other game (except birds), fresh, chilled, or frozen, not specially provided for:	3¢ per lb.

In view of our conclusion we do not deem it necessary to set forth in detail the record made before the trial court. It is sufficient to state that the seven witnesses for the importer testified that frog legs are sold in fish markets and are cooked and eaten in much the same manner as fish; that the texture is similar to lobster claws or the white portion of sturgeon; that the frog legs arrive in this country skinned and frozen; that the frogs are caught by fishermen in Cuba; and that they have one common biological characteristic with fish; viz., both are cold blooded. The Government submitted no evidence.

In overruling the protest of the importer, the trial court held that the testimony of the witnesses was immaterial to the issues of the case that the *eo nomine* provision for frog legs in the Exclusive Trade Agreement with Cuba, *supra*, prevailed over words of general description which might otherwise include the article. . . .

The importer contends that although section 350 of the Tariff Act of 1930 authorizes the President to modify the rates of existing duties, it does not confer upon him the power to change the relative specificity of any tariff provision nor to reclassify any article by removing it from one paragraph of the act and placing it in another.

Frog legs seem to have long been the subject of administrative and judicial interpretation. . . .

In view of the earlier uniform judicial decisions that frog legs are properly classifiable under paragraph 1558, *supra*, and the various reenactments of the statute with no change being made with regard to the classification of merchandise such as that at bar, it must be presumed that there was legislative approval of those decisions. . . .

Despite the able argument advanced by counsel for appellant in support of his principal contention, we find no error in the conclusion of the trial court that the provision for frog legs under paragraph 1558, *supra*, involved in the Exclusive Trade Agreement with Cuba, is not a reclassification of the merchandise by the President, but is a modification of existing duties, which action is authorized by section 350 (a) of the Tariff Act of 1930.

With respect to the other contentions of appellant, the Government properly points out that the *eo nomine* provision for frog legs in the Exclusive Trade Agreement with Cuba must prevail over more general provisions for fish or game, either directly or by similitude, and that since paragraph 1558, *supra*, embraced the merchandise, the Exclusive Trade Agreement with Cuba properly provided for them *eo nomine* therein, citing Sandoz Chemical Works, Inc. v. United States, 25 Cust. Ct. 115, C.D. 1273; and United States v. Canadian National Railways, 29 C.C.P.A. (Customs) 272, C.A.D. 202.

The judgment of the trial court is affirmed.

NOOTKA PACKING CO. v. UNITED STATES

22 C.C.P.A. 464, 470, T.D. 47464 (1975)

GRAHAM, Presiding Judge, delivered the opinion of the court:

Merchandise, consisting of minced razor clam meat, in cans, packed in British Columbia, Canada, was classified by the collector at the port of Seattle,

Wash., as "clams . . . packed in airtight containers" and assessed with duty at 35 per centum ad valorem under paragraph 721 (b) of the Tariff Act of 1930. The importers protested said classification, claiming, inter alia, that the goods were free of duty under paragraph 1761 of said act as shellfish, prepared or preserved. This claim is the only one relied on in this court. From the judgment of the United States Customs Court, First Division, overruling the protest, importers have appealed to this court.

The two competing tariff provisions follow:

> Par. 721. (b) Clams, clam juice, or either in combination with other substances, packed in air-tight containers, 35 per centum ad valorem.
> Par. 1761. Shrimps, lobsters, and other shellfish, fresh or frozen (whether or not packed in ice), or prepared or preserved in any manner (including pastes and sauces), and not specially provided for.

The uncontradicted testimony of the two witnesses for the importers shows that the involved merchandise consists of razor clams which, after shelling, have had the stomachs, entrails and part of the necks removed, and which have been washed, drained and put through a mincer; that this clam meat is put in cans of two sizes, referred to in the record as "half pound" and "picnic" sizes, so as to half fill them; that the cans are then filled with a brine "partly salt and partly fresh water," "for seasoning and delivery," are steamed about 5 minutes to produce a vacuum, and are sealed and cooked for a period of from 1 hour 15 minutes to 1 hour 22 minutes; that the merchandise is shipped in this condition and is ready to eat; that there is no clam juice produced or added to the product. The average size of the meat of one of the clams, after removal from the shell, is $5\frac{1}{2}$ inches, the maximum length shown being 8 inches, and the weight of the same being from $2\frac{1}{2}$ to 5 ounces. The contents of the so-called "half pound" tins is about 5 ounces. An examination of the exhibits representing the merchandise shows that the cans are about one-half full of clam meat, cut into pieces ranging from one-half inch in length to the size of small peas, immersed in a milk-colored juice. No testimony was offered by the Government. . . .

The importer contends that the involved merchandise is not "clams" for the reason that it is something more than clams—processed material obtained from clams—and relies largely upon the decision of this court in United States v. Sheldon & Co., 14 Cust. Appls. 228, T.D. 41708, to support this contention. The importer argues that "The enumeration of 'clams' in the plural is an indication that whole clams, identifiable as individuals, are intended, rather than the processed material obtained from clams."

In support of the Government's contention that the merchandise is dutiable as assessed, three arguments are made: First, that the case of Alexander & Baldwin, Ltd. v. United States, 21 C.C.P.A. (Customs) 558, T.D. 46988, is *stare decisis;* second, that the legislative history of the provisions under consideration indicates that it was the intent of Congress to make the merchandise at bar dutiable as assessed; third, that paragraph 721 (b) is an *eo nomine* provision, and is a more specific description of the merchandise involved than is said paragraph 1761.

The imported merchandise was entered and invoiced as "minced clams." Although cut into pieces, cleaned, and cooked, according to the testimony of the importers, it can be readily identified as parts of clams. Paragraph 721 (b) of the Tariff Act of 1930 provides for "Clams, clam juice, or either in combination with other substances, packed in air-tight containers." It will be observed that this language is not restricted to clams in their raw or natural state, nor is it restricted to entire clams. It includes any clams in any condition, so long as they are clams. "Where a dutiable provision names an article without terms of limitation all forms of the article are thereby included unless a contrary legislative intent otherwise appears." Smillie v. United States, 11 Ct. Cust. Appls. 199, 201, T.D. 38966. In Tower & Sons v. United States, 11 Ct. Cust. Appls. 157, 162, T.D. 38948, boiled down cider was held to come within the statutory designation "cider," as against "fruit juices" and "fruit syrups," the court saying, "when the term 'cider' was written into the provision without words of limitation it must be assumed that it was intended to include all kinds of cider."

To the same effect is Schade v. United States, 5 Ct. Cust. Appls. 465, T.D. 35002, where frozen wheat was involved.

It is apparent that this was the intention of the Congress in enacting this provision. We quote a portion of the report of the Ways and Means Committee of the House of Representatives, relative to H.R. 2667, now the Tariff Act of 1930. Report No. 7, 71st Cong., 1st sess., p.74:

> Special provision is made for the caviar from sturgeon roe, which is the most expensive form of caviar, *and for canned clams*. The latter is a new industry of interest to both coasts of the United States. On the Atlantic coast the competition is from Canada and on the Pacific coast there exists a very important competition from Japan. The rates provided are intended to equalize the cost of production. (Italics ours.)

The mere mincing of the clams, or cleaning them, or cooking them, does not remove them from the designation of clams. The cases are plentiful in support of this proposition. In Neuman & Schwiers Co. et al. v. United States, 4 Ct. Cust. Appls. 64, T.D. 33310, hams, with the bone extracted, and cooked and canned, were held to be hams, and not prepared or preserved meats. In Brown & Co. v. United States, 6 Ct. Cust. Appls. 415, T.D. 35977, soya beans, cooked and salted, and canned, were held to be not "something more than soya beans in the sense that they are something else." In that case the court further said, "That is to say, they are soya beans advanced in condition, but not so far advanced as to be converted into a new article." In that case the court cited many preceding cases, both in this court and in the Supreme Court of the United States, where the same principle obtained.

In Mawer Co. v. United States, 7 Ct. Cust. Appls. 493, T.D. 37108, olives, pitted, stuffed with pimentos, sterilized and soaked and canned, were held to come within the designation "olives," rather than within "edible fruits . . . prepared or preserved." In the recent case of Alexander & Baldwin v. United States, 21 C.C.P.A. (Customs) 558, T.D. 46988, the contest was between paragraphs 721 (b) and 1761, as in the case now before us. While the precise question here involved was not presented there, this court did say in its opinion:

> While it does not appear in the instant case whether the combination of clams and clam juice had undergone a process of cooking, that, in our opinion, as the issue has been here presented, is not material, and we regard this case and that involved in T.D. 46025 as being quite analogous.

The appellants contend that this case is controlled by another line of cases, exemplified by the pistache nuts case, United States v. Sheldon & Co., 14 Ct. Cust. Appls. 228, T.D. 41708. In that case, pistache nuts, roasted and salted, were held by a majority of the court to be edible nuts, prepared or preserved, rather than under the designation "pistache nuts." However, that case did not rest upon the competition between pistache nuts and edible nuts, prepared or preserved, alone, but was based largely upon the fact that the Congress, in enacting the provision for edible nuts, had repeated the expression, "not specially provided for," in such a way as to compel the court to the conclusion that what the Congress had in mind was edible nuts, prepared or preserved, which had not been otherwise specially provided for, rather than as edible nuts which had not been specially provided for.

The appellants also cite two cases, United States v. La Manna et al., 14 Ct. Cust. Appls., 123, T.D. 41647, and United States v. Pacific Trading Co., 14 Ct. Cust. Appls. 131, T.D. 41649. There the competition was between a statutory provision for onions, and another for vegetables, pickled, or packed in salt, brine, oil, or prepared or preserved. In each of these latter cases, the decision rested largely upon the fact that onions had been uniformly in previous acts, and in the act then under consideration, dutiable by the bushel or pound, and it was thought by the court that this, together with a consideration of the legislative history, compelled the conclusion that only onions in their natural state were intended to be included in the *eo nomine* provision for onions. Hence, the onions involved in the cases there at bar, being pickled, were held to be more properly dutiable under the pickled or prepared vegetable provision. These cases were followed by Budlong Pickle Co. v. United States, 16 Ct. Cust. Appls. 174, T.D. 42808.

Other adjudged cases on the subject will be briefly commented upon.

Breman v. United States, 136 Fed. 743, wherein limes, in brine, were held by the court to be classifiable as "fruits in brine" rather than as "limes," is relied upon by appellant. An examination of that case shows that limes in brine were different in character and use from fresh limes; that there was a commercial designation distinguishing limes in brine from fresh limes, and a long established administrative practice distinguishing the same.

The case of United States v. Reiss & Brady, 136 Fed. 741, also relied upon, is one where commercial designation distinguished between "figs" and "fruits preserved." Lacomb, C. J., in disposing of the matter, was of the opinion that in trade and commerce the competing paragraphs described different articles.

Stone & Co. v. United States, 7 Ct. Cust. Appls. 173, T.D. 36492, involved currants, crushed and ground into a mass. These were held to be "fruits, . . . prepared," rather than as "currants." This case approaches closely the matter involved here, and is strongly relied upon. However, it will be noted that the court there said: "The importation has completely lost its identity as currants. It is an indeterminate mass or pulp. It is, in fact, a material prepared or made from currants, the ultimate use of which is in the manufacture of wines. Its general and more diversified uses as currants have thus been destroyed or limited."

No such facts appear here. So far as the record goes, the imported product before us is adaptable to exactly the same uses as would be whole clams. . . .

The case of Kwong Yuen Shing v. United States, 1 Ct. Cust. Appls. 16, T.D. 30774, is brought to our attention. In that case, preserved duck meat, salted, pickled, dried in the sun and packed in tins, and sometimes packed in peanut oil, was held to be "meats prepared or preserved" rather than "poultry dressed." It appears from the opinion of the court that this holding rested upon proof of commercial designation. This further appears from reference to the opinion of this court in United States v. General Hide & Skin Corp., 11 Ct. Cust. Appls. 78, T.D. 38731, where the decision in the Kwong Yuen Shing case, *supra,* is commented upon. In United States v. General Hide & Skin Corp., *supra,* rabbit meat, cooked and canned, was, in the absence of commercial designation, held to be rabbits, and to come within the designation "game" rather than as "meats . . . prepared or preserved."

In this latter case, this court again reiterated its holding "that where an article is designated without words of limitation, that designation will generally include the article in all its forms known to commerce." To the same effect is Shoellkopf, Hartford & MacLagan v. United States, 71 Fed. 694, where the statutory term "paraffine," without limitations and without proof of commercial designation, was held to include all kinds of paraffine.

In Smith v. United States, 168 Fed. 462, meat of the quail, lark, and young chickens, prepared by cooking and packed in airtight cans for preservation, was held to be classifiable as "meats of all kinds, prepared or preserved," rather than as "poultry dressed." This case, also, went off on proof of the established meaning of the word "poultry."

The clear weight of the authorities on the subject is that an *eo nomine* statutory designation of an article, without limitations or a shown contrary legislative intent, judicial decision, or administrative practice to the contrary, and without proof of commercial designation, will include all forms of said article. Such is the situation here, and the trial court properly held the imported goods to be dutiable under said paragraph 721 (b).

It seems inconceivable that the Congress, in attempting to protect the clam industry in the United States, should intend to free list such clams if they were cut into pieces. In our opinion, no such conclusion is required. The imported goods are clams, and should be classified as such.

The judgment of the United States Customs Court is affirmed.

NOTES AND QUESTIONS

1. How can the "common meaning" of terms be determined? Are you impressed with Judge Re's sources to determine the common meaning of the term "screen" in *W & J Sloane*?

2. What does the rule of relative specificity really tell us? Doesn't it merely state a truism, and leave courts to grapple with what they think are more specific descriptions?

3. What is the difference between a cigarette holder and a novelty item in the form of a cigarette holder? How should a 13-½ inches long cigarette holder be classified? Assume: (a) there is a classification for both cigarette holders and for novelty items in the form of cigarette holders; or (b) there is a classification for cigarette holders but not for novelty items in the form of cigarette holders. *See* Novelty Import Co., Inc. et al. v. United States, 285 F. Supp. 160, 55 C.D. 2570 (Cust. Ct. 1965).

4. The cases rely heavily on legislative intention in ascertaining the proper duty classification. How can legislative intention be ascertained? How influential should it be compared with the actual wording of the TSUS?

5. You are a congressman or congresswoman and are voting on whether the following should be included within the customs territory of the United States: (a) U.S. satellites serving as hosts for manufacturing operations; (b) U.S. ships engaged in deep seabed mining and processing.

How would you vote and why? Consider §209 of the Trade and Tariff Act of 1984:

> The return of articles from space shall not be considered an importation, and an entry of such articles shall not be required, if:
> (1) such articles were previously launched into space from the customs territory of the United States aboard a spacecraft operated by, or under the control of, United States persons and owned—
>   (A) wholly by United States persons, or
>   (B) in substantial part by United States persons, or
>   (C) by the United States;
> (2) such articles were maintained or utilized while in space solely on board such spacecraft or aboard another spacecraft which meets the requirements of paragraph (1)(A) through (C) of this section; and
> (3) such articles were returned to the customs territory directly from space aboard such spacecraft or aboard another spacecraft which meets the requirements of paragraph (1)(A) through (C) of this section;
> without regard to whether such articles have been advanced in value or im-

proved in condition by any process of manufacture or other means while in space.

6. Why should the plaintiff in a tariff classification case have to first prove that the classification made is incorrect, and then that the claimed classification is right, as asserted in the *W & J Sloane* case? Why should the presumption be made that the government is correct? Doesn't the current formulation weight the scales of justice against the plaintiff? *Note* the case of Jarvis Clark Co. v. United States, 733 F.2d 873 (Fed. Cir. 1984), which holds that the plaintiff no longer has to overturn the dual presumption.

7. What do you think was the primary reason for the decision in the *Nootka Packing* case? Hasn't the identity of the whole clams been destroyed by the mincing process?

8. How can one tell between a chief use and a fugitive use? Nonhanging plastic flower pots are classified as horticultural implements, on the theory that their chief use is in a horticultural pursuit. Don't flower pots have other uses, such as champagne glasses, pencil holders, or goldfish bowls? Are these "fugitive" uses?

9. Consider the following cases:

(a) merchandise is imported consisting of dangling or jumping fur monkey figures—the Government contends that these items should be classified as "toys," the headnote definition for which reads:

> The term "toy" means an article chiefly used for the amusement of children, whether or not also suitable for physical exercise or for mental development.

The plaintiffs contend that the fur monkeys should be classified as articles in chief value of fur, dutiable, needless to say, at a lower 17%, versus 35%, level. What result? *See* Pico Novelty et al. v. United States, 62 C.D. 3759 (Cust. Ct. 1969).

(b) How should a model dollhouse or parts thereof be classified—as a "toy" or as a "model made to scale"? Would your answer differ depending on the value of the imported dollhouse? What if a collector of rare dollhouses imports a $250,000 dollhouse—is this a toy?

4.   Unassembled or Unfinished Articles; Doctrine of Entireties

General Interpretive Rule 10(h) of the TSUS provides:

> (h) Unless the context requires otherwise, a tariff description for an article covers such article, whether assembled or not assembled, and whether finished or not finished.

General Headnote 10 is a statutory formulation of the doctrine of entireties pursuant to which unassembled parts or components are classified as an assembled or finished product if the following conditions are met at the time of importation:

(1) The parts or components must be designed or intended to be assembled or combined after importation into the article in question.

(2) The parts or components must be packed separately (not commingled) in the same shipment for the same importer.

(3) The article, "constructively" assembled or combined into an entirety, must itself fall within the product description under consideration. In other words, the "constructive" assembly or combining of the imported parts or components alone must produce an article to which the product description applies. The absence of a substantial or essential part would render the doctrine of entireties, as in the case of General Headnote 10(h), inapplicable. In such case, the imported parts or components would have to be classified separately.

A recent interpretation of the rule of the doctrine of entireties is found in Daisy-Heddon, Div. Victor Comptometer v. United States, 600 F.2d 799 (C.C.P.A. 1979), in which the court had to decide whether components of fishing reels, with certain parts lacking, should be classified as reels (dutiable at 23%) or as parts of reels (dutiable at 13.5%). The court held that under the doctrine of entireties the imported articles should be classified as fishing reels, despite the absence of certain parts, because the articles would have been substantially complete reels if imported in an assembled condition. Thus, under the rule of entireties an unassembled article will be classified as the finished article if the components, upon assembly, would constitute a substantially complete article.

The court in *Daisy-Heddon* rejected its earlier interpretation of the doctrine of entireties based on the principle, formulated in Authentic Furniture Products v. United States, 486 F.2d 1062 (C.C.P.A. 1973), that the absence of a substantial or essential part precludes classification of parts or components as the completed article in unfinished form. Under the *Authentic Furniture Products* interpretation, the intent of General Headnote 10(h) could be circumvented inasmuch as the absence of virtually any part of an unassembled article could prevent the assembled product from being used in the manner contemplated. Thus, the court in *Daisy-Heddon* set out certain factors that could be used in determining whether an imported article was substantially complete:

(1) The number of parts omitted as compared to the number of parts included.

(2) The time and effort required to complete the article as compared to the time and effort required to place it in its imported condition.

(3) The costs of the omitted parts as compared to the costs of the included parts.

(4) The importance of the omitted parts to the overall functioning of the completed article.

(5) Trade customs—whether the importation is usually recognized as an unassembled or unfinished article or as a part of that article.

The court did not intend this list to be exhaustive and recognized that additional factors may require consideration, depending on the nature of the imported article.

The doctrine of entireties may be found inapplicable if one or more of the imported components of an article may be used independently. Thus, if a component is found to have an independent use, or an independent identity, the unassembled or unfinished article may not qualify for classification as a completed product. The doctrine of entireties is also inapplicable when components, even though intended to be assembled after importation, are not imported together.

NOTES AND QUESTIONS

1. Under the doctrine of entireties, would a truck cab chassis imported with a truck bed be classified as a truck? What if it is imported without a bed? The *Daisy-Heddon* decision led the U.S. Customs Service to reopen on October 17, 1979, for public comment the question of the correctness of its established practice of classifying imported cab chassis in item 692.20 TSUS, which carried a duty of 4% *ad valorem,* rather than under the provisions in item 692.02 TSUS for automobile trucks valued at $1,000 or more, which carried the proclaimed rate of duty under item 945.69 TSUS of 25% *ad valorem.* In T.D. 80137 (45 Fed. Reg. 35,057, May 23, 1980), the Customs Service found its established practice to be clearly wrong under the guidelines of the *Daisy-Heddon* case and announced that imports of lightweight cab chassis would be classified under item 692.02 TSUS and charged duty under item 945.69 TSUS (25%). This Customs Service decision was upheld by the Court of International Trade in Toyota Motor Sales U.S.A. v. United States, 585 F. Supp. 649 (Ct. Intl. Trade 1984), *aff'd,* No. 84-1326, slip op. (Fed. Cir. Feb. 1, 1985). How can you square *Toyota Motor Sales* with the Webster's Dictionary definition of a truck as a vehicle possessing both a locomotive capacity and a cargo-carrying capability?

2. How should a light truck with two seats bolted to the truck bed facing backwards be classified—as a truck or a car? What is the chief use—for transportation or hauling?

3. Assume that a platinum bracelet mounting and 234 diamonds are shipped in the same package. The mounting contains 234 holes for the insertion of diamonds suitable for mounting in the bracelet. Should the bracelet mounting and diamonds be classified as a bracelet, and assessed as jewelry? *See* United States v. Kronfeld, Saunders, 20 C.C.P.A. 57, T.D. 45679 (1932).

4. What if a combination of machinery designed and used as a composite unit with the single purpose of producing finished welded pipe is imported. Should it be held as an entirety classifiable as electrical welding apparatus? *See* United States v. Mannesmann-Meer, Inc., 54 C.C.P.A. 24, C.A.D. 897 (1966).

5. What if an importation did not comprise a complete breadstick production line since it lacked packaging or wrapping machinery? Should it be held as an entirety? *See* Stella D'oro Biscuit Co. v. United States, 65 C.C.P.A. 52, C.A.D. 1205, 570 F.2d 945 (1978).

6. Should batteries for radios be classified as entireties with radios? *See* United Merchandising v. United States, 48 Cust. Ct. 50, C.D., 2313 (1962). Should cases for radios be classifiable as entireties with radios? *See* Lafayette Radio Electronics v. United States, 57 C.C.P.A. 62, C.A.D. 977, 421 F.2d 751 (1970).

7. Try the following as an example of bringing together the various ideas. The commodity imported was specially designed multistrike film ribbon used in cartridges in daisy-wheel word processing equipment. The government wanted it classified as "other articles not specially provided for of textile materials" (25 cents per pound plus 15% *ad valorem*) or alternatively "parts of typewriters" (9.5% *ad valorem*). Importer wanted it as "other articles not specially provided for of plastics" (8.5% *ad valorem*) or "other parts of office machines" (5.5% *ad valorem*). *See* Kores Manufacturing v. United States, 545 F. Supp. 1303 (Ct. Intl. Trade 1982).

8. Assume you are a judge sitting on the U.S. Court of International Trade. How would you rule on the proper tariff classification of imported plastic germination tray sets, assuming the following facts:

(a) the chief use of the item, which consists of three trays, syphon caps, a catch basin, and a lid, is for the cultivation of edible sprouts from seeds in a soilless medium;

(b) the following alternative classifications exist in the Tariff Schedules of the United States:

(1) TSUS item 772.15, "other" articles chiefly used for preparing food;

(2) TSUS item 666.00, "horticultural implements";

(3) TSUS item 772.20, containers for the packing, transportation, or marketing of merchandise.

C. VALUATION

1. The GATT Customs Valuation Code

The second part of the customs entry process for the importer is valuation. The GATT Code on Customs Valuation greatly simplified the entire area, and should reduce the use of customs valuation procedures as a nontariff barrier to trade. As you read the following selections from the code consider how the treatment of a related party trade transaction might differ from that of an unrelated party sale. The provisions of U.S. law implementing the GATT Code on Customs Valuation (Title II of the Trade Agreements Act of 1979) are included in the Selected Documents Supplement. For background on the code, and particularly for discussion of a European predecessor, the Brussels Definition of Value, *see* Sherman, Reflections on The New Customs Valuation Code, 12 Law & Pol. Intl. Bus. 119 (1980); and S. Sherman and H. Glashoff, A Businessman's Guide to the GATT Customs Valuation Code (1980).

GATT CUSTOMS VALUATION CODE

Articles 1-3, 8 (1979)

PART I—RULES ON CUSTOMS VALUATION

ARTICLE 1

1. The customs value of imported goods shall be the transaction [i.e., the invoice] value, that is the price actually paid or payable for the goods when sold for export to the country of importation adjusted in accordance with the provisions of Article 3, provided:

  (a) that there are no restrictions as to the disposition or use of the goods by the buyer other than restrictions which:
      (i) are imposed or required by law or by the public authorities in the country of importation;
      (ii) limit the geographical area in which the goods may be resold; or
      (iii) do not substantially affect the value of the goods;
  (b) that the sale or price is not subject to some condition or consideration for which a value cannot be determined with respect to the goods being valued;
  (c) that no part of the proceeds of any subsequent resale, disposal or use of the goods by the buyer will accrue directly or indirectly to the seller, unless an appropriate adjustment can be made in accordance with the provisions of Article 8; and
  (d) that the buyer and seller are not related, or where the buyer and seller are related, that the transaction value is acceptable for customs purposes under the provisions of paragraph 2 of this Article.
2. (a) In determining whether the transaction value is acceptable for the purposes of paragraph 1, the fact that the buyer and the seller are related within the meaning of Article 15 shall not in itself be grounds for regarding the transaction value as unacceptable. In such case the circumstances surrounding the sale shall be exam-

ined and the transaction value shall be accepted provided that the relationship did not influence the price. If, in the light of information provided by the importer or otherwise, the customs administration has grounds for considering that the relationship influenced the price, it shall communicate its grounds to the importer and he shall be given a reasonable opportunity to respond. If the importer so requests, the communication of the grounds shall be in writing.

(b) In a sale between related persons, the transaction value shall be accepted and the goods valued in accordance with the provisions of paragraph 1 whenever the importer demonstrates that such value closely approximates to one of the following occurring at or about the same time:

(i) the transaction value in sales to unrelated buyers of identical or similar goods for export to the same country of importation;

(ii) the customs value of identical or similar goods as determined under the provisions of Article 5;

(iii) the customs value of identical or similar goods as determined under the provisions of Article 6;

(iv) the transaction value in sales to unrelated buyers for export to the same country of importation of goods which would be identical to the imported goods except for having a different country of production provided that the sellers in any two transactions being compared are not related.

In applying the foregoing tests, due account shall be taken of demonstrated differences in commercial levels, quantity levels, the elements enumerated in Article 8, and costs incurred by the seller in sales in which he and the buyer are not related that are not incurred by the seller in sales in which he and the buyer are related.

(c) The tests set forth in paragraph 2(b) are to be used at the initiative of the importer and only for comparison purposes. Substitute values may not be established under the provisions of paragraph 2(b).

ARTICLE 2

1. (a) If the customs value of the imported goods cannot be determined under the provisions of Article 1, the customs value shall be the transaction value of identical goods sold for export to the same country of importation and exported at or about the same time as the goods being valued.

(b) In applying this Article, the transaction value of identical goods in a sale at the same commercial level and in substantially the same quantity as the goods being valued shall be used to determine the customs value. Where no such sale is found, the transaction value of identical goods sold at a different commercial level and/or in different quantities shall be used, adjusted to take account of differences attributable to commercial level and/or to quantity, provided that such adjustments can be made on the basis of demonstrated evidence which clearly establishes the reasonableness and accuracy of the adjustment, whether the adjustment leads to an increase or a decrease in the value.

2. Where the costs and charges referred to in Article 8.2 are included in the transaction value, an adjustment shall be made to take account of significant differences in such costs and charges between the imported goods and the identical goods in question arising from differences in distances and modes of transport.

3. If, in applying this Article, more than one transaction value of identical goods is found, the lowest such value shall be used to determine the customs value of the imported goods.

ARTICLE 3

1. (a)   If the customs value of the imported goods cannot be determined under the provisions of Articles 1 and 2, the customs value shall be the transaction value of similar goods sold for export to the same country of importation and exported at or about the same time as the goods being valued. . . .

ARTICLE 8

1. In determining the customs value under the provisions of Article 1, there shall be added to the price actually paid or payable for the imported goods:
   (a)   the following, to the extent that they are incurred by the buyer but are not included in the price actually paid or payable for the goods:
       (i)   commissions and brokerage, except buying commissions;
       (ii)   the cost of containers which are treated as being one for customs purposes with the goods in question;
       (iii)   the cost of packing whether for labour or materials;
   (b)   the value, apportioned as appropriate, of the following goods and services where supplied directly or indirectly by the buyer free of charge or at reduced cost for use in connection with the production and sale for export of the imported goods, to the extent that such value has not been included in the price actually paid or payable:
       (i)   materials, components, parts and similar items incorporated in the imported goods;

  (ii) tools, dies, moulds and similar items used in the production of the imported goods;

  (iii) materials consumed in the production of the imported goods;

  (iv) engineering, development, artwork, design work, and plans and sketches undertaken elsewhere than in the country of importation and necessary for the production of the imported goods;

 (c) royalties and licence fees related to the goods being valued that the buyer must pay, either directly or indirectly, as a condition of sale of the goods being valued, to the extent that such royalties and fees are not included in the price actually paid or payable;

 (d) the value of any part of the proceeds of any subsequent resale, disposal or use of the imported goods that accrues directly or indirectly to the seller.

2. In framing its legislation, each party shall provide for the inclusion in or the exclusion from the customs value, in whole or in part, of the following:

 (a) the cost of transport of the imported goods to the port or place of importation;

 (b) loading, unloading and handling charges associated with the transport of the imported goods to the port or place of importation; and

 (c) the cost of insurance.

2. *United States Customs Evaluation*

Articles in commerce transported into the United States for sale are, of course, subject to U.S. Customs. The following sets out some of the procedures and criteria the U.S. Customs Service employs to evaluate incoming merchandise.

NONTRANSACTION METHODS OF VALUATION

U.S. Customs Service, Customs Valuation (1980)

1. DEDUCTIVE VALUE

If the transaction value of imported merchandise, of identical merchandise, or of similar merchandise cannot be determined, then deductive value is calculated for the merchandise being appraised. Deductive value is the next basis of appraisement to be used, unless the importer designated, at entry summary, computed value as the preferred method of appraisement. If computed value was chosen and subsequently determined not to exist for customs valuation purposes, then the basis of appraisement reverts back to deductive value.

 If an assist is involved in a sale, that cannot be used in determining deductive value. So any sale to a person who supplies an assist for use in connection with the production or sale for export of the merchandise concerned is disregarded for deductive value.

Basically deductive value is the resale price in the United States after importation of the goods, with deductions for certain items. In discussing deductive value, the term "merchandise concerned" is used. The term means the merchandise being appraised, identical merchandise, or similar merchandise. Generally, the deductive value is calculated by starting with a unit price and making certain additions to and deductions in that price.

A.   UNIT PRICE.

One of three prices constitutes the unit price in deductive value. The price used depends on when and in what condition the merchandise concerned is sold in the United States. . . .

B.   ADDITIONS.

Packing costs for the merchandise concerned are added to the price used for deductive value, provided such costs have not otherwise been included. These costs are added, regardless of whether the importer or the buyer incurs the cost.

Packing costs means the cost (1) of all containers and coverings of whatever nature and (2) of packing, whether for labor or materials, used in placing the merchandise in condition, packed ready for shipment to the United States.

C.   DEDUCTIONS.

Certain items are not a part of deductive value. These items must be deducted from the unit price. The items are:

1. Commissions or Profit and General Expenses. Any commission usually paid or agreed to be paid, or the addition usually made for profit and general expenses, applicable to sales in the United States of imported merchandise that is

(a) of the same class or kind as the merchandise concerned;

(b) regardless of the country of exportation;

2. Transportation/Insurance Costs.

The usual and associated costs of transporting and insuring the merchandise concerned

(a) From the country of exportation to the place of importation in the United States, and

(b) From the place of importation to the place of delivery in the United States, provided these costs are not included as a general expense under the preceding paragraph;

3. Customs Duties/Federal Taxes. The customs duties and other Federal taxes payable on the merchandise concerned because of its importation, plus any

Federal excise tax on, or measured by the value of, such merchandise for which sellers in the United States are ordinarily liable; and

4. Value of Further Processing. The value added by the processing of the merchandise after importation, provided sufficient information exists concerning the cost of processing. The price determined for deductive value is reduced by the value further processing, only if the third unit price (the superdeductive) is used as deductive value. (Under the superdeductive, the merchandise concerned is not sold in the condition as imported and not sold before the close of the 90th day after the date of importation, but is sold before the 180th day after the date of importation.) . . .

5. COMPUTED VALUE

The last basis of appraisement is computed value. If customs valuation cannot be based on any of the values previously discussed, then computed value is considered. This value is also the one the importer can select at entry summary to precede deductive value as a basis of appraisement.

Computed value consists of the sum of the following items:

a. Materials, fabrication, and other processing used in producing the imported merchandise

b. Profit and general expenses

c. Any assist, if not included in (a) and (b), and

d. Packing costs.

a. Materials, Fabrication, and Other Processing. The cost or value of the materials, fabrication, and other processing of any kind used in producing the imported merchandise is based (1) on information provided by or on behalf of the producer and (2) on the commercial accounts of the producer, if the accounts are consistent with generally accepted accounting principles applied in the country of production of the goods.

Note: If the country of exportation imposes an internal tax on the materials or their disposition and refunds the tax when merchandise produced from the materials is exported, then the amount of the internal tax is not included as part of the cost or value of the materials.

b. Profit and General Expenses. The producer's profit and general expenses are used, provided they are consistent with the usual profit and general expenses reflected by producers in the country of exportation in sales of merchandise of the same class or kind as the imported merchandise.

Some facts concerning the amount for profit and general expenses should be mentioned:

1. The amount is determined by information the producer supplies and on his commercial accounts, provided such accounts are consistent with generally accepted accounting principles in the country of production.

Note: As a point of contrast, for deductive value the generally accepted principles used are those in the United States, whereas in computed value the generally accepted accounting principles are those in the country of production.

2. The producer's profit and general expenses must be consistent with those usually reflected in sales of goods of the same class or kind as the imported merchandise that are made by producers in the country of exportation for export to the United States. If they are not consistent, then the amount for profit and general expenses is based on the usual profit and general expenses of such producers.

3. The amount for profit and general expenses is taken as a whole. This is the same treatment as occurs, and has been discussed, in deductive value.

Basically, a producer's profit could be low and his general expenses high, so that the total amount is consistent with that usually reflected in sales of goods of the same class or kind. A producer's actual profit figures even if low, will be used, provided he has valid commercial reasons to justify them and his pricing policy reflects usual pricing policies in the industry concerned.

c. Assists. If the value of an assist used in producing the merchandise is not included as part of the producer's materials, fabrication, other processing or general expenses, then the prorated value of the assist will be included in computed value. It is important that the value of the assist is not included elsewhere because no component of computed value should be counted more than once in determining computed value.

Note: The value of any engineering, development, artwork, design work, and plans and sketches undertaken in the United States is included in computed value only to the extent that such value has been charted to the producer.

d. Packing Costs. The cost of all containers and coverings of whatever nature and of packing, whether for labor or material, used in placing merchandise in condition, packed ready for shipment to the United States is included in computed value. . . .

As can be seen, computed value relies to a certain extent on information that has to be obtained outside the United States, that is, from the producer of the merchandise. If a foreign producer refuses to or is legally constrained from providing the computed value information, or if the importer cannot provide such information within a reasonable period of time, then computed value cannot be determined.

6.   VALUE IF OTHER VALUES CANNOT BE DETERMINED

If none of the previous five values can be used to appraise the imported merchandise, then the customs value must be based on a value derived from one of the five previous methods, reasonably adjusted as necessary. The value so determined should be based, to the greatest extent possible, on previously determined values. Only data available in the United States will be used.

Some examples of how the other methods can be reasonably adjusted are:

Identical Merchandise (or Similar Merchandise):

(a) The requirement that the identical merchandise (or similar merchandise) should be exported at or about the same time as the merchandise being appraised could be flexibly interpreted.

(b) Identical imported merchandise (or similar imported merchandise) produced in a country other than the country of exportation of the merchandise being appraised could be the basis for customs valuation.

(c) Customs values of identical imported merchandise (or similar imported merchandise) already determined on the basis of deductive value and computed value could be used.

Deductive Method. The 90-day requirement could be administered flexibly. . . .

NOTES AND QUESTIONS

1. Under current Japanese customs law, imports of chocolate confectionery are subject to *ad valorem* tariff duties. These imports are classified under Customs Tariff Item No. 18.06 in Japan, which includes chocolate and other food preparations (including sugar confectionery) containing cocoa. Pursuant to a GATT concession, a general 35% *ad valorem* duty rate applies to imports of chocolate confectionery from the United States.

On the basis of advertising independently undertaken by Candyman Inc. Japan, the Japanese customs bureau proposes to "uplift" the value of imported chocolate confectionery from its parent in the United States for the purpose of determining the actual tariff duty to be imposed under the aforementioned system. This results in an increase in the effective tariff rate from 35% to 43%.

If you were arguing this case for the U.S. exporter, how persuasive could you be in citing:

(a)   Article 8 of the GATT Customs Valuation Code;
(b)   Article II of the GATT;
(c)   Article VII of the GATT;
(d)   Article XXII of the GATT;
(e)   Article XXIII of the GATT;
(f)   Section 301 of the Trade Act of 1974, citing the "unjustifiable" and "unreasonable" aspects of that provision?

2. Under the export value test used in U.S. customs law prior to the Trade Agreements Act of 1979, export value was deemed to include the value of European Economic Community (EEC) restitutions paid upon the exporta-

tion of certain agricultural products from the EEC. What result under Customs Valuation Code and the Trade Agreements Act of 1979? Assume sugar is exported to the United States with a home market value of 50 units of account, and receives a 10 unit of account restitution upon exportation to the United States. *See* M & M/Mars Snackmaster Div. of Mars., Inc. v. United States, No. 84-5, slip op. (Ct. Intl. Trade 1984).

3. XYZ Corporation, a toy manufacturer and distributor in the United States, imported this month from ABC Corporation, its sister company in Abu Dhabi, 100,000 each of four toy items, representing well-known movie characters. Made of plastic, the toys were manufactured from molds furnished free of charge by XYZ. The costume designer for the movie had flown from his home in Hollywood at the expense of XYZ to consult with ABC personnel on the proper colors for the toys.

At the time of the toys' exportation from Abu Dhabi, ABC was the only manufacturer of plastic toys in that country. The items were the first products produced by ABC, and the company does not plan to manufacture more of the toys for at least six months.

In answering this question, consider the U.S. Customs Classification Document C.S.C. 99-501 *infra*.

XYZ agreed initially to pay $2.00 plus five cents for packing costs for each of the toys. In addition, the sales contract provides that XYZ will pay ABC an additional $1.00 for every item it sells within two years from the toys' date of importation. XYZ must also pay the designer a royalty of ten cents for each of the articles and a selling commission of $10,000 to TNT, a Panama corporation and the parent company of both XYZ and ABC.

a. What is the proper tariff classification of the toys? What is the applicable rate of duty?

b. Explain how the goods should be valued for customs purposes.

c. How could XYZ postpone for six months paying the applicable duty on the items?

(The relevant tariff schedules follow.)

C.S.D. 99-501—CLASSIFICATION: FIGURES INSPIRED BY THE MOVIE "STAR WARS"

United States Customs Service, Classification and Value Division (July 11, 1979)

To: District Director of Customs, Seattle Wash.
From: Director, Classification and Value Division.
Subject: Internal advice request No. 74/78 concerning the tariff classification of the "Darth Vader," "Sand People," "Jawa" and "Chewbacca" Star Wars figures.

Facts.—The above four "Star Wars" figures were classified as other toys not specially provided for in item 737.95, TSUS. The inquirer contends that the four articles are properly classifiable as toy figures of animate objects in item 737.40, TSUS.

Issue.—Was the classification of this merchandise under the provision for other toys not specially provided for in item 737.95, TSUS, correct?

Law and analysis.—Toy figures of animate objects need not necessarily be representations of human beings. They may be either representations of earth beings or other living beings. This interpretation was given in the case of Lewis Galoob Co. v. United States, C.D. 4239 (1971) wherein the court equated the word "animate" with a *living* being [italic ours]. In the main body of the case, the court uses the phrases "human or other living being," from which an inference can be drawn that creatures other than human beings were contemplated as being animate objects, for example, creatures which are life forms on other planets. The court, moreover, refers to the case of Louis Marx & Co. v. United States, 40 Cust. Ct. 610 (1958), for a definition of the word "animate." In the *Marx* case, the court cited the dictionary definition of the word, concluding that an animate object is one representing animals or people, that is, possessing animal life, and that inanimate objects are those which are not endowed with animal life, such as benches, trees, fences, etc.

Insofar as the four aliens from the motion picture "Star Wars" are concerned, they are, with the exception of Darth Vader, animate creatures, recognizable life forms on other planets. They are humanoid or human-like in that they think, play, fight, and communicate to one another. They possess all the traits associated with human beings.

This does not imply that all extra-terrestrial creatures will be considered toy figures of animate objects. Only those which are humanoid in form or those which are similar to earth-type animals, like apes, cats, spiders, etc., will be classifiable as such. Thus the "Ents" toy figure from J. R. Tolkien's Lord of the Rings would not be a figure of an animate object. The "Ents" resemble trees which are not considered animate objects on earth and which therefore are not classifiable as animate objects for tariff classification purposes. As a further example, the wind-up bug like object referred to in headquarters letter Mfg. 492.113 c 004055 dated April 20, 1970, would not be a toy figure of an animate object because there is no easily identifiable counterpart of this bug like creature in the animal kingdom.

Darth Vader is now considered a human in the movie "Star Wars." Underneath the black mask there is presumably the face of a human being as opposed to that of a robot. The Darth Vader figure, therefore, is a doll for tariff classification purposes, classifiable in item 737.22, TSUS.

Holding.—The Darth Vader figure is classifiable as a doll in item 737.22, TSUS.

The other three Star Wars figures were improperly classified as other toys not specially provided for in item 737.95, TSUS. They are classifiable under the provision for other toy figures of animate objects in item 737.40, TSUS.

Please inform the inquirer of this ruling.

GSP	Item	Stat. suffix	Articles	Units of quantity	Rates of duty 1	Rates of duty LDDC	Rates of duty 2
			Subpart E. - Models; Dolls, Toys, Tricks, Party Favors				
			Subpart E headnotes:				
			1. The articles described in the provisions of this subpart (except parts) shall be classified in such provisions, whether or not such articles are more specifically provided for elsewhere in the tariff schedules, but the provisions of this subpart do not apply to—				
			(i) doll carriages, doll strollers, and parts thereof (see part 5C of this schedule);				
			(ii) wheeled goods designed to be ridden by children, and parts thereof (see part 5C of this schedule); or				
			(iii) games and other articles in items 734.15 and 734.20, toy balls (items 735.09-.12), and puzzles and games in item 735.20 (see part 5D of this schedule).				
			2. For the purposes of the tariff schedules, a *"toy"* is any article chiefly used for the amusement of children or adults.				
			Model trains, model airplanes, model boats, and other model articles, all the foregoing whether or not toys; and construction kits or sets for making or assembling such model articles:				
	737.05	00	Models of inventions and of other improvements in the arts, to be used exclusively as models	X	Free		Free

	Item		Description		Rates of Duty		
A	737.07	00	Other models, and construction kits or sets: Rail locomotives and rail vehicles; railroad and railway rolling stock; track, including switching track; rail depots, round houses, signal towers, water towers, and other trackside structures; trolley buses and trolley-bus systems; cable-car systems; highway vehicles; ships and harbor structures; and airplanes and spacecraft; all the foregoing made to scale of the actual article at the ratio of 1 to 85 or smaller	X	6.9% ad val.	5.1% ad val.	45% ad val.
A	737.09	00	Construction kits or sets with construction units prefabricated to precise scale of the actual article	X	8.1% ad val.	5.7% ad val.	45% ad val.
A*	737.15	20	Model trains, model airplanes, model boats, etc. (con.): Other models, and construction kits or sets (con.): Articles described in item 737.07, made to a scale of the actual article at a ratio larger than 1 to 85	X	13.9% ad val.	7.8% ad val.	70% ad val.
		60	Other	X			
A*	737.21	00	Dolls, and parts of dolls including doll clothing: Doll clothing imported separately	X	13.9% ad val.	8% ad val.	70% ad val.
A*	737.22	05	Other Dolls (with or without clothing): Stuffed	No	15.4% ad val.	12% ad val.	70% ad val.
		15	Other: Over 13 inches in height	No			
		25	13 inches and under in height	No			
		40	Parts of dolls	X			

SCHEDULE 7. - SPECIFIED PRODUCTS; MISCELLANEOUS AND NONENUMERATED PRODUCTS (*continued*)

Part 5. - Arms and Ammunition; Fishing Tackle; Wheel Goods; Sporting Goods, Games and Toys

GSP	Item	Stat. suffix	Articles	Units of quantity	Rates of duty		
					1	LDDC	2
			Toy figures of animate objects (except dolls):				
			Not having a spring mechanism:				
			Stuffed:				
A*	737.25	00	Valued not over 10 cents per inch of height	No	21.7% ad val.	11.2% ad val.	70% ad val.
A*	737.30	00	Valued over 10 cents per inch of height	No	7.7% ad val.	5.5% ad val.	70% ad val.
			Not stuffed:				
A	737.35	00	Wholly or almost wholly of metal	No	8.1% ad val.	4.2% ad val.	70% ad val.
A	737.40	00	Other	No	13.6% ad val.	7% ad val.	70% ad val.
			Having a spring mechanism:				
A	737.45	00	Wholly or almost wholly of metal	No	9.7% ad val.	5.8% ad val.	70% ad val.
A*	737.50	00	Other	No	17.1% ad val.	8.8% ad val.	70% ad val.
	737.52	00	Toy books, including coloring books and books the only reading matter in which consists of letters, numerals, or descriptive words	X	Free		Free
A	737.55	00	Toy alphabet blocks; and toy building blocks, bricks, and shapes	X	8.8% ad val.	6% ad val.	70% ad val.
A*	737.60	00	Toy musical instruments	X	12.4% ad val.	6.4% ad val.	70% ad val.

	No.	Stat.	Description		Rate 1	Rate 2	Rate 3
A	737.65	00	Magic tricks, and practical joke articles	X	8.4% ad val.	5.8% ad val.	70% ad val.
A	737.70	00	Confetti, paper spirals or streamers, party favors, and noisemakers	X	4% ad val.	4% ad val.	45% ad val.
			Toys, and parts of toys, not specially provided for:				
A*	737.80	00	Toys having a spring mechanism	No	17.1% ad val.	8.8% ad val.	70% ad val.
			Other:				
	737.85	00	Kites	X	13.9% ad val.	7.8% ad val.	70% ad val.
A*	737.95		Other		13.6% ad val.	7% ad val.	70% ad val.
		15	Toys having a friction or weight operated motor	No			
		25	Toys having an electric motor	No			
			Other (except parts):				
			Wholly or almost wholly of rubber or plastics:				
			Inflatable:				
		36	Toy balloons and punch-balls	X			
		38	Other	X			
		45	Other	X			
		50	Other	X			
		60	Parts	X			

Bibliographical Note

For additional information on customs classification the standard treatise is by R. Sturm, Customs Law and Administration (1980). *See also* P. Feller, U.S. Customs and International Trade Guide (1979); and Feller, "An Introduction to Tariff Classification, 8 Law & Pol. Intl. Bus. 991 (1976).

For additional description of the Customs Valuation Code, *see* Sherman, Reflections on the New Customs Valuation Code, 12 Law & Pol. Intl. Bus. 159 (1980); White, The New Import Valuation Code: A Digest of Customs Rulings, 17 Intl. Law. 729 (1983). On valuation generally, *see* Dickey, A Guide for Pricing Commodities to Enter the Commerce of the United States, 11 Law & Pol. Intl. Bus. 491 (1979).

Chapter VIII

Nontariff Barriers to Trade: Standards and Government Procurement

Nontariff barriers to trade (NTBs) permeate the world of international commerce and are today more significant deterrents to trade than tariffs. The job of classifying the many barriers to the flow of commerce other than tariffs is a difficult one; practices such as harassment of traders through use of the antidumping and countervailing duty laws, along with arbitrary tariff reclassifications and inappropriate valuations could be considered as NTBs. This chapter focuses on two other areas that are more clearly discernible as NTBs—standards and government procurement.

A. TECHNICAL STANDARDS

Technical standards have a major impact on trade, and, in some instances, may totally eliminate imports in a particular product sector. Problems with national technical standards include:

(a) the multiplicity of standards;
(b) the implementation of technical standards criteria upon arrival of the foreign products;
(c) national requirements on domestic in-process testing; and
(d) standards which, while not discriminatory against imports, are prima facie unreasonable.[1]

---

[1] See, in general, Fisher, U.S. Safety Standards as Non-tariff Trade Barriers: The Case of Compressed Gas Cylinders, 19 SAIS Rev. 42 (1975).

Technical standards are often set by administrative agencies and frequently reflect a politically important balance between industrial interests and environmental or consumer interests. Nations, however, have often sought to use these standards as excuses to exclude foreign goods; technical standards, enacted apparently for legitimate reasons, have sometimes also made a market hard for foreign suppliers to penetrate.

There are many examples. There is evidence that at one point U.S. tomato standards, dealing with ripeness and size, etc., were designed to be hard for Mexican growers and easy for U.S. growers to meet. In some periods, the severe auto emission rules for U.S. cars were a barrier to the smaller foreign auto manufacturers who had trouble tooling for this small portion of their output. Rules for metric vs. English system sizes and labelling have had similar effects. To complicate the situation, standards are often made privately, by business or by trade association, especially when they are designed for manufacturing convenience: screw thread sizes, parts labelling, component compatibility provisions, etc.

To rectify the trade-limiting aspects of national standards, the participants in the Multilateral Trade Negotiations consummated the Agreement on Technical Barriers to Trade, excerpts of which follow. (The implementing legislation for ensuring U.S. compliance with this agreement is contained in Title IV of the 1979 Trade Act; that for helping U.S. exporters obtain foreign compliance is the §301 procedure of Title IX of the 1974 Act. (Both are included in the Selected Documents Supplement selections from the Trade Act.)

As you read the Standards Code, consider how the code handles the issues of:

(1)   national treatment;
(2)   the type of standard which, while not discriminatory, is unreasonably high;
(3)   harmonization of national standards;
(4)   transparency in the formulation and application of national standards;
(5)   federalism, i.e., the possibility that states (or provinces, for that matter) might enact standards higher than those of the national (or federal) authorities;
(6)   the role of non-governmental organizations in the preparation and adoption of standards;
(7)   the problems of domestic in-process testing requirements;
(8)   application of obligations to:
      (a)   non-signatories;
      (b)   developing countries; and
(9)   enforcement and sanctions.

Portions of the MTN Standards Code are included in the Selected Documents Supplement.

GATT AGREEMENT ON TECHNICAL BARRIERS TO TRADE

§§2, 5, 13 (1979)

PREAMBLE

Having regard to the Multilateral Trade Negotiations, the Parties to the Agreement on Technical Barriers to Trade, hereinafter referred to as "the Parties" and "this Agreement";

Desiring to further the objectives of the General Agreement on Tariffs and Trade;

Recognizing the important contribution that international standards and certification systems can make in this regard by improving efficiency of production and facilitating the conduct of international trade;

Desiring therefore to encourage the development of such international standards and certification systems;

Desiring however to ensure that technical regulations and standards, including packaging, marking and labelling requirements, and methods for certifying conformity with technical regulations and standards do not create unnecessary obstacles to international trade;

Recognizing that no country should be prevented from taking measures necessary to ensure the quality of its exports, or for the protection of human, animal or plant life or health, of the environment, or for the prevention of deceptive practices subject to the requirement that they are not applied in a manner which would constitute a means of arbitrary or unjustifiable discrimination between countries where the same conditions prevail or a disguised restriction on international trade;

Recognizing that no country should be prevented from taking measures necessary for the protection of its essential security interest;

Recognizing the contribution which international standardization can make to the transfer of technology from developed to developing countries;

Recognizing that developing countries may encounter special difficulties in the formulation and application of technical regulations and standards and methods for certifying conformity with technical regulations and standards, and desiring to assist them in their endeavours in this regard;

Hereby agree as follows. . . .

TECHNICAL REGULATIONS AND STANDARDS

2. *Preparation, adoption and application of technical regulations and standards by central government bodies*

With respect to their central government bodies:

2.1 Parties shall ensure that technical regulations and standards are not prepared, adopted or applied with a view to creating obstacles to international trade. Furthermore, products imported from the territory of any Party shall be accorded *treatment no less favourable than that accorded to like products of national origin* and to like products originating in any other country in relation to such technical regulations or standards. They shall likewise ensure that neither technical regulations nor standards themselves nor their application have the effect of *creating unnecessary obstacles to international trade.*

2.2 Where technical regulations or standards are required and relevant international standards exist or their completion is imminent. Parties shall use them, or the relevant parts of them, as a basis for the technical regulations or standards except where, as duly explained upon request, such international standards or relevant parts are inappropriate for the Parties concerned, for inter alia such reasons as national security requirements; the prevention of deceptive practices; protection for human health or safety, animal or plant life or health, or the environment; fundamental climatic or other geographical factors; fundamental technological problems.

2.3 With a view to *harmonizing* technical regulations or standards on as wide a basis as possible, Parties shall play a full part within the limits of their resources in the preparation by appropriate international standardizing bodies of international standards for products for which they either have adopted, or expect to adopt, technical regulations or standards.

2.4 Wherever appropriate, Parties shall specify technical regulations and standards in terms of performance rather than design or descriptive characteristics.

2.5 Whenever a relevant international standard does not exist or the technical content of a proposed technical regulation or standard is not substantially the same as the technical content of relevant international standards, and if the technical regulation or standard may have a significant effect on trade of other Parties, Parties shall:

2.5.1 publish a notice in a publication at an early appropriate stage, in such a manner as to enable interested Parties to become acquainted with it, that they proposed to introduce a particular technical regulation or standard;

2.5.2 notify other Parties through the GATT secretariat of the products to be covered by technical regulations together with a brief indication of the objective and rationale of proposed technical regulations;

2.5.3 upon request, provide without discrimination, to other Parties in regard to technical regulations and to interested parties in other Parties in regard to standards, particulars or copies of the proposed technical regulation or standard and whenever possible, identify the parts which in substance deviate from relevant international standards;

2.5.4 in regard to technical regulations allow, without discrimination reasonable time for other Parties to make comments in writing, discuss these comments upon request, and take these written comments and the results of these discussions into account;

2.5.5 in regard to standards, allow reasonable time for interested parties in other Parties to make comments in writing, upon request discuss these comments with other Parties and take these written comments and the results of these discussions into account.

2.6 Subject to the provisions in the heading of Article 2.5, where urgent problems of safety, health, environmental protection or national security arise or threaten to arise for a Party, that Party may omit such of the steps enumerated in Article 2.5 as it finds necessary provided that the Party, upon adoption of a technical regulation or standard, shall:

2.6.1 notify immediately other Parties through the GATT secretariat of the particular technical regulation, the products covered, with a brief indication of the objective and the rationale of the technical regulation, including the nature of the urgent problems;

2.6.2 upon request provide, without discrimination other Parties with copies of the technical regulation and interested parties in other Parties with copies of the standard;

2.6.3 allow, without discrimination, other Parties with respect to technical regulations and interested parties in other Parties with respect to standards, to present their comments in writing, upon request discuss these comments with other Parties and take the written comments and the results of any such discussion into account;

2.6.4 take also into account any action by the Committee as a result of consultations carried out in accordance with the procedures established in Article 14.

2.7 Parties shall ensure that all technical regulations and standards which have been adopted are published promptly in such a manner as to enable interested Parties to become acquainted with them. . . .

CONFORMITY WITH TECHNICAL REGULATIONS AND STANDARDS

5.   Determination of conformity with technical regulations or standards by central government bodies

5.1 Parties shall ensure that, in cases where a positive assurance is required that products conform with technical regulations or standards, central government bodies apply the following provisions to products originating in the territories of other Parties:

5.1.1 imported products shall be accepted for testing under conditions no less favourable than those accorded to like domestic or imported products in a comparable situation;

5.1.2 the test methods and administrative procedures for imported products shall be no more complex and no less expeditious than the corresponding methods and procedures, in a comparable situation for like products of national origin or originating in any other country;

5.1.3 any fees imposed for testing imported products shall be equitable in relation to any fees chargeable for testing like products of national origin or originating in any other country;

5.1.4 the results of tests shall be made available to the exporter or importer or their agents, if requested, so that corrective action may be taken if necessary;

5.1.5 the siting of testing facilities and the selection of samples for testing shall not be such as to cause unnecessary inconvenience for importers, exporters or their agents;

5.1.6 the confidentiality of information about imported products arising from or supplied in connexion with such tests shall be respected in the same way as for domestic products.

5.2 However, in order to facilitate the determination of conformity with technical regulations and standards where such positive assurance is required, Parties shall ensure whenever possible, that their central government bodies:

accept test results, certificates or marks of conformity issued by relevant bodies in the territories of other Parties; or rely upon self-certification by producers in the territories of other Parties;

even when the test methods differ from their own, provided they are satisfied that the methods employed in the territory of the exporting Party provide a sufficient means of determining conformity with the relevant technical regulations or standards. It is recognized that prior consultations may be necessary in order to arrive at a mutually satisfactory understanding regarding self-certification, test methods and results, and certificates or marks of conformity employed in the territory of the exporting Party, in particular in the case of perishable products or of other products which are liable to deteriorate in transit.

5.3 Parties shall ensure that test methods and administrative procedures used by central government bodies are such as to permit, so far as practicable, the implementation of the provisions in Article 5.2.

5.4 Nothing in Article 5 shall prevent Parties from carrying out reasonable spot checks within their territories. . . .

INSTITUTIONS, CONSULTATION AND DISPUTE SETTLEMENT

13.   THE COMMITTEE ON TECHNICAL BARRIERS TO TRADE

There shall be established under this Agreement:

13.1 A *Committee on Technical Barriers to Trade* composed of representatives from each of the Parties to this Agreement (hereinafter referred to as "the Committee"). The Committee shall elect its own Chairman and shall meet as necessary but no less than once a year for the purpose of affording Parties to this Agreement the opportunity of consulting on any matters relating to the operation of this Agreement or the furtherance of its objectives and shall carry out such responsibilities as assigned to it under this Agreement or by the Parties;

13.2 Working parties, technical expert groups, panels or other bodies as may be appropriate, which shall carry out such responsibilities as may be assigned to them by the Committee in accordance with the relevant provisions of this Agreement.

13.3 It is understood that unnecessary duplication should be avoided between the work under this Agreement and that of governments in other technical bodies, e.g. Codex Alimentarius. The Committee shall examine this problem with a view to minimizing such duplication. . . .

QUESTIONS

1. To understand the various procedures of the U.S. implementing legislation, trace through what you would do as counsel in each of the following cases:

(a) Your client is a U.S. company that believes that a European standard is discriminatory and is keeping your client's products out of Europe.

(b) Your client is a European company that believes that a U.S. standard is discriminatory and is keeping your client's products out of the U.S.

(c) Your client is a U.S. company that dominates the widget socket industry. The widget industry is dominated by a German company. Always before, the two companies have easily reached agreement on compatible specifications, but negotiations have broken down for a new generation of widgets almost ready for mass production.

(d) Your client is a U.S. environmental group that believes the U.S. has standards that pay inadequate attention to environmental interests. (Or an industrial group that believes the U.S. intervention responded unduly to environmental concerns.)

2. Under the U.S. legislation, how much power does a private party have to compel executive action? What about a foreign party to compel U.S. response?

3. Why does the legislation include §2551? In which of the cases of Question 1 is this provision relevant? Is it wise?

4. What does the legislation say about the right of a foreign firm to appear at a U.S. administrative hearing to set standards? To use §2532 to attack the outcome of such a hearing? For a case raising the issue before §2532 was enacted, see Walter Holm & Co. v. Hardin, 449 F.2d 1009 (D.C. Cir. 1971).

5. Has the United States adequately implemented the international agreement?

6. Is the international agreement meant to be directly applied by courts or to give legal rights to private parties? What are the pros and cons of doing so?

7. How often are national standards likely to fail to measure up to the international standards for standards?

8. How does the Standards Code attempt to avoid conflicts between safety (or health, or the environment) and trade considerations? Is it successful?

9. The Standards Code prohibits the use of standards, test methods, or certification systems that create "unnecessary obstacles to international trade."

Don't all standards, test and certification requirements create obstacles to trade? When are such obstacles "unnecessary"?

10. Does the prohibition of "unnecessary obstacles to international trade" ever mean that the United States cannot adopt higher standards for product safety or automobile emissions than, say, Brazil? Does it mean that whatever levels of health, safety, or environmental protection that the United States chooses to require must be enforced fairly and efficiently? Which meaning should the phrase have?

11. Who decides whether obstacles to trade resulting from standards, test methods, or certification systems are "unnecessary"? What is the result of a finding that a standard creates unnecessary obstacles?

12. How would you evaluate the effect of this dispute settlement procedure on the balance of power between environmental and consumer groups on the one side and industrial groups on the other? Be sure to think about which side is likely to be best represented in the transnational process. And note further that the lessons of the U.S. context are subtle—e.g., the 19th century pattern of business control of state legislatures compared with the late twentieth century pattern of federal legislation preempting stronger pro-consumer and pro-environment state legislation.

13. What is the effect of this dispute settlement procedure on the balance of power between the private sector and the executive (in the United States)?

14. Was it wise to adopt this approach? Consider some of the alternatives:

(a) A provision like §2532 directly enforceable in the courts of each nation by foreign parties. (Note that this would be difficult in nations that give courts a weaker role in administrative rule making.)

(b) Binding international adjudication, perhaps with arrangements for participation by consumer and environmental groups.

15. Suppose the state of California adopts a testing requirement that every automobile imported from Japan be driven into a brick wall at 20 mph. What could the federal government do about this clear violation of the Standards Code (a) before an international complaint is filed; or (b) after an international panel has found the United States to be in violation of its obligations under the Standards Code?

16. The Standards Code requires signatories to accept the results of foreign tests "whenever possible." Who decides when acceptance of foreign tests is or is not possible? What if testing in country A is reliable, and testing in country B is not. If both are GATT Contracting Parties, would it violate U.S. most-favored-nation obligations to accept foreign testing from country A but not from country B?

17. The Standards Code requires signatories to base new standards upon internationally-accepted standards if such international standards exist. This requirement applies except where the international standards are "inappropriate." What constitutes "inappropriateness"? Who decides?

18. Could another signatory bring a complaint under the Standards Code against the U.S. electrical system (110 volts v. 220 volts in most of the rest of the world)? Against the U.S. non-metric system of weights and measures?

Aren't these "unnecessary obstacles to international trade"? What about special standards in response to the danger of earthquakes in California?

19. When is a labelling requirement an "unnecessary obstacle to trade"? Would it be permissible for Canada to require that Chablis wine from California be labeled "American Wine of Chablis Type"—ostensibly to protect consumers from deception?

20. India is a GATT Contracting Party but is not a signatory to the Standards Code. Suppose the United States refuses to accept foreign testing of Indian products, claiming that there is no obligation under the code to accept foreign testing by nonsignatories. Does India have a legitimate complaint that its MFN rights under the GATT have been violated? How would (and should) the GATT handle such an issue?

21. Suppose the government of Sweden, in an effort to reduce national health care costs, proposes to have all high-cholesterol items packaged in red wrappers, all low-cholesterol items in green wrappers, and all other items in yellow wrappers. The publicly stated rationale is that high-cholesterol items tend to cause heart attacks, which in turn places a high cost on Sweden's national health care system. Would a U.S. exporter of confectionery to Sweden have a valid complaint against Sweden under the Standards Code if it were forced to market its produce in a red wrapper? What if the government of Sweden required all of the red wrapper packages to contain a skull-and-crossbones logo?

Bibliographical Note

For additional data on technical standards, *see* Sweeney, Technical Analysis of the Technical Barriers to Trade Agreement, 12 Law & Pol. Intl. Bus. 179 (1980); R. Baldwin, Non-Tariff Distortions of International Trade (1970); on the issue of the application of NTB codes *see* Hufbauer, Erb, and Starr, The GATT Codes and the Unconditional Most-Favored-Nation Principle, 12 Law & Pol. Intl. Bus. 59 (1980).

B. GOVERNMENT PROCUREMENT

Government procurement, or the purchase of goods and services for governmental use,[2] accounts for an increasing amount of commerce, as national authorities increase their policy targets. If national authorities were to purchase only domestic products this would amount to a significant NTB.[3]

---

[2]Government procurement should be distinguished from state trading, which is the commercial activity of state-owned enterprises, or enterprises given special privileges by a government.

[3]In the United Kingdom and the United States, government purchases typically account for one-fifth of the GNP. Twenty-five percent of the world's GNP has been estimated to consist of

Prior to the MTN, government procurement had been omitted from the GATT,[4] and, accordingly, international surveillance as a potential NTB. Not only were national authorities reserving most of their procurements for local suppliers, but they were not even making transparent, or known, their bidding process.[5]

The MTN Government Procurement Code was intended to be a partial remedy for this state of affairs. The key obligation assumed by signatories under the code is that of national treatment. Part II of the code provides that signatories are to provide other signatories treatment no less favorable than that accorded to domestic products and suppliers for specified government agencies. In addition, signatories are not to discriminate among foreign suppliers (Part V), and the code requires fair, consistent, and transparent procedures in government purchasing. Signatories must publish their procurement laws and regulations in publications specified in the code itself. Moreover, intricate substantive standards and publication requirements must be satisfied during all phases of the procurement process.

The code is clearly not a panacea for the NTB that government procurement has become over the years, and the code's limitations abound. First, it applies only to the purchase of products, and service contracts are not included (although services that are "incidental to the supply of products" are). Second, the code applies only to specified government agencies, which vary from signatory to signatory, each of which was the subject of considerable negotiation. Third, national security acquisitions (warlike material) are generally omitted by the signatories.

The Government Procurement Code, like the standards code, applies on a conditional-MFN basis, i.e., its benefits flow only to those accepting its obligations. One may question whether its enforcement mechanism is strong enough—signatories may retaliate only by suspending the application of the accord if a violation of the code is found by the Committee on Government Procurement.

The next round of multilateral trade negotiations will undoubtedly address

---

government procurement. *See* United States Tariff Commission, Report to the Senate Committee on Finance and Its Subcommittee on International Trade Barriers (1972); and Travers, An International Code on Government Procurement—Reality Enhanced by Trade Reform Act of 1974, 10 Pub. Cont. Newsletter No. 4 (July, 1975).

[4] Article II 8(a) expressly provided that the national treatment obligations of the GATT on internal taxation and regulation were not to apply to government procurements. *See also* 8(b). With regard to state-trading, Article XVII (2) provides only that governments should accord "fair and equitable treatment" to suppliers when filling their governmental requirements.

[5] The reasons generally provided by national governments for discrimination in favor of local suppliers were:

(a) national security considerations, or the desire to avoid excessive dependence on foreign suppliers for strategic materials;

(b) promotion of domestic goods, such as employment, and the promotion of domestic technology and industrialization; and

(c) the alleviation of balance of trade problems.

See in general Marks and Malmgren, Negotiating Nontariff Distortions to Trade, 7 Law and Pol. Intl. Bus. 327-399 (1975).

the Government Procurement Code, and possibly expand its coverage to services and other areas. The MTN Agreement on Government Procurement is included in the Selected Documents Supplement, as are the provisions of U.S. law implementing the Code (Title III of the Trade Agreements Act of 1979).

If you were the owner of a small or medium-size business, would you expect to benefit substantially from the code? How would the benefits you might expect compare with those forgone by the waiver of the Buy America Act? Consider the following excerpt from a House report.

HOUSE COMMITTEE ON WAYS AND MEANS, TRADE AGREEMENTS ACT OF 1979

H.R. Rep. No. 317, 96th Cong., 1st Sess. 103-110 (1979)

ANALYSIS OF POTENTIAL BENEFITS TO THE UNITED STATES

INTRODUCTION

Negotiations regarding coverage of the Agreement on Government Procurement were conducted on an entity basis. In other words, negotiations centered on the inclusion or exclusion of specific ministries, departments, and other government agencies. The end result of this process was a set of country offers consisting of lists of covered entities.

Analysis of the coverage of the Agreement is a difficult and imprecise task for a number of reasons. One of the key reasons for this difficulty is the extent to which the structures of governments, and their purchasing practices, vary. Some governments purchase through central purchasing entities while others allow each agency to do its own purchasing. Some governments are highly centralized while some have numerous semiautonomous sub-jurisdictions. Finally, the extent of government incursion in the market place varies among countries. For instance, in most European countries power generating facilities are owned by the government, while in the United States such facilities are generally privately owned.

Statistics on government purchasing are of limited use as an analytical tool. To begin with, very little data is available. Even the United States has only recently begun to maintain procurement data on a centralized and systematic basis. In fact, one of the major benefits of the Agreement is that it will require adherents to maintain detailed statistics on their purchasing practices. The data which is currently available must be viewed in the light of its limitations. It is one year data rather than time series data. As a result these data provide no indication of the constant growth of government purchasing over time. This type of data also masks or unduly highlights such things as large but intermittent purchases. Finally, fluctuating exchange rates make it difficult to pin down the value in dollar terms of offers of purchases which are made using other currencies.

One final consideration which is key to the analysis of the benefits of this Agreement is the currently large disparity in the openness of government procurement markets to foreign products. The United States is trading the equivalent of six to 12 percent tariff in return for the elimination of what amounts in most cases to an administrative embargo by our trading partners. The United States procurement market is already open to any foreign firm that can overcome a relatively modest preference margin. On the other hand, our trading partners, for the most part, only purchase foreign goods when the goods to be procured are not available domestically.

Given the nature of this agreement, it appears that the most useful method of analyzing its economic benefits is to examine the degree to which the United States and our trading partners have agreed to cover government entities and the extent to which comparable entities serving comparable functions are covered.

In general, major signatories have agreed to coverage of most purchases of goods by their central government ministries and departments—excluding national security purchases. While a comparison in dollar terms is not by itself a particularly useful way of measuring reciprocity, the overall picture is as follows. The United States has offered coverage totaling $12.5 billion while our negotiating partners have offered an aggregated coverage totaling approximately $20.7 billion, not including offers by Austria and the developing countries.

On a country basis, offers amount to:	Billion
European Communities	$10.50
Japan	6.90
Canada	1.10
Sweden	1.10
Switzerland	.33
Finland	.26
Norway	.17

It is not possible to calculate in dollar terms the increase in U.S. exports or imports that will result from this Agreement. However, it should be noted that our trading partners will be providing new export opportunities in areas where we are highly competitive. These areas include, inter alia, computers, business machines, laboratory equipment, pharmaceuticals, measuring instruments and, to a limited extent, telecommunications equipment. . . .

From the outset of negotiations it was expected that the telecommunications, heavy electrical, and transportation (mostly railroad) sectors would be problem areas. The U.S. market in these areas is already essentially open to purchasing based on commercial considerations because most of such entities are in the private sector. On the other hand, there is a high degree of government incursion in these areas on the part of our trading partners. The European Communities (EC) was expected to be particularly difficult in the negotiations since it had been unable to agree to the opening of markets in these areas even among its member states. As anticipated, the EC did not offer these entities although the EC did offer the post offices within the Postal-Telegraph-Telephone systems (PTTs) which was an important foot in the door. Our other trading partners followed suit (with the exception, in part, of Japan). As a result, the United States sought to redress this imbalance by withdrawing coverage of:

Department of Transportation;
Department of Energy;
The Bureau of Reclamation;
The Army Corps of Engineers;
The Tennessee Valley Authority; and
GSA's automated Data and Telecommunications Service

In a further balancing move, the United States did not offer coverage of such government chartered corporations as COMSAT, AMTRAK, CONRAIL, or the U.S. Postal Service, which are not bound by the Buy America Act. . . .

Although the U.S. Buy America law will be waived for federal government purchases of covered goods under the Government Procurement Code, no such waiver need be granted for purchases of these same goods by state and local governmental bodies. Agreement on Government Procurement, done Apr. 11, 1979, MTN/NTM/W/211/Rev. 1, Part I, reprinted in Agreements Reached in the Tokyo Round of the Multilateral Trade Negotiations H.R. Doc. No. 153, 96th Cong., 1st Sess. 67-89 (1979). Thus, for those states that currently have their own Buy America acts, the code ostensibly imposes no obligation to open up competitive bidding to foreign contractors.

State Buy America acts have been the subject of litigation on a few occasions during the past two decades. The following case considers the constitutionality of such a state act. In reading it, consider whether the results would be different had the Government Procurement Code been in effect at the time.

K.S.B. TECHNICAL SALES CORP. v. NORTH JERSEY DISTRICT WATER SUPPLY COMMISSION OF THE STATE OF NEW JERSEY

75 N.J. 272, 381 A.2d 774 (1977)

SCHREIBER, J.

This case projects for our review the validity of New Jersey "Buy American" statutes, which generally require use in government purchase contracts of materials produced in this country. The bidding specifications of the North Jersey District Water Supply Commission (Commission) for a water treatment plant contained such a provision. K.S.B. Technical Sales Corp. (K.S.B.), a New York corporation which is a wholly owned subsidiary of a West German manufacturer of pumps and pumping equipment, and Linda Fazio, a taxpayer and resident of the City of Clifton, seek an adjudication that the Buy American condition in the specifications be declared invalid and its statutory foundation unconstitutional. . . .

A brief factual summary is in order. The North Jersey District Water Supply Commission, a governmental agency, was created for the purpose of developing a water supply for municipalities in the northern part of the State. N.J.S.A. 58:5-1 et seq. It has carried out that function and has been distributing water to eight municipalities in Essex, Hudson and Passaic counties. In 1974 the Commission was ordered to comply with a directive of the State Department of Health to construct a water treatment plant to improve the quality of the water. . . . For that purpose the Commission submitted specifications to prospective bidders which included a requirement that "[o]nly manufactured products of the United States, wherever available, shall be used in the work in accordance with municipalities and counties Local Public Contracts Law. . . .

State work is governed by N.J.S.A. 52:32-1 which reads as follows:

> The state shall make provisions in the specifications for all contracts for state work and for work for which the state pays any part of the cost, that only such manufactured and farm products of the United States, whenever available, be used in such work. (N.J.S.A. 52:32-1]

This law has remained unchanged since its adoption in 1932. . . .

The plaintiffs, who, as counsel stated during oral argument, are not particularly concerned with the award of this contract, seek a general declaration that the New Jersey Buy American statute is unconstitutional. The constitutional issues concern the applicability and effect of the General Agreement on Tariffs and Trade made between the United States and foreign countries, the conflict, if any, between the New Jersey Buy American provisions and the foreign affairs power, and the conflict, if any, between the New Jersey Buy American provisions and the Commerce Clause. . . .

I. THE NEW JERSEY BUY AMERICAN STATUTE AND THE FEDERAL GENERAL AGREEMENT ON TARIFFS AND TRADE (GATT)

The General Agreement on Tariffs and Trade (GATT) is a multi-lateral international agreement to which the United States is a party by virtue of executive action. Presidential authority to bind the United States to GATT has been predicated in part on the Reciprocal Trade Agreements Act of 1934 and its successors, 48 Stat. 943 (1934) (currently codified at 19 U.S.C.A. §§1351-1366 (1965 & Supp. 1977)), and in part upon the executive power to conduct foreign affairs. The legal significance of GATT has been considered by all parties as equivalent to that of a treaty. . . .

In the context of this litigation we do likewise. Thus we conclude that GATT is, by virtue of the federal constitution, "the supreme Law of the Land." *See* U.S. Const., Art. VI, cl. 2. A state law must yield when it is inconsistent with or impairs the policy or provisions of a treaty. . . .

Facially the Buy American statute, N.J.S.A. 52:33-2 and 3, appears to be in direct conflict with GATT, Pt. II, Article III, paragraph 4, 62 Stat. 3680 (Vol. 3) (1948), which provides that:

> The products of the territory of any contracting party imported into the territory of any other contracting party shall be accorded treatment no less favourable than that accorded to like products of national origin in respect of all laws, regulations and requirements affecting their internal sale, offering for sale, purchase, transportation, distribution or use.

Both the trial court and the Appellate Division opinions are bottomed on that conclusion. *See also* Territory of Hawaii v. Ho, 41 *Haw.* 565 (Sup. Ct. 1957).

Article III, paragraph 4 of GATT is not, however, all-inclusive. An exception reads as follows:

> The provisions of this article shall not apply to laws, regulations or requirements governing the procurement by governmental agencies of products purchased for governmental purposes and not with a view to commercial resale or with a view to use in the production of goods for commercial sale. [GATT, Pt. II, Art. III, par. 8(a), 62 Stat. 3681 (Vol. 3) (1948)]

The Commission has urged that materials to be acquired in connection with the construction of its proposed water treatment plant fall within the exception clause. The exclusionary requisites are: (1) procurement by a governmental agency, (2) of a product, (3) purchased for governmental purposes, (4) not for commercial sale, and (5) not with a view to use in the production of goods for commercial sale. That the Commission is a governmental agency and that it proposes to acquire products, materials with which to construct and equip the plant, are clear.

The plaintiffs contend, however, that the Commission's construction of a water treatment plant is not for a governmental purpose and that the proposed plant will produce "goods", namely water, for commercial sale. Consideration of these contentions necessitates examination of the Commission, its operations and functions.

We are satisfied that the Commission's activities in harnessing, treating and channeling the water to eight municipalities constitute appropriate governmental functions and purposes. It is transmitting "common" property, potable water, to municipalities for the use of their inhabitants—a necessity upon which their very existence depends. In performing these functions, the Commission, unlike a commercial enterprise, operates at cost. We find, then, that the Commission's purchases of materials and equipment for its water treatment plant are for governmental purposes and not with a view to use in the "production of goods for commercial sale." . . .

II.   THE NEW JERSEY BUY AMERICAN STATUTE AND THE FEDERAL FOREIGN AFFAIRS POWER

Plaintiffs argue that the New Jersey Buy American provisions, N.J.S.A. 52:33-2 and 3, even if found not to conflict with GATT, represent an impermissible intrusion by the State into the field of foreign affairs, an area constitutionally reserved to Congress and the President. The Constitution contains no specific grant to Congress to enact legislation to regulate foreign affairs, but existence of such power stemming from national sovereignty has been acknowledged by the Supreme Court. . . .

Plaintiffs rely primarily upon the Supreme Court opinion in Zschernig v. Miller, 389 U.S. 429, 88 S. Ct. 664, 19 L. Ed. 2d 683 (1968), *reh. den.* 390 U.S. 974, 88 S. Ct. 1018, 19 L. Ed. 2d 1196 (1968), for their position that the Buy American provisions constitute an impermissible state invasion of foreign policy. *Zschernig* involved an Oregon probate law which conditioned the right of a nonresident alien to inherit from Oregon residents upon the alien's ability to demonstrate that his country of origin would grant reciprocal rights to U.S. citizens and would not confiscate personalty passing to the alien claimant. The Supreme Court found that the statute as applied represented an unconstitutional intrusion upon the foreign affairs power. Mr. Justice Douglas, writing for the majority, observed that under similar provisions courts of other states had conducted minute inquiries into the ideological climates of various foreign countries, often disfavoring claimants from Marxist nations. 389 U.S. at 435, 88 S. Ct. at 667, 19 L. Ed. 2d at 689. He further noted that the real desiderata of the Oregon decisions under the statute seemed to be "foreign policy attitudes, the freezing or thawing of the 'cold war' and the like . . ." 389 U.S. at 437, 88 S. Ct. at 669, 19 L. Ed. 2d at 690. In a concurring opinion, Mr. Justice Stewart (joined by Mr. Justice Brennan) stated that "any realistic attempt to apply [the criteria of the statute] would necessarily involve the Oregon courts in an evaluation, either express or implied, of the administration of foreign law, the credibility of foreign diplomatic statements, and the policies of foreign governments." 389 U.S. at 442, 88 S. Ct. at 671, 19 L. Ed. 2d at 693.

It is significant that the Supreme Court in *Zschernig* refused to reexamine its ruling in Clark v. Allen, 331 U.S. 503, 67 S. Ct. 1431, 91 L. Ed. 1633 (1947). In *Clark,* a California statute permitted a nonresident alien to inherit personalty only if there was a reciprocal right on the part of United States' citizens to take on the same terms and conditions as citizens of the other nation. The challenge to the statute grounded on its intrusion into the field of foreign affairs was rejected. In *Zschernig* Mr. Justice Douglas, who had also written the opinion in *Clark,* pointed out that the California reciprocity statute "did not on its face intrude in the federal domain" and would only have "some incidental or indirect effect in foreign countries," 389 U.S. at 433-438, 88 S. Ct. at 667, 19 L. Ed. 2d at 688. *See also* In re Estate of Kish, 52 N.J. 454, 466, 246 A.2d 1 (1968), where Justice Hall upheld the validity of the New Jersey custodial statute, N.J.S.A. 3A:25-10. He construed the statute to prohibit payments to foreign beneficiaries when it was apparent from a routine reading of the foreign country's laws that the beneficiary's receipt was forbidden.

It is quite clear that the New Jersey Legislature, by means of the statutory provisions under review, has not authorized its local units of government to engage in the sensitive business of evaluating the politics of countries whose citizens seek to market their products in this State. The Buy American provisions apply without any discrimination based on the ideology of the seller's country. Nor is there any evidence to suggest that the political climate in a potential foreign bidder's nation has ever motivated the inclusion of the Buy American condition in a invitation for bids or that its inclusion is predicated on an assessment of the internal policies of any foreign country. If refined inquiries into foreign ideologies entered into the decision to apply or not to apply the condition, there would, of course, be little difficulty in finding a constitutional infirmity of the type condemned in *Zschernig*. But the statute in no way requires, nor should it be construed to permit, such inquiries. We can only conclude the statute does not represent the kind of intrusion into the foreign affairs power condemned in *Zschernig*. . . .

In addition to *Zschernig,* the plaintiffs rely heavily on Bethlehem Steel Corp. v. Board of Commrs. of Dept. of W. & P., 276 Cal. App. 2d 221, 80 Cal. Rptr. 800 (Ct. App. 1969). The California court in a 3 to 1 decision declared unconstitutional the California Buy American Act containing an absolute requirement that only materials manufactured in the United States be used. The court likened the California act to the Oregon statute in *Zschernig* and reasoned that the states have no power to affect foreign commerce, an exclusive federal domain. Referring to the numerous treaties and agreements concerned with trade which the United States has entered into with foreign nations, including GATT (noting that it was unnecessary to delve into an analysis of that agreement), the court held that the California statute had more than an incidental or indirect effect on foreign affairs.

The California Buy American Act did not have the restricted sphere and more limited impact of the New Jersey statute. *Compare* N.J.S.A. 52:33-2 and 3 with Cal. Govt. Code §§4300-4305 (West 1966). Unlike the California Code N.J.S.A. 52:33-2 and 3 provide that domestic materials need not be used if the cost is "unreasonable" or it is "inconsistent with the public interest" or it is "impracticable." Nor did the California court consider the express exemption in GATT into which the New Jersey legislation fits. This exemption indicates that the federal government has not foreclosed state action which does not have a significant and direct impact on foreign affairs. Indeed, it would appear that federal policy reflected by the GATT exemption would tolerate state action which is not inconsistent with the overriding federal approach to foreign trade. Moreover, we do not agree that every and any state statute which in any way touches upon foreign affairs is proscribed. States may properly exercise their police powers and in doing so have some permissible effect on foreign trade. Cf. DeCanas v. Bica, 424 U.S. 351, 96 S. Ct. 933, 47 L. Ed. 2d 43 (1976) (upholding a California statute regulating alien employment even though it touches upon the exclusive federal power to regulate immigration). We read *Zschernig* and *Clark* to permit state regulation which does not result demonstrably in a significant and direct impact upon foreign affairs. . . .

Note on Nontariff Barriers to Trade and the Federal System

The materials considered in this chapter highlight the difficulties involved in regulating international trade in a federal system including 50 states and myriad local governments that must procure goods annually. The City of New York alone purchases over $200 million in goods and services each year.

The overarching constitutional law issue is that of preemption of local power by the national government. To what degree may the federal government, taking a national action through the treaty power, occupy the field of commerce? Advocates of strong national power cite art. I, §8 of the Constitution, which grants to the Congress the authority "to regulate commerce with foreign nations, and among the several states," as well as the authority to lay and collect duties. Those championing states' rights cite the Tenth Amendment, which provides that the powers not "delegated to the United States by the Constitution, nor prohibited by it to the states, are reserved to the states respectively, or to the people."

Put another way, the question is whether *Curtiss-Wright*,[6] which gives extensive authority to the president in the area of foreign affairs, coupled with the broad Commerce Clause power in the Constitution, can permit the national government to regulate nontariff barriers to trade in contravention of particular state laws or regulations.

The answers to this question are complicated, with legal and political dimensions. From a legal standpoint, issues of concern include how authority may be delegated to the president to conclude agreements on nontariff barriers to trade without running afoul of the *Schechter* problem of an overly broad statute,[7] and whether the treaties are intended to comprehend an entire area of commerce, or only part of the domain.

From a political standpoint the question is one of sensitivity to the strength

---

[6]United States v. Curtiss-Wright Export, 299 U.S. 304, 57 S. Ct. 216, 81 L. Ed. (1936).
[7]Schechter Poultry v. United States, 295 U.S. 495 (1935), which struck down the National Industrial Recovery Act of 1933.

of the federal system. The states are laboratories for reform and innovation, and a vital part of the federal system. As international trade becomes a larger part of the GNP, states will be increasingly tempted to regulate international as well as domestic commerce to protect the economic interests of their citizens.

NOTES AND QUESTIONS

1. How satisfied are you with the analysis of the New Jersey Supreme Court in *K.S.B. Technical Sales?* Has it articulated a workable standard for determining whether a particular government purchase conflicts with the GATT? *See* Note, State Buy-America Laws—Invalidity of State Attempts to Favor American Producers, 64 Minn. L. Rev. 389 (1980).

2. Suppose you were a Japanese bidder on an advanced United States civilian fiber optics system and your low bid was rejected on national security grounds. Would you have any recompense under current law? For such a case, *see* Meadows, Japan Runs Into America, Inc., Fortune, March 22, 1982, at pp. 56-61.

3. Consider the American Law Institute's Restatement of the Foreign Relations Law of the United States (Revised), Tentative Draft No. 4 (May, 1983), Part VIII. Selected Law of International Economic Relations. Do you think the Restatement fairly summarizes the state of the law following the conclusion of the MTN codes on standards, government procurement, customs valuation, subsidies and import licensing?

§805. INDIRECT BARRIERS TO IMPORTS

(1) Under the General Agreement on Tariffs and Trade, a state party may not apply internal taxes or other restrictions that unreasonably burden imports from other states parties.

(2) Under the law of the United States, restrictions within the scope of Subsection (1) may not be imposed on imports from states that are beneficiaries of such agreements.

4. In addition to the Buy America Act, there are other forms of preferential treatment granted by the U.S. government to American companies, e.g.,

1. preference to procurement from companies in labor surplus areas for the purpose of encouraging employment;
2. set-aside programs for small and minority businesses;
3. requirement under the so-called Berry Amendment to the Department of Defense Appropriations Act that the Defense Department will procure all of its needs for textiles, clothing, shoes, food, stainless steel flatware, certain specialty metals, buses, ships and components thereof from U.S. companies;

4. preference for goods made by prisoners and the blind;
5. 50% differential granted in favor of domestic suppliers of hand tools; and
6. preferences for use of American cargo transportation services.

Aside from the labor surplus area preference, all of these preferences were unaffected by the signing of the Government Procurement Code. How serious would this be to you as a foreign supplier?

5. How does the Government Procurement Code handle:

(a) "public" or "open" tender procedures;
(b) "selective" or "restricted" tender procedures; and
(c) "private contract" or "single tender" procedures, in which the awarding agency contacts only one firm? *See* Part V, §15.

6. The United States Department of Commerce takes the position that its acquisition of $50,000 worth of erasers is not covered by the Government Procurement Code. What result? *See* Part I, §1(b) of the code. What if there are 12 monthly acquisitions during the course of one calendar year—would a foreign signatory be entitled to bid on the tenders for the erasers?

Bibliographical Note

For data on government procurement, *see* Anthony & Hagerty, Cautious Optimism as a Guide to Foreign Government Procurement, 11 Law & Pol. Intl. Bus. 1301 (1979); Pomeranz, Toward a New International Order in Government Procurement, 11 Law & Pol. Intl. Bus. 1263 (1979); Note, Eliminating Nontariff Barriers to International Trade: The MTN Agreement on Government Procurement, 12 N.Y.U. J. Intl. Law & Pol. 315 (1979); Note, Technical Analysis of the Government Procurement Agreement, 11 Law & Pol. Intl. Bus. 1345 (1979); U.S. General Accounting Office, The International Agreement on Government Procurement: An Assessment of Its Commercial Value and U.S. Government Implementation, GAO/NSIAD-84-117 (July 16, 1984).

Chapter IX

Dispute Settlement and Enforcement of GATT Rights

The international legal basis for dispute settlement in the trade area is contained in Articles XXII and XXIII of the GATT, as supplemented by several MTN Round side-agreements. Under these provisions, consultation and ad hoc agreement (as reflected in Article XXII) is the preferred solution to any trade dispute. When that is not possible, the Contracting Parties can, under Article XXIII, authorize the offended nation to retaliate against another nation's failure to honor the GATT by withdrawing or suspending concessions. Usually, a panel is appointed to help resolve the dispute and, if necessary, to prepare it for the Contracting Parties. In addition, the Contracting Parties can, under Article XXV, waive the application of GATT rules in a particular case.[1]

The corresponding U.S. domestic law is §301 of the 1974 Act, updated and modified by §901 of the 1979 Act, and Title III of the Trade and Tariff Act of 1984. Section 301 includes procedures by which a United States exporter that believes itself harmed by a foreign nation's trade action can compel the United States Trade Representative to consider the issue and, if appropriate, to proceed through the relevant international dispute settlement process. The section also authorizes the president to take such responsive action as may be appropriate, including the imposition of retaliatory duties.[2]

In the very early period of the GATT, the formal dispute settlement pro-

---

[1] For general discussions on GATT decision-making, see Hudec's articles, GATT Dispute Settlement after the Tokyo Round: An Unfinished Business, 13 Cornell Intl. L.J. 145 (1980); Retaliation Against "Unreasonable" Foreign Trade Practices: The New Section 301 and GATT Nullification and Impairment, 59 Minn. L. Rev. 461 (1975); and GATT or GABB? The Future Design of the General Agreement on Tariffs and Trade, 80 Yale L.J. 1299 (1971).

[2] See Fisher and Steinhardt, The Enforcement by Private Citizens of United States Rights Under International Trade Agreements in P. Macrory & P. Suchman (eds.), Current Legal Aspects of International Trade Law (1982).

cesses were taken quite seriously. Later on, however, as might be anticipated, the preference for compromise and political solution—as well as, in some cases, for just ignoring the GATT—became much stronger. Thus, the general trend has been from legal decision-making to ad hoc political settlement. But there are several variations on this theme. During the early 1970s, the United States initiated a number of "cases" against foreign governments, probably in an effort to persuade Congress that further trade negotiations would be wise. And the politics of passing the 1979 Act suggested a new effort at making a more regulatory approach work—but this was an approach stretched by over-enthusiasm, given the protectionist sentiment of the early 1980s.

A. THE DESIGNED FRAMEWORK

1. The Article XXIII Nullification or Impairment Procedure

The original GATT framework was relatively legalistic and the standard dis-pute-settlement and sanction pattern was to be that of Article XXIII—a pro-cedure by which a nation aggrieved by another's violation of the GATT would be able to bring a complaint, and, eventually, obtain international authoriza-tion to restrict the offender's exports to the injured nation. The procedure is exemplified in the following sequence, one of the very first examples of the GATT dispute settlement procedure.

GATT, UNITED STATES IMPORT RESTRICTIONS ON DAIRY PRODUCTS

GATT, BISD, 1st Supp. 31 (1952)

THE CONTRACTING PARTIES

Note with regret from the reports submitted to the Seventh Session that the United States Government has not succeeded in its efforts to effect the repeal of Section 104 of the United States Defense Production Act,

Note that, as a result of amendments made to that Act, and also of conse-quent administrative action, it has been possible for the United States Govern-ment to mitigate for some products the restrictions imposed in accordance with Section 104 of that Act,

Note however that Section 104 in its present form still requires the mainte-nance of restrictions inconsistent with the provisions of the General Agreement,

Recognise that, although the measures introduced by the United States Gov-ernment have reduced or eliminated the damage caused to some contracting parties by these restrictions, many contracting parties have indicated that they are still suffering serious damage and that some contracting parties have indicated further that the recent partial relaxation of the restrictions has not improved the position with regard to products in which they are interested,

Confirm the findings made in their resolution of 26 October 1951,

(*a*) that concessions granted by the United States Government to contracting parties under the General Agreement have been nullified or impaired with[in] the meaning of Article XXIII of the General Agreement and that the import restrictions in question constitute an infringement of Article XI of the Agreement and

(*b*) that the circumstances are serious enough to justify recourse to Article XXIII, paragraph 2, by the contracting parties affected, and

Resolve, notwithstanding any recourse that contracting parties may take to Article XXIII while these restrictions are in effect,

1. *to recommend* that the United States Government have regard to the effects of its continued application of these restrictive measures in breach of the General Agreement and continue its efforts to secure the repeal of Section 104 of the Defense Production Act as the only satisfactory solution of this problem, and

2. *to request* the United States Government to report to the Contracting Parties at as early a date as possible and in any case not later than the opening of the Eighth Session of the Contracting Parties on the action which it has taken.

GATT, NETHERLANDS ACTION UNDER ARTICLE XXIII:2 TO SUSPEND OBLIGATIONS TO THE UNITED STATES

GATT, BISD, 1st Supp. 62 (1952)

1. At the Sixth Session the Contracting Parties decided that the import restrictions on dairy products maintained by the United States under Section 104 of the Defense Production Act were contrary to the provisions of the General Agreement and, under the circumstances, were sufficiently serious to justify recourse to paragraph 2 of Article XXIII, by the contracting parties affected. That paragraph provides in part that, if the Contracting Parties consider that the circumstances are serious enough to justify such action, they may authorise a contracting party or parties to suspend the application to any other contracting party or parties of such obligations or concessions under the Agreement as the Contracting Parties determine to be appropriate in the circumstances. Therefore, the Netherlands delegation requested the Contracting Parties, in accordance with Article XXIII:2, to authorise the Netherlands to suspend the application to the United States of its obligations under the Agreement to the extent necessary to allow the Netherlands to impose an upper limit of 57,000 metric tons on imports of wheat flour from the United States during the calendar year 1953. This would constitute an annual reduc-

tion of approximately 15,000 metric tons from the rate of current imports from the United States.

2. The Working Party was instructed by the Contracting Parties to investigate the appropriateness of the measure which the Netherlands Government proposed to take, having regard to its equivalence to the impairment suffered by the Netherlands as a result of the United States restrictions.

3. The Working Party felt that the appropriateness of the measure envisaged by the Netherlands Government should be considered from two points of view: in the first place whether, in the circumstances, the measure proposed was appropriate in character, and secondly, whether the extent of the quantitative restriction proposed by the Netherlands Government was reasonable, having regard to the impairment suffered.

4. Although the Working Party recognised that it was appropriate to consider calculations of the trade affected by the measures and countermeasures in question, it was aware that a purely statistical test would not, by itself, be sufficient and that it would also be necessary to consider the broader economic elements entering into the assessment of the impairment suffered. It was agreed therefore that it would be proper to take into account the contention of the Netherlands Government that the restrictions imposed by the United States had had serious effects on the efforts which were being made by the Netherlands to stimulate its exports to the United States not only of the products subject to the restrictions but of other products as well, and the further contention of the Netherlands Government that the restrictions had affected its efforts to overcome balance-of-payments difficulties with which the country was confronted.

5. The meetings of the Working Party were conducted in a spirit of cooperation. The representatives of the Netherlands and the United States presented statements, including statistical information, for the guidance of the Working Party.

6. The Working Party recognised the difficulties inherent in fixing, with any real precision, the point at which any proposed measure could no longer be considered reasonable. The Working Party was of the view that the size of the measure proposed could not be regarded as unreasonable. However, on the basis of its independent review of the circumstances and of the considerations adduced at this Session, the Working Party decided to recommend a measure somewhat different in magnitude from that proposed by the Netherlands. . . .

GATT, NETHERLANDS MEASURES OF SUSPENSION OF OBLIGATIONS TO THE UNITED STATES

GATT, BISD, 1st Supp. 32 (1952)

Taking Note of the request from the Netherlands Government for the application of paragraph 2 of Article XXIII of the General Agreement, and

Considering information relating to the damage suffered by the Netherlands through limitations on its ability to sell its products in the United States market owing to the restrictions imposed by the United States of America under Section 104 of the Defense Production Act,

THE CONTRACTING PARTIES

Determine

1. that the measure proposed by the Netherlands Government is appropriate in character, and
2. that, having regard to
   (i)   the value of the trade involved,
   (ii) the broader elements in the impairment suffered by the Netherlands, and
   (iii) the statement of the Netherlands Government that its principal objective in proposing the measure in question is to contribute to the eventual solution of the matter in accordance with the objectives and spirit of the General Agreement,
   the limitation by the Netherlands of imports of wheat flour from the United States to 60,000 tons in 1953 would be appropriate within the meaning of Article XXIII, and

Authorise the Netherlands Government to suspend the application to the United States of their obligations under the General Agreement to the extent necessary to allow the Netherlands Government to impose an upper limit of 60,000 metric tons on imports of wheat flour from the United States during the calendar year 1953.

QUESTIONS

1. How effective is a sanction such as that the Netherlands imposed against the United States? What are its costs? What if the situation had been reversed, and there had been a U.S. sanction against the Netherlands?

2. What guidelines might you suggest for the relationship between the retaliatory tariff and the underlying GATT violation?

3. What alternative sanctions can you imagine? Fines? Damage actions by offended industries (rather than governments) against the offending foreign government? What are the pros and cons of such alternatives?

4. It is generally assumed that political feasibility requires that these sanctions be kept under executive governmental control, rather than judicial or international control. Is this assumption correct or not? Why?

2.   The Article XXV Waiver Procedure

In some cases, a nation that expected to violate the GATT would use a different procedure—a request for a waiver under Article XXV. One of the most important such waivers was also one of the earliest, that granted to the United States, arising from U.S. agricultural legislation that violated the GATT, but which the United States believed to be compelled by domestic politics. The waiver decision, which follows, called for annual reports until the offending import restrictions could be eliminated. GATT discussion of one such report follows the document granting the waiver.

GATT, WAIVER GRANTED TO THE UNITED STATES IN CONNECTION WITH IMPORT RESTRICTIONS IMPOSED UNDER SECTION 22 OF THE UNITED STATES AGRICULTURAL ADJUSTMENT ACT (OF 1933), AS AMENDED

GATT, BISD, 3d Supp. 32 (1955)

Having received the request of the United States Government for a waiver of the provisions of Article II and Article XI of the General Agreement with respect to certain actions by the United States Government required by the provisions of Section 22 of the United States Agricultural Adjustment Act (of 1933), as amended, (hereinafter referred to as Section 22) which are not authorized by the Agreement,

Having also received the statement of the United States:

(*a*) that there exist in the United States governmental agricultural programmes (including programmes or operations which provide price assistance for certain domestic agricultural products and which operate to limit the production or market supply, or to regulate or control the quality or prices of domestic agricultural products) which from time to time result in domestic prices being maintained at a level in excess of the prices at which imports of the like products can be made available for consumption in the United States and that under such conditions imports may be attracted into the United States in abnormally large quantities or in such manner as to have adverse effects on such programmes or operations unless the inflow of such imports is regulated in some manner;

(*b*) that the Congress of the United States therefore enacted Section 22 which requires that restrictions in the form either of fees or of quantitative limitations must be imposed on imports whenever the President of the United States finds, after investigation, that such products are being or are practically certain to be imported in such quantities and under such conditions as to render ineffective or materially interfere with any programme or operation undertaken by the United States Department of Agriculture or any agency under its direction with respect to any agricultural commodity or product thereof, or to reduce substantially the amount of any product processed in the United States from any agricultural commodity or product thereof, with respect to which such a programme is being undertaken, and has required the President not to accept any international obligation which would be inconsistent with the requirements of the Section; . . .

Noting:

(*a*) that, to help solve the problem of surpluses of products for which Section 22 import quotas are now in effect, the United States Government has taken positive steps aimed at reducing 1955 crop supplies by lowering support price levels or by imposing marketing quotas at minimum levels permitted by legislation; and that it is the intention of the United States Government to continue to seek a solution of the problem of surpluses of agricultural commodities;

(*b*) the assurance of the United States Government that it will discuss proposals under Section 22 with all countries having a substantial interest prior to taking action, and will give prompt consideration to any representations made to it;

(*c*) that it is the intention of the United States Government promptly to terminate any restrictions imposed when it finds that circumstances requiring the action no longer exist, and to modify restrictions whenever changed circumstances warrant such modification;

The Contracting Parties

Decide, pursuant to paragraph 5 (*a*) of Article XXV of the General Agreement and in consideration of the assurances recorded above, that subject to the conditions and procedures set out hereunder the obligations of the United States under the provisions of Articles II and XI of the General Agreement are waived to the extent necessary to prevent a conflict with such provisions of the General Agreement in the case of action required to be taken by the Government of the United States under Section 22. . . .

Declare that this Decision shall not preclude the right of affected contracting parties to have recourse to the appropriate provisions of Article XXIII, and

Declare, further, that in deciding as aforesaid, they regret that circumstances make it necessary for the United States to continue to apply import restrictions which, in certain cases, adversely affect the trade of a number of contracting parties, impair concessions granted by the United States and thus impede the attainment of the objectives of the General Agreement.

CONDITIONS AND PROCEDURES

1. Upon request of any contracting party which considers that its interests are seriously prejudiced by reason of any import restriction imposed under Section 22, whether or not covered by this Decision, the United States will promptly undertake a review to determine whether there has been a change in circum-

stances which would require such restrictions to be modified or terminated. In the event the review shows such a change, the United States will institute an investigation in the manner provided by Section 22.

2. Should the President of the United States acting in pursuance of Section 22 cause an investigation to be made to determine whether any existing import restriction should be modified, terminated or extended, or whether restrictions should be imposed on the import of any additional product, the United States will notify the Contracting Parties and, in accordance with Article XXII of the General Agreement, accord to any contracting party which considers that its interests would be prejudiced the fullest notice and opportunity, consistent with the legislative requirements of the United States, for representations and consultation.

3. The United States will give due consideration to any representations submitted to it including:

(a) When investigating whether any existing import restriction should be modified, terminated or extended, representations that a greater volume of imports than is permitted under the import restriction would not have the effects required to be corrected by Section 22, including representations that the volume of imports that would have entered in the absence of governmental agricultural programmes would not have such effects;

(b) When investigating with respect to import restrictions on additional products, representations with regard to:
   (i) the effects of imports of any product upon any programme or operation undertaken by the United States Department of Agriculture or any agency under its direction, or upon the domestic production of any agricultural commodity or product thereof for which such a programme or operation is undertaken, including representations that the volume of imports which would have entered in the absence of governmental agricultural programmes will not have the effects required to be corrected by Section 22;
   (ii) the representative period to be used for the determination of any quota;

(c) Representations by any contracting party that the portion of a total quota allotted or proposed to be allotted to it is inequitable because of circumstances that operated to reduce imports from that contracting party of the product concerned during the past representative period on which such import quota is based.

4. As soon as the President has made his decision following any investigation the United States will notify the Contracting Parties and those contracting parties which have made representations or entered into consultations. If the Decision imposes restrictions on additional products or extends or intensifies existing restrictions the notification by the United States will include particulars of such restrictions and the reasons for them (regardless of whether the

restriction is consistent with the General Agreement). At the time of such notification the provisions of the General Agreement are waived to the extent necessary to permit such restrictions to be applied under the General Agreement, subject to the review herein provided and, as declared above, without prejudice to the right of the affected contracting parties to have recourse to the appropriate provisions of Article XXIII.

5. The United States will remove or relax each restriction permitted under this waiver as soon as it finds that the circumstances requiring such restriction no longer exist or have changed so as no longer to require its imposition in its existing form.

6. The Contracting Parties will make an annual review of any action taken by the United States under this Decision. For each such review the United States will furnish a report to the Contracting Parties showing any modification or removal of restrictions effected since the previous report, the restrictions in effect under Section 22 and the reasons why such restrictions (regardless of whether covered by this waiver) continue to be applied and any steps it has taken with a view to a solution of the problem of surpluses of agricultural commodities.

GATT, UNITED STATES IMPORT RESTRICTIONS ON AGRICULTURAL PRODUCTS

GATT, BISD, 27th Supp. 206 (1980)

1. The Working Party on United States Import Restrictions Waiver was established by the Council on 26 March 1980 with the following terms of reference:

> To examine the twenty-second annual report (L/4925) submitted by the Government of the United States under the Decision of 5 March 1955, and to report to the Council.

2. The Working Party met on 28 May and on 23 June 1980 under the Chairmanship of Mr. C. Magnus P. Lemmel (Sweden).

3. In accordance with its terms of reference, the Working Party has examined the twenty-second annual report submitted by the Government of the United States under the Decision of 5 March 1955, on import restrictions in effect under Section 22 of the United States Agricultural Adjustment Act as amended, on the reasons for the maintenance of these restrictions, and on the steps taken with a view to a solution of the problem of agricultural surpluses. On the basis of the report and with the assistance of the representative of the United States, the Working Party has reviewed the action taken by the United States Government under the Decision.

4. The representative of the United States, introducing the report submitted by his Government, said that, since its enactment, Section 22 had been used

sparingly and only as absolutely necessary. He recalled that the utilization of Section 22 powers to establish quotas or import fees was confined exclusively to commodities which were subject to support programs and that import restriction under Section 22 currently in force applied to four groups of commodities: cotton and cotton waste, peanuts, sugar, and dairy products. Summarizing recent developments with respect to the commodity programs and imports controls concerned, he noted that on 31 March 1980, a special temporary import quota had been imposed on upland cotton in addition to the existing quota established under Section 22 authority.

5. With reference to dairy products, the representative of the United States went on to say that important changes had taken place since the last annual report as a consequence of the agreements reached in the MTN. He recalled that his Government had made important concessions in the framework of the MTN with respect to import quotas for certain cheeses and chocolate crumb and to the system of their administration. He stressed that the implementation by the United States of its MTN agreements on dairy products was taking place during a period of particular difficulties, both economically and politically.

6. The representative of the United States furthermore said that his Government had attempted to administer the import restrictions imposed under Section 22 in a fair and open manner and to carry out responsibly its obligations under the waiver. He stated that the United States was prepared to consult with its GATT partners on any problems which might arise. Further, the United States keeps the situation under continuing review and will carefully examine whether the present arrangement should be changed. He noted that the basic United States farm legislation which authorizes and directs the Government to carry out the support programs for the commodities concerned was subject to renewal next year. He was ready to note and convey to his authorities any comments the Working Party would wish to make and was ready to answer any questions.

7. The Working Party was grateful for the introductory comments given by the representative of the United States. Several members, however, expressed concern with the maintenance of this waiver and with the fact that alternative policies had not been pursued. They felt that the annual report did not entirely fulfil the obligations taken by the United States under the Contracting Parties' Decision of 5 March 1955, and in particular those set out in condition 6 of that Decision.

8. A member of the Working Party pointed out that if the problem of surpluses of certain agricultural commodities was a structural one, then the recourse to temporary measures could not result in a positive solution, while, if the problem was one of a conjunctural nature, the measures already taken over twenty-five years had to be regarded as not effective. In both cases, in his view, the waiver was not justified.

9. With reference to the operation of the restriction under the waiver, a further member noted with satisfaction that the list of products subject to import restriction had now been shortened as to cover four commodity groups.

He expressed, however, deep concern over the existing restrictions and over the fact that those temporarily suspended could presumably be reinstated. In his view, more information was needed on the coverage of products which were subjected to action under Section 22, on the terms of suspension for the products which were previously subject to restrictions, and on legal possibilities to remove on a permanent basis those restrictions which were temporarily suspended.

10. A member of the Working Party recalled that during the recently concluded MTN, the United States was prepared to negotiate a dismantling of Section 22 quotas against commitments by other countries to pursue policies aimed at eliminating unfair export practices, and, in particular, export subsidization. He argued that, in his view, that constituted a recognition by the United States that the circumstances under which the waiver was granted had changed, the actual problem not being one of agricultural surpluses but of subsidized exports. He pointed out that a "change in circumstances" was the basis on which the United States in 1955 undertook to terminate or modify its Section 22 quotas, and that, with regard to subsidized exports, the United States has the same protection from such practices as other contracting parties, namely recourse to the provisions of the General Agreement. Additional protection was available to the United States in the form of the Code on Subsidies and Countervailing Duties and in its own domestic legislation.

11. Several members of the Working Party stated that the Government of the United States in its annual report should have paid more attention to changes in those circumstances which had led the Contracting Parties to grant the waiver in 1955. They also suggested, as they had in the past, that the United States Government should consider alternative measures, including adjustment measures, for stabilizing the domestic markets without recourse to quota restrictions on imports.

12. In its examination of the report, the Working Party devoted special attention to the section dealing with dairy products. In this connexion, several members of the Working Party felt that the United States had particularly failed to make progress for this group of commodities in terms of the obligations it accepted when the waiver was granted.

13. A member of the Working Party stated that, in his opinion, a review of the events of the last twenty-five years showed that, at least in the field of dairy products, the United States had pursued a policy not envisaged by the Contracting Parties when the waiver was granted. He said that, by maintaining dairy support prices at levels too high in relation to its obligations under the waiver, the United States had indeed pursued a long-term policy of self-sufficiency in the dairy sector—an option that was not envisaged by the Contracting Parties when they had granted the waiver. In his view, even within existing legislative provisions, the United States could have done much more to hold the rate of increase of dairy support prices to a level that would have reduced dairy surpluses and permitted greater access for imports. He noted that the dairy trade was of crucial importance to the economy of his country. He stated that after twenty-five years the circumstances that existed when the waiver

was granted have substantially changed. Commenting in particular on certain economic features of and developments in the United States dairy industry, he stressed that the report failed to address these changes and the effect that those could have had in supporting some modification or termination of import restrictions. He recalled that at the time the waiver was granted there had been discussion of the use of basic measures, in the context of the search for solutions to the problem of continuing surpluses. He thought that these should be tried again. He noted that other reports by United States Government agencies recognized the possibility for real alternatives to the present severe restrictions on dairy imports and the need to undertake studies in this respect and urged that these be presented. He pointed out that despite continuing increases in consumption of cheese, controls on this product had been tightened. He stated that the annual report also failed to provide an indication as to the future intentions of the United States with respect to complying with the obligations of the waiver, and he requested the representative of the United States to provide such information. . . .

15. With respect to the quota on cheese applied since 1955 by the United States under the provisions of the waiver, a member asked whether in the light of the significant development which had occurred over this period in the export capacity of the milk industry of some countries and of important changes in trade policy relations between certain countries, the United States had a position on the question of the situation of eventual new suppliers, and how the United States intended to treat these suppliers within its cheese quota. Referring more specifically to the case of his country he said that his country, which had a substantial interest in supplying cheese to the US market, was not included in the United States import quota on cheese and that it would like to get an equitable share within this quota. He added that the past performance of his country did not adequately reflect its supplying interests but this was due to special factors as the existence of the quota in which his country had not had a share and the lack of m.f.n. treatment between the United States and his country until 1978. . . .

18. Recalling that casein was currently the subject of a Section 332 enquiry in the United States under the United States Trade Act of 1974, a member of the Working Party asked the United States representative for an indication of the current status of that enquiry. He added that the basic argument used by those favouring import restrictions on casein—that it competes with domestic sales of skimmed milk powder [SMP]—was spurious, competition to SMP sales in the United States coming from increasing United States production of whey powder.

19. Replying to the various points made, the representative of the United States stated that although twenty-five years had elapsed and certain changes had occurred, the underlying problems which had pressed the United States to request a waiver in 1955 still remained. He stressed, however, that the United States had always met its obligations, fulfilled its requirements, and submitted reports as stipulated under the waiver. In reply to the question whether different treatments were applied in the United States to substitutes for dairy prod-

ucts, he said that both animal and vegetable fats were subject to the same requirements in the domestic market. In response to the question concerning a possible introduction of quantitative restrictions on casein under Section 22, the representative of the United States indicated that a recent investigation by the International Trade Commission had concluded that no ground existed at present for introducing such restrictions. Under current legislation, the dairy import quotas may not be expanded except through regular Section 22 procedures initiated by a recommendation by the Secretary of Agriculture to the President that increased imports will not materially interfere with the domestic price support program for milk. With net removals by the Commodity Credit Corporation [CCC] for this marketing year expected to total seven billion pounds, milk equivalent, at a cost to the Government of approximately $1 billion, no such recommendation is possible. Total cost of CCC Dairy program purchases for the 1978-79 fiscal year was $246.7 million. Estimated cost for the present fiscal year ending 30 September 1980 is $1,001.7 million. Special programs for increasing dairy products consumption aim at bringing supply and demand more nearly into balance. Such programs currently in operation include (a) addition of mozzarella cheese to items provided by CCC to the school lunch program; (b) expansion of the food stamp program; (c) increased participation in the women-infants-children (WIC) program, which provides financial assistance to certain disadvantaged groups for increased food purchases, including dairy products; (d) the bonus program, under which certain community welfare programs may obtain extra supplies of certain foods, including dairy products, free of charge after satisfying specified basic procurement requirements; and (e) increased distribution on Indian reservations.

20. Noting that most of the discussion had focussed on dairy products, the representative of the United States pointed out that other countries maintained restrictions on this group of commodities and that most of these restrictions were not even being discussed and consulted upon in the GATT.

21. Referring to a point made by a member of the Working Party, he recalled that the United States had been prepared to negotiate its dairy restrictions in the course of the MTN with a view to finding a global solution to the problems of the dairy sector. It was for that reason that the United States had joined the International Dairy Arrangement. . . .

27. The Working Party noted the various statements made by the representative of the United States. Several members felt, however, that the information contained in the report was not complete and that in its present form it could not provide any longer a basis for a full examination as envisaged under the waiver.

28. Referring to dairy products in particular, some members of the Working Party recalled the importance their governments attached to a satisfactory resolution and termination of the restrictions under the waiver. They stated that the United States should undertake a fundamental reassessment of its dairy import policy, including the levels of permitted dairy imports. The careful reappraisal should be made against the terms and conditions of the waiver granted in 1955. The results of the reappraisal should be included in the next

annual report submitted to the Contracting Parties. They expressed the view that the United States should provide a detailed assessment of how it had performed in the dairy sector in relation to the terms of the waiver. Further, the United States should give particular attention to why they had so far not been able to liberalize, let alone dismantle, the import restrictions maintained under the waiver. The possibility of using alternative measures should also be addressed. They requested information on initiatives which the United States intends to take in order to prevent or moderate production of dairy surpluses in the future and to encourage greater domestic offtake of dairy products. They also requested a clear indication on behalf of the United States, to be included in its next report, about when and how the United States authorities envisaged to terminate the restrictions under the waiver, particularly on dairy products. . . .

31. The Working Party noted that the representative of the United States stated that his country had both lived up to the commitments of the waiver and had fulfilled its requirements faithfully. In his view, the use of import restrictions on agricultural products should be regarded as a global problem, one that the United States could not be expected to try to solve alone. In that spirit, in its next annual report, he expressed the willingness of his authorities to endeavour to provide such further information requested by members of the Working Party. He further stated he would report fully to his authorities the result of the Working Party and transmit all suggestions, comments and questions which had been made. He expressed his thanks to the members of the Working Party for the constructive spirit which had prevailed during the course of the meeting.

32. Members of the Working Party expressed their gratitude to the representative of the United States for his co-operative attitude and the frank way in which he had taken part in the discussion.

QUESTIONS

1. From the viewpoint of the future of the GATT, was it wise for the United States to seek such a waiver in 1955 when it had the strongest economy in the world? Was it politically unavoidable, given relations with Congress and the problematic constitutional status of the GATT?

2. What is the proper role of such a waiver provision? If you were advising a government as to its vote on another nation's request for a waiver, what principles would you use?

3. What is the point of still discussing an annual report, 25 years later? In thinking about this question, consider the different kinds of issues posed in paragraphs 15, 18, 19, 20, and 21.

4. In comparing the formal and real effects of the waiver procedure with those of Article XXIII, what differences do you see? When is it better to use one rather than the other?

B.   CONTEMPORARY PRACTICE—GATT

The following two examples, one based on a U.S. complaint about a European agricultural subsidy, the other on a European complaint about a U.S. export taxation device, show the system at work today.[3] Note that in both cases there was a panel that produced an elaborate and reasoned report, much like a judicial opinion. Nevertheless, each panel was much more oriented toward assisting negotiation than is the typical court—and each panel report left the parties with a need to negotiate further.

1.   *The Canned Peaches Case*

The first case exemplifies a series of problems that have marked U.S.-European agricultural relationships. This particular case was brought after pressure from California fruit growers who faced a sharp drop in exports to the European Economic Community (EEC)—for example, a 71% decline in the export of cling peaches in the 1981-1982 year.[4] The EEC regulations involved amounted to subsidies to canners to allow them to compete while buying their fresh fruit at the high Community price. Some of the regulations reflected the compromises associated with bringing Greece into the Community.

GATT PANEL REPORT ON EEC SUBSIDIES ON RAISINS AND CANNED FRUIT

20 U.S. Export Weekly 1028 (1984)

THE PANEL

I.   INTRODUCTION

1. In a communication dated 19 March 1982, which was circulated to contracting parties in document L/5306, the Government of the United States requested the Contracting Parties to establish a panel to examine a dispute

---

[3]For background, *see* the Draft Understanding Regarding Notification, Consultation, Dispute Settlement and Surveillance negotiated in the Multilateral Trade Negotiations as part of an overall framework agreement. The GATT panel report considered in the following case on EEC subsidies on raisins and canned fruit should be analyzed in light of the procedures outlined for panels in the framework accord.

[4]Statement of R. Peterson, Cling Peach Advisory Board, Senate Committee on Agriculture, Nutrition, and Forestry, Hearings on Agricultural Trade, 98th Cong., 1st Sess. 73 (1983).

between the United States and the European Economic Community regarding production aids granted by the European Economic Community on canned peaches, canned pears, fruit cocktail and dried grapes. The communication indicated that the two parties had engaged in consultations under Article XXIII:1 on 25 February 1982, but that no satisfactory adjustment of the problem could be reached.

2. At its meeting of 31 March 1982 the Council agreed to establish a Panel as requested and authorized its Chairman, in consultation with the Parties concerned, to decide on appropriate terms of reference and to designate the Chairman and Members of the Panel. The European Economic Community requested that the development of terms of reference for the panel be delayed until further consultations had taken place between the two parties with regard to production aids on dried grapes (C/M/156).

3. These consultations under Article XXIII:1 took place on 21 April 1982. As no satisfactory settlement was reached, both parties agreed to the inclusion of dried grapes in the terms of reference of the panel.

4. At the meeting of the Council on 29-30 June 1982, the Chairman of the Council informed the Council that, following consultations with the parties concerned, the composition and terms of the Panel had been agreed as follows:

Composition
Chairman: Mr. J. L. MacNeil
Members: Mr. Bo Henrikson
             Mr. Shi-Hyung Kim

Terms of reference
"To examine, in the light of the relevant GATT provisions, the matter referred to the Contracting Parties by the United States relating to production aids granted by the European Economic Community on the production of canned peaches, canned pears, fruit cocktail and dried grapes (L/5306), and to make such findings as will assist the Contracting Parties in making recommendations or rulings as provided for in Article XXIII."

Following the departure of Mr. Kim from Geneva in January 1983, Mr. Hikang Hyun was nominated to the Panel in agreement with the two parties concerned.

5. At the meeting of the Council on 30 June, 1982, Australia said that it reserved its right to make a representation before the panel. At this meeting the representative of the European Communities said that for the EC, the reference to "relevant GATT provisions" in the panel's terms of reference essentially meant Article XXIV. It was the Panel's understanding that this was only in reference to dried grapes.

6. The Panel met three times with the two parties: on 29 September 1982, 29 October 1982 and 27 February 1984. In addition, the Panel met on numerous occasions between June 1982 and April 1984.

II. FACTUAL ASPECTS

A. EEC REGULATIONS

7. On 14 March 1977, the European Economic Community adopted Council Regulation No. 516/77, which introduced a common organization of the market in the EEC for products processed from fruit and vegetables. For the commodities named in the regulation (OJ No. L73/1 of 21.3.77) a common tariff and levy structure was established and provision was made for the possibility of export refunds. On 30 May 1978, the European Economic Community adopted Council Regulation No. 1152/78 (which amended Regulation No. 516/77) introducing a minimum grower price/production aid system for five types of processed fruits and vegetables. Under this regulation processors of the five products became eligible for a "production aid" if they bought fresh products from growers at at least the minimum specified grower price. The "production aid" would be calculated so as to ". . . make up the difference between the prices of Community products and those of products from non-member countries" (OJ No. L 144/2, 31.5.78). According to the regulation, the purpose of the production aid is to ". . . enable the products in question to be manufactured at a price lower than that which would result from the payment of a remunerative price to producers of the fresh products" (OJ No. L 144/1). Additionally, the aids were intended to ". . . enable (Community products) to be sold at prices which compete with those charged by the major non-member countries" (OJ No. L 144/1). One of the products specified in Regulation No. 1152/78 is "peaches in syrup" (CCT heading no. ex 20.06B).

8. Pursuant to Article 3 b.1 of Regulation No. 516/77, as amended by Regulation No. 1152/78, the "amount of aid shall be so fixed as to make up the difference between the prices of Community products and those of products from non-member countries". The cost of producing EEC products is to be calculated for each product as the minimum price paid for the fresh product adjusted by the trend in processing costs of that product (Article 3b.2). The prices for products from non-member countries are determined taking into account duty-free import prices of the product in question into the EEC and prices obtained in international trade (Article 3b.3). . . .

V. FINDINGS

A. INTRODUCTION

39. The Panel recalled that the United States' complaint was based on two arguments:

> (a) that the aid system constituted, prima facie, nullification and impairment of tariff concessions obtained by the United States on the products in question in 1962, 1967, 1973 and 1979; and

(b) that there was additional evidence which demonstrated that the EEC production aid systems had already caused market distortion and trade injury, thus confirming the existence of nullification and impairment of the tariff concessions concerned. The United States contended that:

(i) the aid offered to processors was such that it eliminated any competitive advantage of product imported from the United States. As a consequence imported products' share of the EC market had decreased.

(ii) that the minimum price granted to EC growers of fresh peaches and fresh pears and primary producers of dried grapes were excessive and that they were stimulating increased plantings of peach and pear trees and of grape vines. It was the United States' assertion that these increased plantings, while not currently causing nullification or impairment, threatened to do so at some time in the future.

(iii) that the production aid system as well as the ancillary provisions of the system for dried grapes had been, and were currently, disrupting normal marketing relationships and had depressed world market prices for dried grapes.

B.   CONSIDERATION OF WHETHER TO ADDRESS THE ISSUE OF DRIED
     GRAPES

40. The Panel noted first that the EC had expressed doubts in the framework of the GATT Council, regarding the appropriateness of including dried grapes in the terms of reference of the Panel. It was the EC's view that this issue was closely linked to the accession of Greece to the Community. Consequently, in the EC's view, the appropriate framework for dealing with this matter was the Working Party established to examine all matters relating to Greek accession. The Panel noted that the EC had notified contracting parties that it intended to modify, in the context of Article XXIV:6, the existing concession on dried grapes.

41. The Panel also noted, however, that its terms of reference, which had been set by the Council, included reference to dried grapes, and that the EC had accepted these terms of reference. The Panel felt obliged to address the issue of whether tariff concessions granted by the EC on dried grapes were being nullified and impaired by the subsidy system. Moreover, the Panel noted that, more than two years after the opening of Article XXIV:6 negotiations, the EC tariff concessions on dried grapes had not been withdrawn or modified and continued to apply to the customs territory of the EC. The Panel was of the view that the mere opening and continuation of Article XXIV:6 negotiations could not curtail the right of contracting parties to invoke existing tariff bindings and to claim that benefits accruing under these tariff bindings had been nullified or impaired by the subsequent introduction of subsidies. The Panel was also of the view that its conclusions could not add to or diminish existing rights and obligations of contracting parties under Article XXIV:6 of the General Agreement.

42. The Panel concluded therefore that it would examine the United States' claim with respect to dried grapes in the same manner as it would for the other

commodities. As regards the emergency action, which the EEC had taken after the establishment of the Panel and notified in October 1982 under Article XIX (document L/5399 and add.) and to which the United States had referred in its submission to the Panel (see above paragraph 22), the Panel was of the view that it was not within its terms of reference to determine whether the introduction of EEC minimum import prices for raisins was consistent with Article XIX or with any other provision of the General Agreement.

C.   CONSISTENCY OF THE EC MEASURES WITH THE PROVISIONS OF THE
GENERAL AGREEMENT

43. The Panel noted that the United States had presented its complaint to the Panel as a case of a "non-violation" nullification and impairment. It was the Panel's understanding that the United States had not contended that the EC production aid system on the four products in question had violated any specific provisions of the General Agreement. The Panel considered that in these circumstances it was not for the Panel to examine the consistency of the EC production aid system with the provisions of the General Agreement. Having noted this the Panel then proceeded to an examination as to whether the EC production aids had nullified or impaired the tariff concessions granted on canned peaches, canned pears, canned fruit cocktail and dried grapes.

D.   NULLIFICATION AND IMPAIRMENT OF THE CONCESSIONS GRANTED TO
THE UNITED STATES ON CANNED PEACHES, CANNED PEARS, CANNED
FRUIT COCKTAIL AND DRIED GRAPES

a. *Nullification or impairment of tariff concessions in the case of a "non-violation" complaint*
44. The Panel first considered the question of whether and to what extent the United States could claim "any benefit accruing to it directly or indirectly under this Agreement" (Article XXIII:1) in respect of the tariff concessions invoked. The Panel noted the EEC's claim that it had withdrawn, in 1973, the tariff concessions granted in 1962 and 1967 on the four product categories concerned. The Panel noted that the EEC had notified in GATT document L/4067 of 6 August 1974 that, with effect from 1 August 1974, the concessions previously granted by the EEC (Schedule XL) had been withdrawn and were replaced by the concessions in the common customs tariff of the European Communities, which had resulted from the Article XXIV:6 negotiations (Schedules LXXII and LXXIIbis). The Panel further noted the EEC legal position that: (1) its GATT tariff bindings on dried grapes had not been extended to Greece, and (2) the United States could not claim initial negotiating rights in respect of all the tariff concessions invoked. However, the Panel noted that the EEC had neither contested the existence of the tariff bindings of 1974/79 invoked by the United States nor the US submission that the EEC tariff bindings on canned peaches, canned pears, fruit mixtures and dried

grapes had been given "as a part of a balance of concessions". The Panel also noted that, pursuant to Articles I and II of the General Agreement, tariff concessions, and the benefits deriving therefrom, have to be accorded on a most favoured nation basis independent of the existence of initial negotiating rights in respect of the tariff concessions concerned. The Panel found, therefore, that the tariff bindings granted by the EEC in 1974/79 on the four product categories concerned had created for the United States "benefits accruing to it directly or indirectly under this Agreement" in terms of Article XXIII:1 of the General Agreement.

45. The Panel then considered whether there was any legal basis in the General Agreement for limiting the rights of contracting parties to bring a "non-violation complaint" under Article XXIII to contracting parties having initial negotiating rights. The Panel found no legal justification in either Article XXIII or past GATT practice for limiting the right of contracting parties to challenge under Article XXIII an alleged nullification or impairment of tariff concessions which have to be applied on a most-favoured-nation basis. The Panel noted that neither past Panel proceedings concerning "non-violation complaints" in respect of tariff concessions (BISD 11/188; 1S/53; 11S/95) nor the parties to this dispute had suggested any such limitation of the rights of contracting parties under Article XXIII. The Panel also noted that the United States had in fact claimed to have initial negotiating rights or substantial interests in the tariff concessions invoked.

46. The Panel considered the definition given to 'nullification or impairment' of tariff concessions in past GATT panel reports which had examined "non-violation complaints" in respect of tariff concessions (BISD 11/193; 1S/58). It agreed with the findings in these reports that nullification or impairment of tariff concessions would exist if the measure in question: (1) could not have reasonably been anticipated by the party bringing the complaint at the time of negotiation of the tariff concessions and (2) the measure resulted in the upsetting of the competitive position of the imported products concerned. In the present case, this meant that nullification or impairment of the tariff concessions would exist if the introduction or increase of the EEC production aids could not have been reasonably anticipated by the United States at the time of the negotiations for the tariff concessions on those products (below under b) and the aid systems had upset the competitive position of imported canned peaches, canned pears, canned fruit cocktail and dried grapes on the EC market (below under c).

b. *Consideration of the existence of reasonable expectations on the part of the United States*

47. The Panel observed that the EC production aids for canned peaches and canned pears had been introduced in 1978 and 1979, respectively, and that no party to the dispute had contended that the United States could have reasonably expected the introduction of these subsidies at the time it had received tariff concessions on these products in 1974. The Panel next observed that the EC production aids for canned peaches had been introduced by

Regulation No. 1152/78 of 30 May 1978 prior to the conclusion of the Geneva (1979) Tariff Protocol on 30 June 1979. In the Panel's view, therefore, the United States should have been aware of the existence of this subsidy and have taken due account of it in the negotiation of the tariff concessions for canned peaches in 1978/79. Since peaches are a principal component of canned fruit cocktail, the Panel found that the United States should also have been aware of any possible effects of these production aids on the economic benefit of the tariff concessions for fruit mixtures negotiated in 1978/79. As regards the EC tariff concessions of 1979 for canned pears, the Panel noted that the production aids had been introduced subsequent to the conclusion of the Geneva (1979) Tariff Protocol and that neither party to the dispute had contended that the EEC Regulation No. 1639/79 of 24 July 1979 could have reasonably been foreseen by the United States at the time it negotiated these tariff concessions.

48. With regard to dried grapes the Panel noted the arguments made by the EC that the tariff concessions of 1979 did not cover Greece's customs territory and that the EC production aids were only a heritage from the earlier national Greek subsidization system of which the United States had been fully aware. It was the EC's view that the previous Greek subsidy system and the EC production aids were financed in a substantially similar manner and extended to the same economic beneficiaries, so that the question of budgetary source was not important for GATT. Since Greece is the only Community producer and the annual increases in the national Greek subsidies prior to Greece's accession to the EC had been greater than the increase due to EC production aids since accession, the EC contested the ability of the United States to claim any kind of 'legitimate expectation' in respect of the tariff concession granted for dried grapes.

49. In considering the various EC arguments relating to the EC tariff concessions on dried grapes, the Panel first recalled its previous finding (above paras. 41 and 44) that the EC tariff bindings of 1974 and 1979 on dried grapes had not been withdrawn. Even if they had not been extended to Greece in terms of Article II of the General Agreement, they continued to apply to the customs territory of the "EEC of nine" to which the United States exported its dried grapes. The Panel therefore found that, even in the absence of tariff concessions granted by Greece in respect of the Greek territory, the granting of the EEC tariff bindings had justified reasonable expectations on the part of the United States in respect of the benefits deriving from these tariff concessions. The Panel also found, however, that Greece had granted grower support prices, storage subsidies and subsidization of processors/exporters already prior to the granting of the EEC tariff concessions on dried grapes in 1974/79. In the Panel's opinion the United States had no reason to assume during the negotiation of the various tariff concessions on dried grapes that—in the case of an accession of Greece to the EEC—Greek raisins would not continue to benefit from such subsidies. The Panel also observed that Greek producers had benefited from duty-free access to the EEC at least since 1974. The Panel

found therefore that the United States should have reasonably anticipated during the tariff negotiations that—in case of an accession of Greece to the EEC—the national Greek subsidy scheme would possibly be replaced by an equivalent EC subsidy scheme for Greek processors. The granting of the EEC tariff bindings on dried grapes in 1974/79 only justified the expectation that the substitution of an EC subsidy scheme for the prior national Greek subsidy scheme would not lead to an unforseeable additional upsetting of the competitive relation between US and Greek dried grapes on the market of the "EEC of nine".

c. *Consideration of the upsetting of the competitive position of canned peaches, canned pears, canned fruit cocktail and dried grapes imported from the United States on the EEC market*

50. The Panel recalled its earlier finding (paragraph 46) that in past GATT practice it had been established that the upsetting of the competitive position of an imported product as a result of a subsequent domestic measure, which could not have reasonably been anticipated by the party bringing the complaint at the time of negotiation of a tariff concession on the imported product, would constitute nullification or impairment of the tariff concessions. The Panel noted that this principle had been established in two cases brought before the GATT: the Report of the Working Party on the Australian subsidy on ammonium sulphate (BISD Vol. II/448, 193) and the Report of the Panel on the treatment by Germany of imports of sardines (BISD 1S/58). . . .

51. The Panel proceeded to an examination as to whether the aid system had upset the competitive relationship between EC and imported canned peaches, canned pears and canned fruit cocktail. The Panel noted that there were two elements to the production aid system for canned fruit: the minimum grower price and the processor aid. The Panel first examined the minimum grower price to see if it had or could upset the competitive relationship between EC processed products and imported processed product.

52. The Panel noted that the United States' claim with regard to the minimum grower prices was that they had stimulated increased production of fresh peaches and pears. The United States claimed that this increased production of fresh product necessarily implied increased production of canned product and therefore a distortion of the competitive relationship between EC and imported canned product. The Panel was of the opinion, however, that even if the minimum grower price had stimulated production of fresh product this need not upset the competitive relationship between EC and imported canned product. The Panel noted that regardless of the supply situation in the fresh fruit market, EC processors were still required to pay growers the minimum price. It was the Panel's opinion that any adverse effects imparted to imported products by the minimum grower price would be to imported fresh product and not to imported canned product.

53. The Panel next addressed the issue of the production aid to see if it had upset the competitive relationship between EC and imported canned peaches,

canned pears and canned fruit cocktail. It noted firstly that the EC had argued that the purpose of the production aid was to reimburse processors for having had to pay a price for fresh product which was higher than that which would otherwise have existed. By this the Panel understood that the purpose of the aid was to compensate the processor for the difference between the minimum grower price and the price which the processor would have paid for the fresh fruit had there been no guaranteed price.

54. The Panel observed that, although the EEC had maintained that the production aid was granted to re-imburse processors for having to pay a higher price for fresh fruit than they would otherwise have to, the production aid for each fruit was actually calculated as the difference between a "computed" EEC price for each canned fruit and the average duty-free price of the corresponding imported products. The "computed" EEC price for each fruit was calculated as the sum of the minimum grower price for fresh fruit in the EEC and the estimated cost of processing fresh fruit into canned fruit in the EEC.

55. The Panel noted, however, that if the cost of producing canned product in non-member countries was lower than that in the EEC (either because of lower processing costs or because of lower prices of fresh fruit) the EEC processor would receive an aid in excess of that which would compensate him for the difference between the minimum grower price and the "free market" price in the EEC. . . . It was the Panel's opinion that in this situation the EEC processor would receive a net subsidy enabling him to improve the price competitiveness of his products viz-a-viz the prices of imported product. This meant that the production aid ensured that EEC product would never be any less competitive than imported product. In addition, the Panel noted that this meant that foreign suppliers would never be able to improve their competitive position in the EEC market even if productivity gains in their industries, or other circumstances, permitted them to lower the cost of producing their product. The Panel noted from the EEC Agricultural Price Statistics . . . that the production aids had always more than compensated the difference between the EEC minimum grower prices and the "free market" prices for fresh peaches and Williams Pears.

56. The Panel next noted that, in fact, the stated objective of Regulation (EEC) No. 1152/78 was to eliminate any price advantage enjoyed by imported product. It noted in particular that Article 3b, paragraph 1, of this regulation stated that "the amount of aid shall be so fixed as to make up the difference between the prices of Community products and those of products from non-member countries". The Panel found that it was difficult to reconcile this Article with either the EC's contention that the aid was intended only to compensate the processor for having had to pay a guaranteed minimum price for fresh fruit or with the possibility that it was ever intended that the processing costs and prices of fresh fruit in non-member countries should serve as reasonable proxies for the equivalent costs and prices in the EC. . . .

VI. Conclusions

70. The Panel unanimously *concluded* that the production aids granted by the EEC since 1978 to processors of peaches and since 1979 to processors of pears nullified or impaired benefits accruing to the United States from tariff concessions granted by the EEC under Article II of the General Agreement in 1974 on canned peaches, canned pears and canned fruit mixtures and in 1979 on canned pears.

71. The Panel examined whether there was any evidence that the United States could have reasonably expected the introduction of the EEC production aids during the negotiation of the tariff concessions on the products concerned. With regard to canned peaches, canned pears and canned fruit mixtures the Panel *concluded* that the United States could not have anticipated the introduction of the subsidy at the time it negotiated concessions on these products in 1973. As regards concessions received in 1979 the Panel *concluded* that the United States should have been aware of the existence of the aid system for canned peaches. Inasmuch as that aid system benefits processors of canned fruit mixtures the United States should have taken due account of it in negotiating concessions of that product. The Panel *concluded* that the United States could not have reasonably foreseen the introduction of the aid system for canned pears. With regard to dried grapes the Panel *concluded* that the United States could have reasonably anticipated during the various tariff negotiations that Greek producers and processors would continue to benefit from support prices, storage subsidies, and subsidization of the selling price of product from governmental agencies. Only to the extent that it could be demonstrated that the EEC subsidy scheme for dried grapes was more than a mere continuation of the prior national Greek subsidy scheme and resulted in an unforeseeable additional upsetting of the competitive relationship between US dried grapes and Greek dried grapes on the market of the "EEC of nine" (i.e. without Greece), could the United States not have reasonably anticipated such additional EC subsidies and competitive distortions resulting therefrom.

72. The Panel considered whether the aid systems for each product upset the competitive relationship between EEC products and those imported from the United States. With regard to canned peaches, canned pears, and canned fruit mixtures the Panel *concluded* that the minimum price granted to growers of fresh peaches and pears did not adversely affect the competitive relationship between EEC and imported canned peaches, pears or fruit cocktail. With regard to the production aids granted on canned peaches, canned pears and canned fruit mixtures the Panel *concluded* that:

> —since the production aids made up any differences between the prices of Community products and those of products from non-member countries, foreign product could never improve its competitivity in the EEC.
> —whenever EEC fresh fruit prices and processing costs for peaches and pears were higher than those in non-EEC countries, EEC processors of peaches and

pears were compensated for the differences in fresh fruit prices and processing costs. To this extent, the EEC production aids more than merely compensated EEC processors for the costs resulting from the granting of a minimum price to growers. The Panel noted that, since their introduction, the production aids had always exceeded that amount necessary to compensate for any increased costs resulting from the minimum grower prices for fresh fruit.

—since the production aid is calculated as the difference between the computed EEC price and the duty-free price of imported product, the bound rates of tariff duty had become an absolute margin of protection for EEC products cancelling any cost and price advantages of foreign competitors.

The Panel *concluded,* therefore, that the production aids granted to processors upset the competitive relationship between EEC and imported canned peaches, canned pears and canned fruit cocktail.

73. With respect to the production aids granted to processors of dried grapes the Panel *concluded* that Greek processors had benefited already prior to 1974 from subsidies by Greek authorities so as to be able to market their product at competitive prices in the EEC. The United States could have reasonably expected at the time of tariff negotiations in 1974 and 1979 that, in case of an accession of Greece to the EC, Greek processors would continue to benefit from no less generous a system. In the light of new factual evidence submitted by the EC at a very late stage of the Panel proceedings, the Panel could not exclude that the market distortions resulting from EEC production aids to the detriment of competing dried grapes imported from the US had also been possible under the prior Greek subsidy scheme. Specifically it could not conclude that the EEC production aids had actually gone beyond what was possible and foreseeable at the time of the tariff negotiations in 1974/79. As regards the three other aspects of the subsidy system for dried grapes, namely the minimum grower price, the storage aids and the compensation for losses on sales by tenders by storage agencies, the Panel could not conclude that there was nullification or impairment on the basis of available evidence.

74. Having established the existence of nullification and impairment of tariff concessions with respect to canned peaches, canned pears, and canned fruit mixtures, the Panel considered what suggestions it could make so as to assist Contracting Parties in their task of formulating recommendations to achieve a satisfactory settlement of the matter. The Panel noted that in past "non-violation" complaints of nullification or impairment of tariff concessions (BISD II/195; 1S/30, 31, 59) the Contracting Parties had recommended that the party against which the finding had been made consider ways and means to remove the competitive inequality brought about by the measure at issue. The Panel was aware of the finding of the Working Party Report on the Australian subsidy on ammonium sulphate that "there is nothing in Article XXIII which would empower the Contracting Parties to require a contracting party to withdraw or reduce a consumption subsidy" . . . and that the "ultimate power of the Contracting Parties under Article XXIII is that of authorizing an affected contracting party to suspend the application of appropriate obligations

or concessions under the General Agreement" (BISD II/195, para. 16). In making the following draft recommendation, the Panel also wishes to emphasize that the recommendation cannot constitute a legal obligation for the EEC to remove or reduce its domestic production subsidies and does not preclude other modes of settling the dispute such as granting of compensation or, in the last resort, a request for authorization of suspension of concessions. The Panel also wishes to emphasize that this recommendation cannot detract from the rights of Contracting Parties under Article XXIV:6 of the General Agreement.

75. The Panel therefore suggests that the Contracting Parties recommend to the EEC that it consider ways and means to restore the competitive relationship between imported US and domestic EC canned peaches, canned pears and canned fruit cocktail which derived from the tariff concessions granted in 1974 on these products and in 1979 on canned pears. In accordance with agreed dispute settlement procedures (BISD 29S/15, para. (viii)), the EEC should be invited to report within a reasonable, specified period on action taken pursuant to this recommendation. . . .

QUESTIONS

1. Why wasn't the EEC subsidy a violation of the GATT?
2. Why should the EEC be penalized for a "nonviolation" nullification and impairment?
3. If you were now advising the EEC, how would you suggest that it revise its subsidy program? Do you think that this decision will actually lead to revision?
4. If you were representing the California growers, would you be satisfied? What would you do next?

2.   *The DISC Case*

No alleged U.S. "subsidy" has been more contentious than the Domestic International Sales Corporation (DISC) legislation.[4] Congress recognized in 1971 that U.S. corporations faced significant competition from foreign companies that were receiving some form of export assistance. Moreover, U.S. companies that engaged in export activities through domestic corporations were treated less favorably than those companies that manufactured products abroad through foreign subsidiaries. With these facts in mind, Congress authorized the creation of DISCs, a legislative concept that has since been replaced by the Foreign Sales Corporation (FSC).

A DISC was structured to mimic certain of the tax consequences available

[4]*See* Jackson, The Jurisprudence of International Trade: The DISC Case in GATT, 72 Am. J. Intl. L. 747, 772 (1978).

by export through a foreign subsidiary. Suppose a U.S. firm exports to Europe through, say, a Swiss sales subsidiary that it wholly owns. It will sell its exports to the Swiss subsidiary, which will then resell them and earn a profit that will be influenced by the initial transfer price as well as by the final sales price and the actual selling expenses. This profit will be taxable by Switzerland, but will not normally be taxable by the United States until actually paid to the U.S. parent in the form of a dividend to that parent. (Even then, there will be a credit allowed for a portion of the taxes paid to Switzerland.) Thus, by leaving the profits in the foreign subsidiary, the parent can defer a portion of the U.S. income tax on the transaction.

The DISC was a U.S. subsidiary, set up as formally as a foreign sales subsidiary, but set up in the United States to obtain similar advantages. Congress established the DISC legislation through Title V of the Revenue Act of 1971 by adding Sections 991 through 997 to the Internal Revenue Code of 1954, as amended. Under the original legislation, one-half of the DISC's income was taxable as a deemed distribution to its shareholder, whether distributed or not, and tax was deferred on the remaining one-half of DISC income until profits were distributed as dividends or were otherwise realized as income.

Concerned about the effectiveness of DISCs, the European Community (EC) requested consultations with the United States within the GATT framework shortly after the DISC legislation was enacted. Unable to convince the U.S. government to repeal the DISC legislation, the EC filed a formal complaint in the GATT in July 1972. The U.S. government responded by filing similar complaints, alleging that the territorial tax systems of France, Belgium, and the Netherlands were illegal. These tax systems, with various technical differences, have consequences comparable to those available through the foreign sales subsidiary already described. After three years of study, a GATT panel issued reports in which the panel concluded that the DISC and the three European territorial tax systems violated the GATT.

In 1981, the GATT Council, which is composed of all 88 member nations of the GATT (the Contracting Parties), adopted the 1976 panel reports. Whatever the validity of the panel findings, the Council essentially agreed to disagree about the merits of the case. The Europeans continued to insist that the DISC violates the GATT.

GATT ACTIVITIES IN 1981: TAX LEGISLATION

52

UNITED STATES TAX LEGISLATION (DISC) . . .

In 1981, the United States and the EEC reached an understanding on disputes between them over taxation of exports which had remained unsettled for nearly ten years.

In May 1973, the European Community had complained to the GATT Council about the operation of the United States Domestic International Sales Corporations (DISC's). Designed as a tax incentive to increase United States exports, the DISC legislation took effect on 1 January 1972. A corporation that qualifies as a DISC benefits from a tax deferral of part of its export income. The European Community argued that the DISC system constituted an exemption of direct taxes in favour of exports and thus conflicted with GATT rules on subsidies.

The Council set up a panel to investigate the EEC complaint. In November 1976, the panel reported to the Council that after reviewing the operation of the DISC scheme in the light of GATT rules, it concluded that the scheme should be regarded as an export subsidy, and that in some cases it had effects which contravened United States obligations under Article XVI:4 of the General Agreement. The panel found there was a prima facie case of nullification or impairment of benefits which other GATT member countries were entitled to expect under the General Agreement.

At the same time as the EEC complained about the DISC scheme, in 1973, the United States also complained to the GATT Council about income tax practices maintained by three EEC member States: France, Belgium and the Netherlands. The United States considered that these three countries' tax practices gave a certain exemption from income taxes on export sales, and were thus contrary to the requirements of the General Agreement.

Separate panels were set up by the Council in early 1976 to examine each of the three complaints by the United States, at the same time as the panel which was to examine the DISC legislation; the same five experts served on all four panels.

Reporting to the Council in November 1976, the panels said the application of the territoriality principle by Belgium and France—and of the world-wide principle by the Netherlands with qualified exemption for foreign income—allowed some part of export profits belonging to an economic process originating in the parent country to be outside the scope of that country's taxes. The panels concluded that all these practices amounted to export subsidies and in some cases had effects which contravened Belgian, French and Dutch obligations under Article XVI:4 of the General Agreement. Each of the three panels found prima facie cases of nullification or impairment of benefits which other GATT member countries were entitled to expect under the General Agreement.

The Council took note of all four panel reports, but could not agree on their adoption. The reports were discussed at several Council meetings over the next five years.

There was no resolution of the issue until December 1981, when the Council considered the reports together with an understanding proposed by the countries principally concerned.

After some discussion, during which several other countries expressed reservations about the long delay in resolving this dispute and also about the meaning of the understanding, the Council adopted all four reports "on the understanding that with respect to these cases, and in general, economic processes (including transactions involving exported goods) located outside the territorial limits of the exporting country need not be subject to taxation by the exporting country and should not be regarded as export activities in terms of Article XVI:4 of the General Agreement. It is further understood that Article XVI:4 requires that arm's-length pricing be observed, i.e., prices for goods in transactions between exporting enterprises and foreign buyers under their or the same control should for tax purposes be the prices which would be charged between independent enterprises acting at arm's length. Furthermore, Article XVI:4 does not prohibit the adoption of measures to avoid double taxation of foreign source income."

Following adoption of the reports, the chairman noted that the Council's decision and understanding "does not mean that the parties adhering to Article XVI:4 are forbidden from taxing the profits on transactions beyond their borders, it only means that they are not required to do so". He noted further that the decision does not modify the existing GATT rules in Article XVI:4 as they relate to the taxation of exported goods. He noted also that this decision did not affect and was not affected by the Tokyo Round Agreement on Subsidies and Countervailing Measures. Finally, he noted that the adoption of the reports, together with the understanding, did not affect the rights and obligations of GATT member states under the General Agreement.

The Council then took note of the chairman's statement, and also of the subsequent statements by several countries that although they had not objected to the Council's decision to adopt the reports, they had objections to the understanding and reserved their rights to raise this issue again both under the General Agreement and under the terms of relevant Tokyo Round agreements to which they were parties.

Note on Foreign Sales Corporations and the Denouement to the GATT DISC Case

On July 25, 1984, Congress passed the FSC legislation, replacing the DISC system, as part of the Deficit Reduction Act of 1984. Congress enacted this new system at the urging of the Reagan administration, which was in turn motivated by a decision to bring the United States tax system into conformity with GATT.

The new FSC provisions, which became effective on January 1, 1985, will allow taxpayers to establish a foreign sales corporation outside the United States through which foreign sales would be made. A portion of the income earned by the FSC would be exempt from U.S. taxation. In order to qualify for FSC benefits, certain management activities must take place outside the United States. Thus, an FSC is very similar to a DISC, but is actually foreign, and therefore more like the traditional foreign sales subsidiary. Exceptions to some of the rules are provided to help small businesses take advantage of the provisions.

QUESTIONS

1. Recognizing that the DISC was a fundamental and conscious export subsidy action on the part of the United States, should the DISC case even have been brought? What was the political purpose of doing so? What about that of bringing the other cases, which attacked a fundamental principle of European tax law that long predated GATT?

2. Should the tax and DISC panel even have decided the issue, or should it have used some evasion technique? For an argument in the latter direction, *see* Hudec, 13 Cornell Intl. L.J. 145, 165-166 (1980). The panel reports themselves (GATT, BISD, 23d Supp. at 98 ff.) are quite complex and technical.

3. Does the FSC resolve the legal problems raised by the trading partners of the United States? Is it consistent with the GATT?

4. Are developing nations likely to benefit from or be harmed by the shift to more consensual decision-making in GATT?

C.   CONTEMPORARY PRACTICE—SECTION 301

Section 301 of The Trade Act of 1974 authorizes the president to "take all appropriate and feasible action" to "enforce the rights of the United States under any trade agreement" or to respond to any foreign practice that is "unjustifiable, unreasonable, or discriminatory and burdens or restricts United States commerce."

The provision was definitively stated in the 1974 Trade Act, but it has roots going much further back, and was modified in both the 1979 and 1984 acts. Under the current procedures, the president may act on his own initiative or on the recommendation of the United States Trade Representative. There is a procedure for petitioning the Office of the United States Trade Representative, and there are statutory schedules that all must follow.

Section 301 gives the president great authority. The words "unjustifiable," "unreasonable," and "discriminatory" are defined quite broadly in the 1984 statute, and reach not only practices that violate the GATT and its codes but also those that violate international guidelines of entities like the Organization for Economic Cooperation and Development (OECD) or the Food and Agricultural Organization of the United Nations (FAO). Some practices may be encompassed even though they violate no international understandings. The president is given wide latitude in choosing a response—with an international agreement formalizing market access often being the typical outcome. Thus, this statute typically becomes a very powerful and very political remedy, without the strict definitions of the statutes examined in earlier chapters.[5]

---

[5] For additional data, *see* Fisher & Steinhardt, Section 301 of the Trade Act of 1974: Protection for U.S. Exporters of Goods, Services, and Capital, Law & Pol. Intl. Bus. 569 (1982). *See also* the implementing regulations at 15 C.F.R. §2006.

The following examples show §301 at work, and suggest the extensive role it may play in the future. The first, involving Canada's refusal to allow an income tax deduction for advertising on United States border radio and television stations, shows the scope of application of the section and the broad range of options available to the president. The second, involving an Argentine limit on cattlehide exports, shows how the section can be used to seek to enforce a trade agreement. And together with the third example, that of steel, it raises the question of whether §301 should be used when more specific remedies are available.

PRESIDENT JIMMY CARTER, MEMORANDUM OF JULY 31, 1980; DETERMINATION UNDER SECTION 301 OF THE TRADE ACT OF 1974; MEMORANDUM FOR THE UNITED STATES TRADE REPRESENTATIVE

45 Fed. Reg. 51,173 (1980)

Under the provisions of section 301(a)(2) of the Trade Act of 1974 (the Trade Act) (19 U.S.C. 2411(a)(2)), I have determined that the action described below is an appropriate and feasible response to the practice of Canada in denying an income tax deduction to Canadian advertisers who contract with U.S. television and radio broadcasting stations located near the U.S.-Canadian border (border broadcasters) for advertising aimed primarily at the Canadian market.

STATEMENT OF REASONS

The Office of the United States Trade Representative initiated an investigation of September 6, 1978 (43 FR 39617) on the basis of a petition filed on behalf of 15 U.S. television licensees. As is reflected in the legislative history to the Trade Act and clarified in the amendment to section 301 in the Trade Agreements Act of 1979 (Pub. L. 96-39, Title IX; 93 Stat. 295), authority to act under section 301 extends to cases involving service industries.

Public hearings were conducted at the request of the petitioner on November 29, 1978, and consultations with the Government of Canada took place on August 15, 1979, in Ottawa. Public hearings relating to the remedies sug-

---

Section 301 of the Trade Act of 1974 and amendments to §301 in Title IX of the Trade Agreements Act of 1979 appear in the Selected Documents Supplement, as do additional amendments to §301 defining its terms more precisely, in Title III of the Trade and Tariff Act of 1984.

gested by the petitioner were held on July 9, 1980, to provide an opportunity for parties who might be affected by such actions to comment.

After considering the recommendation of the United States Trade Representative and the evidence developed in the investigation and the hearings, I have determined that the Canadian tax practice with respect to advertising placed with U.S. border broadcasters is unreasonable and burdens and restricts U.S. commerce, within the meaning of section 301.

The longstanding business relationships between U.S. border broadcasters and their Canadian advertisers were disrupted by the enactment in Canada of Bill C-58 in 1976. The bill, which became section 19.1 of the Canadian Tax Law, was intended to strengthen the Canadian broadcast industry as an aspect of Canadian culture. However, while some Canadian broadcasters have benefitted from the law, it denies the U.S. border broadcasters access to a substantial portion of the advertising market in Canada, amounting to approximately $20 to $25 million annually, to which they previously had had access. The law, in effect, places the cost of attaining its objectives on U.S. companies and thus unreasonably and unnecessarily burdens and restricts U.S. commerce.

Consultations were held between U.S. and Canadian broadcasters and between the U.S. and Canadian government, in order to seek a solution which would address the Canadian cultural development objective without having an adverse impact upon the U.S. broadcasting stations. These consultations were not successful in finding a basis for the negotiation of a mutually acceptable solution.

I have determined that the most appropriate response to the Canadian practice is to propose legislation to the Congress which, when enacted, would mirror in U.S. law the Canadian practice. This legislation would amend the U.S. Internal Revenue Code to deny income tax deductions for the costs of advertising primarily aimed at U.S. audiences and placed on broadcast stations located in a foreign country if a similar deduction under the income tax law of that country is denied for advertising principally aimed at its audience and placed on U.S. broadcast stations.

This measured response is most appropriate because it is directed at those interests in Canada which now benefit from the denial, resulting from enactment of C-58, of Canadian advertising revenues to U.S. border broadcasters.

The proposed U.S. law itself will apply to Canada only as long as, and to the degree that, the Canadian law applies. No disruption of other, unrelated markets will be created which might have adverse effects in other areas of the U.S. economy.

This determination is to be published in the Federal Register.

Jimmy Carter
The White House,
Washington, July 31, 1980.

TANNERS' COUNCIL OF AMERICA, INC.; INITIATION OF INVESTIGATION

46 Fed. Reg. 59,353 (1981)

On October 9, 1981, the Chairman of the Section 301 Committee [Office of the United States Trade Representative] received a petition from the Tanners' Council of America, Inc. alleging that Argentina has defaulted on its 1979 Agreement with the United States to liberalize access to Argentine hides; that the failure to honor this agreement burdens and restricts U.S. commerce; and that Argentina imposes unreasonable restraints on access to raw cattle hides which impede domestic and third country sales of the U.S. leather tanning industry. The petition was filed pursuant to Section 301 of the Trade Act of 1974, as amended (19 U.S.C. 2411 et seq.). On November 24, 1981, the United States Trade Representative decided to initiate an investigation pursuant to 19 U.S.C. 2412(a).

The text of the petition is as follows: . . .

[T]he Tanners' Council of America, Inc. charges that Argentina engages in unfair trade practices detrimental to the domestic leather tanning industry. The Tanners' Council of America is a nonprofit trade association that represents virtually the entire U.S. leather tanning industry. The council claims:

(1) Argentina defaulted on its agreement with the United States on leather and hides. This failure to honor this agreement burdens and restricts U.S. commerce.

(2) Argentina imposes unreasonable restraints on access to raw cattlehides which impedes domestic and third country sales of the U.S. leather tanning industry.

These unreasonable Argentine policies and actions are severely damaging to the U.S. leather tanning industry and have contributed to a sharp growth in U.S. imports of leather and a corresponding decline in U.S. tanning production . . . The Tanners' Council requests a review of the Argentine practices and urges President Reagan to take all appropriate and feasible steps to obtain relief from these unfair trade practices.

Because of the serious nature of the Argentine action—defaulting on an international agreement—the Council urges retaliation under section 301(b), and requests that the President impose restrictions on Argentine leather imports into the U.S.

The Tanners' Council has not filed for other forms of relief available under the Trade Act of 1974 or any other provisions of law. However, since Argentina maintains subsidies on exports of leather, the Council is considering filing countervailing duty action on these practices. The government of Argentina provides two forms of subsidy: A reembolso or direct export payment to exporters of leather, and a system of preferential financing to Argentine exporters of leather.

(1) ARGENTINE DEFAULT

In 1979 the U.S. government negotiated an agreement with the government of
Argentina to liberalize access to Argentine hides. The United States agreed to
grant concessions on imports of Argentine corned beef and cheese and to
reduce U.S. tariffs on cattlehide leather. Argentina agreed to remove its ban
on cattlehide exports, and to replace it with an export tax which would be
reduced to zero in three years. . . .

The U.S. government has honored its commitments under the agreement.
However, the government of Argentina has failed to meet its scheduled commitment for April 1981, and is in default.

Argentina's export tax on cattlehides reduces the price of Argentine hides
relative to world hide prices. This reduction acts as a subsidy for Argentine
exports of cattlehide leather by artificially depressing the price of Argentine
raw material.

During the period of time that Argentina was nominally in compliance with
the agreement, the Argentine government took another measure which effectively negated part of the concession to which Argentina had agreed. Argentina imposed a minimum export price on cattlehides. This minimum export
price was used instead of the transaction price in determining the amount of
tax to be charged on export shipments of hides. Since the minimum export
price was higher than the transaction price, the effective tax was higher than
that which had been agreed.

The Argentine default has had several detrimental effects on the welfare of
the U.S. tanning industry. The failure to comply:

(a) Harms the U.S. industry directly by giving the Argentine leather industry an unfair competitive edge in U.S. and third country markets.

(b) Undermines efforts to liberalize international trade in hides and leather
through agreements with other countries.

(c) Signals to the rest of the world that Argentina can default on an agreement in this sector without eliciting effective U.S. response.

(d) Marks a return to protectionist tendencies in the leather and hide sector. Significant achievements of the agreement were a reversal of these trends
and the encouragement of the hope that free markets would once again prevail
for these products.

(2) ARGENTINA IMPOSES UNREASONABLE RESTRICTIONS ON ACCESS
TO RAW CATTLEHIDES

In 1972, in an effort to promote the development of its leather and leather
products industries, Argentina banned the export of green salted cattlehides.
This ban created a great distortion in the international marketplace. Prices of
U.S. cattlehides tripled in the twelve-month period October 1971 to October

1972. . . . The distortions caused by the Argentine restrictions were never completely corrected but exist to this day.

Furthermore, other developing countries followed the Argentine example and restricted access to their hides and skins. This follow-the-leader action increased the burden on U.S. cattlehide supplies. As a result it was estimated that in 1978, out of a world cattle slaughter approaching 300 million head the United States, although slaughtering but 15% of this total, contributed between 70% and 75% of total international trade in cattlehides.

From the U.S. side, the U.S./Argentine agreement had three objectives:

(a) To add Argentine hides to the international pool of raw material supply. This addition would spread the burden of adjustments to changing supply and demand conditions from total dependence on the U.S. and would minimize hide price fluctuations.

(b) To cause Argentine hides to be more price-responsive to international market conditions. This equalization of raw material prices would reduce the Argentines' competitive advantage in international leather trade.

(c) To set an example for other developing countries to remove restrictions on access to their hides and skins.

Because Argentina has failed to live up to its agreement to remove its restrictions on access to cattlehides, the burden on the U.S. tanning industry continues.

Argentina's restrictions are unreasonable. The Argentine tanning industry is among the most modern in the world. With its plentiful supply of raw material it has no reason to restrict access to it.

BURDENS ON THE U.S. INDUSTRY

Argentina's unreasonable restrictions on cattlehide exports severely damage the U.S. tanning industry in three ways:

(a) The restrictions that Argentina has placed on its exports of cattlehides have artificially depressed prices on its raw material. Since raw material is the largest component of leather prices, the unreasonable restrictions have given Argentina a price advantage in exporting leather to the U.S.

. . . [P]rior to its ban on the exports of cattlehides, Argentina's hides sold at or above U.S. prices. Subsequent to the ban prices of Argentine hides are a fraction of U.S. prices.

(b) Argentina's unreasonable restrictions on the exports of cattlehides damage the U.S. industry by giving an unfair advantage to Argentina in third country markets for leather. . . .

(c) Argentina's unreasonable action in restricting exports of cattlehides has placed an unfair burden on cattlehide markets in the U.S.

The accompanying chart[6] . . . of U.S. cattlehide prices shows the volatility

---

[6]Omitted—EDS.

caused partially by the decreased pool of available cattlehides on world markets. The chart shows two extreme peaks. The first, in 1972-73, illustrates the effect of the initiation of the Argentine ban on the U.S. market. The second, in 1979, was the result of the inability of countries seeking cattlehides to purchase them in countries other than the United States during a period when U.S. supplies were low due to the normal actions of the cattle cycle.

The damages inflicted by Argentina's unreasonable restrictions on exports of cattlehides are quantifiable for the first two types. In the period from 1972 to date, these damages are in the hundreds of millions of dollars in terms of lost trade to U.S. tanning companies.

The third type of damage, while not quantifiable, is possibly more important than the other two. It has created extraordinary capital demands on the U.S. industry and has added to inflationary pressures on leather and leather products in the United States.

. . . [T]he Argentine leather tanning industry is exploiting its default of the agreement and the reduced U.S. duties on leather to increase sharply shipments of leather to the U.S. For the month of July 1981, leather imports from all countries set a new record of $32 million. Of this amount, U.S. leather imports from Argentina were $13.7 million, or 43% of the July total.

In the first seven months of 1981 cattlehide leather imports from Argentina were 83.4% higher than the first seven months of 1980. Leather imports from all sources in the same period were up 49%. These figures show the severe impact of the reductions in duties on the U.S. tanning industry. They further dramatize the extraordinary advantage that Argentina has because of its unfair trade practices.

TANNERS' COUNCIL OF AMERICA, INC.; TERMINATION OF INVESTIGATION

47 Fed. Reg. 53,989 (1982)

The United States Trade Representative, in accordance with the provisions of 15 C.F.R. 2006.6, is terminating the investigation under Section 301 of the Trade Act of 1974 (19 U.S.C. 2411) regarding the Agreement Concerning Hide Exports and Other Trade Matters (the Agreement) between the Governments of the United States and Argentina entered into on August 10, 1979. . . .

In February, 1982, U.S. Government officials began a series of consultations with officials of the Government of Argentina on the issues raised by the Tanners' Council of America [TCA]. A Federal Register notice was published on September 16, 1982 (47 FR 40959) announcing a public hearing on a proposed recommendation to the President concerning termination of the Agreement. The public hearing was held on October 6, 1982 and interested parties were given the opportunity to present their views on that proposal and on all aspects of the investigation. On October 29, 1982, the United States and

Argentina mutually terminated the Agreement effective October 30, 1982, and the President by Proclamation No. 4993 (47 FR 49625, November 2, 1982) increased the column 1 rate of duty on bovine leather (TSUS 121.61) to five percent ad valorem effective October 30, 1982.

On November 9, 1982 the TCA notified the United States Trade Representative by letter of its desire to withdraw its petition.

In view of the above, the investigation of the complaint filed by the Tanners' Council of America, Inc. is terminated.

Jeanne S. Archibald
Chairman, Section 301 Committee.
November 18, 1982.

PRESIDENT RONALD REAGAN, MEMORANDUM FOR THE UNITED STATES TRADE REPRESENTATIVE: DETERMINATION UNDER SECTION 301 OF THE TRADE ACT OF 1974

18 Weekly Comp. of Pres. Docs. 1489 (1982)

Pursuant to Section 301(a)(2) of the Trade Act of 1974 (19 U.S.C. 2411(a)(2)), I have determined that the action described below is an appropriate and feasible response to subsidy practices of the European Community (EC), Belgium, France, Italy, the United Kingdom, Austria and Sweden, which are inconsistent with Articles 8 and 11 of the Agreement on the Interpretation and Application of Articles VI, XVI and XXIII of the General Agreement on Tariffs and Trade (Subsidies Code). With a view toward eliminating the harmful effects of such practices, I am directing the United States Trade Representative (USTR) to: (1) request the United States International Trade Commission to conduct an expedited investigation under Section 201 of the Trade Act of 1974 (19 U.S.C. 2251) with regard to the five specialty steel products subject to the 301 investigation; (2) initiate multilateral and/or bilateral discussions aimed at the elimination of all trade distortive practices in the specialty steel sector; and (3) monitor imports of specialty steel products subject to the 201 proceeding. If during the pendency of the International Trade Commission section 201 investigation imports cause damage which is difficult to repair, consideration would be given to what action, if any, might appropriately be taken on an emergency, interim basis under Section 301 of the Trade Act of 1974, consistent with U.S. international obligations.

STATEMENT OF REASONS

The Office of the USTR initiated investigations under Section 301 on February 26, 1982 (47 F.R. 10107) and on August 9, 1982 (47 F.R. 35387) on the basis of petitions filed by the Tool and Stainless Steel Industry Committee and the United Steelworkers of America. Petitioners principally allege that the EC and the above-mentioned countries have subsidized the production of specialty steel in a manner inconsistent with their obligations under Articles 8 and 11 of the Subsidies Code.

Petitioners' allegations are well founded. The United States believes that subsidies have been provided by the Government of Austria in the form of grants and capitalization, by the Government of Sweden in the form of preferential loans, loan guarantees and grants, and by the European Communities and its member governments in the form of preferential loans, loan guarantees, capital grants, "recapitalization" of financial losses, interest rebate programs, exemptions from taxation, and other practices.

The injury to the domestic industry is clear. The specialty steel industry is an efficient technologically up-to-date and export-oriented branch of the steel industry. Its output is used in a wide range of demanding applications critical to an industrial economy and thus commands a price far higher than ordinary steel. Regarded as an advanced, innovative and competitive industry, specialty steel producers in the United States have tended to be more profitable than the industry as a whole and far more so than most of their major competitors abroad. Nevertheless, the industry is facing an unprecedented challenge to its continued prosperity, and a number of its member firms are fighting for survival.

Part of the problem can be traced to the recession that began in America's basic industries more than two years ago. However, it is clear that since the lifting of import quotas in February 1980, imports have steadily captured a larger share of the U.S. market, further depressing operating rates, employment, prices and revenues. Through the first eight months of 1982, imports were at historically high levels, with import penetration ratios ranging from 11 to more than 50 percent, depending on the product. In every product category, imports now exceed the surge levels established by the Department of Commerce.

The majority of these imports are currently under investigation for unfair trade practices under Section 301, the countervailing duty statute, or the antidumping duty statute. However, they do not cover all important, or potentially important, sources of specialty steel imports. A partial remedy against unfair imports can be rendered meaningless by a substitution of new foreign suppliers for those whose shipments are affected. Thus, the specific subsidy complaints could lead to a remedy that fails to resolve the overall import problem. Moreover, dealing with the specific subsidy problem itself probably would not have a great impact on the world steel trading environment in which our industry must compete. Subsidies are only one of a wide range of trade restrictive and trade distortive practices that many of our trading partners engage in to protect their industries and to stimulate exports. If we are ever to put an end to constant trade disputes in steel, we must stop dealing with discrete import and export issues in isolation and instead begin a coordinated approach to the problem. By combining the Section 201 and Section 301 approaches, the United States hopes to stabilize the immediate import situation and to reverse the global trend toward greater excess capacity, increased subsidization, and closed markets.

This determination shall be published in the Federal Register.

RONALD REAGAN
November 16, 1982

NOTES AND QUESTIONS

1. Are you troubled at giving the president essentially unfettered discretion to choose the commodities on which to impose retaliatory tariffs and to choose whether or not to impose these tariffs on a discriminatory basis or an MFN basis? For an interesting example, *see* United States v. Star Industries, 462 F.2d 557 (C.C.P.A. 1972), *cert. denied*, 409 U.S. 1076 (1972). Is there any alternative to providing so much discretion?

2. As a matter of GATT design (or of voting on an individual case), would you prefer the discriminatory approach or the MFN approach to retaliatory tariffs? Is the issue different from its analogue under GATT Article XIX?

3. Was President Carter right in brushing off the U.S. TV station's complaint about Canadian Bill C-58? Was it really a brush off? Note that in 1984 Congress passed the requested legislation. Do the U.S. stations have any judicial relief against the president? For additional data, *see* Fisher & Steinhardt, Section 301 of the Trade Act of 1974: Protection for U.S. Exports of Goods, Services, and Capital, 14 Law & Pol. Intl. Bus. 569, 639-652 (1982).

4. Did Canada's action in that case violate the GATT? How might this event relate to Congress's effort to bring trade in services under GATT-style rules? For a general example of the latter interest, not specifically tied to the Canadian example, *see* Trade in Services and Trade in High Technology Products, Hearing Before the Subcommittee on Trade of the House Committee on Ways and Means, 97th Cong., 2d Sess. 60 (1982).

5. Do you think the Tanners' Council would have won a countervailing duty proceeding against Argentina? What is the difference between what the tanners must show under the two sections? What about possible remedies?

6. Does the use of a §301 proceeding—which lacks some of the procedural formalities favoring free trade found in the countervailing duty laws—bother you in this case? Or does the existence of an agreement with Argentina really make this situation different from the usual countervailing duty one?

7. How voluntary do you think the final upshot was on Argentina's part? Again, is the trend favorable to developing nations?

8. Should §301 proceedings be pursued simultaneously with countervailing duty proceedings? For a decision that, "in order to avoid redundant remedies

and the waste of limited government resources," they need not be so pursued, *see* Office of the United States Trade Representative, Industrial Union Department, AFL-CIO; Termination of Complaint, 47 Fed. Reg. 42,059 (1982). How would you advise the AFL-CIO if asked about the likely outcome of a legal attack on this determination?

9. In the face of *Industrial Union Department,* why is the government attempting to cumulate §201 and §301 remedies in *Specialty Steel*—given that the issue is one plausibly best covered by the countervailing duty laws? Is this a necessary result of the existence of the Subsidies Code dispute settlement procedure? A way to take advantage of the greater flexibility of the §301 procedure? A way to orient the trade law process toward VRAs and OMAs to obtain greater protection and higher prices? Note that the ITC subsequently found injury pursuant to §201 and the President imposed quantitative restraints and duties on imported specialty steel products.

10. Is §301 likely to become a catch-all absorbing all other domestic trade-law procedures?

11. Could a consumer's group have successfully proceeded against OPEC (before the recent price falls) under §301?

12. Need the government be consistent as between the position it takes in the GATT discussions and that which it takes under domestic law? For an example (the "cattle war") in which the United States gave radically different legal descriptions of a Canadian action in the two contexts, *see* Hudec, Retaliation Against "Unreasonable" Foreign Trade Practices: The New Section 301 and GATT Nullification and Impairment, 59 Minn. L. Rev. 461, 535-539 (1975).

13. If a GATT panel has found against the United States in a trade conflict, how is this finding relevant to a §301 action?

14. Consider the following remarks by Sen. Danforth (R. Mo.) in support of a stronger §301 for the United States.[7] Then consider the definitions provided for §301 in the Trade and Tariff Act of 1984. (Selected Documents Supplement) Do the new definitions make §301 a more viable mechanism for U.S. exporters?

> Mr. President, I am pleased to be joined today by Senator Lloyd Bentsen and an impressive group of our Senate colleagues in introducing the Reciprocal Trade and Investment Act.
>
> This legislation is the product of extensive consultations within the Congress and discussions with the administration, labor, and the private sector. . . . In its current form, the Reciprocal Trade and Investment Act was twice approved and reported out of the Finance Committee in the 97th Congress.
>
> The result is a bill that should serve to further the objectives we all share; namely, the maintenance and expansion of market opportunities abroad for U.S. exports of goods and services, and for foreign investment of the United States. The legislation builds on the broad concept of reciprocity of market access that

---

[7] 129 Cong. Rec. S.636 (1983).

is fundamental to U.S. trade policy. It strengthens enforcement of the legal rights of the United States under existing trade agreements and it sets the stage for the expansion of those international rights through the negotiation of agreements in the service and investment areas. Finally, the bill addresses itself to the problems encountered by high technology industries as a result of Government intervention that distorts international trade in such high growth sectors.

Overall, the bill is designed to liberalize international trade and to curb protectionist pressures in the United States by demonstrating that we will enforce our rights under international agreements. The idea is to close the credibility gap created when we consistently refuse to take protectionist action in spite of the widespread perception that we are the only country practicing what everyone else preaches; namely, free trade. . . .

Through the GATT system, the industrialized world has benefited from over 30 years of relative peace in international trade, along with the gradual reduction of traditional tariff and nontariff barriers to imports. The two fundamental principles of the GATT—the mutual extension of national and most-favored-nation treatment—remain essential elements in the GATT's formula for success.

The United States has, since the inception of the GATT, taken the leadership role in lowering international barriers to trade. Pushing and cajoling our trading partners into accepting each new liberalizing guideline, America has taken pains to employ the GATT's dispute settlement provisions. We have been in the forefront of any negotiations aimed at the reduction of tariff and nontariff barriers.

This leadership role has prompted the United States to set domestic policies relating to trade that are in conformity with GATT and to hope for similar action from our trading partners. The result is an American market with comparatively few import barriers while foreign markets are protected by a wide variety of restrictions. This has put us in a weak position to bargain for mutual concessions by other countries, for there are few American import restrictions left to trade away for market access abroad.

Of our major developed trading partners, Japan retains the most severe barriers to competitive American exports. Protection of the Japanese market is maintained in a variety of ways—some clearly illegal, some not. But regardless of whether these impediments are formal or informal, legal or illegal, the fact is, they work. Moreover, it is clear even to the casual observer of American driving, viewing, and listening habits that Japan has ample access to our market in areas where Japanese firms are competitive.

Our largest single trading partner, Canada, continues to focus its attention on the investment and service areas for its "Canadianization" efforts. Although not traditionally considered under the general GATT framework, these barriers are not only harmful in and of themselves, but also have a significant impact on trade in goods. Investment restrictions imposed by the Foreign Investment Review Agency (FIRA), discriminatory tax practices and similar Government policies have already begun to impede our access to their market.

Finally, the European Communities give one the impression that they are ever on the lookout for new ways of closing their markets. These efforts have been directed at Japan for some time and may well affect our exports in the future. Meanwhile, we are still groping for the means to deal with the impact of EC agricultural export subsidies on competitive U.S. exports to third markets.

The problems we face with respect to market access abroad are equally, if not more, severe in the case of developing nations. Many of these nations continue to benefit from developed country MFN concessions in the past 30 years without being accountable in GATT for reducing their own barriers. Of particular concern are barriers to trade and investment maintained by the Newly Industrialized Countries (NIC's) such as Mexico (not even a GATT member), and Korea and Brazil, which have no desire to "graduate" from their LDC status in GATT terms. [In late 1985 President de la Madrid authorized the beginning of negotiations toward Mexico's entry.—EDS.]

It cannot be surprising then, that many believe the GATT, however essential it is, is not alone sufficient to provide the basis of truly free international trade. It has become clear that national and MFN treatment are inadequate in some circumstances to provide the benefits of the system to the United States, when our market access is so disproportionately greater than others.

Further, while the GATT may work well to combat many traditional barriers to merchandise trade, it still fails to address some of the more sophisticated impediments found in the world today.

For example, the GATT offers no guidance whatever with regard to the free flow of investment and services, an integral part of international trade in today's world. Barriers in these sectors, such as performance requirements, continue to grow abroad in the absence of any firm international guidelines.

Therefore, while the GATT may be necessary to maintain equilibrium in the international trading system, it is by no means sufficient to achieve equitable access for U.S. trade and investment.

Mr. President, the bill under consideration today is designed to set the course for American trade policy that will accomplish our market access objectives by building upon and expanding the international trading system as we know it. . . .

15. Consider the EEC Council Regulation No. 2641/84, September 17, 1984, which follows. What does the regulation mean by illicit commercial practice? Would you consider this EEC regulation to be the functional equivalent of §301 in the ECC context? In what respects does Regulation 2641 differ from §301? Which is more discretionary? Could Regulation 2641 be used to counter what the EEC would consider to be an overly broad §301 or §337 ruling?

COUNCIL REGULATION (EEC) NO 2641/84 OF 17 SEPTEMBER 1984

On the strengthening of the common commercial policy with regard in particular to protection against illlicit commercial practices.

THE COUNCIL OF THE EUROPEAN COMMUNITIES

Having regard to the Treaty establishing the European Economic Community, and in particular Article 113 thereof. . . .

Whereas in the light of experience and of the conclusions of the European Council of June 1982, which considered that it was of the highest importance to defend vigorously the legitimate interests of the Community in the appropriate bodies, in particular GATT, and to make sure the Community, in managing trade policy, acts with as much speed and efficiency as its trading partners, it has become apparent that the common commercial policy needs to be strengthened, notably in the fields not covered by the rules already adopted;

Whereas to this end it is advisable to provide the Community with procedures enabling it:

—to respond to any illicit commercial practice with a view to removing the injury resulting therefrom,

—to ensure full exercise of the Community's rights with regard to the commercial practices of third countries;

Whereas, in particular, the Community should be enabled to remove the injury resulting from third countries' practices whose illicit nature is evident from their incompatibility regarding international trade practices either with international law or with the generally accepted rules. . . .

Whereas the Community must act in compliance with its international obligations and, where such obligations result from agreements, maintain the balance of rights and obligations which it is the purpose of those agreements to establish;

Whereas, in conducting the defence of its commercial interests, the Community needs to have at its disposal a decision-making process which permits rapid and effective action,

HAS ADOPTED THIS REGULATION:

ARTICLE 1

Aims

This Regulation establishes procedures in the matter of commercial policy which, subject to compliance with existing international obligations and procedures, are aimed at:

(a) responding to any illicit commercial practice with a view to removing the injury resulting therefrom;

(b) ensuring full exercise of the Community's rights with regard to the commercial practices of third countries.

ARTICLE 2

Definitions

1. For the purposes of this Regulation, illicit commercial practices shall be any international trade practices attributable to third countries which are incompatible with international law or with the generally accepted rules.

2. For the purposes of this Regulation, the Community's rights shall be those international trade rights of which it may avail itself either under international law or under generally accepted rules.

3. For the purposes of this Regulation, injury shall be any material injury caused or threatened to Community industry.

4. The term "Community industry" shall be taken to mean all Community producers:

—of products identical or similar to the product which is the subject of illicit practices or of products competing directly with that product, or

—who are consumers or processors of the product which is the subject of illicit practices,

or all those producers whose combined output constitutes a major proportion of total Community production of the products in question; however:

(a)   when producers are related to the exporters or importers or are themselves importers of the product alleged to be the subject of illicit practices, the term 'Community industry' may be interpreted as referring to the rest of the producers;

(b)   in particular circumstances, the producers within a region of the Community may be regarded as the Community industry if their collective output constitutes the major proportion of the output of the product in question in the Member State or Member States within which the region is located provided that:

    (i)   where the illicit practice concerns imports into the Community, their effect is concentrated in that Member State or those Member States,

    (ii)   where the illicit practice concerns Community exports to a third country, a significant proportion of the output of those producers is exported to the third country concerned.

ARTICLE 3

Complaint on Behalf of Community Producers

1. Any natural or legal person, or any association not having legal personality, acting on behalf of a Community industry which considers that it has suffered injury as a result of illicit commercial practices may lodge a written complaint.

2. The complaint must contain sufficient evidence of the existence of illicit commercial practices and the injury resulting therefrom. Proof of injury must be given on the basis of the factors indicated in Article 8.

3. The complaint shall be submitted, to the Commission, which shall send a copy thereof to the Member States.

4. The complaint may be withdrawn, in which case the procedure may be terminated unless such termination would not be in the interests of the Community.

5. Where it becomes apparent after consultation that the complaint does not provide sufficient evidence to justify initiating an investigation, then the complainant shall be so informed. . . .

ARTICLE 10

Adoption of Commercial Policy Measures

1. Where it is found as a result of the examination procedure that action is necessary in the interests of the Community in order to:

(a)   respond to any illicit commercial practice with the aim of removing the injury resulting therefrom; or

(b)   ensure full exercise of the Community's rights with regard to the commercial practices of third countries

the appropriate measures shall be determined in accordance with the procedure set out in Article 11.

2. Where the Community's international obligations require the prior discharge of an international procedure for consultation or for the settlement of disputes, the measures referred to in paragraph 3 shall only be decided on after that procedure has been terminated, and taking account of the results of the procedure.

3. Any commercial policy measures may be taken which are compatible with existing international obligations and procedures, notably:

(a) suspension or withdrawal of any concession resulting from commercial policy negotiations;

(b) the raising of existing customs duties or the introduction of any other charge on imports;

(c) the introduction of quantitative restrictions or any other measures modifying import or export conditions or otherwise affecting trade with the third country concerned.

4. The corresponding decisions shall state the reasons on which they are based and shall be published in the Official Journal of the European Communities. Publication shall also be deemed to constitute notification to the countries and parties primarily concerned. . . .

This Regulation shall be binding in its entirety and directly applicable in all Member States.

Done at Brussels, 17 September 1984.

For the Council
The President
P. Barry

16. During the 1982-1984 period, U.S. and EC agricultural interests faced a series of disputes over—for example—a highly subsidized U.S. wheat sale to Egypt, a GATT panel decision that certain EC export subsidies did not violate GATT, U.S. claims that the EC was improperly subsidizing poultry exports, pasta exports, and raisin exports and that these exports were hurting U.S. markets.

In the midst of this unresolved conflict, the EC, faced with enormous agricultural subsidy costs, was considering major revamping of its agricultural program, revamping that would (almost necessarily) increase protection of some items while that of others might be reduced.

What would you do if you

(a) represented a U.S. grain substitute or oilseed firm likely to be hurt by the EC reshuffling?

(b) represented a dairy firm likely to be helped by the same reshuffling?

(c) were the USTR?

(d) were the Secretary of Agriculture?

A description of the EC reference proposal follows.[8] (For additional data, *see* Butler, The Ploughshares War Between Europe and America, 62 Foreign Affairs 105 (1983); Echols, Just Friends: The U.S.-E.E.C. Agricultural Export Subsidies Standoff, Proc. 77th Ann. Mtg., Am. Socy. Intl. L. 119, 1983 (1985).)

THE UNITED STATES AND CHANGES IN THE COMMON AGRICULTURAL POLICY

The Commission of the European Communities has recently made proposals to change the Common Agricultural Policy (CAP), the European Communities' system for ensuring food supply, price stability and supporting farm income. These proposals have been the subject of considerable misunderstanding in the United States where they have been interpreted as an attack on the American farmer. So this note sets out what has been proposed, why it has been proposed and what the effects are likely to be on the American farmer.

WHAT IS THE OBJECTIVE OF THE EC COMMISSION'S PROPOSALS?

The main thrust of the Commission's proposals is:

a) to limit European Community spending on farm support.

b) to discourage surplus farm production.

WHY HAVE THESE PROPOSALS BEEN MADE?

a) because the Community is running out of cash. From 1974 to 1979 expenditure on supporting agricultural markets and guaranteeing prices grew at 23% a year, almost double the rate of growth of EC revenue which amounted in 1982 to some 23 billion dollars. EC agricultural expenditure (roughly two-thirds of this amount) remained relatively steady in 1980-82 largely because prices remained high on world markets. Since then however expenditure has increased sharply—by about 30% in 1983. So the cash is running out.

b) Productivity gains in European agriculture have meant output rising more rapidly than consumption and thus rising surpluses.

THE PROPOSALS

This is the background to the program proposed for the rationalisation of European agriculture. The Commission proposes

a) to extend the application of the guarantee threshold system to more products. The guarantee thresholds discourage surpluses by putting a ceiling on the amount of a crop EC farmers may produce without being forced to contribute to the cost of disposing of the surplus. In the Commission's view it is no longer reasonable or possible to provide an open-ended guarantee to farmers when outlets no longer exist.

b) to accelerate the EC's continuing efforts to *narrow the gap between EC prices and world prices.*

HOW WOULD SOME SPECIFIC PRODUCTS BE AFFECTED?

Milk, which accounts for about one-third of the EC's current farm price support spending, provides an important example of how the new EC proposals are

---

[8]*Reprinted in* Review of Agricultural Exports and Trade, Hearing Before the House Committee on Agriculture, 98th Cong. 1st Sess. 39 (1983).

designed to discourage over-production. The EC Commission has recommended that milk producers be required to pay a supplementary levy on the amount of milk they produce exceeding 101% of their 1981 production. This supplementary levy would be equal to 75% of the EC's milk target price. In addition, the Commission proposed a further 4% levy on all milk produced on intensive dairy farms.

The Commission's proposals would also extend guarantee thresholds for *grains and oilseeds. Sugar* producers would be required to continue paying the full cost of disposing of excess sugar production, as they have done in the past two years.

This proposed EC farm package would therefore

a) restrict the volume of their production on which farmers are entitled to receive a guaranteed price,

b) require EC farmers to foot the bill for their own overproduction, and,

c) reduce the EC-world price gap.

This package represents a major shift in the direction urged for years by U.S. critics of the CAP and should be welcome news for U.S. farmers who have long complained about the European Communities' "extravagant" farm spending.

EXTERNAL EFFECTS

The proposals would require substantial sacrifices from EC farmers and have not generally been well received by them. When the EC is asking its own farmers to make sacrifices and in fact to control their production, the Commission believes that it is not unreasonable for the Community to review its treatment of competing imports provided that this is strictly in accordance with the international trading rules as set out in GATT.

GRAIN SUBSTITUTES

The EC cannot implement a guarantee threshold for grain without stabilising imports of grain substitutes, which displace Community grown cereals in animal feed and have the effect of forcing more EC grain on to the world market. This is not a proposal aimed specifically at the United States. Substitutes are imported from a wide range of sources and action has already been taken on manioc and bran coming from such areas as South East Asia. It is therefore proposed to stabilise the imports of other important substitutes—corn gluten feed and citrus pellets. Imports of corn gluten feed have in fact soared from 700,000 tons to 3 million tons since 1974.

What is being proposed for corn gluten and citrus pellets therefore is *not* banning imports or reducing them, but *stabilising* these imports after discussion with the EC's major suppliers and in full accordance with the GATT rules.

OILS AND FATS TAX

This proposal is frequently presented as an external measure which will impair the duty free access to the EC of soybeans, soymeal and other oilseeds and oilseed products valued at around $4 billion in 1982. This is not so.

First, the tax would be a non-discriminatory sales tax on all oils and fats (excluding butter) consumed in Europe whether produced locally or imported. Imports would not be treated differently from domestic products; this non-discriminatory treatment squares fully with the international trading rules. Imports of soybeans and meal would *not* be affected.

It is extremely doubtful whether the proposed tax would have any discernable effect on the quantity of soybeans imported. First, the low rate of tax proposed combined with the reduction in butter subsidies is not likely to alter consumption patterns of soybean oil or margarine. Second, all other vegetable oils including olive oil whether obtained from imported or domestically produced seeds would be taxed. This would have a proportionally greater effect on the lower priced oils (such as rapeseed oil). Lastly, soybeans are imported very largely for animal feed and not for oil production.

WILL THE U.S. BEAR THE BURDEN OF CAP REFORMS?

This major package of proposals has *not* been designed to shift the burden of adjustment away from European agriculture onto the shoulders of U.S. exporters.

First, soybean exports should not be affected by the proposed tax on vegetable oil.

Second, the stabilisation of imports of corn gluten feed and citrus pellets will be carried out in compliance with GATT rules.

Third, European farmers would bear the major burden of the reforms which would
—reduce price increases for farm products
—fix prices for some surplus commodities for more than one marketing year
—set production quotas with severe penalties for farmers who exceed them
—extend guarantee thresholds
—reduce EC support buying to prop up farm prices
—discontinue many other forms of financial assistance.

The Commission's proposals are a tough package of measures which call for major sacrifices by European farmers but which are unlikely to reduce current levels of U.S. agricultural exports to the EC. In fact, world wide the U.S. farmer stands to benefit from the cutbacks in the production of EC products which compete with U.S. products in third markets.

17. U.S. Sake, a California corporation produces sake in California for sale in the United States and for export. In addition to selling to the growing U.S.-Japanese restaurant market, U.S. Sake would like to export sake to Japan, which is, of course, a highly "educated" market with respect to sake. Currently, 99% of all sake sold in Japan is produced in Japan.

Sake is classified as a wine under the applicable U.S. Treasury Bureau of Alcohol, Tobacco and Firearms (BATF) regulations, and is also classified as a wine by various states. In addition, U.S. Sake belongs to the Wine Institute, a trade association designed to promote U.S. wines. Sake, however, is imported into the United States as a "malt" under the Tariff Schedules of the United States (TSUS), and is derived from rice.

Always eager to gain assistance from the U.S. government, U.S. Sake intends to apply for an export incentive program offered by the U.S. Department of Agriculture's Foreign Agricultural Service.

(1) You are counsel to the president of Japan Sake, a Tokyo corporation that is directly competitive with U.S. Sake in the United States and Japan. Through industry sources, it has come to your attention that USDA is about

to award a substantial export promotion allowance to U.S. Sake for exports to Japan, a matter of some concern since U.S. Sake's products retail at 10% below the price of Japan Sake's goods, and may indeed be currently selling at below the cost of production in overseas markets. What advice will you give to the President of Japan Sake? Should he have Japan Sake go to the Government of Japan to have this matter raised with the United States as a violation of applicable trade agreements?

(2) If you were representing the United States, in your capacity as General Counsel to the Office of the U.S. Trade Representative, how would you defend the U.S. program before any possible GATT panel summoned by Japan to consider the Wine Promotion Allowance?

(3) What if the target market in this problem were not Japan but Burma? How would this fact alter your conclusions?

An outline of the Export Incentive Program for U.S. wines follows:

> This program is designed to assist U.S. wineries in promoting their own brand(s) in specific countries. All varietal and proprietary grape and fruit wines produced by vintners in the United States are eligible under this program. Exports of bulk wines may be included if the foreign bottler maintains the U.S. identity of the products and clearly identifies them as U.S. wine.
>
> *PROMOTIONAL ACTIVITIES.* Promotional activities acceptable in the calculation of promotional expenditures include: in-store demonstrations, point-of-sale materials, wine tastings and consumer or trade advertising. Salaries, international travel, price-off deals and giveaways may not be included.
>
> *CONTRACTS.* Contracts are signed for a three-year term, but may be funded each year to assure funding at appropriate levels. Contractees may claim reimbursement at the end of each marketing year. The marketing years for the purposes of this program are either from October 1 through September 30, or from July 1 through June 30, whichever is more convenient for the participating firm.
>
> *TERMS OF PAYMENT.* FAS payment will be the lesser of the following:
>
> A. Fifty percent of the firm's (and/or third party's) total expenditures for promotion of U.S. wines or
>
> B. The following percentages of the f.a.s. value of a winery's exports to selected countries in the same marketing year, according to the schedule below:

Year in program	FAS payment
1st	10% of Export Sales
2nd	7% of Export Sales
3rd	5% of Export Sales

> N.B., while the Foreign Agricultural Service will be as responsive as possible to applications, budgetary limitations may require proration of our funds if the response to this program remains high.

18. A mid-1970s American Society of International Law study panel on trade institutions focused on the following topics.

1. the need for continuous formulation of trade rules;
2. the overall structure of trade institutions;
3. the role of the developing countries in tariff and non-tariff negotiations;
4. the application of Most-Favored-Nation treatment;
5. the scope of trade institution coverage;
6. voting;
7. dispute resolution;
8. amendment procedures;
9. staff services; and
10. the implementation of institutional reform—how we get "from here to there" in the area of institutional reform.

Am. Socy. Intl. L., Re-Making the System of World Trade: A Proposal for Institutional Reform 13 (1976).

How might the list be different today?

19. How do you think the GATT structure could be improved? Should the membership of the GATT and the codes negotiated under its aegis be congruent? What sorts of reforms might be instituted to make the GATT relate more effectively to other international economic institutions such as the OECD, IMF, and UNCTAD?

20. The next chapter deals with the regulation of trade and the problems of developing countries (LDCs). Many LDCs have described the GATT as a "rich man's club." Are you satisfied with the treatment of developing countries by the GATT? Do you think the GATT codes you have studied so far on subsidies, dumping, government procurement, standards and customs valuation have dealt fairly with LDCs? Should the GATT be expanded to regulate international commodity markets of concern to LDCs through export quota arrangements, buffer stock agreements, and multilateral contracts? Mexico, an LDC struggling with tremendous foreign debt problems, finally joined the GATT in 1985. How will membership in the GATT be of assistance to Mexico?

21. Should the GATT be expanded to regulate trade in services (such as shipping, aviation, insurance, or tourism) or foreign investment? Note the two-edged sword here: while expanded jurisdiction could permit more trade-offs, too many subjects could bog down the organizations. Note that the next round of GATT negotiations may focus on services. To what extent are the principles used to regulate goods under the GATT relevant to trade in services?

22. How should international trade disputes be settled—on a juridical basis, or by using a negotiating or political approach expressing the relative strength of the parties?

23. Are the sanctions used by the GATT—withdrawal of substantially equivalent concessions—strong enough to insure compliance with the agreement or its subcodes? How would you compare the problem of imposing sanctions under the GATT with other areas of international relations?

Chapter X

Trade and Developing Nations

More than anyone else, Raúl Prebisch has brought to the fore the idea that the international trade system (and the rest of the international economic system as well, as will be seen in later chapters) should be reshaped to the benefit of developing nations (LDCs).

STATEMENT BY MR. RAÚL PREBISCH, SECRETARY-GENERAL OF THE UNITED NATIONS CONFERENCE ON TRADE AND DEVELOPMENT*

2 Trade & Dev. Poly. Statements 76, U.N. Doc. E/CONF. 46/141 (1964)

MR. PREBISCH.

The starting-point of this Conference is a clear political concept which has apparently ceased to be a subject of controversy: that the prosperous countries of the world should not neglect the problems of the economic periphery, where two-thirds of the world's population live in very precarious conditions. But there is a basic difference between recognition of this concept and its translation into a vigorous policy of international co-operation designed to bring about rapid development in this very vast part of the world. Never before has there been an opportunity like the present of quickly solving, thanks to the enormous potential of contemporary technology, the problem of poverty and its inherent evils in the developing countries. Yet never before have such distressing tensions, as those which beset the developing world, emerged on such a huge scale. . . .

*Third Plenary Meeting, March 24, 1964.

The "attainable minimum" . . . could . . . be summed up in six main points.

Firstly, primary commodities should be given easier access in the markets of the major industrial centres, and be assured a reasonable share in the growth of their consumption.

Secondly, the purchasing power generated by the export earnings of developing countries should be increased and stabilized, either by commodity agreements designed to influence prices, or by a compensatory financing mechanism which, in many cases, might eventually be more effective than the mere adjustment of prices, especially for those products in respect of which it would not be advisable to influence prices for the reasons explained in my report.

The third type of measure relates to the export of industrial products by developing countries. Here we deal with the problem of restrictions presently hampering the normal expansion of such exports, as well as with the need, over a limited period, for a preferential policy with regard to the remaining manufactures, subject to a reasonable list of exceptions, to assist new industries of developing countries in finding external markets, this being essential if the persistent tendency to disequilibrium is to be corrected.

The fourth point relates to import substitution. Not all the disequilibrium of trade can be corrected by means of increased exports or better prices. Import substitution must continue, in so far as possible, through the formation of groups of developing countries, since this will permit such substitution to be carried out in a more rational manner than at present.

The fifth measure relates to trade with the socialist countries under long term agreements, in order to use the great import potential of those countries, resulting from their present rate of economic growth. It may not be possible to solve this problem at present other than by means of bilateral agreements. However there is reason to hope that expansion of trade of socialist countries with the rest of the world will make it possible to move from bilateralism to multilateralism, since multilateral compensation is greatly restricted when trade is limited to a small number of goods and only a few countries. The greater the increase in the number of countries, and in the scope of trade, the greater will be the possibility of evolving towards multilateral trade, which is most desirable in view of the well-known drawbacks of the bilateral system.

The sixth point relates to trade in "invisibles", and the need to reduce the burden of servicing external debt by readjusting loan periods and terms. This is urgently required in many countries. Similarly, measures will also have to be taken regarding freight and insurance, as a means of improving the balance of payments and correcting the tendency to disequilibrium. . . .

The fundamentally sound idea has been put forward, and is still being stressed, that countries must develop through their own efforts. However, these efforts must be allowed to take the form of an increase in exports, which is the only form they can take in the international economic field. There is therefore a need for a policy of continuing and accelerated expansion of exports which, in turn, will accelerate the development of these countries.

A fruitful dialogue is now about to commence, in the course of which we must concentrate on basic problems and avoid marginal issues which may divert us from the questions with which the developing countries are primarily concerned. I should like to indicate briefly how people in the periphery view these problems at present. We believe that developing countries must not be forced to develop inwardly—which will happen if they are not helped to develop outwardly through an appropriate international policy. We also deem it undesirable to accept recommendations which tend to lower mass consumption in order to increase capitalization, either because of the lack of adequate foreign resources or because such resources are lost owing to adverse trends in terms of trade.

I believe that to force these countries to develop inwardly would have serious consequences, not only economically and socially, but also politically. However, I do not wish to point to the dire handwriting on the wall.

On the contrary, I wish to stress the great opportunity we have of solving the basic problems of the developing world. It would be tragic if this opportunity, accentuated by the great potential of modern technology were to be wasted. We must make use of this potential and we must learn to influence technological and economic forces and also to influence the forces of history in order to channel the profound emotional pressures which have been accumulating in the developing countries. Those countries have a great task before them. However, they are not merely called upon to solve their own economic problems. They can contribute a great deal because they have a concept of life and of human values which will, I am sure, enable them to contribute decisively to resolving basic incompatibilities between technological and spiritual values.

Many developing countries bear the deep imprint of thousands of years of civilization. They could do much to ensure that, in our efforts to control economic forces, we do not subordinate man to the demands of technology or of purely economic processes, but enable him to free himself from economic need, from poverty, and from his inherent ills, so that he may improve his life and achieve that full life which, in the developing countries has until now been traditionally enjoyed by only a few.

Even though relatively little of substance has happened on the level of international trade regulation, Prebisch's ideas have shaped an enormous range of discussions and institutions. These have included extensive debates in the United Nations and proposals in the United Nations Conference on Trade and Development (UNCTAD), which has met regularly and has become a developing nation counterbalance to the Organisation for Economic Co-operation and Development.[1]

[1] For further background, *see* Krishnamurti, Multilateral Trade Negotiations and the Developing Countries, 2 Third World Q. 251 (1980), as well as the text of the Brandt Commission report, published as North-South: A Program for Survival (1980). *See also* J. Sewell and J. Mathieson, North-South Relations in J. Pechman (ed.), Setting National Priorities: Agenda for the 1980s (1980).

QUESTIONS

1. Considering that the developed nations (DCs) are unlikely to agree to more than a small part of the New International Economic Order, why do the LDCs persist in repeating their demands in so many different contexts?

2. Would there be better models than UNCTAD for the negotiation of new North-South arrangements? In thinking about this question, go beyond the accurate but standard arguments that in organizations like the U.N., that are relatively powerless, the LDCs play a major role, while in institutions like the IMF and the World Bank, where there is actual power, the LDCs have a much weaker role. Consider also other approaches with which you may be familiar, such as the Brandt Commission, working groups in GATT, or the committee structure of the Law of the Sea negotiations.

3. Viewed from a U.S. perspective, the developing countries are pressing for a redistribution of economic, and, a fortiori, political power. Functional areas such as trade, technology, resource transfers, private investment, and the law of the sea are involved, among others. It could be argued that the United States possesses three broad policy alternatives—cooperation, confrontation, or isolation. What are the economic and political consequences of each alternative for different groups here and abroad, and which is the preferable route for the United States to follow?

4. Is Prebisch's idealism the only way to support southern interests in northern politics or are there other ways—following the pattern of the most successful GATT negotiations of the 1950s and 1960s—to appeal to a form of self-interest and define northern constituencies that might actually support southern interests? In arguing for a development and trade preference program for the Caribbean Basin, President Reagan emphasized its effects on political instability and on migration. Is this a wise alternative? What about the OPEC model of economic pressure based on a resource cartel controlled by developing nations?

5. Much of the current trade debate turns on the issue of "reciprocity" between the United States and trading partners. Do you think the United States should seek reciprocity from developing countries? What if these countries keep out U.S. imports? What if the import restraints are mandated by the IMF as "conditionality" for an IMF loan?

6. Should those developing nations that are most deeply in debt to the banks be given special trade privileges to help them earn the foreign exchange needed to pay their debts?

A. EXPORT GENERATION AND IMPORT SUBSTITUTION

One of the central issues in the UNCTAD program is the need for developing nations to industrialize by manufacturing exports for the world market, not just for their own internal market.

These two approaches, export generation and import substitution, often contrast sharply with one another. They tend to lead to different policies and to appeal to different constituencies. With export generation, low tariffs are preferred so that industries can have inexpensive access to raw materials; with import substitution, high tariffs may be preferred to protect relatively small and inefficient industries. The constituency for import substitution is frequently (as it was in the pre-Civil War United States) urban while that for export generation may be rural. Perhaps for this reason, import substitution economies often have artificially low food prices (like Egypt) and export generation economies often have artificially high food prices (like Japan).

Realistically, every economy does some of each—and , to some extent, the two alternate in intellectual fashion. The UNCTAD program was formulated with the Latin American model especially in mind, and at a time when new export industries were clearly needed. Latin America had had a generation of import substitution—and was nearly running out of reasonable opportunities for such substitution. Hence the initial UNCTAD agenda emphasized export generation—and particularly the ways that developed nations could make it easier for developing nations to increase the value of their exports.

As the next U.N. excerpt shows, however, the choices are still a matter of dispute.

U.N., ACCELERATED DEVELOPMENT IN SUB-SAHARAN AFRICA: AN ASSESSMENT BY THE OAU, ECA, AND ADB SECRETARIATS

U.N. Doc. E/ECA/CM.8/16 (1982)

I. INTRODUCTION

1. In July 1979, the Assembly of Heads of State and Government of the Organization of African Unity adopted the Monrovia Strategy for the Economic Development of Africa on the recommendations of African Ministers responsible for economic development and planning. The recommendations of the Ministers were themselves based on proposals already worked out by sectoral conferences such as the Conference of African Ministers of Industry, the Conference of African Ministers of Trade and the Conference of African Ministers of Transport, Communications and Planning.

2. In order to devise a plan of action for the implementation of that Strategy, the Heads of State and Government held an extraordinary summit in Lagos, Nigeria, in April 1980, devoted exclusively to economic development problems of Africa and adopted the Lagos Plan of Action[1] for the Economic Development of Africa. The Plan was presented to the United Nations General Assembly at its eleventh special session in September 1980 and is now an

[1] Organization of African Unity, Lagos Plan of Action for the Economic Development of Africa, 1980-2000.

integral part of the International Development Strategy for the Third United Nations Development Decade.

3. Concerned about the dim prospects projected for sub-Saharan African countries in the 1980s and beyond, as presented in the World Development Report, 1979,[2] the African Governors of the World Bank and the International Monetary Fund in September 1979 requested the World Bank to prepare "a special paper on the economic development problems of these countries and an appropriate programme for helping them." The response to that request is the report entitled "Accelerated development in sub-Saharan Africa: An agenda for action",[3] which was published in 1981.

4. Following the publications of the World Bank report, a joint staff working group of the OAU, ECA and ADB secretariats, set up for the purpose of reviewing the report, prepared, in September 1981, a paper containing some preliminary reflections. The paper was presented to the meeting of the African Governors of the Bank. At that meeting, the Governors decided that further discussion of the report should be held in Africa and that a special meeting should be organized by ADB, ECA, and OAU for that purpose.

5. The aim of this paper, which has been prepared by the resumed meeting of the joint secretariat working group in Addis Ababa in January 1982, is to assist in a better understanding of the goals, objectives and characteristics of the report in the light of the requirements of the Lagos Plan of Action.

6. Accordingly the paper discusses the contrasting goals, objectives and characteristics of the two documents, examines the broad economic policy issues raised by the report, reviews the report's treatment of sectors; and concludes with a highlight of the findings of the group.

II.   GOALS, OBJECTIVES AND CHARACTERISTICS

A.   THE LAGOS PLAN OF ACTION

7. The Lagos Plan of Action was adopted by African Heads of State and Government against the background of two decades of stagnation in output; worsening balance of payments brought about by deteriorating terms of trade; increasing payments for the import of high-level skills, capital goods, spare parts and equipment, raw material inputs, marketing, shipping and insurance services; widespread unemployment and mass poverty; and a painful realization that past policies are not viable and sustainable if the objectives of self-reliance, eradication of mass poverty, reduction of widespread unemployment, equitable distribution of the benefits of development and economic growth, sovereignty over natural resources and equitable participation in international decision-making processes are to be pursued and achieved.

---

[2] World Bank, World Development Report, 1979 (New York, Oxford University Press, 1979).
[3] Accelerated Development in Sub-Saharan Africa: An Agenda for Action, The World Bank, Washington, D.C., 1981.

8. The Plan is designed to restructure the economy of Africa, based on the twin principles of national and collective self-reliance and self-reliant and self-sustaining development. Restructuring implies not only the necessary change in the composition of goods and services by gradually increasing the shares of industrial products in the national and regional basket of goods and services but also internalizing the sources of the supply of producer goods (capital equipment, spare parts, and machines and raw material inputs), high-level skills for natural resources exploration, evaluation and extraction, products and process design, industrial and other production organization and management, project identification, analysis and implementation, research and development, education and training, marketing, banking, shipping and financial services; changing the pattern of external trade and changing the ownership of enterprises not only between the public and private sectors but also between indigenous and foreign ownership.

9. The principles of self-reliance and self-sustainment imply the increasing dependence of economic growth and development on internal demand stimuli and the gradual substitution of domestic for imported factor inputs. Collective self-reliance implies the pooling of resources—manpower, markets, institutions, finance etc.—at the subregional, regional and other multinational levels for the purpose of effectively achieving those objectives enumerated above.

10. Within this framework, the Plan emphasizes the imperative need for the countries of the region individually and collectively to have a thorough knowledge of the natural resource base of their economies not only for the purpose of determining the industrial products which they can produce but also for designing appropriate strategies for the types of high-level skills which they can import in the short run and must produce in the long run.

11. The Plan is based on an integrated approach which covers different economic and social activities and takes into account the interdependence of these activities. In this connexion, the Plan recognizes two leading production sectors—food and agriculture and industry. The industrial sector is designed to make possible the supply of the bulk of industrial inputs required for agricultural production, processing, storage and transportation. The food and agriculture programme (which includes forest products and industrial fibres) is designed to provide not only inputs into the processing industries but also markets for industrial products. And the industrial programme goes much further; it is intended to cover building materials and metal and engineering products which make heavy use of capital goods. Emphasis is also laid on the need to attack the present paradox of the African region with its enormous energy resources and its heavy dependence on energy imports, by developing science and technology and human resources relevant not only to the development of industry, agriculture, transport and communications but to the local evaluation, extraction and refining of natural resources which constitute the base of all production.

12. The Plan underscores the importance of involving all agents of development and change: private enterprises; public enterprises; trade unions; cham-

bers of commerce, agriculture, industry and mines, etc.; universities and other institutions of learning and research in the process of development and growth.

13. The Plan recognizes the importance of regional economic co-operation and integration as necessary instruments for pursuing the objectives of national and collective self-reliance and accordingly spells out clearly the steps to be taken for strengthening economic co-operation and integration efforts.

14. While the importance of external assistance is recognized, the Heads of State and Government were convinced that ". . . outside contributions should only supplement our own efforts, they should not be the mainstay of our development".

15. In outlining and adopting the Lagos Plan of Action, member States were fortified by one important fact; that not one of today's developed countries developed by depending excessively on external sources for the supply of the strategic inputs into their processes of generating and sustaining development and economic growth. Indeed, the development and economic growth of these countries were based on the development of their national markets for the supply of factor inputs and production of final goods and services. The decision to export usually came later on. This approach has been adopted irrespective of political and ideological orientation.

B.   ACCELERATED DEVELOPMENT IN SUB-SAHARAN AFRICA: AN AGENDA FOR ACTION

16. The authors of the World Bank report recognize the existence of the Lagos Plan of Action and claim to build on it. According to them the report "deals with short- to medium-term responses to Africa's current economic difficulties. It focusses on how growth can be accelerated and how the resources to achieve the longer-term objectives set by the African Governments can be generated, with the support of the international community". In short, the main objective of the report is to design a short- to medium-term strategy that will assist member States to generate the resources necessary to implement the goals and objectives of the Lagos Plan of Action.

17. The Strategy proposed is based on a diagnosis of the economic situation of sub-Saharan Africa as it has evolved over the past two decades. Basically, the findings are the following: slow over-all economic growth; sluggish agricultural performance coupled with rapid rates of population increase; balance-of-payments and fiscal crises, overextended public sector, and scarcities of financial resources, skilled manpower and organizational capacities.

18. However, according to the World Bank, the picture is not uniformly bleak: vastly more Africans are in schools and most are living longer, roads, ports and new cities have been built and new industries developed; technical and managerial positions, formerly occupied by foreigners, are now held by Africans. In general, the authors agree that "for most African countries, and for a majority of the African population, the record is grim and it is no exaggeration to talk of crisis". Indeed, as they put it, "slow over-all economic

growth, sluggish agricultural performance coupled with rapid rates of population increase, and balance-of-payments and fiscal crises—these are dramatic indicators of economic trouble".

19. As far as the causes of the present crises are concerned, the report identifies internal and external factors. Internal factors comprise constraints based on "structural" factors that evolved from historical circumstances or from the physical environment and they include underdeveloped human resources, the economic disruption that accompanied decolonization and postcolonial consolidation, climatic and geographic factors hostile to development and rapidly growing population. External factors consist of adverse trends in the international economy which include, particularly since 1974, "stagflation" in the industrialized countries, higher energy prices, the relatively slow growth of trade in primary products and adverse terms of trade especially for copper and iron ore. The authors conclude their analysis of sources of lagging growth by asserting that the internal "structural" problems and the external factors have been exacerbated by domestic policy inadequacies comprising trade and exchange-rate policies which have over-protected industry, held back agriculture and absorbed much administrative capacity; too little attention being paid to administrative constraints in mobilizing and managing resources for development, particularly since planning, decision-making and management capacities were weak; and a consistent bias against agriculture in price, tax, and exchange-rate policies.

20. Since the majority of Africans are engaged in agriculture and this sector has performed badly during the past two decades, the solution to African problems lies in prosperous agriculture. Therefore, the report contends that sub-Saharan Africa now needs to concentrate on agriculture with a view to increasing exports so as to earn the foreign exchange required for the implementation of the Lagos Plan of Action. Furthermore, the report offers a prescription: if sub-Saharan Africa is to change the present economic situation, it must concentrate on production, and agriculture is necessarily the centrepiece of any production-oriented strategy. The main elements of such a strategy are: concentration of resources on small holders; reform of incentive structures to ensure better prices; more open and competitive marketing system; and greater availability of consumer goods in some instances; a focus in the medium term, on making existing programmes work better and on rehabilitation of existing infrastructure, small-scale irrigation, and rural roads; a major effort in research on crops [and] livestock; and expansion of pest control and related activities to reduce post-harvest losses.

21. The report also acknowledges that productive activities can take place in other sectors as well. Thus, the authors discuss energy, industry (manufacturing, utilities, construction), non-fuel minerals, and transport and communications. The importance of human resources is also discussed. However, they maintain that most of the activities in the other sectors are to be supportive of agriculture.

22. To implement the agriculture-based and export-oriented strategy, three

major policy actions are recommended: more suitable trade and exchange-rate policies; increased efficiency of resource use in the public sector; and improvement in agricultural policies. Other aspects of the strategy include the reduction of size of the public sector and the encouragement of small-scale enterprises, co-operatives, and the promotion of the participation of foreign private capital.

23. Finally, the report maintains that the agricultural-based and export-oriented development strategy is an essential beginning to a process of long-term transformation, a prelude to industrialization, which in addition to rapid population, expanding urbanization, soil conservation, reforestation, fuelwood consumption and regional co-operation and integration is regarded as a longer-term issue.

C.   SOME PRELIMINARY OBSERVATIONS

24. In their diagnostic analyses of the economic problems of Africa, there is no doubt that the two documents have a lot in common. However, while the Lagos Plan of Action sees external factors as having played a major role in producing the present unsatisfactory situation, the World Bank Report gives internal factors a greater role.

25. The World Bank claims that its strategy is designed to deal with short-to medium-term economic problems of sub-Saharan Africa as well as assist in generating resources Africa needs. It gives the impression that the Lagos Plan of Action is only a long-term strategy whose main objective is to create an African Economic Community by the year 2000. It is important to stress that, although the Lagos Plan of Action has as its ultimate aims the creation of an African Economic Community, such ultimate objective is based on a series of short- to medium-term activities.

26. The emphasis of the World Bank report is on Africa continuing to feed external markets. As far as the Lagos Plan of Action is concerned, national and collective self-reliance and self-reliant and self-sustaining development and economic growth imply the development of national, subregional and regional markets.

27. While the World Bank report identifies agriculture as the motor of all African countries, the Lagos Plan of Action recognizes that the motor of any country will depend on the content and nature of its natural resource endowment. . . .

QUESTIONS

1. Which approach is preferred under classical free trade theory? What other economic or policy arguments would you make on each side of the controversy?

2. If you were emphasizing a product-cycle theory of international trade,

how would it affect your relative preference between export-generation and import-substitution?

3. What are the LDC national policies needed for export-generation? For import-substitution? Which LDC political constituencies would be most likely to favor export-generation? Which import substitution? In thinking about this question consider the tariff debates in pre-Civil War United States. Also, consider such examples as Japan's postwar development based on export generation *a l'outrance* supported by a rural-based political system or the Soviet Union's import-substitution style New Economic Program imposed by an urban elite.

4. What are the DC and international trade law policies that would be most favorable to developing nations under each of the two approaches? What are the implications for DC economic adjustment and safeguards strategy? Which approach is implicit in each of the provisions of the New International Economic Order ideas?

5. In the face of a DC economic crisis, such as that of the early 1980s, is an export strategy feasible for the LDCs?

6. Is the emphasis on increasing exports more than a fad that is likely to be reversed every generation or so? For good background, *see* Hirschman, The Political Economy of Import-Substituting Industrialization in Latin America in C. Nisbet (ed.), Latin America, Problems in Economic Development (1969).

7. Some developing nations are applying domestic content laws to high-tech areas requiring that products like computers or pharmaceuticals be manufactured by local firms or by nationally owned firms. When is such a policy wise?

B. PREFERENCES

The UNCTAD arguments went beyond the obvious—and quite accurate—point that trade barriers were high against many potential LDC exports.

First, the barrier was argued to be systematically, not just accidentally, discriminatory against developing nations. During the first negotiating rounds, the GATT nations had reduced those tariffs on which reciprocity with other developed nations was possible—meaning, generally, advanced manufactures (automobiles, machine tools, computers, etc.). In contrast, for the easy-entry industries, which would be the starting points for the LDCs (textiles, shoes, etc.), trade barriers were relaxed much less. Precisely because they were easy-entry industries, these industries were only marginally profitable in the DCs and the DCs had no incentive to lower trade barriers to give one another access to these industries. Neither, at least early on, would the LDCs have anything to trade off in return for an opening of DC markets for their exports.

The trend was to the contrary—the DCs would protect such industries from possible LDC ("low-wage") competition. Thus, trade barriers would automatically survive to restrict LDC exports of intermediate manufactures—and the LDCs daring enough to try to compete in a high-tech area would have to match the most efficient DC industry!

A second argument went to the "effective protection" concept—the concept that the level of effective protection afforded a *process* (as opposed to a *product*) might be significantly greater than that appearing on the face of the tariff schedules. Consider the following example, based on an assumed difference in tariffs between a raw material (say, leather) and a finished product (say, shoes):

Item	World price	"Tariff"	Internal price
leather	$ 5.00	10%	$ 5.50
(manufacturing process)	$ 5.00	effectively 90%	$ (9.50)
shoes	$10.00	50%	$15.00

By imposing a much larger tariff on shoes than on leather, the nation has provided greater effective protection to its shoemakers. The difference in tariffs on shoes and leather permits a great increase in the domestic price for shoes compared with a small increase in the domestic cost of leather (both as compared to world markets). The result is that a domestic firm spending $9.50 for assembly and marketing can compete successfully with a foreign firm spending a little more than half that amount. (For an inverse example arising earlier on in the production process, *see* the Tanners' case, *supra* Chapter IX, at 485: the Argentine export restrictions on raw hides were intended to give their tanners an advantage compared with foreign tanners.)

UNCTAD's most important response to these concerns was to call for preferences: DC tariffs that would be smaller (or ideally zero) for imports from LDCs than for imports from DCs. Thus, Australia, say, would levy no tariff on imports of certain products manufactured in India, while its tariff for similar products manufactured in Europe would be 20%. The Indian manufacturer could be roughly 20% less efficient and still seize the Australian market from Europe.

In spite of many economic counterarguments,[2] the idea of preferences caught on. The United States included part of a "generalized system of preferences" (GSP) in Title V of the 1974 Trade Act. Europe and other developed nations enacted their own versions, often more generous than that of the United States.

The U.S. legislation, updated in §1111 of the 1979 Act and Title V of the 1984 Act, includes a number of noneconomic provisions, such as those restricting GSP treatment to nations that violate specific congressional concerns such

---

[2] *See,* e.g., Meier, UNCTAD Proposals for International Economic Reform, 19 Stan L. Rev. 173 (1967).

as the fight against narcotics. Its core, however, reflects several difficult problems, exemplified in the following materials. The *Texas Instruments* case shows the problem of distinguishing a developing-nation product when different production steps are performed in different nations. The presidential report shows the hard economics issues—basically deriving from the likelihood that preferences will help the strongest eligible nations much more than they will help the weakest. It also shows the practical difficulties of the "competitive needs" exclusion—a way to make sure that a single national industry doesn't gain all the benefit of GSP or hurt a U.S. industry. And the Oswald statement shows the problems faced by U.S. competitors. Finally, the *Mast* case, which should be compared with *Texas Instruments,* shows a traditional provision that encourages labor-intensive border industry, somewhat like that sought by preferences.

TEXAS INSTRUMENTS, INC. v. UNITED STATES

681 F.2d 778 (C.C.P.A. 1982)

Rich, J.

This appeal is from the decision of the United States Court of International Trade (court below) granting the Government's motion for summary judgment and denying Texas Instrument's (TI) cross-motion for summary judgment, holding that TI's importation was not entitled to duty-free entry pursuant to the Generalized System of Preferences (GSP), 19 U.S.C. 2461 et seq., 520 F. Supp. 1216, 2 C.I.T. 36 (1981). We reverse.

BACKGROUND

The imported goods are electronic camera parts, called "cue modules," and consist of a flexible circuit board having attached thereto three integrated circuits (IC's), one photodiode, one capacitor, one resistor, and a jumper wire (which is merely extra lead length cut from the resistor). . . .

The cue modules were classified as "other" parts of photographic cameras under Tariff Schedules of the United States (TSUS), item 722.34, as modified by T.D. 68-9, and assessed with a 10% ad valorem duty. Appellant agreed that the goods were properly classified, but argued that they should have received duty-free treatment under the GSP in accordance with TSUS General Headnote 3(c).[1]

---

[1]General Headnote 3(c)(ii), 19 U.S.C. §1202, reads, in relevant part:

Whenever an eligible article is imported into the customs territory of the United States directly from a country or territory listed in subdivision (c)(i) of this headnote, it shall receive duty-free treatment, unless excluded from such treatment by subdivision (c)(iii) of this headnote, provided that, in accordance with regulations promulgated by the Secretary of the Treasury:

(A) The sum of (1) the cost or value of the materials produced in the beneficiary

The pertinent facts were described by the court below as follows:

> Certain items were imported into Taiwan where they were then assembled into the ICs and photodiodes. These items consisted of silicon slices containing a multitude of fabricated electronic chips, lead frame strips, mold compound, gold wire on spools and chip mounting material, either epoxy or gold preforms. The chips were separated by a "scribe and break" operation. Subsequently, each chip was mounted (and by use of epoxy or gold preform made to adhere conductively) to a section of a lead frame strip. Pieces of gold wire were used to provide an electrical connection from various areas on the chip to various areas on each lead frame strip section. Plastic mold compound was then liquified and molded under pressure over each section of lead frame strip containing a bonded and connected chip (or, in one instance, two bonded and connected chips). After the mold compound hardened into a protective covering, the lead frame strips were trimmed and severed into a multitude of individual devices. The devices, at this stage, were finished ICs and photodiodes.

Additionally, we note that the principal parts of the cue module, and materials such as gold wire, epoxy, and molding compounds, including those utilized in Taiwan to construct the IC's and photodiodes, were imported into Taiwan from the United States.

The court below, granting the Government's motion for summary judgment, held that the "value of the IC's and photodiodes cannot be included in the figures for the 'cost of material' and 'direct costs of processing' to determine whether these figures are not less than 35 percent of the appraised value of the cue modules." The court opined that the "use of the term 'article' to refer to imported merchandise, and use of the term 'material' to refer to the value added [sic] requirement for the 'eligible article' in the BDC [beneficiary developing country], clearly demonstrate the Congressional intent to differentiate between 'articles' on the one hand and 'materials' on the other hand."

Referencing 19 C.F.R. 10.177(a),[2] which limits inclusion in the 35 percent of appraised value (not "value added") figure to, among other things, "material" which was either wholly the growth, product, or manufacture of the BDC or substantially transformed in the BDC into a new and different article of commerce, the court stated that, "while the assembly of fabricated components, rather than materials, may be relevant in determining whether the 'eligible

---

developing country, plus (2) the direct costs of processing operations performed in such country is not less than 35 percent of the appraised value of such article at the time of its entry into the customs territory of the United States; . . .

See 19 U.S.C. §2463(b)(2).

[2] 19 C.F.R. 10.177(a) reads:

(a) *"Produced in the beneficiary developing country" defined.* For purposes of §§10.171 through 10.178, the words produced in the beneficiary developing "country" refer to the constituent materials of which the eligible article is composed which are either:

(1) Wholly the growth, product, or manufacture of the beneficiary developing country; or

(2) Substantially transformed in the beneficiary developing country into a new and different article of commerce.

article' was a product of the BDC, assembly of fabricated components is not relevant respecting the 35 percent value added [sic] requirement." The court concluded that, "the GSP statute and pertinent regulations preclude the inclusion of fabricated components produced outside the BDC and assembled in the BDC in the 'cost or value of the materials produced in the beneficiary developing country' to determine the 35 percent value added [sic] requirement. Consequently, *the value of the ICs and photodiodes cannot be included in the figures for the 'cost of materials' and 'direct costs of processing'* to determine whether these figures are not less than 35 percent of the appraised value of the cue modules." (Emphasis ours.) . . .

The court below never reached the issue of substantial transformation, holding that a mere assembly of fabricated components *cannot,* within the meaning of the GSP and as a matter of law, create a "material" to be utilized in the production of an "article." . . .

We find nothing in the GSP statutes or related rules to support this limitation on what may be considered a "material," nor is it determinative that Congress chose to distinguish an "eligible article" from that which comprises it by utilizing the different terms "article" and "material." We, therefore, hold that the decision of the court below was in error, and we turn to the substantial transformation issue outlined above. . . .

The question presented to us by the "substantial transformation" issue, not addressed by the court below, is a mixed question of technology and customs law, mostly the latter. In essence, the defendant's position, adopted by the court below, is that the making of the IC's and photodiodes was mere assembly of prefabricated components. The following are our principal reasons for disagreeing with the Government's position, adopted by the court below.

(1) One element allegedly imported into Taiwan was IC "chips." Chips were not imported. Silicon slices were imported. These were not ready to be assembled into anything in Taiwan and were never assembled into anything. The slices—carrying many hundreds of IC or photodiode elements, to be sure, but in unfinished or unseparated and "unpackaged" form—had to be further manufactured before chips ready for *assembly* came into existence. This involved the steps of careful scribing and production of the chips from the integral slices. The Government arguments attempt to equate chips and finished (i.e., "packaged") IC's as though, for practical purposes, they are interchangeable. The record is to the contrary. . . .

In light of the aforesaid explanations of what was actually done to the materials imported into Taiwan, we have no doubt there was compliance with the provision of 19 CFR 10.177(a)(2), "material which had been substantially transformed in the beneficiary developing country into a new and different article of commerce." We therefore respectfully disagree with the conclusion of the court below that the IC's and the photodiodes, as completed ready for assembly into the imported articles, were components "produced outside the BDC." We hold they were, on the contrary, materials produced in the beneficiary developing country and entitled to be included in computing the 35% of the appraised value of the imported cue modules.

The Government also argues, however, that agreement with appellant's position would frustrate the purpose of the GSP, which is to promote—

> . . . "diversification," "development," and "industrialization" of BDC's, and, on the other hand, to assure that the benefits of GSP would accrue to BDC's rather than to developed countries. Clearly, the purpose was to promote manufacturing operations which convert materials into articles, as opposed to a further extension of labor intensive assembly operations which have already been promoted under the "807.00 program."

The Government continues, saying that "It is evident that the GSP program was intended to make developing countries self-sufficient rather than continue the chain of dependency that mere assembly operations may foster." It is concluded that, "while the utilization of the non-BDC cost of fabricated components, in determining whether the 35% value added [sic] requirement . . . was fulfilled, would generally benefit the BDC with possible expension [sic] of trade, it would . . . frustrate the *major purpose* of our GSP. . . ."

Given our holding that the IC's and photodiodes were the result of extensive manufacturing operations in Taiwan which converted materials into articles, as distinguished from mere assembly, that there was "substantial transformation" into new and different articles of commerce, and granting that a statute must be so interpreted as to implement its legislative purpose, we conclude that our decision in the case is harmonious with the legislative purpose. The facts of record indicate that a number of employees were needed, and had to be technically trained in numerous skills to "convert materials into articles" in the manner we have described above, laying the groundwork for the acquisition of even higher skills and more self-sufficiency.

Accordingly, the Court of International Trade's order granting defendant's motion for summary judgment, denying plaintiff's motion for summary judgment, and dismissing the action is *reversed.* . . .

PRESIDENT JIMMY CARTER, REPORT TO THE CONGRESS ON THE FIRST FIVE YEARS' OPERATION OF THE U.S. GENERALIZED SYSTEM OF PREFERENCES (GSP)

House Committee on Ways and Means, 96th Cong., 2d Sess. (1980)

1.   OVERVIEW

A.   THE ORIGINS OF THE U.S. GENERALIZED SYSTEM OF PREFERENCES

Title V of the Trade Act of 1974 authorized the United States to grant generalized tariff preferences to certain imports from developing countries for ten years. With the implementation of its scheme on January 1, 1976, the United States became the twenty-third developed country to extend such preferences.

The concept of a generalized system of tariff preferences was formally introduced in Geneva at the first United Nations Conference on Trade and Development (UNCTAD) in 1964. Convened to examine the means for increasing the economic wealth of developing countries through trade rather than aid, UNCTAD became a major forum for review of the principal trade and development problems facing developing countries. At UNCTAD I developing countries claimed that one of the major impediments to accelerated economic growth and development was their inability to compete on an equal basis with developed countries in the international trading system.

For many developing countries, export earnings constitute not only the primary source of investment funds needed for development but also the means for financing imports of food and other basic commodities required to maintain existing standards of living. The extension of tariff preferences to goods from developing countries provides a means for helping them increase exports, diversify their economies and lessen their dependence on foreign aid.

In 1967 the United States announced its readiness to explore the possibility of establishing a generalized system of preferences. At the second UNCTAD conference in New Delhi in early 1968 the United States joined other participants in supporting a resolution to establish a mutually acceptable system of preferences.

The most-favored-nation (MFN) clause of Article 1 of the General Agreement on Tariffs and Trade (GATT) provides that trade be conducted on the basis of non-discrimination. In order to permit the implementation of generalized preferences, the developed countries, including the United States, requested and were granted a 10 year waiver from Article 1 of the GATT in June 1971. The preferential trading relationships between Britain and France and their former colonies, as well as between the United States and the Philippines and Cuba, provided precedents for such a move. These preferences were "grandfathered" into Article 1 of the GATT.

Following the granting of the Article 1 waiver, the European Community (EC) implemented its system on July 1, 1971. Soon after, GSP programs were implemented by Japan (August 1971); Norway (October 1971); Denmark, Finland, Ireland, New Zealand, Sweden and the United Kingdom (January 1972); Switzerland (March 1972); and Austria (April 1972). Australia introduced its GSP program in January 1974, Canada implemented its system in July 1974 and the U.S. GSP program was introduced in January 1976. The more developed socialist countries of Eastern Europe also have introduced preferential measures in favor of developing countries.

During the recently concluded Tokyo Round of Multilateral Trade Negotiations (MTN) the United States maintained that the GSP was a temporary, non-reciprocal program and therefore outside the scope of the MTN. The United States and other countries, however, recognized the need to address in the MTN the legal basis for continuing to grant generalized tariff preferences to developing countries. In anticipation of the 1981 expiration of the GATT waiver, the developing countries sought in the MTN to "bind" the GSP preference margins under the GATT. Although the binding of margins of preference was not acceptable to the donor countries, agreement was reached in the

MTN Framework Group on an "enabling clause" which provides the legal basis for "special and differential treatment" for developing countries. This agreement explicitly includes generalized systems of preferences, as defined by the 1971 GATT waiver. The enabling clause, which has no expiration date, replaces the waiver for all practical purposes. Developed countries may, if they choose, continue their GSP programs indefinitely; however, there is no obligation to do so. U.S. statutory authority for the GSP expires January 3, 1985. [It was renewed in Title V of the 1984 Trade Act.]

B.   THE GENERALIZED SYSTEMS OF PREFERENCES OF OTHER DEVELOPED COUNTRIES

Eleven GSP programs involving nineteen member countries of the Organization for Economic Cooperation and Development (OECD) currently are in place. Nearly 150 developing countries benefit from the resulting preferential tariff treatment. The GSP programs are generally similar and have the following elements: . . .

(4) All programs contain safeguard limitations. The GSP programs of the EC and Japan contain ceiling limits on the value of trade that is granted GSP treatment. These ceilings may be set at low levels to limit preferential imports of sensitive items. Trade in excess of these ceilings is charged normal MFN duties. The U.S. GSP contains the competitive need formula. Competitive need is designed to phase out GSP benefits as developing countries become internationally competitive in specific products, as well as to provide some measure of protection to domestic industries. The United States' program has a petitioning procedure under which products can be added to, or removed from, the list of GSP eligible products. The other GSP programs also have mechanisms to add products and "escape clause" procedures to withdraw import-sensitive products from GSP treatment. . . .

In terms of "burden sharing" the United States grants duty-free treatment on a smaller share of dutiable imports from beneficiaries than do the EC, Japan or other donor countries. On the other hand, the ceiling limitations under the EC and Japanese GSP programs create some uncertainty regarding the tariff treatment that will apply to certain GSP products.

3.   EVALUATION OF THE U.S. GENERALIZED SYSTEM OF PREFERENCES

A.   IMPACT OF THE U.S. GENERALIZED SYSTEM OF PREFERENCES ON BENEFICIARY DEVELOPING COUNTRIES' TRADE AND DEVELOPMENT

The objectives of the GSP are to encourage the diversification of developing country economies, spur the process of development and lessen developing countries' dependence on foreign aid. It is difficult to evaluate fully the extent to which the U.S. GSP in fact has accomplished these objectives since it only has been in operation since 1976 and more time is required for investment and trade patterns to change. Nevertheless, the quantitative and qualitative analysis outlined in this report provides some indication of the GSP's impact on developing country economies since the implementation of the program.

Between 1976 and 1978, GSP duty-free imports increased at an average annual rate of 28.5 percent from $3.2 billion to $5.2 billion. This growth rate has been affected by changes in the composition of the GSP product list and the loss of GSP duty-free treatment due to competitive need exclusions. Another indicator of the growth in GSP trade can be calculated using the fixed set of all products which have been on the GSP list since the program began and which have not been affected by competitive need. GSP duty-free imports of these items have grown at an average annual rate of 17 percent compared to an average growth rate of 22 percent for imports of all items from GSP beneficiaries.

While GSP benefits have increased since the implementation of the program, the distribution of these benefits among beneficiaries has been uneven. . . . The most competitive beneficiaries from Latin America and Asia, which are the United States' principal developing country trading partners overall, are also the major GSP beneficiaries under the U.S. scheme. . . .

During the early UNCTAD negotiations for the GSP it was recognized that the least developed were unlikely to be important beneficiaries of an industrial tariff preference program. Consequently, it was agreed that special measures should be introduced to favor these countries. Initially little was done to provide special treatment for the least developed. However, Norway subsequently introduced GSP duty-free treatment on all imports from the least developed and the European Community last year exempted the least developed from tariffs and quotas on almost all items included in its GSP. Although the United States is statutorily precluded from taking such steps, the United States on January 1, 1980, implemented its full MTN tariff reductions on many products from the least developed. For all other countries these tariff reductions are being phased in over a period of several years.

Beneficiary country views on the U.S. program were solicited in connection with the preparation of this report. Countries were asked to assess the impact of GSP on their economies—particularly the extent to which it has fostered economic development in terms of export expansion and new investment and employment. In addition, countries were asked to compare their utilization of the U.S. and other donor country programs and comment on the U.S. competitive need criteria, the product coverage of the U.S. GSP and various administrative and operational aspects of the U.S. program. Some 100 replies were received, ranging from extensive official comments in the cases of Hong Kong, Israel and Mexico, to more informal responses by government officials, export promotion organizations and individual exporters.

Overall Economic Impact on Beneficiaries

As might be expected, those countries which have been most successful in utilizing the U.S. program generally emphasized its positive effect on their economic development. In this category of major beneficiaries, Taiwan, Korea, Malaysia, Singapore, Israel and India acknowledged a direct relationship between GSP and domestic economic development. In addition, some smaller countries with more modest GSP benefits, such as Haiti, Honduras, Sri Lanka and Kenya, also viewed GSP as contributing to their overall economic growth. A majority of the countries, however, believed GSP played only a marginal role in their development process. Many of these countries confirmed that GSP had contributed to growth and diversification and that in many cases GSP exports were growing more rapidly than non-GSP exports, but they did not view the GSP as a significant factor in their overall economic development. Several countries with relatively open market economies, such as Hong Kong and Chile, believed their free-trade philosophy was more instrumental than GSP preferences in fostering economic growth.

A considerable number of Near Eastern, Asian and African countries which have only marginal trade ties with the United States thought the U.S. program has had no impact on their economies. It should be noted that many of these countries have long-standing trade links with the EC and benefit significantly from the EC's Lome program of trade preferences and aid which covers 58 African, Caribbean and Pacific countries. Among the African respondents which have made little use of the U.S. GSP program, several signaled a desire to utilize the U.S. scheme more fully as a means of diversifying export markets and lessening dependence on Europe. . . .

Several countries cited the planning problems resulting from the "on-again-off-again" nature of competitive need. This occurs when two or three beneficiary countries together supply total imports of a particular item and alternate between losing and regaining GSP eligibility for the product from year to year. India suggested that stability could be improved by reducing the frequency of competitive need exclusions and product modifications from the current annual basis to once every three years. Finally, all countries urged that the present discretionary process of redesignating a country for GSP eligibility once it has fallen below a competitive need limit be made automatic, given the automaticity with which competitive need removes GSP eligibility. Several countries likened the practice of discretionary non-redesignation to implicit graduation. . . .

In addition to the frequent references to competitive need, there were numerous comments on the substance of the U.S. product list. Many beneficiary countries—especially the least developed—viewed the U.S. product list as too restricted and irrelevant to their present export capabilities. In particular, textiles and apparel, footwear, handicraft and folklore items, and certain agricultural products were cited as categories of goods that should be added to the U.S. program, at least when they come from the least developed countries if it is not feasible for competitive reasons to include them from all beneficiary sources. Generally, these are the categories of products in which the poorer countries have a comparative advantage in exporting to developed markets. Many countries maintained that unless these products can be added to GSP, there is little likelihood of achieving a better distribution of program benefits among the least developed countries. While aware that many of these products are considered to be import-sensitive in the United States, lesser developed beneficiaries maintain that their modest export potential could in no way constitute a threat to competing U.S. production. They note that most other GSP donors, including the EC and Japan, include these goods in their GSP schemes and that this has not had an adverse impact on their economies.

Beneficiary country comparisons between the U.S. program and those of the EC and Japan varied considerably. All concurred that the duty-free treatment of the U.S. system was preferable to what at times amounted to marginal tariff cuts and quotas in the EC and Japanese programs. In addition, all commentators supported the openness and simplicity of operation of the U.S. scheme which they contrasted with the highly complex EC program. There were favorable comments on the annual product review procedure for requesting product additions to GSP, although many countries believed the data requested in petitions was too extensive and often difficult to obtain. Countries generally appreciated the availability of information on the U.S. program.

OSWALD, STATEMENT BEFORE THE SUBCOMMITTEE ON INTERNATIONAL TRADE: REVIEW OF THE U.S. GENERALIZED SYSTEM OF PREFERENCES

Senate Committee on Finance, 96th Cong., 2d Sess. (1980)

Statement of Dr. Rudolph Oswald, Director, Department of Research, American Federation of Labor and Congress of Industrial Organizations . . . September 20, 1979: . . .

It is important to review who are the real beneficiaries of industrialization and whether the working people of the countries are receiving the benefits, or whether the multinationals and powerful elites are the major beneficiaries. Sad to say, it is our experience that most of the benefits have gone to multinational firms and power elites. In many cases, the preference system has helped feed the export-led development which has not proved beneficial to the people even of those countries. Real wages have actually declined in some countries where the "miracles" of development are heralded. Furthermore, the problem of economic distortion for U.S. production and jobs has grown. . . .

But any set of data understates the true impact of GSP for three reasons: One, the impact of imports does not stop with the removal of GSP. Imports continue. Only the tariff is reimposed. The fact that GSP exists encourages initial foreign production of the item for exports to the U.S. Instead of U.S. investment, foreign investments are made. Subsequently, U.S. capacity becomes obsolete and is allowed to go idle and U.S. production may cease entirely. Third, as one type of item is removed from GSP another may be added. A current proposed list of deletions and additions demonstrates the continually shifting program. . . . The result is that no single figure gives a realistic picture of the effect of GSP imports.

Title V of the Trade Act of 1974 includes limitations which seek to avoid disruption to U.S. production and provide benefits to those countries that truly need it. Section 501 and 503 of the Trade Act made it clear that the President had the authority to choose countries and products for the list for this unilateral benefit. However, in making these decisions, three major standards were clearly stated:

(1) The President was to show "due regard" for the impact on U.S. producers, (Section 501 (3)).

(2) The President was to limit the granting of benefits to products which were not *"import-sensitive"* (Section 503).

(3) An elaborate *"competitive need"* formula was devised to make sure that countries which could compete in world trade would not get all the benefits. (Section 504) . . .

The direction to omit import-sensitive items has not been administered effectively. Instead, countries' desires for exports to the U.S. seem to outweigh clear evidence that injury in the U.S. has taken place or may occur. Where market penetration is great, dumping has been found, escape clause actions are pending and/or trade adjustment assistance has been granted, import-sensitivity clearly exists. But a number of products involved in such cases are still on the list. . . .

Note that the next case arises under pre-preference legislation that goes back to long before the preferences debate, but may prove to serve some of the same purposes:

UNITED STATES v. MAST INDUSTRIES, INC.

668 F.2d 501 (C.C.P.A. 1981)

MILLER, J.

This is an appeal from the judgment of the United States Court of International Trade ("trial court") sustaining the claim of appellee, Mast Industries, Inc. ("Mast"), that certain fabric components (of women's pants) manufactured in the United States and subjected to buttonholing and pocket slitting operations abroad were entitled to a duty allowance for the cost or value of the components under item 807.00 of the Tariff Schedules of the United States ("TSUS").[2] We affirm.

[2]The relevant statutory provisions are as follows:

TSUS, Schedule 8, Part I, Subpart B—Articles Advanced or Improved Abroad
Subpart B headnotes: . . .

3. Articles assembled abroad with components produced in the United States.—The following provisions apply only to item 807.00: . . .

The Merchandise

Involved are four entries of two styles of women's pants, style 4083 and style 4086. The fabric components of the pants were cut to shape in the United States for Mast, then shipped to a factory in El Salvador together with all other necessary components, such as thread and buttons, where they were finished into completed garments. In addition to being sewn together, certain of the components were subjected to buttonholing and pocket slitting. As to those components, the Customs Service disallowed item 807.00, TSUS, treatment, and that determination was contested by Mast.

At trial, Mast's production manager, Salvatore Fasciana, explained how the buttonholes and slash pockets were made. When a pedal was depressed, a Reece S-2 buttonholer clamped a fabric component to the machine bed, sewed around the buttonhole area, and automatically cut the buttonhole slit. The machine cycle time for each buttonhole was approximately 2.5 hundredths of a minute (1.5 seconds). During assembly of the pockets, a Singer 112W140 sewing machine simultaneously cut a slit in the rear quarter panel component and sewed the welt piece and facing piece to either side of the slit. Small diagonal cuts were then made at each end of the welt; the welt, the facing, and the two parts of the pocket bag (which were previously sewn to the welt and facing) were turned through the slit to the wrong side of the rear quarter panel. The welt seam was then top stitched, the pocket components were turned back through the slit to the right side of the fabric, the pocket bag was stitched together, and the pocket was again turned through the slit. . . .

Witnesses also testified that the buttonholes should be made before the buttons are set (sewn on) to insure that the buttons line up, and that buttonholes and pocket slits improved the commercial value of the pants, enabling them to conform to the specifications.

The issue before us is whether the Court of International Trade correctly

---

(b) The duty on the imported article shall be at the rate which would apply to the imported article itself, as an entirety without constructive separation of its components, in its condition as imported if it were not within the purview of this subpart. If the imported article is subject to a specific or compound rate of duty, the total duties shall be reduced in such proportion as the cost or value of such products of the United States bears to the full value of the imported article.

Item		
807.00	Articles assembled abroad in whole or in part of fabricated components, the product of the United States, which (a) were exported in condition ready for assembly without further fabrication, (b) have not lost their physical identity in such articles by change in form, shape, or otherwise, and (c) have not been advanced in value or improved in condition abroad except by being assembled and except by operations incidental to the assembly process such as cleaning, lubricating, and painting.	A duty upon the full value of the imported article, less the cost or value of such products of the United States (see headnote 3 of this subpart.)

decided that: (1) the precut fabric components shipped by Mast to El Salvador and there subjected to buttonholing or pocket slitting, "were exported in condition ready for assembly without further fabrication," item 807.00(a), TSUS; and (2) those components were not "advanced in value or improved in condition abroad except by . . . operations incidental to the assembly process such as cleaning, lubricating, and painting," item 807.00(c), TSUS.

I.   QUESTION OF FURTHER FABRICATION

The government relies on Zwicker Knitting Mills v. United States, 67 C.C.P.A. 37, C.A.D. 1240, 613 F.2d 295 (1980), to support its position that buttonholing and pocket slitting constituted further fabrication necessary before the components could be assembled. In that case, the trial court (82 Cust. Ct. 34, 37, C.D. 4786, 469 F. Supp. 727, 729 (1979)) found that glove shells were knitted in the United States on machines which could not close the fingertips. The open-fingered glove shells, precut palms, and, in one entry, a separate piece of yarn were sent to Haiti, where a piece of yarn was passed through the top row of loops at each fingertip to lock the loops and thereby fix the knitting so that it would not unravel. The shells were paired and shaped, and the precut palms were sewn on the shells. This court held that the glove shells were not entitled to an item 807.00 duty allowance because the Haitian "tipping" operation constituted "further fabrication," item 807.00(a).

The trial court distinguished *Zwicker,* stating:

> *Zwicker* involved a fingertipping operation performed abroad on glove shells exported from the United States minus the fingertips. And, unlike the situation at bar which involved only a *separation* or *removal* for an opening in fabricated material, the *Zwicker* operation involved an *addition* of material to close the fingertips. It was this *addition* of material which influenced the courts in *Zwicker* to find that the tipping operation constituted a "further fabrication" of the gloves which is proscribed by item 807.00(a).

. . . 515 F. Supp. at 47. We are persuaded that *Zwicker* is distinguishable not merely because it involved an addition of material, while the present case involves a separation, but, more importantly, because in *Zwicker* the glove shells were only partially *fabricated* in the United States by knitting. Locking the loops at the tip of each finger to prevent unraveling was a part of the knitting process of the glove shell not completed in the United States, and one that was required to complete the component prior to shaping and attaching the precut palms. Therefore, the tipping operation was a continuation of the knitting process and constituted further fabrication of the component. In the present case, the components were cut to shape in the United States, and, at that point, were fabricated components ready to immediately enter into the assembly process. *See* General Instrument Corp. v. United States, 61 C.C.P.A. 86, 89, C.A.D.1128, 499 F.2d 1318, 1321 (1974).

Nevertheless, on the basis of evidence that the buttonholes had to be made before the buttons were sewn on the pants and that the pockets could not be assembled without the pocket slit, the government argues that the operations in question constituted further fabrication which was necessary and prior to completing the assembly of the garments. However, although such operations were necessary to complete the assembly process, they did not complete the manufacturing process by which the cut-to-shape fabric components were fabricated. *Cf. Zwicker, supra.* Moreover, the government's position is at odds with the decision in Miles v. United States, *supra* [567 F.2d 979 (C.C.P.A. 1978)]. In *Miles,* this court held that burning slots and holes into 55 foot steel Z-beams, which were assembled as center sills of boxcars, was incidental to the assembly process. The holes were necessary to install wear plates and support plates, to allow passage of brake pipe, and to allow insertion of the draft keys which fix the couplers to the yokes. Although the making of the slots and holes was a prerequisite to assembly, that did not disqualify the Z-beams under item 807.00(a).

Accordingly, we hold that the buttonholing and pocket slitting operations were not further fabrication within the meaning of item 807.00(a).

II. THE INCIDENTAL-TO-ASSEMBLY QUESTION

Since we agree with the government that buttonholing and pocket slitting advanced the value and improved the condition of the assembled components, it is necessary to determine whether these operations were "incidental to the assembly process."

In seeking to distinguish Miles v. United States, *supra,* the government argues that item 807.00(c), "was intended to encompass those operations which solely related to the assembly process and which were of a minor nature." It contends that the slots and holes in *Miles* "possessed a function and utility that *only* related to assembly"; whereas, the buttonholes and pocket slits involved here have "essential functions and utility that possess *absolutely no relationship to the assembly process,*" *viz.,* to allow closure of certain portions of the pants and entry and exit to the pocket. Because these operations created features in the garments which had a utility independent from the assembly process, it is argued that they could not be "merely incidental" to assembly. . . . We are persuaded that the government urges too narrow a construction of the statute. Indeed, the statute sets forth "painting" of a component as an example of permissible operations incidental to assembly. Painting could serve both to enhance the appearance of an article and to protect it from corrosion—each an independent utility. It is difficult to visualize a situation where the sole purpose of painting would be to facilitate assembly, or even where painting would be essential to the assembly process.

We note that the government's "independent utility" theory is also unsupported by case law. In *Miles,* whether the slots and holes in the Z-beams had utility outside the assembly process was not considered, although slots in the end of each beam allowed the insertion (and presumably the removal) of draft keys for fixing the couplers to the yokes. This utility survived the assembly process. There appears to be no reasonable distinction under the statute between holes which allow insertion of draft keys and holes which allow insertion of buttons. . . .

The apparent legislative intent was to not preclude operations that provide an "independent utility" or that are not essential to the assembly process; rather, Congress intended a balancing of all relevant factors to ascertain whether an operation of a "minor nature" is incidental to the assembly process. Relevant factors in this case include:

(1) Whether the cost of the operation relative to the cost of the affected component and the time required by the operation relative to the time required for assembly of the whole article were such that the operation may be considered "minor." *See Miles, supra* at 36, 567 F.2d at 982. (Here, the time required for each operation compared to the overall time required for assembly of the article was minor. The same is true of the cost of each operation relative to the cost of each affected component. For example, the least expensive component in which a buttonhole was placed in style 4083 was the side pocket flap lining, with a United States cost of $0.020. By contrast, the buttonholing cost was 0.0075 colones, or $0.003.)

(2) Whether the operations in question were necessary to the assembly process, as were the slots and holes in *Miles*. (The government acknowledges that placing buttonholes and making the pocket slit were prerequisites to other assembly steps.)

(3) Whether the operations were so related to assembly that they were logically performed during assembly. (Buttonholing and pocket slitting were closely related to the assembly process. Both involved taking needle and thread to fabric, as in the assembly process. Both were done with special sewing machines. The relationship of these operations to assembly is further demonstrated by the availability of alternative closures and pockets which may obviously be incorporated into pants through operations which are solely assembly operations.)[7]

Applying these factors to the facts before us, we hold that the buttonholing and pocket slitting operations were "incidental to the assembly process."

The judgment of the trial court is affirmed.

NOTES AND QUESTIONS

1. Were preferences really a good idea? Whose employment is given away? Why were they so widely adopted? For information on the current operation,

---

[7]Another factor not addressed by the parties would be whether economic or other practical considerations dictate that the operations be performed concurrently with assembly.

see Fisher and Samolis, Trade and Developing Countries, Law and Practice of U.S. International Trade Regulation (C. Johnston ed. 1986).

2. Do preferences violate the GATT? Do the 1966 amendments (Articles XXXVI and XXXVII) resolve the issue in favor of legitimacy? One early GATT working group that considered Australia's preference system (in the context of an Austrialian request for a waiver) told it in essence: "You're violating GATT—but don't stop!" Report of Working Party, Adopted 28 March 1966, BISD 14th Supp. at 162. During the discussion, the following special principles were suggested:

(i) apprehension was expressed concerning the danger that the exclusion of a particular country from preferences in respect of a particular item as a result of the (possibly arbitrary) application of the principle of competitive need could divert trade from one source to another among the less-developed countries themselves;

(ii) the scheme should take into account differences in levels of development among less-developed countries;

(iii) the benefits to less-developed countries from the proposed preferences would be modest in comparison with those enjoyed by certain developed countries already benefiting from preferences in the Australian market; the list of products should be expanded and the quota limits to the preferences removed;

(iv) the less-developed countries pointed out that the principle of the infant economy, rather the infant industry, should be the guiding principle in this connexion, and that all exports of less-developed countries should be granted preferences;

(v) the benefits to less-developed countries from the Australian scheme would not only be modest but could have been conferred in large measure through reduction of tariffs on a most-favoured-nation basis;

(vi) the definition of semi-manufactured and manufactured products, which the Australian representative had put forward, was considered imprecise for the purpose of the scheme;

(vii) disappointment was expressed that the Australian Government was unable to provide domestic production figures on some items appearing in the list of products since these figures were relevant to the subject under discussion.

3. Are you impressed with the "effective protection" argument advanced by the developing countries? When is the DC's use of higher duties on finished products not a reasonable way to protect workers in value-added industries?

4. Based on the president's report and Dr. Oswald's statement, what do you think have been the failures of preferences? Could the U.S. law be revised to give more benefit to LDC's per unit cost to U.S. employment? If so, how?

5. Dr. Oswald's argument that U.S. multinational enterprises (MNEs) have been prime beneficiaries of the GSP raises a fundamental question concerning the equity of the program from the standpoint of the U.S. worker. Assume that a U.S. MNE moves part of its widget production to Brazil to benefit from GSP, while its competitor in the United States chooses not to make such a move. Should U.S. labor pay the price for the MNE's mobility of capital? Is

there any alternative policy that might be followed here? What is the interrelationship of international tax policy here with trade policy? As we will see in Chapter XVIII, taxation provisions are a matter of great importance in terms of where the MNE chooses to locate.

6. The presidential report hinted at one impact of the competitive needs exception: an on-off cycle for certain more successful middle-income developing nations who would export heavily under GSP for one year, lose GSP rights the following year and see their exports plummet, and then regain eligibility in another year, repeating the cycle. Does the 1984 Amendment resolve this problem? For additional interpretation of the competitive needs exception, *see* Florsheim Shoe Co. v. United States, 744 F.2d 787 (Fed. Cir. 1984).

7. Would Dr. Oswald's concerns be met by "graduation" from the program of the most advanced developing countries? If, say, Brazil were to be dropped from the program, but Bangladesh kept on GSP, would the MNE be as likely to relocate? Shouldn't the program be reshaped, in any event, towards the so-called Fourth World, the least developed countries?

8. Is there any way to avoid the problem described in *Texas Instruments*? What are the implications for industry structure in the developing nations? For an argument that the European version of the rule effectively favors multinationals over developing nation indigenous industry, *see* McQueen, Lomé and the Protective Effect of Rules of Origin, 16 J.W.T.L. 119 (1982). For another example of the rules of origin problem, *see* Belcrest Linens v. United States, 741 F.2d 1368 (Fed. Cir. 1984) (pillowcases made partly in China and partly in Hong Kong), and for a response to a federal rule designed to restrict the possibility of restructuring different textile steps to take advantage of quota patterns, *see* Mast Industries v. Regan, 596 F. Supp. 1567 (C.I.T. 1984).

9. Is the approach described in the *Mast Industries* case presented in the text an alternative to be preferred to preferences? Why or why not? Why, do you think, was TSUS item 807.00 politically feasible? Although the provision effectively exports employment, it has been in the code for a long time and was inserted as a normal housekeeping item, comparable to the personal travelers' exempt amount. It is this provision that ensures that tariffs are not levied on an item manufactured in the United States and exported for later reimport— for example, if a foreign auto manufacturer were to export to the United States cars containing U.S.-made engines. Compare TSUS item 806.30 covering metal exported from the United States and processed already.

C.   COMMODITY AGREEMENTS

The other trade component of the UNCTAD program was the commodity agreement, a concept with which you are already familiar from the *Natural Rubber* case, *supra* Chapter III. Developing-world political support for the concept grew significantly in the wake of OPEC's success in raising oil prices in 1973. One result was the following resolution, UNCTAD's proposal for a common fund for commodities, a fund that was, in fact, created in 1980.[3] This background is supplemented by excerpts discussing the operation of commodity agreements.

UNITED NATIONS CONFERENCE ON TRADE AND DEVELOPMENT, RESOLUTION 93(IV)

U.N. Doc. TD/217 (1976)

INTEGRATED PROGRAMME FOR COMMODITIES

THE UNITED NATIONS CONFERENCE ON TRADE AND DEVELOPMENT,

Recalling the Declaration and the Programme of Action on the Establishment of a New International Economic Order as well as the Charter of Economic Rights and Duties of States, which lay down the foundations of the new international economic order, General Assembly resolution 623 (VII) of 21 December 1952 and the recommendation contained in annex A.II.1 of the Final Act adopted at the first session of the Conference, . . .

Decides to adopt the following Integrated Programme for Commodities:

I. Objectives

With a view to improving the terms of trade of developing countries and in order to eliminate the economic imbalance between developed and developing countries, concerted efforts should be made in favour of the developing countries towards expanding and diversifying their trade, improving and diversifying their productive capacity, improving their productivity and increasing their export earnings, with a view to counteracting the adverse effects of inflation, thereby sustaining real incomes. Accordingly the following objectives are agreed:

1. To achieve stable conditions in commodity trade, including avoidance of excessive price fluctuations, at levels which would:

(a) be remunerative and just to producers and equitable to consumers;

(b) take account of world inflation and changes in the world economic and monetary situations;

(c) promote equilibrium between supply and demand within expanding world commodity trade;

2. To improve and sustain the real income of individual developing countries through increased export earnings, and to protect them from fluctuations in export earnings, especially from commodities;

---

[3] Articles of Agreement for a Common Fund, adopted June 27, 1980, open for signature October 1, 1980, U.N. Doc. TD/IPC/CONF/L.15, reprinted in 19 I.L.M. at 896 (1980).

3. To seek to improve market access and reliability of supply for primary products and the processed products thereof, bearing in mind the needs and interests of developing countries;

4. To diversify production in developing countries, including food production, and to expand processing of primary products in developing countries with a view to promoting their industrialization and increasing their export earnings;

5. To improve the competitiveness of, and to encourage research and development on the problems of, natural products competing with synthetics and substitutes, and to consider the harmonization, where appropriate, of the production of synthetics and substitutes in developed countries with the supply of natural products produced in developing countries;

6. To improve market structures in the field of raw materials and commodities of export interest to developing countries;

7. To improve marketing, distribution and transport systems for commodity exports of developing countries, including an increase in their participation in these activities and their earnings from them.

II.   Commodity Coverage

The commodity coverage of the Integrated Programme should take into account the interests of developing countries in bananas, bauxite, cocoa, coffee, copper, cotton and cotton yarns, hard fibres and products, iron ore, jute and products, manganese, meat, phosphates, rubber, sugar, tea, tropical timber, tin, and vegetable oils, including olive oil, and oilseeds, among others, it being understood that other products could be included. . . .

III.   International Measures of the Programme . . .

2. It is also agreed to take the following measures, to be applied singly or in combination, including action in the context of international commodity arrangements between producers and consumers, in the light of the characteristics and problems of each commodity and the special needs of developing countries:

(a) Setting up of international commodity stocking arrangements;

(b) Harmonization of stocking policies and the setting up of coordinated national stocks;

(c) Establishment of pricing arrangements, in particular negotiated price ranges, which would be periodically reviewed and appropriately revised, taking into account, *inter alia*, movements in prices of imported manufactured goods, exchange rates, production costs and world inflation, and levels of production and consumption;

(d) Internationally agreed supply management measures, including export quotas and production policies and, where appropriate, multilateral long-term supply and purchase commitments;

(e) Improvement of procedures for information and consultation on market conditions;

(f) Improvement and enlargement of compensatory financing facilities for the stabilization, around a growing trend, of export earnings of developing countries;

(g) Improvement of market access for the primary and processed products of developing countries through multilateral trade measures in the multilateral trade negotiations, improvement of schemes of generalized preferences and their extension beyond the period originally envisaged, and trade promotion measures;

(h) International measures to improve the infrastructure and industrial capacity of developing countries, extending from the production of primary commodities to their processing, transport and marketing, as well as to the production of finished manufactured goods, their transport, distribution and exchange, including the establishment of financial, exchange and other institutions for the remunerative management of trade transactions;

(i) Measures to encourage research and development on the problems of natural products competing with synthetics and consideration of the harmonization, where appropriate, of the production of synthetics and substitutes in developed countries with the supply of natural products produced in developing countries;

(j) Consideration of special measures for commodities whose problems cannot be adequately solved by stocking and which experience a persistent price decline.

3. The interests of developing importing countries, particularly the least developed and the most seriously affected among them, and those lacking in natural resources, adversely affected by measures under the Integrated Programme, should be protected by means of appropriate differential and remedial measures within the Programme.

4. Special measures, including exemption from financial contributions, should be taken to accommodate the needs of the least developed countries in the Integrated Programme.

5. Efforts on specific measures for reaching arrangements on products, groups of products or sectors which, for various reasons, are not incorporated in the first stage of application of the Integrated Programme should be continued.

6. The application of any of the measures which may concern existing international arrangements on commodities covered by the Integrated Programme would be decided by governments within the commodity organizations concerned.

IV. Procedures and Time-Table

1. The Secretary-General of UNCTAD is requested to convene a negotiating conference open to all members of UNCTAD on a common fund no later than March 1977. . . .

ERB AND FISHER, U.S. COMMODITY POLICY: WHAT RESPONSE TO THIRD WORLD INITIATIVES?*

9 Law & Poly. Intl. Bus. 479 (1977)

Necessary Attributes of Viable Commodity Agreements

Apart from the questions of desirability and appropriate mechanism, is the need to determine the objectives of each particular commodity agreement. A viable agreement is a dynamic form of international organization that must possess certain systemic attributes in order to be successful. It must have a flexible market reallocation system, flexible pricing arrangements, a sound enforcement system, and a program for structural reform of the market.

1.   MARKET REALLOCATION

The first systemic attribute any commodity agreement should possess is a mechanism to permit exporters to obtain larger market shares if they are efficient and lower cost producers. An agreement based on the buffer stock mechanism would appear to impose the fewest restraints on individual trans-actions and maximize reallocation towards more efficient producers. On the other hand, a buffer stock may not be desirable in a given situation if the product involved is not storable and resources are not available on an international level to stock or carry the product.

Export quota commodity agreements, on the other hand, may result in two forms of serious resource misallocation. First, at the time national export quotas are set, the largest quotas may not go to the lowest cost producers but, instead, to those who have the most economic power and are the best bargainers. Even a technical solution based on historical market performances may not reflect the lowest cost producers, because cost performance is always in flux and new producers can enter the market, as is now taking place in the copper industry. The second allocational error may occur during the course of the agreement if quotas are not adjusted to reflect changing cost conditions.

The key to success in a commodity agreement based on export quotas is constant reallocation of market shares in the direction of efficient, lower cost producers and other countries able and willing to fill designed, basic quota shares. Such arrangements should contain, for example, provisions for the entry of new producers and frequent reviews of basic quotas, waivers, and techniques for reallocation of annual shortfalls. Flexible quota provisions serve the interest of consumer countries by maximizing the amounts of the commodity placed on the market, and placate revisionist countries, which believe, perhaps justifiably, that their share of the market should be larger. . . .

2.   PRICE MECHANISM

The pricing system of a commodity agreement frequently will become a bone of contention between consumer and producer countries. The latter may want to use the agreement as a resource transfer mechanism, while consumers may seek to check price fluctuations but go no further. A viable pricing system should adequately deal with four different issues. First, each commodity agreement should be designed to ensure adequate countervailing power for consumers, so that the accord does not become simply a price-raising cartel. Secondly, a pricing system should evolve that will reflect the price movements in the various submarkets, if any, of the commodity. In the case of the International Coffee Agreement, for example, a sophisticated, selective pricing mechanism was established with separate floor and ceiling price levels for each of the four submarkets of coffee; Colombian milds, other milds, unwashed arabicas, and robustas. Thirdly, the price ranges should be wide enough to permit some price movement for the product, while checking extreme price instability. Finally, the levels of the price range should be flexible and capable of responding to long-term market pressures. This does not mean acceptance of indexation of prices keyed to an external index of prices for unrelated industrial goods. Rather, it means a moving price range keyed to the fundamentals of supply and demand for the product under regulation. Efforts must constantly be made to relate prices to supply and demand, otherwise any arrangement will lose touch with the reality of the current market situation. . . .

3.   ENFORCEMENT

Assignment of export quotas is one thing; enforcement is another. The history of commodity agreements suggests that exporting countries will frequently cheat on each other if consumer countries are not participating in a viable enforcement scheme designed to keep them honest. In the case of coffee, for example, a sophisticated form of export enforcement developed which, over time, sharply curtailed the overshipment of export quotas. A commodity agreement should thus contain provisions designed to control direct shipments between member countries and transshipment through non-member countries.

4.   STRUCTURAL REFORM

Structural reform has often been the most neglected part of commodity agreement systems, but in the long run, may be the most important. Steps should be taken in the commodity agreement to correct the underlying market problems which necessitated the agreement in the first place. These could include programs to limit or expand national output, depending on the nature of the problem. The 1962 International Coffee Agreement, for example, sought to meet the structural problem of inadequate demand through the establishment of a producer financed fund for the promotion of coffee consumption. Marketing, product improvements, increased processing, and diversification into other areas of production are increasingly being accepted as organization objectives by producer associations and producer-consumer groups.

UNITED STATES DEPARTMENT OF STATE, INTERNATIONAL COMMODITY AGREEMENTS

Dept. State Bull., Nov. 1981, at 34

SUMMARY

In 1976, the less-developed countries (LDCs) undertook a major effort sponsored by the U.N. Conference on Trade and Development (UNCTAD IV) to organize international agreements for their important commodity exports. They hoped that such agreements would help stabilize and/or enhance their earnings.

The resulting UNCTAD integrated program for commodities has not succeeded significantly in altering the terms of trade for commodity producers, and little prospect remains that it will succeed in doing so. Theoretically, such agreements could produce modest benefits by facilitating the commitment of a more appropriate level of resources to production over time. It has proven extremely difficult to realize these benefits in practice, however, due to the continuing vagaries of supply and demand and continuing competition for market shares.

Raising commodity prices to artificially high levels attracts added production, both from agreement members and from nonmembers. It also discourages consumption and encourages substitution. These powerful reactions all work toward creating surpluses of targeted commodities and explain why commodity agreements have been unable to sustain higher price levels. In fact, price stabilization efforts can themselves stimulate output if producers believe that their risk of low prices has been decreased.

Recent commodity agreements have tried several means for dealing with market competition problems: keeping price goals modest, signing up all major producers, and enrolling importer nations, which agree not to increase their purchases from nonmembers. It has been a practical impossibility to include all producers and potential producers of major commodities, however. It has also been difficult to get importers to agree with producers on appropriate stabilization mechanisms and price levels for the agreements.

Competition from synthetics and substitutes has been an even more intractable problem. Modern technology has produced major competitors for nearly every commodity, from synthetic rubber and plastics to high-fructose corn sweetener and glass-fiber telephone cable. Only the beverages—coffee, tea, and cocoa—have so far escaped serious inroads from synthetics and substitutes.

Commodity agreements have also exhibited some serious limitations as an aid mechanism. Their benefits are distributed on the basis of commodity production, rather than need, so they assist only indirectly in reaching economic, political, or social goals within the recipient country. They also encourage added production, which either boosts donor costs or dilutes benefits.

There is little prospect that international commodity agreements can overcome their inherent limitations and provide greater benefits for commodity exporters in the future. Prices can be expected to continue to fluctuate widely around the trends dictated by demand, competition, and long-term production costs.

HISTORY OF AGREEMENTS IN CORE COMMODITIES

The 10 core commodities listed by UNCTAD IV (cocoa, coffee, copper, cotton, hard fibers—sisal, abaca, and coir—jute, rubber, sugar, tea, and tin) share some important characteristics: all have volatile prices, and all are produced mainly in the LDCs. Each, however, has distinctive characteristics. . . .

SUGAR

Several factors contribute to the volatile price pattern in the world sugar markets:

Production varies unpredictably with weather and periodic outbreaks of crop disease.

The supply response to price increases has lagged and may overshoot because it takes several years to bring on efficient new production and the associated large-scale refining capacity.

Demand for sugar is inelastic, magnifying the price impact of supply problems.

Much of the world's sugar production and consumption is insulated from price changes by subsidies, leaving the remaining sugar to trade in a relatively thin market where price responses are amplified.

The developed non-Communist countries currently produce about 30% of the world's sugar (mostly from subsidized sugar beets). Developing countries produce about 40%, and the Communist countries produce about 30%.

Sugar consumption is no longer increasing in many of the developed non-Communist economies, because consumption levels are already high and substitute sweeteners are becoming more important. High-fructose corn sweetener is displacing millions of tons of sugar in the United States, Japan, and Canada. Furthermore the European Community's (EC) common agricultural policy has stimulated production of millions of tons of European beet sugar, which is being exported under subsidy.

Markets in the U.S.S.R. and Eastern Europe are approaching saturation. Sugar consumption is already high in the developing countries which export sugar. Only among the developing-nation importers is per capita sugar consumption still increasing in line with consumer incomes.

Sugar was one of the first commodities for which control via international agreement was tried. Under the Chadbourne plan of 1931, the chief world exporters agreed to restrict exports and gradually reduce stocks over a 5-year period. However, heavy stocks and declining consumption depressed prices, while nonmember production more than offset the members' export cutbacks.

A broader International Sugar Agreement, signed in 1937, included the United States, the United Kingdom, and much of Europe and set quotas for their domestic production. The agreement was never tested because World War II intervened. It was not until well after the war that low sugar prices again became a serious concern.

The 1954 edition of the International Sugar Agreement included most of the major exporters and importers. It had a price range of 3.25-4.35¢ per pound, protected by export quotas. The Suez crisis in 1956 sent prices above 6¢, but a large 1957-58 world sugar crop pushed prices to the floor level. The agreement was renewed in 1958, and Brazil and Peru, the two major exporters that had remained outside the agreement, were brought in. Production increased again in 1959, consumption faltered, and stocks continued to rise. In 1961, after the United States stopped imports of Cuban sugar in an anti-Castro move, Cuba demanded a huge increase in its export quota. The agreement broke down when the other exporters refused the demand.

The International Sugar Agreement was revised in 1969 and reactivated for a 5-year period until it was finally terminated in 1973. The agreement was undercut by the need to offer attractive quotas to attract new members, by subsidized sugar production in the developed countries, and by an uncertain mechanism for limiting Cuban sugar reexported through Communist countries. Prices varied from 3.2¢ in 1969 to 9.5¢ in 1973.

After termination of the agreement, prices peaked again in 1974, averaging 30¢ a pound, and then fell back to about 8¢ for several years. These low prices led to the current agreement, which went into effect in 1978.

The current International Sugar Agreement comprises 59 producing and consuming nations including the United States. The agreement has been committed to keeping sugar prices within a specified range, currently 13-23¢ per pound. Producer nations agree to apply export quotas when prices are low, and consuming nations agree to limit imports of nonmember sugar. When prices are high, exporting member stocks totaling 2.5 million tons are released according to a prearranged price schedule. The agreement cut export quotas by 12½%—or 2.2 million metric tons—for both 1978 and 1979, when sugar prices averaged 7.8¢ and 9.9¢ per pound, respectively. In 1980, with the national stocks drawn down, sugar prices rose well above 40¢ per pound.

Despite broad producer and consumer membership, the International Sugar Agreement faces serious problems. Expanded production of high-fructose corn sweetener and its lineal descendents will displace millions of tons of sugar from key markets in the years ahead. The EC is likely to continue major exports of subsidized beet sugar in the world markets, because it will be reluctant to join the agreement without a quota that recognizes those exports. In addition, the World Bank projects that sugar production will increase more rapidly than consumption in the developing countries over the next decade. The general outlook for sugar stability is poor. . . .

NATURAL RUBBER

Rubber price fluctuations arise primarily from the demand side, in sharp contrast to most other crops. The major use of rubber has been in automotive products, and prices have been very sensitive to changes in general economic activity. Natural rubber demand has also been dramatically affected by the relative price and availability of synthetic rubber.

Sales of elastomers have been growing at roughly 6.5% per year since the early 1950s. Until recently, however, synthetic rubber gained most of the market growth, expanding at more than 9% a year. Natural rubber production grew at less than 3% annually. Recently, the demand for natural rubber has been stimulated by the demand for radial tires, which require a high proportion of natural rubber, and by higher oil prices, which increase the cost of synthetic rubber. The impact of high energy prices on autos and driving is expected to hold back elastomer demand during the coming decade. Even so, natural rubber production may not keep up with demand unless additional investments are made in the next few years.

Rubber production is centered in Southeast Asia, with 80% coming from Malaysia, Indonesia, and Thailand. Sri Lanka, India, Liberia, and Nigeria have accounted for another 12%. Most rubber is now produced on small farms rather than on large plantations.

Rubber has a long history of international market control efforts. The Stevenson plan was inaugurated in 1922, restricting rubber exports from Ceylon, Malaya, and the Straits Settlement (all British dependencies). Rubber prices increased sharply at first. However, growers in other areas stepped up plantings sharply. By 1927, when the plan was dropped, the British dependencies' share of the rubber market had declined from about 70% to 54%, with no long-term increase in price. But temporarily higher prices had stimulated the development of synthetic rubber and the rubber reclaiming industry.

The Depression and larger world plantings kept rubber prices low through 1934 and produced the International Rubber Regulation Agreement. This agreement at first raised prices, at the cost of building producer stocks. Rubber demand increased significantly in the next few years, carrying prices up with it and permitting the liquidation of those stocks. The agreement continued in force until the Japanese conquest of rubber-producing areas catalyzed an explosive increase in the synthetic rubber industry.

Perhaps because of the direct competition from synthetic rubber, there were no further rubber agreements until 1979, when negotiations for the International Natural Rubber Agreement were concluded. It entered into force provisionally in late 1980 and will enter into force definitively when full financing of the large 550,000-metric ton buffer stock is assured. This could occur as early as mid-1981; then, if warranted by market conditions, the buffer stock could begin market operations to defend a price range of 150-270 Malaysian/ Singapore cents per kilo (approximately 32-58 U.S. cents per pound). The World Bank expects natural rubber prices to fluctuate around a level of 52¢ per pound (in 1977 dollars) through 1990. . . .

COMMODITY AGREEMENT MECHANISMS

International commodity agreements have been used since the 1920s in a wide variety of situations. By using one of two mechanisms—buffer stocks and export quotas—most agreements have attempted to control the amount of a commodity reaching the market. The buffer stock mechanism requires a fund that can be used to buy up stocks of the commodity when prices slump; the stocks are sold when prices rise above agreement objectives. Export quotas defend a price floor, reducing total supply by limiting the amount of the commodity that each member nation is permitted to market. Export controls generally require producing nations to stockpile or limit production individually, but stockpiling can be costly and limiting production can be politically painful. Some producers may elect to remain outside an agreement. The cooperation of consuming-country members may strengthen a commodity agreement; consumers can be asked to agree not to import commodities marketed in violation of the agreement. Some commodity agreements contain consultative provisions intended to facilitate planning and minimize price fluctuation due to faulty assessment of demand. Market-development measures sometimes are included.

Not all commodities lend themselves equally well to the commodity agreement concept. The most fundamental success factor is relative inelasticity of demand: the less elastic the demand, the more producer revenues can be raised by withholding supply. Otherwise, falling sales volume can offset price gains. Other success factors include perishability, transportation costs, industry concentration, the range of production costs, and the existence of a homogeneous product and organized international market. Low storage and transportation costs generally enhance an agreement's chances for success (bananas and fresh meat would be poor candidates for a buffer stock agreement). Success also depends on the proportion of a product's production that reaches the market; so an industry with fewer and more concentrated producers likely would have a greater market share than one with widely dispersed production. It also helps if producers' costs are generally equal, so that no one group of producers feels it can afford to expand its market share through price competition.

THE INTEGRATED PROGRAM FOR COMMODITIES

The integrated program for commodities had an immediate goal of establishing international agreements covering the 10 "core" commodities of special importance to the Third World. The integrated program for commodities also planned eventual development of measures for eight additional commodities: bananas, bauxite, iron ore, manganese, meat, phosphates, tropical timber, and vegetable oils. Integrated programs for commodities operations were to be financed by a common fund, projected at $6 billion, to be contributed by both importer and exporter governments. About $4.5 billion of the fund was earmarked for buffer stock operations. The remainder was to be used for lending operations in support of other commodities for which buffer stocks were not considered suitable.

After 4 years, the integrated program for commodities has made little progress. Only one new agreement has been signed since the UNCTAD IV conference—the International Natural Rubber Agreement. It entered into force in 1980, and its buffer stock will probably become operational in 1981. The sugar and coffee agreements, already in effect at the time of the UNCTAD conference, have been renewed but face market conditions that make their long-term economic effectiveness questionable. The International Cocoa Agreement has been renewed but without the largest producer (Ivory Coast) and the largest consumer (the United States). Negotiations are underway to replace the fifth International Tin Agreement, which is due to expire in June 1982. The International Wheat Agreement remains in effect, but only as a consultative mechanism, without economic provisions. Prices for the 10 core commodities have continued to fluctuate widely.

Enthusiasm for the common fund has waned among the LDCs, because the fund's size is much smaller than originally envisioned ($750 million instead of $6 billion). The fund has been scaled down drastically because only a few commodity agreements now seem likely to associate with it and because attention has shifted from stabilization of commodity prices to stabilization of commodity export earnings. The latter goal requires less intervention, because lower prices often are associated with increased supply rather than reduced demand.

Has the integrated program for commodities failed? Or will it merely require more time to develop than UNCTAD IV envisioned? Does recent experience with commodity agreements indicate eventual success? Have flaws emerged in commodity agreement designs? Is intransigence on the part of consumers or producers to blame for the integrated program for commodities' slow progress? Should the Third World redouble its efforts on the integrated program for commodities or turn to other means of increasing its income?

These questions bear importantly on the development strategies and potential of many Third World nations and on the interests of developed ones as well. Ultimately, these questions will be assessed in the broadest possible economic, political, and sociological terms. However, the primary focus of this paper is economic constraints shaping the potential of commodity agreements to affect international markets and producer incomes.

STABILIZATION SUCCESS OF COMMODITY AGREEMENTS

Even a quick reading of commodity agreements history suggests that international commodity agreements have produced little price stability. Economic studies strongly support this conclusion. Alton D. Law in International Commodity Agreements (Toronto, 1975.) determined that the average coffee price fluctuation was at least 50% greater during the agreement years of 1965-72 than in the preceding nonagreement period of 1950-63. For sugar, he found the fluctuation at least 75% greater for 12 recent years of control than for 11 noncontrol years, even eliminating the years when the U.S-Cuban confrontation disrupted the sugar market. Only in wheat and tea did Law find more stable prices during the tenure of international agreements—and the wheat stability resulted primarily from national stockpiling by the United States and Canada. Gordon W. Smith and George R. Schink, writing on The International Tin Agreement: A Reassessment in The Economic Journal of December 1976, concluded that the U.S. tin stockpile has lent far more stability to the tin market than has the International Tin Agreement, in large part because it is many times larger than the agreement's tin buffer stock.

Those commodities with the most volatile market fundamentals—least elastic demand, longest supply response lags, greatest vulnerability to business cycles, etc.—have had volatile price patterns even when commodity agreements have been in effect. Tea, on the other hand, has had a relatively stable and uneventful price history both with and without a commodity agreement.

LIMITATIONS OF STABILIZATION SCHEMES

The potential gains to be had from stabilization are relatively modest and enormously difficult to achieve.

In the first place, stabilization gains depend importantly on committing a more appropriate level of resources to production over time. It is extremely difficult, however, to determine the correct level at any given moment. Demand for many commodities swings in pronounced and erratic cycles. With other commodities, supply is the more important variable. For most, the overall market is growing, slowly—and judgments of when to add new production are extremely important. Production of most commodities must be developed in sizable units to achieve economies of scale, and this, too, complicates stabilization. Once such resources as ore deposits, groves of trees, and specialized processing machinery have been committed, they have little alterative use in the short or even medium term. Even with an international agreement, it is difficult to improve resource efficiency.

Any benefits achieved from stabilization must also be balanced against the costs involved. To the extent that they rely on export controls, commodity agreements may raise production costs by locking in the production patterns that exist at the time of negotiation. In order to maintain peak efficiency, these patterns normally would tend to change with new technology, new opportunities for resources, new entrants into the industry, and other factors. The recent shift of cotton production from the developed to the developing countries is such a change, which might well have been hindered by a strong commodity agreement. If the agreements encourage less efficient use of a nation's resources, that loss of efficiency must be balanced against the gains in stability.

Finally, of course, producer proponents of commodity agreements need to bear in mind that the benefits of stability in a commodity are shared between producers and consumers. Ezriel Brook and Enzo Grilli indicate in an article, Commodity Price Stabilization and the Developing World, in Finance and Development, March 1977, that the source of market instability is a key factor in the distribution of these benefits, with producers gaining the principal benefits only when instability results from production factors.

On a more pragmatic level, stabilization itself can affect resource commitment and lead to increased—and sometimes surplus—production. Effective stabilization in the short run reduces producers' risks—and thus encourages them to expand output to the point where their variable costs are covered by the minimum price. This phenomenon has been frequently documented in connection with agricultural price-support policies in the developed nations (notably the United States). It is also noted in a World Bank study of the international jute market. This tendency toward increased production undermines even the most limited goal that has been outlined for commodity agreements—protecting exporters with a floor price.

Because agreements require a political consensus, the economic foundation of some agreements is shaky from the start. Export quotas are often the first area of compromise, because producing nations threaten not to join unless they receive attractive quotas. The second area of compromise, of course, is price objectives. Producers argue for higher prices; consumers for lower. For example, the recently renewed cocoa agreement has not been signed by Ivory Coast, the largest producer, because the price range is too low, while the United States, as the largest consumer, refuses to join because it believes the price is too high and that consequently the agreement will be overwhelmed by surplus cocoa. Some may have believed the price range was unrealistic but signed the agreement anyway to avoid seeming obstructionist. They may have assumed the costs to them would be small, because such agreements have a history of breaking down.

Competition among producers has probably been the most important factor in the collapse of stabilization efforts. Producer incomes, of course, are determined not only by prices but also by sales volume. So even when the agreement sets a price range, producers continue to compete for market shares. Often producing nations are under balance-of-payments pressure. Sometimes they attempt to market some of their production by subterfuge outside the agreement. Market pressure almost always comes from producers who are not party to the agreement.

HAVE COMMODITY AGREEMENTS ENHANCED PRODUCER PRICES?

Economic theory holds that raising commodity prices to artificially high levels will attract additional production, encourage substitution, and cut back quantities demanded. These reactions create surpluses, and they basically explain why the price increases achieved by international commodity agreements have been limited to the short run. In fact, many of the short-term gains have turned into long-term losses.

Historically, price enhancement was tried first by individual companies, which found they lacked the market power to maintain high prices. It has been tried by cartels of companies, which found their prices undercut by producers outside the cartels. It has been tried by governments, which found themselves undercut by producers in other nations. It has been tried by groups of producer nations, which found their markets invaded by nonmember nations. Finally, it has been tried by broad alliances of producer and consumer nations, which have not yet discovered mutual interests strong enough to survive long-term pressures.

Jere R. Behrman, writing Stabilizing Prices Through International Buffer Stock Commodity Agreements in National Development, May 1980, found that most of the organized international arrangements that have attempted to raise prices have been unsuccessful. He documented 51 attempts, which lasted a median $2\frac{1}{2}$ years each. Even those which have been successful in the short run have not lasted long; 4 years has been their median duration. These relatively successful efforts have been associated with "higher concentrations of production and foreign trade"; more inelastic demand; fewer possibilities of short-term substitution; small cost differences among producers; and less government involvement. . . .

CONCLUSIONS AND POLICY IMPLICATIONS

The prices of primary commodities probably will continue to fluctuate widely in response to demand, competition, and long-term production costs. Recent international commodity agreements have not succeeded beyond the limited goal of protecting modest price floors for relatively short time periods, and there is little prospect that future commodity agreements will be more effective. Even if an agreement got full government financing, competition among producers for increased market shares and external competition from substitutes might drive costs to politically untenable levels. Moreover, the benefits of true stabilization are seldom sufficient to overcome the diversity of interests among affected nations.

There is virtually no evidence to indicate that primary commodities can be utilized to generate much larger amounts of development capital for LDCs. The International Tin Agreement is often pointed to as the most successful of the agreements. It has effectively defended its floor price over a long period (aided by Malaysia's ability to shut down its gravel-pump tin production when prices are unattractive). The real price of tin has also trended upward, albeit erratically. However, tin producers have often been squeezed between rising labor costs and the prices of competing materials. If tin is, indeed, the outstanding success story among recent international commodity agreements, then such agreements hardly seem to offer LDCs a powerful force for economic growth.

Based on analysis of supply and demand projections for primary commodities and on the lack of success in UNCTAD's integrated program for commodities, expansion of manufacturing appears to be a far more promising development strategy than reliance on exports of primary products under the aegis of international commodity agreements. In "The Changing Composition of Developing Country Exports," staff working paper 314 of January 1979, the World Bank notes that LDC exports have shifted dramatically toward manufactured goods in the last 15 years. Manufactures now account for nearly half of LDCs' non-oil exports. If the expansion of manufacturing continues over the next few years, the World Bank projects it will lead to an export growth rate for LDCs roughly equal to that of the rest of the World. The Bank notes that the greatest success to date has been achieved by the most advanced LDCs, but that this situation is changing rapidly as increasing numbers of LDCs move toward manufacturing. . . .

NOTES AND QUESTIONS

1. How would you tell whether a commodity agreement was designed to increase prices or just to stabilize them?

2. Why would a consumer nation ever participate in a commodity agreement?

3. What does the commonness of a common fund add to the separate commodity agreements? Ease of creation of individual agreements? Reduction of financial requirements? (Remember that the price fluctuations of different commodities may be unsyncronized if they depend on weather conditions, but are likely to be synchronized to the extent they depend on the world business cycle.) For more background on the common fund, together with a full text, see Amerasinghe, The Common Fund for Commodities, 7 Intl. Trade L.J. 231 (1982-1983).

4. In negotiating an individual commodity agreement, what would be

your points of concern? Consider the questions of setting buying and selling prices (or parallel rules for whatever alternative intervention procedures are chosen), allocation of the costs of purchasing the commodity inventory, decision-making for the different kinds of decisions, enforcement against participants who violate the rules, responses if major nations refuse to participate.

5. What additional issues are posed for a common fund? Consider whether there should be standards or principles for the individual commodity agreements to be associated with the fund and also the way to respond if one of the associated funds should go bankrupt.

6. What sort of implementing legislation is needed for a commodity fund? Consider at least the appointment of the representative, appropriation of the funding, and application of specific rules.

7. One agreement negotiated under the Integrated Programme for Commodities covers tropical timber, and includes conservation-oriented provisions and technical forest management assistance procedures, as well as efforts to move processing activities from developed to developing nations. *See* Obrecht, A Kind of Woodpec, Far E. Econ. Rev., at 59 (Dec. 15, 1983). How would the special problems of making this agreement succeed differ from those of making a regular commodity agreement succeed?

8. Can you envision commodity agreements as breeders of white collar crime and consumer fraud? Under the coffee agreement, limitations are placed in consumer member countries on imports from non-members, and no bags without certificates of origin from member countries are permitted. For a description of the so-called tourist coffee phenomena under the coffee accord, *see* Fisher, Enforcing Export Quota Commodity Agreements: The Case of Coffee, 12 Harv. Intl. L.J. 401 (1971), and B. Fisher, The International Coffee Agreement: A Study in Coffee Diplomacy, Chapter 6 (1972).

9. By 1982, in spite of the agreement described in the Department of State Bulletin, the world sugar price had fallen to around 8 cents a pound and the U.S. government had greatly reduced the level of imports permitted under its domestic law quota system. What would this action do to other parties? Is it consistent with the agreement? In United States Cane Sugar Refiners' Assn. v. Block, 544 F. Supp. 883 (Ct. Intl. Trade 1982), the court rejected *ultra vires* arguments based on domestic law and then said the following about the agreement:

> Moreover, plaintiff's contention that the quotas are inconsistent with the International Sugar Agreement (ISA) is similarly untenable. Article 58 of the ISA requires a developed importing member only to "adopt such measures compatible with its domestic legislation as it deems appropriate to its own circumstances" to ensure access to its markets. Article 58 obviously does not prohibit the United States from maintaining or imposing restrictions on imports. Additionally, plaintiff is incorrect in the statement that "[t]he only restrictions on importation [in the ISA] are against the importation of sugar which has been exported in violation of the Agreement." On the contrary, Article 57 of the ISA requires

that when the world price falls below a certain level, importing members of the ISA are to limit their imports from non-members.

Was the court correct?

10. Based on the data available to you, would you regard the ISA as a success? For detailed criticism and serious reform proposals, *see* Smith, Prospects for a New International Sugar Agreement, 17 J.W.T.L. 308 (1983).

11. Why, do you think, have governments—and the EC—been quite successful (in the sense of actually raising prices) in their domestic price support programs for agricultural commodities, but have nearly always failed when working at any broader level?

12. Does the EC Common Agriculture Policy model suggest any steps toward redesigning commodity arrangements to be more "successful"?

13. As, say, a member of Congress, would you favor any form of commodity arrangement?

Bibliographical Note

For further information on commodity agreements, *see* Frank, Toward a New Framework for International Commodity Policy, Finance and Development (June 1976); Bilder, The International Coffee Agreement: A Case History in Negotiation, 28 L. & Contemp. Prob. 328 (1963); W. Fox, Tin: The Working of a Commodity Agreement (1974).

Note on Food Aid and Economic Development

The interrelationships between trade and economic development are complicated, and particularly so in the food area. The moral and ethical starting point is that in many of the poorer countries of the world people are starving or living at only slightly above the subsistence level. The issue of food aid, therefore, assumes central importance to the poorer developing countries.

Food aid is administered through national and international bureaucracies. At the international level the World Food Program (WFP) provides food aid and strives to promote economic development. Through 1976 the WFP had provided about $1.36 billion in aid through its project. The governing body of the WFP is the UN and its specialized agency in this area, the Food and Agriculture Organization of the United Nations.

At the national level, the major U.S. food aid program falls under P.L. 480 and operates out of the Department of Agriculture. Some of the aid is provided under special credit terms; some is simply given away as a grant. The total planned for FY 1985 was $1.9 billion, about $500 million of which was for Africa.

The United States may be the world's granary, but unlimited food aid is an impossibility. First, the United States needs to promote its commercial agricultural exports to earn foreign exchange to import products such as petroleum. Second, the developing countries themselves would prefer agricultural self-sufficiency rather than accepting doles from the DCs, and food aid may depress food prices and discourage local agriculture. The FAO Principles of Surplus Food Disposal, for example, require that food surplus disposal should not interfere with the normal channels of commerce.

Some have advocated use of U.S. "food power" as leverage not only in the interest of East-West trade but also in that of North-South trade with OPEC nations to "break the cartel." Others have urged the barter of food for oil.

As of the mid-1980s the United States possessed huge reserves of food, deriving from its domestic agricultural subsidy program. The use of these stocks as food aid for the LDCs has an obvious humanitarian appeal, but could undermine commercial markets for U.S. exporters, lead to allegations of unfair subsidization of agricultural exports and "dumping" by U.S. trading partners, and deter agricultural development by LDCs. The issue has been made more difficult by the strength of the U.S. dollar, which has made many U.S. agricultural products noncompetitive. Moreover, the United States was also exploring ways to subsidize agricultural exports by special financing arrangements, or by combining surplus grain with market grain to reduce the effective export price. Such practices accompanied bidding wars between the United States and the European Community to obtain markets in areas like Egypt and Algeria.

For more on the interrelationship between food aid and LDC trade policy *see* D. Paarlberg, Farm and Food Policy (1980).

QUESTIONS

1. Was the 1983 Caribbean Basin Economic Recovery Act (P.L. 98-67, Title II, August 5, 1983), which gave very limited special preferences to goods coming in from that area, a wise concept from the trade viewpoint? Note that only a small amount of goods were covered by this preference that were not already covered by GSP—but this preference was enacted for ten years, while the future of the GSP after 1985 was, at the time, uncertain.

2. How is your thinking about commodity arrangements affected by the fact that DCs are the major exporters of some commodities, e.g., wheat?

3. What is likely to be the impact on economic development of the following examples taken from earlier chapters:

(a)   the rice controversy described in the chapter on countervailing duties?
(b)   the question of countervailing against EXIM and AID loans to developing nations?
(c)   the Article XIX "escape clause" discussion?

4. If the leader of a developing nation asked your advice on whether or not to join the GATT, what would you say? What special factors might push you one way or the other?

5. What bargaining power do developing nations have in the trade and commodity area? Consider China's seven-month suspension of agricultural imports from the United States to attempt to improve U.S. market access for its textiles. The result was a July 1983 quota agreement. The U.S. textile industry regarded this agreement as unduly favorable to China, brought charges of a subsidy system inherent in China's exchange rate policy, and achieved a new quota system in December with a new system for negotiation of further input restraints. *See* Manning, A China Puzzle, Far E. Econ. Rev. 74 (Nov. 24, 1985) and Nations, Reagan Cuts His Cloth, id. at 44 (Dec. 29, 1983).

6. What might LDCs be able to do cooperatively in the event that the DCs make their markets even less available? Consider, for example, mutual preference arrangements or an LDC bank to even out fluctuations in export earnings, averaging the variations of different commodities and exports to create some level of predictability. In thinking about this question, consider the trade numbers presented in Chapter I. Consider also the ways in which the role and benefit of a developing nation's economic community—such as the Central America Common Market or the Association of South East Asian Nations—would be likely to differ from those of the EC.

7. In Title V of the Trade and Tariff Act of 1984 Congress extended the GSP program until July 4, 1993. Why do you suppose the Congress renewed the GSP (*see* Selected Documents Supplement), despite the opposition to the program from organized labor in the United States?

8. If you represented a European agricultural exporter hurt by the new United States agricultural export grant program, how would you proceed? How would you deal with the United States argument that Europe had subsidized such exports first and that the United States program was merely reestablishing fairness? What would you do if you represented the nation that was benefiting from the subsidy?

Chapter XI

Antitrust Issues in International Trade

Because the different parts of international antitrust law[1] are quite discrete, this book divides the antitrust area into several parts and treats each along with the other doctrines to which it is most closely related. This chapter presents the trade-related antitrust issues, which generally arise in two ways. In one, a group of competitors attempts to combine to monopolize a particular export or import market. In the other, one or a few firms attempt unfairly to gain an advantage over other competitors in a particular export or import market.

The chapter begins with the questions of the extent to which a nation's view of antitrust law, typically thought of as a way to protect the consumer, should be applied to transactions involving various combinations of foreign or domestic consumers and foreign or domestic firms. It then turns to the legal problems posed when different nations have conflicting views of the law applicable to a particular transaction, for example, when a foreign nation urges firms to monopolize or when a firm (licitly or corruptly) persuades a foreign government to give it an advantage over a United States competitor. Courts have typically resolved these problems through the antitrust act of state doctrine, a doctrine that, like much else in the area of conflict of laws, is evolving from a set of formal and absolute principles to a balancing test. Finally, the chapter focuses on direct interplays between trade and antitrust principles; interplays reflected in a variety of statutes that combine antitrust and trade concerns.

---

[1] For sources, see Department of Justice, Antitrust Guide for Industrial Operations, Jan. 26, 1977 (Reprinted in part in Selected Documents Supplement); James Atwood and Kingman Brewster, Antitrust and American Business Abroad (1981); Earl Kintner and Mark Joelson, An International Antitrust Primer (1974); the special international antitrust issue: 18 Stan. J. Intl. L. 241 (Summer 1982); Hawk, International Antitrust Policy and the 1982 Acts: The Continuing Need for Reassessment, 51 Fordham L. Rev. 201 (1982); W. Fugate, Foreign Commerce and the Antitrust Laws (1982); and see generally P. Areeda, Antitrust Law, Vols. 1-7 (1977-1986).

A.   ANTITRUST LAW AND ITS FORMAL TERRITORIAL SWEEP

Those students who have not taken an antitrust course tend to come at international antitrust with some fear. It turns out, however, that the antitrust principles raised in most international antitrust contexts are actually relatively simple—what prove complex are rather the international aspects.

The substantive principles of U.S. antitrust that are most important for this text are the Sherman Act of 1890 (15 U.S.C. §§1-7 (1982)) §§1 and 2:

§1.   TRUSTS, ETC., IN RESTRAINT OF TRADE ILLEGAL

Every contract, combination in the form of trust or otherwise, or conspiracy, in restraint of trade or commerce among the several States, or with foreign nations, is declared to be illegal. . . .

Every person who shall make any contract or engage in any combination or conspiracy declared by sections 1 to 7 of this title to be illegal shall be deemed guilty of a misdemeanor, and, on conviction thereof, shall be punished by fine not exceeding fifty thousand dollars, or by imprisonment not exceeding one year, or by both said punishments, in the discretion of the court.

§2.   MONOPOLIZING TRADE A MISDEMEANOR; PENALTY

Every person who shall monopolize, or attempt to monopolize, or combine or conspire with any other person or persons, to monopolize any part of the trade or commerce among the several States, or with foreign nations, shall be deemed guilty of a misdemeanor, and, on conviction thereof, shall be punished by fine not exceeding fifty thousand dollars, or by imprisonment not exceeding one year, or by both said punishments, in the discretion of the court.

The U.S. courts have generally worked toward an economic interpretation of this legislation, interpreting §1 as forbidding those agreements that raise prices to the consumer or perhaps produce economic misallocation, and interpreting §2 as forbidding certain exercises of monopoly power that have similar bad effects. The Clayton Act of 1914 (15 U.S.C. §§12 et seq.) (1982) adds detail, particularly with respect to mergers. The Robinson-Patman Act of 1936, (15 U.S.C. §§13 and 21 (1982)), which prohibits price discrimination among customers, attempts to protect small business and adds a more populist theme that has proven hard to integrate with the rest of antitrust law or theory.

Beyond these substantive principles several procedural points deserve attention. The first derives from the fact that it is almost always impossible to prove convincingly that a particular action has, say, actually affected a price. Antitrust law, therefore, includes a complex set of presumptions to manipulate the burden of proof: *per se* principles, rules of reason and the like—and much of the actual domestic case law amounts to choices of particular burdens of proof. Second—and particularly important in the international context—the U.S.

law looks both to standard enforcement by Department of Justice or Federal Trade Commission action (usually in the form of a civil law prosecution rather than of a criminal law prosecution) and to private attorney-general enforcement by injured private parties seeking treble damages. The implication is that, unless U.S. law is changed, these injured private parties can sometimes bring antitrust suits in politically sensitive situations in which the Department of Justice might well have exercised discretion not to prosecute.

In the case of the horizontal trade agreements considered in this chapter, foreign antitrust law will not generally be explicitly different from U.S. law. Even though the U.S. laws date from an era of populist suspicion of largeness—and could probably not be passed in the face of today's lobbyists—the concepts of avoiding the misuse of monopoly and of avoiding conspiracy are broadly shared. Thus, the European antitrust law—while most eager to avoid those trade restraints that affect the flow of goods across the old national boundaries within Europe—includes provisions roughly analogous to those of the Sherman Act, as, for example, the following from the Treaty of Rome (1957) that established the EEC (Common Market):

ARTICLE 85

1. The following shall be prohibited as incompatible with the Common Market: all agreements between enterprises, all decisions by associations of enterprises and all concerted practices which are apt to affect trade between the Member States and which have as their object or effect the prevention, restriction or distortion of competition within the Common Market, in particular those consisting in:

(a) the direct or indirect fixing of purchase or selling prices or of any other trading conditions;

(b) the limitation or control of production, markets, technological development or investment;

(c) market-sharing or the sharing of sources of supply;

(d) the application of unequal conditions to parties undertaking equivalent engagements in commercial transactions, thereby placing them at a competitive disadvantage;

(e) making the conclusion of a contract subject to the acceptance by the other party to the contract of additional obligations, which, by their nature or according to commercial usage have no connection with the subject of such contract.

2. Any agreements or decisions prohibited pursuant to this Article shall be null and void.

3. The provisions of paragraph 1 may, however, be declared inapplicable in the case of:

—any agreements or groups of agreements between enterprises,
—any decisions or groups of decisions by associations of enterprises, and
—any concerted practices or groups of concerted practices,

which contribute to the improvement of the production or distribution of goods or to the promotion of technological or economic progress while reserving to consumers an equitable share in the profit resulting therefrom, and which:

(a) neither impose on the enterprises concerned any restrictions not indispensable to the attainment of the above objectives;

(b) nor enable such enterprises to eliminate competition in respect of a substantial proportion of the goods concerned.

ARTICLE 86

Any abusive exploitation by one or more enterprises of a dominant position within the Common Market or within a substantial part of it shall be deemed to be incompatible with the Common Market and shall be prohibited, in so far as trade between Member States could be affected by it.

Such abusive exploitation may, in particular, consist in:

(a) the direct or indirect imposition of any inequitable purchase or selling prices or of any other inequitable trading conditions;

(b) the limitation of production, markets or technological development to the prejudice of consumers;

(c) the application of unequal conditions to parties undertaking equivalent engagements in commercial transactions, thereby placing them at a competitive disadvantage.

(d) making the conclusion of a contract subject to the acceptance by the other party to the contract of additional obligations which by their nature or according to commercial usage have no connection with the subject of such contract.

ARTICLE 87

1. Within three years after this Treaty comes into force, the Council, acting by unanimous vote on a proposal of the Commission and after the Assembly has been consulted, shall issue the necessary regulations or directives to put into effect the principles set out in Articles 85 and 86.

If such regulations or directives have not been adopted within the specified time-limit, they shall be laid down by the Council acting by a qualified majority vote on a proposal of the Commission and after the Assembly has been consulted.

2. The regulations or directives referred to in paragraph 1 shall be designed, in particular:

(a) to ensure observance, by the institution of fines or penalties, of the prohibitions referred to in Article 85(1), and in Article 86;

(b) to determine the particulars of the application of Article 85(3), taking due account of the need, on the one hand, of ensuring effective supervision and, on the other hand, of simplifying administrative control to the greatest possible extent;

(c) to specify, where necessary, the extent to which the provisions contained in Articles 85 and 86 are to be applied in the various economic sectors;

(d) to define the respective tasks of the Commission and of the Court of Justice in giving effect to the provisions referred to in this paragraph;

(e) to determine the relationship between municipal law, on the one hand, and the provisions of this Section or any other provisions issued pursuant to this Article, on the other hand.

The regulation required by Article 87 was passed as EEC Regulation 17 of 1962. This regulation spells out the procedures for enforcing Articles 85 and 86, and establishes procedures under which some agreements may be exempted in accord with Article 85(3).

The similarity among national antitrust systems fails to obtain, however, as the economic basis of the various national principles diverge. Still less can such similarity be asserted—and this is the basis of major conflicts considered in this chapter—when a nation encourages monopoly or cartel within a specific industry. Many nations, even those with a basic commitment to antitrust principles, have done this in the hope of strengthening their export position or in order to strengthen a particular industry.

Early on, the United States courts were very hesitant to extend their antitrust principles to reach foreign acts, even when those acts affected domestic consumers, but this position was reversed in the following case, *Alcoa*. Note that this case has essentially the same prestige as a Supreme Court opinion; it had been referred to Judge Learned Hand because so many members of the Supreme Court excused themselves. The materials following *Alcoa*, a decision of the Commission of the European Communities posing essentially the same issue, and a recent U.S. statute seeking to clarify some aspects of extraterritorial jurisdiction, are included to provide perspective on the *Alcoa* principles—principles that have often been strongly attacked as reaching extravagantly far. The examples in the Antitrust Guide for International Operations (Selected Documents Supplement) provide additional perspective. These guidelines, issued in March 1977, have no formal binding force, but do give an indication of the Department of Justice's enforcement policy.

UNITED STATES v. ALUMINUM CO. OF AMERICA [ALCOA]

148 F.2d 416 (1945)

HAND, J.

This appeal comes to us by virtue of a certificate of the Supreme Court, under the amendment of 1944 to §29 of 15 U.S.C.A. The action was brought under §4 of that title, praying the district court to adjudge that the defendant, Aluminum Company of America, was monopolizing interstate and foreign commerce, particularly in the manufacture and sale of "virgin" aluminum ingot, and that it be dissolved; and further to adjudge that that company and the defendant, Aluminum Limited, had entered into a conspiracy in restraint of such commerce. . . .

At the date of judgment there were fifty-one defendants who had been served and against whom the action was pending. We may divide these, as the district judge did, into four classes: Aluminum Company of America, with its wholly owned subsidiaries, directors, officers and shareholders. (For convenience we shall speak of these defendants collectively as "Alcoa," that being the name by which the company has become almost universally known.) Next, Aluminum Limited, with its directors, officers and shareholders. (For the same reason we shall speak of this group as "Limited" [this was a Canadian firm].) . . .

For these reasons [omitted] we conclude that "Alcoa" was not a party to the "Alliance," and did not joint in any violation of §1 of the Act, so far as concerned foreign commerce.

Whether "Limited" itself violated that section depends upon the character of the "Alliance." It was a Swiss corporation, created in pursuance of an agreement entered into on July 3, 1931, the signatories to which were a French corporation, two German, one Swiss, a British, and "Limited." The original agreement, or "cartel," provided for the formation of a corporation in Switzerland which should issue shares, to be taken up by the signatories. This corporation was from time to time to fix a quota of production for each share, and each shareholder was to be limited to the quantity measured by the number of shares it held, but was free to sell at any price it chose. The corporation fixed a price every year at which it would take off any shareholder's hands any part of its quota which it did not sell. No shareholder was to "buy, borrow, fabricate or sell" aluminum produced by anyone not a shareholder except with the consent of the board of governors, but that must not be "unreasonably withheld." Nothing was said as to whether the arrangement extended to sales in the United States; but Article X, known as the "Conversion Clause," provided that any shareholder might exceed his quota to the extent that he converted into aluminum in the United States or Canada any ores delivered to him in either of those countries by persons situated in the United States. This was confessedly put in to allow "Limited" to receive bauxite or alumina from "Alcoa," to smelt it into aluminum and to deliver the aluminum to "Alcoa." . . .

The agreement of 1936 abandoned the system of unconditional quotas, and substituted a system of royalties. Each shareholder was to have a fixed free quota for every share it held, but as its production exceeded the sum of its quotas, it was to pay a royalty, graduated progressively in proportion to the excess; and these royalties the "Alliance" divided among the shareholders in proportion to their shares. . . . Although this agreement, like its predecessor, was silent as to imports into the United States, when that question arose during its preparation, as it did, all the shareholders agreed that such imports should be included in the quotas. The German companies were exempted from royalties—for obvious reasons—and that, it would seem, for practical purposes put them out of the "cartel" for the future, for it was scarcely possible that a German producer would be unable to dispose of all its production, at least within any future period that would be provided for. The shareholders continued this agreement unchanged until the end of March, 1938, by which time it had become plain that, at least for the time being, it was no longer of service to anyone. Nothing was, however, done to end it, although the German shareholders of course became enemies of the French, British and Canadian shareholders in 1939. The "Alliance" itself has apparently never been dissolved; and indeed it appeared on the "Proclaimed List of Blocked Nationals" of September 13, 1944.

Did either the agreement of 1931 or that of 1936 violate §1 of the Act? The answer does not depend upon whether we shall recognize as a source of liability a liability imposed by another state. On the contrary we are concerned only with whether Congress chose to attach liability to the conduct outside the United States of persons not in allegiance to it. That being so, the only question open is whether Congress intended to impose the liability, and whether our own Constitution permitted it to do so: as a court of the United States, we cannot look beyond our own law. Nevertheless, it is quite true that we are not to read general words, such as those in this Act, without regard to the limitations customarily observed by nations upon the exercise of their powers; limitations which generally correspond to those fixed by the "Conflict of Laws." We should not impute to Congress an intent to punish all whom its courts can catch, for conduct which has no consequences within the United States. American Banana Co. v. United Fruit Co., 213 U.S. 347, 357, 29 S. Ct. 511, 53 L. Ed. 826, 16 Ann. Cas. 1047; . . . On the other hand, it is settled law—as "Limited" itself agrees—that any state may impose liabilities, even upon persons not within its allegiance, for conduct outside its borders that has consequences within its borders which the state reprehends; and these liabilities other states will ordinarily recognize. . . .

Two situations are possible. There may be agreements made beyond our borders not intended to affect imports, which do affect them, or which affect exports. Almost any limitation of the supply of goods in Europe, for example, or in South America, may have repercussions in the United States if there is trade between the two. Yet when one considers the international complications likely to arise from an effort in this country to treat such agreements as unlawful, it is safe to assume that Congress certainly did not intend the Act to cover them. Such agreements may on the other hand intend to include imports into the United States, and yet it may appear that they have had no effect upon them. That situation might be thought to fall within the doctrine that intent may be a substitute for performance in the case of a contract made within the United States; or it might be thought to fall within the doctrine that a statute should not be interpreted to cover acts abroad which have no consequence here. We shall not choose between these alternatives; but for argument we shall assume that the Act does not cover agreements, even though intended to affect imports or exports, unless its performance is shown actually to have had some effect upon them. Where both conditions are satisfied, the situation certainly falls within such decisions as United States v. Pacific & Artic R. & Navigation Co., 228 U.S. 87, 33 S. Ct. 443, 57 L. Ed. 742; Thomsen v. Cayser, 243 U.S. 66, 37 S. Ct. 353, 61 L. Ed. 597, Ann. Cas. 1917D, 322 and United States v. Sisal Sales Corporation, 274 U.S. 268, 47 S. Ct. 592, 71 L. Ed. 1042.

It is true that in those cases the persons held liable had sent agents into the United States to perform part of the agreement; but an agent is merely an animate means of executing his principal's purposes, and, for the purposes of this case, he does not differ from an inanimate means; besides, only human agents can import and sell ingot.

Both agreements would clearly have been unlawful, had they been made within the United States; and it follows from what we have just said that both were unlawful, though made abroad, if they were intended to affect imports and did affect them. Since the shareholders almost at once agreed that the agreement of 1931 should not cover imports, we may ignore it and confine our discussion to that of 1936: indeed that we should have to do anyway, since it superseded the earlier agreement. The judge found that it was not the purpose of the agreement to "suppress or restrain the exportation of aluminum to the United States for sale in competition with 'Alcoa'." By that we understand that he meant that the agreement was not specifically directed to "Alcoa," because it only applied generally to the production of the shareholders. If he meant that it was not expected that the general restriction upon production would have an effect upon imports, we cannot agree, for the change made in 1936 was deliberate and was expressly made to accomplish just that. It would have been an idle gesture, unless the shareholders had supposed that it would, or at least might, have that effect. The first of the conditions which we mentioned was therefore satisfied; the intent was to set up a quota system for imports.

The judge also found that the 1936 agreement did not "materially affect the . . . foreign trade or commerce of the United States"; apparently because the imported ingot was greater in 1936 and 1937 than in earlier years. We cannot accept this finding, based as it was upon the fact that, in 1936, 1937 and the first quarter of 1938, the gross imports of ingot increased. It by no means follows from such an increase that the agreement did not restrict imports; and incidentally it so happens that in those years such inference as is possible at all, leads to the opposite conclusion. . . . [T]he proportion of imports to domestic ingot was about 15.6 per cent for the first period and about 12.6 per cent for the second. We do not mean to infer from this that the quota system of 1936 did in fact restrain imports, as these figures might suggest; but we do mean that nothing is to be inferred from the gross increase of imports. We shall dispose of the matter therefore upon the assumption that, although the shareholders intended to restrict imports, it does not appear whether in fact they did so. Upon our hypothesis the plaintiff would therefore fail, if it carried the burden of proof upon this issue as upon others. We think, however, that, after the intent to affect imports was proved, the burden of proof shifted to "Limited." In the first place a depressant upon production which applies generally may be assumed, ceteris paribus, to distribute its effect evenly upon all markets. Again, when the parties took the trouble specifically to make the depressant apply to a given market, there is reason to suppose that they expected that it would have some effect, which it could have only by lessening what would otherwise have been imported. If the motive they introduced was over-balanced in all instances by motives which induced the shareholders to import, if the United States market became so attractive that the royalties did not count at all and their expectations were in fact defeated, they to whom the facts were more accessible than to the plaintiff ought to prove it, for a prima facie case had been made. Moreover, there is an especial propriety in demand-ing this of "Limited," because it was "Limited" which procured the inclusion in the agreement of 1936 of imports in the quotas.

There remains only the question whether this assumed restriction had any influence upon prices, Apex Hosiery Co. v. Leader, 310 U.S. 469, 60 S. Ct. 982, 84 L. Ed. 1311, 128 A.L.R. 1044. To that Socony-Vacuum Oil Co. v. United States, 310 U.S. 150, 60 S. Ct. 811, 84 L. Ed. 1129, is an entire answer. It will be remembered that, when the defendants in that case protested that the prosecution had not proved that the "distress" gasoline had affected prices, the court answered that that was not necessary, because an agreement to withdraw any substantial part of the supply from a market would, if carried out, have some effect upon prices, and was as unlawful as an agreement expressly to fix prices. The underlying doctrine was that all factors which contribute to determine prices, must be kept free to operate unhampered by agreements. For these reasons we think that the agreement of 1936 violated §1 of the Act. . . .

RESTRICTIVE PRACTICES RE CARTEL IN ANILINE DYES

[1969] 8 C.M.L.R. (R.P. Supp.) Issue No. 3 at D23

The Commission of the European Communities, in the light of the Treaty instituting the European Economic Community (especially Article 85) and of Regulation 17 of 6 February 1962 (especially Articles 3 and 15), took a deci-sion on 31 May 1967 to institute proceedings of its own motion, under Article 3 of Regulation 17, against various producers of colouring matter after finding that there had been simultaneous price increases which were applied on iden-tical conditions within the Common Market.

The Commission has heard the parties concerned in accordance with Article 19 (1) of Regulation 17 and of Regulation 99/63/EEC.

The Consultative Committee on Cartels and Monopolies gave its opinion under Article 10 of Regulation 17 on 8 and 9 July 1969.

I

[1] Following information supplied by the professional bodies of the leather industry, the textile industry, the dyeing industry and the printing industry of

several Common Market countries concerning the occurrence of simultaneous price increases by various producers of colouring matter, the Commission carried out several series of investigations in the six member-States relating to the successive price increases of 1964, 1965 and 1967, under Article 14 of Regulation 17.

These investigations allowed it to find the following facts:

(a) between 7 and 20 January 1964 a uniform increase of 15 per cent. in the prices of most dyestuffs with an aniline base, except for certain categories (such as pigments and pigmentary preparations, sulphur blacks and dyestuffs intended for food, biology and the manufacture of cosmetics), took place in Italy, Holland, Belgium and Luxembourg:

(b) on 1 January 1965, the same increase 15 per cent. was extended to Germany; on that day, nearly all manufacturers applied in that country, as well as in those countries already touched by the 1964 increase, a uniform increase of 10 per cent. in the price of dyestuffs and pigments which had been excluded from the first increase;

(c) on 16 October 1967, an increase of 8 per cent. in the price of all dyestuffs was applied by nearly all producers in Germany, Holland, Belgium and Luxembourg; the increase was 12 per cent. in France; it was not made in Italy.

[2] These three increases were made, in circumstances to be described below, by the following producers:

—Badische Anilin- und Soda-Fabrik AG (B.A.S.F.) of Ludwigshafen (Germany),

—Cassella Farbwerke Mainkur AG of Frankfurt am Main (Germany),

—Farbenfabriken Bayer AG of Leverkusen (Germany),

—Farbwerke Hoechst AG of Frankfurt am Main (Germany),

—Société Française des Matières Colorantes S.A. (Francolor) of Paris (France),

—Aziende Colori Nazionali Affini S.p.A. (A.C.N.A.) of Milan (Italy),

—S.A. Ciba of Basel (Switzerland),

—J. R. Geigy S.A. of Basel (Switzerland),

—Sandoz S.A. of Basel (Switzerland),

—Imperial Chemical Industries Ltd. (I.C.I.) of Manchester (Great Britain). . . .

[6] The investigations made by the Commission have revealed that the successive price increases and the conditions in which they were carried out cannot be explained by the oligopolistic structure of the market but are indeed the consequence of a concerted practice. . . .

[9] Informational contacts between the producers were made several times, especially in meetings in Basel and London. It appears from the record of one of these meetings, held in Basel on 18 August 1967, attended by all the producers in question except for A.C.N.A., that not only was the question of the prices of colouring matter discussed but also that the company J. R. Geigy S.A. announced as appears from the record, "that it was seriously considering

increasing its sales prices to its customers before the end of that year" and, as appears from the decision of the Bundeskartellamt of 28 November 1967, "that it would increase the price of its dyestuffs by 8 per cent. on 16 October 1967".

[10] It is clearly apparent in these various circumstances that the increases in price found by the Commission are at the very least the effect of concerted practices within the meaning of Article 85 (1); there is, therefore, no need to examine whether the increases are the result of an agreement.

[11] The proof of the existence of concerted practices has been made with regard to the various producers, whether established inside or outside the Common Market, and not with regard to their subsidiaries or representatives. The orders to make the increases sent to these latter were imperative. Even had they been able freely to determine their prices, it would have been impossible for them to absorb an increase of 12 to 18 per cent. in the prices paid by them without passing on at least a large part of the increase in their own sales prices. Consequently, it is to the producers and not to their subsidiaries or representatives that the concerted practices are to be imputed.

[12] These concerted practices restrict competition within the Common Market. Indeed, having as their object the application by all the undertakings concerned, on almost identical dates and for the same categories of products, of identical rates of price increase, they directly fix the sales prices of the various dyestuffs marketed by each of the undertakings within the Common Market.

The Commission, for these reasons, decides:

1. The concerted practices consisting in fixing the rates of price increase and conditions of application of such increases in the colouring matter sector, which resulted in price increases in 1964, 1965 and 1967 [,] . . . constitute infringements of the provisions of Article 85 (1) of the Treaty instituting the E.E.C. . . .

2. There shall be imposed:

—on Badische Anilin- und Soda-Fabrik AG (B.A.S.F.) of Ludwigshafen (Germany) a fine of 50,000 units of account;

—on Cassella Farbwerke Mainkur AG of Frankfurt am Main (Germany) a fine of 50,000 units of account;

—on Farbenfabriken Bayer AG of Leverkusen (Germany) a fine of 50,000 units of account;

—on Farbwerke Hoechst AG of Frankfurt am Main (Germany) a fine of 50,000 units of account;

—on S.A. Française des Matières Colorantes (Francolor) of Paris (France) a fine of 50,000 units of account;

—on Aziende Colori Nazionali Affini S.p.A. of Milan (Italy) a fine of 40,000 units of account;

—on S.A. Ciba of Basel (Switzerland) a fine of 50,000 units of account;

—on J. R. Geigy S.A. of Basel (Switzerland) a fine of 50,000 units of account;

—on Sandoz S.A. of Basel (Switzerland) a fine of 50,000 units of account;
—on Imperial Chemical Industries Ltd. (I.C.I.) of Manchester (Great Britain) a fine of 50,000 units of account.

These sums should be paid to the Commission within three months of notification of the present decision. . . .

As regards the companies S.A. Ciba, J. R. Geigy S.A., Sandoz S.A. and Imperial Chemical Industries Ltd., it may equally well be notified to the office of one of their subsidiaries established within the Common Market. . . .

FOREIGN TRADE ANTITRUST IMPROVEMENTS ACT OF 1982, §402—TITLE IV OF THE EXPORT TRADING COMPANY ACT OF 1982

P.L. 97-290, 15 U.S.C. §6a (1982)

AMENDMENT TO SHERMAN ACT

Sec. 402. The Sherman Act (15 U.S.C. 1 et seq.) is amended by inserting after section 6 the following new section:

Sec. 7. This Act shall not apply to conduct involving trade or commerce (other than import trade or import commerce) with foreign nations unless—

"(1)   such conduct has a direct, substantial, and reasonably foreseeable effect—

"(A) on trade or commerce which is not trade or commerce with foreign nations, or on import trade or import commerce with foreign nations; or

"(B) on export trade or export commerce with foreign nations, of a person engaged in such trade or commerce in the United States; and

"(2)   such effect gives rise to a claim under the provisions of this Act, other than this section.

If this Act applies to such conduct only because of the operation of paragraph (1)(B), then this Act shall apply to such conduct only for injury to export business in the United States".

[Section 403 amends the Federal Trade Commission Act in parallel fashion.]

NOTES AND QUESTIONS

1. What, precisely, is Judge Hand's test for extraterritorial application of the Sherman Act? Are you convinced by his burden-of-proof logic?

2. Which of the following violate the Sherman Act? Under *Alcoa*? Under the Foreign Trade Improvements Act of 1982?

(a) An agreement among U.S. auto manufacturers to fix U.S. auto prices when the agreement was negotiated and signed in Canada?

(b) One among European auto manufacturers to fix U.S. prices when the agreement was negotiated and signed in Europe?

(c) One among European auto manufacturers to fix European prices that has side effects on the U.S. price?

3. What about an agreement by U.S. auto manufacturers to fix prices in Europe? How are the issues here different from those of *Alcoa*? *See* Pfizer, Inc. v. Government of India, 434 U.S. 308 (1978) (foreign government a person for purposes of act)—which is essentially overruled by P.L. 97-393 (Dec. 29, 1982).

4. Suppose the U.S.manufacturers, except Chrysler, agreed to cooperate to exclude Chrysler from the European market? *See* Todhunter-Mitchell & Co. v. Anheuser-Busch, 375 F. Supp. 610 (E.D. Pa. 1974), *modified,* 383 F. Supp. 586 (E.D. Pa. 1974).

5. What if they agreed to cooperate to exclude a Japanese manufacturer from that market? How are the issues and policies in these cases different from those of *Alcoa*? Of *Pfizer*? For a comparable case, finding no Sherman Act violation in exclusion of plaintiff from Canadian bank card market, *see* Natl. Bank of Canada v. Interbank Card Assn., 666 F.2d 6 (2d Cir. 1981).

6. In what respects, if any, are the principles of *Aniline* different from those of *Alcoa*?

7. Is there any alternative to the *Alcoa* position?

8. As you understand them now and taking into account prices, effects on consumers, effects on foreign business, and effects on U.S. business, what are the relative economic and political objectives of the U.S. antitrust laws? The U.S. trade laws? Is there (inevitably) (sometimes) (never) conflict between the two sets of statutes?

B.   WAYS TO LIMIT INTERNATIONAL CONFLICT OVER ANTITRUST POLICY

International law has developed several concepts for jurisdiction over an international action; these are spelled out in American Law Institute, Restatement of the Foreign Relations Law of the United States (Revised) (Tentative Draft No. 5, 1985):

§402.   BASES OF JURISDICTION TO PRESCRIBE

Subject to §403, a state has jurisdiction to prescribe law with respect to

(1) (a) conduct a substantial part of which takes place within its territory; (b) the status of persons, or interests in things, present within its territory; (c) con-

duct outside its territory which has or is intended to have substantial effect within its territory;

(2) the activities, status, interests or relations of its nationals outside as well as within its territory; or

(3) certain conduct outside its territory by persons not its nationals which is directed against the security of the state or a limited class of other state interests.

Section 403 presents a rule of reasonableness in the exercise of jurisdiction.

Although the limits of these principles are a matter of judgment and therefore subject to debate, the principles themselves are broadly shared. They help courts avoid international conflict by providing a basis to abstain from dealing with a controversy better resolved abroad.

Even with the broadly shared principles, however, antitrust law still offers serious potential for conflict. The clear underlying U.S. position is to reach all restraints of trade that affect the price to the U.S. consumer or affect exports of U.S. firms. (EC law is parallel on at least the first point.) Thus, U.S. antitrust law can come into conflict with a foreign government's decision to permit or grant a monopoly within its own territory, a decision that is sometimes actively sought by the potential monopolist.

Because both nations' legal principles can plausibly be applied in such cases, U.S. courts have had to turn to different doctrines to resolve these cases. The traditional doctrine was the act of state doctrine, which attempts to respond directly to foreign government concerns.

1.   The Antitrust Act of State Doctrine

a. Traditional Form

In its traditional form, the U.S. antitrust act of state doctrine prohibited any consideration of a case that would call into question a foreign "act of state," e.g., an official act that would establish the rights of the parties according to the foreign law. The following case is illustrative of the doctrine.

OCCIDENTAL PETROLEUM CORP. v. BUTTES GAS & OIL CO.

331 F. Supp. 92 (C.D. Cal.), *aff'd*, 461 F.2d 1261 (9th Cir. 1971), *cert. denied*, 409 U.S. 950 (1972)

PREGERSON, J.

This is a private antitrust suit for treble damages and an injunction, brought by Occidental Petroleum Corporation and its wholly owned subsidiary Occidental of Umm al Qaywayn against the Clayco Petroleum Corporation

("Clayco") and its president, Clayman, and the Buttes Gas and Oil Company ("Buttes") and its officers Boreta and Smith. The complaint charges the defendants with conspiracy in restraint of trade, conspiracy to monopolize, and attempted monopoly, all with respect to "the exploration, development and exploitation of petroleum reserves of the territorial waters of the Trucial States." The plaintiffs and the defendant corporations are holders of offshore oil concessions granted by two adjacent sheikdoms in the Persian Gulf. Defendants are charged with instigating a presently pending international dispute over sovereign rights to a portion of the Gulf—allegedly covering the richest area of plaintiffs' concession—with the result that plaintiffs have been prevented from enjoying the fruits of their concession. . . .

Plaintiffs assert that, pursuant to their efforts to develop and exploit the petroleum reserves underlying the offshore waters of the Trucial States in the Persian Gulf, they obtained in 1969 a concession from the Ruler of Umm al Qaywayn, one of the Trucial States, granting plaintiffs the exclusive right to explore for, extract, and sell oil underlying the territorial and offshore waters of Umm al Qaywayn. It was plaintiffs' purpose to import into the United States for refining any oil extracted pursuant to this concession. Owing to the unavailability of the Suez Canal, such importation would be made through Pacific Coast seaports in California. The concession agreement is by its own terms to terminate if oil is not discovered in "commercial quantities" . . . in the concession area within four years of the concession's effective date.

Immediately prior to their obtaining the concession from Umm al Qaywayn, plaintiffs allege, defendants Buttes and Clayco had themselves unsuccessfully attempted to negotiate such a concession. Subsequent to plaintiffs' success with Umm al Qaywayn, Buttes and Clayco allegedly negotiated, in December, 1969, a comparable concession by the Ruler of the Trucial State Sharjah, covering its territorial and offshore waters.

The mainland areas of Sharjah and Umm al Qaywayn are situated contiguously at the southeastern end of the Persian Gulf. Sharjah, moreover, asserts sovereignty to the island of Abu Musa, located 38 miles off the coast of its mainland. Plaintiffs allege that at the time defendants' concession was granted by Sharjah, it claimed a territorial waters domain of three miles, including a belt extending that distance seaward from the low water mark of Abu Musa. The territorial waters perimeter off Abu Musa allegedly constituted a boundary between the Sharjah and Umm al Qaywayn concession areas that was acknowledged by both states. A map indicating this boundary is attached to the complaint, and plaintiffs allege that confirmatory copies of this map were included in the two concession agreements when each was submitted to and approved by the British Foreign Office, pursuant to a treaty still in force between Britain and the Trucial States.

Still friendly in the beginning of 1970, plaintiffs and Buttes agreed to exchange information gleaned from seismic tests to be made of the seabed and subsoil underlying their respective concession areas. The results of plaintiffs' tests indicated the presence of oil in extensive quantities at a point within their alleged concession area nine miles seaward from the low water mark of Abu Musa. Plaintiffs proceeded to prepare to drill in this area, expending several million dollars for that purpose by the time the complaint was filed.

The complaint alleges that after learning in March, 1970 of the apparent richness of plaintiffs' concession area, defendants entered into and acted upon a conspiracy to misappropriate plaintiffs' rights to the oil underlying the Persian Gulf nine miles off Abu Musa. The execution of this conspiracy, as alleged, involved a multi-faceted international intrigue whose detail, relevant to the grounds of the instant motion to dismiss, is set out in the margin in the words of the complaint.[11] Briefly stated, after unsuccessfully submitting to the British Political Agent in the Trucial States a plan whereby Buttes would drill for oil in a portion of the Occidental-Umm al Qaywayn concession area, defendants "induced and procured" the Ruler of Sharjah to claim ownership of the oil-rich portion of plaintiffs' concession area by preparing and submitting to the British Agent a concession amendment and two decrees, one of the latter fraudulently backdated to represent that prior to the granting of plaintiffs' concession by Umm al Qaywayn, Sharjah had claimed territorial waters extending *twelve* miles seaward from the low water mark of its territory, including Abu Musa. These representations did not convince the British Foreign Office, which ordered the Ruler of Sharjah to desist and acknowledged the authority of the Occidental-Umm al Qaywayn concession. Defendants allegedly then enlisted the aid of other sovereigns: they "induced and procured" the National Iranian Oil Company, in May, 1970, to claim Iranian sovereignty over Abu Musa and the waters twelve miles seaward therefrom; and defendants thereafter further "induced and procured" the British Foreign Office to request that plaintiffs refrain from their imminent drilling operations until the claims of Sharjah and of the Iranian Company could be resolved. British ships and aircraft menaced plaintiffs' personnel and equipment on the drilling site, and on June 1, 1970, members of the Royal Navy forcibly boarded plaintiffs' equipment. Two days later the Ruler of Umm al Qaywayn directed plaintiffs not to drill in the disputed area; this order, which had the effect of suspending plaintiffs' intended drilling operations under their concession, was allegedly the consequence of threats of exile and acts of military intimidation by British forces made to the Ruler of Umm al Qaywayn. The threats against the Ruler of Umm al Qaywayn, and his order to plaintiffs, were allegedly "direct consequences, fully intended and expected by the defendants, of the conflicting and fraudulent claims with regard to the island of Abu Musa and its territorial waters, which the defendants had induced and procured." . . .

---

[11]"22. Plaintiffs are informed and believe and thereon allege that to that end and for that purpose, defendants combined and conspired with each other to do, and pursuant to said combination and conspiracy did, among others, the following acts under the following circumstances:

"(a) Undertook falsely to claim and fraudulently to appropriate, under color of their aforesaid agreement with the Ruler of Sharjah, all exploratory rights anywhere within an area bounded by a line twelve nautical miles seaward from the low water mark on the island of Abu Musa, notwithstanding the rights previously granted plaintiffs up to a line only three miles seaward from Abu Musa. . . .

The intended upshot of this intrigue, the complaint alleges, is that following the withdrawal of the British from the Persian Gulf area in 1971 defendants will arrange with the Ruler of Sharjah to extract oil and gas from areas covered by plaintiffs' concession.

To remedy the injury suffered from this conspiracy, the plaintiffs request treble their damages of $100 million—the estimated worth of the oil in the concession area—as well as extensive equitable relief, to wit, an injunction restraining defendants or any persons operating in concert with them from disputing the validity of the Occidental concession as alleged in the complaint, from interfering with plaintiffs' operations in the waters of the Trucial States, and from extracting oil from the area of the Occidental concession; in the alternative to this last demand, plaintiffs request the impressment of a trust for their benefit upon any revenues derived by defendants or those acting for them from any part of the plaintiffs' concession area.

The Buttes defendants urge five arguments to defeat the complaint. First, they assert that this court lacks jurisdiction of the subject matter of the action under the antitrust laws because the complaint fails to allege a substantial anti-competitive effect upon United States commerce. Second, defendants urge, subject matter jurisdiction is lacking because the complaint sets forth an international boundary dispute, which is not amenable to decision in the courts of the United States. Third, defendants claim that Sharjah, Umm al Qaywayn, Iran, and Great Britain are parties whose joinder is necessary under Rule 19 (a) of the Federal Rules of Civil Procedure, and without whose presence the action should be dismissed pursuant to section (b) of Rule 19—in more traditional language, that the four sovereigns are "indispensable" to the action. Fourth, the defendants contend that since the complaint attacks activities undertaken to influence governmental conduct, this case is not within the subject matter of the antitrust laws, as interpreted by the Supreme Court in Eastern R. R. Presidents Conference v. Noerr Motor Freight, Inc., 365 U.S. 127, 81 S. Ct. 523, 5 L. Ed. 2d 464 (1961), and United Mine Workers of America v. Pennington, 381 U.S. 657, 85 S. Ct. 1585, 14 L. Ed. 2d 626 (1965). Fifth and finally, defendants argue that because the conspiracy and damage complained of are based upon the conduct of several sovereigns, this court is barred from adjudicating plaintiffs' claims by the act of state doctrine.

EFFECT ON AMERICAN COMMERCE

The Buttes defendants first contend that jurisdiction of this case requires "a substantial anti-competitive effect on American commerce," and that such an

---

"23. Beginning May 27, 1970, plaintiffs' personnel and equipment, standing ready near the Occidental concession to commence drilling operations, were menaced and threatened by armed surface ships and airplanes of the British Armed Forces. On June 1, 1970, plaintiffs' seagoing equipment was boarded under force by the British Royal Navy. On June 3, 1970, over his protest and acting under the threat of exile, and after his home had been buzzed by airplanes of the British Royal Air Force and surrounded by British soldiers, the Ruler of Umm Al Qaywayn directed plaintiffs not to drill in the area claimed to be within the territorial waters of Sharjah and Iran. Plaintiffs were forced to abandon indefinitely their plans to commence drilling operations."

effect has not been demonstrated by the complaint. On this basis the court is urged to dismiss the complaint for want of subject matter jurisdiction. . . .

The interference with plaintiffs' business of extracting and importing oil into the United States, alleged in the complaint, is certainly a "direct" effect on our foreign commerce. On this basis, the court is disposed to hold that the complaint alleges a sufficient effect on foreign commerce. Moreover, since the standard urged by defendants is largely coterminous with the scope of proof required to establish plaintiffs' section 1 case on the merits, dismissal now on the grounds that that standard has not been met would be premature. In urging dismissal, defendants stress such factors as the smallness of the Buttes Company in relation to plaintiff Occidental Petroleum Corporation, the confined geographical area of plaintiffs' concession, the presently speculative value of that concession, and the presence in the Persian Gulf of numerous other companies extracting oil for importation into the United States. These are matters that would appear to bear upon proof of plaintiffs' claims of antitrust violations; they cannot serve at this stage to defeat jurisdiction.

BOUNDARY DISPUTE

The remaining points of the Buttes defendants' motion reflect the unconventional nature of this lawsuit, as one arising out of the claims and acts of a number of foreign states. The initial and broadest contention posed respecting these circumstances is that the complaint demands that the court decide the boundary dispute pending between the two Trucial States whose concessionaires are the principal parties to this case; therefore, defendants say, the complaint fails for want of subject matter jurisdiction.

The determination of foreign states' boundaries is certainly not a permissible function of this court. In our system, the questions of what are a country's boundaries, or of what nation has sovereignty over a certain piece of territory, are not for the judiciary to decide; they are political questions, upon which the courts must be guided and bound by the pronouncements of the executive. . . .

Although the factual setting and the relief demanded in this case center around the territorial dispute between Sharjah and Umm al Qaywayn, the complaint does not require an explicit or implicit adjudication of those states' rights to the disputed territory. Plaintiffs seek, essentially, to prove a conspiracy, unlawful under the antitrust laws, in the clouding of the boundary question, and to remedy the injury done them by that conspiracy. Their claim is, as it were, framed in tort rather than as a suit to quiet title. Absent is any requirement that this court undertake a determination of foreign boundaries— a task that the court is admittedly neither suited nor authorized to pursue. The instant ground of the motion to dismiss must be denied.

"INDISPENSABLE PARTIES"

The Buttes defendants next assert that Sharjah, Umm al Qaywayn, Great Britain, and Iran are, in the traditional language, "indispensable parties" to this case. [The court decided against the Buttes defendants on this point and ruled that the action "need not be dismissed pursuant to Rule 19, Fed. R. Civ. P."]

FOREIGN GOVERNMENT ACTION

The final two points of this motion are addressed to the peculiar nature of the conspiracy alleged in this case. As detailed above, the defendants are charged, exclusively, with "inducing and procuring" assorted executive acts by foreign states; and it is plainly these acts that allegedly have caused and threatened to cause the damage plaintiffs seek to remedy. The Buttes defendants contend that the foregoing circumstances preclude the court from adjudicating this case. Two doctrines are relied upon: the limitation of antitrust jurisdiction articulated in [*Noerr, supra*], and the rule of judicial abstention known as the act of state doctrine. The two rules spring from different considerations.

In *Noerr,* the Supreme Court unanimously decided that "the Sherman Act does not prohibit two or more persons from associating together in an attempt to persuade the legislature or the executive to take particular action with respect to a law that would produce a restraint or a monopoly." 365 U.S. at 136, 81 S. Ct. at 529. This interpretation of the Sherman Act was reaffirmed, with further elucidation, in United Mine Workers of America v. Pennington, 381 U.S. 657, 85 S. Ct. 1585, 14 L. Ed. 2d 626 (1965). Since *Noerr* and *Pennington* construed the Sherman Act with reference to influencing American state and federal officials, the threshold question here is whether the teaching of those cases is applicable when foreign governments are involved.

There is no direct authority on this question. The Buttes defendants, however, contend that *Noerr* was implicitly extended to cover the solicitation of foreign governments, in Continental Ore Co. v. Union Carbide & Carbon Corp., 370 U.S. 690, 82 S. Ct. 1404, 8 L. Ed. 2d 777 (1962). *Continental Ore* was an antitrust case in which a subsidiary of Union Carbide had allegedly boycotted the plaintiff in the course of exercising discretionary authority as the purchasing agent of the Canadian government. The Court distinguished *Noerr* on ground that "[r]espondents were engaged in private commercial activity, no element of which involved seeking to procure the passage or enforcement of laws." 370 U.S. at 707, 82 S. Ct. at 1415. Defendants insist that in distinguishing *Noerr* only on its facts, the Court in *Continental Ore* decided sub silentio that the rule of *Noerr* would have applied had there been solicitation of foreign government action. At least one commentator agrees precisely. However, an at least equally tenable interpretation of *Continental Ore* is that the Court deemed it unnecessary, in view of the facts, to decide the legal question at all.

Examination of the premises underlying *Noerr* indicates that the case's rationales do not readily fit into a foreign context, such as the facts of this case. One of the roots of the *Noerr* decision was a desire to avoid a construction of the antitrust laws that might trespass upon the First Amendment right of petition. 365 U.S. at 138, 81 S. Ct. 523. The constitutional freedom "to petition the

Government" carries limited if indeed any applicability to the petitioning of foreign governments.[26] A second basis of *Noerr* is a concern with insuring that, "[i]n a representative democracy such as this," law-making organs retain access to the opinions of their constituents, unhampered by collateral regulation. 365 U.S. at 137, 81 S. Ct. 523, 529. *Noerr* has been held inapplicable to situations in which this relationship has not been deemed threatened.

The persuasion of Middle Eastern states alleged in the present case is a far cry from the political process with which *Noerr* was concerned.

In sum, the interests asserted in this case are dissimilar to those that Noerr was concerned with safeguarding; therefore, the wholesale application of that exception to the Sherman Act appears inappropriate. However, other considerations become prominent when acts of foreign governments are brought to bar—considerations reflecting a prudent allocation of competence between the American judiciary and executive in the field of foreign relations. The act of state doctrine is the relevant and dispositive principle on this motion to dismiss.

In Underhill v. Hernandez, 168 U.S. 250, 252, 18 S. Ct. 83, 84, 42 L. Ed. 456 (1897), the Supreme Court first definitively held that "the courts of one country will not sit in judgment on the acts of the government of another, done within its own territory." This "classic American statement of the act of state doctrine" was reaffirmed by the court most recently in Banco Nacional de Cuba v. Sabbatino, 376 U.S. 398, 416-418, 84 S. Ct. 923, 934, 11 L. Ed. 2d 804 (1964). In the *Sabbatino* case, the bases of the doctrine were at last explicitly elaborated. The act of state doctrine, it was held, is not required by international law. 376 U.S. at 421-422, 84 S. Ct. 923. Nor is it compelled by notions of sovereign authority, although they "do bear upon the wisdom of employing" it. *Id.* Finally, the doctrine is not required by the Constitution. 376 U.S. at 423-424, 84 S. Ct. 923.

> The act of state doctrine does, however, have "constitutional" underpinnings. It arises out of the basic relationships between branches of government in a system of separation of powers. It concerns the competency of dissimilar institutions to make and implement particular kinds of decisions in the area of international relations. The doctrine as formulated in past decisions expresses the strong sense of the Judicial Branch that its engagement in the task of passing on the validity of foreign acts of state may hinder rather than further this country's pursuit of goals both for itself and for the community of nations as a whole in the international sphere. 376 U.S. at 423, 84 S. Ct. at 938.

In sum, the doctrine is a reflection of the executive's primary competency in foreign affairs, and an acknowledgment of the fact that in passing upon foreign governmental acts the judiciary may hinder or embarrass the conduct of our foreign relations. *See* 376 U.S. at 427-428, 431-433, 84 S. Ct. 923.

---

[26]One authority extracts from *Noerr* and *Continental Ore* the notion that the antitrust laws do not apply to petitioning a *democratic* government. P. Areeda, Antitrust Analysis ¶187 & n. 206 (1967). This interpretation, not presently adopted herein, would in any event not cover much of the conduct alleged in the instant complaint.

Consideration of the act of state doctrine's relevance to the present case begins with one of the early act of state cases, American Banana Co. v. United Fruit Co., 160 F. 184 (C.C.S.D.N.Y.) *aff'd,* 166 F. 261 (2nd Cir. 1908), *aff'd* 213 U.S. 347, 29 S. Ct. 511, 53 L. Ed. 826 (1909). The facts of that case are strikingly similar to those now before the court. A private defendant was sued under the Sherman Act for destruction of plaintiff's fledgling banana business in Panama and Costa Rica. The gravamen of the complaint was that the defendant had instigated and procured Costa Rican soldiers to seize and maintain control of plaintiff's plantation and supplies. The trial court dismissed the complaint, stating, "[i]t is impossible to adjudicate this matter without sitting in judgment on the right of Costa Rico [sic] to do what was done . . . this court has no power to sit in judgment on the validity or legality of the act of any sovereign independent nation." 160 F. at 188. The circuit court of appeals affirmed, using the following language:

> Upon principle and authority, it follows that Costa Rica is entitled to immunity from any investigation of its sovereign acts by this court. The plaintiff, however, asserts that this immunity is only an immunity from suit which has no bearing upon the defendant's liability. But, as we have seen, the immunity is far broader than this. The validity of an act adopted by a sovereign state cannot be inquired into at all—directly or collaterally—by the courts of another state. Relief must be sought in the courts of the former state or through diplomatic channels. 166 F. at 266.

On certiorari, the result was the same, Justice Holmes writing:

> The substance of the complaint is that, the plantation being within the de facto jurisdiction of Costa Rica, that state took and keeps possession of it by virtue of its sovereign power. But a seizure by a state is not a thing that can be complained of elsewhere in the courts. . . .

and then citing Underhill v. Hernandez (as had the two lower courts). 213 U.S. at 357-358, 29 S. Ct. at 513.

The significance of the *American Banana* case has been somewhat obscured by virtue of the fact that Justice Holmes's opinion expounds at some length a restrictive view of Sherman Act jurisdiction, based upon the situs of primary conduct. This aspect of the opinion has been distinguished in subsequent international antitrust cases, *e.g.,* United States v. Sisal Sales Corp., 274 U.S. 268, 276, 47 S. Ct. 592, 71 L. Ed. 1042 (1927); Continental Ore Co. v. Union Carbide & Carbon Corp., *supra,* 370 U.S. at 704-705, 82 S. Ct. 1404. But as those two cases intimate, and as other analyses clearly establish, the holding of *American Banana* that has endured is that the act of state doctrine bars a claim for antitrust injury flowing from foreign sovereign acts allegedly induced and procured by the defendant. This holding would appear directly to control the present case.

Plaintiffs say that they do not complain of the acts of foreign states set forth in the complaint, but rather only of defendants' conduct in "catalyzing" those acts. This construction of the case is at odds with plaintiffs' papers in at least two crucial respects. In the first place, plaintiffs have in another phase of this motion dubbed the states involved in the present Persian Gulf controversy as co-conspirators. The implication to be drawn from this allegation is that plaintiffs do question the conduct of those states under the antitrust laws—an inquiry which the act of state doctrine surely bars. Second, the complaint charges that several of Sharjah's acts were violative of international law. This claim, too, is barred from American courts by the act of state doctrine— specifically by the *Sabbatino* decision. *See* 376 U.S. at 428, 430-431, 84 S. Ct. 923, 11 L. Ed. 2d 804. Indeed, this portion of plaintiffs' pleading appears designed expressly to avoid the anticipated effect of the doctrine, by invoking an exception to it, which will be discussed shortly.

There is, moreover, a further dimension to this case's implication of foreign acts of state. Because a private antitrust claim requires proof of damage resulting from forbidden conduct, . . . plaintiffs necessarily ask this court to "sit in judgment" upon the sovereign acts pleaded, whether or not the countries involved are considered co-conspirators. That is, to establish their claim as pleaded plaintiffs must prove, *inter alia,* that Sharjah issued a fraudulent territorial waters decree, and that Iran laid claim to the island of Abu Musa at the behest of the defendants. Plaintiffs say they stand ready to prove the former allegation by use of "internal documents." But such inquiries by this court into the authenticity and motivation of the acts of foreign sovereigns would be the very sources of diplomatic friction and complication that the act of state doctrine aims to avert. *See Sabbatino, supra,* 376 U.S. at 423-424, 431-433, 84 S. Ct. 923. . . .

It thus appears prima facie that the act of state doctrine precludes further adjudication of the present case. Plaintiffs, however, offer several further arguments against this result. They first contend that the doctrine has been sapped of its vitality and rationale by the so-called "Sabbatino Amendment," 22 U.S.C. §2370(e) (2). [The Sabbatino amendment, set forth by the court below, was passed in reaction to the *Sabbatino* case, *supra.* In that case the Supreme Court held that a Cuban expropriation should not be tested against international law standards for expropriation, but should rather be recognized on act of state grounds.]

At issue is the significance of the "Sabbatino Amendment" vis-a-vis the act of state doctrine in general. From the plain wording and history of the legislation, that issue is easy to resolve. The statute prescribes, in relevant part:

> Notwithstanding any other provision of law, no court in the United States shall decline on the ground of the federal act of state doctrine to make a determination on the merits giving effect to the principles of international law in a case in which a claim of title or other right to property is asserted by any party including a foreign state (or a party claiming through such state) based upon (or traced through) a confiscation or other taking after January 1, 1959, by an act of that state in violation of the principles of international law . . . : *Provided,* That

this subparagraph shall not be applicable . . . (2) in any case with respect to which the President determines that application of the act of state doctrine is required in that particular case by the foreign policy interests of the United States and a suggestion to this effect is filed on his behalf in that case with the court. . . .

. . . This pleading is insufficient to invoke the Sabbatino Amendment for several reasons. In the first place, the charge of an attempted confiscation, invalid under international law, has not been directed against the other acts of state—by Sharjah and also by Iran, Umm al Qaywayn, and Great Britain— adjudication of which would form an integral part of plaintiffs' case. Moreover, the portion of the complaint here in issue does not itself fall within the Sabbatino Amendment's ambit, for the simple reason that the complaint refers to an "attempted confiscation," whereas the statute applies only to a "confiscation or other taking." It is clear from a reading of the complaint as a whole that the conduct of Sharjah did not amount to an effective confiscation; rather, plaintiffs were allegedly deprived of the enjoyment of their concession only by the cooperative effect of a number of acts of state, of which Sharjah's claims were not the most efficacious. This is not a situation at which the Sabbatino Amendment was aimed.

Plaintiffs next contend that Sharjah and Umm al Qaywayn do not qualify as "states" under the act of state doctrine, because they have delegated to Britain ultimate authority over their foreign relations. The authority cited by plaintiffs indicates a contrary result. In Carl Zeiss Stiftung v. V.E.B. Carl Zeiss, Jena, 293 F. Supp. 892 (S.D.N.Y.1967), aff'd, 433 F.2d 686 (2nd Cir. 1970), the act of state doctrine was held applicable to Wuerttemberg, one of the constituent states of West Germany. After citing cases that had accorded act of state treatment to similar national subdivisions, the district court noted that Wuerttemberg "has had the power to engage in foreign relations with the consent of the Government of West Germany and has done so. See Article 32, West German Constitution. . . . " 293 F. Supp. at 910; aff'd, 433 F.2d at 703. Under the holding of the Zeiss case and the authority on which it relied, the application of act of state to the Trucial States would appear to follow a fortiori. Previously recognized as independent sovereigns by Britain, the Trucial States acceded supervision over their foreign relations to the latter only by a series of treaties. H. Albaharna, The Legal Status of the Arabian Gulf States 70-74 (1968). While the precise international status of these sheikdoms is at present unique and difficult to characterize, see id. ch. 8, their degree of international personality is obviously greater than that, say, of Wuerttemberg. Bearing in mind especially the foreign affairs roots of the act of state doctrine, the court concludes that the doctrine applies to Sharjah and Umm al Qaywayn.

Nor is this conclusion disturbed, as regards Sharjah, by plaintiffs' assertion that some of the conduct of its Ruler was motivated by "his own personal gain and benefit." Compl. ¶22(c). Jimenez v. Aristeguieta, 311 F.2d 547 (5th Cir.

1962), relied on by plaintiffs, holds only that crimes committed by a chief of state outside or in violation of his official authority are not acts of state. *Id.* at 557-558. Contrariwise, the complaint clearly indicates that the Ruler of Sharjah acted at all times in his official capacity and on behalf of his state. In these circumstances, as the *Jimenez* case itself holds, the act of state doctrine applies. *Id.* at 557.

CONCLUSION

For the reasons elaborated above, the act of state doctrine precludes this court from further adjudication of the instant complaint. The Buttes defendants in their briefs have contended that this defect of the complaint is jurisdictional. But it is clear from Ricaud v. American Metal Co., 246 U.S. 304, 308, 38 S. Ct. 312, 62 L. Ed. 733 (1918), quoted with approval in *Sabbatino,* 376 U.S. at 418, 84 S. Ct. 923, that this is not so; rather, the questioning of sovereign acts by the complaint results in its failure to state a claim upon which relief may be granted. *American Banana, supra,* 166 F. at 267. . . .

The Buttes defendants' motion to dismiss will be granted for failure to state a claim upon which relief may be granted.

NOTES AND QUESTIONS

1. As a policy matter, what is it about the foreign government participation in *Occidental Petroleum* that makes the U.S. court willing to let stand what looks like a severe injustice to the plaintiff? (For the later evolution of this controversy in the United States, *see* Occidental of Umm al-Qaywayn v. A Certain Cargo of Petroleum, 577 F.2d 1196 (5th Cir. 1978), *cert. denied,* 441 U.S. 928 (1979), which resolved essentially the same dispute by saying that any territorial issue posed a political question beyond the competence of a national court.)

2. What about the argument that the defendant did something wrong, even if a foreign government was involved, or as one British lawyer argued: "conspire with the great and plead act of state."? *See* Buttes Gas & Oil v. Hammer, [1975] 1 Q.B. 557, 568, *rev'd on later approval,* [1981] 3 W.L.R. 787. For a U.S. example, *see* Hunt v. Mobil Oil, 550 F.2d 68 (2d Cir. 1977), *cert. denied,* 434 U.S. 984 (1977).

3. Suppose the foreign government gave a firm permission to monopolize a market, but did not direct it to do so. Does that firm have an act of state defense? For a clear negative, *see* Continental Ore v. Union Carbide, 370 U.S. 690 (1962). For an extreme application, *see* Linseman v. World Hockey Assn., 439 F. Supp. 1315 (D. Conn. 1977) (hockey player's effort to contest Canadian-based—but international—league's age restriction upheld on basis that rule was not "compelled" by Canadian government).

4. Suppose the foreign government directed a U.S. firm to conduct an action *in the United States* that would, save for any act of state considerations, violate U.S. antitrust law. Is the firm protected? *See* Interamerican Refining v. Texas Maracaibo, 307 F. Supp. 1291 (D. Del. 1970), *but see* Antitrust Guide, Case K.

5. Should *Noerr-Pennington* protect a firm against a U.S. Department of Justice civil investigation demand to provide communication that it has made to a *foreign* government? For negative answers, *see* Associated Container Transportation (Australia) v. United States, 705 F.2d 53 (2d Cir. 1983); Australia/Eastern U.S.A. Shipping Conf. v. United States, 537 F. Supp. 807 (D.D.C. 1982). For a case going the other way on *Noerr-Pennington*, but in a private treble damage contract, *see* Coastal States Marketing v. Hunt, 694 F.2d 1358 (5th Cir. 1983).

b.   Contemporary Form

To understand the current evolution of the act of state doctrine, it is important to remember that the policy problems of respecting foreign government sensitivities and the State Department's freedom of maneuver in foreign policy come up in a number of other areas. Of relevance here are three contexts: (1) whether to extend the territorial scope of United States law to reach a foreign action (traditionally an issue of territorial jurisdiction), (2) whether to abstain from jurisdiction explicitly out of fear of offending a foreign government (traditionally an act of state issue), and (3) whether to abstain from making a foreign government a defendant (traditionally a sovereign immunity question).

Under *Occidental Petroleum*, the antitrust act of state doctrine appears relatively inflexible and hard-edged. The three contexts of the previous paragraph are also kept rigorously separate. The following case, *Timberlane*, brings a more flexible balancing test to the area, and, to some extent, combines the territorial scope and abstention issues. The case is an extremely important one that has been widely followed in the antitrust area and also in other areas like trademark law in which different nations may impose conflicting rules.

At the same time that *Timberlane* was changing the act of state doctrine, Congress was changing the sovereign immunity area, through the Foreign Sovereign Immunities Act of 1976, P.L. 94-583, 90 Stat. 2891 (1976), 28 U.S.C. §§1602 et seq. (Supp. IV 1981), which made it clear that suits against foreign governments were authorized when those governments were acting in a commercial context. The *IAM* case, the next major case after *Timberlane*, shows a court struggling with this evolving structure in a situation—suit against the OPEC cartel—in which many of the economic arguments and some of the formal legal arguments favored jurisdiction, but in which such an exercise of jurisdiction would have been extremely sensitive politically. The court rested its decision on the political question doctrine—and it is conceivable that such a political question doctrine will, along with a *Timberlane* balancing test, ultimately replace the antitrust act of state doctrine.

TIMBERLANE LUMBER CO. v. BANK OF AMERICA

549 F.2d 597 (9th Cir. 1976)

Сноу, J.

Four separate actions, arising from the same series of events, were dismissed by the same district court and are consolidated here on appeal. The principal action is Timberlane Lumber Co. v. Bank of America (Timberlane action), an antitrust suit alleging violations of sections 1 and 2 of the Sherman Act (15 U.S.C. §§1, 2) and the Wilson Tariff Act (15 U.S.C. §8). This action raises important questions concerning the application of American antitrust laws to activities in another country, including actions of foreign government officials. The district court dismissed the Timberlane action under the act of state doctrine and for lack of subject matter jurisdiction. The other three are diversity tort suits brought by employees of one of the Timberlane plaintiffs for individual injuries allegedly suffered in the course of the extended anti-Timberlane drama. Having dismissed the Timberlane action, the district court dismissed these three suits on the ground of forum non conveniens. We vacate the dismissals of all four actions and remand.

I.   THE TIMBERLANE ACTION

The basic allegation of the Timberlane plaintiffs is that officials of the Bank of America and others located in both the United States and Honduras conspired to prevent Timberlane, through its Honduras subsidiaries, from milling lumber in Honduras and exporting it to the United States, thus maintaining control of the Honduran lumber export business in the hands of a few select individuals financed and controlled by the Bank. The intent and result of the conspiracy, they contend, was to interfere with the exportation to the United States, including Puerto Rico, of Honduran lumber for sale or use there by the plaintiffs, thus directly and substantially affecting the foreign commerce of the United States.

PROCEDURAL BACKGROUND

Some of the defendants moved to dismiss the Timberlane action. After a hearing and the submission of memoranda, affidavits, and depositions by both sides, the district court granted the motion in a brief judgment entered on March 20, 1974. The court gave as its reason "that it is prohibited under the act of state doctrine from examining the acts of a foreign sovereign state; and in any event, that there is no direct and substantial effect on United States foreign commerce," the latter apparently being deemed a prerequisite for jurisdiction. No specific findings of fact were announced, nor were any more extensive conclusions of law stated.

CAST OF CHARACTERS

There are three affiliated plaintiffs in the Timberlane action. Timberlane Lumber Company is an Oregon partnership principally involved in the purchase and distribution of lumber at wholesale in the United States and the importation of lumber into the United States for sale and use. Danli Industrial, S.A., and Maya Lumber Company, S. de R.L., are both Honduras corporations, incorporated and principally owned by the general partners of Timberlane. Danli held contracts to purchase timber in Honduras, and Maya was to conduct the milling operations to produce the lumber for export. (Timberlane, Danli, and Maya will be collectively referred to as "Timberlane.") . . .

FACTS AS ALLEGED

The conspiracy sketched by Timberlane actually started before the plaintiffs entered the scene. The Lima family operated a lumber mill in Honduras, competing with Lamas and Casanova, in both of which the Bank had significant financial interests. The Lima enterprise was also indebted to the Bank. By 1971, however, the Lima business was in financial trouble. Timberlane alleges that driving Lima under was the first step in the conspiracy which eventually crippled Timberlane's efforts, but the particulars do not matter for this appeal. What does matter is that various interests in the Lima assets, including its milling plant, passed to Lima's creditors: Casanova, the Bank, and the group of Lima employees who had not been paid the wages and severance pay due them. Under Honduran law, the employees' claim had priority.

   Enter Timberlane, with a long history in the lumber business, in search of alternative sources of lumber for delivery to its distribution system on the East Coast of the United States. After study, it decided to try Honduras. In 1971, Danli was formed, tracts of forest land were acquired, plans for a modern log-processing plant were prepared, and equipment was purchased and assembled for shipment from the United States to Danli in Honduras. Timberlane became aware that the Lima plant might be available and began negotiating for its acquisition. Maya was formed, purchased the Lima employees' interest in the machinery and equipment in January 1972, despite opposition from the conspirators, and re-activated the Lima mill.

   Realizing that they were faced with better-financed and more vigorous competition from Timberlane and its Honduran subsidiaries, the defendants and others extended the anti-Lima conspiracy to disrupt Timberlane's efforts. The primary weapons employed by the conspirators were the claim still held by the Bank in the remaining assets of the Lima enterprise under the all-inclusive mortgage Lima had been forced to sign and another claim held by Casanova. Maya made a substantial cash offer for the Bank's interest in an effort to clear its title, but the Bank refused to sell. Instead, the Bank surreptitiously conveyed the mortgage to Casanova for questionable consideration, Casanova paying nothing and agreeing only to pay the Bank a portion of what it collected. Casanova immediately assigned the Bank's claim and its own on similar terms to Caminals, who promptly set out to disrupt the Timberlane operation.

Caminals is characterized as the "front man" in the campaign to drive Timberlane out of Honduras, with the Bank and other defendants intending and carrying responsibility for his actions. Having acquired the claims of Casanova and the Bank, Caminals went to court to enforce them, ignoring throughout Timberlane's offers to purchase or settle them. Under the laws of Honduras, an "embargo" on property is a court-ordered attachment, registered with the Public Registry, which precludes the sale of that property without a court order. Honduran law provides, upon embargo, that the court appoint a judicial officer, called an "intervenor" to ensure against any diminution in the value of the property. In order to paralyze the Timberlane operation, Caminals obtained embargoes against Maya and Danli. Acting through the intervenor, since accused of being on the payroll of the Bank, guards and troops were used to cripple and, for a time, completely shut down Timberlane's milling operation. The harassment took other forms as well: the conspirators caused the manager of Timberlane's Honduras operations, Gordon Sloan Smith, to be falsely arrested and imprisoned and were responsible for the publication of several defamatory articles about Timberlane in the Honduran press.

As a result of the conspiracy, Timberlane's complaint claimed damages then estimated in excess of $5,000,000. Plaintiffs also allege that there has been a direct and substantial effect on United States foreign commerce, and that defendants intended the results of the conspiracy, including the impact on United States commerce. . . .

The defendants argue—as the district court apparently held—that the injuries allegedly suffered by Timberlane resulted from acts of the Honduran government, principally in connection with the enforcement of the security interests in the Maya plant, which American courts cannot review. Such an application of the act of state doctrine seems to us to be erroneous. Even if the *coup de grace* to Timberlane's enterprise in Honduras was applied by official authorities, we do not agree that the doctrine necessarily shelters these defendants or requires dismissal of the Timberlane action.

The leading modern statement of the act of state doctrine appears in Banco Nacional de Cuba v. Sabbatino, 376 U.S. 398, 84 S. Ct. 923, 11 L. Ed. 2d 804 (1964). Despite contrary implications in *Underhill* and *American Banana,* the Court concluded that the doctrine was not compelled by the nature of sovereignty, by international law, or by the text of the Constitution. 376 U.S. at

421-23, 84 S. Ct. 923. Rather, it derives from the judiciary's concern for its possible interference with the conduct of foreign affairs by the political branches of the government:

> The doctrine as formulated in past decisions expresses the strong sense of the Judicial Branch that its engagement in the task of passing on the validity of foreign acts of state may hinder rather than further this country's pursuit of goals both for itself and for the community of nations as a whole in the international sphere.

Id. at 423, 84 S. Ct. at 938. The Court recognized that not every case is identical in its potential impact on our relations with other nations. For instance:

> [S]ome aspects of international law touch much more sharply on national nerves than do others; the less important the implications of an issue are for our foreign relations, the weaker the justification for exclusivity in the political branches.

Id. at 428, 84 S. Ct. at 940. Thus the Court explicitly rejected "laying down or reaffirming an inflexible and all-encompassing rule." *Id.* Whether forbearance by an American court in a given situation is advisable or appropriate depends upon the "balance of relevant considerations." *Id. . . .*

The touchstone of *Sabbatino*—the potential for interference with our foreign relations—is the crucial element in determining whether deference should be accorded in any given case. We wish to avoid "passing on the validity" of foreign acts. *Sabbatino,* 376 U.S. at 423, 84 S. Ct. 923. Similarly, we do not wish to challenge the sovereignty of another nation, the wisdom of its policy, or the integrity and motivation of its action. On the other hand, repeating the terms of *Sabbatino, id.* at 428, 84 S. Ct. at 940, "the less important the implications of an issue are for our foreign relations, the weaker the justification for exclusivity in the political branches."

While we do not wish to impugn or question the nobility of a foreign nation's motivation, we are necessarily interested in the depth and nature of its interest. The Restatement (Second) of Foreign Relations Law of the United States §41 (1965) makes an important distinction on this basis in limiting the deference of American courts:

> [A] court in the United States . . . will refrain from examining the validity of an act of a foreign state by which that state has exercised its jurisdiction *to give effect to its public interests.* [Emphasis added.]

The "public interest" qualification is intentional and significant in the context of Timberlane's action, as a comment to §41 makes plain:

> *Comment d. Nature of act of state.* An "act of state" as the term is used in this Title involves the public interests of a state as a state, as distinct from its interest in

providing the means of adjudicating disputes or claims that arise within its territory. . . . A judgment of a court may be an act of state. Usually it is not, because it involves the interests of private litigants or because court adjudication is not the usual way in which the state exercises its jurisdiction to give effect to public interests.

Id. at 127.

On the basis of the foregoing analysis, we conclude that the court below erred in dismissing the instant suit on the authority of Occidental Petroleum Corp. v. Buttes Gas & Oil Co., 331 F. Supp. 92, 108-13 (C.D. Cal. 1971), *aff'd,* 461 F.2d 1261 (9th Cir.), *cert. denied,* 409 U.S. 950, 93 S. Ct. 272, 34 L. Ed. 2d 221 (1972). The actions of the Honduran government that are involved here— including the application by its courts and their agents of the Honduran laws concerning security interests and the protection of the underlying property against diminution—are clearly distinguishable from the sovereign decrees laying claim to off-shore waters that were at issue in *Occidental Petroleum, see* 331 F. Supp. at 99-101 & n.11. Here, the allegedly "sovereign" acts of Honduras consisted of judicial proceedings which were initiated by Caminals, a private party and one of the alleged co-conspirators, not by the Honduran government itself. Unlike the *Occidental Petroleum* plaintiffs, *see id.* at 110, Timberlane does not seek to name Honduras or any Honduran officer as a defendant or co-conspirator, nor does it challenge Honduran policy or sovereignty in any fashion that appears on its face to hold any threat to relations between Honduras and the United States. In fact, there is no indication that the actions of the Honduran court and authorities reflected a sovereign decision that Timberlane's efforts should be crippled or that trade with the United States should be restrained. *Compare* Alfred Dunhill of London, Inc. v. The Republic of Cuba, 425 U.S. at 695, 96 S. Ct. 1854. Moreover, and once again unlike the situation in *Occidental Petroleum, see* 331 F. Supp. at 109-10 n.28, plaintiffs here apparently complain of additional agreements and actions which are totally unrelated to the Honduran government. These separate activities would clearly be unprotected even if procurement of a Honduran act of state were one part of defendants' overall scheme. Continental Ore Co. v. Union Carbide & Carbon Corp., 370 U.S. at 704-05, 82 S. Ct. 1404; United States v. Sisal, 274 U.S. at 275-76, 47 S. Ct. 592.

Under these circumstances, it is clear that the "act of state" doctrine does not require dismissal of the Timberlane action.

EXTRATERRITORIAL REACH OF THE UNITED STATES ANTITRUST LAWS

There is no doubt that American antitrust laws extend over some conduct in other nations. There was language in the first Supreme Court case in point, American Banana Co. v. United Fruit Co., 213 U.S. 347, 29 S. Ct. 511, 53 L. Ed. 826 (1909), casting doubt on the extension of the Sherman Act to acts outside United States territory. But subsequent cases have limited *American Banana* to its particular facts, and the Sherman Act—and with it other antitrust laws—has been applied to extraterritorial conduct. *See, e.g.,* Continental Ore Co. v. Union Carbide & Carbon Corp., 370 U.S. 690, 82 S. Ct. 1404, 8 L. Ed. 2d 777 (1962); United States v. Sisal Sales Corp., 274 U.S. 268, 47 S. Ct. 592, 71 L. Ed. 1042 (1927); United States v. Aluminum Co. of America, 148 F.2d 416, (2d Cir. 1945) (the *"Alcoa"* case). The act may encompass the foreign activities of aliens as well as American citizens. *Alcoa, supra;* Swiss Watch, 1963 Trade Cases ¶70,600; United States v. General Electric Co., 82 F. Supp. 753 (D.N.J. 1949), *judgment implementing decree,* 115 F. Supp. 835 (D.N.J. 1953).

That American law covers some conduct beyond this nation's borders does not mean that it embraces all, however. Extraterritorial application is understandably a matter of concern for the other countries involved. Those nations have sometimes resented and protested, as excessive intrusions into their own spheres, broad assertions of authority by American courts. *See* A. Neale, The Antitrust Laws of the United States of America 365-72 (2d ed. 1970); Assn. of the Bar of the City of New York, National Security and Foreign Policy in the Application of American Antitrust Laws to Commerce with Foreign Nations 7-18 (1957); Zwarensteyn, The Foreign Reach of the American Antitrust Laws, 3 Am. Bus. L.J. 163, 165-69 (1965). Our courts have recognized this concern and have, at times, responded to it, even if not always enough to satisfy all the foreign critics. *See Alcoa,* 148 F.2d at 443; Swiss Watch, 1965 Trade Cases ¶71,352 (modification of order); General Electric, 115 F. Supp. at 878 (implementation of decree). In any event, it is evident that at some point the interests of the United States are too weak and the foreign harmony incentive for restraint too strong to justify an extraterritorial assertion of jurisdiction.

What that point is or how it is determined is not defined by international law. Miller, Extraterritorial Effects of Trade Regulation, 111 U. Pa. L. Rev. 1092, 1094 (1963). Nor does the Sherman Act limit itself. In the domestic field the Sherman Act extends to the full reach of the commerce power. United States v. South-Eastern Underwriters Assn., 322 U.S. 533, 558, 64 S. Ct. 1162, 88 L. Ed. 1440 (1944). To define it somewhat more modestly in the foreign commerce area courts have generally, and logically, fallen back on a narrower construction of congressional intent, such as expressed in Judge Learned Hand's oft-cited opinion in *Alcoa,* 148 F.2d at 443:

> [T]he only question open is whether Congress intended to impose the liability and whether our own Constitution permitted it to do so: as a court of the United States we cannot look beyond our own law. Nevertheless, it is quite true that we are not to read general words, such as those in this Act, without regard to the limitations customarily observed by nations upon the exercise of their powers; limitations which generally correspond to those fixed by the "Conflict of Laws." We should not impute to Congress an intent to punish all whom its courts can catch, for conduct which has no consequences within the United States.

It is the effect on American foreign commerce which is usually cited to support extraterritorial jurisdiction. *Alcoa* set the course, when Judge Hand declared, *id.*:

> [I]t is settled law . . . that any state may impose liabilities, even upon persons not within its allegiance, for conduct outside its borders that has consequences within its borders which the state reprehends; and these liabilities other states will ordinarily recognize.

Despite its description as "settled law," *Alcoa's* assertion has been roundly disputed by many foreign commentators as being in conflict with international law, comity, and good judgment. Nonetheless, American courts have firmly concluded that there is some extraterritorial jurisdiction under the Sherman Act.

Even among American courts and commentators, however, there is no consensus on how far the jurisdiction should extend. The district court here concluded that a "direct and substantial effect" on United States foreign commerce was a prerequisite, without stating whether other factors were relevant or considered. The same formula was employed, to some extent, by the district courts in the *Swiss Watch* case, 1963 Trade Cases ¶70,600, in United States v. R. P. Oldham Co., 152 F. Supp. 818, 822 (N.D. Cal. 1957), and in *General Electric,* 82 F. Supp. at 891. It has been identified and advocated by several commentators. *See, e.g.,* W. Fugate, Foreign Commerce and the Antitrust Laws 30, 174 (2d ed. 1973); J. Van Cise, Understanding the Antitrust Laws 204 (1973 ed.). *See also* Report of the Attorney General's National Committee to Study the Antitrust Laws 76 (1955) ("substantial anticompetitive effects"); Restatement (Second) of Foreign Relations Law of the United States §18.[18]

Other courts have used different expressions, however. *See, e.g.,* Thomsen v. Cayser, 243 U.S. 66, 88, 37 S. Ct. 353, 360, 61 L. Ed. 597 (1917) ("the combination affected the foreign commerce of this country"); *Alcoa,* 148 F.2d at 444 ("intended to affect imports and exports [and] . . . is shown actually to

---

[18] Restatement §18 reads:

A state has jurisdiction to prescribe a rule of law attaching legal consequences to conduct that occurs outside its territory and causes an effect within its territory, if either

(a) the conduct and its effect are generally recognized as constituent elements of a crime or tort under the law of states that have reasonably developed legal systems, or

(b)(i) the conduct and its effect are constituent elements of activity to which the rule applies; (ii) the effect within the territory is substantial; (iii) it occurs as a direct and foreseeable result of the conduct outside the territory; and (iv) the rule is not inconsistent with the principles of justice generally recognized by states that have reasonably developed legal systems.

The "direct" and "substantial" requirements come from (b)(ii) and (iii). Comment *a* to this section specifically indicates, however, that this rule applies only to aliens, since United States citizens may be bound by nationality, and govern only where there has been no significant conduct within the United States, since otherwise territorial jurisdiction could be asserted. The proposed section of the new §402 printed above at pp. 563-564 will replace Restatement §18.

have had some effect on them"); United States v. Imperial Chemical Industries, Ltd., 100 F. Supp. 504, 592 (S.D.N.Y. 1951) ("a conspiracy . . . which
affects American commerce"); United States v. Timken Roller Bearing Co.,
83 F. Supp. 284, 309 (N.D. Ohio 1949), *modified and affirmed,* 341 U.S. 593, 71
S. Ct. 971, 95 L. Ed. 1199 (1951) ("a direct and influencing effect on trade").
See also citations in 1 J. von Kalinowski, Antitrust Law and Trade Regulation
§5.02[2], at 5-120.

Different standards have been urged by other commentators. Julian von
Kalinowski, *id.* at 5-122, advocates a "direct *or* substantial" effect test—"any
effect that is not *both* insubstantial and indirect" should support jurisdiction, a
view that was adopted by the district court in Occidental Petroleum v. Buttes
Gas & Oil Co., 331 F. Supp. 92, 102-03 (C.D. Cal. 1971), *affirmed on other
grounds,* 461 F.2d 1261 (9th Cir.), *cert. denied,* 409 U.S. 950, 93 S. Ct. 272, 34 L.
Ed. 2d 221 (1972). James Rahl turns away from a flat requirement of effects
by concluding that the Sherman Act should reach a restraint either "(1) if it
occurs *in the course of* foreign commerce, *or* (2) if it *substantially affects* either
foreign or interstate commerce." Rahl, Foreign Commerce Jurisdiction of the
American Antitrust Laws, 43 Antitrust L.J. 521, 523 (1974). In essence, as
Dean Rahl observes, "[t]here is no agreed black-letter rule articulating the
Sherman Act's commerce coverage" in the international context. *Id.*

Few cases have discussed the nature of the effect required for jurisdiction,
perhaps because most of the litigated cases have involved relatively obvious
offenses and rather significant and apparent effects on competition within the
United States. *Id.*; P. Areeda, Antitrust Analysis 129 n.455 (1974). It is probably in part because the standard has not often been put to a real test that it
seems so poorly defined. William Fugate, who has identified the "direct and
substantial" standard as the rule, has described the meaning of that phrase as
being "quite broad." W. Fugate, *supra,* at 174. What the threshold of significance is, however, has not been identified. Nor is it quite clear what the
"direct-indirect" distinction is supposed to mean. It might well be, as was said
in the context of transnational securities regulation:

> Although courts have spoken in terms of the *Restatement* and of congressional
> policy, findings that an American effect was direct, substantial, and foreseeable,
> or within the scope of congressional intent, have little independent analytic sig-
> nificance. Instead, cases appear to turn on a reconciliation of American and
> foreign interests in regulating their respective economies and business affairs. . . .

Note, American Adjudication of Transnational Securities Fraud, 89 Harv. L.
Rev. 553, 563 (1976).

Implicit in that observation, as it is in several of the cases and commentaries
employing the "effects" test, is the suggestion that factors other than simply
the effect on the United States are weighed, and rightly so. As former Attorney
General (then Professor) Katzenbach observed, the effect on American commerce is not, by itself, sufficient information on which to base a decision that

the United States is the nation primarily interested in the activity causing the effect. "[A]nything that affects the external trade and commerce of the United States also affects the trade and commerce of other nations, and may have far greater consequences for other than for the United States." Katzenbach, Conflicts on an Unruly Horse, 65 Yale L.J. 1087, 1150 (1956).

The effects test by itself is incomplete because it fails to consider other nations' interests. Nor does it expressly take into account the full nature of the relationship between the actors and this country. Whether the alleged offender is an American citizen, for instance, may make a big difference; applying American laws to American citizens raises fewer problems than application to foreigners. As was observed in Pacific Seafarers, Inc. v. Pacific Far East Line, Inc., 131 U.S. App. D.C. 226, 404 F.2d 804, 815 (1968), *cert. denied*, 393 U.S. 1093, 89 S. Ct. 872, 21 L. Ed. 2d 784 (1969):

> If . . . [American antitrust] policy cannot extend to the full sweep of American foreign commerce because of the international complications involved, then surely the test which determines whether United States law is applicable must focus on the nexus between the parties and their practices and the United States, not on the mechanical circumstances of effect on commodity exports or imports.

American courts have, in fact, often displayed a regard for comity and the prerogatives of other nations and considered their interests as well as other parts of the factual circumstances, even when professing to apply an effects test. To some degree, the requirement for a "substantial" effect may silently incorporate these additional considerations, with "substantial" as a flexible standard that varies with other factors. The intent requirement suggested by *Alcoa*, 148 F.2d at 443-44, is one example of an attempt to broaden the court's perspective, as is drawing a distinction between American citizens and non-citizens.

The failure to articulate these other elements in addition to the standard effects analysis is costly, however, for it is more likely that they will be overlooked or slighted in interpretating past decisions and reaching new ones. Placing emphasis on the qualification that effects be "substantial" is also risky, for the term has a meaning in the interstate antitrust context which does not encompass all the factors relevant to the foreign trade case.

A tripartite analysis seems to be indicated. As acknowledged above, the antitrust laws require in the first instance that there be *some* effect—actual or intended—on American foreign commerce before the federal courts may legitimately exercise subject matter jurisdiction under those statutes. Second, a greater showing of burden or restraint may be necessary to demonstrate that the effect is sufficiently large to present a cognizable injury to the plaintiffs and, therefore, a civil *violation* of the antitrust laws. *Occidental Petroleum*, 331 F. Supp. at 102-03; Beausang, The Extraterritorial Jurisdiction of the Sherman Act, 70 Dick. L. Rev. 187, 191 (1966). Third, there is the additional question which is unique to the international setting of whether the interests of, and links to, the United States—including the magnitude of the effect on American foreign commerce—are sufficiently strong, vis-á-vis those of other nations, to justify an assertion of extraterritorial authority.

It is this final issue which is both obscured by undue reliance on the "substantiality" test and complicated to resolve. An effect on United States commerce, although necessary to the exercise of jurisdiction under the antitrust laws, is alone not a sufficient basis on which to determine whether American authority *should* be asserted in a given case as a matter of international comity and fairness. In some cases, the application of the direct and substantial test in the international context might open the door too widely by sanctioning jurisdiction over an action when these considerations would indicate dismissal. At other times, it may fail in the other direction, dismissing a case for which comity and fairness do not require forebearance, thus closing the jurisdictional door too tightly—for the Sherman Act does reach some restraints which do not have both a direct and substantial effect on the foreign commerce of the United States. A more comprehensive inquiry is necessary. We believe that the field of conflict of laws presents the proper approach, as was suggested, if not specifically employed, in *Alcoa* in expressing the basic limitation on application of American laws:

> [W]e are not to read general words, such as those in this Act, without regard to the limitations customarily observed by nations upon the exercise of their powers; limitations which generally correspond to those fixed by the "Conflict of Laws."

148 F.2d at 443. The same idea is reflected in Restatement (Second) of Foreign Relations Law of the United States §40:

> Where two states have jurisdiction to prescribe and enforce rules of law and the rules they may prescribe require inconsistent conduct upon the part of a person, each state is required by international law to consider, in good faith, moderating the exercise of its enforcement jurisdiction. . . .

The act of state doctrine discussed earlier demonstrates that the judiciary is sometimes cognizant of the possible foreign implications of its action. Similar awareness should be extended to the general problems of extraterritoriality. Such acuity is especially required in private suits, like this one, for in these cases there is no opportunity for the executive branch to weigh the foreign relations impact, nor any statement implicit in the filing of the suit that that consideration has been outweighed.

What we prefer is an evaluation and balancing of the relevant considerations in each case—in the words of Kingman Brewster, a "jurisdictional rule of reason." . . .

The elements to be weighed include the degree of conflict with foreign law or policy, the nationality or allegiance of the parties and the locations or principal places of business of corporations, the extent to which enforcement by either state can be expected to achieve compliance, the relative significance of effects on the United States as compared with those elsewhere, the extent to which there is explicit purpose to harm or affect American commerce, the foreseeability of such effect, and the relative importance to the violations charged of conduct within the United States as compared with conduct abroad.[31] A court evaluating these factors should identify the potential degree of conflict if American authority is asserted. A difference in law or policy is one likely sore spot, though one which may not always be present. Nationality is another; though foreign governments may have some concern for the treatment of American citizens and business residing there, they primarily care about their own nationals. Having assessed the conflict, the court should then determine whether in the face of it the contacts and interests of the United States are sufficient to support the exercise of extraterritorial jurisdiction.[34]

We conclude, then, that the problem should be approached in three parts: Does the alleged restraint affect, or was it intended to affect, the foreign commerce of the United States? Is it of such a type and magnitude so as to be cognizable as a violation of the Sherman Act? As a matter of international comity and fairness, should the extraterritorial jurisdiction of the United States

---

[31] Restatement (Second) of Foreign Relations Law of the United States §40 states that a court should act

> in the light of such factors as
> (a) vital national interests of each of the states,
> (b) the extent and the nature of the hardship that inconsistent enforcement actions would impose upon the person,
> (c) the extent to which the required conduct is to take place in the territory of the other state,
> (d) the nationality of the person, and
> (e) the extent to which enforcement by action of either state can reasonably be expected to achieve compliance with the rule prescribed by that state.

President (then Professor) Brewster lists these variables:

> (a) the relative significance to the violations charged of conduct within the United States as compared with conduct abroad; (b) the extent to which there is explicit purpose to harm or affect American consumers or Americans' business opportunities; (c) the relative seriousness of effects on the United States compared with those abroad; (d) the nationality or allegiance of the parties or in the case of business associations, their corporate location, and the fairness of applying our law to them; (e) the degree of conflict with foreign laws and policies, and (f) the extent to which conflict can be avoided without serious impairment of the interests of the United States or the foreign country. K. Brewster, [Antitrust and American Business Abroad (1958)] at 446.

[34] In requiring district courts to assess the conflicting contacts and interests of those nations involved, we do not thereby assign them the same task which the "act of state" doctrine prohibits them from undertaking. As . . . *comment d.* to §41 of the Restatement, Second, Foreign Relations Law of the United States (1963) . . . makes clear, there is an important distinction between examining the validity of the "public interests" which are involved in a sovereign policy decision amounting to an "act of state" and evaluating the relative "interests" which each state may have "in providing the means of adjudicating disputes or claims that arise within its territory." Our "jurisdictional rule of reason" does not in any way require the court to question the "validity" of "foreign law or policy." Rather, the legitimacy of each nation's interests is assumed. It is merely the relative involvement and concern of each state with the suit at hand that is to be evaluated in determining whether extraterritorial jurisdiction should be exercised by American courts as a matter of comity and fairness.

be asserted to cover it? The district court's judgment found only that the restraint involved in the instant suit did not produce a direct and substantial effect on American foreign commerce. That holding does not satisfy any of these inquiries. . . .

We, therefore, vacate the dismissal and remand the Timberlane action. . . .

The balancing factors for extraterritorial jurisdiction are listed in more detail in Mannington Mills v. Congoleum Corp., 595 F.2d 1287 at 1297-1298 (3d Cir. 1979):

    1. Degree of conflict with foreign law or policy;

    2. Nationality of the parties;

    3. Relative importance of the alleged violation of conduct in this country compared to that abroad;

    4. Availability of a remedy abroad and the pendency of litigation there;

    5. Existence of intent to harm or affect American commerce and its foreseeability;

    6. Possible effect upon foreign relations if the court exercises jurisdiction and grants relief;

    7. If relief is granted, whether a party will be placed in the dilemma of being forced to perform an act illegal in either country or being under conflicting requirements by both countries;

    8. Whether the court can make its order effective;

    9. Whether an order for relief would be acceptable in this country if made by the foreign nation under similar circumstances;

    10. Whether a treaty with the affected nations has addressed the issue.

INTERNATIONAL ASSOCIATION OF MACHINISTS AND AEROSPACE WORKERS (IAM) v. ORGANIZATION OF PETROLEUM EXPORTING COUNTRIES (OPEC)

649 F.2d 1354 (9th Cir. 1981)

Choy, J.

I. Introduction

The members of the International Association of Machinists and Aerospace Workers (IAM) were disturbed by the high price of oil and petroleum-derived products in the United States. They believed the actions of the Organization of the Petroleum Exporting Countries, popularly known as OPEC, were the cause of this burden on the American public. Accordingly, IAM sued OPEC and its member nations in December of 1978, alleging that their price-setting activities violated United States anti-trust laws. IAM sought injunctive relief and damages. The district court entered a final judgment in favor of the defendants, holding that it lacked jurisdiction and that IAM had no valid anti-trust claim. We affirm the judgment of the district court on the alternate ground that, under the act of state doctrine, exercise of federal court jurisdiction in this case would be improper. . . .

The defendants refused to recognize the jurisdiction of the district court, and they did not appear in the proceedings below. Their cause was argued by various amici, with additional information provided by court-appointed experts. The district court ordered a full hearing, noting that the Foreign Sovereign Immunities Act (FSIA) prohibits the entry of a default judgment against a foreign sovereignty "unless the claimant establishes his claim or right to relief by evidence satisfactory to the court." 28 U.S.C. §1608(e). . . .

At the close of the trial, the district judge granted judgment in favor of the defendants. The court held, first, that it lacked jurisdiction over the defendant nations under the Foreign Sovereign Immunities Act.

The court further held that even if jurisdiction existed in the first instance, the antitrust action failed because foreign sovereigns are not persons within the meaning of the Sherman Act and because there was no proximate causal connection between OPEC activities and domestic price increases. The court also decided that default judgment could not properly lie against the non-appearing defendants, and that the defendants had not waived their immunity. . . .

III. DISCUSSION

A. SOVEREIGN IMMUNITY

In the international sphere each state is viewed as an independent sovereign, equal in sovereignty to all other states. It is said that an equal holds no power of sovereignty over an equal. Thus the doctrine of sovereign immunity: the courts of one state generally have no jurisdiction to entertain suits against another state. This rule of international law developed by custom among nations. Also by custom, an exception developed for the commercial activities of a state. The former concept of absolute sovereign immunity gave way to a restrictive view. Under the restrictive theory of sovereign immunity, immunity did not exist for commercial activities since they were seen as non-sovereign.

In 1976, Congress enacted the FSIA and declared that the federal courts will apply an objective nature-of-the-act test[6] in determining whether activity is commercial and thus not immune: "The commercial character of an activity shall be determined by reference to the nature of the course of conduct or particular transaction or act, rather than by reference to its purpose." 28 U.S.C. §1603(d).

---

[6]The categorization of activity as commercial or non-commercial is a source of controversy. Two different tests arose to determine the character of state activity. One focused on the *purpose* of the activity, the other on the *nature* of the activity. The purpose test, which asks whether the act in

A critical step in characterizing the nature of a given activity is defining exactly what that activity is. The immunity question may be determined by how broadly or narrowly that activity is defined. In this case, IAM insists on a very narrow focus on the specific activity of "price fixing." IAM argues that the FSIA does not give immunity to this activity. Under the FSIA a commercial activity is one which an individual might "customarily carr[y] on for profit." H.R. Rep. No. 94-1487, 94th Cong., 2d Sess. 16, *reprinted in* [1976] U.S. Code Cong. & Ad. News 6604, 6615. OPEC's activity, characterized by IAM as making agreements to fix prices, is one which is presumably done for profit; it is thus commercial and immunity does not apply.

The Court below defined OPEC's activity in a different way: "[I]t is clear that the nature of the activity engaged in by each of these OPEC member countries is the establishment by a sovereign state of the terms and conditions for the removal of a prime natural resource—to wit, crude oil—from its territory." 477 F. Supp. at 567. The trial judge reasoned that, according to international law, the development and control of natural resources is a prime governmental function. *Id.* at 567-78. The opinion cites several resolutions of the United Nations' General Assembly, which the United States supported, and the United States Constitution, Art. 4, §3, cl.2, which treat the control of natural resources as governmental acts.

IAM argues that the district court's analysis strays from the path set forth in the FSIA. The control of natural resources is the purpose behind OPEC's actions, but the act complained of here is a conspiracy to fix prices. The FSIA instructs us to look upon the act itself rather than underlying sovereign motivations.

The district court was understandably troubled by the broader implications of an anti-trust action against the OPEC nations. The importance of the alleged price-fixing activity to the OPEC nations cannot be ignored. Oil revenues represent their only significant source of income. Consideration of their sovereignty cannot be separated from their near total dependence upon oil. We find that these concerns are appropriately addressed by application of the act of state doctrine. While we do not apply the doctrine of sovereign immunity, its elements remain relevant to our discussion of the act of state doctrine.

B.   THE ACT OF STATE DOCTRINE . . .

It has been suggested that the FSIA supersedes the act of state doctrine, or that the amorphous doctrine is limited by modern jurisprudence. We disagree.

---

question was undertaken for sovereign ends, is subjective. The nature test, which focuses on the nature of the act itself, is objective. The purpose test grants broader immunity, since even the most commercial activity could have an underlying governmental purpose. For example, the purchase of furniture is objectively a commercial act. If the furniture is purchased for a state's embassy, however, under the purpose test, the act is sovereign and immunity applies. The problem with the purpose test is that the expectations of the furniture seller relying on the commercial appearance of the activity would be frustrated if the foreign government could claim immunity and disclaim its obligation to pay. Only the objective test would protect the seller's reliance on the nature and appearance of the purchase as commercial activity subject to domestic laws.

Congress in enacting the FSIA recognized the distinction between sovereign immunity and the act of state doctrine. *See, e.g.,* H.R. Rep. No. 94-1487, 94th Cong., 2d Sess. 20 n.1, *reprinted in* [1976] U.S. Code Cong. & Ad. News 6619 n.1 ("The Committee has found it unnecessary to address the act of state doctrine in this legislation"); *see generally* Jurisdiction of U.S. Courts in Suits Against Foreign States: Hearings on H.R. 11315 Before the Subcomm. on Admin. Law and Governmental Relations of the House Comm. on the Judiciary, 94th Cong., 2d Sess. 29-57 (1976); Immunities of Foreign States; Hearings on H.R. 3493 Before the Subcomm. on Claims & Governmental Relations of the Committee on the Judiciary, 93d Cong., 1st Sess. 20 (1973) (the FSIA "in no way affects existing law concerning the extent to which the 'act of state' doctrine may be applicable in similar circumstances"). Indeed, because the act of state doctrine addresses concerns central to our system of government, the doctrine must necessarily remain a part of our jurisprudence unless and until such time as a radical change in the role of the courts occurs.

The act of state doctrine is not diluted by the commercial activity exception which limits the doctrine of sovereign immunity. While purely commercial activity may not rise to the level of an act of state, certain seemingly commercial activity will trigger act of state considerations. As the district court noted, OPEC's "price-fixing" activity has a significant sovereign component. While the FSIA ignores the underlying purpose of a state's action, the act of state doctrine does not. This court has stated that the motivations of the sovereign must be examined for a public interest basis. *Timberlane,* 549 F.2d at 607. When the state *qua state* acts in the public interest, its sovereignty is asserted. The courts must proceed cautiously to avoid an affront to that sovereignty. Because the act of state doctrine and the doctrine of sovereign immunity address different concerns and apply in different circumstances, we find that the act of state doctrine remains available when such caution is appropriate, regardless of any commercial component of the activity involved.

In addition to the public interest factor, a federal court must heed other indications which call for act of state deference. The doctrine does not suggest a rigid rule of application. In the *Sabbatino* case, the Supreme Court suggested a balancing approach:

> some aspects of international law touch more sharply on national nerves than do others; the less important the implications of an issue are for our foreign relations, the weaker the justification for exclusivity in the political branches. 376 U.S. at 428, 84 S. Ct. at 940.

The decision to deny access to judicial relief is not one we make lightly. In Timberlane Lumber Co. v. Bank of America, 549 F.2d 597, 606 (9th Cir. 1976), this court noted that "not every case is identical in its potential impact on our relations with other nations." The "touchstone" or "crucial element" is the potential for interference with our foreign relations. *Timberlane,* 549 F.2d at 607. This court has stated:

we do not wish to challenge the sovereignty of another nation, the wisdom of its policy, or the integrity and motivation of its action. On the other hand, repeating the terms of *Sabbatino,* "the less important the implications of an issue are for our foreign relations, the weaker the justification for exclusivity in the political branches." *Id.* (Citations omitted.)

There is no question that the availability of oil has become a significant factor in international relations. The growing world energy crisis has been judicially recognized in other cases. *See, e.g.,* Occidental of UMM al Qaywayn, Inc. v. A Certain Cargo of Petroleum, 577 F.2d 1196 (5th Cir. 1978), *cert. denied,* 442 U.S. 928, 99 S. Ct. 2857, 61 L. Ed. 2d 296 (1979) (dismissing an action to determine rights to oil in the Persian Gulf as raising a nonjusticiable political question); Hunt v. Mobil Oil Corp., 550 F.2d 68, 78 (2d Cir.) *cert. denied,* 434 U.S. 984, 98 S. Ct. 608, 54 L. Ed. 2d 477 (1977) (affirming, on the basis of the act of state doctrine, dismissal of anti-trust claim where the act complained of was part of "a continuing and broadened confrontation between the East and West in an oil crisis which has implications and complications far transcending those suggested by appellants"). The record in this case contains extensive documentation of the involvement of our executive and legislative branches with the oil question. IAM does not dispute that the United States has a grave interest in the petro-politics of the Middle East, or that the foreign policy arms of the executive and legislative branches are intimately involved in this sensitive area. It is clear that OPEC and its activities are carefully considered in the formulation of American foreign policy.

The remedy IAM seeks is an injunction against the OPEC nations. The possibility of insult to the OPEC states and of interference with the efforts of the political branches to seek favorable relations with them is apparent from the very nature of this action and the remedy sought. While the case is formulated as an anti-trust action, the granting of any relief would in effect amount to an order from a domestic court instructing a foreign sovereign to alter its chosen means of allocating and profiting from its own valuable natural resources. On the other hand, should the court hold that OPEC's actions are legal, this "would greatly strengthen the bargaining hand" of the OPEC nations in the event that Congress or the executive chooses to condemn OPEC's actions. *Sabbatino,* 376 U.S. at 432, 84 S. Ct. at 942.

A further consideration is the availability of internationally-accepted legal principles which would render the issues appropriate for judicial disposition. As the Supreme Court stated in *Sabbatino,*

It should be apparent that the greater the degree of codification or consensus concerning a particular area of international law, the more appropriate it is for the judiciary to render decisions regarding it, since the courts can then focus on the application of an agreed principle to circumstances of fact rather than on the sensitive task of establishing a principle not inconsistent with the national interest or with international justice. 376 U.S. at 428, 84 S. Ct. at 940.

While conspiracies in restraint of trade are clearly illegal under domestic law, the record reveals no international consensus condemning cartels, royalties, and production agreements.[9] The United States and other nations have supported the principle of supreme state sovereignty over natural resources. The OPEC nations themselves obviously will not agree that their actions are illegal. We are reluctant to allow judicial interference in an area so void of international consensus. An injunction against OPEC's alleged price-fixing activity would require condemnation of a cartel system which the community of nations has thus far been unwilling to denounce. The admonition in *Sabbatino* that the courts should consider the degree of codification and consensus in the area of law is another indication that judicial action is inappropriate here.

The district court was understandably reluctant to proceed on the complaint below and the act of state doctrine provides sound jurisprudential support for such reluctance. While the act of state doctrine does not compel dismissal as a matter of course, in a case such as this where the controlling issue is the legality of a sovereign act and where the only remedy sought is barred by act of state considerations dismissal is appropriate.

IV.   CONCLUSION

The act of state doctrine is applicable in this case. The courts should not enter at the will of litigants into a delicate area of foreign policy which the executive and legislative branches have chosen to approach with restraint. The issue of whether the FSIA allows jurisdiction in this case need not be decided, since a judicial remedy is inappropriate regardless of whether jurisdiction exists. Similarly, we need not reach the issues regarding the indirect-purchaser rule, the extra-territorial application of the Sherman Act, the definition of "person" under the Sherman Act, and the propriety of injunctive relief.

The decision of the district court dismissing this action is affirmed.

NOTES AND QUESTIONS

1. How would *Timberlane* have come out under the *Occidental Petroleum* approach? For a leading case in accord with *Timberlane, see* International Investment Development v. Mitsui & Co., 671 F.2d 876 (5th Cir. 1982), *vacated and remanded on other grounds,* 460 U.S. 1007 (1983).

2. Is *Timberlane* wise in converting to a balancing test? Do you trust courts to make this kind of balance wisely? Are the uncertainties of a balancing test likely to create difficulty in advising a client caught in the middle between two

---

[9]The amici suggest that production quotas and royalties are accepted sovereign practices, *citing,* inter alia, the Connally Hot Oil Act, 15 U.S.C. §715; United States' payment to farmers not to produce wheat; and Japan's voluntary reduction of TV and automobile production to maintain prices.

national policies? Do the *Mannington Mills* factors provide much additional predictability?

3. Is *Timberlane* wise in the complex relationship it creates between the jurisdictional test and the act of state balancing test? Does it trouble you that some of the same factors will be relevant to both tests?

4. Given courts' natural overemphasis on their own national interests, will the *Timberlane* approach ever lead to a decision denying jurisdiction in a non-sensitive case? Note that it did so in *Timberlane* itself on remand, 574 F. Supp. 1453 (N.D. Cal. 1983), *aff'd*, 749 F.2d 1378 (9th Cir. 1984).

5. Will U.S. law permit antitrust suits against a foreign government trading corporation? In Outboard Marine v. Pezetel, 461 F. Supp. 384 (D. Del. 1978) jurisdiction was granted over a Polish Foreign Trade Organization selling golf carts to the United States, the court saying:

> [D]efendant's characterization of this litigation as "the spectacle of one nation's courts sitting in judgment of another nation's sovereign policies" to specifically measure "the legality of Polish economic and trade policies by the yardstick of American economic and trade policies" does not substantiate its act-of-state argument. The Court cannot agree that this action is the kind contemplated by Justice Harlan when he wrote "some aspects of international law touch much more sharply on national nerves than do others." *Sabbatino, supra,* 376 U.S. at 428, 84 S. Ct. at 940. The sale of goods within the United States is not perceived as impinging on the political system of Poland. Even if Poland were directly involved, any political embarrassment appears highly remote since there can be no genuine insult to sovereignty when a foreign enterprise undertaking to do business in a given market place is subject to the nondiscriminatory laws of that market place. Consequently, the Court concludes that jurisdiction over Pezetel is well founded and application of the act-of-state doctrine unwarranted.

6. Is *IAM* faithful to *Timberlane*?

7. How seriously would you take footnote 9 of *IAM* as a statement about the antitrust law of voluntary restraints and about *Consumer's Union*?

8. Is our law effectively one of respecting the monopolies of the powerful and overriding those of the weak? If so, is the result unavoidable?

9. Brazil has typically marketed sugar and produced and marketed alcohol (made in industrial form from sugar) through a state agency, the Institute for Sugar and Alcohol, which operates as a separate commission of appointed public and private officials from the industry, the unions, etc., and in fact sets its own policies. It has the explicit power to set prices in Brazil.

Assume that, with the new interest in gasohol (a mixture of alcohol and gasoline) as an automobile fuel, the Institute entered into "special marketing arrangements," signed in London, with and at the instigation of several foreign oil companies that distributed in the United States. The "special marketing arrangements" included price-fixing provisions for sale anywhere in the world of alcohol used for gasohol.

What are the factors determining who should win the inevitable suit by U.S.

buyers of gasohol (with the Foreign Sovereign Immunities Act providing the statutory basis for jurisdiction over the Brazilian institute)? If you were the judge, how would you handle the problems of evaluating the extent of Brazilian government political involvement in the action, in order to determine whether or not the act was commercial? For a European Commission decision upholding EC jurisdiction in a similar situation, *see* Re: The Application of the Federación Nacional de Cafeteros de Columbia [1983] 1 C.M.L.R. 703.

10. Which of the following could be a violation of the U.S. antitrust laws:

(a)   a cartel of foreign oil companies;
(b)   a cartel of foreign state-owned oil companies;
(c)   a cooperative, created under national law, of all of a nation's producers of cocoa;
(d)   a producer cartel consisting of the National Marketing Boards of cocoa for Ghana, Brazil, Ivory Coast, Malaysia, and Argentina?

2. *Beyond Accommodation*

In spite of the effort to accommodate foreign concerns, U.S. courts have sometimes been willing to take jurisdiction over the opposition of foreign governments, and, as a result, have created diplomatic and political reaction. An example is the uranium litigation of the late 1970s, in which the controversy became extremely serious.

Commonwealth uranium producers, acting with the encouragement of their governments, worked toward a uranium cartel in the early 1970s. Some of the operations of this cartel were revealed by a document acquired and leaked by the Australian Friends of the Earth during the course of contract litigation involving Westinghouse. Westinghouse had made a series of commitments to provide a lifetime supply of uranium to those who bought its nuclear reactors. When caught by rising prices, it sought relief from these contracts. The numbers were enormous—Westinghouse had committed itself to provide about a third of the world's consumption of uranium at a price of about $8 per pound—and the price went up to about $40 per pound.

As a part of a multicontinent legal saga,[2] Westinghouse sued the Commonwealth uranium manufacturers in Chicago. Most defaulted and asked their governments to file amicus briefs explaining that U.S. courts did not have jurisdiction. The Chicago court rejected these arguments and issued default judgments.

Foreign reactions to this litigation were immediate and severe. Great Britain passed "claw-back" legislation, opening its courts to suits by its firms to recoup treble damages in certain cases. As did a number of other nations, it also

---

[2] *See* Wood and Carrera, The International Uranium Cartel: Litigation and Legal Implications, 14 Tex. Intl. L.J. 59 (1979).

restricted the flow of information to U.S. courts. In an effort to make peace, the United States and some foreign governments reached agreements to consult when such issues arose. Following is the key *Uranium* decision and an excerpt from the British statute.

IN RE URANIUM ANTITRUST LITIGATION: WESTINGHOUSE ELECTRIC CORP. v. RIO ALGOM, LTD.

617 F.2d 1248 (7th Cir. 1980)

CAMPBELL, J.

In October of 1976, plaintiff-appellee, Westinghouse Electric Corporation, filed a complaint alleging anti-trust violations against twenty-nine foreign and domestic uranium producers. All of the defendants were duly served with process; however, nine foreign defendants chose not to appear. On February 2, 1977, the District Court entered defaults pursuant to Rule 55(a) of the Federal Rules of Civil Procedure against each of the nine defaulting defendants. In August 1977, Westinghouse moved for entry of final judgment against the defaulters on the issue of liability. On January 3, 1979, the District Court granted the motion for entry of default judgment against the defaulting defendants.

On January 12, 1979, Westinghouse moved *ex parte* for a temporary restraining order and for a preliminary injunction seeking to require the defaulting defendants to give twenty days' prior notice to the Court of any transfers of assets in excess of $10,000 out of the United States. In support of the motion, counsel for Westinghouse submitted an affidavit stating that several of the defaulters, and particularly Rio Tinto Zinc Corp. Ltd. of London, held substantial assets in the United States through wholly owned subsidiaries. Westinghouse counsel further stated that there was reason to believe that those assets were being, or were about to be, removed from the United States to avoid execution on the default judgment entered on January 3, 1979.

On January 15, 1979, the District Court temporarily restrained transfers [by means of a temporary restraining order—TRO] in excess of $10,000 pending a hearing on January 24. On the latter date, the District Court entered the preliminary injunction sought by Westinghouse.

Notice of the TRO was served on the defaulting defendant, Rio Tinto Zinc Corp. (RTZ), in London, on January 17, 1979. Rio Algom Limited in Canada was served with notice of the TRO that same day. It was later learned that within hours after notice of the TRO, RTZ instructed employees of its subsidiaries to transfer as much money as possible out of American bank accounts and into Canada. Approximately three million two hundred thousand dollars were transferred from the accounts of Atlas Alloys to Rio Algom Limited in Canada. Neither the plaintiff nor the District Court were given notice of these transfers, in apparent violation of the TRO and the subsequent preliminary injunction.

On January 25, 1979, Atlas Alloys moved for an exemption from the preliminary injunction, seeking to make arms length purchases of steel or metal products in the ordinary course of business in amounts of less than $40,000. Approximately one month later, Atlas Alloys gave twenty days' advance notice that it intended to pay its defaulting parent, Rio Algom Limited approximately $1.6 million dollars, which had been owed to Rio Algom Limited for some time. Westinghouse moved to enjoin the proposed transfer and sought to require Atlas Alloys to pay the funds into a trust account under the jurisdiction of the District Court. The District Court heard argument on the question and indicated that a ruling would be forthcoming shortly. In the interim, Atlas Alloys transferred about $1.2 million dollars to its defaulting parent by means of writing 124 separate checks for amounts slightly less than $10,000. On March 27, 1979, the District Court enjoined the transfer of the $1.6 million dollars, and required that the funds be deposited in a trust account with the Court. The Court also found that five out of six of Atlas Alloys' top officers and directors were also officers and directors of the defaulting defendant, Rio Algom Limited. The District Court further found that the monies which Atlas Alloys sought to transfer out of the United States to its parent, Rio Algom Limited in Canada, were assets of Rio Algom Limited here in the United States and that the entirety of Atlas Alloys is an asset of Rio Algom Limited.

On March 27 and April 2, 1979, Atlas Alloys gave further notice of its intent to make transfers of an additional $168,000 to its defaulting parent. Westinghouse again moved to enjoin these transfers, and to have the monies deposited in a trust account. At this time Westinghouse also moved for further injunctive relief against Atlas Alloys based on the discovery of Atlas Alloys' practice of transferring funds out of the United States by means of checks written for amounts slightly under $10,000. At that point Atlas Alloys had written 481 checks for a total of $3.9 million dollars to its defaulting parent.

On May 4, 1979, the District Court entered a third injunction. The Court enjoined the proposed transfer of $168,000 from Atlas Alloys and, based on evidence of the transfers to Rio Algom Limited, the Court granted further injunctive relief requiring that all transfers of funds be approved by the Court upon twenty days' prior written notice, regardless of amount. . . .

This appeal arises out of an Order of September 17, 1979, in which the District Court denied motions filed by the answering defendants seeking to postpone any hearing on damages as to the defaulting defendants until after trial on the merits. The appellants claim that the January 3, 1979, entry of default judgment and the subsequent determination to proceed to a damages hearing are an abuse of discretion by the District Judge. . . .

In addition to these issues raised by the appellants, a significant issue has been raised by amici curiae. The amici request that this Court remand the case to the District Court to conduct an analysis of the international ramifications of this case in order to determine whether subject matter jurisdiction exists, and whether it should be exercised. Because the concerns of the amici curiae call into question the Court's jurisdiction, those matters must be resolved at the outset.

I. JURISDICTION

The governments of Australia, Canada, South Africa and the United Kingdom of Great Britain and Northern Ireland[11] have filed briefs as amici curiae. The principal thrust of the amici's briefs is to call into question the jurisdiction of the United States District Court over this controversy. We view the jurisdictional issue as two-pronged: (1) does subject matter jurisdiction exist; and (2) if so, should it be exercised? . . .

In its complaint Westinghouse alleges that twenty domestic and nine foreign corporations conspired to fix the price of uranium in the world market. The alleged meetings at which Westinghouse claims prices were agreed upon took place in France, Australia, South Africa, Illinois, the Canary Islands and England. At the present state of this litigation, there has been no opportunity for fact-finding.[20] We must therefore accept all properly pleaded allegations as true for purposes of determining jurisdiction. Accordingly, the picture which emerges is one of concerted conduct both abroad and within the United States intended to affect the uranium market in this country. While the governments of the foreign participants in this alleged conspiracy are actively and admittedly sympathetic to the economic determinism of the defaulters, there is no claim that the alleged conduct of the defaulters is mandated by those governments. We therefore conclude that Westinghouse's allegations against the defaulters do fall within the jurisdictional ambit of the Sherman Act, as defined in *Alcoa*.

The amici, in particular the United Kingdom contend that *Alcoa* is "no longer to be accepted by United States Courts as 'settled law' ", in light of the recent opinions of the United States Courts of Appeals in Timberlane Lumber Co. v. Bank of America, N.T. & S.A., 549 F.2d 597 (9th Cir. 1976) and Mannington Mills, Inc. v. Congoleum Corporation, 595 F.2d 1287 (3rd Cir. 1979). In those cases the Courts were faced with a dismissal of an antitrust claim brought by an American company against an American corporation for conduct in a foreign country; and against a foreign subsidiary of an American corporation for illicit conduct abroad. Each Court began its analysis with the

[11] Four Australian companies are in default: Conzinc Rio Tinto of Australia Ltd., Mary Kathleen Uranium Ltd., Pancontinental Mining Ltd., and Queensland Mines Ltd. Two British companies are in default: Rio Tinto Zinc Corp. Ltd. and RTZ Services Ltd. Two South African companies are in default: Nuclear Fuels Corporation of South Africa, and Anglo-American Corporation of South Africa Ltd. One Canadian corporation is in default: Rio Algom Limited.

[20] Indeed, so long as the nine defaulting foreign corporations refuse with specific support of their respective Governments to appear and contest the allegations of the complaint, including those upon which jurisdiction is asserted, they have made it virtually impossible to arrive at any further findings.

questions of whether the complaint stated a claim and whether subject matter jurisdiction existed. Both Courts answered those questions in the affirmative. In each case the Court reversed the District Court and remanded the case for a determination as to whether jurisdiction should be exercised. The Third Circuit set forth factors for the District Court to consider in resolving that question. Those factors were employed by the Court in *Mannington Mills.*

The United Kingdom relies primarily on the comment in *Timberlane* that "The effects test by itself is incomplete because it fails to consider other nations' interests." This amicus curiae contends the critical discussion of the *Alcoa* effects test has undermined its continuing viability as the standard of extraterritorial jurisdiction of the Sherman Act. We do not read *Timberlane* so broadly. The "jurisdictional rule of reason" espoused in *Timberlane* is that while an effect on American commerce is the necessary ingredient for extraterritorial jurisdiction, considerations of comity and fairness require a further determination as to "whether American authority *should* be asserted in a given case." The clear thrust of the *Timberlane* Court is that once a district judge has determined that he has jurisdiction, he should consider additional factors to determine whether the exercise of that jurisdiction is appropriate.

We conclude that nothing in *Timberlane* is inconsistent with our determination that Westinghouse's allegations of concerted conduct by foreign and domestic corporations are sufficient to confer jurisdiction on the District Court, under *Alcoa.* We turn now to the question of whether jurisdiction should be exercised in the present case.

In this case, unlike the situation in *Timberlane* and *Mannington Mills,* there has been a determination by the District Court as to whether jurisdiction should be exercised. In the order of January 3, 1979, and the order of September 17, 1979, the District Judge considered the unique circumstance presented in this case, and determined, in the exercise of his discretion, to proceed. Our task is to decide whether he abused his discretion in reaching that conclusion. We find that he did not.

In granting the requested default judgment, the District Court considered three factors: the complexity of the present multi-national and multi-party action; the seriousness of the charges asserted; and the recalcitrant attitude of the defaulters.[30] The District Judge concluded that those factors all weighed heavily in favor of proceeding to judgment and damages.

The amici suggest that the District Court abused its discretion by not considering the factors set out in *Mannington Mills* in reaching this determination. While the considerations recommended in that case certainly provide an adequate framework for such a determination, we can hardly call the failure to employ those precise factors an abuse of discretion. First, the *Mannington Mills* factors are not the law of this Circuit. Second, even assuming their adoption by

---

[30] Indeed, it was asserted by counsel for Westinghouse during oral argument that one defaulter simply tore up the complaint in the presence of the process server.

this Court, the circumstances here are distinct from those found in *Timberlane* and *Mannington Mills*. In those cases the defendants appeared and contested the jurisdiction of the District Court. In the present case, the defaulters have contumaciously refused to come into court and present evidence as to why the District Court should not exercise its jurisdiction. They have chosen instead to present their entire case through surrogates. Wholly owned subsidiaries of several defaulters have challenged the appropriateness of the injunctions and shockingly to us, the governments of the defaulters have subserviently presented for them their case against the exercise of jurisdiction. If this Court were to remand the matter for further consideration of the jurisdictional question, the District Court would be placed in the impossible position of having to make specific findings with the defaulters refusing to appear and participate in discovery. We find little value in such an exercise.

We conclude that given the posture of this case, and the circumstances before the District Court, the Judge did not abuse his discretion in proceeding to exercise his jurisdiction. We therefore decline to remand the case to the District Court as requested by the amici curiae.

[Discussion upholding default judgment, injunction, and damages, and partial dissent on these issues omitted.]

UNITED KINGDOM, PROTECTION OF TRADING INTERESTS ACT

1980, Ch. 11

An Act to provide protection from requirements, prohibitions and judgments imposed or given under the laws of countries outside the United Kingdom and affecting the trading or other interests of persons in the United Kingdom. [20th March 1980]

Be it enacted by the Queen's most Excellent Majesty, by and with the advice and consent of the Lords Spiritual and Temporal, and Commons, in this present Parliament assembled, and by the authority of the same, as follows: . . .

4. A court in the United Kingdom shall not make an order under section 2 of the Evidence (Proceedings in Other Jurisdictions) Act 1975 for giving effect to a request issued by or on behalf of a court or tribunal of an overseas country if it is shown that the request infringes the jurisdiction of the United Kingdom or is otherwise prejudicial to the sovereignty of the United Kingdom; and a certificate signed by or on behalf of the Secretary of State to the effect that it infringes that jurisdiction or is so prejudicial shall be conclusive evidence of that fact.

5.—(1) A judgment to which this section applies shall not be registered under Part II of the Administration of Justice Act 1920 or Part I of the Foreign

Judgments (Reciprocal Enforcement) Act 1933 and no court in the United Kingdom shall entertain proceedings at common law for the recovery of any sum payable under such a judgment.

(2) This section applies to any judgment given by a court of an overseas country, being—

(a)   a judgment for multiple damages within the meaning of subsection (3) below:

(b)   a judgment based on a provision or rule of law specified or described in an order under subsection (4) below and given after the coming into force of the order; or

(c)   a judgment on a claim for contribution in respect of damages awarded by a judgment falling within paragraph (a) or (b) above.

(3) In subsection (2)(a) above a judgment for multiple damages means a judgment for an amount arrived at by doubling, trebling or otherwise multiplying a sum assessed as compensation for the loss or damage sustained by the person in whose favour the judgment is given.

(4) The Secretary of State may for the purposes of subsection (2)(b) above make an order in respect of any provision or rule of law which appears to him to be concerned with the prohibition or regulation of agreements, arrangements or practices designed to restrain, distort or restrict competition in the carrying on of business of any description or to be otherwise concerned with the promotion of such competition as aforesaid. . . .

6.—(1) This section applies where a court of an overseas country has given a judgment for multiple damages within the meaning of section 5(3) above against—

(a)   a citizen of the United Kingdom and Colonies; or

(b)   a body corporate incorporated in the United Kingdom or in a territory outside the United Kingdom for whose international relations Her Majesty's Government in the United Kingdom are responsible; or

(c)   a person carrying on business in the United Kingdom,

(in this section referred to as a "qualifying defendant") and an amount on account of the damages has been paid by the qualifying defendant either to the party in whose favour the judgment was given or to another party who is entitled as against the qualifying defendant to contribution in respect of the damages.

(2) Subject to subsection (3) and (4) below, the qualifying defendant shall be entitled to recover from the party in whose favour the judgment was given so much of the amount referred to in subsection (1) above as exceeds the part attributable to compensation; and that part shall be taken to be such part of the amount as bears to the whole of it the same proportion as the sum assessed by the court that gave the judgment as compensation for the loss or damage

sustained by that party bears to the whole of the damages awarded to that party.

(3) Subsection (2) above does not apply where the qualifying defendant is an individual who was ordinarily resident in the overseas country at the time when the proceedings in which the judgment was given was instituted or a body corporate which had its principal place of business there at that time.

(4) Subsection (2) above does not apply where the qualifying defendant carried on business in the overseas country and the proceedings in which the judgment was given were concerned with activities exclusively carried on in that country.

(5) A court in the United Kingdom may entertain proceedings on a claim under this section notwithstanding that the person against whom the proceedings are brought is not within the jurisdiction of the court. . . .

NOTES AND QUESTIONS

1. Had the act of state question been raised more sharply in Chicago, how should it have come out? Would your pre- and post-*Timberlane* answers differ? For additional data on the cartel, *see* Stewart, Canada's Role in the International Uranium Cartel, 35 Intl. Org. 657 (1981).

2. Suppose a foreign firm obtains a judgment against a U.S. firm under the Protection of Trading Interests Act. How is that judgment likely to be treated in the United States?

3. What will be the actual effect of the U.K. act? For the full text and an exchange of diplomatic notes, *see* 21 I.L.M. 834 (1982).

4. Could the U.S. government reach a "settlement agreement" with Canada or other Commonwealth nations that would terminate Westinghouse's ability to pursue the Chicago action? Is this the implication of Dames & Moore v. Regan, 453 U.S. 654 (1981)? Should the executive have such a power? If the government has the power, would it be wise to exercise it?

5. Should private litigants be restricted in their ability to initiate antitrust proceedings in cases in which those proceedings have international implications? Consider the following three possibilities suggested in 1983: (1) requiring U.S. government consent for a private party suit against a foreign government; (2) eliminating treble damages in international cases; (3) creating a statutory mechanism for foreign governments to participate. 44 A.T.T.R. 847 (1983). What about authorizing the court to dismiss if it determines that the interests of the United States in the action are outweighed by those of foreign nations? *See* the bill introduced by Senator DeConcini (D. N.M.) in 1985, under which the attorney general could give testimony on these various interests, 48 A.T.T.R. 341 (1985). What are the costs and benefits of such changes in the law?

6. Suppose a defendant in a U.S. international antitrust case seeks a foreign court decree prohibiting plaintiff from suing in the United States. Should the

U.S. court issue a preventive injunction prohibiting defendants from seeking such a decree? *See* Laker Airways v. Sabena, 731 F.2d 909 (D.C. Cir. 1984). For a thoughtful comparison of this case with *Timberlane, see* Meesen, Antitrust Jurisdiction under Customary International Law, 78 A.J.I.L. 783 (1984).

C.   TRADE—ANTITRUST RELATIONSHIPS

In general, antitrust law has focused on protecting the consumer from the high prices that monopoly and conspiracy might bring. In contrast, trade law has focused on protecting industry from the low prices that foreign competition might bring. The potentially sharp conflict is dulled in practice. With respect to exports, there is relatively little problem, because the antitrust laws are not thought of as protecting foreign consumers. It is with respect to imports that the conflict might become acrimonious—but many of the real world examples arise in the context of suits by one competitor against another alleging an unfair method of competition. There is a continuity between those practices (like dumping) regarded as unfair in the international context and those practices (like pricing low to drive a competitor out of business) regarded as unfair in the domestic antitrust context. As will be seen, both bodies of law have been complicated by the enactment of several bodies of repetitive legislation.

1.   *The Export Side*

The trade law logic of increasing exports and their profitability can arguably be pursued without conflicting with the antitrust goal of protecting competition on the domestic market. There has, therefore, been a tradition of permitting export cartels while attempting to reduce the chance that these cartels would become covers for cartels affecting the domestic market. The Webb-Pomerence Act sought this goal in 1918; the 1982 Export Trading Act extended the concept.

On October 8, 1982, President Reagan signed the Export Trading Company Act of 1982, P.L. 97-290. The act is designed to increase U.S. exports by facilitating the formation of export trading companies (ETCs). An ETC is defined in the act as a person, partnership, association, or similar organization that is organized and operated principally for the purposes of exporting U.S. products and services.

A significant change effected by the act is the modification of U.S. antitrust laws applicable to U.S. export trade. Although for years export trade associations have been able to export goods (not services) collectively, only 30 such associations have ever been formed, due in part to uncertainty about the antitrust implications of their activities.

Under the act, however, an ETC may apply for an antitrust certificate which, if granted, will give the holder protection from any criminal and civil antitrust actions brought under federal or state laws. The applications must be reviewed by both the Departments of Commerce and Justice and a final determination must be made within 90 days, although the procedure can be shortened to require the determination within 30 days. Both the application and the certificate holder's future conduct will be judged by the act's *new* antitrust standards, explained below. Also, the act permits an ETC to engage in the export of services, as well as goods.

To receive the certificate, an ETC applicant must establish that the export trade activities and methods of operation specified in its application will:

(1) result in neither a substantial lessening of competition or restraint of trade within the United States, nor a substantial restraint of the export trade of any competitor of the applicant;

(2) not unreasonably enhance, stabilize, or depress prices within the United States of the goods, wares, merchandise, or services of the class exported by the applicant;

(3) not constitute unfair methods of competition against competitors engaged in the export of goods, wares, merchandise, or services of the class exported by the applicant; and

(4) not include any act that may reasonably be expected to result in the sale for consumption or resale within the United States of the goods, wares, merchandise, or services exported by the applicant.

Once the certificate is issued and as long as the ETC operates within its terms and scope, the ETC will be immune from criminal and civil antitrust actions under both federal and state laws. The only exception to this blanket immunity would be private party lawsuits in which a challenger could allege violation of the antitrust standards set forth above. In such a lawsuit, a certificated ETC would have several advantages because of: the challenger's heavy burdens to prove a substantial lessening of competition and to overcome the legal presumption provided by the act that the ETC's certified conduct is lawful; the short two-year statute of limitations; possible award of only actual or single (not treble) damages; and full reimbursement of the ETC's litigation costs and reasonable attorneys' fees if the ETC prevails against the challenger.

If the ETC elects not to apply for a certificate (or if it holds a certificate but violates the terms), its conduct will be subject to the sanctions of federal and state antitrust laws, including treble damages. It is important to note, however, that the court's jurisdictional reach in any antitrust action against an ETC for its export transactions has been clarified by Title IV of the act. It amends the Sherman Act and Federal Trade Commission Act to clarify that an ETC's conduct in other than import trade (i.e., export trade, or wholly foreign transactions) must have a "direct, substantial, and reasonably foreseeable effect" on commerce in the United States in order for an antitrust suit to be brought in a U.S. court and judged by substantive U.S. antitrust law.

While Title IV of the act (the Foreign Trade Antitrust Improvements Act, excerpted *supra* after the *Aniline* case) clarifies the jurisdictional test for a challenger's suit, it does not make it any harder to prove the claim. By contrast, an antitrust certificate creates substantial obstacles for, and thereby protects against, antitrust lawsuits. In sum, an antitrust certification may not be a necessity for an ETC, but it insures against meritless, potentially costly harassment suits by disgruntled competitors.

QUESTIONS

1. Would you expect the export cartel concept to work well when the foreign market is competitive (as in, say, consumer electronics)?

2. What about its application when the foreign market is controlled by a few foreign firms (as might be the case for certain patented chemicals or pharmaceuticals)?

3. When, then, does an export cartel ever provide economic advantage? For a thoughtful analysis, pointing out the two clear exceptions—cases where the exporting nation is the world's only supplier and cases, exemplified by cinema exports, in which the export cartel achieves marketing economies of scale—*see* Larson, An Economic Analysis of the Webb-Pomerene Act, 13 J. Law & Econ. 461 (1970).

4. Do you think the new act will make any more difference than the old one?

5. Suppose France enacted an export trading company act. Would the firms participating in an export trading company organized under that act be liable to suit under U.S. antitrust law?

6. Is the U.S. Export Trading Company Act consistent with the GATT?

7. Suppose the Japanese government permits a number of firms to pool their resources in a cooperative R & D program, which would be jointly controlled and whose research results would be available to the participating firms, but only the participating firms. Although the U.S. law is not entirely clear, such a pool (if everything is in the United States) may be a violation of the antitrust laws if the technology involved is very important and the participating firms represent a very large share of the industry. Assuming such conditions to be satisfied, when, if ever, would antitrust prosecution against the Japanese group be possible under U.S. law? What relief might be available under the trade acts?

8. Suppose such a cooperative research program were formed by United States firms, and a Japanese firm sought and was refused the opportunity to participate in the program?

2.   The Import Side

As noted above, in the import context the trade acts and the antitrust laws both tend to focus on arguably unfair practices by foreign competitors against

U.S. firms. The two bodies of law reflect different traditions and goals, and firms can be caught in the middle. In the winter of 1983, for example, the Justice Department was investigating complaints that the Japanese semiconductor industry had a cartel to force up the price of chips at the same time that part of the U.S. industry was arguing that they were forcing down prices unfairly. These tensions are reflected in the interpretation of that legislation in which Congress has sought to provide a special international analogue of domestic antitrust law.

a. Section 337

The provision exemplified in the following case is §337, 19 U.S.C. §1337 (*see* §341 of the 1974 Act and §1105 of the 1979 Act), which prohibits "unfair methods of competition" and "unfair acts" in the import trade. This section[3] has traditionally been used to exclude goods that infringe a patent or trademark and will be considered in Chapter XIV in connection with technology transfer. During the late 1970s, however, the U.S. International Trade Commission, which administers the provision, sought to give it a much broader application on the basis of its parallelism to the Federal Trade Commission's analogous statutory authority. The issue posed by the case then is how to relate this broad grant of authority with overlapping more specific trade procedures.

USITC, IN THE MATTER OF CERTAIN WELDED STAINLESS STEEL PIPE AND TUBE

Investigation No. 337-TA-29 (1978)

COMMISSION DETERMINATION AND ACTION

The United States International Trade Commission ("Commission") having instituted an investigation pursuant to its Notice of Investigation issued on February 16, 1977;

And, having heard this matter in accordance with the provisions of 19 U.S.C. 1337 (section 337) and 5 U.S.C. 551-559;

Has determined* that there is in this investigation a violation of section 337 by reason of the importation or sale or both (as the case may be) by persons named in this order of certain welded stainless steel pipe and tube at prices lower than the average variable cost of production of said product without

---

[3] Those who have studied antitrust will note that the section offers the same kind of anticompetitive potential as does the Robinson-Patman Act or even some Federal Trade Commission actions.

* Vice Chairman Joseph O. Parker and Commissioner Catherine Bedell dissenting as to the determination of violation of section 337 and are not participating in the issuance of the subject order.

commercial justification; that an order directing these persons to cease and
desist from this practice should be issued in lieu of a direction under section
337(d); that the articles concerned be excluded from entry into the United
States; that such order has none of the effects listed under section 337(f) such
that the order should not be issued; and that during the period of Presidential
consideration of this order under section 337(g), the articles concerned shall be
entitled to entry free of bond.

Therefore, the Commission hereby issues the following [cease and desist]
order as its action in this matter: . . .

II.   CONDUCT PROHIBITED

No respondent manufacturer shall sell for export to the United States, without
commercial justification, any welded stainless steel pipe and tube manufactured in Japan at a price that is below the reasonably anticipated marginal
cost. In determining whether costs are "reasonably anticipated," the Commission will assume that prices above average variable cost, as calculated by
methods that are reasonably consistent for each respondent manufacturer from
year to year, are above reasonably anticipated marginal cost. . . .

The Antidumping Act and Section 337

Respondents argued that this investigation ought to be dismissed or suspended because a current investigation under the Antidumping Act of 1921
and this investigation are duplicative. They dwelled at length on this similarities between the two proceedings, and there are some. However, we believe it
is particularly appropriate to distinguish clearly the many important differences between the two statutes, and the significantly varied results which can,
quite logically, be obtained. Because of these differences, the argument is without merit.

The Department of Justice has also contended that this Commission should
defer to the Treasury Department whenever we determine that our investigation under Section 337 of the Tariff Act of 1930 involves only below cost sales.
While it is somewhat understandable for the Department of Justice to be
asserting their own pre-eminence in matters of Antitrust law, it is disturbing to
find them attempting to limit our jurisdiction under this statute. This continuing opposition to Commission actions clearly within the purview of section 337
is hardly the kind of "advice and information" envisioned by section
337(b)(2). The Justice Department arguments are not worthy of serious consideration because section 337 has been "in addition to any other provisions of
law" since it was passed in 1922.

There are many obvious differences between the dumping investigation currently under way at the Department of the Treasury with respect to welded
stainless steel pipe and tube from Japan and this case under section 337. For
example, the Treasury investigation covers many more products than our
investigation. Treasury looks at a specific six-month period and examines a
percentage of sales to compare with their determined fair value. The Commis-

sion, in this particular case, examined sales for a 36-month period. The respondents in our case are not the same as those in the Treasury proceeding either.

Even more significant is the very nature of the investigation itself. Treasury investigations under the Antidumping law are not adversary proceedings. There is no opportunity for cross-examination on the question of less than fair value sales. Respondents seemed to be arguing before the Commission that the tentative findings of the Treasury Department in its investigation of welded stainless steel pipe and tube from Japan were somehow conclusive evidence that respondents could not be pricing below average variable cost. Some of the margins found by Treasury were as high as 42%, so the factual assertion is at best questionable.

A careful examination of the two statutes will note two important differences. First, in section 337, an element of intent is a significant factor, while it plays no role whatsoever in the Antidumping Act. Second, and most important, is the question of harm caused by the unfair acts. Under the Antidumping Act, the only question is "whether an industry in the United States is being or is likely to be injured, or is prevented from being established, by reason of the importation of such merchandise into the United States." Under section 337, much broader questions are raised. The unfair acts or unfair methods of competition must have— ". . . the effect or tendency . . . to destroy or substantially injure an industry, efficiently and economically operated, in the United States, or to prevent the establishment of such an industry, or to restrain or monopolize trade and commerce in the United States, . . ." The portions of the statutes quoted above have only one common phrase where the meanings of the two are clearly identical, and that refers to preventing the establishment of such an industry. The standards are the same in that respect, but, since establishment of an industry is not an issue in this case, it need not be further analyzed.

The critical addition under 337 is the possibility that an effect or tendency of substantial injury is not required if there is an "effect or tendency . . . *to restrain or monopolize trade and commerce in the United States.*" Thus, when injury to the domestic industry does not exist, but a restraint or monopolization of trade and commerce in the United States does exist, Section 337 applies where the Antidumping Act does not. As we will show, this case demonstrates this difference between the two laws, because the result we reach now is impossible under the Antidumping Act. Our result depends solely on having found a tendency to restrain trade.

Unfair Methods of Competition or Unfair Acts

It is generally accepted that Section 337 embraces a broad variety of unfair trade practices. Moreover, Congress intended to allow the Commission wide discretion in applying the statute. It behooves the Commission, however, to formulate rational and generally acceptable reasons for treating certain practices as unfair.

Respondents argue that the Commission has never based a finding of unfair method or act solely on the price-cost comparison. It is important, therefore, to decide whether a practice of unreasonably low pricing constitutes an unfair method or act within the meaning of Section 337.

The basis contention in this case is that some respondents have sold below even their marginal cost of production. Since any allegations of joint action, combination, contract or conspiracy were stricken by the Presiding Officer, the basic charge is that each respondent engaged in a separate, unilateral pricing policy designed to exclude competitors from the United States market. It is then important to examine the arguments for proscribing such unilateral pricing schemes.

The presiding officer relied heavily on section 3 of the Robinson-Patman Act as the basis for prohibiting predatory business practices. That law makes it unlawful "to sell or contract to sell goods at unreasonably low prices for the purpose of destroying competition or eliminating a competitor." Section 3 is a little-used criminal statute. While it does not attempt to define what constitutes "unreasonably low prices," the Supreme Court provided some illumination in United States v. National Dairy Corp., 372 U.S. 29, 33-34, (1963):

> The history of §3 of the Robinson-Patman Act indicates that selling below cost, unless mitigated by some acceptable business exigency, was intended to be prohibited by the words "unreasonably low prices." In proscribing sales at "unreasonably low prices for the purpose of destroying competition or eliminating a competitor" we believe that Congress condemned sales made below cost for such purpose. . .
>
> Whether "below cost" refers to "direct" or "fully distributed" cost or some other level of cost computation cannot be decided in the abstract.

Hence, when prices fall too far below production costs, and the only business exigency is an intent to drive out competitors, there is a clear violation of section 3.

Certainly section 337 is broad enough to cover these predatory pricing schemes, since it is designed to apply the protection of domestic trade regulation to the unique circumstances of international trade. We therefore hold that a violation of section 337 may occur when foreign competitors engage in unreasonably low pricing with an intent, either individually or collectively, to destroy competition in the United States market.

It is unnecessary for this Commission to adopt an inflexible test of what constitutes "unreasonably low prices". In each industry there are peculiar methods of accounting, cost computation, and cost distribution, such that any absolute test would be meaningless. Each case must be examined individually to determine whether, under the circumstances, prices are unreasonably low.

Evidence presented in this case indicates that stainless steel pipe and tube producers incur substantial costs which bear a direct relationship to their volume of output. The most important of these are raw materials and labor. These costs ("variable costs") increase significantly as output grows. Hence, increased output will not significantly reduce the percentage of such costs attributable to each unit of production. These are referred to by economists as marginal costs. They represent the additional cost of producing each additional unit of output. For various reasons, exact marginal costs are difficult to isolate and are usually applied to cases such as this on the basis of some average, hence the term "average variable costs" (AVC). If a company sells below AVC it is unable to recover the amount expended to maintain or increase production. In short, it is more profitable to close down than to continue selling below AVC.

Producers of welded stainless steel pipe and tube also incur fixed costs, or those which remain relatively constant despite changes in output. These fixed costs include overhead, taxes, plant costs, and some sales costs. For the most part, fixed costs are long range costs which can be computed in advance. Thus, it is ordinarily quite possible to determine the percentage of fixed costs borne by each product—but, that percentage declines as output increases.

When fixed costs are added to AVC, the sum is Average Total Cost (ATC). Hence, when we refer to "pricing below ATC", we are referring to prices which may recoup variable costs, but do not recoup fixed costs. "Pricing below AVC" would indicate that even variable costs are not being recovered. It is only when prices dip below AVC that each sale means *greater* losses. By contrast, pricing below ATC does not mean mounting business losses; it merely means long term investment costs are not being recovered.

Presumably sales below either ATC or AVC could be unreasonably low for the purposes of section 337. In either case, the effect might very well be to drive others out of business, or at least to force them out of production temporarily. It only becomes significant to understand the difference between these two practices when we recognize that complainants in this case presented no independent evidence of predatory intent. Instead, they relied on inferences of such intent gleaned from numerous cases, and strengthened by the fact that respondents made no showing of a contrary intent.

Given the fact that any sales below ATC might be unreasonable, the presiding officer adopted a rule that predatory intent could only be inferred where prices fell lower than AVC. He cited Utah Pie Co. v. Continental Baking Co., 386 U.S. 687 (1967), as well as other authorities, to support the use of such an inference. More importantly, he cited the rule of thumb laid down in the article by Professors Areeda and Turner. The rule, in short, states that sales below average variable cost raise a conclusive presumption of predatory pricing. The uncontested testimony of the only expert economist on this record is that pricing below AVC is inevitably predatory.

The presiding officer, however, did not adopt a *per se* rule. He held instead that in this case the presumption of intent must be rebuttable, due to the number of variables in the international steel market which justify a rule "flexible enough to allow a defendant to demonstrate its price was commercially justified."

On the other hand, it is reasonable to draw a line between AVC and ATC, and to consider AVC the threshhold at which a presumption of predatory intent arises. This is so because of the significantly greater number of plausible justifications for pricing between ATC and AVC than for pricing below AVC. Considerable evidence indicates that a serious situation of excess capacity prevails in the domestic market. Hence, there may be a rational business decision that the market cannot sustain normal prices at current output, and that it would be better to put off recovering fixed costs in favor of maintaining long standing customers, keeping faithful employees, and assuring the vitality of the industry. In a product such as steel, where crucial defense and security reasons argue for a strong industry, the latter consideration may be forced upon respondents by government policy.

For all these reasons, we hold that sales below a respondent's average variable costs of production raise a rebuttable presumption of predatory intent, while sales above AVC but below average total costs must be supported by evidence of subjective intent before this Commission can find them to be unfair within the meaning of section 337.

We do not consider this rule to depend upon a showing of monopoly power. Rather, it is sufficient to conclude from surrounding economic circumstances that respondents could engage in such a course of unreasonable sales persistently. In the absence of some proof that respondents possess monopoly power, it is permissible to apply the above rule when there is a sustained practice of sales below AVC sufficient to indicate a party's ability to incur mounting losses in the course of a predatory scheme.

Having found an unfair method or act by reason of pricing below AVC on a sustained basis, we are required by Section 337 to consider whether this unfair method has one of three "effects or tendencies." Of these, we find and determine that the unfair method or act we have found in this case has a tendency to restrain trade and commerce in the United States.

In applying the statutory criteria to this case, complainants make two arguments, both of which we find without merit. The first is that we may derive an inference that the pricing practices we have found necessarily cause injury (the so-called double inference test). The staff makes a similar argument, that the practice involved inherently restrains trade as well as causes injury to competitors. Section 337 will not support the double inference. It contains a separate requirement of injury, either to competition or to competitors. The party with the burden of proof must show by substantial, probative and reliable evidence that either injury or a restraint of trade is taking place, or that there is a tendency toward them. A restraint of trade is demonstrated affirmatively by any number of factors including the commercial context.

Secondly, complainants argued there was actual injury to an efficiently and economically operated domestic industry. We agree with the presiding officer that market shares are not such as to indicate that the industry as a whole is being substantially injured and we adopt his findings of fact on this question.

However, complainants did point to one aspect of this case which shows a tendency to restrain trade. In their brief to the Commission, they suggested that imports from Japan of welded stainless steel pipe and tube have a large and increasing share of total imports into the United States.

Section 337 is not merely a statute to protect competitors but also a statute to preserve competition. In this case the evidence in the record on imports establishes that the tendency of the unfair practices of the respondents has been to exclude from the United States market welded stainless steel pipe and tube manufactured in countries other than Japan. Such evidence is contained in complainants' exhibit 14. This exhibit compares imports of welded stainless steel pipe and tube from Japan with total imports. In 1973, imports from Japan constituted 89 percent of total imports. In 1974, the Japanese share was reduced to 70 percent. In 1975, it increased to 82 percent, and in 1976 Japanese imports represented 87 percent of total imports. The unfair pricing that we have found began seriously in mid-1975 and has continued with greater frequency in 1976 than in 1975. In our opinion it is the unfair practice which is enabling Japanese firms to regain the market share they lost in 1974 to imports from other countries. We conclude from this exhibit that firms which are engaging in unfair pricing are the ones who receive the advantage of an increased total share for Japanese firms of imports to the United States. In summary, the information in complainants' exhibit 14 demonstrates that the tendency of the unfair method or act has been to exclude imports from other countries.

For the purposes of this proceeding under Section 337, it is unimportant that imports as a whole constitute a relatively small percentage of the domestic market, because the record shows that they are a significant competitive factor without which competition in the United States would be restrained. The Department of Justice also takes the position that "imports have had a re-straining effect on price" in the domestic market. We agree.

Lawful competition between firms handling imported products is essential to maintain a healthy competitive environment in the U.S. market. Thus, competition between products from Japan and from other countries must exist. When competitors are excluded from the U.S. market, as they are in this case, by a means contrary to law, they are being excluded not by our competitive process but by a means which would not be permitted to any competitor, foreign or domestic.

Imports are an essential part of U.S. trade and commerce. Imports are protected from restraints in trade and commerce under the Sherman, Wilson Tariff, and Clayon Acts as well as the Federal Trade Commission Act.

Simply stated, what we have found here is that the sale by certain respondents of stainless steel pipe and tube in the U.S. market at prices below AVC is an unfair act which has the tendency to restrain trade and commerce in the United States by substantially reducing the domestic market share of other foreign competitors.

STATEMENT OF PRESIDENT CARTER

THE WHITE HOUSE
WASHINGTON

To Chairman Daniel Minchew

Pursuant to Section 337(g)(2) of the Tariff Act of 1930, as amended, I have decided to disapprove of the Commission's determination concerning Certain Welded Stainless Steel Pipe and Tube, Investigation No. 337-TA-29. Enclosed is a copy of my determination.

Sincerely,

Jimmy Carter

The Honorable Daniel Minchew
Chairman
United States International
    Trade Commission
Washington, D.C. 20436

DETERMINATION. In this case, the Commission found a tendency to restrain trade and commerce in the United States on the ground that sales below the average variable costs of production tended to reduce the domestic market share of other foreign competitors. The Commission did not base its finding on injury to the domestic welded stainless steel pipe and tube industry. The Commission cited a factual determination that total import penetration into the domestic market had increased only from 12.2% in 1972 to 12.7% in 1976. The primary effect of approving the cease and desist order would therefore likely be limited to a shifting among foreign suppliers of their share of the present level of imports into the domestic market. This result would provide little or no benefit to the United States welded stainless steel pipe and tube industry or its employees. Nor would it significantly promote competition in the domestic industry.

Sales below cost of welded stainless steel pipe and tube have been the subject of two antidumping investigations by the Department of the Treasury, one in 1972, and another which proceeded simultaneously with the Commission's Section 337 investigation. As a result of its more recent investigation, which involved six producers accounting for approximately 85% of Japanese imports into the United States, the Treasury Department found that four firms had sales at more than minimal margins below fair value. Sales from those four firms have been referred to the Commission for an injury determination under the Antidumping Act. The Treasury Department's determination under the Antidumping Act therefore provides adequate protection against unfair trade practices described in this petition. In fact, the cease and desist order's prohibition of unjustified sales below the variable cost of production provides a more difficult standard for petitioners to satisfy than that contained in the Antidumping Act of 1921, as amended, which prohibits injurious sales below the total cost of production.

In this case, the Commission did not suspend its investigation after notifying the Secretary of the Treasury of the potential applicability of the Antidumping Act to the same subject matter. This resulted in overlapping investigations and determinations. As a result of this duplication, the imposition of the cease and desist order would be viewed by our trading partners as a precedent and a departure from internationally agreed procedures for dealing with below cost sales. Such a result would be an irritant in relations between the United States and those governments whose firms are being subjected to duplicative investigations, often at considerable expense to the parties and governments concerned. If allowed to stand, the cease and desist order would be viewed by foreign governments as undesirable harassment of their producers and as an unjustified burden on international trade. It would invite retaliation against United States exports, would complicate our current efforts to negotiate revisions of the international trading rules, and would thus be detrimental to the national economic interest and to the international economic relations of the United States.

NOTES AND QUESTIONS

1. In *Certain Welded Stainless Steel*, why weren't the petitioners content to pursue antidumping proceedings? What are the differences in standards? Decision-makers? Remedies?

2. If you were President Carter, what would you have done when the case reached you? For more information on §337 during this era, *see* Symposium, 8 Ga. J. Intl. & Comp. L. 27 (1978); Fisher, Protection Against Unfair Foreign Competition: Section 337 of the Tariff Act of 1930, 13 Va. J. Intl. Law 158 (1972); and Kaye and Plaia, Developments in Unfair Trade Practices in International Trade: A Review of the Third and Fourth Years under Section 337 as amended by the Trade Act of 1974, 61 J. Pat. Off. Socy. 115 (1979).

3. How does the 1979 Act change the relation between §337 and the antidumping laws? The result if *Certain Welded Stainless Steel* were to come up now?

4. How should the ITC treat a Department of Justice intervention like that in *Certain Welded Stainless Steel*? Suppose Justice intervened similarly in antidumping settlement negotiations under §734 of the Tariff Act of 1930 as amended by §101 of the 1979 Act? Would it be possible to comply with both the antidumping laws and the antitrust laws?

b.   Other Import Antitrust Legislation

The other legislation is, on its face, much closer to traditional antitrust principles. One provision, the Wilson Tariff Act, is essentially a restatement of the Sherman Act in the import context. Another is the 1916 Antidumping Act, which, unlike the 1921 Act, was designed specifically against predatory dumping.

The impact of these laws is explored in the massive Japanese Electronics Products Antitrust Litigation, excerpted below. This suit was built on the theory that defendant Japanese firms conspired to charge high prices in Japan so they could afford to charge low prices in the United States and undercut U.S. competitors—a theory that the plaintiffs sought to read into both the above laws as well as the Sherman Act. They also sought to apply the Robinson-Patman Act, a law that prohibits price discrimination, initially to protect small retailers against the buying power of larger competitors. The suit outlived a number of judges; at the time this book went to press, the Supreme Court had granted certiorari.

IN RE JAPANESE ELECTRONIC PRODUCTS ANTITRUST LITIGATION (I): ZENITH RADIO CORP. v. MATSUSHITA ELECTRIC INDUSTRIAL CO., LTD.

723 F.2d 238 (3d Cir. 1983), *cert. granted,* 53 U.S.L.W. 3696 (1985)

GIBBONS, J.

The plaintiffs, National Union Electric Corporation (NUE) and Zenith Radio Corporation (Zenith), appeal from an order of the District Court for the Eastern District of Pennsylvania granting summary judgment in favor of all twenty-four defendants on their respective complaints. The NUE complaint, filed in the District of New Jersey in December 1970, names as defendants seven Japanese television manufacturers, nine of their subsidiaries, and one Japanese trading company. The Zenith complaint, filed in the Eastern District of Pennsylvania in September 1974, names as defendants all of those named in the NUE complaint, a few additional subsidiaries, and two American companies: Motorola, Inc., a manufacturer of consumer electronic products, and Sears Roebuck & Co., a retailer. On January 10, 1975, the Judicial Panel on Multidistrict Litigation transferred the NUE case to the Eastern District of Pennsylvania, pursuant to 28 U.S.C. §1407 (1976 & Supp. V 1981), for coordinated or consolidated pre-trial proceedings with the Zenith case. The defendants and the charges made against them are described more particularly hereafter. Although counterclaims filed by several of the defendants are pending unresolved in the district court, we have jurisdiction over the grant of summary judgment on the NUE and Zenith claims because that court, pursuant to Fed.R.Civ.P. 54(b), directed the entry of a final judgment as to fewer than all claims. We conclude that as to most of the defendants the record discloses material issues of disputed fact which made the entry of summary judgment improper. Thus we reverse, except as hereafter noted.

I. THE PARTIES AND THE CHARGES

NUE is the corporate successor to Emerson Radio Co., a manufacturer of radio and television receivers, which ceased production of television receivers in February 1970 when it could no longer conduct that activity profitably. NUE claims that it was forced from the market by the unlawful activities of the defendants. Zenith is still a major manufacturer of television receivers. It claims that it has incurred operating losses and lost profits because of the unlawful activities of the defendants.

Both plaintiffs allege a conspiracy to drive all American manufacturers of television receivers out of business by a "scheme to raise, fix and maintain artifically *high* prices for television receivers sold by defendants in Japan and, at the same time, to fix and maintain *low* prices for television receivers exported to and sold in the United States." Preliminary Pretrial Memorandum, App., vol. 3, at 712. Both plaintiffs charge that such activity violates sections 1 and 2 of the Sherman Act, 15 U.S.C. §§1,2 (1982), and section 73 of the Wilson Tariff Act, 15 U.S.C. §8 (1982). Both complaints also charge that the pricing activity complained of violates the Antidumping Act of 1916, 15 U.S.C. §72 (1982). Zenith's complaint alleges sales at depressed prices not only of television receivers, but of radios, phonographs, tape and audio equipment, and electronic components. Zenith also alleges price discrimination among purchasers in violation of section 2(a) of the Robinson-Patman Act, 15 U.S.C. §13(a) (1982), and as to two Japanese defendants, a violation of section 7 of the Clayton Act, 15 U.S.C. §18 (1982), by acquiring interests in American manufacturers of consumer electronic products formerly owned by Motorola, Inc. and Sears, Roebuck & Co. Both NUE and Zenith seek treble damages and injunctive relief.

Of the twenty-four defendants, fifteen are named in both suits, seven in the Zenith action only, and two in the NUE action only. Among the principal Japanese defendants, Mitsubishi Corporation is a trading company, Matsushita Electric Industrial Co., Ltd. (MEI), Toshiba Corporation, Hitachi, Ltd., Sharp Corporation, Sanyo Electric Co., Ltd., Sony Corporation and Mitsubishi Electric Corporation (MELCO) are manufacturers of television receivers and other consumer electronic products. Many of the subsidiaries of these Japanese corporations are also joined as defendants. The section 7 Clayton Act charge addresses two transactions engaged in by Sears Roebuck & Co. and Motorola, Inc., respectively, with individual Japanese defendants. Sears Roebuck & Co., one of this country's largest retailers of consumer electronic products, at one time was a twenty-five percent owner of Warwick Electronics, Inc., a manufacturer of television receivers for private label retail customers.

Warwick, in 1976, was acquired by a Sanyo Electric Co. subsidiary in which Sears retained a twenty-five percent interest. Motorola, Inc., a manufacturer of consumer electronic products, sold its television manufacturing business and its trademark "Quasar" to MEI in 1974.

We deal in this opinion with charges based on the Sherman Act, section 1, and the Wilson Tariff Act, both of which are directed at combinations or conspiracies, and which, in granting summary judgment, the district court treated as co-equal in scope. We also deal with the charges that the defendants monopolized and attempted to monopolize in violation of section 2 of the Sherman Act. We deal as well with the charges that some defendants violated the Robinson-Patman Act by giving or receiving price discriminations. Finally, we deal with the charge that the Warwick and Motorola transactions violated section 7 of the Clayton Act. Only the section 1 Sherman Act and the Wilson Tariff Act charges require proof of a combination or conspiracy. Evidence bearing on those conspiracy charges, however, is relevant to the nonconspiracy charges in many instances. As described in the plaintiffs' Preliminary Pretrial Memorandum and noted above, "the conspiracy involved an unlawful, concerted scheme to raise, fix and maintain artificially *high* prices for television receivers sold by defendants in Japan and, at the same time, to fix and maintain *low* prices for television receivers exported to and sold in the United States." App., vol. 3, at 712. . . .

[Discussion of evidentiary issues omitted.]

2.   THE NUE-ZENITH THEORY OF THE CASE. . .

NUE and Zenith charge that the defendants conspired to fix and maintain artificially high prices for their products sold in Japan, while maintaining artificially low prices for those products in the United States, to the injury of American television manufacturers.

In ruling on the summary judgment motions the trial court assumed, correctly, that there is evidence in the record from which a fact-finder could conclude that the defendant Japanese manufacturers sold comparable television sets in the Unites States at prices significantly below the prices charged in the Japanese home market. Such a differential, even if regarded as consciously parallel business behavior, obviously would not establish a violation of section 1 of the Sherman Act or of the Wilson Tariff Act.[4] NUE and Zenith therefore

---

[4]15 U.S.C. §8:

> Every combination, conspiracy, trust, agreement, or contract is declared to be contary to public policy, illegal and void when the same is made by or between two or more persons or corporations, either of whom, as agent or principal, is engaged in importing any article from any foreign country into the United States and when such combination, conspiracy, trust, agreement, or contract is intended to operate in restraint of lawful trade, or free competition in lawful trade or commerce, or to increase the market price in any part of the United States of any article or articles imported or intended to be imported into the United States, or of any manufacture into which such imported article enters or is intended to enter.—Eds.

also charge that the Japanese manufacturers, who in the aggregate had manufacturing capacity in excess of what could be absorbed by the Japanese home market at a desirable price, entered into an agreement or understanding to stabilize prices in that market. While such an agreement or understanding was unlawful under Japanese law, standing alone it would normally be beyond the reach of American law. NUE and Zenith contend, however, that its necessary effect was to make it possible for the conspirators to sell at prices in the American market below the prices at which they could successfully compete.

The defendants urge that even if there was such a home market horizontal price-fixing agreement it would not be a violation of American law so long as their behavior in the American market was nonconspiratorial and pro-competitive. NUE and Zenith do not agree that a price-fixing conspiracy in Japan, having the effect of permitting each of its members to cut prices in the American market, is beyond the reach of American antitrust law. That question is not free from doubt. *See, e.g.,* Timberlane Lumber Co. v. Bank of America, N.T. & S.A., 549 F.2d 597, 608-15 (9th Cir. 1976). NUE and Zenith urge, however, that the question is not presented here, because they also charge that the defendants entered into certain agreements respecting the export of consumer electronic products. One feature of these alleged agreements was that each manufacturer would confine itself to sales to five companies in the United States. Other features were secret rebates and sales at prices that produced losses. The effect of those agreements, they urge, was to reduce, if not eliminate, competition among the Japanese manufacturers in the American market, and permit the full effect of the support derived from home market price stabilization to be concentrated upon competition with American manufacturers.

A horizontal allocation of customers in the American market would, of course, be a violation of section 1 of the Sherman Act. United States v. Topco Associates, Inc., 405 U.S. 596, 92 S. Ct. 1126, 31 L. Ed. 2d 515 (1972). It would not ordinarily be one for which primary line competitors like NUE and Zenith could seek recovery under section 4 of the Clayton Act, however, since it would leave them free to compete for all customers, and tend to insulate them from competition. Thus it would not injure their business or property. When coupled with a home market price stabilization conspiracy in Japan, however, the effect on them would be different. Price stabilization in Japan coupled with customer allocation in the United States would tend to permit separate Japanese manufacturers to concentrate their predatory tactics on separate selected American mass merchandisers, insulated from price competition at home and from Japanese competition here. The full brunt of the support derived from home market price stabilization could thus be concentrated against the American manufacturers competing for sales to the retailers in question. We hold that if the evidence would permit a finding that there was a conspiracy having these features, it would support the conclusion that there were Sherman Act and Wilson Tariff Act violations for which NUE and Zenith may recover under section 4 of the Clayton Act.

In so holding we reject the contention, advanced principally by MELCO, that the NUE and Zenith complaints do not charge conduct which as a matter of customary international law is within the jurisdictional reach of American antitrust law. We have in this court adopted the test, first articulated in United States v. Aluminum Co. of America, 148 F.2d 416, 443-45 (2d Cir.1945), that the Sherman Act reaches conduct abroad which is intended to and does have an impact on United States commerce. *See* Mannington Mills, Inc. v. Congoleum Corp., 595 F.2d 1287, 1291-92 (3d Cir. 1979). Even if we were to refine the *Mannington Mills* test so as to apply the Sherman Act only to conduct which has a *substantial* effect on United States commerce, the NUE and Zenith allegations would amply satisfy such a test. They charge foreign conduct which in conjunction with American conduct impinged severely on primary-line competition in consumer electronic products in the American market.

3.   EVIDENCE SUPPORTING THE NUE-ZENITH CONSPIRACY THEORY

In Part V C [omitted], we reserved ruling on the relevancy of evidence we found otherwise admissible. To the extent that we refer to it hereafter, we hold that evidence to be relevant under Rule 402 and admissible under Rule 403.

a.   Evidence Relating to the Japanese Home Market

It is undisputed that the Japanese television receiver manufacturing industry originated with the utilization by Japanese manufacturers of American technology, and that the encoding system adopted in Japan, that of the National Television Standards Committee, is compatible with that used in the United States. This encoding system differs from the Phase Alternating Line encoding system used in Germany, and the Sequential Color and Memory System used in France and the Soviet Union. 494 F. Supp. at 1204. There are technical differences, acknowledged in the opinion filed simultaneously herewith on the 1916 Antidumping Act claim. But, as that opinion makes clear, the similarities are more significant than the differences.

There is also evidence from which a fact-finder could conclude that although American technology in television receivers is substantially compatible with Japanese broadcast standards, there are governmentally imposed barriers to competition by American or other non-Japanese manufacturers in the Japanese home market. That evidence is contained in the Nehmer, DePodwin, Yamamura and Haley Reports, discussed in Part V C, *supra* [omitted]. The barriers include high tariff rates, discriminatory ocean freight rates, the Japanese commodity tax, import deposits, limitations on foreign investment in Japan, safety and design standards involving cumbersome inspection and testing procedures, and Japanese government procurement practices. 513 F. Supp. at 1183-84. Besides these governmentally erected barriers to entry, there is evidence of structural barriers to entry arising from the traditional methods of organization of Japanese businesses in *keiretsu,* which effectively control channels of distribution. 513 F. Supp. at 1185. The evidence respecting entry barriers to manufacturers whose products are technically compatible with Japanese broadcast standards would support an inference that a home-market horizontal price-fixing agreement among the Japanese manufacturers was a technically feasible project, because the parties to such an agreement would be protected from price competition from non-parties.

There is also evidence from which a fact-finder could conclude that Japanese manufacturers of consumer electronic products had relatively higher fixed costs than did their American counterparts, resulting from Japanese employment practices, and from Japanese financing practices. Japanese manufacturers are expected to maintain the permanence and stability of their workforce. They also customarily have higher debt-equity ratios, and thus greater fixed obligations. Saxonhouse Report, App., vol. 7, at 2891-92. A fact-finder could reasonably infer that higher fixed costs provide a strong incentive to utilize manufacturing capacity at the highest possible rate.

The evidence also would permit a finding that the manufacturer defendants, individually and in the aggregate, created plant capacity which exceeded what could reasonably be absorbed by the Japanese home market for consumer electronic products at a desirable price. DePodwin Report, App., vol. 5, Part III. A fact-finder could reasonably infer, from the existence of such excess capacity, that those manufacturers had strong incentives to dispose of the products of this excess capacity in a market outside Japan. Since, however, unlimited price competition in all markets in an industry characterized by excess capacity would be likely to produce losses, a reasonable inference could be drawn that if it were feasible to avoid price competition in one such market, efforts might be made to do so. Because the Japanese home market may be sheltered from outside competition by the entry barriers referred to above, it would not be unreasonable to believe that such collusion was possible.

The evidence also would permit a finding that the Japanese consumer electronic industry was in the years in issue characterized by concentration in a small number of dominant manufacturers, and that those manufacturers belonged to industry trade associations which met at regular intervals and exchanged information about plant capacity, inventories and pricing. These included the Electronic Industries Association of Japan, the TV Export Council, the Market Stabilization Council, and others. Evidence of concentration among a small number of manufacturers, and of their common membership in industry trade associations which met regularly and exchanged information, would support the inference that there were opportunities for concert of action with respect to home market price stabilization. Such concert of action would make possible export sales at prices sufficiently low to absorb excess capacity.

To the foregoing can be added the evidence in Part VI of the DePodwin Report tending to show that fairly consistently each defendant sold comparable models in the Japanese market at prices higher than they were being sold in the United States. That parallel conduct over a long time permits an inference that each manufacturer was confident that it would be able to support low price sales in the export market by higher price sales at home.

The evidence relating to the Japanese home market to which we have referred thus far, while having some tendency to make the existence of a conspiracy to stabilize home market prices more probable than if there were no such evidence, is probably not, standing alone, sufficient to support a conspiracy finding. What it suggests is a set of economic circumstances providing a strong incentive for horizontal price stabilization, the feasibility of such a program, an opportunity to meet for the purpose of agreeing on it, and pricing activity in the export market consistent with the existence of such an agreement. Were this the only evidence, we would probably agree that a finding of conspiracy would be impermissibly speculative.

Besides the foregoing circumstantial evidence, however, we have considerable direct evidence that there was agreed-upon price stabilization in Japan. That evidence includes the findings of the Japanese Fair Trade Commission which in Part V C 4 above we have held to be admissible for the truth of the matters reported upon. The report in the Market Stabilization case finds that the six respondents in that case agreed to stabilize the domestic market by establishing high prices and enforcing that agreement among the parties. The report in the 1967 MEI case finds that MEI took steps to require that its Japanese wholesalers maintain high resale prices. Moreover the evidence of what transpired at certain meetings, which in Part V E we have held to be admissible, tends to show that the participation of the defendants in various trade groups led to agreements on price stabilization. There is, moreover, direct evidence of the exchange of production and inventory statistics which would be necessary for the functioning of a horizontal price stabilization agreement. . . .

We hold, therefore, that on this record a fact-finder could reasonably infer the existence, among some Japanese manufacturers, of an agreement to stabilize prices in the Japanese home market, thereby deriving profits which would support sales at low prices in the United States. The direct and circumstantial evidence of a price stabilization conspiracy in the home market is reinforced by the conclusions of several of the NUE-Zenith economist experts, who, after studying the industry, opine that there was a price-fixing cartel in operation. *See* Nehmer Report; DePodwin Report. . . .

b. Evidence Relating to Exports to the United States

We have already noted the Japanese manufacturers' high fixed costs, higher debt-equity ratios (Saxonhouse Report, App., vol. 7, at 2887), and more stable workforce. A fact-finder could reasonably infer that these conditions created an incentive to find a market for excess capacity. We have also noted that Japanese and American television standards are compatible. Thus, among the developed countries likely to be a market for excess capacity of the Japanese manufacturers, the United States was the market with the greatest potential. This evidence would permit a fact-finder to infer that the Japanese manufacturers had a strong incentive to find a market for excess capacity in the United States. Moreover, when considered in light of the evidence respecting price stabilization in the home market, it would permit a fact-finder to infer a motive to sell at prices low enough to eliminate competition in the United States market by American firms. The trial court reasoned that "[n]o defendant, or any other businessman for that matter, would have any motivation for entering a conspiracy to sell at low prices." 513 F. Supp. at 1238. On this record a fact-finder could find such a motive. Moreover a fact-finder could find, from the evidence of price stabilization in Japan, that the Japanese manufacturers, if they acted in concert, had the ability to carry out a predatory export raid on the American market sustained by home market profits. There is record evidence that the Japanese Ministry of International Trade and Industry (MITI) plays an important role in the supervision of Japanese firms engaging in exports. The purpose of that supervision is to discourage the sale of Japanese products in other countries at prices which might result in charges of dumping, charges which might encourage the erection in those countries of trade barriers against Japanese products. With the apparent encouragement of MITI, the seven principal Japanese manufacturers of television receivers between 1963 and 1973 became signatories of formal written agreements which established minimum prices for television receivers sold for export to the United States. Similar agreements were made with respect to radio receivers and tape equipment. At the same time the seven manufacturers were members of the Japan Machinery Exporters' Association, an export trade association which required all its members to register the names of all customers who purchased television receivers for the United States market, and which, after 1967, limited the number of customers so registered to five. While the minimum price agreements appear to have been encouraged, if not mandated, by MITI, a fact-finder could conclude that the five-company rule was the result of non-governmental action.

Putting aside for the moment the role of the Japanese government, an agreement fixing minimum prices for the American market would ordinarily be a per se violation of section 1 of the Sherman Act. Thus the United States might sue to enjoin enforcement of such an agreement, or a purchaser might seek damages under section 4 of the Clayton Act. Since, however, the effect of a horizontal agreement among manufacturers to set minimum prices would in isolation protect non-party competitors like NUE and Zenith from competition, they could not, absent other circumstances, bring a section 4 suit, because they could not show the requisite injury to their business or property. . . . Likewise, a horizontal agreement to allocate customers in the American market would ordinarily be a per se violation of section 1. United States v. Topco Associates, Inc., 405 U.S. 596, 606-12, 92 S. Ct. 1126, 1133-35, 31 L. Ed. 2d 515 (1972). But again, such an agreement would not, absent other circumstances, produce an injury to the business or property of a non-party competitor.

There is record evidence, however, of other circumstances suggesting that NUE and Zenith may have been injured in their business or property from the existence of what they refer to as an export cartel. First, there is evidence from which a fact-finder might conclude that the minimum prices agreed upon were in fact dumping prices. That evidence includes the finding made in investigations under the Antidumping Act of 1921 (Part V C 2) and several expert opinions (Part V D). The collusive establishment of dumping prices could support an inference of collective predatory intention to harm American competitors. Next, there is substantial evidence that with the exception of Sony, the defendant manufacturers and their subsidiaries engaged in various schemes to rebate part of the sales price to a number of mass marketing retail customers in the United States. The evidence would permit a finding that efforts were made to conceal this activity both from MITI and from the United States Customs Service, and a finding that at least some of the manufacturers knew that other were engaged in rebating but did not report it to either government. There is expert opinion evidence that export sales generally were at prices which produced losses, often as high as twenty-five percent on sales. Long-term sales below cost are circumstantial evidence from which one can draw an inference of intentional predatory pricing. Finally, there is evidence that the five-company rule operated at a time when a fact-finder might conclude that there was a horizontal price-fixing agreement in Japan. Thus a fact-finder might reasonably infer that the allocation of customers in the United States, combined with price-fixing in Japan, was intended to permit concentration of the effects of dumping upon American competitors while eliminating competition among the Japanese manufacturers in either market. . . .

[Discussion of individual defendants omitted.]

4.   PROOF OF INJURY ARISING FROM VIOLATION OF THE ANTITRUST LAWS

Defendants claim that any damage which may have been sustained by NUE and Zenith could not have been caused by the conspiracy alleged. Their argument is that the minimum prices set in the MITI-sponsored manufacturers' export agreements would tend to insulate the plaintiffs from competition. . . .

Since, however, the MITI-sponsored agreements are relied on as evidence of a conspiracy to sell at predatory prices, we need not address this argument.

5.   THE DEFENSE OF SOVEREIGN COMPULSION

MELCO urges that all the Japanese manufacturer defendants are entitled to summary judgment because the activities of those defendants in Japan were undertaken at the direction of the Japanese Government, as an integral part of its trade policy toward the United States. MELCO's theory is that MITI mandated agreements fixing minimum export prices in order to accommodate United States concerns about dumping and to prevent the development of retaliatory trade barriers against Japanese products. We may assume, without deciding, that a government-mandated export cartel arrangement fixing minimum export prices would be outside the ambit of section 1 of the Sherman Act. *See, e.g.,* International Association of Machinists and Aerospace Workers

v. Organization of Petroleum Exporting Countries, 649 F.2d 1354, 1358-59 (9th Cir.1981), *cert. denied*, 454 U.S. 1163, 102 S. Ct. 1036, 71 L. Ed. 2d 319 (1982). On this record, summary judgment on that ground is not possible for several reasons.

First, we note that NUE and Zenith rely on the minimum price agreements primarily as evidence of a low export price conspiracy. Moreover, it cannot be said with any degree of certainty that the minimum prices, claimed by the NUE and Zenith experts to be dumping prices, were in fact determined by the Japanese Government. It is possible to conclude that the government merely provided an umbrella under which the defendants gained an exemption from Japanese antitrust law, and fixed their own export prices. Second, there is abundant evidence suggesting that many defendants departed from the agreed-upon minimums and took steps to conceal their departure from MITI. Thirdly, there is no record evidence suggesting that the five-company rule originated with the Japanese Government. Finally the evidence about price stabilization in the Japanese home market suggests unequivocally that this activity violated the laws of Japan.

Clearly, therefore, a summary judgment in defendant's favor on the defense of sovereign compulsion would be improper.

7.   CONCLUSION AS TO THE CONSPIRACY

We conclude that there was sufficient evidence to raise a genuine issue of material fact as to participation in the conspiracy alleged by NUE and Zenith by all of the defendants except Sony Corporation, Motorola, Inc., and Sears Roebuck & Co. Such a conspiracy would violate section 1 of the Sherman Act and the Wilson Tariff Act, and would be a basis for liability to NUE and Zenith under section 4 of the Clayton Act. Thus the summary judgment in favor of defendants must, except to the extent indicated, be reversed. . . .

C.   THE ROBINSON-PATMAN CLAIMS

1.   DISCRIMINATION BETWEEN JAPANESE AND AMERICAN CUSTOMERS

NUE and Zenith both pleaded Robinson-Patman Act[5] counts based on the fact that the defendants sold consumer electronic products in the Japanese home market at prices significantly higher than those charged for products of

---

[5] 15 U.S.C. §13(a)(1982):

> It shall be unlawful for any person engaged in commerce, in the course of such commerce, . . . to discriminate in price between different purchasers of commodities of like grade and quality, where either or any of the purchases involved in such discrimination are in commerce, where such commodities are sold for use, consumption, or resale within the United States . . . and where the effect of such discrimination may be substantially to lessen competition or tend to create a monopoly in any line of commerce, or to injure, destroy, or prevent competition with any person who either grants or knowingly receives the benefit of such discrimination, or with customers of either of them. . . .—Eps.

like grade and quality in the United States. As noted in Part II A above, Judge Higginbotham dismissed these counts for failure to state a claim upon which relief could be granted. 402 F. Supp. at 246-51. Section 2(a) applies "where either or any of the purchases involved in such discrimination are in commerce, where such commodities are sold for use, consumption, or resale within the United States. . . ." 15 U.S.C. §13(a) (1982). NUE and Zenith urged that only one sale of a commodity need be for use, consumption, or resale within the United States. After carefully analyzing the less than pellucid statutory language, and the available statutory history of section 2(a) and its predecessors, the trial court concluded that both sales must be for use within the United States. *Id.* at 248.

Essentially for the reasons set forth in Judge Higginbotham's opinion, we agree that Count V of the NUE and Count IV of the Zenith complaints were properly dismissed for failure to state a claim on which relief may be granted.

IN RE JAPANESE ELECTRONIC PRODUCTS ANTITRUST LITIGATION (II): ZENITH RADIO CORP. v. MATSUSHITA ELECTRIC INDUSTRIAL CO., LTD.

723 F.2d 319 (1983)

Seitz, J.

The procedural history of this complex antitrust litigation has been set forth in the immediately preceding opinion. As described in that opinion, plaintiffs are Zenith Radio Corporation [Zenith] and National Union Electric Corporation [NUE]. Defendants are various Japanese and American companies. This opinion addresses plaintiffs' claims under section 801 of the Revenue Act of 1916, commonly known as the Antidumping Act of 1916 [1916 Act], 15 U.S.C. §72 (1976).

I

Plaintiffs' complaints charge that from as early as 1960 to the filing of the complaints, defendants, individually and collectively, have engaged in illegal dumping by selling consumer electronics products [CEPs] in the United States at prices substantially lower than in Japan. Dumping is "price discrimination between purchasers in different national markets." J. Viner, Dumping: A Problem in International Trade 4 (1923, reprinted in 1966). Analysis of plaintiffs' dumping claims in this case thus requires a price comparison between imported CEPs sold in the United States and CEPs sold in Japan.

The 1916 Act makes it illegal to dump imported goods on the United States market with the purpose of destroying or injuring United States industry. The relevant text of the 1916 Act provides:

> It shall be unlawful for any person importing or assisting in importing any articles from any foreign country into the United States, commonly and systematically to import, sell, or cause to be imported or sold such articles within the United States at a price substantially less than the actual market value or wholesale price of such articles . . . in the principal markets of the country of their production . . . *Provided,* That such act or acts be done with the intent of destroying or injuring an industry in the United States. 15 U.S.C. §72 (1976). . . .

The first element necessary to a finding of dumping under the 1916 Act is proof that a price differential exists between two comparable products, one of which is imported or sold in the United States and the other of which is sold in the exporting country. During discovery, the district court required plaintiffs to pair models of CEPs sold in the United States with comparable models sold in Japan and to supply the model-by-model price comparisons on which they intended to base their dumping claims.

After plaintiffs filed their model-by-model price comparisons, defendants moved for summary judgment. Defendants argued that the models paired in plaintiffs' price comparisons were not comparable under the 1916 Act because of the technical differences that existed between them. Plaintiffs opposed defendants' motion by submitting affidavits that stated that the differences between the paired models were technically insignificant. Plaintiffs, however, do not dispute the existence of the technical differences.

The 1916 Act requires that the prices of products imported or sold in the United States be compared to the "actual market value or wholesale price of such articles" sold in the exporting country. The standard of comparability is not defined in the Act. The quoted language, however, should be interpreted in a manner consistent with the legislative purpose behind the enactment. The primary aim of the 1916 Act is to prohibit anticompetitive pricing.[4] Specifically, the Act prohibits price differentials which do not reflect legally significant product differences. It therefore becomes necessary to determine what constitutes a legally significant difference.

The district court correctly held that the 1916 Act does not require a comparison only between identical products. The history of the phrase "actual market value or wholesale price of such articles" supports this holding. That phrase is a term of art borrowed directly from the Tariff Act of 1913, and is defined in that Act: "the words 'value,' or 'actual market value,' or 'wholesale price,' whenever used in this Act, or in any law relating to the appraisement of imported merchandise, shall be construed to be the actual market value or wholesale price of *such, or similar* merchandise comparable in value therewith, as defined in this Act." Tariff Act of 1913, sec. III, ¶R, 38 Stat. 114, 189 (1913) (emphasis added).

---

[4] In requesting that Congress enact a law prohibiting dumping, Secretary of Commerce William Redfield explained that the law should not prohibit the pricing practices of normal competition, but only those based on predatory motive. Annual Report of the Secretary of Commerce 43 (1915). The legislative history suggests that the majority party in Congress at the time passed the Act to deal with unfair competition, and we will interpret the Act in light of its motivating purpose. We are not unaware, however, that protectionist sentiment ran high in Congress and the country at the time. *See Zenith, supra,* 494 F. Supp. at 1217-23.

The district court also correctly rejected plaintiffs' argument that products are comparable under the 1916 Act as long as they are functional equivalents or in the same generic category. Such an expansive reading of the comparability requirement would be inconsistent with the intent of Congress to distinguish legitimate from anticompetitive pricing. Prohibiting price differentials between two non-identical products that serve the same function but appeal to different consumer preferences is as likely to interdict competitive as anticompetitive pricing. We would certainly expect the price of a television encased in a cabinet of fine mahogany to be different from the price of a television encased in a cabinet of inexpensive plastic, yet the mahogany and plastic sets are arguably functional equivalents.

The district court nevertheless held that most of the CEPs paired in plaintiffs' price comparisons were not comparable under the 1916 Act. According to the district court, the proper standards for measuring the technical differences between the CEPs were consumer use and preference, marketability, and commercial interchangeability. 494 F.Supp. at 1241. The district court held that the technological "significance" of these differences, and the accompanying differences in production costs, were irrelevant as a matter of law. *Id.* Because certain technical differences made CEPs sold in Japan inoperable in the United States, and vice versa, the court concluded that the CEPs were noncomparable. We cannot agree with this holding.

The technical differences between the television receivers sold in the United States and Japan are required by the different broadcast frequencies and the different power supplies available in the two countries. Similarly, the technical differences between non-television products sold in the United States and Japan are required by the different power supplies and the different radio frequency bands that the two countries assign to their FM radio transmissions. Thus, the only differences that we consider here between the products paired in plaintiffs' price comparisons result from the fact that the products sold in Japan have technical components that make them work in Japan, and those sold in the United States have technical components that make them work in the United States. Considered in terms of consumer utility—i.e., consumer use and preference, marketability, and commercial interchangeability—the purchaser of a CEP in Japan buys the same thing as the purchaser of a CEP in the United States, an operable CEP. Because the two consumers purchase the same thing, we would, absent other factors, expect them to pay the same price. The technical differences at issue, measured as a matter of consumer utility, cannot explain a price differential, and thus the two products are, absent other differences, comparable under the 1916 Act. . . .

D.   PRICE DIFFERENTIAL

Assuming for the purposes of this appeal that the CEPs paired in plaintiffs' model-by-model price comparisons are comparable under the 1916 Act, plaintiffs must show that defendants sold CEPs in the United States at prices that were "substantially less" than the prices at which comparable CEPs were sold in Japan. Plaintiffs have produced several sources of evidence on this issue, all of which we have concluded are a proper part of this summary judgment record. . . .

E.   SPECIFIC INTENT ISSUE

The 1916 Act does not require that all imports sold in the United States be priced at or above the home-market prices of comparable goods. To sustain a claim under the 1916 Act, plaintiffs must show that defendants priced the CEPs that they imported or sold in the United States with the "intent of destroying or injuring an industry in the United States." 15 U.S.C. §72. We now consider whether evidence in this summary judgment record creates a genuine issue of fact as to whether defendants acted with the specific intent required by the 1916 Act. In considering the evidence of intent, we address separately plaintiffs' conspiracy and individual dumping claims.

1.   Conspiracy Claims

Plaintiffs' complaints allege that defendants conspired to dump CEPs on the United States market. To prove such an agreement, plaintiffs rely on substantially the same evidence relied on to prove the conspiracy to sell products at artificially high prices in Japan and artificially low prices in the United States, as described in our preceding opinion. Proof of this agreement, however, requires evidence that defendants agreed to sell at dumping prices, evidence not required to create a genuine issue of fact as to the conspiracy.

To make out a claim that defendants conspired under the antitrust laws, plaintiffs need only show that defendants conspired with general intent to restrain trade. United States v. United States Gypsum Co., 438 U.S. 422, 445, 98 S. Ct. 2864, 2877, 57 L. Ed. 2d 854 (1978). However, a showing of general intent does not necessarily constitute a prima facie showing of the specific intent required by the 1916 Act. *See id.* (distinguishing general from specific intent). After reviewing the record in this case, we hold that the evidence supporting plaintiffs' theory that defendants entered into the alleged conspiracy also creates a genuine issue of fact as to whether defendants agreed to dump CEPs on the United States market with the specific intent to destroy or injure an industry in the United States.

Evidence supporting plaintiffs' conspiracy theory would support an inference of predation in the United States market. This evidence is offered to show that the Japanese defendants agreed to stabilize prices at artificially high levels in Japan, insulating themselves by agreement from price-cutting competition at home. There is also evidence that defendants at the same time entered into an agreement to sell the fruits of the excess capacity of the Japanese CEP industry in the United States at low prices. We assume that the minimum price agreement, of which all the Japanese defendants were members, was mandated by the Ministry of International Trade and Industry [MITI].

Plaintiffs offer this evidence to show that defendants used the prices in that agreement as reference prices. Finally, plaintiffs point to evidence that defendants sought to conceal sales below MITI prices by a system of secret rebating.

The Japanese defendants also allegedly eliminated the possibility of price-cutting competition among themselves in the United States by agreeing to the Five-Company Rule and other customer allocation rules promulgated by the Japanese Machinery Exporters Association [JMEA], of which all the principal Japanese defendants were members. Those rules allocated to each member of the JMEA not more than five customers in the United States and prevented any two members from selling to the same customer. By thus allocating the market, defendants allegedly brought to bear the full force of their low-price conspiracy on their United States competitors in an effort to drive them out of the market.

NOTES AND QUESTIONS

1. How does *Zenith* (I) and (II)s' basic argument differ from one against "targeting"? Under this court's interpretation, could one effectively undercut the regular countervailing duty procedure? Might this court's interpretation be correct in an industry with a very steep learning curve?

2. Is the *Zenith* (I) court's application of *Alcoa* and *Timberlane* correct? How might you argue either way?

3. Is the court's interpretation of the similarity standard of the 1916 Act correct? How then does the cause of action under the 1916 statute differ from that under the 1921 Act?

4. Under the *Zenith* (I) and (II) court's approach, what are the precise differences—if any—between the coverages of the Sherman Act, the Wilson Tariff Act, the Robinson-Patman Act, the Antidumping Act of 1916, and the Antidumping Act of 1921? Does the existence of the latter three acts make you concerned about applying the broader acts to this context?

5. Is it possible that a foreign firm could be caught in a situation in which it could not sell in the United States at *any* price without violating some U.S. law (or being uncompetitive)? If so, what laws, if any, are best revised and how? Antitrust? Antidumping of 1916? Antidumping of 1921? Something else?

6. Is there any way to prohibit dumping without creating a conflict with the Sherman Act? In what ways might accommodation be eased? Revision of injury requirements? Elimination of the settlement option of the antidumping laws?

7. Should the existence of imports be taken into account in evaluating the anticompetitive effects of a merger of domestic firms? The Assistant Attorney General for Antitrust and the Secretary of Commerce fought publicly over this issue in the context of a proposed steel merger in the spring of 1984, and consideration was also being given to the recognition of imports in the merger guidelines. *See also* FTC, Consent Order, General Motors Corp. and Toyota Motor Corp., Docket C-3132, 49 Fed. Reg. 18,289 (1984).

8. In granting cert. in *Zenith* (I) and (II) the Supreme Court restricted its review to two questions, one going to the appellate court's reversal of summary judgment for defendants in a case based on " 'parallel' acts and other circumstantial evidence," and one described at 53 U.S.L.W. 3696 (1985):

REVIEW GRANTED

ANTITRUST

Matsushita Electric Industrial Co., Ltd. v. Zenith Radio Corp.

Ruling below (a/k/a In re Japanese Electronic Products Antitrust Litigation, 723 F.2d 238, 723 F.2d 319):

. . . May U.S. court (a) disregard duly issued statement of friendly foreign government attesting that certain export controls observed by its nationals were compelled by that government, (b) permit trier of fact to adjudicate veracity of such official government statement, or (c) hold such government-mandated conduct to constitute or be "feature" of conspiracy in violation of U.S. antitrust laws?

How would you answer this question? What different doctrines discussed in this chapter might be relevant? How might the doctrines be modified to apply to this context?

On March 26, 1986, the Supreme Court announced its decision in the case and reversed the Third Circuit, deciding in favor of the Japanese manufacturers, 106 S. Ct. 1348 (1986).

Chapter XII

The Use of Trade Controls for Political Purposes

The trade restrictions discussed to this point derive from a combination of economic motivations. There is another major category of trade restrictions, imposed much more explicitly, but with motivations usually other than protectionist. These include a desire to avoid participation in foreign wrongdoing, a desire to avoid providing technology or assistance to one's enemies, a desire to demonstrate political disapproval, and a desire to resist foreign manifestations of political disapproval.

A. THE FOREIGN CORRUPT PRACTICES ACT

1. Direct Effect

The United States Foreign Corrupt Practices Act of 1977 (FCPA) (15 U.S.C. §§78dd-1 et seq. (Supp. V. 1981)) criminalizes bribery of foreign officials (beyond the "grease" level of small payments to low-level officials). This act supplements efforts by several U.S. government agencies in the mid-1970s to reach bribery under such legal authority, primarily the duty to report income accurately to the Internal Revenue Service and the Securities and Exchange Commission's creation of a duty to report corruption to shareholders. The FCPA has been very controversial. Many have criticized it as extending U.S. moral principles extraterritorially and as making it harder for U.S. business to compete for export sales. Supporters respond that foreign corruption might extend into the nation, that foreign corruption often robs the poorest in a developing nation, and that it creates an entangling web, which, like that in Iran under the Shah, ultimately hurts U.S. interests.

The following materials present a report on a survey of corporate attitudes toward the act and provide a sense of international attitudes toward corporate bribery.

COMPTROLLER GENERAL, REPORT TO THE CONGRESS: IMPACT OF FOREIGN CORRUPT PRACTICES ACT ON U.S. BUSINESS

AFMD-81-34, March 4, 1981

PERSPECTIVE

Beginning in 1973—as a result of the work of the Office of the Watergate Special Prosecutor—the Securities and Exchange Commission (SEC) became aware of a pattern of conduct involving the use of corporate funds for illegal domestic political contributions. Subsequent SEC investigations and enforcement actions revealed that instances of undisclosed questionable or illegal corporate payments, both domestic and foreign, were widespread.

SEC announced a program in 1975 whereby companies could voluntarily disclose questionable activities. Under this program more than 450 corporations admitted making questionable or illegal payments exceeding $300 million.

PASSAGE OF THE FOREIGN CORRUPT PRACTICES ACT

The disclosures of widespread corporate bribery of foreign officials initiated the congressional action which eventually resulted in the December 19, 1977, passage of the Foreign Corrupt Practices Act of 1977 (Public Law 95-213— title I). Reports that accompanied the House and Senate versions of the act clearly indicated that the Congress perceived corporate bribes to foreign officials as (1) unethical, (2) unnecessary to the successful conduct of business, and (3) harmful to our relations with foreign governments.

In addition to addressing the bribery issue, the Congress also responded to SEC's recommendation that legislation be enacted that would enhance the accuracy of corporate books and records and strengthen corporate systems of internal accounting control. These legislative changes were intended to operate in tandem with the act's other provisions to deter corporate bribery. SEC found that millions of dollars had been inaccurately recorded in corporate books and records to facilitate making bribes. The falsification of these records was known to corporate employees and often to top management.

REQUIREMENTS OF THE ACT

The Foreign Corrupt Practices Act is a significant and far-reaching law regulating the conduct of American business in foreign countries. However, it covers a much broader area than is suggested by its title. The act is not limited to companies doing business abroad, nor is it restricted to corrupt payments. It contains significant internal accounting control objectives and recordkeeping requirements that go beyond corrupt foreign payments.

The act contains two important segments: (1) an antibribery prohibition and (2) standards for maintaining records and objectives for systems of internal accounting control. The antibribery provision applies to SEC registrants and domestic concerns, as well as to officers, directors, employees, or agents acting on behalf of such companies. The accounting standards apply only to SEC registrants. "SEC registrants" are defined as all U.S. companies that have a class of securities registered with SEC and/or file reports with SEC under the Securities Exchange Act of 1934. A "domestic concern" is defined as (1) any U.S. citizen, national, or resident or (2) any business entity (other than an SEC registrant) that either has its principal place of business in the United States or is organized under the laws of any U.S. State, territory, commonwealth, or possession.

Antibribery Provisions

The act prohibits both SEC registrants and domestic concerns from corruptly offering or giving anything of value to

—a foreign official, including any person acting in an official capacity for a foreign government;
—a foreign political party official or political party; or
—a candidate for foreign political office.

The above prohibitions relate to offers or payments made to influence these officials in order to help a registrant or domestic concern obtain or retain business or direct business to any person.

The act also prohibits the offering or paying of anything of value to any person if it is known or if there is reason to know that all or part of the payment will be used for the above prohibited actions. This provision covers situations when intermediaries, such as foreign affiliates or agents, are used to channel payoffs to foreign officials.

The potential penalties for violating the antibribery provisions are severe. SEC registrants and domestic concerns (other than an individual) can be fined up to $1 million. Individuals who are domestic concerns and any officer, director, or stockholder who acts on behalf of a registrant or domestic concern and who willfully violates the law can be fined up to $10,000 and imprisoned for not more than 5 years. The law prohibits companies from directly or indirectly paying a fine imposed on an individual.

Accounting Provisions

These provisions, which apply only to SEC registrants, contain requirements for recordkeeping and internal accounting controls. They were adopted in response to SEC and congressional discoveries that foreign bribery was accomplished mainly by (1) off-the-books slush funds and (2) transactions inaccurately recorded on a firm's books.

The recordkeeping standard requires that a company's books, records, and accounts, in reasonable detail, accurately and fairly reflect its transactions and the disposition of its assets. The internal accounting control provision requires that a company's system of internal accounting controls be sufficient to provide reasonable assurances that certain control objectives are met.

SEC registrants and any person authorized to control the direction, management, and policies of a corporation who willfully violate the accounting provisions are subject to the general penalties imposed by the Securities Exchange Act of 1934. These penalties include a fine of up to $10,000 and imprisonment for up to 5 years, or depending upon the circumstances, a violation may result in an SEC civil enforcement action.

SHARED RESPONSIBILITY FOR ENFORCEMENT

SEC and the Department of Justice share responsibility for enforcing the act. SEC is responsible for conducting investigations of SEC registrants suspected of violating the antibribery and accounting provisions. SEC can bring civil actions against these violators and/or refer them to Justice for criminal prosecution. Justice is also responsible for proceeding civilly and criminally against domestic concerns alleged to have violated the antibribery provisions. . . .

CORPORATE CODES OF CONDUCT HAVE BEEN GREATLY AFFECTED

Written codes of conduct are policies defining the standards of acceptable business conduct for corporate employees. Ninety-eight percent of our questionnaire respondents reviewed their policies to see if they were adequate in light of the act's requirements.

Over 60 percent of the respondents reported that these reviews had resulted in changes not only in what the policies said, but also in how they were communicated. Also, more than 50 percent reported making changes during the turbulent 4-year period before passage of the act; 25 percent did not find it necessary to make any further changes as a result of the act.

What effect the changes in the codes will have in reducing questionable payments is difficult to determine. However, more than 70 percent of the respondents believed that the act has effectively reduced questionable foreign payments by U.S. companies. . . .

THE COST OF COMPLYING WITH THE ACT'S ACCOUNTING PROVISIONS IS PERCEIVED TO EXCEED BENEFITS

As discussed above, corporate systems of internal accounting control have undergone extensive change. In many cases, however, these compliance efforts were perceived as costing more than the benefits received.

About 55 percent of the questionnaire respondents reported that their compliance efforts have resulted in costs that exceeded the benefits. The remaining 45 percent did not believe this to be the case. For the respondents who reported that the costs incurred exceeded the benefits, the extent of the cost burden varied as follows:

—50 percent believed the burden has increased their accounting and auditing costs by 11 to 35 percent.

—22 percent reported that the burden has increased their accounting and auditing costs more than 35 percent.

—28 percent estimated the cost burden at less than 11 percent. . . .

THE ACT IS PERCEIVED AS ADVERSELY AFFECTING U.S. OVERSEAS BUSINESS

As with the accounting provisions, the antibribery provisions may have created a cost burden. More than 30 percent of the questionnaire respondents engaged in foreign business said they had lost overseas business as a result of the act. In addition, over 60 percent perceived that—assuming all other conditions were similar—American companies could not successfully compete against other companies abroad that were bribing.

These beliefs are neither supported nor rejected by hard verifiable data. Attempts to quantify the act's impact have had only limited success. Due to the sensitivity of the foreign bribery issue and the complexities inherent in international trade, conclusive evidence of the act's impact on U.S. foreign business may never be forthcoming. However, the perceptions by themselves are important.

The act's adverse impact on U.S. corporate foreign sales has been attributed to a number of factors. In particular, business has charged that American companies are forgoing legitimate export opportunities because certain aspects of the act's antibribery provisions are ambiguous. In addition, the lack of an international antibribery agreement may be giving foreign competitors an advantage in international markets.

Throughout its deliberations on the act, the Congress was inundated with statements that corporate bribery to obtain overseas business was unnecessary. Then Secretary of the Treasury Blumenthal, testifying before one congressional committee, stated that

> Paying bribes . . . is simply not necessary to the successful conduct of business in the United States or overseas. My own experience as Chairman of the Bendix Corp. was that it was not necessary to pay bribes to have a successful export sales program.

Other governmental officials held similar views. Then SEC Chairman Hills stated that in every industry in which companies were bribing, other companies of equal size in that industry proclaimed that they saw no need to engage in such practices. Then Secretary of Commerce Richardson was quoted as saying that, in a number of instances, payments were made not to outcompete foreign competitors but rather to gain an edge over other U.S. manufacturers.

BUSINESS' PERCEPTION OF THE ACT'S IMPACT ON OVERSEAS SALES

Although the majority of our questionnaire respondents reported that the act has had little or no effect on their overseas business, more than 30 percent of our respondents engaged in foreign business reported they had lost overseas business as a result of the act. In addition, over 60 percent reported that, assuming all other conditions were similar, American companies could not successfully compete abroad against foreign competitors that were bribing.

Almost all the respondents that reported decreases in business stated that the act had discouraged foreign buyers and agents from doing business with their firms. In some countries, the use of foreign agents is a recommended practice; in other countries, it is necessary. About 45 percent of the respondents that reported lost business stated that the act has limited the number of countries in which they do business. The impact on overseas business was felt more by respondents from the top 500 companies. Whereas 25 percent of the respondents from the second 500 reported decreases in business, about 42 percent of the top 500 respondents reported losses.

How much the act can affect a company's overseas sales is influenced by many factors, including:
—The country in which the company conducts its business.
—The type of product or service it sells.
—The identity of the purchasers (government versus non-government).
—The business practices of its competitors.
—The honesty of foreign government officials.
—Whether or not the company previously made questionable payments to obtain foreign business.

Our respondents believed that companies in the construction and aircraft industries were more likely to be adversely affected by the act. Because of these perceptions, we sent additional questionnaires to a number of leading companies in these industries. The response rate of these two samples was slightly lower than that of our overall sample; 13 of 20 aircraft companies and 15 of 25 construction firms responded. However, those responding supported the perception that the aircraft and construction industries have been significantly affected by the act; 54 percent reported that the act had adversely affected their overseas business.

The loss of business by construction companies was reiterated in a recent Wall Street Journal article which implied that the firms hardest hit were large international construction companies dealing mainly with foreign governments or government-run industries. According to the article, some construction companies have stated that in certain countries, it is impossible even to get on the bidding lists without paying what amounts to an entry fee to a local agent who has good connections with the government in power. What impact this has had is hard to tell. However, industry statistics show that in 1977, the United States ranked fourth in worldwide construction and industrial project activity; in 1979, the United States ranked seventh. Further, one construction firm has alleged that it lost a $40 million overseas contract because its foreign competitor made a payment to a foreign official. . . .

COUNCIL OF EUROPE: RECOMMENDATION ON ECONOMIC CRIME

21 I.L.M. 884 (1982)

THE COMMITTEE OF MINISTERS, under the terms of Article 15.*b* of the Statute of the Council of Europe.

Considering that the considerable growth of economic activity in Council of Europe member states and the development of international economic relations often give rise to the commission of criminal offences;

Considering that economic crime:

—causes loss to a large number of people (partners, shareholders, employees, competitors, customers, creditors), to the community as a whole and even to the state, which has to bear a heavy financial burden or suffers a considerable loss of revenue;

—harms the national and/or international economy;

—causes a certain loss of confidence in the economic system itself;

Considering the substantial legal problems caused by this form of crime at both national and international level;

Considering the desirability of, first of all, seeking to prevent such crime by means of civil, commercial and administrative law measures;

Considering that civil, commercial and administrative law should, wherever necessary, be strengthened or supplemented by the criminal law;

Considering that effective control of economic crime would redress the balance in the system of criminal justice in relation to conventional offences, thus increasing public confidence in the working of the system;

Convinced that it is in the best interest of Council of Europe member states to develop joint criminal-policy principles against this evil and to improve their mutual assistance in this field without delay;

Having regard to the conclusions of the 8th Conference of European Ministers of Justice, held in Stockholm in 1973;

Having regard to the proceedings of the 12th Conference of Directors of Criminological Research Institutes, held in Strasbourg in 1976,

I. Recommends that the governments of member states review their legislation on business activity in the light of the need to promote a coherent and comprehensive set of standards, easily understandable to all concerned, as well as a legal system flexible enough to cope with such economic crime as may occur as a result of future economic and technological development;

II. Recommends, in particular, that the governments of member states:

1. devote greater attention to preventing economic crime, with particular reference to statutory provisions concerning the following matters:

—The minimum funds necessary for setting up and/or running a commercial company,

—the conditions to be observed and particulars to be supplied for the entry of commercial companies in special registers kept by the state,

—the book-keeping of commercial companies and supervision thereof by appropriate bodies,

—the periodic inspection of companies by government departments and the conduct of administrative enquiries concerning companies where grave irregularities are suspected;

2. examine the possibility of entrusting an ombudsman with the task of protecting the public, particularly consumers, from abuses and malpractices in the business world;

3. improve co-operation between the authorities responsible for economic crime control;

4. inform the public of its rights and of the remedies available to it against economic crime and, by facilitating access to the authorities, encourage the public to turn to them for protection;

5. encourage trade associations and other groups in the business world to draw up codes of business ethics;

III. Recommends that the governments of member states:

1. take steps to facilitate the detection of economic offences and the institution of criminal proceedings, in particular by:

—setting up police units specialising in economic crime control,

—setting up, under prosecuting authorities, sections specialising in economic cases,

—providing specialised training for police and other investigative bodies dealing with economic crime, such training being associated, where appropriate, with satisfactory career structures,

—giving victims of economic crime the right to enforce their claims personally in the criminal proceedings or, if they already enjoy this right, by making their task easier,

—examining the possibility of allowing certain victims' associations to be parties to criminal proceedings;

2. take all steps required to ensure swift and efficient criminal justice in the field of economic crime, in particular by:

—providing specialised training for judges dealing with economic cases,
—revising the rules of secrecy for certain professions (e.g. banking),
—permitting or encouraging other public authorities to provide the criminal authorities with information needed for criminal proceedings,
—examining the possibility of adopting the concept of criminal liability of corporations or at least of introducing other arrangements serving the same purposes in respect of economic offences,
—encouraging authorities responsible for prosecuting economic offences to avoid excessive delays;

3. review their legislation on criminal penalties for economic offences with a view to:

—appropriate use being made of custodial penalties in the case of serious offences,
—making fines correspond better to the financial situation of offenders and to the seriousness of the economic offences committed and seeking legislative or other means to prevent a fine from being paid by a third person, particularly the person for whose benefit the offence was committed,
—professional disqualifications being introduced as main penalties and compensation of victims being made a penalty in appropriate cases;

IV. Recommends that the governments of member states:

—keep detailed statistics on economic crime to facilitate criminological research and reinforce the prevention and punishment of such crime.
—encourage and promote research into the causes, manifestations and consequences of economic crime and into the efficacy of preventive and punitive measures in this field;

V. Recommends that the governments of member states intensify their cooperation at international level, in particular by:

—signing and ratifying the European Conventions on Mutual Assistance in Criminal Matters and on Extradition, the Protocols thereto and any other international instrument facilitating the prosecution and punishment of economic crime,
—examining the desirability of harmonising the rules of mutual assistance in criminal matters more closely in the Council of Europe and determining the field of application of member states' criminal law in the repression of economic crime in particular with a view to a revision of domestic laws restricting assistance;

VI. Recommends that the governments of member states widely circulate among the appropriate authorities the report of the European Committee on Crime Problems (CDPC) on economic crime.

APPENDIX TO RECOMMENDATION NO. R (81) 12

LIST OF ECONOMIC OFFENCES

Owing to the generally recognised difficulty of giving an exact definition of economic crime, it was found necessary to delimit the concept by means of a list of offences. . . .

The offences referred to in the recommendation are the following:

1. cartel offences;
2. fraudulent practices and abuse of economic situation by multinational companies;
3. fraudulent procurement or abuse of state or international organisations' grants;
4. computer crime (e.g. theft of data, violation of secrets, manipulation of computerised data);
5. bogus firms;
6. faking of company balance sheets and book-keeping offences;
7. fraud concerning economic situation and corporate capital of companies;
8. violation by a company of standards of security and health concerning employees;
9. fraud to the detriment of creditors (e.g. bankruptcy, violation of intellectual and industrial property rights);
10. consumer fraud (in particular falsification of and misleading statements on goods, offences against public health, abuse of consumers' weakness or inexperience);
11. unfair competition (including bribery of an employee of a competing company) and misleading advertising;
12. fiscal offences and evasion of social costs by enterprises;
13. customs offences (e.g. evasion of customs duties, breach of quota restrictions);
14. offences concerning money and currency regulations;
15. stock exchange and bank offences (e.g. fraudulent stock exchange manipulation and abuse of the public's inexperience);
16. offences against the environment.

NOTES AND QUESTIONS

1. Is it wise to prohibit U.S. firms from corrupt practices abroad? What are the arguments in favor of doing so? What are the arguments in favor of not doing so?

2. What are the problems in the language of the act, insofar as you can identify them from the above materials? How much can you resolve and clarify these problems? Is any revision wise? Why, do you think, hasn't it occurred yet?

3. If you were drafting a regulation or an act, how would you handle the following situations?

(a)   gifts in the $5 to $100 range to a foreign official?
(b)   buying an expensive dinner for a foreign official?
(c)   contributions to a foreign political party?
(d)   contributions to a charity suggested by a foreign official?

4. Does the European document affect your position on extraterritoriality? What about the fact that most nations have laws against corruption? Which of the enforcement methods described in the European statement appear wise? What different approaches would you urge for the various kinds of corruption listed in the appendix to the European statement?

5. Should the FCPA, which explicitly authorizes enforcement only by the SEC and the Justice Department, be interpreted as authorizing a parallel private damage action by a firm alleging that a competitor gained a contract by bribery? Most commentators assume not.

6. How much might the act be clarified if cases actually went to trial rather than settlement? Practically the only published cases are United States v. McLean, 738 F.2d 655 (5th Cir. 1984) (restriction on criminal prosecution of employee in absence of such prosecution of employer); and SEC v. World-Wide Coin Investments, 567 F. Supp. 724 (N.D. Ga. 1983).

7. Suppose the United States were to negotiate an international agreement against corrupt business practices. What might be the appropriate substantive provisions? What sorts of enforcement might be appropriate?

For additional data on the Foreign Corrupt Practices Act, *see* Symposium, 9 Syracuse J. Intl. L. & Com. 235 (1982); Trooboff, Proposed Amendment of the Foreign Corrupt Practices Act of 1977, 77 A.J.I.L. 340 (1983).

2.   Possible Antitrust Implications

It is generally agreed that no tort-style private cause of action is implicit in the FCPA. Nevertheless, litigants have frequently sought to use the FCPA to bolster a suit under another statute. The following case exemplifies this approach in the antitrust area. As will be recalled from the preceding chapter, a firm that loses a foreign government sale because its competitor bribed the foreign official might attempt a treble-damage antitrust action, based on the argument that the firm and the foreign official conspired in restraint of trade. Such a suit will normally be met with an act of state defense—the FCPA provides the plaintiff with a new argument that the congressional policy against corruption should be taken into account in interpreting the act of state defense.

CLAYCO PETROLEUM CORP. v. OCCIDENTAL PETROLEUM CORP.

712 F.2d 404 (9th Cir. 1983), *cert. denied,* 104 S. Ct. 703 (1984)

PER CURIAM.

This appeal arises from an antitrust suit filed by Clayco Petroleum Corporation and Bruce Clayman, the founder and principal shareholder of Clayco against Occidental Petroleum Corporation, Occidental of Umm Al Qaywayn, Inc. and Armand Hammer (Occidental) charging Occidental with making secret payments to an official of Umm Al Qaywayn in order to obtain unlawfully an off-shore oil concession. The district court dismissed the action on the basis of the act of state doctrine. We affirm.

I.   FACTS AND PROCEDURAL CONTEXT

Plaintiffs commenced this action alleging violations of section 1 of the Sherman Act, 15 U.S.C. §1, section 2(c) of the Robinson-Patman Act, 15 U.S.C. §13(c), sections 16720 and 17045 of the California Business and Professions Code, and the common law. The crux of the complaint is that Occidental conspired to make and made secret payments in England and Switzerland totalling $417,000 to Sheikh Sultan bin Ahmed Muallah (Sultan), Umm Al Qaywayn's Petroleum Minister and son of its ruler, Sheikh Ahmed al Mualla (Ahmed). The complaint further alleges that only through these unlawful and anti-competitive actions did defendants secure the valuable off-shore oil concession. More specifically, plaintiffs allege that in September 1969, Ahmed agreed that Clayco would receive the concession, but instead, on November 18, 1969, he awarded the concession to defendant Occidental of Umm Al Qaywayn, Inc., Occidental Petroleum's subsidiary.

Plaintiffs allege that the first information they obtained regarding why they lost the concession became available in December 1978. The December 11, 1978, edition of the Oakland Tribune contained a story which said that Occidental had distributed about $30 million under "questionable legal circumstances," and that Dr. Armand Hammer, Occidental's chief executive officer, had personally disbursed $217,000 to Sultan in a London hotel room in 1969. The article also reported that a second payment of $200,000 was made to Sultan in Switzerland. The article stated, "Hammer paid the initial $217,000 as part of a $1.7 million deal with the sheikdom . . . for an oil and gas concession."

In 1977, the Securities and Exchange Commission (SEC) commenced an action against Occidental alleging violations of the Securities Exchange Act of 1934 and rules promulgated thereunder, based on illegal or questionable payments made by Occidental. Securities and Exchange Commission v. Occidental Petroleum Corp., No. 77-0751, (D.D.C. filed May 3, 1977). Occidental consented to the entry of a permanent injunction and agreed to conduct an internal investigation of the alleged illegal payments and to prepare for the SEC and Occidental's stockholders a special report describing such payments. Report of the Special Committee of the Board of Directors of Occidental Petroleum Corporation, Investigated Payments and Accounting Practices of Occidental Petroleum Corporation (April 17, 1978) (the Payments Report).

The Payments Report was filed and revealed various illegal payments. A Source Memorandum annexed to the Payments Report further recites that Occidental's $200,000 payment in Switzerland was of "uncertain legality" and was inaccurately described and documented on Occidental's books.

Plaintiffs allege that these $417,000 in payments plus "entertainment" expenses constituted bribes to induce Sultan and his father to award the concession to Occidental. Plaintiffs contend that Occidental, its subsidiary, and Dr. Hammer conspired to prevent competition and to deprive plaintiffs of the concession. . . .

The district court granted defendants' motion to dismiss, based on the act of state doctrine. The court stated that an exercise of sovereignty—the award of the offshore oil concession—was implicated in the case, and that adjudication would interfere with United States foreign policy. The court noted that plaintiffs' obligation to prove that they were damaged by defendants' conduct would necessitate review of the ethical validity of the sovereign's conduct. The court also refused to apply a commercial exception to the act of state doctrine.

II. ISSUES

The appellants raise numerous challenges to the district court's application of the act of state doctrine. In essence, appellants argue first that this case is outside the purview of the act of state doctrine; and second, that the foreign sovereign action involved fits within "corruption" or "commercial" exceptions to the doctrine. . . .

Appellants also contend that the passage of the Foreign Corrupt Practices Act of 1977 (FCPA), 15 U.S.C. §§78dd-1 et seq. (Supp. V. 1981), created an exception to the act of state doctrine which should apply in this case.[3]

The FCPA prohibits bribery of a foreign official for the purpose of obtaining or retaining business. 15 U.S.C. §§78dd-1, 78dd-2. The Act provides for severe criminal penalties including fines and imprisonment. 15 U.S.C. §§78dd-2(b),

---

[3] Neither the Supreme Court nor a court of appeals has spoken on this issue. The district court in Dominicus Americana Bohio v. Gulf & Western, 473 F. Supp. 680, 690 (S.D.N.Y. 1978), held, at least in the alternative, that there is a "corruption exception" to the act of state doctrine. No truly supportive authority, however, is cited by the court for that proposition. The district court in Sage International, Ltd. v. Cadillac Gage Co., 534 F. Supp. 896 (E.D. Mich. 1981), said in dictum that "there is a likelihood that the doctrine could be avoided were the allegations such as to call for review of foreign sovereign corruption charges." *Id.* at 910. The court also said in dictum that "in spirit and practice, the Act [FCPA] supports the notion that act of state concerns are subjugated to interests in stemming foreign corrupt practices." *Id.* n. 26.

78ff. In addition, the Attorney General may bring a civil action to enjoin impending violations. 15 U.S.C. §78dd-2(c).

The FCPA was intended to stop bribery of foreign officials and political parties by domestic corporations. Bribery abroad was considered a "severe" United States foreign policy problem; it embarrasses friendly governments, causes a decline of foreign esteem for the United States and casts suspicion on the activities of our enterprises, giving credence to our foreign opponents. H.R. Rep. No. 640, 95th Cong., 1st Sess. 5 (1977).[4] The FCPA thus represents a legislative judgment that our foreign relations will be bettered by a strict anti-bribery statute. There is also no question, however, that any prosecution under the Act entails risks to our relations with the foreign governments involved. Note, Sherman Act Jurisdiction and the Acts of Foreign Sovereigns, 77 Colum. L. Rev. 1247, 1261 (1977); Department of State Responses to October 5, 1981 Inquiry by Congressman Timothy E. Wirth, Chairman U.S. House of Representatives Subcommittee on Telecommunications, Consumer Protection, and Finance of the Committee on Energy and Commerce at 10-11, 13, 18, 20.

The Justice Department and the SEC share enforcement responsibilities under the FCPA. They coordinate enforcement of the Act with the State Department, recognizing the potential foreign policy problems of these actions. *See* Testimony of Ernest B. Johnston, Jr., Department of State Before the Subcommittee on Telecommunications, Consumer Protection and Finance, House Committee on Energy and Commerce, December 16, 1981 at 11; Department of State Responses to October 5, 1981 Inquiry, *supra,* at 12, 13. Executive bodies have discretion in bringing any action. *E.g.* United States v. Cox, 342 F.2d 167, 193 (5th Cir. 1965) (Wisdom, J., concurring), *cert. denied,* 381 U.S. 935, 85 S. Ct. 1767, 14 L. Ed. 2d 700 (1965). Therefore, any governmental enforcement represents a judgment on the wisdom of bringing a proceeding, in light of the exigencies of foreign affairs. Act of state concerns are thus inapplicable since the purpose of the doctrine is to prevent the judiciary from interfering with the political branch's conduct of foreign policy. . . .

Here, however, we are faced with a private lawsuit, rather than a public enforcement action. It is the screening of governmental proceedings, with State Department consultation, which distinguishes FCPA enforcement from private suits. . . . Hence, in private suits, the act of state doctrine remains necessary to protect the proper conduct of national foreign policy. We therefore reject appellants' contention, which is not supported by the legislative history, that in enacting the FCPA, Congress intended to abrogate the act of state doctrine in private suits based on foreign payments.

For the reasons above, we hold that the act of state doctrine applies, and that appellants do not come within any exception to the doctrine. The decision of the trial court dismissing the action is therefore affirmed.

---

[4] It may be that the revelation of bribery, more than bribery itself, causes these problems. H.R. Rep. No. 640, 95th Cong. 1st Sess. 5(1977).

QUESTIONS

1. Is this case consistent with *Timberlane?*
2. If you were drafting legislation to restrict private international antitrust actions, how would you deal with the situation exemplified by *Clayco?*

3.   Possible Corporate Law Implications

In the corporate law area, there have also been efforts to use the FCPA to obtain support for a private cause of action. Here, the typical suit is by shareholders against management believed to have participated in illegal payments. The following case exemplifies such as a suit; it is built on two legal theories that, although similar in policy substance, differ analytically.

One legal theory is that of the shareholder derivative suit, a suit in which the shareholders bring a suit against directors or management on behalf of the corporation, usually based on an argument that these directors or management have hurt the corporation and that they are unwilling to represent the corporate interest against themselves. The suit is formally one between the corporation and the allegedly offending directors or management, and recovery (save for legal fees) would go to the corporation.

The other legal theory is built on the idea that the directors defrauded the shareholders by failing to disclose the corrupt payments. As with any suit for fraud, there has to be an action in reliance; here, presumably, the shareholders' action in voting for or against retention of particular directors. The international scope of this body of law, which relies heavily on federal statutes, together with the subtleties of what constitutes a fradulent statement and an action in reliance, will be considered again in Chapter XVI.

GAINES AND FITZPATRICK v. HAUGHTON

645 F.2d 761 (9th Cir. 1981), *cert. denied*, 454 U.S. 1145 (1982)

ELY, J.

Ora E. Gaines, the plaintiff-appellant herein, appeals from an order of dismissal and summary judgment for defendants (Lockheed Aircraft Corporation and a number of former and present directors and officers of Lockheed) in a shareholder lawsuit alleging both derivative claims of breach of fiduciary duty/waste of corporate assets and class action claims of federal securities violations. Gaines assigns a variety of errors by the District Court and seeks partial summary judgment and/or remand.

FACTS

From as early as 1961 to as late as 1975, Lockheed engaged in the practice of hiring "consultants" and "foreign sales agents" and paying them large fees and commissions in connection with foreign sales of Lockheed aircraft and equipment. Approximately $30-38 million was paid directly to foreign governments and officials during this period.[1] Shortly after the existence of these clandestine, "off the books" questionable payments was revealed by Securities and Exchange Commission (SEC) and United States Senate proceedings in July-August 1975, Gaines—an individual Lockheed shareholder—commenced his lawsuit in the United States District Court for the Central District of California. Gaines' complaint, filed on February 24, 1976, asserts two derivative causes of action on behalf of the corporation and two class action counts on behalf of the shareholders.

The derivative causes of action—based on California law since Lockheed is a California corporation—allege that the individual defendants breached their fiduciary duty to the corporation and "wasted" corporate assets by authorizing, employing, and affirmatively concealing corrupt business practices (i.e., the practice of paying large "sales commission," "consulting fees," and outright bribes to foreign purchasers, foreign government officials, and their agents) which resulted in "no use or benefit to Lockheed whatsoever" (Complaint, ¶43(a), see id. ¶¶43(c), (e), 44) and tarnished Lockheed's image and goodwill. See id. ¶¶17, 30. The class action counts—based on federal securities law—allege that defendants-appellees (hereinafter "appellees") violated the filing and proxy requirements of §§13(a) and 14(a) of the Securities Exchange Act of 1934, as amended ("the 1934 Act"), 15 U.S.C. §§78m & 78n, by (1) failing to disclose the existence and details of the questionable foreign payments to the shareholders in proxy solicitation materials each year from 1961-74, and (2) by filing materially false and misleading annual and other periodic financial reports on behalf of Lockheed.

Gaines' federal class action claims seek a permanent injunction barring Lockheed from making further improper or undisclosed payments, filing materially false or misleading proxy materials or periodic financial reports, or maintaining any undisclosed accounts. Gaines also seeks a declaration invalidating past elections, removing certain directors, appointing a special master to investigate the payments made, approving new proxy materials, requiring amendment of prior filings, and requiring an accounting of payments made. Gaines does not seek any damages in his §13(a) or §14(a) claims.

The *derivative* causes of action seek restitution and money damages for "any

---

[1] There are no allegations that Lockheed made improper payments to *domestic* officials or that any federal criminal laws were violated by the foreign payments. *See* Special Review Committee Report at 7-15. The Foreign Corrupt Practices Act of 1977, Pub. L. No. 95-213, 91 Stat. 1494, codified at 15 U.S.C. §§78m, 78dd-1, 78dd-2, 78ff, was signed into law after the conclusion of the scenario herein. *See generally Comment,* The Foreign Corrupt Practices Act of 1977: A Solution or a Problem?, 11 Cal. W. Intl. L.J. 111, 137-39 (1981).

and all" disbursements and expenditures in connection with the alleged corrupt business practices and improper foreign payments, including interest, attorneys' fees, and punitive damages.

Apart from the commencement of Gaines' lawsuit, the revelation of Lockheed's foreign payments in July-August 1975 precipitated several other events.[6] On February 2, 1976, the Lockheed board of directors appointed a Special Review Committee [7] (SRC), whose investigation was assisted by the New York law firm Shearman & Sterling and the accounting firm Arthur Anderson & Co. and was directed by the SRC's counsel, former United States District Judge Arnold Bauman. On April 13, 1976, and in response to an SEC complaint, see SEC v. Lockheed Aircraft Corp., [1975-1976 Transfer Binder] Fed. Sec. L. Rep. ¶95,509 (C.C.H.) (D.D.C. 1976), Lockheed entered into a consent decree and permanent injunction which enjoined future improper payments, improper accounting methods, and other forms of concealment; required amendment of prior SEC fillings; provided for an internal corporate investigation and report procedures to be conducted under SEC supervision; and ordered other remedial actions. On June 23, 1978, Lockheed agreed to a consent order of the Federal Trade Commission containing even more sweeping prohibitions than those contained in the SEC permanent injunction. See In re Lockheed Corp., [1976-79 Transfer Binder] Trade Reg. Rep. (C.C.H.) ¶21,454 (F.T.C. Dkt. C-2942, Aug. 17, 1978).

The SRC conducted a fourteen-month investigation, interviewed more than 250 witnesses, and issued a report (dated May 16, 1977) to the Lockheed board, the SEC, and the United States District Court for the District of Columbia on May 26, 1977. The SRC report, which concluded that Lockheed had, with the approval and participation of several senior executives, make $30-38 million in questionable and "off the books" foreign payments, was distributed to all Lockheed shareholders on June 10, 1977. The SRC report contained a "secret" two-volume appendix prepared by Judge Bauman, which the District Court placed under a protective order on June 10, 1977.

On April 20, 1977, the Lockheed board appointed a Special Litigation Committee (SLC), and delegated to it the full power and authority of the board of directors with respect to the then-pending derivative lawsuit. The SLC, composed of four non-defendant outside directors, retained independent outside counsel and, over a period of ten months, considered the factual and legal merit of Gaines' lawsuit. In its March 14, 1978 report, the SLC detailed

---

[6]For a description of the SEC's general response to the disclosure of questionable foreign payments by American corporations, see Note, Disclosure of Payments to Foreign Government Officials Under the Securities Acts, 89 Harv. L. Rev. 1848, 1850-53 (1976).

[7]The original members of the SRC were four nonmanagement Lockheed directors: Messrs. D.M. Cochran, J.K. Horton, F.M. Vinson, and R.W. Haack. On April 14, 1976, after Gaines commenced his lawsuit, four independent outside directors joined the Lockheed board and were appointed to the SRC. These directors, who later became the Special Litigation Committee, were: J.P. Downer (executive vice president of Atlantic Richfield Co.), H.I. Flournoy (dean of Center for Public Affairs of the University of Southern California), E.L. Hazard (former chairman of Continental Group, Inc.), and J.W. Newman (former chairman of Dun & Bradstreet Cos.).

the factual background of Gaines' lawsuit, enumerated and analyzed a series of factors it deemed definitive of Lockheed's interest in pursuing the suit,[11] and unanimously concluded that "sound business judgment as to the interests of Lockheed in light of the circumstances and legal considerations here present leads directly and clearly to the conclusion that the claims asserted in the derivative cases should not be pursued against any of the defendants." Special Litigation Committee Report at 41. Consistent with its decision that the pursuit of the derivative litigation was not in the best interests of the corporation or its shareholders, on March 14, 1978, the SLC directed its counsel to seek dismissal of the derivative claims. Shortly thereafter, Lockheed authorized counsel to seek dismissal of the federal class action claims. These motions were filed in the District Court on April 17, 1978. . . .

DISCUSSION

I. THE BUSINESS JUDGMENT RULE AND CORPORATE DECISIONS TO TERMINATE DERIVATIVE LITIGATION

In Lewis v. Anderson, 615 F.2d 778 (9th Cir. 1979), *cert. denied*, 449 U.S. 869, 101 S. Ct. 206, 66 L. Ed. 2d 89 (1980), this court decided that, as a matter of California law, a corporation's board of directors may delegate to a disinterested "special litigation committee" the business judgment authority to dismiss a shareholder derivative lawsuit brought on behalf of the corporation against some of the directors. While *Lewis* is not identical to the instant case—*Lewis* determined only the legal *authority* of the delegation and exercise of the "business judgment rule"; did not pass on the factual determination of whether the committee acted in good faith; and involved derivative *federal* securities claims—it lends strong support to the District Court's holding on this issue.

Drawing on analogous decisions by intermediate appellate courts in California—for the California Supreme Court had not (and still has not) faced the precise issue *sub judice* —this court in *Lewis* amplified the general common law

---

[11] These factors included the following:

1. whether or not each defendant's conduct has been such as to give rise to a cause of action by Lockheed against him;

2. the legal and practical difficulties of sustaining any possible cause of action;

3. the cost to Lockheed in resources of time and money of pursuing any particular claim;

4. the likelihood that, if successful, Lockheed would realize a significant recovery;

5. the effect that dismissal or pursuit of the claims would have on Lockheed's reputation and standing in the business community and elsewhere;

6. the effect the dismissal or pursuit of the claims would have on the morale and adherence to current business practices of Lockheed's employees;

7. the extent to which, if at all, continued litigation would result in disclosures of facts and suppositions harmful to Lockheed and its stockholders as well as to the national interest; and

8. the extent to which, if at all, Lockheed would be damaged by protracted and embittered litigation with its officers past and present.

Special Litigation Committee Report at 9-10.

"business judgment rule" in two important respects.[17] First *Lewis* held that a board of directors' general management responsibility and discretion—including the decision whether to pursue a cause of action—may be delegated to a committee of directors. The committee's *good faith* decision that dismissing a derivative action would be in the best interests of the corporation, even if that decision is negligent, bars any further legal action by the shareholder. 615 F.2d at 780, 783-84. The second, and related, holding of *Lewis* is that even when "a majority of the board is charged with wrongdoing in the very action sought to be dismissed," *id.* at 782, they may appoint a committee of disinterested directors "to make an independent determination of the merits of the [derivative] action." *Id.* The application of the business judgment rule to boards of directors with "interested" majorities is not improper because "the directors who are accused of wrongdoing have not decided to dismiss the case," *id.*, a committee of disinterested directors has. See *Gall v. Exxon Corp.*, 418 F. Supp. 508, 517 (S.D.N.Y. 1976).

Gaines contends, however, that various factors require remand to the District Court for further findings of fact on the appropriateness and sufficiency of the investigative procedures chosen and pursued by the SLC. Specifically, Gaines argues that Lockheed's delay in establishing the SLC until a year after this suit was commenced is attributable to shopping around for a "friendly" committee. Gaines also alleges that the participation of two "deeply involved" directors in the formation and investigation of the SRC sufficiently tainted the investigative structure and procedures by the later SLC to preclude summary judgment on this issue. Gaines also asserts that the District Court applied an erroneous legal standard in determining the propriety of the SLC's exercise of business judgment.

While we are mindful of the need to scrutinize carefully the mechanism by which directors delegate to a minority committee the business judgment authority to terminate derivative litigation, particularly when the lawsuit is directed against some or a majority of the directors, we find that Gaines has not raised a triable issue of fact on this issue. The record establishes beyond question that the SLC was composed of independent outside directors whose investigation and recommendations were not tainted by the attenuated

---

[17] For a discussion of corporate director's business judgment authority to, *inter alia*, terminate derivative litigation, *see* Burks v. Lasker, 441 U.S. 471, 478, 480, 485, 99 S. Ct. 1831, 1837, 1838, 1840, 60 L. Ed. 2d 404 (1979), *rev'g* 567 F.2d 1208 (2d Cir. 1978); United Copper Securities Co. v. Amalgamated Copper Co., 244 U.S. 261, 263-64, 37 S. Ct. 509, 510-11, 61 L. Ed. 1119 (1917) (Brandeis, J.); Corbus v. Alaska Treadwell Gold Mining Co., 187 U.S. 455, 463, 23 S. Ct. 157, 160 47 L. Ed. 256 (1903); Galef v. Alexander, 615 F. 2d 51, 57-62 (2d Cir. 1980); Genzer v. Cunningham, 498 F. Supp. 682, 686-89 (E.D. Mich. 1980); Maldonado v. Flynn, 485 F. Supp. 274 (S.D.N.Y. 1980); Abbey v. Control Data Corp., 460 F. Supp. 1242, 1243-46 (D. Minn. 1978), *aff'd*, 603 F.2d 724 (8th Cir. 1979), *cert. denied*, 444 U.S. 1017, 100 S. Ct. 670, 62 L. Ed. 2d 647 (1980); Gall v. Exxon Corp., 418 F. Supp. 508, 514-17 (S.D.N.Y. 1976); Findley v. Garrett, 109 Cal. App. 2d 166, 174, 240 P.2d 421, 426 (1952); Auerbach v. Bennett, 47 N.Y.2d 619, 419 N.Y.S.2d 920, 393 N.E.2d 994 (1979); 3A W. Fletcher, Cyclopedia of the Law of Private Corporations §1039, at 37-38 (perm. ed. 1975).

involvement of "interested" directors in the formation and preliminary investigation of the SRC. The record also establishes beyond question that the SLC's investigatory procedures were adequate. *See generally* Radobenko v. Automated Equipment Corp., 520 F.2d 540, 543-44 (9th Cir. 1975). Moreover, we hold that the legal standard employed by the District Court in reviewing the SLC's decision to terminate the litigation comports with this court's statement in *Lewis* that even a negligent decision to dismiss an action is legally dispositive, so long as it is made in good faith. *See* 615 F.2d at 783-84. Accordingly, we conclude that remand is unnecessary. The District Court's order of summary judgment for appellees on this issue is affirmed.

II.   THE DISMISSAL OF THE §14(a) CLAIM

Gaines contends that the District Court's Rule 12(b)(6) dismissal of his §14(a) claim was erroneous because his complaint adequately states a cause of action for equitable relief under §14(a) of the 1934 Act. Gaines challenges both of the District Court's alternative bases for dismissal—that Gaines lacked "standing" to bring a nonderivative action because he himself had not granted a proxy in reliance on the allegedly misleading solicitation materials and that Gaines' complaint failed to allege the requisite "transactional causation" or "causal nexus." Resolution of these issues requires a brief overview of the §14(a) cause of action.

Section 14(a) of the 1934 Act, 15 U.S.C. §78n(a), provides:

> It shall be unlawful for any person, by the use of the mails or by any means or instrumentality of interstate commerce or of any facility of a national securities exchange or otherwise, *in contravention of such rules and regulations as the Commission may prescribe* as necessary or appropriate in the public interest or for the protection of investors, to solicit or to permit the use of his name to solicit any proxy or consent or authorization in respect to any security (other than an exempted security) registered pursuant to section 78*l* of this title.

(Emphasis added.) The pertinent SEC regulation, 17 C.F.R. §240.14a-9 (1980), provides:

> (a) No solicitation subject to this regulation shall be made by means of any proxy statement, form of proxy, notice of meeting or other communication, written or oral, containing any statement which, at the time and in the light of the circumstances under which it is made, is false or misleading with respect to any material fact, or which omits to state any material fact necessary in order to make the statements therein not false or misleading or necessary to correct any statement in any earlier communication with respect to the solicitation of a proxy for the same meeting or subject matter which has become false or misleading.
>
> (b) The fact that a proxy statement, form of proxy or other soliciting material has been filed with or examined by the Commission shall not be deemed a

finding by the Commission that such material is accurate or complete or not false or misleading, or that the Commission has passed upon the merits of or approved any statement contained therein or any matter to be acted upon by security holders. No representation contrary to the foregoing shall be made.

Note: The following are some examples of what, depending upon particular facts and circumstances, may be misleading within the meaning of this section.

(a) Predictions as to specific future market values.

(b) Material which directly or indirectly impugns character, integrity or personal reputation, or directly or indirectly makes charges concerning improper, illegal or immoral conduct or associations, without factual foundation.

(c) Failure to so identify a proxy statement, form of proxy and other soliciting material as to clearly distinguish it from the soliciting material of any other person or persons soliciting for the same meeting or subject matter.

(d) Claims made prior to a meeting regarding the results of a solicitation.

"The purpose of §14(a) is to prevent management or others from obtaining authorization for corporate action by means of deceptive or inadequate disclosure in proxy solicitation." J.I. Case Co. v. Borak, 377 U.S. 426, 431, 84 S. Ct. 1555, 1559, 12 L. Ed. 2d 423 (1964). The Supreme Court has recognized an implied private cause of action under that section in favor of stockholders and investors who have been injured as a result of false or misleading proxy solicitations. *Id.* at 430-31, 84 S. Ct. at 1558-59. *See* Mills v. Electric Auto-Lite Co., 396 U.S. 375, 377, 90 S. Ct. 616, 618, 24 L. Ed. 2d 593 (1970). . . .

B.   *Transactional Causation and Materiality*

Gaines' §14(a) claim is ultimately premised on appellees' failure to disclose "corrupt and improper foreign payments" and related corporate misconduct to the Lockheed shareholders in the proxy solicitation materials for director elections each year from 1961 to 1975. The real issue in this appeal is whether, and in what circumstances, management's failure to disclose particular conduct to the shareholders states a §14(a) cause of action. . . .

Many corporate actions taken by directors in the interest of the corporation might offend and engender controversy among some stockholders.[18] Investors share the same diversity of social and political views that characterizes the polity as a whole. The tenor of a company's labor relations policies, economic decisions to relocate or close established industrial plants, commercial dealings with foreign countries which are disdained in certain circles, decisions to develop (or not to develop) particular natural resources or forms of energy technology, and the promulgation of corporate personnel policies that reject (or embrace) the principle of affirmative action, are just a few examples of busi-

---

[18] Illegal foreign payments cases clearly involve state law questions of breach of fiduciary duties. They should not be dealt with under the general disclosure provisions of the federal securities laws where it is apparent, as here, that the nondisclosure of such payments had little, if any, impact on the plaintiff's dealings in the corporation's stock. Several recent cases involving illegal foreign payments have adopted this rationale in dismissing the plaintiff's cause of action for failure to state a claim under §13(a) or §14(a).

ness judgments, soundly entrusted to the broad discretion of the directors, which may nonetheless cause shareholder dissent and provoke claims of "wasteful," "unethical," or even "immoral" business dealings. Should corporate directors have a duty under §14(a) to disclose all such corporate decisions in proxy solicitations for their re-election? We decline to extend the duty of disclosure under §14(a) to these situations. While we neither condone nor condemn these and similar types of corporate conduct (including the now-illegal practice of questionable foreign payments), we believe that aggrieved shareholders have sufficient recourse to state law claims against the responsible directors and, if all else fails, can sell or trade their stock in the offending corporation in favor of an enterprise more compatible with their own personal goals and values.

Absent credible allegations of self-dealing by the directors or dishonesty or deceit which inures to the direct, personal benefit of the directors—a fact that demonstrates a betrayal of trust to the corporation and shareholders and the director's essential unfitness for corporate stewardship—we hold that director misconduct of the type traditionally regulated by state corporate law need not be disclosed in proxy solicitation for director elections.

NOTES AND QUESTIONS

1. Does the court adequately recognize the shareholder's interest in ensuring that a management is not corrupt? Is the case consistent with the SEC's position that the securities laws require that corruption be disclosed, a position that was the statutory basis for the initial investigation in the case?

2. What precisely is the shareholder's interest in ensuring that the management is not corrupt?

3. Is the position of either of the just presented cases faithful to Congress's intent? How would you argue for and against the positions of the courts?

4. Suppose the people of a nation sue their former chief executive to recover allegedly corrupt earnings. Should the U.S. courts grant recovery? Note that such a suit against the Shah's family was envisaged as part of the Iranian settlement, but was rejected by the New York courts. *See* Islamic Republic of Iran v. Pahlevi, 478 N.Y.S.2d 597 (Ct. App. 1984).

5. Should Swiss bank secrecy be modified to decrease the use of that nation's banking system for the storage and transfer of corruptly acquired funds? How could this be negotiated?

6. Please assume that Byteboards, Inc., a U.S. firm, has—almost certainly by corrupt means—obtained enormously favorable concessions on the tax, labor, construction, and environmental arrangements for a large new electronic printed circuit fabrication facility in Southeast Asia. As a result of the cost savings associated with these concessions, Byteboards has been able to displace a large portion of the competing domestic and foreign manufacturer's sales of printed circuits.

Several of these U.S. and foreign manufacturers, along with the U.S. Printed Circuit Manufacturers' Association, have filed a complaint with the ITC under §337, alleging the necessary damage to trade, and putting forward the ideas that the import of goods made under significantly lower health and safety and environmental regulations amounts to an unfair trade practice and that acquisition of these advantages by corrupt means also amounts to an unfair trade practice. They hope to exclude Byteboards' boards.

Before facing the merits of the individual case, the members of the ITC are planning a discussion of the idea of extending ITC jurisdiction to these new areas. As a new appointee of the ITC, please outline your position on the jurisdictional issues posed by this case, so that you can present it to your colleagues.

B. THE EXPORT ADMINISTRATION ACT

The United States has several bodies of export control law, exemplified by the following materials. The laws serve a number of purposes—ranging from efforts to avoid supplying strategic military technology to the Soviet Union to efforts to avoid supplying advanced nuclear technology to nonnuclear nations. In addition, they serve foreign policy purposes—ranging from implementation of United Nations embargos against South Africa to implementation of national policy goals against disfavored nations such as Nicaragua and Iran. These laws are administered by a variety of bureaucracies, some in Commerce, some in State, and some in Defense—and some even international. They have spawned an extremely complex and detailed body of regulation that significantly restricts and complicates the export of high-tech products.

The United States has attempted to apply some of these bodies of law extraterritorially—the legal problems of doing so (and of a firm caught in the middle) will be examined in Chapter XVII. The *Edler* case, which follows, shows some of the difficulties of applying one of the older statutes, the Mutual Security Act of 1954, which is oriented toward the export of weapons themselves. The Export Administration Act, 50 U.S.C. App. §§2401 et seq., which creates an elaborate licensing procedure for many other goods and particularly for multipurpose goods, has received much more publicity, because of debates in 1983 and 1984 surrounding its renewal. Even continuing resolutions ultimately expired, and, for some time, the regulations were issued under the authority of the International Economic Emergency Powers Act, 50 U.S.C. §§1701 et seq., but the legislative deadlock was broken and the program reenacted, in modified form, in 1985.

These bodies of law pose a number of difficult issues. Some are relatively technical—for example, the precise definition of which materials should be controlled on national security grounds, taking into account such issues as foreign availability. This particular problem has traditionally pitted industry against the government, as have the associated procedures—industry fears that delay will often mean a lost sale. Another group of issues is based on the fear of circumvention through foreign transshipment, issues typically faced by prohibiting any export contacts with domestic or foreign firms found to have been involved in circumvention.

The foreign policy regulations raise a much broader category of questions. The central one is effectiveness—when will an embargo lead a foreign government to change its policies, and when will it instead create a siege mentality that actually strengthens commitment to the policy? What if an embargo appears more likely to hurt the foreign populace than to contribute to changing the foreign leaders' policies? Debate here is often extremely sloppy, with people (in both parts of the political spectrum) making arguments with respect to the embargos against Cuba and Nicaragua that they would reject when considering an embargo against South Africa.

Bibliographical Note

For additional data on these restrictions, *see* Marcuss and Mathias, U.S. Foreign Policy Export Controls: Do They Pass Muster Under International Law? 2 Intl. Tax & Bus. Law. 1 (1984); Hunt, Multilateral Cooperation in Export Controls—The Role of COCOM, 14 U. Tol. L. Rev. 1285 (1983); Abbott, Linking Trade to Political Goals: Foreign Policy Export Controls in the 1970s and 1980s, 65 Minn. L. Rev. 739 (1981); Mehlman et al., United States Restrictions on Exports to South Africa, 73 A.J.I.L. 581 (1979); Bettauer, The Nuclear Non-Proliferation Act of 1978, 10 Law & Poly. Intl. Bus. 1105 (1978); National Academy of Sciences, Scientific Communication and National Security (1982).

UNITED STATES v. EDLER INDUSTRIES, INC.

579 F.2d 516 (9th Cir. 1978)

ELY, J.

Edler Industries, Incorporated, and Vernon Edler appeal from their convictions for exporting, without a license, technical data relating to articles on the United States Munitions List. 22 U.S.C. §1934 (1970) (repealed 1976); . . . [of comparable import is a new version of the statute, 22 U.S.C. §2777.] Edler Industries was sentenced to pay a fine of $25,000. Vernon Edler received a two-year sentence, suspended on the condition that he serve ten weekends in a jail-type institution, remain on probation for five years, and donate 1200 hours of work to a charitable organization.

I

Most of the facts are not seriously disputed. About 1950 Edler Industries began in Newport Beach, California, as a small machine shop and gradually evolved into a manufacturing and engineering firm in the aerospace industry. Vernon Edler, the founder and president of the corporation, guided the business affairs of the firm and had frequent contacts with its engineers and technicians. The corporation acquired expertise in tape wrappings, a process for creating durable lightweight materials by wrapping specially impregnated cloth around a form, further impregnating it with other materials, and curing it under pressure and heat. It also developed a capacity to produce carbon/carbon composites through application of some of the same techniques. Both types of materials have important applications for rocket and missile components, particularly in nozzles. Their light weight is valuable, and they are ablative, wearing away under the pressure and heat of the rocket exhaust at a predictable rate. Edler Industries worked on the Polaris and other government missile programs; consequently, its officers and employees were familiar with missile components.

The techniques utilized by Edler Industries do not constitute classified information, and they have various civilian uses. Carbon/carbon technology is, for example, utilized in the manufacture of golf club shafts.

French missile companies eager to master this technology first contacted Edler Industries in 1968. Edler and the Societe d'Etude de la Propulsion par Reaction negotiated an agreement for a technical assistance program. Edler then sought approval from the Office of Munition Control of the State Department (OMC). OMC denied the request, but Edler nevertheless continued to provide assistance.

In January 1974 Edler Industries reached an agreement with a second French firm, the Societe Europeene de Propulsion (SEP), for the provision of technical assistance and data related to a tape wrapping program. In March 1974 Edler executed a similar agreement with SEP for carbon/carbon materials. SEP engineers visited Edler's Newport Beach plant, and Edler employees toured SEP's missile and rocket plant in Bordeaux. Edler filed applications with OMC for licenses covering the two programs, stating that the agreements would not become effective without OMC approval. OMC again rejected the requests in October 1974 on the basis that the exportation of this particular technical knowledge contravened United States policy. Edler, despite its prior representation, began implementing the programs shortly after the execution of the agreements. By the time OMC issued its disapproval, the tape wrapping program was completed, and, in spite of OMC's action, Edler continued to fulfill its carbon/carbon agreement.

Employees of Edler Industries demonstrated to SEP the techniques they used and experimented with the application of those techniques to the different materials used by SEP in France. They observed and commented on the techniques employed by SEP. They produced sample pieces in configurations similar to those utilized in missiles but not specifically designed for any particular missile. SEP was engaged in the production of rockets, a fact known to Edler personnel. Only on one minor occasion was there any indication that SEP might use the information supplied by Edler for nonmilitary purposes. The witnesses at trial generally agreed that the technology furnished by Edler had direct missile applications.

II

The Mutual Security Act of 1954 authorizes the President to control the "export and import of arms, ammunition, and implements of war, including technical data relating thereto." 22 U.S.C. §1934(a) (1970). The President is expressly empowered to designate which articles, including relevant technical data, constitute arms, ammunition, and implements of war. *Id.* Pursuant to this statute the Department of State has promulgated regulations to restrict the international traffic in arms. *See* 22 C.F.R. §§121-130 (1977). One of the regulatory requirements is that an exporter of arms first obtain a license for exportation from the State Department. *Id.* §§123.01, 125.04, 125.05.

22 C.F.R. §125.01 (1977) provides a three-part definition for the term "technical data." The only portion that is relevant here provides:

> "[T]echnical data" means: (a) Any unclassified information that can be used, or be adapted for use, in the design, production, manufacture, repair, overhaul, processing, engineering, development, operation, maintenance, or reconstruction of arms, ammunition, and implements of war on the U.S. Munitions List. . . .

Invoking the First Amendment, appellants emphasize the great potential breadth of the definition. The basic principles of the diesel engine, for example, constitute unclassified information that can be used in the manufacture of military trucks, which are included in category VII(d) of the U.S. Munitions List. *Id.* §121.01.

Export controls regulate the transmission of unclassified information by mail, hand carriage, participation in foreign symposia, and domestic plant visits. *Id.* §125.03. An exemption to the license requirement exists for published unclassified technical data, provided the exporter follows prescribed procedures. The person seeking publication, however, has the burden of obtaining governmental approval prior to publication. *Id.* §125.11(a)(1) n. 3; *see* United States v. Van Hee, 531 F.2d 352, 356 (6th Cir. 1976). In the context of the regulatory framework, an expansive interpretation of technical data relating to items on the Munitions List could seriously impede scientific research and publishing and the international scientific exchange.

III . . .

Edler has advanced a colorable claim that the First Amendment furnishes a degree of protection for its dissemination of technological information. We deem it unnecessary in this case to resolve the precise scope of that protection. Assuming the full applicability of the First Amendment, invalidation of the federal controls on munitions is unwarranted because of the narrow statutory construction that we adopt. . . .

As we have indicated, section 1934 and the definition of technical data are susceptible of an overboard interpretation. Their expansive language may be construed to restrict not only the export of arms and information directly leading to the production of articles on the Munitions List, but also the interchange of scientific and technical information that of itself is without any substantial military application. A broad statutory reading, however, is neither necessary nor proper. In our opinion, technical data must relate in a significant fashion to some item on the Munitions List. Moreover, adequate notice to the potential exporter requires that the relationship be clear. The Senate Committee on Foreign Relations described section 1934 as allowing control of munitions, "including relevant technical data." S. Rep. No. 1799, 83d Cong., 2d Sess.—, *reprinted in* [1954] U.S. Code Cong. & Admin. News, pp. 3175, 3244. Presumably, Congress intended that the technical data subject to control would be directly relevant to the production of a specified article on the Munitions List, not simply vaguely useful for the manufacture of arms.

A careful reading of the regulations also suggests that the broad definition of technical data contained in 22 C.F.R. §125.01 is not to be taken literally. The exemptions from licensing listed in 22 C.F.R. §125.11 (1977) are specific, referring to items such as training manuals, firearms of less than .50 caliber, and editorial revisions of technical data previously approved for export.

In addition, we note that the successor statute to the Mutual Security Act of 1954 evinces a congressional intent to delineate narrowly the scope of information subject to arms controls. The replacement for section 1934, 22 U.S.C. §2778 (1976), provides for presidential control of "defense articles and defense services." *Id.* §2778(a)(1). Although the President retains the authority to designate what information constitutes defense services for the purpose of section 2778, *id.* §§2778(a)(1), 2794(7), the act supplies a fairly narrow definition of defense services for the remaining provisions. Under 22 U.S.C. §2794(4) (1976) defense services include technical assistance and "defense information . . . used for the purposes of making military sales." The term "defense information" refers in part to items such as documents, plans, or prototypes that relate to specified defense articles. *Id.* §2403(e).

The sole appellate case dealing with technical data under section 1934 lends some support to our narrow interpretation of the term. In United States v. Van Hee, 531 F.2d 352 (6th Cir. 1976), the defendant exported information to Portugal for the production of an armored amphibious military vehicle essentially identical to one manufactured in the United States. The Department of State had denied an export license for the vehicle. The Sixth Circuit held that the exported information, which consisted of blueprints and the technical expertise of Americans who travelled to Portugal, constituted technical data for which an export license was required. *Id.* at 356-57. While noting the broad regulatory definition of technical data, the court emphasized the close connection between the data and the amphibious vehicle, an article designated in the Munitions List. *Id.* at 356.

We conclude, therefore, that section 1934 and the accompanying regulations prohibits only the exportation of technical data significantly and directly related to specific articles on the Munitions List. The prohibition includes the provision of technical assistance for the foreign manufacture of articles that, if manufactured domestically, would be on the Munitions List. If the information could have both peaceful and military applications, as Edler contends that its technology does, the defendant must know or have reason to know that its information is intended for the prohibited use. *Cf.* Gorin v. United States, 312 U.S. 19, 27-28, 61 S. Ct. 429, 85 L. Ed. 488 (1941) (*scienter* requirement shelters Espionage Act, ch. 30, §§1, 2, 40 Stat. 217 (1917) (current version at 18 U.S.C. §793 (1976)), from impermissible vagueness). These limitations are necessary both to adhere to the purpose of the Act and to avoid serious interference with the interchange of scientific and technological information.

As construed, section 1934 and the regulations do not interfere with constitutionally protected speech. Rather, they control the conduct of assisting foreign enterprises to obtain military equipment and related technical expertise. So confined, the statute and regulations are not overbroad. For the same reasons the licensing provisions of the Act are not an unconstitutional prior restraint on speech.

One additional First Amendment argument is presented. This is that the Government may not constitutionally prohibit the exportation of Edler's technology because that technology is widely distributed in the United States. The District Court properly rejected Edler's position. Given the unquestionable legitimacy of the national interest in restricting the dissemination of military information, the claim of public availability in the United States is not a defense recognized by the Constitution. *Cf.* Zemel v. Rusk, 381 U.S. 1, 85 S. Ct. 1271, 14 L. Ed. 2d 179 (1965) (Government may prevent person from travelling to particular country). The State Department regulations, we should note, do grant a public availability defense, subject to certain conditions. Technical data is exempt from the export license requirements if it is both published and available to the general public. 22 C.F.R. §125.11(a) (1977). To claim such an exemption an exporter must comply with the certification standards contained in 22 C.F.R. §125.22 (1977). *See* United States v. Van Hee, *supra,* 531 F.2d at 356.

While, under the facts present here, the trial court correctly refused to recognize appellants' public availability defense, the court did not have the benefit of our interpretation of technical data. It rejected a second defense raised at trial by both appellants, which was that the information furnished by Edler Industries had a number of nonmilitary uses. We believe evidence concerning nonmilitary applications is relevant to the question of *scienter, i.e.,* whether a defendant knew or should have known that the recipient of the exported information would use the information to produce or operate Munitions List articles.

The District Court also refused to permit the defense to develop the proposition that the assistance given to SEP would not, of itself, suffice for the manufacture of rocket nozzle components. Any information that would in any way help in a process that led to the final product, the court stated, came under the definition of technical data. Such a reading of the statute and regulations is far too broad, as such evidence bears on the significance of the relationship between information and Munitions List items.

Accordingly, because the case was tried on an incorrect interpretation of the scope of section 1934 and the pertinent regulations, the judgments of conviction are reversed and the cause is remanded for a new trial consistent with this opinion.

Reversed and remanded.

NOTES AND QUESTIONS

1. Are you satisfied with the logic of the case? Was defendent really in doubt about the applicability of the law? If this is a void-for-vagueness situation, why isn't the statute held unconstitutional?

2. Which forms of limitation on technical data export are likely to be wise? Possible? Consider the range of examples: computer software, technical conferences, employment or education of foreign nationals, transnational consulting contracts, the genetic information of a microorganism . . .

3. What about goals? National security as in the above example? Arms-control-style national security as in nuclear weapons information? Protection of the national fisc as in efforts to ensure that subsidized research produces employment here rather than abroad? Simple mercantilism? Retaliation to any of the above?

4. Suppose you represented a foreign firm that wished to buy a U.S. silicon chip manufacturing machine and had been told that the Export Administration Act banned export of the machine. What would you do if you believed that the restraint was imposed to protect a U.S. industry rather than to protect national security?

5. Although they will not be discussed in this text, there are many other emerging issues with respect to transborder data flow. Consider a few examples: foreign requests under the Freedom of Information Act, differing privacy

rules for data files with personal aspects, dependence on a distant computer for emergency or security matters, economic nationalism to obtain employment from building the computer data base, etc. *See generally,* "Transborder Data Flow," 16 Stan. J. Intl. Law 1 (1980).

6. What about nonresearch export restriction such as on hazardous products? Drugs that have not yet been approved? Materials in short supply in the United States?

7. When should a labor union be entitled to boycott shipping for political purposes? Start with Jacksonville Bulk Terminals v. Intl. Longshoremen's Assn., 457 U.S. 702 (1982).

Bibliographical Note

For other cases exploring export restrictions, *see* Nuclear Pacific v. Department of Commerce, (No. C84-49R, W.D. Wash., June 8, 1984), noted in 79 A.J.I.L. 460 (1985) (upholding judicial authority to review EAA regulation extended under IEEPA); Daedalus Enterprises v. Baldridge, 563 F. Supp. 1345 (D.D.C. 1983) (government delaying an export license application for 29 months); Natural Resources Defense Council v. Nuclear Regulatory Commission, 647 F.2d 1345 (D.C. Cir. 1981) (export of nuclear reactor); United States v. Salem Carpet Mills, 632 F.2d 1259 (5th Cir. 1980) (export of flammable fabric).

C.   COUNTERING EMBARGO

The previous materials suggested the concept of foreign policy embargos, such as those against Iran and South Africa. The United States is not the only nation to have embargoed trade for political purposes. One of the most important and complex examples of other embargos is the Arab boycott of Israel, a collective (but sporadically enforced) refusal to purchase from firms that have done business with Israel. During the 1970s, the United States decided to respond to this embargo. One part of that response is the law that is the subject of the following case. This law was passed under very unusual circumstances: in essence it and its regulations were written in a negotiation between the Business Roundtable and the American Jewish Congress, and then enacted and promulgated without significant change. For additional information *see* Saltour, Regulation of Foreign Boycotts, 33 Bus. Law. 559 (1978); and the Symposium, The Arab Boycott and the International Response, 8 Ga. J. Intl. & Comp. L. 529 (1978).

BRIGGS & STRATTON CORP. v. BALDRIDGE

539 F. Supp. 1307 (E.D. Wis.), *aff'd*, 728 F.2d 915 (7th Cir. 1984)

GORDON, J.

This action challenges the constitutionality of certain provisions of the Export Administration Act of 1979, 50 U.S.C. App. §2401 et seq., and certain regulations which make it unlawful "to comply with, further, or support any boycott fostered or imposed by a foreign country against a country which is friendly to the United States. . . ." 50 U.S.C. App. §2407(a)(1). In this case, the boycott is that of the League of Arab States against Israel and those companies doing business with Israel. The plaintiffs contend that the act and regulations violate their rights under the first, fifth, and ninth amendments. The parties have submitted a stipulation of facts and have fully briefed cross motions for summary judgment.

I. FACTUAL BACKGROUND

On December 11, 1954, the council of the League of Arab States approved a resolution calling for an economic boycott of Israel. Since that time, a boycott of varying effectiveness has been conducted by members of the League. To implement the boycott, the League formed

> . . . the Central Boycott Office, with headquarters presently in Damascus, Syria, which facilitates communications among the boycott offices of the individual boycotting states and makes recommendations concerning enforcement of the boycott to the individual states. Stipulation of Facts, ¶6.

The boycott is not confined to actual trade with Israel. It also applies to dealings with companies that have been "blacklisted" for activities "deemed to be inconsistent with the purported 'General Principles for the Boycott of Israel' (June 1972), published by the Central Boycott Office and the League of Arab States." Stipulation, ¶8. These so-called "principles" are lengthy and intricate, but it is safe to conclude generally that a firm may be blacklisted if it trades with Israel or if it has a relationship with a firm that trades with Israel. *See* stipulation, exh. A, General Principles for the Boycott of Israel (1972), pp. 23–80. The ban on dealing with blacklisted companies has included bans on the importation of products manufactured by, or products containing components manufactured by, such companies. Decisions to blacklist a company are made haphazardly, however, and there are several factors that may result in continued trade with a company despite activity that could be deemed inconsistent with boycott principles. Stipulation ¶23.

"Israel is a country friendly to the United States and is not itself the object of any form of boycott pursuant to United States law or regulation." Stipulation ¶7. In the mid-1970s, Congress became concerned about Arab efforts to pressure American companies into participating in the boycott of Israel; several examples of such pressure were cited. *See* S. Rep.No.95-104, 95th Cong., 1st Sess. 16-18 (1978) (Senate Report); Subcomm. on Oversight and Investigations of the House Comm. on Interstate and Foreign Commerce, 94th Cong., 2d Sess., Report of the Arab Boycott and American Business 10-11, 41-42 (Subcomm. Print 1976) (Boycott Report).

Congress eventually enacted anti-boycott legislation an an amendment to the Export Administration Act. *See* Pub. L. No.95-52, 91 Stat. 235 (1977); the anti-boycott rules were reenacted as part of the Export Administration Act of 1979, Pub. L. No. 96-72, 93 Stat. 503 (codified at 50 U.S.C. App. §2401 et seq. (Supp. III 1979)). Congress was assisted in the preparation of this legislation by representatives of American business, including the Business Roundtable, and representatives of several American Jewish organizations. *See* Senate Report, p. 78; H.R. Rep. No. 95-190, 95th Cong., 1st Sess. 5 (1977), *reprinted in* 1977 U.S. Code Cong. & Ad. News 362, 366 (House Report). The defendants in this action are the four highest ranking officials of the United States charged with enforcing the act. Their enforcement duties are set forth in the stipulation. *Id.* at ¶¶10-13.

Briggs & Stratton is a manufacturer of internal combustion engines; its engines are incorporated as power components in the end products of other manufacturers. Mr. Hamilton is vice-president for international sales for Briggs. Briggs does not manufacture or sell end products; it only manufactures components for end products. Thus the vast majority of its sales are to end product manufacturers who place the Briggs engines into their products.

Briggs' customers usually manufacture their products in large quantities using assembly line techniques. Their products are designed for a particular engine model and the design is not readily alterable. The parties stipulate:

> Manufacturers in Australia, England, France, Germany, Japan, the United States and other countries sell products powered by Briggs engines to customers all over the world. The Arab countries are a segment and only a minor volume segment of this worldwide market. Because Briggs has been placed on some Arab country blacklists, and because of the standardization by its customers on a particular engine model, a number of its customers have notified it that they can no longer use its engines as components of products they will ship not only to the Arab countries but to all other countries as well." Stipulation, ¶4.

The parties also agree that there are other, foreign manufacturers of engines with sufficient capacity to supply the foreign market for these engines.

In May, 1977, Briggs received a letter from Georges A. K. Kabbabe, a distributor of Briggs' products in Syria. Stipulation, exh. B. Mr. Kabbabe wrote that a request for an import license for Briggs' products had been refused because Briggs was on a blacklist. He enclosed a letter from the Syrian "Economical Department" that contained seven items which Briggs was to answer. The translation of the seven items reads:

1. Has the company now or in the past main or branch factories or combinating factories in Israel.

2. Has the company now or in the past general offices in Israel for its regional or international works.

3. Has it granted now or in the past the right of utilizing its name or trade marks or patents to persons or establishments or Israel works inside or outside Israel.

4. Does it share in or own now or in the past shares in Israel works or establishments inside or outside Israel.

5. Does it now or did it offer in the past any technical assistance to any Israeli work or establishment.

6. Does it represent now or did it represent in the past any Israel establishment or work inside or outside Israel.

7. What are the companies which it shares in or with, their nationality and the size or rate of this share. Stipulation, exh. C.

Briggs responded to the letter, answering all seven questions in the negative. *See* stipulation, exh. D. This response was eventually not accepted, however, for Briggs had failed to have its response authenticated by an Arab consular officer, as the letter required. *See* stipulation, exh. E. The parties agree that by the time Briggs received the request for authentication, the regulations challenged at bar prohibited Briggs from responding. Stipulation, ¶15.

Subsequent to its failure to return the authenticated response to the questionnaire, Briggs was blacklisted by Syria, Saudi Arabia, Bahrain, Oman, and Kuwait, all members of the Arab League. *See* stipulation, exhs. F & I. Briggs believes that it was blacklisted because of its failure to answer the questionnaire. Stipulation, ¶17. This is consistent with the Arab League's General Principles, *see* stipulation, exh. A; ¶15, First, g; p.24. Briggs has been removed from the blacklist, however, and its products are currently accepted in all Arab League states. Stipulation, ¶18 and exhs. G & H.

The government acknowledges that the effect on Briggs of being blacklisted is significant:

Briggs' sales to persons who in turn export their products incorporating Briggs' engines to states which are members of the League of Arab States amounted to in excess of $15,000,000 in Briggs' most recently completed fiscal year ended June 30, 1980. Briggs believes that such sales for the fiscal year ending June 30, 1981 would exceed $15,000,000 but for the fact that some members of the League of Arab States have blacklisted Briggs. Briggs is making active efforts further to increase such sales and believes that there are good prospects for such increases. Such sales are profitable and currently account for the employment of in excess of 100 persons by Briggs in the United States. . . . Stipulation, ¶1.

This litigation focuses on specific provisions of the anti-boycott legislation and the regulations implementing it. The crucial portion of the statute reads:

(a)(1) . . . [T]he President shall issue regulations prohibiting any United States person, with respect to his activities in the interstate or foreign commerce of the

United States, from taking or knowingly agreeing to take any of the following actions with intent to comply with, further, or support any boycott fostered or imposed by a foreign country against a country which is friendly to the United States and which is not itself the object of any form of boycott pursuant to United States law or regulation: . . .

(D) Furnishing information about whether any person has, has had, or proposes to have any business relationship (including a relationship by way of sale, purchase, legal or commercial representation, shipping or other transport, insurance, investment, or supply) with or in the boycotted country, with any business concern organized under the laws of the boycotted country, with any national or resident of the boycotted country, or with any other person which is known or believed to be restricted from having any business relationship with or in the boycotting country. Nothing in this paragraph shall prohibit the furnishing of normal business information in a commercial context as defined by the Secretary [of Commerce]. 50 U.S.C. App. §2407.

The parties have stipulated:

> Commerce Department officials have advised . . . Briggs that . . . any answer made by . . . Briggs which is responsive to the request [of the Syrian Economical Department] would contravene the Regulations herein described and that defendants would, upon learning that any information had been furnished by Briggs or on its behalf, in contravention of the Regulations, so construed, seek to impose one or more of the . . . penalties [described in paragraphs 10-12]. Stipulation, ¶14.

II. THE REGULATIONS' PRESUMPTION OF INTENT

The plaintiffs primarily object to the regulations promulgated by the Commerce Department on the issue of intent. These regulations read:

> (e) *"Intent".* (1) Part 369 prohibits a United States person from taking or knowingly agreeing to take certain specified actions with intent to comply with, further, or support an unsanctioned foreign boycott.
>
> (2) A United States person has the intent to comply with, further, or support an unsanctioned foreign boycott when such a boycott is at least one of the reasons for that person's decision whether to take a particular prohibited action. So long as that is at least one of the reasons for his action, a violation occurs regardless of whether the prohibited action is also taken for non-boycott reasons. Stated differently, the fact that such action was taken for legitimate business reasons does not remove that action from the scope of this part if compliance with an unsanctioned foreign boycott was also a reason for the action. . . .
>
> (6) Actions will be deemed to be taken with intent to comply with an unsanctioned foreign boycott if the person taking such action knew that such action was required or requested for boycott reasons. On the other hand, the mere absence of a business relationship with a blacklisted person or with or in a boycotted country does not indicate the existence of the requisite intent. . . . 15 C.F.R. §369.1(e).

Briggs argues that the regulations read the intent element out of the statute, making the answering of a questionnaire a violation, even though Briggs does not have the "intent to comply with, further, or support the boycott." Briggs points to paragraph 21 of the stipulation, part of which reads:

> Briggs has in the past and intends in the future to trade with persons in Israel and in all other respects conduct its business without regard to such purported "General Principles [for the Boycott of Israel].". . .

In the report expressing approval of the present language, the Senate committee made clear that it wished to prohibit the conduct described at bar.

> [The act] prohibits furnishing information about whether any person has, has had, or proposes to have any business relationship with or in the boycotted country, with any business concern organized under the laws of the boycotted country, with any national or resident of the boycotted country, or with any other person known or believed to be restricted from having any business relationship with or in the boycotted country. The purpose of this provision is to prohibit U.S. persons from supplying information about whether they have business dealings with boycotted countries or blacklisted persons where such information is supplied with intent to comply with, further, or support a boycott. However, nothing in paragraph 4A(a)(1) is to prohibit the furnishing of normal business information in a commercial context as defined by the Secretary of Commerce.
>
> The most common example of prohibited information in the present context is a boycott questionnaire designed to elicit information about dealings with the boycotted country or blacklisted persons. The boycott questionnaire typically has no legitimate business purpose. It is intended to establish categories of eligibility for dealings with the boycotting country based on the subject's dealings with third parties. This provision prohibits the supply of that information in such a context." Senate Report, pp.39-40.

The above plainly states Congress' meaning when it included the "intent" language in the statute. The plaintiffs maintain that answering a boycott questionnaire does not manifest intent to support the boycott if the person supplying the information does not agree with the boycott and does not intend to abide by it. However, I believe that Congress viewed answering a questionnaire from the boycott office as acting with intent "to comply with the boycott" by supplying the boycott officials with information. The regulations promulgated are consistent with Congress' meaning and the statute enacted. . . .

III.   THE RATIONALITY OF THE REGULATORY SCHEME

The plaintiffs contend that the Commerce Department regulations are irrational as they apply to Briggs and therefore void. Briggs argues that the boycott authorities send out questionnaires haphazardly and seek information that either is not useful or is readily available from public sources. Briggs maintains that once a company fails to answer an inquiry, the boycott authorities consider whether that firm's products are readily available from other sources. If they are, the company is blacklisted. Thus Briggs argues that by prohibiting answers to such inquiries, the Commerce Department has simplified the task of the boycotters and shifted commerce to foreign competitors. Briggs argues that this is irrational.

The government argues that the regulations prohibiting the furnishing of information cannot be viewed in isolation. As the Senate Report states:

> [T]he committee strongly believes that the United States should not acquiesce in attempts by foreign governments through secondary and tertiary boycotts to embroil American citizens in their battles against others by forcing them to participate in actions which are repugnant to American values and traditions. Accordingly, the bill reported by the committee directly attacks attempts to interfere with American affairs while creating mechanisms for more subtle and flexible pressure against the other dimensions of foreign boycotts. *Id.* at 21.

A major provision of the act is the "refusal to deal" section, 50 U.S.C. App. §2407(a)(1)(A), which authorizes the issuance of regulations prohibiting Americans from intentionally refusing to do business with entities associated with boycotted countries. Congress intended the prohibition on passing information to reinforce this provision and others.

> The prohibition on furnishing information about another person's race, religion, sex, or national origin would reinforce the anti-discrimination provisions of the bill. Similarly, the prohibition on furnishing information about who does and proposes to do business with a boycotted country or blacklisted person would bolster the refusal to deal provisions of the bill. Both are necessary to prevent a boycotting country from using U.S. persons to supply information necessary to boycott enforcement. Senate Report, p.25.

Questionnaires such as that received by Briggs were a major focus of Congress' prohibition on the passing of information. *See* Senate Report, pp.39-40 (quoted *ante*).

Congress recognized that the information sought would often be available from other sources, but it determined that the prohibition should include such matters.

> Such information may very well be available through other sources, including information innocently supplied by U.S. firms in the course of ordinary business transactions. And in that regard the bill does explicitly permit the furnishing of normal business information in a commercial context. . . . But there is little justification for permitting U.S. persons to supply information when they know it is being sought for boycott enforcement purposes. To do so would be to sanction active complicity in boycott implementation. Senate Report, p.25.

Considering this context, I cannot find the Commerce Department regulations to be an irrational implementation of the legislation. The regulations adequately translate Congress' concerns about cutting off the flow of information to boycotters. As a result, Briggs did not answer a questionnaire from the boycott office, the only purpose of which was to seek information to aid the boycott effort. I believe that the regulations are "reasonably related to the purposes of the . . . legislation." Thorpe v. Housing Authority of the City of Durham, 393 U.S. 268, 280-81, 89 S. Ct. 518, 525-26, 21 L. Ed. 2d 474 (1969). Accordingly, they do not violate the due process clause.

Briggs oversimplifies the case by arguing that failure to answer the questionnaire triggers a blacklisting. The parties have indeed stipulated that Briggs was blacklisted subsequent to its failure to answer the inquiry. Stipulation, ¶16. However, Briggs had a problem exporting to Syria prior to receiving the questionnaire, *see* stipulation, exh. B, and it has also been taken off of the blacklist, even though it has not answered the questionnaire. At the time of the stipulation, its products were being accepted throughout the nations of the Arab League. Stipulation, ¶18. Thus the effect of the regulations on American trade is not nearly so cut and dried as Briggs argues.

I also reject Briggs' argument that the regulations permit a firm to supply information in the absence of a questionnaire that it cannot supply if it gets one. Example (ix) following the intent regulation reads:

> U.S. company A is on boycotting country Y's blacklist. In an attempt to secure its removal from the blacklist, A wishes to supply to Y *information which demonstrates that A does at least as much business in Y and other countries engaged in a boycott of X as it does in X.* A intends to continue its business in X undiminished and in fact is exploring and intends to continue exploring an expansion of its activities in X without regard to Y's boycott.
>
> A may furnish the information, because in doing so it has no intent to comply with, further, or support Y's boycott. 15 C.F.R. §369.1(e), Examples of Intent. (Emphasis added).

Briggs' interpretation of this example goes too far. The example merely permits a company on its own initiative to demonstrate non-discriminatory conduct. *See* 15 C.F.R. §369.1(e), Note to the examples. Example (ix) cannot be read to condone a company unilaterally providing a variety of information to a boycott agency. For example, I believe that the regulations quite reasonably prohibit a company from currying favor with boycott officials by unilaterally telling them that it will not trade with the boycotted country.

[Discussion of constitutional issues omitted. For additional discussion of constitutional views, *see* Trane Co. v. Baldrige, 552 F. Supp. 1378 (W.D. Wis. 1983).]

QUESTIONS

1. Had you been a U.S. legislator, what would have affected your vote for or against the response to the Arab boycott?

2. Does the case close with the actual international legal issues presented by the antiboycott rules? Is there any way those issues could have been raised under U.S. law?

3. What about the fact that the detailed regulations turn out to include more form than substance—e.g., it is a violation for a firm explicitly to identify to an Arab nation which employees proposed for a project in that nation are Jewish, but it is all right for the firm to pass out visa applications (for return to the Arab nation) that ask the same question. *See* 15 C.F.R. §369.3.

4. Could the Arab boycott be dealt with under the antitrust laws? *See* United States v. Bechtel Corp., 1979—1 Trade Cas. (C.C.H.) ¶¶62,429 & 62,430 (N.D. Cal. 1979). Note also that there is an elaborate body of antiboycott tax law, whose guiding principle is that tax advantages should not accrue to a firm from complying with the boycott, and the firm must even calculate an "international boycott factor." 1976 Tax Reform Act, §§1061-1064, P.L. 94-455.

5. What do the materials and issues raised in this chapter tell you about applying economic pressure against *apartheid?* Consider possible suits under existing law and possible new legislation. And consider efforts to restrict trade as well as efforts to compel U.S. subsidiaries to withdraw from South Africa. (The materials in Chapter XVII will be relevant to efforts to encourage U.S. subsidiaries to remain in South Africa and avoid discrimination in their own policies.)

PART 2

TECHNOLOGY IN INTERNATIONAL COMMERCE

Chapter XIII

The Territorial Structure of Intellectual Property Rights

Part I of this text explored the international flow of goods; in Part II we look at a different kind of flow, that of ideas and technology. Most of the legal issues in this area involve various forms of intellectual property, such as patents, trademarks, and copyrights, and typically relate to the flow of technology within a corporate structure or between a corporation and its licensees. This form of technology flow is a natural consequence of the product cycle theory discussed in Chapter I. This form of technology transfer, however, is only one of many—technology flow in the form of education, scientific communication, and public international cooperation may produce fewer legal controversies but is often more important, especially in areas like agriculture and medicine.

In this chapter, the different legal forms of intellectual property are treated together. From a legal viewpoint, each of these forms of property is simply a power to exclude: to keep someone else from practicing the invention or using the trademark or reproducing the copyrighted text. Moreover, the international structures of the different areas are closely parallel.

Nevertheless, there are major differences that should be noted between the two examples that the text emphasizes: patent rights and trademarks. The patent right is purely a creature of statutory law and protects the right to manufacture, sell, or use a product or, in some cases, a process. Although there are minor differences in detail from nation to nation, the right to control the invention lasts for a limited period, typically around 17 years, and completely expires after that time. In some nations certain specific products such as pharmaceuticals are not patentable, and in a few nations a firm loses control over a patented idea unless it actually practices the idea.

Trademark rights, in contrast, derive (in Anglo-American nations) from a common law tort right to protect one's trade reputation against inferior goods

671

passed off as one's own. The statutory structure systematizes and details this right. In contrast to the patent case, trademark protection can theoretically last forever, although one has actually to use the trademark in order to obtain the protection.

These accidental differences reflect more fundamental policy differences. The patent monopoly is intended as an incentive to invention (although its real-world effectiveness for this purpose is sometimes unclear). The value of the monopoly—and therefore of the patent—depends on the economic improvement associated with the invention. The requirements that the invention will be disclosed in the patent application and that it will be available to all at the end of the patent term are central to the economic wisdom of granting the monopoly. For the trademark, the social function of the monopoly—of preventing passing off and ensuring authenticity of goods—is one that reasonably requires continued protection. And the value of this monopoly depends on the brand image carried by the product; the monopoly loses its value unless the mark is known to the public.

There are many other forms of intellectual property, such as copyright and plant breeder's rights. Their existence reflects a strong sense, especially in civil law nations, that creators have a moral right to control over their product; hence, for example, the expansion of artists' rights over use of their work. But a less formal kind of intellectual property should also be mentioned—that of trade secrets and know-how. Some inventions are not patentable, and some innovators have chosen secrecy rather than a legal route to protect their invention. Examples range from the formula for certain soft drinks or candy bars to "tricks of the trade" used in high-tech manufacturing. There is no analogue of the patent system for these properties, which are protectable only indirectly such as through contracts with employees or through what amount to actions against theft. The international flow of these ideas can present legal difficulties different from those of the regular patent area.

QUESTIONS

1. If you were starting legal systems afresh, to which of these forms of intellectual property would you provide legal protection? Patents? Trademarks?

2. How might you answer this question differently if you were from a socialist nation? From a developing nation?

3. How would you decide whether a specific intellectual property system is benefiting a specific nation?

4. Suppose you were counsel to a hotel chain seeking to set up the analogue of franchised local hotels in a nation with no trademark law. What special difficulties would you face, and how might you resolve them?

A. NATIONAL SYSTEMS

In most circumstances, both patent and trademark rights apply only to infringement within the nation granting the right. Hence, it is quite plausible for an idea to be patented in one nation and not another or for one firm to hold a specific trademark in one nation and for another firm to hold the same trademark in another nation. This territoriality leaves only very limited protection against foreign practice of an invention. In general, the existing treaty structure is only strong enough to permit an inventor or initial trademark user the opportunity to obtain parallel coverages in all nations in which he or she is interested. Arrangements to protect an inventor from imports coming from places where they were legitimately made are left to national law.

The following cases show the territorial extension that contemporary courts give to intellectual property concepts. The first case, *Deepsouth*, shows how sharply the United States courts will refuse to provide extraterritorial protection for a patent. (This case was effectively reversed by §101 of the Patent Law Amendments Act of 1984, P.L. 98-622, 35 U.S.C. §271.)

The law for trademarks is much less settled, as suggested by the two cases that follow *Deepsouth*. Footnote 22 of *Wells Fargo*, the first case following *Deepsouth*, describes the traditional cases, *Steele* and *Vanity Fair*, that had long defined working boundaries for extraterritorial application of trademark law— but, in the wake of *Timberlane*, the trend is toward a balancing test rather than the factor analysis suggested by the earlier cases. This is the lesson of *Wells Fargo*, which involved a global copying of the Wells Fargo mark. And, as shown in *American Rice*, the last of the cases in this group, U.S. courts are now willing to protect U.S. competitors against copying in foreign markets—and do not necessarily defer to the decisions of foreign trademark offices.

DEEPSOUTH PACKING CO. v. LAITRAM CORP.

408 U.S. 518 (1972)

Mr. Justice WHITE delivered the opinion of the Court.

The United States District Court for the Eastern District of Louisiana has written:

> Shrimp, whether boiled, broiled, barbecued or fried, are a gustatory delight, but they did not evolve to satisfy man's palate. Like other crustaceans, they wear their skeletons outside their bodies in order to shield their savory pink and white flesh against predators, including man. They also carry their intestines, commonly called veins, in bags (or sand bags) that run the length of their bodies. For shrimp to be edible, it is necessary to remove their shells. In addition, if the vein is removed, shrimp become more pleasing to the fastidious as well as more palatable.

Such "gustatory" observations are rare even in those piscatorially favored federal courts blissfully situated on the Nation's Gulf Coast, but they are properly recited in this case. Petitioner and respondent both hold patents on machines that devein shrimp more cheaply and efficiently than competing machinery or hand labor can do the job. Extensive litigation below has established that respondent, the Laitram Corp., has the superior claim and that the distribution and use of petitioner Deepsouth's machinery in this country should be enjoined to prevent infringement of Laitram's patents. *Laitram Corp. v. Deepsouth Packing Co.*, 443 F.2d 928 (5th Cir. 1971). We granted certiorari, 404 U.S. 1037, 92 S. Ct. 702, 30 L. Ed. 2d 728 (1972), to consider a related question: Is Deepsouth, barred from the American market by Laitram's patents, also foreclosed by the patent laws from exporting its deveiners, in less than fully assembled form, for use abroad? . . .

The lower court's decision that Laitram held valid combination patents entitled the corporation to the privileges bestowed by 35 U.S.C. §154, the keystone provision of the patent code. "[F]or the term of seventeen years" from the date of the patent, Laitram had "the right to exclude others from making, using, or selling the invention throughout the United States. . . ." The §154 right in turn provides the basis for affording the patentee an injunction against direct, induced, and contributory infringement, 35 U.S.C. §283, or an award of damages when such infringement has already occurred, 35 U.S.C. §284. Infringement is defined by 35 U.S.C. §271 in terms that follow those of §154:

> (a) Except as otherwise provided in this title, whoever without authority makes, uses or sells any patented invention, within the United States during the term of the patent therefor, [directly] infringes the patent.
>
> (b) Whoever actively induces infringement of a patent shall be liable as an infringer.
>
> (c) Whoever sells a component of a patented machine, manufacture, combination or composition, or a material or apparatus for use in practicing a patented process, constituting a material part of the invention, knowing the same to be especially made or especially adapted for use in an infringement of such patent, and not a staple article or commodity of commerce suitable for substantial noninfringing use, shall be liable as a contributory infringer.

As a result of these provisions the judgment of Laitram's patent superiority forecloses Deepsouth and its customers from any future use (other than a use approved by Laitram or occurring after the Laitram patent has expired) of its deveiners "throughout the United States." The patent provisions taken in conjunction with the judgment below also entitle Laitram to the injunction it has received prohibiting Deepsouth from continuing to "make" or, once made, to "sell" deveiners "throughout the United States." Further, Laitram may recover damages for any past unauthorized use, sale, or making "throughout the United States." This much is not disputed.

But Deepsouth argues that it is not liable for every type of past sale and that a portion of its future business is salvageable. Section 154 and related provisions obviously are intended to grant a patentee a monopoly only over the United States market; they are not intended to grant a patentee the bonus of a favored position as a flagship company free of American competition in international commerce. Deepsouth, itself barred from using its deveining machines, or from inducing others to use them "throughout the United States," barred also from making and selling the machines in the United States, seeks to make the parts of deveining machines, to sell them to foreign buyers, and to have the buyers assemble the parts and use the machines abroad.[5] Accordingly, Deepsouth seeks judicial approval, expressed through a modification or interpretation of the injunction against it, for continuing its practice of shipping deveining equipment to foreign customers in three separate boxes, each containing only parts of the $1^3/_4$-ton machines, yet the whole assemblable in less than one hour. The company contends that by this means both the "making" and the "use" of the machines occur abroad and Laitram's lawful monopoly over the making and use of the machines throughout the United States is not infringed.

Laitram counters that this course of conduct is based upon a hypertechnical reading of the patent code that, if tolerated, will deprive it of its right to the fruits of the inventive genius of its assignors. "The right to make can scarcely be made plainer by definition . . . ," Bauer v. O'Donnell, 229 U.S. 1, 10, 33 S. Ct. 616, 617, 57 L. Ed. 1041 (1913). Deepsouth in all respects save final assembly of the parts "makes" the invention. It does so with the intent of having the foreign user effect the combination without Laitram's permission. Deepsouth sells these components as through they were the machines themselves; the act of assembly is regarded, indeed advertised, as of no importance.

The District Court, faced with this dispute, noted that three prior circuit courts had considered the meaning of "making" in this context and that all three had resolved the question favorably to Deepsouth's position. . . . The District Court held that its injunction should not be read as prohibiting export of the elements of a combination patent even when those elements could and predictably would be combined to form the whole.

> It may be urged that . . . [this] result is not logical . . . But it is founded on twin notions that underlie the patent laws. One is that a combination patent protects only the combination. The other is that monopolies—even those conferred by patents—are not viewed with favor. These are logic enough. 310 F. Supp. 926, 929 (1970).

---

[5] Deepsouth is entirely straightforward in indicating that its course of conduct is motivated by a desire to avoid patent infringement. Its president wrote a Brazilian customer:

> We are handicapped by a decision against us in the United States. This was a very technical decision and we can manufacture the entire machine without any complication in the United States, with the exception that there are two parts that must not be assembled in the United States, but assembled after the machine arrives in Brazil.

Quoted in Laitram Corp. v. Deepsouth Packing Co., 443 F.2d 928, 938 (5th Cir. 1971).

The Court of Appeals for the Fifth Circuit reversed, thus departing from the established rules of the Second, Third, and Seventh Circuits. In the Fifth Circuit panel's opinion, those courts that previously considered the question "worked themselves into . . . a conceptual box" by adopting "an artificial, technical construction" of the patent laws, a construction, moreover, which in the opinion of the panel, "[subverted] the Constitutional scheme of promoting 'the Progress of Science and useful Arts' " by allowing an intrusion on a patentee's rights, 443 F.2d, at 938-939, citing U.S. Const., Art. I, §8.

III

We disagree with the Court of Appeals for the Fifth Circuit. Under the common law the inventor had no right to exclude others from making and using his invention. If Laitram has a right to suppress Deepsouth's export trade it must be derived from its patent grant, and thus from the patent statute. We find that 35 U.S.C. §271, the provision of the patent laws on which Laitram relies, does not support its claim.

Certainly if Deepsouth's conduct were intended to lead to use of patented deveiners inside the United States its production and sales activity would be subject to injunction as an induced or contributory infringement. But it is established that there can be no contributory infringement without the fact or intention of a direct infringement. "In a word, if there is no [direct] infringement of a patent there can be no contributory infringer." Mercoid Corp. v. Mid-Continent Co., 320 U.S. 661, 677, 64 S. Ct. 268, 276, 88 L. Ed. 376 (1944) (Frankfurter, J., dissenting on other grounds). . . .

The statute makes it clear that it is not an infringement to make or use a patented product outside of the United States. 35 U.S.C. §271. . . . Thus, in order to secure the injunction it seeks, Laitram must show a §271(a) direct infringement by Deepsouth in the United States, that is, that Deepsouth "makes," "uses," or "sells" the patented product within the bounds of this country. . . .

We cannot endorse the view that the "substantial manufacture of the constituent parts of [a] machine" constitutes direct infringement when we have so often held that a combination patent protects only against the operable assembly of the whole and not the manufacture of its parts. "For as we pointed out in Mercoid v. Mid-Continent Investment Co. [320 U.S. 661, 676, 64 S. Ct. 268, 276] a patent on a combination is a patent on the assembled or functioning whole, not on the separate parts." Mercoid Corp. v. Minneapolis-Honeywell Regulator Co., 320 U.S. 680, 684, 64 S. Ct. 278, 280 (1944). . . .

It was this basic tenet of the patent system that led Judge Swan to hold in the leading case, Radio Corp. of America v. Andrea, 79 F.2d 626 (2d Cir. 1935), that unassembled export of the elements of an invention did not infringe the patent.

> [The] relationship is the essence of the patent.
> . . . No wrong is done the patentee until the combination is formed. His

monopoly does not cover the manufacture or sale of separate elements capable of being, but never actually, associated to form the invention. Only when such association is made is there a direct infringement of his monopoly, and not even then if it is done outside the territory for which the monopoly was granted. *Id.,* at 628. . . .

We reaffirm this conclusion today.

IV

It is said that this conclusion is derived from too narrow and technical an interpretation of the statute, and that this Court should focus on the constitutional mandate

[t]o promote the Progress of Science and useful Arts, by securing for limited Times to Authors and Inventors the exclusive Right to their respective Writings and Discoveries . . . ," Art. I, §8,

and construe the statute in a manner that would, allegedly, better reflect the policy of the Framers.

We cannot accept this argument. The direction of Art. I is that *Congress* shall have the power to promote the progress of science and the useful arts. When, as here, the Constitution is permissive, the sign of how far Congress has chosen to go can come only from Congress. We are here construing the provisions of a statute passed in 1952. The prevailing law in this and other courts as to what is necessary to show a patentable invention when a combination of old elements is claimed was clearly evident from the cases when the Act was passed; and at that time *Andrea,* representing a specific application of the law of infringement with respect to the export of elements of a combination patent, was 17 years old. When Congress drafted §271, it gave no indication that it desired to change either the law of combination patents as relevant here or the ruling of *Andrea.* Nor has it on any more recent occasion indicated that it wanted the patent privilege to run farther than it was understood to run for 35 years prior to the action of the Court of Appeals for the Fifth Circuit.

In conclusion, we note that what is at stake here is the right of American companies to compete with an American patent holder in foreign markets. Our patent system makes no claim to extraterritorial effect; "these acts of Congress do not, and were not intended to, operate beyond the limits of the United States," Brown v. Duchesne, 19 How., at 195, 15 L. Ed. 595 (1856), and we correspondingly reject the claims of others to such control over our markets. *Cf.* Boesch v. Graff, 133 U.S. 697, 703, 10 S. Ct. 378, 380, 33 L. Ed. 787 (1890). To the degree that the inventor needs protection in markets other than those of this country, the wording of 35 U.S.C. §§154 and 271 reveals a congressional intent to have him seek it abroad through patents secured in countries where his goods are being used. Respondent holds foreign patents; it does not adequately explain why it does not avail itself of them.

V

In sum: the case and statutory law resolves this case against the respondent. When so many courts have so often held what appears so evident—a combination patent can be infringed only by combination—we are not prepared to break the mold and begin anew. And were the matter not so resolved, we would still insist on a clear congressional indication of intent to extend the patent privilege before we could recognize the monopoly here claimed. Such an indication is lacking. Accordingly, the judgment of the Court of Appeals for the Fifth Circuit is reversed and the case is remanded for proceedings consistent with this opinion.

It is so ordered.

Reversed and remanded.

Mr. Justice BLACKMUN, with whom THE CHIEF JUSTICE, Mr. Justice POWELL, and Mr. Justice REHNQUIST join, dissenting. . . .

With all respect, this seems to me to be too narrow a reading of 35 U.S.C. §§154 and 271(a). In addition, the result is unduly to reward the artful competitor who uses another's invention in its entirety and who seeks to profit thereby. Deepsouth may be admissive and candid or, as the Court describes it, . . . "straightforward," in its "sales rhetoric" . . . but for me that rhetoric reveals the very iniquitous and evasive nature of Deepsouth's operations. I do not see how one can escape the conclusion that the Deepsouth machine was *made* in the United States, within the meaning of the protective language of §§154 and 271(a). The situation, perhaps, would be different were parts, or even only one vital part, manufactured abroad. Here everything was accomplished in this country except putting the pieces together as directed (an operation that, as Deepsouth represented to its Brazilian prospect, would take "less than one hour"), all much as the fond father does with his little daughter's doll house on Christmas Eve. To say that such assembly, accomplished abroad, is not the prohibited combination and that it avoids the restrictions of our patent law, is a bit too much for me. The Court has opened the way to deny the holder of the United States combination patent the benefits of his invention with respect to sales to foreign purchasers. . . .

WELLS FARGO & CO. v. WELLS FARGO EXPRESS CO.

556 F.2d 406 (9th Cir. 1977)

CHOY, J.

A show-down over rights to the storied name "Wells Fargo" is the subject of this trademark infringement and unfair competition action. Two American corporations challenge the use of the name, in the United States and abroad, by two other corporations, one of which is foreign. . . .

At the heart of plaintiffs' allegations is the claim that a group headed by Herman Heymann, a German national who resides in Gibraltar, has deliberately and wrongfully attempted to appropriate the "Wells Fargo" name both in Europe as well as in the United States. Defendant Wells Fargo Express Company, A.G. ("A.G."), a Liechtenstein corporation, was incorporated in 1967 by Heymann to engage in the business of loaning money and is the foreign defendant dismissed by the district court below. In the course of its activities, A.G. had acquired various European and American subsidiaries. While none of the European subsidiaries has been named in the instant action, an American subsidiary, Wells Fargo Express Company ("Express"), is a named defendant.

Plaintiff Wells Fargo & Company, a California corporation, is engaged in various businesses in the United States and abroad, most notably as Wells Fargo Bank. In addition to world-wide banking and trust services, the company is also involved in toy manufacture, the restaurant trade, and the travel agency business. In each of these endeavors, it makes use of trade names, trademarks, and service marks which consist—in whole or in part—of the name "Wells Fargo," and which are registered in the United States under the Lanham Act, [the Trademark Act of 1946], 15 U.S.C. §§1051-1127, and in various foreign countries. The other plaintiff, Baker Industries, Inc., is a Delaware corporation which owns and has registered the "Wells Fargo" trademark for use in its business of providing armored car and other protective services. . . .

II. Subject Matter Jurisdiction Over A.G.'s Activities

The Lanham Act grants a registrant a civil right of action against "[a]ny person who shall . . . use in commerce," in any improper manner detailed therein, a registered trademark. 15 U.S.C. §1114(a)(1). For purposes of the Act, "commerce" is sweepingly defined as "all commerce which may lawfully be regulated by Congress." *Id.* §1127. Section 1121 provides the federal courts with subject matter jurisdiction over causes of action arising under the Act. . . .

A. A.G.'S FOREIGN ACTIVITIES

The district court ruled that the Lanham Act was generally limited to causes of action arising out of American activities. It held that foreign activities could be reached only if the following three factors were present:

> (1) Defendant's conduct must have had a substantial effect on United States commerce; (2) defendant must be a United States citizen, as the United States has broad powers to regulate the conduct of its citizens in foreign countries; (3) there must be no conflict with trademark rights established under the foreign law.

358 F. Supp. at 1077. Although it is somewhat unclear, it appears that the district court's test required that all of the factors be present. This conclusion

follows from the court's holding that, even if A.G. and Express be viewed as one corporation, the court would decline jurisdiction because A.G.'s "purely foreign activities have no substantial effect on commerce in the United States and there would exist a conflict between the trademark laws of the United States and the trademark laws of foreign countries." *Id.*

In so holding, the district court carefully analyzed the three cases which have discussed whether foreign activities may be reached under the Lanham Act. Steele v. Bulova Watch Co., 344 U.S. 280, 73 S. Ct. 252, 97 L. Ed. 252 (1952); Vanity Fair Mills, Inc. v. T. Eaton Co., 234 F.2d 633 (2d Cir.), *cert. denied,* 352 U.S. 871, 77 S. Ct. 96, 1 L. Ed. 2d 76 (1956); Ramirez & Feraud Chili Co. v. Las Palmas Food Co., Inc., 146 F. Supp. 594 (S.D. Cal. 1956), *aff'd per curiam,* 245 F.2d 874 (9th Cir. 1957), *cert. denied,* 355 U.S. 927, 78 S. Ct. 384, 2 L. Ed. 2d 357 (1958). It did not, however, have before it this court's recent decision in Timberlane Lbr. Co. v. Bank of America, N. T. & S. A., 549 F.2d 597 (9th Cir. 1976). In *Timberlane,* we set down a "jurisdictional rule of reason" to govern the extraterritorial reach of the Sherman Act which, like the Lanham Act, contains sweeping jurisdictional language. *Compare* 15 U.S.C. §§1 & 2 *with* 15 U.S.C. §§1114(a)(1) & 1127.

Our review of the cases on which the district court relied,[22] and the extensive analysis of extraterritoriality undertaken by us in *Timberlane, see* 549 F.2d at

---

[22] In Steele v. Bulova Watch Co., 344 U.S. 280, 73 S. Ct. 252, 97 L. Ed. 252 (1952), Steele was an American citizen who imported watch parts from the United States into Mexico and there affixed to the completed watches the name "Bulova." Sales were confined to Mexico, but some purchasers of the watches carried them into the United States. By the time the case reached the Supreme Court, the Bulova Watch Company had secured the cancellation of Steele's Mexican trademark. In holding that the district court had jurisdiction under the Lanham Act to award relief, the Court reasoned that Congress could constitutionally regulate the foreign activities of American citizens, 344 U.S. at 285-86, 73 S. Ct. at 252; that the Lanham Act evidenced a congressional intent to exercise its power to the fullest, *id.* at 285-87, 73 S. Ct. 252; that Steele's foreign activities adversely affected Bulova's "trade reputation in markets cultivated by advertising here as well as abroad," *id.* at 286, 73 S. Ct. at 256; and that, owing to the cancellation of the Mexican trademark, the question "whether a valid foreign registration would affect either the power to enjoin or the property of its exercise" was not before the Court, *id.* at 289, 73 S. Ct. at 257. Contrary to the district court's reading of *Bulova,* the Supreme Court does not appear to have required a "*substantial* effect on commerce *in* the United States," 358 F. Supp. at 1076 (emphasis added).

In Vanity Fair Mills, Inc. v. T. Eaton Co., 234 F.2d 633 (2d Cir. 1956), the defendant was a Canadian corporation which had registered the name "Vanity Fair" in Canada. Plaintiffs, holders of that trademark in the United States, brought an action against the Canadian use of the name. Defendant's use of the name extended to the United States only in a few mail order sales and advertisements which crossed the border. Observing that the "Lanham Act itself gives almost no indication of the extent to which Congress intended to exercise its power in this area," the court nevertheless held that Congress did not intend that the infringement remedies of the Act should reach "acts committed by a foreign national in his home country under a presumably valid trademark registration in that country." 234 F.2d at 642. Plaintiffs were, however, allowed to amend their complaint to challenge only the United States sales and advertisements. *Id.* at 647-48.

The facts of Ramirez & Feraud Chili Co. v. Las Palmas Food Co., 146 F. Supp. 594, 601-02 (S.D. Cal. 1956), *aff'd per curiam,* 245 F.2d 874 (9th Cir. 1957), are very similar to those of the *Bulova* case. *Ramirez* presented an even stronger case for coverage than did *Bulova,* however, because defendants, American citizens, produced their counterfeit labels in the United States and sold their merchandise to American residents after affixing the labels in Mexico to goods produced there.

608-15, lead us to the conclusion that the district court's denial of subject matter jurisdiction under the Lanham Act must be vacated. First, it seems clear that, just as in the interstate context, the extraterritorial coverage of the Lanham Act should be gauged not so much by the locus of the activity sought to be reached—as the district court below held, *see* 358 F. Supp. at 1076—as by the nature of its effect on that commerce which Congress may regulate. *See Bulova,* 344 U.S. at 286, 73 S. Ct. 252.

Next, although foreign activities must of course have *some* effect on United States foreign commerce before they can be reached, we disagree with the district court's requirement that that effect must be "substantial." *Bulova* contains no such requirement. And, as we noted in *Timberlane,* since the origins of the "substantiality" test apparently lie in the effort to distinguish between intrastate commerce, which Congress may not regulate as such, and interstate commerce, which it can control, it may be unwise blindly to apply the factor in the area of foreign commerce over which Congress has exclusive authority. *See Timberlane,* 549 F.2d at 612.

Finally, while we agree with the district court that each of the three factors which it cited—degree of effect on United States commerce, the citizenship of defendants, and the existence of a conflict with foreign trademark registrations—are indeed relevant to the resolution of the jurisdictional issue, contrary to the apparent view of the district court, the absence of one of the factors is not necessarily determinative of the issue. Rather, each factor is just one consideration to be balanced in the "jurisdictional rule of reason" of comity and fairness adopted by us in *Timberlane:*

> The elements to be weighed include the degree of conflict with foreign law or policy, the nationality or allegiance of the parties and the locations or principal places of business of corporations, the extent to which enforcement by either state can be expected to achieve compliance, the relative significance of effects on the United States as compared with those elsewhere, the extent to which there is explicit purpose to harm or affect American commerce, the foreseeability of such effect, and the relative importance to the violations charged of conduct within the United States as compared with conduct abroad. A court evaluating these factors should identify the potential degree of conflict if American authority is asserted. A difference in law or policy is one likely sore spot, though one which may not always be present. Nationality is another; though foreign governments may have some concern for the treatment of American citizens and businesses residing there, they primarily care about their own nationals. Having assessed the conflict, the court should then determine whether, in the face of it, the contacts and interests of the United States are sufficient to support the exercise of extraterritorial jurisdiction.

549 F.2d at 614-15 (footnotes omitted).

In the instant case, it appears that plaintiffs have been successful in securing the invalidation of some, but not all, foreign registrations held by A.G. and its

European subsidiaries.[23] While A.G. and its affiliates are alien corporations, they may indeed be conducting some commercial activity in the United States either themselves or through the Express entity. Moreover, A.G.'s activities may have some effect on both plaintiffs' domestic business and Wells Fargo Bank's heavily-advertised international affairs, and plaintiffs do maintain that A.G.'s scheme has all along been purposeful and deliberate.

We are, however, not prepared to say that some or all of A.G.'s foreign activities may be reached under the Lanham Act. Therefore, we vacate the dismissal of the district court and remand the issue to it for the opportunity to apply the *Timberlane* test to the jurisdictional facts which plaintiffs can establish.

AMERICAN RICE, INC., v. THE ARKANSAS RICE GROWERS COOPERATIVE ASSN.

701 F.2d 408 (5th Cir. 1983)

WISDOM, J.

In this interesting and unusual trademark dispute, we are asked to explore the extraterritorial reach of the Lanham Act, 15 U.S.C. §1051 et seq. The district court, 532 F. Supp. 1376 (1982), concluded that it was not powerless to prevent the acts complained of, despite the facts that the sales of the products bearing the allegedly infringing marks were consummated in a foreign country, Saudi Arabia, and none of those products found their way back into the United States. Finding also that there was a likelihood of confusion between the competing products, the district court issued a preliminary injunction, enjoining the defendant from any acts likely to cause confusion in the Saudi Arabian consuming public. We affirm.

I

The plaintiff, American Rice, Inc. ("ARI"), and defendant, Arkansas Rice Growers Cooperative Association ("Riceland"), in this trademark suit are farmers' marketing cooperatives that process, mill, package, and market rice for their member-patrons. ARI is based in Houston, Texas, and counts among its members 1700 farmers in Arkansas, Louisiana, and Texas. Riceland's

---

[23] At last report of plaintiffs, the tally in foreign encounters stood as follows: Plaintiff Wells Fargo & Company has met with great success in West Germany and Austria against A.G., and in Italy and France against A.G.'s wholly-owned Irish subsidiary. Lesser success is reported in Liechtenstein against A.G. itself, and proceedings in Great Britain and South Africa against A.G., and in Spain against A.G.'s partially-owned Spanish subsidiary, were still awaiting resolution. Plaintiff Baker Industries has seemingly fared less well, losing to A.G. in Great Britain and to A.G.'s Spanish subsidiary in Spain. . . .

14,000 members are located in Arkansas, Louisiana, Mississippi, and Missouri. Both cooperatives are actively engaged in selling rice under a number of brands in the United States and abroad.

In 1975, ARI purchased Blue Ribbon Mills, a company that had been exporting its rice to Saudi Arabia since 1966, and was assigned that company's trademarks. Included among those trademarks were the word marks "Blue Ribbon", "Chopstick", and "Abu Bint", and the design mark of a girl. Since the takeover of Blue Ribbon, ARI has continued to market rice under these marks with the assistance of its brokerage firm, Alpha Trading and Shipping Agencies, Ltd. ("Alpha"). Alpha is ARI's exclusive agent in Saudi Arabia, and is licensed by ARI to use the mark "Abu Bint" and to assist it in the on-going efforts to obtain a trademark registration in that country. ARI has attempted to register the "Abu Bint" mark since 1972, when a Saudi official rejected the application.

At the time of the injunctive order, ARI owned two federal registrations for the girl design trademark, and Texas trademark registrations, in both English and Arabic, of the word mark "Abu Bint". The plaintiff contends, and the trial court found, that "Abu Bint" translates into English as "of the girl" or "girl brand". The girl design marks, which are featured prominently on ARI's rice bags sold in Saudi Arabia, show the head and torso of a young oriental woman holding a bowl of rice and chopsticks. The color combination is red, yellow, and black. The words "chopstick" and "rice" appear in large, oriental-style writing, and the words "golden parboiled" are set into the table of the girl design. "Abu Bint" is printed at the top of each bag in Arabic script, and the logo and full name of ARI appear at the bottom in smaller English print.

ARI's rice is referred to only as Abu Bint in Saudi Arabia, and not as Chopstick brand. The reason for this, as the district court stated, is that the largely illiterate Saudi Arabian public distinguishes rice brands on the basis of the design on the package. The high incidence of illiteracy also explains why the plaintiff does not advertise, but relies instead on promotional schemes. ARI sells its rice in merchant "offices" where Saudis are permitted to view samples and place their orders. The rice is typically purchased in large quantities, 25 o · 100 pound burlap bags.

Like ARI, Riceland sells its rice in 25 and 100 pound burlap bags through a system of merchants. The defendant initially marketed the rice in bags displaying a lion design, but in 1974 the company entered into an agreement with a Saudi merchant and began selling its product under the name "Abu Binten" or "Twin Girl". The colors appearing on the Twin Girl bags are red, yellow and black, the same colors used by ARI.[3] Four years later, in 1978, Riceland introduced a third brand called "Bintal-Arab" or "daughter of the Arabs". Although the mark Bint al-Arab is owned by a Saudi merchant, Alamoudi, Riceland contends that it possesses the exclusive right to use the

[3]Riceland has obtained a registration for its Twin Girl mark in the United States, and the district court did not find that use of this mark constituted an infringement.

mark outside of Saudi Arabia.[4] The Bint al-Arab design portrays a young Arab woman outlined by a black seal. Arabic script is on the top of the seal and Roman lettering is on the bottom. The predominant colors are green, yellow, and black. Below the seal are the English words "extra long grain, parboiled American RICE," and at the bottom of the bag is the Riceland logo. In 1981, at the request of Alamoudi, Riceland modified its Bint al-Arab label and changed the color scheme to red, yellow, and black. The seal was also enlarged and the girl's facial features were altered.

Following the change in the Bint al-Arab label, Riceland began packaging, on a "private label" basis, another variety of rice called "Gulf Girl" in Arabic. The brand once again featured a label with a design of a girl and the colors red, yellow, and black. The girl is portrayed between black Arabic script, from the waist up, her hair uncovered. Unlike the young woman displayed on the Bint al-Arab rice bags, the Gulf Girl is western in appearance.

Even before the Gulf Girl mark was introduced, evidence admitted at the hearing showed that Saudi Arabian merchants, longshoremen, and consumers occasionally confused the defendant's Bint al-Arab brand with the plaintiff's Abu Bint rice. Riceland bags were shipped to and accidentally mixed with ARI bags at a merchant's warehouse. And one witness testified that he heard the owner of the Bint al-Arab mark, Alamoudi, attempt to tell a customer looking for Abu Bint that Bint al-Arab was the same rice.

ARI filed suit against Riceland on October 15, 1981, alleging trademark infringement in violation of the common law and the Lanham Act, 15 U.S.C. §1051 *et seq.*, false designations of origin in violation of 15 U.S.C. §1125(a), and deceptive trade practices in violation of the Texas Deceptive Trade Practice Act, Tex. Bus. & Com. Code Ann. §§17.41-.63 (Vernon Supp. 1980-81). ARI's complaint sought preliminary and permanent injunctive relief, loss of profits, damages, and costs. An evidentiary hearing on the plaintiff's motion for a preliminary injunction was held on February 5, 1982, and on March 2 the motion was granted, enjoining the defendant from the use of certain trademarks and trade dress in connection with the sale of rice in Saudi Arabia. The district court concluded its memorandum opinion and order by finding:

> that plaintiff has presented evidence demonstrating its substantial likelihood of success at trial on the merits. Likelihood of confusion is due to the introduction of the red, yellow and black Bint al-Arab and the Gulf Girl labels. Defendant packages and sells the same product, rice, as plaintiff does. They both reach the same market. They both use the same advertising approach, although plaintiff has introduced a significant number of promotional items. There is some evidence of defendant's intent. There is some evidence of actual confusion. The designs of all three labels have similar characteristics. In light of the consuming public, careful distinction between the brands of a common product probably

---

[4]Riceland attempted to register the Bint al-Arab mark for use on rice by filing a trademark application in the United States Patent and Trademark Office in November 1978. ARI opposed the application, and the opposition proceeding was stayed pending the outcome of this litigation.

would not be expected. Thus, plaintiff has carried its burden on this element in regard to these two labels.

532 F. Supp. at 1388. The district court also enjoined the defendant from using its green Bint al-Arab label because it, too, was similar to the plaintiff's Abu Bint mark, and its continued use would permit Riceland to retain part of the goodwill misappropriated from ARI.

II

The Lanham Act provides a trademark registrant a civil right of action against "[a]ny person who shall . . . use in commerce" a colorable imitation of a registered mark in connection with the sale, offering for sale, or distribution of goods. 15 U.S.C. §1114(1)(a). "Commerce" is sweepingly defined as "all commerce which may lawfully be regulated by Congress." *Id.* §1127. Section 1121 provides the federal courts with subject matter jurisdiction over causes of action arising under the Act.

The extraterritorial reach of American law is no new subject to federal courts. It has been examined extensively in the context of the Sherman Act, 15 U.S.C. §§1 & 2, and courts have proposed a variety of tests for determining when district courts should entertain claims involving extraterritorial conduct. . . .

Although cases brought under the Lanham Act have been fewer than those under the Sherman Act, we are not without guidance in determining when a federal court has jurisdiction to entertain an infringement action involving commerce between the United States and a foreign market. The leading case is Steele v. Bulova Watch Co., 1952, 344 U.S. 280, 73 S. Ct. 252, 97 L. Ed. 252. . . .

Bulova stands for the proposition that "a United States district court has jurisdiction to award relief to an American corporation against acts of trademark infringement and unfair competition consummated in a foreign country by a citizen and resident of the United States." 344 U.S. at 281, 73 S. Ct. at 253, 97 L. Ed. at 322. Because Steele's Mexican trademark was cancelled before the case was decided, the Supreme Court did not reach the question whether enjoining use of Steele's mark would be an affront to Mexican sovereignty. The Court did note, however, that the Lanham Act did not constrict prior law, and cited the earlier case of George W. Luft Co., Inc. v. Zande Cosmetic Co., Inc., 2 Cir. 1944, 142 F.2d 536, *cert. denied,* 1944, 323 U.S. 756, 65 S. Ct. 90, 89 L. Ed. 606. There, both parties were engaged in the manufacture and sale of cosmetics, and the defendant's mark, "Zande", first used in 1935, was found to infringe the plaintiff's mark, "Tangee", introduced in 1920. The district court granted a broad injunction, and prohibited the defendant from showing its right, established under foreign laws, to use the trade-name. The Second Circuit modified the breadth of the injunction, and held that such evidence would prohibit the district court from affecting the defendant's shipment to those countries where it had established a *superior* right to the trademark. As the Court stated:

> Nor can we perceive upon what theory a plaintiff can recover damages for acts in the United States resulting in a sale of merchandise in a foreign country under a mark to which the defendant has established, over the plaintiff's opposition, a legal right of use in that country. Consequently, neither the injunction nor the accounting should cover activities of the defendants, either here or abroad, concerned with sales in countries where the defendants have established rights superior to the plaintiff's. . . .

142 F.2d at 541.

We conclude that under *Bulova* and *Luft* certain factors are relevant in determining whether the contracts and interests of the United States are sufficient to support the exercise of extraterritorial jurisdiction. These include the citizenship of the defendant, the effect on United States commerce, and the existence of a conflict with foreign law. *See* Vanity Fair Mills v. T. Eaton Co., 2 Cir. 1956, 234 F.2d 633, 642, *cert. denied,* 1956, 352 U.S. 871, 77 S. Ct. 96, 1 L. Ed. 2d 76. The absence of any one of these is not dispositive. Nor should a court limit its inquiry exclusively to these considerations. Rather, these factors will necessarily be the primary elements in any balancing analysis.

Riceland contends that the district court erred when it found that it was not deprived of the power to issue equitable relief, even though the ultimate sale of the defendant's Bint al-Arab and Gulf Girl brands occurred in Saudi Arabia and none of its products found their way back into the United States. Our reading of *Bulova* and *Luft* convinces us that no error was committed. It is undisputed that the defendant is an American corporation, based in Stuttgart, Arkansas, engaged in both interstate and foreign commerce. It is also clear, contrary to Riceland's assertions, that the defendant's Saudi Arabian sales had more than an insignificant effect on United States commerce. Each of Riceland's activities, from the processing and packaging of the rice to the transportation and distribution of it, are activities within commerce. And by unlawfully selling its products under infringing marks in Saudi Arabia, Riceland diverted sales from ARI, whose rice products are also processed, packaged, transported, and distributed in commerce regulated by Congress. Merely because the consummation of the unlawful activity occurred on foreign soil is of no assistance to the defendant. As the Supreme Court stated in *Bulova,* "we do not deem material that petitioner affixed the mark 'Bulova' in Mexico City rather than here, or that his purchases in the United States when viewed in isolation do not violate any of our laws. They were essential steps in the course of business consummated abroad; acts in themselves legal lose that character when they become part of an unlawful scheme." 344 U.S. at 287, 73 S. Ct. at 256, 97 L. Ed. at 325-26. There is also no requirement that the defendant's products bearing the infringing marks make their way back into the United States. *See* Paco Rabanne, Etc. v. Norco Enterprises, Inc., 2 Cir. 1982, 680 F.2d 891; Hecker H—O Co. v. Holland Food Corp., 2 Cir. 1929, 36 F.2d 767.

Riceland argues that even if its sales adversely affected commerce, the district court should have refrained from issuing an injunction because its acts were lawful in Saudi Arabia. The mark Bint al-Arab was created and is owned in that country by the merchant Alamoudi. It has been in use since 1978 for rice, when Riceland became a private label supplier to Alamoudi, and since 1977 for cooking oil. Under the Saudi Arabian Trade Marks Registration Code, any individual who uses a mark for more than a year before its registration by anyone else has at least a concurrent right to use that mark. Because ARI's Abu Bint mark is as yet unregistered in Saudi Arabia, the defendant points out, and because Alamoudi used the Bint al-Arab mark for more than one year, Alamoudi has a vested right to use the mark, and through him, Riceland. The district court's decision to enjoin the defendant's use of the infringing marks, therefore, interferes with the laws of another nation and runs contrary to the principles of international comity.

We cannot accept the defendant's contention. At best, Riceland has shown that Alamoudi, not it, has a concurrent right to use the Bint al-Arab mark. According to the defendant's own translation of the Saudi Arabian Trade Marks Registration Code, any right which Alamoudi may have acquired is "personal, non-inheritable and non-transferable to third parties".[10] Even were we to accept Riceland's contention that it possesses a concurrent right to use the mark, that right is not superior, as *Luft* requires, to the plaintiff's right. *See Luft,* 142 F.2d at 541. The defendant has not established, over the plaintiff's opposition, a legal right of use in Saudi Arabia. ARI has sought a Saudi registration for its Abu Bint mark since 1972, and the application is currently before that country's courts. Absent a determination by a Saudi court that Riceland has a legal right to use its marks, and that those marks do not infringe ARI's Abu Bint mark, we are unable to conclude that it would be an affront to Saudi sovereignty or law if we affirm the district court's injunction prohibiting the defendant from injuring the plaintiff's Saudi Arabian commerce conducted from the United States.

Riceland's reliance on Vanity Fair Mills, Inc. v. T. Eaton Co., 2 Cir. 1956, 234 F.2d 633, is misplaced. There the defendant, a Canadian corporation,

---

[10]Chapter 2, Paragraph 19 of the Saudi Trade Marks Code provides as follows:

Anyone whose trade mark is registered shall be deemed to be its sole owner, and the right of calling the ownership of such a trade mark into question shall abate if the person who registers the said trade mark uses it continually for at least five years as of the date of registration, provided that no proper legal action is brought against such person in regard to such registration. *However, if anyone proves that he has the said trademark and utilized it, continually for one year prior to registration, before anybody else, then he shall acquire the right to take hold of such a trademark, and such right shall be personal, non-inheritable and non-transferable to third parties.* (emphasis added.)

registered in 1915 the trademark "Vanity Fair" in Canada. The plaintiffs, holders of the same trademark in the United States since 1914, and doing business under that name in Canada since 1917, attempted to register the mark in Canada in 1919. The application was rejected, however, because of the defendant's prior registration. In 1954, the plaintiffs brought suit in New York to enjoin the Canadian use of the name. The only contact the defendant had with the United States was a sales office in New York, and except for a few mail order sales into the United States through this office, the passing off occurred in Canada. "The crucial issue in the case was the validity of the defendant's Canadian trademark registration under Canadian trademark law". 234 F.2d at 646. Although the defendant's conduct had a substantial effect on American commerce, the Court found *Bulova* distinguishable and held that Congress did not intend that the Lanham Act reach "acts committed by a foreign national in his home country under a presumably valid trademark registration in that country". 234 F.2d at 642. In refusing to determine the validity of the Canadian registration, the court followed the act of state doctrine, applicable when exclusive rights are conferred by the act of a foreign sovereign, the ramifications of which we may avoid. Here, unlike in *Vanity Fair,* the defendant possesses no superior foreign right to use the trademarks in question. And here, unlike in *Vanity Fair,* the defendant is an American corporation. "No principle of international law bars the United States from governing the conduct of its own citizens upon the high seas or even in foreign countries when the rights of other nations are not infringed. Congress has the power to prevent unfair trade practices in foreign commerce by citizens of the United States, although some of the acts are done outside the territorial limits." Scotch Whisky Association v. Barton Distilling Co., 7 Cir. 1973, 489 F.2d 809, 812. *See also* Kerios, Territoriality and International Copyright Infringement Actions, Copyright Law Symposium No. 22, at 53, 65 (1977).

QUESTIONS

1. Under what principle of patent law would Deepsouth have been liable if it had completed manufacture of the machines in the United States? What if it had sold them to someone who used them in the United States?

2. Assume that Laitram, which has a U.S. monopoly and invented the machine, charges a significantly higher price for U.S. sales of its machine than does Deepsouth for foreign sales. As a result, foreign shrimp fishers and packers may be able to underprice domestic ones. Any relief for the U.S. firms? For Laitram, which may be forced to lower its prices in the United States (where it has patent protection) as well as abroad (where it does not have patent protection)?

3. Suppose the patent in *Deepsouth* were on the method rather than on the machine itself. Could Deepsouth have assembled the machines in the United States without infringing the patent, (as long as it didn't test them)? For an

affirmative answer in such a situation, *see* John Mohr & Sons v. Vacudyne, 354 F. Supp. 1113 (N.D. Ill. 1973).

4. Are *Wells Fargo* and *Deepsouth* consistent? *American Rice* and *Deepsouth?*

5. To the extent these cases differ, how might you explain those differences? Specific factors? A patent versus trademark distinction?

6. In *Bulova*, discussed in both *Wells Fargo* and *American Rice* (*see supra* pp. 678 and 682), why did Bulova brave the jurisdictional questions of that case rather than pursue its right (to be examined later in this chapter) to have imports of the watches stopped at the border?

7. Is *Wells Fargo* fair in its interpretation of *Timberlane?* Of *Bulova?*

8. Is it wise to extend the jurisdictional flexibility of *Timberlane* to this area?

9. In both *Wells Fargo* and *American Rice,* the U.S. court appeared ready to contradict a foreign decision on a trademark question in the foreign nation. Is this wise? Unavoidable? What would you do if you represented a firm that appeared about to be caught in the middle of inconsistent decrees?

B. THE TREATY STRUCTURE

There is an international treaty structure designed to tie together the rights to territorial intellectual property protection. The key provision, found in a host of treaties for different kinds of intellectual property, is that nationals of each treaty party are guaranteed the right to apply for protection in any nation as if they were nationals of that nation. This provision is supplemented by minimum standards for the particular type of intellectual property involved.

This treaty structure makes it possible for a firm to obtain coverage in a number of different nations—but the firm must, in general, apply separately in each nation. The global structure has proceeded only a little beyond this point. The Paris Convention for the Protection of Intellectual Property gives an inventor a defined period to file in a series of nations without having its first filings count as publication that would, under some nations' laws, disqualify the invention from patentability. And the Patent Cooperation Treaty of 1970 (28 U.S.T. 7645, T.I.A.S. No. 8733), implemented in the United States by P.L. 94-131 (codified at 35 U.S.C. §§351-376) is beginning to move toward ways to avoid having to repeat the search of prior inventions from nation to nation. Moreover, Europe is moving toward greater unity. Even there, however, when one obtains a "European patent," available with a single application, what is received is in essence a bundle of national patents, for the nations were unable to agree upon a precise common alignment of the content to be given the patent right. *See* Beier, The European Patent System, 14 Vand. J. Transnatl. L. 1 (1981).

The following materials provide excerpts from the Paris Convention, one of the international treaties, and from *Vanity Fair,* which interprets that convention.

PARIS CONVENTION FOR THE PROTECTION OF INDUSTRIAL PROPERTY OF MARCH 20, 1883 [PARIS UNION]

As revised at Stockholm on July 14, 1967, T.I.A.S. No. 6923 (1970)

ARTICLE 1

[Establishment of the Union; Scope of Industrial Property]

(1) The countries to which this Convention applies constitute a Union for the protection of industrial property.

(2) The protection of industrial property has as its object patents, utility models, industrial designs, trademarks, service marks, trade names, indications of source or appellations of origin, and the repression of unfair competition.

(3) Industrial property shall be understood in the broadest sense and shall apply not only to industry and commerce proper, but likewise to agricultural and extractive industries and to all manufactured or natural products, for example, wines, grain, tobacco leaf, fruit, cattle, minerals, mineral waters, beer, flowers, and flour.

(4) Patents shall include the various kinds of industrial patents recognized by the laws of the countries of the Union, such as patents of importation, patents of improvement, patents and certificates of addition, etc.

ARTICLE 2

[National Treatment for Nationals of Countries of the Union]

(1) Nationals of any country of the Union shall, as regards the protection of industrial property, enjoy in all the other countries of the Union the advantages that their respective laws now grant, or may hereafter grant, to nationals; all without prejudice to the rights specially provided for by this Convention. Consequently, they shall have the same protection as the latter, and the same legal remedy against any infringement of their rights, provided that the conditions and formalities imposed upon nationals are complied with. . . .

ARTICLE 3

[Same Treatment for Certain Categories of Persons as for Nationals of Countries of the Union]

Nationals of countries outside the Union who are domiciled or who have real and effective industrial or commercial establishments in the territory of one of the countries of the Union shall be treated in the same manner as nationals of the countries of the Union.

ARTICLE 4

[A to I. *Patents, Utility Models, Industrial Designs, Marks, Inventors' Certificates:* Right of Priority.—G. *Patents:* Division of the Application]

A.—(1) Any person who has duly filed an application for a patent, or for the registration of a utility model, or of an industrial design, or of a trademark, in one of the countries of the Union, or his successor in title, shall enjoy, for the purpose of filing in the other countries, a right of priority during the periods hereinafter fixed.

(2) Any filing that is equivalent to a regular national filing under the domestic legislation of any country of the Union or under bilateral or multilateral treaties concluded between countries of the Union shall be recognized as giving rise to the right of priority.

(3) By a regular national filing is meant any filing that is adequate to establish the date on which the application was filed in the country concerned, whatever may be the subsequent fate of the application.

B.—Consequently, any subsequent filing in any of the other countries of the Union before the expiration of the periods referred to above shall not be invalidated by reason of any acts accomplished in the interval, in particular, another filing, the publication or exploitation of the invention, the putting on sale of copies of the design, or the use of the mark, and such acts cannot give rise to any third-party right or any right of personal possession. Rights acquired by third parties before the date of the first application that serves as the basis for the right of priority are reserved in accordance with the domestic legislation of each country of the Union.

C.—(1) The periods of priority referred to above shall be twelve months for patents and utility models, and six months for industrial designs and trademarks.

(2) These periods shall start from the date of filing of the first application; the day of filing shall not be included in the period.

(3) If the last day of the period is an official holiday, or a day when the Office is not open for the filing of applications in the country where protection is claimed, the period shall be extended until the first following working day.

ARTICLE 4bis

[*Patents:* Independence of Patents Obtained for the Same Invention in Different Countries]

(1) Patents applied for in the various countries of the Union by nationals of countries of the Union shall be independent of patents obtained for the same invention in other countries, whether members of the Union or not.

(2) The foregoing provision is to be understood in an unrestricted sense, in particular, in the sense that patents applied for during the period of priority are independent, both as regards the grounds for nullity and forfeiture, and as regards their normal duration.

(3) The provision shall apply to all patents existing at the time when it comes into effect.

(4) Similarly, it shall apply, in the case of the accession of new countries, to patents in existence on either side at the time of accession.

(5) Patents obtained with the benefit of priority shall, in the various countries of the Union, have a duration equal to that which they would have, had they been applied for or granted without the benefit of priority. . . .

ARTICLE 4^{quater}

[*Patents:* Patentability in Case of Restrictions of Sale by Law]
The grant of a patent shall not be refused and a patent shall not be invalidated on the ground that the sale of the patented product or of a product obtained by means of a patented process is subject to restrictions or limitations resulting from the domestic law.

ARTICLE 5

[A. *Patents:* Importation of Articles; Failure to Work or Insufficient Working; Compulsory Licenses.—B. *Industrial Designs:* Failure to Work; Importation of Articles.—C. *Marks:* Failure to Use; Different Forms; Use by Co-proprietors.—D. *Patents, Utility Models, Marks, Industrial Designs:* Marking]
A.—(1) Importation by the patentee into the country where the patent has been granted of articles manufactured in any of the countries of the Union shall not entail forfeiture of the patent.

(2) Each country of the Union shall have the right to take legislative measures providing for the grant of compulsory licenses to prevent the abuses which might result from the exercise of the exclusive rights conferred by the patent, for example, failure to work.

(3) Forfeiture of the patent shall not be provided for except in cases where the grant of compulsory licenses would not have been sufficient to prevent the said abuses. No proceedings for the forfeiture or revocation of a patent may be instituted before the expiration of two years from the grant of the first compulsory license.

(4) A compulsory license may not be applied for on the ground of failure to work or insufficient working before the expiration of a period of four years from the date of filing of the patent application or three years from the date of

the grant of the patent, whichever period expires last; it shall be refused if the patentee justifies his inaction by legitimate reasons. Such a compulsory license shall be non-exclusive and shall not be transferable, even in the form of the grant of a sub-license, except with that part of the enterprise or goodwill which exploits such license. . . .

ARTICLE 5quater

[*Patents:* Importation of Products Manufactured by a Process Patented in the Importing Country]

When a product is imported into a country of the Union where there exists a patent protecting a process of manufacture of the said product, the patentee shall have all the rights, with regard to the imported product, that are accorded to him by the legislation of the country of importation, on the basis of the process patent, with respect to products manufactured in that country. . . .

ARTICLE 9

[*Marks, Trade Names:* Seizure, on Importation, etc., of Goods Unlawfully Bearing a Mark or Trade Name]

(1) All goods unlawfully bearing a trademark or trade name shall be seized on importation into those countries of the Union where such mark or trade name is entitled to legal protection.

(2) Seizure shall likewise be effected in the country where the unlawful affixation occurred or in the country into which the goods were imported.

(3) Seizure shall take place at the request of the public prosecutor, or any other competent authority, or any interested party, whether a natural person or a legal entity, in conformity with the domestic legislation of each country.

(4) The authorities shall not be bound to effect seizure of goods in transit.

(5) If the legislation of a country does not permit seizure on importation, seizure shall be replaced by prohibition of importation or by seizure inside the country.

(6) If the legislation of a country permits neither seizure on importation nor prohibition of importation nor seizure inside the country, then, until such time as the legislation is modified accordingly, these measures shall be replaced by the actions and remedies available in such cases to nationals under the law of such country. . . .

ARTICLE 10bis

[*Unfair Competition*]

(1) The countries of the Union are bound to assure to nationals of such countries effective protection against unfair competition.

(2) Any act of competition contrary to honest practices in industrial or commercial matters constitutes an act of unfair competition.

(3) The following in particular shall be prohibited:

1. all acts of such a nature as to create confusion by any means whatever with the establishment, the goods, or the industrial or commercial activities, of a competitor;
2. false allegations in the course of trade of such a nature as to discredit the establishment, the goods, or the industrial or commercial activities, of a competitor;
3. indications or allegations the use of which in the course of trade is liable to mislead the public as to the nature, the manufacturing process, the characteristics, the suitability for their purpose, or the quantity, of the goods.

VANITY FAIR MILLS, INC. v. THE T. EATON CO.

234 F.2d 633 (2nd Cir. 1956)

WATERMAN, J. . . .

Plaintiff, Vanity Fair Mills, Inc., is a Pennsylvania corporation, having its principal place of business at Reading, Pennsylvania. It has been engaged in the manufacture and sale of women's underwear under the trade-mark "Vanity Fair" since about the year 1914 in the United States, and has been continuously offering its branded merchandise for sale in Canada since at least 1917. Plaintiff has publicized its trade-mark "Vanity Fair" on feminine underwear in the United States since 1914, and since 1917 has regularly expended large sums of money in advertising and promoting its trade-mark both in the United States and Canada. As a result of the high quality of plaintiff's merchandise, and its extensive sales promotion and advertising, the name "Vanity Fair" has become associated throughout the United States and Canada with plaintiff's products.

Beginning in 1914 plaintiff has protected its trade-mark rights by registrations with the United States Patent Office of the trade-mark "Vanity Fair" as applying to various types of underwear. It has been continuously manufacturing and selling feminine underwear under these trade-mark registrations since about the year 1914.

Defendant, The T. Eaton Company, Limited, is a Canadian corporation engaged in the retail merchandising business throughout Canada, with its principal office in Toronto, Ontario. It has a regular and established place of business within the Southern District of New York. On November 3, 1915, defendant filed with the proper Canadian official an application for the registration in Canada of the trade-mark "Vanity Fair," claiming use in connection with the sale of "Women's, Misses' and Children's Coats, Suits, Cloaks, Waists, Dresses, Skirts, Corsets, Knitted Goods, Gloves, Hosiery, Boots & Shoes, Outer Garments, and other Wearing Apparel." On November 10, 1915, the proper Canadian official granted defendant's application for the registration of that mark. Plaintiff asserts that this registration applies only to feminine outerwear, and that in any event it is merely a "paper registration" because of non-use. In 1919 plaintiff sought to register the trade-mark "Vanity Fair" in Canada for "ready made underwear," but its application was rejected as a matter of course because of the prior registration of defendant. In 1933 defendant, in reply to a request of the Canadian Registrar of Trade-Marks, listed "women's underwear, corsets, girdles and other foundation garments" as the goods in connection with which it had actually been using the mark "Vanity Fair," and its registration was modified accordingly. Plaintiff alleges that defendant, by this informal procedure, amended its trade-mark registration in Canada to include, for the first time, feminine underwear.

During the years 1945-1953 the defendant ceased to use its own "Vanity-Fair" trade-mark, purchased branded merchandise from the plaintiff, and sold this merchandise under advertisements indicating that it was of United States origin and of plaintiff's manufacture. These purchases by defendant from plaintiff were made through defendant's New York office. In 1953 defendant resumed the use of its own trade-mark "Vanity Fair" and, simultaneously, under the same trade-mark, sold plaintiff's branded merchandise and cheaper merchandise of Canadian manufacture. Defendant at this time objected to plaintiff's sales of its branded merchandise to one of defendant's principal competitors in Canada, the Robert Simpson Company. The Simpson Company discontinued purchases of plaintiff's branded merchandise after being threatened with infringement suits by defendant.

Plaintiff alleges that these acts constitute a conspiracy on the part of the corporate defendant and its officers and agents to appropriate for their own benefit plaintiff's registered and common-law trade-mark. It asserts that defendant, by purchasing plaintiff's branded merchandise for a period of years and advertising and selling such merchandise as plaintiff's goods, attempted to associate plaintiff's trade-mark with itself, and, that purpose having been accomplished, defendant then began using the trade-mark "Vanity Fair" in connection with its own inferior feminine underwear, discontinued purchases from plaintiff, and threatened its competitors in Canada with infringement suits if they continued to sell plaintiff's branded merchandise in Canada.

Finally, plaintiff asserts that defendant has advertised feminine underwear in the United States under the trade-mark "Vanity Fair," and that it has sold such underwear by mail to customers residing in the United States.

The complaint seeks injunctive relief against the use by defendant of the trade-mark "Vanity Fair" in connection with women's underwear both in Canada and the United States, a declaration of the superior rights of the plaintiff in such trade-mark, and an accounting for damages and profits. . . .

I. THE INTERNATIONAL CONVENTION

Plaintiff asserts that the International Convention for the Protection of Industrial Property (Paris Union), 53 Stat. 1748 (1883, as revised 1934), T.S. No. 941, to which both the United States and Canada are parties, is self-executing; that by virtue of Article VI of the Constitution it is a part of the law of this country which is to be enforced by its courts; and that the Convention has created rights available to plaintiff which protect it against trade-mark infringement and unfair competition in foreign countries. Plaintiff would appear to be correct in arguing that no special legislation in the United States was necessary to make the International Convention effective here, but it erroneously maintains that the Convention created private rights *under American law* for acts of unfair competition occurring in foreign countries.

The International Convention is essentially a compact between the various member countries to accord in their own countries to citizens of the other contracting parties trade-mark and other rights comparable to those accorded their own citizens by their domestic law. The underlying principle is that foreign nationals should be given the same treatment in each of the member countries as that country makes available to its own citizens. In addition, the Convention sought to create uniformity in certain respects by obligating each member nation "to assure to nationals of countries of the Union an effective protection against unfair competition."[1]

The Convention is not premised upon the idea that the trade-mark and related laws of each member nation shall be given extraterritorial application, but on exactly the converse principle that each nation's law shall have only territorial application. Thus a foreign national of a member nation using his trade-mark in commerce in the United States is accorded extensive protection here against infringement and other types of unfair competition by virtue of United States membership in the Convention. But that protection has its source in, and is subject to the limitations of, American law, not the law of the foreign national's own country. Likewise, the International Convention provides protection to a United States trade-mark owner such as plaintiff against unfair competition and trade-mark infringement in Canada—but only to the extent that Canadian law recognizes the treaty obligation as creating private rights or has made the Convention operative by implementing legislation. Under Canadian law, unlike United States law, the International Convention was not effective to create any private rights in Canada without legislative implementation. However, the obligations undertaken by the Dominion of Canada under this treaty have been implemented by legislation, most recently by the Canadian Trade Marks Act of 1953, 1-2 Elizabeth II, Chapter 49. If plaintiff has any rights under the International Convention (other than through §44 of the Lanham Act, discussed below), they are derived from this

---

[1] Paris Convention for the Protection of Intellectual Property, Article 10[bis]—EDS.

Canadian law, and not from the fact that the International Convention may be a self-executing treaty which is a part of the law of this country. . . .

[Discussion of those Lanham Act extraterritorial application of trademark issues described in *Wells Fargo* and *American Rice* omitted here.]

B. SECTION 44 OF THE LANHAM ACT

Plaintiff's alternative contention is that §44 of the Lanham Act, which is entitled "International Conventions," affords to United States citizens all possible remedies against unfair competition by foreigners who are nationals of convention countries, including the relief requested in this case. Subsection (b) of §44 specifies that nationals of foreign countries signatory to certain named conventions (including the Paris Union signed by Canada) are "entitled to the benefits . . . [of the Act] to the extent . . . essential to give effect to [the Conventions]." Subsection (g) then provides that the trade names of persons described in subsection (b), i.e., nationals of foreign countries which have signed the conventions, "shall be protected without the obligation of filing or registration whether or not they form parts of marks", and subsection (h) provides that the same persons "shall be entitled to effective protection against unfair competition. . . ." Finally, subsection (i) provides that "citizens or residents of the United States shall have the same benefits as are granted by this section to persons described in subsection (b) . . ." Thus §44 first implements the international agreements by providing certain foreign nationals with the benefits contained in those agreements, then, in subsection (i), places American citizens on an equal footing by providing them with the same benefits. . . . [The court reviewed the specific benefits provided by §44.] It will be noted that all of these benefits are internal to the United States in the sense that they confer on foreign nationals certain rights in the United States. None of them could have extraterritorial application, for all of them relate solely to the registration and protection of marks within the United States.

We now come to the two remaining benefits specified in §44, and the ones upon which plaintiff relies: the provision in subsection (g) protecting tradenames without the obligation of filing or registration, and the provision in subsection (h) entitling eligible foreign nationals "to effective protection against unfair competition" and making available "the remedies provided in this chapter for infringement of marks . . . so far as they may be appropriate in repressing acts of unfair competition." Here again, we think that these benefits are limited in application to within the United States. It is true that they are not expressly so limited, but it seems inconceivable that Congress meant by this language to extend to all eligible foreign nationals a remedy *in the United States against unfair competition occurring in their own countries.* Moreover, if §44 were so interpreted, it would apply to commerce which is beyond the Congressional power to regulate, and a serious constitutional question would be created. In the absence of any Congressional intent to provide remedies of such extensive application, we interpret §44 in a manner which avoids constitutional questions and which carries out the underlying principle of the International Conventions sought to be implemented by §44—the principle that each nation shall apply its national law equally to foreigners and citizens alike.

Since United States citizens are given by subsection (i) of §44 only the same benefits which the Act extends to eligible foreign nationals, and since the benefits conferred on those foreign nationals have no extraterritorial application, the benefits accorded to citizens by this section can likewise have no extraterritorial application. . . .

NOTES AND QUESTIONS

1. Is *Vanity Fair*'s interpretation of the convention and its implementation correct? The position may be changing. In London Film Productions v. Intercontinental Communications, 580 F. Supp. 47 (S.D.N.Y. 1984), alleged infringement in Chile of British copyright was held triable in New York. *But see* C-Cure Chemical Co. v. Secure Adhesives, 571 F. Supp. 808 (W.D.N.Y. 1983), following *Vanity Fair.*

2. Why didn't Vanity Fair bring its law suit in Canada?

3. Suppose a trademark "pirate" goes to a foreign nation and registers a trademark before the "legitimate" holder goes to the trouble of filing. Later, when the legitimate holder seeks to develop that market, it finds itself faced with a suit for infringement, which, can, of course, be settled for a price. What recourse does it have?

4. Suppose the situation of question 3 were to occur in the United States to the detriment of a foreign legitimate trademark holder? You probably want to begin with 15 U.S.C. §§1052(d) 1091, and 1126; and with Toho Co. v. Sears, Roebuck, 645 F.2d 788 (9th Cir. 1981).

5. What changes are required for the law to be able to work reasonably in the situation described in questions 3 and 4?

6. How might the law handle the more innocent situation—which has happened—in which two firms, starting in different nations, use trademarks that can be easily confused with each other and expand their marketing areas until, all of a sudden, a problem arises? *See* Pioneer Hi-Bred Corn v. Hy-Line Chicks, [1978] 2 N.Z.L.R. 50.

7. Suppose you can't be sure whether a situation is piracy or innocent confusion?

C.   IMPORT RESTRICTIONS

For a major invention, an inventor (often through his or her employer) applies for parallel patents in several different jurisdictions. The inventor may then transfer a license—the right to practice the monopoly in a particular nation—to another firm or to one of its affiliates or subsidiaries. This license may be exclusive (the only one granted) or nonexclusive (one of several that are or may be granted) and it may be royalty-free or for a stated royalty.

1. Patented or Trademarked Products

The following case presents an example of this pattern, and develops its implication—that the holder of the patent in one jurisdiction can use that patent to exclude goods from another jurisdiction, even though they were made legitimately in that jurisdiction.

GRIFFIN v. KEYSTONE MUSHROOM FARM, INC.

453 F. Supp. 1283 (E.D. Pa. 1978)

LORD, J.

Plaintiff in this patent infringement suit is the holder of United States Patents Nos. 3,386,705 and 3,791,593 for a composting machine and certain parts of composting machinery, respectively. Defendant, which has counterclaimed for declaratory judgment with regard to the patent suit and for breach of contract, now moves for partial summary judgment on the infringement claims and on its counterclaim for declaratory judgment of non-infringement. Accepting as the factual record the account of events presented by the defendant in its affidavits and exhibits, we find the defense to infringement deficient as a matter of law and will deny the motion.

The plaintiff holds patents for these inventions in Italy as well as in the United States. He had granted before 1975 an exclusive license to Longwood Manufacturing Corporation to make, use and sell the patented composting machine in the United States, and he granted on July 28, 1975, an exclusive license to Celeste Carminati to practice in Italy and in other European Economic Community nations the art patented under the laws of Italy. The defendant's president purchased a composting machine from Carminati, *f.o.b. Genoa,* in late 1975, and the defendant purchased two more machines from Carminati in 1976, *f.o.b. Genoa.* The defendant, a mushroom grower and supplier of equipment and materials to mushroom farmers in Pennsylvania, has used the first-purchased of these composters in its own business and has sold the other two. Infringement of the United States patent is alleged on the basis of the use and sale of these three machines.

Defendant concedes for purposes of this motion that the United States patents in suit are valid and enforceable, that the three machines embody the patented inventions and that the plaintiff had granted an exclusive licensing agreement for practicing them in this country. It has advanced two legal grounds for this motion, both of which rely on its purchase of the machines in Italy from Carminati to defeat the plaintiff's infringement action.

The defendant's first contention is that its purchase of the machines from Carminati, who was authorized under Italian law to sell them, released these articles from the patent monopoly. In support of this argument the defendant relies on the clear and indisputable proposition that "upon familiar principles the authorized sale of an article which is capable of use only in practicing the patent is a relinquishment of the patent monopoly with respect to the article sold." United States v. Univis Lens Co., 316 U.S. 241, 249, 62 S. Ct. 1088, 1093, 86 L. Ed. 1408 (1942). . . .

We find this case to be controlled by the decision in Boesch v. Graff, 133 U.S. 697, 10 S. Ct. 378, 33 L. Ed. 787 (1890). There Graff, who held patents relating to lamp burners both in this country and in Germany, sued the defendant Boesch for infringement of the United States patent by selling infringing burners in the United States. Boesch defended on the ground that he had bought at least some of the burners in Germany from one Hecht before importing them into the United States. The Supreme Court acknowledged that Hecht was authorized to make and sell these burners in Germany because he had made preparations for manufacturing them before Graff applied for the patent and because the Imperial Patent Law of Germany at that time permitted persons who had already used or prepared to use an invention at the time application for a patent for that invention was made to continue to practice the patented art notwithstanding the granting of the patent. Boesch contended that Hecht's authorization freed the burners manufactured by him from the patent monopoly and that he therefore purchased them free of that monopoly. The Court deemed Hecht's authorization under German law immaterial and concluded that the right granted him thereunder could not authorize "purchasers from him . . . to sell the articles in the United States in defiance of the rights of patentees under a United States patent." Id. at 703, 10 S. Ct. at 380.

Defendant seeks to distinguish Boesch by limiting the scope of its authority to its precise facts, i.e., Hecht's permission to manufacture as a pre-patent application producer, which status does not exist under the United States patent laws. The defendant concedes that the Supreme Court's decision was correct in deciding against one whose right did not come from a patentee, as it must in this country, but it asserts that the Boesch rationale does not extend to this case because it obtained its authority to practice the patented art from Carminati, who was a licensee under the Italian patent.

This distinction between the ways in which Hecht and Carminati became authorized to practice the patent art is untenable under the Boesch opinion because the Court considered the question before it to be:

> . . . whether a dealer residing in the United States can purchase in another country articles patented there, from a person authorized to sell them, and import them to and sell them in the United States, without the license or consent of the owners of the United States patent.

Id. at 702, 10 S. Ct. at 380. The source of the alleged infringer's authorization under foreign law thus was without significance in the Court's reasoning. Accordingly, the Second Circuit concluded in a somewhat more recent case that a "sale by a German patentee of a patented article may take it out of the monopoly of the German patent" but could not protect the defendant from an allegation of infringement by use in the United States. Daimler Manufacturing Co. v. Conklin, 170 F. 70, 72 (2d Cir. 1909), *cert. denied,* 216 U.S. 621, 30 S. Ct. 575, 54 L. Ed. 641 (1910).

The second string to defendant's bow in this motion is that the "special facts" of this case take it out of the general rule of *Boesch*. The heart of this argument is that the plaintiff owned concurrent United States and Italian patents and had entered into analogous licensing agreements concerning the same inventions, and that holding the sale and use of the three imported composting machines at issue to infringe the United States patents in this case would give plaintiff a windfall "double recovery." . . .

The "double recovery" theory advanced by the defendant fails principally in that it misconceives the underlying theory of patent infringement under the United States patent laws. The conceptual basis of that system is that the patentee has a certain bundle of rights—*i.e.,* to exclude others from making, using or selling the patented invention, and to control at the first stage the exceptions to that exclusion by the granting of licenses. Infringement of that right "is essentially a tort" against the patentee. . . . The sale or use of each machine in both countries represents potentially two separate torts against the plaintiff and infringes potentially on two separate sets of rights held by him (assuming the conceptual underpinnings of the Italian patent law to conform to those of our own). The non-tortiousness of defendant's conduct in Italy cannot enter into an adjudication of the plaintiff's rights in this country. That the plaintiff has been or can be compensated by Carminati, thereby making the sale and defendant's acts in Italy non-tortious, therefore cannot compromise his discrete right to exclusive practice of the patented art in the United States.

The defendant further argues that judgment for the plaintiff would unjustly enrich him by allowing recovery of two royalties, but this argument miscasts the analogy. If the plaintiff had arranged for ownership of the Italian and American patents to be vested in two different persons (most conveniently, by setting up a corporation in each nation to own the patents granted under that country's laws), the facts here presumably would create a right under *Boesch* and Daimler Manufacturing Co. v. Conklin to two different royalties—one due the Italian patentee from Carminati, the other owing to the American patentee from the defendant for use and/or sale here. Defendant's second theory apparently would create no exception to this doctrine under those facts. We fail to perceive why the plaintiff's ownership of both bundles of rights should compromise those rights, nor do we see why this fact should award a windfall, the avoidance of liability for infringement in the United States, to defendant.

Furthermore, there is nothing in the defendant's argument which would undercut the basic thrust of the *Boesch* decision, *i.e.,* that the "sale of articles in the United States under a United States patent cannot be controlled by foreign laws," 133 U.S. at 703, 10 S. Ct. at 380. The Court itself has recently reaffirmed and in fact broadened this doctrine in Deepsouth Packing Co., Inc. v. Laitram Corp., . . . where it stated that a foreign patent system can have no effect in American markets generally. . . .

Griffin v. Keystone Mushroom represents a somewhat settled area of patent law; the following decision (and the appeals court decision vacating it) represents the much less settled question for trademark law. For further background, *see* Takamatsu, Parallel Importation of Trademarked Goods: A Comparative Analysis, 57 Wash. L. Rev. 433 (1982).

BELL & HOWELL: MAMIYA CO. v. MASEL SUPPLY CO. (I)

548 F. Supp. 1063 (E.D.N.Y. 1982)

NEAHER, J.

This trademark case brings into sharp focus the commercially significant question of whether an American company, which is engaged on an exclusive basis in the business of importing and selling trademarked goods of foreign manufacture under United States trademark rights owned by it, may enjoin another's unauthorized, competitive sale in the United States of the same identically trademarked goods, which were made and placed in the stream of international commerce by the foreign manufacturer, who did not intend that such goods be sold here. The action is now before the Court on plaintiff's motion for a preliminary injunction, following the issuance of a temporary restraining order, which has remained in effect with the consent of the parties. Based upon the facts which do not appear to be seriously disputed, the Court is of opinion that a preliminary injunction should be granted.

Plaintiff, formerly named Bell & Howell: Mamiya Company, and now named Osawa & Co., is a Delaware corporation. It is the registered owner of United States trademark registrations for three "MAMIYA" marks, and, on a purportedly exclusive basis, it imports and sells in this country medium format photographic equipment under these marks. The equipment is manufactured in Japan by the Mamiya Camera Co. ("Mamiya Co."), a Japanese company, sold by Mamiya Co. to a Japanese trading company, J. Osawa & Co. Ltd. ("Osawa Japan"), and then sold by the latter to plaintiff.

By agreement with Mamiya Co., Osawa Japan holds the exclusive right to distribute MAMIYA medium format equipment worldwide, except in Japan, which Mamiya Co. has reserved for itself. By a further oral agreement with plaintiff, Osawa Japan has named it the exclusive American distributor of these cameras. Osawa Japan owns all of the stock of Osawa & Co. (USA), Inc. ("Osawa USA"), a New York corporation which owns 93% of plaintiff's stock. Mamiya Co. of Japan holds the remaining 7%.

It appeared from the papers, and is now established that defendant Masel Supply Co. and another company had imported from Hong Kong (without opposition by U.S. Customs) non-counterfeit MAMIYA medium format cameras which they purchased from someone other than plaintiff and then resold in the United States, without authorization from plaintiff. There is no question that the equipment sold by defendant was made by Mamiya Co. and distributed by Osawa Japan. Defendant simply contends that no likelihood of confusion, dilution or unfair competition can arise from its sales of imported MAMIYA cameras in competition with plaintiff's sales of the same goods.

Despite the importance of the question raised, there are only a few certain landmarks. These are Justice Holmes' brief decision for the Supreme Court in A. Bourjois & Co. v. Katzel Co., 260 U.S. 689, 43 S. Ct. 244, 67 L. Ed. 464 (1923), rev'g, 275 F. 539 (2d Cir. 1921), rev'g, 274 F. 856 (S.D.N.Y. 1920), and the two congressionally imposed restrictions on the importation of trademarked goods contained in the Act of September 21, 1922, ch. 356, title iv, §526, 42 Stat. 975, superseded by section 526 of the Tariff Act of 1930 (codified at 19 U.S.C. §1526), and in section 42 of the Lanham Act (codified at 15 U.S.C. §1124). Understandably, these have been subjected to extremely close scrutiny by practitioners and scholars, who have expressed widely divergent views about their significance. With the important exception of United States v. Guerlain, Inc., 155 F. Supp. 77 (S.D.N.Y. 1957), vacated and remanded, 358 U.S. 915, 79 S. Ct. 285, 3 L. Ed. 2d 236 (1958), action dismissed, 172 F. Supp. 107 (S.D.N.Y. 1959), the legal journals have been the main battleground. Now this case has brought the sufficiency of those views to the fore.

In essence, plaintiff relies on the fact that it is the registered owner of the United States trademark registrations for the MAMIYA marks and on an unrestrictive reading of Bourjois v. Katzel, supra. Apart from its particular facts, the significance of which has fueled much of the debate, the Bourjois decision undeniably established for American trademark law the principle of the territoriality of trademarks, viz., that

> the protection of a trademark in a certain country depends exclusively on the law of that country, and that the effects of a trademark ownership by use or registration in a country do not reach beyond the borders of that country, II S. Ladas, Patents, Trademarks, and Related Rights 1340 (1975),

and thus rejected the principle of trademark "universality" which the Second Circuit had sustained in decisions going back to Appollinaris Co., Ltd. v. Scherer, 27 F. 18 (C.C.S.D.N.Y. 1886). Under the "universality" principle, goods manufactured abroad under a trademark and then imported and sold in the United States were held not to infringe the rights of the owner of the

American trademark, simply because the goods were genuine and the public, therefore, was undeceived. In *Bourjois v. Katzel* the Supreme Court held that an exclusive American distributor of a foreign-made, trademarked product, who possessed the American trademark rights by assignment from the foreign manufacturer, could maintain an infringement suit against one who imported and sold the foreign manufacturer's product under the trademark in competition with the plaintiff.

Defendant acknowledges the continued validity of Bourjois v. Katzel, but focusing on its facts, and one in particular, contends that the case does not render the situation here a true case of trademark infringement. Defendant points out that the plaintiff in Bourjois v. Katzel was apparently unconnected with the foreign manufacturer and originator of the trademark, beyond having been the manufacturer's exclusive American distributor and having acquired from it the American trademark rights. Defendant contrasts this with the more extensive affiliations that exist among plaintiff, its ultimate parent Osawa Japan, and Mamiya Co., which relate to the manufacture and worldwide distribution of MAMIYA medium format photographic equipment. Piercing the "veils" of Osawa USA's 93% ownership of plaintiff and Osawa Japan's sole ownership of Osawa USA, it argues in essence that where the American trademark owner is subject to common ownership or control with the owner and users of the trademark in foreign nations, or forms part of a unified international enterprise engaged in the production and worldwide distribution of the trademarked product—descriptions it urges fit plaintiff—there can be no likelihood of confusion, false designation of origin, dilution or unfair competition for which relief can be granted.

For support, defendant relies on the reasoning of the district court in United States v. Guerlain, Inc., *supra,* which upheld the government's antitrust, Sherman Act §2 monopolization claims against three trademark owners who were the exclusive United States distributors for three French perfumers, and who utilized the customs statute, 19 U.S.C. §1526, *supra,* to block the importation of perfumes from the French companies to which they were related. Defendant also draws on the somewhat similar reasoning apparent in the United States Customs Service's current interpretation and administration of the related customs and trademark laws, 15 U.S.C. §1124 and 19 U.S.C. §1526, which are directed against the importation of foreign-made goods bearing trademarks registered in the United States. 19 C.F.R. Part 133 (1980). *See* J. Atwood, Import Restrictions on Trademarked Merchandise—The Role of the United States Bureau of Customs, 59 T.M.R. 301 (1969). . . .

That leaves the case, then, to be decided upon the fundamental question of trademark law, whether or not the defendant's use of the MAMIYA marks on medium format photographic equipment is likely to cause confusion with the plaintiff's use of the mark.

It is clear that such a substantial likelihood of confusion exists in this case. The business of selling MAMIYA goods in the United States is the plaintiff's business. It is the legitimate owner of the MAMIYA marks. Its ownership of those marks, conversely, "indicates in law," Bourjois v. Katzel, *supra,* 260 U.S. at 692, 43 S. Ct. at 245 that the goods came from plaintiff. It is plaintiff that defines the warranty and provides the repair services for the cameras it sells. The cameras defendant sells lack that warranty. No proof supports defendant's contention that the public associates the MAMIYA marks with the Japanese manufacturer, even assuming that such proof could alter the legal consequence of the assignment of the marks to plaintiff. For it must be recognized that plaintiff is not a mere shell but the legitimate and actual owner of the business of selling MAMIYA medium format products in this country.

There remains the contention that there can be no likelihood of confusion because plaintiff is part of an international organization distributing MAMIYA products. The business of the plaintiff in this country is different from that of Osawa Japan elsewhere in the world and that of Mamiya Co. in Japan. It is plaintiff's warranty and assurances of quality that are signified by the MAMIYA marks in this country. Defendant's use of those marks carries with it none of these assurances.

Accordingly, this Court concludes that a substantial likelihood of confusion has been demonstrated and that an injunction against defendant's sale of trademarked MAMIYA cameras should issue. The parties are directed to settle the form of the preliminary injunction on or before October 15, 1982.

So ordered.

BELL & HOWELL: MAMIYA CO. v. MASEL SUPPLY CO. (II)

719 F.2d 42 (2d Cir. 1983)

PIERCE, J.

II. DISCUSSION

To obtain a preliminary injunction in this circuit, a party must make "a showing of (a) irreparable harm and (b) either (1) likelihood of success on the merits or (2) sufficiently serious questions going to the merits to make them a fair ground for litigation and a balance of hardships tipping decidedly toward the party requesting the preliminary relief." Jackson Dairy, Inc. v. H.P. Hood & Sons, Inc., 596 F.2d 70, 72 (2d Cir. 1979) (per curiam); . . .

Applying these principles to the instant case, we hold that the district court's grant of preliminary injunctive relief must be vacated. As stated above, the district court concluded that "a substantial likelihood of confusion exists in this case." Bell & Howell: Mamiya Co. [I], 548 F. Supp. at 1079. However, there is an absence of factual support in the district court's opinion for this conclusion which apparently related to the irreparable injury prong of the preliminary injunction test. Whether irreparable injury exists is a determination to be made in the first instance by the district court. On the basis of the present record, irreparable injury may well not be present herein since there would appear to be little confusion, if any, as to the origin of the goods and no significant likelihood of damage to BHMC's reputation since thus far it has not been shown that Masel's goods, which have a common origin of manufacture with BHMC's goods, are inferior to those sold by BHMC and are injuring BHMC's reputation. Further, it does not appear that the lack of warranties accompanying MAMIYA cameras sold by Masel amounts to irreparable injury, since the consumer can be made aware by, among other things, labels on the camera boxes or notices in advertisements as to whether the cameras are sold with or without warranties. Thus, less drastic means would appear to be available to avoid the claimed confusion. Further, should there be an ultimate decision in BHMC's favor, it could seek relief through a permanent injunction, an accounting, or an award of damages. For purposes of our review, it suffices that thus far irreparable injury has not been demonstrated, and, consequently, it was an abuse of discretion for the district court to issue the preliminary injunction. . . .

NOTES AND QUESTIONS

1. Is the *Keystone Mushroom* result economically rational? Is the *Mamiya* result?

2. Are the two situations distinguishable on policy grounds? Consider the following excerpt from Osawa & Co. v. B & H Photo, 589 F. Supp. 1163, 1972 (S.D.N.Y. 1984), a case that granted an injunction:

> The universality principle upon which the older cases had been decided was flawed in several related respects. First, it failed to recognize that legal rights within one sovereignty are creatures of that sovereignty's law. The establishment by A of legal rights to exclusivity in one country could obviously not satisfactorily be squared with B's establishment of exclusive right in a second country, if either right (much less if both) were thought to extend across the world universally. The principle was perhaps based on an idealistic view of the world as a single marketplace. That view, however, did not conform to reality or to international treaty. While it might have been possible to imagine the development of a unified world marketplace, organized on the same set of assumptions that have dominated the creation of a single marketplace among the United States, the development between nations did not occur in that fashion. . . .
>
> A second flaw, an outgrowth of the first, is the failure to recognize that, within one country, a mark may represent a factually different goodwill from that which the mark signifies elsewhere. A few examples illustrate the importance of the distinction between the goodwill associated simply with the product name and that of the domestic distributor.
>
> (a) Suppose a manufacturer makes in Japan and sells under his trademark X a fine computer; the reputation of the X mark is high in the country of manufac-

ture and in certain other countries, where it is distributed and serviced under equally high standards. However, the U.S. distributor and owner of mark X conducts its business in a shoddy way: fails to inspect the equipment for damage upon importation; handles it without care in distribution; fails to stock and make available a broad inventory of needed parts and attachments; fails to provide user instruction programs; establishes no maintenance and repair service; provides grudging, slow and incompetent warranty service or no warranty at all. It is readily perceived that mark X will have an altogether different value and significance in the U.S. than elsewhere, because the mark does not merely identify the manufacturer; it signifies the goodwill (or in this example the badwill) of the U.S. owner.

(b) Keeping the same basic example but altering certain facts, suppose the local owner of the X mark earned an excellent reputation not only by selling quality equipment under the mark but also by conscientiously providing all the peripheral services whose absence was noted in (a). Then the mark will come to represent an excellent public reputation. It is easy to see, in connection with the present dispute, how the reputation attached to the mark of a conscientious domestic distributor could be seriously injured if strangers were free to import and sell the computer under its brand name. For they would be trading on X's earned *domestic* reputation and would have no incentive to insure the continuing goodwill of the mark. Purchasers from the grey market importers, although buying essentially the same equipment, might receive damaged goods, unsatisfactory warranty protection or inadequate service, etc. The reputation of the X mark would inevitably be damaged at the markholder's expense for deficiencies over which he had no control.

(c) The point is still more clearly made if the foreign markholder and the domestic markholder seek to develop the goodwill in different directions. Suppose that the mark had originally applied to conservative, costly, French high fashions and continued to be used only in that manner in the U.S. with great success, but that in the meantime the French trademark owner finds for whatever reasons that his profits are dwindling in the French market and decides to use the famous mark on a new line of low-priced clothes of daring fashion catering to the young and wild. Third parties then import the cheap, young and wild clothes bearing their "genuine" French mark to the U.S., where the mark has been developed by its local owner as a status symbol catering to the wealthy and conservative. If the U.S. mark owner were powerless to prevent the marketing of the new French line in the U.S. under his mark, he would promptly suffer a destruction, or in any event a drastic alteration, of the goodwill associated with his U.S. mark.

These examples illustrate that a mark may have not only a separate legal basis but also a different factual significance in each separate country where the local mark owner has developed an independent goodwill. That is the basis of the territoriality principle recognized by Justice Holmes in the *Bourjois* decisions. The principle has become still more solidly implanted in United States law by the 1962 amendment to §32 of the Lanham Act, 15 U.S.C. 1114, which repealed the requirement that a plaintiff in a trademark action show confusion as to "source of origin" of the goods. *See* Syntex Laboratories, Inc. v. Norwich Pharmacal Co., 437 F.2d 566, 568 (2 Cir. 1971).

The universality decisions were superficially and deceptively consistent with the trademark doctrine of "exhaustion." Under this doctrine, as applied within the borders of a sovereignty, a markholder may no longer control branded goods after releasing them into the stream of commerce. After the first sale, the brandholder's control is deemed exhausted. Down-the-line retailers are free to display and advertise the branded goods. Secondhand dealers may advertise the branded merchandise for resale in competition with the sales of the markholder (so long as they do not misrepresent themselves as authorized agents). See Prestonettes, Inc. v. Coty, 264 U.S. 359, 44 S. Ct. 350, 68 L. Ed. 731 (1924); Trail Chevrolet, Inc. v. General Motors Corp., 381 F.2d 353 (5 Cir. 1967); Chrysler Corp. v. Thayer Plymouth Center, Inc., 303 F. Supp. 543 (C.D. Cal. 1969). See generally 3A R. Callman, The Law of Unfair Competition, Trademarks, and Monopolies §21.17 (4 ed. 1983). The application of the exhaustion concept to international trade seemed to suggest that once the original mark owner had lost control of the marked goods by releasing them into commerce, his assignee in a foreign country could not logically own rights superior to those of the assignor. The right of control seemed exhausted.

This reasoning is flawed, however, where the assignee of the mark in the second country has developed a separate, factually independent goodwill. If no such independent goodwill has been developed, then in spite of recognition of territorial limits, arguably there might be no infringement. If the U.S. mark represents nothing more than a foreign outpost of the goodwill associated with the original mark, it might well be argued that exhaustion has taken place with the release into commerce and that no infringement occurs on unauthorized importation. See Derenberg, [Territorial Scope and Status of Trademarks and Good Will, 47 Va. L. Rev. 753 (1961)] But where, as here, the U.S. assignee has developed a separate goodwill factually independent from that of the mark originator, whatever exhaustion occurred with the original release into commerce was the exhaustion of a legally distinct and factually different mark.

3. Do you think the courts adequately consider the antitrust issues in these situations? (The antitrust issues will be discussed in detail in Chapter XIV.)

4. How would you now advise a client in the *Mamiya* or "gray market" situation? Note that, in 1984, the Customs Service and the Patent and Trademark Office began a new study of the area. See Request for Economic Data on Parallel Imports, 49 Fed. Reg. 21,453 (1984). To further complicate the issue, the Court of International Trade has claimed jurisdiction over the issue and upheld the Customs Service's rules permitting gray market imports under some circumstances. See Vivitar Corp. v. United States, 585 F. Supp. 1419 (Ct. Intl. Trade 1984) (jurisdiction) and 593 F. Supp. 420 (Ct. Intl. Trade 1984) (merits); 761 F.2d 1552 (Fed. Cir. 1985) (customs regulations permitting entry of goods valid but not controlling; plaintiff free to pursue parallel remedy in U.S. district court and to seek exclusion order if that remedy granted). Although imports were also permitted in El Greco Leather Prod. v. Shoe World, 599 F. Supp. 1380 (E.D.N.Y. 1984), these rules were questioned in *Osawa, supra*. The ITC, moreover, has held that such imports may violate §337, Certain Alkaline Batteries, Investigation 337-7A-165, U.S.I.T.C. Pub. 1616 (Nov. 1984). The ITC *Batteries* decision was, however, disapproved by the president on January 4, 1985. 50 Fed. Reg. 1,655 (1985).

5. Suppose a foreign firm is attempting to sell a product that *may*—the issue isn't clear—infringe a U.S. patent. As a result of the *Boesch/Keystone Mushroom* doctrine, no U.S. distributors will buy the product. What form of action can the firm bring to test the U.S. patent? *See* Enka B.V. of Arnhem, Holland v. E.I. duPont de Nemours, 519 F. Supp. 356 (D. Del. 1981) (suit for declaratory judgment that patent not infringed dismissed on basis of lack of case or controversy).

2. Products of a Patented Process

Import restrictions associated with process patents present special issues. As explained in *University Patents,* the following case, under U.S. law, infringement does not lie against an imported product that was made abroad by means of a patented process. Nevertheless, *Sealed Air,* the case following *University Patents,* shows how a proceeding to exclude can be brought before the International Trade Commission under §§1337 and 1337a. The particular case may strike you as highly protective of the U.S. patent holder, but U.S. firms holding process patents generally believe that the ITC remedies are less effective than infringement proceedings, and are seeking change in the patent laws to allow infringement to be brought against the product of a process patent. The laws of many nations do permit such infringement suits, but a provision authorizing them in the United States was dropped at the last minute from the 1984 Patent Law Amendments Act for unspecified reasons. *See* 130 Cong. Rec. 14248-14249 (1984).

UNIVERSITY PATENTS, INC. v. QUESTOR CORP.

517 F. Supp. 676 (D. Colo. 1981)

KANE, District Judge.

Plaintiff's complaint, filed originally in Massachusetts and moved here on a change of venue, alleges that defendant infringed two patents owned by the plaintiff in violation of 35 U.S.C. §271. Jurisdiction is based on 28 U.S.C. §1338(a). One of the patents, No. 3,237,319, a product patent, is not at issue in this motion. The other patent, No. 3,402,411, a process patent, is the subject of this motion. Defendant moved for partial summary judgment, seeking to have the portion of the complaint dealing with the process patent dismissed. Briefs and affidavits have been submitted and the motion is now ripe for determination. I grant defendant's motion.

In U.S. Patent No. 3,402,411 the patentee claims a patent of the process of making boots having a pressure-compensating ankle support. The patented process consists of three steps: "providing a flexible ankle support shaped envelope, sealing a high viscosity material in said envelope and assembling said sealing envelope and boot." Defendant does not manufacture any boots in the United States, but does import ski boots from a wholly owned Italian subsidiary for distribution in the United States. The dispute here stems from defendant's importation of replacement ski-boot liners, which it distributes to retailers and customers, who then insert the liners into old ski boots' plastic shells.

A process patent may only be infringed by processes carried out in the United States. Clairol, Inc. v. Brentwood Industries, Inc., 193 U.S.P.Q. 683, 687 (C.D. Cal. 1976) (citing Deepsouth Packing Co. v. Laitram Corp., 406 U.S. 518, 92 S. Ct. 1700, 32 L. Ed. 2d 273 (1972), and other cases). "It is settled that the sale of a product made from a process does not infringe a patent on that process." Koratron Co. v. Lion Uniform, Inc., 449 F.2d 337, 338 (9th Cir. 1971) (citing Merrill v. Yeomans, 94 U.S. 568, 24 L. Ed. 235 (1877), and other cases). Defendant's manufacturing activities in Italy, followed by sales in the United States, are therefore not sufficient grounds for patent infringement.

Defendant also cannot be guilty of contributory infringement unless someone has directly infringed on the patent. Deepsouth Packing Co. v. Laitram Corp., 406 U.S. at 526, 92 S. Ct. at 1706. Defendant is therefore entitled to partial summary judgment unless either it or someone else directly infringed on the patent in the United States. Plaintiff only asserts that defendant has induced others to perform the third step of the patented process: "assembling said sealing envelope and boot;" it does not argue that anyone in the United States has engaged in the first two steps of its patented process: "providing a flexible ankle support shaped envelope" or "sealing a high viscosity material in said envelope." Plaintiff therefore fails to state a claim for infringement of the patent because "[a] patent for a method or process claim is not infringed unless all of the steps or stages of the process are used." Englehard Industries, Inc. v. Research Instrumental Corp., 324 F.2d 347, 351 (9th Cir. 1963), *cert. denied*, 377 U.S. 923, 84 S. Ct. 1220, 12 L. Ed. 2d 215 (1964) (citing Royer v. Coupe, 146 U.S. 524, 13 S. Ct. 166, 36 L. Ed. 1073 (1892) and other cases); Roberts Dairy Co. v. United States, 530 F.2d 1342, 1354 (Ct. Cl. 1976).

It is ordered that defendant's motion for partial summary judgment is granted. It is further Ordered that all claims relating to U.S. Patent No. 3,402,411 are dismissed from this civil action. Each party to bear its own costs.

SEALED AIR CORP. v. U.S. INTERNATIONAL TRADE COMMISSION

645 F.2d 976 (C.C.P.A. 1981)

MARKEY, J.

This is a consolidated appeal from the June 29, 1979 determination of the United States International Trade Commission (ITC) terminating investigation No. 337-TA-54, "Certain Multicellular Plastic Film" (film). All respondents save one were found in violation of section 337 of the Tariff Act of 1930, as amended by the Trade Act of 1974, by reason of the importation of the film into, or its sale in, the United States. We affirm.

On May 12, 1978, Sealed Air Corporation (Sealed Air) filed a complaint with the ITC, alleging violations of Section 337 of the Tariff Act of 1930, as amended (19 U.S.C. §1337), by the importation into the United States, or subsequent sale, of film manufactured in a foreign country by processes that allegedly infringed method claims 1 and 2 of U.S. Letters Patent 3,416,984 ('984).

After a January 1979 evidentiary hearing, a Commission Administrative Law Judge (ALJ) concluded that the claims were invalid under 35 U.S.C. §103 [patent requirement of non-obviousness] and recommended that no violation of 19 U.S.C. §1337 be found. The ALJ determined that the ITC had jurisdiction over all respondents.

Manufacturers named and served were: Tong Seae Industrial Co., Ltd. (Tong Seae) of Taiwan; Conform Plastics Ltd. (Conform) of New Zealand; and Unipak (H.K.) Ltd. (Unipak) of Hong Kong. Importers named and served were Polybubble, Inc. (Polybubble) and Peter Darlington, d/b/a Solar Pool Covers (Darlington).

Unipak neither answered the complaint nor participated in discovery. Conform filed a response but did not participate in discovery or in the hearing. Darlington participated in discovery but not in the hearing. Neither Conform nor Darlington is represented in this appeal.

A June 26, 1978 mailing of the complaint and other papers by the ITC to Unipak resulted in a return receipt stamped July 6, 1978. Unipak admittedly received Sealed Air's request for discovery and declined to participate. Four shipments of film into the United States were made by Unipak, with Polybubble as the importer.

On December 7, 1978, upon motion by Sealed Air, the ALJ issued Order No. 6, finding Unipak in default and ruling that "without further notice to Unipak, the facts may be found to be as alleged in the complaint and notice of investigation."

The Commission: (1) reversed the ruling of invalidity; (2) found Tong Seae's process non-infringing; and (3) sustained the finding of jurisdiction with respect to Unipak. Conform and Unipak were found to have infringed claims 1 and 2 of the '984 patent. All respondents except Tong Seae were held in violation of 19 U.S.C. §1337.

Polybubble, as an importer of Unipak's products, and Tong Seae challenge the ruling that the '984 patent is valid. Sealed Air challenges the determination of non-infringement by Tong Seae. Unipak challenges the determination that it is subject to the jurisdiction of the ITC. . . .

[The court affirmed the validity of the '984 patent.]

(3) JURISDICTION

Unipak having failed to respond to the complaint, and having refused to participate in discovery, the ITC entered an order excluding the relevant products of Unipak from entry into this country. Unipak has appealed, asserting that it was given inadequate notice of the investigation and had insufficient contacts with the United States to support the jurisdiction of the ITC. That assertion is based on an incorrect view of the nature of ITC's jurisdiction.

The order was not entered against Unipak personally. The sole effect upon Unipak is that the relevant product cannot be imported into the United States until it is established that it has not been made by the patented process. The order is directed against, and only against, certain "multicellular plastic material manufactured abroad in accordance with the process disclosed by claims 1 and 2 of U.S. Letters Patent 3,416,984." An exclusion order operates against goods, not parties. Accordingly, that order was not contingent upon a determination of personal or "*in personam*" jurisdiction over a foreign manufacturer. The Tariff Act of 1930 (Act) and its predecessor, the Tariff Act of 1922, were intended to provide an adequate remedy for domestic industries against unfair methods of competition and unfair acts instigated by foreign concerns operating beyond the *in personam* jurisdiction of domestic courts. *See,* In re Orion Co., 22 C.C.P.A. 149, 163, 71 F.2d 458, 467, 21 U.S.P.Q. 563, 571 (1934). Authority to provide such remedy is grounded in Congress' plenary constitutional power to regulate foreign commerce, a portion of which power Congress delegated to the ITC under 19 U.S.C. §1337. That Congress has wide discretion concerning procedures for barring imports has been judicially confirmed in numerous cases.

The ALJ and the ITC found that the ITC had *in personam* jurisdiction over Unipak. That finding was unnecessary, although there is evidence to support such a finding. The *subject matter* jurisdiction of the ITC over "the importation of articles into the United States", §1337(a), and its authority to exclude "the articles concerned", §1337(d), are fully adequate. Similarly, the sale in the United States of a foreign manufacturer's articles, by the "owner", "importer", or "consignee" of those articles is clearly within the subject matter jurisdiction of the ITC under §1337(a). Hence the ITC, upon investigation and determination of a violation, could exclude products sold by a domestic owner/importer/consignee, under its subject matter jurisdiction, whether or not it named the foreign manufacturer as a respondent or gave notice to that foreign manufacturer.

When the imported product is alleged to infringe patent claims drawn to a product, the truth of that allegation can be tested by comparison of the product with the claims. When, as here, the imported product is alleged to have been made by a process that infringes patent claims drawn to a process of making the product, determination of the literal truth of that allegation requires comparison of the process employed by the foreign manufacturer with the claims. Thus, in the former instance a product found to be itself an infringement, and all products identical to it, may be excluded, without regard to which foreign manufacturer was exporting it to the United States, and without regard to how it was made. Apparently recognizing that, in the instance of a process claim, the personal involvement of the manufacturer and the process it employed is determinative, that is, that the same product might be made by several manufacturers employing different processes, Sealed Air named Unipak in the complaint as a respondent, and ITC sent Unipak a copy of the complaint, a notice of its investigation, a copy of its rules of practice, and other papers. Thereafter, the ITC determined that *in personam* jurisdiction over Unipak was required to support its order excluding Unipak's products.

The ITC's mistaken belief that it required *in personam* jurisdiction was not determinative of the result, and its decision must be affirmed where the result is correct, notwithstanding its reliance on a wrong ground or a wrong reason. SEC v. Chenery Corp., 318 U.S. 80, 88, 63 S. Ct. 454, 459, 87 L. Ed. 626 (1942).

In In re Orion Co., *supra,* this court noted the broad mandate of Congress to regulate acts of importation stating:

> So long as such regulation was within constitutional limitations, as we have seen it was, the wisdom of the methods provided by the Congress is a political, not a judicial, question. The importer has no right to complain as to the operation of the machinery, for the act of importation, even to our citizens, is not a vested right, but an act of grace. Buttfield v. Stranahan, 192 U.S. 470, [24 S. Ct. 349, 48 L. Ed. 525] (1904).

Because the Act does not require personal or *in personam* jurisdiction over a foreign manufacturer before its goods may be excluded from entry into this country, Unipak's allegations of inadequate notice and insufficient contacts are irrelevant, and its principal argument, directed solely at a jurisdictional question, must fail.

Though its subject matter jurisdiction is sufficient, the ITC is a creature of statute. Hence it must follow established procedures in making a determination that a violation of the Act has occurred, and may exclude a product only after completion of such procedures.

To enable it to carry out its duties in connection with investigations authorized by law, ITC was granted the right to summon witnesses, to take testimony, and to require the production of documents and other evidence pertaining to a pending investigation. In addition, Congress authorized the ITC to adopt such reasonable procedures, rules, and regulations as it deems necessary to carry out its functions and duties.

Accordingly the ITC has duly promulgated rules of practice. Rule 210.21 requires each respondent to affirmatively respond to each allegation in the complaint, and to set forth a concise statement of the facts constituting each ground of defense within twenty days from the date of service of the complaint and notice of investigation. More particularly, Rule 210.21(b)(1) provides that where it is asserted in defense that an article imported or sold by a respondent is not covered by, or produced under, a process covered by the claims of a U.S. patent involved, a showing of such noncoverage for each involved claim in each U.S. patent in question shall be made by appropriate allegations.

Rule 210.21(d) addresses the consequences of the failure of a respondent to comply with Rule 210.21:

> (d) Default. Failure of a respondent to file a response within the time provided for in subsection (a) of this section may be deemed to constitute a waiver of its right to appear and contest the allegations of the complaint and of the notice of investigations, and to authorize the presiding officer, without further notice to that respondent, to find the facts to be alleged in the complaint and notice of investigation and to enter a recommended determination (or a determination if the Commission is the presiding officer) containing such findings.

Unipak does not contest the validity of the quoted rule provision on "Default". It merely argues that petitioner offered no evidence during the investigation to establish a violation of 19 U.S.C. §1337.

As above indicated, where, as here, the subject patent claims relate to a process and the practice of that process is not discernable from an examination of the product, cooperation of the respondent is necessary if the ITC is to carry out, in a normal manner, its mandate to investigate. ITC's obligation to conduct an investigation and to reach a determination, however, does not and cannot depend upon cooperation from named respondents. There must be, and there are, consequences attendant upon a respondent's refusal to respond.

The record establishes that Unipak denied the ITC its cooperation. Indeed, Unipak arrogantly and intransigently refused to participate in the proceeding from which it now appeals.

Unipak's response to Sealed Air's Request for Interrogatories was a letter dismissing the Interrogatories as "needlessly long, detailed and in many cases irrelevant," and announcing that such request "should be passed to the Hong Kong courts before requiring a Hong Kong corporation to respond." Unipak expressly refused to provide any evidence of its manufacturing process in writing. It limited its "cooperation" to an offer to testify before the ITC at a time and date "mutually convenient," *provided* that subject matter it may consider confidential would not be disclosed to Sealed Air or to the respondents, and *provided further* that it be guaranteed the total expenses it would incur in sending representatives to appear before the ITC. Unipak concluded by reserving to itself its "right" to continue exportation of its products into the U.S.

In view of Unipak's failure to respond to the complaint and notice of investigation, coupled with its failure to participate in discovery, the ITC was fully justified in discharging, in the only way it could, its obligation to issue a determination on whether importation and sale of Unipak's product was in violation of 19 U.S.C. §1337. The alternative would have been to allow Unipak to frustrate the ITC's investigation, while it continued to ship its products into the U.S. to the injury of efficiently operated domestic industries. If the ITC were precluded from applying its "default" rule, when confronted with a foreign manufacturer's adamant refusal to participate, and refusal to provide indispensible evidence of noninfringement, the ITC's determination would be postponed indefinitely and the ITC would be deprived of the means to perform its functions under the statute, clearly frustrating the intent of Congress. This court can see no basis for placing that lethal weapon in the hands of foreign manufacturers. . . .

Having determined the existence of a violation of the law, that is, of unfair methods of competition or unfair acts in the importation of certain multicellular film products into the U.S., having the effect or tendency to destroy or substantially injure an efficient and economically operated domestic industry, the ITC was faced with two alternatives.

The ITC could exclude all such products from entering the U.S., contingent upon Unipak's or other foreign manufacturer's or the importer's petition for an ITC proceeding to determine whether entry should be allowed. That remedy risked unfairness to a foreign manufacturer entitled to entry, for example, one whose process might be found non-infringing, the unfairness being denial of importation for the period necessary to make that finding.

Alternatively, the ITC could allow Unipak and other foreign manufacturers to continue to ship, and importers continue to import, all such products into the U.S. until Sealed Air could file another complaint against Unipak and new complaints against each other such foreign manufacturer or importer, the ITC could institute investigations in each case, and violations could be found. That alternative risked unfairness to American industry injured by importation during the period necessary to reach those determinations.

The ITC chose to resolve the issue in favor of American business. In paragraph 3 of its Determination, ITC referred to its consideration of the effect of its Order upon the public health and welfare, competitive conditions in the United States economy, the production of like or directly competitive articles in the United States, and the interests of United States consumers. In sum, ITC determined whether the public interest lies in excluding or not excluding the goods involved. There has been no showing that the present ITC Order is in any way inconsistent with its mandate. In view of the ITC's expertise in evaluating the likelihood of injury to American business, and absent a showing of loss of protectable rights, it is not the function of a court to substitute a different remedy of its own design for that chosen by the ITC, or to substitute its view of the public interest for that of the ITC.

The ITC's determination and order are affirmed.

NIES, J., with whom BALDWIN, J., joins, concurring with respect to Appeal No. 79-35 and dissenting with respect to Appeal No. 80-4.

By affirming that the Tong Seae process would not, if practiced in the United States, infringe U.S. Patent No. 3,416,984 owned by the complainant Sealed Air, this court has no alternative but to vacate the order below and remand for the ITC's determination of violation of 19 U.S.C. §1337 based on the evidence with respect to the processes of others. An exclusion order must be supported by factual findings based on reliable, probative, and substantial evidence (5 U.S.C. §556(d)) which establish the material facts required under

19 U.S.C. §1337 for issuance of the order. In this case, the order is unsupported by the ITC's analysis and reliance on any evidence. In violation of the directive of the Supreme Court, every precedent as to the scope of appellate review, and without a glance at the Administrative Procedure Act, the majority substitutes its own findings to uphold the order. I respectfully dissent.

The ITC based its determination that there was a violation of 19 U.S.C. §1337 (and §1337a) in the importation of Unipak's products on findings that it had *in personam* jurisdiction over Unipak, a company located in the British Crown Colony of Hong Kong, which was sent a notice of investigation and complaint by mail, and that Unipak "defaulted" by failing to answer the complaint and "refused" to participate in discovery. Unipak challenges the determination of violation based on these findings.

The majority holds *in personam* jurisdiction over Unipak is unnecessary for the issuance of an exclusion order against its products. Disregarding the ITC's findings, the majority makes its own by relying ambiguously on Unipak's "default", Unipak's arrogance and intransigence, and interjecting its own review of the evidence concerning the Unipak process to show a prima facie case of infringement.[1] SEC v. Chenery Corp., 318 U.S. 80, 63 S. Ct. 454, 87 L. Ed. 626 (1943), relied upon by the majority, prohibits rather than endorses the substitution of the court's findings to sustain the order below.

UNIPAK'S DEFAULT AND INTRANSIGENCE

On June 26, 1978, the ITC instituted an investigation relating to multicellular plastic film used for swimming pool covers based on a complaint filed by Sealed Air, a U.S. corporation, on May 12, 1978, which named two domestic importers (Darlington and Polybubble) and three foreign manufacturers, Tong Seae (Taiwan), Conform (New Zealand), and Unipak (Hong Kong) as respondents. On June 29, 1978, the ITC sent notices of investigation with copies of the subject complaint to all named respondents. Answers were filed by all except Unipak. A receipt initialled by some unknown recipient was returned to the ITC, which indicates acceptance of the mailing to Unipak, on July 6, 1978. Unipak denies that it received these documents and alleges that the correspondence was misaddressed.

In any event, Unipak acknowledges receiving interrogatories from counsel for Sealed Air shortly thereafter and a copy of Sealed Air's "Discovery Statement."

On August 3, 1978, Unipak responded to Sealed Air with copies to all other named respondents and to appropriate persons in the ITC and other Government agencies. Unipak acknowledged receiving Sealed Air's interrogatories but denied receiving the complaint from the ITC. It questioned the authority

---

[1] Technically, the use of the process could "infringe" only if practiced in the United States. For convenience, the term "infringement" is used in this opinion in the broader sense to include practice abroad.

of the ITC outside the United States. It advised that requests concerning the investigation must be processed through the Hong Kong courts. It objected to the interrogatories as needlessly long, detailed and in many cases irrelevant and refused to disclose confidential information in writing. It offered to give testimony to the ITC provided certain matters were treated confidentially and its expenses were guaranteed. It denied the allegations of the complaint "totally," and reserved its right to continue exportation of products to the U.S.A. Unipak further advised that Polybubble (a named respondent/importer) was under the duty to defend Unipak against all claims arising out of the importation of Unipak's products into the United States.

Sealed Air's counsel did not reply to this letter. However, on August 31, 1978, the attorney for the ITC undertook to do so, enclosing the complaint and a copy of the ITC rules. He advised that there were no motions regarding discovery; that Sealed Air had stated its intentions were to inspect the facilities of the foreign respondents in order to determine whether or not there was infringement of the subject patent and proposed to use an independent technical expert, qualified under a protective order in effect, to analyze technical confidential data.

He further advised that "there is presently pending a motion for default against your firm dated August 14, 1978, pursuant to Rule 210.21(d) for failure to file a response to the complaint."

On October 15, 1978, Unipak acknowledged receipt (on October 12, 1978) of the August 31 letter from ITC's counsel, as well as receipt in the interim of the first mailing. Unipak continued to protest the jurisdiction of the ITC and the charge that it used the Sealed Air process in its three layer film, objected to any finding that it was in default, and again offered to cooperate in the investigation through the Hong Kong courts or before the ITC if its expenses were paid.

On December 7, 1978, the Administrative Law Judge (ALJ) made the following findings:

> Motion No. 54-4 is granted to the extent that the following findings are made:
> 1. The Commission has jurisdiction over Unipak.
> 2. Unipak has failed to file a response to the complaint within the time provided for in Rule 21(a) of the Commission's Rules, and is therefore found to be in default under Rule 21(d). Unipak's failure to file a response is deemed to constitute a waiver of its right to appear and contest the allegations of the complaint and of the notice of investigation. Without further notice to Unipak, the facts may be found to be as alleged in the complaint and notice of investigation, and a recommended determination may be made containing such findings.
> Further findings and a recommended decision will be reserved, so that the findings relating to Unipak will not be inconsistent with the evidentiary record made in this case.

The ultimate findings by the ALJ were that the subject patent was invalid and there was, accordingly, no violation in the importation of multicellular plastic film into the United States, but that if the patent were valid, Unipak and another foreign manufacturer, Conform, would be in violation of 19 U.S.C. §1337 by default.

The Commission on June 29, 1979, reached a contrary conclusion as to the validity of the patent. After review of an extensive record developed by Sealed Air and Tong Seae, the Commission then determined that the extrusion process practiced by Tong Seae for making multicellular plastic film did not infringe the process covered by claims 1 and 2 of Sealed Air's patent which utilizes sheets of plastic as the starting material. Having found U.S. Patent 3,416,984 valid but not infringed by the Tong Seae process, the Commission relied upon the non-participation by Unipak and Conform for its exclusion order: . . .

4.   THE CONFORM AND UNIPAK PROCESSES INFRINGE

The ALJ recommended that the processes employed by Conform and Unipak in manufacturing multicellular plastic film be found to infringe claims 1 and 2 of the '984 patent. We concur. Neither Conform nor Unipak participated in discovery. Conform was subject to evidentiary sanctions. With respect to Conform, the ALJ ruled that an inference was to be drawn that the testimony, documents, or other evidence sought from that firm by complainant would be adverse to Conform. With respect to Unipak, the ALJ ordered that without further notice to that firm, the facts could be found to be as alleged in the complaint and the notice of investigation. In view of these firms' refusal to participate in discovery and the ALJ's finding that the Commission has jurisdiction over them, we agree with the ALJ that, on the record of this investigation, the processes used by Conform and Unipak in manufacturing multicellular plastic film infringe the '984 patent.

I can see no other conclusion than that the findings of the ALJ and the ITC rest solely on the basis of an erroneous interpretation of the law, without any evaluation of the evidence.

The majority characterizes Unipak's conduct as arrogant and intransigent. I find the objections of Unipak entirely in order. Only the most formalistic tribunal would not deem Unipak's initial letter sufficient to avoid a default. Even though insufficient as a complete answer, it raised a jurisdictional defense which fairness required be ruled upon, with additional time being given for answer thereafter. Moreover, in view of our treaty obligations with Hong Kong,[4] the holding of *in personam* jurisdiction would have required taking into account the time periods and service requirements under the Treaty, before default sanctions can be imposed.

THE SCOPE OF THE ORDER

The majority modifies the effect of the order below by placing Unipak in the same position as every other foreign manufacturer of multicellular plastic film

---

[4]Hague Convention on the Service Abroad of Judicial and Extrajudicial Documents, 20 U.S.T. 361.

who was not a party to the proceeding. All multicellular plastic film products, except those of Tong Seae, are blocked until a determination is made by the ITC in a subsequent proceeding that they are made by a non-infringing process.

I have previously expressed my views that the ITC may not issue an exclusion order broader than the investigation it noticed and conducted. In this case, it is particularly offensive that the ITC has invoked sanctions against an entire industry throughout the world on the basis of technical "defaults" by two named respondents.

What has occurred here results from broad judicial construction, not congressional action. This court endorsed the concept that patent infringement without other unfair acts, such as false advertising or unfair pricing (both alleged by complainant here but not found below) constitutes an unfair method of competition within the meaning of 19 U.S.C. §1337. Such "other acts" which originally were considered an inherent requirement in the statute pinpointed who were violators. Assuming that the judicial interpretation which finds patent infringement *per se* enough under §1337 is correct, it does not follow that orders may issue against an industry. The ITC is engaged in adjudication, not industry-wide rule-making, in the type of proceeding here under review.

NOTES AND QUESTIONS

1. Can you find any basis, besides statutory quirk, for the difference in outcome between these two cases? In thinking about this question, note that the two statutes imply somewhat different remedies, and also use different decisionmakers.

2. Are you troubled by the fact that §337 asks the ITC—whose expertise is in determining injury to U.S. business—to evaluate patent infringement? (Consider that the courts find something like 40% of all patents they consider to be invalid.) How else might you set up the statutory structure? There is a voluminous history here—and there were even periods when the ITC excluded goods on patent infringement grounds while the validity of the patent was being tested in litigation in the regular courts. For good general discussions of §337 issues, *see* Symposium, Section 337 and the International Trade Commission, 10 A.P.L.A. Q.J. 111 (1982); Symposium, 8 Ga. J. Intl. & Comp. L. 27 (1978); and Fisher, Protection Against Unfair Foreign Competition: Section 337 of The Tariff Act of 1930, 13 Va. J. Intl. L. 158 (1972).

3. Is *Sealed Air*'s exercise of jurisdiction to enjoin future imports consistent with prior law? Constitutional? Wise?

4. What would you do if you were in Unipak's position and feared revealing proprietary information to your U.S. competitor?

5. Is *Sealed Air* consistent with the GATT?

6. In dealing with commercial piracy, when is §337 likely to be most effec-

tive? Trademark protection law in the nation of origin? Possibly a new GATT code? What about criminalizing "trafficking in counterfeit goods or services?" *See* the Trademark Counterfeiting Act of 1984, §1502, P.L. 98-473, 18 U.S.C. §2320.

7. Suppose that fresh produce were imported wrapped with a film made by means of the patented process. Should Sealed Air be entitled to exclude it? For discussion of a comparable issue in Great Britain, *see* Beecham Group v. Bristol Laboratories, [1978] Pat. Cas. 153,204, which contains dicta suggesting that a patent on a pharmaceutical intermediate would be infringed by foreign use of that intermediate "in the manufacture of [an imported] semi-synthetic penicillin, but not of a wholly different product like, say, glue."

8. Assume you are general counsel for the Ideal Toy Company, which produces and markets in the United States the mind-twisting device known as Rubik's Cube. Your particular task as general counsel is to solve the following trade problem for the Ideal Toy Company. The Copycat Toy Company, which is located in Japan, seeing the popularity of Ideal's Rubik's Cube, has begun to market the same kind of mind-twisting device in the United States. Copycat also calls its device the "Rubik's Cube," although it did not invent the device. Assume the following additional facts to be true:

a. Copycat's Rubik's Cube is manufactured and exported exclusively from Japan;

b. Copycat is receiving a direct cash grant from the government of Japan, the amount to be paid to increase in direct proportion to export sales by Copycat;

c. Copycat is allowed to depreciate its production equipment on an "accelerated depreciation" basis;

d. Copycat is given a rebate upon export by the Japanese government equal to the amount of the commodity tax assessed on all its Cubes sold in Japan;

e. the government of Japan has a policy of absorbing the losses of all companies that export through so-called recapitalization;

f. Copycat sells its Rubik's Cube in Japan for the yen equivalent of $5.00 per Cube; it sells the same product in the United States for $4.50 per Cube; its cost of production in Japan is $3 per Cube; it exports the Cube also to the United Kingdom for $4.75 per Cube.

g. Ideal Toy Company obtained a patent from the U.S. Patent Office on the Rubik's Cube in 1978 and a trademark on the Cube in 1980;

h. the U.S. Customs Service classified the Rubik's Cube as an educational device, thus bearing no duty; there is an alternative duty classification, however, for "toys," which bears a duty of 17.5%. The headnote for toys in the Tariff Schedule of the United States (T.S.U.S.) reads: "items for the amusement of children or adults";

i. both Japan and the United States belong to the GATT.

j. the market penetration in the United States of Copycat's product has risen from 0 in 1980 to 20% of the U.S. Rubik's Cube market in 1982. Ideal

Toy's net profits since 1980 have increased by 25%, despite the increased import penetration. Calculations indicate, however, that employment would have been about 400 workers higher had Ideal kept the whole Rubik's Cube market.

You have been asked by the president of the Ideal Toy Company to advise the board of directors in a memorandum on the applicable U.S. remedies to the Copycat market invasion that might exist pursuant to the foreign patent and trademark laws of the United States. You are expected to address not only the alternative routes for relief that might exist but also the efficacy of the remedies that could be obtained and the likelihood of success. How would your advice differ if the Rubik's Cubes were produced and exported from Taiwan? Hungary?

Chapter XIV

The International Licensing of Technology and Associated Antitrust Issues

A. THE STANDARD PATTERN

The *Keystone Mushroom* case demonstrates (*see* Chapter XIII), as noted, a standard procedure for exploitation of international property rights. The inventing firm obtains patent coverage in several markets and may then license the patent rights in a specific nation to another entity or to its own subsidiary or affiliate. Under the principle of *Keystone Mushroom,* the firm is free to protect its home market from competition by the foreign affiliate. And, in general, this is legitimate under the antitrust laws, for it is a normal incident of the patent structure—even though a contract to accomplish the same thing would sometimes violate the antitrust laws.

QUESTIONS

1. Is there any sense to the distinction between passive use of the patent laws to divide territories (as in *Keystone Mushroom*) and active agreement to divide territories? Is a distinction of this type unavoidable in light of the fundamental tension between the patent law authorization of a monopoly and the antitrust law prohibition of monopoly?

2. Suppose the territorial division were based upon a license of a *process* patent, in which the license restricted transnational sale of the goods made with the process. OK? *See* United States v. Studiengesellschaft Kohle, 670 F.2d 1122 (D.C. Cir. 1981) (not a violation).

3. What about the parallel trademark issue? *See* the case discussed in *Mamiya,* p.703 *supra,* United States v. Guerlain, 155 F. Supp. 77 (S.D.N.Y. 1957),

whose force is limited by the fact that the Department of Justice moved for vacation during appeal.

B.   DEVELOPING-NATION CONCERNS

When a developing-nation (LDC) firm acquires technology from the developing world, a frequent pattern is for the license holder to be a subsidiary of the developed nation (DC) firm that invented the concept. Through the patent, the subsidiary gains a monopoly in the LDC, and can perhaps, depending on the availability of substitutes, price accordingly. It can then take its profits out in a number of—sometimes disguised—forms: actual dividends paid by the subsidiary to the parent, royalties for the technology, fees for management and training contracts, or artificial pricing of the components or intermediate materials transferred between parent and subsidiary. And in the face of all this, the LDC subsidiary is frequently unable to export to the DC market, which is protected by the *Keystone Mushroom* doctrine.

In response to these problems, LDCs have undertaken a major legal effort to control these terms of technology transfer. Japan did this during the 1950s and 60s, clearly with enormous success. Its Ministry of International Trade and Investment reviewed all technology licenses and often rejected them (or provided bargaining backbone) on grounds that the technology was too expensive or available elsewhere cheaper or that unwise export restrictions were included. *See* Layton, Japan and the Introduction of Foreign Technology: A Blueprint for Less Developed Countries, 18 Stan. J. Intl. L. 171 (1982). Latin America looked at this approach, and the Andean Pact, a regional economic group, accepted it in Decision 24 of 1970 (Selected Documents Supplement). The concept has remained part of the Andean Pact's intellectual core ever since, although in practice, the member nations of the Andean Group have imposed less stringent requirements than stated in the Decision. The concept has also become part of the global United Nations Conference on Trade and Development (UNCTAD) agenda, albeit a part on which agreement appears unlikely.

It is in great part the United States that is responsible for this failure of agreement. The United States has emphasized the idea that development depends on private investor access to the LDCs—and thus argues that any limitation on patent rights would be counterproductive. It would hurt more by deterring private investment than it would help by improving the terms for the developing nation of the investment that occurred. And some in Europe have also taken a very doctrinaire natural law approach to intellectual property rights that leaves them unwilling to compromise on the issue.

The following materials, which include an early empirical analysis supporting the Andean position, provide a good sample of the issues involved in the debate. They should be read together with Articles 18-26 of Decision 24.

THE JUNTA DEL ACUERDO DE CARTAGENA, TRANSFER OF TECHNOLOGY—POLICIES RELATING TO TECHNOLOGY OF THE COUNTRIES OF THE ANDEAN PACT: THEIR FOUNDATIONS

Chapter 2, Item 19 of the Provisional Agenda, United Nations Conference on Trade and Development (3d Sess.), Santiago, Chile, April 13, 1972

EMPIRICAL RESULTS AND THEIR INTERPRETATION

14. In order to understand the terms of the commercialization of technology, diverse studies were undertaken on the subject in the Andean countries between 1968 and 1971. These studies included an evaluation of contracts for the purchase of know-how, an investigation of the structure and implications of the present patent system and a financial analysis of the price effects of technology embodying imported intermediate products. The results, in summary form, of these studies are presented below:

A. ANALYSIS OF CONTRACTS FOR THE COMMERCIALIZATION OF TECHNOLOGY

15. In the five Andean countries 451 contracts belonging to various sectors were evaluated. The country breakdown was as follows:

Country	N° of contracts	N° of sectors of economy
Bolivia	35	4 including "others"
Colombia	140	4
Chile	175	13
Ecuador	12	5
Peru	89	2 including "others"

16. The clauses analysed in these contracts raise important economic and legal issues about the extent to which private contracting (*Contratación privada*) reaches into areas where private economic benefits derived by some or all of the parties involved are in conflict with the overall economic and social interests of the country where they operate. Some answers to this type of questions have long been provided in the industrialized world through antimonopoly and antitrust legislation as well as through the establishment of public regulatory agencies. Many developing countries have still to demonstrate an awareness of these issues and their implications for their private and public economic interests. Furthermore, the terms and conditions to be discussed below raise questions about the concept of liberty or sovereignty to contract among unequals. In a bargaining structure with very unequal participants, with limited information and imperfect overall market conditions the sovereignty of the "technology consumers" becomes a concept of very limited applicability.

B.   EXPORT RESTRICTIVE CLAUSES

17. One of the most frequent clauses encountered in contracts for the commercialization of technology is one prohibiting export. Such restrictive practices generally limit the production and sale of goods produced through the use of foreign technology solely to the territory of the receiving country. Some allow exports to specific neighbouring countries only. Of the total of 451 contracts analysed by the secretariat of the Andean Pact, 409 contained information about exports which is summarised in the table below:

Country	Total number of contracts	Total prohibition of exports	Exports permitted only in certain areas	Exports permitted to the rest of the world
Bolivia	35	27	2	6
Colombia	117	90	2	25
Ecuador	12	9	—	3
Peru	83	74	8	1
TOTAL	247	200	12	35

18. In Chile out of 162 contracts about which information was available, 117 prohibited any form of exportation altogether. Of the remaining 45, the majority limited exports to certain countries. The exact number of these partial exports permits could not be estimated from the data provided by Chile. Thus, in the four countries for which precise figures were available about 81 per cent of the contracts prohibited exports altogether and 86 per cent had some restrictive clause on exports. In Chile about 73 per cent of the contracts prohibited exports altogether.

19. An analysis of the above data indicates that no significant differences exist among the stipulations in contracts for the commercialization of technology entered into by firms in the countries considered here. For example, contracts with complete prohibition of exports as a percentage of the total number of contracts about which information was available were as follows:

Bolivia	77%
Colombia	77%
Chile	73%
Ecuador	75%
Peru	89%

20. With the exception of contracts entered into by firms in Peru, where figures were high owing to the large number of contracts relating to the pharmaceutical sector in the sample taken, the rest indicate similar percentages. In terms of sectorial comparisons the following figures were noted with regard to the various forms of export restrictions:

Textiles	88%
Pharmaceuticals	89%
Chemicals	78%
Food and Beverages	73%
Others	91%

21. Restrictive clauses affecting exports are stipulated on the basis of relative bargaining power, in the light of market conditions relating to alternative sources of supply of technology. Despite the different sizes and relative strengths of firms in the Andean countries, the concessions obtained by these firms in their negotiations with foreign transnational corporations that sell industrial technology do not differ greatly. The bargaining power of a relatively large firm in Medellin, Colombia, in dealing with a transnational corporation does not seem to differ very much from a smaller firm in Cochabamba, Bolivia. There appears to be a "critical" level of bargaining power, and this will depend, in part, on government policies.

22. An analysis according to ownership indicated that 92 per cent of the contracts prohibited the exportation of goods produced with foreign technology in the cases where the technology purchasing firms were locally owned. And this occurred at a time when the Andean nations, with the establishment of their common market, were trying to integrate economies by increasing intra-regional trade. Agreements reached between governments are, in the case of the commercialization of technology, greatly influenced by the terms reached among private firms whose relative bargaining power is totally unequal. Also, efforts by UNCTAD and individual governments to achieve preferential treatment for the exports of manufacturing goods from developing countries have to be considered within a market structure which does not permit such exports through explicit restrictive clauses. Technology, an indispensable input in industrial development, becomes, through its present form of commercialization, a major factor limiting such development.

23. The absence of such export-prohibiting clauses will not, of course, lead necessarily to actual exports. Everything depends on the productive and marketing capacities of the firms, their relative competitive position in external markets, their export horizon, etc. Yet, contractually assumed export possibilities, even if they do not constitute a sufficient condition, nevertheless constitute a necessary condition for such export capabilities. What is more, such clauses can severely inhibit the long process necessary for firms to develop export orientation and capacities.

C.   TIE-IN CLAUSES RELATING TO INTERMEDIATE PRODUCTS AND PRICE EFFECTS

24. A large percentage of the contracts for the commercialization of technology include obligatory terms requiring intermediate and capital goods to

be purchased from the same source as that of know-how. For example, more than two-thirds of the contracts about which information was available in Bolivia, Colombia, Ecuador and Peru had such tie-in clauses.

25. Even in the absence of such explicit terms, control through ownership or technological requirements and specifications, stemming from the nature of the know-how sold, could determine quite uniquely the source of intermediate products. Thus, as in the case of tie-in arrangements in loans, benefits for the supplier and costs for the purchaser are not limited only to the payments expressly stipulated such as royalties or interest. They also include implicit charges through the various forms of margins in the concomitant or tied sale of other goods and services. Furthermore, at the aggregate level, flows of technology among countries determine the associated flow of intermediates, equipment and capital.

26. This structure of the market for intermediates and other inputs which are tied to the sources of technology and/or capital, has significant repercussions on the strategy of import substitution pursued by the majority of developing countries. Such a strategy has, in fact, implied an increasing dependence on imports of capital goods and intermediate products. Only a few countries well ahead in their development process, like Argentina, Mexico and Brazil, have achieved in certain sectors significant "backward linkages" in domestic production. Others, however, find that inputs account for an increasing share in their total import bill as industrialization advances.

27. For example, in Colombia two-thirds of the total import bill in 1968 comprised imports of materials, machinery and equipment for the industrial sector, while the other one-third was accounted for by final products for consumption and intermediate goods for the agricultural sector. A similar dependence and a similar structure of imports are to be expected for Chile and Peru and other countries at a comparable stage of industrial development.

28. For the whole of Latin America it has been estimated that during the period 1960-65 about $1,870 million were spent annually for the importation of machinery and equipment. These imports amounted to 31 per cent of the total import bill of the area. They also constituted about 45 per cent of the total amount spent by Latin America on capital goods during the same period. For individual countries this relationship amounted to 28 per cent for Argentina, 35 per cent for Brazil, 61 per cent for Colombia, and 80 per cent for Chile.

29. As far as intermediates are concerned, industry samples in Colombia have indicated that imported materials represented in 1968 between 52 and 80 per cent of total materials used by firms in parts of the chemical industry. In the case of rubber products the corresponding ratio was 57.5 per cent and in the pharmaceutical industry 76.7 per cent. It was only in textiles that the ratio of imported intermediates to total materials used fell to 2.5 per cent. Similar figures were reported for Chile. For example, imported intermediate products amounted to more than 80 per cent of total materials used in the pharmaceu-

tical industry and between 35 and 50 per cent of total sales of the Chilean firms involved. This heavy dependence on imports of intermediates and capital goods has important repercussions on the recipient countries if one considers the fact that the bulk of such imports is either exchanged between affiliated firms and/or tied to the purchase of technology. For example, it has been estimated that about one-third of the total imports of machinery and equipment in Latin America are made by foreign-owned subsidiaries. If one defines as "overpricing" the following ratio:

$$\frac{100 \times (\text{FOB prices on imports in Andean countries} - \text{FOB prices in different world markets})}{(\text{FOB prices in different world markets})}$$

the results for the countries members of the Andean Pact presented the following indicators:

In the Colombian pharmaceutical industry a sample taken indicated that the weighted average overpricing of products imported by foreign-owned subsidiaries amounted to 155 per cent while that of national firms was 19 per cent. The absolute amount of overpricing in the case of the foreign firms studied was equivalent to six times the royalties and twenty-four times the declared profits. For national firms the absolute amount of overpricing did not exceed one fifth of the declared profits. Smaller samples taken in the same industry in Chile indicated an overpricing of imported products in excess of 500 per cent while for the majority of them the range was between 30 and 500 per cent. Similarly, in Peru samples in the same industry presented overpricing that in most cases ranged between 20 and 300 per cent while in the case of some products overpricing exceeded 300 per cent. In all three countries the overpricing noted in the imports of foreign-owned firms was considerably higher than that of nationally-owned ones. Evidently foreign technology and capital suppliers have indicated in these cases a preference for realizing their returns in an implicit form through transfer pricing rather than explicitly through royalty payment and/or profit remittances. . . .

NOTES AND QUESTIONS

1. If you were the responsible minister in a developing nation, would you favor adoption of a patent law at all? Would it encourage innovation? *See generally,* Haar, Revision of the Paris Convention; A Realignment of Private and Public Interests in the International Patent System, 8 Brooklyn J. Intl. L. 77 (1982); Note, The United States Position on Revising the Paris Convention: Quid Pro Quo or Denunciation? 5 Fordham Intl. L.J. 411 (1982).

2. Are the LDCs asking for more than a reasonable global view of antitrust law would give them? What are the situations permitted under antitrust law that appear likely to be prohibited under Decision 24?

3. What bargaining chips do the LDCs have, in the individual case or in the global negotiation, to open the DC market past patent and trademark barriers?

4. The U.S. executive has adamantly resisted the UNCTAD technology transfer approach, and Congress said in the 1984 Trade and Tariff Act that the United States should "encourage developing countries . . . to provide effective means under which foreign nationals may secure, exercise, and enforce exclusive intellectual property rights," (§501). What reasons can you give for this U.S. concern? Which U.S. interests are helped or hurt by the absence of a strong foreign intellectual property system?

5. Would you expect Decision 24 to help or hurt Andean economic development? It is said that European firms, more used to government intervention and review, are less deterred than U.S. ones. For general discussion, *see* Armstrong, Political Components and Practical Effects of the Andean Foreign Investment Code, 27 Stan. L. Rev. 1597 (1975).

6. Suppose that the Andean Pact has hired you as a consultant. As you know, it has the problem that goods manufactured by Andean technology licensees are often barred from export to the United States by U.S. patents, even though the U.S.-owned Andean counterpart patents have been licensed to the Andean companies. The Andean leaders are considering a recommendation to the Andean nations that laws be passed that would extraterritorially prohibit U.S. firms from using U.S. patents to bar U.S. import of goods produced in the Andean area when these goods have been produced pursuant to licenses of counterpart local patents granted by the same or a parent firm. Please advise them on the wisdom and effectiveness of such laws—or on any alternative courses of action that might help them.

7. A critic of the current international patent system has proposed a new LDC patent treaty. The new treaty would intentionally favor research conducted in the developing world. It would also create a single LDC patent, valid immediately in all participating nations, in order to strengthen the incentives for such research.

Thus, the proposed system would create two forms of patent. The preferred patent, issued to an LDC corporation or inventor (or to a DC corporation that had carried out the relevant research within the developing world), would provide 17 years of protection. The less preferred patent, available to all others, would provide only nine years of protection. Both types of patent would be issued by a new LDC integrated patent organization, and would immediately provide protection in all participating developing nations. (The participating LDCs would withdraw from the current international patent treaty that prohibits discrimination against nationals of foreign parties in the issuance of patents.)

Please give your judgment of this concept, explaining problems and benefits, including any additional points that might wisely be included in the treaty concept, and presenting a recommendation for or against the concept.

C. TERRITORIAL DIVISION AND ANTITRUST ENFORCEMENT PROBLEMS

The same territorial character of the patent monopoly that helps restrict LDC exports can also be used, as noted above, to create a pattern of market division. In essence, two firms can use patent rights to give each other a monopoly in half the world market rather than to compete in the entire world. Although the patent rules may help avoid antitrust liability, too elaborate and explicit a use of such patents may, at some point, amount to an antitrust violation. Drawing this patent-antitrust line intelligibly is not easy.

It is not surprising, then, that the two leading U.S. cases on this concept, *Timkin* and *ICI*, (*see* following) both raise difficult substantive antitrust questions. In *Timkin*, the antitrust violation was, in essence, an agreement among a number of affiliates to divide markets through trademark restrictions exactly parallel to the patent restrictions we've just seen. In *ICI*, the violation lay in an agreement between duPont and ICI to divide markets for a series of products through the territorial exclusion capabilities of patents. Beyond these technical policy questions, the cases also raise significant enforcement questions, emphasized in the following excerpts. (Note that the intra-corporate conspiracy aspects of the first case may be significantly affected by Copperweld v. Independence Tube, 104 S. Ct. 2731 (1984).)

TIMKEN ROLLER BEARING CO. v. UNITED STATES

341 U.S. 593 (1951)

Mr. Justice BLACK delivered the opinion of the Court.

The United States brought this civil action to prevent and restrain violations of the Sherman Act by appellant, Timken Roller Bearing Co., an Ohio corporation. The complaint charged that appellant, in violation of §§1 and 3 of the Act, combined, conspired and acted with British Timken, Ltd. (British Timken), and Societe Anonyme Française Timken (French Timken) to restrain interstate and foreign commerce by eliminating competition in the manufacture and sale of antifriction bearings in the markets of the world. After a trial of more than a month the District Court made detailed findings of fact which may be summarized as follows:

As early as 1909 appellant and British Timken's predecessor had made comprehensive agreements providing for a territorial division of the world markets for antifriction bearings. These arrangements were somewhat modified and extended in 1920, 1924 and 1925. Again in 1927 the agreements were substantially renewed in connection with a transaction by which appellant and one Dewar, an English businessman, cooperated in purchasing all the stock of British Timken. Later some British Timken stock was sold to the public with the result that appellant now holds about 30% of the outstanding shares while Dewar owns about 24%. In 1928 appellant and Dewar organized French Timken and since that date have together owned all the stock in the French company. Beginning in that year, appellant, British Timken and French Timken have continuously kept operative "business agreements" regulating the manufacture and sale of antifriction bearings by the three companies and providing for the use by the British and French corporations of the trademark "Timken." Under these agreements the contracting parties have (1) allocated trade territories among themselves; (2) fixed prices on products of one sold in the territory of the others; (3) cooperated to protect each other's markets and to eliminate outside competition; and (4) participated in cartels to restrict imports to, and exports from, the United States.

On these findings, the District Court concluded that appellant had violated the Sherman Act as charged, and entered a comprehensive decree designed to bar future violations. 83 F. Supp. 284. The case is before us on appellant's direct appeal under 15 U.S.C. §29. . . .

Appellant next contends that the restraints of trade so clearly revealed by the District Court's findings can be justified as "reasonable," and therefore not in violation of the Sherman Act, because they are "ancillary" to allegedly "legal main transactions," namely, (1) a "joint venture" between appellant and Dewar, and (2) an exercise of appellant's right to license the trademark "Timken."

We cannot accept the "joint venture" contention. . . .

Nor can the restraints of trade be justified as reasonable steps taken to implement a valid trademark licensing system, even if we assume with appellant that it is the owner of the trademark "Timken" in the trade areas allocated to the British and French corporations. Appellant's premise that the trade restraints are only incidental to the trademark contracts is refuted by the District Court's finding that the "trade mark provisions [in the agreements] were subsidiary and secondary to the central purpose of allocating trade territories." Furthermore, while a trademark merely affords protection to a name, the agreements in the present case went far beyond protection of the name "Timken" and provided for control of the manufacture and sale of antifriction bearings whether carrying the mark or not. A trademark cannot be legally used as a device for Sherman Act violation. Indeed, the Trade Mark Act of 1946 itself penalizes use of a mark "to violate the antitrust laws of the United States."

We also reject the suggestion that the Sherman Act should not be enforced in this case because what appellant has done is reasonable in view of current foreign trade conditions. The argument in this regard seems to be that tariffs, quota restrictions and the like are now such that the export and import of antifriction bearings can no longer be expected as a practical matter; that appellant cannot successfully sell its American-made goods abroad; and that the only way it can profit from business in England, France and other countries is through the ownership of stock in companies organized and manufacturing there. This position ignores the fact that the provisions in the Sherman Act against restraints of foreign trade are based on the assumption, and reflect the policy, that export and import trade in commodities is both possible and desirable. Those provisions of the Act are wholly inconsistent with appellant's argument that American business must be left free to participate in international cartels, that free foreign commerce in goods must be sacrificed in order to foster export of American dollars for investment in foreign factories which sell abroad. Acceptance of appellant's view would make the Sherman Act a dead letter insofar as it prohibits contracts and conspiracies in restraint of foreign trade. If such a drastic change is to be made in the statute, Congress is the one to do it. . . .

Mr. Justice DOUGLAS, Mr. Justice MINTON and I believe that the decree properly ordered divestiture. Our views on this point are as follows: Appellant's interests in the British and French companies were obtained as part of a plan to promote the illegal trade restraints. If not severed, the intercompany relationships will provide in the future, as they have in the past, the temptation and means to engage in the prohibited conduct. These considerations alone should be enough to support the divestiture order. . . .

Nevertheless, a majority of this Court, for reasons set forth in other opinions filed in this case, believe that divestiture should not have been ordered by the District Court. . . . As so modified, the judgment of the District Court is affirmed.

It is so ordered.

Mr. Justice BURTON and Mr. Justice CLARK took no part in the consideration or decision of this case.

Mr. Justice REED, with whom THE CHIEF JUSTICE joins, concurring.

It seems to me there can be no valid objection to that part of the opinion which approves the finding of the District Court that the Timken Roller Bearing Company has violated §§1 and 3 of the Sherman Act. It may seem strange to have a conspiracy for the division of territory for marketing between one corporation and another in which it has a large or even a major interest, but any other conclusion would open wide the doors for violation of the Sherman Act at home and in foreign fields. My disagreement with the opinion is based on the suggested requirement that American Timken divest itself of all interest in British Timken and French Timken as required by paragraph VIII of the decree. . . . My reasons for this disagreement follow.

There are no specific statutory provisions authorizing courts to employ the harsh remedy of divestiture in civil proceedings to restrain violations of the Sherman Act. Fines and imprisonment may follow criminal convictions, 15 U.S.C. §1, and divestiture of property has been used in decrees, not as punishment, but to assure effective enforcement of the laws against restraint of trade.

Since divestiture is a remedy to restore competition and not to punish those who restrain trade, it is not to be used indiscriminately, without regard to the type of violation or whether other effective methods, less harsh, are available. That judicial restraint should follow such lines is exemplified by our recent rulings in United States v. National Lead Co., 332 U.S. 319, where we approved divestiture of some properties belonging to the conspirators and denied it as to others, pp. 348-353. While the decree here does not call for confiscation, it does call for divestiture. I think that requirement is unnecessary. . . .

Mr. Justice FRANKFURTER, dissenting.

The force of the reasoning against divestiture in this case fortifies the doubts which I felt about the Government's position at the close of argument and persuades me to associate myself, in substance, with the dissenting views expressed by MR. JUSTICE JACKSON. Even "cartel" is not a talismanic word, so as to displace the rule of reason by which breaches of the Sherman Law are determined. Nor is "division of territory" so self-operating a category of Sherman Law violations as to dispense with analysis of the practical consequences of what on paper is a geographic division of territory. . . .

Of course, it is not for this Court to formulate economic policy as to foreign commerce. But the conditions controlling foreign commerce may be relevant here. When as a matter of cold fact the legal, financial, and governmental policies deny opportunities for exportation from this country and importation into it, arrangements that afford such opportunities to American enterprise may not fall under the ban of a fair construction of the Sherman Law because comparable arrangements regarding domestic commerce come within its condemnation.

Mr. Justice JACKSON, dissenting.

I doubt that it should be regarded as an unreasonable restraint of trade for an American industrial concern to organize foreign subsidiaries, each limited to serving a particular market area. If so, it seems to preclude the only practical means of reaching foreign markets by many American industries. . . .

The philosophy of the Government, adopted by the Court, is that Timken's conduct is conspiracy to restrain trade solely because the venture made use of subsidiaries. It is forbidden thus to deal with and utilize subsidiaries to exploit foreign territories, because "parent and subsidiary corporations must accept the consequences of maintaining separate corporate entities," and that consequence is conspiracy to restrain trade. But not all agreements are conspiracies and not all restraints of trade are unlawful. In a world of tariffs, trade barriers, empire or domestic preferences, and various forms of parochialism from which we are by no means free, I think a rule that it is restraint of trade to enter a foreign market through a separate subsidiary of limited scope is virtually to foreclose foreign commerce of many kinds. It is one thing for competitors or a parent and its subsidiaries to divide the United States domestic market which is an economic and legal unit; it is another for an industry to recognize that foreign markets consist of many legal and economic units and to go after each through separate means. I think this decision will restrain more trade than it will make free.

After *Timken*, the firm moved to coalesce all its operations into a single corporate operation with the assent of the Department of Justice. Even the

British minority shareholders were bought out. (*See* Markley, How Timken Coordinates Its Worldwide Manufacturing and Marketing, Export Trade, Apr. 25, 1960, p.10.)

The duPont-ICI sequence, which follows, began with the agreement, described in the first of the excerpts, to exchange U.S. and British patent rights on related products in such a way, roughly, that duPont could protect itself from ICI competition in the United States, and ICI could protect itself from duPont competition in Great Britain. Whether such a use of patents should be regarded as an antitrust violation is clearly the central antitrust policy issue in the sequence.

Enforcement of the U.S. decision was complicated by the fact that ICI had transferred its patent rights to British Nylon Spinners (BNS), a British firm, in which it held a 50% interest and over which the United States courts lacked *in personam* jurisdiction. Thus, the stage was set for the problem that is the focus of the later excerpts. How could the U.S. court define an equitable decree when certain of the patent rights were thus beyond its reach? What should or could the British courts do in response? What ultimate competitive benefits could a decree bring, and should the U.S. court try to keep the two firms' obligations under the decree symmetrical?

UNITED STATES v. IMPERIAL CHEMICAL INDUSTRIES, LTD. (I)

105 F. Supp. 215 (S.D.N.Y. 1952)

RYAN, J. . . .

We have found that the patents and processes agreements "did, in operation, result in restraints of United States trade." DuPont agreed to restrict its use of United States patents by undertaking not to ship products manufactured under these patents to the territory assigned exclusively to ICI. To make this restriction effective, duPont was also required to impose like limitations on the shipments of anyone whom it might license under its United States patents. Insofar as shipments to Great Britain were concerned, the restrictions imposed by agreement were further implemented by the granting to ICI of exclusive licenses under the British counterparts of the United States patents. Thus, the exclusionary right under the British patents was applied against imports from the United States, and the basic understanding by which ICI recognized the United States as the exclusive territory of duPont was in turn observed by the granting of an exclusive license to duPont in the United States. This kept the patented products manufactured in the United States out of the market of Great Britain, and the like products manufactured in Great Britain out of the United States.

The agreement between ICI and duPont also brought about a situation by which the United States patents of both were placed in the hands of duPont.

This was a pooling of patents for a purpose in restraint of foreign trade. This use of patent rights was condemned in United States v. Line Material Co., 1948, 333 U.S. 287, 311, 68 S. Ct. 550, 92 L. Ed. 701, when employed as a means to effect price fixing arrangements. Line Material was, like the instant suit, brought under Section 1 and neither monopoly nor domination was charged. We have held that when patents are pooled to carry out a division of territories, it is equally as unlawful as when they are unified to effect price fixing.

The remedy of compulsory licensing is not to be restricted to monopoly situations. An effect of compulsory licensing is to grant to the public a right to use the patented invention and thus remove an impediment to competition. The wrong it is designed to correct arises from the misuse of lawful patent rights pursuant to an unlawful agreement. Such misuse creates an extension of the patent monopoly. Here, we have had proof of a wrong—unlawful restraints on our trade—accomplished by agreement between ICI and duPont. It was made possible of performance by the voluntary abstention from trade by one in the exclusive territory of the other, and the restrictive provisions in patent licenses and in technology exchanged. We may hope to compel an abandonment of limitations in the exchange of patents and technology which are used to violate the anti-trust laws only by decreeing that ICI and duPont grant to all others what they have heretofore granted to each other. It may be that the decree will permit them to make better and more profitable terms for the additional grants than they have heretofore demanded *inter sese*. . . .

. . . We are also concerned with increasing the possibility of competition between ICI, duPont and others who might desire to enter the field. The unquestionable right of ICI to determine whether or not it will manufacture under its American patents, to select its licenses, and to determine whether licenses granted shall be exclusive or non-exclusive, has been exercised to implement the allotment of territories. Compulsory licensing will be a cure and not a punishment for this.

It has been contended on duPont's behalf that compulsory licensing should not be decreed because it would not "cause duPont to export and would not affect in any way the result of past failure on the part of duPont to export." Perhaps this is so, and it leads us to observe that neither would a simple injunctive provision in the decree produce this result. But compulsory licensing will enable others to manufacture and put them in a position where they will be able to export. The application of this remedy might serve as an impetus to a sincere desire on duPont's part to enter the export field on an active and competitive basis.

To us, it seems that an effective method to establish competitive conditions is to decree compulsory licensing of all patents which were licensed among the conspirators and which were put to use in the production of products which were common to some, if not to all. It has rightly been observed that "as long as the patentee is free to grant or withhold a patent license at his pleasure, the striking down of one set of restrictive conditions attached to a patent license may lead only to the adoption of another set of conditions which achieve the same effect." Compulsory Patent Licensing, 56 Yale Law Journal, 1946, p. 82.

With the compulsory licensing provisions with respect to patents, there must follow similar licensing provisions with respect to know-how affecting these patents and the products made under them. This must be so because it has been found that the exchange of know-how—as well as that of patents—served as a direct means for the accomplishment of the unlawful restraints; and because the supplying of such know-how and technology is necessary to the efficient use of the licensed patents and to the production by the licensee of products comparable in quality and cost of production to that of the licensor. The Government has asked that the compulsory licensing of know-how and technology be extended to include all "usable" processes—those processes now being used and applied and those which have been found to be of possible use but which are not currently being applied. The objection to the inclusion of "usable" processes because of difficulties in ferreting out those processes which have been tried only to be abandoned, and those known to be possible but never used, seems to us more fanciful than real. We have been impressed by the evidence throughout that the defendants function as extremely efficient and competently managed industrial organizations. The records of these "usable" processes will be available to them for disclosure; and it will be so decreed. . . .

The provisions for fixation of reasonable royalties will follow substantially the provisions in anti-trust suits in which similar relief has been decreed. . . . The royalties are to be determined by the court, when agreement has not been privately reached, on petition from the applicant and on proof submitted by the applicant and the defendant involved.

The Government does not seek a decree directing ICI to grant compulsory licenses of its British patents. The Government requests that ICI be required to grant immunity under its foreign patents which correspond to the United States patents which we have made subject to compulsory licensing. . . . We have had testimony offered on behalf of ICI by an expert in British law that a provision for granting immunities is contrary to British public policy and that a British court will not enforce such a provision in the judgment of a court of a foreign jurisdiction. As to this, we observe that, acting on the basis of our jurisdiction in personam, we are merely directing ICI to refrain from asserting rights which it may have in Britain, since the enforcement of those rights will serve to continue the effects of wrongful acts it has committed within the United States affecting the foreign trade of the United States.

We are not unmindful that under British law there are restrictions upon exports from the United States by reason of the existence of the British patents owned by ICI. The exclusion of unlicensed imports and the prohibition of unlicensed sales is enforceable because of the legal rights which attach to a British patent.

We accept as correct the statements in the brief of ICI that: "Under United States law if a product is patented, sale into the United States of that product constitutes clear infringement of the rights of the American patentee. Such sale will therefore subject the vendor to a suit for infringement even though his acquisition of the patented article abroad (and his use and sale of it there) may be wholly lawful. Boesch v. Graff, 1890, 133 U.S. 697, 10 S. Ct. 378, 33 L. Ed. 787. This is true even though the vendor may hold the foreign patent on the article in question. . . .

We accept as correct the statements in the brief of ICI:

> In the British Empire the law is even more stringent. The owner of a British patent may bar the importation of any product patented in Great Britain and also any product made by any process where the process is patented under British law. It is clear that a patent on a process essential to the production of a product is infringed by sale of an imported product made abroad by that process. Von Heyden v. Neustadt, 1880, 14 Ch. D. 230; United Horse Nail Co. v. Stewart and Co., 1885, 2 R.P.C. 122, 133-134; Saccharin Corp., Ltd. v. Anglo-Continental Chemical Works, Ltd., 1900, 17 R.P.C. 307, 318-319; Terrell, The Law and Practice Relating to Letters Patent for Inventions (London, 1934), pp.173-177.
>
> There is no requirement under American law which required duPont to license ICI under its United States patents or ICI to license duPont under its British patents. To the extent that each retained the right under the laws of its respective country to assert patents against imports, this resulted in no limitation upon such imports which in any way exceeded the limitation that would have existed had there been no agreement at all.

But as we have heretofore observed these lawful rights were employed as means to accomplish the unlawful purpose of their underlying agreement.

While it is true that these rights exist independent of any provision in the patents and processes agreements, they were granted to ICI by the disclosure or assignment of inventions by duPont pursuant to the terms of these agreements. Inventions were also licensed by ICI to duPont for its exclusive use and exploitation in the United States in accordance with the agreements. In the first instance the patents were employed to restrain duPont's exports to Great Britain, in plain violation of American anti-trust laws; in the second instance, the patents were used as a means to prevent ICI exports to the United States and placed a restraint upon the foreign trade of Great Britain, in violation of her declared policy, if not her laws. It does not seem presumptious for this court to make a direction to a foreign defendant corporation over which it has jurisdiction to take steps to remedy and correct a situation, which is unlawful both here and in the foreign jurisdiction in which it is domiciled. Two evils have resulted from the one understanding of ICI and duPont—restraints upon the foreign trade and commerce of the United States as well as on that of Great Britain. It is not an intrusion on the authority of a foreign sovereign for this court to direct that steps be taken to remove the harmful effects on the trade of the United States.

We recognize that substantial legal questions may be raised with respect to our power to decree as to duPont's foreign patents as well as those issued to ICI. Here, we deal with the regulation of the exercise of rights granted by a foreign sovereign to a domestic corporate defendant and to a foreign corporate defendant. Our power so to regulate is limited and depends upon jurisdiction *in personam;* the effectiveness of the exercise of that power depends upon the recognition which will be given to our judgment as a matter of comity by the courts of the foreign sovereign which has granted the patents in question.

Where we have required ICI to grant immunity under British patents which are the counterpart of duPont's United States patents, the payment of reasonable royalty upon imports of articles manufactured under them into Great Britain shall be paid to ICI.

Full recognition is hereby given to the inherent property rights granted by the British patent to exclude from Great Britain merchandise covered by the patent. Since a license under the corresponding United States patent conveys no right to ship into Great Britain articles manufactured in the United States under the patent, no royalty shall be collectible by duPont upon such items as are destined for export to Great Britain. . . .

The history of the basic British nylon patents reveals a studied and continued purpose on the part of ICI and duPont to remove these patents from within the scope of any decree which might ultimately be made by this court. . . . These British patents were issued to duPont. By the agreement of March 30, 1939, ICI received an exclusive license under them; in January, 1940, ICI granted irrevocable and exclusive rights to make nylon yarn from nylon polymer (which is manufactured by ICI) to British Nylon Spinners, Ltd. (BNS). ICI has a stock interest of 50% in BNS, the remaining 50% is held by Courtaulds, Inc. BNS is in the business of manufacturing and distributing nylon yarn. Not content with this arrangement and with the deliberate purpose to "materially reduce the risk of any loss of rights" as a result of this suit . . . , duPont pursuant to the nylon agreement of 1946 assigned the basic British nylon patents to ICI. It is now urged that we may not decree with reference to these British patents so as to direct ICI to remove restrictions on imports into Great Britain of nylon polymer or nylon yarn from the United States. It is argued that the sum total of all these agreements is not to create by itself any restrictions against American imports, and that those which exist arise from the right to be free from competition which is inherent in the British patents and cannot possibly be repugnant to the American anti-trust laws.

BNS is not before this court; although they were knowing participants in acts designed to thwart the granting of full relief, we may not direct our decree to them. The lack of majority stock ownership in ICI likewise prevents control of the future acts of BNS by this means; however, we are not without some remedy still available.

Objection is raised by ICI that we are without power to decree that the British nylon patents may not be asserted to prevent the importation of nylon polymer and nylon yarn into Great Britain because BNS has rights which exist independent of those possessed by ICI. This overlooks the circumstances under which BNS acquired its rights to these patents by licenses from ICI. . . . Throughout all these negotiations it appears that BNS was advised of the dealings between ICI and duPont concerning the British nylon patents. Both ICI and duPont are parties to the instant suit; they were advised in fact and realized that the further use and control of the rights pertaining to the British nylon patents were subject to a decree of this court to be entered in this suit. We find that in fact Courtaulds and BNS were also fully advised of this situation. The first, or "manufacturing sub-license" which BNS received granted to it no greater rights than had been acquired by ICI; it was subject to the same infirmities as existed against ICI. The second license granted after the assignment of the patents to ICI did not come to BNS as an innocent party. BNS, again, knew exactly what it was receiving; its rights are wholly subject to the inherent vices of the agreements through which they were acquired. We have found them to be tainted with the illegality of the unlawful conspiracy; of this probability BNS was informed. The circumstances surrounding the execution of the assignment to ICI in December, 1946, makes this clear (Op. 198, Ex. 708). It is also recorded that on October 17, 1946, "Courtaulds appreciated the difficulty in which all parties were placed consequent upon the American litigation and were, therefore, willing to accede to a modification of the duPont/I.C.I. Nylon License Agreement." . . . On October 28, 1946, Courtaulds undertook to "take all steps in their power to secure that British Nylon Spinners also raise no objection to the conclusion by ICI of the new agreement . . . ."

We do not hesitate therefore to decree that the British nylon patents may not be asserted by ICI to prevent the importation of nylon polymer and of nylon yarn into Great Britain. What credit may be given to such an injunctive provision by the courts of Great Britain in a suit brought by BNS to restrain such importations we do not venture to predict. We feel that the possibility that the English courts in an equity suit will not give effect to such a provision in our decree should not deter us from including it.

In any event it appears that BNS would have the right under Section 63 of the Patents Act of 1949, as the exclusive licensee to bring suit for infringement against an importer of yarn and staple fiber. There would then be a speedy determination of the effectiveness of the immunity provision of the decree with reference to these products. If the British courts were not to give credit to this provision, no injury would have been done; if the holding of the British courts were to the contrary, a remedy available would not have been needlessly abandoned. . . .

Judge Ryan's opinion was received with no small interest by an English court. BNS brought suit in England to enjoin ICI's compliance with the U.S. court's order. Of particular interest to the English court was the possible issue of extraterritoriality raised in the U.S. decision. BNS obtained an interlocutory injunction against ICI's compliance. The following is the text of the British

Court of Appeals' decision denying ICI's appeal for dismissal of the injunction. At a later trial on the merits, it was ruled that ICI was bound by British law to perform its contract. *See* British Nylon Spinners, Ltd. v. Imperial Chem. Indus., Ltd., [1954] All E.R. 88 (Ch.).

BRITISH NYLON SPINNERS, LTD. v. IMPERIAL CHEMICAL INDUSTRIES, LTD.

[1952] 2 A.E.R. 780

SIR RAYMOND EVERSHED, M.R.

The agreement of December 31, 1946, was an agreement whereby the defendant company acquired outright from du Pont de Nemours the patents (among others) which are specified in the schedule to the order, and one of the terms of the final judgment of the district judge, was that this agreement was thereby cancelled and terminated. That, however, was not all, for in a later part of the same judgment, Imperial Chemical Industries, Ltd. (the defendant company) was forbidden to make, among other things, "any disposition of foreign patents" (i.e., patents foreign to the United States of America and including the patents now in suit) unless it required, as a condition of the grant, that the grantee agreed in writing to hold its licence subject to certain rights of immunity, viz., the rights of American manufacturers of these nylon products freely to import and vend in the United Kingdom articles manufactured in accordance with the patents or with comparable patents. The effect of any such condition, if insisted on, would, obviously, be to derogate in a most serious way from the value of the exclusive licences which the defendant company was under contract to grant to the plaintiff company. Further, if the defendant company were to re-assign these various patents to du Pont de Nemours, as directed by the judgment of the district judge, it would, in fact, disable itself altogether thenceforward from granting licences in the terms which it had contracted to grant. The present proceedings have, therefore, been brought by the plaintiff company, in effect, to enforce what it claims to be its contractual rights under the contract of March, 1947, and by way of interim relief (seeing that the ninety days specified in the order of the district judge, are about to expire) the plaintiff company seeks to restrain the defendant company from executing an assignment in obedience to that order. Upjohn, J., granted an injunction, pending the trial, restraining the defendant company from so doing.

This is an interlocutory matter, and, therefore, it is inappropriate for the court to say more about the case or its merits than is necessary to make clear the grounds of the conclusion which it reaches. It is plain from what I have said that there is here a question of what is sometimes called the comity which subsists between civilised nations. In other words, it involves the extent to which the courts of one country will pay regard and give effect to the decisions and orders of another country. I certainly should be the last to indicate any lack of respect for any decision of the district courts of the United States, but I think that in this case there is raised a somewhat serious question whether the order, in the form that it takes, does not assert an extraterritorial jurisdiction which the courts of this country cannot recognise, notwithstanding any such comity. Applied conversely, I conceive that the American courts would likewise be slow (to say the least) to recognise an assertion on the part of the British courts of jurisdiction extending, in effect, to the business affairs of persons and corporations in the United States. In a judgment which the district judge delivered in May, 1952 (the second of his opinions in the proceedings to which I have referred), it is plain that the learned judge carefully considered this matter, and, indeed, as Upjohn, J., pointed out, expressed his own doubts whether, in giving effect, as he felt it his duty to do, to the implications of the Sherman Act, he might not be going beyond the normally recognised limits of territorial jurisdiction. But he said: "It is not an intrusion on the authority of a foreign sovereign for this court to direct that steps be taken to remove the harmful effects on the trade of the United States."

If by that passage the learned judge intended to say (as it seems to me that he did) that it was not an intrusion on the authority of a foreign sovereign to make directions addressed to that foreign sovereign, or to its courts, or to nationals of that foreign power, effective to remove (as he says) "harmful effects on the trade of the United States", I am bound to say that, as at present advised, I find myself unable to agree with it. Questions affecting the trade of one country may well be matters proper to be considered by the government of another country. Tariffs are sometimes imposed by one country which obviously affect the trade of another country, and the imposition of such tariffs, as it seems to me, is a matter for the government of the particular country which imposes them. And if that observation of the learned judge were conversely applied to directions designed to remove harmful effects on the trade, say, of Great Britain or British nationals in America, I should be surprised to find that it was accepted as not being an intrusion on the rights and sovereign authority of the United States. On the other hand, there is no doubt that it is competent for the courts of a particular country, in a suit between persons who are either nationals or subjects of that country or are otherwise subject to its jurisdiction, to make orders in personam against one such party, directing it, for example, to do something or to refrain from doing something in another country affecting the other party to the action. As a general proposition, that would not be open to doubt, but the plaintiff in this case is neither a subject nor a national of the United States, nor (unlike the defendant company) was it a party to the proceedings before the district judge, nor is it otherwise subject to his jurisdiction.

What the precise relationship, commercially or otherwise, is between the plaintiff company and the defendant company we have not at this stage of the proceedings considered, and I proceed on the assumption (and I am not to be taken as hinting that the contrary is the fact) that the plaintiff is an independent trade corporation and entitled to be treated as independent of the defend-ant company. Being so independent, it has beyond question, according to the laws of England, certain rights, certain choses in action, by virtue of the con-tract of 1947, which the courts of this country, in exercise of the laws which they claim to be entitled to administer, will in this country protect and enforce. Broadly speaking, the contract of March, 1947, being an English contract, made between English nationals and to be performed in England, the right which the plaintiff company has may be described as its right, under the contract, to have it performed and, if necessary, to have an order made by the courts of this country for its specific performance. That is a right, or, in other words, a species of property (seeing, particularly, that it is related to patents) which is English in character and is subject to the jurisdiction of the English courts, and it seems to me that the plaintiff company has, at least, established a prima facie case for saying that it is not competent for the courts of the United States, or of any other country, to interfere with those rights or to make orders, the observance of which by our courts would require that our courts should not exercise the jurisdiction which they have and which it is their duty to exercise in regard to those rights.

I think, however, that the matter goes somewhat further. I have said that the subject-matter of the contract of December, 1946, is a number of English and Commonwealth patents. An English patent is a species of English prop-erty of the nature of a chose in action and peculiar in character. By English law it confers on its proprietor certain monopoly rights, exercisable in Eng-land. A person who has an enforceable right to a licence under an English patent appears, therefore, to me to have, at least, some kind of proprietary interest which it is the duty of our courts to protect. And, certainly, so far as the English patents are concerned, it seems to me, with all deference to the judgment of the district judge, to be an assertion of an extra-territorial jurisdic-tion which we do not recognise for the American courts to make orders which would destroy or qualify those statutory rights belonging to an English na-tional who is not subject to the jurisdiction of the American courts.

As regards the patents other than the English patents, viz., Australian, Indian, New Zealand, South African, Irish or other patents, a possible distinc-tion can, of course, be drawn, since the patents in those countries are a species of property in those countries, and an effective right to use those patents would, if necessary, have to be asserted in those countries. But no special point has been made before us as regards the Australian and other non-English patents, and, for present purposes, I do not understand that it is suggested, if the injunction goes as regards the English patents, that it should not go to the full extent of the patents specified in the schedule to the order of Upjohn, J. We must, in the absence of some evidence to the contrary, assume that the law in these other countries is the same as it is here, and, apart from what I might call the particular rights quoad the particular non-English patents, there re-mains the general contractual right which relates to all the patents and is derived from the English contract of March, 1947.

I think it undesirable that I should say more, except to re-affirm the proposition that the courts of this country will, in the natural course, pay great respect and attention to the superior courts of the United States of America, but I conceive that it is none the less the proper province of English courts, when their jurisdiction is invoked, not to refrain from exercising that jurisdiction if they think that it is their duty so to do for the protection of rights which are peculiarly subject to their protection. In so saying, I do not conceive that I am offending in any way against the principles of comity which apply between the two countries, and, like Upjohn, J., I take some comfort from the doubts which the district judge himself entertained about the extent to which his order might go, if carried to its logical conclusion.

DENNING, L. J.

I agree. It would be a serious matter if there was a conflict between the orders of the courts of the United States and the orders of the courts of this country. The writ of the United States does not run in this country, and, if due regard is had to the comity of nations, it will not seek to run here. But, as I read this judgment of the United States court, there is a saving clause which prevents any conflict, because, although the defendant company has been ordered to do certain acts by the United States court, nevertheless there is a provision which says that nothing in the judgment shall operate against the company for action taken in complying with the law of any foreign government or instrumentality thereof to which the defendant company is for the time being subject. In view of that saving clause I hope that there will be no conflict between the orders. I agree that the appeal should be dismissed.

ROMER, L.J.: I also agree.

Appeal dismissed.

Finally, ICI petitioned in the U.S. courts for a grant of immunity under the duPont nylon patents. In the following decision Judge Ryan denied the petition.

UNITED STATES v. IMPERIAL CHEMICAL INDUSTRIES, LTD. (II)

1954 Trade Cases (C.C.H.) ¶67,739

RYAN, J. . . .

ICI moves for an order directing duPont to grant to ICI pursuant to the provisions of Article IX-4 of the judgment entered herein "an unrestricted, nonexclusive, royalty-free immunity under any existing nylon patent . . . to import into the United States of America, . . . nylon filaments and bristles . . . and nylon flakes and molding powders, which shall have been lawfully manufactured outside the United States."

By Article IX-4 of the judgment, it was decreed that "to the extent they have the legal right to do so, duPont and ICI shall: . . . (b) grant to any person (including ICI and duPont) making written request therefor, in consideration of a reasonable royalty, an unrestricted, non-exclusive immunity under any existing or new patent to import into the United States any common chemical product lawfully manufactured outside the United States; . . . "

DuPont has refused to grant the request of ICI for immunities on the first two groups of the nylon products so scheduled. It has predicated this refusal upon the fact that ICI, by reason of its prior assignment to BNS of British nylon patents covering nylon yarn (group 3 of the scheduled nylon products) is presently unable to grant like immunities to duPont for the importation of nylon yarn into Great Britain.

DuPont urges in support of its refusal that the immunities grant directed by Article IX-4 is intended to be reciprocal and indivisible with respect to the three groups of products flowing from the several basic nylon patents. It contends that since it has not obtained immunities from ICI on all three groups of nylon common chemical products in their entirety, it should not be directed to grant to ICI immunities on the first two groups. Its position is that the immunities contemplated by the judgment were intended to embrace "whole patents" rather than "products."

On the other hand, ICI urges that the provision for immunities was intended to apply to the separate common chemical products rather than to "whole patents" or all the products produced under a given basic patent. It contends, therefore, that it rightly requested and should receive immunities from duPont on the first two groups only, and it points out that it has made this limited request since it may grant reciprocal immunities to duPont only on these two groups. ICI argues that to interpret Article IX-4 as providing for the grant of immunities only if the recipient itself has the legal right to grant complete immunities under a particular patent (as duPont would read it), is to take all meaning from the phrase "to the extent that it has the legal right to do so."

ICI SUPPORTED BY GOVERNMENT

The Government's position is substantially in accord with that taken by ICI. The Government contends that since a purpose of the judgment was to remove obstacles to free trade between the United States and Great Britain, opportunity is here presented to encourage such trade as to some nylon products, although not as to all, and that the present disability of ICI to grant immunities with respect to one group of nylon products—yarn—only, should not result in the continuance of restrictions on United States' commerce in the nylon products embraced in the other groups. It agrees with ICI that the request now made by the latter is consistent with the provisions of Article IX-4.

PURPOSE OF JUDGMENT TO FACILITATE TRADE

A purpose of the judgment was to encourage and facilitate trade between Great Britain and the United States. The provisions of the article in question dealing with the importation and exportation of various products flowing from the several basic nylon patents were intended to accomplish this end. The grants were intended, however, to be reciprocal and to embrace immunities on patents and their use in their entirety and not on products produced under a particular patent. Unless duPont is as free to export to Great Britain as ICI is to export to the United States, the granting of royalty-free immunities to ICI to export to this country without such a corresponding grant to duPont with respect to Great Britain would not be carrying out the broad purpose of the judgment; such a result was not contemplated or intended by Article IX or any article of the judgment.

It is no answer to say that nevertheless obstacles to free trade between these two countries would be removed by the granting of immunities on some of the nylon products. This does not justify splitting up and dividing products based on the same patents—a step which would be neither just nor equitable, nor in conformity with the purpose of the Article.

It is possible, as ICI and the Government point out, that BNS may by enforcing its claim under the assignment of British nylon patents from ICI forever foreclose ICI from granting duPont immunities on nylon yarn. Such a course of action, if pursued by BNS, would permanently bar the exchange of reciprocal immunities on all nylon products, thus limiting the coverage of the immunity provisions and narrowing the original, broad purpose of Article IX-4 of the judgment. That this regrettable situation might develop was not entirely unforeseen at the time of the drafting of these provisions of the judgment. It was with this in mind that reassignment of the British nylon patents to duPont by ICI was decreed by an *in personam* direction, revoking an assignment which it was found had been made in 1946 with a purpose on the part of both duPont and ICI, and in which BNS participated, to thwart any adverse judgment which might be entered.

IMMUNITY APPLIES TO ALL NYLON GROUPS

The fact that now ICI finds itself able, and that it is willing, to grant duPont reciprocal immunities on two groups of nylon products is without significance in view of the interpretation here given to the immunities provisions of Article IX. The broad immunity covering all nylon common chemical products under basic nylon patents in their entirety contemplated by the judgment will not now be read so as to apply to some and not all of these products. Until ICI can grant duPont complete reciprocal immunities on all three groups of nylon products, it may not require immunities to be granted by duPont on these two groups.

The application of ICI for the granting of immunities on nylon products exclusive of yarn is at the present time denied without prejudice to a renewal when and if ICI finds itself in a position to grant reciprocal immunities to duPont as to all nylon products.

Settle order on notice.

NOTES AND QUESTIONS

1. If the various components of the Timkin Company had been genuinely separate but had each held the trademark rights for specific nations as in the real case, would they have been entitled to protect their markets against imports from one another?

2. Was competition increased as a result of the ultimate decision? Assuming there was an antitrust violation, was there any practical alternative to divestiture in this case? In other words, is not the Supreme Court responsible for the failure of enforcement?

3. Could Judge Ryan have logically issued a decree very different from that which he actually chose?

4. Did ICI want to win the suit brought against it by Courtaulds?

5. Suppose the patent rights had not been transferred to Courtaulds. Do you think that ICI would have granted admission to U.S. products? What if it had resisted to the point that Justice had to use contempt procedures? Would the U.K. courts have helped Justice?

6. Was Judge Ryan right in his 1954 decision?

7. Can this enforcement problem be avoided?

8. Suppose executives are careless in talking about the market division obtainable through patent procedures (while the corporate lawyers, of course, are careful to emphasize that this market division is only an indirect effect of legitimate patent licensing procedures). Is there an antitrust violation? *See* United States v. Westinghouse Electric Corp., 648 F.2d 642 (9th Cir. 1981).

D. OTHER INTERNATIONAL ANTITRUST-INTELLECTUAL PROPERTY ISSUES

A new generation of technology issues is emerging with the growing interest of many nations in encouraging and controlling their own high-technology industries. Although there are not yet many relevant cases, or even directly relevant legislation, traditional legislation and regulation are being applied in patterns like the following:

a. subsidization of one's own high-technology industry—and countervailing against other's subsidies;

b. protection of one's own market to give one's high-technology firms a chance to work down the learning curve faster than foreign firms—and diplomacy to break down similar foreign barriers;

c. direct restrictions on technology flow and on the benefits of research in order to give one's own firms competitive advantage;

d. encouragement of cooperative research ventures;

e. domestic content requirements for high-technology areas.

Most of these today have to be analyzed by traditional means—the following hypotheticals suggest a few of the issues. For more information, *see* Barton, Technology Trade, Proc. 77th Ann. Mtg., Am. Soc. Intl. L. 130 (1983); and Coping with Technological Protectionism, 62 Harv. Bus. Rev. 91 (1984).

QUESTIONS

1. Assume that France, without disapproval by European Economic Community authorities, has sought to give strong research and development support to one of its recently nationalized firms, a (mythical) biotechnology firm, DNA, S.A., which has long sold yeasts and fermentation equipment worldwide. Under what appears to be French policy, this firm is given special R & D funds (in spite of the fact that it has not been making a profit), and French purchasers are informally encouraged to deal with it rather than with competitors. Moreover, the firm itself, which has a French monopoly on certain key winemaking components, has begun to discourage members of the French wine industry from dealing with others.

Your client, Yeastco, has been developing processes for genetic manipulation of wine yeast, and has research laboratories in both California and France. The client has just told you, however, that the French research laboratory is facing difficulties, which the client suspects derive from actions of DNA. Key employees are leaving and and it has suddenly become impossible to obtain sample research materials from French vineyards. This problem is serious, because Yeastco was hoping to build components of French yeasts into its yeast used for markets in other nations.

What actions would you advise? Suppose that so far it is only your firm's sales in France and ability to do research for world-wide markets that have been hurt.

2. A number of developed nations have a breeders' rights system, and the seed industries of these nations will accordingly not release their seeds for use without appropriate compensation. Does it follow that nations (typically LDCs) that are the source of wild varieties should not permit export of these varieties without compensation? Should developing nations enact a breeders' rights system? *See* Barton, The International Breeder's Rights System and Crop Plant Innovation, 216 Science 1071 (1982).

PART 3

REGULATING
INTERNATIONAL INVESTMENT

Chapter XV

Capital Transfers

This chapter turns to a third major international economic flow—that of capital. Its goal is to explain the various motivations for and forms of international investment. It also presents the macroeconomic regulations affecting that flow, particularly those associated with international bank loans. Later chapters will explore the protection of the individual investor, the regulation of the multinational firm, and the resolution of disputes between a multinational firm and its host nation.

A. LEGAL FORMS OF CAPITAL FLOW

Just as for a national capital market, there can be many possible forms and instruments for international capital flow. Among the most important legal forms (which are not directly correlated with the economic forms) are the following:

Bank loans to governments or individuals. These are loans made by the regular banking system, usually denominated in a hard currency, generally dollars, from banks to governments or individuals. In recent years, these have been granted for relatively short terms, but typically rolled over regularly. The International Bank for Reconstruction and Development (IBRD or World Bank) and the various regional development banks also make such loans. For the private banks, the counter-balancing deposits include those from OPEC treasuries as well as from domestic investors in the United States and Europe, and perhaps from developing nation elites investing a return flow of funds.

751

This market is international, with the banks lending funds to one another in what is usually called the "Eurodollar market," a market that grew from a few billion dollars in the mid 1960s to over $600 billion around 1980. Interest rates are usually defined in terms of points above LIBOR, the London interbank loan rate set as a market rate for these bank-to-bank loans.

Bond issues by governments or corporations. These are issues of long-term (10 to 30 years), generally fixed-rate securities by the more successful developing nations, by major corporations, and by international lending agencies such as the IBRD. The investors, whose identities are carefully concealed in the issue process, may include at least some OPEC interests and certainly include many developed-world institutional investors. These loans are typically made through syndicates of European investment banking houses.

Stock issues of corporations. These are the sale of equity interests in private corporations to an investor in a nation other than that of incorporation. They can take the form of "portfolio" investment, in which the investor gains no significant control over the corporation, a situation exemplified by a small investor's purchase of a few shares of stock in a foreign corporation. They can also take the form of "direct" investment in which a corporation acquires a controlling interest in or substantial control of a foreign corporation, either through purchasing stock in a going concern or through creating a new corporation under local law as an affiliate or subsidiary.

International branch operation. This is the direct purchase of foreign assets, such as land or a factory. This is not economically different from creating a subsidiary to conduct the same operation, but is clearly legally different. A firm's choice of legal pattern depends on such factors as the tax benefits of foreign incorporation and the desire or not to place the home corporation's assets at risk in the foreign operation. In general, the foreign subsidiary's earnings are not taxable at home until they have been declared as dividends (a position quite logical in the legally similar case of portfolio investment), while the branch's earnings are immediately taxable at home. And while a firm will usually want to create a subsidiary to limit the parent corporation's liability, a bank may have to operate through a branch in order to create the confidence derived from making its entire assets available for settlement of obligations arising within the jurisdiction.

Some of the variations in the above reflect economic differences. Anyone studying the corporation is familiar with the spectrum of financing patterns beginning with bank loans and moving through bonds to equity investment, and the way the extent of economic control associated with the loan increases along that spectrum while the priority of payment obligations, both in bankruptcy and during the firm's ongoing existence, correspondingly decreases. And there are clear economic differences between loans to a nation's government and loans to a private (or semipublic) entity within that nation—loans that may create an economic allocation different from that which the government would have chosen.

The economic and the legal forms, however, fail to correspond in the case of branch and subsidiary investment, which are very different legally, but need not differ economically. When these investment forms bring control, they are economically indistinguishable from each other—and they are radically different economically from portfolio investment, which, almost by definition, does not bring control. Economically, the real question is whether the transnational operation is being operated as a single unit, something which can be achieved with either a branch or a subsidiary. The economics depends on management structure; under some management strategies local management may be given so much control (whether the local arrangement is that of branch or subsidiary) that the corporation is not operated as an entity anyway.

"Company law," as corporation law is known in most of the world, deserves very careful attention in any actual case. In most nonsocialist nations, company law permits a foreign corporation to create a wholly owned subsidiary. Formalities may require that a national sit on the board of directors or its analogue, or that token shares of stock be held locally, but control is usually achievable.

Nevertheless, there are surprises. Most nations define separate legal regimes for companies with few shareholders and for those with many shareholders. This reflects the U.S. distinction between close corporations and publicly owned corporations. In Germany, for example, the publicly owned corporation has several layers of management and boards, and also provides for employee participation (*mitbestimmung*). Moreover, in many foreign nations, shares are held in bearer fashion (typically through banks for physical safety) rather than there being a central registry, as is typical in the United States. This foreign approach reflects the investor's interest in privacy against the government, an interest reinforced by such historical examples as Nazi efforts to discriminate against Jewish shareholders. The approach also requires governments to use withholding to collect taxes on dividends.

Later chapters will explore techniques of direct investment and the legal issues arising from such investment. This chapter emphasizes bank lending, as exemplified by the credit agreement in the Selected Documents Supplement, which should be consulted at this point. This particular credit agreement is designed for a loan made by a group of banks, each of which makes a share of the loan. The loan uses a variable interest rate; and it gives the borrower flexibility in deciding how much to borrow at any specific time. The following questions refer to this credit agreement.

QUESTIONS

1. How is the amount lent to be set? The interest rate? The share of each bank?

2. Do you think the provisions of Art. VIII of the credit agreement assuring payment in dollars should be legally enforceable? (You will want to reconsider this question after learning about the International Monetary Fund's (IMF's) Article VIII 8(2)(b) (*infra*, p.768) and after reading the *Weston Banking Corp.* case (*infra*, p.780) both later in this chapter.

3. Can you explain the division of issues between Arts. IX and X?

4. Should the sovereign immunity waiver of Art. XIV be held effective? What are the pro and con arguments?

5. Notice the Events of Default in Art. XI: How is the existence of default determined? And by whom?

6. What is the effect of Art. XI(d)?

7. What law governs this agreement? What are the arguments for and against upholding the provisions?

8. Could a country's decision to suspend payments on a loan be considered an act of state and therefore not controlled by the terms of the loan agreement? For background, *see Allied Bank, infra*, p.801.

Bibliographical Note

For more data in this area, *see* R. Rendell, International Financial Law; Lending, Capital Transfers and Institutions (1980); Eskridge, *Les Jeux Sont Faits:* Structural Origins of the International Debt Problem, 25 Va. J. Intl. L. 281 (1985); and Pigott, The Historical Development of Syndicated Eurocurrency Loan Agreements, 10 Intl. Bus. L. 199 (1982).

B.   MACROREGULATION OF BANKING AND CAPITAL FLOWS

There is a special international legal structure dealing with the macroeconomic issues arising from portfolio and bank investment and from trade imbalances. This international monetary law helps assure that such capital flows—and economic restrictions to respond to them—distort trade as little as possible. Its key institution, the IMF, has also been focusing increased attention on ways to avoid loan defaults that might affect the international banking system.

1.   *Public Law of the International Monetary System*

An international monetary regime can be defined as a set of rules and institutions for the macroeconomic coordination of the various national economies—

for responding to the fact that the fiscal (government budget surplus or deficit) and monetary (interest-rate and monetary control operations) policies of different nations interact, and the policy designed to influence one nation's economy may end up having a cross-effect on other nations' economies. (These are the "Keynesian" issues discussed in Chapter I.)

The old pre-Depression gold standard system is probably the simplest example. At that time, it was assumed that a nation's currency had to be backed by gold. In many nations, paper currency was a transferrable right to obtain a certain quantity of gold or silver from the national central bank. And national law directed that the amount of currency in circulation bear a defined ratio to the amount of gold or silver in the central bank's coffers. International adjustment was then easy and automatic. Suppose a nation ran a balance of payments deficit because it imported more than it exported. It would then have to settle this deficit in gold. This would require it to reduce the amount of currency in circulation, thus decreasing domestic prices and making its goods more competitive internationally. Ideally, equilibrium would be restored.

There is a question as to whether the gold standard ever actually worked like this oversimplified description. And it was ended during the Depression, when nations arbitrarily devalued their currencies (in terms of gold) in order to make their exports more competitive and to thus export unemployment. Of more fundamental importance, political expectations changed—automatic adjustment processes became no longer politically acceptable and it became necessary to allow governments to intervene in their economies in accordance with Keynesian theories.

Hence, the Bretton Woods system, created at the end of World War II, attempted both to give governments greater freedom to intervene in their economies and to avoid competitive devaluations. The central concept was to fix currency rates vis-à-vis one another by international agreement. An institution was created, the International Monetary Fund (IMF), which would, by a weighted voting procedure, authorize changes in the agreed rates in the event of "fundamental disequilibrium." This approach was intended to complement the new GATT system. Ideally, if a nation began falling behind others in employment levels, it would respond by changing its currency value rather than by imposing trade restrictions. Hence free trade could be achieved while giving weaker economies a chance.

The obvious question was how currency values were to be maintained at a fixed relationship, even though governments might engage in inconsistent economic policies. The answer was through a duty of exchange market intervention. When its currency fell more than a defined percentage in comparison with others, a nation was obliged to buy its currency and sell the foreign currencies in order to maintain the desired relationship. And a nation whose currency rose above the margin was to sell that currency and buy others.

The practical limiting factor was the nation's store of foreign hard currency, a major component of its currency "reserves." A creditor nation could always print more of its own currency to sell to maintain the price relationship. But a debtor nation had to buy its currency and sell foreign currency. Its reserves of foreign currency, therefore, determined how long it could defend a defined price. The IMF system provided a number of ways to increase these reserves or "international liquidity." They all depended on the fact that dollars, say, were useful reserve assets when in U.K. hands, even though they were not in U.S. hands. Thus, a simple swap arrangement—mutual promises by the United States and the United Kingdom on demand to exchange so many billion dollars in returns for pounds or vice versa—could increase the effective foreign reserve assets of each.

Although swaps were widely used, the original and core method was a more formalized variant relying on the same logical principle. This was a "drawing"—the borrowing of foreign currency (in return for national currency) from a pool of currencies held by the IMF and deposited with that institution. When a nation joined, it contributed a certain amount of its currency, in proportion to an amount known as its "quota," that determined voting and borrowing rights. It could later, as it needed to, draw foreign currency from the pool supplied by other participants. It naturally had to repay the borrowing over several years, and it also had to satisfy the IMF that its economic policies would help it do so—the "conditionality" issue.

In a next step, the IMF created the Special Drawing Right (SDR), an even more abstract variant of the swap. SDRs are given a value defined in terms of a package of currencies and are allocated to the members of the IMF in proportion to their quotas. Each member is obliged to provide its own currency (up to a defined limit) in return for other nations' SDRs. Thus, looked at inversely, each SDR is a right to obtain a specified amount of any other nation's currency, and therefore a useful reserve asset. As a right to obtain currency, it is parallel to the old paper money right to obtain gold and thus comes close to an international currency—although the SDR still takes the mechanical form of a centralized book of accounts rather than that of distributed pieces of paper.

The Bretton Woods system collapsed in the early 1970s, in a process described in part in the *Yoshida* case, Chapter III *supra*. There were several reasons. One was the perceived need to change the relative value of the dollar as the United States ran a long-term balance of payments deficit, deriving in part from the Vietnam War. Under the technicalities of the system, the United States could not do this alone, for other currencies were defined in terms of the dollar. The second reason was a series of exchange crises—as a nation's currency began to fall, speculators could estimate how long the government would be able to support it. At some point, the "run on the bank" would begin. Everyone would seek to sell the currency, and the nation's central bank would expend billions to keep up the currency. Then the markets would close, and the IMF would authorize a new exchange rate. As the Eurodollar market grew along with international capital flows, these crises became more frequent and more severe.

The result was to give up the obligation to maintain fixed exchange rates and to go to "floating" ones. This deprived the IMF of its traditional raison d'etre—but the organization remained in existence to help nations maintain the exchange rates they desired for economic purposes, to help the developed nations coordinate economic policy, and to make loans to and provide economic supervision of debtor nations. These roles are described more fully in the following.

J. GOLD, FINANCIAL ASSISTANCE BY THE INTERNATIONAL MONETARY FUND: LAW AND PRACTICE

IMF Pamphlet Series No. 27, 2d Edition (1980)

GENERAL ASPECTS

ARTICLES OF AGREEMENT AND MEMBERSHIP

The International Monetary Fund is an intergovernmental organization in which, on October 1, 1984, there were 148 members. Membership is confined to states that control their external relations and are able and willing to perform the obligations imposed on members by the Articles of Agreement. The Articles were drafted at the Bretton Woods Conference held in July 1944. The treaty has been amended twice. . . .

Except as otherwise authorized by the Articles, the financial activities of the Fund are conducted between the Fund and a member through the medium of its treasury, central bank, stabilization fund, or other similar fiscal agency. The financial activities of the Fund are complex. The main activity is the Fund's financial assistance to a member in balance of payments difficulty by providing it with SDRs or the currencies of other members in support of an economic and financial program that is designed to overcome the difficulty. The Fund's financial, supervisory, and regulatory functions relate to the balance of payments. The Fund is concerned with other fields of economic activity, such as trade and development, but its jurisdiction to approve or disapprove measures stops at the borders of those fields. The Fund collaborates closely, however, with the organizations that have jurisdiction over these other activities.

In order that a member may use the Fund's resources, its economic and financial program must be consistent with the purposes of the Fund. A major purpose is the achievement of a multilateral system of payments and transfers for current international transactions in order to promote international trade and the benefits that flow from it. A multilateral system means the absence of exchange restrictions, multiple currency practices, and discriminatory currency arrangements. The idea is that, in international trade and in other current international transactions, residents and nonresidents should be as free to use currencies as they are to use a domestic currency within the domestic economy. . . .

RESOURCES OF THE FUND: SUBSCRIPTIONS . . .

The general resources, which will be referred to in the rest of this paper simply as resources, are derived mainly from subscriptions, loans, . . . and income. The subscriptions of members are the main source of the Fund's holdings in the first instance. Each member is assigned a quota expressed in SDRs, and its subscription is equal to its quota. In the past, 75 per cent of the normal original subscription of a member was payable in its currency and the rest was payable in gold. Under the Second Amendment, SDRs or the currencies of other members are substituted for the proportion formerly payable in gold, because, except in rare situations, gold is no longer used in obligatory payments to or by the Fund.

A member's quota is a fundamental datum in its relations with the Fund, governing or affecting, among other things, its voting power, the amount of SDRs it receives in allocations, and the amount of financial assistance it can obtain from the Fund. Both the absolute amount of a quota and its proportion of total quotas are important for members. This importance becomes painfully apparent when the adjustment of quotas is considered in the general reviews that must take place at intervals not longer than five years. The protracted and strenuous negotiations that take place on the adjustment of quotas can retard the necessary augmentation of the Fund's resources. An increase in quota gives rise to an obligation to pay an additional subscription equal to the increase. The further subscription is payable in proportions, prescribed by the Fund, in the member's own currency and in SDRs or the currencies of other members. The Fund's holdings of SDRs come from its receipt of them from members in its various financial activities. The Fund cannot allocate SDRs to itself on the occasion of an allocation to members or at any other time. . . .

RESOURCES OF THE FUND: BORROWING

The second main source of the Fund's holdings is loans. The extent to which the Fund may borrow is unlimited in the sense that the Fund has full freedom to decide whether and how much to borrow. The Fund has authority to agree with a member that it shall lend its currency if the Fund deems it appropriate to replenish its holdings of the currency because it is needed for financing the Fund's transactions. The Fund also has authority to borrow a member's currency from other sources inside or outside the member's territories. No qualification is placed on the sources from which these borrowings may be made. The authority is wide enough, therefore, for the Fund to borrow from private lenders, including commercial banks. If, however, the Fund wishes to borrow the currency of a member from some source other than the member itself, the

Fund must seek the concurrence of the member. The Articles insist on the necessity for concurrence in order to ensure that the Fund's entry into the capital market is not inconsistent with the member's management of its currency and does not interfere with the member's own ability to borrow. No member is required to lend to the Fund or to concur in loans of its currency to the Fund from other sources. . . .

EXCHANGE TRANSACTIONS

The Articles recognize that a member may make a purchase from the Fund under a stand-by or similar arrangement or without one of these arrangements, but in modern practice arrangements predominate except under certain special policies. A member may request a purchase if it has a need based on its balance of payments, or its reserve position (for example, uncomfortably low reserves), or unfavorable developments in its reserves (for example, an impending discharge of substantial indebtedness). The Fund may challenge a request for good cause, such as the absence of need, but the occasion does not arise because a member consults the Managing Director and the staff before submitting a request. A stand-by or similar arrangement makes this kind of consultation unnecessary before a purchase is initiated under the arrangement if the member is observing the terms of the arrangement.

When making a purchase, the member pays an equivalent amount in its own currency to the Fund. The transaction is never a loan according to legal analysis. The Articles rigorously avoid the language of loans and repayments and refer instead to purchases and repurchases. The closest analogy to the transaction of purchase and sale of currency between a member and the Fund is an exchange transaction in which a party buys foreign exchange from a commercial bank and pays for it with the domestic currency. The analogy is not exact. For example, the transaction with the Fund gives rise to an obligation resembling an obligation of reversal. The purchasing member must repurchase its own currency paid to the Fund in the transaction, but not necessarily with the same kinds of resources that it purchased. . . .

The Fund pays remuneration, on the basis of a formula, to members whose currencies have been used in its transactions. Originally, the formula was based on the simple fact of the net use of the ideal currency subscription of 75 per cent of quota, but the formula is now more sophisticated. The main source of revenue from which remuneration is paid is the periodic charges levied by the Fund on the holdings of currencies obtained from purchasing members in their transactions with the Fund.

STAND-BY AND EXTENDED ARRANGEMENTS

It has been seen that a member can request an immediate purchase of SDRs or currencies from the Fund without having received a stand-by or extended arrangement, or it can request an arrangement, which will give the member an assurance that it will be able to enter into transactions with the Fund should the need arise. The original concept of the stand-by arrangement placed more emphasis on its precautionary character, but in more recent years most members requesting an arrangement have had an immediate need for resources. Precautionary arrangements continue to be approved, and in some circumstances a member has no realistic expectation that it will need to use the Fund's resources, but the member wishes to have testimony given to the world of its creditworthiness. The Fund has been willing to approve symbolic stand-by arrangements for this purpose. . . .

A stand-by (or extended) arrangement is approved by the Fund after negotiations between a mission composed of officials of the Fund's staff, who act under the instructions of the Managing Director, and the member's representatives. The negotiations can be protracted, but need not be. From them, a "letter of intent" emerges, signed usually by the Minister of Finance or the Governor of the central bank, or by both, in which the intentions and policies of the member that constitute its program are set forth for the period of the arrangement. The Fund formulates the stand-by arrangement by reference to certain aspects of the letter of intent. The main purpose of this reference is to select those aspects of the program that are to be performance criteria and to ensure that the member will have access to the Fund's resources under the arrangement only if the performance criteria are being observed. The Managing Director submits the request and proposed stand-by arrangement to the Executive Board, with its recommendation for approval of the request, and memoranda prepared by the staff, and the Executive Board takes its decision. The Executive Board, it should be said, is composed of Executive Directors appointed or elected by members, and is the organ of the Fund that is in continuous session. A preoccupation of the Executive Board, the Managing Director, and the staff mission is that the program should be consistent with the "conditionality" that is appropriate to the member's circumstances.

The various intentions and policies of a member that make up its program may be drafted in more or less precise terms. Some of those that are precise will be made performance criteria that apply to purchases in the credit tranches beyond the first credit tranche [roughly, 25 percent of the member's quota]. Performance criteria are certain elements in the program that are formulated in arithmetic or other objective terms. Formulation in this way is insisted on in order to avoid undermining the assurance that a member requires in support of its program. If performance criteria were not objective, the member might conclude that the Fund could impede purchases under the stand-by arrangement by decisions motivated by subjective or discretionary considerations. Performance criteria also give the Fund the assurance that it has reasonable safeguards for the proper use of its resources, as is required by Article I(v). The practice of employing performance criteria developed because the Fund has a duty to see that a proper use is made of its resources, and a greater element of risk may be present when the assurance of future use is given. In fact, when the technique of the stand-by arrangement was being discussed, its legality was questioned for this reason. As a result, the earliest stand-by arrangements were for short periods. Performance criteria were introduced at a later stage of the Fund's practice. . . .

There is no single code of performance criteria for all cases. One performance criterion that is always used is a ceiling on the expansion of credit by the central bank or the banking system, supported in most cases by a ceiling on the expansion of bank credit to the government or the public sector. Balance of payments problems often arise from national overspending, so that it becomes necessary to ensure that aggregate demand for goods and services is brought into line with output. Ceilings on the expansion of domestic credit help to regulate aggregate demand and to enhance the effectiveness of financial policies, including the channeling of sufficient credit to meet the needs of the private sector. If the policies on credit could have detrimental effects on employment and growth, policies must be devised to encourage savings and investment as well as a proper direction of investment.

Almost all stand-by arrangements include performance criteria that deal with the avoidance of all restrictions on payments and transfers for current international transactions as well as restrictions on imports for balance of payments reasons. If existing restrictions have resulted in substantial arrears in payments for current international transactions, a schedule for the aggregate reduction of them may be established as a performance criterion. If external debt service is a present or prospective burden on the balance of payments of undue proportions, limits on the amount and maturity of new short- and medium-term debt may be made a performance criterion. If the exchange rate for the member's currency is not consistent with underlying economic conditions, a performance criterion may take the form of minimum levels of net foreign exchange reserves, the effect of which is to restrain the use of reserves in intervention in the exchange market to support the exchange rate. . . .

To promote the efficacy of performance criteria, a stand-by arrangement, if it does not fall within the exception mentioned in the next paragraph, provides for the phased availability of the amount covered by the arrangement. The Fund has no general rule for determining the installments but adapts the phasing to the member's circumstances, including the urgency of its need for resources. . . .

CONDITIONALITY

The fundamental and distinctive characteristic of the Fund's financial assistance is the Fund's doctrine of conditionality. Four strands are woven into it. First, to qualify for the use of the Fund's resources in order to deal with a balance of payments problem, a member must be prepared to pursue policies that are designed to overcome its problem. The policies are often referred to as policies of adjustment of the balance of payments or as a stabilization program. The objective of the program is a balance of payments position that can be sustained over a medium term such as five to eight years ahead. A member's willingness to undertake a program is not a concession to the Fund. Adjustment is inevitable for any member that does not have the means to neglect adjustment. The conditionality of the Fund helps a member to achieve adjustment with the financial, technical, and moral support of the Fund. Second, the policies must be consistent with the purposes of the Fund. For example, the policies should enable the member to avoid the introduction of restrictions on trade and payments for balance of payments purposes and if possible eliminate existing restrictions, because restrictions are likely to intensify and not correct the distortions that give rise to the need for adjustment, and are likely to be harmful to other members. Third, the policies must be designed to overcome the member's problem within a moderate ("temporary") period. Fourth, the policies must be likely to result in augmenting the member's monetary reserves so that it will be able to repurchase its currency from the Fund in accordance with the principle that use of the Fund's resources must be temporary in order that they can revolve for the benefit of all members.

Conditionality developed as a characteristic of the Fund's financial assistance without any reference to it in the Fund's original Articles. It became clear that the international monetary system needed an institution that could apply policies of conditionality without giving intolerable offense to its members. An effort to perform this function by another government would be resisted by a borrowing government as a trespass on its sovereignty. Private banks would seem to be even more officious if they made the attempt. Even regional organizations might find it embarrassing to call for truly corrective policies, because the action might appear inconsistent with the spirit of neighborliness. . . .

The purpose of conditionality is not to change the basic character or the organization of a member's economy. For example, the degree to which the economy is under government ownership or control is accepted as part of the framework within which a program of adjustment must be made to fit. Similarly, the social objectives or priorities of a member are accepted as beyond negotiation, subject to the proviso that the policies to promote them will permit the member to achieve a sustainable balance of payments position. In short, the Fund does not seek to modify the political or social policies of a member. The character of the Fund is determined by its technical tasks, the principle of universal membership, and the uniform treatment of all members. . . .

It is sometimes said that conditionality is progressively more severe as the amounts made available ascend through the upper credit tranches. This proposition is doubtful because conditionality always has the same objective, the conquest of a member's balance of payments difficulty. It could even be argued that in many instances conditionality is less severe when more resources are made available. It may be easier for a government to give effect to a program over a longer period. Stand-by or extended arrangements for the longer periods that have become a feature of the Fund's practice in recent years tend to be associated with substantial amounts in terms of quota. The apparent truism that more time means more ease is not always true, however, because a program for a longer period may require a perseverance that is politically difficult to maintain.

The word "harsh" is sometimes attached to particular operations involving conditionality. The inevitable determinant of the severity of a program, however it may be measured, is the intensity of a member's problem. Conditionality should be regarded as harsh only if it were to go beyond what was necessary to overcome a problem within the period that was reasonable in the circumstances, but this view does not mean that what is necessary in accordance with this criterion is always beyond controversy.

In discussing with a member a program that would meet the test of conditionality in the member's circumstances, the Fund does not insist that there is only one route by which adjustment can be reached. The purpose of the discussion is to elucidate the different policies that could be pursued to reach this objective and to leave it to the member to choose the policies it prefers.

Performance criteria must not be equated with conditionality, because some of the policies that the Fund recommends are not, or cannot be, given the form of performance criteria. Nevertheless, performance criteria are an important element in conditionality, and much of the debate on this topic centers on them.

Performance criteria normally involve macroeconomic or aggregate variables, such as the financing requirement of the government, or the volume of external borrowing, or credit expansion within the economy. The Fund avoids performance criteria formulated in terms of microeconomic variables, such as the prices of commodities or services, particular subsidies, or particular taxes, although the Fund is interested in the internal consistency of a program and the measures that a member plans to take to meet performance criteria. In special circumstances, the Fund is willing to treat quantities related to some of these economic elements as performance criteria.

Concentration on the broadest economic aggregates that suffice to achieve adjustment enables the Fund to observe its policy of avoiding involvement in the distribution of the burden of adjustment among the different sections of society. But conditionality does affect sections of society, particularly in their incomes, and it gives rise, therefore, to fervent public and professional debate. Criticisms that have been made of conditionality have been based on its compatibility with the current state of the world economy, or on the economic theories implicit in conditionality as applied by the Fund, or on other aspects of the Fund's practice.

Conditionality has been criticized as too strict in the upper credit tranches because major changes of policy are expected within too short a period, with consequential political difficulties. Other criticisms have been that conditionality is too standardized, is correlated too closely with the features of the market economies of developed countries, limits growth unduly because of the emphasis on restraining demand, is not predictable when applied to individual members, and is undertaken in return for an inadequate amount of resources.

Criticisms such as those that have been mentioned would be valid if justified. Mr. Witteveen, the former Managing Director of the Fund, and Mr. de Larosière, the present Managing Director, have analyzed and replied to many of them.[5] This is not the occasion to rehearse their replies or to examine the extent to which the criticisms may be justified, but some general comments may be useful. It will be observed that some of the criticisms, such as those involving standardization and unpredictability, go in opposite directions. For political reasons and because other sources of financing may be available in substantial amounts in these days, a member may defer an approach to the Fund, so that the Fund becomes in fact as well as in theory the lender of last resort. When that stage is reached the member's difficulties may have become so acute that only a more rigorous program than would have been necessary for adjustment at an earlier date will solve the member's difficulties. Cases of this kind foster the impression that the Fund's resources are used only when a desperate situation arises, and that conditionality is always burdensome. These impressions tend to deter an approach to the Fund when difficulty is impending or at an early stage of difficulty, with the result that it becomes even harder to dispel them.

The Fund has responded to the problems that would be created by too rapid an adjustment by supporting programs of longer duration than one year, and by providing in some policies for repurchase over a longer span of time than the three to five years of the credit tranche policy. A similar attitude on the part of the Fund was responsible for its practice of approving stand-by arrangements for successive periods of a year, but in some instances progress under these arrangements was punctuated with intervals of retrogression. In recent years, programs formulated for a longer period, supported by stand-by or extended arrangements, have appeared to give greater hope for success in some circumstances. This practice not only spreads the burden of adjustment over time, but also broadens the range of policies from which a member may choose and gives it greater flexibility in determining when to introduce measures. The stand-by arrangement for one year continues to be appropriate for situations in which the disequilibrium is moderate and can be substantially corrected within that period, and for situations in which something of a holding action is advisable until a broader program can be formulated. Conditionality is the subject of debate, and even controversy, not only because of its effects on the policies of members but also because the national and international economic environment is in constant change and produces new problems for which solutions are not readily apparent. Nevertheless, conditionality

---

[5] See "Fund's Conditional Assistance Promotes Adjustment Programs of Members, Witteveen States" (an address by H. Johannes Witteveen, Managing Director, delivered May 8, 1978 in London before the 1978 Euromarkets Conference on Financing in LDCs: The Role of Public and Private Institutions), IMF Survey, Vol. 7 (May 22, 1978), pp. 145-50; and "Developing Nations' Mounting Problems Demand Bold Action, de Larosière Says" (an address by J. de Larosière, Managing Director, delivered May 11, 1979 before the Fifth Session of the UN Conference on Trade and Development in Manila), IMF Survey, Vol. 8 (May 21, 1979), pp. 149-52.

is accepted in principle by most governments, although it is often resisted in the form of its proposed application to them. This attitude is reminiscent of the definition of idealism as a code of conduct for others. The reluctance of some governments to adopt programs of adjustment should not obscure the fact that the strategy of other governments is to pursue the policies they would wish to follow in any event by enlisting the endorsement of the Fund and by presenting it publicly as a demand.

Bibliographical Note

There are many sources on the IMF, but one of the best is A. Hooke, The International Monetary Fund (1982). The debate on conditionality has also generated an extensive literature. For examples, *see* T. Killich (ed.), The Quest for Economic Stabilization: The IMF and the Third World (1984), and The IMF and Stabilization; Developing Country Experience (1984); Guitián, Fund Conditionality, Evaluation of Principles and Practices (IMF Pamphlet No. 38, 1981); Johnson & Salop, Distributional Aspects of Stabilization Programs in Developing Countries, 27 IMF Staff Papers 1 (1980); Frental & O'Donnell, The "Stabilization Programs" of the International Monetary Fund and their Internal Impacts, R. Fagen (ed.), Capitalism and the State in U.S.-Latin American Relations (1979).

QUESTIONS

1. How would you feel about conditionality as a political official in a borrowing nation? As a banker lending to that nation?
2. How successful do you expect IMF conditionality programs to be in ensuring that countries are able to repay loans? In the long run, isn't the ability of the countries to repay the loans dependent on their success in developing their economies?
3. In its efforts to encourage a borrowing nation to improve its balance of payments, what are the differences—for the nation, for economic efficiency, and for the rest of the world—between encouraging the nation to work more to cut imports or encouraging it to work more to increase exports? Note that the IMF has generally chosen the former approach on the assumption that it will operate more quickly.
4. To what extent does the IMF function in effect as a cartel of private banks, imposing conditions on Third World nations that the banks themselves desire, but are unable to enforce? In considering this, recognize that the IMF has regularly been involved in debt reschedulings since the mid-1970s, when international commercial banks sought to impose conditionality on Peru and failed.

5. The IMF's ability to adapt to changing circumstances and create new roles to fill was mentioned in the materials. Recently, the IMF has taken on the role of encouraging private banks, particularly the smaller regional ones, to continue lending to seriously indebted countries. This advocacy usually occurs after the IMF has reached an agreement with the debtor nation. *See* The IMF and Central Banks Flex Their Muscles, Euromoney, January, 1983, at 36.

2.   *Private Law Implications*

Two important private law issues derive directly from the international monetary system. The first is the "gold clause," the approach a private creditor uses to protect itself from fluctuating exchange rates. The debt is denominated not as a duty to pay so many dollars but as a duty to pay the current dollar equivalent of so much gold, or so many Swiss francs, or the creditor's choice between several sums specified in different currencies, or even so many SDRs. Courts will almost always respect a relevant currency choice for an actual international transaction, such as the use of dollars or of Swiss francs for a U.S. sale to Switzerland. However, this is not always the case when the transaction is domestic—governments argue that they need to have the right to overrule these clauses in order to make their domestic economic regulation effective. The U.S. Supreme Court, for example, thus upheld the New Deal regulations making gold clauses (in a domestic context) unenforceable, *see* Norman v. Baltimore & Ohio R.R. Co., 294 U.S. 240 (1935). This position—which was also taken in many other nations—is likewise being globally reversed (by statute in the United States) in the new era of floating exchange rates.[1]

The second private law issue is that of "exchange restrictions." In order to avoid modifying their currency values and in order to protect limited stores of hard currency, nations often apply such exchange controls. On the debtor nation side, the most common one is to centralize all exchange transactions; a government agency accumulates all the hard currency and rations it out for the purposes it finds most important. Other options include multiple exchange rates. In the early 1970s, France, for example, was running a balance of payments deficit at a time it wanted to maintain a high interest rate. The high interest rate would attract investment funds, bidding up the exchange rate and hurting the nation's trade balance. France, therefore, separated the two markets through careful regulations designed to allow the "financial [investment] franc" to be bid up while the "commercial [trade] franc" floated down to help clear the balance of trade market. And in a third variation, the United States imposed direct regulations in the 1960s. Creditor nations use different systems.

---

[1] E.g., P.L. 95-147 (Secretary of Treasury authorization), October 28, 1977. Note, however, that in Trans World Airlines v. Franklin Mint, 104 S. Ct. 1776 (1984), the Court regarded the air carrier's Warsaw Convention liability "limit" for lost cargo of 250 gold French francs per kilogram as not rising with the freed post-1978 unofficial price of gold.

German and Swiss laws, for example, have frequently required investors or banks to pay a special tax on foreign deposits or to make special reserve deposits against these deposits. The result is that the banks offer a lower interest rate on such accounts, which are thereby discouraged.

These rules can create great difficulties for an investor who wants to repatriate its income or its principal. The IMF generally dislikes such rules, but does have a procedure for approving them (a nearly automatic procedure requiring affirmative action for a veto). And when the rules are approved, other nations are not to assist in evading them, as explained in the following case.

BANCO FRANCES E BRASILEIRO, S. A. v. DOE

36 N.Y.2d 592 (1975)

JASEN, J.

The principal question before us is whether a private foreign bank may avail itself of the New York courts in an action for damages for tortious fraud and deceit and for rescission of currency exchange contracts arising from alleged violations of foreign currency exchange regulations.

Plaintiff, a private Brazilian bank, brings this action for fraud and deceit, and conspiracy to defraud and deceive, against 20 "John Doe" defendants whose identities are unknown to it. The gravamen of plaintiff's complaint is that these defendants over a period of approximately six weeks participated, in violation of Brazilian currency regulations, in the submission of false applications to Banco-Brasileiro of Brazil, which the plaintiff relied upon, resulting in the improper exchange by the bank of Brazilian cruzeiros into travelers checks in United States dollars totaling $1,024,000. . . .

It is an old chestnut in conflict of laws that one State does not enforce the revenue laws of another. By way of rationale, an analogy is drawn to foreign penal laws, extrastate enforcement of which is denied (*see* The Antelope, 10 Wheat. [23 U.S.] 66, 123, 6 L. Ed. 268) to deny recognition to foreign tax assessments, judicially expanded also to include foreign currency exchange regulations. The analogy, reformulated in the Restatement (Restatement, Conflict of Laws, §§610, 611), but interestingly withdrawn in the Restatement Second (§89), traces from Lord Mansfield's now famous dictum in an international smuggling case that "no country ever takes notice of the *revenue* laws of another." (Holman v. Johnson, 1 Cowp. 341, 343.) But the modern analog of the revenue law rule is justifiable neither precedentially nor analytically.

Holman v. Johnson was an action for goods had and received. The plaintiffs, Frenchmen, sold and delivered tea to the defendant in France. The tea was then smuggled into England by the defendant in violation of the revenue laws. In an action for the price, Lord Mansfield's holding was simply to the effect that a French court would not invalidate a sale of tea by a Frenchman in France made in violation of an English prohibition. The decision was concerned largely with the impact of foreign revenue laws on international commerce, but the quoted dictum became the basis in this country for denying foreign tax authorities the right to collect taxes assessed by them. But certainly that case and earlier (e.g., Boucher v. Lawson, 95 Eng. Rep. 53) and later (e.g., Planché v. Fletcher, 1 Dougl. 250) dicta in other cases denying extraterritorial effect to forum defenses, should not have been relied upon to deny forum effect to foreign claims.

Nor is the rule analytically justifiable. Indeed, much doubt has been expressed that the reasons advanced for the rule, if ever valid, remain so. (E.g., Leflar, Extrastate Enforcement of Penal and Governmental Claims, 46 Harv. L. Rev. 193.) But inroads have been made. In interstate cases, for example, where the rule made least sense, administrative tax assessments are increasingly equated with tax judgments . . . and on that basis generally afforded full faith and credit. . . . Some do consider that, in light of the economic interdependence of all nations, the courts should be receptive even to extranational tax and revenue claims as well, especially where there is a treaty involved, but also without such constraint. (Scoles, Interstate and International Distinctions in Conflict of Laws in the United States, 54 Cal. L. Rev. 1599, 1607-1608.) Indeed, there may be strong policy reasons for specially favoring a foreign revenue regulation, using that term in its broadest sense, especially one involving currency exchange or control.

In the international sphere, cases involving foreign currency exchange regulations represent perhaps the most important aspect of the revenue law rule. This assumes, of course, that a currency exchange regulation, normally not designed for revenue purposes as such, but rather, to prevent the loss of foreign currency which in turn increases the country's foreign exchange reserves, is properly characterizable as a revenue law. (*Contra,* Kahler v. Midland Bank [1950] A.C. 24; Dicey, Conflict of Laws [7th ed.], p. 920.) At any rate, it is for the forum to characterize such a regulation and in this State the question would appear to have been resolved for the present at least by Banco do Brasil v. Israel Commodity Co., 12 N.Y.2d 371, 377, 239 N.Y.S.2d 872, 875, 190 N.E.2d 235, 237, *cert. den.* 376 U.S. 906, 84 S. Ct. 657, 11 L. Ed. 2d 605, . . .

But even assuming the continuing validity of the revenue law rule and the correctness of the characterization of a currency exchange regulation thereunder, United States membership in the International Monetary Fund (IMF) makes inappropriate the refusal to entertain the instant claim. The view that nothing in article VIII (§2, subd. [b]) of the Bretton Woods Agreements Act (60 U.S. Stat. 1401, 1411)* requires an American court to provide a forum for a private tort remedy, while correct in a literal sense (*see* Banco do Brasil v.

---

*There it is provided in relevant part: "Exchange contracts which involve the currency of any member and which are contrary to the exchange control regulations of that member maintained or imposed consistently with this Agreement shall be unenforceable in the territories of any member. In addition, members may, by mutual accord, cooperate in measures for the purpose of making the exchange control regulations of either member more effective."

Israel Commodity Co., *supra,* p. 376, 239 N.Y.S.2d p. 874, 190 N.E.2d p. 236), does not represent the only perspective. Nothing in the agreement prevents an IMF member from aiding, directly or indirectly, a fellow member in making its exchange regulations effective. And United States membership in the IMF makes it impossible to conclude that the currency control laws of other member States are offensive to this State's public policy so as to preclude suit in tort by a private party. Indeed, conduct reasonably necessary to protect the foreign exchange resources of a country does not offend against international law. (Restatement, 2d, Foreign Relations Law of the United States, §198, comment *b.*) Moreover, where a true governmental interest of a friendly nation is involved—and foreign currency reserves are of vital importance to a country plagued by balance of payments difficulties—the national policy of co-operation with Bretton Woods signatories is furthered by providing a State forum for suit.

The *Banco do Brasil* case relied upon by the Appellate Division is quite distinguishable. There the Government of Brazil, through Banco do Brasil, a government bank, sought redress for violations of its currency exchange regulations incident to a fraudulent coffee export transaction. Here, the plaintiff is a private bank seeking rescission of the fraudulent currency exchange transactions and damages. And no case has come to our attention where a private tort remedy arising from foreign currency regulations has been denied by the forum as an application of the revenue law rule and we decline so to extend the *Banco do Brasil* rationale. Thus, in the instant case we find no basis for reliance upon the revenue law rule to deny a forum for suit. Moreover, where the parties are private, the "jealous sovereign" rationale is inapposite (*cf.* Loucks v. Standard Oil Co., 224 N.Y. 99, 102-103, 120 N.E. 198, 199 [Cardozo, J.]) even as it might seem inapposite in the *Banco do Brasil* situation where the sovereign itself, or its instrumentality, asks redress and damages in a foreign forum for violation of the sovereign's currency laws. (*But cf.* Moore v. Mitchell, 2 Cir., 30 F.2d 600, 603 [L. Hand, J., concurring].)

Perutz v. Bohemian Discount Bank in Liquidation, 304 N.Y. 533, 110 N.E.2d 6, is consistent with an expansive application of the IMF agreement to which we here ascribe (*cf.* Kolovrat v. Oregon, 366 U.S. 187, 196-198, 81 S. Ct. 922, 6 L. Ed. 2d 218), although there it is true defensive use of foreign currency exchange regulation was made and upheld by this court. But interestingly, in *Perutz,* in contrast to the instant case, political relations at the time were not conducive to comity which nevertheless was extended. . . .

Finally, subsequent to the commencement of this action, a penalty was levied by the Central Bank of Brazil, and paid by the plaintiff, on account of the alleged fraudulent currency exchange transactions. Therefore, our decision today is without prejudice to a proper application by plaintiff to Special Term to allege by supplemental pleading such sum as an element of special damages on the third cause of action. (C.P.L.R. 3025, subd. [b]; *cf.* Morrison v. National Broadcasting Co., 19 N.Y.2d 453, 280 N.Y.S.2d 641, 227 N.E.2d 572.)

Accordingly, the order of the Appellate Division should be modified in accordance with the views here expressed and the action remitted to the Supreme Court, New York County.

WACHTLER, J. (dissenting). . . .

I believe that the relief sought here, albeit indirectly through plaintiff bank, is an aspect of the Brazilian government's sovereign management of the economy of its own country. This is not a matter involving the resolution of private rights only as those rights are defined under the laws of a foreign State. Were that so our courts would not withhold judicial sanction even if the definition of such private rights were somewhat different from our own, "unless some sound reason of public policy makes it unwise for us to lend our aid" (Loucks v. Standard Oil Co., 224 N.Y. 99, 110, 120 N.E. 198, 201).

There is no allegation in this complaint that defendants intended to or succeeded in defrauding plaintiff of foreign currency exchange in the private rights sense. On the contrary, from all that appears, defendants obtained no more United States dollars in consequence of their alleged fraud than they would have been entitled to receive at the then currently effective exchange rate for the Brazilian cruzeiros which they exchanged with plaintiff bank. The gravamen rather is that the fraud and deceit practiced by the defendants induced plaintiff bank to violate Brazilian currency exchange regulations, thereby exposing that bank to consequent penalties which would be imposed by the Brazilian Government.

It has long been recognized that the courts of one jurisdiction will not enforce the tax laws, penal laws, or statutory penalties and forfeitures of another jurisdiction. "The rule that the courts of no country execute the penal laws of another applies, not only to prosecutions and sentences for crimes and misdemeanors, but to all suits in favor of the state for the recovery of pecuniary penalties for any violation of statutes for the protection of its revenue, or other municipal laws." (Wisconsin v. Pelican Ins. Co., 127 U.S. 265, 290, 8 S. Ct. 1370, 1374, 32 L. Ed. 239; . . .) Under the principle of territorial supremacy, fundamental to the community of nations, courts refuse to enforce any claim which in their view is a manifestation of a foreign State's sovereign authority (Dicey & Morris, Conflict of Laws [8th ed.], p. 160; cf. Judge Learned Hand's concurring opinion in Moore v. Mitchell, 2 Cir., 30 F.2d 600). The proper question is whether in the particular instance the claim sought to be enforced is a manifestation of such sovereign authority.

In previous cases our court held that governmental foreign exchange regulation may present an aspect of the exercise of sovereign power by a foreign State to implement its national fiscal policy. Thus, in Banco do Brasil v. Israel Commodity Co. (*supra*), we decided that our courts were not open to enforce a Brazilian foreign currency exchange regulation. Although the regulation in that case was characterized as a revenue measure, the essence of the matter was that we declined to enforce what we considered to be an exercise of Brazil's sovereign power. Whether a regulation denominated "currency exchange regulation" has or does not have a revenue-producing effect, it must be presumed to have been adopted to accomplish fiscal regulation and ultimate economic objectives significantly similar to, if not identical with, the objectives which underlie what would be characterized as revenue measures—namely, governmental management of its economy by a foreign country. Accordingly, the result is not determined by the threshold appearance of the particular law sought to be enforced or whether such law be denominated by the foreign government as a penal law or a revenue law or otherwise. The bottom line is that the courts of one country will not enforce the laws adopted by another country in the exercise of its sovereign capacity for the purpose of fiscal regulation and management.

Although our earlier decisions in Perutz v. Bohemian Discount Bank in Liquidation, 304 N.Y. 533, 110 N.E.2d 6, and Industrial Export & Import Corp. v. Hongkong & Shanghai Banking Corp., 302 N.Y. 342, 98 N.E.2d 466, may appear to be to the contrary, a studied analysis dispels this apparent inconsistency. These cases merely refine the traditional conflict-of-laws rule by holding that the provisions of any international agreement to which the United States is a party supplement, and to that extent, supersede the traditional rule. For instance, the Bretton Woods Agreements Act (U.S. Code, tit. 22, §286), authorizes United States membership in the International Monetary Fund (60 U.S. Stat. 1401; 2 U.S. Treaty Developments, Dec. 27, 1945, T.I. A.S. 1501). Another example of such a treaty is article VIII (§2, subd. [b]) of the International Monetary Fund Agreement (60 U.S. Stat. 1411) making exchange contracts which are contrary to the exchange control regulations of a member (Brazil is a member) unenforceable in the territory of another member (United States). So in *Perutz* (*supra*), relying on the provisions of the Bretton Woods Agreements Act we refused to enforce a private agreement contrary to Czechoslovakian exchange control regulations. Similarly, in *Industrial Export & Import Corp.* (*supra*), we refused to enforce a private contract contrary to the currency regulations of China on the basis of a separate agreement between the United States and China. Thus, by treaty provision what would otherwise have been the applicable rule of judicial nonrecognition of sovereign acts of a foreign State may be modified in the area of currency exchange control to require courts in the member States (including courts in the United States) to recognize foreign currency regulation as a *defense*.

Nothing in the Bretton Woods Agreements Act or in any other agreement between the United States and Brazil of which we are aware, however, mandates a complete abrogation of the normal conflicts rule or requires our courts *affirmatively* to enforce foreign currency regulation, as we are invited to do in the present case. This distinction was expressly recognized and held to be dispositive in *Banco do Brasil* (*supra*), in which we said (12 N.Y.2d p. 376, 239 N.Y.S.2d p. 874, 190 N.E.2d p. 237): "An obligation to withhold judicial assistance to secure the benefits of such contracts [i.e., those violative of the foreign currency control regulation] does not imply an obligation to impose tort penalties on those who have fully executed them." (See Dicey & Morris, Conflict of Laws [8th ed.], *op. cit.*, p. 161, n. 19; pp. 898-900.)

The appellant seeks to distinguish our decision in *Banco do Brasil* on the ground that the plaintiff in that case was recognized as an instrumentality of the Brazilian Government. I find this unpersuasive. As Judge Cardozo noted in the *Loucks* case (*supra*), a statute will be deemed to reflect the Sovereign's interest if it "awards a penalty to the state, or to a public officer in its behalf, or to a member of the public, suing in the interest of the whole community to redress a public wrong . . . The purpose must be, not reparation to one aggrieved, but vindication of the public justice." (Loucks v. Standard Oil Co., *supra*, 224 N.Y. pp. 102-103, 120 N.E. p. 198; cf. Huntington v. Attrill, *supra*, 146 U.S. pp. 673, 681-682, 13 S. Ct. 224). Whenever vindication of the public interest is sought at the instance of a third person, as here by plaintiff bank, of necessity such third party must show "aggrievement" or no cause of action will lie. But any such formulation is incomplete.

The core of the issue here is enforcement of a Brazilian currency exchange regulation. The only "reparation" sought by this plaintiff is for damages sustained in consequence of violation of that regulation—penalties to be imposed on it by the Brazilian Government plus associated injury to its business and reputation in consequence of such violation. Damages which are wholly attributable to violation of such a regulation, although alleged to have been occasioned by defendants' fraud, do not convert the action to one solely for private reparation. The ultimate economic reality, of granting relief to the plaintiff bank, would be the imposition on defendants of sanctions for violation of currency exchange control.

I recognize that this case is not an instance of recourse sought by a foreign country in our courts for the direct enforcement of its foreign currency exchange regulations, as would be the case were the Brazilian Government seeking here to recover penalties from either Banco-Brasileiro or from the defendants. The rights of private parties will be significantly affected; it is alleged that plaintiff bank has suffered and will suffer detriment in its private capacity in consequence of the fraud and deceit of defendants. The resolution of the issue posed by the motion to dismiss does not depend on the incidental, inescapable fact that private rights have already been, and would be affected by the judicial relief sought. Rather, the determinative factor is that the primary objective and the ultimate practical effect of the relief sought would be the enforcement of the currency regulation system of a foreign country. Our courts are not open for the accomplishment of that end, and that it may be sought through private intermediaries does not change the result. It matters not whether enforcement is sought directly or indirectly (Dicey & Morris, Conflict of Laws [8th ed.], *op. cit.*, pp. 160-161).

I consider the plaintiff's complaint as an attempt to utilize the judicial machinery of our courts to enforce the exercise of the sovereign power by the Government of Brazil. I believe that our courts, under traditional and established principle, are not available for this purpose.

The majority, however, argues that the time may have come for a change in what historically has been the applicable rule. I recognize that strong arguments can be mounted for a change in view of the increased frequency and importance of international commerce and the significantly different perspective in today's world in which one nation views another nation and its interests. In my opinion, however, the responsibility for any change lies with our Federal Government rather than with the highest court of any single State. Change, if at all, in my view, would better come at the hands of the State Department and the Congress, through the negotiation of international agreement or otherwise in the discharge of the constitutional responsibility of the Federal Government "to regulate commerce with foreign nations" (cf. Bretton Woods Agreements Act). A fitting sense of judicial restraint would dictate that the courts of no single State should enunciate a change, however large that State's relative proportion of foreign commerce may be, particularly since the authoritative effect thereof would necessarily be confined to the borders of that State.

Accordingly, I believe the order of the Appellate Division should be affirmed.

The *Banco Frances* case, applying the IMF treaty, shows a principle suitable to exchange control restrictions. These restrictions do not necessarily prohibit all payment; it is understandable for the sake of an orderly international monetary system that they not be undercut by foreign judicial action. Another equally intelligible principle evolved and was recently restated in the following case, *Vishipco*. This principle holds that a bank with international branches should not, in general, be able to resist liability to a depositor who invested in a branch that was since closed.

As this body of law evolved, it evaluated the impact of the foreign government's policy in expropriation or act of state terms, typically relying heavily on whether a conceptual "situs" or location of the debt was in the foreign nation. In *Vishipco* as in Garcia v. Chase Manhattan Bank, 735 F.2d (2d. Cir. 1984), the situs was found to be no longer in the foreign nation; for an example in which the situs was in the foreign nation and the bank did not have to pay, *see* Perez v. Chase Manhattan Bank, 61 N.Y.2d 460, 463 N.E.2d 5 (1984).

Perhaps without realizing it, the courts had stated two inconsistent principles for the situation when the situs is no longer foreign. Suppose the foreign government enacts an exchange control rule that freezes deposits in local branches of foreign banks—the *Banco Frances* principle calls on foreign courts to honor that rule; the *Vishipco* rule calls on them to dishonor it. Yet, this is precisely the situation posed in some of the emergency regulations issued in response to the debt crisis. And the situation of a nation refusing to honor its debts poses much the same policy issue. *Weston*, the case after *Vishipco*, shows the difficulty the courts have with the conflict. For another example *see* Libra Bank v. Banco Nacional de Costa Rica, 570 F. Supp. 870 (S.D.N.Y. 1983).

VISHIPCO LINE v. CHASE MANHATTAN BANK

660 F.2d 854 (2d Cir. 1981), *cert. denied*, 459 U.S. 976 (1982)

MANSFIELD, J.

Plaintiffs appeal from a judgment of the United States District Court for the Southern District of New York entered after a non-jury trial by Judge Robert L. Carter on December 5, 1980, dismissing their claims against Chase Manhattan Bank, N.A. ("Chase"), for breach of contract. The ten corporate plaintiffs—Vishipco Line, Ha Nam Cong Ty, Dai Nam Hang Hai C.T., Rang Dong Hang Hai C.T., Mekong Ship Co. Sarl, Vishipco Sarl, Thai Binh C.T., VN Tau Bien C.T., Van An Hang Hai C.T., and Cong Ty U Tau Sao Mai—are Vietnamese corporations which maintained piastre demand deposit accounts at Chase's Saigon branch in 1975. Invoking diversity jurisdiction, they claim that Chase breached its deposit contracts with them when it closed the doors of its Saigon branch on April 24, 1975, to escape from the Communist insurgents and subsequently refused to make payment in New York of the amount owed. The individual plaintiff—Ms. Nguyen Thi Cham—is a Vietnamese citizen who purchased a six-month two hundred million piastre certificate of deposit ("CD") from Chase's Saigon branch on November 27, 1974, and claims that Chase is in breach for refusing to cash the CD in dollars in New York.

We reverse. Chase was clearly obligated to pay plaintiffs the amounts it owed them. None of the affirmative defenses raised by Chase to its conceded obligations to plaintiffs can be sustained. Under Rule 44.1, plaintiffs' failure to introduce evidence of their right to recovery under Vietnamese law governing deposit obligations is not a ground for dismissal of their claims. The evidence was sufficient to give Tran Dinh Truong standing to represent the corporate plaintiffs in this lawsuit. The record does not support Chase's claim that the new Vietnamese government became the successor in interest to the corporate plaintiffs or that the individual plaintiff Ms. Nguyen Thi Cham is disqualified from bringing her action because the funds used to buy her CD may not have been her own. Chase's defenses of impossibility and *force majeure* fail because it remained liable to discharge obligations incurred through its branch, which were never assumed by the new Vietnamese government. The present worthlessness of the South Vietnamese piastre is no barrier to recovery. Under New York law which governs, the dollar value of Chase's obligation to the corporate plaintiffs must be determined as of the date when it closed its branch without giving them the opportunity to withdraw sums owed them rather than the date of judgment. The individual plaintiff, Ms. Cham, is entitled to recover the value in dollars of her CD on its due date.

From 1966 until April 24, 1975, Chase operated a branch office in Saigon. Among its depositors were the ten corporate plaintiffs, which were principally engaged at that time in providing shipping services to the U.S. Government in Southeast Asia, and the individual plaintiff, who owned a 200 million piastre

CD issued by Chase's Saigon branch. Chase's operations in Saigon came to an end at noon on April 24, 1975, after Chase officials in New York determined that Saigon would soon fall to the Communists. After closing the branch without any prior notice to depositors, local Chase officials balanced the day's books, shut the vaults and the building itself, and delivered keys and financial records needed to operate the branch to personnel at the French Embassy in Saigon. Saigon fell on April 30th, and on May 1st the new government issued a communique which read as follows:

> All public offices, public organs, barracks, industrial, agricultural and commercial establishments, banks, communication and transport, cultural, educational and health establishments, warehouses, and so forth—together with documents, files, property and technical means of U.S. imperialism and the Saigon administration—will be confiscated and, from now on, managed by the revolutionary administration.

Shortly thereafter, the French embassy turned over records from the Chase branch to the new government. . . .

[Discussion of proof of foreign law, capacity, and standing omitted.]

Chase next argues that the Vietnamese decree confiscating the assets which maritime corporations such as the corporate plaintiffs had left behind had the effect of seizing the piastre deposits at issue in this case. As a result, according to Chase, the corporate plaintiffs may not sue to recover the deposits because they no longer own them, and the act of state doctrine bars any challenge to the validity of the governmental seizure. We disagree. There is no evidence that plaintiffs' existence as corporate entities was terminated. Moreover, it is only by way of a strained reading of the Vietnamese confiscation announcement that one can even argue that choses in action were meant to be included. The plain meaning of the statement that "the Saigon-Gia Dinh Management Committee quickly took over the management of all maritime transportation *facilities* abandoned by their owners (emphasis supplied)" is that the seizures involved physical assets only and did not reach whatever claim the corporate plaintiffs might have on their departure for payment of the amounts owed to them by Chase.

More importantly, however, upon Chase's departure from Vietnam the deposits no longer had their situs in Vietnam at the time of the confiscation decree. As we have said in the past, "[f]or purposes of the act of state doctrine, a debt is not 'located' within a foreign state unless that state has the power to enforce or collect it." Menendez v. Saks and Co., 485 F.2d 1355, 1364 (2d Cir. 1973), *rev'd on other grounds sub nom.* Alfred Dunhill of London, Inc. v. Republic of Cuba, 425 U.S. 682, 96 S. Ct. 2201, 48 L. Ed. 2d 815 (1976). The rule announced in Harris v. Balk, 198 U.S. 215, 25 S. Ct. 625, 49 L. Ed. 1023 (1905), continues to be valid on this point: the power to enforce payment of a debt depends on jurisdiction over the debtor. Since Chase had abandoned its Saigon branch at the time of the Vietnamese decree, and since it had no separate corporate identity in Vietnam which would remain in existence after its departure, the Vietnamese decree could not have had any effect on its debt to the corporate plaintiffs. As one qualified commentator has observed:

> The situs of a bank's debt on a deposit is considered to be at the branch where the deposit is carried, but if the branch is closed, . . . the depositor has a claim against the home office; thus, the situs of the debt represented by the deposit would spring back and cling to the home office. If the situs of the debt ceased to be within the territorial jurisdiction of [the confiscating state] from the time the branch was closed, then at the time the confiscatory decree was promulgated, [the confiscating state would] no longer [have] sufficient jurisdiction over it to affect it. . . . [U]nder the act of state doctrine, the courts of the United States are not bound to give effect to foreign acts of state as to property outside the acting state's territorial jurisdiction. Heininger, Liability of U.S. Banks for Deposits Placed in Their Foreign Branches, 11 Law & Pol. Intl. Bus. 903, 975 (1979) (footnotes omitted) ("Heininger").

These principles have been recognized in New York. *See* Manas y Pineiro v. Chase Manhattan Bank, N.A., 106 Misc. 2d 660, 434 N.Y.S.2d 868 (Sup. Ct. N.Y. Cty. 1980), where the court held that for the purpose of the act of state doctrine the situs of a debt depends on whether the parties and the *res* were in the foreign country at the time of confiscation. Since in our case Chase's branch in Saigon was neither open nor operating at the time of the confiscation and had in fact been abandoned prior to that time, the Vietnamese decree was ineffective as against Chase's debt to the plaintiffs.[4] . . .

Chase next argues that under Vietnamese law its failure to repay plaintiffs' deposits in the period prior to May 1, 1975, was not a breach of its deposit contract, because the conditions prevailing in Saigon at the time rendered payment impossible. In support of this argument, Chase cites various sections of the South Vietnamese Civil Code which excuse performance under various extenuating circumstances, as well as the provisions included in the deposit contracts used by the Saigon branch which purported to discharge the bank's responsibility for losses to depositors resulting from a variety of unexpected and uncontrollable sources.

This argument must be rejected for the reasons that impossibility of performance in Vietnam did not relieve Chase of its obligation to perform elsewhere. By operating in Saigon through a branch rather than through a separate corporate entity, Chase accepted the risk that it would be liable elsewhere for obligations incurred by its branch. As the official referee in the *Sokoloff* case (Harrison Tweed, of the Milbank Tweed firm) summarized the law:

> [W]hen considered with relation to the parent bank, [foreign branches] are not independent agencies; they are, what their name imports, merely branches, and

---

[4]Neither *Manas* nor *Menendez* were cited to this Court by counsel despite the fact that Chase's counsel here and in *Manas* were the same.

are subject to the supervision and control of the parent bank, and are instrumentalities whereby the parent bank carries on its business. . . . *Ultimate liability for a debt of a branch would rest upon the parent bank.* Sokoloff v. National City Bank, 130 Misc. 66, 73, 224 N.Y.S. 102, 114 (Sup. Ct. N.Y. Cty. 1927) (emphasis added).

U.S. banks, by operating abroad through branches rather than through subsidiaries, reassure foreign depositors that their deposits will be safer with them than they would be in a locally incorporated bank. Heininger, *supra,* at 911-12. Indeed, the national policy in South Vietnam, where foreign banks were permitted to operate only through branches, was to enable those depositing in foreign branches to gain more protection than they would have received had their money been deposited in locally incorporated subsidiaries of foreign banks. Chase's defenses of impossibility and *force majeure* might have succeeded if the Saigon branch had been locally incorporated or (more problematically) if the deposit contract had included an explicit waiver on the part of the depositor of any right to proceed against the home office. But absent such circumstances the Saigon branch's admitted inability to perform did not relieve the Chase of liability on its debts in Saigon, since the conditions in Saigon were no bar to performance in New York or at other points outside of Vietnam. Nor has Chase shown that the Vietnamese government took steps to assume or cancel its branch liabilities. The May 1st decree nationalizing the Vietnamese banking industry only provided that "[a]ll . . . banks . . . will be confiscated and from now on managed by the revolutionary administration." In addition, during discovery Chase, in response to the following interrogatory:

"Interrogatory 4. When the assets were seized did the Government of Vietnam agree to pay the depositors at the Saigon Branch?"
replied
"Chase lacks the knowledge necessary to answer this interrogatory."

The evidence therefore can only be read as showing that the Vietnamese government confiscated the assets abandoned by Chase in Saigon, but did not thereby affect Chase's liabilities to its depositors. Under these circumstances, Justice (then Judge) Cardozo's opinion in *Sokoloff* fifty years ago applies:

> The defendant's liability was unaffected by the attempt to terminate its existence and the seizure of its assets. . . . Plaintiff did not pay his money to the defendant, and become the owner of this chose in action, upon the security of the Russian assets. He paid his money to a corporation organized under our laws upon the security of all its assets, here as well as elsewhere. Everything in Russia might have been destroyed by fire or flood, by war or revolution, and still the defendant would have remained bound by its engagement. Sokoloff v. National City Bank, 239 N.Y. 158, 167, 145 N.E. 917 (1924).

As one commentator has summarized the law:

> The defenses of frustration and impossibility were . . . rejected at an early stage in the *Sokoloff* proceedings, and do not appear to have been successfully raised in

subsequent cases involving foreign branches of U.S. banks. Rather, the well-established path from branch to home office has been followed, even if the branch has been closed, to establish an alternative means for performance. Heininger, *supra,* at 1003-04.

A bank which accepts deposits at a foreign branch becomes a debtor, not a bailee, with respect to its depositors. In the event that unsettled local conditions require it to cease operations, it should inform its depositors of the date when its branch will close and give them the opportunity to withdraw their deposits or, if conditions prevent such steps, enable them to obtain payment at an alternative location. *See, e.g.,* Sokoloff v. National City Bank, *supra,* 130 Misc. at 71, 224 N.Y.S. at 112; Heininger, *supra,* at 1009-10. In the rare event that such measures are either impossible or only partially successful, fairness dictates that the parent bank be liable for those deposits which it was unable to return abroad. To hold otherwise would be to undermine the seriousness of its obligations to its depositors and under some circumstances (not necessarily present here) to gain a windfall.

Chase's next argument, that under New York law its non-payment must be excused because no demand was ever made prior to the closing of its Saigon branch, must also be rejected. No Vietnamese law was offered on this issue. Nor is Chase's contention supported by New York law. It is not settled that a demand is not necessary where the branch in which the deposit was maintained (or by which the CD was issued) has been closed. 10 Am. Jur. 2d Banks & Banking §450 (1963); Sokoloff v. National City Bank, 250 N.Y. 69, 80-81, 164 N.E. 745 (1928) (where Petrograd branch of National City Bank ceased to exist because of Soviet seizure, this made "demand useless and unnecessary" and no demand was required since it "would manifestly be futile"). Similarly, reliance on New York cases suspending or excusing performance during times of war fails, since Chase, which was ultimately liable for the debt, was never barred by the wartime conditions in Vietnam from making payment outside of Vietnam. Finally, Chase, as a national bank, can find no comfort in the provisions of §138 of the New York Banking Law, which purport to limit in various ways the liability of *state* bank and trust companies for deposits made in overseas branches. By its own terms, §138 is unavailable to Chase in this case, because it only applies to state, not national, banks. If this unavailability has the effect of placing national banks like Chase at a competitive disadvantage vis-a-vis state banks, as Chase alleges, the solution lies with Congress, not the judiciary.

Chase argues that, even if all its other affirmative defenses fail, plaintiffs cannot recover because the judgment-day rule, under which obligations to pay foreign currencies (in this case piastres) must be converted prior to payment into dollars at the rate of exchange prevailing on the day judgment is entered, applies to this case and precludes any recovery, since the piastre is now worthless. We disagree. As a federal court sitting in diversity, we must apply the currency-conversion rule employed by the courts of New York, which has followed the breach-day rule for many years. Therefore, plaintiffs are entitled to recover an amount in dollars which reflects the exchange rate between dollars and South Vietnamese piastres at the time of breach, plus statutory interest.

It is true that federal courts sitting in *non*-diversity cases have rather consistently adopted the judgment-day rule. . . . However, this rule is substantive rather than procedural (there is no Federal Rule of Procedure on the subject) and therefore cannot be followed by federal courts sitting in diversity in states which apply the breach-day rule. *See generally* Compania Engraw Commercial E. Industrial S. A. v. Schenley Distillers Corp., 181 F.2d 876, 879 (9th Cir. 1950). Absent a federal rule, *see* Ely, The Irrepressible Myth of Erie, 87 Harv. L. Rev. 693, 698 (1974), the choice between conflicting state and federal practice must be made with a view toward fulfilling "the twin aims of the *Erie* rule: discouragement of forum-shopping and avoidance of inequitable administration of the laws." Hanna v. Plumer, 380 U.S. 460, 468, 85 S. Ct. 1136, 1142, 44 L. Ed. 2d 8 (1968). A plaintiff attempting to collect on an obligation denominated in a foreign currency that has appreciated significantly since the date the obligation was incurred would be tempted to forum-shop if he could rely on the federal courts to apply the judgment-day rule even in a diversity case. Conversely, a defendant faced with a state suit demanding payment of an obligation denominated in a currency that had depreciated significantly since the date it was incurred would be tempted to seek removal to a federal court whenever possible in order to utilize a federal judgment-day rule. *Hanna* must therefore be read as barring use of the federal judgment-rule here. In addition, it would be inequitable to allow a party to benefit or suffer from the existence of diversity jurisdiction in cases involving obligations denominated in foreign currencies when a similarly situated non-diverse party would not face such a consequence. *See generally* Morris, English Judgments in Foreign Currency: A "Procedural" Revolution, 41 Law & Contemp. Prob. 44, 48 (Spr. 1977); Becker, The Currency of Judgment, 25 Am. Jur. Comp. L. 152, 158 & n.31 (1977) ("Becker"). The New York law of currency conversion must therefore be applied.

With one or two rare exceptions not applicable here. . . . New York has long favored the breach-day rule.[7] . . .

---

[7]Advocates of the judgment-day rule argue that it avoids inconsistent results, depending on whether the suit is brought in the United States or in the courts of the country in whose currency the obligation is denominated:

> Suppose that in X, a foreign nation, the plaintiff delivers a dress to the defendant in return for the latter's promise to pay him 100 units of X currency. The defendant does not pay as promised. Suppose furthermore that . . . local law governs the contract and that if suit had been brought in X the plaintiff would have recovered 100 units of X currency which at the time of breach were worth 25 U.S. dollars. Suit, however, is brought some years later in Y, a State of the United States, and by the time that the Y court renders judgment the X currency has depreciated to the point where 100 units of X currency are worth only 10 U.S. dollars. Even at this time, however, the X courts would only give the plaintiff judgment for 100 units of their currency since, with exceptions too rare to mention, courts do not take account of fluctuations in the value of their own local currency. Therefore, the Y

. . . Until the New York courts choose to change their position on this question, we are bound to apply the breach-day rule, and do so here.

Reversed and remanded for further proceedings consistent with the foregoing.

See also Vishipco Line v. The Chase Manhattan Bank, No. 84-7778, slip op. (2d Cir. Feb. 4, 1985).

WESTON BANKING CORP. v. TURKIYE GARANTI BANKASI, A.S.

57 N.Y.2d 315, 442 N.E.2d 1195 (1982)

JASEN, J.

On this appeal, we are asked to decide whether, in light of the Act of State doctrine and the Bretton Woods Agreement, a Panamanian bank can maintain an action in this State against a Turkish bank on the basis of a promissory note that designates New York as the proper jurisdiction for resolution of any disputes. A secondary issue presented by this appeal is whether there was proper service of process on the defendant.

The promissory note which plaintiff, Weston Banking Corporation, a Panamanian banking corporation, seeks to enforce was signed by representatives of the defendant on July 9, 1976 in Istanbul, Turkey. Pursuant to its terms, defendant bank undertook an obligation to repay plaintiff principal in the

---

court should give judgment for the equivalent in United States dollars at the time of judgment of 100 units of X currency. Only in this way can uniformity of result be assured. The plaintiff, in other words, should be given judgment in Y for $10.

Restatement (Second) of Conflict of Laws §144, Comment d (1971).

On the other hand, New York decisions reflect a conviction that the breach-day rule is the best method of making the plaintiff whole, since it puts him back in the position which he would have occupied had the defendant performed in a timely fashion, giving the plaintiff the value in U.S. dollars of the foreign currency as of the date when he should have been paid. However, the breach-day rule is favorable to a plaintiff only when the foreign currency in which the obligation was originally measured has depreciated with respect to the defendant's currency (here the dollar) during the period since the breach. If it has appreciated, the judgment rule will be more favorable.

Prior to 1975 it had long been the English rule that all court-awarded judgments were to be made in pounds sterling converted at the time of breach. *See, e.g.,* In re United Railways of Havana and Regla Warehouses Ltd., [1961] A.C. 1007. In a series of decisions culminating in Miliangos v. George Frank (Textiles) Ltd., [1976] A.C. 443, however, the breach-day rule has been replaced in England by what might roughly be called a payment-day rule, which permits the plaintiff to recover either the nominal value of the obligation in the foreign currency itself or in pounds at the payment-day conversion rate. One commentator has urged that New York could and should adopt a similar rule. Becker, *supra,* at 157-59. An extended debate on the subject has subsequently appeared in English legal periodicals. *See, e.g.,* Knott, Foreign Currency, 43 Mod. L. Rev. 18 (1980); Bowles & Whelan, Judgments in Foreign Currencies: Extension of the Miliangos Rule, 42 Mod. L. Rev. 452 (1979); Bowles & Phillips, Judgments in Foreign Currencies: An Economist's View, 39 Mod. L. Rev. 196 (1976).

amount of 500,000 Swiss francs, plus interest calculated at 9% per annum. The interest was to be paid semiannually and the principal was due on July 9, 1979. The note also provided that: "Payment of principal and interest shall be made at the offices of the CHEMICAL BANK . . . New York City, New York, U.S.A., by means of a cable transfer to Switzerland in Lawful currency of the Swiss Federation." Such payments were to be "made clear of all restrictions of whatsoever nature imposed thereon by, outside of bilateral or multilateral payment agreements or clearing agreements which may exist at the time of payment and free and clear of and without deductions for any taxes, levies, imposts, deductions . . . imposed . . . by the Republic of Turkey".

Under the terms of the note, the defendant designated Chemical Bank, International Division, New York City, as its legal domicile and accepted the jurisdiction of New York courts "in the event of Judicial or extrajudial [*sic*] claim or summons of any nature". The holder was also given the option to bring suit against the maker in the Turkish courts. The final paragraph of the note indicates that the note "is issued under communique number 164, published by the Ministry of Finance."

Communique No. 164 amended Decree No. 17 of the Turkish Ministry of Finance. The decrees allow banks in Turkey to open convertible Turkish lira deposit accounts (CTLDs) when the bank obtains foreign currency by borrowing or through deposits. The bank is required under Turkish law to transfer the foreign currency to the Central Bank of Turkey. The Central Bank credits the privately owned bank with the equivalent amount of Turkish lira. These amounts are then available for investment by the banks. This program was apparently designed to encourage Turkish banks to seek foreign investments and to help stabilize the Turkish balance of payments by making available to the Turkish government more foreign currency. The banks benefited because the Turkish government covered any costs incurred by a fluctuation in the exchange rates between the currencies.

In July, 1976, the defendant Turkish bank borrowed 500,000 Swiss francs from the plaintiff bank and used these funds to establish a CTLD. As the interest became due, payments were made in Swiss francs at Chemical Bank's International Division in New York City. However, when the note was presented for payment in July, 1979, defendant refused to pay the principal on the ground that the then existing Turkish banking regulations barred it from paying back the loan in Swiss francs. . . .

It is not disputed that the defendant failed to pay the principal amount due plaintiff. Nor is the validity of the underlying note disputed. The heart of the defenses raised is that Turkish monetary regulations enacted subsequent to the date of the note make it legally impossible for the defendant bank to repay the loan in Swiss francs and that plaintiff's only "recourse is to be repaid in Turkish lira." Furthermore, the defendant contends that the promulgation of this regulation is an act of State and as such is beyond the review of New York courts. Similarly, defendant argues that the policy of the United States, as incorporated in the Bretton Woods Agreement (U.S. Code, tit. 22, §286; 59

U.S. Stat 512; 60 U.S. Stat 1411), is to refrain from any interference with the monetary regulations of signatory countries. . . .

Turning then to the facts of this case, we must determine whether the note and the regulation which defendant contends restricts the repayment of the promissory note require application of the Act of State doctrine. The note was executed in Istanbul, Turkey, and states that it is "issued under communique number 164" of the Turkish Ministry of Finance. Defendant contends that this makes the note subject to all Turkish monetary controls, even those enacted subsequent to the date of the note. Plaintiff, on the other hand, points out that Communique No. 164 merely authorizes Turkish banks to engage in this type of transaction and that the note specifies that repayment is not subject to regulation by the Turkish government. We would add that the note requires payment to be made at Chemical Bank in New York City and designates New York law to be controlling.

We conclude that on these facts the Act of State doctrine does not constitute a defense to plaintiff's action to recover on this note. A debt is not located within a foreign State unless it has the power at the instance of an interested party to enforce or collect it. (Zeevi & Sons v. Grindlays Bank [Uganda], 37 N.Y.2d 220, 228, 371 N.Y.S.2d 892 (1975), *cert. denied,* 423 U.S. 866 (1975); Republic of Iraq v. First Natl. City Bank, 353 F.2d 47, 51 (2d Cir. 1965), *cert. denied,* 382 U.S. 1027 (1966)). Here, the debt is equally capable of being enforced against the defendant's assets in New York as it is capable of being enforced against its assets in Turkey, and the State of Turkey has no power to enforce collection of this debt. The mere fact that this suit might have been commenced in Turkey, instead of New York, does not bar the action. Indeed, the note provides that New York shall be the proper jurisdiction for dispute resolution. Such a provision naturally contemplates enforcement of any judgment which would resolve the dispute. Thus, the Act of State doctrine does not bar this action.

Whether or not extraterritorial effect will be given to the Turkish regulation depends on whether it controls the issue presented to this court and whether it is consistent with the policies of this State. (Zeevi & Sons v. Grindlays Bank [Uganda], *supra,* 37 N.Y.2d at pp. 227-228, 371 N.Y. S.2d 892, 333 N.E.2d 168; Republic of Iraq v. First Natl. City Bank, *supra,* at p. 51.) The initial inquiry must be to ask what the regulation provides.

Defendant has provided the court with translated and certified copies of all pertinent Turkish law and plaintiff has raised no claim concerning the propriety of these documents. Our reading of those regulations, whether individually or as representative of a continuous Turkish monetary policy, indicates that there is no per se ban imposed on all Turkish banks preventing them from paying this type of promissory note with foreign currency. The record indicates that the directive of the Ministry of Finance does not bar payment of the note, but, rather, establishes a program under which CTLDs could be restructured through the Turkish Central Bank. Defendant's own counsel in responding to plaintiff's inquiry about the effect of the restructuring program stated:

"The Central Bank is obligated to pay interest only after CTLDs are included in the restructuring under the CTLD Credit Agreement. All CTLDs not included in the restructuring will remain obligations of the commercial banks in Turkey with which they are made." Plaintiff denies ever agreeing to have this note included in the restructuring program. Defendant makes no claim and offers no proof to the contrary; in fact, the record is devoid of any indication that the regulations on which defendant relies are applicable to this note.

Thus, we need not reach the question of whether these regulations comport with this State's policy so that they should be given extraterritorial application. It is sufficient to note that defendant has failed to introduce any documentation to support its contention that Turkish law forbids the payment of a promissory note designating that payment shall be made in Swiss francs at a bank incorporated in the United States.

This failure of proof also reaches to the validity of defendant's claim that the Bretton Woods Agreement bars this action. The Bretton Woods Agreement (U.S. Code, tit. 22, §286; 59 U.S. Stat 512; 60 U.S. Stat 1411) is an international treaty to which both the United States and Turkey are signatories. The purpose of the Agreement, as stated in article I (60 U.S. Stat 1401), is to promote international monetary co-operation, exchange stability and "[t]o assist in the establishment of a multilateral system of payments in respect of current transactions between members and in the elimination of foreign exchange restrictions which hamper the growth of world trade." (Art I. [iv].)

The defendant relies on article VIII (§2, subd. [b]) of the Agreement as a defense to this action, which provides that "[e]xchange contracts which involve the currency of any member and which are contrary to the exchange control regulations of that member maintained or imposed consistently with this Agreement shall be unenforceable in the territories of any member." This article renders unenforceable any agreement involving the currency of a member State which is contrary to "that member's" currency control regulations. The promissory note involved here obligated the defendant to repay the plaintiff the principal sum loaned in Swiss francs and not Turkish lira.

Were the currency regulations to ban payment in foreign currencies when a CTLD was liquidated, a different case would have been presented. In this case, however, the regulation merely permits a Turkish bank to restructure the debt. As we previously stated, there is no proof, in this record, that if the debt were not restructured, the bank would be barred from repaying the plaintiff in Swiss francs as required by the terms of the note. Therefore, although we recognize the validity of the Bretton Woods Agreement and its potential controlling effect over international currency transactions, on the record before us, we do not find it to be applicable. . . .

[Dismissal of service of process omitted.]

Accordingly, the order of the Appellate Division should be affirmed.

MEYER, J. (dissenting).

The International Monetary Fund (Bretton Woods) Agreement of 1945 (60 U.S. Stat 1401, TIAS 1501) to which the United States and Turkey are signatories, the mandate of section 11 of the Bretton Woods Agreements Act (59 U.S. Stat 516; U.S. Code, tit. 22, §286b) that "the first sentence of article VIII, section 2(b), of the Articles of Agreement of the Fund . . . shall have full force and effect in the United States", the legislative history of that Congressional enactment, the supremacy clause of the United States Constitution and the decision of the United States Supreme Court in Kolovrat v. Oregon, 366 U.S. 187, 81 S. Ct. 922, 6 L. Ed. 2d 218 establish beyond peradventure that the applicability of the first sentence of article VIII (§2, subd. [b] presents a question of Federal not State law. . . .

If article VIII (§2, subd. [b]) applies, neither the Act of State doctrine referred to by the majority and the Appellate Division nor the intention of the parties to free it from Turkish regulation, relied upon by the Appellate Division, are relevant. The starting point for analysis is rather the Appellate Division's statement (86 A.D.2d 544, 545, 446 N.Y.S.2d 67) that "Communique No. 164, under which the note was issued, imposes no conditions on repayment; it simply authorizes issuance of a note payable in foreign currency" and the statement of the majority in this court (pp. 325-326, 456 N.Y.S.2d 688, 442 N.E.2d 1199) "that defendant has failed to introduce any documentation to support its contention that Turkish law forbids the payment of a promissory note designating that payment shall be made in Swiss francs at a bank incorporated in the United States." Does the record bear out those conclusions? . . .

[Judge Meyer concludes that Turkish law does forbid the payment, and then that the contract is an exchange contract and does involve Turkish currency.]

Because, as the foregoing discussion shows, the note in suit is governed by Turkish regulations and the Bretton Woods Agreement and the Bretton Woods Agreements Act proscribe enforcement of the note by the courts of this State in contravention of those regulations, I would grant defendant's cross motion for summary judgment dismissing the complaint.

NOTES AND QUESTIONS

1. Do you think you can tell an "exchange contract" from a contract that simply happens to involve foreign exchange? (This is the most common judicial method for evading the IMF rule.)

2. Do you find *Banco Frances*'s modification of the old penal judgment concepts wise?

3. Why isn't *Vishipco* governed by Article VIII(2)(b) of the IMF Agreement?

4. Note that the Milbank Tweed firm that represented Vishipco had also been involved in the *Sokoloff* case cited by the court. Did this hurt its position? What could it have done?

5. Should a U.S. court ever issue judgments in foreign currency?

6. Does *Vishipco* give a lucky few a way to evade foreign exchange control rules?

7. Suppose that it were clear in *Weston* that the Turkish laws were meant to be applicable and mandatory. Would you decide the case the way Judge Meyer urges? What are the arguments and possible approaches each way?

8. When it imposed the Iranian asset freeze in 1980, the United States registered that freeze as a formal exchange control rule. Would this make the freeze more enforceable in Europe? *See* R. Edwards, Extraterritorial Application of the U.S. Iranian Assets Control Regulations, 45 Am. J. Intl. L. 870 (1981).

9. Suppose an exchange control rule purported to apply to outstanding letters of credit. What approaches might you take to resolving the strong conflict of policies? For interesting examples, *see* Zeevi & Sons v. Grindlays Bank [Uganda], 37 N.Y.2d 220, 371 N.Y.S.2d 892 (1975), *cert. denied*, 423 U.S. 866 (1975); and United City Merchants (Investments) v. Royal Bank of Canada, [1982] 2 A.E.R. 720.

10. Suppose that after signing a loan agreement and borrowing under it, Ruritania passed an exchange control law that prohibited payment of the loan, and a lending bank sought to collect on the loan out of Ruritanian assets in your court's jurisdiction. What holding? *See* Libra Bank v. Banco Nacional de Costa Rica, 570 F. Supp. 870 (S.D.N.Y. 1983).

C. PREVENTION AND MANAGEMENT OF DEFAULT

The international system just described assists nations in managing their monetary systems and in foreign enforcement of their exchange control regulations. The international banking crises of the last several years, however, have produced a further generation of regulations. Some of these are designed to assist banks in avoiding problem loans; some, just beginning to be developed, are designed to provide fairness among different creditors, and perhaps to assist debtor nations to avoid default.

1. *Domestic Regulation of International Capital Flows*

Details of banking regulation differ radically from nation to nation. Most have specific requirements affecting, for example, the ratio of loans to capital, together with various forms of auditing, disclosure, and self-regulation procedures. These are enforced by a variety of agencies, including, in the United States, the Treasury, the Federal Deposit Insurance Corporation, and the Federal Reserve. Most of these regulations are designed primarily to affect domestic transactions and the inherent safety of the bank. Only a few apply explicitly to international transactions.

United States regulations largely rely on market mechanisms to control banking activities in the sense that many are reporting requirements designed to increase information available to investors and depositors.

Before enactment of a new five-point plan in 1983, the international lending activities of U.S. banks were largely controlled by the following rules, which still apply:

(1) United States banks are subject to the statutory lending limit in 12 U.S.C. §84, which limits lending to any person to 10 percent of the bank's unimpaired capital and surplus. Other regulations, e.g., 12 C.F.R. §932.5, go on to define what is a separate person for the purposes of the statute:

(d) *Loans to foreign governments, their agencies, and instrumentalities.* (1) Notwith-standing paragraphs (a), (b), and (c) of this section, loans or extensions of credit to foreign governments, their agencies, and instrumentalities will be combined with one another under section 84 only if they fail to meet either of the following tests at the time the loan or extension of credit is made:

(i) The borrower has resources or revenue of its own sufficient over time to service its debt obligations ("means" test);

(ii) The purpose of the loan or extension of credit is consistent with the pur-poses of the borrower's general business ("purpose" test).

(2) In order to show that the "means" and "purpose" tests have been satisfied, a bank shall, at a minimum, assemble and retain in its files the following items:

(i) A statement (accompanied by supporting documentation) describing the legal status and the degree of financial and operational autonomy of the borrow-ing entity.

(ii) Financial statements for the borrowing entity for a minimum of three years prior to the date the loan or extension of credit was made or for each year less than three that the borrowing entity has been in existence.

(iii) Financial statements for each year the loan or extension of credit is out-standing.

(iv) The bank's assessments of the borrower's means of servicing the loan or extension of credit, including specific reasons in support of that assessment. The assessment shall include an analysis of the borrower's financial history, its pres-ent and projected economic and financial performance, and the significance of any financial support provided to the borrower by third parties, including the borrower's central government. If the government's support exceeds the borrow-er's annual revenues from other sources, it will be presumed that the "means" test has not been satisfied. No such presumption will be made, however, because of a guarantee by the central government of the borrower's debt.

(v) A loan agreement or other written statement from the borrower which clearly describes the purpose of the loan or extension of credit. The written representation will ordinarily constitute sufficient evidence that the "purpose" test has been satisfied. However, when, at the time the funds are disbursed, the bank knows or has reason to know of other information suggesting that the borrower will use the proceeds in a manner inconsistent with the written repre-sentation, it may not, without further inquiry, accept the representation.

The Comptroller of the Currency and the Federal Reserve Board also issue minimum capital guidelines for use in examining banks. *See* Comptroller of the Currency and Federal Reserve Board, Release of June 13, 1983, reprinted at 22 I.L.M. 930 (1983).

(2) There is also an accounting principle that requires banks to write off interest due from a borrower once it is 90 days overdue. Normally, a bank will treat such an interest payment as paid on its books, whether or not it has been received, until the 90-day limit has been reached.

The importance of this principle was demonstrated in the spring of 1984, when a rescheduling of Argentine debt was negotiated just in time to save banks from having to write off significant losses against their first-quarter earnings. The regulation also implies that when U.S. banks enter into negotiations over debt rescheduling with a sovereign borrower, they will have a strong interest in the maintenance of interest payments in order to prevent losses from appearing on their domestic income statements.

(3) The Securities and Exchange Commission has imposed disclosure standards on bank holding companies with foreign loans. These include Article 9 of Regulation S-X and Staff Accounting Bulletins 49 and 49A. Through these standards bank holding companies are required to disclose information regarding large foreign loans outstanding.

(4) An Interagency Country Exposure Review Committee, established by the three banking regulatory agencies in 1979, evaluates the risk associated with foreign loans and ranks foreign borrowers into six categories from strong to weak. This evaluation is then incorporated into the regulator's bank supervision.

The Regulations discussed in (1)-(4) were supplemented in late 1983 by the five-point program of the following legislation.

INTERNATIONAL LENDING SUPERVISION ACT OF 1983

P.L. 98-181, 97 Stat. 1153 (1983)

Sec. 901. . . .

DECLARATION OF POLICY

Sec. 902. (a)(1) It is the policy of the Congress to assure that the economic health and stability of the United States and the other nations of the world shall not be adversely affected or threatened in the future by imprudent lending practices or inadequate supervision.

(2) This shall be achieved by strengthening the bank regulatory framework

to encourage prudent private decisionmaking and by enhancing international coordination among bank regulatory authorities.

(b) The Federal banking agencies shall consult with the banking supervisory authorities of other countries to reach understandings aimed at achieving the adoption of effective and consistent supervisory policies and practices with respect to international lending. . . .

STRENGTHENED SUPERVISION OF INTERNATIONAL LENDING

Sec. 904. (a) Each appropriate Federal banking agency shall evaluate banking institution foreign country exposure and transfer risk for use in banking institution examination and supervision.

(b) Each such agency shall establish examination and supervisory procedures to assure that factors such as foreign country exposure and transfer risk are taken into account in evaluating the adequacy of the capital of banking institutions.

RESERVES

Sec. 905. (a)(1) Each appropriate Federal banking agency shall require a banking institution to establish and maintain a special reserve whenever, in the judgment of such appropriate Federal banking agency—

(A) the quality of such banking institution's assets has been impaired by a protracted inability of public or private borrowers in a foreign country to make payments on their external indebtedness as indicated by such factors, among others, as—

(i) a failure by such public or private borrowers to make full interest payments on external indebtedness;

(ii) a failure to comply with the terms of any restructured indebtedness; or

(iii) a failure by the foreign country to comply with any International Monetary Fund or other suitable adjustment program; or

(B) no definite prospects exist for the orderly restoration of debt service.

(2) Such reserves shall be charged against current income and shall not be considered as part of capital and surplus or allowances for possible loan losses for regulatory, supervisory, or disclosure purposes.

(b) The appropriate Federal banking agencies shall analyze the results of foreign loan rescheduling negotiations, assess the loan loss risk reflected in rescheduling agreements, and, using the powers set forth in section 908 (regarding capital adequacy), ensure that the capital and reserve positions of

United States banks are adequate to accommodate potential losses on their foreign loans.

(c) The appropriate Federal banking agencies shall promulgate regulations or orders necessary to implement this section within one hundred and twenty days after the date of the enactment of this title.

ACCOUNTING FOR FEES ON INTERNATIONAL LOANS

Sec. 906. (a)(1) In order to avoid excessive debt service burdens on debtor countries, no banking institution shall charge, in connection with the restructuring of an international loan, any fee exceeding the administrative cost of the restructuring unless it amortizes such fee over the effective life of each such loan.

(2)(A) Each appropriate Federal banking agency shall promulgate such regulations as are necessary to further carry out the provisions of this subsection.

(B) The requirement of paragraph (1) shall take effect on the date of the enactment of this section.

(b)(1) Subject to subsection (a), the appropriate Federal banking agencies shall promulgate regulations for accounting for agency, commitment, management and other fees charged by a banking institution in connection with an international loan.

(2) Such regulations shall establish the accounting treatment of such fees for regulatory, supervisory, and disclosure purposes to assure that the appropriate portion of such fees is accrued in income over the effective life of each such loan.

(3) The appropriate Federal banking agencies shall promulgate regulations or orders necessary to implement this subsection within one hundred and twenty days after the date of the enactment of this title.

COLLECTION AND DISCLOSURE OF CERTAIN INTERNATIONAL LENDING DATA

Sec. 907. (a) Each appropriate Federal banking agency shall require, by regulation, each banking institution with foreign country exposure to submit, no fewer than four times each calendar year, information regarding such exposure in a format prescribed by such regulations.

(b) Each appropriate Federal banking agency shall require, by regulation, banking institutions to disclose to the public information regarding material foreign country exposure in relation to assets and to capital.

(c) The appropriate Federal banking agencies shall promulgate regulations or orders necessary to implement this section within one hundred and twenty days after the date of the enactment of this title.

CAPITAL ADEQUACY

Sec. 908. (a)(1) Each appropriate Federal banking agency shall cause banking institutions to achieve and maintain adequate capital by establishing minimum levels of capital for such banking institutions and by using such other methods as the appropriate Federal banking agency deems appropriate.

(2) Each appropriate Federal banking agency shall have the authority to establish such minimum level of capital for a banking institution as the appropriate Federal banking agency, in its discretion, deems to be necessary or appropriate in light of the particular circumstances of the banking institution.

(b)(1) Failure of a banking institution to maintain capital at or above its minimum level as established pursuant to subsection (a) may be deemed by the appropriate Federal banking agency, in its discretion, to constitute an unsafe and unsound practice within the meaning of section 8 of the Federal Deposit Insurance Act.

(2)(A) In addition to, or in lieu of, any other action authorized by law, including paragraph (1), the appropriate Federal banking agency may issue a directive to a banking institution that fails to maintain capital at or above its required level as established pursuant to subsection (a).

(B)(i) Such directive may require the banking institution to submit and adhere to a plan acceptable to the appropriate Federal banking agency describing the means and timing by which the banking institution shall achieve its required capital level.

(ii) Any such directive issued pursuant to this paragraph, including plans submitted pursuant thereto, shall be enforceable under the provisions of section 8(i) of the Federal Deposit Insurance Act to the same extent as an effective and outstanding order issued pursuant to section 8(b) of the Federal Deposit Insurance Act which has become final.

(3)(A) Each appropriate Federal banking agency may consider such banking institution's progress in adhering to any plan required under this subsection whenever such banking institution, or an affiliate thereof, or the holding company which controls such banking institution, seeks the requisite approval of such appropriate Federal banking agency for any proposal which would divert earnings, diminish capital, or otherwise impede such banking institution's progress in achieving its minimum capital level.

(B) Such appropriate Federal banking agency may deny such approval where it determines that such proposal would adversely affect the ability of the banking institution to comply with such plan.

(C) The Chairman of the Board of Governors of the Federal Reserve System and the Secretary of the Treasury shall encourage governments, central banks, and regulatory authorities of other major banking countries to work toward maintaining and, where appropriate, strengthening the capital bases of banking institutions involved in international lending.

FOREIGN LOAN EVALUATIONS

Sec. 909. (a)(1) In any case in which one or more banking institutions extend credit, whether by loan, lease, guarantee, or otherwise, which individually or in the aggregate exceeds $20,000,000, to finance any project which has as a major objective the construction or operation of any mining operation, any metal or mineral primary processing operation, any fabricating facility or operation, or any metal-making operations (semi and finished) located outside the United States or its territories and possessions, a written economic feasibility evaluation of such foreign project shall be prepared and approved in writing by a senior official of the banking institution, or, if more than one banking institution is involved, the lead banking institution, prior to the extension of such credit.

(2) Such evaluation shall—

(A) take into account the profit potential of the project, the impact of the project on world markets, the inherent competitive advantages and disadvantages of the project over the entire life of the project, and the likely effect of the project upon the overall long-term economic development of the country in which the project is located; and

(B) consider whether the extension of credit can reasonably be expected to be repaid from revenues generated by such foreign project without regard to any subsidy, as defined in international agreements, provided by the government involved or any instrumentality of any country.

(b) Such economic feasibility evaluations shall be reviewed by representatives of the appropriate Federal banking agencies whenever an examination by such appropriate Federal banking agency is conducted. . . .

(2) No private right of action or claim for relief may be predicated upon this section.

QUESTIONS

1. Whom does the 10% limit protect?

2. Would the limit allow a bank to lend 9% of its capital to the Republic of Mexico and another 9% to Pemex, the Mexican state-owned oil company? What additional data might you want before writing an opinion letter on this question?

3. What about the rules on accounting for fees? Why do you think they are there?

4. Do you think these regulations are likely to help prevent the next wave of overlending, whatever that wave may be (developing nations, oil tankers, etc.)?

5. How might this direction of regulation evolve in light of the trend toward

banking deregulation and the new competition in the domestic financial industry?

For examples of the new regulations issued in accordance with the statute, see the group issued by Treasury, the Federal Reserve, and the Federal Deposit Insurance Corporation at 49 Fed. Reg. 5,587 (February 13, 1984). And for additional background, *see* Lichtenstein, U.S. Banks and the Eurocurrency Markets; The Regulatory Structure, 99 Banking L.J. 484 (1982); and Greenberg, The Eurodollar Market: the Case for Disclosure, 71 Cal. L. Rev. 1492 (1983).

2.   *Management of Default*

In spite of all the efforts just described, a number of nations have been unable to meet the payments on their loans, and have negotiated reschedulings. These are typically handled in two separate negotiations, one at the "Paris Club" in which the public creditors, including the IMF and the World Bank, agree on terms of extension, and a second, less formal one in which private banks agree to a rollover, or perhaps to the advancement of new loans to meet current interest payments. The process and its implications are described in the following excerpts.

A NIGHTMARE OF DEBT: A SURVEY OF INTERNATIONAL BANKING

The Economist, March 20, 1982, Supp. p.9

LIVING WITH A NIGHTMARE

Rescheduling Poland's debts has been the most traumatic experience western bankers have known since the first surplus Opec dollar trickled through their fingers. It has forced them to rethink all the traditional assumptions on which they built their international lending. This survey looks at some of the questions the banks should be asking themselves during their introspective post-mortem. Although their international lending may have grown too fast in the past, the danger now is that it will grow too slowly in the future.

If all the dollars Poland owes to western banks were laid end to end they would encircle the globe 57 times. A dozen of those circumferences were due to be paid back in 1981. With Poland's economy working at half-cock there was no way it could meet its obligations. The 501 western banks to whom this Comecom country owed money had a simple choice. Either they waved good-bye to their Polish loans and took the blow immediately on the chin (which would have savagely lopped their profits in 1981) or they agreed to reschedule Poland's debts in order to give it more time to pay. Both the Poles and the bankers always wanted to take the rescheduling option, but they played a dangerous and often bizarre game before they allowed themselves to admit it.

Rescheduling a country's debts is always a long and cumbrous process. In Poland's case there was a new dimension—the relentless spotlight of publicity thrown on to the private discomfort of the crepuscular bankers. They began to wish that the ordinary process of rescheduling could be made to look less extraordinary. They began to wish they had not been persuaded to lend so much to eastern Europe in the first place. They began to wish they had never left home.

For the bankers Poland extended Lord Keynes's oft-quoted comment that if you owe your bank a hundred pounds you have a problem, but that if you owe a million, it has. They discovered that if you owe your bank a billion pounds everybody has a problem. And everybody is interested in how you solve it. . . .

The writing had been on the wall for some time. The bankers, shielded by the IMF, had chosen not to read it. When countries like Jamaica, Turkey or Sudan did not like the IMF's economic medicine doled out as a pre-condition for rescheduling their private bank debts, it was the IMF that was the focus of their wrath. The banks, while urging the IMF to be tough, stayed in the political shadows.

Poland, however, is not (yet) a member of the IMF. The bankers were alone and fully exposed to any political brickbats. Moreover, the two occasions—in Zaire and Peru—when the banks attempted to impose economic conditions themselves had been dismal never-to-be-repeated failures. There was no way they could monitor and enforce their own conditions. In the absence of the IMF, how were they to tell Poland what to do? And if they did not tell Poland what to do what hope was there that they would ever get their money back?

THE POLISH BOGEY

"We will pay every penny we owe", insisted Bank Handlowy's first vice president Mr Jan Woloszyn in June, 1980, "and we will pay on time". Nine months later an unruffled Mr Woloszyn was standing before serried rows of dark-suited international bankers in the City of London to announce, effectively, that Poland was broke.

The news, delivered on a wintry March day in the elegant surroundings of the Plaisterers' Hall, came as no surprise to most of Poland's bankers. As long ago as 1975, Mr Gabriel Eichler, Bank of America's east European economist had written a paper concluding "without radical changes, Poland will find itself facing severe financial and economic problems." Other voices echoed the same tune.

Yet the lending went on. Between 1976 and 1980, Poland's foreign debt more than doubled. Although some American banks started to draw back there was no shortage of Japanese and Europeans to take their place. Stuffed with petrodollars, they were anxious to open up new markets. Encouraged by generous backing from western export credit agencies, and comforted by the belief that, if the worst came to the worst Russia would always pick up the tab (the so-called "umbrella theory"), many bankers saw Comecon as the growth area of the future. The economists' warnings were brushed aside: "Why should we hold back", one was told, "when Citibank, Barclays and the rest are getting in there? After all, they're not idiots."

By 1979 Poland was moving to the top of the agenda in bankers' lunchtime conversations. The sparse statistical evidence available already pointed to the failure of the country's heavy industrialisation programme. The western recession dampened demand for Polish copper and coal, but Polish imports continued unabated. Riots and strikes thwarted the attempts of Warsaw's planners to raise prices and suppress demand.

Many banks were still, however, viewing Poland's problems as temporary. In March, 1979, Poland signed a $550m syndicated loan, led by Bank of America. Originally targeted for $500m, the loan was oversubscribed. As late as November, an International Herald Tribune survey concluded that "bankers see short-run problems in Poland . . . but the long-term view is bullish".

Behind the scenes, Polish officials were now discreetly (so as not to alarm the bankers) sounding out western governments for more credits. In defiance of the gentleman's agreement between western export credit agencies, France's agency, Coface, agreed to a bilateral rescheduling of FFr1.25 billion ($208m) in December, 1979. The German government refused a rescheduling but offered modest amounts of new money.

This kept Warsaw going until early in 1980, but by April Bank Handlowy was telling the bankers it needed more money. Separate approaches were made to Bank of America and to Dresdner Bank to organise big loans.

By now the bankers were becoming alarmed; "We knew", commented one, "that this was a semi-disguised rescue package." The Poles' projected $1.4 billion current-account deficit for 1979 had proved wildly inaccurate: the actual deficit was more than double that amount. And few bankers had any belief in the $1.3 billion deficit forecast for 1980.

The two banks had the greatest difficulty in scraping up the cash. Bank of America was forced to scale down its original target of $500m to $375m, and only achieved that with the help of $80m from the Moscow Narodny Bank and the Polish bank, Pekao.

The DM1.2 billion ($500m) German loan was cobbled together only under heavy pressure from the finance ministry ("quite exceptional" circumstances according to one senior German banker) and after the promise of a government guarantee covering 40% of it.

Desperate Jan

By now Poland's cash-flow problems were obvious. Yet the Polish finance ministry still refused to face reality. At a meeting in Dresdner Bank's plush Frankfurt offices, in the middle of January, 1981, Mr Jan Woloszyn and other Bank Handlowy officials were advised to "restructure" their debt and to call in some merchant bankers to sort out the tangled maze of borrowings. Mr

Woloszyn would not hear of it. "Even using the word restructuring was out of the question", says one banker of that time. "He was convinced that the markets were still soft enough to give Poland new loans."

At meetings with western bankers in Europe and New York over the next six weeks, Mr Woloszyn persisted in his request for a new $1 billion "jumbo" loan. He drew a blank. Nervous bankers were even withdrawing Poland's short-term credit facilities as they came up for renewal. By the beginning of March the Poles could see that within a few weeks the kitty would be empty. They had no choice but to call a meeting.

Ignoring advice from several bankers to discuss rescheduling quietly, Bank Handlowy organised a large presentation in London. Representatives of over 70 banks were given "a sketchy and ill-prepared projection of Poland's financing needs for 1981". Mr Woloszyn's request for a new $1 billion loan, along with a rescheduling, fell on deaf ears. Bankers scurried back to their offices to reduce their Polish exposure as fast as they could.

Poland's main bankers then took the initiative. With Chase Manhattan as initial co-ordinator, a 20-bank "multi-national task force" of Poland's main creditor banks was set up. At a meeting in Lloyds Bank International's City headquarters on the last day of March, 1981, the task force told the Poles that it would, henceforth, be the sole medium for negotiations between Warsaw and its 501 creditor banks.

Despite the Polish economic planning commissioner Mr Henryk Kisiel's assertion that the Poles would "spit blood" to pay their debts, there were alarming reports of overdue payments. "It's a fact", said one New York banker baldly, "Poland is in default." Luckily no big bank wanted to call the default and trigger the hundreds of cross-default clauses on other Polish loans. With few Polish assets available to seize, it could do little to help repayment.

Polish negotiators, led by Bank Handlowy's Mr Jan Woloszyn and the deputy finance minister Mr Zbigniew Karcz, requested a deferral of all principal repayments due between March 27th and June 30th to allow time for talks. This triggered the first of a series of squabbles between the western banks.

There was an immediate split between those (such as the Swiss, led by Union Bank of Switzerland) who insisted on timely repayment of short-term debts (under 12 months) and those (including the West Germans) willing to take a softer line. Some Americans were all for charging penal interest rates on any overdue principal.

At a tense meeting in London in mid-April, the West German view prevailed. Second-quarter payments were rolled over. The meeting established a working party of five banks to prepare an outline of rescheduling terms. In addition, an international committee of bank economists was formed to monitor the Polish economy.

Two weeks later the working group met the Poles in New York. Mr Woloszyn demanded that the bankers follow the precedent set by government creditors in Paris 10 days earlier and reschedule all principal due in 1981 together with interest. No dice, said the bankers. "The one principle which we stuck to right the way through", recalls one Austrian banker, "was that there should be no rescheduling of interest." And only debt due after the end-March "cut-off" date would be considered for rescheduling.

By May 20th, when the full task force met again at Dresdner Bank's Frankfurt offices, the working group had drafted a short five-page memorandum. It proposed rescheduling 95% of the $2.4 billion due in the last nine months of 1981 over seven and a half years including four years' grace. Interest would be set at $1^3/4\%$ over Libor (which recently was floating around $16^3/4\%$) with a stiff penalty of $2^3/4\%$ for late payments. In addition there would be a 1% renegotiation fee.

At the meeting there were sharp differences between those who wanted much tougher "conditionality"—more data on the Polish economy and an economic recovery plan—and those who were prepared to endorse the memorandum in the interests of getting a quick agreement.

Furthermore, Chase Manhattan was now insisting (through Citibank and Bank of America, the two American task force members) that two loans totalling $525m to the state-owned mining company, Kombinat Gorniczo-Hutniczy w Lubine, to finance copper production, should be treated separately. These were, Chase argued, project-finance loans with their own foreign currency earnings to support repayment.

Few were prepared to buy this argument. A number of bankers claimed that one of Chase's original reasons for structuring the loans in this way had been to convince the New York banking regulators that the money had not gone to the Polish government, and that it was not therefore exceeding its limits on lending to any single borrower. Most of the specific conditions attached to the loan had not been kept. "There was only the shadow of a project loan left", commented one British banker.

Schwartz's showdown

The meeting broke up in disagreement, with a decision to refer the memorandum itself to the 501 creditor banks through their national task forces. By and large the Europeans were prepared to go along with the terms; the Americans were not. At a meeting of the American task force on June 11th in New York, feelings ran high. Mr Frederick Schwartz, of Bankers Trust, accused the Europeans of "steam-rolling" the agreement out of fear for their own balance sheets. Poland had never complied with economic conditions before; moreover, the Poles' latest forecasts for the balance of payments were a mixture of "pure propaganda and wild economic projections".

This time, said Mr Schwartz, the banks must be tough. A paper drawn up by Bankers Trust in conjunction with a few other hard-line American banks proposed much stricter legal language for the agreement, full disclosure of Poland's eastern-block debt and its maturity, and verification of the numbers and data presented by Bank Handlowy to the banks' economic committee as preconditions of any signing of a final agreement.

On a wave of anti-European invective the American banks "totally and absolutely rejected" the working group's May 20th proposals and Mr Schwartz of Bankers Trust was voted into the chair in place of Bank of America.

The stage was set for a ding-dong battle at the next meeting of the full multi-national task force two weeks later in the Banque Nationale de Paris's sedate headquarters on the Boulevard des Italiens. Mr Schwartz told the Europeans that only the American banks had any real experience of rescheduling, and "we're not going to be pushed around." This aggressive attack caused a complete uproar. Work was brought to a halt. Even Citibank, the other American task force member, was embarrassed.

The Europeans recognised that stiffer monitoring provisions might be needed. But they were anxious above all to get an agreement in place. They felt Mr Schwartz was calling for pie in the sky.

Over the next month, the gap was narrowed by informal bargaining and private meetings. The big split (in which the Americans were threatening to try for a separate agreement) was averted. At the next full task force meeting on July 22nd in Zurich, the bankers closed ranks. Poland would be required to develop a consultative group to work with the economic steering committee, and provide quarterly progress reports once the agreement was in place. The sensitive question of eastern-block debt was handled by asking the Poles to provide numbers but no exact sources. Finally, all interest payments must be current by the deadline for the signing of a full agreement, December 10th.

Chase Manhattan's claim for preferential treatment was thrown out. However, its loans (to satisfy regulators and shareholders) were shoved into a separate category.

The task was now to get the memorandum accepted by the Poles. Initial reaction from Mr Marian Krzak, the Polish finance minister, seemed favourable. "The proposals form a good basis for discussion", he commented after the Zurich meeting.

Stalling and haggling

The bankers' optimism proved short-lived. At a series of meetings in August and early September, little progress was made towards agreement. "There was just a lot of stalling and haggling", recalls one. "Each time we thought we'd got agreement on something, the Poles would go back on it at the next meeting."

The Poles proved astute negotiators. Often, after meetings, an individual banker would be approached by one of the Poles trying to drive a wedge between the hard and soft liners. By the middle of August, some bankers were in favour of caving in to Polish demands for softer terms—lowering the spread to $1\frac{1}{2}\%$ and boosting the amount of principal to be rescheduled. However, when they consulted individual banks in their national caucuses, the mood was against it.

The gap between debtor and creditors seemed unbridgeable. A meeting of the full task force slated for September 17th was put off until the 28th because the Poles were unready to respond. When the meeting finally got under way in the *fin de siècle* offices of Creditanstalt-Bank-verein in the heart of Vienna, the Polish negotiators, Mr Woloszyn and Mr Karcz, were evasive. Almost none of the economic data requested at the Zurich meeting in July was forthcoming. The bankers' frustration had reached fever pitch. They were in no mood for further stalling.

After a day of fruitless negotiations some members of the American delegation suggested a meeting in Warsaw with the finance minister Mr Krzak to try to break the deadlock. The Poles were taken aback at this sudden demand for an appointment "at ten o'clock the following morning". They objected. There were no scheduled flights to Warsaw the following day; Mr Krzak was "busy with affairs of state". The Americans replied that they had "a private plane waiting at Vienna airport, and that Mr Krzak had better cancel his appointments or there might not be a state left to run."

So, in the early hours of Tuesday, September 29th, seven bleary-eyed bankers climbed aboard the aeroplane chartered by Creditanstalt and bound for Warsaw. When they arrived in Mr Krzak's offices the bankers were blunt. "We said that if he didn't sign the memorandum that afternoon the banks would declare a default. There would be no more loans to Poland for 25 years. The consequences for the whole of east-west trade would be incalculable."

Mr Krzak's line was that his negotiators had not kept him fully informed of the gravity of the situation. "He gave us the impression that the Polish negotiators had overplayed their hand." Some of the bankers were sceptical. "It was a smart move", says one, "to pretend he really hadn't been informed".

In any event, Mr Krzak got the message. When Mr Woloszyn and Mr Karcz arrived back in Warsaw (in more leisurely fashion, by a scheduled flight) the following day, September 30th, they signed.

With the basic terms agreed, the detailed work on the final rescheduling (a mammoth 150-page document) got under way. The London firm of lawyers Coward Chance was drafted in to work out the fine print and accountants Peat Marwick Mitchell were dispatched to Poland to reconcile Bank Handlowy's accounts with those of the banks.

The most pressing problem was to catch up on outstanding interest arrears. Poland owed some $500m (largely in interest arrears), and many banks doubted it could find it on its own. In the middle of November, with the December 10th deadline fast approaching, Dresdner Bank called an informal meeting in Frankfurt. "We discussed whether a last-ditch loan to cover interest would be made if required to get a signature. The unanimous answer was no."

When martial law was declared on December 13th, some bankers unguardedly expressed optimism about Poland's economic future. But when Dresdner Bank received a telex on December 17th asking for a new loan of £350m the bankers knew that for them nothing had changed. They were ready with an immediate reply—"nothing doing".

Interest payments continued to trickle in slowly—though not without allegations that some groups (particularly the Austrians and Swiss) were getting favourable treatment. Poland reaffirmed its wish to sign the agreement and Bank Handlowy said it would get up to date on all 1981 interest payments by February 15th.

Meanwhile, the draft rescheduling agreement had been seen and approved by all 501 banks but by the end of February Poland was still not up to date on its payments and ready to sign. Even if Poland meets the new end-March deadline there can be no let-up for any of the actors in the drama. They will soon have to sit down and start the whole process again for Poland's 1982 debts.

SOFTLY, SOFTLY AT THE PARIS CLUB

The Economist, March 20, 1982, Supp. p.27

"The Paris Club is so flexible it must have been invented by the British", is the view of one senior IMF official closely involved with the workings of this group of creditor governments. The club has no formal rules and no legal status. It does not even necessarily meet in Paris. The Peruvian negotiations in 1968 took place in London, but most often its get-togethers are in the former Hotel Majestic on the Avenue Kléber—the equivalent of Carey Street for the developing world.

The Paris Club meetings bring together the official creditors of a country that has requested to reschedule its external debts. The meetings are chaired by the French treasury and supported by a small secretariat from the treasury.

Since Argentina became the club's first visitor in 1956 there have been 56 different negotiations involving about 20 debtor countries (some of them coming to Paris more than twice). However, the club is so ill-defined that there are borderline cases. Turkey, as a member of the OECD, has had its official debts rescheduled within the OECD—but in Paris at meetings chaired by the head of the French delegation.

Again, Paris Club reschedulings are generally carried out after the debtor has been to see the IMF and taken one of its economic packages. IMF officials often attend Paris Club meetings (along with representatives of the World Bank, the OECD and Unctad) as observers. When Poland rescheduled its official debts in May, 1981, it was not a member of the IMF. There was no stabilisation programme and no IMF observer at the meetings.

Paris Club meetings (like commerical bankers' reschedulings) are tailored to suit individual debtors. Hard and fast rules are few but Mrs Hardy's study[1] of official reschedulings has identified some.

- Paris Club meetings are delayed until the last possible moment—when the debtor is in substantial arrears and in imminent danger of default.

[1] *See* Hardy, Rescheduling Developing Country Debts, 131 The Banker 33-44 (July 1981)—Eds.

This cliffhanging approach is meant to show debtors that rescheduling is not a soft option, and not a surrogate form of aid.

* Only the principal OECD creditor governments are invited to attend. Other governments can sit in as observers (like that of Brazil which is owed $1.5 billion by Poland—more than Italy or Japan).
* The debt to be rescheduled is limited to officially guaranteed export credits and straight government loans. Exporters who have extended unguaranteed trade credits are left to fend for themselves. The banks do not look after their interests either. For exporters, obtaining bank finance has become a sort of insurance against rescheduling.
* The terms of rescheduling almost always involve stretching out the maturities on about 80% of existing debt at market rates of interest. Very rarely is new money provided to repay old debts (refinancing).

Within this framework there is plenty of scope for one debtor country to get a better deal than others. Mrs Hardy shows that the cost to creditor governments of reschedulings varies considerably from case to case. This has left negotiators (and especially the French) vulnerable to accusations of favouritism. Comparison of the terms obtained in 1966 by Indonesia and Ghana shows that western governments—who politically favoured Indonesia—reflected that favouritism in the terms of the two countries' reschedulings.

Paris Club deals are not necessarily accompanied by a rescheduling of private bank debt. When they are, they precede the bankers' meetings. In the recent case of Rumania, the commercial bankers (approached first by the Rumanians) insisted that a Paris Club agreement be reached first.

Creditor governments get scared of being accused of being lenient to debtors and thereby allowing them to pay off private banks (effectively with OECD taxpayers' money). Hence their (usual) insistence that no other creditor should obtain more favourable terms than they.

The IMF also frets that its loans enter a country only to re-emerge out of the back door as a repayment to private banks. Like a red rag to a bull was the statement earlier this year from Peru's central bank president, Mr Richard Webb. "IMF money", he said, "is cheap and in 1982 we need to borrow substantially"—a lot of it to service existing commerical bank debt. Peru duly requested a $1 billion loan from the IMF a few weeks later.

Mutual mistrust and jockeying for position among creditors often seems the dominant force behind reschedulings. The smug assurance of one French treasury official that the Paris Club "has a civilising mission to help debtor countries recognise the nature of their problems and the kind of international help they require" rings hollow.

The following case turned on the act of state doctrine: Could a foreign bank, which was effectively the instrument of a foreign power, unilaterally restructure its debt owed to, inter alia, American banks when the situs of the debt is not the foreign country but the United States? The court ruled it could not.

ALLIED BANK INTL. v. BANCO CREDITO AGRICOLA DE CARTAGO

757 F.2d 518 (2d Cir. 1985)

MESKILL, J.:

This matter is before us on rehearing. We vacate our previous decision dated April 23, 1984. We reverse the dismissal of the cause by the United States District Court for the Southern District of New York, Griesa, J. We also reverse the district court's denial of plaintiff-appellant Allied Bank International's (Allied) motion for summary judgment. Both district court rulings were predicated solely on the act of state doctrine. Because that doctrine is not applicable, we remand to the district court for entry of summary judgment for Allied.

I

Allied is the agent for a syndicate of thirty-nine creditor banks. Defendants appellees are three Costa Rican banks that are wholly owned by the Republic of Costa Rica and subject to the direct control of the Central Bank of Costa Rica (Central Bank). Allied brought this action in February 1982 to recover on promissory notes issued by the Costa Rican banks. The notes, which were in default, were payable in United States dollars in New York City. The parties' agreements acknowledged that the obligations were registered with Central Bank which was supposed to provide the necessary dollars for payment.

The defaults were due solely to actions of the Costa Rican government. In July 1981, in response to escalating national economic problems, Central Bank issued regulations which essentially suspended all external debt payments. In November 1981, the government issued an executive decree which conditioned all payments of external debt on express approval from Central Bank. Central Bank subsequently refused to authorize any foreign debt payments in United States dollars, thus precluding payment on the notes here at issue. In accordance with the provisions of the agreements, Allied accelerated the debt and sued for the full amount of principal and interest outstanding.

The Costa Rican banks moved the district court to dismiss the complaint, claiming lack of subject matter jurisdiction due to sovereign immunity, lack of in personam jurisdiction and insufficiency of process and service. Allied moved for summary judgment. The sole defense raised by appellees in response was the act of state doctrine.

The district court denied all of the motions. 566 F. Supp. 1440 (S.D.N.Y. 1983). Reasoning that a judicial determination contrary to the Costa Rican directives could embarrass the United States government in its relations with the Costa Rican government, the court held that the act of state doctrine barred entry of summary judgment for Allied.

While the action was still pending before the district court, the parties began to negotiate a rescheduling of the debt. In July 1982, the suit was dismissed by agreement after the parties stipulated that no issues of fact remained with respect to the act of state doctrine issue. In September 1983, appellees, Central Bank and the Republic of Costa Rica signed a refinancing agreement with the coordinating agent for Costa Rica's external creditors. Fidelity Union Trust Company of New Jersey, one of the members of the Allied syndicate, did not accept the agreement. On behalf of Fidelity, the only creditor that refused to participate in the restructuring, Allied has prosecuted this appeal. The refinancing went into effect nonetheless and appellees have been making payments to the remaining thirty-eight members of the syndicate.

II

In our previous decision, we affirmed the district court's dismissal. We did not address the question of whether the act of state doctrine applied because we determined that the actions of the Costa Rican government which precipitated the default of the Costa Rican banks were fully consistent with the law and policy of the United States. We therefore concluded that principles of comity compelled us to recognize as valid the Costa Rican directives.

Our interpretation of United States policy, however, arose primarily from our belief that the legislative and executive branches of our government fully supported Costa Rica's actions and all of the economic ramifications. On rehearing, the Executive Branch of the United States joined this litigation as *amicus curiae* and respectfully disputed our reasoning. The Justice Department brief gave the following explanation of our government's support for the debt resolution procedure that operates through the auspices of the International Monetary Fund (IMF). Guided by the IMF, this long established approach encourages the cooperative adjustment of international debt problems. The entire strategy is grounded in the understanding that, while parties may agree to renegotiate conditions of payment, the underlying obligations to pay nevertheless remain valid and enforceable. Costa Rica's attempted unilateral restructuring of private obligations, the United States contends, was inconsistent with this system of international cooperation and negotiation and thus inconsistent with United States policy.

The United States government further explains that its position on private international debt is not inconsistent with either its own willingness to restructure Costa Rica's intergovernmental obligations or with continued United States aid to the economically distressed Central American country. Our previous conclusion that the Costa Rican decrees were consistent with United States policy was premised on these two circumstances.

In light of the government's elucidation of its position, we believe that our earlier interpretation of United States policy was wrong. Nevertheless, if, as Judge Griesa held, the act of state doctrine applies, it precludes judicial examination of the Costa Rican decrees. Thus we must first consider that question.

III

The act of state doctrine operates to confer presumptive validity on certain acts of foreign sovereigns by rendering non-justiciable claims that challenge such acts. The judicially created doctrine is not jurisdictional; it is "a rule of decision under which an act meeting the definition . . . is binding on the court." Restatement (Revised) of Foreign Relations Law §428 comment c (Tent. Draft No. 4, 1983); Empresa Cubana Exportadora de Azucar y Sus Derivados v. Lamborn & Co., 652 F.2d 231, 239 (2d Cir. 1981). The applicability of the doctrine is purely a matter of federal law. Banco Nacional de Cuba v. Sabbatino, 376 U.S. 398, 427, 84 S. Ct. 923, 939, 11 L. Ed. 2d 804 (1964). . . .

The Supreme Court has been quite careful to avoid the creation of "an inflexible and all-encompassing rule" to govern the application of the doctrine; "the less important the implications of an issue are for our foreign relations, the weaker the justification for exclusivity in the political branches." *Sabbatino*, 376 U.S. at 428, 84 S. Ct. at 940. The doctrine demands a case-by-case analysis of the extent to which in the context of a particular dispute separation of powers concerns are implicated. Texas Trading & Milling Corp. v. Federal Republic of Nigeria, 647 F.2d 300, 316 n. 38 (2d Cir. 1981), *cert. denied*, 454 U.S. 1148, 102 S. Ct. 1012, 71 L. Ed. 2d 301 (1982).

This analysis must always be tempered by common sense. *See* Tabacalera Severiano Jorge, S.A. v. Standard Cigar Co., 392 F.2d 706, 715 (5th Cir.), *cert. denied*, 393 U.S. 924, 89 S. Ct. 255, 21 L. Ed. 2d 260 (1968). The doctrine does not necessarily "preclude judicial resolution of all commercial consequences" that result from acts of foreign sovereigns performed within their own borders. Arango v. Guzman Travel Advisors Corp., 621 F.2d 1371, 1380-81 (5th Cir. 1980). But, obviously, where the taking is wholly accomplished within the foreign sovereign's territory, "it would be an affront to such foreign government for courts of the United States to hold that such act was a nullity." *Tabacalera*, 392 F.2d at 715. Furthermore, under such circumstances, the court's decision would almost surely be disregarded within the borders of the foreign state.

The extraterritorial limitation, as inevitable conjunct of the foreign policy concerns underlying the doctrine, dictates that our decision herein depends on the situs of the property at the time of the purported taking. The property, of course, is Allied's right to receive repayment from the Costa Rican banks in accordance with the agreements. The act of state doctrine is applicable to this dispute only if, when the decrees were promulgated, the situs of the debts was in Costa Rica. Because we conclude that the situs of the property was in the United States, the doctrine is not applicable.

As the Fifth Circuit explained in *Tabacalera,* the concept of the situs of a debt for act of state purposes differs from the ordinary concept. It depends in large part on whether the purported taking can be said to have "come to complete fruition within the dominion of the [foreign] government." *Tabacalera,* 392 F.2d at 715-16. In this case, Costa Rica could not wholly extinguish the Costa Rican banks' obligation to timely pay United States dollars to Allied in New York. Thus the situs of the debt was not Costa Rica.

The same result obtains under ordinary situs analysis. The Costa Rican banks conceded jurisdiction in New York and they agreed to pay the debt in New York City in United States dollars. Allied, the designated syndicate agent, is located in the United States, specifically in New York; some of the negotiations between the parties took place in the United States. The United States has an interest in maintaining New York's status as one of the foremost commercial centers in the world. Further, New York is the international clearing center for United States dollars. In addition to other international activities, United States banks lend billions of dollars to foreign debtors each year. The United States has an interest in ensuring that creditors entitled to payment in the United States in United States dollars under contracts subject to the jurisdiction of United States courts may assume that, except under the most extraordinary circumstances, their rights will be determined in accordance with recognized principles of contract law.

In contrast, while Costa Rica has a legitimate concern in overseeing the debt situation of state-owned banks and in maintaining a stable economy, its interest in the contracts at issue is essentially limited to the extent to which it can unilaterally alter the payment terms. Costa Rica's potential jurisdiction over the debt is not sufficient to locate the debt there for the purposes of act of state doctrine analysis. *Cf.* United Bank Ltd. v. Cosmic International, Inc., 542 F.2d 868, 874 (2d Cir. 1976).

Thus, under either analysis, our result is the same: the situs of the debt was in the United States, not in Costa Rica. Consequently, this was not "a taking of property within its own territory by [Costa Rica]." *Sabbatino,* 376 U.S. at 428, 84 S. Ct. at 940. The act of state doctrine is, therefore, inapplicable.

IV

Acts of foreign governments purporting to have extraterritorial effect—and consequently, by definition, falling outside the scope of the act of state doctrine—should be recognized by the courts only if they are consistent with the law and policy of the United States. United States v. Belmont, 301 U.S. 324, 332-33, 57 S. Ct. 758, 761-62, 81 L. Ed. 1134 (1937); Banco Nacional de

Cuba v. Chemical Bank, 658 F.2d at 908-09 . . . . Thus, we have come full circle to reassess whether we should give effect to the Costa Rican directives. We now conclude that we should not.

The Costa Rican government's unilateral attempt to repudiate private, commercial obligations is inconsistent with the orderly resolution of international debt problems. It is similarly contrary to the interests of the United States, a major source of private international credit. The government has procedures for resolving intergovernmental financial difficulties. *See, e.g.,* Foreign Assistance Act of 1961, Pub. L. No. 87-195, 75 Stat. 424 (1961) (codified as amended in scattered sections of 22 U.S.C.). With respect to private debt, support for the IMF resolution strategy is consistent with both the policy aims and best interests of the United States.

Recognition of the Costa Rican directives in this context would also be counter to principles of contract law. Appellees explicitly agreed that their obligation to pay would not be excused in the event that Central Bank failed to provide the necessary United States dollars for payment. This, of course, was the precise cause of the default. If we were to give effect to the directives, our decision would vitiate an express provision of the contracts between the parties.[4]

The Costa Rican directives are inconsistent with the law and policy of the United States. We refuse, therefore, to hold that the directives excuse the obligations of the Costa Rican banks. The appellees' inability to pay United States dollars relates only to the potential enforceability of the judgment; it does not determine whether judgment should enter. *See* Weston Banking Corp. v. Turkiye Garanti Bankasi A.S., 86 A.D.2d 544, 446 N.Y.S.2d 67, 69, *aff'd*, 57 N.Y.2d 315, 442 N.E.2d 1195, 456 N.Y. S.2d 684 (1982).

V

The parties agreed below that no questions of material fact remained as to Allied's motion for summary judgment. The act of state doctrine was the only defense raised by the Costa Rican banks to Allied's motion and the only

---

[4] Each agreement specifically provided:

7. Events of Default:
If any of the following events of default should occur and is not remedied within a period of 30 days as of the date of occurrence, the Agent Bank may, by a written notice to the Borrower declare the promissory notes to be due and payable. In such an event, they shall be considered to be due without presentment, demand, protest or any other notice to the Borrower, all of which are expressly waived by this agreement:
7.1 Any payment of principal or interest under this transaction shall not have been paid on its maturity date. If the Borrower shall not effect any payment of principal or interest on the promissory notes at maturity, due solely to the omission or refusal by the Central Bank of Costa Rica to provide the necessary U.S. Dollars, such an event shall not be considered to be an event of default which would justify the demandability of the obligation, during a period of 10 days after such maturity date.

ground for the district court's denial of that motion. Moreover, the doctrine was the sole basis for the district court's dismissal of the action. We hold today that the act of state doctrine is not applicable to this litigation. Therefore, the district court's rulings cannot stand.

We vacate our previous decision, reverse the district court's denial of Allied's motion for summary judgment and its dismissal of the action and direct the district court to enter judgment for Allied.

COMMITTEE ON BANKING, FINANCE, AND URBAN AFFAIRS OF THE U.S. HOUSE OF REPRESENTATIVES, TO INCREASE THE U.S. QUOTA IN THE INTERNATIONAL MONETARY FUND AND RELATED MATTERS

98th Cong., 1st Sess. (1983)

ANNEX TO THE TESTIMONY OF W.R. KLINE BEFORE THE SUBCOMMITTEE ON INTERNATIONAL TRADE, INVESTMENT, AND MONETARY POLICY, APRIL 16, 1983

PROPOSALS FOR DEBT REFORM

Most analysts agree that orderly servicing of the $700 billion in external debt of developing and Eastern European countries will be contingent on world economic recovery in 1983-86. But a growing number go further: they argue that the debt is already unmanageable and that, either regardless of the extent of world recovery or because they expect it to be weak, the only way to defuse the systemic threat of the debt is to reduce its real burden for developing countries. Their plans typically involve an internationally coordinated stretch-out of the debt and reduction in its interest burden.

Proposals

The principal reform proposals under discussion in the United States are those by Peter Kenen of Princeton University, Senator Bill Bradley (D-New Jersey), Congressman Charles Schumer (D-New York), and financier Felix Rohatyn. A unique proposal has also been suggested by Norman Bailey of the National Security Council. In addition, some British bankers have been calling for new institutional changes.

Kenen/Bradley. The proposal by Peter Kenen (and in many regards the approach advocated by Senator Bradley) would establish a new International Debt Discount Corporation. This agency would buy up LDC debt held by banks at a discount of 10 cents on the dollar. It would pay the banks in long term bonds. It would become the creditor of the developing country, taking over the debt in question. It could afford to grant a modest reduction in the interest rate payable by the developing country, because of the 10 percent discount at which the debt would be purchased from banks. In addition, it would renegotiate the debt to longer maturities. Its program would not be optional: once a country entered into a program with it, all bank claims on the country would be forced into inclusion in its program. (Otherwise banks would sell off only the weakest loans.)

Rohatyn. Drawing on the analogy of a worldwide Municipal Assistance Corporation—the entity created to revive New York City from bankruptcy—Felix Rohatyn proposes that LDC debt be stretched out to long term maturities of 25 to 30 years, and its interest reduced to perhaps 6 percent. The schedule of principal repayments would be designed so that interest plus principal payments would be no more than 25 to 30 percent of exports annually. The agency for this conversion could be the International Monetary Fund, the World Bank, or a totally new agency. Such an agency would buy the claims of the banks with long term bonds it would issue. Rohatyn recognizes that the conversion to long term low interest loans would impose a loss on banks, and that the division of the loss between bank stockholders, taxpayers, and countries would have to be resolved. He argues that against this loss, banks would achieve greater security of their assets, and that regulators could permit them to spread out their write-downs over a long period of time. Rohatyn also envisions the need for the U.S. government to be prepared to purchase preferred shares in banks as a means of providing them with an infusion of capital in the event that foreign countries seek to intimidate the U.S. with financial blackmail by threatening outright repudiation of debt.

Schumer. Congressman Schumer proposes that bank loans be converted to long term, low interest loans, with the guidance of the IMF. This conversion would be directly by the banks and debtor countries, with no new international intermediary: the banks would still be the creditors. Where such conversion is not agreed to, the US Executive Director in the IMF would be instructed to vote against any IMF loans. The conversion program would set repayments at a manageable fraction of export earnings. Schumer's plan also calls for increased loan loss reserves when debts are not paid on time—unless restructuring is part of an IMF-negotiated conversion of short term to long term loans; establishment of an insurance fund with a small surcharge on renegotiated debt; and country ceilings on short term loans.

Others. Norman Bailey of the U.S. National Security Council has proposed that LDC debt be replaced with a form of equity asset ("exchange participation note") entitling the holder to a specified share in the country's export earnings. Congressman Jacobs (D-Indiana) has proposed the "Reckless Risk Recovery Act of 1983," which would require that banks owning loans in countries that do not meet payment schedules and subsequently receive loans from the U.S. government or the IMF reimburse the U.S. Treasury for a pro rata share of such loans.

Finally, some British bankers (including officials of Barclays Bank and Morgan Grenfell) have advocated a discounting device whereby banks could sell off their rescheduled LDC debts to central banks or other agencies in order to obtain liquidity for use in other lending, domestic and foreign. Such purchases by central banks could be in the form of bonds issued to the private banks, eligible for discounting for cash if the banks experienced illiquidity. In some versions those bonds would bear no interest so that their eventual sale would only be at a significant discount, causing a loss for the bank—and reflecting the sentiment that banks should pay a price for mistaken loans.

Evaluation

Most of these reform proposals share the following flaws.

(1) Diagnosis. The proposals all diagnose the current debt situation as unmanageable. In effect, they judge the LDCs to be insolvent, not just illiquid. But unless world economic conditions are extremely depressed for the next three or four years, this debt should be manageable, as discussed in the main testimony.

(2) Adverse Impact. Most of the proposals constitute a counterproductive, panic-based action that would tend to turn good debt into bad debt. These schemes would tend to choke off new bank lending to LDCs. Few banks will be prepared to lend new money if the likelihood is high that such money will be subsequently mandated into a program requiring the loss of 10 cents on the dollar, or converted into a low interest asset. Yet the choking off of new loans would precipitate precisely the crisis that the authors of such proposals fear. Countries such as Brazil need more than rollover of existing loans: they need infusion of new loans to cover at least a major portion of the interest due on old loans. Most of the reform proposals would make sense only in an environment in which there are expected to be no new loans whatsoever but maturities are being lengthened; they do not address the need for new lending.

(3) Impact on Bank Capital. Several of the proposals appear naive in that they do not address their dire implications for bank capital. Even a 10 percent write-off would mean a 30 percent cut in capital for the large banks (or somewhat less, allowing for profits and tax effects). More ambitious debt relief such as Rohatyn's and Schumer's would quite likely cause bank losses exceeding capital.

(4) Requirement of Public Capital. New international agencies would have to have massive capital to take over significant LDC debt. If only half of the $700 billion debt were taken over, and if capital backing were full, and if paid-in capital were 10 percent of total, industrial countries would have to autho-

rize contingent liability for $350 billion and actually pay in $35 billion to give an international agency capital backing to take over the debt. Such magnitudes are wildly beyond any contributions made to multilateral institutions in recent years. As for Schumer's proposal, which does not involve an international agency, it is extraordinary in requiring an outright loss by banks, without providing them in return even the increased security that would be achieved by switching their claims from LDCs to an official entity.

(5) Moral Hazard. The establishment of a new international entity to stretch out maturities of LDC debt and reduce its interest burden would inevitably pose serious "moral hazard" problems of inducing changes in action that are to the self-interest of the debtor at the expense of the creditor and taxpayer. With such an entity in place there would be a strong incentive for any LDC to seek debt relief even when it would be possible with appropriate adjustment policies to continue to meet orderly debt payments. It would be a structural flaw in the system to build in an incentive to debt servicing disruption. It is for this reason that debt reschedulings have typically been carried out only when the alternative was imminent default.

Conclusion

Increasing attention is being attracted by proposals for sweeping debt reform. However, their adoption could be counterproductive. Case by case negotiation with countries in debt servicing difficulty remains a preferable alternative.

And finally, a concluding word on the debt crisis.

THE BANKER'S SONG

Far Eastern Economic Review, August 11, 1983

Thanks to the Review for the excellent continuing coverage of Indonesia's financial and economic woes. It certainly has helped me, as a financial and insurance consultant, to focus on specific areas where risk factors have increased and liabilities should be kept covered more than ever.

It also inspired—in fact, in the shower—the following lament which I offer as my contribution to the international banking community:

> My money is over the ocean,
> My money is over the sea,
> My money is over the ocean;
> Oh bring back my money to me.

CHORUS:
Bring back, oh bring back,
Oh bring back my money to me,
      to me.
Pay back, please pay back,
Complete with my management fee.
Collateral never existed
To any meaningful degree;
'Twas really all wishful thinking
On somebody's part, if not me.
      Bring back, . . .
The principal has been re-scheduled
By new governmental decree;
The interest can't be recovered
From debtors far over the sea.
      Bring back, . . .
So went my depositors' money,
Somebody has shaken the tree;
I cannot recover the honey,
Nobody to blame now, but me.
      Bring back, . . .

Harjo Nimpoeno
Jakarta

Bibliographical Note

For additional information *see* the remainder of the hearings from which the
W. R. Cline excerpt is taken; and the Senate Banking Committee Hearings on
International Debt, 98th Cong., 1st Sess., February 14-17, 1983.

QUESTIONS

1. How is the order of negotiation important as between public and private
creditors?

2. How does this procedure differ from a Chapter 11 Bankruptcy (with the
IMF effectively playing the decisive role, because of its control over conditionality)?

3. What will happen if this is done in many cases? Is each case a precedent
for the next?

4. Is the *Allied Bank* case correct? Consistent with *Vishipco? Weston?* Would it
matter whether or not the loan agreement had the kinds of covenants and
waivers of sovereign immunity included in the credit agreement in the Selected Documents Supplement? For background, describing earlier acrimony

among the various creditors, *see* Step by Step through the Costa Rica Sage, Euromoney, August 1982, p.33.

5. Is the court's treatment of the act of state doctrine wise? Consistent with *Timberlane?* For cases going the opposite way on the act of state issue in this context, *see* Braka v. Bancomer, S.A., 589 F. Supp. 1465 (S.D.N.Y. 1984); and Braka v. Multibanco Comermex, S.A., 589 F. Supp. 802 (S.D.N.Y. 1984).

6. Is the *Allied Bank* approach fair among different creditors? Does the result help or hurt a "cooperative adjustment of international debt problems?"

7. Is there value in the court's effort to define the "situs" of the debt, or is this effectively a way of avoiding the policy issues? Whether or not you are sympathetic with the analytical approach, do you find the result of the approach reasonable, as you look at the various cases in this chapter?

8. Is the court right, in the paragraph citing *Weston,* in distinguishing the enforceability of a judgment from entry of a judgment?

9. Is the case consistent with IMF Article VIII, §2(b)?

10. Which of the bail-out techniques described in the Kline Annex are likely to be effective? To be enacted? Who pays the price in each case?

11. Is there any way to bail out the debtor governments without bailing out the banks?

12. How important is judicial enforceability in causing nations to pay their debts?

13. Suppose that control and avoidance of the international debt crisis became a basis of controversy between the European nations and Japan on the one hand and the United States on the other. The United States, moved by a combination of laissez-faire economic conservatism and of congressional opposition to bailing out of international banks, refused to support new formal international arrangements.

Europe and Japan, however, took a very different view, and urged the banks to form an international cartel to protect themselves against debt default. Under the terms of this cartel—which the banks of the involved nations would be only too happy to organize—the participating international banks would agree to help one another in the event that developing nations' defaults would bring any one of them near bankruptcy. And, in a much more important and controversial clause, the banks would agree on a common policy of restricting payouts to depositors in the event that this would be the only way for all to avoid bankruptcy. As a lawyer for a U.S. bank, what would you now recommend to your management?

Chapter XVI

Investor Nation Regulation
of Portfolio Investment

Regulation of portfolio investment—typically carried out through such forms as corporate stocks and bonds—has followed a very different path from that of bank lending. Following the stock market collapse of 1929, the United States enacted two statutes, the Securities Act of 1933 and the Securities Exchange Act of 1934 (15 U.S.C. §§77a-77aa; 15 U.S.C. §§78a-78bb, respectively)—designed to reassure investors and restore confidence in the stock market.

These statutes rely primarily upon disclosure through registration statements and prospectuses filed with the Securities and Exchange Commission (SEC) and, under certain circumstances, made available to the investor. The material disclosed in these statements, which must meet standards defined by the SEC, is designed to enable investors and financial analysts to obtain accurate information about the issuer (i.e., borrower). With this information available, the quality of the securities offerings should be self-regulating, and there should be no need for the government directly to regulate the terms of securities offerings, as it does in a few nations.

The securities industry itself generally operates through "underwriters," securities firms that buy a block of securities from the company making the public offering, and that then resell the securities to the public through a national network. Thus, when a company, say General Motors, wishes to raise new capital on the securities market, it authorizes a stock offering through its own corporate procedures and sells the entire package to the underwriters, who pass it on to institutional investors and the public. The entire arrangement is carefully negotiated in advance—part of the expertise of the underwriter lies in estimating the likelihood that the securities will actually sell at a specific price.

After their sale to the public, the securities enter the "secondary market," the market in which a holder (who might have acquired the securities in an original offering) may resell them, either on a stock exchange or on the less centralized national market. These markets serve speculative functions—but also contribute to initial investment. A person is much more likely to make such an initial investment (which usually directly supports the acquisition of productive resources) if that person can reasonably expect to be able to resell the security later should he or she so wish.

The situations in which the disclosures must be made are defined in quite technical ways—and the securities statutes are particularly difficult to follow because they place many of the important criteria and standards in the definitions. But they are designed basically to encompass a "public offering," i.e., one in which the securities are offered to more than a very few individuals who are well informed about the specific firm. Typically, this public offering will either be by the firm itself selling a large package of securities for the sake of raising capital, or by the inside investors, entrepreneurs, and executives who hold large blocks of stock that they wish to resell to the public. In both cases a registration statement will be required. And, in addition, various statements are required upon registration on a stock exchange. Finally, some of the regulations look to indirect enforcement. Thus, the leading stock exchanges have their own standards as to what to accept; the SEC can and does rely in part upon those rules to protect investors.

A.   INTERNATIONAL ASPECTS OF REGISTRATION REQUIREMENTS AND THEIR ANALOGUES

If it is to protect U.S. investors, the registration and disclosure requirements must extend to at least some international transactions. Consider the following situations:

1. A U.S. firm, publicly traded in the United States or listed on a U.S. stock exchange, makes an offering of securities in Europe to raise additional capital.

2. A European firm makes a public offering in the United States or seeks listing on a U.S. stock exchange.

3. A European firm sells a few shares of a European public offering to U.S. citizens who are living in Europe and who purchase the securities in Europe through brokers in Europe.

4. A very few of the shares purchased in Europe, as in example 3, are brought back to the United States.

5. The pattern of example 4 reaches the point that there are a significant number of U.S. shareholders. (Note that this can relatively easily happen with respect to Canada and securities purchased on the Toronto stock exchange.)

In each of the five cases, the question is whether or not registration under U.S. law should be required. Assuming that the key purpose of the law is to protect U.S. investors, the answer is relatively obvious in each case. The most difficult definitional problem, however, is how to draw the line between case 4 and case 5 in a way that does not penalize the foreign firm that accidentally has a few U.S. shareholders but does not open the door to effective evasion of U.S. law.

Consider the following SEC approach to these tasks.

17 C.F.R. §240.12g3-2 EXEMPTIONS FOR AMERICAN DEPOSITARY RECEIPTS AND CERTAIN FOREIGN SECURITIES

(a) Securities of any class issued by any foreign private issuer shall be exempt from section 12(g) [registration requirement] of the Act if the class has fewer than 300 holders resident in the United States. This exemption shall continue until the next fiscal year end at which the issuer has a class of equity securities held by 300 or more persons resident in the United States. For the purpose of determining whether a security is exempt pursuant to this paragraph, securities held of record by persons resident in the United States shall be determined as provided in Rule 12g5-1 [ownership rules] except that securities held of record by a broker, dealer, bank or nominee for any of them for the accounts of customers resident in the United States shall be counted as held in the United States by the number of separate accounts for which the securities are held. The issuer may rely in good faith on information as to the number of such separate accounts supplied by all owners of the class of its securities which are brokers, dealers, or banks or a nominee for any of them.

(b)(1) Securities of any foreign private issuer shall be exempt from section 12(g) of the Act if the issuer, or a government official or agency of the country of the issuer's domicile or in which it is incorporated or organized:

(i) Shall furnish to the Commission whatever information in each of the following categories the issuer since the beginning of its last fiscal year (A) has made or is required to make public pursuant to the law of the country of its domicile or in which it is incorporated or organized, (B) has filed or is required to file with a stock exchange on which its securities are traded and which was made public by such exchange, or (C) has distributed or is required to distribute to its security holders;

(ii) Shall furnish to the Commission a list identifying the information referred to in paragraph (b)(1)(i) of this section and stating when and by whom it is required to be made public, filed with any such exchange, or distributed to security holders;

(iii) Shall furnish to the Commission, during each subsequent fiscal year, whatever information is made public as described in (A), (B) or (C) of paragraph (b)(1)(i) of this section promptly after such information is made or required to be made public as described therein;

(iv) Shall, promptly after the end of any fiscal year in which any changes occur in the kind of information required to be published as referred to in the list furnished under paragraph (b)(1)(ii) of this section or any subsequent list, furnish to the Commission a revised list reflecting such changes; and

(v) Shall furnish to the Commission in connection with the initial submission the following information to the extent known or which can be obtained without unreasonable effort or expense: the number of holders of each class of equity securities resident in the United States, the amount and percentage of each class of outstanding equity securities held by residents in the United States, the circumstances in which such securities were acquired, and the date and circumstances of the most recent public distribution of securities by the issuer or an affiliate thereof.

(2) The information required to be furnished under paragraphs (b)(1)(i) and (b)(1)(ii) of this section shall be furnished on or before the date on which a registration statement under section 12(g) of the Act would otherwise be required to be filed. Any issuer furnishing information under paragraph (b)(1)(i) of this section shall notify the Commission that it is furnished under that paragraph.

(3) The information required to be furnished under this paragraph (b) is information material to an investment decision such as: the financial condition or results of operations; changes in business; acquisitions or dispositions of assets; issuance, redemption or acquisitions of their securities; changes in management or control; the granting of options or the payment of other remuneration to directors or officers; and transactions with directors, officers or principal security holders. . . .

(5) The furnishing of any information or document under paragraph (b) of this rule shall not constitute an admission for any purpose that the issuer is subject to the Act. . . .

(d) The exemption provided by paragraph (b) of this rule shall not be available for the following securities:

(1) Securities of a foreign private issuer that has or has had during the prior eighteen months any securities registered under section 12 of the Act [registration for securities listed on exchanges] or a reporting obligation (suspended or active) under section 15(d) of the Act [follow-on reporting requirements for public issue];

(2) Securities of a foreign private issuer issued in a transaction to acquire by merger, consolidation, exchange of securities, or acquisition of assets, another issuer that had securities registered under section 12 of the Act or a reporting obligation (suspended or active) under section 15(d) of the Act; . . .

NOTES AND QUESTIONS

1. How well does the SEC draw the lines involved?

2. If you were a U.S. issuer borrowing in Europe, how would you assure yourself that the securities did not find their way back to the United States? For a sample approach, a "90-day lockup," based on temporary certificates along with certifications that the purchaser is not a U.S. national or resident, see Nathan, Special Problems Arising as a Result of Trading in Multiple Markets, 4 J. Comp. Corp. L. & Sec. Reg. 225 (1982).

3. How comfortable would you be if you represented the board of a European firm that had large numbers of bearer shares outstanding (shares circulating without any central registry so that the firm does not know who its shareholders are)?

4. Why is the SEC so sensitive to foreign concerns in saying that it will not

take jurisdiction should the relevant foreign statements be filed rather than saying that it is taking jurisdiction and then requiring the relevant statements? *See* 21 The Record of the Association of the Bar of the City of New York 240 (1966).

5. How well would the procedures be adapted to sovereign loans, such as bonds issued by a foreign government on a U.S. security market?

6. As treasurer of a foreign private firm, when would you prefer to approach the U.S. capital market by selling securities under these procedures, and when would you prefer to take out a bank loan under the procedures described in the previous chapter? Are the differences rationally related to the various economic and institutional differences in the risks involved?

B.   EXTRATERRITORIAL APPLICATION OF JUDICIALLY ENFORCED PROVISIONS

The securities acts include not just registration requirements but also a substantive law enforced by civil actions in the regular federal courts. The key provisions are the following statute and rule adopted under it:

SECURITIES AND EXCHANGE ACT OF 1934, 15 U.S.C. §78j

REGULATION OF THE USE OF MANIPULATIVE AND DECEPTIVE DEVICES

Sec. 10.   It shall be unlawful for any person, directly or indirectly, by the use of any means or instrumentality of interstate commerce or of the mails, or of any facility of any national securities exchange—

(a) To effect a short sale, or to use or employ any stop-loss order in connection with the purchase or sale, of any security registered on a national securities exchange, in contravention of such rules and regulations as the Commission may prescribe as necessary or appropriate in the public interest or for the protection of investors.

(b) To use or employ, in connection with the purchase or sale of any security registered on a national securities exchange or any security not so registered, any manipulative or deceptive device or contrivance in contravention of such rules and regulations as the Commission may prescribe as necessary or appropriate in the public interest or for the protection of investors.

17 C.F.R. §240.10b-5

RULE 10b-5. EMPLOYMENT OF MANIPULATIVE AND DECEPTIVE DEVICES

It shall be unlawful for any person, directly or indirectly, by the use of any means or instrumentality of interstate commerce, or of the mails, or of any facility of any national securities exchange,

(1) to employ any device, scheme, or artifice to defraud,

(2) to make any untrue statement of a material fact or to omit to state a material fact necessary in order to make the statements made, in the light of the circumstances under which they were made, not misleading, or

(3) to engage in any act, practice, or course of business which operates or would operate as a fraud or deceit upon any person, . . .

You have already seen this section in Gaines and Fitzpatrick v. Haughton (*supra*, pp. 645-652) in Chapter XII. The section has given rise to a "federal common law" of corporations in which civil actions are available to an investor who has lost money and can bring his or her complaint under the ambit of 10b-5. The idea of fraud and deceit is very broad, so the potential scope of this section is also broad, and it becomes a way to bring a number of corporate issues into federal court. At the same time, concerns for federalism have led the Supreme Court to exercise special care in defining the scope of rights under this provision.

Although 10b-5 is the leading example, there are a number of other comparable provisions that can lead to parallel forms of lawsuit, including, for example, restrictions that profits made by corporate insiders on purchases and sales made within a six-month period must be given to the company for the benefit of all investors. At the time that these provisions were enacted, their domestic impact may not have been fully realized—and their international impact was considered only indirectly and opaquely. This impact lay dormant until the following case. In analyzing the case, note that two separate jurisdictional tests are involved. One, raising issues that should by now be familiar, goes to United States jurisdiction over a transaction with mixed domestic and foreign elements. The other, spelled out in the securities laws in terms of use of the means of interstate commerce, goes to the domestic question of jurisdiction in the federal courts as opposed to the state courts. On a rehearing en banc, the district court was reversed. That decision is set out following the first.

SCHOENBAUM v. FIRSTBROOK (I)

405 F.2d 200 (2d Cir. 1968)

LUMBARD, J.:

Plaintiff, an American shareholder of Banff Oil Ltd., a Canadian corporation, brought this shareholder derivative action to recover under Section 10(b) of the Securities Exchange Act of 1934, 15 U.S.C. 78j(b) and Rule 10b-5, 17 C.F.R. §240.10b-5 (1967), for damages to the corporation resulting from the sales, in Canada, of Banff treasury stock to defendants Aquitaine of Canada, Ltd., and Paribas Corporation. Plaintiff alleged that the defendant corporations and Banff's directors, who are the individual defendants in this action, conspired to defraud Banff by making Banff sell treasury shares at the market price which the defendants, who had inside information not yet disclosed to the public, knew did not represent the true value of the shares.

Defendants moved pursuant to Rules 12(c) and 56, Fed. R. Civ. P., for summary judgment, and under Rule 12(b) to dismiss the complaint on the ground that the Court lacked jurisdiction over the subject matter. Judge Cooper, refusing to permit plaintiff to carry out a program of discovery, entered judgment for defendants, holding that the Court lacked jurisdiction because the Securities and Exchange Act does not have extraterritorial application, and that plaintiff failed to state a cause of action under §10(b) and Rule 10b-5. 268 F. Supp. 385 (S.D.N.Y. 1967).

We find that the district court had subject matter jurisdiction but affirm the judgment below because, while plaintiff's complaint alleges a breach of fiduciary duty by Banff's directors in authorizing sales of treasury shares at too low a price, these allegations fail to state a cause of action under §10(b) of the Exchange Act.

THE FACTS

Banff is a Canadian corporation and conducts all of its operations within Canada. Its common stock is registered with the SEC and traded upon both the American Stock Exchange and the Toronto Stock Exchange. In February 1964, Aquitaine Company of Canada, Ltd., acquired control of Banff through a tender offer to Banff shareholders in the United States and Canada. Aquitaine is a wholly owned subsidiary of a French corporation, Societe National des Petroles d'Aquitaine, which in turn is a subsidiary of Enterprises for Research and Activities in Petroleum (ERAP), a French governmental oil agency.

In March 1964, Banff and Aquitaine entered into an agreement to conduct joint oil explorations. In October 1964, Banff entered into a "farmout agreement" with Socony Mobil under which Banff and Aquitaine would receive a 50% interest in 160,000 acres in the Rainbow Lake area of Alberta, Canada, in return for paying the total cost of drilling two exploratory wells. The Rainbow area is a desolate wilderness region over 100 miles from the nearest all-weather road or railway. At least sixteen wells had previously been drilled in the general vicinity by six different oil companies, and all had been abandoned as failures. Because of the difficulty of conducting explorations in this region and the highly speculative prospects for success Socony Mobil was willing to give up a half interest merely for drilling two test wells.

Banff received a 5% interest and Aquitaine received a 45% interest, pursuant to their joint exploration agreement, with the drilling costs to be paid 10% by Banff and 90% by Aquitaine. On December 11, 1964 Banff's Board of Directors, the three Aquitaine representatives abstaining, voted to offer to sell 500,000 shares of Banff treasury stock to Aquitaine at the current market price allegedly for the purpose of financing Banff's share of the exploration expenses. On January 5, 1965, Aquitaine's president wrote to Banff that "our Chairman and Managing Director . . . has agreed to your . . . proposal." On January 26, Banff issued a press release announcing that Aquitaine "intended to purchase" 500,000 shares of common stock at the price of $1.35 per share, the closing price on the Toronto Stock Exchange on December 11, 1964. Actual delivery of the shares took place March 16, 1965.

Exploration in the Rainbow area commenced toward the end of 1964. On February 6, 1965, the test well flowed oil to the surface on a drillstem test. This information was released to the public on February 8. The well reached total depth on March 17, 1965, the day after delivery on the Aquitaine purchase. On March 18, Banff issued a press release indicating that the discovery well was completed and that no further information would be disclosed in the immediate future. A further release on April 20 explained that the company was taking advantage of the Alberta law permitting it to withhold information on its discovery for one year to reduce competition from other companies in bidding on government oil lands in the discovery area. The release stated "The Board feels that this discovery is of great significance to the company but it is too early to have any idea of the areal extent."

After the discovery, further exploration activity was undertaken. In September 1965, a press release announced the formation of a company, in which Banff has a $3\frac{1}{3}\%$ interest and Aquitaine has a 30% interest, to build a pipeline into the area. To finance its activities, Banff's Board of Directors authorized negotiation of sales of treasury shares of common stock at $6.75 per share or more. Paribas Corporation—a Delaware corporation doing business in New York and a wholly owned subsidiary of Banque de Paris et des Pays-Bas, a French banking institution—negotiated a purchase of 270,000 shares of Banff Common at $7.30 per share, the current price on the Toronto Stock Exchange, on behalf of Banque de Paris et des Pays-Bas pour le Grand Duche de Luxembourg, another subsidiary of Banque de Paris. The issue was to be placed with "ten European professional investors." A verbal offer was made by Paribas on November 19, 1965. A written offer was mailed by Paribas from New York and was accepted by Banff in Canada on November 22. Payment and delivery took place in Canada January 24, 1966.

THE ALLEGATIONS IN THE COMPLAINT

The complaint alleged that "For some time prior to February 6, 1965, Aquitaine and the other defendants knew Banff had exceptionally valuable oil properties located in the Rainbow Lake area in Alberta, Canada." It alleged that the Aquitaine purchase of 500,000 treasury shares at $1.35 per share took place March 15, 1965, and that the Paribas purchase of 270,000 shares at $7.30 on January 24, 1966 was on behalf of "affiliates, business associates and friends" of Aquitaine and its parent companies, and that defendants withheld information until March 16, 1966 in order to purchase the treasury shares at an artificially low market price, paying to Banff about $10,000,000 less than the stock's fair market value.[1]

The individual defendants are all of Banff's directors. They allegedly conspired with the corporate defendants and approved of, participated in or acquiesced in the transactions with the corporate defendants.

SUBJECT MATTER JURISDICTION

Plaintiff predicated subject matter jurisdiction upon Section 27 of the Securities and Exchange Act, 15 U.S.C. §78aa, which gives the district courts exclusive jurisdiction over all "actions at law brought to enforce any liability or duty created by this title or the rules and regulations thereunder." The district court concluded that the Act has no extraterritorial application, and that therefore no liability arose under the Act with regard to the sales in question, which took place in Canada between foreign buyers and sellers. The court found nothing to rebut the presumption that the Act was intended to apply only to transactions within the territorial limits of the United States. It also stated that the presumption was reinforced by the "specific mandate" of Section 30(b), 15 U.S.C. §78dd(b), which provides that the Act does not apply "to any person insofar as he transacts a business in securities without the jurisdiction of the United States. . . ."

We disagree with the district court's conclusion. We believe that Congress intended the Exchange Act to have extraterritorial application in order to protect domestic investors who have purchased foreign securities on American exchanges and to protect the domestic securities market from the effects of improper foreign transactions in American securities. In our view, neither the usual presumption against extraterritorial application of legislation nor the specific language of Section 30(b) show Congressional intent to preclude application of the Exchange Act to transactions regarding stocks traded in the United States which are effected outside the United States, when extraterritorial application of the Act is necessary to protect American investors.

Section 2 of the Exchange Act, 15 U.S.C. §78b, states that because transactions in securities are affected with "a national public interest" it is "necessary to provide for regulation and control of such transactions and of practices and matters related thereto, . . . necessary to make such regulation and control reasonably . . . complete state commerce and to insure the maintenance of fair and honest markets in such transactions."

The Act seeks to regulate the stock exchanges and the relationships of the investing public to corporations which invite public investment by listing on such exchanges. . . .

Banff common stock is registered and traded on the American Stock Exchange. To protect United States shareholders of Banff common stock, Banff is

---

[1] Banff common stock traded at prices as high as $18 per share in 1966.

required to comply with the provisions of the Securities Exchange Act concerning financial reports to the SEC, §13, 15 U.S.C. §78m; proxy solicitation, §14, 15 U.S.C. §78n, and reports of insider holdings, §16, 15 U.S.C. §78p. Similarly, the anti-fraud provision of §10(b), which enables the Commission to prescribe rules "necessary or appropriate in the public interest or for the protection of investors" reaches beyond the territorial limits of the United States and applies when a violation of the Rules is injurious to United States investors. "Acts done outside a jurisdiction, but intended to produce and producing detrimental effects within it, justify a state in punishing the cause of the harm as if [the actor] had been present at the [time of the detrimental] effect, if the state should succeed in getting him within its power." Strassheim v. Daily, 221 U.S. 280, 285, 31 S. Ct. 558, 560, 55 L. Ed. 735 (1911).

The Commission has recognized the broad extraterritorial applicability of the Act and has specifically exempted certain foreign issuers from the operation of Sections 14 and 16 of the Act, when enforcement would be impractical. . . .

The provision contained in Section 30(b) does not alter our conclusion that the Exchange Act has extraterritorial application. In our view, while section 30(b) was intended to exempt persons conducting a business in securities through foreign securities markets from the provisions of the Act, it does not preclude extraterritorial application of the Exchange Act to persons who engage in isolated foreign transactions.

Section 30, entitled "Foreign Securities Exchanges,"[3] deals with the extent to which the Act applies to persons effecting securities transactions through foreign exchanges. Section 30(a) empowers the SEC to regulate all brokers and dealers who use the mails or interstate commerce, for the purpose of effecting a transaction in American securities on exchanges outside the United States. 2 Loss, Securities Regulation, 1170 n.2 (2d ed. 1961). It was intended to prevent evasion of the Act through transactions on foreign exchanges. *See* Hearings on S. Res. 89 (72d Cong.), and S. Res. 56 and S. Res. 97 (73d Cong.) before the Committee on Banking and Currency, 73d Cong., 2d Sess. part 15, pp.6569, 6578-79 (1934).

Section 30(b) states that the Act does not apply in the absence of SEC rule to prevent evasion of the Act to "any person insofar as he transacts a business in securities without the jurisdiction of the United States." The language of

---

[3]"Section 30. (a) It shall be unlawful for any broker or dealer, directly or indirectly, to make use of the mails or of any means or instrumentality of interstate commerce for the purpose of effecting on an exchange not within or subject to the jurisdiction of the United States, any transaction in any security the issuer of which is a resident of or is organized under the laws of, or has its principal place of business in, a place within or subject to the jurisdiction of the United States, in contravention of such rules and regulations as the Commission may prescribe as necessary or appropriate in the public interest or for the protection of investors or to prevent the evasion of this title.

"(b) The provisions of this title or of any rule or regulation thereunder shall not apply to any person insofar as he transacts a business in securities without the jurisdiction of the United States, unless he transacts such business in contravention of such rules and regulations as the Commission may prescribe as necessary or appropriate to prevent the evasion of this title."

§30(b) must be construed in light of the purpose of the subsection, and the definitions of terms contained in §3(a) of the Act.

The purpose of this subsection is to permit persons in the securities business to conduct transactions in securities outside of the United States without complying with the burdensome reporting requirement of the Act and without being subject to its regulatory provisions, except insofar as the Commission finds it necessary and appropriate to regulate such transactions to prevent evasion of the Act. It is also designed to take the Commission out of the business of regulating foreign security exchanges unless the Commission deems regulation necessary to prevent evasion of the domestic regulatory scheme. The exemption relieves the Commission of the impossible task of enforcing American securities law upon persons whom it could not subject to the sanctions of the Act for actions upon which it could not bring its investigatory powers to bear.

If §30(b) had been meant to exempt every transaction by any person outside of the United States it would have been drafted to state that the Act does not apply to "any transaction in any security outside the jurisdiction of the United States," a phrase used in §30(a). The drafters used the phrase "any person insofar as he transacts a business in securities without the jurisdiction of the United States" in §30(b) because it is a term which would exempt the business transactions not only of brokers and dealers but also of banks. The term "brokers and dealers," used in §30(a), could not be used because the definitions of "broker" and "dealer" in §§3(a) (4) and 3(a) (5), 15 U.S.C. §78c(a) (4) and (5), specifically exclude "banks" as defined in §3(a) (6), 15 U.S.C. §78c(a) (6). It is precisely the terminology that appears in §30(b), when construed in light of §3(a) (4) and (5) that exempts brokers and dealers and banks otherwise subject to the Act insofar as they conduct transactions not subject to §30(a) outside the United States, even though their United States transactions are subject to the Act.

In Kook v. Crang, 182 F. Supp. 388 (S.D.N.Y. 1960) the Court properly held that §30(b) exempted from the margin requirements of Section 7(c) of the Act, 15 U.S.C. §78g(c), sales to a United States citizen of Canadian stock in Canada by a Canadian broker, since the transactions were outside of the United States and part of the Canadian firm's business in securities. 2 Loss, Sec. Reg. 1292 n.15 (2d ed. 1961). The Court found in §30(b) a Congressional intent to exempt from application of the Act transaction of a business in securities outside the United States.

This holding was extended in Ferraioli v. Cantor, C.C.H. Fed. Sec. L. Rep. ¶91, 615 (S.D.N.Y. 1965) to exempt an isolated transaction, not part of a business in securities, the private sale in Canada of controlling shares of a New York corporation in which plaintiff was a minority shareholder, on the ground that the Exchange Act does not have extraterritorial application. The Court reasoned that if Congress specifically exempted foreign business in securities it intended to exempt isolated transactions as well. We disagree with this reasoning.

We find that the language and purpose of §30(b) show that it was not meant to exempt transactions that are conducted outside the jurisdiction of the United States unless they are part of a "business in securities." Indeed, since Congress found it necessary to draft an exemptive provision for certain foreign transactions and gave the Commission power to make rules that would limit this exemption, the presumption must be that the Act was meant to apply to those foreign transactions not specifically exempted.

We hold that the district court has subject matter jurisdiction over violations of the Securities Exchange Act although the transactions which are alleged to violate the Act take place outside the United States, at least when the transactions involve stock registered and listed on a national securities exchange, and are detrimental to the interests of American investors. *See* Ford v. United States, 273 U.S. 593, 619-624, 47 S. Ct. 531, 71 L. Ed. 793 (1927); United States v. Pizzarusso, 388 F.2d 8 (2d Cir. Jan. 9, 1968); United States v. Aluminum Company of America, 148 F.2d 416, 443-444 (2d Cir. 1945).

However, the district court found that the only harm alleged was to the foreign corporation on whose behalf plaintiff brought the action. We do not agree. A fraud upon a corporation which has the effect of depriving it of fair compensation for the issuance of its stock would necessarily have the effect of reducing the equity of the corporation's shareholders and this reduction in equity would be reflected in lower prices bid for the shares on the domestic stock market. This impairment of the value of American investments by sales by the issuer in a foreign country, allegedly in violation of the Act, has in our view, a sufficiently serious effect upon United States commerce to warrant assertion of jurisdiction for the protection of American investors and consideration of the merits of plaintiff's claim. . . .

USE OF INTERSTATE COMMERCE

There can be no violation under Section 10 unless a rule of the Commission is contravened "directly or indirectly," by the use of any means or instrumentality of interstate commerce or of the mails, or of any facility of any national securities exchange. *See generally* 3 Loss, Sec. Reg. 1519-1524 (2d ed. 1961). The trial court found that the transactions in question were essentially Canadian, with insufficient contacts with the United States to fall within §10(b) of the Act. We are uncertain whether the Court's finding was directed at the issues of extraterritorial application of the Exchange Act or at the jurisdictional requirements of §10. In either case we disagree with its conclusion. We have already discussed the reasons why a foreign purchase or sale of treasury shares by a corporation has sufficient effect upon interstate commerce to warrant extraterritorial application of the Exchange Act.

The present question is not whether this limited use of the mails and the facilities of interstate commerce would be a sufficient basis for subject matter jurisdiction over a foreign transaction which would otherwise be exempt from the Act, *see* Kook v. Crang, *supra,* but whether, once it has been determined , that the Act applies to a particular foreign transaction, there is a use of the mails or interstate commerce sufficient to meet the requirement of §10(b). We find that defendant's affidavits show a use of interstate commerce or the mails sufficient to bring both transactions within the scope of Section 10(b).

Since defendants admit that the Aquitaine purchase was delayed pending the successful conclusion of negotiations with the Treasury Department regarding tax rulings and negotiations with the American Stock Exchange regarding the listing of the additional shares, we find, on this record, that these negotiations were a part of the scheme for the sale of treasury stock to Aquitaine. And since it appears that, as plaintiff alleges, these negotiations with United States government and stock exchange officials must have made some use of the mails or other facilities of interstate commerce, there was at the very least use of interstate commerce[7] or the mails sufficient to bring the sales transactions within the scope of Section 10(b). Hooper v. Mountain States Securities Corp., 282 F.2d 195, 204 (5th Cir. 1960), *cert. denied,* 365 U.S. 814, 81 S. Ct. 695, 5 L. Ed. 2d 693 (1961).

The Paribas transaction likewise involved negotiations which must have taken place in part in the United States or made some use of the mails or interstate commerce. Furthermore, the purchase agreement was mailed from Paribas in New York to Banff in Canada; this in itself would establish a use of the mails sufficient to meet the requirement of Section 10.

RULE 10b-5

Plaintiff's theory of its cause of action is that "Banff was defrauded by its directors and controlling shareholder who combined to force it to sell treasury shares at the prevailing market price when they knew that the price was an artificially low one." In other words, plaintiff contends that defendants violated §10(b) and Rule 10b-5 by causing Banff to issue shares to defendant corporations at the current market price at a time when all the defendants knew that Banff had made an oil discovery which, if known to the public, would have raised the market price considerably. For purposes of the motion the court below rejected plaintiff's claim of the existence of a conspiracy and defendants' claims that at the time of the transaction they did not have material information and assumed that at the time of the sales in question the buyers and Banff's directors all knew that Banff had made a valuable discovery. We agree with the district court's conclusion that plaintiff failed to state a cause of action under Rule 10b-5 because there was no fraud and the allegations amounted to nothing more than breach of fiduciary duty by the controlling shareholder and directors. . . .

---

[7]The term "interstate commerce," as used in the Exchange Act, encompasses commerce "between any foreign country and any State." §3(a)(17), 15 U.S.C. §78c(a)(17).

We do not see how Banff's directors, in authorizing sales of treasury stock in arm's length transactions in which all parties possessed the same information, can properly be characterized as participating in a "manipulative or deceptive device or contrivance" in connection with a sale so as to fit within §10(b) merely because some shareholders now consider the sale price too low. Plaintiff's claim fails to state a cause of action under §10(b) because it does not show that the corporation was deceived. The directors, who were authorized to act on behalf of the corporation in these transactions, were all concededly in full possession of the material information, and we find no basis, on the facts before us, for refusing to impute their knowledge to the corporation.

A corporation can act only through its agents and officers and can know only what its agents and officers know. . . . If the persons entitled in the ordinary course to participate in authorizing a securities transaction on behalf of the corporation have not been fully informed, it may be said that the corporation has not been fully informed. . . . In general, if the corporation's agents have not been deceived, neither has the corporation. However, as in other situations governed by agency principles, knowledge of the corporation's officers and agents is not imputed to it when there is a conflict between the interests of the officers and agents and the interests of the corporate principal. . . . Therefore, a corporation may be defrauded in a stock transaction even when all of its directors know all of the material facts, if the conflict between the interests of one or more of the directors and the interests of the corporation prevents effective transmission of material information to the corporation, in violation of Rule 10(b)-5(2). . . .

While the purchaser in the Aquitaine transaction had three representatives on Banff's board of directors and was Banff's controlling shareholder, the Aquitaine representatives on the Banff board abstained from the authorization vote and shareholder ratification by Aquitaine was not required for the sale. Under these circumstances, we cannot refuse to impute the directors' knowledge to the corporation on the ground that directors participating in the corporate decision had a conflicting personal interest in the transaction. . . . Since the directors were all fully informed and since only the non-interested directors participated in the vote authorizing the sale, there is no deception of the corporation and no violation of §10(b) and Rule 10b-5 even though it may be that the directors, by authorizing sales of shares for inadequate consideration, may have breached their fiduciary duty to the corporation.

Section 10(b) does not encompass all corporate wrongs involving securities transactions. . . .

The judgment is affirmed.

HAYS, J. (concurring in part and dissenting in part):

I concur in Judge Lumbard's distinguished opinion on the issue of jurisdiction.

I am constrained to dissent on the point of the applicability to the facts of this case of the provisions of Section 10(b) and, more particularly, Rule 10b-5.

Defendants are alleged to have caused Banff to sell treasury shares at a price far below the fair price of such shares. In doing so defendants took advantage of their special relationship to Banff by reason of which they knew of Banff's discovery of extremely valuable oil reserves,—information which was clearly material to the purchase of the securities.

The complaint alleges a scheme to defraud the corporation by transferring corporate property to the corporation's majority stockholder and to an affiliate of the majority stockholder for a vastly inadequate consideration. My brothers do not absolve the defendants of fraud by calling their action a breach of fiduciary duty. There is no reason for making that distinction since such a breach of fiduciary duty as is here alleged clearly constitutes fraud.

The majority "do not see how Banff's directors . . . can properly be characterized as participating in a 'manipulative or deceptive device or contrivance' in connection with a sale so as to fit within §10(b) merely because some shareholders now consider the sale price too low." This statement completely disregards allegations of the complaint which are based upon matters of record and which establish that the treasury stock was sold at a price which did not reflect in any way the value of the recently discovered oil reserves. Whatever reason there may be for denying plaintiffs' recovery in this case it certainly cannot be because their complaint is deficient in its allegation that Banff was bilked of some millions of dollars by the transactions in question.

Rule 10b-5 makes it unlawful for any person

"(1) to employ any device, scheme, or artifice to defraud" or

"(3) to engage in any act, practice, or course of business which operates . . . as a fraud . . . upon any person, in connection with the purchase or sale of any security."

The acts in which defendants are alleged to have engaged clearly fall within the literal language of both of these subdivisions of Rule 10b-5.

The purpose of Section 10(b) and Rule 10b-5 is apparent from their language. That purpose is simply to prevent in interstate commerce the perpetration of fraud in connection with the sale of securities.

"Quite obviously the broad purpose of this legislation was to keep the channels of interstate commerce, the mail, and national security exchanges pure from fraudulent schemes, tricks, devices, and all forms of manipulation." . . .

Reluctance to see the federal courts involved in this broad field cannot justify rejection of a case that comes so clearly within the ambit of the statute as does the case which we are now considering.

The majority believe that the complaint fails to "state a cause of action under §10(b) because it does not show that the corporation was deceived" since the directors "who were authorized to act on behalf of the corporation in these transactions, were all concededly in full possession of the material information" and the knowledge of the directors is to be "imputed to the corporation."

Endowing a corporation with a fictitious "personality," so that, for example, it has "knowledge," is a useful device for the analysis of many problems. But it can also constitute a trap for the unwary when they ascribe reality to the fictions. What the majority is actually saying is that since the directors *were* the corporation for the purposes of the questioned transactions the corporation must have known what the directors knew, or, in other words, the directors knew what the directors knew. There is, of course, no justification for interposing the corporate fiction between the directors and the minority stockholders who were the victims of the directors' fraudulent actions. In order to establish fraud it is surely not necessary to show that the directors deceived themselves. It must be enough to show that they deceived the shareholders, the real owners of the property with which the directors were dealing. Deception of the shareholders (with the exception of the majority stockholder which was a party to the transactions) is established by showing that the directors withheld from them information that would have revealed the true value of the treasury stock.

The directors cannot take refuge behind the law permitting the information as to the discovery of the reserves to be withheld for one year. Such a law does not constitute a license to the directors to deal with the property as if no such discovery had been made. To argue to the contrary would be to argue that the directors could give the oil reserves away, as they in fact did in part, by selling the treasury stock at a price which did not reflect the value of the reserves.

What we have here then is a scheme by which the directors of Banff gave to the controlling stockholder[2] and an affiliated corporation some millions of dollars worth of the corporation's property. A plainer case of fraud would be hard to find.

SCHOENBAUM v. FIRSTBROOK (II)

405 F.2d 215 (2d Cir. 1968), *cert. denied,* 395 U.S. 906 (1969)

HAYS, J.

After a panel opinion in this case was issued a petition for rehearing en banc was granted. Additional briefs were submitted including an amicus brief by the Securities and Exchange Commission. On consideration by the full court the order of the district court granting summary judgment for the defendants is affirmed as to the defendant Paribas Corporation and reversed as to the other defendants.

The petition for rehearing sought reconsideration only of the issue of whether the defendants were entitled to summary judgment under Rules 12(c)

---

[2]The abstention of the "Aquitaine directors" on the vote for the sale to Aquitaine is hardly worthy of mention. As I said in my dissenting opinion in Alleghany Corporation v. Kirby, 344 F.2d 571 (2d Cir. 1965), *cert. dismissed as improvidently granted,* 384 U.S. 28, 86 S. Ct. 1250, 16 L. Ed. 2d 335 (1966): "No one who knows anything about the conduct of corporate enterprise considers that the major stockholder's withdrawal from the room when a vote is taken amounts to anything more than an empty ceremonial."

and 56 of the Federal Rules of Civil Procedure. The court en banc has not reviewed the decision announced by Chief Judge Lumbard on the issue of jurisdiction over the subject matter and that decision stands as the holding of the court. . . .

PLAINTIFF'S CAUSE OF ACTION UNDER SECTION 10-b AND RULE 10b-5 OF THE SECURITIES EXCHANGE ACT OF 1934 . . .

In the present case it is alleged that Aquitaine exercised a controlling influence over the issuance to it of treasury stock of Banff for a wholly inadequate consideration. If it is established that the transaction took place as alleged it constituted a violation of Rule 10b-5, subdivision (3) because Aquitaine engaged in an "act, practice or course of business which operates or would operate as a fraud or deceit upon any person, in connection with the purchase or sale of any security." Moreover, Aquitaine and the directors of Banff were guilty of deceiving the stockholders of Banff (other than Aquitaine). . . .

The order of the district court is reversed as to all defendants except Paribas and the case is remanded for further proceedings consistent with this opinion.

QUESTIONS

1. How did the stock sale to Aquitaine hurt any U.S. investors?

2. What is the court's standard for the extraterritorial application of U.S. law? Does it appear reasonable?

3. Does the court's decision appear to infringe on the right of Canada to regulate its own corporations in the way it reasonably chooses? Is it fair for a Canadian firm to have to consider both Canadian and U.S. views of the rights of minority shareholders?

4. Is the impact of the Aquitaine sale on minority shareholders something likely to be reasonably permitted by any nation's corporate law? What about the practices permitted by the Alberta law described in Schoenbaum (I)?

5. Are you satisfied with the way the court read Section 20 (b)?

6. What about the way the court read 10b-5 itself?

Building on *Schoenbaum* (I) and (II), the courts, particularly the Second Circuit, quickly built an elaborate structure, generally regarded as well summarized in the following cases. The first, *Leasco Data,* extends *Schoenbaum* (I) and (II) to reach a situation in which, according to the complaint, part of the fraud occurred in the United States, and the defrauded party, a corporation, was U.S. owned, even though the sale occurred abroad and the defrauded corporation was technically not a U.S. firm.

The second case, *Bersch,* which deals with a global fraud affecting plaintiffs all over the world, presents the current standards for taking jurisdiction on the basis of effects on the United States. (There is another case, discussed below, but not presented here, IIT v. Vencap, Ltd., 519 F.2d 1001 (2d Cir. 1975), involving the inverse question of jurisdiction over a securities fraud originating in the United States and affecting foreign plaintiffs.) For additional background *see* the Restatement of the Foreign Relations of the United States (Revised) §416, Tentative Draft No. 6 (1985). But you should treat the case not only as raising the classical issues of extraterritoriality but also as raising a practical question: how can the courts and enforcement authorities of different nations cooperate in stopping a global fraud and in providing as equitable a recovery as possible to those who were defrauded?

LEASCO DATA PROCESSING EQUIPMENT CORP. v. MAXWELL

468 F.2d 1326 (2d Cir. 1972)

FRIENDLY, J. . . .

I.   THE FACTS CLAIMED BY LEASCO

The gist of the complaint is that the defendants conspired to cause Leasco to buy stock of Pergamon Press Limited ("Pergamon"), a British corporation controlled by defendant Robert Maxwell, a British citizen, at prices in excess of its true value, in violation of §10(b) of the Securities Exchange Act and the SEC's sufficiently known Rule 10b-5. According to Leasco, and—as we shall not always repeat—we here state only Leasco's version, the first contact occurred early in 1969 when Maxwell came to Great Neck, N.Y., where Leasco then had its principal office, and proposed to Saul Steinberg, Chairman of Leasco, that Pergamon and Leasco engage in a joint venture in Europe. Maxwell falsely told Steinberg that Pergamon had a computerized typesetting plant in Ireland and gave Steinberg the most recent Pergamon annual report, which contained untruthful and misleading statements of Pergamon's affairs. Steinberg telephoned Maxwell in London to decline the joint venture; Maxwell invited him to come there to discuss areas of possible cooperation. . . .

. . . On what is now before us it is impossible to say that conduct in the United States was not "an essential link," Mills v. Electric Auto-Lite Co., 396 U.S. 375, 385, 90 S. Ct. 616, 24 L. Ed. 2d 593 (1970), in leading Leasco into the contract of June 17, 1969. And that contract, signed in the United States, was "an essential link" in inducing Leasco to make the open-market purchases, whether these were triggered by a call from London to New York, as Leasco contends, or by a conversation in England, as defendants assert. Putting the matter in another way, if defendants' fraudulent acts in the United States significantly whetted Leasco's interest in acquiring Pergamon shares, it would be immaterial, from the standpoint of foreign relations law, that the damage resulted, not from the contract whose execution Maxwell procured in this country, but from interrelated action which he induced in England or, for that matter, which Leasco took there on its own. As said in a leading English case, "In order to establish a coherent chain of causation it is not necessary that the precise details leading up to the accident [here the loss] should have been reasonably foreseeable," Hughes v. Lord Advocate, [1963] A.C. 837, 852. We have approved this with the qualification, doubtless intended, that the damage was within the area where the defendant had unlawfully created a risk of loss. . . .

Up to this point we have established only that, because of the extensive acts alleged to have been performed in the United States, considerations of foreign relations law do not preclude our reading §10(b) as applicable here. The question remains whether we should. Appellants have three lines of defense: they claim (1) that §10(b) has no application to transactions in foreign securities not on an organized American market; (2) that if it does, it has no application when such transactions occur outside the United States; and (3) that in any event it can have no application when the purchaser is not a citizen of the United States. . . .

Since Congress . . . meant §10(b) to protect against fraud in the sale or purchase of securities whether or not these were traded on organized United States markets, we cannot perceive any reason why it should have wished to limit the protection to securities of American issuers. The New Yorker who is the object of fraudulent misrepresentations in New York is as much injured if the securities are of a mine in Saskatchewan as in Nevada. Defendants have pointed to nothing in the legislative history which would indicate an intention that the language of §10(b) should be narrowed so as not to protect him.

We likewise cannot see any sound reason for believing that, in a case like that just put, Congress would have wished protection to be withdrawn merely because the fraudulent promoter of the Saskatchewan mining security took the buyer's check back to Canada and mailed the certificate from there. In the somewhat different yet closely related context of choice of law, the mechanical test that, in determining the *locus delicti,* "The place of wrong is in the state where the last event necessary to make an actor liable for an alleged tort takes place," Restatement of the Conflict of Laws §377 (1934), has given way, in the case of fraud and misrepresentation, to a more extensive and sophisticated analysis. See Restatement (Second) of the Conflict of Laws §148 (1971).

Our case, however, is not the simple one thus hypothesized. In that instance not only the fraudulent misrepresentation but the issuance of the check and the receipt of the securities occurred in the United States, although the check was deposited and the security mailed in Canada. Here it was understood from the outset that all the transactions would be executed in England. Still we must ask ourselves whether, if Congress had thought about the point, it would not have wished to protect an American investor if a foreigner comes to the United States and fraudulently induces him to purchase foreign securities abroad—a purpose which its words can fairly be held to embrace. While, as

earlier stated, we doubt that impact on an American company and its shareholders would suffice to make the statute applicable if the misconduct had
occurred solely in England, we think it tips the scales in favor of applicability
when substantial misrepresentations were made in the United States.

This brings us to appellants' third line of defense, namely, that the purchaser was not an American but a Netherlands Antilles corporation. . . .

It seems quite arguable from all this that Leasco N.V. is holding the shares
merely as trustee for Leasco, which has the beneficial interest and is bound to
reimburse Leasco N.V. for the latter's expenditures. If that were so, defendants' contention that the true purchaser was a foreigner would be drained of
force. But even if Leasco N.V. is the beneficial owner, it would be elevating
form over substance to hold that this entails a conclusion that the purchases
did not have a sufficient effect in the United States to make §10(b) apply.
Whether Leasco N.V. is merely a financial conduit, as plaintiffs assert, or was
planned to conduct an active business, as some of the SEC filings indicate, it
was wholly-owned and its debt securities were guaranteed by Leasco and were
convertible with Leasco common stock. We see no need to enter into the
debate whether, as defendants contend and plaintiffs deny, Leasco obtained
substantial tax and other advantages through the incorporation of Leasco
N.V. and the use of the latter to acquire the Pergamon shares. Whatever may
be the rule where the defrauded American investor chooses, deliberately and
unilaterally, to have the purchase consummated abroad by a foreigner, here
the situation was quite different. The Maxwell group expressly agreed in its
written contract that Leasco could "at its election" have the offer made "by a
wholly-owned subsidiary of Leasco or a wholly-owned subsidiary of such subsidiary," "providing Leasco shall remain responsible for the due performance"
of the obligation to acquire the shares. This clause specifically covered Leasco
N.V., which was part and parcel of Leasco in every realistic sense. In acceding
to this provision the defendants themselves recognized that Leasco, the United
States company, remained at all times intimately involved in the transaction;
the foreign entity was accepted by both sides as the alter ego of the American.
The case is quite different from another hypothetical we posed at argument,
namely, where a German and a Japanese businessman met in New York for
convenience, and the latter fraudulently induced the former to make purchases of Japanese securities on the Tokyo Stock Exchange. . . .

We therefore hold that the motions to dismiss for lack of subject matter
jurisdiction were properly denied.

BERSCH v. DREXEL FIRESTONE, INC.

519 F.2d 974 (2d Cir.), *cert. denied,* 423 U.S. 1018 (1975)

FRIENDLY, J.

These appeals from orders of Judge Carter in an action in the District Court
for the Southern District of New York again bring before us the question of the

territorial reach of the federal securities laws with which we have previously dealt in Schoenbaum v. Firstbrook, 405 F.2d 200 (2d Cir.), *rev'd on the merits,* 405 F.2d 215 (2d Cir. 1968) (en banc), *cert. denied sub nom.,* Manley v. Schoenbaum, 395 U.S. 906, 89 S. Ct. 1747, 23 L. Ed. 2d 219 (1969), and Leasco Data Processing Equipment Corp. v. Maxwell, 468 F.2d 1326 (2d Cir. 1972). Apart from differences in the facts, there is the added complexity that whereas *Schoenbaum* was a derivative action by stockholders of a Canadian corporation and *Leasco* an action by two corporate plaintiffs, the suit here is a class action on behalf of thousands of plaintiffs[2] preponderantly citizens and residents of Canada, Australia, England, France, Germany, Switzerland, and many other countries in Europe, Asia, Africa, and South America.

I. THE BASIC FACTS

The securities transactions giving rise to this litigation go back to 1969. The securities were the common stock of defendant I.O.S., Ltd. (IOS), an international sales and financial service organization principally engaged in the sale and management of mutual funds and complementary financial activities organized under the laws of Canada, having had its main business office in Geneva, Switzerland. It is now in the hands of liquidators appointed in November, 1973, by the Supreme Court of New Brunswick pursuant to the Canadian Winding-Up Act, Revised Statutes of Canada, 1970, ch. W-10.[4]

[2] The exact size of the plaintiff class has not yet been determined with any precision. In his original complaint, plaintiff Bersch, on the basis of an "estimate" that the average class member purchased 100 shares, alleged that there were approximately 100,000 potential class members. Apparently based on the alleged fact, revealed by discovery, that the average American purchaser bought 3,906 shares, and certain other information derived from the settling defendants, Bersch has now lowered his estimate of the size of the potential class to 25,000. On the record before us it is not possible to ascertain whether this new estimate is reasonable. On its face, if one were to assume that foreign purchasers on average subscribed for as many shares as discovery allegedly has revealed with respect to Americans, then even the 25,000 figure would be a significant overestimate. However, plaintiff's 3,906 average purchase estimate is based in part upon an erroneously high computation of the total number of shares allegedly purchased by Americans. Elimination of an apparently inadvertent double counting error with respect to one major purchaser lowers the total shares purchased by the alleged 386 American purchasers from 1,507,578 to 844,683. Moreover, even after elimination of this error, the average purchase figure is still deceptively high since one of the American purchasers which plaintiff lists in support of his allegations—the IOS Foundation of Delaware—purchased some 662,895 shares. Exclusion of these shares from the averaging would reduce the average American purchase to around 200 shares, and extrapolation of this to the foreign purchasers would result in a class of some 50,000.

[4] The liquidation proceedings against IOS were initiated on August 30, 1973, before Mr. Justice Dickson of the Supreme Court of New Brunswick, Canada, on the petition of the Public Trustee of the Province of Ontario, as creditor of IOS. Subsequently two additional petitions for the liquidation of IOS were filed, one by another creditor, and one by a shareholder. *See* In re I.O.S., Ltd., 7 N.B.R.(2d) 316 (S. Ct. 1973), *amended on appeal,* 7 N.B.R.(2d) 311 (S. Ct. App. Div. 1973). We are told that the filing of the first petition "followed and was in great measure the result of conferences among the governments of Canada and the Provinces of Quebec and Ontario, the regulatory authorities of Luxembourg and of the United States Securities and Exchange Commission." Affidavit of Herbert M. Wachtell, p.4 n.*, April 16, 1974. During those conferences it was apparently agreed, inter alia, that liquidation of the various interconnected business entities that made up the multi-national IOS complex would be sought by or with the assistance of the

Prior to 1968 the stock of IOS and its subsidiaries had been held by its organizer, defendant Bernard Cornfeld, his associates, and their employees. Although Cornfeld had always been free to sell his IOS shares, and in fact had disposed of significant amounts of these over the prior nine year period, his employees had been denied the right to sell their holdings and no organized market for IOS shares existed. Within the company the price of the stock was set by a theoretical formula value; the stock was used as a means of partial compensation and was granted to employees as a performance incentive, it being commonly understood by the employees that the company would eventually be taken public and they might then "cash in". A plan was developed wherein each of IOS's principal subsidiaries would first separately be taken public; finally common shares of IOS itself would be sold. In 1968 IOS floated 600,000 shares of one of its principal subsidiaries, IOS Management Ltd., a Canadian registered concern. The shares were offered at $12.50; trading opened at $75; and by March 1969 they had reached a peak of around $180. Subsequent to this sale, no doubt in part due to the success of this offering and more importantly to growing salesman dissatisfaction in light of a successful offering by a recently created competitor, the decision was made to abandon the original plan and to take IOS public as soon as appeared feasible. The planning of this offering was constrained by the framework set out in an Order Accepting Offer of Settlement entered by the SEC on May 23, 1967. Paragraph 4 of this order provided in pertinent part:

> Upon entry of the Order based on this Stipulation, IOS and all its affiliates shall cease all sales of securities to United States citizens or nationals wherever located, except for (i) offers and sales outside of the United States (and its territories, possessions or commonwealth subject to the jurisdiction of the United States) to officers, directors and full-time personnel of IOS and its subsidiaries. . . .

Three separate distributions of IOS common stock were proposed. The largest was to be a primary offering of 5,600,000 newly issued shares underwritten by six of the defendants (hereafter the Drexel group)—two American banking houses, Drexel Firestone, Inc. and Smith, Barney & Co., having their principal offices in the United States but also having offices in Europe, and four foreign underwriting houses, Banque Rothschild; Hill Samuel & Co. Limited; Guinness Mahon & Co. Limited; and Pierson Heldring & Pierson, having their principal offices abroad. The 5,600,000 shares were to be and were in fact sold under a prospectus outside the United States to foreign nationals residing in Europe, Asia and Australia. Prospectuses were printed abroad in English, French, and German and delivered to the purchasers outside the

---

relevant government or regulatory authorities of the corporate domiciles of the various key corporations. We are further told that it was agreed at the conference that an informal international committee made up of representatives of the various governments and regulatory authorities referred to above "would periodically meet and generally oversee the liquidation process."

United States. A secondary offering of 1,450,000 shares, underwritten by defendant J. H. Crang & Co., a Toronto investment house (Crang), was made in Canada by a prospectus conforming to the laws of Canada and its provinces; all of these shares were sold in Canada and none was sold to Americans resident there. The third distribution, whence this action springs, was a secondary offering of 3,950,000 shares by defendant Investors Overseas Bank Limited of Nassau, the Bahamas, an IOS subsidiary (IOB). The prospectus stated, as had that of the Drexel Group, that the shares "are not being offered in the United States of America or any of its territories or possessions or any area subject to its jurisdiction" and was "being made to approximately 25,000 persons who are either (1) employees or sales associates of the Company, (2) certain clients presently holding investments in managed funds or other products of the Company, or (3) persons who have had a long-standing professional or business relationship with the Company."

The offerings were made at the same price, $10 per share, and at approximately the same time. Each prospectus referred to the two other offerings. Reference was made to plans to list the IOS stock on various stock exchanges, none of these being in the United States. The Drexel Group and IOB prospectuses were substantially identical. Although the Crang prospectus was somewhat different insofar as compliance with particular Canadian securities regulations was sought, all three contained balance sheets of IOS and various subsidiaries as of December 31, 1968, and income statements for the five years then ended, and a report of defendant Arthur Andersen & Co. (Andersen), an international accounting firm with its principal office in the United States, that, subject to usual qualifications, the statements fairly presented the financial condition of the company as of December 31, 1968, and for the five years then ended. The Drexel and IOB prospectuses stated that the offerings had not been registered under United States securities laws. The offerings were successful in the limited sense of being fully subscribed, but after stabilizing briefly at $14 the price of the shares drifted downward until April 1970 when it collapsed through the $10 level and three weeks later the shares apparently were virtually unsaleable. The plight of the purchasers was further aggravated when control of IOS passed into the hands of Robert L. Vesco, currently a resident of Costa Rica, and a defendant in a substantial number of actions for fraud pending in this circuit.

II. The Proceedings in the District Court and this Court

The complaint in this action alleging violations of the Securities Act of 1933 and the Securities Exchange Act of 1934, and also containing allegations which can be read as charging common law fraud, was filed in December 1971 by Howard Bersch, a United States citizen living in New York, who had purchased 600 shares of IOS common distributed as part of the IOB underwriting. Characterizing the three underwritings as the "IOS Public Offering",

Bersch alleged he was bringing the action individually and on behalf of all persons who purchased stock in each of the offerings, estimated to approximate 100,000. The complaint contained the allegations usual when a plaintiff desires designation of his action as a class action under Fed. R. Civ. P. 23(b)(3). It alleged that the underwriters "impliedly represented to the public that IOS was a suitable company for public ownership" when, in part as a result of the refusal of other investment houses to participate, they should have known that it was not. It also contained more particularized charges, e.g., that the prospectuses failed to reveal illegal activities by IOS and its officers which had seriously damaged the company, that the books and records of IOS and its subsidiaries and affiliates were in such a chaotic condition that it was impossible to determine from them an accurate picture of IOS's financial position, and that during the months preceding the offering various IOS officials, including Cornfeld, had touted IOS' prospects. It charged that the underwriters in the Drexel Group had failed to use due diligence with regard to their prospectus, and that Andersen had failed to observe generally accepted accounting principles in connection with its audit with the result that the financial statements were false and misleading in various respects unnecessary to detail here. . . .

The district court rendered its opinion on November 26, 1974. The first question it addressed was whether the 1969 IOS Public Offering fairly could be viewed as one, two, or three distinct offerings. Depending upon whether one focused "on the purposes of the offering and the interaction of its prime movers, upon the character of the offerings themselves, or upon the structure of the selling arrangement and the identity and locus of the purchasers," each of these views was considered at least arguable. The court concluded that the three offerings were sufficiently integrated that they should be considered as one for the purpose of determining subject matter jurisdiction. It then found subject matter jurisdiction because of three factors:

(1) The amount of activity in the United States, almost entirely in connection with the Drexel offering, by the underwriters, their counsel and accountants (Price Waterhouse & Co.), and IOS.

(2) Sales to Americans, estimated at 386 individuals, even though "the defendants appear to have made an attempt to prevent any sales to Americans" and none occurred through the Drexel Group or Crang offerings.

(3) Generally adverse effects upon the American securities markets from the collapse in the price of the IOS shares offered. . . .

With this background we turn to the three elements a combination of which led the district judge to conclude that subject matter jurisdiction existed with respect not only to the relatively few Americans who had purchased IOS shares but to the many thousands of foreign purchasers whom plaintiff sought to represent. We think it will be useful to consider the first and third elements on which the court relied before we take up the second.

Assuming that there were no American purchasers and that the underwriting related, for example, to a large foreign industrial company clearly identified with a foreign country rather than with the United States, e.g., Rolls-Royce, Mercedes-Benz or Fiat, we do not believe the activities in the United States . . . would justify an American court in taking jurisdiction in a suit for damages by foreign plaintiffs. The fraud, if there was one, was committed by placing the allegedly false and misleading prospectus in the purchasers' hands. Here the final prospectus emanated from a foreign source—London or Brussels in the case of the Drexel offering, Toronto in the case of the Crang offering, and apparently the Bahamas and Geneva in the case of the IOB offering. Not only do we not have the case where all the misrepresentations were communicated in the nation whose law is sought to be applied as in Illustration 2 of §17 of the Restatement (2d) of Foreign Relations Law at 45, *see Leasco*, 468 F.2d at 1334 n.3, or the case where a substantial part of them were, as in *Leasco* itself, but we do not even have the oft-cited case of the shooting of a bullet across a state line where the state of the shooting as well as of the state of the hitting may have an interest in imposing its law. At most the acts in the United States helped to make the gun whence the bullet was fired from places abroad; alternatively proper action in the United States would have prevented the gun's ever being sent abroad. We are indeed holding in IIT v. Vencap, Ltd., 519 F.2d 1001 (2d Cir. 1975) decided this day, that Congress did not mean the United States to be used as a base for fraudulent securities schemes even when the victims are foreigners, at least in the context of suits by the SEC or by named foreign plaintiffs. But as we there point out, that holding itself goes beyond any case yet decided, and we see no reason to extend it to cases where the United States activities are merely preparatory or take the form of culpable nonfeasance and are relatively small in comparison to those abroad. We thus conclude that the action and inaction which here occurred in the United States would not of itself confer subject matter jurisdiction with respect to foreign plaintiffs even if we assume *arguendo* that the three underwritings may be considered for this purpose as one.

We turn next to the third ground on which the district court predicated subject matter jurisdiction—the adverse general effect of the collapse of IOS in the United States. This was based on an affidavit by Morris Mendelson, Associate Professor of Finance at the Wharton School of the University of Pennsylvania. Professor Mendelson's principal conclusions were that:

(1) The aftermath of the Drexel offering "was a debacle of monumental proportions which resulted in a deterioration of investor confidence in American underwriters at home and, particularly, abroad," and increased the problems of United States corporations in seeking to raise capital abroad.

(2) "The false and misleading prospectus issued in connection with the Public Offering impaired investors' confidence and trust and contributed to a steep decline in the purchase of United States securities by foreigners" with attendant adverse effects on the balance of payments and the price of American securities generally.

(3) Loss of investor confidence in IOS led to large redemption of shares in

the mutual funds controlled by it, notably Fund of Funds Limited, which required the funds to sell substantial parts of their portfolios, mainly United States securities, with consequent depression of prices.

(4) Part of the attraction of American securities to foreigners has been the superior disclosures afforded by SEC registration requirements. The collapse of IOS after the offering undermined this confidence since IOS was "identified as an American company in the minds of investors", the Drexel underwriting was led by an American firm and the accountants, Andersen, were American.

(5) The collapse of IOS after the offering "contributed to a breakdown in the entire structure of building up an offshore investing industry whereby funds of European investors were channeled into American securities markets."

Although appellants attack certain of Professor Mendelson's conclusions as erroneous or exaggerated, we do not doubt that the collapse of IOS after the offering had an unfortunate financial effect in the United States. Nevertheless we conclude that the generalized effects described by Professor Mendelson would not be sufficient to confer subject matter jurisdiction over a damage suit by a foreigner under the anti-fraud provisions of the securities laws.

This branch of plaintiff's arguments goes back to Mr. Justice Holmes' statement in Strassheim v. Daily, 221 U.S. 280, 284-85, 31 S. Ct. 558, 55 L. Ed. 735 (1911), which was relied on by Judge L. Hand in United States v. Aluminum Co. of America, 148 F.2d 416, 443 (2d Cir. 1945), and by Chief Judge Lumbard in *Schoenbaum, supra,* 405 F.2d at 206:

> Acts done outside a jurisdiction, but intended to produce and producing detrimental effects within it, justify a state in punishing the cause of the harm as if he had been present at the effect, if the state should succeed in getting him within its power.

See Restatement (2d) of Foreign Relations Law §18, "Jurisdiction to Prescribe with Respect to Effect within Territory". The statement, however, must be read in context. The indictment at issue in Strassheim v. Daily charged that Daily, in Illinois, had connived with the warden of a Michigan prison to defraud the prison's Board of Control by substituting worn and second-hand machinery for the new machinery that had been ordered, and the Court declined to upset, on a petition for habeas corpus, an order extraditing Daily from Illinois to Michigan. This principle would support subject matter jurisdiction if a defendant, even though acting solely abroad, had defrauded investors in the United States by mailing false prospectuses into this country, *see* ALI Proposed Federal Securities Code (Draft No. 3, April, 1974) §1604(a)(1)(A) & Comment (3)(b) at 165-66, or if, as in *Schoenbaum,* the number of shares of a company traded on American exchanges was increased by a sale to insiders without adequate consideration at least when this is imperfectly disclosed, *cf.* Popkin v. Bishop, 464 F.2d 714 (2d Cir. 1972). But it does not support subject matter jurisdiction if there was no intention that the securities should be offered to anyone in the United States, simply because in the long run there was an adverse effect on this country's general economic interests or on American security prices. Moderation is all. This, we think, is what Judge Hand had in mind in the remarks in his [*Alcoa*] opinion quoted in the margin.[33] These considerations are particularly pertinent in view of the limitations in §17(a) of the 1933 Act to acts in "the offer or sale of any securities" and in §10(b) of the 1934 Act to acts "in connection with the purchase or sale of any security." This means to us that there is subject matter jurisdiction of fraudulent acts relating to securities which are committed abroad only when these result in injury to purchasers or sellers of those securities in whom the United States has an interest, not where acts simply have an adverse effect on the American economy or American investors generally. Also we do not think that a combination of the district court's first and third grounds, neither sufficient in itself, supports a result different from that which would be proper if each subsisted alone.

IV. SUBJECT MATTER JURISDICTION—AMERICANS

We find it rather strange that this large record, with appendices alone running to more than 1200 pages, leaves us in serious doubt about one simple fact that seemingly could have been established quite readily. That is how plaintiff Bersch came to buy 600 shares of IOS that were part of the 3,950,000 share IOB offering.

Bersch was Vice-President and Secretary of Saja Associates Ltd., a privately-held business management and consulting firm, whose principal client was IOS, having an office in a building on Madison Avenue in New York City. . . .

If the record is thus murky on how Bersch came to subscribe, it is even murkier about how other American residents did. Appellant Andersen repeatedly says that the only information on this is a statement in an affidavit of Bersch:

> I was not the only American residing here who purchased IOS stock. . . . Among the New Yorkers purchasing the IOS securities were: Christine Cullen, Naydyne Nelson, Claire Pipolo, David Ellner, Elliott Adler, Robin Leach, Robert Sutner, Raymond Grant, Simme Arthur, Hyman Feld, and Morton Schiowitz.

But this is simply not so. Much more information is furnished in a series of letters from IOS to the SEC in the fall of 1970. These indicate that sales aggregating 41,936 shares were made to 22 American residents, all having

---

[33] There may be agreements made beyond our borders not intended to affect imports, which do affect them, or which affect exports. Almost any limitation of the supply of goods in Europe, for example, or in South America, may have repercussions in the United States if there is trade between the two. Yet when one considers the international complications likely to arise from an effort in this country to treat such agreements as unlawful, it is safe to assume that Congress certainly did not intend the Act to cover them.

relationships with IOS or its affiliates as employees, lawyers, directors or consultants. Although Andersen loudly claims that Bersch and other American residents bought the shares when they knew they should not have, we find nothing in the record to support this. The IOB prospectus does not exclude American employees residing in the United States and, as indicated above, see note 7 and accompanying text, the SEC 1967 order does not clearly do so. We note also that several of the subscribers were members of law firms that had represented IOS or its affiliates; it is scarcely to be thought that they would have subscribed for shares which they knew were not intended to and could not lawfully be made available to them.

We see no reason why there would not be subject matter jurisdiction with respect to such persons on the part of defendants IOS and Cornfeld who were responsible for the IOB offering. This type of situation—the dispatch from abroad of misleading statements to United States residents—would be closely analogous to that in which jurisdiction was upheld in Strassheim v. Daily, *supra*, and in the [*Alcoa*] case and one which would be considered an appropriate subject of United States jurisdiction under §18 of the Restatement (2d). To be sure, it may turn out that particular individuals never saw the statements or, because of their knowledge, were not misled. But at the present stage we must assume that there was some mailing of prospectuses into the United States and some reliance on them. The same result should also follow with respect to Andersen; action in the United States is not necessary when subject matter jurisdiction is predicated on a direct effect here and Andersen allowed its report on the 1968 financial statements to be used in the IOB offering as much as in the two others. Subject matter jurisdiction with respect to the Drexel Group defendants is more debatable; this depends on whether their activities, whether in the United States or abroad, can be considered as essential to the carrying out of the IOB offering and thus of the purchases here at issue. On the material before the district judge we think they can properly be, although this would be open to disproof at a trial. *Cf. Leasco*, 468 F.2d at 1330. Whether the same is true with respect to Crang is more debatable since the IOB offering was far more dependent on the large Drexel offering throughout the world than on the much smaller Canadian offering by Crang, but in view of our approval of the court's holding of lack of in personam jurisdiction over Crang, we need not decide this.

Plaintiff asserts that, in addition to purchases by Americans resident in the United States, there were significant purchases by Americans resident abroad. Whether Congress intended that such persons should be entitled to obtain damages for violation of the securities laws is a different and closer question from that on which we have just ruled. We think the answer would be in the negative if none of the defendants engaged in significant activities within the United States, as defendants, with apparent soundness, claim to be the case with respect to the IOB offering considered alone. Congress surely did not mean the securities laws to protect the many thousands of Americans residing in foreign countries against securities frauds by foreigners acting there, and we see no sufficient reason to believe it would have intended otherwise simply because an American participated so long as he had done nothing in the United States. However, in Judge Carter's view the IOB offer to American citizens residing abroad would not have occurred but for the primary offering which involved the many documented activities of most of the defendants in the United States. There was enough basis for this to justify a holding of subject matter jurisdiction as regards American citizens residing abroad, with respect to IOS and Andersen. Despite the paucity of physical acts on its part in the United States, the head and front of its alleged offending was its decision to allow its 1968 report to be used in all three prospectuses, including the IOB prospectus, and this must have emanated from its headquarters in the United States. We are of the same view with respect to the Drexel group. While merely preparatory activities in the United States are not enough to trigger application of the securities laws for injury to foreigners located abroad, they are sufficient when the injury is to Americans so resident. We here assume that, for reasons stated in the preceding paragraph . . . proof will disclose a significant causal relationship between the Drexel offering and the IOB offering. The case with respect to Crang is weaker but, since we sustain the judge's ruling of lack of *in personam* jurisdiction, we need not reach it. This leaves Cornfeld; the question of how far the alleged defrauding of American citizens abroad resulted from acts which he did or caused in the United States had best be left for development at a trial. We again invite attention to our observation in *Leasco:*

> We add that if a trial should disclose that the allegedly fraudulent acts of any of the defendants within the United States were non-existent or so minimal as not to be material, the principles announced in this opinion should be applied to the proven facts; the issue of subject matter jurisdiction persists.

468 F.2d at 1330.

We have thus concluded that the anti-fraud provisions of the federal securities laws:

(1) Apply to losses from sales of securities to Americans resident in the United States whether or not acts (or culpable failures to act) of material importance occurred in this country; and

(2) Apply to losses from sales of securities to Americans resident abroad if, but only if, acts (or culpable failures to act) of material importance in the United States have significantly contributed thereto; but

(3) Do not apply to losses from sales of securities to foreigners outside the United States unless acts (or culpable failures to act) within the United States directly caused such losses.

Other fact situations, such as losses to foreigners from sales to them within the United States, are not before us. We freely acknowledge that if we were asked to point to language in the statutes, or even in the legislative history, that compelled these conclusions, we would be unable to respond. The Congress that passed these extraordinary pieces of legislation in the midst of the depression could hardly have been expected to foresee the development of offshore funds thirty years later. We recognize also that reasonable men might conclude that the coverage was greater, or less, than has been outlined in this opinion and in IIT v. Vencap, Ltd., 519 F.2d 1001 (2d Cir. 1975) this day decided. Our conclusions rest on case law and commentary concerning the application of the securities laws and other statutes to situations with foreign elements and on our best judgment as to what Congress would have wished if these problems had occurred to it.

V.   CLASS ACTION

If what was before us was a single action with only named plaintiffs of the three sorts above described or three separate actions on behalf of the respective classes, we could promptly proceed to decision. Unhappily that is not the case. Appellants contend that once we have determined that the federal securities laws do not apply to the sales to foreign purchasers, they must be stricken from the class. Plaintiff says that all that is before us is whether the action may be maintained on behalf of some of the purchasers and that, since we have decided it can be, that is the end of the matter; alternatively, if we should reach the issue, the district court could entertain the claims of the foreign plaintiffs as pendent claims for common law fraud. . . .

The management of a class action with many thousands of class members imposes tremendous burdens on overtaxed district courts, even when the class members are mostly in the United States and still more so when they are abroad.[47] Also, while an American court need not abstain from entering judgment simply because of a possibility that a foreign court may not recognize or enforce it, the case stands differently when this is a near certainty. This point must be considered not simply in the halcyon context of a large recovery which plaintiff visualizes but in those of a judgment for the defendants or a plaintiffs' judgment or a settlement deemed to be inadequate. As Judge Frankel stated in his order permitting the case to proceed as a class action: "if defendants prevail against a class they are entitled to a victory no less broad than a defeat would have been."

---

[47] This is illustrated by the problem of notice. On the facts of this case one must have pause over sending notices only in English, as was directed in connection with the proposed settlement. The fact that the Drexel prospectus stated "[t]he English language version . . . shall control any question arising from its translation into other languages," thereby apprising non-English speaking purchasers that the English language might possibly become relevant to the final determination of their rights, in no way justifies notice only in English. On the other hand, if notice is to be sent in several languages, can the court simply delegate responsibility to insure accuracy?

Here the record contains uncontradicted affidavits that England, the Federal Republic of Germany, Switzerland, Italy, and France would not recognize a United States judgment in favor of the defendant as a bar to an action by their own citizens, even assuming that the citizens had in fact received notice that they would be bound unless they affirmatively opted out of the plaintiff class, and another affidavit recites that several hundred claims, including those of at least eighteen Americans, against defendant Cornfeld are pending in Switzerland[49] and that at least ninety have been settled. The affidavits are consistent with the conclusion in Von Mehren and Trautman, Recognition of Foreign Adjudications: A Survey and a Suggested Approach, 81 Harv. L. Rev. 1601 (1968), that European courts are far less inclined to recognize foreign judgments than are American courts applying the principles of Hilton v. Guyot, 159 U.S. 113, 202-03, 16 S. Ct. 139, 40 L. Ed. 95 (1895). We do not find it a satisfactory answer that here the defendants may be protected by the running of the statute of limitations in foreign countries. Nothing like a complete survey has been made and apparently the statute will not run in France until 1999. Moreover, in a situation like this, defendants should be entitled to a decision concerning the claims of foreign plaintiffs early in the progress of the litigation. . . .

We therefore direct that the district court eliminate from the class action all purchasers other than persons who were residents or citizens of the United States.

QUESTIONS

1. Should the *Leasco* court have been quite so ready to read through the corporate form of Leasco, N.V.? Why should the U.S. investor be entitled to have both the tax advantages of Netherlands Antilles incorporation and the securities law advantages of the United States? Or is the situation really no different from that in *Schoenbaum* (I) and (II)?

2. In *Bersch*, what logical basis is there for distinguishing between the jurisdictional standards applicable to Americans resident in America and Americans resident abroad? What about Americans resident abroad and foreign citizens resident in the same nations?

3. Is there anything to be said for such complex and detailed tests? Why shouldn't the court simply balance factors in the pattern of antitrust cases such as *Timberlane, supra,* p.576?

4. Are the actions at stake in these two cases likely to be legitimate under

---

[49] A criminal proceeding was instituted in November, 1971 against Cornfeld, Swiss law permits intervention by civil parties in a criminal proceeding, and pursuant to such intervention at least 395 claimants of 22 nationalities have sought full reparations for any damages they may have suffered as a result of their purchases. . . .

any nation's corporate laws? Why are the cases brought in the United States rather than elsewhere?

5. Is the *Bersch* result on extraterritoriality explained by the class action character of the case? Are the policy issues on extraterritoriality really different from those on the class action?

6. Do these cases help you in advising a foreign corporate client as to when it should be careful not only to avoid fundamental fraud but also to comply with more technical U.S. requirements?

C.   THE FUTURE OF THE *SCHOENBAUM* DOCTRINE

Several pressures might work to modify the *Schoenbaum* doctrine of relatively extensive extraterritorial jurisdiction for securities fraud. First of all, this area has not had a *Timberlane* to convert into a balancing test the (relatively) sharp-edged tests just described. Second, the Supreme Court has sought to restrict the expansion of 10b-5 in places where it arguably infringes on state law. These issues are both posed in the following case, IIT v. Cornfeld.

To understand *Cornfeld*, it is useful to begin by noting that, as already mentioned, the Second Circuit decided still a third case, IIT v. Vencap, Ltd., 519 F.2d 1001 (2d Cir. 1975) at roughly the same time as *Leasco* and *Bersch*. This case held that the security laws reached to the "manufacturing of fraudulent securities devices for export." This concept, the reverse of protecting the U.S. investor, provides the underlying basis for jurisdiction in *Cornfeld.*

But *Cornfeld* also raises the substantive issues that troubled the Supreme Court, issues close to those that divided the original panel opinion from the en banc opinion in *Schoenbaum*, and the key case is Santa Fe Industries v. Green, 430 U.S. 462 (1977), in which minority shareholders were held unable to use 10b-5 to attack a domestic transaction somewhat similar to that of *Schoenbaum*. In *Santa Fe*, the Supreme Court relied on the absence of a misrepresentation in the case before it:

[T]he cases do not support the proposition, adopted by the Court of Appeals below and urged by respondents here, that a breach of fiduciary duty by majority stockholders, without any deception, misrepresentation, or nondisclosure, violates the statute and the Rule. [*Santa Fe Industries,* at 476.]

Shareholders in such a position are thus remanded to state law remedies.

Nevertheless, the Second Circuit has sought to narrow the impact of *Santa Fe* by defining "deception" quite broadly in Goldberg v. Meridor, 567 F.2d 209 (2d Cir.), *cert. denied,* 434 U.S. 1069 (1978). Under *Meridor,* there can be a 10b-5 action if the insiders harm a group of shareholders and there is nondisclosure or misleading disclosure. There may also have to be reliance on the misrepresentation; this typically means that the harmed shareholders would have had a chance to vote on the corporate action or bring a suit against it, had they known what was being done.

IIT v. CORNFELD

619 F.2d 909 (2d Cir. 1980)

FRIENDLY, J.

I. IIT's Transactions in King-related Securities

Many members of the cast of characters in this case are not new to our courtroom. Plaintiff-appellant IIT, an International Investment Trust, was organized under the laws of the Grand Duchy of Luxembourg in 1961. Before it and its liquidators were forced to spend most of their time in court,[3] IIT provided an investment vehicle by which fundholders could participate in a portfolio of securities chosen and managed by allegedly "[q]ualified professional investment counsel." IIT was controlled and managed by IIT Management Company, S.A. (Management), a Luxembourg corporation, which was in turn controlled by its parent Investors Overseas Services, Ltd. (IOS), first a Panamanian and then a Canadian corporation whose "troubled existence", *see* 519 F.2d at 1003, has spawned many actions besides the present one. Both Management and IOS were operated out of Geneva, Switzerland, although plaintiffs allege that "all the top persons" controlling the once vast financial empire were Americans, notably Bernard Cornfeld and Edward M. Cowett. The transactions which form the basis of IIT's complaint occurred before Cornfeld lost control of IOS to Robert Vesco.

IIT currently has 144,496 fundholders residing in 154 countries. Some 218 reside in the United States, although it is unclear how many of these are American citizens. At the height of its prosperity in the late 1960s and early 1970s, IIT held assets worth $375 million, about forty percent of which were in American securities. This prosperity, however, was short-lived. Late in 1972 the Securities and Exchange Commission charged that Vesco was looting the assets of the IOS funds and, in the wake of the resulting scandal, the Grand Duchy of Luxembourg placed all Luxembourg investment funds under supervision of the Bank Control Commissioner. One year later, upon petition of that Commissioner, the Luxembourg district court declared IIT an involuntary

---

[3]. . . The liquidators of IIT list no less than thirteen actions which they have litigated or are litigating on IIT's behalf in federal district courts from Puerto Rico to Colorado.

bankrupt. Georges Baden, Jacques Delvaux, and Ernest Lecuit, were appointed liquidators of the fund and are co-plaintiffs in this action.

The transactions giving rise to the present case, which occurred between January 16 and October 26, 1969, involved three series of acquisitions by IIT of securities related to a complex of companies controlled by one John M. King, an American oil and gas entrepreneur based in Denver. King allegedly controlled King Resources Company (KRC), a publicly traded Maine corporation, and The Colorado Corporation (TCC), a private company largely owned by him. Both the public side of the King complex (KRC) and the private side (TCC) bought and sold natural resource properties and offered a variety of investments in the nature of tax shelters. The two companies had numerous subsidiaries. One of these, King Resources Capital Corporation, N.V. (KRCC), a wholly-owned Netherlands Antilles subsidiary of KRC, figures prominently in this case. Like IIT, King and his companies have fallen on hard times, but were not named as defendants in this action because stays were issued by courts in bankruptcy proceedings involving them.

IIT's first acquisition of King-related securities occurred between January 16 and October 26, 1969, during which period IIT bought about $8 million face value of KRCC subordinated convertible debentures. The debentures had been issued in Europe on November 27, 1968, to raise $15 million in the eurodollar market. This offering was closely coordinated with a domestic offering of an additional $25 million in debentures of KRC which occurred on November 26. The KRCC debentures were guaranteed by KRC and convertible into KRC common stock. The bulk of IIT's purchases were made abroad, although IIT alleges it purchased $50,000 face value of the debentures through defendant Arthur Lipper Corporation (Lipper) in the United States. IIT sold its KRCC debentures between July 28, 1970 and February 5, 1971 at a loss of $8,765,698.

IIT's second acquisition of King-related securities was the purchase between January 16 and March 20, 1969, of 200,000 shares of KRC common stock. IIT purchased its shares in the United States over-the-counter market for $16.8 million, availing itself of the brokerage services Lipper performed for IIT and the other members of the IOS complex. These shares were sold between October 6 and November 4, 1970, at a loss of approximately $14 million.

IIT's final acquisition of King-related securities was a July, 1969 purchase of a $12 million 15 year convertible note from TCC. IIT alleges that the purpose of this loan was to make TCC a seemingly attractive merger partner for KRC, although no such merger took place. TCC defaulted on the note and has never paid any principal or interest to IIT. As noted, TCC is now in bankruptcy. . . .

According to the complaint and various affidavits and memoranda submitted by plaintiffs in the district court, the three . . . transactions outlined above were the result of a conspiracy to defraud IIT between those in control of IOS and Management, together with Lipper and those in control of the King complex. The King empire allegedly required "continuous injections of vast sums of cash to survive," some of which it obtained from IIT's purchases. For their part, the IOS and Management defendants received personal kick-backs, opportunities to join in KRC tax avoidance schemes, and the ability to over-value King-related assets so as to increase their management fees and performance bonuses. Lipper, the United States broker for the IOS complex, was allegedly involved in all three transactions. Its recompense included not only the sizable commissions it gained from the IOS brokerage business but also a special right, allegedly given in connection with the TCC note transaction, to purchase 10,000 shares of TCC stock at what was thought to be a bargain price. Lipper and individuals at Lipper also allegedly partook of KRC investment and tax avoidance schemes involving projects as diverse as the development of Sinai oil properties and the leasing of jet aircraft. . . .

III. THE DISTRICT COURT'S REASONS FOR FINDING LACK OF SUBJECT-MATTER JURISDICTION

Judge Goettel began his discussion of subject-matter jurisdiction by rejecting the argument that Rule 10b-5 applied to the transactions here in question because of their effects within the United States. Distinguishing *Schoenbaum, supra,* because the victim in that case was a corporation whose shares were listed on the American Stock Exchange, with a substantial minority of American shareholders, he cited *Bersch, supra,* as holding that an unparticularized deleterious effect on the American economy from lessened ability to attract offshore investment funds did not provide the necessary effect, 519 F.2d at 989, and *Vencap, supra,* as holding that such effect was not provided "simply because half of one percent" of the shares of the allegedly defrauded fund were "held by Americans." 519 F.2d at 1017. In this the judge was clearly right, and we need say no more about "effects" as a basis of subject-matter jurisdiction save in one respect noted in Part V below.

Turning to jurisdiction based on acts within the United States, the judge focused on the complicity of Management in all the fraudulent transactions. He thought that "[s]o long as the derivative action is one alleging total complicity on the part of foreign management, the ultimate focus of the theory remains a deception of foreign fundholders by foreign 'directors'." 462 F. Supp. at 224. "Since virtually all the fundholders were foreign nationals residing in foreign countries, the deception, if it could be proved, *must* have occurred outside of the United States." *Id.* (emphasis in original). Furthermore, insofar as our decision in Goldberg v. Meridor, 567 F.2d 209 (2d Cir. 1977), *cert. denied,* 434 U.S. 1069, 98 S. Ct. 1249, 55 L. Ed. 2d 771 (1978), relied, as regards causation, on the ability of the deceived shareholders to have sought injunctive relief if they had known the facts, the court thought this case to differ from "a domestic case", 462 F. Supp. at 223, because, for reasons not clearly stated and somewhat contradicted by fn. 35 on p.224, it assumed that any such suit would have had to be brought in Luxembourg. This would place "the plaintiffs in a curious position in that by establishing their right to an injunction under Luxembourg law, they could prove 10b-5 materiality; simultaneously, however, they would be offering a good reason not to apply Rule 10b-5 to the transactions, since the availability of relief under foreign law would then be at least partially evident." Viewing the action as one that had "its genesis abroad . . . with a group of foreign managers of a foreign investment trust violating what would appear to be their fiduciary duties to their fundholders, and the foreign managers merely enlisting the aid of American aiders and abettors", 462 F. Supp. at 225, the court found no basis for subject-matter jurisdiction, even as to transactions consummated within the United States, *see id.* at 224 n.34.

We see no sufficient ground for this characterization of the transactions here at issue. Our decision in Goldberg v. Meridor, *supra,* did not find the nub of the action to be the directors' breach of fiduciary duty to the shareholders, *see* 567 F.2d at 221; indeed, that was the very ground that had been ruled out by Santa Fe Industries, Inc. v. Green, 430 U.S. 462, 97 S. Ct. 1292, 51 L. Ed. 2d 480 (1977). The holding rather was that, as we said in speaking of *Schoenbaum,* an action under Rule 10b-5 can lie if "there is deception of the corporation (in effect, of its minority shareholders) when the corporation is influenced by its controlling shareholder to engage in a transaction adverse to the corporation's interests (in effect, the minority shareholders' interests) and there is nondisclosure or misleading disclosures as to the material facts of the transaction." 567 F.2d at 217. The basic principle was that where the directors are parties to the fraud, deception, as stated by Chief Judge Seitz in Pappas v. Moss, 393 F.2d 865, 869 (3d Cir. 1968), "is fairly found by viewing this fraud as though the 'independent' stockholders were standing in the place of the defrauded corporate entity. . . ." The relevance of the wrongdoing of the directors and managers is in relieving the corporation of having their knowledge attributed to it. The judge was thus mistaken in viewing all the American participants, even including the King group, as mere aiders and abettors of Management in perpetrating a fraud on IIT. While that is a fair description of the asserted role of Andersen, the underwriter defendants and perhaps even Lipper, the members of the King complex and other defendants were claimed to have been perpetrators of a fraud upon the fundholders, and the three sets of defendants here before us could be held, on proper allegations, for aiding and abetting a deception originating in the United States. An actual participant in a fraud is no less a principal because someone else originated the plan. IIT and its liquidators are complaining of deception practices on IIT by both the King complex, whose acts were primarily in the United States, and Management, whose acts were mainly outside it, both allegedly aided and abetted by the defendants here before us, without any attribution to IIT of knowledge on the part of Management. The ability of such a victim to maintain such an action was decided in *Goldberg,* we see no reason to depart from that decision, and we shall discuss subject-matter jurisdiction in that light.

IV.   Subject-Matter Jurisdiction: the King Resources Common and TCC Convertible Note Transactions

So viewing the case, we have no difficulty in finding subject-matter jurisdiction with respect to IIT's purchases of the KRC common stock and the TCC convertible note. Apart from the fact that these were securities of American corporations, the transactions were fully consummated within the United States. . . . We see nothing foreign in this transaction except that the purchaser was a foreigner and the orders were transmitted from abroad, by a devious method whereby Management advised the Montreal Trust Company in Toronto, the custodian of IIT's securities, to receive the KRC common stock through its sub-custodian, with payment to Lipper's London office to be made by IIT's cash custodian, Credit Suisse. None of our cases or any others intimate that foreigners engaging in security purchases in the United States are not entitled to the protection of the anti-fraud provisions of the securities laws. . . .

V.   Subject-Matter Jurisdiction: the KRCC Convertible Debentures

The defendants stress that IIT purchased its KRCC eurodollar convertible debentures, except perhaps for the $50,000 purchased from Lipper, in the European after-market. They argue that lack of jurisdiction over these purchases follows from our conclusion in *Bersch, supra,* 519 F.2d at 993, that the anti-fraud provisions of the federal securities laws "[d]o not apply to losses from sales of securities to foreigners outside the United States unless acts (or culpable failures to act) within the United States directly caused such losses", since with the exception noted all purchases were made abroad. When the quoted statement is read in the context of the facts in *Bersch,* it does not have the effect contended.

The first difference is that in *Bersch* we were dealing wholly with foreign securities. All three of the offerings were of common stock of IOS, Ltd., a Canadian corporation having its center of activities in Geneva, Switzerland. The prospectuses for the primary offering of the shares underwritten by the Drexel group for the 5,600,000 share offering and for the secondary 3,950,000 share offering by IOB, of which the shares involved in the action were a part, stated that the shares "are not being offered in the United States of America or any of its territories or possessions or any area subject to its jurisdiction"; the secondary offering of 1,450,000 shares underwritten by J.H. Crang & Co. of Toronto was sold entirely in Canada. Here the primary offering was of $25,000,000 of KRC debentures, United States securities offered in the American market. The offering of $15,000,000 of KRCC eurodollar bonds was, in substance, an integral part of this financing. There is abundant evidence that the United States and foreign offerings were closely coordinated; while this was also true of the three offerings in *Bersch*, 519 F.2d at 980, there none of the offerings was of an American security or was made domestically to anywhere near the same extent as the coordinated debenture offerings, $25,000,000 in the United States and $15,000,000 abroad, in this case. Although the eurodollar debentures were nominally the obligations of a wholly owned Netherlands Antilles subsidiary of KRC, this corporation was inserted into the total offering simply because European investors were reluctant to purchase debentures issued directly by an American corporation, since interest payments would then be subject to United States withholding tax. The Netherlands Antilles corporation had no operating assets, the debentures issued by it were guaranteed by KRC, and they were convertible into KRC common stock. We have previously refused to be deterred from considering the real facts by the interposition of a foreign subsidiary of this kind. *Leasco, supra*, 468 F.2d at 1337-38.

The fact that we are dealing here with debentures which in substance were American rather than foreign securities has bearings of several sorts. The first goes back to the effects test. We think Congress would have been considerably more interested in assuring against the fraudulent issuance of securities constituting obligations of American rather than purely foreign business. Our statement in *Vencap, supra*, 519 F.2d at 1017: "We do not think Congress intended to allow the United States to be used as a base for manufacturing fraudulent security devices for export, even when these are peddled only to foreigners" applies with even greater force when, as here, the securities are essentially American. Our very next sentence, *id.*, "This country would surely look askance if one of our neighbors stood by silently and permitted misrepresented securities to be poured into the United States" reads with particular strength on a situation where the securities are essentially of the pourer's own nationals. This concern is only partially diminished by the fact that the prospectus for the eurodollar offering stated that the securities were not registered under the Securities Act of 1933 and were not being offered within the United States or to Americans, and by the SEC's grant of no-action treatment under the 1933 Act. None of this amounts to saying that if fraud had been committed in the United States in connection with the issuance of the debentures, American courts would look away. See *Bersch, supra*, 519 F.2d at 986.

Here there was also greater relative American participation than in *Bersch* in other respects. While two of the six underwriters of the primary offering in *Bersch* were American banking houses, these had European offices from which they apparently did much of their work, and all the others and the underwriters of the two secondary offerings were foreigners. Here Dempsey-Tegeler & Company, Inc., an American firm, was the sole lead underwriter of the dollar offering and co-lead underwriter of the eurodollar offering along with a Luxembourg bank.

Perhaps most important of all, a consequence of the KRCC debentures being essentially of an American security is that the activities occurring in the United States, which on their surface may appear similar to those held in *Bersch* to be "merely preparatory" and thus insufficient to have "directly caused" loss to foreigners, assume a different aspect. The fact that the drafting of the final prospectus in *Bersch* was done in Europe was not just "a formal or ultimate act . . . staged in Europe", as the *Bersch* district court found, 389 F. Supp. at 446, 457. The *Bersch* prospectus was mainly drafted in Europe because that was where IOS' records and principals were. Here the prospectus was wholly drafted in the United States because the offering, for largest part in form and for all in substance, was of securities of an American based corporation. Similarly while there was some domestic accounting work in *Bersch*, 389 F. Supp. at 456, most of the field work was and in the nature of things had to be done abroad. Here all the accounting work was and had to be done in the United States. Similarly the fact that the prospectuses in *Bersch* were printed in Europe while those in this case (including the prospectus for the eurodollar offering) were printed in the United States, while not of particular significance in and of itself, reflects the fact that in *Bersch* the work on the prospectuses had mainly been done in Europe, so that Europe was the natural place for printing, whereas here most of the work had been done in the United States and there was no reason to ship the prospectus elsewhere for printing. In sum while many of the acts in the United States in this case were similar to those in *Bersch*, the relativity is entirely different because of the lack here of the foreign activity so dominant in *Bersch*, 519 F.2d at 987 ("We see no reason to extend [jurisdiction] to cases where the United States activities . . . are relatively small in comparison to those abroad.") Determination whether American activities "directly" caused losses to foreigners depends not only on how much was done in the United States but also on how much (here how little) was done abroad.

We see little force in defendants' argument that sustaining jurisdiction here will somehow affront Luxembourg. The problem of conflict between our laws and that of a foreign government is much less when the issue is the enforcement of the anti-fraud sections of the securities laws than with such provisions as those requiring registration of persons or securities. The primary interest of Luxembourg is in the righting of a wrong done to an entity created by it. If our anti-fraud laws are stricter than Luxembourg's, that country will surely not be offended by their application. If they are weaker—which is not seriously suggested—the liquidators made their choice, doubtless at least in part because of difficulty in securing personal jurisdiction in Luxembourg, and after Andersen attacked their capacity, . . . they obtained a second order from the Luxembourg district court reaffirming their right, so far as Luxembourg was concerned, to bring suit on behalf of the fundholders. The defendants with whom we are here concerned acted in the United States and cannot fairly object to having their conduct judged by its laws. . . .

NOTES AND QUESTIONS

1. Is *Cornfeld* consistent with *Leasco* and *Bersch*? Implied by them? This extension (to manufacturing securities frauds for export) has often been criticized. Is this criticism reasonable?

2. If the more refined analysis of *Cornfeld* were applied back to the *Schoenbaum* (I) facts, would it still be appropriate for the U.S. court to take jurisdiction?

3. All questions of technical jurisdiction aside, is it not reasonable for a U.S. court to give jurisdiction to the representative of a foreign court that has undeniable jurisdiction over some aspects of the cases and a plausible claim to have the right and duty to marshal assets from throughout the world?

4. Is there any sense in taking rules written to draw a line between federal and state jurisdiction and applying them to derive a line between federal and foreign jurisdiction? What about the possibility of a foreign action in a U.S. state court?

5. Would a reasonable rule (or perhaps the actual rule being applied covertly) be to take jurisdiction in a securities fraud case wherever any remaining assets can be found? For an example implicitly suggesting such a rule, *see* SEC v. Kasser, 548 F.2d 109 (3d Cir. 1977), *cert. denied sub nom.* Churchill Forest Industries (Manitoba) v. SEC, 431 U.S. 938 (1977).

6. Why is the U.S. extension of extraterritorial jurisdiction in this area producing much less international conflict than in the antitrust area?

7. What kinds of cooperation would you propose for dealing with future securities fraud? How much are the forms administrative rather than judicial?

8. Suppose the parties to a securities transaction specify application of foreign law and decision in a foreign court. When should a U.S. court decline jurisdiction? *See* AVC Nederland B.V. v. Atrium Investment Partnership, 740 F.2d 148 (2d Cir. 1984).

9. Suppose that AMSUB is the Panamanian subsidiary of a multinational U.S. manufacturing firm, ZEECO. As is typical of Panamanian subsidiaries, this subsidiary holds profits from various foreign operations to protect them from U.S. taxes. In what may be a somewhat unusual pattern, AMSUB has been investing these funds in Eurobonds issued by developing nations. One of these nations, Guatador, has recently faced severe difficulties in making payments on its bonds, and the value of the bonds has fallen sharply. There are strong indications that Guatador misrepresented its financial situation at the time of the Eurobond borrowing and that the prospectus circulated by the European underwriting from whom AMSUB bought the bonds contained significant misrepresentations. (The bonds, of course, were not registered in the United States.)

ZEECO has approached you to ask about a 10b-5 suit by AMSUB and ZEECO in the United States against Guatador and the European underwriter (assuming that *in personam* jurisdiction will be available against the latter). What would you say?

10. Assume that the international controversy over the Westinghouse Uranium litigation continues to become nastier and nastier. Several key congressmen, incensed over various foreign efforts to keep evidence away from U.S. courts and to avoid the effects of U.S. treble-damage judgments, have introduced a new bill. This proposed legislation would amend the U.S. securities legislation to require that any foreign firm that is named as a defendant in any public or private U.S. antitrust litigation and fails to produce evidence that it is directed to provide by the U.S. court shall be required to file the information publicly as a condition of registration (or of exemption from the duty to register, where that is the wording of the security laws) of its securities for sale in the United States. In short, the legislation proposes making access to the U.S. securities market conditional on compliance with the information requests of U.S. courts.

You are chairperson of a special study group for the New York Bar Association, whose task is to comment on this legislative proposal. That study group's preliminary discussions make it clear that the memorandum, if it is to have any political weight at all, will have to deal with both the wisdom of the specific legislative proposal and the underlying problem of evidence in the extraterritorial application of U.S. antitrust law. What would you say?

Bibliographical Note

For further information, *see* W. Surrey and D. Wallace, A Lawyer's Guide to International Business Transactions, 2d ed. (1977); Thomas, Internationalization of the Securities Markets: An Empirical Analysis, 50 Geo. Wash. L. Rev. 155 (1982); Hacker & Rotunda, The Extraterritorial Regulation of Foreign Business Under the U.S. Securities Laws, 59 N.C.L. Rev. 643 (1981); Johnson, Application of Federal Securities Laws for International Securities Transactions, 45 Alb. L. Rev. 890 (1981); Liftin, The Extraterritorial Reach of the Federal Securities Code: An Analysis of Section 1905, 32 Vand. L. Rev. 495 (1979); Comment, Extraterritorial Effect of the Registration Requirements of the Securities Act of 1933, 24 Vill. L. Rev. 729 (1979).

Chapter XVII

Regulating the Multinational

In the portfolio investment area just examined, nations have relatively similar goals—no nation wants to encourage fraud. But, as the transnational investment takes the different form of direct corporate investment, room for disputes becomes much greater. The home and host nations will have significantly different interests and may also have significantly different philosophies. This chapter briefly explores some of the potential conflicts. It begins by looking at the economic basis for multinational investment, explores a selection of host nation responses, turns to a selection of actual conflicts, and then reviews an effort at negotiating an international code to avoid these conflicts.

A. THE ECONOMICS OF MULTINATIONAL INVESTMENT

In international investment two polar strategies can be discerned. In one, the savers of one economy invest on a net basis in assets of another economy, typically through international loans, bonds, and portfolio investment. In the other, a firm opens a branch or subsidiary in another nation. The former of these is generally explainable by macroeconomic considerations. In the case of the latter, however, there is often cross-investment (e.g., the U.S. auto industry investing in Europe while the parallel European industry is investing in the United States) so that explanations have to look to the theory of the firm.

The net investment situation, already explored in Chapter XV, is exemplified by OPEC investments in the Eurodollar market and the banks' parallel investment in developing nations. To the extent that the banks are following economic considerations here, they are helping move capital from the Mid-east, where its economic rate of return (as reflected in the interest rate) was low, to other economies, where its economic rate of return would be higher. Because of differences in economic opportunities to use capital, the marginal return on capital varies from place to place, and capital will flow to the place where its return is highest. By tariffs or currency adjustments, a nation may be able to influence that rate of return to modify the flow of capital. Although these factors alone do not explain cross-investment, note that portfolio diversification can explain some such cross-investment. It is reasonable for European investors, facing currency-exchange risks, to want to place some of their assets in dollars, which pose a different foreign exchange risk, while U.S. investors, for the same reason, place some of their assets in foreign currencies.

The direct investment situation is more complex. In general, one would expect a local firm to do better than a foreign-controlled firm. Putting the question a little more sharply: why can't a French firm, in France, using capital borrowed from the United States, always out-compete a U.S. firm that has to pay the same amount for its capital but is probably never able to understand French operation as well as the local firm? And, going still further in a reflection of Chapter I's product-cycle analysis, why can't a U.S. firm obtain the greatest economic return in applying its new technology to the French market by licensing that technology to a French firm that understands the market?

The answer to these questions lies in a quasimonopoly or in an economy of integration that is not fully reflected in the usual licensing arrangements. If the local economy does not yet have the trained entrepreneurs and staff needed for the project, then foreign direct investment is likely to be essential. If the technology is evolving so rapidly that management arrangements are a more practical way to transfer it than are a series of separately negotiated contracts, then the administratively integrated operation has a comparative advantage that explains its emergence and survival. If economies of scale transcend the market available in any single nation, efficiency may lead to the IBM or automotive industry pattern where different production steps (e.g., those for computer chips or transmissions or assembly) are carried out in different nations, each on a scale intended to meet a multinational or global market. And there are other economies of integration that are less defensible economically. The multinational (MN), with its well-understood credit rating, may be more easily able to raise new capital than its local competitor. Or the extractive MN may be able to take advantage of tax breaks in ways unavailable to a less vertically integrated operation.

What is clear is that the evolution of the multinational corporation is, in practically every case, closely coupled with some form of market power. The areas in which MNs and international investment have become most important are the extractive industries (where market power and tax advantages are especially relevant), the manufacturing industries where economies of scale have gone beyond the nation, and the high-technology, oligopolistic industries such as pharmaceuticals, chemicals, and electronics. Although MNs do play a role in relatively special situations such as international commodity trading in, say, sugar or bananas, there are relatively few in the more competitive parts of the agricultural or textile industries. The economic genesis of the MN raises many of the same questions as does the antitrust issue of international vertical integration.

As everywhere, there are tax considerations. Although the details are beyond the scope of this book, foreign branches of U.S. firms are directly taxed by the host nation and taxed currently by the United States, subject to the foreign tax credit—a credit calculated by a formula designed to provide at least partial recognition of the income taxes paid the foreign government. In a subsidiary arrangement, however, the foreign subsidiary's earnings are generally not taxed by the United States until dividends are paid to the parent, and the foreign tax credit then becomes available. In exceptional cases, such as the "controlled foreign corporation," designed to restrict use of foreign corporations for tax deferral, a dividend will be deemed distributed. In the general case, however, a firm is able to defer taxes by leaving profit in foreign subsidiaries.

These arrangements under the Internal Revenue Code, already complex, are complicated by tax treaties, which sometimes establish special limits on withholding and the like. Hence, one finds the elaborate networks of subsidiaries in tax haven nations.

Bibliographical Note

For sources on the more general economic theory of international investment, and particularly of the multinational, *see* N. Hood, Economics of Multinational Enterprise (1979); C. Kindleberger, The International Corporation (1970), and American Business Abroad (1969); Caves, Industrial Economics of Foreign Investment; The Case of the International Corporation, 5 J.W.T.L. 303 (1971). And for the very influential *dependencia* critique of the multinational, *see* J. Caporaso, (ed.), Dependence and Dependency in the Global System, 32 International Organization (special issue, No. 1) (Winter 1978).

For additional information on the international tax area, *see*, in addition to the primary sources, Fisher, The Multinationals at Bay: The Foreign Taxation Provision of the Tax Reduction Act of 1975, 10 J. Intl. L. & Econ. 61 (1975) and The Multinationals and the Crisis in United States Trade and Investment Policy, 53 B.U.L.Q. 308 (1973); W. Gifford, International Tax Planning (2d ed. 1979); D. Tillinghast, Tax Aspects of International Transactions (2d ed. 1984).

B.   HOST-NATION REGULATION

There are many reasons why host nations regulate foreign investment—all the reasons why they regulate domestic investment, along with some special ones. Foreign investment often seems both a real and a psychological infringement on sovereignty. Note how strongly the United States has reacted to a little OPEC investment and then consider the situation of Canada in which over 50% of many industries (and much more in some industries) is foreign (mostly U.S.) owned. Moreover, there are special concerns that the foreign firm will operate without adequate consultation or to the detriment of local interests in such areas as labor policy or willingness to create export revenues for the host nation.

At the same time, foreign investment is often seen as a way of bringing technology and employment. Nations thus have a variety of laws dealing with foreign investment. Some seek to attract it, as through tax holidays and special privileges like those that U.S. cities and states use to attract industry. Some, in contrast, seek to regulate it. These may control the areas of investment, for example, to keep foreign investment out of sensitive areas like telecommunications or the media; they may control the terms of investment, as through restricting rates at which profits may be expropriated; or they may protect specific local concerns such as that of labor.

One of the most important examples, which reflects a major developing world tradition and with which you are already familiar, is Andean Pact Decision 24 (Selected Documents Supplement). For a quite different approach, consider the following excerpt, which demonstrates Canada's effort to gain increased control over an economy so open to its powerful neighbor. The Foreign Investment Review Act was repealed in the summer of 1985 by the Investment Canada Act, 1985 c.20 (June 30, 1985).

FOREIGN INVESTMENT REVIEW ACT

21-22 Eliz. 2 c.46, 1973-1974 [repealed]

An Act to provide for the review and assessment of acquisitions of control of Canadian business enterprises by certain persons and of the establishment of new businesses in Canada by certain persons . . .

PURPOSE OF ACT

2.(1) This Act is enacted by the Parliament of Canada in recognition by Parliament that the extent to which control of Canadian industry, trade and commerce has become acquired by persons other than Canadians and the effect thereof on the ability of Canadians to maintain effective control over their economic environment is a matter of national concern, and that it is therefore expedient to establish a means by which measures may be taken under the authority of Parliament to ensure that, in so far as is practicable after the enactment of this Act, control of Canadian business enterprises may be acquired by persons other than Canadians, and new businesses may be established in Canada by persons, other than Canadians, who are not already carrying on business in Canada or whose new businesses in Canada would be unrelated to the businesses already being carried on by them in Canada, only if it has been assessed that the acquisition of control of those enterprises or the establishment of those new businesses, as the case may be, by those persons is or is likely to be of significant benefit to Canada, having regard to all of the factors to be taken into account under this Act for that purpose.

(2) In assessing, for the purposes of this Act, whether any acquisition of control of a Canadian business enterprise or the establishment of any new business in Canada is or is likely to be of significant benefit to Canada, the factors to be taken into account are as follows:

(*a*) the effect of the acquisition or establishment on the level and nature of economic activity in Canada, including, without limiting the generality of the foregoing, the effect on employment, on resource processing, on the utilization of parts, components and services produced in Canada, and on exports from Canada;

(*b*) the degree and significance of participation by Canadians in the business enterprise or new business and in any industry or industries in Canada of which the business enterprise or new business forms or would form a part;

(*c*) the effect of the acquisition or establishment on productivity, industrial efficiency, technological development, product innovation and product variety in Canada;

(*d*) the effect of the acquisition or establishment on competition within any industry or industries in Canada; and

(*e*) the compatibility of the acquisition or establishment with national industrial and economic policies, taking into consideration industrial and economic policy objectives enunciated by the government or legislature of any province likely to be significantly affected by the acquisition or establishment.

One European approach to the challenge of the multinationals was the so-called Vredeling Proposal, which sought to give European Economic Community labor unions an improved bargaining position in dealing with MNs. In a draft of the proposal, presented to the Council of the European Community on October 24, 1980, the situation confronting European labor unions and its remedy were described as follows:

1. As a result of changes in the structure of undertakings, the procedures for consulting and disclosing information to employees are often no longer consistent with these new structures. Whereas firms have become more complex in that they have grown or expanded their operations by setting up subsidiaries or establishments in a given country, or even in several foreign countries, their employees continue to be informed and consulted only at local level (shop, works or sector of activity).

2. It therefore follows that decisions which may have serious repercussions for employees at local level may well have been considered and taken at a much higher level (in the same country or even abroad). Even local employers may be ignorant of the motives behind such decisions. Generally speaking, disclosure of information to employees is still confined to the affairs of the local business entity, with the result that the workers concerned are only able to obtain a partial or even incorrect picture of the affairs of the concern as a whole.

3. Recent events have merely confirmed that this situation has particularly serious implications for the employees of firms operating in several countries, since the application of labour law (and even more so the law relating to employees' representative bodies) is usually confined to the territory of a given country. The powers of these bodies, like those of the trade unions, do not normally extend beyond national frontiers. Thus, the procedures by which employees in a given country are informed or consulted only have effect within the legal framework of that country, only benefit the employees in that State and generally only relate to activities carried out in that State when they are not confined to a particular subsidiary or establishment.

Provision should be made for additional information to be supplied to employers in each Member State relating to their company's transnational operations so that they can provide their employees with a clear and complete picture of the activities and performance of the concern as a whole *in the various countries in which it is established.* There is also a need for provisions that would enable employees' representatives to approach management at the level of the decision-making centre in another country where this management alone is in a position to inform and consult them in accordance with the provisions of the directive.

4. Similar information and consultation problems can arise in undertakings operating exclusively at national level when procedures for informing and consulting employees are inconsistent with the structure of the entity whose decisions affect their interests, for instance when a firm expands its business operations by opening a number of establishments in one country and the bodies representing its employees continue to operate only at the level of the individual shop, works or establishment. However, a more common situation is that where a dominant undertaking may have several subsidiaries in the same country while the bodies representing its employees are not organized at the highest level. There is a need for provisions to enable the managers of these establishments or subsidiaries to inform and consult their employees in the proper manner even where the decision affecting their interests is taken not by them but by management at a higher level. Employees' representatives should also be allowed to approach the central management if it alone is in a position to inform and consult them in accordance with the provisions of the Directive.

In a Community in which national economies are closely interlinked and in which undertakings are undergoing structural changes by availing themselves of the right of establishment guaranteed by the EEC Treaty, it is essential that all undertakings with a sizeable workforce and a relatively complex structure, in particular those operating on a transnational basis, should have the same rights and the same responsibilities.

A legal framework for the disclosure of information to and consultation with employees will therefore constitute a stepping-stone to the creation of a uniform operating environment for all undertakings in the Community. The current economic climate, which has necessitated far-reaching and difficult structural changes in industry and has had very serious social repercussions, highlights the importance of a Community initiative in this field. Against this background, the requirement that all firms should inform and consult their employees on the basis of their overall operations assumes particular importance.

Furthermore, it should be remembered that all the Member States already have information and consultation procedures of their own, although the legal nature of these arrangements and their effectiveness in practice vary from one country to the next. A Community instrument should not interfere with existing systems which have already gone part of the way towards solving the problem. Procedures already put in place by national legislation or on a voluntary basis, for example those modelled on the OECD guidelines [discussed in Part D, *infra*], should—where possible—be integrated into the Community system. These arrangements should also be flexible enough to take account of systems based on agreements between the two sides of industry and those that have force of law.

The same objectives as those enshrined in international instruments that are not legally binding, such as the OECD guidelines and the ILO Tripartite Declaration, will be followed with regard to the activities of transnational firms, but they will be achieved in a Community context by means of methods appropriate to the Community's peculiar circumstances and needs.

The initial 1980 draft regulation of the Vredeling proposal drew severe criticism from business interests and particularly from U.S. business interests. Objections included fears that the regulation would be extraterritorial in its effect on foreign management of European subsidiaries, that local management would be undercut by a "by-pass" provision permitting labor to go over the heads of local management to reach more senior foreign officials on occasion, and that confidential information might be revealed. The opposition was particularly effective during consultations before the European Parliament, and the draft regulation was renegotiated within the Community.

DRAFT VREDELING DIRECTIVE

[1984] 1 C.M.L.R. 732

PROPOSAL FOR A COUNCIL DIRECTIVE ON PROCEDURES FOR INFORMING AND CONSULTING EMPLOYEES

Submitted by the Commission to the Council in amended form on 13 July 1983.

SECTION I

DEFINITIONS AND SCOPE

Article I

For the purposes of this Directive, the following definitions shall apply:
(a) *Parent undertaking and subsidiary:* an undertaking within the Community is

a parent undertaking when another undertaking is its subsidiary according to the legislation applicable to the parent undertaking and the criteria of Article 1 of Directive 83/349/EEC;[1]

an undertaking outside the Community is a parent undertaking when another undertaking is its subsidiary according to the legislation applicable to that subsidiary and the criteria of Article 1 of Directive 83/349/EEC.

(b) *Establishment:* an entity, geographically separate from, but not legally independent of, the undertaking of which it is a part, in particular a workshop, branch, agency, factory or office.

(c) *Decision-making centre:* the place where an undertaking has its central administration.

(d) *Management:* the person or persons responsible for the management of an undertaking under the national legislation to which it is subject.

(e) *Employees' representatives:* the employees' representatives provided for by the laws or practice of the member-States, with the exception of members of administrative, managing or supervisory bodies of companies who sit on such bodies or certain member-States as employees' representatives.

SECTION II

INFORMATION AND CONSULTATION PROCEDURES IN TRANSNATIONAL
UNDERTAKINGS

Article 2

1. This Directive relates to procedures for informing and consulting the employees:

—of a subsidiary in the Community when a total of at least 1,000 workers is employed in the Community by the parent undertaking and its subsidiaries taken as a whole,

—of an undertaking having in the Community one or more establishments when a total of at least 1,000 workers is employed in the Community by the undertaking taken as a whole.

2. When the decision-making centre of an undertaking is located in a non-member country, its management may be represented in the Community by an agent who is responsible for fulfilling the requirements regarding information and consultation laid down by this Directive. In the absence of such an agent the management of each subsidiary concerned in the Community shall be held responsible for the obligations arising from Articles 3 and 4.

Article 3

1. At least once a year, at a fixed date, the management of a parent undertaking shall forward general but explicit information giving a clear picture of the activities of the parent undertaking and its subsidiaries as a whole to the

---

[1] A directive on accounting rules—EDS.

management of each of its subsidiaries in the Community, with a view to the communication of this information to the employees' representatives as provided in paragraph 4. For the same purpose, the management of the parent undertaking shall forward to the management of each subsidiary concerned specific information on a particular sector of production or geographical area in which the subsidiary is active.

2. This information shall relate in particular to:

(a)   structure;
(b)   the economic and financial situation;
(c)   the probable development of the business and of production and sales;
(d)   the employment situation and probable trends;
(e)   investment prospects.

3. Where the information provided for in paragraph 2 is brought up to date after the date fixed in accordance with paragraph 1, and communicated in implementation of the relevant legislation to shareholders and creditors, the management of the parent undertaking shall also forward it to the management of its subsidiaries, with a view to its communication to the employees' representatives.

4. The management of each subsidiary shall be required to communicate the information referred to in paragraphs 2 and 3 without delay to the employees' representatives, with the exception of secret information as defined in Article 7(1). The employees' representatives may ask the management for oral explanations of the information communicated. The management is required to provide such explanations, and, if necessary, to make it clear what information is to be treated as confidential under the terms of Article 7(2).

5. If the management of the subsidiary fails to fulfill its obligation to communicate the information required to its employees' representatives within 30 days of the date fixed, referred to in paragraph 1, or of the date of communication in the case of the updated information referred to in paragraph 3, the representatives of the employees of the subsidiary may approach in writing the management of the parent undertaking. That undertaking shall be obliged to communicate the relevant information without delay to the management of the subsidiary.

6. The terms of this Article shall apply equally where the parent undertaking is at the same time the subsidiary of another parent undertaking, unless that undertaking itself meets the obligations resulting from this Article.

7. Member-States shall provide for appropriate penalties for failure to comply with the obligations laid down in this Article.

Article 4

1. Where the management of a parent undertaking proposes to take a decision concerning the whole or a major part of the parent undertaking or of a subsidiary in the Community which is liable to have serious consequences for the interests of the employees of its subsidiaries in the Community, it shall be

required to forward precise information to the management of each subsidiary concerned in good time before the final decision is taken with a view to the communication of this information to the employees' representatives in the manner provided in paragraph 3. This information shall relate in particular to:

—the grounds for the proposed decision,
—the legal, economic and social consequences of such decision for the employees concerned,
—the measures planned in respect of such employees.

2. Decisions liable to have serious consequences may in particular relate to:

(a)   the closure or transfer of an establishment or major parts thereof;
(b)   substantial restrictions or modifications of the activities of the undertaking;
(c)   major modifications with regard to organisation, working practices or production methods, including modifications resulting from the introduction of new technologies;
(d)   the introduction of long-term co-operation with other undertakings or the cessation of such co-operation;
(e)   measures relating to workers' health and to industrial safety.

3. Without prejudice to Article 7(1), the management of each subsidiary concerned shall be required to communicate in writing without delay the information referred to in paragraph 1, with the exception of secret information as defined in Article 7(1), to the employees' representatives, to ask for their opinion, granting them a period of at least 30 days from the day on which the information is communicated, and to hold consultations with them with a view to attempting to reach agreement on the measures planned in respect of the employees. The provisions of the second subparagraph of Article 3(4)shall apply *mutatis mutandis.*

4. Where the obligations laid down in paragraph 3 are not fulfilled, member-States shall ensure that employees' representatives have the right to appeal to a tribunal or other competent national authority for measures to be taken within a maximum period of 30 days to compel the management of the subsidiary to fulfil its obligations.

5. The proposed decision referred to in paragraph 1 shall not be implemented before the opinion of the employees' representatives is received or failing that before the end of the period granted according to paragraph 3.

6. Where information concerning a decision within the meaning of paragraph 1 is withheld because it is secret within the meaning of Article 7(1), the management of the subsidiary is nonetheless required, at least 30 days before putting into effect any decision directly affecting conditions of work or employment, to hold consultations with the employees' representatives with a view to attempting to reach agreement on the measures planned in respect of the employees.

7. The terms of this Article shall apply equally where the parent undertaking is at the same time the subsidiary of another parent undertaking, unless that undertaking itself meets the obligations resulting from this Article.

8. Member-States shall provide for appropriate penalties for failure to comply with the obligations laid down in this Article.

Article 5

1. Where, in a member-State a body representing employees exists at a level higher than that of the subsidiary, the information referred to in Article 3 relating to the employees of all the subsidiaries thus represented shall be given to that body.

2. The consultation provided for in Article 4 shall take place under the same conditions with the representative body referred to in paragraph 1 if the representatives of the employees whose terms of employment or working conditions are directly affected by the decision agree to transfer their right to be consulted to the higher level.

3. A body representing all the employees of the parent undertaking and its subsidiaries within the Community may be created by means of agreements to be concluded between the management of the undertaking concerned and the employees' representative. If such a body is created, paragraphs 1 and 2 shall be applicable.

4. Member-States may limit the obligations laid down in Articles 3 and 4 to subsidiaries which, in respect of the number of employees, fulfil the conditions for the election or designation of a collegiate body representing the employees.

5. Member-States may provide that the information and consultation procedures referred to in Article 3(4) and (5) and Article 4(3) to (6) may take place directly with the employees, without prejudice to the application of the other provisions of this Directive.

Article 6

1. The provisions of Articles 3, 4 and 5 shall apply *mutatis mutandis* to the procedures for informing and consulting the employees' representatives in the undertakings referred to in the second indent of Article 2(1).

2. For the purposes of this Article, the terms "parent undertaking" and "subsidiary" shall be replaced by the terms "undertaking" and "establishment" respectively.

SECTION III

SECRECY AND CONFIDENTIALITY

Article 7

1. The management of an undertaking shall be authorised not to communicate secret information. Information may only be treated as secret which, if

disclosed, could substantially damage the undertaking's interests or lead to the failure of its plans.

2. Employees, their representatives and the experts to whom they refer shall not reveal to third parties any information which has been given to them in confidence.

3. Member-States shall ensure that a tribunal or other competent national authority can settle disputes concerning the secret character of any information withheld in application of paragraph 1, or the confidential character of the information referred to in paragraph 2.

4. Member-States shall provide for appropriate penalties for failure to comply with the obligations laid down in this Article.

SECTION IV

FINAL PROVISIONS

Article 8

1. This Directive shall be without prejudice to measures taken pursuant to Directive 75/129/EEC [governing collective redundancies] and Directive 77/187/EEC [governing employees' rights on transfer of a business operation] or to the freedom of the member-States to apply or introduce laws, regulations or administrative provisions which are more favourable to employees.

2. In implementing this Directive, member-States may lay down special provisions for undertakings and establishments whose direct and main objectives are:

(a)   political, religious, humanitarian, charitable, educational, scientific or artistic, or

(b)   related to public information or expression of opinion.

Such special provision must be limited to that which is necessary to ensure that such undertakings enjoy the freedom to which they are entitled under the national laws to which they are subject.

3. This Directive shall be without prejudice to the application of national laws concerning bankruptcy, winding up proceedings, arrangements, compositions or other similar proceedings in so far as these proceedings result from judicial decisions.

Article 9

The member-States shall introduce the laws, regulations and administrative provisions necessary to comply with this Directive not later than 1 July 1987. They shall forthwith inform the Commission thereof.

Article 10

Within two years from the date referred to in Article 9, member-States shall forward to the Commission all necessary information to enable it to draw up a report on the application of this Directive for submission to the Council.

Article 11

This Directive is addressed to the member-States.

Bibliographical Note

For additional data on the Vredeling proposal, *see* Kolvenbach, EEC Directive on Information and Consultation of Employees (Vredeling-Proposal), 10 Intl. Bus. Law. 365 (1982); and Walker, The Vredeling Proposal: Cooperation Versus Confrontation in European Labor Relations, 1 Intl. Tax & Bus. Law. 177 (1983).

On differing types of host-nation regulations and their effect generally, *see* B. Fisher & J. Turner, Regulating the Multinational Enterprises (1983); Cordova, Workers' Participation in Decisions with Enterprises: Recent Trends and Problems, 121 Intl. Lab. Rev. 125 (1982); Singer, The Distribution of Gains between Investing and Borrowing Countries, 40 Am. Econ. Rev. 473 (1950); R. Hawkins & J. Walter, The Multinational Corporation, in R. Amacher et al. (eds.), Challenges to a Liberal International Economic Order 159 (1979); Symposium, Canadian Regulation and Restriction of American Investment 1 B.U. Intl. L.J. 1 (1982).

QUESTIONS

1. Note that, in practice, Canada's Foreign Investment Review Act (FIRA), which had gone on to create an administrative review (and possible veto) procedure for those investment transactions found to be within the act, was often interpreted as authorizing the Canadian government to impose conditions on the specific investment. If you had been the minister of industry, trade, and commerce, what kinds of conditions would you have considered?

2. Would such conditions violate the GATT? (In 1982, the United States government announced that it would initiate a GATT Art. XXIII claim on this point.)

3. Should the Canadian Act have been applicable to a U.S. sale of a Canadian business by one U.S. firm to another? For an affirmative answer, *see* Dow Jones & Co. v. Attorney-General of Canada, 113 D.L.R.3d 395 (1980). Does this extension of jurisdiction infringe U.S. rights? As a Canadian minister, what principles would you find relevant in reviewing such a transaction?

4. What parts of the Vredeling proposal, as amended, are most likely to be offensive to foreign firms. Secrecy provisions? The duty to consult at all?

5. How much does the Vredeling approach actually help labor in Europe?

6. Consider Articles 1 to 13 and 27-37 of the Andean Pact's Decision 24 (Selected Documents Supplement). What is their likely intention? Will they actually achieve it?

7. Under what circumstances is it wise to have a special regime for foreign investment, rather than simply to make sure that foreign investors follow local law?

8. Should laws like these follow the Most-Favored-Nation principle—or would it be wise, for example, for Canada to treat U.S. and French investment differently or for a developing nation to treat OPEC and developed world investment differently?

9. In what areas might you be particularly concerned about foreign investments into the United States? Defense issues? Agricultural land ownership? (reporting required under 7 U.S.C. §§3501-3508), TV station control? (*See* Noe v. FCC, 260 F.2d 739 (D.C. Cir. 1958), *cert. denied,* 359 U.S. 924 (1959)).

10. Should Fourteenth Amendment principles that have led to a number of fairly broad protections for individual resident aliens be applied as well for the protection of foreign investors?

11. Suppose you wanted to create a special regime to favor and encourage the foreign investor in the United States? What would you do?

12. In whatever package of tax holidays and concessions you develop in response to the previous question, how much would you fear competition from other investment-hungry nations? How does the situation differ from that of local U.S. governments bidding for a new industry?

13. If a developing nation grants a tax holiday to a subsidiary of a U.S. firm, should the benefit of the foreign tax credit be reduced accordingly?

C.   HOME-NATION REGULATION—AND CONSEQUENT DISPUTE PATTERNS

Home nations often also impose special regulations on their firms' foreign branches and subsidiaries. These can range from the regulation implicit in the international sections of the tax code, through details of bookkeeping (a very important part of the Foreign Corrupt Practices Act), and efforts to shape the influence of the investment on the nation's balance of payment. Some of these rules can create severe complications, either for the competitive position of the foreign subsidiary or for political relations between the different nations.

Of the range of such rules and conflicts, three will be considered here: those of employment regulation, those of extraterritorial export regulations, and those of franchise regulations (and the associated vertical antitrust issue generally). These examples are representative of many possible conflicts but are chosen for their subject matter variety. They are also chosen to exemplify different dispute resolution procedures. In the first case, a U.S. court decided on its own extraterritorial authority; in the second, a dispute was ultimately resolved by diplomatic means; and, in the third situation, arbitration is frequently preferred to litigation.

1. Employment Regulation

Probably the most common problem for the MN is that of labor regulation— a problem already exemplified in the Vredeling proposal just examined. Consider the following case as an example of policy conflict (the case was reversed on the grounds that the practice involved did not amount to discrimination within the sense of Title VII, but it offers the clearest available exposition of the problem).

BRYANT AND LILLIBRIDGE v. INTERNATIONAL SCHOOLS SERVICES, INC.

502 F. Supp. 472 (D.N.J. 1980), *rev'd*, 675 F.2d 562 (3d Cir. 1982)

DEBEVOISE, J.

I. PARTIES AND PROCEEDINGS

Plaintiffs in these consolidated actions, Theresa O. Lillibridge and Dotti D. Jernigan Bryant, instituted suit under Title VII of the Civil Rights Act of 1964, as amended, 42 U.S.C. §2000e, et seq. ("Title VII"). Plaintiffs charge that the practice of defendant, International Schools Services, Inc. ("ISS"), of awarding to its overseas teachers two kinds of employment contracts having substantially different compensation and benefit provisions constituted unlawful discrimination against plaintiffs on the basis of sex.

ISS is a private, non-profit corporation organized under the laws of the District of Columbia, with its headquarters in Princeton, New Jersey. ISS works by contract with overseas governments or corporations to operate schools for children of American employees overseas. The services it provides are educational consulting, school operation, education staffing, purchasing, procurement and financial management.

The case was tried without a jury, and decision was reserved. This opinion constitutes this Court's findings of fact and conclusions of law.

II. FINDINGS OF FACT

A. THE ISS CONTRACTS

The American School in Isfahan, one of the schools ISS operated, was established in 1973, pursuant to a contract between ISS and Bell Helicopter. The contracts which Bell Helicopter and other companies performed for the Iranian government required the presence of the companies' employees overseas in Iran. These employees brought their families. It was ISS's responsibility, under its contract, to establish a school and employ and supervise the staff of the school where the children of these employees would be educated. ISS initially contracted with Bell Helicopter to operate the American School; for 1976 and thereafter, ISS contracted directly with the Iranian government to operate the school.

The school term for the American School ran from September of one year through June of the next year, and the staff went on annual leave for the summer months. The American School operated until January 6, 1979, when it was permanently closed due to the revolution in Iran which began in late 1978.

All of the staff at the American School were compensated according to the same base salary scale, which varied depending upon (1) teaching experience and (2) educational achievement. The base salary scale is not an issue in this case. . . .

Teachers at the American School taught under two kinds of contracts—local-hire contracts and ISS-sponsored contracts. Regardless of the kind of contract, the duties of the teachers did not differ. Persons who had ISS-sponsored contracts received additional allowances. . . .

The extra benefits paid under the ISS-sponsored contracts were comparable to extra benefits which business corporations under contract with the Iranian government paid to United States citizens they recruited to work in Iran. ISS specifically patterned its benefits upon those provided by Bell Helicopter.

Teachers having ISS-sponsored contracts were hired in the United States and in Isfahan; teachers having local-hire contracts were hired only in Isfahan.

B.   BRYANT'S EMPLOYMENT BY ISS

Bryant was married to Marc Jernigan in 1974 and was an elementary school teacher by profession. She expected to accompany her husband to Iran, where he was to be employed by Grumman. She learned of ISS from a Grumman employee and wrote to ISS at Princeton, New Jersey, informing it of her expected arrival in Isfahan, Iran, in October 1975. ISS sent her application forms, which she completed and returned in early May, 1975. Receiving no response, Bryant made inquiry by letter dated July 30, 1975, again addressing her letter to ISS at Princeton. On September 22, 1975, ISS replied, stating that all positions were filled and advising her to communicate with the School superintendent upon her arrival in Isfahan.

When Bryant arrived in Isfahan in November, 1975, a Grumman employee introduced her to Michael White, the principal of the American School's Middle School. He already had her résumé and hired her forthwith as a substitute teacher, paid on a daily basis. In April 1976, ISS hired Bryant on a full-time basis and entered into a local-hire contract with her. The contract recited that

Bryant was entitled to participate in the benefit program attached to the letter agreement. There was no attachment to the letter agreement. She was not informed of the fact that there were two kinds of contract, nor was she given a copy of the School's personnel manual.

While she was a substitute teacher she had heard of certain allowances being paid to some of the teachers.

After her employment under a local-hire contract commenced, Bryant asked the American School's assistant superintendent, Ralph Englesby, whether she would receive these allowances. He replied in the negative and, during the course of their discussion, informed her, "You can sue for them."

At a faculty meeting at the end of the 1975-76 school year which Bryant attended, Dr. Howard Wire, Superintendent of the American School, was asked about the disparity between payments under local-hire contracts and ISS-sponsored contracts. Apparently there was a discussion of an EEOC case entitled *Michele Dick v. Telemedia,* in which a woman married to a man who worked in Iran was awarded damages for unpaid benefits on the grounds that she, as a married woman, had suffered from discriminatory treatment vis-a-vis married men. Dr. Wire defended ISS's policy of awarding contracts with different benefits. Asked by one of the women if it wouldn't be smart to go to the United States to sue ISS, Dr. Wire stated that "I wouldn't do so if I were you while you and your husband are employed here." . . .

Both before commencement of this action and during the course of this litigation ISS has articulated several different bases for distinguishing between persons receiving ISS-sponsored contracts and persons receiving local-hire contracts. It is abundantly clear that ISS did not succeed in perfecting its rationale until the closing phases of this law suit. However, even though ISS never clearly expressed what it was doing either to itself or to others, the evidence suggests that in fact ISS's criterion for awarding contracts was a subjective one, namely, whether the teacher came to Iran and remained there for the primary purpose of teaching at the American School or whether the teacher came to Iran and remained there primarily for some other purpose. In the former situation the teacher was awarded an ISS-sponsored contract and in the latter situation the teacher was awarded a local-hire contract.

ISS decided what was the teacher's primary purpose for coming to or remaining in Iran on the basis of whether the teacher's spouse was employed by Bell Helicopter or Grumman or perhaps some other American company in Iran. Such employment by the spouse would lead ISS to conclude that the would-be teacher and her/his spouse were induced to come to Iran by the spouse's employment and that, presumably, the couple was already receiving benefits comparable to the ones offered by ISS to attract teachers to Iran.

Bryant and Lillibridge claim that ISS's method of awarding two types of contracts discriminated against them on the basis of sex, in violation of Title VII. Specifically, they maintain that the benefits policy resulted in disparate treatment and/or had a disparate impact on them—married females whose spouses were not employed by ISS.

ISS maintains that its benefits policy was applied equally to males and females and therefore could not result in disparate treatment. Moreover, ISS maintains that its policy did not have a disparate impact on females. . . .

IV.   EXTRATERRITORIAL APPLICATION OF TITLE VII

ISS urges that Title VII does not apply extraterritorially and that, therefore, the Court lacks subject matter jurisdiction. ISS advances the following reasons in support of its position:

First, as in the case of the National Labor Relations Act, 29 U.S.C. §141, et seq., Title VII contains no clear affirmative expression setting forth the territorial jurisdiction of the Act. The National Labor Relations Act does not apply outside the territorial jurisdiction of the United States, RCA OMS, Inc., 202 N.L.R.B. 228 (1973); GTE Automatic Electric, Inc., 226 N.L.R.B. 1222 (1976). ISS concludes that by analogy Title VII should be given the same limited construction.

Second, prior to the enactment of Title VII various other labor laws were narrowly construed to preclude extraterritorial application. Foley Bros., Inc. v. Filardo, 336 U.S. 281, 69 S. Ct. 575, 93 L. Ed. 680 (1949); Benz v. Compania Naviera Hidalgo, 353 U.S. 138, 77 S. Ct. 699, 1 L. Ed. 2d 709 (1957); McCulloch v. Sociedad Nacional, 372 U.S. 10, 83 S. Ct. 671, 9 L. Ed. 2d 547 (1963). ISS argues that it would be illogical to think that Congress would grant EEOC the same investigatory powers as it granted to the NLRB and, at the same time, give EEOC greater territorial jurisdiction unless Congress specifically so provided.

Third, ISS contends that §206(d) of the Fair Labor Standards Act, 29 U.S.C. §201, et seq. (commonly known as the Equal Pay Act), should be read *in pari materia* with Title VII. The Equal Pay Act does not apply outside the territorial jurisdiction of the United States, 29 U.S.C. §213(f), and, again, ISS argues that it would be illogical to think that Congress meant to limit the jurisdiction of the Equal Pay Act and not Title VII when the two are to be read in harmony with one another.

Fourth, ISS asserts that given the sensitive nature of international affairs, to apply Title VII extraterritorially without an affirmative Congressional expression to do so is unwarranted.

Fifth, ISS seeks comfort from the recent case of Rossi v. Brown, 24 E.P.D. ¶31,238 (D.C. Cir. 1980).[2] The issue in the *Rossi* case was whether an agreement with the Republic of the Philippines constituted a treaty, which would form the basis for permissible discrimination against the plaintiff. Section 106 of Public Law No. 92-129[3] prohibited discrimination against United States

---

[2]This case was ultimately resolved against the plaintiff on quite different statutory construction grounds. Weinberger v. Rossi, 456 U.S. 25 (1982)—EDS.

[3]§106 of Pub. L. 92-129 provided:

 Unless provided by treaty, no person shall be discriminated against by the Department of Defense or by any officer or employee thereof, in the employment of civilian personnel

citizens in the employment of civilian personnel on United States military bases overseas unless such discrimination is permitted by treaty. ISS stated, in a letter memorandum to the Court, "Title VII was intended to offer protection against discrimination to civilian applicants and employees of the military. . . . It has been so construed in Johnson v. Alexander, 572 F.2d 1219 (8th Cir. 1978), *cert. den.,* 439 U.S. 986, 99 S. Ct. 579, 58 L. Ed. 2d 658 (1978), *reh'g den.,* 439 U.S. 1135, 99 S. Ct. 1061, 59 L. Ed. 2d 98 (1979). . . . Given the application of Title VII to civilian employees of the Armed Services, the existence of Section 106 of Public Law No. 92-129, and its legislative history, make no sense *unless* it were intended by Congress that Title VII *not* apply extraterritorially."

The short answer to all of ISS's arguments against giving extraterritorial effect to Title VII is that Congress has spoken on the subject and that a fair interpretation of the statutory language leads to the conclusion that Title VII is to be given extraterritorial effect.

The question whether an act applies extraterritorially is a matter of statutory construction, for it is well settled that Congress has the power to extend the reach of its laws to American citizens outside the geographical boundaries of the United States. Foley Bros. v. Filardo, *supra;* Blackmer v. United States, 284 U.S. 421, 52 S. Ct. 252, 76 L. Ed. 375 (1932). The provision of Title VII exempting certain entities, 42 U.S.C. §2000e-1, provides in pertinent part:

> This subchapter shall not apply to an employer with respect to the employment of *aliens outside any State,* or to a religious corporation. . . . (Emphasis added.)

By negative implication, since Congress explicitly excluded aliens employed outside of any state, it must have intended to provide relief to non-aliens, i.e., American citizens, outside of any state by an employer otherwise covered by the Act. Love v. Pullman Co., 12 E.P.D. ¶11,225 (D. Colo. 1976).

The *Love* case dealt with the extent to which Canadian porters (aliens) were protected by Title VII and concluded that when such porters operated in the United States they were entitled to relief. In a footnote, the Court explained:

> This discussion assumes that the porters in Montreal were not American citizens. American citizens who were employed by Pullman in Canada are entitled to full relief without any subtraction. This conclusion rests on the negative inference of §702 of the Civil Rights Act of 1964. 42 U.S.C. §2000e-1. Since Congress explicitly excluded aliens employed outside of any state, it must have intended to provide relief to American citizens employed outside of any state in an industry affecting commerce by an employer otherwise covered under the act. Nothing in the legislative history addresses this specific point, but neither is it contra-indi-

---

at any facility or installation operated by the Department of Defense in any foreign country because such person is a citizen of the United States or is a dependent of a member of the Armed Forces of the United States. As used in this section, the term "facility or installation operated by the Department of Defense" shall include, but shall not be limited to, any officer's club, non-commissioned officers' club, post exchange, or commissary store.

cated. Equal Employment Opportunity Commission, Legislative History of Titles VII and XI of Civil Rights Act of 1964. Our research has revealed no cases directly in point. An additional support for this interpretation comes from the international or extraterritorial application of the antitrust laws. *See, e.g.,* Continental Ore Co. v. Union Carbide & Carbon Corp., 370 U.S. 690 [82 S. Ct. 1404, 8 L. Ed. 2d 777] (1962). *Id.* at n.4. . . .

Thus, I conclude that Title VII has extraterritorial effect and was applicable to ISS's employment practices in Iran. . . .

VIII.   "ACT OF STATE" AND "FOREIGN COMPULSION" DEFENSES

ISS asserts that its policies and practices in awarding contracts to teachers at the American School in Isfahan were immunized from attack on Title VII grounds by the act of state doctrine and by the defense of foreign compulsion. The act of state doctrine precludes inquiry into the validity of a foreign sovereign's act and requires American courts to respect private claims based on the contention that the damaging act of another nation violates American law. Mannington Mills, Inc. v. Congoleum Corp., 595 F.2d 1287, 1292-1293 (3d Cir. 1979). The foreign compulsion defense, developed in the context of antitrust litigation, shields from liability the acts of parties carried out in obedience to the mandate of a foreign government, Interamerican Refining Corp. v. Texaco Maracaibo, Inc., 307 F. Supp. 1291, 1296 (D. Del. 1970).

It is ISS's contention that the conduct which lies at the heart of plaintiff's claims was mandated by Iranian authorities, that the insistence by these authorities that ISS not pay benefits to teachers which would duplicate benefits being received by the teachers' spouses constituted an act of state and the basis of the defense of foreign compulsion.

Long before it entered into a contractual relationship with the Iranian government, ISS allocated its ISS-sponsored contracts and its local-hire contracts on the basis of the primary purpose which motivated its employees to come to or remain in Iran. Continuation of this policy after ISS began contracting with the Iranian government instead of Bell Helicopter insured compliance with the government's requirement that there be no double payments of benefits to spouses working in Iran for companies under contract with the Iranian government. Inasmuch as I have concluded that ISS's policy in this regard did not violate Title VII, there is no need to decide whether this requirement of the Iranian authorities who negotiated the contract with ISS rose to the level of an act of state.

It was not the policy against payment of double benefits or the primary purpose basis for awarding contracts which I found violated Title VII; I found that ISS violated Title VII by failing to advise persons hired locally of its basis for awarding contracts and by determining an employee's primary purpose for being or remaining in Iran by means of criteria which had the effect of discriminating against married women. There was nothing in Iranian law and there were no requirements of the Iranian authorities which compelled ISS to conceal its policies from persons hired locally, or to base its determination of primary purpose on the employment status of its teachers' spouses. Those were actions and policies of ISS and neither reflected sovereign decisions of the Iranian government nor were compelled by the Iranian government. Thus those actions and policies are not protected by the act of state doctrine or the defense of foreign compulsion. Mannington Mills, Inc. v. Congoleum Corp., *supra*, at 1293; Timberlane Lbr. Co. v. Bank of America, N.T. & S.A., 549 F.2d 597, 608 (9th Cir. 1976). . . .

NOTES AND QUESTIONS

1. What is the point in distinguishing between employment of U.S. citizens abroad and employment of foreign nationals abroad?

2. How would the case have come out if the government of Iran had prohibited all employment of women as teachers within Iran?

3. Is the opinion really responsive to *Timberlane*? Should it be? For a good discussion of the area, *see* Kirschner, The Extraterritorial Application of Title VII of the Civil Rights Act, 34 Lab. L.J. 394 (1983).

4. Taking this case as a general example, how should the following analogous cases come out?

(a) Discrimination against a U.S. citizen abroad, in possible violation of the Age Discrimination in Employment Act of 1967? *See* Cleary v. United States Lines, 728 F.2d 607 (3d Cir. 1984) (the lower court opinion at 555 F. Supp. 1251 (D.N.J. 1983) also helpful); Zahourek v. Arthur Young & Co., 567 F. Supp. 1453 (D. Colo. 1983); Linsky v. Heidelberg Eastern, 470 F. Supp. 1181 (E.D.N.Y. 1979).

(b) Possible Title VII discrimination against a U.S. citizen abroad due to local law excluding women from certain heavy jobs?

(c) Possible Title VII discrimination against a U.S. national due to local law prohibiting the employment of Jewish people in the nation?

(d) Application of a code of conduct in opposition to South Africa's apartheid policy? *See* Sullivan, Agents for Change: The Mobilization of Multinational Companies in South Africa, 15 L. & Poly. Intl. Bus. 427 (1983).

(e) Possible violation of U.S. minimum wage laws? Assuming you come out differently on this one, how would you explain the difference? Where would you come out on safety rules? Pension rights? Labor union rules?

5. How would you advise a company caught in the middle in one of these situations? Must it suspend operations in the foreign nation?

6. What about the reciprocal case? Suppose a Japanese subsidiary in the United States is alleged to discriminate against women in executive positions in the United States, reflecting a pattern of predominantly male executives in the home branches in Japan? *See* Sumitomo Shoji America v. Avagliano, 457

U.S. 176 (1982); Note, International Law—Employment Discrimination, 13 Ga. J. Intl. & Comp. L. 159 (1983).

7. When is it fair to apply U.S. law *both* to U.S. subsidiaries of foreign firms and foreign subsidiaries of U.S. firms?

2.   *The Export Administration Act and the Gas Pipeline Case*

The United States has on a number of occasions sought to apply its law to foreign activities of U.S. corporations. You have already seen examples in the antitrust area, and there have been others, such as the balance of payments regulations issued under the Trading with the Enemy Act during the 1960s.

The most politically controversial examples have arisen from regulations under the Export Administration Act. Executive actions have gone beyond the direct export context, discussed in Chapter XII, to attempt to reach foreign operations of firms affiliated with the United States. A controversy that shows the legal arguments and problems quite clearly is that surrounding the United States effort in 1982 to discourage Soviet construction of a pipeline to transport natural gas to Western Europe. The United States feared that this pipeline would make Western Europe dependent on Soviet gas and directed that foreign subsidiaries of U.S. firms, as well as certain foreign firms using U.S. technology, should not export relevant materials to the Soviet Union. A number of European subsidiaries had already entered contracts to export such materials.

As demonstrated in the first excerpt below, Europe resisted this exercise of U.S. jurisdiction. There were even court cases in Europe dealing with the firm caught between conflicting demands. The second excerpt, *Fruehauf,* exemplifies these cases but arose from an earlier similar conflict and deals more fundamentally with the issues than do the later cases. Finally, as shown in the last excerpt of the group, a speech by President Reagan, the conflict was settled politically.

EUROPEAN COMMUNITIES: COMMENTS ON THE U.S. REGULATIONS CONCERNING TRADE WITH THE U.S.S.R.

21 I.L.M. 891 (1982)

I.   INTRODUCTION

1. On June 22, 1982, the Department of Commerce at the direction of President Reagan and pursuant to Section 6 of the Export Administration Act amended Sections 376.12, 379.8 and 385.2 of the Export Administration

Regulations. These amendments amounted to an expansion of the existing U.S. controls on the export and re-export of goods and technical data relating to oil and gas exploration, exploitation, transmission and refinement.

The European Community believes that the U.S. regulations as amended contain sweeping extensions of U.S. jurisdiction which are unlawful under international law. Moreover, the new Regulations and the way in which they affect contracts in course of performance seems to run counter to criteria of the Export Administration Act and also to certain principles of U.S. public law.

2. The main thrust of the Regulations may be summarized as follows:

First of all, persons within a third country may not re-export machinery for the exploration, production, transmission or refinement of oil and natural gas, or components thereof, if it is of U.S. origin, without permission of the U.S. Government.

Moreover, any person subject to the jurisdiction of the United States[1] is required to get prior written authorization by the Office of Export Administration for export or re-export to the U.S.S.R. of non-U.S. goods and technical data related to oil and gas exploration, production, transmission and refinement.

Finally, no person in the U.S. *or in a foreign country* may export or re-export to the U.S.S.R. foreign products directly derived from U.S. technical data relating to machinery etc. utilized for the exploration, production or transmission or refinement of petroleum or natural gas or commodities produced in plants based on such U.S. technical data.

This prohibition applies in three alternative situations, namely:

—if a written assurance was required under the U.S. export regulations when the data were exported;

—if any person subject to the jurisdiction of the U.S.A. . . . receives royalties or other compensation for, or has licensed, the use of the technical data concerned, regardless of when the data were exported from the U.S.;

—if the recipient of the U.S. technical data has agreed (in the licensing agreement or other contracts) to abide by U.S. export control regulations.

3. The following comments will discuss *firstly* the international legal aspects of the U.S. measures, including (a) the generally recognized bases on which jurisdiction can be founded in international law and (b) other bases of jurisdiction which might be invoked by the U.S. Government; *secondly* the rules and principles as laid down in U.S. law, in particular the Export Administration Act, and as applied by U.S. Courts, which would seem to be at variance with the Amendments of June 22, 1982.

---

[1]Now defined as (i) Any person wherever located who is a citizen or resident of the United States; (ii) any person actually within the United States; (iii) any corporation organized under the laws of the United States; or (iv) any partnership, association, corporation or other organization, wherever organized or doing business, that is owned or controlled by persons specified in paragraphs (i), (ii) or (iii).

II.   THE AMENDMENTS UNDER INTERNATIONAL LAW

A.   GENERALLY ACCEPTED BASES OF JURISDICTION IN INTERNATIONAL LAW

4. The U.S. measures as they apply in the present case are unacceptable under international law because of their extra-territorial aspects. They seek to regulate companies not of U.S. nationality in respect of their conduct outside the United States and particularly the handling of property and technical data of these companies not within the United States.

They seek to impose on non-U.S. companies the restriction of U.S. law by threatening them with discriminatory sanctions in the field of trade which are inconsistent with the normal commercial practice established between the U.S. and the E.C.

In this way the Amendments of June 22, 1982, run counter to the two generally accepted bases of jurisdiction in international law; the territoriality and the nationality principles.[2]

5. The *territoriality principle* (i.e. the notion that a state should restrict its rule-making in principle to persons and goods within its territory and that an organization like the European Community should restrict the applicability of its rules to the territory to which the Treaty setting it up applies) is a fundamental notion of international law, in particular insofar as it concerns the regulation of the social and economic activity in a state. The principle that each state—and *mutatis mutandis* the Community insofar as powers have been transferred to it—has the right freely to organize and develop its social and economic system has been confirmed many times in international fora. The American measures clearly infringe the principle of territoriality, since they purport to regulate the activities of companies in the E.C., not under the territorial competence of the U.S.

6. The *nationality principle* (i.e. the prescription of rules for nationals, wherever they are) cannot serve as a basis for the extension of U.S. jurisdiction resulting from the Amendments, i.e. (i) over companies incorporated in E.C. Member States on the basis of some corporate link (parent-subsidiary) or personal link (e.g. shareholding) to the U.S.; (ii) over companies incorporated in E.C. Member States, either because they have a tie to a U.S.-incorporated company, subsidiary or other "U.S. controlled" company through a licencing agreement, royalty payments, or payment of other compensation, or because they have bought certain goods originating in the U.S.

7. *ad (i)* The Amendments in two places purport to subject to U.S. jurisdiction companies, wherever organized or doing business, which are subsidiaries of U.S. companies or under the control of U.S. citizens, U.S. residents or even persons actually within the U.S. This implies that the United States is seeking to impose its corporate nationality on companies of which the great majority

---

[2]See Restatement (2nd) of the Foreign Relations Law of the U.S. (1972), paras. 17 and 30 respectively.

are incorporated and have their registered office elsewhere, notably in E.C. Member States.

Such action is not in conformity with recognized principles of international law. In the Barcelona Traction Case, the International Court of Justice declared that two traditional criteria for determining the nationality of companies; i.e. the place of incorporation and the place of the registered office of the company concerned, had been "confirmed by long practice and by numerous international instruments". The Court also scrutinized other tests of corporate nationality, but concluded that these had not found general acceptance. The Court consequently placed primary emphasis on the traditional place of incorporation and the registered office in deciding the case in point. This decision was taken within the framework of the doctrine of diplomatic protection, but reflects a general principle of international law.

8. *ad (ii)* The notion inherent in the subjection to U.S. jurisdiction of companies with no tie to the U.S. whatsoever, except for a technological link to a U.S. company, or through possession of U.S. origin goods, can only be that this technology or such goods should somehow be considered as unalterably "American" (even though many of the patents involved are registered in the Member States of the European Community). This seems the only possible explanation for the U.S. Regulations given the fact that national security is not at stake here. . . .

Goods and technology do not have any nationality and there are no known rules under international law for using goods or technology situated abroad as a basis of establishing jurisdiction over the persons controlling them. . . .

10. The practical impact of the Amendments to the Export Administration Regulations is that E.C. companies are pressed into service to carry out U.S. trade policy towards the U.S.S.R., even though these companies are incorporated and have their registered office within the community which has its own trade policy towards the U.S.S.R.

The public policy ("ordre public") of the European Community and of its Member States is thus purportedly replaced by U.S. public policy which European companies are forced to carry out within the E.C., if they are not to lose export privileges in the U.S. or to face other sanctions. This is an unacceptable interference in the affairs of the European Community.

11. Furthermore, it is reprehensible that present U.S. Regulations encourage non-U.S. companies to submit "voluntarily" to this kind of mobilization for U.S. purposes. . . .

III.   THE AMENDMENTS UNDER U.S. LAW

A.   U.S. REACTIONS TO MEASURES SIMILAR TO THE JUNE 22 AMENDMENTS

15. If a foreign country were to take measures like the June 22 Amendments, it is doubtful whether they would be in conformity with U.S. law and they would therefore probably not be recognized and enforced by U.S. courts.

The kind of mobilization of E.C. companies for U.S. purposes to which the Community objects was subject to strong American reactions and legislative counter-measures, when U.S. companies were similarly mobilized for the foreign policy purposes of other states.

The anti-foreign-boycott provisions of Section 8 of the Export Administration Act are testimony to that. In the same way as the U.S. could not accept that its companies were turned into instruments of the foreign policy of other nations, the E.C. cannot accept that its companies must follow another trade policy than its own within its own territorial jurisdiction.

It is noteworthy that the anti-boycott provisions of the Export Administration Act can be invoked in response to a boycott that takes a less direct form than the June 22 Amendments, namely a boycott which merely tries to dissuade persons from dealing with a third country by refusing to trade with such persons. An export restriction patterned on the June 22 Amendments, in contrast, would directly prohibit a person from dealing with a particular country under the threat of government-imposed penalties. Therefore, the latest Amendments would appear to be even more far-reaching than a boycott which might give rise to the application of the anti-boycott provisions. . . .

This being the reaction of the U.S. legislator and judiciary to foreign measures comparable to its own measures of June 22, the U.S. Government should not have inflicted these measures on the E.C. companies concerned in the virtual knowledge that these measures would be regarded as unlawful and ineffective by public authorities in the E.C.

B.   CONFLICTS OF JURISDICTION AND ACCOMMODATION OF INTEREST

17. In cases where the conflicting exercise of jurisdiction to prescribe leads to conflicts of enforcement jurisdiction between states, each state, according to para. 40 of the Restatement (2nd) Foreign Relations Law of the U.S., is required by international law to consider, in good faith, moderating the exercise of its enforcement jurisdiction. In this connection the following factors should be considered:

(a)   vital national interests of each of the states;
(b)   the extent and the nature of the hardship that inconsistent enforcement actions would impose upon the person;
(c)   the extent to which the required conduct is to take place in the territory of the other state;
(d)   the nationality of the other person. . . .

18. Over the past years various U.S. Courts of Appeal have pronounced themselves in favour of this "balancing of interests" approach.

In the case of the Timberlane Co. v. Bank of America, Judge Choy suggested that comity demanded an evaluation and balancing of relevant factors, and continued: "The elements to be weighed include the degree of conflict with foreign law or policy, the nationality or allegiance of the parties, and the locations or principal places of businesses or corporations, the extent to which enforcement by either state can be expected to achieve compliance, the relative significance of effects on the United States as compared with those elsewhere, the extent to which there is explicit purpose to harm or affect American commerce, the foreseeability of such effect, and the relative importance to the violations charged of conduct within the United States as compared with conduct abroad."

A similar approach was followed in *Mannington Mills* and is set out in paragraph 40 of the Second Restatement.

19. Although this "balancing of interest" approach applies in the first place to courts, there are good reasons why the U.S. Government should exercise such restraint already at the rule-making stage. . . .

23. Whatever approach is adopted by the U.S. Government in balancing U.S. interests against the interests of the European Community, the following considerations have been neglected.

—The interest of the European Community in regulating the foreign trade of the nationals of the Member States in the territory to which the Community Treaties apply is paramount over any foreign policy purposes that a third country may have.

—The conduct required by the Amendments is to take place largely in territory to which the E.C. Treaties apply and not in U.S. territory.

—The nationality and other ties of many persons whose conduct is purportedly regulated by the June 22 Amendments link them primarily to E.C. Member States and not to the U.S.

—There are justified expectations on the part of E.C. companies which are seriously hurt by the U.S. measures.

C. CRITERIA UNDER SECTION 6(B) OF THE EXPORT ADMINISTRATION ACT

24. It can hardly be claimed that the U.S. measures satisfy the criteria laid down in the Export Administration Act, and therefore it is doubtful whether the restrictions are properly applied in terms of U.S. law. Criterion 1 refers to the probability that the controls will achieve the intended foreign policy purposes. Soviet Authorities have clearly stated their intention to deliver gas to Western Europe as scheduled, and there is little reason to doubt their ability to do so, even without American or European equipment since the existing Soviet pipeline system already has sufficient spare capacity, at least to cover the requirements of the early phases of the programme of deliveries. If the pipeline is built with Soviet technology and the gas flows on time, these U.S. export controls are at best ineffectual, and may well be self-defeating, as instruments of foreign policy.

25. Criterion 3 requires that the reaction of other countries to the imposition or expansion of such export controls be taken into account. In view of the

extra-territorial application, and retroactive effect of the U.S. measures, the European Community cannot fail to denounce the measure as unlawful under international law; and in view of their damaging economic and political consequences, has already protested in the strongest terms.

26. Criterion 4 requires consideration of the effects of the proposed controls on the export performance of the United States. Here again, confirmation of the U.S. measures despite criterion 4 would involve complete disregard for damaging effects not only immediately, but also in the longer term, owing to the grave doubts that are bound to arise in the future about the U.S. as a reliable supplier of equipment under contract, or as a reliable partner in technology-licensing arrangements. This danger has already been pointed out to the President of the United States by the U.S. Chamber of Commerce.

D.   COMPENSATION FOR DAMAGE RESULTING FROM U.S. MEASURES

27. The U.S. measures inasmuch as they refer to exports from countries outside the U.S. are all the more objectionable, as they affect contracts that were free from restrictions imposed by the U.S. Authorities at the time of their conclusion.

The main contractors of the Siberian pipeline, a number of major sub-contractors and suppliers as well as other exporters, will suffer substantial economic and financial losses for which no compensation is provided. For many sub-contractors who for the most part have nothing to do with American goods or technology for gas transport, the practical consequences of the Amendments will be particularly severe and may actually force them out of business. Lay-offs of a considerable number of workers will result in any case from the Amendments.

28. The idea that compensation is due in case private property or existing contracts are seriously affected by government action is also familiar in the U.S. legal system. If U.S. Government takes private property by eminent domain it has to compensate the owner. The Supreme Court has indicated many times that if regulatory legislation virtually deprives a person of the complete use and enjoyment of his property the law of eminent domain applies.

Justice Brandeis has written: "It is true that the police power embraces regulations designed to promote public convenience or the general welfare. . . . But when particular individuals are singled out to bear the cost of advancing the public convenience, that imposition must bear some reasonable relation to the evils to be eradicated or the advantages to be secured."[3] It is self-evident that for European contractors and sub-contractors within the E.C. the cost imposed upon them by the Amendments does not bear a reasonable relation to the advantage of furthering American export policy.

---

[3]Nashville C. and St. L. Ry. v. Walters, 294 U.S. 405, 429 (1935).

RAOUL MASSARDY ET AUTRES, SOC. FRUEHAUF-FRANCE v. ME. SOLVET ET SOC. ANON. DES AUTOMOBILES BERLIET

Cour d'appel de Paris (14e Ch.), (85) II *Gazette du Palais* 86 (1965)

THE COURT.

Ruling on the timely appeal by William Grâce, Alex Ananyos, the Fruehauf Corporation, S.A., Richard Cronan, and R.-D. Rowan against a decision rendered on 16 February 1965 by the president of the Tribunal de Commerce of Corbeil-Essones, and together with appellant's submissions of March 5 and April 2, those of appellees Raoul Massardy, Georges Massardy, and Paul Godbille of April 1, of intervenor Automobiles Berliet, S.A., on April 1, and finally of Solvet, receiver and also an intervenor, of April 3, 1965;

Considering that Fruehauf-France, S.A. was founded in 1946 with its headquarters (*siege*) at Ris-Orangis (Seine-et-Oise) with the object of building trailers, semi-trailers, and merchandise under the Fruehauf mark in France for export;

Considering that its social capital, currently fixed at 7,500,000 Francs, is divided into 150,000 shares of which ⅔ are held by a group of shareholders residing in the United States and ⅓ by French shareholders;

Considering that its Board (*Conseil d'administration*) was, until recently, composed similarly, being under the presidency of Raoul Massardy, the Director General, and including on one hand the five appellants, with the Fruehauf Corporation (whose seige is in Detroit and not at Ris-Orangis as was indicated by error in the appeal papers) represented by its permanent delegate Richard Cronan, and on the other hand the three French appellees;

Considering that on December 24, 1964, Automobiles Berliet placed with Fruehauf-France a 1,785,310 Franc order for sixty Fruehauf 25- and 40-ton semitrailers and sixty Pacific tractors, which were to be delivered beginning February 15, 1965 and were destined for export to the People's Republic of China;

Considering that on January 12, 1965, in New York, Alex Aranyos, President of Fruehauf International, which appears to coordinate the relations of the various Fruehauf corporations, told Francois Godbille, the Assistant Director General of Fruehauf-France, that United States authorities had started an investigation of this sale which was against its regulations, and added that, "we are under order to suspend performance of this contract unless we have a license from the Department of the Treasury, which, it has told us, would not be in accord with current policy;"

Considering that Francois Godbille argued that Fruehauf-France's future would be compromised by the cancellation of such an important order that involved merchandise designed and manufactured in France, whose prefinancing had been arranged by a specialized French credit source, and that could be equally well furnished by competing enterprises;

But considering that on January 28, 1965, Francois Godbille received a telegram containing the following language: "We hereby formally order you to cancel the contract and to reduce the possible losses to the minimum;"

Considering that on February 11, 1965, Raoul Massardy asked Paul Berliet if it would be possible to agree to rescind the contract in light of the moral and material harm "to our American friends" that would arise from its performance; and that the next day Berliet replied that he did not see any way to accept such a recission and would hold Fruehauf-France fully responsible for any direct or indirect damages that might be caused by its default;

Considering that on February 13, 1965, Raoul Massardy submitted a letter of resignation as President-Director General, because of these difficulties which set him in opposition to the majority of the Board and because of the gravity of the situation for Fruehauf-France, and that the three French directors applied to the President of the Tribunal de Commerce of Corbeil, who authorized them to summon the five American directors before him for the purpose of appointing a receiver (*mandataire de justice*) to direct the corporation for a set period, to complete orders in progress, and to call a meeting of the shareholders at an appropriate time;

Considering that this summons was delivered to the appellants on February 15, 1965, who, the same day, held a Board meeting in order to name a director, a President-Director General, and an Assistant Director General;

Considering that on February 16, 1965, the President of the Tribunal de Commerce, noting essentially that Fruehauf-France had no legal organs of management and that failure to carry out its commitments would put its existence in peril, appointed Solvet as receiver (*administrateur provisoire*), for a period of three months or until otherwise ordered, with the responsibility to manage the assets and the liabilities of said corporation and in particular to carry out orders in progress;

Considering further that on February 18, 1965, the Board, meeting without appellees, took note of Raoul Massardy's resignation, named Pierre Chérét as director and President-Director General, and continued Francois Godbille in his position as Assistant Director General; and that on March 4, 1965, the appellees summoned appellants before the Tribunal de Commerce of Corbeil to have these actions voided;

Considering that appellant American directors argued to the court that the judge lacked jurisdiction in the absence of emergency and that he could not, without prejudice to the parent interfere in the management of a corporation to impose the views of the minority shareholders on the majority;

Considering that appellees who support the confirmation of the order in question have summoned as intervenors Automobiles Berliet S.A., who left the issue to justice while asking to protect its position in the event that the balance of the order were not delivered on time in accordance with the contract, and Solvet, who asked the court to decide as it chose on the appeal on the merits but to supply a certificate of its decision;

Considering that, in principle, there is no emergency power to substitute, even temporarily, a receiver for the decision-making organs of a corporation, that this rule can be overridden only in exceptional circumstances when, for example, the normal functioning of the corporation can no longer be assured, it is threatened by ruin, or its management is manifestly hindered by grave dissension among those involved, and that the issue of whether there is enough urgency to confer jurisdiction can thus not be examined without considering the cogency of the relief sought;

Considering that in the case at hand, the judge erred in relying upon the absence of management of Fruehauf-France, for in fact the corporation continued to have a full, regularly named Board, capable of replacing the resigning President-Director General, who was in fact replaced on February 18, 1965, only five days after his resignation, regardless of the criticisms that appellees today make of this appointment in court;

But considering that the evidence introduced during the discussion and not seriously contravened reveals not only the evident importance to Fruehauf-France of performing this contract with Societe Berliet, its principal customer who obtains about 40% of its exports from it, but above all the catastrophic consequences which would have occurred at the promised delivery time, and would still follow today from the cancellation of the contract, because the buyer would apparently be able to recover full reparation from its supplier for its commercial losses, estimated at more than 5,000,000 Francs following upon the rupture of its negotiations with China;

Considering that these consequences, whose cost neither Fruehauf Corporation nor Fruehauf-International have offered to cover, would be of such a character as definitively to ruin Fruehauf-France's financial equilibrium and moral credit and cause its disappearance and the layoff of more than 600 workers; that these circumstances establish the urgency and the legal basis for the protective measures anticipated, considering that in order to name a receiver, the judge acting in an emergency must consider social interests in preference to personal interests of particular partners, even if they are in the majority, and further, that it is in no way clear that this appointment is contrary to the real interests of the appellants;

Considering always that the general instructions given to the receiver should not impose on him actions where he alone is in a position to evaluate the corporation's viewpoint in an individual case;

Considering that in the absence of new issues, the court has no power to prolong Solvet's authority beyond the time set by the lower court judge nor to anticipate calling a shareholders' meeting;

For these reasons,—holds the appeal and the interventions receivable;— rejects the appeal and sustains the interventions;—gives the intervenor the certificates requested;—confirms the order of February 16, 1965 in so far as it names Solvet a receiver of Fruehauf-France for a period of three months with the duty of managing the corporation's assets and liabilities;—directs Grâce, Aranyos, Fruehauf-Corporation, Cronan, and Rowen, to pay the expenses of the hearing, the appeal and the interventions, with the proper amounts awarded to Bonnet, Garnier, and Naret, as lawyers, upon their legal application.

Excerpts from two paragraphs of the Avocat-General's (Nepveu) statement deserve quotation:

> Here, certainly, American capital holds the majority position. In pure capitalist doctrine, it is the master of the situation and its decisions are orders. However, we are in France in a period of fundamental change of the national economy. Banking credits or credit facilities exist as a result of the intellectual potential of the transaction; French banks currently play a primordial role in this credit. Local personnel, of whom there are many at Fruehauf-France, contribute also to the importance of this transaction, whose difficulties risk creating a certain perturbation in a key industry of the national economy. All these are also social interests that must be protected.
>
> What justifies your intervention? It is the defense and protection of the organism named Fruehauf-France, which operates in France, where it plays an important productive role with these 650 employees threatened with unemployment, with the support of important French banks, notably of the Banque de France. . . .

PRESIDENT RONALD REAGAN, EAST-WEST TRADE RELATIONS AND THE SOVIET PIPELINE SANCTIONS[3]

83 Dept. State Bull. 28 (1983)

Since taking office, I have emphasized to our allies the importance of our economic as well as our political relationship with the Soviet Union. In July of 1981 at the economic summit meeting in Ottawa, Canada, I expressed to the heads of state of the other major Western countries and Japan my belief that we could not continue conducting business as we had. I suggested that we forge a new set of rules for economic relations with the Soviet Union which would put our security concerns foremost. I wasn't successful at that time in getting agreement on a common policy.

Then, in December of 1981, the Polish Government, at Soviet instigation, imposed martial law on the Polish people and outlawed the Solidarity union. This action showed graphically that our hopes for moderation in Soviet behavior were not likely to be fulfilled.

In response to that action, I imposed an embargo on selected oil and gas equipment to demonstrate our strong opposition to such actions and to penalize this sector of the Soviet economy which relies heavily on high technology, much of it from the United States. In June of this year I extended our embargo

---

[3] President Reagan's radio address to the nation on November 13, 1982.

to include not only U.S. companies and their products but subsidiaries of U.S. companies abroad and on foreign licensees of U.S. companies.

It's no secret that our allies don't agree with this action. We stepped up our consultations with them in an effort to forge an enduring, realistic, and security-minded economic policy toward the Soviet Union. These consultations have gone on over a period of months.

I'm please today to announce that the industrialized democracies have this morning reached substantial agreement on a plan of action. The understanding we've reached demonstrates that the Western alliance is fundamentally united and intends to give consideration to strategic issues when making decisions on trade with the U.S.S.R.

As a result, we have agreed not to engage in trade arrangements which contribute to the military or strategic advantage of the U.S.S.R. or serve to aid preferentially the heavily militarized Soviet economy. In putting these principles into practice, we will give priority attention to trade in high technology products, including those used in oil and gas production. We will also undertake an urgent study of Western energy alternatives, as well as the question of dependence on energy imports from the Soviet Union.

In addition, we've agreed on the following immediate actions.

First, each partner has affirmed that no new contracts for the purchase of Soviet natural gas will be signed or approved during the course of our study of alternative Western sources of energy.

Second, we and our partners will strengthen controls on the transfer of strategic items to the Soviet Union.

Third, we will establish without delay procedures for monitoring financial relations with the Soviet Union and will work to harmonize our export credit policies.

The understanding we and our partners have reached and the actions we are taking reflect our mutual determination to overcome differences and strengthen our cohesion. I believe this new agreement is a victory for all the allies. It puts in place a much needed policy in the economic area to complement our policies in the security area.

As I mentioned a moment ago, the United States imposed sanctions against the Soviet Union in order to demonstrate that their policies of oppression would entail substantial costs. Now that we've achieved an agreement with our allies which provides for stronger and more effective measures, there is no further need for these sanctions, and I am lifting them today. . . .

QUESTIONS

1. Legally, how does the position of the United States in the antipipeline embargo differ from that in its antiboycott legislation?

2. In light of *Fruehauf,* how would you advise a European subsidiary of a U.S. firm caught in the middle in the pipeline situation?

3. How well reasoned do you find the *Fruehauf* analysis?

4. The United States and Europe reached a negotiated settlement in the pipeline case. What approaches would you suggest for avoiding similar problems in the future?

5. Would you support revision of the Export Administration Act so as to ban the U.S. government from actions that affect contracts already in force? Limitations on such actions were included in the Export Administration Act renewal that passed Congress in mid-1985 (§108(*l*), Pub. L. No. 99-64, (1985)).

6. Is the Vredeling proposal consistent with the positions expressed in the European Communities' pipeline memorandum?

Bibliographical Note

For additional information, *see* Note, Extraterritorial Application of the Export Administration Act of 1979 Under International and American Law, 81 Mich. L. Rev. 1308 (1983).

3.   *Franchise and Vertical Antitrust Law*

The economics of vertical relationships and integration is often very difficult to analyze in antitrust terms. The analysis generally turns on foreclosure:—if a company acquires a major supplier, for example, it may deprive other firms of the opportunity to compete for sales to it. Whether competition will be decreased depends, however, on whether the firm has competitive power and whether it is in any way able to increase that power by the acquisition (a concept many economists would deny). Moreover, there may be several reasonably competitive patterns—camera brands, for example, competing against one another, with essentially all brands sold in the same stores, while autos compete with just a few brands per store and the quality of the store makes up part of the product that is sold.

There are only a few international antitrust cases, however, that illuminate the comparative advantage of the multinational corporation—for example, in which a U.S. firm might argue that its competitor's arrangement with a foreign licensee or foreign supplier gives the competitor an advantage that violates the antitrust laws. Presumably, there would be no serious argument unless the firm involved had a near monopoly in one of the markets, perhaps attempting to use control over a foreign source of supply to gain control over the U.S. market. For one of the few examples, *see* Calnetics v. Volkswagen of America, 532 F.2d 674 (9th Cir.), *cert. denied,* 429 U.S. 940 (1976).

The franchise area provides a different kind of insight into vertical relationships. Here, the typical conflict is between two entities in the vertical distribution chain, and the risk is that the larger may take advantage of the smaller. As a result, most nations give franchise operators and distributors special protection against their suppliers. The pattern varies from nation to nation; in many civil law nations it is nearly impossible to terminate an agency or distribution relationship without incurring substantial liabilities. United States laws are somewhat more restrained, as exemplified by the Auto Dealers' Day in Court Act (15 U.S.C. §1222):

> An automobile dealer may bring suit against any automobile manufacturer engaged in commerce . . . and shall recover the damages by him sustained . . . by reason of the failure of said automobile manufacturer . . . to act in good faith in performing or complying with any of the terms or provisions of the franchise, or in terminating, canceling, or not renewing the franchise with said dealer: *Provided,* that in any such suit the manufacturer shall not be barred from asserting in defense of any such action the failure of the dealer to act in good faith.

Because they must work together on a continuing basis, dealers and manufacturers rarely sue each other except after termination of the arrangement. Conflicts are worked out—under the possibility that the franchise will not be renewed. Usually there is a lawsuit only if that threat is exercised, and the law suit will include claims under statutes like those just quoted as well as antitrust claims. The dealer may argue, for example, that it was being forced out so the manufacturer could take over the franchise or that the manufacturer was using its power over the dealer to require it to buy associated products at unfair prices. And reflecting the desire to work out problems on a less adversarial basis—but also effectively transferring jurisdiction to resolve disputes—franchise agreements often include arbitration clauses.

QUESTIONS

1. Do you think that arbitration is better than use of the courts in an international franchise context? What are the pros and cons? Which is likely to be more responsive to differences in national views of franchise and antitrust law? For discussion *see* Mitsubishi Motors Corp. v. The Soler Chrysler-Plymouth Inc., 105 S. Ct. 3346 (1985).

2. Your client is a small foreign manufacturer that has been supplying widgets to a national U.S. retailer. The retailer acquires your client's competitor, and cuts your client out. What would you do? How would your answer depend on whether or not there was an arbitration clause?

3. Is there any argument that a nation would violate the GATT if it imposed its franchise rules in a way that severely complicated life for foreign sellers?

4. How might you attempt to coordinate regulation in the bankruptcy area,

where courts in one or several nations seek to distribute assets held in one or several nations to creditors in one or several nations according to priority rules that may differ from nation to nation? *See* Bankruptcy Reform Act of 1978, §304; Israel-British Bank (London) v. FDIC, 536 F.2d 509 (2d Cir. 1976), *cert. denied sub nom.* Bank of the Commonwealth v. Israel-British Bank (London), 429 U.S. 978 (1976); Banque de Financement v. First National Bank of Boston, 568 F.2d 911 (2d Cir. 1977).

5. In resolving these international jurisdictional issues, when is the act of state approach best? The international law jurisdictional test approach? The *Timberlane* approach?

6. How do you think the U.S. Supreme Court would decide a *Fruehauf*-type case of a foreign-owned firm in the United States faced with a foreign directive to breach a contract?

D.   POSSIBLE INTERNATIONAL RESOLUTIONS

Procedural and jurisdictional approaches can resolve some of these disputes. Sometimes, however, it is necessary to deal directly with substance, and there is a growing effort to achieve international codes of conduct to govern transnational corporate behavior. These are being pursued in quantity in a number of international forums, particularly the United Nations. The typical pattern has been for developing nations to seek a code much along the lines of Andean Pact Decision No. 24. The developed nations, particularly the United States, have resisted this direction. Sometimes they have emphasized the importance of foreign investment as a method of economic development; sometimes they have simply sought to weaken proposals for a code. The United States, under competitive pressure from the Foreign Corrupt Practices Act, has sought international agreement against corruption.

In spite of these tensions, there have been some agreements; the OECD Guidelines, reproduced in the Selected Documents Supplement, are among the most important. The Economist article that follows is intended to describe the political context of the Guidelines. As shown in the succeeding excerpt, they have also been the basis for new kinds of dispute settlement. Other examples include the 1977 International Labour Organization Tripartite Declaration of Principles Concerning Multinational Enterprises and Social Policy, and the 1980 UNCTAD Set of Multilaterally Agreed Equitable Principles and Rules for the Control of Restrictive Business Practices, reproduced in the Selected Documents Supplement, and the pending U.N. Code of Conduct for Transnational Corporations (UN Doc. E/C. 10/1983/c/2 (1983), *reprinted in* 22 I.L.M. 177 (1983), and *see also* Draft Code of Conduct on Transnational Corporations, 23 I.L.M. 616 (1984).

MULTINATIONAL MUMMERY

The Economist, p.61, June 26, 1976

THE NEW OECD CODE OF CONDUCT FOR MULTINATIONAL COMPANIES IS UNNECESSARILY WEAK

With trumpet and drums, the rich countries grouped in the Organisation for Economic Co-operation and Development this week brought out their code of conduct for multinational companies. It is the outcome of some twenty years' thinking, on and off—mainly off—but all it deserved was a tin whistle.

The drafts of the code that were circulating last winter were mild enough. They said firmly that the code was to be a voluntary one. This is sensible. Many third world countries would like the code that the United Nations plans to draw up (by early 1978, it hopes) to be legally enforceable. But there is no prospect the rich countries will agree—and without their agreement, any code will merely spell out, probably in extreme terms, things that any country is free individually to pass into law tomorrow morning if it wishes. The OECD drafts, again unlike those that the tougher members of the third world are hoping for, were also sensible in not seeking to lay down such fierce standards that the multinational goose would simply decide to lay its eggs at home. But these early OECD drafts nonetheless set a respectable standard of conduct for the multinationals; one that good companies would meet fairly easily, but that could well worry some not so good.

In contrast the code that ministers approved at the OECD meeting in Paris this week had been systematically bowdlerised to make observance easier. The trade unions of the OECD countries were already unhappy at the scant attention paid to their views in the early drafts; the best thing they could find to say for the final version (and the Nordic unions were unhappy even to say this) was that it was a first step to something tougher.

The changes of substance were not all significant. The spirit they were made in is. Three examples of that spirit, and one could cite a great many more:

• Even the implication that a concentration of economic power could (not must, just perhaps sometimes could), in itself, be too great has been excised.

• Multinationals were asked, in the earlier drafts, to observe labour-relations standards at least as favourable as those of "good local" employers—as most, in fact, do. This has become "comparable" employers: i.e., if your competitors are bastards go ahead and be one too?

• The multinationals are still asked to supply more information than most do today. But this request has been toned down with special care.

The one section that has been notably strengthened is the one on bribery— a subject of special concern to the United States. Indeed Mr. Kissinger in Paris repeated an earlier proposal that the United Nations should promptly set to work on a binding agreement on the issue—with some other Kissinger propos-

als, a useful smokescreen for the fact that the chief footdragger over the whole
OECD code has been the American government (with some Trojan-horse help
recently from the AFL-CIO, which in March rejoined the OECD's trade-
union advisory committee). But don't blame America alone: under its . . .
wing, the British and West German governments, ever so keen on corporate
responsibility and disclosure at home, also found it convenient to appease their
own multinationals, as, more naturally, did the Japanese. But for the Nordic
governments, with the voice of Sweden and backing from the Dutch, the
code's last plastic teeth would have been drawn.

   A good thing too, many respectable multinationals would say. Many of
their good friends, including this newspaper, must disagree. If you don't want
silly codes, miles in advance of the real world, then don't provide ammunition
for those who do by taking the (nonmandatory) teeth out of sensible codes
which are just that little bit ahead of some people's practice that sensible codes
ought to be.

SMITH, BADGER REVISITED: IMPLICATIONS FOR THE IMPLEMENTATION OF THE TRANSFER OF TECHNOLOGY CODE

1 Intl. Tax & Bus. Law. 117, 125-130 (1983)

II.   THE BADGER CASE

The Badger case[40] has been called an "historic precedent" in that it was the
first time the [OECD] Guidelines were successfully invoked and their implementation machinery effectively utilized against an MNE [Multinational En-
terprise] operating in an OECD member country. The case arose in January,
1977, when Badger, Inc., an American MNE headquartered in Cambridge,
Massachusetts and owned by Raytheon, Inc., ordered the closure of its Belgian
subsidiary, Badger Belgium N.V. The subsidiary did not supply adequate
notice of the closing to its employees, and its assets were insufficient to satisfy
the termination payments to which the employees were entitled under Belgian
law. The employees could have drawn upon a fund financed by employer's
contributions to satisfy a substantial part of their claims. However, their belief
that the U.S. parent had manipulated Badger's income to induce its bankruptcy persuaded them to forego payment from the fund and to insist as a
matter of principle that Badger International make good the shortfall. The
employees felt that to do otherwise would be to allow a financially robust
MNE to rely on the legal technicality of separate incorporation to shift its
social and moral obligations to the Belgian community. When Badger Inter-

---

[40] *See generally* R. Blanpain, The Badger Case and the OECD Guidelines for Multinational
Enterprises at 51-132 (1977).

national refused to supplement its subsidiary's assets in order to accommodate the staff termination indemnities, the employee's union contacted TUAC [Trade Union Advisory Committee—a labor group associated with the OECD] with a view to invoking the Guidelines.

The question raised by the Badger case was whether a parent corporation was obliged by virtue of the Guidelines to pay that part of the severance indemnities which its wholly owned and controlled subsidiary could not meet and which it was not required to pay under the law of either the host or home countries. Badger International contended that the obligation under the Guidelines to mitigate the adverse effects caused by the closure of an enterprise applied only to the local entity and not to the multinational as a unit. This position brought directly into question the scope of the Guidelines and the proper interpretation of paragraph 8 of their Introduction. . . .

TUAC played an active role in attempting to settle the Badger case outside the OECD framework, and when that failed, in guiding the case through the OECD consultation procedures to a favorable outcome. Despite this shift in tactics, TUAC's objective to effect a negotiated settlement amid mounting pressure on Badger remained constant. Outside the OECD, TUAC's attempt to resolve the dispute involved coordinated activities at the national level among representatives of labor, management, and the Belgian Government, at the bilateral level between the Belgian and U.S. Governments, and at the international level through the involvement of foreign trade unions, the international trade union movement, and Badger International's management. Although efforts at these levels failed to produce a settlement, they nonetheless had a cumulative effect that facilitated resolution of the dispute once resort to the OECD became unavoidable.

At the bilateral level, TUAC appealed directly to the Belgian and U.S. Governments. The Belgian Government's involvement in the case was the key to the employee's success, and will be examined below. As part of its approach to the U.S. Government, TUAC asked the Belgian Prime Minister to try to persuade the U.S. Government to cooperate. TUAC calculated that the Badger case's potential repercussions would be perceived in Washington as jeopardizing American interests in maintaining a liberal investment climate in Europe, and therefore as warranting action. Although the U.S. Government was responsible for encouraging American MNEs to comply with the Guidelines, its earlier insistence on the voluntary nature of the Guidelines foreclosed the possibility of its active intervention. Thus, while the State Department went so far as to suggest that Badger reconsider its position in the light of the Guidelines, in the end the Government "could hardly do more than play an informative role." The U.S. Government had apparently determined that America's broader interest in preserving a tranquil investment environment in Europe was best served by maintaining a low profile in the dispute.

A second course of action attempted to force Badger to settle by focusing trade union pressure on the company's affiliates operating in Europe. TUAC's ties to its constituent unions and to the International Trade union movement ensured the necessary trade union backing outside Belgium. TUAC urged its member unions in Britain and Denmark, where Badger affiliates resided, to intervene on behalf of their fellow workers in Belgium. The Dutch unions, for instance, were asked to adopt the position that Badger, The Hague was implicated in Badger's violation of the Guidelines due to the dependency of the Antwerp affiliate on The Hague office. It followed that Badger, The Hague shared responsibility with the American parent to pay the indemnity owed the dismissed Belgian employees. TUAC also coordinated with the World Confederation of Labor whose representative took the case to the American Embassy in Brussels while its Federation of Non-Manual Workers informed Badger headquarters of the Federation's view on the social obligations of Badger International in regard to the severance pay. In the end, trade union pressure was sufficient to bring about a meeting with Badger's management on February 21, 1977, but it was not enough to compel the multinational to change its position.

Having made little headway in settling the dispute through these conventional means, the unions decided to resort to the OECD consultation procedures. The Secretary General of TUAC introduced the Badger case to CIME [Committee on International Investment and Multinational Enterprise—a management group associated with the OECD] in a note of March 24, 1977 that reviewed the facts and the efforts that had been made to effect a solution. The Secretary General emphasized the significance of Badger as a test case for the credibility and future effectiveness of the Guidelines. He noted that "[a]s a result of developments in the Badger case, the Belgian trade unions and political authorities, as well as the employers' organizations and foreign enterprises in Belgium, are confronted with a situation that directly challenges the authority of the OECD and its Member Governments." He warned that the absence of tangible results would be seen by Belgian public opinion "as an attack on the legislation and current practice regarding employment and labor relations in Belgium" and as a loophole in the OECD Guidelines and consultation procedures.

The OECD consultation mechanism was officially triggered by the Belgian Ambassador to the OECD in his request on March 18 for an exchange of views concerning the interpretation of the sections of the Guidelines relevant to the Badger case. At the ensuing CIME meeting on March 31, 1977, the Belgian Government's view that the parent company was under a duty to assist the local entity in observing its obligations was amplified by Professor Dr. M. Eyskens, the Belgian Secretary of State for Regional Economic Development. His presence at the meeting underlined the importance attached to the proceedings by the Belgian government. Following Dr. Eyskens' presentation, the Committee held a discussion in which twelve countries participated. The Committee accepted the Belgian Government's version of the facts and used it as an illustration to facilitate examination and clarification of the Guidelines' text. In view of its mandate, CIME tried not to focus on the merits of the case or pass upon the conduct of the parties to the dispute. The Committee's conclusions were not immediately and formally released as an official opinion. Instead, their dissemination was left largely to the Belgian Government, which moved quickly to press its interpretation of events on the media. A month after the CIME consultation, the conclusions drawn from the debate by the Belgian Government were published in the OECD Observer, the Organization's monthly magazine. It was not until the publication of the 1979 CIME review report to the OECD Council that the official views of the Committee regarding the Badger case were made known. By this time, the outcome of the meeting had already been profusely hailed by the Belgian news media "as a moral condemnation of the Badger company."

CIME's conclusions amounted to an endorsement of the Belgian Government's position, and can be reduced for present purposes to three propositions. First, "[t]o the extent that parent companies actually exercise control over the activities of their subsidiaries they have a responsibility for the observance of the Guidelines by those subsidiaries." Second, "multinational and domestic enterprises are subject to the same expectations in respect of their conduct wherever the Guidelines are relevant for both." Third, the question of the responsibility of parent companies for certain financial obligations of their subsidiaries "as a matter of good management practice . . . consistent with observance of the Guidelines, could arise in special circumstances," particularly in those "relating to important changes in the operations of a firm and the cooperation as to the mitigation of resulting adverse effects." In other words, the Guidelines may place moral obligations on a parent company that exceed what is strictly required by law. Based on the outcome of the CIME consultation, meetings among representatives of the Belgian Government, Badger's international management, and the unions took place under the chairmanship of Secretary of State Eyskens. The meetings ended in a negotiated settlement favorable to the former Badger employees. . . .

QUESTIONS

1. Does the OECD Code face any of the more difficult issues posed by the Vredeling proposal?

2. Was Canada's FIRA consistent with it? What about the U.S. position in the Siberian pipeline dispute?

3. Has CIME effectively become an international court? How relevant were the Code's principles to the resolution of the Badger controversy? The fundamental appeal of the workers' position? The availability of the CIME?

4. How important is the difference between "binding" and "voluntary" guidelines?

5. Note that the OECD and U.N. contexts are not the only places in which components of an effective code of conduct might be negotiated. What approaches and forums might you consider for the following:

    a.   Coordination issues that lead to awkward conflicts but are fundamentally neutral as between the firm and governments—examples include harmonization of accounting principles;

    b.   Issues in which a government can take advantage of and possibly hurt other nations—e.g., child labor laws, "pollution havens," or perhaps bank secrecy havens;

    c.   Issues in which the regulator's personal interest may be opposed to his or her nation's public interest—e.g., anticorruption rules;

    d.   Issues in which global optimization and the short-term interests of specific nations may be really in conflict—e.g., industrial policy, efforts to prevent runaway shops;

    e.   Issues of the political role of multinationals, such as the possible adverse effects on democracy that are frequently alleged by critics.

6. In a joint venture, local and foreign entities join in the firm's legal control and sometimes its practical control. When is this approach likely to be helpful in avoiding or resolving disputes?

7. In what ways does the effective statelessness of some MNs make dispute settlement easier or harder?

8. Now, what would be the possibility and the wisdom of requiring those subsidiaries of U.S. firms operating in South Africa to live up to specified labor standards? In what ways is this approach better or worse than prohibiting the firms from operating in South Africa?

Bibliographical Note

For additional information, *see* Wallace, International Codes and Guidelines for Multinational Enterprises: Update and Selected Issues, 17 Intl. Law. 435 (1983); Coombe, Multinational Codes of Conduct and Corporate Accountability: New Opportunities for Corporate Counsel, 36 Bus. Law. 11 (1980); Sanders, The Implementation of International Codes of Conduct for Multinational Enterprises, 28 Neth. Intl. L. Rev. 318 (1981); Symposium: Codes of Conduct for Transnational Corporations, 30 Am. U. L. Rev. 903 (1981); R. Blanpain, The OECD Guidelines for Multinational Enterprises and Labour Relations 1976-1979 (1979) and The Badger Case and the OECD Guidelines for Multinational Enterprises (1977); Symposium, Multinational Corporations, 11 Stan. J. Intl. Stud. (1976); Note, The United Nations Code of Conduct for Transnational Corporations: Establishing a New Modus Vivendi? 1 B.U. Intl. L.J. 88 (1982).

Chapter XVIII

Investment Disputes

The relationship between a foreign-based corporation and a host nation is almost designed to encourage disputes. At the beginning of the relationship, the bargaining power usually lies almost entirely with the corporation. In a few cases the corporation has little choice but to invest, for example, when it is interested in a host-nation market that is protected by high tariffs or by domestic content provisions. But in general and particularly if the corporation is planning to extract or manufacture goods for export, it does not have to invest in a particular nation. It may even be in a position of choosing among different nations that compete against one another to offer the most favorable investment terms. Even without corruption or a subservient government, then, the initial terms of an investment contract are likely to favor the corporation.

Everything changes after the corporation has actually made its investment. It has now brought in assets—and the host government can at any time seize those assets to enforce a new decree or policy. Even with the best faith, disputes become likely—labor relations might not work out or a new government might want to change its tax policy in a way not envisioned at the time of the investment. And, looking back, the commitments made by the government to the firm at the time of investment may now look unduly favorable to the firm. This will almost certainly be the case (at least politically) in extractive industries. Once the oil has been found and the risk is past, the rate of return appears high; it is easy to forget that that rate of return must cover the cost of dry wells as well as of successful ones.

The result is almost always renegotiation. In this process, the host nation always has the practical alternative of expropriating the corporation, a possibility that greatly affects the relative bargaining positions of the two. It is no surprise that most long-term contracts, for example, the oil concessions in the Middle East, have been regularly modified in favor of the host nation. The initial contractual allocation of profits was very favorable to the firms; over time the contract was renegotiated so as to favor the host nation. This occurs even without revolutionary change in the host nation; if that nation changes in a revolutionary fashion—Mexico in 1917, Cuba in 1959, or Iran in 1979—reallocations are likely to be much more dramatic, and expropriation very common.

This chapter explores these interrelated questions of dispute settlement and expropriation. It does not seek to explore the closely related international law doctrines of act of state and sovereign immunity. This chapter seeks rather to examine the practical business issues and solutions that have evolved. It emphasizes the arbitration arrangements designed to restrain disputes short of expropriation, the insurance arrangements that a firm can use to protect itself from arbitration, and the emerging network of international treaties designed to assist the investment process and to avoid investment disputes.

A. DISPUTE SETTLEMENT PROCEDURES

The lawyer's obvious way to control disputes is to create dispute settlement procedures. But the problem arises at once of choosing among legal systems. Relying upon the host nation's legal system appears unfair to the investor, because that nation's government is so interested in the outcome. Even so, this system is the obvious basis of settlement and the one that would automatically be used in the developed world. But sometimes one cannot be confident of the courts. And the courts of almost any legal system would feel bound to follow new legislation—and host-nation law might be changed in a way that is extremely unfavorable to the firm. Although a firm might seek alternatively to contract for application of foreign law, this is often unacceptable to the nation. Moreover, some issues undoubtedly should be handled flexibly by local law.

In the face of these dilemmas, which go to both choice of law and choice of forum, the traditional solution, except in Latin America, has been to negotiate a procedure for settling disputes through arbitration. Note that this form of arbitration, typically between a private firm and a sovereign government, can raise great political difficulties. There is usually a somewhat ambiguous provision for choice of law, designed to leave the nation reasonable flexibility in changing the law, but also to protect the firm from seriously adverse legal changes. The arbitration agreement was once spelled out ad hoc in the initial investment agreement or concession; more recently, many firms and nations are adopting a new international procedure, the International Centre for the Settlement of Investment Disputes (ICSID).

Latin American nations, however, have generally resisted this approach, arguing that a foreign investor should be treated no differently from a domestic investor. Since the domestic investor has no access to special dispute settlement arrangements, neither should the foreign investor. Hence, all these arbitration agreements are rejected, and the investor is asked as well to accept a "Calvo clause," a provision under which it promises not to call in diplomatic pressure in the event of a dispute. As will be seen below, the Calvo clause has often failed to achieve its goal.

1. Arbitration Procedure

One of the most important recent arbitrations is the *Topco* case excerpted below. The arbitrations resulted from 1973 and 1974 nationalizations of oil concessions originally granted in 1955. The arbitration award was issued in 1977 by a French arbitrator over the opposition of the Libyan government, and was ultimately honored (with a compromise amount) by that government. *See* Von Mehren & Kourides, International Arbitrations between States and Foreign Private Parties: The Libyan Nationalization Cases, 75 A.J.I.L. 476 (1981).

TEXAS OVERSEAS PETROLEUM CO. AND CALIFORNIA ASIATIC OIL CO. v. THE GOVERNMENT OF THE LIBYAN ARAB REPUBLIC

17 I.L.M. 3 (1978)

Dupuy, Sole Arbitrator.

INTRODUCTION

On September 1, 1973 and February 11, 1974, the Libyan Arab Republic promulgated decrees purporting to nationalize all of the rights, interests and property of Texaco Overseas Petroleum Company and California Asiatic Oil Company (the "Companies") in Libya granted to them jointly under 14 Deeds of Concession. The Companies objected to the decrees and claimed that such action by the Libyan Government violated the terms and conditions of their Deeds of Concession.

Exercising their rights under their Deeds of Concession, the Companies requested arbitration and appointed an arbitrator. The Libyan Government refused to accept arbitration and did not appoint an arbitrator. Pursuant to the arbitration provision in their Deeds of Concession, the Companies requested the President of the International Court of Justice to appoint a sole arbitrator to hear and determine the disputes. The Libyan Government opposed such request and filed a memorandum with the President contending, *inter alia,* that the disputes were not subject to arbitration because the nationalizations were acts of sovereignty. This memorandum represented the only appearance by the Libyan Government in the arbitration proceedings.

After considering the Libyan Government's objections, the President of the International Court of Justice, on December 18, 1974, appointed René-Jean Dupuy, Secretary General of The Hague Academy of International Law and Professor of Law at the University of Nice, as the Sole Arbitrator. Professor Dupuy named Jean-Pierre Sortais, Professor of Law at the University of Nice, as the Registrar of the Arbitral Tribunal.

Resolving first the procedural aspects of the Arbitration, the Sole Arbitrator then determined that the initial stage of the Arbitration should be devoted to the question whether he had jurisdiction to hear and determine the disputes. He invited the parties to submit memorials in support of their positions and the Companies submitted their Memorial on the Jurisdiction of the Sole Arbitrator on June 16, 1975. It should be noted that although the Libyan Government did not submit a memorial during the jurisdictional or merits phase of the Arbitration, the Sole Arbitrator did specifically consider at each phase of the arbitral proceedings the arguments raised by the Libyan Government in its memorandum referred to above.

On November 27, 1975, the Sole Arbitrator delivered a Preliminary Award deciding that he had jurisdiction to hear and determine the disputes between the parties. The Preliminary Award was delivered in the French language and the following version . . . is the Companies' authorized English translation.

The Sole Arbitrator immediately proceeded to the next phase of the Arbitration to determine the merits of the disputes. The damages portion of the Arbitration was reserved for a later phase if necessary. The Sole Arbitrator again invited the parties to submit memorials in support of their positions and the Companies submitted their Memorial on the Merits on February 28, 1976. On June 15 and 16, 1976, the Arbitral Tribunal held oral hearings in Geneva at which time the Companies presented their case and responded to a series of questions asked by the Sole Arbitrator.

On January 19, 1977, the Sole Arbitrator delivered an Award on the Merits in favor of the Companies. The Sole Arbitrator held that (a) the Deeds of Concession are binding on the parties, (b) by adopting the measures of nationalization, the Libyan Government breached its obligations arising under the Deeds of Concession and (c) the Libyan Government is legally bound to perform the Deeds of Concession and to give them their full force and effect. The Award on the Merits was delivered in the French language and the following version . . . is the Companies' authorized English translation.

AWARD ON THE MERITS . . .

33. As Dr. F. A. Mann wrote (Studies in International Law (1973), at 223):

. . . [I]n regard to treaties between international persons, the nature and subject matter of which frequently are not substantially different from contracts between international and private persons, those legal rules have been, or are capable of being, and, in any event, must be developed. The law which is available for application to the one type of contractual arrangement can, without difficulty, be applied to the other group of contracts.

Commenting on this point in a recent article ("Contrats entre Etats et Personnes Privées Etrangères: The Theoretical Approach towards the Law Governing Contracts between States and Private Persons", Rev. Belge D.I. 562 (1975), at 564-565), Professor Mann writes further:

> Although normally the law of a given State will govern the State contract, precisely years ago another possible solution was suggested. It was said that a contract between a State and an alien private person could be "internationalized" in the sense of being subjected to the only other legal order known to us, namely public international law. This does not mean or was ever intended to mean that the State contract should be considered to be a treaty or should be governed by public international law in the same way as transactions between States. It simply means that by exercising their right to choose the applicable legal system the parties may make public international law the object of their choice. Certainly French law is designed normally to apply to French people or French transactions. Certainly public international law is designed to apply as a rule to States and the transactions between them. But nothing prevents a contract between the German State and a Dutch firm to be submitted to French law. Similarly, the fact that one party is not a State should not prevent the contract from being submitted to public international law. It would thus become subject to the mandatory rules of public international law. No mandatory law of any national system as such could touch it. If the parties desire this, why should we put any obstacle in their way? . . . Of course, we must guard against abuse. For this reason the teachings of private international law in general are to the effect that the choice of the legal system adopted by the parties must be reasonable, free from capriciousness, supported by rational, legitimate grounds. These conditions will be fulfilled if one party to the contract is a State or, one may add, a State corporation, though for reasons of social policy private persons contracting among themselves should be precluded from choosing a legal system other than a national one. The public international law thus applicable within a limited field would normally be found in the general principles accepted by civilized nations. . . .

35. This Tribunal therefore holds that it is established that the Deeds of Concession in dispute are within the domain of international law and that this law empowered the parties to choose the law which was to govern their contractual relations.

2. SECOND QUESTION

36. Under what circumstances was the choice of applicable law made and what consequences should be derived therefrom as to the internationalization of the Deeds of Concession in dispute?

(a) In its final version, the clause designating the applicable law or the choice of law established by Clause 28 of the Deeds of Concession reads as follows:

> This concession shall be governed by and interpreted in accordance with the principles of the law of Libya common to the principles of international law and, in the absence of such common principles, then by and in accordance with the general principles of law, including such of those principles as may have been applied by international tribunals. . . .

40. As the Tribunal has already observed . . . the internationalization of contracts entered into between States and foreign private persons can result in various ways which it is now time to examine. . . .

42. International arbitration case law confirms that the reference to the general principles of law is always regarded to be a sufficient criterion for the internationalization of a contract. One should remember, in this respect, the awards delivered in Lena Goldfields v. U.S.S.R. in 1930, Petroleum Development Ltd. v. Sovereign of Abu Dhabi in 1951, and International Marine Oil Company v. Sovereign of Qatar in 1953, and in Sapphire International Petroleum Ltd. v. N.I.O.C., all cases in which the arbitrators noted a reference to the general principles of law in order to reach their conclusions as to the internationalization of the contract.

It should be noted that the invocation of the general principles of law does not occur only when the municipal law of the contracting State is not suited to petroleum problems. Thus, for example, the Iranian law is without doubt particularly well suited for oil concessions but this does not prevent the contracts executed by Iran from referring very often to these general principles. The recourse to general principles is to be explained not only by the lack of adequate legislation in the State considered (which might have been the case, at one time, in certain oil Emirates). It is also justified by the need for the private contracting party to be protected against unilateral and abrupt modifications of the legislation in the contracting State: it plays, therefore, an important role in the contractual equilibrium intended by the parties.

43. This evolution toward the internationalization of contracts was foreseeable: indeed, in its judgments in the cases relating to the *Serbian and Brazilian Loans* and on the occasion of the examination of the criteria which could be adopted for the determination of the applicable law, the Permanent Court of International Justice laid down a rule of great flexibility:

> The Court which has before it a dispute involving the question as to the law which governs the contractual obligations at issue, can determine what this law is only by reference to the actual nature of these obligations and to the circumstances attendant upon their creation, though it may also take into account the expressed or presumed intention of the Parties. ([1929] P.C.I.J., Ser. A, No. 20, at 41.)

The three criteria laid down by the Permanent Court of International Justice and derived from the nature of the obligations, the circumstances of their creation and the will of the parties, converge, in the instant case, to reverse the presumption which was established, in another connection, by the judgments of 1929, a presumption to which reference was made already . . . and according to which a State cannot, from the outset, be presumed "to have made the substance of its debt and the validity of the obligations accepted by it in respect thereof, subject to any law other than its own".

44. Another process for the internationalization of a contract consists in inserting a clause providing that possible differences which may arise in respect of the interpretation and the performance of the contract shall be submitted to arbitration.

Such a clause has a twofold consequence:

—on the one hand, as this Tribunal has already noted . . . the institution of arbitration shall be that established by international law.

—on the other hand, as regards the law applicable to the merits of the dispute itself, the inclusion of an arbitration clause leads to a reference to the rules of international law.

Even if one considers that the choice of international arbitration proceedings cannot by itself lead to the exclusive application of international law, it is one of the elements which makes it possible to detect a certain internationalization of the contract. The *Sapphire International Petroleum Ltd.* award is quite explicit: "If no positive implication can be made from the arbitral clause, it is possible to find there a negative intention, namely to reject the exclusive application of Iranian law" (35 Intl. L.R. 136 (1963), at 172); this is what led the arbitrator in that case, in the absence of any explicit reference to the law applicable, not to apply automatically Iranian law, thus dismissing any presumption in its favor. It is therefore unquestionable that the reference to international arbitration is sufficient to internationalize a contract, in other words, to situate it within a specific legal order—the order of the international law of contracts.

45. (c) A third element of the internationalization of the contracts in dispute results from the fact that it takes on a dimension of a new category of agreements between States and private persons: economic development agreements (*see* Bourquin, Arbitration and Economic Development Agreements, 15 Bus. Law. 860 (1960); A. A. Fatouros, Government Guarantees to Foreign Investors (1962); Hyde, Economic Development Agreements, 105 Recueil des Cours de l'Académie de Droit International de la Haye ("R.C.A.D.I.") 267 (1962), and Verdross, The Status of Foreign Private Interests Stemming from Economic Development Agreements with Arbitration Clauses, in Selected Readings on Protection by Law of Private Foreign Investments 117 (1964)).

Several elements characterize these agreements: in the first place, their subject matter is particularly broad: they are not concerned only with an isolated purchase or performance, but tend to bring to developing countries investments and technical assistance, particularly in the field of research and exploitation of mineral resources, or in the construction of factories on a turnkey basis. Thus, they assume a real importance in the development of the country where they are performed: it will suffice to mention here the importance of the obligations assumed in the case under consideration by the concession holders in the field of road and port infrastructures and the training on the spot of qualified personnel. The party contracting with the State was thus associated with the realization of the economic and social progress of the host country.

In the second place, the long duration of these contracts implies close cooperation between the State and the contracting party and requires permanent installations as well as the acceptance of extensive responsibilities by the investor.

Finally, because of the purpose of the cooperation in which the contracting party must participate with the State and the magnitude of the investments to which it agreed, the contractual nature of this type of agreement is reinforced: the emphasis on the contractual nature of the legal relation between the host State and the investor is intended to bring about an equilibrium between the goal of the general interest sought by such relation and the profitability which is necessary for the pursuit of the task entrusted to the private enterprise. The effect is also to ensure to the private contracting party a certain stability which is justified by the considerable investments which it makes in the country concerned. The investor must in particular be protected against legislative uncertainties, that is to say the risks of the municipal law of the host country being modified, or against any government measures which would lead to an abrogation or rescission of the contract. Hence, the insertion, as in the present case, of so-called stabilization clauses: these clauses tend to remove all or part of the agreement from the internal law and to provide for its correlative submission to *sui generis* rules as stated in the *Aramco* award, or to a system which is properly an international law system. From this latter point of view, the following considerations should be noted, which were mentioned in the *Sapphire* award, and which stress the interest of the internationalization of the contract:

> Such a solution seems particularly suitable for giving the guarantees of protection which are indispensable for foreign companies, since these companies undergo very considerable risks in bringing financial and technical aid to countries in the process of development. It is in the interest of both parties to such agreements that any disputes between them should be settled according to the general principles universally recognized and should not be subject to the particular rules of national laws. . . . (35 Intl. L.R. 136 (1963), at 175-176.) . . .

70. It is therefore necessary to examine in the light of these principles whether the nationalization measures decreed by the Libyan Government with respect to the plaintiffs disregard any specific commitment undertaken by that Government, a commitment which should have been sufficient to protect the plaintiffs from such a decision.

The Deeds of Concession entered into by the parties do not include any provision by which the Libyan Government limited its recourse to nationalization. However, Clause 16 of the Deeds of Concession contains a stabilization clause with respect to the rights of the concession holder. As consideration for the economic risks to which the foreign contracting parties were subjected, the Libyan State granted them a concession of a minimum duration of 50 years and, more specifically, containing a non-aggravation clause, Clause 16, which provided:

> The Government of Libya will take all steps necessary to ensure that the company enjoys all the rights conferred by this concession. The contractual rights expressly created by this concession shall not be altered except by mutual consent of the parties.

Another paragraph was added to this provision under the Royal Decree of December 1961 and became an integral part of the contract on the basis of the Agreement of 1963. It provides:

> This Concession shall throughout the period of its validity be construed in accordance with the Petroleum Law and the Regulations in force on the date of execution of the agreement of amendment by which this paragraph (2) was incorporated into the concession agreement. Any amendment to or repeal of such Regulations shall not affect the contractual rights of the Company without its consent.

71. Such a provision, the effect of which is to stabilize the position of the contracting party, does not, in principle, impair the sovereignty of the Libyan State. Not only has the Libyan State freely undertaken commitments but also the fact that this clause stabilizes the petroleum legislation and regulations as of the date of the execution of the agreement does not affect in principle the legislative and regulatory sovereignty of Libya. Libya reserves all its prerogatives to issue laws and regulations in the field of petroleum activities in respect of national or foreign persons with which it has not undertaken such a commitment. Clause 16 only makes such acts invalid as far as contracting parties are concerned—with respect to whom this commitment has been undertaken—during the period of applicability of the Deeds of Concession. Any changes which may result from the adoption of new laws and regulations must, to affect the contracting parties, be agreed to by them. This is so not because the sovereignty of Libya would be reduced, but simply by reason of the fact that Libya has, through an exercise of its sovereignty, undertaken commitments under an international agreement, which, for its duration, is the law common to the parties.

Thus, the recognition by international law of the right to nationalize is not sufficient ground to empower a State to disregard its commitments, because the same law also recognizes the power of a State to commit itself internationally, especially by accepting the inclusion of stabilization clauses in a contract entered into with a foreign private party. . . .

NOTES AND QUESTIONS

1. Does the award reflect the probable original intentions of the parties?
2. If you were now representing a host government in drafting a concession

agreement, what changes might you consider in the arbitral submission or choice of law clauses used in *TOPCO*?

3. Is the concept of "internationalization" a wise one? What are the implications of internationalization? What should be the prerequisites for the internationalization of a contract? For a case setting in a somewhat different context, a very loose standard, *see* Revere Copper and Brass v. OPIC, 17 I.L.M. 1321 (1978).

4. How would or should an award like this be enforced? Should a national court regard it as equivalent to a final award? Would you read the concession, under U.S. law, as creating a waiver of immunity for the purposes of the Foreign Sovereign Immunity Act? For a U.S. example, *see* Ipitrade International, S.A. v. Federal Republic of Nigeria, 465 F. Supp. 824 (D.D.C. 1978); for a French analogue, *see* Procureur de la République v. S.A. Société LIAMCO, 106 Journal du Droit International 857 (Trib. gr. inst. 1979); and in Switzerland: Decision of the Federal Supreme Court in Libya v. Libyan American Oil Co., reprinted at 20 I.L.M. 151 (Bundesgericht 1980).

5. After seeing this case, are you more or less sympathetic to the Latin American position? Is the Latin American position feasible only when one is both a substantial host nation for foreign investment and a substantial home nation for such investment? (This kind of reciprocity characterizes the developed nations, which apply among themselves what amounts to the Latin American position.)

6. Why is this dispute settlement and enforcement procedure so different from that that has evolved for international bank loans, described in Chapter XV?

2.   *ICSID*

During the 1960s, the International Bank for Reconstruction and Development (IBRD or World Bank) assisted the negotiation of a convention creating the International Centre for the Settlement of Investment Disputes (ICSID). The World Bank is an international organization created after World War II and working first for the reconstruction of Europe and later for the economic advancement of the developing nations. It viewed the Centre as a way to assist the growth of foreign investment, and therefore economic development, in the developing nations.

The facility it created is actually a framework—a set of arbitration rules and procedures, together with a stand-by panel of arbitrators. Thus, on request, a panel can be convened relatively quickly. The Convention, excerpted below, includes default choice-of-law rules and also includes detailed provisions on the enforcement of its judgments.

At first there were relatively few cases; moreover, very few Latin American nations participated. Some of the few cases, in addition, were pursued very slowly, involving procedural steps over many years. By the beginning of the 1980s, however, decisions were beginning to be published. These include

AGIP Co. v. Popular Republic of the Congo, 21 I.L.M. 726 (1982); and Benvenuti et Bonfant v. People's Republic of the Congo, 21 I.L.M. 740 (1982).

INTERNATIONAL BANK FOR RECONSTRUCTION AND DEVELOPMENT, CONVENTION ON THE SETTLEMENT OF INVESTMENT DISPUTES BETWEEN STATES AND NATIONALS OF OTHER STATES

Articles 1, 25-27, 36-37, 41-48, 53-55 (1966)

The Contracting States

Considering the need for international cooperation for economic development, and the role of private international investment therein;

Bearing in mind the possibility that from time to time disputes may arise in connection with such investment between Contracting States and nationals of other Contracting States;

Recognizing that while such disputes would usually be subject to national legal processes, international methods of settlement may be appropriate in certain cases;

Attaching particular importance to the availability of facilities for international conciliation or arbitration to which Contracting States and nationals of other Contracting States may submit such disputes if they so desire;

Desiring to establish such facilities under the auspices of the International Bank for Reconstruction and Development;

Recognizing that mutual consent by the parties to submit such disputes to conciliation or to arbitration through such facilities constitutes a binding agreement which requires in particular that due consideration be given to any recommendation of conciliators, and that any arbitral award be complied with; and

Declaring that no Contracting State shall by the mere fact of its ratification, acceptance or approval of this Convention and without its consent be deemed to be under any obligation to submit any particular dispute to conciliation or arbitration,

Have agreed as follows:

CHAPTER I. INTERNATIONAL CENTRE FOR SETTLEMENT OF INVESTMENT DISPUTES

SECTION 1. ESTABLISHMENT AND ORGANIZATION

Article 1

(1) There is hereby established the International Centre for Settlement of Investment Disputes (hereinafter called the Centre).

(2) The purpose of the Centre shall be to provide facilities for conciliation and arbitration of investment disputes between Contracting States and nationals of other Contracting States in accordance with the provisions of this Convention. . . .

CHAPTER II.   JURISDICTION OF THE CENTRE

Article 25

(1) The jurisdiction of the Centre shall extend to any legal dispute arising directly out of an investment, between a Contracting State (or any constituent subdivision or agency of a Contracting State designated to the Centre by that State) and a national of another Contracting State, which the parties to the dispute consent in writing to submit to the Centre. When the parties have given their consent, no party may withdraw its consent unilaterally.

(2) "National of another Contracting State" means:

(a) any natural person who had the nationality of a Contracting State other than the State party to the dispute on the date on which the parties consented to submit such dispute to conciliation or arbitration as well as on the date on which the request was registered pursuant to paragraph (3) of Article 28 or paragraph (3) of Article 36, but does not include any person who on either date also had the nationality of the Contracting State party to the dispute; and

(b) any juridical person which had the nationality of a Contracting State other than the State party to the dispute on the date on which the parties consented to submit such dispute to conciliation or arbitration and any juridical person which had the nationality of the Contracting State party to the dispute on that date and which, because of foreign control, the parties have agreed should be treated as a national of another Contracting State for the purposes of this Convention.

(3) Consent by a constituent subdivision or agency of a Contracting State shall require the approval of that State unless that State notifies the Centre that no such approval is required.

(4) Any Contracting State may, at the time of ratification, acceptance or approval of this Convention or at any time thereafter, notify the Centre of the class or classes of disputes which it would or would not consider submitting to the jurisdiction of the Centre. The Secretary-General shall forthwith transmit such notification to all Contracting States. Such notification shall not constitute the consent required by paragraph (1).

Article 26

Consent of the parties to arbitration under this Convention shall, unless otherwise stated, be deemed consent to such arbitration to the exclusion of any other remedy. A Contracting State may require the exhaustion of local administrative or judicial remedies as a condition of its consent to arbitration under this Convention.

Article 27

(1) No Contracting State shall give diplomatic protection, or bring an international claim, in respect of a dispute which one of its nationals and another Contracting State shall have consented to submit or shall have submitted to arbitration under this Convention, unless such other Contracting State shall have failed to abide by and comply with the award rendered in such dispute.

(2) Diplomatic protection, for the purposes of paragraph (1), shall not include informal diplomatic exchanges for the sole purpose of facilitating a settlement of the dispute. . . .

CHAPTER IV. ARBITRATION

SECTION 1. REQUEST FOR ARBITRATION

Article 36

(1) Any Contracting State or any national of a Contracting State wishing to institute arbitration proceedings shall address a request to that effect in writing to the Secretary-General who shall send a copy of the request to the other party.

(2) The request shall contain information concerning the issues in dispute, the identity of the parties and their consent to arbitration in accordance with the rules of procedure for the institution of conciliation and arbitration proceedings.

(3) The Secretary-General shall register the request unless he finds, on the basis of the information contained in the request, that the dispute is manifestly outside the jurisdiction of the Centre. He shall forthwith notify the parties of registration or refusal to register.

SECTION 2. CONSTITUTION OF THE TRIBUNAL

Article 37

(1) The Arbitral Tribunal (hereinafter called the Tribunal) shall be constituted as soon as possible after registration of a request pursuant to Article 36.

(2) (a) The Tribunal shall consist of a sole arbitrator or any uneven number of arbitrators appointed as the parties shall agree.

(b) Where the parties do not agree upon the number of arbitrators and the method of their appointment, the Tribunal shall consist of three arbitrators, one arbitrator appointed by each party and the third, who shall be the president of the Tribunal, appointed by agreement of the parties. . . .

SECTION 3. POWERS AND FUNCTIONS OF THE TRIBUNAL

Article 41

(1) The Tribunal shall be the judge of its own competence.

(2) Any objection by a party to the dispute that that dispute is not within

the jurisdiction of the Centre, or for other reasons is not within the competence of the Tribunal, shall be considered by the Tribunal which shall determine whether to deal with it as a preliminary question or to join it to the merits of the dispute.

Article 42

(1) The Tribunal shall decide a dispute in accordance with such rules of law as may be agreed by the parties. In the absence of such agreement, the Tribunal shall apply the law of the Contracting State party to the dispute (including its rules on the conflict of laws) and such rules of international law as may be applicable.

(2) The Tribunal may not bring in a finding of *non liquet* on the ground of silence or obscurity of the law.

(3) The provisions of paragraphs (1) and (2) shall not prejudice the power of the Tribunal to decide a dispute *ex aequo et bono* if the parties so agree.

Article 43

Except as the parties otherwise agree, the Tribunal may, if it deems it necessary at any stage of the proceedings,

(a) call upon the parties to produce documents or other evidence, and

(b) visit the scene connected with the dispute, and conduct such inquiries there as it may deem appropriate.

Article 44

Any arbitration proceeding shall be conducted in accordance with the provisions of this Section and, except as the parties otherwise agree, in accordance with the Arbitration Rules in effect on the date on which the parties consented to arbitration. If any question of procedure arises which is not covered by this Section or the Arbitration Rules or any rules agreed by the parties, the Tribunal shall decide the question.

Article 45

(1) Failure of a party to appear or to present his case shall not be deemed an admission of the other party's assertions.

(2) If a party fails to appear or to present his case at any stage of the proceedings the other party may request the Tribunal to deal with the questions submitted to it and to render an award. Before rendering an award, the Tribunal shall notify, and grant a period of grace to, the party failing to appear or to present its case, unless it is satisfied that that party does not intend to do so.

Article 46

Except as the parties otherwise agree, the Tribunal shall, if requested by a party, determine any incidental or additional claims or counter-claims arising directly out of the subject-matter of the dispute provided that they are within the scope of the consent of the parties and are otherwise within the jurisdiction of the Centre.

Article 47

Except as the parties otherwise agree, the Tribunal may, if it considers that the circumstances so require, recommend any provisional measures which should be taken to preserve the respective rights of either party.

SECTION 4.   THE AWARD

Article 48

(1) The Tribunal shall decide questions by a majority of the votes of all its members.

(2) The award of the Tribunal shall be in writing and shall be signed by the members of the Tribunal who voted for it.

(3) The award shall deal with every question submitted to the Tribunal, and shall state the reasons upon which it is based.

(4) Any member of the Tribunal may attach his individual opinion to the award, whether he dissents from the majority or not, or a statement of his dissent.

(5) The Centre shall not publish the award without the consent of the parties. . . .

SECTION 6.   RECOGNITION AND ENFORCEMENT OF THE AWARD

Article 53

(1) The award shall be binding on the parties and shall not be subject to any appeal or to any other remedy except those provided for in this Convention. Each party shall abide by and comply with the terms of the award except to the extent that enforcement shall have been stayed pursuant to the relevant provisions of this Convention.

(2) For the purposes of this Section, "award" shall include any decision interpreting, revising or annulling such award pursuant to Articles 50, 51 or 52.

Article 54

(1) Each Contracting State shall recognize an award rendered pursuant to this Convention as binding and enforce the pecuniary obligations imposed by that award within its territories as if it were a final judgment of a court in that State. A Contracting State with a federal constitution may enforce such an award in or through its federal courts and may provide that such courts shall treat the award as if it were a final judgment of the courts of a constituent state.

(2) A party seeking recognition or enforcement in the territories of a Con-

tracting State shall furnish to a competent court or other authority which such State shall have designated for this purpose a copy of the award certified by the Secretary-General. Each Contracting State shall notify the Secretary-General of the designation of the competent court or other authority for this purpose and of any subsequent change in such designation.

(3) Execution of the award shall be governed by the laws concerning the execution of judgments in force in the State in whose territories such execution is sought.

Article 55

Nothing in Article 54 shall be construed as derogating from the law in force in any Contracting State relating to immunity of that State or of any foreign State from execution.

NOTES AND QUESTIONS

1. If you were representing an investor, what advantages and disadvantages would you see in the ICSID procedure as compared with arbitration in the *TOPCO* pattern? As compared with litigation in host nation courts? Litigation in home nation courts? What if you were representing the host nation?

2. How likely, do you think, is it that this arbitration format really does offer the advantages of speed and simplicity? What about possible confidentiality? Expertise?

3. Why, do you think, does the convention apply only when there is specific consent of the parties to the dispute (as opposed to application to any investment dispute between a member nation and a firm from another member nation)? Would you favor extension to all such investment disputes save those specifically excluded?

4. Is the ICSID choice of law provision more or less favorable to the investor than that of *TOPCO*?

5. How would you enforce an award made under ICSID? *See, as an example,* Benvenuti & Bonfant v. Government of the People's Republic of the Congo, 20 I.L.M. 877 (1981).

6. Suppose you represented a foreign government that had consented to submission of a specific dispute to ICSID and the investor sued you in the United States courts. Result? *See* Maritime Intl. Nominees Establishment v. The Republic of Guinea, 693 F.2d 1094 (D.C. Cir. 1982), *cert. denied,* 104 S. Ct. 71 (1983).

Bibliographical Note

For additional information on arbitration and ICSID, *see,* in addition to the material cited above, Delaume, Economic Development and Sovereign Immunity, 79 A.J.I.L. 319 (1985) and ICSID Arbitration and the Courts, 77 A.J.I.L. 784 (1983); Brower, Jurisdiction over Foreign Sovereigns: Litigation v. Arbitration, 17 Intl. Law. 681 (1983); Delaume, Arbitration with Governments: "Domestic" v. "International" Awards, 17 Intl. Law. 687 (1983); Brodus, Settlement of Disputes Arising out of Investment in Developing Countries, 11 Intl. Bus. Law. 213 (1983); Delaume, State Contracts and Transnational Arbitration, 75 A.J.I.L. 784 (1981); Laline, The First "World Bank" Arbitration (*Holiday Inns* v. *Morocco*)—Some Legal Problems, 51 Brit. Y.B. Intl. L. 1980 123 (1982).

B. EXPROPRIATION AND INSURANCE

Expropriation is most likely when a revolutionary government comes to power or when a serious investment dispute cannot be settled by means such as those just described. It is always an intensely political act, comparable to a seizure of church lands, a major nationalization, or a major land reform. This both complicates the application of law and creates an incentive to find alternative ways to control the risk, as through insurance.

1. The Legal and Political Approach to Expropriation

There is an elaborate, but highly contested, body of international law governing expropriation. It is generally assumed that a nation always has the right to expropriate a firm, national or foreign, save perhaps in the presence of a stabilization clause in the founding agreement between the nation and the firm. There may be a limitation that the taking be for public purposes. The most controversial substantive issues go to the duty of compensation, with developed nations (DCs) holding to a standard of "prompt, adequate, and just compensation," while developing nations (LDCs) urge a more flexible standard.

But underlying this dispute, there is a jurisdictional dispute reflected in the Calvo clause concept already discussed at p.899. The traditional DC view has been that an expropriation that does not meet proper compensation standards is a violation not only of the rights of the individual investor, but also of the rights of that investor's home nation. The private issue, of the type faced by ICSID, becomes an "international tort," to be handled through international diplomatic pressure. It is this diplomatic pressure (once actual gunboat pressure) that LDCs specifically resist, and that is the target of the Calvo clause. That clause, however, has been formally ineffective, for the investor's home nations generally regard the investor's waiver of diplomatic jurisdiction as binding on the investor—but not on its government, which did not accept the waiver.

In practice, these technical legal issues are seldom sharply posed. Home nation courts usually rely on such doctrines as act of state and sovereign immunity to avoid consideration of international investment disputes. Thus, although those who have been expropriated often attempt to obtain jurisdiction wherever the expropriating government has assets or the expropriated goods are sold, these efforts are only rarely successful. The compensation issue is almost always blurred. The expropriating nation will usually make some form of counterclaim, e.g., that the expropriated firm gained its position fraudulently, that it owes back taxes, or that it has allowed its physical assets to deteriorate to the point that they are not worth their accounting value (a number that is itself subject to great dispute). The expropriating nation will also usually design a special legal procedure for the expropriation—and the question whether this procedure is fair becomes part of the problem. Moreover, the nation is very unlikely to have the hard currency needed to make actual payment even if it wanted to (and this sort of purpose is one that is hard to borrow for!). Hence, the nation will probably offer payment in long-term bonds, possibly even with some condition attached, such that the bonds become due only as foreign exchange becomes available to the nation.

The diplomatic issues are often blurred as well. Nearly every major international investment dispute ends with a "lump-sum settlement," typically reached years after the expropriation, when tempers have cooled and, very possibly, after governments have changed as well. A lump sum agreement is an arrangement between the investor's nation and the host nation in which a compromise amount is recognized and, in form, paid to the investor's nation, which may then pay it on to the investor.

In fact, the investor's nation is often the effective source of the funds. Sometimes, as with some of the disputes with Eastern European nations after World War II, the United States "freezes" the bank accounts of the foreign nation and its nationals, meaning that the funds may not be withdrawn (save sometimes for specified amounts for personal needs). When such a dispute is settled, the settlement is often in the amount of the frozen accounts, which are then unblocked. See R. Lillich and B. Weston, International Claims: Their Settlement by Lump-Sum Agreements 216-240 (1975). Sometimes, as with the 1941 settlement of Mexican oil expropriation claims, the amount comes at least in part from foreign aid. See 5 Dept. State Bull. 399-403 (1941). Sometimes, as with the 1976 Marcona settlement (see Gantz, The Marcona Settlement: New Forms of Negotiation and Compensation for Nationalized Property, 71 A.J.I.L. 474 (1977)), the home nation helps the host nation borrow the needed capital. And sometimes, as with the Iranian hostage settlement of 1981, the amount comes in part from frozen assets and in part from the host nation itself. The Iranian settlement also included complex escrow procedures to ensure parallel release of the hostages and of the frozen sums. And it included detailed provisions for arbitration of the many specific investor disputes. See the settlement documents at 20 I.L.M. 223 (1981) and the arbitration material at 23 I.L.M. 1 (1984).

Such a settlement obviously requires substantial diplomatic interference with normal individual dispute settlement. Thus, although its duty to pay compensation to the investor in settling a major international dispute is not clear, the U.S. government clearly has the right to freeze property for bargaining chip purposes, to compromise an investor's claim against a foreign government as part of a diplomatic settlement, and even to take a case out of the courts in order to submit it to international dispute settlement procedures. *See,* e.g., Dames & Moore v. Regan, 453 U.S. 654 (1981).

Bibliographical Note

The literature in this area is enormous. Among the best sources are the Lillich and Weston volume referred to above, Rogers, Of Missionaries, Fanatics, and Lawyers: Some Thoughts on Investment Disputes in the Americas, 72 A.J.I.L. 1 (1978); Vagts, Coercion and Foreign Investment Rearrangements, 72 A.J.I.L. 17 (1978); Gantz, The Marcona Settlement: New Forms of Negotiation and Compensation for Nationalized Property, 71 A.J.I.L. 474 (1977). And for the recent U.S. position, *see* the letter by D. Robinson, the legal advisor, to Professor Henkin, the reporter for the Foreign Relations Restatement, printed in 83 Dept. State Bull. 52 (June 1983).

2. *Investment Insurance*

It is quite understandable that firms would like insurance against the expropriation risk. In the United States such insurance is available through the Overseas Private Investment Corporation (OPIC), a semiautonomous entity created by the Foreign Assistance Act of 1969 as a continuation of an earlier Agency for International Development (AID) program. OPIC provides insurance against losses due to currency exchange controls as well as due to expropriation.

The OPIC insurance system is rather complicated but can be suggested in the following diagram:

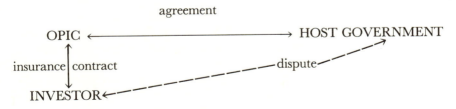

The insurance contract between OPIC and the investor provides, for a fee, the actual insurance coverage. Disputes under the contract are to be resolved by arbitration (note that this is arbitration between the investor and the U.S. agency about the investment dispute, not arbitration between the investor and the host government).

The agreement between OPIC and the host government is required by statute; its fundamental provision is the host government's acceptance of OPIC's claim to subrogation—the right to compensation from the host government for the funds that it has had to pay to the investor. This right is actually exercised; OPIC's predecessor agency in AID, for example, once found itself attempting to operate a textile mill in Nigeria that it had acquired under the terms of war-risk insurance. And similarly, a firm using the exchange control insurance will be expected to give the soft currency (that it cannot otherwise convert) to the government, which can then use it for embassy housekeeping expenses and, effectively, convert it against the host government's will.

The following text of an agreement on investment guaranties between the United States and the People's Republic of China (PRC) exemplifies the kind of protections the U.S. government seeks for U.S. investment abroad.

1980 AGREEMENT BETWEEN THE UNITED STATES AND THE PEOPLE'S REPUBLIC OF CHINA ON INVESTMENT GUARANTIES

October 30, 1980, [1980]—U.S.T.—, T.I.A.S. No. 9924

The American Ambassador to the Chinese Vice Minister of Foreign Affairs

Embassy of the
United States of America

Note No. 438   Beijing, October 30, 1980

Excellency:

I have the honor to refer to conversations which have recently taken place on the basis of equality and mutual benefit between representatives of the Government of the United States of America and of the Government of the People's Republic of China relating to investments in the People's Republic of China and to investment insurance (including reinsurance) and investment guaranties which are administered by the Overseas Private Investment Corporation ("OPIC"), an independent government corporation organized under the laws of the United States of America. On behalf of the Government of the United States of America, I also have the honor to confirm the following understandings reached as a result of those conversations:

ARTICLE 1

As used herein, the term "Coverage" shall refer to any investment insurance (including reinsurance) against loss from political risk or to any investment guaranty which is issued in accordance with this Agreement by OPIC or by any successor United States Government agency, OPIC and any such successor being hereinafter referred to as the "Issuer" to the extent of its interest as insurer or reinsurer in any Coverage.

ARTICLE 2

The procedures set forth in this Agreement shall apply only with respect to Coverage of investments relating to projects or activities approved by the Government of the People's Republic of China.

ARTICLE 3

(a) If the Issuer makes payment to any investor under Coverage, the Government of the People's Republic of China shall, subject to the provisions of Article 4 hereof, recognize the transfer to the Issuer of any currency, credits, assets, or investment on account of which payment under such Coverage is made, as well as the succession of the Issuer to any right, title, claim, or cause of action existing, or which may arise, in connection therewith, subject to existing legal obligations.

(b) The Issuer shall assert no greater rights than those of the transferring investor with respect to any interests transferred or succeeded to under this paragraph. The Government of the United States of America does, however, reserve its rights to assert a claim in its sovereign capacity under international law.

ARTICLE 4

To the extent that the laws of the People's Republic of China partially or wholly invalidate or prohibit the acquisition from a covered investor of any interest in any property within the territory of the People's Republic of China by the Issuer, the Government of the People's Republic of China shall permit such investor and the Issuer to make appropriate arrangements pursuant to which such interests are transferred to an entity permitted to own such interests under the laws of the People's Republic of China.

ARTICLE 5

Amounts in the lawful currency of the People's Republic of China, including credits thereof, acquired by the Issuer by virtue of such Coverage shall be accorded treatment by the Government of the People's Republic of China no less favorable as to use and conversion than the treatment to which such funds would be entitled in the hands of the covered investor. Such amounts and credits shall be freely available for use by the Government of the United States of America to meet its expenditures in the territory of the People's Republic of China. Such amounts and credits may also be transferred by the Issuer to any person or entity agreed by the Government of the People's Republic of China for use by such person or entity in the territory of the People's Republic of China.

ARTICLE 6

(a) Any dispute between the Government of the United States of America and the Government of the People's Republic of China regarding the interpretation of this Agreement or which, in the opinion of one of the Governments, involves a question of public international law arising out of any investment or project or activity relating to such investment for which Coverage has been issued shall be resolved, insofar as possible, through negotiations between the two Governments. If at the end of three months following the request for negotiations the two Governments have not resolved the dispute by agreement, the dispute, including the question of whether such dispute presents a question of public international law, shall be submitted, at the initiative of either Government, to an arbitral tribunal for resolution in accordance with Article 6(b). . . .

ARTICLE 7

The two Governments, desiring reciprocity, agree that, in the event the Government of the People's Republic of China is authorized under its laws to issue coverage for investments in any project or activity within the United States of America under a program similar to the investment incentive program to which this Agreement relates, there shall be, upon the request of either Government, an exchange of notes to make applicable, with respect to such investments made in the United States of America, provisions equivalent to those of this Agreement. . . .

Accept, Excellency, the renewed assurances of my highest consideration.

Leonard Woodcock
Ambassador of the United States
to the People's Republic
of China

His Excellency
Zhang Wenjin
Vice Minister of Foreign Affairs
Beijing, People's Republic of China

The OPIC program has long been controversial, a controversy reflected in the history of OPIC. The program began with AID; its transfer to OPIC reflected a Nixon administration effort to "privatize" it, an effort that also led to some reinsurance of OPIC's risks with other insurance firms, including the Soviet Union's Black Sea and Baltic Company!

The controversy revolves around a number of much broader issues—each of which brings its own constituencies and politics:

(a) Does OPIC in practice favor big business at the expense of small business?
(b) Does it really contribute to economic development or is it merely a help to business?
(c) Does it reach the poorest nations?
(d) Is it needed to help U.S. business compete with other national systems?
(e) Does it encourage the flow of jobs abroad?
(f) And does it encourage or discourage State Department intervention in foreign economic disputes?

NOTES AND QUESTIONS

1. How does Article 6 of the treaty affect the PRC's liabilities? The investor's rights?

2. Is the international agreement really needed?

3. Would you, as counsel for a host nation, seek to encourage or to discourage a foreign investor to acquire OPIC insurance?

4. In what ways do the OPIC arbitration decisions affect the expropriating nation? Should the OPIC arbitration doctrines be the same as those of international law?

5. What should OPIC do if an investor appears to have seriously antagonized a government, which then expropriated it? *See* International Telephone & Telegraph Sud America v. OPIC, 13 I.L.M. 1307 (1974).

6. What problems do you see in combining OPIC insurance with ICSID dispute settlement? Note that a nation's nonpayment of an arbitration award is a typical "event of recovery" under an OPIC insurance contract.

7. Under what circumstances might you use both EXIM and OPIC insurance? Would you choose to do so or would the coverages effectively overlap?

8. How does the incidence of the costs of reimbursing expropriated U.S. investors differ depending on whether or not OPIC insurance is used? (Note that this question becomes even more complex if the tax effects of an unreimbursed loss are considered along with the estimates of likely lump-sum settlement terms with and without investment insurance.)

9. If you were in the State Department, what would you tell a complaining investor who might have acquired OPIC insurance but didn't and then took the loss?

10. Do you think a global investment insurance system is likely to be widely approved? For a current program, *see* World Bank: [draft] Convention Estab-

lishing the Multilateral Investment Guarantee Agency, Seoul, Oct. 11, 1985, reprinted in 24 I.L.M. 1598 (1985).

11. Would a global investment insurance system be wise? What are the arguments each way?

12. Is labor's concern with OPIC well founded? Suppose it were clear that there really was a subsidy involved?

13. Recognizing that it is somewhat late for dealing with the debt problems of the mid-1980s, would investment insurance (national or international) for bank loans be wise?

Bibliographical Note

For additional information, *see* T. Meron, Investment Insurance in International Law (1976); Senate Committee on Foreign Relations, Hearings on Overseas Private Investment Corporations, 97th Cong., 1st Sess. (1981); House Committee on Foreign Affairs, Hearings on Extension and Revision of Overseas Private Investment Insurance Programs, 97th Cong., 1st Sess. (1981); Note, Encouraging Investment in LDC's: The United States Investment Guaranty Program, 8 Brooklyn J. Intl. L. 365 (1982); Koven, Expropriation and the "Jurisprudence" of OPIC, 22 Harv. Intl. L.J. 269 (1981); Adams, The Emerging Law of Dispute Settlement Under the United States Investment Insurance Program, 3 Law & Poly. Intl. Bus. 101 (1971).

C. INVESTMENT TREATIES

In the face of all the uncertainties involving international investment, a number of nations, including the United States, have been working to negotiate networks of "bilateral investment treaties." These treaties vary in detail, but generally require each nation to give the other's firms either Most-Favored-Nation treatment or the equivalent of national treatment, frequently restrict the kinds of investment control of laws that the nation may require, may define terms of compensation in the event of expropriation, and typically set up detailed dispute settlement procedures. An example is presented in the Selected Documents Supplement, and is the basis of the following questions.

QUESTIONS

1. After accepting the treaty, would either Panama or the United States be free to enact a law like the Canadian FIRA? To join the Andean Pact? To enact a Vredeling-style law? To enact a domestic content requirement?

2. Under what circumstances would a U.S. court be likely to apply the treaty? Would the treaty have any influence on extension of a U.S. embargo to a Panama subsidiary?

3. Would the treaty help with any of the detailed disputes discussed in the previous chapter?

4. If you were representing a U.S. firm considering an investment in Panama, what provisions, if any, would appear important to you?

5. If you were voting in the U.S. Senate, would you support or oppose the treaty? Why? What if you were playing a similar role in Panama?

6. Why, do you think, would Panama accept such a treaty?

7. Should there be a single global treaty comparable to this treaty, a sort of GATT for investment? What might its provisions reasonably be?

8. Suppose that in the current negotiations toward an international code of conduct for multinationals some of the LDCs that are particularly oriented toward economic development through foreign investment are willing to commit themselves to a clause stating

> Host nations hereby recognize international legal duties to expropriate property only for public use, to pay prompt, adequate, and just compensation, and not to discriminate against foreign investors in such expropriations.

In return for this commitment, which reflects the goals of some developed world nations, several such nations are willing to make the code of conduct legally binding in international law. Might such a compromise be wise?

9. Suppose several mutually sympathetic nations were to coordinate their efforts against an expropriating government. What might they wisely do?

10. Why is the United States so much more sympathetic to this approach than to the global code of conduct approach?

Bibliographical Note

For other treaty examples, *see* the Panama-Switzerland Treaty of October 19, 1983, 22 I.L.M. 1255 (1983) and the Asian-African Legal Consultative Committee, Models for Bilateral Agreements on Promotion and Protection of Investments, 23 I.L.M. 237 (1984). For additional information, *see* Bergman, Bilateral Investment Protection Treaties: An Examination of the Evolution and Significance of the U.S. Protection Treaty, 16 N.Y.U.J. Intl. L. & Poly. 1 (1983); Juillard, Les conventions bilaterales d'investissement conclus par la France, 106 J. Droit Intl. 274 (1979); Sachs, The "New" U.S. Bilateral Investment Treaties, 2 Intl. Tax & Bus. Law. 192 (1984); Coughlin, The U.S. Bilateral Investment Treaty: An Answer to Performance Requirements? in B. Fisher and J. Turner (eds.) Regulating the Multinational Enterprise National and International Challenges (1983).

TABLE OF CASES

923

INDEX